THE
COLLINS
SHORTER
SCHOOL
DICTIONARY

Collins Educational
An imprint of HarperCollins*Publishers*

To my father, the late Gerald McIlwain, who would have enjoyed
being involved in the preparation of this dictionary.

First published 1992 by Collins Educational
An imprint of HarperCollins*Publishers*
77–85 Fulham Palace Road, London W6 8JB

© Harper Collins Publishers Ltd, John McIlwain 1992

Reprinted 1992, 1993, 1994, 1995 (twice), 1996, 1997 (three times), 1998

ISBN 0 00 317653 3

Typeset by Barbers Ltd, Wrotham, Kent

Printed and bound in Great Britain by The Bath Press, Bath.

Contents

Editorial Consultant

John McIlwain BA, PGCE
with additional material by Tony Bisson BA, LGSM

Acknowledgements

The editorial consultant and publisher wish to acknowledge the work of the editors and compilers of The Collins School Dictionary which provided the basis for this book. Through their work we have been able to use the 20-million word collection of current English texts held on computer in the University of Birmingham.

Grateful thanks are due to Tony Bisson who read the first draft, made many valuable suggestions and supplied most of the supplementary material. Thanks are also due to Mark Prowse, Sylvia Lewis and Will Jones who offered helpful advice in the planning of this book.

A word to the teacher

The aim of this dictionary is to help you and your pupils in four ways:

– by including as much information as possible appropriate to the needs of later KS2 and KS3 pupils
– by communicating this information simply and clearly
– by taking into account the demands of the National Curriculum
– by encouraging pupils to become involved with the words in this dictionary on a more than 'look-it-up, shut-the-book' basis.

In pursuit of these aims, some innovations have been introduced. The essential element of the pupils' material is The Survival Guide (pp v - vii) comprising explanations of abbreviations and phrases used throughout the dictionary, a sample page and other advice. Pupils must be encouraged (if not ordered!) to use it until they know the information well. There are other pages at the beginning and end of the dictionary which contain further information on language and the use of libraries. At certain points there are questions for pupils to answer, with dictionary games and lists that we hope they, and you, will find helpful.

The dictionary incorporates the following policies which represent a departure from many other 'mainstream' dictionaries, and in particular from The Collins School Dictionary from which this dictionary grew:

1 Some entries are knowingly 'over-simplified' in the interests of readability where it is felt that the pupil's understanding is not affected.
2 To avoid complexity, where a word is extremely well-known, e.g. *off*, an example of usage rather than a definition is given.
3 For the same reason, the term 'selected meanings' is used in places to show that well-known meanings have been omitted as being unnecessary to define.
4 For conciseness, the pronoun 'their' is used instead of the grammatically correct but more cumbersome 'his or her'.
5 The main dictionary has two novel features:
– there are eight spoof headwords with definitions.
– each page includes a relevant 'nugget' of information, etc. about language.

Our aim throughout is to support you in your efforts to help pupils to use a dictionary effectively and to cultivate their interest in the wider aspects of language.

The publishers would be very pleased to know what features of this dictionary have proved useful or otherwise, and would welcome your comments and suggestions for consideration in the preparation of future editions.

The Survival Guide

Try this Survival Test. In it are abbreviations and expressions used throughout the dictionary, with examples of their use. You need to understand them all, so that the dictionary can give you maximum help. Check your answers on the inside of the back cover of the dictionary.

Survival Test

What do these mean?

1 **e.g.** (Many cars in Britain come from abroad, *e.g.* the Volvo.)

2 **i.e.** (William I was a Norman, *i.e.* he came from Normandy.)

3 **etc.** (The shop sold fridges, irons, kettles, *etc.*)

4 **activity** (Fishing is an *activity* often done with a rod and line.)

5 **item** (A shirt is an *item* of clothing.)

6 **structure** (The Eiffel Tower is the tallest *structure* in central Paris.)

7 **condition** (Poverty is the *condition* of being poor.)

8 **substance** (Flour and salt are two *substances* you might find in a kitchen.)

9 **device** (A mousetrap is a *device* for catching mice.)

10 **elsewhere** (You can find a list of abbreviations *elsewhere* in this dictionary.)

11 **method** (Throwing water is not always the best *method* of putting a fire out.)

12 **process** (Cooking is a *process* by which food is heated so that it can be eaten.)

13 **situation** (The *situation* in the Sudan is causing concern.)

14 **state** (Perfection is the *state* of being absolutely correct in every detail.)

15 **hence** (box: Latin buxus = box tree; *hence* a wooden container.)

16 **attitude** (Laziness is an *attitude* of not wanting to do much work.)

17 **the act of** (Pulling the trigger is *the act of* firing a gun.)

18 **by means of** (She escaped *by means of* the toilet window.)

19 **refers to** (The word 'philatelic' *refers to* the collecting of stamps.)

20 **the case** (If that is *the case*, then I was wrong to say what I said.)

21 **therefore** (You have worked hard and *therefore* will receive good marks.)

22 **apparatus** (Marconi invented an *apparatus* for sending messages.)

23 **via** (They went from Bristol to London *via* Birmingham.)

24 **degree** (To what *degree* were you hurt in the accident?)

now turn over

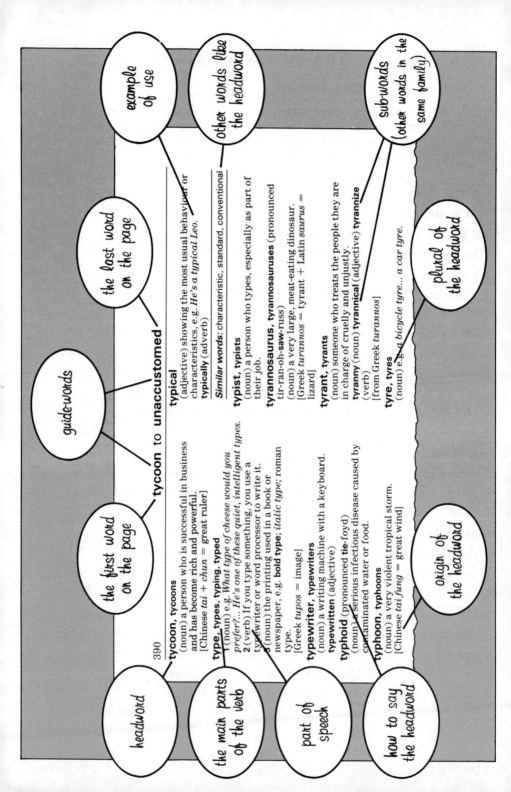

390

tycoon to **unaccustomed**

tycoon, tycoons
(noun) a person who is successful in business and has become rich and powerful.
[Chinese *tai* + *chun* = great ruler]

type, types, typing, typed
1 (noun) e.g. *What type of cheese would you prefer?... He's one of these quiet, intelligent types.*
2 (verb) If you type something, you use a typewriter or word processor to write it.
3 (noun) the printing used in a book or newspaper, e.g. **bold type**; *italic type*; roman type.
[Greek *tupos* = image]

typewriter, typewriters
(noun) a writing machine with a keyboard.
typewritten (adjective)

typhoid (pronounced **tie-foyd**)
(noun) a serious infectious disease caused by contaminated water or food.

typhoon, typhoons
(noun) a very violent tropical storm.
[Chinese *tai fung* = great wind]

typical
(adjective) showing the most usual behaviour or characteristics, e.g. *He's a typical Leo.*
typically (adverb)
Similar words: characteristic, standard, conventional

typist, typists
(noun) a person who types, especially as part of their job.

tyrannosaurus, tyrannosauruses (pronounced tir-ran-oh-**saw**-russ)
(noun) a very large, meat-eating dinosaur.
[Greek *turannos* = tyrant + Latin *saurus* = lizard]

tyrant, tyrants
(noun) someone who treats the people they are in charge of cruelly and unjustly.
tyranny (noun) **tyrannical** (adjective) **tyrannize** (verb)
[from Greek *turannos*]

tyre, tyres
(noun) e.g. *a bicycle tyre... a car tyre.*

Annotations:
- guide-words
- the first word on the page
- the last word on the page
- example of use
- other words like the headword
- sub-words (other words in the same family)
- headword
- the main parts of the verb
- part of speech
- how to say the headword
- origin of the headword
- plural of the headword

Other words and phrases used in this dictionary

formal
e.g. consume (verb; formal)
This means that 'consume' is likely to be used in writing and official language rather than in everyday speech, e.g. *Official figures show that 6500 tons of breakfast cereal were consumed by the Army last year.*

informal
e.g. scoff (verb; informal)
This means that scoff is used in everyday speech but not in serious speech or official language, e.g. *'Don't scoff all those bangers, Sid!'*

plural noun
e.g. trousers (plural noun)
This means that the word is not generally used in the singular.

phrasal verb
e.g. hang about (phrasal verb)
This means that the two words may be used together in a phrase for that meaning of the verb.

prefix
e.g. centi- (prefix)
A prefix is the beginning part of a word attached to root words to form words with something in common – in this case to do with the number 100, e.g. centipede, centimetre, centigrade.

suffix
e.g. -ology (suffix)
A suffix is the end part of a word used with beginnings to form words with something in common – in this case to do with the study of a subject, e.g. geology, psychology.

comparative
e.g. better (adjective, adverb; comparative)
The comparative of an adjective or adverb is used when two things are being compared, e.g. *This one is better than that one; I feel better; My dog is faster than yours; She ran faster than I did.*

superlative
e.g. best (adjective, adverb; superlative)
The superlative of an adjective is used to show that something is at the extreme when more than two things are involved, e.g. *This one is the best; my dog is fastest.*

Abbreviations

AA	Automobile Association
AB	able-bodied seaman
AD	*anno domini* (Latin = in the year of Our Lord) e.g. AD 55 = 55 years after Christ's birth
AIDS	Acquired Immune Deficiency Syndrome
AGM	annual general meeting
a.m.	*ante meridiem* (Latin = before noon) morning
anon.	anonymous (used after a poem etc. when the name of the writer is not known)
A.P.R.	annual percentage rate (used by banks etc. to show what interest they charge if you borrow money from them)
ASCII	American Standard Code for Information Exchange – the computer language standard to most types of computer
BA	Bachelor of Arts (a first university degree)
B.A.	British Airways
B.B.	Boys' Brigade
BBC	British Broadcasting Corporation
BC	Before Christ (44 BC = 44 years before the birth of Christ)
BDR	Bundesrepublik Deutschland (Germany)
BR	British Rail
B.Sc.	Bachelor of Science (a first university degree)
BST	British Summer Time
BO	body odour
B.T.	British Telecom
°C	degrees Centigrade or Celsius
CB	citizens' band radio
CBE	Commander (of the Order) of the British Empire
cc	cubic centimetre(s)
c.c.	carbon copy (used at the foot of a letter to indicate that a copy has been sent to someone else)
CD	compact disc
cf.	confer = compare (used in reference books to direct the reader to other relevant parts of the book)
CID	Criminal Investigation Department
cl	centilitre(s) (100 cl = 1 litre)
cm	centimetre(s) (100 cm = 1 metre)
CND	Campaign for Nuclear Disarmament
co.	company, e.g. Bloggs & Co. Ltd.
c/o	care of, e.g. in an address – Sid James, c/o T. Hancock, Railway Cuttings, East Cheam, Surrey
COD	cash on delivery – you pay for your goods at the time you receive them
CV	curriculum vitae – the details of a person's career
cwt	hundredweight(s) (1 cwt = 112lbs = 50 kg; 20 cwt = 1 ton)
dB	decibel(s) (a unit of measure for sound)
DAT	digital audio tape
D-I-Y	do-it-yourself
DJ	disc jockey
DNA	deoxyribonucleic acid (the material from which all human cells are made)

EC	European Commission (formerly European Economic Commission)
e.g.	*exempli gratia* (Latin = for example)
ER	*Elizabeth Regina* (Latin = Queen Elizabeth)
ESP	extra-sensory perception (e.g. telepathy)
Esq.	esquire (e.g. John Smith Esq. = Mr John Smith)
etc.	*et cetera* (Latin = and other similar things)
°F	degrees Fahrenheit
FBI	Federal Bureau of Investigation
FM	frequency modulation
G	gigabyte
g	gram or grams (1000 g = 1 kilogram)
GB	Great Britain
GCSE	General Certificate of Secondary Education
GI	government issue (an American private soldier)
GMT	Greenwich Mean Time (the standard time in Britain)
GP	general practitioner (a local doctor)
ha	hectare (1 ha = 10,000 m² = 0.4 acres)
HM	His or Her Majesty (e.g. HM The Queen)
HMS	His or Her Majesty's Ship
h.p.	horse power
HP	hire purchase (paying for something by regular small payments)
HQ	headquarters
HRH	His or Her Royal Highness (e.g. HRH The Princess Royal)
i.e.	*id est* (Latin) = that is (used to give more detail about something)
ID	identification (ID card = identity card)
IQ	intelligence quotient (a measure of a certain sort of intelligence)
JP	Justice of the Peace (a magistrate)
K	1000 or £1000
KB or k	kilobyte (1 KB =1024characters)
kg	kilogram (1 kg = 1000 grams)
kHz	kiloHerz (a measure of radio wave frequency)
km	kilometre (1 km = 1000 metres)
kW	kiloWatt (a measure of electrical current)
l	litre or litres
lab	laboratory
lb	pound (weight)
lbw	leg before wicket
L.E.D.	light-emitting diode
LP	a long-playing record
Ltd	Limited (e.g. Reid & Sons Ltd – the name of a limited company)
m	metre
MA	Master of Arts (a higher university degree)
MBorMb	megabyte (1 MB = 1,048,576 characters)
MBE	Member of the British Empire
MD	Doctor of Medicine
MEP	Member of the European Parliament
Messrs	*messieurs* (French) (e.g. Messrs Redmond & Co Ltd)
mg	milligram (1000 mg = 1 gram)
mHz	megaHerz (a unit of radio wave frequency)
MOR	middle of the road (used to describe 'easy listening' music)
ml	millilitre (1000 ml = 1 litre)
mm	millimetre (1000 mm = 1 metre)

MOT	Ministry of Transport (the test for older vehicles)
MP	Member of Parliament
m.p.g.	miles per gallon
m.p.h.	miles per hour
Ms	used before a woman's name (e.g. Ms Mary Christmas) when you do not know or do not wish to indicate if she is married
MS	manuscript
MS	multiple sclerosis
M.Sc.	Master of Science (a higher university degree)
Mr	a shorter version of mister
Mrs	a shorter version of the old-fashioned mistress (now means a married woman)
NATO	North Atlantic Treaty Organization
NB	*nota bene* (Latin = note well; a reminder to look at something carefully)
NHS	National Health Service
no.	*numero* (Latin = number)
OAP	old-age pensioner
OBE	Order of the British Empire
o.n.o.	or nearest offer (used in advertisements)
oz.	ounce(s)
p	pence
p.	page
p.a.	*per annum* (Latin = each year)
P.A.	public address system (loudspeakers for a large event)
PC	Police Constable or personal computer
PE	physical education
pH	a measure of how acid something is (potential for hydrogen)
Ph.D.	Doctor of Philosophy (an advanced university degree)
plc	public limited company (a company which is publicly owned through shares on the stock market)
p.m.	*post meridiem* (Latin = after noon) afternoon
pp.	pages
p.&p.	postage and packing
PPS	*post post scriptum* (Latin = after after writing) used to add a second extra message after a P.S.
PR	public relations
PS	*post scriptum* (Latin = after writing) used to add an extra message to a letter after the signature
PTA	parent-teacher association
PTO	please turn over
PVC	polyvinyl chloride - a type of plastic
RAC	Royal Automobile Club
RAF	Royal Air Force
RAM	random access memory – the part of a computer's memory that the user fills up
RE	religious education
Revd	Reverend (the title of a clergyman) e.g. the Revd H. Smoke
RGN	Registered General Nurse
RIP	*requiescat in pace* (Latin = May he/she rest in peace; used in connection with a dead person)
RN	Royal Navy
ROM	read-only memory – the part of a computer's memory that contains its basic systems.
r.p.m.	revolutions per minute (how fast an engine turns)

RSVP	*Répondez s'il vous plaît* (French = please reply; written at the end of an invitation)
s.a.e.	stamped, self-addressed envelope
SI	Système Internationale d'Unités – a system of units for measurement of all physical things.
SS	sailing ship or steamship
TA	Territorial Army
TNT	Trinitrotoluene
TUC	Trades Union Congress
TV	television
UFO	unidentified flying object
UHF	ultra high frequency
UHT	ultra-heat-treated (a type of processed milk)
UK	United Kingdom
UV	ultra-violet
UN	United Nations
USA	United States of America
v.	*versus* (Latin = against) e.g. Man City v. Spurs
VCR	video cassette recorder
VD	venereal disease
v.g.c.	very good condition (used in advertisements)
VHF	very high frequency
vs.	*versus* (Latin = against) e.g. Hibs vs. Hearts
WC	water closet (lavatory)
WI	Women's Institute
WPC	Woman Police Constable
w.p.m.	words per minute (the speed that a person can type or do shorthand)
WRAC	Women's Royal Army Corps
WRAF	Women's Royal Air Force
WRNS	Women's Royal Naval Service (known as the Wrens)
YMCA	Young Men's Christian Association
YWCA	Young Women's Christian Association

A very short history of the English language

If time machines were possible, travellers would go back only a little way before they found themselves unable to understand the language being spoken in the United Kingdom. Even 400 years ago, in Shakespeare's time, differences in pronunciation and dialect might make English seem like a foreign tongue.

Our knowledge of the language spoken in these islands begins with the Celts who came here from Europe at least 3000 years ago. We now use very few **Celtic** words (e.g. ass, bog, brook) but many place-names come from the words the Celts used for rivers and water: Avon, Exe and Ouse.

In 55BC the Romans invaded and their language, **Latin,** was used here for more than 400 years until the Roman legions had to return to Italy to defend the main part of their empire. Although some Latin words survived among the Celts, it was the next settlers who brought the language which was to become the basis of our English tongue.

The Angles, Saxons and Jutes migrated from roughly the area we now call Germany and settled largely in southern England as farmers, taking over much of the best land so that the Celts either worked for them or chose to move westwards, settling in Cornwall, Wales and Ireland, where their influence is still strong.

For 500 years **Anglo-Saxon** was the dominant language here though it was influenced by the Vikings who brought their **Norse** tongue from the Scandinavian regions. They settled mainly in the north of England but their language gradually merged with Anglo-Saxon into what we now call **Old English.**

In 1066, William, Duke of Normandy, invaded England and began to form a centralized system of government. **French** became the language of the ruling group while Old English was looked down on as a language for the peasants. In fact French was not in those days as unlike Old English as you might expect; William's Normans were originally Norsemen and the languages therefore had much in common.

Inevitably, French and Old English began to merge into what we now call **Middle English** and in the 14th century even at government level it was accepted as our language.

You should be aware, though, that throughout all these centuries, the influence of the Roman Catholic Church was very powerful in Europe. Being based in Rome, it used Latin for its rituals, communications and education. Consequently, the Latin language contributed thousands of words to the ever-growing English vocabulary.

Languages throughout Europe went through an upheaval when, in the 15th and 16th centuries, there was a renewal of interest in the culture of Ancient Greece. This Renaissance was quickened by the introduction of printing (including William Caxton's first English printing house of 1476) and by a great desire for new ideas and scholarly study. **Greek** became an influence on all European languages and the spread of learning meant that every language gave something to its neighbours. A desire to standardize pronunciation and spelling was now widespread and from this period we can date what we now call **Modern English.**

Our language continues to change and we can assume that our time travellers would again be in difficulty if they travelled a couple of hundred years ahead. You might like to discuss how the language has changed even in your lifetime and what will be the main reasons for further changes in the ways we speak, read and write.

These are the main languages from which the words in this dictionary originate:
Afrikaans, Anglo-French, Arabic, Aramaic, Aztec, Czech, Dutch, Gaelic, German, Greek, Hebrew, Hindi, Inuit, Irish Gaelic, Italian, Javanese, Latin, Malay, Middle English, North American Indian, Old English, Old Norse, Portuguese, Sanskrit, South American Indian, Spanish, Tamil, Urdu

A

a
(indefinite article) e.g. *a book.*

aback
(adverb) If you are taken aback, you are very surprised and slightly shocked.

abacus, abacuses
(noun) a frame with beads that slide along rods, used for calculating.
[Greek *abax* = board covered with sand for doing sums on]

abandon, abandons, abandoning, abandoned
1 (verb) If you abandon someone or something, you leave them or give them up permanently.
2 (noun) If you do something with abandon, you do it in a rather wild uncontrolled way.
[Old French *a bandon* = under outside control]

Similar words: (verb) desert, forsake, quit

abate, abates, abating, abated
(verb) to become less, e.g. *The storm abated and the rain stopped.*
abatement (noun)
[French *abattre* = to beat down]

abattoir, abattoirs (pronounced **ab**-a-twah)
(noun) a place where animals are killed for meat.
[a French word]

abbess, abbesses
(noun) the woman in charge of all the nuns in a convent.

abbey, abbeys
(noun) a large church with a community of monks or nuns attached to it.

abbot, abbots
(noun) the monk or priest in charge of all the monks in a monastery.
[Latin *abbat* from Aramaic *abba* = father]

abbreviate, abbreviates, abbreviating, abbreviated
(verb) to make a word or phrase shorter.
[Latin *brevis* = brief]

abbreviation, abbreviations
(noun) a short form of a word or phrase.

abdicate, abdicates, abdicating, abdicated
(verb) If a king or queen abdicates, they give up the position of being king or queen.
abdication (noun)
[Latin *abdicare* = to renounce]

abdomen, abdomens
(noun) the part of the body below the chest, containing stomach and intestines; the belly.
abdominal (adjective)

abduct
(verb) to kidnap.

abhor, abhors, abhorring, abhorred
(verb; formal) to hate something.
abhorrence (noun) **abhorrent** (adjective)
[Latin *abhorrere* = to shudder at]

abide, abides, abiding, abided
1 (verb) If you can't abide something, you dislike it very much.
2 If you abide by a decision, agreement or law, you accept it and act in accordance with it.
3 If something abides, it remains or continues to happen for a long time.
[Old English *bidan* = to wait]

ability, abilities
(noun) Your ability to do something is the quality of intelligence or skill that you have that enables you to do it, e.g. *the ability to read.*

Similar word: competence

ablaze
(adjective) on fire or in flames.

able, abler, ablest
1 (adjective) If you are able to do something, you can do it.
2 Someone who is able is clever or talented.

Similar words: (sense 1) capable, fit; (sense 2) capable, competent

able-bodied
(adjective) physically fit and with no injuries or disabilities.

abnormal
(adjective) unusual or peculiar, e.g. *The X-ray showed up an abnormal growth.*
abnormally (adverb)

abnormality, abnormalities
(noun) something that is not normal or usual.

aboard
(preposition, adverb) on a ship or plane.

abode, abodes
(noun; old-fashioned) a home.

abolish, abolishes, abolishing, abolished
(verb) to put an end to something officially, e.g. *Hanging for murder was abolished in the 60s.*
abolition (noun)
[Latin *abolere* = to destroy]

Similar words: do away with, scrap

abominable
(adjective) very unpleasant or shocking.
abominably (adverb) **abomination** (noun)

aborigine, aborigines (pronounced ab-or-**rij**-in-ee)
(noun) someone descended from the people who lived in Australia before Europeans arrived.
aboriginal (adjective)
[Latin *aborigines* = the people who lived in Italy before the Romans]

abort, aborts, aborting, aborted
(verb) If a plan or activity is aborted, it is stopped before it is finished.

The letter A began as a picture of an ox head. Look at A upside-down. Aleph meant ox.

abortion
(noun) If a pregnant woman has an abortion, the pregnancy is ended and the baby dies.
[Latin *aborire* = to miscarry]

abortive
(adjective) unsuccessful, e.g. *an abortive attempt.*

abound, abounds, abounding, abounded
(verb) If things abound, there are very large numbers of them.
[Latin *abundare* = to overflow]

about
(preposition, adverb) e.g. *It's about time.*

above
(preposition, adverb) e.g. *above the door.*

above board
(adjective) completely open, honest, and legal, e.g. *Was the deal above board?*
[originating from the difficulty of cheating at cards with your hands above the table]

abrasion, abrasions
(noun) an area where your skin has been broken or scraped.

abrasive
1 (adjective) An abrasive substance is rough and can be used to clean hard surfaces.
2 unpleasant and rude, e.g. *an abrasive manner.*
[Latin *abradare* = to scrape away]

abreast
(adverb) side by side, e.g. *We marched four abreast.*

abridge, abridges, abridging, abridged
(verb) to abridge, for example, a piece of writing means to make it shorter.

abridgement
(noun) a shortened word using the first and last letter of the original, e.g. **Mr** Mann, **Dr** Spock.

abroad
(adverb) in a foreign country.

abrupt
1 (adjective) sudden, quick, and unexpected, e.g. *The interview came to an abrupt end.*
2 rude, unfriendly and impolite.
abruptly (adverb) **abruptness** (noun)
[Latin *abruptus* = broken off]

abscess, abscesses (pronounced **ab**-sess)
(noun) a painful swelling that contains pus.

abscond, absconds, absconding, absconded
(verb) to leave suddenly and secretly, usually after doing something wrong, e.g. *The boys absconded from the detention centre.*
[Latin *abscondere* = to hide away]

abseil, abseils, abseiling, abseiled
(verb) If you abseil down a cliff or mountain, you go down it by sliding down a rope.
[German *ab* = down + *Seil* = rope]

absent, absents, absenting, absented
1 (adjective) not present in a place or situation.
2 (verb; formal; pronounced ab-**sent**) If you absent yourself, you keep away from a place.
absence (noun)

Similar words: (adjective) away, elsewhere

absentee, absentees
(noun) someone who is not present in a place when they should be there.

absent-minded
(adjective) rather vague and forgetful.
absent-mindedly (adverb)
absent-mindedness (noun)

absolute
1 (adjective) total and complete, e.g. *absolute secrecy.*
2 having complete and unlimited power and authority, e.g. *an absolute ruler.*
absolutely (adverb)
[Latin *absolutus* = freed]

absolve, absolves, absolving, absolved
(verb) To absolve someone of something means to state officially that they are not guilty of it or not to blame for it; to pardon.
absolution (noun)
[Latin *absolvere* = to free]

absorb, absorbs, absorbing, absorbed
1 (verb) to soak up a liquid or gas.
2 To absorb a shock, change or effect means to deal with it or cope with it.
absorbent (adjective) **absorption** (noun)
[Latin *absorbere* = to suck]

Similar words: digest, assimilate, take in

absorbed
(adjective) If you are absorbed in something, it has all your attention.

abstain, abstains, abstaining, abstained
1 (verb) If you abstain from something, you do not do it or have it, e.g. *to abstain from alcohol.*
abstinence (noun)
2 If you abstain in a vote, you do not vote.
abstainer (noun) **abstention** (noun)

Similar words: (sense 1) refrain, deny yourself

abstract
1 (adjective) based on thoughts and ideas rather than physical objects or events.
2 Abstract art is a style of art which uses shapes rather than representing people or objects.
3 Abstract nouns refer to qualities or ideas rather than to physical objects, e.g. thought.
[Latin *abstractus* = removed]

absurd
(adjective) ridiculous and stupid.
absurdly (adverb) **absurdity** (noun)

Similar words: ludicrous, preposterous, ridiculous

abundance
(noun) Something that exists in abundance exists in large numbers, e.g. *an abundance of fish.*
abundant (adjective) **abundantly** (adverb)

Similar words: plenty, wealth

abuse, abuses, abusing, abused
1 (noun; pronounced ab-**yooce**) insults and rude words directed towards someone.

If an abbreviation uses the first and last letters of a word, it does not need a full stop: Mr Dr Mrs

2 the wrong use of something, e.g. *the abuse of power... drug abuse.*
3 (verb) [pronounced ab-**yooze**] to speak insultingly to someone.
4 to treat someone cruelly and violently.

Similar words: (noun: sense 1) misuse, ill-treatment, harm
(verb: sense 4) ill-treat, misuse

abusive
(adjective) rude, offensive, and unkind.
abusively (adverb) **abusiveness** (noun)

abysmal (pronounced ab-**biz**-mul)
(adjective) very bad indeed, e.g. *abysmal wages.*
abysmally (adverb)

abyss, abysses
(noun) a very deep hole.
[Greek *abussos* = bottomless]

academic, academics
1 (adjective) Academic work is work done in a school, college, or university.
2 (informal) of little importance, e.g. *The result of the match was now academic.*
3 (noun) someone who teaches or does research in a college or university.
academically (adverb)

academy, academies
1 (noun) a school or college, usually one that specializes in one particular subject, e.g. *the Royal Academy of Music.*
2 a society of scientists, artists, writers, or musicians, e.g. *the Royal Academy.*
[Greek *akadēmeia*, the name of the grove where the philospher Plato taught]

accelerate, accelerates, accelerating, accelerated
(verb) to go faster.
acceleration (noun) **accelerator** (noun)

accent, accents
1 (noun) a way of pronouncing a language, e.g. *She has a Scottish accent.*
2 a mark placed above or below a letter in some languages, which affects the way the letter is pronounced, e.g. *é* in *frappé.*
3 an emphasis on something, e.g. *This season's accent is on longer skirts.*
accentuate (verb)

accept, accepts, accepting, accepted
1 (verb) If you accept something, you say yes to it or take it from someone.
2 If you accept a situation, you realize that it cannot be changed, e.g. *The astronaut accepts danger as part of his job.*
3 If you accept a statement or story, you believe that it is true, e.g. *Accept that you were wrong.*
4 If a group accepts you, they treat you as one of the group.
acceptance (noun) **acceptable** (adjective)
acceptably (adverb) **acceptability** (noun)
[Latin *ad* = to + *capere* = to take]

access
(noun) the right or opportunity to use something or to enter a place.
[Latin *accessus* = an approach]

accessible
1 (adjective) easily reached or seen, e.g. *The cave was accessible only at low tide.*
2 easily understood and used, e.g. *I want to make computers more accessible to ordinary people.*
accessibility (noun)

accessory, accessories
1 (noun) an extra part.
2 Someone who helps another a person commit a crime is an accessory to the crime.

accident, accidents
1 (noun) a chance event in which something goes wrong.
2 Something that happens **by accident** happens by chance.
accidental (adjective) **accidentally** (adverb)
[Latin *accidere* = to happen]

Similar words: unplanned, unintentional

acclaim, acclaims, acclaiming, acclaimed
1 (verb; formal) To acclaim someone or something means to praise them a lot, e.g. *The speech was acclaimed by everyone present.*
2 (noun) great praise.
acclamation (noun)
[Latin *acclamare* = to shout applause]

accommodate, accommodates, accommodating, accommodated
1 (verb) to provide someone with a place to sleep, live, or work.
2 If a place can accommodate a number of things or people, it has enough room for them.
[Latin *accommodare* = to make something fit in]

accommodation
(noun) a place provided for someone to sleep, work or live in.

Similar words: board, lodging, lodgings, housing

accompany, accompanies, accompanying, accompanied
1 (verb) to go with someone.
2 If you accompany a singer or musician, you play the piano or another instrument while they sing or play the main tune.
accompaniment (noun) **accompanist** (noun)
[Old French *compaing* = companion]

accomplice, accomplices
(noun) a person who helps someone else to commit a crime.
[Latin *complex* = associate]

Similar words: partner, accessory

accomplish, accomplishes, accomplishing, accomplished
(verb) to succeed in doing something.
accomplishment (noun)
[Latin *complere* = to fill up]

accomplished
(adjective) very talented at something, e.g. *She is an accomplished musician.*

accord
1 (noun) agreement.
2 (phrase) If you do something **of your own**

Repeat quickly: It took twenty talented teachers to teach him his ten times table.

accord, you do it willingly and not because you have been forced to do it.

accordingly
(adverb) in a way that is suitable for the circumstances, e.g. *The singer changed her image and her hairstyle changed accordingly.*

according to
1 (preposition) If something is true according to a particular person, that person says that it is true, e.g. *The Gospel according to St John.*
2 If something is done according to a plan, that plan is used as the basis for it.

accordion, accordions
(noun) a musical instrument shaped like an expanding box. It is played by squeezing the two sides together while pressing the keys on it.

account, accounts, accounting, accounted
1 (noun) a written or spoken report of something.
2 (plural noun) Accounts are records of money spent and received by a person or business.
3 (noun) If you have a bank account, you can leave money and take it out when you need it.
4 **On account of** means because of.
5 If something must **on no account** be done, it must not be done under any circumstances.
6 (verb) To account for something means to explain it, e.g. *If she wasn't feeling well, that might account for her strange mood.*
[Old French *acconter* = to count]

accountable
(adjective) If you are accountable for something, you are responsible for it and have to explain your actions, e.g. *A ship's captain is accountable for the safety of his crew.*
accountability (noun)

accountant, accountants
(noun) a person whose job is to keep or inspect financial records.

accumulate, accumulates, accumulating, accumulated
(verb) If you accumulate things, you gather or collect them over a period of time. When things accumulate, they come together in one place.
accumulation (noun) **accumulative** (adjective)
[Latin *cumulus* = heap]

accurate
(adjective) completely true, correct or precise.
accurately (adverb) **accuracy** (noun)
[Latin *accurare* = to perform carefully]

Similar words: exact, precise, correct, true

accusative
(noun, adjective) In the grammar of some languages, the accusative is the form of a noun when it is the direct object of a verb.

accuse, accuses, accusing, accused
(verb) If you accuse someone of doing something wrong, you say that they have done it.
accusation (noun) **accuser** (noun)
[Latin *causa* = lawsuit]

accustomed
(adjective) If you are accustomed to something, you are used to it.

ace, aces
1 (noun) In a pack of cards, an ace is a card with a single symbol on it.
2 (adjective; informal) good or skilful, e.g. *an ace marksman.*
3 (noun) In tennis, an ace is a serve so good that the other player cannot hit the ball.
[Latin *as* = a unit]

ache, aches, aching, ached
1 (verb) If you ache, you feel a continuous dull pain in a part of your body.
2 If you are aching for something or aching to do something, you want it very much.

achieve, achieves, achieving, achieved
(verb) to do something successfully or to cause it to happen.
[Old French *achever* = to bring to a conclusion]

Similar words: accomplish, attain, realize, fulfil

achievement, achievements
(noun) something which you succeed in doing, especially after a lot of effort.

acid, acids
1 (noun) Acids are watery liquids of many different types. They can cause chemical changes, e.g. colour change, production of gas. Acidity is measured in pH numbers. Water has a pH of 7 and acids have a pH of less than this. Acids have many industrial, medical and household uses. They are the chemical opposites of alkalis.
2 (adjective) Acid tastes are sharp or sour.
3 a short name for lysergic acid diethylamide, a very powerful and dangerous hallucinatory drug.
acidic (adjective) **acidity** (noun)
[Latin *acidus* = sour]

acid rain
(noun) rain polluted by acid in the atmosphere which has come from factories etc.

acknowledge, acknowledges, acknowledging, acknowledged
1 (verb) If you acknowledge a fact or situation, you agree or admit that it is true.
2 If you acknowledge someone, you show that you have seen and recognized them.
3 If you acknowledge a message etc., you tell the person who sent it that you have received it.
acknowledgement or **acknowledgment** (noun)

Similar words: (sense 1) accept, admit

acne (pronounced **ak**-nee)
(noun) painful, lumpy spots that cover someone's face.
[Greek *akme* = point or spot]

acorn, acorns
(noun) the fruit of the oak tree, a pale oval nut in a cup-shaped base.

acoustic (pronounced a-**koo**-stik)
1 (adjective) relating to sound or hearing.
2 An acoustic guitar does not have its sound amplified electronically.
[Greek *akouein* = to hear]

Mary and **I** went to the cinema with Dad. Dad took Mary and **me** to the cinema.

acquaint, acquaints, acquainting, acquainted
1 (verb) If you say you are acquainted with someone, you mean you know them slightly but not well.
2 If you are acquainted with the facts, you know about them.
[Latin *accognoscere* = to know perfectly]

acquaintance, acquaintances
(noun) someone you know slightly but not well.

acquire, acquires, acquiring, acquired
(verb) to obtain something.
[Latin *quaerere* = to seek or to get]
acquisition (noun)

acquit, acquits, acquitting, acquitted
(verb) If someone is acquitted of a crime, they have been tried in a court and found not guilty.
acquittal (noun)

Similar words: clear, absolve

acre, acres
(noun) a unit for measuring areas of land.
(1 acre = 4047 square metres.)
[Old English *æcer* = field]

acrid
(adjective) sharp and bitter, e.g. *the acrid smell of burnt wood.*

acrobat, acrobats
(noun) an entertainer who does gymnastic tricks.
acrobatic (adjective) **acrobatics** (plural noun)
[Greek *akrobates* = someone on tiptoe]

acronym, acronyms
(noun) a word made up of the initial letters of a phrase, e.g. *P.L.U.T.O. = pipeline under the ocean.*

across
(preposition, adverb) e.g. *across the road.*

act, acts, acting, acted
1 (verb) to do something, e.g. *We have to act now.*
2 to behave in a particular way, e.g. *She was acting strangely.*
3 If one thing acts as something else, it does the job of the second thing, e.g. *We hired a student to act as our interpreter.*
4 If you act in a play or film, you play a part.
5 (noun) a single thing that someone does, e.g. *an act of violence.*
6 An Act of Parliament is a law passed by the government.
7 In a play, ballet, or opera, an act is one of the main parts that it is divided into.
8 In a TV or stage show, an act is one of the separate short performances in it by different performers.
[Latin *actum* = something done]

Similar words: (noun: sense 5) action, deed

action, actions
1 (noun) something you do for a particular purpose, e.g. *The police took action to stop the demonstration.*
2 a physical movement.
3 In law, an action is a legal proceeding.

4 fighting in a war or battle, e.g. *He was killed in action.*

activate, activates, activating, activated
(verb) to cause something to start working, e.g. *Goldfinger activated the bomb.*

Similar words: set in motion, trigger

active
1 (adjective) Active people are full of energy and are always busy doing things.
2 happening now, e.g. *The project is under active discussion.*
3 In grammar, a verb in the active voice is one where the subject does the action, rather than having it done to them, e.g. **active:** I hit; **passive:** I am hit.
actively (adverb)

activist, activists
(noun) a person who tries to bring about political and social change.

activity, activities
1 (noun) a situation in which a lot of things are happening at the same time.
2 Something that you do for pleasure, e.g. *outdoor activities and hobbies.*
3 The activities of a group or organization are the things that they do.

actor, actors
(noun) a man or woman whose profession is acting in plays, TV or films.

actress, actresses
(noun) a woman whose profession is acting.

actual
(adjective) real or genuine, and not imaginary.
actually (adverb)

acupuncture
(noun) the treatment of illness or pain by sticking small needles into special places in a person's body. It originates from China.
[Latin *acus* = needle + *puncture*]

acute
1 (adjective) severe or intense, e.g. *acute pain.*
2 very bright and intelligent, e.g. *an acute mind.*
3 An acute angle is less than 90°.
4 In French and some other languages, an acute accent is an upward-sloping line placed over a vowel to indicate a change in pronunciation, as in the word *café.*

ad, ads
(noun; informal) an advertisement.

Adam's apple
(noun) a piece of cartilage forming a lump that sticks out at the front of the neck.
[from the story that a piece of the forbidden apple got stuck in Adam's throat]

adapt, adapts, adapting, adapted
1 (verb) If you adapt to a new situation, you change so that you can deal with it successfully.
2 If you adapt something, you change it so that it is suitable for a new purpose or situation.
adaptable (adjective) **adaptation** (noun)

What nouns match these verbs: act see tell sell marry speak? (e.g. do – deed)

adaptor, adaptors; also spelled **adapter**
(noun) a type of electric plug which can be used
to connect two or more plugs to one socket.

add, adds, adding, added
(verb) e.g. *Two and two adds up to four.*

adder, adders
(noun) a small poisonous snake with a black
zigzag pattern on its back; also called a viper.
[Middle English *a naddre*]

addict, addicts
(noun) someone who cannot stop doing
something, e.g. taking drugs.
addicted (adjective) **addiction** (noun)
[Latin *addicere* = to agree to]

addictive
(adjective) If a drug is addictive, the people who
take it find that they cannot stop taking it.

addition, additions
1 (noun) something that has been added to
something else, e.g. *The last addition to the
house was in the early 18th century.*
2 the process of adding numbers together.
additional (adjective) **additionally** (adverb)

additive, additives
(noun) something that is added to something else
for a particular purpose, e.g. *Additives are put
into food to make it last longer, to colour it, etc.*

address, addresses, addressing, addressed
1 (noun) e.g. *30, Dogg Road, Wuffborough,
Berkshire.*
2 a speech to a group of people.
3 (verb) to deal with a situation or problem.

adenoids
(plural noun) the soft lumpy tissue at the back of
the nose and throat.

adequate
(adjective) enough in amount or good enough for
a purpose, e.g. *an adequate answer.*
adequately (adverb) **adequacy** (noun)
[Latin *adaequare* = to make equal]

Similar words: sufficient, satisfactory

adhere, adheres, adhering, adhered
(verb) to stick firmly.

adhesive, adhesives
1 (noun) any substance that is used to stick
things together, e.g. glue.
2 (adjective) sticky and able to stick to things.

ad infinitum (pronounced **add** in-fin-**nite**-um)
(adverb) again and again, e.g. *Your father heard
it from his father, and so on ad infinitum.*
[Latin = to infinity]

adjacent (pronounced ad-**jay**-sent)
(adjective; formal) If two things are adjacent,
they are next to each other, e.g. *She sat on a
chair adjacent to mine.*

adjective, adjectives (see page 427)
(noun) a word that adds to the description given
by a noun. For example, in 'They live in a large,

white, Georgian house', 'large', 'white', and
'Georgian' are all adjectives.
adjectival (adjective)
[Latin *adjicere* = to throw to]

adjourn, adjourns, adjourning, adjourned
(pronounced aj-**urn**)
(verb) If a meeting or trial is adjourned, it stops
for a time, e.g. *The trial was adjourned until the
next morning.*
adjournment (noun)
[Old French *à* = to + *jour* = day]

**adjudicate, adjudicates, adjudicating,
adjudicated**
(verb; formal) to make an official decision about
a question or dispute.
adjudication (noun) **adjudicator** (noun)
[Latin *judicare* = to act as judge]

adjust, adjusts, adjusting, adjusted
1 (verb) If you adjust something, you slightly
change its position or alter it in some other way.
2 If you adjust to a new situation, you get used to
it, often by slightly changing your attitude.
adjustable (adjective) **adjustment** (noun)

ad-lib, ad-libs, ad-libbing, ad-libbed
(verb) to say something that has not been
prepared before, e.g. *Ronald had lost his script,
so he had to ad-lib, with disastrous results.*
ad-lib (noun)
[Latin *ad libitum* = according to desire]

**administer, administers, administering,
administered**
1 (verb) to be responsible for managing an
organization.
2 to administer the law or administer justice
means to put it into practice and apply it.
3 If medicine or a punishment is administered to
someone, it is given to them.
administration (noun) **administrative** (adjective)
administrator (noun)

admirable
(adjective) very good and deserving to be
admired.
admirably (adverb)

admiral, admirals
(noun) the commander of a navy holding the
highest naval rank.
[Arabic *amir* = commander]

admire, admires, admiring, admired
(verb) to like, respect and approve of someone or
something.
admiration (noun) **admirer** (noun)
admiring (adjective) **admiringly** (adverb)
[Latin *admirare* = to wonder at]

admission, admissions
1 (noun) If you are allowed admission to a place,
you are allowed to go in.
2 If you make an admission of something bad, for
example guilt or laziness, you agree, often
reluctantly, that it is true.

admit, admits, admitting, admitted
1 (verb) to agree, often reluctantly, that
something is true.
2 to allow someone or something to enter a place.

What verbs match these adjectives: pure clean simple noble? (e.g. dark – darken)

3 If you are admitted to hospital, you are taken there to stay until you are better.
[Latin *ad* = to + *mittere* = to send]

admittance
(noun) the right to enter a place.

adolescent, adolescents
(noun) a young person who is no longer a child but who is not yet an adult.
adolescence (noun)
[Latin *adolescere* = to grow up]

adopt, adopts, adopting, adopted
(verb) If you adopt a child that is not your own, you take them into your family as your son or daughter.
adoption (noun)
[Latin *adoptare* = to choose for oneself]

adorable
(adjective) sweet, pretty and attractive.

adore, adores, adoring, adored
(verb) If you adore someone, you feel deep love and admiration for them.
adoration (noun)
[Latin *adorare* = to pray to]

adorn, adorns, adorning, adorned
(verb) to decorate or make beautiful, e.g. *The desk was adorned with a vase of fresh flowers.*
adornment (noun)

adrenalin or **adrenaline** (pronounced a-**dren**-al-in)
(noun) a hormone produced by your body when you are angry, nervous or excited. It makes your heart beat faster, and gives you energy.

adrift
1 (adjective, adverb) If a boat is adrift, it is floating on the water without being controlled.
2 If a plan goes adrift, it goes wrong.

adult, adults
(noun) a fully developed person or animal.
[Latin *adolescere* = to grow up]

adultery
(noun) sexual intercourse between a married person and someone they are not married to.
adulterer (noun) **adulterous** (adjective)

advance, advances, advancing, advanced
1 (verb) to move forward.
2 (noun) a forward movement, especially by an army.
3 progress in something, e.g. *Steam power was a great technological advance.*
4 (adjective) done or happening before an event, e.g. *We had no advance warning.*
5 (phrase) If you do something **in advance**, you do it before something else happens.
advancement (noun)

Similar words: (noun: sense 3) progress, development

advantage, advantages
1 (noun) a benefit or something that puts you in a better position.
2 In tennis, the umpire says 'Advantage' to indicate the first point won after deuce.
3 (phrase) If you **take advantage of** someone, you treat them unfairly for your own benefit.

4 If you **take advantage of** something, you make use of it.
advantageous (adjective)

advent
1 (noun) The advent of something is its start or its coming into existence, e.g. *This process was impossible before the advent of computers.*
2 the season just before Christmas in the Christian calendar.
[Latin *advenire* = to come]

adventure, adventures
(noun) an event that is unusual, exciting, and perhaps dangerous.
adventurous (adjective) **adventurer** (noun)
[Latin *advenire* = to happen]

adverb, adverbs (see page 428)
(noun) a word that adds information about a verb or a following adjective or other adverb, for example, saying, how, when or where something is done. e.g. *It moved slowly. They want it now. Please come here;* 'slowly', 'now', and 'here' are all adverbs.
adverbial (adjective)
[Latin *adverbium* = added word]

adverse
(adjective) unfavourable to you or opposite to what you want or need, e.g. *adverse weather.*
adversely (adverb)

adversity, adversities
(noun) a time of danger or difficulty.

advert, adverts
(noun; informal) an advertisement.

advertise, advertises, advertising, advertised
(verb) to tell people, in a newspaper or poster, or on TV, about something for sale.
advertiser (noun) **advertising** (noun)
advertisement (noun)
[Latin *advertere* = to turn one's attention to]

Similar words: publicize, promote, push, plug

advice
(noun) an opinion or suggestion from someone about what you should do.
[Latin *ad visum* = according to one's view]

Similar words: guidance, counselling, instruction

advisable
(adjective) sensible and likely to achieve the result you want, e.g. *It is advisable to take out medical insurance.*
advisability (noun)

advise, advises, advising, advised
1 (verb) If you advise someone to do something, you tell them that you think they should do it.
2 (formal) If you advise someone of something, you inform them of it.
adviser (noun) **advisory** (adjective)

Similar words: (sense 1) recommend, counsel, guide

aerial, aerials (pronounced **air**-ee-al)
1 (adjective) happening in the air or above the ground, e.g. *aerial photography.*

Adverbs end- *lly* only if the original adjective ended with *l*; faithfully, really BUT sincerely, merely.

2 (noun) a device for receiving television or radio signals.

aerobatics
(noun) skilful movements by a small aeroplane, e.g. diving and making loops.
aerobatic (adjective)

aerobics
(noun) a type of fast physical exercise, often to music.

aerodrome, aerodromes
(noun; rather old fashioned) a place where aeroplanes can land and take off.

aeronautics
(noun) the science of designing and building aircraft.
aeronautical (adjective)

aeroplane, aeroplanes
(noun) a vehicle with wings and engines that enable it to fly.

aerosol, aerosols
(noun) a metal container in which liquid is kept under pressure so that it can be forced out as a spray.

aerospace
(adjective) involved in making and designing aeroplanes, rockets and spacecraft.

affair, affairs
1 (noun) an event or series of events, e.g. *The wedding was a quiet affair.*
2 (plural noun) Your affairs are your private and personal life, e.g. *She meddled in his affairs.*
[Old French *afaire* = to do]

affect, affects, affecting, affected
(verb) If something affects you, it influences you or changes you in some way.
[Latin *afficere* = to act upon]

Similar words: influence, change

affection, affections
(noun) a feeling of love and fondness for someone.

affectionate
(adjective) full of love, care and fondness for someone, e.g. *an affectionate parent.*
affectionately (adverb)
[Latin *affiliare* = to adopt as a son]

affirmative
(adjective) a word or gesture that means yes.

afflict, afflicts, afflicting, afflicted
(verb) If pain, illness or sorrow afflicts someone, it causes them to suffer, e.g. *He had been afflicted with blindness.*
affliction (noun)
[Latin *affligere* = to knock against]

affluent
(adjective) having a lot of money and possessions.
affluence (noun)
[Latin *affluere* = to flow towards]

afford, affords, affording, afforded
1 (verb) If you can afford to do something, you have enough money to do it.

2 If you cannot afford something to happen, it would be harmful if it happened, e.g. *We can't afford to give another goal away.*
[Old English *geforthian* = to promote]

afloat
(adverb, adjective) floating on water.

afraid
(adjective) frightened.
[*affraied*, past participle of *affray* = to frighten]

Similar words: fearful, scared, anxious, apprehensive

African, Africans
1 (adjective) belonging or relating to Africa.
2 (noun) someone who comes from Africa.

afro, afros
(noun, adjective) a hairstyle in which hair is a great mass of very small curls.

aft
(adverb, adjective) towards the back of a ship or boat, e.g. *The guns were moved aft for safety.*

after
(preposition, adverb) e.g. *After lunch comes tea.*

afterbirth
(noun) the placenta and other membranes that come out of a female's womb soon after she has given birth.

afternoon, afternoons
(noun) e.g. *I'll see you this afternoon.*

afterwards
(adverb) after an event, date, or time.

again
(adverb) e.g. *Once again, it's hello from me!*

against
(preposition) e.g. *We are up against a good team.*

age, ages, ageing, aged
Selected meanings:
1 (phrase) When you **come of age**, you become legally an adult.
2 (noun) the quality of being old, e.g. *Age has great status in some cultures.*
3 (verb) to grow old or to appear older.
4 (noun) a particular period in history, e.g. *the Bronze Age.*
5 (plural noun; informal) Ages means a very long time, e.g. *I haven't seen you for ages.*

aged
1 (rhymes with **raged**) having a particular age, e.g. *women aged 60 and over.*
2 (pronounced ay-jid) very old, e.g. *his aged aunt.*

agency, agencies
(noun) an organization or business which provides services on behalf of other businesses, e.g. *an advertising agency.*
[Latin *agere* = to do]

agenda, agendas
(noun) a list of items to be discussed at a meeting.
[a Latin word meaning 'things to be done']

agent, agents
1 (noun) someone who arranges work or business for other people, e.g. for actors or singers.
2 someone who works for their country's secret service.

aggravate, aggravates, aggravating, aggravated
1 (verb) To aggravate a bad situation means to make it worse.
2 (informal) If someone or something aggravates you, they make you annoyed.
aggravating (adjective) **aggravation** (noun)
[Latin *aggravare* = to make heavier]

aggregate, aggregates
(noun) a total that is made up of several smaller amounts, e.g. *City won the cup tie on aggregate.*

aggression
(noun) violent and hostile behaviour.
aggressor (noun)
[Latin *aggressare* = to attack]

aggressive
1 (adjective) full of anger, hostility and violence.
2 determined and eager to succeed, e.g. *The aggressive salesman put his foot in the door.*
aggressively (adverb) **aggressiveness** (noun)

Similar words: (sense 1) hostile, belligerent, truculent

aggrieved
(adjective) upset and angry about the way you have been treated.

aghast (pronounced a-**gast**)
(adjective) shocked and horrified.
[Middle English *agast* = frightened]

agile
1 (adjective) able to move quickly and easily, e.g. *He was as agile as a monkey.*
2 quick and intelligent, e.g. *an agile mind.*
agilely (adverb) **agility** (noun)

agitated
(adjective) worried or shaken.
agitation (noun) **agitator** (noun) **agitate** (verb)

agnostic, agnostics
(noun, adjective) someone who believes that it is impossible to know definitely whether God exists or not.
agnosticism (noun)
[Greek *agnōstos* = unknown]

ago
(adverb) in the past, e.g. *We met two years ago.*

agony
(noun) very great physical or mental pain.
agonizing or **agonising** (adjective)
[Greek *agōnia* = struggle]

agree, agrees, agreeing, agreed
1 (verb) If you agree with someone, you have the same opinion as them.
2 If you agree to do something, you say that you will do it.
3 If two stories or totals agree, they are the same.
4 Food that doesn't agree with you makes you ill.
agreeable (adjective) **agreement** (noun)

agriculture
(noun) farming.
agricultural (adjective)
[Latin *ager* = field + *cultura* = culture]

aground
(adverb) If a boat goes aground, it is stuck in shallow water.

ahead
1 (adverb) in front, e.g. *She looked ahead.*
2 more advanced than someone or something else, e.g. *His research is ahead of the rest.*
3 in the future, e.g. *We need to plan ahead.*

aid, aids, aiding, aided
1 (noun) money or equipment that is provided for people in need, e.g. *foreign aid.*
2 help or support, e.g. *a report compiled with the aid of experts.*
3 something that makes a task easier, e.g. *Tapes and videos can be useful teaching aids.*
4 (verb; formal) to help or support someone.
[Latin *adjutare* = to help]

AIDS
(noun) a disease which destroys the body's natural system of immunity to diseases.
(acronym for 'acquired immune deficiency syndrome')

ailment, ailments
(noun) a minor illness.

aim, aims, aiming, aimed
1 (verb) If you aim an object or weapon at someone or something, you point it at them.
2 to plan to do something.
3 (noun) Your aim is what you intend to achieve.

Similar words: (verb: sense 1) point, direct, level
(verb: sense 2) aspire, intend
(noun:) goal, intention, purpose, ambition, intent, objective, aspiration, object, end, target

aimless
(adjective) having no clear purpose or plan.
aimlessly (adverb) **aimlessness** (noun)

air, airs, airing, aired
1 (noun) the mixture of oxygen and other gases which we breathe and which forms the earth's atmosphere.
2 (phrase) If a radio or TV programme is **on the air**, it is being broadcast.
3 (verb) to dry clothes gently in an enclosed space.
[Greek *aēr* = the lower atmosphere]

airborne
(adjective) in the air and flying, e.g. *The plane's wheels lifted off and we were airborne.*

air-conditioning
(noun) a system of providing cool, dry, clean air in buildings in summer, and warm air in winter.
air-conditioned (adjective)

aircraft
(noun) any vehicle which can fly.

aircraft carrier, carriers
(noun) a warship with a deck on which aircraft take off and land.

airfield, airfields
(noun) an open area of ground with runways where aircraft take off and land.

air force, forces
(noun) the part of a country's armed services that fights using aircraft, e.g. the R.A.F.

air gun, guns
(noun) a gun which fires pellets by air pressure.

Pun. St Peter: 'How did you get up to heaven?' — New Arrival: 'Flu!'

air hostess, hostesses
(noun) a woman whose job is to look after
passengers on an aircraft.

airing cupboard, cupboards
(noun) a warm, dry cupboard, usually containing
a hot-water tank, in which you can dry clothes.

airline, airlines
(noun) a company which provides air travel.

air mail
(noun) the system of sending letters etc. by air.

airman, airmen
(noun) a man who serves in an air force.

airport, airports
(noun) a place where people go to catch planes.

air raid, raids
(noun) an attack by enemy aircraft, in which
bombs are dropped.

airship, airships
(noun) a large, light aircraft, consisting of a rigid
balloon filled with gas and powered by an
engine, with a passenger compartment beneath.

airtight
(adjective) not letting air in or out.

air traffic control
(noun) an organization that directs air traffic by
giving instructions to pilots by radio about their
course and height.

aisle, aisles (rhymes with **mile**)
(noun) a long narrow gap that people can walk
along between rows of seats or shelves, e.g. in
church or in a cinema.
[Latin *ala* = wing]

ajar
(adjective) a door or window that is ajar is
slightly open.
[Old English *on char* = on the turn]

à la carte (rhymes with **tart**)
(adjective, adverb) An à la carte menu gives a
choice of dishes for each course of a meal.
[French phrase meaning 'according to the card']

alarm, alarms, alarming, alarmed
1 (noun) a feeling of fear, anxiety, and worry,
e.g. *She looked round in alarm.*
2 an automatic device used to warn people of
something, e.g. *fire alarms*
3 (verb) If something alarms you, it makes you
worried and anxious.
alarming (adjective)
[Italian *all'arme* = to arms]

alas
(interjection) sadly or unfortunately, e.g. *I am,
alas, unable to give you any marks for this.*

Albanian
1 (adjective) belonging to Albania.
2 (noun) someone who comes from Albania.

albatross, albatrosses
(noun) a large, white seabird with the largest
wingspan of any bird in the world.
[Portuguese *alcatraz* = pelican]

album, albums
1 (noun) a book in which you keep a collection of
things such as photographs or stamps.
2 another name for a long-playing record (L.P.)

alcohol
(noun) any drink that can make people drunk;
also the colourless, flammable liquid found in
these drinks, produced by fermenting sugar.

alcoholic, alcoholics
1 (adjective) An alcoholic drink contains alcohol.
2 (noun) someone who is addicted to alcohol.
alcoholism (noun)

alcove, alcoves
(noun) an area of a room set back slightly from
the main part.
[Arabic *al-qubbah* = arch]

alert, alerts, alerting, alerted
1 (adjective) paying full attention to what is
happening, e.g. *an alert guard dog.*
2 (noun) a situation in which people prepare
themselves for danger, e.g. *a nuclear alert.*
3 (verb) If you alert someone to a problem or
danger, you warn them of it.
alertness (noun)

Similar words: (adjective) watchful, vigilant, attentive

algae (pronounced **al-jee**)
(plural noun) plants without roots, leaves or
stems that grow in water or on damp surfaces.
[Latin *alga* = seaweed]

algebra
(noun) a branch of maths in which symbols and
letters are used instead of numbers, to express
general relationships between quantities.
algebraic (adjective)
[Arabic *al-jabr* = reunion]

algorithm, algorithms
(noun) a mathematical procedure for solving a
particular problem.
[from *al-Khuwarizmi*, the name of a 9th-century
Arab mathematician]

alias, aliases (pronounced **ay-lee-ass**)
(noun) a false name used by a criminal, e.g.
James Smith, alias John Jones.
[Latin *alias* = otherwise]

Similar word: pseudonym

alibi, alibis (pronounced **al-li-bye**)
(noun) evidence proving that you were
somewhere else when a crime was committed.
[Latin *alibi* = elsewhere]

alien, aliens (pronounced **ay-lee-an**)
1 (adjective) not normal, and therefore strange
and slightly frightening, e.g. *a totally alien
environment and culture.*
2 (noun) someone who is not a citizen of the
country in which he or she lives.
3 In science fiction, an alien is a creature from
outer space.
[Latin *alienus* = foreign]

alike
1 (adjective) similar.

When 'the' comes before a word beginning with a vowel, it is pronounced 'thee': the air, the oak.

2 (adverb) If people or things are treated alike, they are treated in a similar way.

alive
1 (adjective) living.
2 lively and active, and full of interest.

alkali, alkalis
(noun) Alkalis are watery liquids of many different types. They can cause chemical changes, e.g. colour change. How alkaline something is, is measured in pH numbers. Water has a pH of 7 and alkalis have a pH of more than this. Alkalis have many industrial, medical and household uses. They are the chemical opposites of acids.
alkaline (adjective) **alkalinity** (noun)
[Arabic *al-qili* = ashes]

all
(adjective, adverb) e.g. *Put it all back.*

Allah
(proper noun) the Muslim name for God.

allege, alleges, alleging, alleged (pronounced a-**lej**)
(verb) If you allege that something is true, you say it is true but do not provide any proof, e.g. *They alleged that she had stolen the ring.*
allegation (noun) **alleged** (adjective)

allegiance, allegiances (pronounced al-**lee**-jenss)
(noun) loyal support for a person or organization, e.g. *My allegiance is to Spurs.*

alleluia, alleluias (pronounced al-li-**loo**-yah)
(interjection, noun) an exclamation of praise and thanks to God.
[a Hebrew word]

allergic, (pronounced al-**er**-jic)
(adjective) When someone is allergic to something, they become ill when they eat it or are exposed to it.
allergy (noun)

alley, alleys
(noun) a narrow passage between buildings.
[Old French *aler* = to go]

alliance, alliances
(noun) a group of people, organizations, or countries working together for similar aims.

Similar words: association, league, union

allied
(adjective) united by political or military agreements, e.g. *the Allied forces.*

alligator, alligators
(noun) a large reptile, similar to a crocodile, with powerful jaws, sharp teeth and a strong tail.
[Spanish *el lagarto* = lizard]

alliteration
(noun; literary) the use of several words together which all begin with or include the same sound, e.g. 'the forest's ferny floor'.
alliterative (adjective)

allocate, allocates, allocating, allocated
(verb) If you allocate something, you decide that it should be given to a person or place, or used for a particular purpose, e.g. *Modern houses had been allocated to people with young children.*
allocation (noun)

allotment, allotments
(noun) a piece of land which people can rent, usually to grow vegetables on.

allow, allows, allowing, allowed
1 (verb) If you allow something to happen, you let it happen.
2 If you allow a period of time or an amount of something, you set it aside for a particular purpose, e.g. *Allow 4 metres for the skirt... She allowed two hours for the journey.*
allowable (adjective)

allowance, allowances
1 (noun) money that is given regularly to someone for a particular purpose. Pocket money is a sort of allowance.
2 (phrase) If you **make allowances** for something, you take it into account in your plans or actions, e.g. *They made no allowances for his age.*

alloy, alloys
(noun) a mixture of two or more metals.
[Old French *aloier* = to combine]

all right or alright
(adjective) e.g. *Are you all right, Mrs Day?*
[Some people say that **all right** is the only correct spelling.]

all-rounder, all-rounders
(noun) someone who is good at lots of different things, especially in sport.

ally, allies, allying, allied (pronounced **al**-eye)
1 (noun) a person, organization or country that helps and supports another.
2 (verb) [pronounced al-**lie**] If you ally yourself with someone you agree to help and support each other.

almighty
1 (adjective) very great or serious, e.g. *She made the most almighty fuss.*
2 (proper noun) The Almighty is a name for God.

almond, almonds
(noun) a pale, brown, oval nut.

almost
(adverb) very nearly, but not completely.

Similar words: nearly, all but, practically, virtually

alone
(adjective, adverb) not with other people or things.

Similar words: solitary, lonely, unaccompanied

along
(preposition) e.g. *She ran along the road.*

aloof
(adjective) separate from someone or something, distant, and not involved with them.

aloud
(adverb) When you read or speak aloud, you speak loudly enough for other people to hear you.

Similar words: out loud, audibly

Some poets like to use *alliteration*, i.e. repeating the same consonant sound several times in a line.

alphabet, alphabets
(noun) a set of letters in a fixed order.
alphabetical (adjective) **alphabetically** (adverb)
[from *alpha* + *beta*, the first two letters of the
Greek alphabet]

already
(adverb) in the process of, e.g. *The teacher had
already started when the girl came in.* (Not to be
confused with **all ready**, e.g. *We were all ready to
go, but the car wouldn't start.*

alright another spelling of **all right.**

alsatian
(noun) a breed of rough-haired dog, often used as
a guard dog.

also
(adverb) as well, e.g. *Bill was also with us.*

altar, altars
(noun) a special table in a church or temple used
for religious services.

alter, alters, altering, altered
(verb) to change.
alteration (noun)

alternate, alternates, alternating, alternated
1 (verb; pronounced ol-turn-**ate**) If one thing
alternates with another, the two things regularly
occur one after the other.
2 (adjective; pronounced ol-**turn-ut**) If an
event happens on alternate days, it happens on
the 1st day but not the 2nd, on the 3rd day but
not the 4th, and so on, e.g. *We meet on alternate
Mondays.*
alternately (adverb) **alternation** (noun)

alternative, alternatives
1 (noun) something that you can do or have
instead of something else, e.g. *Margarine is an
alternative to butter.*
2 (adjective) Alternative plans etc. can happen
instead of what is already planned.
alternatively (adverb)

although
(conjunction) in spite of the fact of, e.g. *Although
we were poor, we were happy.*

altitude, altitudes
(noun) height above sea level, e.g. *The plane
climbed to an altitude of 31,000 feet.*
[Latin *altus* = high]

altogether
(adverb) completely, e.g. *It was altogether too
hard for me.* (Not to be confused with **all
together**, e.g. *The children were all together in
the kitchen).*

aluminium
(noun) a light silvery-white metal used to make
aircraft and other equipment.

always
(adverb) all the time; for ever, e.g. *I shall always
love you.* (Not to be confused with **all ways**, e.g.
They found that all ways to town were blocked.)

amateur, amateurs
(noun) someone who does something as a hobby
rather than as a job and is not paid.
[Latin *amator* = lover]

amateurish
(adjective) not skilfully made or done.
amateurishly (adverb)

amazing
(adjective) very surprising, remarkable or
difficult to believe.
amaze (verb) **amazement** (noun)
amazingly (adverb)

Similar words: incredible, fabulous, wonderful

ambassador, ambassadors
(noun) a person sent to a foreign country as the
representative of their own government.

ambiguous
(adjective) a word or phrase that is ambiguous
has more than one meaning. e.g. *I shall waste no
time reading your book* is an ambiguous
statement.
ambiguously (adjective) **ambiguity** (noun)

ambition, ambitions
(noun) If you have an ambition to achieve
something, you want very much to do it.

ambitious
1 (adjective) Someone who is ambitious has a
strong desire for success, power, and wealth.
2 An ambitious plan or project is on a large scale
and requires a lot of effort and work, e.g. *an
ambitious development programme.*

amble, ambles, ambling, ambled
(verb) to walk slowly in a relaxed manner.
[Latin *ambulare* = to walk]

ambulance, ambulances
(noun) a vehicle for taking sick and injured
people to hospital.

ambush, ambushes, ambushing, ambushed
(verb) to attack someone after hiding and lying
in wait for them.
[Old French *embuschier* = to hide in a wood]

ameba (noun) another spelling of **amoeba**

amen
(interjection) A word said by Christians at the
end of a prayer. It means 'so be it'.
[a Hebrew word]

amenable (pronounced am-**mee**-na-bl)
(adjective) willing to listen to comments and
suggestions, or to co-operate with someone, e.g.
He was amenable to running the errand.
amenably (adverb) **amenability** (noun)

amend, amends, amending, amended
1 (verb) to change something slightly, e.g. *Last
year the rules were amended.*
2 (plural noun) If you make amends for
something bad that you have done, you say you
are sorry and try to make up for it in some way.
amendment (noun)

amenity, amenities (pronounced am-**mee**-nit-ee)
(noun) something that is available for the public
to use, such as sports facilities, a cinema or a
shopping centre.

From Alpha to Omega (first and last letters of the Greek alphabet) means 'from beginning to end'.

American, Americans
1 (adjective) belonging to the United States, or to the whole of North, South and Central America.
2 (noun) someone who comes from the U.S.A.

amiable
(adjective) pleasant, friendly and kind, e.g. *He was in an amiable mood.*
amiably (adverb) **amiability** (noun)

amicable
(adjective) friendly.
amicably (adverb)
[Latin *amicus* = friend]

ammunition
(noun) anything that can be used in fighting, especially that can be fired from a gun or other weapon, e.g. bullets, rockets, and shells.

amnesty
(noun) an official pardon for political or other prisoners, or a chance to hand in something illegal without being punished, e.g. *The New York police had a weapons amnesty.*
[Greek *amnestos* = forgetting]

amoeba, amoebas or amoebae (pronounced am-**mee**-ba; also spelled **ameba**)
(noun) the smallest kind of living creature, with one cell, which reproduces by dividing into two.
[Greek *amoibē* = change]

amok (pronounced a-**muk**)
(phrase) If a person or animal **runs amok**, they behave in a violent and uncontrolled way.
[a Malay word]

among or **amongst**
(preposition) surrounded by; included with.

Similar words: amid, amidst

amount, amounts, amounting, amounted
1 (noun) how much there is of something.
2 (verb) If something amounts to a particular total, all the parts of it add up to that total, e.g. *fees which amounted to £2,000...*

Similar words: (noun) quantity, measure, degree

amp, amps
(noun) An amp is the same as an ampère, a unit of electrical current, named after the French physicist A.M. Ampère.

amphibian, amphibians
(noun) a creature that lives partly on land and partly in water, e.g. frogs, toads and newts.

amphibious
1 (adjective) living partly on land and partly in water.
2 An amphibious vehicle is able to move on both land and water.
[Greek *amphibios* = having a double life]

ample
(adjective) If there is an ample amount of something, there is more than enough of it.
amply (adverb)

amplifier, amplifiers
(noun) a piece of equipment in a sound system that causes sounds or signals to become louder.

amplify, amplifies, amplifying, amplified
(verb) If you amplify a sound, you make it louder.
amplification (noun)

amputate, amputates, amputating, amputated
(verb) To amputate an arm or a leg means to cut it off in a surgical operation.
amputation (noun)
[Latin *putare* = to trim]

amuse, amuses, amusing, amused
1 (verb) If something amuses you, you think it is funny.
2 If you amuse yourself, you find things to do which stop you from being bored.
amusement (noun) **amused** (adjective) **amusing** (adjective)

an
(indefinite article) e.g. *an elephant.*

anaesthetic, anaesthetics (pronounced an-niss-**thet**-ik; also spelled **anesthetic**)
(noun) a substance that stops you feeling pain. A general anaesthetic puts you to sleep, and a local anaesthetic makes one part of your body go numb.
anaesthetist (noun) **anaesthetize** (verb)
[Greek *anaisthēsia* = lack of feeling]

anagram, anagrams
(noun) word or phrase formed by reordering the letters of another word or phrase e.g. 'Triangle' is an anagram of 'integral'.

analogy, analogies (pronounced an-al-o-jee)
(noun) a comparison showing that two things are similar in some ways.
analogous (adjective)

analyse, analyses, analysing, analysed
(verb) to investigate something carefully to understand it or find out what it is made up of.
analysis (noun)
[Greek *analusis* = dissolving]

anatomy
1 (noun) the study of the structure of the human body or of the bodies of animals.
2 An animal's anatomy is the structure of its body.
anatomical (adjective) **anatomically** (adverb)
[Greek *anatemnein* = to dissect]

ancestor, ancestors
(noun) Your ancestors are previous members of your family from whom you are descended.
ancestral (adjective)
[Latin *antecessor* = one who goes before]

ancestry
(noun) Your ancestry consists of the people from whom you are descended, e.g. *American citizens of Irish ancestry.*

Similar word: pedigree

anchor
(noun) a heavy, hooked object that is lowered by a chain from a boat into the water to keep the boat in one place.

anchorage, anchorages
(noun) a place where a boat can safely anchor.

a before a word beginning with a vowel becomes an, e.g. an umbrella, an artistic pupil.

ancient (pronounced **ayn**-shent)
1 (adjective) existing or happening in the distant past, e.g. *ancient Greece and Rome.*
2 very old or having a very long history, e.g. *an ancient Roman Catholic family.*

anecdote, anecdotes
(noun) a short, entertaining story about a person or event.
anecdotal (adjective)
[Greek *anekdotos* = unpublished]

anemometer, anemometers
(noun) an instrument used for recording the speed and direction of winds.

anesthetic another spelling of **anaesthetic**

angel, angels
(noun) spiritual beings that some people believe live in heaven and act as messengers for God.
angelic (adjective)
[Greek *angelos* = messenger]

anger, angers, angering, angered
1 (noun) the feeling of being angry.
2 (verb) If something angers you, it makes you feel angry.

Similar words: (noun) fury, rage, wrath
(verb) enrage, infuriate, incense, madden

angle, angles
1 (noun) the distance measured in degrees between two lines at the point where they join together. It is a measure of how far one line must turn to become another.
2 the direction from which you look at something, e.g. *The house was photographed from all angles.*
3 (phrase) If something is **at an angle**, it is not in a vertical or horizontal position, e.g. *an old table leaning at an angle.*

Anglican, Anglicans
(noun, adjective) a member of one of the Protestant churches which includes the Church of England.
[Latin *Anglicus* = English]

angling
(noun) the sport of fishing.
angler (noun)
[Old English *angul* = fish-hook]

Anglo-
(prefix) involving England or Britain, e.g. *the Anglo-Irish treaty.*

Anglo-Saxon
(noun) another name for **Old English.**

angry, angrier, angriest
(adjective) very cross or annoyed.

Similar words: furious, enraged, infuriated

anguish
(noun) extreme mental or physical suffering.
anguished (adjective)
[Old French *angoisse* = strangling]

angular
(adjective) Angular things have straight lines and sharp points, e.g. *his angular face.*

animal, animals
(noun) any living being except a plant, or any mammal except a human being.
[Latin *anima* = life or soul]

Similar words: brute, beast, creature

animate
(adjective) Something which is animate has life, in contrast to inanimate things like stones or machines that do not have life.

animated
1 (adjective) lively and interesting, e.g. *an animated discussion.*
animatedly (adverb)
2 An animated film has been made using animation, e.g. *an animated cartoon.*
animate (verb)

animation
1 (noun) a method of film-making in which a series of drawings is photographed. When the film is projected, the characters in the drawings appear to move, e.g. a cartoon.
animator (noun)
2 Someone who has animation shows liveliness in the way they speak and act, e.g. *She talked with animation about her scooter.*

animosity, animosities
(noun) a feeling of strong dislike and anger towards someone.

ankle, ankles
(noun) the joint, made up of 7 bones, which connects your foot to your leg.

annex; also spelled **annexe**
1 (noun) an extra building which is joined to or nearby a larger main building.
2 (verb) to take possession of land by force, e.g. *In 1938 Hitler annexed Austria.*

annihilate, annihilates, annihilating, annihilated (pronounced an-**nye**-ill-ate)
(verb) to destroy completely.
annihilation (noun)
[Latin *annihilare* = to bring to nothing]

anniversary, anniversaries
(noun) a date which is remembered or celebrated because something special happened on that date in a previous year.
[Latin *anniversarius* = returning annually]

announce, announces, announcing, announced
(verb) If you announce something, you tell people about it publicly or officially, e.g. *The Prime Minister announced his resignation.*
announcement (noun) **announcer** (noun)
[Latin *nuntius* = messenger]

Similar words: broadcast, proclaim

annoy, annoys, annoying, annoyed
(verb) If someone or something annoys you, they irritate you and make you fairly angry.
annoyance (noun) **annoyed** (adjective)

annual, annuals
1 (adjective) happening every year or once a year, e.g. *her annual holiday.*

When is it a good thing to lose your temper? When it is a bad one.

2 happening or calculated over a period of one year, e.g. *an annual income of £12,000.*
3 (noun) a book or magazine published regularly once a year.
4 a plant that grows and dies within a year.
annually (adverb)
[Latin *annus* = year]

anonymous
(adjective) If something is anonymous, nobody knows who did it or who is responsible for it, e.g. *The donor preferred to remain anonymous.*
anonymously (adverb) **anonymity** (noun)

anorak, anoraks
(noun) a warm, waterproof jacket, with a hood.
[an Inuit (Eskimo) word]

another
(pronoun, adjective) e.g. *just another one.*

answer, answers, answering, answered
1 (verb) If you answer someone, you reply to them using words or actions or in writing.
2 (noun) a reply.
3 (phrase) If you say that someone has **a lot to answer for,** you mean that they are responsible for a lot of trouble.

Similar words: (verb) respond (noun) response

ante-
(prefix) before.

antelope, antelopes
(noun) a deer-like animal.

antenna, antennae or antennas
1 (noun) the two long, thin parts attached to the heads of insects etc. which they use to feel with. (plural: antennae)
2 an aerial for radio etc. (plural: antennas).

anthem, anthems
(noun) a hymn written for a special occasion such as a coronation, e.g.*the National Anthem.*

anthology, anthologies
(noun) a collection of poems, songs, or extracts from literature written by various authors and published in one book.
[Greek *anthologia* = flower gathering]

anthropology
(noun) the study of human beings and their society and culture.
anthropological (adjective) **anthropologist** (noun)
[Greek *anthrōpos* = human being]

anti-
(prefix) opposed to, against, or opposite to something, e.g. *an anti-nuclear demonstration.*

antibiotic, antibiotics
(noun) drug or chemical that is used in medicines to kill bacteria and cure infections, e.g.penicillin.

antibody, antibodies
(noun) Antibodies are proteins produced in the blood which protect against disease.

anticipate, anticipates, anticipating, anticipated
(verb) If you anticipate an event, you are expecting it and are prepared for it, e.g. *The secretary had anticipated the question.*
anticipation (noun)
[Latin *anticipare* = to take before]

anticlockwise
(adjective, adverb) moving in the opposite direction to the hands of a clock.

antics
(plural noun) funny or silly ways of behaving.

anticyclone, anticyclones
(noun) an area of high air pressure which usually causes settled weather.

antidote, antidotes
(noun) a chemical substance that works against the effect of a poison.

antifreeze
(noun) a substance added to the water in a car radiator to stop it freezing.

antiperspirant, antiperspirants
(noun) a substance which stops you sweating when you put it on your skin.

antiquated
(adjective) very old-fashioned and out of date.
antiquity (noun)

antique, antiques (pronounced an-**teek**)
1 (noun) an object from the past that is collected because of its value, beauty or interest.
2 (adjective) from or concerning the past, e.g. *antique furniture.*

antiseptic
(noun) substance used to kill germs.

antisocial
1 (adjective) Antisocial behaviour is annoying or upsetting to other people, e.g. *Smoking is often antisocial in confined spaces.*
2 An antisocial person is unwilling to meet and be friendly with other people.

antler, antlers
(noun) the horns on the head of a male deer.

antonym, antonyms
(noun) a word which means the opposite of another word, e.g.'Hot' is the antonym of 'cold'.
[*anti-* = opposite + Greek *onoma* = name]

anus, anuses
(noun) the opening at the end of the digestive system where solid waste leaves the body.

anvil, anvils
(noun) a heavy iron block on which hot metal is beaten into shape.

anxiety, anxieties
(noun) nervousness or worry.

anxious
1 (adjective) nervous or worried.
2 If you are anxious to do something or anxious that something should happen, you very much want to do it or want it to happen.
anxiously (adverb)

any
(adverb, pronoun) e.g. *Have you any more?*

anybody
(pronoun) e.g. *Is anybody here?*

What is the antonym of 'synonym'?

anyhow
1 (adverb) in any case.
2 in a careless or untidy way, e.g. *They were packed together anyhow.*

anyone
(pronoun) e.g. *Anyone for tennis?*

anything
(pronoun) e.g. *Anything will do, please.*

anyway
(adverb) e.g. *Anyway, as I was saying...*

anywhere
(adverb) e.g. *Go anywhere you like.*

apart
1 (adverb, adjective) When something is apart from something else, there is a space or a distance between them, e.g. *They lived apart from each other... The cars were two feet apart.*
2 (adverb) If you take something apart, you separate it into pieces.

Similar words: (sense 1) separate, asunder

apartheid (pronounced a-**part**-hate)
(noun) In South Africa, apartheid is the government policy and laws which keep people of different races apart.
[an Afrikaans word]

apartment, apartments
(noun) a set of rooms for living in, usually on one floor of a building.

apathetic
(adjective) not interested in anything.
apathetically (adverb)

Similar words: indifferent, uninterested, half-hearted

apathy (pronounced **ap**-path-ee)
(noun) a state of mind in which you do not care about anything.
[Greek *apathēs* = without feeling]

ape, apes, aping, aped
1 (noun) primate with a very short tail or no tail, closely related to man, e.g. gorilla, chimpanzee.
2 (verb) If you ape someone's speech or behaviour, you imitate it.

aperture, apertures (pronounced **app**-er-chure)
(noun) a narrow hole or opening. It is also the setting of a camera lens according to the amount of light available, e.g. *f 8, f16.*

apex, apexes or **apices**
(noun) The apex of something is its pointed top.

aphid, aphids
(noun) a small insect that feeds by sucking the juices from plants.

aphorism, aphorisms
(noun) a short, clever sentence that expresses a general truth, e.g. *More haste, less speed.*

apiary, apiaries (pronounced **ape**-yer-ee)
(noun) a place where bees are kept.
[Latin *apis* = bee]

apologize, apologizes, apologizing, apologized;
also spelled **apologise**
(verb) to say you are sorry for something you have said or done.

apology (noun) **apologetic** (adjective)
apologetically (adverb)

apostle, apostles
(noun) The Apostles are the twelve disciples who were chosen by Christ.
apostolic (adjective)
[Greek *apostolos* = messenger]

apostrophe, apostrophes
(pronounced ap-**poss**-troff-ee)
(noun) a punctuation mark used to show that one or more letters have been missed out of a word, e.g. *he's = he is.* Apostrophes are also used with -s at the end of a noun to show that what follows belongs to the noun, e.g. *my brother's books.* If the noun has an -s at the end because it is plural, you just add the apostrophe, e.g. *the twins' books.*

appalling
(adjective) shockingly bad, e.g. *They lived in appalling conditions.*
appal (verb)
[Old French *apalir* = to turn pale]

apparatus
(noun) the equipment used for a particular task.
[Latin *apparare* = to make ready]

apparent
1 (adjective) seeming real rather than actually being real.
2 clear and obvious, e.g. *It became apparent that she wasn't going to turn up.*
apparently (adverb)
[Latin *apparere* = to appear]

apparition, apparitions
(noun) something that you think you see but that is not really there.

appeal, appeals, appealing, appealed
1 (verb) If you appeal for something, you make a serious and urgent request for it, e.g. *The police appealed for calm as the crowd panicked.*
2 If you appeal to someone in authority against a decision, you formally ask them to change it.
3 If something appeals to you, you find it attractive or interesting.
4 (noun) the quality something has which people find attractive or interesting, e.g. *What is the appeal of water polo?*
appealing (adjective)

appear, appears, appearing, appeared
1 (verb) to move into view.
2 When an actor or actress appears in a film, play or show, they take part in it.
3 If something appears to be a certain way, it looks that way, e.g. *He appeared to be having a good time.*
appearance (noun)

Similar words: (sense 1) show, emerge, turn up

appendicitis (pronounced app-end-i-**site**-uss)
(noun) a painful illness in which a person's appendix becomes infected.

appendix, appendices
1 (noun) a small closed tube forming part of your digestive system. It is not used.

The apostrophe ' is used when a word or pair of words is shortened: don't, wouldn't, let's, o'er....

2 An appendix to a book is extra information that is placed after the end of the main text.
[a Latin word meaning 'appendage']

appetite, appetites
1 (noun) the desire to eat.
2 a strong desire for something and enjoyment of it, e.g. *He has an amazing appetite for work.*
[Latin *appetere* = to desire]

appetizing or **appetising**
(adjective) Food that is appetizing looks and smells good, and makes you want to eat it.

applaud, applauds, applauding, applauded
1 (verb) When people applaud, they clap their hands in approval or praise.
2 to praise something.
[Latin *applaudere* = to clap]

applause
(noun) clapping by a group of people.

apple, apples
(noun) a round fruit with smooth skin and firm white flesh.

appliance, appliances
(noun) any device or machine that is designed to do a particular job, especially in the home, e.g. *A fridge is an electrical appliance.*

applicable
(adjective) relevant, e.g. *This rule is applicable only to Year 8.*

applicant, applicants
(noun) someone who is applying for something, e.g. *There were 20 applicants for the job.*

application, applications
1 (noun) a formal request for something, usually in writing, e.g. *Put in an application for it.*
2 The application of a rule, system, or skill is the use of it in a particular situation.
3 To do something with application means to do it with a lot of hard work and concentration.

applied
(adjective) to do with or designed for practical use, e.g. *applied mathematics.*

apply, applies, applying, applied
1 (verb) to ask for something formally, usually by writing a letter.
2 If you apply a rule, system or skill, you use it in a situation or an activity, e.g. *She applied her common sense to the problem.*
3 If something applies to a person or a situation, it is relevant to that person or situation, e.g. *The rule applies only to car drivers.*
4 If you apply something to a surface, you put it on, e.g. *Apply the glue to the corners.*

appoint, appoints, appointing, appointed
1 (verb) If you appoint someone to a job or position, you formally choose them for it.
2 If you appoint a time or place for something to happen, you decide when or where it will happen.
appointed (adjective)
[Old French *apointier* = to arrange]

appointment, appointments
1 (noun) an arrangement you have with someone to meet or visit them.
2 the choosing of a person to do a particular job.
3 a job or position of responsibility, e.g. *She has applied for an appointment in London.*

Similar words: (sense 1) engagement, date, booking

appraisal
(noun) careful thought and opinion about someone or something.
appraise (verb)

appreciate, appreciates, appreciating, appreciated
1 (verb) to recognize the good qualities of something, e.g. *She appreciates good food.*
2 to understand a situation or problem.
3 If you appreciate something that someone has done for you, you are grateful to them for it, e.g. *I really appreciate your coming to visit me.*
appreciative (adjective)
4 to increase in value, e.g. *The value of the old car appreciated by 50% in six months.*
appreciation (noun)
[Latin *pretium* = price]

apprentice, apprentices
(noun) a person who, for a period of time, learns a skill or trade by working with a craftsman and attending college.
apprenticeship (noun)
[Old French *aprendre* = to learn]

approach, approaches, approaching, approached
1 (verb) to come nearer.
2 (noun) the process of coming closer, e.g. *In October, we felt the approach of winter.*
3 (verb) If you approach someone about something, you ask them about it.
4 (noun) An approach to a situation or problem is a way of thinking about it or dealing with it, e.g. *A calm approach to chess works best.*
5 a road or path that leads to a place, e.g. *the station approach.*

appropriate, appropriates, appropriating, appropriated
1 (adjective) suitable or acceptable, e.g. *Jeans are not appropriate for a formal dinner party.*
2 (verb) to take something without permission.
appropriately (adverb) **appropriation** (noun)
[Latin *appropriare* = to make one's own]

approval
1 (noun) agreement given to a plan or request, e.g. *The plan has government approval.*
2 admiration for someone, e.g. *Janet looked at her young son with approval.*

Similar words: (sense 1) authorization, blessing, OK

approve, approves, approving, approved
1 (verb) If you approve of something, you think that it is right or good.
2 If you approve of someone, you like them and think they are all right, e.g. *My parents approve of my new girlfriend.*

....The apostrophe is used to show how the noun that follows relates to its owner: my friend's house.

3 If someone in a position of authority approves a plan or idea, they formally agree to it.
approved (adjective) **approving** (adjective)
[Latin *probare* = to test]

Similar words: (sense 1) applaud, commend (sense 3) authorize

approximate
(adjective) almost accurate or exact, e.g. *The approximate value of the house is £90,000.*
approximately (adverb) **approximate** (verb)
[Latin *proximus* = nearest]

Similar words: close, near, rough

apricot, apricots
(noun) a small, soft, yellowish-orange fruit.
[Latin *praecox* = early ripening]

April
(noun) the 4th month of the year.

apron, aprons
1 (noun) a piece of clothing worn over the front of normal clothing to protect it.
2 a hard-surfaced area in front of an aircraft hangar or terminal building.
3 part of the stage which juts into the audience.
[Middle English *a napron* = small table cloth]

apt
1 (adjective) suitable or relevant, e.g. *It was a very apt remark for that situation.*
2 having a particular tendency to do something, e.g. *He's apt to make silly remarks in public.*
3 You can describe a person as apt when they have an ability to learn quickly, e.g. *an apt pupil.*

aptitude
(noun) the ability to learn quickly and to do something well, e.g. *She has an aptitude for maths.*

aqualung, aqualungs
(noun) a piece of equipment used by divers to enable them to breathe under water.

aquarium, aquaria or aquariums
(noun) a glass tank in which fish are kept.
[Latin *aqua* = water]

aquatic
1 (adjective) living or growing in water.
2 involving water, e.g. *aquatic sports.*

aqueduct, aqueducts
(noun) a bridge carrying water.

Arab, Arabs
(noun) a member of a group of people who used to live in Arabia but who now live throughout the Middle East and North Africa.

Arabic
(noun) a language spoken by many people in the Middle East and North Africa.

arable
(adjective) Arable land has crops grown on it.

arbitrate, arbitrates, arbitrating, arbitrated
(verb) When someone arbitrates between two people or groups who are in disagreement, they consider the facts and decide who is right.
arbitration (noun) **arbitrator** (noun)

arc, arcs
1 (noun) a smoothly curving line.
2 In geometry, an arc is a section of the circumference of a circle.
[Latin *arcus* = bow]

arcade, arcades
1 (noun) a covered passageway, usually where there are shops or market stalls.
2 An amusement arcade is a place where there are slot machines, video games, etc.

arch
1 (noun) a structure that has a curved top supported on either side by a pillar or wall.
2 (adjective) most important, e.g. *Moriarty was the arch-enemy of Sherlock Holmes.*

archaeology or archeology (pronounced ar-kee-ol-loj-ee)
(noun) the study of the past by digging up and examining the remains of buildings, tools, etc.
archaeological (adjective) **archaeology** (noun)
[Greek *arkhaios* = ancient]

archbishop, archbishops
(noun) a bishop of the highest rank in a Christian Church.

archeology another spelling of archaeology.

archery
(noun) a sport in which people shoot at targets with bows and arrows.

architect, architects (pronounced ar-kit-tekt)
(noun) a person who designs buildings.
[Greek *arkhitektōn* = chief builder]

architecture
(noun) the art or practice of designing buildings.
architectural (adjective)

archive, archives (pronounced ar-kive)
(noun) a collection of documents and records about the history of a family, organization, etc.

arctic
(adjective) very cold indeed, e.g. *arctic temperatures.*
[Greek *arktos* = bear; originally it referred to the northern constellation of the Great Bear]

ardent
(adjective) full of enthusiasm and passion, e.g. *She was an ardent Rangers fan.*
ardently (adverb)
[Latin *ardere* = to burn]

arduous (pronounced ard-yoo-uss)
(adjective) tiring and needing a lot of effort.

area, areas
1 (noun) a particular part of a place, country or the world, e.g. *a run-down area of London.*
2 The area of a piece of ground or a surface is the amount of space that it covers, measured in, for example, square feet or square metres.
3 An area of knowledge, interest or activity is a particular kind of subject or activity.
[a Latin word meaning 'piece of flat ground']

Similar words: (sense 1) district, locality, neighbourhood, vicinity, zone

---

We take these words from Arabic: assassin orange algebra zero alcohol sofa mattress magazine.

arena, arenas
(noun) a place where sports and other public events take place.
[Latin *harena* = sand, hence the sandy centre of an amphitheatre where gladiators fought]

Argentinian, Argentinians (pronounced ar-jen-**tin**-ee-an)
1 (adjective) belonging to Argentina.
2 (noun) someone who comes from Argentina.

argon
(noun) a chemical element found as a colourless, odourless gas in the air.

argue, argues, arguing, argued
1 (verb) If you argue that something is the case, you give reasons why you think it is so, e.g. *Some people argue that the NHS should be abolished.*
2 to disagree, sometimes in an angry way.
[Latin *arguere* = to make clear or to accuse]

argument, arguments
1 (noun) a disagreement between people which causes a quarrel.
2 a point or a set of reasons that you use to try to convince people about something.
argumentative (adjective)

arid
(adjective) Arid land is very dry because it has very little rain.
aridity (noun)

arise, arises, arising, arose, arisen
1 (verb) When something, for example a problem, arises, it begins to exist.
2 to stand up from a sitting, kneeling or lying position, e.g. *Arise, Sir Lancelot!*

aristocrat, aristocrats
(noun) someone whose family has a high social rank, and who has a title, e.g. Lord Snooty.
aristocratic (adjective) **aristocracy** (noun)
[Greek *aristos* = best]

arithmetic
(noun) the part of maths to do with the addition, subtraction, multiplication and division of numbers.
arithmetic (adjective) **arithmetically** (adverb)
[Greek *arithmos* = number]

ark
1 (noun) the boat built by Noah for his family and the animals during the Flood.
2 The Ark of the Covenant was the symbol of the presence of God to the Hebrew people. It was a box covered with gold.
[sense 2 – Latin *arca* = box]

arm, arms
1 (noun) the part of the body between the shoulder and the wrist.
2 (plural noun) Arms are weapons used in a war.

armada, armadas (pronounced ar-**mah**-da)
(noun) a large fleet of warships.
[a Spanish word; *The Spanish Armada, 1588.*]

armadillo, armadillos
(noun) a mammal from South America covered with strong bony plates like armour.
[a Spanish word meaning 'little armed man']

armchair, armchairs
(noun) a comfortable chair with a support on each side for your arms.

armed
1 (adjective) carrying a weapon or weapons.
2 If you are armed with, e.g. information, skill or a tool, you have it ready to be used, e.g. *Armed with spanners he went to mend his bike.*

armistice, armistices (pronounced ar-**miss**-tiss)
(noun) an agreement in a war to stop fighting.
[Latin *arma* = weapons + *sistere* = to stop.]

armour
(noun) metal clothing worn in the past for protection in battle.
armoured (adjective)

armour-plate
(noun) a heavy, tough steel used for protecting warships and tanks.

armpit, armpits
(noun) the area under the arm where the arm joins the shoulder.

army, armies
(noun) a large group of soldiers for fighting on land.
[Latin *armata* = armed forces]

aroma, aromas
(noun) a strong, pleasant smell.
aromatic (adjective)
[a Greek word meaning 'spice']

around
(preposition, adverb) e.g. *Look around you.*

arouse, arouse, arousing, aroused
1 (verb) If something arouses a feeling in you, it makes you begin to have this feeling, e.g. *The letter aroused in me a strong feeling of jealousy.*
2 When something or someone arouses you from sleep, they wake you up.
arousal (noun)

arrange, arranges, arranging, arranged
1 (verb) If you arrange to do something, you make plans for it.
2 If you arrange something for someone, you make it possible for them to have it or do it, e.g. *The bank manager has arranged a loan for me.*
3 If you arrange objects, you set them out in a particular position, e.g. *The chairs were arranged in a circle.*
arrangement (noun)
[Old French *arangier* = to put in a row]

array, arrays
(noun) a large number of different things displayed together, e.g. *an array of models.*
[Old French *arayer* = to arrange]

arrears
(plural noun) amounts of money that you owe, e.g. *She had 3 months' arrears in rent.*
[Old French *arere* = backwards]

arrest, arrests, arresting, arrested
1 (verb) If the police arrest someone, they take them into custody to decide whether to charge them with an offence.
2 (noun) the act of taking a person into custody.

3 (verb) to stop something happening, e.g.
Doctors tried to arrest the disease with drugs.
4 If something arrests your attention, it interests
or surprises you so that you stop and look at it.
arresting (adjective)
[Latin *restare* = to remain]

Similar words: (verb: sense 1) detain, stop

arrival, arrivals
1 (noun) the act or time of arriving, e.g. *The
arrival of the plane was delayed.*
2 something or someone who has arrived, e.g. *We
welcomed all the new arrivals.*

arrive, arrives, arriving, arrived
1 (verb) to reach the end of a journey.
2 When you arrive at a decision or conclusion,
you reach it or decide on it, e.g. *The committee
arrived at their decision last night.*
3 to begin to happen, e.g. *The holidays arrived.*

arrogant
(adjective) conceited and showing little feeling
for anyone else.
arrogantly (adverb) **arrogance** (noun)
[Latin *arrogare* = to lay claim to]

arrow, arrows
1 (noun) a pointed weapon shot from a bow.
2 a sign showing a direction.

arsenic
(noun) a strong poison used in insecticides etc.

arson
(noun) the crime of deliberately setting fire to
something, especially a building.

art, arts
1 (noun) the creation of objects such as paintings
and sculptures.
2 (plural noun) The arts are literature, music,
painting and sculpture considered together.
3 (noun) An activity is an art when it requires a
lot of skill or ability, e.g. *the art of cookery.*

artefact, artefacts (pronounced **ar**-tif-fact)
(noun) any ornament, tool or other object that is
made by people.

artery, arteries
(noun) one of the tubes that carry blood from the
heart to the rest of the body.
arterial (adjective)

arthritis
(noun) a type of illness in which the joints in the
body become swollen and painful.
arthritic (adjective)

artichoke, artichokes
(noun) a type of root vegetable.
[Arabic *al-kharshuf* = artichoke]

article, articles
1 (noun) a particular object or item, e.g. *She
bought three articles of clothing.*
2 a piece of writing in a newspaper or magazine.
3 In English grammar 'a' and 'the' are articles: 'a'
(or 'an') is the indefinite article; 'the' is the
definite article.

articulate, articulates, articulating, articulated
1 (verb) to express in words what you think or
feel, e.g. *He could not articulate his grief.*
2 to speak clearly and distinctly.
articulation (noun)
3 (adjective) able to express yourself well in
words.

articulated
(adjective) An articulated lorry has two sections,
a cab and a detachable trailer.
[Latin *articulatus* = jointed]

artificial
1 (adjective) created by people rather than
occurring naturally, e.g. *artificial flowers.*
2 pretending to have attitudes and feelings
which other people realize are not real, e.g. *the
artificial smile of the game show host.*
artificially (adverb) **artificiality** (noun)

artificial intelligence
(noun) the study of how to make computers do
things considered to be human activities,
especially thinking, talking and seeing.

artillery
1 (noun) large, powerful guns such as cannons.
2 the branch of an army which uses large,
powerful guns.

artist, artists
(noun) a person who draws or paints or produces
other works of art.
artistic (adjective) **artistically** (adverb)

artiste, artistes (pronounced ar-**teest**)
(noun) a professional entertainer, e.g. a singer or
a dancer.
[a French word meaning 'artist']

as
(conjunction, preposition) e.g. *as usual.*

asbestos
(noun) a grey heat-resistant material used in the
past to make fireproof articles.
[Greek *asbestos* = inextinguishable]

ascend, ascends, ascending, ascended
(pronounced ass-**end**)
(verb; formal) to move or lead upwards, e.g.
stairs ascending to the attic.
ascent (noun)

ash, ashes
1 (noun) a type of hardwood tree.
2 the powdery remains of anything that has been
burnt.

ashamed
(adjective) feeling embarrassed or guilty.

ashore
(adverb) on land or onto the land.

Asian
1 (adjective) belonging to Asia.
2 (noun) someone who comes from Asia, usually
India, Pakistan, Bangladesh or Sri Lanka.

aside, asides
1 (adverb) If you move something aside, you
move it to one side.
2 (noun) a comment, usually in a play, that is not
part of the conversation or dialogue.

Cal and cle are sometimes confused at the ends of words. Usually cal ends adjectives, cle ends nouns....

ask, asks, asking, asked
1 (verb) to put a question or request.
2 (phrase) If you say that someone is **asking for trouble**, you mean that they are doing something that will get them into trouble.

asleep
(adjective) sleeping.

asparagus
(noun) a vegetable with long soft-tipped shoots that is cooked and eaten.

aspect, aspects
(noun) An aspect of something is one of its distinctive features, e.g. *The most interesting aspect of photography is developing your prints.*
[Latin *aspicere* = to look at]

asphalt
(noun) a mixture of tar, oil and small stones used for road surfaces and playgrounds.

asphyxiate, asphyxiates, asphyxiating, asphyxiated
(verb) If a person is asphyxiated, they cannot breathe or cannot get enough oxygen.
asphyxiation (noun)
[Greek *asphuxira* = stopping of the pulse]

aspirate, aspirates, aspirating, aspirated
(verb) to pronounce a word with an 'h' sound at the beginning.

aspiration, aspirations
(noun) Someone's aspiration is their desire and ambition.

aspire, aspires, aspiring, aspired
(verb) to have an ambition to achieve something, e.g. *She had always aspired to become a nurse.*
aspiring (adjective)

aspirin, aspirins
(noun) a drug used to relieve pain, fever, etc.

ass, asses
1 (noun) a donkey.
2 You might call someone an ass if you think they are stupid.

assassin, assassins
(noun) someone who has murdered a political or religious leader.
[Arabic *hashshashin* = people who eat the drug hashish; from a medieval Muslim sect who ate hashish and went about murdering Crusaders]

assassinate, assassinates, assassinating, assassinated
(verb) to murder a political or religious leader.
assassination (noun)

assault, assaults, assaulting, assaulted
1 (noun) a violent physical attack on someone.
2 (verb) to attack someone violently.
[Latin *assalire* = to leap upon]

assemble, assembles, assembling, assembled
1 (verb) to gather together.
2 to fit the parts of something together.
[Latin *simul* = together]

assembly, assemblies
1 (noun) a group of people who have gathered together for a meeting.
2 The assembly of an object is the fitting together

of its parts, e.g. *Read these instructions for the assembly of a barbecue.*

assembly line, lines
(noun) an arrangement of machines in a factory, in which each machine makes one part of a product. The product is passed along from machine to machine.

assent, assents, assenting, assented
(pronounced as-**sent**)
1 (noun) If you give your assent to something, you say yes to it.
2 (verb) to agree to something.
[Latin *sentire* = to feel or to think]

assertive
(adjective) speaking and behaving in a forceful way, so that people pay attention to you and your opinions.
assert (verb) **assertively** (adverb) **assertiveness** (noun)
[Latin *asserere* = to join to oneself]

assess, assesses, assessing, assessed
(verb) to consider something carefully and make a judgement about it.
assessment (noun) **assessor** (noun)
[Latin *assidere* = to sit beside]

Similar words: appraise, evaluate, size up

asset, assets
1 (noun) a person or thing that is considered useful, e.g. *As goalkeeper, he was a major asset to the team. As a winger, he was useless.*
2 (plural noun) The assets of a person or company are all the things they own that could be sold to raise money.
[Latin *satis* = enough]

assignment, assignments
(noun) a task that someone is given to do.
assign (verb)
[Latin *signare* = to mark out]

assimilate, assimilates, assimilating, assimilated
1 (verb) If you assimilate ideas or experiences, you learn and understand them.
2 When people are assimilated into a group or community, they become part of it.
assimilation (noun)
[Latin *assimilare* = to make alike]

assist, assists, assisting, assisted
(verb) to help someone do something.
assistance (noun)
[French *assister* = to be present]

assistant, assistants
(noun) someone whose job is to help another person in their work.

associate, associates, associating, associated
1 (verb) If you associate one thing with another, you connect the two things in your mind.
2 If you associate with a group of people, you spend a lot of time with them, e.g. *He spent his youth associating with criminals.*
3 (noun) Your associates are the people you work with or spend a lot of time with.
[Latin *associare* = to join with]

....Cal: critical practical tropical mechanical
....Cle: article vehicle cubicle particle

association, associations
1 (noun) an organization for people who have similar interests, jobs or aims.
2 An association between two things is a link that you make in your mind between them, e.g. *The name has many strange associations.*

assonance
(noun) similarity of sounds, for example in poetry. The vowels are the same but the consonants are not, e.g. slumber, blunder.

assorted
(adjective) Assorted things vary in size, shape, and colour, e.g. *assorted sweets.*

assortment, assortments
(noun) a group of similar things that vary in size, shape and colour.

assume, assumes, assuming, assumed
(verb) If you assume that something is true, you accept that it is true even though you lack convincing evidence, e.g. *They assumed that he was rich just because he had a flashy car.*
assumption (noun)
[Latin *assumere* = to take up]

assurance, assurances
1 (noun) something said about a situation intended to make people less worried, e.g. *The Government gave assurances about the safety of nuclear power after the grass turned red.*
2 a feeling of confidence, e.g. *He was speaking now with more assurance.*
3 Life assurance is a type of insurance that pays money to your dependants if you die before a certain age.

assure, assures, assuring, assured
(verb) If you assure someone that something is true, you tell them that it is true.
[Latin *adsecurare* = to secure or to make sure]

assured
(adjective) very confident, e.g. *the assured voice of a man who inspires confidence in others.*

asterisk, asterisks
(noun) the symbol '*' used in printing etc.
[Greek *asterikos* = small star]

astern
(adverb) backwards or at the back of a boat, e.g. *Engines full astern!*

asteroid, asteroids
(noun) one of the large number of very small planets that move around the sun between the orbits of Jupiter and Mars.
[Greek *asteroeidēs* = starlike]

asthma (pronounced **ass**-ma)
(noun) a chest disorder which causes wheezing and difficulty in breathing.
asthmatic (adjective)
[Greek *azein* = to breathe hard]

astonish, astonishes, astonishing, astonished
(verb) If something astonishes you, it surprises you very much.
astonished (adjective) **astonishing** (adjective)
astonishingly (adverb) **astonishment** (noun)

astound, astounds, astounding, astounded
(verb) to shock and amaze.
astounded (adjective) **astounding** (adjective)

astray
1 (phrase) To **lead someone astray** means to influence them to do something wrong.
2 If something **goes astray**, it gets lost.

astride
(preposition) with one leg on either side of something, e.g. *He was sitting astride a chair.*

astrology
(noun) the study of the sun, moon and stars to predict the future or to analyse someone's character.
astrological (adjective) **astrologer** (noun)

astronaut, astronauts
(noun) a person who operates a spacecraft.
[Greek *astron* = star + *nautēs* = sailor]

astronomical
1 (adjective) relating to astronomy.
2 extremely large in amount or value, e.g. *The house was sold for an astronomical price.*
astronomically (adverb)

astronomy
(noun) the scientific study of stars and planets.
astronomer (noun)

astute
(adjective) clever and quick at understanding situations and behaviour, e.g. *She will make an astute businesswoman.*
[Latin *astutus* = cunning]

asylum, asylums (pronounced ass-**eye**-lum)
1 (noun; old-fashioned) An asylum was a hospital for mental patients.
2 Political asylum is protection given by a government to someone who has fled from their own country for political reasons.
[Greek *asulon* = refuge]

asymmetrical or **asymmetric**
(pronounced ay-sim-**met**-ri-kl)
(adjective) not symmetrical.
asymmetry (noun)

at
(preposition) e.g. *At last we've found you!*

atheist, atheists (pronounced **ayth**-ee-ist)
(noun) someone who believes there is no God.
atheistic (adjective) **atheism** (noun)
[Greek *atheos* = godless]

athlete, athletes
(noun) someone who is good at sport.
[Greek *athlos* = contest]

athletic
(adjective) strong, healthy and good at sports.

athletics
(noun) Sporting events such as running, jumping and throwing are called athletics.

atlas, atlases
(noun) a book of maps.
[from the giant *Atlas* in Greek mythology, who supported the sky on his shoulders]

atmosphere, atmospheres
1 (noun) the air and other gases that surround a

Some poets use *assonance*, i.e. repeating the same vowel sounds in a line or stanza.

planet; also the air in a particular place, e.g. *the atmosphere is polluted ... a smoky atmosphere.*
2 The atmosphere of a place is its general mood, e.g. *a slightly sinister atmosphere.*
atmospheric (adjective)

atom, atoms
(noun) the smallest part of an element that can take part in a chemical reaction.
atomic (adjective)
[Greek *atomos* = indivisible]

atomizer, atomizers; also spelled **atomiser**
(noun) a device for turning a liquid such as perfume into a fine spray.

atrocious
(adjective) extremely bad, e.g. *He spoke French with an atrocious accent.*
atrociously (adverb)

atrocity, atrocities
(noun) an extremely cruel and shocking act.

attach, attaches, attaching, attached
(verb) to join or fasten two things together.

attached
(adjective) If you are attached to someone, you are very fond of them.

attachment, attachments
1 (noun) a feeling of love and affection.
2 an extra part for a tool or machine.

attack, attacks, attacking, attacked
1 (verb) to use violence against someone, trying to hurt or kill them.
2 (noun) a violent physical action against someone.
3 (verb) to criticize strongly, e.g. *He attacked the press for misleading the public.*
4 If a disease or chemical attacks something, it damages or destroys it, e.g. *Radiation can attack cancer cells.*
5 (noun) An attack of an illness is a short time in which you suffer badly with it.
6 (verb) In a game such as football or hockey, to attack means to get the ball into a position from which a goal can be scored.
attacker (noun)

Similar words: (verb: sense 1) assault, set about (noun: sense 2) assault

---

attain, attains, attaining, attained
(verb; formal) to achieve something, e.g. *He eventually attained high office.*
attainable (adjective) **attainment** (noun)

attempt, attempts, attempting, attempted
1 (verb) If you attempt to do something, you try to do it.
2 (noun) an act of trying to do something, e.g. *The injured man made an attempt to walk.*

attend, attends, attending, attended
1 (verb) If you attend an event, you go to it.
2 To attend school, church or hospital means to go there regularly.

3 If you attend to something, you deal with it, e.g. *I had some business to attend to.*
4 to listen carefully to what is being said.
attendance (noun)
[Latin *attendere* = to stretch towards]

attendant, attendants
(noun) someone whose job is to serve people in, for example a shop, museum or garage.

attention, attentions
(noun) the thought, care or interest that you give to something, e.g. *She was the centre of attention... The roof needs attention.*
attentive (adjective) **attentively** (adverb)
attentiveness (noun)

attic, attics
(noun) a room at the top of a house.

attitude, attitudes
(noun) Your attitude to someone or something is the way you think and feel about them and behave towards them.

attract, attracts, attracting, attracted
1 (verb) If something attracts people, it interests them and makes them want to go to it, e.g. *The show attracted large crowds this year.*
2 If someone attracts you, you like and admire them, e.g. *What attracted me to her was her sense of humour.*
3 If something attracts something else, it pulls it towards it, like a magnet.
[Latin *trahere* = to pull]

attraction, attractions
1 (noun) a feeling of liking someone very much, e.g. *physical attraction.*
2 something that people visit for interest or pleasure, e.g. *The Tower of London is one of England's major tourist attractions.*

attractive
1 (adjective) interesting and possibly advantageous, e.g. *an attractive idea.*
2 pleasant to look at or be with, e.g. *an attractive girl... an attractive personality.*
attractively (adverb) **attractiveness** (noun)

aubergine, aubergines
(pronounced oh-ber-jeen)
(noun) a dark purple, pear-shaped vegetable with shiny skin and pale flesh.
[Arabic *al-badindjan* = aubergine]

auburn
(adjective) Auburn hair is reddish brown.
[Old French *alborne* = blond]

auction
(noun) a public sale where goods are sold to the person who offers the highest price.
auctioneer (noun)
[Latin *auctio* = increasing]

audacious
(adjective) very daring.
audaciously (adverb) **audacity** (noun)

audible
(adjective) loud enough to be heard.
audibly (adverb) **audibility** (noun)
[Latin *audire* = to hear]

What are some of the creatures you could compare to a good athlete?

audience, audiences
(noun) a group of people watching or listening to a performance.
[Latin *audientia* = hearing]

audio
(adjective) used in recording and reproducing sound, e.g. *audio equipment*.

audio-visual
(adjective) involving both recorded sound and pictures, e.g. *audio-visual aids for teaching*.

audition, auditions
(noun) a short performance given by an actor or musician, to decide if they are suitable for a part in a play or film or for a place in an orchestra.
[Latin *auditus* = act of hearing]

August (pronounced **aw**-gust)
(noun) the 8th month of the year.
(from the name of the Roman emperor *Augustus*)

aunt, aunts
(noun) Your aunt is the sister of your mother or father, or the wife of your uncle.

au pair, pairs (pronounced oh **pair**)
(noun) a young foreign person who lives with a family to help with the children and housework and to learn the language.
[French words meaning 'on equal terms']

austere
(adjective) plain and simple, and without luxury, e.g. *the austere life of the monk*.
austerity (noun)
[Latin *austerus* = sour]

Australian
1 (adjective) belonging to Australia.
2 (noun) someone who comes from Australia.

Austrian, Austrians
1 (adjective) belonging to Austria.
2 (noun) someone who comes from Austria.

authentic
(adjective) real and genuine.
authentically (adverb) **authenticity** (noun)
[Latin *authenticus* = coming from the author]

author, authors
(noun) the writer of a book, article, etc.

authority, authorities
1 (noun) the power to control people, e.g. *the authority of the State... He spoke with authority*.
2 (plural noun) The authorities are the people who have the power to make decisions.
3 Someone who knows a lot about something, e.g. *She is a world authority on African fish*.
authoritative (adjective) **authoritatively** (adverb)

authorize, authorizes, authorizing, authorized;
also spelled **authorise**
(verb) to give official permission for something to happen.
authorization (noun)

auto-
(prefix) 'self' or 'same'.

autobiography, autobiographies
(noun) an account of someone's life which they have written themselves.
autobiographical (adjective)

autocue, autocues
(noun) a piece of equipment that displays words for a newsreader, TV presenter, etc to read while looking at the camera.

autograph, autographs
(noun) the signature of a famous person.
[Greek *auto* = self + *graphos* = written]

automatic, automatics
1 (adjective) An automatic machine is programmed to perform tasks without needing a person to operate it, e.g. *The airliner was flying on automatic pilot*.
2 (noun) a gun that has a mechanism for continuous reloading and firing.
3 a car in which the gears change automatically.
automatically (adverb) **automate** (verb)
automation (noun)

Similar words: (adjective) mechanical, mechanized

automobile, automobiles
(noun; American) a car.
[Greek *auto-* + *mobile* = self-moving]

autumn, autumns
(noun) the season between summer and winter.
autumnal (adjective)

available
1 (adjective) Something that is available can be obtained, e.g. *now available in paperback*.
2 Someone who is available is ready for work or free for people to talk to, e.g. *The Minister was not available for comment*.
availability (noun)

Similar words: (sense 1) obtainable, accessible

avalanche, avalanches (pronounced av-a-lansh)
(noun) a huge mass of snow and ice that falls down a mountainside.

avenge, avenges, avenging, avenged
(verb) If you avenge something harmful that someone has done to you or your family, you punish or harm the other person in return, e.g. *He was determined to avenge his father's death*.
avenger (noun)

avenue, avenues
(noun) a street, especially one with trees along it.
[French *avenir* = to approach]

average
1 (noun) a result obtained by adding several amounts together and then dividing the total by the number of different amounts, e.g. *Six girls hit a total of 24 rounders, an average of 4 each*.
2 (adjective) standard, normal or usual, e.g. *the average day's work*.
[Italian *avaria* = damage to ships or cargo; the loss was shared equally among all concerned]

Similar words: ordinary, middling

avert, averts, averting, averted
1 (verb) If you avert an unpleasant event, you prevent it from happening.
2 If you avert your eyes from something, you turn your eyes away from it.
[Latin *avertere* = to turn from]

47 scholars worked for 4 years to translate the Authorized Version of the Bible (1611).

aviary, aviaries
(noun) a large cage or group of cages in which birds are kept.
[Latin *avis* = bird]

aviation
(noun) the science of flying aircraft.

avid
(adjective) eager and enthusiastic for something.
avidly (adverb)

avocado, avocados
(noun) a pear-shaped fruit, with dark green skin, greenish-yellow flesh, and a large stone.
[South American Indian *ahuacatl* = testicle]

avoid, avoids, avoiding, avoided
1 (verb) If you avoid doing something, you make a deliberate effort not to do it.
2 If you avoid someone, you keep away from them.
avoidable (adjective) **avoidance** (noun)

Similar words: (sense 1) evade, shirk, dodge

await, awaits, awaiting, awaited
(verb) If you await something, you expect it.

awake, awakes, awaking, awoke, awoken
1 (adjective) not sleeping, e.g. *wide awake.*
2 (verb) to wake up, e.g. *I awoke suddenly.*

award, awards, awarding, awarded
1 (noun) a prize etc. for doing something well.
2 (verb) If you award someone something, you give it to them formally or officially.
[Old French *eswarder* = to decide]

aware
(adjective) If you are aware of something, you know about it or realize that it is there.
awareness (noun)

away
(adverb), e.g. *Throw it away.*

awe
(noun; formal) a feeling of great respect mixed with amazement and sometimes fear.
awesome (adjective)
[Old German = fear]

awful
1 (adjective) very unpleasant or very bad.
2 (informal) very great, e.g. *It took an awful lot of courage to shout 'Come on Spurs' at Highbury.*
awfully (adverb)

Similar words: (sense 1) ghastly, nasty, lousy

awkward
(adjective) clumsy and uncomfortable.
[Old Norse *ofugr* = turned the wrong way]

awoke the past tense of **awake**.

axe, axes, axing, axed
1 (noun) a tool for chopping wood.
2 (verb) to end something, e.g. *Lord Beeching axed many railways in the 1960s.*

axiom, axioms
(noun) a statement or saying that is generally accepted to be true.
axiomatic (adjective)
[Greek *axios* = worthwhile]

axis, axes (pronounced **ak**-siss)
1 (noun) an imaginary line through the centre of something, around which it moves.
2 the horizontal or vertical information side of a graph.

axle, axles
(noun) the bar connecting a pair of wheels on a vehicle.

aye or **ay** (rhymes with **lie**)
In some dialects of English, especially in Northern England and Scotland, aye means yes.

azure
(adjective) bright blue.

B

babble, babbles, babbling, babbled
(verb) to talk in a confused or excited way.

baboon, baboons
(noun) an African monkey with a pointed face, large teeth and a long tail.
[Old French *baboue* = grimace]

baby, babies
(noun) a child in the first year or two of life.
babyhood (noun) **babyish** (adjective)

Similar words: babe, infant

baby-sit, baby-sits, baby-sitting, baby-sat
(verb) To baby-sit for someone means to look after their children while that person is out.
baby-sitter (noun) **baby-sitting** (noun)

bachelor, bachelors
(noun) a man who has never been married.
bachelorhood (noun)
[Old French *bacheler* = young man]

back, backs, backing, backed
Selected meanings:
1 (noun) e.g. *My dad's back often aches... at the back of our house.*
2 (adverb) e.g. *He stepped back... I went back to sleep... back in 1978.*
3 (adjective) e.g. *the back wheels of the car.*
4 (verb) e.g. *Back your car in here... I backed Red Rum to win the Grand National... She backed the business with her money.*
5 (phrase) If you do or say something nasty **behind someone's back**, you do it without letting them know about it.
6 If you **put someone's back up**, you do or say something that annoys them.

back down
(phrasal verb) to withdraw and give up.

back out
(phrasal verb) to decide not to do what you had promised or agreed.

Letter B probably began as a picture of a house. Beth was the word for house.

back up
1 (phrasal verb) If you back up a claim or story, you produce evidence to show that it is true.
2 If you back someone up, you support them against their critics or enemies.
3 If you back up your work on a computer, you make a second copy of a file, in case the original is lost.
back-up (noun)

backbone, backbones
(noun) the column of linked bones along the middle of a person's or animal's back.

Similar words: spine, vertebrae

backfire, backfires, backfiring, backfired
1 (verb) If a plan backfires, it produces an opposite result to the one intended.
2 When a car backfires, there is a small but noisy explosion in its exhaust pipe.

background, backgrounds
1 (noun) Your background is the kind of family you come from and the education you have had, e.g. *She comes from a working-class background.*
2 The background to an event consists of the circumstances which surround it.
3 The background in a picture consists of the less noticeable things in it behind the main scene.

backhand, backhands
(noun, adjective) a stroke in tennis, squash or badminton, etc. made with the back of your hand facing in the direction that you hit the ball.

backing, backings
1 (noun) support or help, e.g. *This move has the backing of the government.*
2 The backing to a pop song is the music that accompanies it, e.g. *a backing group.*

backlog, backlogs
(noun) a number of tasks that have accumulated and that must be dealt with, e.g. *A backlog of work kept her late at the office.*

backpack, backpacks
(noun) a large bag or rucksack that hikers or campers carry on their backs.

backside, backsides
(noun; informal) the buttocks, the part of the body that you sit on.

Similar words: bottom, rear, rump

backstroke
(noun) a swimming stroke in which you lie on your back.

backward
1 (adjective) A backward country does not have modern industries or technology.
2 A backward child has not made as much progress in learning as children of the same age.
backwardness (noun)

Similar words: (sense 2) slow, retarded

backwards
(adverb), e.g. *to move backwards.*

bacon
(noun) meat from the back or sides of a pig, which has been salted and sometimes smoked.

bacteria
(plural noun) very tiny organisms which live in air, water, soil, plants and the bodies of animals. Some bacteria provide food for plants; others cause diseases such as typhoid.
bacterial (adjective)
[Greek *baktērion* = little rod; some bacteria are rod-shaped]

bad, worse, worst
(adjective) e.g. *bad news... a bad cut... bad meat.*
badly (adverb) **badness** (noun)

Similar words: evil, wicked, wrong, sinful, rotten, decayed, off, putrid

baddy, baddies
(noun; informal) a bad man in a film, TV programme, etc.

badge, badges
(noun) a piece of plastic, metal, etc., with a design or message on it that you can pin to your clothes.

badger, badgers, badgering, badgered
1 (noun) a nocturnal wild animal.
2 (verb) to keep asking someone questions or pestering them to do something, e.g. *The fans badgered the stars for their autographs.*

badminton
(noun) a game with rackets and shuttlecock, first played at Badminton in Gloucestershire.

baffle, baffles, baffling, baffled
(verb) If something baffles you, you cannot understand it or cannot think of an answer to it.
baffled (adjective) **baffling** (adjective)
bafflingly (adverb) **bafflement** (noun)

baggage
(noun) all the suitcases and bags used when travelling.
[Old Norse *baggi* = bundle]

baggy, baggier, baggiest
(adjective) Baggy clothing hangs loosely because it is too big.

bagpipes
(plural noun) a musical instrument played by squeezing air out of a leather bag through pipes, on which a tune is played.

bail, bails, bailing, bailed
1 (noun) a sum of money paid to a court to allow an accused person to go free until the time of their trial, e.g. *He was released on bail.*
2 Bails are the two pieces of wood placed on top of stumps to form the cricket wicket.
3 (verb) If you bail water from a boat, you remove it using a container.
[noun: sense 1 – Old French *bail* = custody
noun: sense 2 – Old French *baile* = cross-beam
verb: sense 3 – Old French *baille* = bucket]

bail out or bale out
(phrasal verb) To bail out of an aircraft means to jump out of it with a parachute.

Nouns of assembly. Have you heard of: a cete of badgers; a skulk of foxes; a muster of peacocks?

bailiff, bailiffs
(noun) a law officer who enforces the decision of a court, especially by removing someone's property if they fail to pay a fine etc.

bairn, bairns
(noun) In Scotland and Northern England a child is often called a bairn.
[Old Norse *barn* = child]

bait
1 (noun) a small amount of food placed on a hook or in a trap, to tempt a fish or wild animal to eat it so that it gets caught.
2 something intended to tempt a person to do something,
3 (verb) To bait somebody is to upset them by teasing and tormenting them.
[Old Norse *beita* = to hunt]

bake, bakes, baking, baked
(verb) to cook food in an oven without using liquid or fat.
baker (noun) **bakery** (noun).

balaclava, balaclavas
(noun) a close-fitting woollen hood. Balaclava is a place in Russia; at a battle there in the Crimean War in 1854, British soldiers wore these hoods to protect themselves from the cold.

balance, balances, balancing, balanced
1 (verb) to remain steady and not fall over.
2 (noun) the state of being upright and steady, e.g. *She nearly lost her balance.*
3 (verb) If you balance the books, you make sure that no more money is spent than is earned.
4 (noun) The balance in someone's bank account is the amount of money that they have in it.
5 When you have paid part of the cost of something, the balance is the amount still remaining to be paid.
6 an instrument for weighing, e.g. chemicals.
7 (phrase) When something is **in the balance**, it is uncertain whether it will happen or continue.
[Latin *bilanx* = having two scales]

balcony, balconies
1 (noun) a platform on the outside of a building with a wall or railing round it.
2 an area of seating upstairs in a theatre or cinema.
[Italian *balcone* = balcony]

bald, balder, baldest
(adjective) A bald person has little or no hair on the top of their head.
baldly (adverb) **baldness** (noun)
[Middle English *ballede* = having a white patch]

bale, bales, baling, baled
1 (noun) a large quantity of, for example cloth, paper or hay tied in a tight bundle.
2 (verb) If you bale water from a boat, you remove it using a container; also spelled **bail**

bale out see bail out

ball, balls
1 (noun) spherical object used in games.
2 The rounded part where your toes join your foot or your thumb joins your hand.
3 a large formal social dance.

4 (phrase; informal) Someone who is **on the ball** is alert and quick to understand what is going on.
5 If you are **having a ball**, you are enjoying yourself very much.
[sense 1 – Old Norse *bollr* = round object
sense 2 – French *baler* = to dance]

Similar words: (sense 1) globe, orb, sphere

ballad, ballads
(noun) a long song or poem which tells a story.
[Old French *ballade* = song for dancing to]

ballast
(noun) heavy material placed in a ship to make it more stable.

ball bearings
(plural noun) small metal balls placed between the parts of a wheel or a machine to allow them to move smoothly against each other.

ballerina, ballerinas
(noun) a female ballet dancer.

ballet, ballets (pronounced **bal**-lay)
(noun) a type of very skilled artistic dancing with carefully planned movements.
[Italian *balletto* = little dance]

ballistic
(adjective) fired from a gun or launcher, e.g. *ballistic missile.*
[Latin *ballista* = giant catapult, from Greek *ballein* = to throw]

ballgame
(phrase; informal) If we say something is a **different ballgame,** we mean that it is very different indeed.
[a ballgame is a game of American football or baseball]

balloon, balloons
1 (noun) an inflatable rubber bag used as a toy or decoration.
2 a large, strong bag filled with gas or hot air, sometimes carrying passengers in a basket or compartment underneath.
[Italian *ballone* = large round object]

ballot, ballots
(noun) a secret vote to choose a candidate in an election or express an opinion.
[Italian *ballotta* = little round object; in medieval Venice votes were cast by dropping pebbles or balls into a box]

ballpoint
(noun) a pen with a ball at the tip.

ballroom, ballrooms
(noun) a very large room used for dancing.

balsa
(noun) a lightweight wood from South America used, for example, to make models.
[Spanish *balsa* = raft]

bamboo
(noun) a tall tropical plant with hard, hollow stems used for making furniture. It is a species of giant grass. The young shoots can be eaten.
[Dutch *bamboes* from Malay *mambu* = bamboo]

Pun. He became a baker only because he kneaded the dough.

ban, bans, banning, banned
(verb) If something is banned, it is no longer
allowed, e.g. *Smoking is banned here.*
[Old English *bannan* = to proclaim aloud]

Similar words: forbid, bar, prohibit, outlaw

banana, bananas
(noun) a long, curved, yellow fruit.
[from a West African language, via Portuguese]

band, bands
1 (noun) a group of musicians or any group of
people who have joined together for a particular
purpose, e.g. *a band of outlaws.*
2 a narrow strip of something used to hold things
together or worn as a decoration, e.g. *a rubber
band... a head band.*
bandsman (noun)

band together
(phrasal verb) to join together for a particular
purpose.

bandage, bandages, bandaging, bandaged
1 (noun) a strip of cloth wrapped round a wound
to protect it.
2 (verb) to wrap a wound etc. in a bandage.

bandit, bandits
(noun; old-fashioned) a member of an armed
gang who lived by robbing travellers.
[Italian *bandito* = man who has been outlawed]

bandy-legged
(adjective) having legs that curve outwards at
the knees.

bang, bangs, banging, banged
(verb, noun), e.g. *I banged my thumb... The
firework went off with a loud bang.*

banger, bangers
1 (noun; informal) a sausage.
2 an old car in poor condition.
3 a small firework that makes a loud noise.

Bangladeshi, Bangladeshis (pronounced
bang-glad-**desh**-ee)
1 (adjective) belonging to Bangladesh.
2 (noun) someone who comes from Bangladesh.

bangle, bangles
(noun) an ornamental band or chain.
[Hindi *bangri* = bracelet]

banish, banishes, banishing, banished
(verb) to send someone away, usually out of the
country.
banishment (noun)
[Old French *banir* = or ban]

Similar words: exile, deport, transport

banister, banisters; also spelled **bannister**
(noun) a rail along the side of a staircase.

banjo, banjos or banjoes
(noun) a musical instrument with a long neck, a
hollow circular body, and four or more strings
which you pluck or strum.

bank, banks, banking, banked
1 (noun) a place where you can keep your money,
which lends money and offers other financial
services.

2 (verb) When you bank money, you pay it into a
bank.
banker (noun) **banking** (noun)
3 (noun) a store of something kept ready for use,
e.g. *a blood bank... a databank.*
4 the raised ground along the edge of a river etc.
5 the sloping side of an area of raised ground.
6 (verb) If you bank on something happening,
you expect it and rely on it.
7 When a plane banks, it tilts in order to turn.
[senses 1-3 – Italian *banca* = bench (a
money-changer's table)
senses 4-7 – Old Norse *banki* = ridge or bank]

bank holiday, holidays
(noun) a public holiday when banks are closed
by law.

banknote, banknotes
(noun) a piece of paper money.

bankrupt
(adjective) without enough money to pay debts.
bankruptcy (noun)
[Italian *banca* = bank + *rotta* = broken]

banner, banners
(noun) a piece of cloth with writing or a design
on it, stretched high above the ground or carried
in a procession.
[Old French *baniere* = flag]

bannister another spelling of **banister**

banquet, banquets
(noun) a grand, formal dinner.
[Old French *banquet,* = little bench]

baptize, baptizes, baptizing, baptized; also
spelled **baptise**
(verb) In the Christian religion, when someone is
baptized, water is sprinkled on them, or they are
immersed in water, as a sign that they have
become a Christian.
baptism (noun)
[Greek *baptein* = to dip in water]

bar, bars, barring, barred
1 (noun) a room in a pub or hotel; the counter on
which drinks are served.
2 a small shop or stall where you can buy food
and drink, e.g. *a sandwich bar.*
3 a long, straight piece of metal, e.g. *an iron bar.*
4 a piece of something made in a rectangular
shape, e.g. *a bar of soap.*
5 (verb) If you bar a door, you place something
across it to prevent it being opened.
6 If you bar someone's way, you stop them going
somewhere by standing in front of them.
7 (noun) The bars in a piece of music are the
many short parts of equal length that the piece is
divided into.
8 (phrase) If there are **no holds barred** in a
competition, there are no rules observed.

bar code
(noun) a series of black vertical lines of different
thicknesses appearing on most items sold in
shops. These can be 'read' by a computer light
pen and contain all the necessary information
about the product to go on the customer's receipt
or into the shop's records.

A banker needs these words: account cheque creditor deposit balance deficit debit overdraft loan.

barbarian, barbarians
(noun) a member of a wild and uncivilized tribe in former times.
[Greek *barbaros* = foreigner, originally 'person saying *bar-bar*']

barbaric or **barbarous**
(adjective) cruel or brutal.
barbarity (noun) **barbarism** (noun)

barbecue, barbecues
(noun) a grill with a charcoal fire on which you cook food, usually outdoors.
[a West Indian word meaning 'framework']

barbed wire
(noun) strong wire with sharp points sticking out of it, used to make fences or barricades.

barber, barbers
(noun) a man who cuts men's hair.
[Old French *barbe* = beard]

bare, bares, baring, bared
1 (adjective) not covered.
2 (verb) If you bare something, you uncover it, e.g. *She bared her teeth... He bared his arm.*
3 (adjective) The bare minimum or bare essentials means the very least that is needed.
[Old English *bær* = naked]

bareback
(adverb, adjective) riding a horse without using a saddle, e.g. *The gipsy rode bareback.*

barefoot
(adjective, adverb) not wearing anything on your feet, e.g. *She always walked barefoot.*

barely
(adverb) only just, e.g. *The drunk could barely stand.*

bargain, bargains, bargaining, bargained
1 (noun) a deal between two people or groups about what each will do, pay or receive, e.g. *They struck a bargain about the horse.*
2 (noun) Something which is sold at a low price and is good value.
3 (verb) to discuss the price of something before it is sold.
4 (phrase) **Into the bargain** means as well or in addition, e.g. *He was a good man, and a clever one into the bargain.*
[Old French *bargaigner* = to trade]

bargain for
(phrasal verb) to be prepared for something, e.g. *I didn't bargain for being snowballed.*

barge, barges, barging, barged
1 (noun) a boat with a flat bottom used for carrying heavy loads, especially on canals.
2 (verb; informal) to push in a rough way.

bark, barks, barking, barked
1 (noun) the noise that a dog makes.
2 (verb) e.g. *Stop barking, Fido!*
3 (phrase; informal) If you say that **someone's bark is worse than their bite**, you mean they are not so unpleasant or hostile as they seem.
4 If someone is **barking up the wrong tree**, they are going the wrong way about a problem.
5 (noun) the tough material on the outside of a treetrunk.

barley
(noun) a cereal that is grown for food, also used for making beer and whisky.

bar mitzvah
(noun) A Jewish boy's bar mitzvah is a ceremony that takes place on his 13th birthday, after which he is regarded as an adult.
[a Hebrew phrase meaning 'son of the law']

barmy, barmier, barmiest
(adjective; informal) mad or very foolish.

barn, barns
(noun) a farm building used for storage.
[Old English *bere ærn* = barley room]

barnacle, barnacles
(noun) a small shellfish that fixes itself to rocks and to the bottom of boats.

barometer, barometers
(noun) an instrument that measures atmospheric pressure and shows when the weather is changing.
[Greek *baros* + *metron* = weight measurer]

baron, barons
(noun) a member of the lowest rank of the nobility. (feminine: **baroness)**
baronial (adjective)

barracks
(noun) a building where soldiers live.
[Spanish *barraca* = hut]

barrage, barrages
1 (noun) A barrage of questions or complaints is a lot of them all coming at the same time.
2 continuous artillery fire over a wide area, intended to keep the enemy from moving.
3 an artificial barrier to control the flow of water, e.g. *the Thames barrage.*
[French *barrer* = to obstruct]

barrel, barrels
1 (noun) a wooden container for liquids.
2 the long cylindrical part of a gun through which the bullet or shell is fired.
3 (phrase) If you are **scraping the bottom of the barrel**, you are using the last remaining and least satisfactory resources.
[Old French *baril* = barrel]

barren
(adjective) Barren land has soil of such poor quality that plants cannot grow on it.
barrenness (noun)

Similar words: infertile, desert

barricade, barricades, barricading, barricaded
1 (noun) a temporary barrier to stop people or vehicles getting past.
2 (verb) If you barricade yourself inside a room or building, you put something heavy against the door to stop people getting in.
[Old French *barriquer* = to block with barrels]

barrier, barriers
1 (noun) a fence or wall that prevents people, vehicles, etc. going from one area to another.
2 something that prevents two people or groups from agreeing or communicating, or prevents

A soldier needs these words: regiment arms squad posting parade drill battalion cavalry infan

something from being achieved, e.g. *The talks were hindered by the language barrier.*
[French *barrière* = bar]

Similar words: (sense 1) barricade, bar, railing

barrister, barristers
(noun) a lawyer who can speak in a higher court on behalf of the defence or the prosecution.

barrow, barrows
1 (noun) a cart, in particular a large covered cart from which fruit etc. is sold in the street.
2 a mound of earth or stones built over a grave in prehistoric times.
[sense 1 – Old English *bearwe* = carrier
sense 2 – Germanic *berg* = hill or mountain]

barter, barters, bartering, bartered
(verb) If you barter goods, you exchange them rather than selling them for money.

base, bases, basing, based
1 (noun) the lowest part of something, often the part which supports the rest.
2 a place from which operations or activities are organized, directed and supplied.
3 (verb) To base something on something else means to use the second thing as a foundation or starting point for the first, e.g. *The film is based on a story by Roald Dahl.*
4 (noun) In chemistry, a base is any compound that reacts with an acid to form a salt.
5 In mathematics, a base is a system of counting and expressing numbers. The decimal system uses base 10, and the binary system uses base 2.
[Greek *basis* = base]

Similar words: (noun: sense 1) bottom, foot, foundation

baseball
(noun) an American rounders game played by two teams of 9 players. Each player hits a ball with a bat and tries to run round 4 bases, before the other team can get the ball back.

basement, basements
(noun) a floor of a building below the ground.

bash, bashes, bashing, bashed
1 (verb; informal) to hit hard.
2 (phrase) If you **have a bash** at something, you try to do it.

bashful
(adjective) shy and easily embarrassed.
bashfully (adverb) **bashfulness** (noun)

basic, basics
1 (adjective) The basic aspects of something are the most important ones. e.g. *They never solved the basic economic problems.*
2 (plural noun) The basics are the most important aspects of something, e.g. *For a year I learned the basics of French.*
3 (noun) BASIC is a computer language. [see below]
basically (adverb)

Similar words: (adjective) elementary, fundamental, key, primary

basin, basins
1 (noun) a deep food bowl.
2 The basin of a river is the whole of the area around from which water runs into it.

basis, bases
(noun) the main idea behind something from which it can be developed, e.g. *This was the basis of the final design.*
[Greek *basis* = foundation or pedestal]

Similar words: foundation, nitty-gritty

bask, basks, basking, basked
(verb) to enjoy sitting or lying in the sun.
[Old Norse *bathask* = to bathe oneself]

basket, baskets
(noun) a container made of woven cane.

basketball
(noun) a game in which two teams, usually of 5 players, try to score points by throwing a ball through circular nets high up at each end of the court.

bass, basses (rhymes with **lace**)
(noun) a musical instrument that provides the rhythm and lowest notes for a rock group or jazz band. A bass may be either a guitar or a very large member of the violin family: see **double bass**.
[Italian *basso* = low]

bassoon, bassoons
(noun) a large woodwind instrument.

bat, bats, batting, batted
1 (noun) a piece of wood used for hitting a ball.
2 (verb) In cricket, when someone is batting, it is their turn to try to hit the ball and score runs.
3 (noun) a small, flying nocturnal animal.
[senses 1-2 – Old English *batt* = club or stick
sense 3 – Middle English *bakke* = bat]

batch, batches
(noun) a group of things of the same kind produced or dealt with together.
[originally referring to a batch of loaves baked together; Old English *bacan* = to bake]

bath, baths, bathing, bathed
1 (noun) a large container, usually for water to wash or swim in.
2 (verb) to wash in a bath.

bathe, bathes, bathing, bathed
1 (verb) to swim or play in the sea, a river, etc.
2 When you bathe a wound, you wash it gently.
bather (noun) **bathing** (noun)

bathroom, bathrooms
(noun) a room to take a bath in.

batik
(noun) a process in which designs are printed on cloth by putting wax on parts of it, so that these parts are not coloured when the rest is dyed.
[Javanese *mbatik* = painting]

baton, batons
1 (noun) a light, thin stick that a conductor uses to direct an orchestra or choir.
2 a short stick passed from one runner to another in a relay race.
[a French word]

BASIC is an acronym for Beginner's All-Purpose Symbolic Instruction Code.

batsman, batsmen
(noun) In cricket, the person who is batting.

batter, batters, battering, battered
1 (verb) to hit heavily many times, e.g. *The ship was being battered by the waves.*
battering (noun)
2 (noun) a mixture of flour, eggs and milk, used to make, for example pancakes, or to coat food such as fish before frying it.

battery, batteries
1 (noun) an apparatus for storing and producing electricity.
2 a group of heavy guns.
3 (adjective) A battery hen is one of a large number of hens kept in small cages for the mass production of eggs.
[Old French *batterie* = a beating]

battle, battles, battling, battled
1 (noun) a fight between armies, ships or planes; also a struggle between two people or groups, e.g. *the battle of the sexes.*
2 a determined attempt to obtain or achieve something, e.g. *the battle for women's rights.*
3 (verb) to struggle or fight.
[Latin *battalia* = military exercises]

battlefield, battlefields
(noun) a place where a battle is or was fought.

battlements
(plural noun) a wall round the top of a castle, with gaps for guns or arrows to be fired through.

battleship, battleships
(noun) a large, heavily armoured warship.

batty, battier, battiest
(adjective; informal) crazy or eccentric.

bawl, bawls, bawling, bawled
(verb; informal) to shout loudly and harshly.

bay
1 (noun) part of a coastline where the land curves inwards, e.g. *the Bay of Biscay.*
2 a space or area used for a particular purpose, e.g. *a loading bay... a sick bay.*
3 (phrase) If you **keep something at bay**, you prevent it from reaching you, e.g. *The invaders were kept at bay.*
[senses 1-2 – Old French *baie*
sense 3 – Old French *abaiier* = to bark or howl]

Similar words: (sense 1) cove, gulf, inlet

bayonet, bayonets
(noun) a sharp blade that can be fixed to the end of a rifle and used for stabbing.
[after *Bayonne* in France, where it originated]

bay window, windows
(noun) a window that sticks out from the outside wall of a house.

be, am, is, are; was, were; been, being
(auxiliary verb) e.g. *Well, I'll be blowed!*

beach, beaches
(noun) an area of sand or pebbles by the sea.

Similar words: seaside, shore, seashore, coast

beacon, beacons
(noun) In the past a beacon was a light or fire on a hill, which acted as a signal or warning.
[Old English *beacen* = sign]

bead, beads
(noun) a small piece of coloured glass, wood, or plastic with holes through its centre, strung together to make necklaces and bracelets.
[Old English *bed* = prayer; beads on a string were used for counting prayers]

beady
(adjective) Beady eyes are small, bright and rather mean looking.

beagle, beagles
(noun) a short-haired breed of dog.

beak, beaks
(noun) the hard part of a bird's mouth.
[Old French *bec* = beak]

beaker, beakers
(noun) a tall cup for drinking out of.
[Old Norse *bikarr* = cup]

beam, beams, beaming, beamed
1 (verb) to smile broadly.
2 a band of light from, for example, a torch.
3 a long, thick bar of wood, concrete or metal, especially one that supports a roof.

bean, beans
1 (noun) the pods of a climbing plant, or the seeds inside these pods, eaten as a vegetable, e.g. the seeds from which coffee is made.
2 (phrase; informal) If someone is **full of beans**, they are very lively and energetic.
3 If you **spill the beans**, you give away a secret.

bear, bears, bearing, bore, borne
1 (noun) a large, strong, wild animal with thick fur and sharp claws.
2 (verb) to carry or support, e.g. *His ankle was now strong enough to bear his weight.*
3 to accept and deal with something difficult, e.g *It was painful, but he bore it in silence.*
4 If you can't bear someone or something, you dislike them very much.
5 (formal) When a plant or tree bears flowers, fruit or leaves, it produces them.
6 To bear left or bear right means to turn gently.
7 If someone **bears a grudge** towards someone else, they continue to feel angry towards them.
bearable (adjective) **bearably** (adverb)

bear down
(phrasal verb) If something large bears down on you, it moves quickly towards you.

bear out
(phrasal verb) To bear someone out or to bear out their story means to support what they are saying, e.g. *These claims are not borne out by the evidence.*

bear up
(phrasal verb) If you bear up when you are having problems, you remain brave and cheerful.

bear with
(phrasal verb) If you ask someone to bear with you, you are asking them to be patient.

There are several rivers named Avon in England. Avon is an old Celtic word meaning water.

beard, beards
(noun) the hair that grows on a man's face.
bearded (adjective)

beast, beasts
1 (noun; old-fashioned) an animal, especially a large one.
2 (informal) If you call someone a beast, you mean that they are unkind, cruel or spiteful.
[Latin *bestia* = animal]

beat, beats, beating, beaten
1 (verb) to hit hard and repeatedly, e.g. *His father used to beat him... The rain was beating against the window.*
2 to mix food using a fork or a whisk.
3 (noun) The beat of your heart is its regular pumping action.
4 The beat of a piece of music is its main rhythm.
5 (phrase) If you **beat time** to a piece of music, you move your hand or foot up and down in time with the music.
6 (verb) to defeat someone in a race, etc.
7 (informal) If something beats you, you cannot understand it, e.g. *It beats me where they get the money from.*
8 (noun) A police officer's beat is the area which they walk around when on duty.
beater (noun) **beating** (noun)

Similar words: (verb: sense 1) thrash, batter, pound
(verb: sense 6) conquer, overcome, defeat, lick, trounce

beat down
(phrasal verb) When the sun beats down, it is very hot and bright.

beat up
(phrasal verb) to hit or kick someone violently until they are severely hurt.

beautician, beauticians
(noun) a person whose job is giving people beauty treatments.

beautiful
(adjective) very attractive or pleasing.
beautifully (adverb) **beautify** (verb)

Similar words: glamorous, gorgeous, lovely, exquisite

beauty, beauties
(noun) the quality of being beautiful.
[Old French *biau* = beautiful]

beaver, beavers
(noun) an amphibious rodent with a big, flat tail. Beavers build dams in streams.

because
(conjunction, preposition) e.g. *The cricket stopped because of bad light.*
[Middle English *bi + cause* = by cause of]

beckon, beckons, beckoning, beckoned
(verb) to signal with your hand that you want someone to come to you.

become, becomes, becoming, became
1 (verb) To become something means to start feeling or being that thing, e.g. *She became very angry... We became good friends.*
2 (old-fashioned) If something becomes you, it suits you, e.g. *Blue doesn't become you, Neil.*
becoming (adjective)
[Old English *becuman* = to happen]

bed, beds, bedding, bedded
1 (noun) e.g. *She didn't make her bed... the garden beds were filled with flowers.*
2 (phrasal verb) To **bed down** means to settle down for the night or to make something really secure in the earth.

bedclothes
(plural noun) the sheets and covers on a bed.

bedraggled
(adjective) in a messy state, after being soaked or handled roughly.

bedridden
(adjective) too ill to get out of bed.

bedroom, bedrooms
(noun) a room used for sleeping in.

bedsitter, bedsitters
(noun) a rented, furnished room in a house, where you can live and sleep.

bedspread, bedspreads
(noun) a cover put over a bed, on top of the sheets and blankets.

bee, bees
1 (noun) a flying insect.
2 (phrase) If you have a **bee in your bonnet** about something, you can't stop thinking or talking about it.

beech, beeches
(noun) a deciduous hardwood tree.

beef
(noun) the meat of a cow, bull or ox.
[Old French *boef* = ox or bull]

beefburger
(noun) a flat disc of minced beef, seasoned and fried, often eaten in a bun.

beefy, beefier, beefiest
(adjective; informal) strong and muscular.

beehive, beehives
(noun) a structure in which bees live.

beer
(noun) an alcoholic drink brewed from malted barley and flavoured with hops.

beet
(noun) a plant with an edible root and leaves, e.g. *sugar beet.*

beetle, beetles
(noun) a flying insect with hard forewings which cover its body when it is not flying.
[Old English *bitan* = to bite]

beetroot, beetroots
(noun) a round, dark red root vegetable.

before
(adverb, preposition, conjunction) e.g. *Haven't we met before?*

Similar words: earlier, formerly, previously, sooner

∴ is a short way of writing 'because' when you are taking notes.

befriend, befriends, befriending, befriended
(verb) to act in a kind and helpful way to someone and so become friends with them.

beg, begs, begging, begged
1 (verb) to ask very earnestly.
2 to ask for food or money.

Similar words: beseech, implore, plead

beggar, beggars
(noun) someone who lives by asking people for money or food.

begin, begins, beginning, began, begun
(verb) to start.
beginning (noun)

Similar words: launch, start, commence

beginner, beginners
(noun) someone who has just started learning.

Similar words: learner, novice, recruit

begrudge, begrudges, begrudging, begrudged
(verb) If you begrudge someone something, you are angry or envious because they have it, e.g. *I begrudge paying him when he hasn't worked.*

behalf
(phrase) To do something **on someone else's behalf** means to do it for them or as their representative.
[Old English *be* = by + *halfe* = side]

behave, behaves, behaving, behaved
1 (verb) to act in a particular way, e.g. *He has been behaving very strangely lately.*
2 To behave yourself means to act correctly or properly.
behaviour (noun)

behead, beheads, beheading, beheaded
(verb) to cut someone's head off.
beheading (noun)

behind
(preposition, adverb, noun) e.g. *Look out behind you!... He kicked my behind.*
[Old English *behindan* = at a place in the rear]

beige (pronounced **bayj**)
(noun, adjective) pale brown.
[a French word, referring to undyed wool]

being, beings
(noun) a living creature, e.g. *alien beings.*

belch, belches, belching, belched
1 (verb) to make a sudden noise in your throat because air has risen up from your stomach.
2 to send out smoke or fire in large amounts.

belfry, belfries
(noun) the part of a church tower housing the bells.
[Old French *berfrei* = tower; because towers often had bells, this word became *belfrey*]

Belgian, Belgians
1 (adjective) belonging to Belgium.
2 (noun) someone who comes from Belgium.

belief, beliefs
(noun) a feeling of certainty that something exists or is true.

believe, believes, believing, believed
1 (verb) to accept that something is true.
2 If you believe in something, you are in favour of it, e.g. *He continued to believe in democracy.*
believable (adjective) **believer** (noun)

bell, bells
1 (noun) e.g. *The bell rang so I went to the door.*
2 (phrase; informal) If something **rings a bell**, it reminds you of something, though you cannot remember exactly what.

belligerent, belligerents
(adjective) hostile and aggressive.
belligerently (adverb) **belligerence** (noun)
[Latin *bellum gerere* = to wage war]

bellow, bellows, bellowing, bellowed
1 (verb) When an animal such as a bull bellows, it makes a loud, deep, roaring noise.
2 to shout in a loud, deep voice.

belly, bellies
1 (noun) the stomach or the front of the body below the chest.
2 An animal's belly is the underpart of its body.
[Old English *belig* = bulge or bag]

belong, belongs, belonging, belonged
(verb) If something belongs to you, it is yours.

belongings
(noun) Your belongings are the things you own.

beloved (pronounced bil-**luv**-id)
(adjective) A beloved person or thing is one that you feel a great affection for.

Similar words: adored, cherished, dear

below
(preposition, adverb) under; lower down.

belt, belts, belting, belted
1 (noun) a strip of leather etc. that is fastened round the waist to hold trousers or a skirt up.
2 In a machine, a belt is a circular strip of rubber that drives moving parts or carries objects along.
3 (verb; informal) to hit very hard.
4 If someone is **belting along**, they are moving very fast.
5 (noun) an area around a city, e.g. *the Green Belt... the commuter belt.*

bench, benches
1 (noun) a long seat, usually made of wood.
2 a long, narrow table in a factory, workshop, or laboratory.

Similar words: (sense 1) form, pew

bend, bends, bending, bent
1 (verb) e.g. *She bent my spoon... Bend down to tie your shoes up.*
2 (noun) e.g. *Bends in the road can be dangerous.*
3 (phrase) If someone is **bending over backwards** to help you, they are trying very hard to help.
4 If you **bend the rules**, you interpret them in a way that allows you to do what you want.
5 (phrase; informal) If you say that someone is round the bend, you mean that they are slightly or completely mad.

Similar words: (verb, noun) bow, curve, flex

What prize did the men who invented door-knockers win? The Nobel prize.

beneath
(preposition) underneath

benefactor, benefactors
(noun) a person who helps someone by giving them money or other support.
[Latin *bene facere* = to do well]

Similar words: patron, sponsor

beneficial
(adjective) Something that is beneficial is good for people, e.g. *the beneficial effects of exercise.*
beneficially (adverb)
[Latin *beneficium* = kindness]

Similar words: advantageous, profitable, favourable

benefit, benefits, benefiting, benefited
1 (noun) The benefits of something are the advantages that it brings to people, e.g. *I am not sure if the benefits of modern technology make up for the disadvantages.*
2 (verb) If you benefit from something, it helps you.
3 (phrase) If you do something **for someone's benefit**, you do it specially for them or so that they will notice.
4 (noun) money given by the government to people who are poor, ill or unemployed.
[Latin *benefactum* = good deed]

Similar words: (noun) asset, good, profit, gain (verb) profit, gain

benevolent
(adjective) kind and helpful.
benevolence (noun) **benevolently** (adverb)
[Latin *bene volere* = to wish well]

bent
1 (phrase) If you are **bent on** doing something, you are determined to do it.
2 (adjective; informal) If someone is bent, they are dishonest.

bequeath, bequeaths, bequeathed, bequeathing
(verb; formal) If someone bequeaths money or property to you, they give it to you in their will, so that it is yours after they have died.
[Old English *becwethan* = to say about]
bequest (noun)

bereaved
(adjective; formal) You say that someone is bereaved when a close relative of theirs has recently died.
bereavement (noun)
[Old English *bereafian* = to take forcible possession of something]

beret, berets (pronounced ber-ray)
(noun) a circular flat hat with no brim.
[French, from Latin *birettum* = cap]

berry, berries
(noun) small, round fruit from bushes or trees.

berserk
(phrase) If someone **goes berserk**, they lose control of themselves and become very violent.
[Icelandic *berserkr*, a kind of Viking who wore a shirt (*serkr*) from the skin of a bear (*björn*), who worked himself into a frenzy before battle]

berth, berths
1 (noun) a space in a harbour where a ship stays when it is being loaded or unloaded.
2 In a boat, train, or caravan, a berth is a bed.

beseech, beseeches, beseeching, beseeched or besought
(verb; literary) to beg or plead with someone. e.g. *I beseech you to go with her.*
beseeching (adjective) **beseechingly** (adverb)

beside
1 (preposition) next to.
2 (phrase) If you are **beside yourself** with anger or excitement, you are very angry or excited.

Similar words: adjacent to, alongside

besides
(preposition, adverb) in addition, e.g. *What languages do you know besides English?*

besiege, besieges, besieging, besieged
(verb) to surround a place during a battle and wait for the people inside to surrender, e.g. *The Greeks used a wooden horse in besieging Troy.*

best
(adjective, adverb; superlative) e.g. *good better* **best**; *well better* **best**

Similar words: finest, top, first-rate

best man
(noun) At a wedding the best man acts as the bridegroom's attendant and supporter.

best seller, sellers
(noun) a book which has sold very many copies.

bet, bets, betting
1 (verb) If you bet on a future event, you make an agreement which means you receive money if something happens and lose money if it does not.
2 You say **I bet** to indicate that you are sure that something is or will be so, e.g. *I bet she won't turn up.*
3 (phrase) **You bet** is an emphatic way of saying yes.
betting (noun)

betray, betrays, betraying, betrayed
1 (verb) If you betray someone who trusts you, you do something which harms them, such as helping their enemies.
2 If you betray a secret, you tell it to someone you should not tell it to.
betrayal (noun) **betrayer** (noun)
[Old English *be* = completely + Old French *trair* = to deliver up]

Similar words: (sense 1) double-cross, give away (sense 2) give away

better
(adjective, adverb; comparative) e.g. *good* **better** *best; well* **better** *best*

Similar words: finer, greater, superior

between
(preposition, adverb) e.g. *between the goalposts.*

beverage, beverages
(noun; formal) another name for a drink.
[Old French *beivre* = to drink]

beware
(verb) used to tell someone of possible danger,
e.g. *Beware of the dog.*

Similar words: be careful, look out, watch out

bewildered
(adjective) confused
bewilder (verb) **bewildering** (adjective)
bewilderment (noun)

beyond
(preposition) on the other side of.
[Old English *begeondan* = beyond]

bi-
(prefix) twice or two.

biannual
(adjective) occurring twice a year.
biannually (adverb)
[Latin *bis* = twice + *annus* = year]

bias
(noun) Someone who shows bias favours one
person or thing unfairly in preference to others.

Similar words: discrimination, prejudice

biased or **biassed**
(adjective) favouring one person or thing
unfairly in preference to others, e.g. *He was
stupid to think the ref was biased.*

Similar words: prejudiced, one-sided, bigoted

Bible, Bibles
(noun) The Bible is the sacred book of the Jewish
and Christian religions.
biblical (adjective)
[Greek *biblia* = the books]

bibliography, bibliographies
(noun) a list of books on a particular subject. At
the back of a book, it is a list of other books etc.
which the author has used.
bibliographical (adjective)
[Greek *biblos* = book + *graphein* = to write]

bicentenary, bicentenaries
(noun) the 200th anniversary of an event.
bicentennial (adjective)
[Latin *bis* = two + *centum* = hundred]

biceps
(noun) the large muscles on the upper arms.

bicker, bickers, bickering, bickered
(verb) to argue about unimportant things.

bicycle, bicycles
(noun) a two-wheeled pedal vehicle.
[Latin *bis* = two + Greek *kuklos* = wheel]

bid, bids, bidding, bade, bidden, bid
1 (noun) an attempt to obtain or do something,
e.g. *He made a bid to climb Everest.*
2 an offer to buy something for a certain price.
3 (verb) If you bid for something at an auction,
you offer to pay a certain price for it. (past
tense: bid)
4 (old-fashioned) If you bid someone good

morning, you say good morning to them. If you
bid them farewell, you say goodbye to them.
(past tense: bade)

bidder
(phrase) a person who bids at an auction.

bide, bides, biding, bided
(phrase) If you **bide your time**, you wait for a
good opportunity before doing something.

bidet, bidets (pronounced **bee**-day)
(noun) a low basin in a bathroom which you sit
astride to wash the anus and sexual organs.
[French = small horse]

biennial
1 (adjective) happening every two years.
2 (noun) a plant that lives for two years.
biennially (adverb)
[Latin *bis* = two + *annus* = year]

big, bigger, biggest
(adjective) e.g. *Big Ben.*
biggish (adjective) **bigness** (noun)

Similar words: large, considerable, sizeable,
substantial

bigot, bigots
(noun) someone who has strong and
unreasonable opinions which they refuse to
change.
bigoted (adjective) **bigotry** (noun)

bike, bikes
(noun; informal) a bicycle or motorcycle.

bikini, bikinis
(noun) a woman's two-piece swimming costume.

bilingual
(adjective) involving or speaking two languages,
e.g. *bilingual street signs... The children were
brought up to be bilingual.*
bilingually (adverb) **bilingualism** (noun)
[Latin *bis* = two + *lingua* = tongue]

bill, bills
1 (noun) a written statement of how much is
owed for goods or services.
2 In America, a bill is a piece of paper money, e.g.
a dollar bill.
3 In Parliament, a bill is a formal statement of a
proposed new law, e.g. *a new Health bill.*
4 A bird's bill is its beak.
[senses 1-3 – Latin *bulla* = document]

billion, billions
(noun) a thousand million (1,000,000,000)
(Formerly, a billion was a million million)
billionth (adjective)

binary (pronounced **by**-nar-ee)
(adjective) The binary system expresses
numbers using only two digits, 0 and 1.
[Latin *binarius* = two together]

bind, binds, binding, bound
1 (verb) to tie up with rope or string.
2 When a book is bound, the pages are joined
together and the cover is put on.

binder, binders
(noun) a hard cover with metal rings inside, used
to hold loose pieces of paper.

Can you distinguish between *biannual* and *biennial*?

bingo
(noun) a game in which each player has a card with numbers on. Someone calls out numbers and if you are the first person to have all your numbers called you win a prize.

binoculars
(plural noun) an instrument with two eyepieces which you look through to see distant objects.
[Latin *bis* = two + *ocularis* = of the eye]

biochemistry
(noun) the study of the chemistry of living things.
biochemical (adjective) **biochemically** (adverb)
biochemist (noun)
[Greek *bios* = life + Arabic *kimiya* = change]

biodegradable
(adjective) capable of being rotted naturally by the action of bacteria, e.g. *More and more plastics are becoming biodegradable.*
[Greek *bios* = life + Latin *degradare* = to reduce to a lower status]

biography, **biographies**
(noun) an account of someone's life, written by someone else. [Compare **autobiography**.]
biographer (noun) **biographical** (adjective)
[Greek *bios* = life + *graphein* = to write]

biology
(noun) the study of living things.
biological (adjective) **biologically** (adverb)
biologist (noun)
[Greek *bios* + *logos* = life study]

birch, **birches**
(noun) a tall deciduous tree.

bird of prey, **birds of prey**
(noun) a bird that kills other birds and small animals for food, e.g. eagle, hawk, owl.

biro
(noun) a ballpoint pen.
[from Lazlo and Georg Biro, the first people to produce the pens.]

birth, **births**
1 (noun) the emergence of a baby from its mother's womb at the beginning of its life.
2 the beginnings of something, e.g. *the birth of the motor car age.*

birthday, **birthdays**
(noun) the anniversary of a person's birth.

birthmark, **birthmarks**
(noun) a mark on someone's skin that has been there since they were born.

biscuit, **biscuits**
(noun) a small baked type of cake.
[Old French *bes* + *cuit* = twice-cooked]

bisect, **bisects**, **bisecting**, **bisected**
(verb) to bisect a line, angle, or area means to divide it in half.
[Latin *bis* = two + *secare* = to cut]

bishop, **bishops**
1 (noun) a high-ranking clergyman in some Christian Churches.

2 In chess, a bishop is a piece that is moved diagonally across the board.
[Greek *episkopos* = overseer]

bison
(noun) a large hairy animal, related to cattle, with a large head and shoulders, formerly common in North America.

bit, **bits**
1 (noun) a small piece.
2 In computing, a bit is the smallest unit of information held in a computer's memory. It is either 1 or 0. Several bits form a byte.
[shortened form of **bi**nary dig**it**]
3 a metal bar that fits in a horse's mouth, attached to the reins to help control the horse.
4 (verb) the past tense of **bite**.
[Old English *bita* = piece bitten off]

Similar words: (sense 1) fragment, piece, part, scrap

bitch
(noun) a female dog.

bite, **bites**, **biting**, **bit**, **bitten**
(verb) e.g. *Does your dog bite?*
[Old English *bitan* = to bite]

bitter, **bitterest**
1 (adjective) feeling angry and resentful.
2 A bitter disappointment makes people feel angry or unhappy for a long time afterwards.
3 In a bitter argument or war, people argue or fight fiercely and angrily.
4 A bitter wind is an extremely cold wind.
5 sharp and unpleasant to taste.
6 (noun) beer with a slightly bitter taste.
bitterly (adverb) **bitterness** (noun)
[Old English *bitan* = to bite]

Similar words: (adjective: sense 1) sour, resentful
(adjective: sense 5) sour, acid, acrid, sharp

blab, **blabs**, **blabbing**, **blabbed**
(verb; informal) When someone blabs, they give away secrets by talking carelessly.

black, **blacker**, **blackest**
(noun, adjective) e.g. *as black as coal.*
blackness (noun) **blacken** (verb)

black belt, **belts**
(noun) a high level of skill in judo or karate; also a person who has achieved this level.

blackberry, **blackberries**
(noun) Blackberries are small black fruit that grow on prickly bushes called brambles.

blackbird, **blackbirds**
(noun) a common European bird.

blackboard, **blackboards**
(noun) a board for writing on with chalk.

blackcurrant, **blackcurrants**
(noun) a small, dark purple fruit.

blackhead, **blackheads**
(noun) a very small black spot on the skin caused by a pore being blocked with dirt.

blackmail, **blackmails**, **blackmailing**, **blackmailed**
(verb) If someone blackmails another person, they threaten to reveal something unpleasant

about that person unless they are given money, or something is done that they want doing.

blackmail (noun) **blackmailer** (noun)

black market

(noun) If something is bought or sold on the black market, it is bought or sold illegally.

blackout, blackouts

(noun) If you have a blackout, you temporarily lose consciousness.

black out (verb)

black sheep

(noun) The black sheep of a family is a member of it who makes the others feel ashamed.

blacksmith, blacksmiths

(noun) a person whose job is making things out of metal, including horseshoes.

bladder, bladders

(noun) Your bladder is the part of your body where urine is held until it leaves the body.

blade, blades

1 (noun) the sharp part of a knife, axe or saw.
2 The blades of a propeller are the long, thin parts that turn round.
3 a single piece of grass.
[Old Norse *blath* = leaf]

blame, blames, blaming, blamed

1 (verb) If someone blames you for something bad that has happened, they say that you caused it or are responsible for it.
2 (noun) the responsibility for causing or letting something bad happen.
[Medieval Latin *blasphemare* = to reproach, from Greek *blasphēmein*]

Similar words: (verb) accuse, charge, hold responsible

blameless

(adjective) innocent.

bland, blander, blandest

(adjective) mild, tasteless and dull, e.g. *bland food... a bland reply.*
blandly (adverb)
[Latin *blandus* = flattering]

blank, blanker, blankest

1 (adjective) empty; with nothing on.
2 (noun) If your mind or memory is a blank, you cannot think of anything or remember anything.
3 (phrase) If you **draw a blank** when you are looking for something, you fail to find it.
[Old French *blanc* = white]

blanket, blankets

1 (noun) a thick cloth put on a bed.
2 A blanket of snow is a thick covering of it.
[Old French *blancquete* = little white thing]

blank verse

(noun) poetry in which the lines do not rhyme and which has 10 syllables to the line.

blare, blares, blaring, blared

(verb) to make a loud, unpleasant noise, e.g. *The radio was blaring.*

blaspheme, blasphemes, blaspheming, blasphemed

(verb) to say rude or disrespectful things about God, or to use God's name as a swear word.
blasphemy (noun) **blasphemous** (adjective)
[Greek *blapsis* = evil + *phēmein* = to speak]

blast, blasts, blasting, blasted

1 (verb) to make a hole with an explosion.
2 (noun) a big explosion.
3 a sudden, strong rush of air or wind.
4 a short, sharp sound made by a whistle etc.
5 (phrase) If a machine is working **at full blast**, it is working at its top speed or to its full capacity.

blastoff

(noun) the time when a rocket leaves the ground.

blatant

(adjective) done in an obvious way, without any attempt to hide, e.g. *a blatant foul.*
[*blattant* = extremely noisy; invented by Edmund Spenser in 1596 to describe a monster in 'The Faerie Queen']

blaze, blazes, blazing, blazed

1 (noun) a large, hot fire.
2 A blaze of light is a lot of very bright light.
3 A blaze of publicity or attention is a lot of it.
4 (verb) to burn strongly and brightly.
5 If your eyes are blazing, they look very bright because you are angry or excited.
[Old English *blæse* = bright flame]

blazer, blazers

(noun) a jacket, often part of a uniform.

bleach, bleaches, bleaching, bleached

1 (verb) To bleach material or hair means to make it white or pale by using a chemical.
2 (noun) a chemical used to make material white or to clean things thoroughly and kill germs.
[Old English *blæcan* = to make pale]

bleak, bleaker, bleakest

(adjective) cold, bare and exposed to the wind.
[Old English *blac* = pale]

bleary

(adjective) If your eyes look bleary, they are red and watery, usually because you are tired.
blearily (adverb)

bleat, bleats

(noun) the sound of a sheep or goat.

bleed, bleeds, bleeding, bled

(verb) to lose blood.

bleep, bleeps

(noun) a short high-pitched sound made by an electrical device such as an alarm.

blend, blends, blending, blended

1 (verb) to mix together.
2 (noun) a mixture, usually pleasant.
[Old Norse *blanda* = to mix]

blender, blenders

(noun) a machine used for mixing liquids and foods at high speed.

bless, blesses, blessing, blessed or blest

(verb) When a priest blesses people or things, he asks for God's favour and protection for them.
[Old English *blædsian* = to sprinkle with sacrificial blood]

....Blank verse is unrhymed lines of ten syllables each, i.e. five two-syllable feet!

blessed (pronounced **bless**-id)
1 (adjective) Often used to describe something we are glad about, e.g. *We felt a blessed sense of relief as the storm passed.*
2 (pronounced **blest**) to have a particular quality or skill, e.g. *I am blessed with good sight.*

blessing, blessings
1 (noun) something good that you are thankful for, e.g. *Good health is a great blessing.*
2 (phrase) If something is done **with someone's blessing**, they approve of it and support it, e.g. *The young couple got engaged with their parents' blessing.*

blew past tense of **blow**.

blind, blinds, blinding, blinded
1 (adjective) Someone who is blind cannot see.
2 A blind corner is one where drivers and cyclists cannot see what is coming.
3 (verb) If something blinds you, you become unable to see.
4 (noun) a roll of cloth or paper that you pull down over a window to keep out the light.
blindly (adverb) **blindness** (noun)

blindfold, blindfolds
(noun) a cloth tied over someone's eyes.

blinding
(adjective) so bright that it hurts your eyes, e.g. *There came a blinding flash.*

blind spot
(noun) If you have a blind spot about something, you cannot or will not understand it.

blink, blinks, blinking, blinked
(verb) to close your eyes rapidly for a moment.

blinkers
1 (noun) pieces of leather placed at the side of a horse's eyes so that it can see ahead only.
2 (phrase) If you say that someone is **wearing blinkers**, you mean they are seeing only their own point of view.
blinkered (adjective)

bliss
(noun) complete happiness.
blissful (adjective) **blissfully** (adverb)

blister, blisters
(noun) a swelling on your skin containing watery liquid, caused by a burn or rubbing.
[Old French *blestre* = swelling or pimple]

blistering
(adjective) Blistering heat is very hot.

blitz
(noun) a sudden, intensive bombing attack by aircraft on a city or town.
[German *Blitzkrieg* = lightning war]

blizzard, blizzards
(noun) a heavy snowstorm with strong winds.

bloated
(adjective) much larger than normal, often because there is a lot of liquid or gas inside.

block, blocks, blocking, blocked
1 (noun) a large building of flats or offices.
2 an area of land or buildings with streets on all its sides, e.g. *to walk round the block.*
3 a large rectangular piece, e.g. *a concrete block.*
4 If you have a mental block about something, you are briefly unable to remember it.
5 (verb) To block a road, channel or pipe means to put something across so that nothing can pass.
blockage (noun)
[French *bloc* = block]

Similar words: (noun: sense 3) bar, brick, chunk, square
(verb: sense 5) obstruct, clog, bung, choke

block capitals or **block letters**
(noun) simple, clear, capital letters.

bloke, blokes
(noun; informal) a man.

blonde, blondes
1 (adjective) Blonde hair is pale yellow in colour. The spelling 'blond' is used for men's hair.
2 (noun) a woman with blonde hair.
[Latin *blondus* = yellow]

blood
(noun) the red liquid pumped by the heart round the bodies of humans and other mammals.

blood bank, banks
(noun) a store of blood kept until it is needed for use in hospitals.

bloodcurdling
(adjective) very frightening and horrible, e.g. *a bloodcurdling shriek.*

blood donor, donors
(noun) someone who gives blood from their body to be used for blood transfusions.

bloodshed
(noun) When there is bloodshed, people are killed or wounded.

bloodshot
(adjective) If a person's eyes are bloodshot, the white parts have become red because tiny blood vessels have burst in their eyes.

blood sport, sports
(noun) sports such as hunting, shooting and fishing, in which animals are killed.

bloodstained
(adjective) covered with blood.

bloodstream
(noun) the blood as it flows round the body.

bloodthirsty
(adjective) eager to use violence or to see other people use violence.

blood transfusion, transfusions
(noun) a process in which blood is injected into the body of someone who has lost a lot of blood, for example through injury.

blood vessel, vessels
(noun) the narrow tubes in your body through which your blood flows.

bloody, bloodier, bloodiest
1 (adjective, adverb) a common swear word, used to express anger or annoyance.
2 covered with blood.

How do you spell 'blind pig'? – Blnd pg ...(because it's got no eyes!)

bloom, blooms, blooming, bloomed
1 (noun) a flower on a plant.
2 (verb) When a plant blooms, it makes flowers.
[Old Norse *blom* = flower]

blossom, blossoms, blossoming, blossomed
1 (noun) the growth of flowers on a tree.
2 (verb) When a tree blossoms, it makes blossom.
3 When a person blossoms, they develop attractive qualities and become happy and successful.

blot, blots, blotting, blotted
1 (noun) a drop of ink that has been spilled.
2 A blot on someone's reputation is a mistake or bad behaviour that spoils their good name.

blot out
(phrasal verb) To blot something out means to be in front of it and prevent it from being seen, e.g. *A huge dust cloud blotted out the sun.*

blotch, blotches
(noun) a discoloured area or stain.
blotchy (adjective)

blotting paper
(noun) paper used for drying ink blots.

blouse, blouses
(noun) a light garment, like a shirt, usually worn by a girl or a woman.
[a French word]

blow, blows, blowing, blew, blown
1 (verb) When the wind blows, the air moves.
2 (noun) If you receive a blow, you are hit.
3 something that makes you very disappointed or unhappy, e.g. *Losing his job was a great blow.*
4 (phrase) If people **come to blows**, they start fighting.

blow over
(phrasal verb) If trouble or an argument blows over, it comes to an end.

blow up
1 (phrasal verb) to destroy something with an explosion.
2 to fill something with air.
3 To blow up a photograph means to enlarge it.

blowlamp, blowlamps
(noun) a hand-held gas burner that produces a flame, used, for example, to heat metal or to burn off old paint.

blowout, blowouts
1 (noun) a sudden uncontrolled escape of gas or oil from a well.
2 a sudden loss of air from a burst tyre.

blubber
(noun) the thick insulating layer of fat beneath the skin of animals such as whales and seals.

blue, bluer, bluest
1 (adjective, noun) a colour
2 (phrase) If something happens **out of the blue**, it happens suddenly and unexpectedly.
bluish or **blueish** (adjective)

bluebell, bluebells
(noun) a woodland plant.

bluebottle, bluebottles
(noun) a large fly with a shiny, dark-blue body.

blueprint, blueprints
(noun) a photographic print of an architect's or engineer's plan.

blues
(noun) a type of music that is similar to jazz, but is always slow and sad.

bluetit, bluetits
(noun) a common small bird.

bluff, bluffs, bluffing, bluffed
1 (noun) an attempt to make someone believe that you will do something when you do not really intend to do it.
2 (phrase) If you **call someone's bluff**, you tell them to do what they are threatening to do, because you are sure they will not really do it.
3 (verb) If you are bluffing, you are trying to make someone believe you will do something, although you do not really intend to do it.
[Dutch *bluffen* = to boast]

blunder, blunders
(noun) a silly mistake.
[Old Norse *blunda* = to close one's eyes]

blunt, blunter, bluntest
1 (adjective) A blunt object has a rounded point or edge, rather than a sharp one.
2 If you are blunt, you say exactly what you think, without trying to be polite.

Similar words: (sense 2) outspoken, abrupt, tactless

blur, blurs
(noun) a shape or area which you cannot see clearly because it has no distinct outline or because it is moving very fast.
blurred (adjective)

blurb
(noun) The blurb about a product is information about it written to make people interested in it.
[invented in the 20th century by Gelett Burgess, an American humorist]

blurt out, blurts out, blurting out, blurted out
(verb) to say something suddenly, after trying to keep quiet or keep it a secret, e.g. *She suddenly blurted out, 'I'm not going and I don't care!'*

blush, blushes, blushing, blushed
(verb) If you blush, your face becomes redder because you are ashamed or embarrassed.
[Old English *blyscan* = to glow]

Similar words: colour, flush, redden

blustery
(adjective) Blustery weather is rough and windy.

boar, boars
(noun) a male wild pig, or a male domestic pig used for breeding.

board, boards, boarding, boarded
1 (noun) a long, flat piece of wood.
2 a piece of wood or stiff cardboard to play games on.
3 The board of a company or organization is the group of people who control it.
4 (verb) to get on a train, ship or aircraft.
5 (phrase) If you are **on board** a train, ship or aircraft, you are on it or in it.

He is always blowing his own trumpet. You might know someone like this. What does it mean?

6 If you **take on board** an idea etc. you become fully aware of it.

Similar words: (verb: sense 3) committee, council, panel

board up
(phrasal verb) If you board up a door or window, you cover it by fixing pieces of wood across it.

boarder, boarders
(noun) a pupil who lives at boarding school during term time.

boarding school, schools
(noun) a school where the pupils live during term time.

boast, boasts, boasting, boasted
(verb) If you boast about your possessions or achievements, you talk about them proudly, especially to impress other people.
boastful (adjective) **boastfully** (adverb)

Similar words: brag, crow, blow your own trumpet

boat, boats
1 (noun) a vehicle for travelling across water.
2 (phrase) When people are **in the same boat**, they are all in the same unpleasant situation.

bob, bobs, bobbing, bobbed
(verb) When something bobs, it moves up and down, e.g. *The boat bobbed gently on the lake.*

bobble, bobbles
(noun) a small ball of material used for decorating clothes or furniture.

body, bodies
1 (noun) Your body is either all your physical parts or just the trunk, excluding head and limbs.
2 a person's dead body.
3 The main part of a car or aircraft, excluding the engine.
bodily (adjective and adverb)

Similar words: (sense 1) figure, form, frame, build, physique

bodyguard, bodyguards
(noun) a person or group of people employed to protect someone.

bodywork
(noun) the outer part of a motor vehicle.

boffin
(noun; informal) a name for a scientist or clever person.

bog, bogs
(noun) an area of land which is wet and spongy.
[Gaelic *bogach* = swamp]

Similar words: marsh, swamp

bogged down
(adjective) If you are bogged down in something, you cannot make progress.

boggle, boggles, boggling, boggled
(verb) If your mind boggles at something, you find it difficult to imagine or understand e.g. *My mind boggles when I try to think about where the universe ends.*

bogus
(adjective) not genuine; fake.
[from the name of a machine that made counterfeit money]

boil, boils, boiling, boiled
1 (verb) When a hot liquid boils, bubbles appear in it and it starts to change into vapour.
2 (phrase) Example: *The team's good results* all **boil down to** *our goalkeeper being world-class.* This means that the goalkeeper is the only important reason for the good results.
3 (noun) a red swelling on your skin.
[Latin *bullire* = to bubble]
boiler (noun)

boisterous
(adjective) noisy, lively and rather rough.
boisterously (adverb) **boisterousness** (noun)

Similar words: riotous, rowdy

bold, bolder, boldest
1 (adjective) not afraid of risk or danger.
2 clear and noticeable, e.g. *bold handwriting.*
boldly (adverb) **boldness** (noun)
[Old Norse *ballr* = dangerous or terrible]

Similar words: (sense 2) conspicuous, eye-catching

bollard, bollards
(noun) a short, thick post used to keep vehicles out of a road, track or traffic lane.

bolt, bolts, bolting, bolted
1 (noun) a metal object which screws into a nut and is used to fasten things together.
2 a metal bar that you slide across a door in order to fasten it.
3 (verb) to escape or run away.
4 To bolt food means to eat it very quickly.
5 (phrase) If you are sitting or standing **bolt upright**, you are sitting or standing very straight.
[Old English *bolt* = arrow]

bomb, bombs, bombing, bombed
1 (noun) a container that explodes when it hits something or is activated by a timing mechanism.
2 Nuclear weapons are sometimes referred to as the bomb, e.g. *Ban the bomb!*
3 (verb) to drop or leave bombs.
bomber (noun)
[Greek *bombos* = a booming sound]

bombshell, bombshells
(noun) a sudden piece of very unpleasant news.

bond, bonds, bonding, bonded
1 (noun) a close relationship between people, e.g. *the bond between mother and child.*
2 a certificate which records that you have lent money to the government or to a business and that it will repay you the loan with interest.
3 (literary) chain or rope used to tie a prisoner.
4 In a scientific sense, a bond is the link between two atoms, the particles of which all substances are made.
5 (verb) When two things bond or are bonded, they become closely linked or attached.
[Old Norse *band* = something that binds]

Similar words: (noun: sense 1) link, connection, tie

What do these organs do? liver pancreas lungs brain stomach.

bone, bones
1 (noun) Bones are the hard parts that form the skeleton of a person's or animal's body.
2 (phrase) If you **make no bones** about doing something, especially something unpleasant or difficult, you do not hesitate or have any doubts about doing it.
boneless, bony, bonier, boniest (adjectives)

bonfire, bonfires
(noun) an outdoor fire.
[from 'bone' + 'fire'; bones were used as fuel in the Middle Ages]

bongos
(plural noun) small drums, usually in pairs.

bonnet, bonnets
1 (noun) the metal cover over a car's engine.
2 a baby's or woman's hat tied under the chin.
[Old French *bonet* = hat]

bonny, bonny, bonnier, bonniest
(adjective; Scottish and Northern English) nice to look at, e.g. *a bonny wee lass.*
[Old French *bon* = good]

bonus, bonuses
1 (noun) an amount of money added to your usual pay.
2 a good thing that you get in addition to everything else, e.g. *Having Hick playing in the team was an unexpected bonus.*
[Latin *bonus* = good]

boo, boos, booing, booed
(verb) to shout disapproval.

booby prize, prizes
(noun) a prize given to the person who comes last in a competition.

booby trap, traps
(noun) a trap which is hidden or disguised and which is set off by being touched.

book, books, booking, booked
1 (noun) a number of pages inside a cover.
2 An organization's books are records of money that it has earned and spent.
3 (verb) When you book, e.g. a room, you arrange to have it or use it at a particular time.
4 to record that someone has committed an offence, e.g. speeding
5 (phrase) If you are **in someone's bad books,** they are annoyed with you. If you are **in their good books,** they are pleased with you. {Old English *boc;* from Old Germanic *boks* = (beech books used to be written on beech bark)]

bookcase, bookcases
(noun) a piece of furniture with shelves for books.

booking, bookings
(noun) an arrangement to book, e.g. a hotel room.

book-keeping
(noun) the keeping of a record of the money spent and received by a business.

booklet, booklets
(noun) a small book with a paper cover.

bookmaker, bookmakers or **bookie**
(noun) a person who makes a living by taking people's bets and paying them when they win.

bookmark, bookmarks
(noun) a piece of card etc. to mark your place in a book.

bookplate, bookplates
(noun) a label pasted inside the cover of a book to identify its owner.

bookworm, bookworms
1 (noun) a person who is very fond of reading.
2 a type of insect that feeds on the binding paste of books.

boom, booms, booming, boomed
1 (noun) a rapid increase in something, e.g. *the population boom of the late 1940s.*
2 (verb) When something booms, it increases rapidly, e.g. *Profits are booming.*
3 (noun) a loud, deep, echoing sound, e.g. *the boom of the bass drum.*
4 (verb) to make a loud deep echoing sound, e.g. *'Nonsense!' he boomed.*

boomerang, boomerangs
(noun) a curved piece of wood thrown as a weapon by Australian aborigines balanced so that it returns to the thrower.
[an Australian Aboriginal word]

boost, boosts, boosting, boosted
1 (verb) to cause something to improve or increase, e.g. *The new machine should boost production by 20%.*
2 (noun) an improvement or increase, e.g. *a boost to the economy.*
booster (noun)

boot, boots, booting, booted
1 (noun) a high-sided type of shoe.
2 (verb) to kick something or someone very hard.
[Old French *bote* = boot]

bootleg
(adjective) A bootleg recording of a live performance is one which is made without permission.

booze, boozes, boozing, boozed (informal)
1 (noun) alcoholic drink.
2 (verb) to drink alcohol.
boozer (noun) **boozy** (adjective)
[Old Dutch *busen* = to drink too much]

border, borders, bordering, bordered
1 (noun) the dividing line between countries.
2 a strip or band round the edge of something.
3 In a garden, a border is a long flower bed.
[Old French *bordure*, from Germanic *bort* = the side of a ship]

border on
(phrasal verb) If something borders on a particular condition, it is almost in that condition, e.g. *This work borders on the pathetic.*

borderline
(adjective) only just acceptable as a member of a class or group, e.g. *a borderline case.*

bore, bores, boring, bored
1 (noun) someone or something that becomes tedious and uninteresting.
2 (verb) to make a hole with a drill etc.
3 the past tense of **bear.**
[verb: Old English *borian* = to pierce]

What have the Earl of Sandwich and the Duke of Wellington contributed to our language?

born
1 (verb) When a baby is born, it comes out of its mother's womb at the beginning of its life.
2 (adjective) You use born to mean that someone has a natural ability to do something well, e.g. *He is a born writer*.
[Old English *boren*, past participle of *beran* = to bear]

borough, boroughs (pronounced bur-uh)
(noun) a town or district that has its own borough council with controlling powers.
[Old English *burg* = fortified place]

borrow, borrows, borrowing, borrowed
(verb) to use someone else's property for a period of time, with permission.
borrower (noun)

borstal, borstals
(noun; old-fashioned) a prison for young criminals. They are now officially known as 'youth custody centres'.
[from *Borstal*, the village in Kent where the first borstal was set up]

bosom, bosoms
(noun) A woman's bosom is her breasts.

boss, bosses, bossing, bossed
1 (noun) the person in charge of an organization.
2 (verb) If someone bosses you around, they keep telling you what to do.
[Dutch *baas* = master]

bossy, bossier, bossiest
(adjective) A bossy person enjoys telling other people what to do.
bossily (adverb) bossiness (noun)

botany
(noun) the scientific study of plants.
botanic (adjective) botanical (adjective)
botanist (noun)
[Greek *botane* = plant]

both
(adverb, pronoun) e.g. *Both Mum and Dad are Irish.*

bother, bothers, bothering, bothered
1 (verb) If you do not bother to do something, you do not do it because it involves too much effort or it seems unneccessary.
2 (verb) to be concerned about something.
3 to interrupt someone when they are busy.
4 (noun) trouble, fuss or difficulty.
bothersome (adjective)
[Old Irish *bodhraim* = to deafen, hence to bewilder or confuse with noise]

bottle, bottles, bottling, bottled
(noun) a container for keeping liquids in.
[Medieval Latin *butticula* = a little cask]

bottle up
(phrasal verb) If you bottle up strong feelings, you do not express or show them.

bottleneck, bottlenecks
(noun) a difficult stretch of road where traffic jams occur.

bottom, bottoms
1 (noun) the lowest part of something.
2 (phrase) If you **get to the bottom of** something, you find out the real truth about it.
bottomless (adjective)

bough, boughs (rhymes with now)
(noun) a large branch of a tree.
[Old English *bog* = arm or twig]

bought past tense and past participle of buy.

boulder, boulders
(noun) a large, rounded rock.

bounce, bounces, bouncing, bounced
(verb) When an object bounces, it springs back from something after hitting it.
bouncy (adjective)

bound, bounds, bounding, bounded
1 (adjective) If you say that something is bound to happen, you mean that it is certain to happen.
2 If a plane, ship or bus is bound for a place, it is going there.
3 (plural noun) Bounds are limits which restrict what can be done, e.g. *out of bounds*.
4 (noun) a large leap.
5 (verb) to move quickly with large leaps.
6 past tense and past participle of bind.
[adjective; sense 2 – Old Norse *buinn* = prepared
noun; sense 3 – Old French *bunde* = boundary
verb; sense 5 – Old French *bondir* = to jump]

boundary, boundaries
1 (noun) a line that separates one area from other areas.
2 In cricket, the boundary is the edge of the pitch. If a batsman hits the ball beyond this line, he scores a boundary, i.e. 4 runs.

boundless
(adjective) without end or limit, e.g. *The terrier's energy was boundless.*

bouquet, bouquets (pronounced boo-**kay**)
(noun) an arranged bunch of flowers.
[a French word from Old French *bosc* = forest]

bout, bouts
1 (noun) If you have a bout of something such as an illness, you have it for a short time, e.g. *He is recovering from a bout of 'flu.*
2 a boxing or wrestling match.

boutique, boutiques (pronounced boo-**teek**)
(noun) a small shop that sells fashionable clothes, shoes or jewellery.
[a French word]

bow, bows, bowing, bowed (rhymes with now)
1 (verb) to bend your body downwards briefly to show respect or to receive applause.
2 (noun) the front part of a ship.
[sense 1 – Old English *bugan* = to bend
sense 2 – Dutch *boeg* = shoulder]

bow, bows (rhymes with low)
1 (noun) a knot with two loops and two loose ends.
2 a weapon used for shooting arrows.
3 a long piece of wood with horsehair stretched along it, which you move to play a string instrument, e.g. a violin.
[Old English *boga* = arch or bow]

bowel, bowels
(noun) the tubes in the lower part of the body, through which waste from digested food goes on its way to being excreted through the anus.
[Latin *botellus* = little sausage]

bowl, bowls, bowling, bowled
1 (noun) a cooking container.
2 a large heavy ball used in bowls or tenpin bowling.
3 (verb) In cricket, to bowl means to throw the ball with a straight arm towards the batsman.
bowler (noun)
[noun: sense 1 – Old English *bolla* = cup
noun: sense 2 – French *boule* = ball]

bow-legged
(adjective) Someone who is bow-legged has legs that curve outwards at the knees.

bowling
(noun) a game in which you roll a heavy ball down a wooden lane towards a group of wooden pins and try to knock them down.

bowls
(noun) a game in which heavy balls, weighted so that they do not run straight, are rolled over a green to end up as near as possible to a small ball called the jack.
[French *boule* = ball]

bow tie, ties (rhymes with **low**)
(noun) a man's tie in the form of a bow, worn as part of formal evening dress.

bow window, windows (rhymes with **low**)
(noun) a curving window that sticks out from the wall.

box, boxes, boxing, boxed
1 (noun) a container.
2 On a form, a box is a rectangular space which you have to fill in.
3 In a theatre, a box is a small, separate area of seats for a small number of people.
4 (verb) to fight someone according to the rules of boxing.
[noun: sense 1 – Latin *buxus*, = the box tree; hence a wooden container]

box in
(phrasal verb) If you are boxed in, you cannot move away, because you are surrounded.

boxer, boxers
1 (noun) a man or boy who boxes.
2 a breed of dog.

boxing
(noun) a male sport in which two people fight using their fists, wearing padded gloves.

box office, offices
(noun) the place where tickets are sold in a theatre or cinema.

boy, boys
(noun) a male child.
boyhood (noun) **boyish** (adjective)
boyishly (adverb)

Similar words: lad, youngster, youth

boycott, boycotts, boycotting, boycotted
(verb) If you boycott something you refuse to

have anything to do with it, e.g. *He urged them to boycott the election.*
[from Captain C.C. Boycott (1832-97), an Irish land agent who so offended his tenants that they refused to pay their rents]

boyfriend, boyfriends
(noun) A girl or woman's boyfriend is the man or boy with whom she is having a romantic or sexual relationship.

bra, bras
(noun; informal) a piece of underwear worn by a woman to support her breasts. The formal word is **brassière**, a French word meaning 'restraint'.

brace, braces, bracing, braced
1 (verb) to stiffen your body to steady yourself or avoid falling over, e.g. *The taxi braked and the passenger braced himself with his foot.*
2 to prepare to face something unpleasant, e.g. *She braced herself to read the letter.*
3 (plural noun) Braces consist of a pair of straps to hold up trousers.
4 (noun) an object fastened to something to straighten or support it, e.g. a brace for teeth.
5 Two things of the same kind, e.g. *a brace of pheasants.*
[Old French *brace* = two arms]

bracelet, bracelets
(noun) a chain or band worn on the wrist.
[Old French *bracel* = little arm]

bracken
(noun) a plant like a large fern that grows on hills and in woods.

bracket
1 (noun) a pair of written marks, ( ) or [ ], placed round a word, expression or sentence that is not part of the main text, or to show that the items inside the brackets belong together.
2 a range of ages or prices, *e.g. the 14-16 age bracket ... It's out of our price bracket.*
3 a piece of metal or wood fastened to a wall to support, for example, a shelf.
bracketed (adjective)

brag, brags, bragging, bragged
(verb) to talk in a boastful way.
braggart (noun)

Braille
(noun) a system of printing for blind people. Letters are shown by raised dots that can be felt with the fingers. It was invented by Frenchman Louis Braille in the 19th century.

brain, brains
1 (noun) Your brain is the mass of nerve tissue inside your head that controls your body and enables you to think and feel; also used to refer to your mind and the way that you think.
2 (phrase) If you **pick someone's brains**, you get ideas or information from them.
3 **The brains behind** something is the person organizing it.
[Old English *brægen* = brain]

brainwash, brainwashes, brainwashing, brainwashed
(verb) If people are brainwashed into believing

What have bunsen burners, biros, cardigans and diesel engines got in common?

something, they accept it because it has been said to them over and over again.
brainwashing (noun)

brainwave, brainwaves
(noun; informal) a sudden, clever idea.

brainy, brainier, brainiest
(adjective; informal) clever.

brake, brakes, braking, braked
1 (noun) a device for making a vehicle stop or slow down.
2 (verb) to stop or slow down by using brakes.

bramble, brambles
(noun) a thorny bush that produces blackberries.

bran
(noun) the ground husks (grain casings) left over after flour has been made from wheat grains.

branch, branches, branching, branched
1 (noun) Branches are the parts of a tree that grow out from its trunk.
2 A branch of a business etc. is one of its offices, shops or local groups.
[Old French *branche*, from Latin *branca* = paw or foot]

branch out
(phrasal verb) to start a new, different activity.

brand, brands, branding, branded
1 (noun) a particular make of something, e.g. *Towser's favourite brand of dog food is Muncho.*
2 (verb) When an animal is branded, a mark is burned on its skin to show who owns it.
3 If you are branded as something bad, you have a reputation for it, e.g. *He was branded a traitor.*
[Old English *brand* = piece of burning wood]

brand-new
(adjective) completely new.

brandy
(noun) a strong alcoholic drink, distilled from wine.
[Dutch *brandewijn* = burnt wine]

brass
1 (noun, adjective) a yellowish metal alloy made from copper and zinc.
2 In an orchestra, the brass section consists of wind instruments such as trumpets, trombones, and French horns.

brat, brats
(noun; informal) an annoying child.

brave, braver, bravest; braves, braving, braved
1 (adjective) willing to do dangerous things.
2 (verb) If you brave a difficult or dangerous situation, you put up with it to achieve something, e.g. *Farmers braved the winter weather to rescue the sheep.*
bravely (adverb) **bravery** (noun)
[Italian *bravo* = courageous or wild]

Similar words: (adjective) courageous, fearless, plucky, heroic, valiant

brawl, brawls, brawling, brawled
1 (verb) to fight in a rough, uncontrolled way.
2 (noun) a rough, uncontrolled fight.

brawn
(noun) physical strength, e.g. *He is all brawn and no brain.*
brawny (adjective)
[Old French *braon* = slice of meat]

bray, brays, braying, brayed
1 (noun) the sound a donkey makes.
2 (verb) e.g. *The donkey brayed loudly.*

bread
(noun) a food made from flour and water, usually leavened with yeast, and baked.

breadth
(noun) the distance between the two sides of something; similar to 'width'.
[Old English *brad* = broad]

break, breaks, breaking, broke, broken
Selected meanings:
1 (verb) e.g. *If you slip, you will break your leg... Don't break your promise... Your voice is breaking, Tom.*
2 (noun) e.g. *I'll see you at break... Take a weekend break with British Rail.*
3 (phrase) to **break a fall**: to weaken its effect.
4 to **break the news**: to give a piece of bad news to someone.
breakable (adjective) **breakage** (noun)
[Old English *brecan* = to break]

Similar words: (verb) smash, shatter, snap, fracture

break down
1 (phrasal verb) to stop working because of a fault, e.g. *This pump has broken down.*
2 to start crying.

break in
1 (phrasal verb) to get into a building by force.
2 To break in a young horse means to train it.
break-in (noun)

break off
(phrasal verb) to stop suddenly what you are saying or doing.

break out
(phrasal verb) If something like a fight or disease breaks out, it begins suddenly.

break up
(phrasal verb) to finish a school term.

breakdown, breakdowns
1 (noun) the failure of a car, machine, etc.
2 If someone has a breakdown, they become so depressed that they cannot cope with life.

breaker, breakers
(noun) Breakers are big sea waves.

breakfast, breakfasts
(noun) the first meal of the day.
[You *break your fast*, or stop *not* eating.]

breakneck
(adjective; informal) Going at breakneck speed is travelling dangerously fast.

breakthrough, breakthroughs
(noun) a sudden, important development, e.g. *a breakthrough in the peace talks.*

breakwater, breakwaters
(noun) a wall protecting a harbour from the sea.

Which animals bleat? neigh? low? bellow? howl? trumpet? chatter? bell?

breast, breasts
(noun) A woman's breasts are the two soft, round fleshy parts on her chest, which secrete milk after she has had a baby.

breaststroke
(noun) a front swimming stroke.

breath, breaths
1 (noun) the air you take into your lungs and let out again when you breathe.
2 (phrase) **out of breath**: breathing with difficulty.
3 to **hold your breath**: to stop breathing for a short time.
4 If something **takes your breath away**, it is very surprising or beautiful.
5 If you say something **under your breath**, you say it in a very quiet voice.
[Old English *bræth* = odour or vapour]

breathalyse, breathalyses, breathalysing, breathalysed
(verb) to test a driver to see if they have been drinking.
breathalyser (noun)

breathe, breathes, breathing, breathed
(verb) to take air in and out of the lungs.

breathless
(adjective) out of breath.
breathlessly (adverb) **breathlessness** (noun)

breed, breeds, breeding, bred
1 (noun) one particular type of an animal group.
2 (verb) Someone who breeds animals or plants keeps them to produce more animals or plants with particular qualities.
3 to mate and produce offspring.

breeze, breezes
(noun) a gentle wind.
[probably Old Spanish *briza* = north-east wind]

brew, brews, brewing, brewed
1 (verb) to make tea or coffee with hot water.
2 to make beer by boiling and fermenting malt and hops.
3 If an unpleasant situation is brewing, it is about to happen, e.g. *There's trouble brewing in the factory.*
brewer (noun)

brewery, breweries
(noun) a place where beer is made.

bribe, bribes, bribing, bribed
(noun) money or something valuable given to an official to persuade them to make a favourable decision.
bribery (noun)
[Old French *briber* = to beg]

bric-a-brac
(noun) small ornaments or pieces of furniture that are not worth very much.
[French phrase *à bric et à brac* = at random]

brick, bricks
(noun) a block of baked clay used for building.
bricklayer (noun)

bride, brides
(noun) a woman getting married.
bridal (adjective)

bridegroom, bridegrooms
(noun) a man getting married.

bridesmaid, bridesmaids
(noun) a girl or woman who helps and accompanies a bride on her wedding day.

bridge, bridges
1 (noun) a structure built over a river, road, railway, etc. so that vehicles and people can cross.
2 A ship's bridge is the high part from which it is steered and controlled.
3 a card game for 4 players based on whist.
[Old Norse *bryggja* = gangway]

bridle, bridles
(noun) a set of straps round a horse's head and mouth so that the rider can control it.

brief, briefer, briefest; briefs, briefing, briefed
1 (adjective) lasting only a short time.
2 (verb) to give someone all the instructions and information about a task.
briefly (adverb) **briefing** (noun)
[Old French *bref* = short]

Similar words: short, momentary, quick, fleeting

briefcase, briefcases
(noun) a small, flat case for carrying papers.

bright, brighter, brightest
1 (adjective) strong and noticeable, e.g. *a bright light... a bright colour.*
2 clever, e.g. *my brightest pupil... a bright idea.*
3 cheerful, e.g. *a bright smile.*
brightly (adverb) **brightness** (noun)
brighten (verb)

Similar words: (sense 1) bold, vivid, brilliant, dazzling

brilliant
1 (adjective) shining extremely brightly.
2 extremely clever.
brilliantly (adverb) **brilliance** (noun)
[French *brillant* = shining]

brim, brims
1 (noun) the wide part of a hat.
2 (phrase) **filled to the brim**: filled right to the top.
[Old Norse *barmr* = edge]

bring, brings, bringing, brought
(verb) e.g. *He brings the coal in.*

bring about
(phrasal verb) to cause something to happen, e.g. *Air pollution may bring about global warming.*

bring off
(phrasal verb) to succeed in doing something.

bring up
1 (phrasal verb) To bring up children means to look after and teach them while they grow up.
2 to mention something, e.g. *I'm glad you have brought that up.*
3 to be sick, e.g. *The dog brought up its dinner.*

brisk, brisker, briskest
(adjective) quick and efficient.
briskly (adverb) **briskness** (noun)

bristle, bristles, bristling, bristled
1 (noun) strong animal hairs used in brushes.

What can't you hold for ten minutes though it is lighter than a feather?

2 (verb) If the hairs on an animal's body bristle, they rise up because it is frightened.
bristly (adjective)

British
(adjective) belonging or relating to the United Kingdom of Great Britain and Northern Ireland.

Briton, Britons
(noun) someone who comes from the United Kingdom of Great Britain and Northern Ireland.

brittle
(adjective) easily breakable.
brittleness (noun)

broad, broader, broadest
1 (adjective) wide, e.g. *a broad avenue.*
2 If someone has a broad accent, the way that they speak makes it very clear where they come from, e.g. *She had a broad Yorkshire accent.*
broadly (adverb)

broadcast, broadcasts, broadcasting, broadcast or broadcasted
1 (verb) to appear on TV or radio.
2 to broadcast something means to send it out by radio waves, to be seen on TV or heard on radio.
3 (noun) a programme etc. on radio or TV, e.g. *an outside broadcast.*
broadcaster (noun) **broadcasting** (noun)

broaden, broadens, broadening, broadened
(verb) to grow broader, or make something broader.

broad-minded
(adjective) tolerating behaviour that other people might find upsetting or immoral.

broadsheet
(adjective) Broadsheet newspapers are bigger and more serious than the tabloid press.

broccoli
(noun) a vegetable with green stalks and green or purple flower buds.
[an Italian word meaning 'little sprouts']

brochure, brochures (pronounced broh-sher)
(noun) a booklet with pictures giving information.
[French *brocher* = to bind books]

broke
1 (verb) past tense of **break**.
2 (adjective; informal) having no money.

Similar words: (adjective) bankrupt, penniless

broken past participle of **break**.

bronchitis
(noun) an illness in which your bronchial tubes (wind pipe) become infected, making you cough.

brontosaurus, brontosauruses
(noun) a very large, 4-footed, herbivorous dinosaur, with a long neck and a long tail.

bronze
(noun) a yellowish-brown metal alloy which is a mixture of copper and tin.

brooch, brooches (rhymes with coach)
(noun) a piece of jewellery with a pin at the back for attaching to a dress or blouse.
[Old French *broche* = long needle]

brood, broods, brooding, brooded
1 (noun) a family of baby birds.
2 (verb) to keep thinking about something in a serious or unhappy way.

brook, brooks
(noun) a stream.

broom, brooms
(noun) a long-handled brush.

broth
(noun) a soup, usually with vegetables in it.

brother, brothers
(noun) Your brother is a boy or man who has the same parents as you. Your **half-brother** has one parent the same as you, and one parent different. If your parents get divorced and re-marry other people, your **stepbrother** would be a child of the people they marry.
brotherly (adjective)

brother-in-law, brothers-in-law
(noun) A brother-in-law is the brother of someone's husband or wife, or their sister's husband.

brought past tense and past participle of **bring**.

brow, brows
1 (noun) the forehead.
2 Your brows are your eyebrows or the ridge of the forehead.
3 The brow of a hill is the top of it.

brown, browner, brownest
(adjective, noun) a colour.

browned off
(adjective; informal) feeling bored or miserable.

brownie, brownies
(noun) a junior member of the Girl Guides.

browse, browses, browsing, browsed
1 (verb) to look in a casual way at, for example, a book or the things in a shop.
2 When animals, e.g. deer, are browsing, they are nibbling at the young shoots and leaves of trees.
[sense 2 – French *broust* = bud or young shoot]

bruise, bruises
(noun) a purple mark that appears on your skin after something has hit it.
[Old English *brysan* = to crush]

brunette, brunettes
(noun) a girl or woman with dark brown hair.
[French *brunet* = dark or brownish]

brush, brushes, brushing, brushed
1 (noun) an object with bristles used for cleaning, painting or tidying hair.
2 (verb) e.g. *She brushed her hair.*

brussels sprout, sprouts
(noun) a vegetable that looks like a tiny cabbage.

brutal
(adjective) Brutal behaviour is cruel and violent, e.g. *their brutal treatment of prisoners.*
brutally (adverb) **brutality** (noun)

brute, brutes
1 (noun) A person who is a brute is rough and insensitive.

Britain is England and Wales; Great Britain is England, Wales and Scotland; for United Kingdom add N. Ireland.

2 (adjective) Brute force is strength alone, without any skill.
brutish (adjective)
[Latin *brutus* = heavy or stupid]

bubble, bubbles
(noun) a ball of air in a liquid.

bubbly
1 (adjective) full of bubbles.
2 full of life and energy.

buck, bucks, bucking, bucked
1 (noun) the male of various animals, including the deer and the rabbit.
2 (verb) If a horse bucks, it jumps straight up in the air with all 4 feet off the ground.
3 (phrase; informal) If you **pass the buck**, you pass the blame for something to someone else.
[Old English *bucca* = male goat]

bucket, buckets
(noun) a container with a handle.

buckle, buckles, buckling, buckled
1 (noun) a fastening on the end of a belt etc.
2 (verb) to become bent because of severe heat or pressure, e.g. *The bumper buckled in the crash.*
[Latin *buccula* = helmet strap]

bud, buds, budding, budded
1 (noun) a small, tight swelling on a tree or plant which becomes a flower or a cluster of leaves.
2 (verb) When a tree or plant buds, new buds appear on it.
3 (phrase) To **nip something in the bud** means to put an end to it at an early stage.

budding
(adjective) young and promising, e.g. *Little Roger is a budding poet.*

budge, budges, budging, budged
(verb) If something will not budge, you cannot move it.

budgerigar, budgerigars or **budgie**
(noun) a small, brightly coloured pet bird.
[Australian aboriginal *budgeri* + *gar* = good cockatoo]

budget, budgets, budgeting, budgeted
1 (noun) a plan showing how much money will be available and how it will be spent.
2 (verb) If you budget for something, you plan your money carefully, so you can afford it.
budgetary (adjective)
[Old French *bougette* = small leather bag]

buffalo, buffaloes
(noun) a wild animal like a large cow with long curved horns, also called a bison.
[Greek *boubalos* = wild ox]

buffer, buffers
(noun) Buffers on a train or at the end of a railway line are metal discs on springs that reduce shock when they are hit.

buffet, buffets (pronounced **boof**-ay)
1 (noun) a café at a station.
2 a cold meal laid out for people to choose from.
[a French word meaning 'sideboard']

bug, bugs, bugging, bugged
1 (noun) an insect, especially one that infests houses or beds.
2 a small error in a computer program which means that it will not work properly.
3 (informal) a virus or minor infection, e.g. *I've picked up a stomach bug.*
4 (verb) If a place is bugged, microphones are hidden to pick up what people are saying.

Similar words: (noun: sense 3) germ, virus, infection

bugle, bugles
(noun) a brass instrument like a small trumpet.
bugler (noun)

build, builds, building, built
1 (verb) to make something from its parts.
2 (noun) Your build is the shape of your body.
builder (noun)

Similar words: (verb) construct, erect, assemble

building, buildings
(noun) a structure with walls and a roof.

building society, societies
(noun) an organization in which people invest money, or borrow from it to buy a house, or both.

build-up, build-ups
(noun) A build-up is a gradual increase in something, e.g. *a build-up of nuclear weapons.*

built-up
(adjective) A built-up area is one where there are many buildings.

bulb, bulbs
1 (noun) the glass part of an electric lamp.
2 an onion-shaped root that grows into a flower or plant.
[Greek *bolbos* = onion]

bulge, bulges, bulging, bulged
(verb) to stick out from a surface.

bulk, bulks
1 (noun) a large mass of something, e.g. *the dark bulk of the building.*
2 The bulk of something is most of it, e.g. *The bulk of the population is poor and homeless.*
3 (phrase) To buy something **in bulk** means to buy it in large quantities.
[Old Norse *bulki* = cargo]

bulky, bulkier, bulkiest
(adjective) large and heavy, e.g. *a bulky load.*

bull, bulls
(noun) the male of some species of animals, including cattle, elephants, seals and whales.

bulldog, bulldogs
(noun) a breed of dog with a large square head and short hair.

bulldozer, bulldozers
(noun) a large, powerful tractor with a broad blade in front, used for moving earth or knocking things down.

bullet, bullets
(noun) a small piece of metal fired from a gun.
[French *boulette* = small ball]

What kind of person is: a bull in a china shop a wolf in sheep's clothing a dog in the manger?

bulletin, bulletins
1 (noun) a short news report on radio or TV.
2 a leaflet or small newspaper regularly
produced by a group or organization.
[Italian *bulletino* = small Papal edict]

bullion
(noun) bars or lumps of gold or silver.
[Old French *bouillir* = to boil; metals are refined
by being heated]

bullock, bullocks
(noun) a young neutered bull.

bully, bullies, bullying, bullied
1 (noun) someone who uses strength or power to
hurt or frighten other people.
2 (verb) to hurt or frighten weaker people.
[a 16th century word meaning 'fine fellow or
hired ruffian']

bump, bumps, bumping, bumped
(verb) to knock into something with a jolt.
bumpy (adjective)

Similar words: lump, hump, bulge

bump off
(phrasal verb; informal) to kill.

bump into
(phrasal verb) to meet by chance.

bumper, bumpers
1 (noun) Bumpers are bars on the front and back
of a vehicle which protect it if there is a collision.
2 (adjective) A bumper crop or harvest is larger
than usual.

bunch, bunches
(noun) a group of people or things.

bundle, bundles, bundling, bundled
1 (noun) a number of things tied together or
wrapped up in a cloth etc.
2 (verb) to push someone quickly and roughly,
e.g. *They bundled him into a van.*

bung, bungs, bunging, bunged
1 (noun) a piece of wood, cork, or rubber used to
close a hole in, for example, a barrel.
2 (verb; informal) If you bung something
somewhere, you put it there quickly and
carelessly, e.g. *Bung it in the shed!*

bungalow, bungalows
(noun) a one-storeyed house.
[Hindi *bangla* = house]

bunged up
(adjective; informal) blocked.

bungle, bungles, bungling, bungled
(verb) To bungle something means to make
mistakes and fail to do it properly.
bungler (noun)

bunk, bunks
1 (noun) a bed fixed to a wall, usually with two
layers.
2 (informal) If you describe something written or
spoken as bunk, you mean it is silly or untrue.
3 (phrase; informal) If someone **does a bunk**, they
leave a place without telling anyone.

bunker, bunkers
1 (noun) On a golf course, a bunker is a large hole
filled with sand.
2 A coal bunker is a storage place for coal.
3 an underground shelter, protected from
bombing and gunfire, e.g. *Hitler's bunker.*

bunsen burner, burners
(noun) a kind of gas burner used in laboratories,
invented by R.W. von Bunsen (1811-99), a
German scientist.

buoy, buoys (pronounced **boy**)
(noun) a floating object anchored to the seabed,
marking a channel or warning of an obstruction.

buoyant
1 (adjective) able to float.
2 lively and cheerful, e.g. *in a buoyant mood.*
buoyancy (noun)
[Spanish *boyar* = to float]

burble, burbles, burbling, burbled
(verb) to make an indistinct, continuous bubbling
sound; also to talk on and on.

burden, burdens
(noun) a heavy load.
burdensome (adjective)
[Old English *byrthen* = load or weight]

bureau, bureaux (pronounced **byoo**-roh)
1 (noun) a writing desk with shelves and
drawers.
2 an office that provides a service, e.g. *a travel
bureau... The Federal Bureau of Investigation.*
[a French word meaning 'desk' or 'office']

burger
(noun; informal) short for beefburger or
hamburger.

burglar, burglars
(noun) a thief who breaks into a building.
burglary (noun) **burgle** (verb)

burly, burlier, burliest
(adjective) having a broad body and strong
muscles.
[Middle English *borli* = stately or imposing]

Similar words: beefy, brawny

burn, burns, burning, burned or **burnt**
(verb) e.g. *I burned my hand on the stove.*

Similar words: blaze, flame, incinerate

burp, burps, burping, burped
(verb) to make a noise because air from the
stomach has been forced up through the throat.

burrow, burrows
(noun) a tunnel or hole in the ground dug by a
rabbit or other small animal.

bursar, bursars
(noun) a person who manages the money and
administration in a school or college.
[Latin *bursa* = purse]

burst, bursts, bursting, burst
1 (verb) When something bursts, it splits open
because of pressure from inside it.
2 If you burst into a room, you enter it suddenly.

3 to happen suddenly and with force, e.g. *Mrs Lee burst into tears.*
4 (noun) A burst of something is a short period of it, e.g. *a burst of speed... a burst of rifle fire.*

bury, buries, burying, buried
(verb) When a dead person is buried, their body is put into a grave and covered with earth.
burial (noun)
[Old English *byrgels* = tomb]

bus, buses
(noun) a large vehicle that carries passengers.
[Latin *omnibus* = for all; buses were originally called omnibuses]

bush, bushes
1 (noun) a large plant with many stems branching out from ground level.
2 The wild, uncultivated parts of some hot countries are referred to as 'the bush'.

bushy, bushier, bushiest
(adjective) Bushy hair or fur grows very thickly.

business, businesses
1 (noun) an organization which produces or sells goods or provides a service.
2 work relating to the buying and selling of goods and services, e.g. *I'm in business.*
3 a general word for an event, situation, or activity, e.g. *This whole business has upset me.*
4 (phrase) If a company goes **out of business**, it finishes because it is not making any money.
5 If someone **has no business** to do something, they have no right to do it.
businessman (noun) **businesswoman** (noun)
[Old English *bisignis* = attentiveness]

Similar words: (sense 1) company, enterprise, concern, firm

busker, buskers
(noun) someone who plays music for money in the street or in some other public place.

bust, busts, busting, bust or busted
1 (noun) a statue of someone's head and shoulders, e.g. *a bust of Shakespeare.*
2 A woman's bust is her chest and her breasts.
3 (verb; informal) to break.
4 (adjective; informal) broken, e.g. *The TV's bust.*
5 (informal) If a business goes bust, it becomes bankrupt and closes down.
[noun: sense 1 – Italian *busto* = sculpture]

bustle, bustles, bustling, bustled
1 (verb) to move in a busy, hurried way.
2 (noun) busy, noisy activity.
[from an old word *buskle* meaning 'to prepare energetically']

Similar word: (noun) activity

busy, busier, busiest
1 (adjective) in the middle of doing something.
2 full of activity, e.g. *The shop was busy.*
busily (adverb)
[Old English *bisig* = busy]

Similar words: (sense 1) employed, engaged, occupied

busybody, busybodies
(noun) someone who interferes in other people's affairs.

but
(conjunction) e.g. *I'd like to, but it's fattening.*
[Old English *butan* = without or except]

butcher, butchers
(noun) a shopkeeper who sells meat.
[Old French *bouchier* = butcher]

butt, butts, butting, butted
1 (noun) the thick end of a weapon's handle.
2 (verb) to ram hard with the head.
[noun: *butt* = buttock
verb: Old French *boter* = to strike]

butt in
(phrasal verb) to interrupt rudely.

butter
(noun) a yellow substance made from cream, which is spread on bread and used in cooking.

buttercup, buttercups
(noun) a wild plant with bright yellow flowers.

butterfly, butterflies
1 (noun) an insect with large, colourful wings.
2 a front swimming stroke.

button, buttons, buttoning, buttoned
1 (noun) a disc sewn on to clothing which is passed through a buttonhole to act as a fastener.
2 a small switch on a piece of equipment that you press to operate the equipment.
3 (verb) If you button a piece of clothing, you fasten it using buttons.

buy, buys, buying, bought
(verb) to obtain something by paying for it.
buyer (noun)

buzz, buzzes, buzzing, buzzed
(verb) e.g. *The bees buzzed in the garden.*
buzzer (noun)

Similar words: drone, hum

buzzword
(noun; informal) the word or idea that is fashionable or important at the moment.

by
(preposition, adverb) e.g. *We drove by his house.*

by-election
(noun) the voting to choose an MP in a single district, because of the death, resignation, etc.
[compare: **general election**]

bypass, bypasses
(noun) a main road which takes traffic round a town rather than through it.

bystander, bystanders
(noun) someone who sees something happen but does not take part in it.

byte, bytes
(noun) a unit of storage in a computer, comprising 8 bits.

What happens to a boy who misses the last bus? He catches it when he gets home.

C

cab, cabs
1 (noun) a taxi.
2 where the driver sits in a lorry, bus or train.
[French *cabriolet* = light two-wheeled carriage.]

cabbage, cabbages
(noun) a large, green, leafy vegetable.
[Norman French *cabache* = head]

cabin, cabins
1 (noun) a bedroom in a ship.
2 In a plane, the cabin is the area where the
passengers sit.
3 a small house, usually in the country and often
made of wood.
[Latin *capanna* = hut]

cabinet, cabinets
1 (noun) a small cupboard.
2 The cabinet in a government is a group of
ministers who advise the leader and help decide
policies.

cable, cables, cabling, cabled
1 (noun) a strong, thick rope or chain.
2 a bundle of wires with a rubber covering,
which carries electricity.
3 (verb) If you cable someone, you send them a
message or money by telegram.
[Latin *capulum* = horse's halter]

cable car, cars
(noun) a vehicle pulled by a moving cable, for
taking people up mountains.

cable television
(noun) a special television service which people
receive by cable not by aerial.

cackle, cackles, cackling, cackled
(verb) to laugh harshly.

cacophony (pronounced kak-**koff**-fon-nee)
(noun; formal) a loud, unpleasant noise, e.g. *Dad
thinks Heavy Metal is a cacophony.*
cacophonous (adjective)
[Greek *kakos* + *phōnē* = bad sound]

cactus, cacti or cactuses
(noun) a thick, fleshy plant that grows in deserts
and is usually covered in spikes.

cadet, cadets
(noun) a young person being trained in the army,
navy, air force or police.

cadge, cadges, cadging, cadged
(verb) If you cadge something from someone,
you get it from them and don't give them
anything in return, e.g. *He cadged money from
his aunt then gambled it away.*
cadger (noun)

café, cafés (pronounced **kaf**-fay)
(noun) a place where you can buy light meals,
snacks and drinks.

cafeteria, cafeterias (pronounced
kaf-fit-**ee**-ree-ya)
(noun) a self-service restaurant.

caffeine (pronounced **kaf**-feen)
(noun) a chemical found in coffee, tea, cola
drinks and cocoa, which makes you more active
and keeps you awake.

cage, cages
(noun) a boxlike structure made of wire or bars
in which birds or animals are kept.
caged (adjective)
[Latin *cavea* = enclosure]

cagey (pronounced **kay**-jee)
(adjective; informal) cautious and not direct or
open, e.g. *He's being very cagey about things.*
cagily (adverb) **caginess** (noun)

cagoule, cagoules (pronounced ka-**gool**)
(noun) a light, waterproof jacket with hood.

cajole, cajoles, cajoling, cajoled
(verb) to persuade.
[French *cajoler* = to coax]

cake, cakes
1 (noun) a sweet food made by baking flour,
eggs, fat and sugar.
2 (phrase; informal) If something is a **piece of
cake**, it is very easy to do.
[Old Norse *kaka* = oatcake]

calamity, calamities
(noun) a disaster.
calamitous (adjective)
[Latin *calamitas* = injury]

calcium (pronounced **kal**-see-um)
(noun) a soft, white chemical element found in
bones and teeth.
[Latin *calx* = lime]

calculate, calculates, calculating, calculated
(verb) to work something out, usually by
arithmetic.
calculation (noun)
[Latin *calculus* = stone or pebble. The Romans
used to count with pebbles]

calculating
(adjective) carefully planning situations to get
what you want, e.g. *a cold, calculating criminal.*

calculator, calculators
(noun) a small electronic machine used for doing
mathematical calculations.

calendar, calendars
(noun) a chart showing the date of each day in a
particular year.
[Latin *kalendae*, the day of the month on which
interest on debts was due]

calf, calves
1 (noun) a young cow, elephant, giraffe, whale
etc.
2 the thick part of the leg below the knee.
[sense 1 – Old English *cælf* = calf
sense 2 – Old Norse *kalfi*]

call, calls, calling, called
(verb, noun) e.g *If in doubt, call for help... We are
calling him Walter... a telephone call.*

Letter C is probably based on a weapon, perhaps a boomerang.

call off
(phrasal verb) If you call something off, you cancel it.

call up
(phrasal verb) If someone is called up, they are ordered to join the army, navy or air force.

call box, boxes
(noun) a telephone kiosk.

calligraphy
(noun) the art of beautiful handwriting.
[Greek *kalos* + *graphein* = beautiful writing]

callous
(adjective) cruel; showing no concern for other people's feelings.
callously (adverb) **callousness** (noun)

Similar words: heartless, unfeeling, hard

calm, calmer, calmest; calms, calming, calmed
1 (adjective) Someone who is calm is quiet and does not show any worry or excitement.
2 If the weather or the sea is calm, it is still because there is no strong wind.
3 (verb) to make someone less upset or excited.
calmly (adverb) **calmness** (noun)
[Latin *cauma* = heat of the day]

Similar words: (adjective) cool, unflappable
(verb) quieten, soothe

Calor gas
(noun; a trademark) liquid butane gas in metal bottles, used for cooking and heating.

calorie, calories
(noun) a unit of measurement for the energy value of food, e.g. *a diet of 1,500 calories a day.*
calorific (adjective)
[Latin *calor* = heat]

calves the plural of **calf.**

calypso, calypsos (pronounced kal-**lip**-soh)
(noun) a type of song from the West Indies, with a topical subject and a lively rhythm.

camel, camels
(noun) a large mammal with either one or two humps on its back, living in hot desert areas.
[Hebrew *gamal* = camel]

camera, cameras
(noun) a piece of equipment for taking photographs or films.
[Latin *camera* = vault]

camouflage (pronounced **kam**-mof-flahj)
(noun) a disguise using the same appearance as the surroundings.
[Italian *camuffare* = to disguise or to deceive]

camp, camps, camping, camped
1 (verb) When you camp, you sleep in a tent.
camper (noun) **camping** (noun)
2 (noun) a collection of buildings used for a particular group of people such as soldiers or prisoners.
3 (adjective) Camp acting is very exaggerated in style.
[Latin *campus* = field]

campaign, campaigns (pronounced kam-**pane**)
(noun) a planned set of actions aimed at achieving a particular result, e.g. *the campaign against world hunger.*
campaigner (noun) **campaign** (verb)

Similar words: movement, crusade

campus, campuses
(noun) the area of land and the buildings that make up a university, college or school.

can, could
(verb) e.g. *We can certainly try... She could not move.*

can, cans
(noun) a metal container.
canned (adjective)
[Old English *canne* = vessel for liquid]

Canadian, Canadians
1 (adjective) belonging to Canada.
2 (noun) someone who comes from Canada.

canal, canals
(noun) a man-made channel of water.
[Latin *canalis* = channel or water-pipe]

canary, canaries
(noun) a small, yellow bird often kept as a pet.
[They are found in the Canary Islands.]

cancel, cancels, cancelling, cancelled
(verb) If you cancel something that has been arranged, you stop it from happening.
cancellation (noun)
[Latin *cancellare* = to cross out]

cancer, cancers
(noun) a serious disease in which abnormal cells in the body increase rapidly, producing growths.
cancerous (adjective)
[Latin *cancer* = crab]

Similar word: tumour

candid
(adjective) speaking honestly and openly.
candidly (adverb) **candour** (noun)
[Latin *candidus* = white]

candidate, candidates
1 (noun) A candidate for a job is a person who is being considered for that job.
2 a person taking an examination.
candidacy (noun)
[Latin *candidatus* = white-robed. In Rome, a candidate wore a white toga]

candle, candles
(noun) a stick of hard wax with a wick through the middle, used to provide light.
[Latin *candere* = to shine with a white light]

candlestick, candlesticks
(noun) a holder for a candle.

candy, candies
(noun) Americans call sweets 'candy'.
[Arabic *qand* = cane sugar]

cane, canes, caning, caned
1 (noun) the long, hollow stems of a plant such as bamboo.

Are you sure about the different meanings of: cancel – postpone; artist – artiste; caddie – caddy?

2 (noun) To cane someone means to beat them with a cane as a punishment.
[Greek *kanna* = reed]

canine, canines (pronounced **kay**-nine)
1 (adjective) relating to dogs.
2 (noun) A canine tooth is one of two pointed teeth near the front of the mouth in humans and some animals.
[Latin *canis* = dog]

canister, canisters
(noun) a container with a lid.
[Greek *kanastron* = wicker basket]

cannabis
(noun) a plant, parts of which are used to make a hallucinatory or intoxicating drug. Taking cannabis is illegal and can be dangerous in that it alters behaviour and can lead to the taking of stronger drugs.

canned
1 (adjective) Canned food is preserved in cans.
2 Canned music or laughter on a TV or radio show is recorded beforehand.

cannibal, cannibals
(noun) a person who eats the flesh of other human beings.
cannibalism (noun).

cannibalize, cannibalizes, cannibalizing, cannibalized; also spelled **cannibalise**
(verb) to take parts from one machine to repair another.

cannon, cannons
(noun) a large gun firing metal balls.
[Italian *canna* = tube]

canoe, canoes (pronounced ka-**noo**)
(noun) a narrow boat that is paddled along.
canoeing (noun) **canoeist** (noun)
[Spanish *canoa* = boat]

canon, canons
(noun) a member of the clergy, senior to a vicar.
[Greek *kanōn* = measuring rod or rule]

canopy, canopies
(noun) a cover used for shelter or decoration, e.g. *a throne with a silk canopy.*
[Greek *kōnōpeion* = bed with a mosquito net]

cantankerous
(adjective) quarrelsome and bad-tempered.

canteen, canteens
(noun) the part of a factory etc. where the workers can go to eat.
[Italian *cantina* = cellar]

canter, canters, cantering, cantered
(verb) When a horse canters, it moves at a speed between a gallop and a trot.

canvas, canvases
1 (noun) strong, heavy cotton or linen cloth used for making things such as sails, tents, and bags.
2 A canvas is a piece of canvas on which an artist does a painting.
[Latin *cannabis* = hemp]

canvass, canvasses, canvassing, canvassed
(verb) to talk to people, trying to win their support or their votes.

(possibly, from canvas: counters being tossed in a canvas sheet)

canyon, canyons
(noun) a narrow river valley with steep sides.

cap, caps, capping, capped
1 (noun) a soft, flat hat.
2 the lid or top of a bottle.
3 (verb) To cap something means to put something on top of it, e.g. *a cake capped with a cherry.*
[Latin *cappa* = hood]

capable
(adjective) able to do something, e.g *She is a capable woman... He is capable of anything.*
capably (adverb) **capability** (noun)
[Latin *capabilis* = able to take in]

capacity, capacities (pronounced kap-**pas**-sit-tee)
(noun) the amount that something can hold, e.g. *a tank with a capacity of 10 gallons.*

cape, capes
1 (noun) a short cloak with no sleeves.
2 a large piece of land sticking out into the sea, e.g. *the southern cape of India.*

capital, capitals
1 (noun) The capital of a country is its main city or town where the government meets.
2 a large letter used to start a sentence or name.
3 a sum of money that you save or invest to gain interest.
4 (adjective) involving or requiring the punishment of death, e.g. *capital punishment.*
[Latin *caput* = head]

capitalism
(noun) an economic and political system where business and industry are owned by private individuals and not by the state.
capitalist (adjective and noun)

capsize, capsizes, capsizing, capsized
(verb) If a boat capsizes, it turns upside down.

capsule, capsules
1 (noun) a small soluble container with powdered medicine inside which you swallow.
2 the part of a spacecraft in which astronauts travel.
[Latin *capsula* = little box]

captain, captains
1 (noun) the officer in charge of a ship or plane.
2 an army officer.
3 the leader of a sports team.
[Latin *caput* = head]

Similar words: (sense 1) skipper, commander, master

caption, captions
(noun) a title or description printed underneath a picture or photograph.
[Latin *captio* = seizure; a caption seizes your attention]

captive, captives
(noun) a prisoner who has been captured.
captivity (noun) **captor** (noun)

The names of counties and states begin with capital letters: Yorkshire Cornwall Georgia Kansas.

capture, captures, capturing, captured
(verb) to take someone prisoner.
[Latin *capere* = to take]

car, cars
(noun) a road vehicle.
[Latin *carra* = wagon]

caramel, caramels
1 (noun) a sweet made from sugar, butter and
milk.
2 burnt sugar for colouring or flavouring food.

caravan, caravans
1 (noun) a vehicle which can be pulled by a car,
in which people live or spend their holidays.
2 a group of people and animals travelling
together, usually across a desert.
[Persian *karwan* = desert travellers]

carbohydrate, carbohydrates
(noun) an organic compound containing carbon,
hydrogen and oxygen, found in food such as
sugar and bread. Carbohydrate gives you slowly
releasing energy.

carbon
(noun) a chemical element that is pure in
diamonds and also found in coal. All living things
contain carbon.
[Latin *carbo* = charcoal]

carbon copy, copies
1 (noun) a copy of a piece of writing made using
carbon paper.
2 (informal) someone who looks very similar to
someone else, e.g. *She's a carbon copy of her
grandmother.*

carbon dioxide
(noun) a colourless, odourless gas that humans
and animals breathe out. It is used in industry,
e.g. in fizzy drinks and in fire extinguishers.

carbon monoxide
(noun) a colourless, poisonous gas. It forms part
of vehicle exhaust fumes.

carcass, carcasses; also spelled **carcase**
(noun) the body of a dead animal.

card, cards
1 (noun) a piece of stiff paper, plastic, etc.
Playing cards are marked for use in card games.
2 (phrase) If something is **on the cards**, it is very
likely to happen.
[Greek *khartēs* = papyrus leaf]

cardboard
(noun) thick, stiff paper.

cardigan, cardigans
(noun) a knitted jacket that fastens up the front,
named after the Earl of Cardigan (1797-1868).

cardinal, cardinals
1 (noun) one of the high-ranking members of the
Roman Catholic clergy who elect and advise the
Pope.
2 (adjective) extremely important, e.g. *The
family is a cardinal feature of our society.*
[Latin *cardo* = hinge. When something is
important, other things hinge on it]

cardinal number, numbers
(noun) a whole number, e.g. *1, 2, 3.* [compare
ordinal numbers].

cardinal point, points
(noun) The cardinal points are the main points of
the compass: north, south, east and west.

care, cares, caring, cared
1 (verb) If you care about something, you are
concerned about it and interested in it.
2 If you care about someone, you feel affection
towards them.
3 If you care for someone, you look after them.
4 (noun) If you do something with care, you do it
with close attention, e.g. *Handle with care.*
5 (phrase) Children who are **in care** are living in a
children's home etc, often because their parents
are dead or cannot look after them properly.
6 If something is sent to you **care of** another
person, it goes to the other person to be passed
on to you, e.g. *Dr. Angus Galbraith, care of Ritz
Hotel, London.*
[Germanic *kara* = grief]

Similar words: (verb: sense 3) attend, nurse, tend

career, careers, careering, careered
1 (noun) Someone's career is the series of jobs
that they have in life, usually in the same
occupation, e.g. *his career as a journalist.*
2 (verb) to move very quickly, often out of
control, e.g. *A car careered round the corner.*
[Latin *carraria* = paved road]

carefree
(adjective) having no worries or responsibilities.

careful
(adjective) acting sensibly and with care,
carefully (adverb) **carefulness** (noun)

Similar words: cautious, watchful, wary

careless
(adjective) doing something badly without
enough attention, e.g. *Her work is careless.*
carelessly (adverb) **carelessness** (noun)

Similar words: thoughtless, haphazard, negligent,
slapdash, sloppy, neglectful

caretaker, caretakers
(noun) a person whose job is to look after a large
building such as a school.

cargo, cargoes
(noun) the goods carried on a ship or plane.
[Spanish *cargar* = to load up]

Similar words: freight, load

carnation, carnations
(noun) a plant with long stems and white, pink
or red flowers, often worn for decoration.
[Latin *carnatio* = fleshiness; carnations were
originally flesh-coloured]

carnival, carnivals
(noun) a special occasion with entertainments
such as processions and dancing.

We take these words from Persian: bazaar caravan divan pyjamas shawl.

carnivore, carnivores
(noun) an animal that eats meat.
carnivorous (adjective)

carol, carols
(noun) a religious song sung at Christmas.

carp, carps, carping, carped
1 (noun) a large, edible, freshwater fish.
2 (verb) to complain about unimportant things.
[sense 1 – Latin *carpa* = carp
sense 2 – Old Norse *karpa* = to boast]

carpenter, carpenters
(noun) a person whose job is making and
repairing wooden structures.
(compare **joiner**)
carpentry (noun)
[Latin *carpentarius* = wagon-maker]

carpet, carpets
(noun) a type of floor covering.
carpeted (adjective)
[Latin *carpeta* = carded wool]

carriage, carriages
1 (noun) one of the separate sections of a
passenger train.
2 an old-fashioned vehicle for carrying
passengers, usually pulled by horses.
[Old French *carier* = to convey]

carriageway, carriageways
(noun) one of the separated sides of a road which
traffic travels along in one direction only.

carried away
(phrasal verb) If you get carried away, you are
so excited that you do not behave sensibly.

carrier bag, bags
(noun) a bag made of plastic or paper, which is
used for carrying shopping in.

carrot, carrots
(noun) a root vegetable.

carry, carries, carrying, carried
1 (verb) to hold something and take it
somewhere.
2 A person or animal that carries a germ is
capable of passing it on to other people or
animals, e.g. *Rats carry nasty diseases.*
3 If a sound carries, it can be heard far away,
e.g. *His voice carried right to the back row.*
[Old French *carier* = to take by vehicle]

Similar words: bear, convey, take

carry on
(phrasal verb) to continue.

carry out
(phrasal verb) To carry something out means to
do and complete it, e.g. *They carried out a
survey.*

cart, carts
(noun) a vehicle with wheels, used to carry
goods and often pulled by horses or cattle.
[Old Norse *kartr* = carriage]

cartilage
(noun) strong, flexible body tissue found around
the joints and in the nose and ears.
[Latin *cartilago* = gristle]

cartography (pronounced kahr-**tog**-raf-fee)
(noun) the art of drawing maps.
cartographer (noun)
[Greek *khartès* = papyrus leaf + *graphein* = to
write or to draw]

carton, cartons
(noun) a cardboard or plastic box.

cartoon, cartoons
1 (noun) a drawing which is funny or makes a
political point.
2 an animated film.
cartoonist (noun)
[Italian *cartone* = sketch on stiff paper]

cartridge, cartridges
1 (noun) a tube containing a bullet and an
explosive substance, used in guns.
2 a plastic tube of ink for a pen.
[French *cartouche* = cartridge]

cartwheel, cartwheels
(noun) an acrobatic movement.

carve, carves, carving, carved
1 (verb) To carve an object means to cut it out of
a substance such as stone or wood.
2 To carve meat means to cut slices from it.
[Old English *ceorfan* = to cut into]

Similar words: (sense 1) sculpt, engrave, whittle

cascade, cascades
(noun) a waterfall or group of waterfalls.
[Italian *cascare* = to fall]

case, cases
1 (noun) a particular situation, event, or
example, e.g. *It was a case of 'finders keepers'.*
2 a container for something, or a suitcase, e.g. *a
glasses case.*
3 Doctors sometimes refer to a patient as a case.
4 Detectives refer to a crime as a case.
5 In an argument, the case for an idea is the facts
and reasons used to support it.
6 In law, a case is a trial or other legal inquiry.
7 In grammar, the case of a noun or pronoun is
the form of it which shows its relationship with
other words in a sentence, e.g. 'He' is the
nominative case. 'Him' is in the accusative case.
8 You say **in case** to explain something that you
do because a particular thing might happen, e.g.
I've got some money in case we need it.
[Latin *casus* = event]

Similar words: (sense 1) instance, circumstance

cash
(noun) money in the form of notes and coins
rather than cheques.
[Italian *cassa* = money-box]

cashier, cashiers
(noun) the person that customers pay in a shop
or get money from in a bank.

cash register, registers
(noun) a machine in a shop which records sales
and is where the money is put.

casino, casinos (pronounced kass-**ee**-noh)
(noun) a place where people go to play gambling
games such as roulette, blackjack, poker.

Can you find out which author created The Dong with the Luminous Nose and The Quangle Wangle?

cask, casks
(noun) a wooden barrel.
[Spanish *casco* = helmet]

casket, caskets
(noun) a small decorative box for jewellery etc.
[Old French *cassette* = little box]

casserole, casseroles
(noun) meal made by cooking a mixture of meat and vegetables slowly in an oven; also the pot a casserole is cooked in.
[Old French *casse* = ladle or dripping pan]

cassette, cassettes
(noun) a small box of tape for cassette recorders.
[Old French *cassette* = little box]

cassette recorder, recorders
(noun) a machine for recording and playing cassette tapes.

cast, casts, casting, cast
1 (noun) The cast of a play or film is all the people who act in it.
2 (verb) To cast something means to throw it.
3 to cast your vote means to vote.
4 (noun) A **plaster cast** is plaster of Paris poured round e.g. a broken arm, and set hard.
[Old Norse *kasta* = to throw]

Similar words: (noun: sense 1) actors, company

cast off
1 (phrasal verb) to untie a boat from its mooring.
2 In knitting, to cast off means to take stitches off the needle and finish the edge of the knitting.

cast on
(phrasal verb) In knitting, to cast on stitches means to make them on a needle.

caster sugar or **castor sugar**
(noun) a very fine, white sugar used in cooking.

cast iron
1 (noun) iron which is made into objects by casting. It contains carbon.
2 (adjective) A cast-iron excuse or guarantee is absolutely certain and firm.

castle, castles
1 (noun) a large, ancient building with walls or ditches round it to protect it from attack.
2 In chess, a castle is the same as a rook, moving in straight lines but not diagonally.
[Latin *castellum* = little fort]

castor, castors; also spelled **caster**
(noun) a small wheel fitted to furniture so that it can be moved easily.

casual
1 (adjective) careless or without interest, e.g. *a casual glance... He had a casual attitude.*
2 Casual clothes are suitable for informal occasions.
3 Casual work is not regular or permanent, e.g. *Most theme parks employ casual labourers at peak season.*
casually (adverb) **casualness** (noun)
[Latin *casualis* = happening by chance]

Similar words: (sense 1) nonchalant, unconcerned

casualty, casualties
(noun) a person killed or injured in an accident or war.

cat, cats
1 (noun) a furry animal often kept as a pet, or a larger mammal e.g. lion, tiger (the 'big cats').
2 (phrase) If you **let the cat out of the bag**, you reveal a secret, often by mistake.
[Latin *cattus* = cat]

catalogue, catalogues, cataloguing, catalogued
1 (noun) a book containing a list of goods that you can buy in a shop or through the post, together with prices and illustrations.
2 an organized list of items in a collection, library, etc.
3 (verb) To catalogue a collection of things means to list them in a catalogue.
[Greek *katalegein* = to list]

catalyst, catalysts (pronounced **kat**-a-list)
(noun) In chemistry, a catalyst is a substance that speeds up a chemical reaction without changing itself.
[Greek *kataluein* = to dissolve]

catamaran, catamarans
(noun) a sailing boat with two parallel hulls connected to each other.
[Tamil *kattumaram* = tied logs]

catapult, catapults.
(noun) a Y-shaped object used for shooting stones.
[Greek *kata-* + *pallein* = to hurl down]

catarrh (pronounced kat-**tahr**)
(noun) mucus in your nose and throat.
[Greek *katarrhein* = to flow down]

catastrophe, catastrophes (pronounced kat-**tass**-trof-fee)
(noun) a terrible disaster.
catastrophic (adjective)
[Greek *katastrephein* = to overturn]

catch, catches, catching, caught
Selected meanings:
1 (verb) e.g. *Can you catch that ball?... I'll catch the train... She has caught my cold... Try to catch the waiter's eye.*
2 (noun) e.g. *Put the catch on the door... Good catch, Smithers! He's out.*
3 If, for example, a special offer has a catch in it, there is a hidden problem with it.
4 (phrase) If you **catch someone's eye**, they notice you.
[Latin *captiare* = to take captive]

Similar words: bag, entrap, ensnare, snare, capture, seize, apprehend, take prisoner, contract, go down with, develop

catch on
1 (phrasal verb) to understand something.
2 If something catches on, it becomes popular, e.g. *Jeans really caught on in the 50s.*

catch out
(phrasal verb) to trick someone or trap them.

Adverbial pun. 'We must bury the cat,' she said, gravely.

catch up
(phrasal verb) to draw level with someone by moving slightly faster than them.

catching
(adjective) spreading very quickly, e.g. *Is measles catching?*

catch phrase, phrases
(noun) a phrase that is often used by a famous person, and is therefore popular and well-known.

catchy, catchier, catchiest
(adjective) A catchy tune is attractive and easily remembered.

categorical
(adjective) absolutely certain and direct, e.g. *a categorical denial.*
categorically (adverb)

category, categories
(noun) a set of things with something similar or in common.

cater, caters, catering, catered
(verb) to provide people with what they need, especially food.
caterer (noun)
[Medieval English *catour* = buyer]

caterpillar, caterpillars
(noun) the larva of a butterfly or moth.
[Old French *catepelose* = hairy cat]

cathedral, cathedrals
(noun) the main church in an area that has a bishop in charge of it.
[Greek *kathedra* = seat; bishop's throne]

Catholic, Catholics
1 (noun, adjective) usually, a member of the Roman Catholic church.
2 (adjective) If you have catholic tastes, for example in music, you like several different types of music.
[Greek *katholikos* = universal]

cat's-eye, cat's-eyes
(noun; a trademark) small pieces of glass or plastic set into a road to reflect light so that drivers can see the road at night.

cattle
(plural noun) cows and bulls kept by farmers.

catty, cattier, cattiest
(adjective) unpleasant and spiteful.
cattiness (noun)

caught
past tense and past participle of **catch**.

cauldron, cauldrons
(noun) a large, round metal cooking pot.
[Latin *caldarium* = hot bath]

cauliflower, cauliflowers
(noun) a large leaf vegetable.
[Italian *caoli* + *fiore* = cabbage flowers]

cause, causes, causing, caused
1 (noun) the thing that makes something happen, e.g. *What was the cause of the man's death?*
2 an aim or principle which a group of people are working for, e.g. *The money went towards a good cause.*

3 (verb) to make something happen, e.g. *They were causing a disturbance.*
causal (adjective)
[Latin *causa* = cause or reason]

Similar words: (verb) bring about, give rise to, lead to

caution, cautions
1 (noun) great care which you take to avoid danger, e.g. *They proceeded with caution.*
2 a warning, e.g. *They were let off with a caution.*
cautionary (adjective)
[Latin *cavere* = to beware]

cautious
(adjective) acting very carefully to avoid danger.
cautiously (adverb) **cautiousness** (noun)

cavalry
(noun) the part of an army that uses armoured vehicles or horses.

cave, caves, caving, caved
1 (noun) a large hole in rock.
2 (verb) If a roof caves in, it collapses inwards.
[Latin *cavus* = hollow]

caveman, cavemen
(noun) Cavemen were prehistoric people who lived in caves.

cavern, caverns
(noun) a large cave.
cavernous (adjective)

cavity, cavities
(noun) a small hole in, for example, a tooth.

CD an abbreviation for 'compact disc'.

cease, ceases, ceasing, ceased
(verb) If something ceases, it stops happening.
[Latin *cedere* = to yield]

cease-fire, cease-fires
(noun) an agreement to stop between groups that are fighting each other.

ceaseless
(adjective) going on without stopping.
ceaselessly (adverb)

cedar, cedars
(noun) a large, evergreen tree with wide, flattish branches and needle-shaped leaves.
[Greek *kedros* = cedar or juniper]

ceiling, ceilings
1 (noun) the top surface of a room.
2 a top limit for things such as prices, e.g. *They put a ceiling on wage increases.*

celebrate, celebrates, celebrating, celebrated
(verb) If you celebrate something, you do something special and enjoyable in honour of it, e.g. *We celebrated our victory.*
celebration (noun) **celebratory** (adjective)
[Latin *celeber* = renowned]

celebrated
(adjective) famous, e.g. *a celebrated actress.*

celebrity, celebrities
(noun) a famous person.

celery
(noun) a vegetable with long, pale green stalks.
[Greek *selinon* = parsley]

Cat proverbs. A cat may look at a king. When the cat's away the mice will play.

cell, cells
1 (noun) In biology, a cell is the smallest part of an animal or plant that can exist by itself.
2 a small room which a prisoner is locked in.
3 a device that produces electricity using energy from chemicals, heat or light.
cellular (adjective)
[Latin *cella* = monk's cell]

cellar, cellars
(noun) an underground room below a building.
[Latin *cellarium* = foodstore]

cello, cellos (pronounced **chel**-loh)
(noun) a large, stringed musical instrument.
cellist (noun)

Celsius (pronounced **sel**-see-yuss)
a scale for measuring temperature, in which water freezes at 0 degrees (0°C) and boils at 100 degrees (100°C). It is named after Anders Celsius (1701-44), who invented it. Celsius means the same as Centigrade.

cement, cements
(noun) a fine powder made from limestone and clay, which is mixed with sand and water to make mortar or concrete.
[Latin *caementum* = quarried stone]

cemetery, cemeteries
(noun) a place where dead people are buried.
[Greek *koimētērion* = a place for sleeping]

censor, censors, censoring, censored
(verb) If someone censors a book or film, they cut or ban the whole or parts of it that are considered unsuitable for the public.
censorship (noun)

census, censuses
(noun) an official survey of the population of a country.

cent, cents
(noun) a unit of money in the USA and in some other countries. (In the USA, 100 cents = 1 dollar).
[Latin *centum* = hundred]

centenary, centenaries (pronounced sen-**teen**-er-ee)
(noun) the 100th anniversary of something.

centi-
(prefix) used to form words that have 'hundred' as part of their meaning, e.g. *century, centimetre, centipede, centurion.*
[Latin *centum* = hundred]

Centigrade
another name for the Celsius temperature scale.

centilitre, centilitres
(noun) a unit of liquid volume (100 cl = 1 litre).

centimetre, centimetres
(noun) a unit of length (1 cm = 10 millimetres; 100 cm = 1 metre).

centipede, centipedes
(noun) a small, wormlike creature with a body in segments and many pairs of legs.
[Latin *centum* + *pedes* = a hundred feet]

central
1 (adjective) in or near the centre of something.

2 main or most important, e.g. *the central character in the book.*
centrally (adverb) **centrality** (noun)

central heating
(noun) a system of heating in which water or air is heated in one place and travels through pipes and radiators round the building.

centre, centres, centring, centred
1 (noun) the middle.
2 A centre is a building where people go for activities, meetings or help, e.g. *an arts centre.*
3 (verb) To centre something means to move it so that it is balanced or at the centre of something else, e.g. *He centred himself on the raft.*
4 If something centres on or around a particular thing, that thing is the main subject of attention, e.g. *The workers' demands centred around pay.*
[Latin *centrum* = the point of a pair of compasses]

Similar words: (noun: sense 1) heart, hub, middle

centre of gravity, centres of gravity
(noun) The centre of gravity in an object is the point at which it balances perfectly.

centurion, centurions
(noun) a Roman officer in charge of 100 soldiers.

century, centuries
1 (noun) a period of 100 years.
2 a score of 100 runs at cricket.
[Latin *centum* = hundred]

cereal, cereals
1 (noun) a plant that produces edible grain, such as wheat, maize, oats or rice.
2 a food made from grain, often eaten with milk for breakfast.
[Latin *cerealis* = concerning the growing of grain, from Ceres, goddess of agriculture]

ceremony, ceremonies
(noun) a set of formal actions performed at a special occasion or important public event, e.g. *a wedding ceremony.*
ceremonial (adjective and noun)
ceremonially (adverb)
[Latin *caerimonia* = holy ritual]

Similar words: rite, ritual

certain
1 (adjective) definite and with no doubt at all, e.g. *He is certain to make a big score.*
2 You use certain to refer to a specific person or thing, e.g. *We met on a certain day.*
certainty (noun)
[Latin *certus* = sure]

certainly
1 (adverb) without doubt, e.g. *There will certainly be a good harvest.*
2 of course, e.g. *'May I borrow your pen?'–'Certainly.'*

certificate, certificates
(noun) a document stating particular facts about something important, e.g. *a marriage certificate.*

What's the difference between a jeweller and a prison warder? One sells watches, the other .....

certify, certifies, certifying, certified
(verb) to declare formally that something is true.
[Latin *certus* + *facere* = to make sure]

chaffinch, chaffinches
(noun) a small European bird with black and white wings. The male has a reddish body.

chain, chains
1 (noun) metal rings connected together in a line.
2 a series of things, e.g. a *chain of events*.
[Latin *catena* = chain]

chain reaction, reactions
(noun) a rapid series of events in which each event causes the next one.

chain saw, saws
(noun) a power saw with teeth fixed in a chain.

chain-smoke, chain-smokes, chain-smoking, chain-smoked
(verb) to smoke cigarettes continually.
chain-smoker (noun)

chain store, stores
(noun) a large shop that is part of a chain of shops owned by one company.

chair, chairs
1 (noun) a seat with a back and 4 legs.
2 another word for chairman or chairperson
[Greek *kathedra* = seat]

chair lift, lifts
(noun) a line of chairs that hang from a moving cable and carry people up a mountain.

chairman, chairmen
1 (noun) The chairman of a meeting is the person in charge who decides when each person may speak.
2 The chairman of a company or committee is the head of it.
chairperson (noun) **chairwoman** (noun)

chalet, chalets (pronounced **shall**-lay)
(noun) a wooden house with a sloping roof, especially in a mountain area or a holiday camp.

chalk, chalks
(noun) a soft, white rock consisting of calcium carbonate and containing minute fossils. It is often used for writing or drawing on a blackboard.
chalky (adjective)
[Greek *khalix* = pebble]

challenge, challenges, challenging, challenged
1 (noun) something that is new and exciting but requires a lot of effort, e.g. *Mt Everest presented a challenge to Hillary and Tensing.*
2 (verb) If someone challenges you, they suggest that you compete with them in some way, e.g. *He challenged me to a race.*
3 If you challenge something, you question whether it is correct or true, e.g. *He challenged my answer.*
4 If someone, e.g. a soldier, challenges you, they order you to stop and identify yourself.
challenger (noun) **challenging** (adjective)

chamber, chambers
1 (noun) a large room, especially one used for formal meetings, e.g. *the Council Chamber.*
2 a hollow place or compartment inside

something, especially inside an animal's body or inside a gun.
[Greek *kamara* = vault]

chambermaid, chambermaids
(noun) a woman who works in a hotel cleaning and tidying the bedrooms.

champagne, champagnes (pronounced sham-**pain**)
(noun) a sparkling white wine, called after the region of France where it is made.

champion, champions
1 (noun) a person who wins a competition.
2 A champion of a cause or principle is someone who supports or defends it, e.g. *She is a champion of human rights.*
[Latin *campus* = battlefield]

championship, championships
(noun) a competition to find the champion of a sport, e.g. *the British Open Golf Championship.*

chance, chances, chancing, chanced
1 (noun) The chance of something happening is how possible or likely it is.
2 an opportunity, e.g. *She left before I had a chance to explain.*
3 (verb) If you chance something, you try it although you are taking a risk.
chancy (adjective; informal)
[Old French *cheoir* = to occur]

Chancellor of the Exchequer
(noun) The Chancellor of the Exchequer is the minister responsible for finance and taxes.

change, changes, changing, changed
Selected meanings:
1 (verb) When something changes or when you change it, it becomes different.
2 When you change, you put on different clothes.
3 To change money means to exchange it for smaller coins of the same total value, or to exchange it for foreign money.
4 (noun) small coins rather than notes, e.g. *Have you got change for a fiver?*
changeless (adjective)
[Latin *cambire* = to swap or to barter]

Similar words: (verb) adapt, alter, transform, convert
(noun) adjustment, alteration

changeable
(adjective) likely to change all the time.

Similar words: inconsistent, unpredictable, erratic, unreliable, fickle, variable

channel, channels
1 (noun) a wavelength used to receive programmes broadcast by a TV or radio station; also the station itself, e.g. *He switched to another channel.*
2 a passage along which water flows.
3 The Channel or the English Channel is the stretch of sea between England and France.
[Latin *canalis* = pipe]

chant, chants, chanting, chanted
1 (noun) a group of words repeated over and over again, e.g. *a football chant.*

Some words do not change to make a plural, e.g. cod deer salmon sheep trout cannon chassis.

2 (verb) to say or sing something over and over again.
[Latin *cantare* = to sing]

chaos (pronounced **kay**-oss)
(noun) a state of total disorder and confusion.
chaotic (adjective)
[Greek *khaos* = formlessness]

chap, chaps, chapping, chapped
1 (noun; informal) a man.
2 (verb) If your skin chaps, it becomes dry and cracked, usually as a result of cold or wind.
[noun: from *chapman* an old word meaning 'customer' or 'tradesman']
chapped (adjective)

chapel, chapels
1 (noun) a section of a church or cathedral with its own altar, used for private prayer or smaller services.
2 a type of small church.
[Latin *capella* = small cloak; originally used of the place where St Martin's cloak was kept as a relic]

chapter, chapters
(noun) a part of a book.
[Latin *capitulum* = little head]

character, characters
1 (noun) The character of a person is all the qualities which form their personality.
2 A person or place that has character has an interesting, attractive or admirable quality, e.g. *an old house of great character.*
3 the people in a film, play or book.
[Greek *kharaktēr* = engraver's tool]

Similar words: (sense 1) identity, nature, personality

characteristic, characteristics
1 (noun) a quality that is typical of a particular person or thing, e.g. *Impatience is one of his worst characteristics.*
2 (adjective) typical of a particular person or thing, e.g. *Stone walls are characteristic of this area.*
characteristically (adverb)

Similar words: (noun) property, feature, quality (adjective) distinctive, distinguishing

charcoal
(noun) a form of carbon made by burning wood without air, used as a fuel and also for drawing.

charge, charges, charging, charged
1 (verb) If someone charges you money, they ask you to pay it for something that you have bought or received, e.g. *They charged £2 admission.*
2 (noun) a formal accusation that a person is guilty of a crime and has to go to court.
3 (phrase) To be **in charge of** someone or something means to be responsible for them and be in control of them.
4 (verb) To charge a battery means to pass an electrical current through it to make it store electricity.
5 to rush forward, often to attack someone, e.g. *The bull charged at the farmer.*
[Old French *chargier* = to load]

chariot, chariots
(noun) a two-wheeled open vehicle pulled by horses, used in ancient times for racing and fighting.
[Old French *char* = light vehicle]

charity, charities
(noun) an organization that raises money to help, e.g. people who are ill, in need or disabled.
charitable (adjective)
[Latin *caritas* = love or affection]

charm, charms
1 (noun) an attractive and pleasing quality that some people and things have, e.g. *narrow, cobbled streets full of charm.*
2 a small ornament worn on a bracelet.
3 a magical spell or an object that is supposed to bring good luck.
[Latin *carmen* = song or incantation]

charming
(adjective) very pleasant and attractive, e.g. *a charming girl... a charming house.*
charmingly (adverb)

chart, charts
1 (noun) a diagram or table showing information.
2 a map of sea or stars.
[Greek *khartēs* = papyrus]

chase, chases
(verb) If you chase someone or something, you run or go after them to catch them or drive them away.
[Old French *chacier* = to hunt]

Similar words: pursue, run after

chassis (pronounced **shas**-ee)
(noun) the frame on which a vehicle is built.
[French *chassis* = window-frame]

chastise, chastises, chastising, chastised
(verb) to tell someone off for something they have done wrong.

chat, chats, chatting, chatted
(verb) to talk to someone in a friendly way.
chatty (adjective)

Similar words: gossip, natter, chatter

chat up
(phrasal verb; informal) If you chat up a member of the opposite sex, you talk to them in a friendly way, because you are attracted to them.

chatter, chatters, chattering, chattered
1 (verb) to talk very fast.
2 If your teeth are chattering, they are knocking together because you are cold or frightened.

chatterbox, chatterboxes
(noun; informal) a person who talks too much.

chauffeur, chauffeurs (pronounced **show**-fur)
(noun) a person whose job is to drive another person's car.
[French *chauffeur* = stoker or fireman]

chauvinist, chauvinists (pronounced **show**-vin-ist)
1 (noun) a person who thinks their country is

From which characters of myth and legend do these words come? panic stentorian tantalize vulcanize

always right. Nicolas Chauvin was an extreme French patriot.
2 A male chauvinist is a man who believes that men are superior to women.
chauvinistic (adjective) **chauvinism** (noun)

cheap, cheaper, cheapest
(adjective) costing very little money, and usually of poor quality.
cheaply (adverb)
[Old English *ceap* = price or bargain]

Similar words: inexpensive, reasonable, cut-price

cheat, cheats, cheating, cheated
(verb) If someone cheats, they do wrong or unfair things to win or to obtain something that they want.

Similar words: swindle, deceive, double-cross

check, checks, checking, checked
1 (noun) Checks are different coloured squares which form a pattern.
2 In chess, check is a position in which a player's king is threatened with capture.
3 (verb) To check something means to examine it to make sure that everything is all right.

check in
(phrasal verb) When you check in at a hotel or airport, you arrive and sign your name or show your ticket.

check out
1 (phrasal verb) When you check out of a hotel, you pay the bill and leave.
2 If you check something out, you inspect it and find out whether everything is right about it.

check up on
(phrasal verb) To check up on someone means to find out if they are doing what they should be doing, or if what they have said is true.

checkmate
(noun) In chess, checkmate is the end of the game, where one player cannot stop their king being captured in the next move.
[Arabic *shah mat* = the King is dead]

checkout, checkouts
(noun) a counter in a supermarket where the customers pay for their goods.

checkup, checkups
(noun) an examination by a doctor to see if your health is good.

cheek, cheeks
1 (noun) Your cheeks are the sides of your face below your eyes.
2 speech or behaviour that is rude or disrespectful, e.g. *I've had enough of your cheek.*

Similar words: (sense 2) impertinence, insolence, nerve, impudence

cheeky, cheekier, cheekiest
(adjective) rather rude and disrespectful, often in an amusing way.

cheer, cheers, cheering, cheered
(verb) to shout with approval.

cheer up
(phrasal verb) to feel more cheerful.

cheerful
(adjective) happy and in good spirits.
cheerfully (adverb) **cheerfulness** (noun)

Similar words: bright, breezy, jolly, cheery, merry

cheerio
(interjection) a friendly way of saying goodbye.

cheery, cheerier, cheeriest
(adjective) happy and cheerful, e.g. *a cheery smile.*

cheese, cheeses
(noun) a hard or creamy food made from the thick, soft part of milk (curds) that separates from the watery part (whey) when milk turns sour.
[Latin *caseus* = cheese]

cheesecake, cheesecakes
(noun) a dessert consisting of a layer of biscuit covered with a mixture of cream cheese and a sweet filling.

cheetah, cheetahs
(noun) one of the largest members of the cat family. It has a black-spotted light brown coat. It is found in Africa and is the fastest land animal.
[Sanskrit *citra* + *kaya* = speckled body]

chef, chefs
(noun) a head cook in a restaurant or hotel.

chemical, chemicals
1 (adjective) involved in chemistry or using chemicals, e.g. *the chemical composition of water... a ban on chemical weapons.*
2 (noun) Chemicals are substances manufactured by chemistry.
chemically (adverb)
[Greek *khēmeia* = alchemy]

chemist, chemists
1 (noun) a person who is qualified to make up drugs and medicines prescribed by a doctor.
2 A chemist is also a person qualified in chemistry who works in industry or in a university, e.g. *a research chemist at ICI.*

chemistry
(noun) the scientific study of substances and the ways in which they change when they are combined with other substances.

cheque, cheques
(noun) a printed form on which you write an amount of money that you have to pay. You sign the cheque and your bank pays the money from your account.

chequebook, chequebooks
(noun) a book of printed cheques.

cherry, cherries
(noun) a small, juicy fruit, grown on trees, with a red or black skin and a stone in the centre.

chess
(noun) a board game for two people.
chessboard (noun)

chest, chests
1 (noun) a large wooden box with a hinged lid.

CH can represent these sounds: chorus champion chef.

2 the front part of your body between your shoulders and your waist.
3 (phrase; informal) If you **get something off your chest**, you tell someone about it because it has been worrying you.
[Latin *cista* = box or basket]

chestnut, chestnuts
1 (noun) a reddish-brown nut from the chestnut tree that grows inside a prickly green casing. Some chestnuts can be eaten.
2 (adjective) reddish-brown in colour.

chest of drawers, chests of drawers
(noun) a piece of furniture used for storing clothes.

chew, chews, chewing, chewed
(verb) to use your teeth to break food up in your mouth before swallowing it.
chewing gum (noun)

chick, chicks
(noun) a young bird, especially a young chicken.

chicken, chickens, chickening, chickened
1 (noun) a bird kept on a farm for its eggs and meat; also the meat of this bird, e.g. *We're having chicken for dinner.*
2 (adjective; informal) cowardly or easily scared.
3 (verb; informal) If you chicken out of something, you do not do it because you are afraid or cautious.

chickenfeed
(noun; informal) Example: *'To get £10 for that picture is chickenfeed'* means that £10 is far too little to receive for the picture.

chickenpox
(noun) an illness which produces a fever and blister-like spots on the skin.

chief, chiefs
1 (noun) the leader of a group or organization.
2 (adjective) most important, e.g. *the chief reason for resigning... the chief steward.*
chiefly (adverb)

chilblain, chilblains
(noun) a sore, itchy swelling, usually on the foot or hand, caused by poor circulation of the blood.

child, children
1 (noun) a young person.
2 (phrase; informal) If you say that something is **child's play**, you mean it is very easy.

Similar words: kid, juvenile, youngster, minor, nipper, toddler, tot, offspring, descendant

childhood
(noun) Someone's childhood is the time of their life during which they are a child.

childish
(adjective) immature and foolish, e.g. *He was annoyed by her childish behaviour.*
childishly (adverb) **childishness** (noun)

Similar words: babyish, infantile, juvenile, puerile

childminder, childminders
(noun) a person who is qualified and paid to look after other people's children while they are at work.

childproof
(adjective) A childproof device is one designed to stop children from hurting themselves on it or damaging it.

chill, chills, chilling, chilled
1 (verb) to make something cold, e.g. *White wine should be chilled.*
2 If something chills you, it makes you feel worried or frightened.
3 (noun) a feverish cold.

chilly, chillier, chilliest
(adjective) rather cold, e.g. *a chilly afternoon.*

chime, chimes, chiming, chimed
(verb) When a bell chimes, it makes a clear ringing sound.
[Old English *chymbe* = bell]

chimney, chimneys
(noun) a vertical pipe etc. through which smoke or gases from a fire escapes.
[Greek *kaminos* = fireplace or oven]

chimney sweep, sweeps
(noun) a person whose job is cleaning the soot out of chimneys.

chimpanzee, chimpanzees
(noun) a small ape with dark fur that lives in forests in Central Africa.

chin, chins
(noun) the part of your face below your mouth.

china
(noun) China is items like cups, saucers, and plates made from very fine clay.

Chinese
1 (adjective) belonging to China.
2 (noun) the language spoken by people from China.

chink, chinks
(noun) a small, narrow opening, e.g. *a chink in the curtains... a chink of light.*

chip, chips
1 (noun) Chips are strips of fried potato.
2 In electronics, a chip is a tiny piece of silicon inside a computer which is used to form electronic circuits.
3 a small piece broken off an object, or the mark made when a piece breaks off, e.g. *a mug with a chip in it.*
4 (phrase) If you say that someone is **a chip off the old block**, you mean they are very like one of their parents in behaviour.
5 Someone who has **a chip on their shoulder** behaves aggressively because they have a grudge or feel sensitive about something.

chiropodist, chiropodists (pronounced kir-rop-pod-dist)
(noun) a person whose job is treating people's feet, cutting nails, corns, etc.
chiropody (noun)
[Greek *kheir* = hand + *podes* = feet]

Why is a horse-chestnut called a conker? It might be from the French word *conque* – a shell.

chirp, chirps, chirping, chirped
(verb) to make a short, high-pitched sound,
e.g. *birds chirping in the trees.*

chirpy, chirpier, chirpiest
(adjective; informal) lively and cheerful.

chisel, chisels
(noun) a tool with a long metal blade and a sharp
edge at the end used for cutting and shaping
wood, stone or metal.
[Latin *caesus* = a cut]

chlorine (pronounced **klaw**-reen)
(noun) a poisonous gas with a strong, unpleasant
smell, used to disinfect water and to make bleach.

chlorophyll (pronounced **klor**-rof-fil)
(noun) a green colouring in plants which traps
the energy from sunlight.
[Greek *khlōros* = green]

chock, chocks
(noun) a block or wedge for placing behind
wheels or heavy objects to stop them moving.

chock-a-block or **chock-full**
(adjective) completely full.

chocolate, chocolates
1 (noun) a sweet food made from cacao seeds.
2 (adjective) dark brown.
[Aztec *xococ* + *atl* = bitter water]

choice, choices
(noun) something that you choose, e.g. *Who is
your choice for leader of the party?*

Similar words: selection, variety, alternative, option.

choir, choirs (pronounced **kwire**)
(noun) a group of singers, e.g. in a church.

choke, chokes, choking, choked
1 (verb) If you choke, you stop being able to
breathe properly because something is blocking
your windpipe, e.g. *He choked on his drink.*
2 If things choke a place, they fill it so much that
it is blocked or clogged up, e.g. *The town was
choked with traffic.*

cholesterol (pronounced kol-**less**-ter-rol)
(noun) a substance found in all animal fats,
tissues and blood.
[Greek *kholē* = bile + *stereos* = hard]

choose, chooses, choosing, chose, chosen
(verb) To choose something means to decide to
have it or do it.

Similar words: pick, select, opt for, take

choosy, choosier, choosiest
(adjective) fussy and difficult to satisfy.

chop, chops, chopping, chopped
1 (verb) to cut with quick, heavy strokes using
an axe or a knife.
2 (noun) a small piece of lamb or pork containing
a bone, usually cut from the ribs.

chopper, choppers
(noun; informal) a helicopter.

choppy, choppier, choppiest
(adjective) Choppy water has a lot of waves
because the weather is windy.

chopsticks
(plural noun) a pair of thin sticks used by people
in the Far East for eating food.

chord, chords
1 (noun) a group of 3 or more musical notes
played together.
2 In geometry, a chord is a straight line
connecting two points on a curve.
[Greek *khordē* = gut or string]

chore, chores
(noun) an unpleasant job that has to be done,
e.g. *I don't like household chores.*
[Old English *cierr* = job]

choreography (pronounced kor-ree-**og**-raf-fee)
(noun) the composing of dance steps and
movements for a show or film.
choreographer (noun) **choreograph** (verb)
[Greek *khoreia* = dance + *graphein* = to write]

chortle, chortles, chortling, chortled
(verb) to laugh with amusement. [see below]

chorus, choruses, chorusing, chorused
The chorus of a song is a part which is repeated
after each verse.
[Greek *khoros* = chorus]

Christ
(noun) Christ is the name for Jesus. Christians
believe that Jesus is the son of God.

christen, christens, christening, christened
(verb) When a baby is christened, it is named by
a clergyman in a religious ceremony as a sign
that it is a member of the Christian church.

Christian, Christians
1 (noun) a person who believes in Jesus Christ
and his teachings.
2 (adjective) good, kind, and considerate, e.g. *She
was a very Christian woman.*
Christianity (noun)

Christian name, names
(noun) The first names of a person, e.g. James
Richard Smith's Christian names are James
Richard.

Christmas, Christmases
(noun) the Christian festival celebrating the
birth of Christ, on December 25th.

chrome (pronounced **krome**)
(noun) metal plated with chromium.

chromosome, chromosomes
(noun) In biology, a chromosome is one of a
number of rod-shaped parts in the nucleus of a
cell which contains genes that determine the
characteristics of an animal or plant.
[Greek *khrōma* = colour + *sōma* = body]

chronic (pronounced **kron**-nik)
1 (adjective) never stopping, or lasting a very
long time, e.g. *He has chronic asthma.*
2 (informal) very bad, severe or unpleasant,
e.g. *It was a really chronic film.*
chronically (adverb)

chronological (pronounced kron-nol-**loj**-i-kl)
(adjective) arranged in the order in which things

Lewis Carroll first used the term 'portmanteau word'. One of his is chortle (from chuckle and snort)....

happened, e.g. *The dates are listed in chronological order.*
chronologically (adverb)
[Greek *Khrōnos* = time + legein = to say]

chrysalis, chrysalises (pronounced **kriss-sal-liss**)
(noun) a butterfly or moth when it is developing from being a caterpillar to being a fully grown adult. It has a hard protective covering.

chubby, chubbier, chubbiest
(adjective) plump and round, e.g. *a chubby baby.*

chuck, chucks, chucking, chucked
(verb; informal) to throw.

chuckle, chuckles, chuckling, chuckled
(verb) When you chuckle, you laugh quietly.

chug, chugs, chugging, chugged
(verb) When a machine or engine chugs, it makes a continuous, dull, thudding sound.

chum, chums
(noun; informal) a friend.

chunk, chunks
(noun) a thick piece of something solid.
chunky (adjective)

Similar words: block, hunk, lump, knob

church, churches
1 (noun) a building where Christians go for religious sevices and worship.
2 In the Christian religion, a Church is one of the groups with their own particular beliefs, customs, and clergy, e.g. *the Methodist Church.*
[Greek *kuriakon* = master's house]

churchyard, churchyards
(noun) an area of land around a church, often used as a graveyard.

churn out
(phrasal verb) If you churn things out, you produce them quickly in large numbers, e.g. *We are all churning out ideas for the next show.*

cider
(noun) an alcoholic drink made from apples.
[Hebrew *shekhar* = strong drink]

cigar, cigars
(noun) a roll of dried tobacco leaves which people smoke.
[Mayan *sicar* = to smoke]

cigarette, cigarettes
(noun) a tight roll of tobacco covered in thin paper which people smoke, now known to cause cancer and other illnesses.

cinder, cinders
(noun) small pieces of burnt material left after, for example, wood or coal has burned.

cinema, cinemas
(noun) a place where people go to watch films.
[Greek *kinema* = motion]

circle, circles, circling, circled
1 (noun) a completely regular, round shape.
2 In a theatre or cinema, the circle is an area of seats on an upper floor.

circuit, circuits (pronounced **sir**-kit)
1 (noun) any closed line or path, often circular, e.g. a racing track.
2 An electrical circuit is a complete route around which an electric current can flow.

circular, circulars
1 (adjective) in the shape of a circle.
2 (noun) a letter or advertisement sent to a lot of people at the same time.
circularity (noun)

circulate, circulates, circulating, circulated
1 (verb) When something circulates or when you circulate it, it moves easily around an area, e.g. *Open a window and let the air circulate.*
2 When you circulate something among people, you pass it round or tell it to all the people, e.g. *A letter was circulated to all the club members.*

circulation, circulations
1 (noun) The circulation of a newspaper or magazine is the number of copies that are sold of each issue.
2 Your circulation is the movement of blood through your body.

circumference, circumferences
(noun) The circumference of a circle is its outer line or edge; also the length of this line.

circumstance, circumstances
(noun) The circumstances of a situation or event are the conditions that affect what happens, e.g. *the circumstances of the accident.*
[Latin *circumstare* = to surround]

circus, circuses
(noun) a show given by a travelling group of entertainers such as clowns, acrobats and specially trained animals.
[Latin *circus* = circle]

cistern, cisterns
(noun) a tank in which water is stored, for example, in the roof of a house.
[Latin *cista* = box]

citizen, citizens
(noun) The citizens of a country or city are the people who live in it or belong to it.
citizenship (noun)

citric acid
(noun) a type of weak, water-soluble acid, found especially in citrus fruits.

citrus fruit, fruits
(noun) juicy, sharp-tasting fruits such as oranges, lemons and grapefruit.

city, cities
1 (noun) a large town where many people live and work, usually containing a cathedral.
2 The City is the part of London which contains the main British financial institutions such as the Stock Exchange.
[Latin *civitas* = state or citizenship]

civic
(adjective) relating to a city or citizens, e.g. *Southampton Civic Centre.*

civil engineering
(noun) the design and construction of roads, bridges and public buildings.

....More portmanteau words: motel pulsar smog transistor

civilian, civilians
(noun) a person not in the armed forces.

civilization, civilizations; also spelled civilisation
1 (noun) A civilization is a society which has a highly developed organization, culture and way of life, e.g. *ancient Greek civilization.*
2 an advanced state of social organization, culture and way of life.

civilize, civilizes, civilizing, civilized; also spelled civilise
(verb) To civilize a society or group of people means to educate them and develop their social organization, culture and way of life.
civilized (adjective)

civil service
(noun) the staff who work in government departments responsible for the administration of towns, counties or the whole country.
civil servant (noun)

civil war, wars
(noun) a war between groups of people who live in the same country.

claim, claims, claiming, claimed
1 (verb) If you claim that something is true or is the case, you say that it is, although some people may not believe you, e.g. *He claimed to be sober.*
2 If you claim something, you ask for it because it belongs to you or you have a right to it, e.g. *She claimed her lost anorak.*
[Latin *clamare* = to cry out]

clamber, clambers, clambering, clambered
(verb) If you clamber somewhere, you climb there with difficulty.

clammy, clammier, clammiest
(adjective) unpleasantly damp and sticky, e.g. *cold, clammy hands.*
[Old English *clæman* = to smear]

clamp, clamps, clamping, clamped
1 (noun) an object with movable parts used to hold two things firmly together.
2 (verb) To clamp things together means to fasten them or hold them firmly with a clamp.
3 To clamp down on something means to become stricter in controlling it, e.g. *The police are clamping down on bicycle thefts.*
4 **Wheel clamps** are sometimes used by police to prevent illegally parked cars from moving.
[Old English *clamm* = a punishment clamp for the feet.]

clan, clans
(noun) a group of families related to each other by being descended from the same ancestor; a word used especially in Scotland.

clanger, clangers
(phrase; informal) If you **drop a clanger**, you make an embarrassing mistake.

clap, claps, clapping, clapped
1 (verb) to hit your hands together loudly to show your appreciation.
2 If you clap someone on the back or shoulder, you hit them in a friendly way.
3 (noun) A clap of thunder is a sudden loud noise of thunder.

clarify, clarifies, clarifying, clarified
(verb) to make something clear and easier to understand, e.g. *Would you clarify the last point you made?*
clarification (noun)
[Latin *clarus* + *facere* = to make clear]

clarinet, clarinets
(noun) a woodwind instrument with a straight tube and a single reed in its mouthpiece.
clarinettist (noun)

clarity
(noun) The clarity of something is how clear it is, e.g. *I can see with great clarity, now I have new glasses.*
[Latin *clarus* = clear]

clash, clashes, clashing, clashed
1 (verb) If people clash with each other, they fight or argue.
2 Ideas or styles that clash do not go together, e.g. *Those pink socks clash with your green jeans.*
3 If two events clash, they happen at the same time so that you cannot go to both.
4 When metal objects clash, they hit each other with a loud noise.

clasp, clasps, clasping, clasped
1 (verb) to hold something tightly or fasten it, e.g. *He sat clasping his knees.*
2 (noun) a fastening such as a hook or catch.

class, classes
1 (noun) a group of people or things of a particular type or quality, e.g. *the middle class.*
2 a group of pupils or students taught together.
3 Someone who has class is elegant in appearance or behaviour.

Similar words: (sense 1) group, category, order, set

classic, classics
1 (adjective) typical, and therefore a good example of something, e.g. *The place has a classic country village atmosphere.*
2 of very high quality, e.g. *a classic film.*
3 (noun) something of the highest quality, e.g. *The book 'Animal Farm' is a classic.*
5 Classics is the study of the literature of ancient Greece and Rome.
[Latin *classicus* = of the first rank]

classical
1 (adjective) traditional in style, form and content, e.g. *classical ballet.*
2 characteristic of the style of ancient Greece and Rome, e.g. *classical architecture.*
3 Classical music is serious music considered to be of lasting value.
classically (adverb)

classify, classifies, classifying, classified
(verb) to arrange things into groups with similar characteristics, e.g. *Books are classified according to subject.*
classification (noun) **classified** (adjective)

classroom, classrooms
(noun) e.g. *The teacher entered the classroom.*

Eric Blair was George Orwell's real name. Who are/were Samuel Clemens, Harry Webb, Marion Morrison?

clatter, clatters, clattering, clattered
(noun) a loud rattling noise made by hard things hitting each other.

clause, clauses
1 (noun) a section of a legal document.
2 In grammar, a clause is a group of words with a subject and a verb, which may be a complete sentence or one of the parts of a sentence.
[Latin *clausa* = end of sentence]

claustrophobia (pronounced klos-trof-**foe**-bee-ya)
(noun) a fear of being in enclosed spaces.
claustrophobic (adjective)
[Latin *claustrum* = cloister + Greek *phobos* = fear]

claw, claws, clawing, clawed
1 (noun) An animal's claws are hard, curved nails at the end of its feet.
2 The claws of a crab or lobster are the two jointed parts, used for grasping things.

clay
(noun) a type of soft, sticky earth that is baked to make pottery and bricks.
[Old English *clæg* = mud]

clean, cleaner, cleanest; cleans, cleaning, cleaned
1 (adjective) free from dirt etc.
2 Clean jokes are decent and not offensive.
3 (verb) to keep free from dirt, dust, germs, etc.
4 (phrase; informal) If you **come clean**, you admit something that you have been keeping secret.
cleanly (adverb) **cleaner** (noun)

cleanliness (pronounced **klen**-lin-ness)
(noun) the habit of keeping yourself and your surroundings clean.

cleanse, cleanses, cleansing, cleansed
(pronounced **klenz**)
(verb) to make something completely clean and free from impurities.

clear, clearer, clearest; clears, clearing, cleared
1 (adjective) easy to understand, see or hear, e.g. *a clear explanation.*
2 easy to see through, e.g. *clear water.*
3 free from obstructions or unwanted things, e.g. *cross when the road is clear.*
4 (verb) To clear an area means to remove unwanted things from it.
5 When fog or mist clears, it disappears.
6 If you clear a fence or other obstacle, you jump over it without touching it.
7 If someone is cleared of a crime, they are proved to be not guilty.
clearly (adverb) **clarity** (noun)
[Latin *clarus* = clear or bright]

clear out
1 (phrasal verb; informal) to leave, e.g. *Clear out of here and leave me alone!*
2 If you clear out a room or cupboard, you tidy it and throw away unwanted things.

clear up
1 (phrasal verb) If you clear up, you tidy a place.
2 When a problem or misunderstanding is cleared up, it is solved or settled.

3 When the weather clears up, it becomes brighter.

clearing, clearings
(noun) an area in a forest that has no trees.

clench, clenches, clenching, clenched
(verb) When you clench your fist, you curl your fingers up tightly.

clergyman, clergymen
(noun) a male minister of the Christian church, e.g. vicar, canon, bishop.

clerical
(adjective) relating to work done in an office, e.g. *This is a job requiring clerical skills.*

clerk, clerks (pronounced **klark**)
(noun) a person whose job is keeping records or accounts in an office, bank or law court.
[Latin *clericus* = priest]

clever, cleverer, cleverest
1 (adjective) intelligent and quick to understand things.
2 very effective or skilful, e.g. *a book with a clever plot... a clever device.*
cleverly (adverb) **cleverness** (noun)

Similar words: (sense 1) brainy, smart, bright, brilliant, intelligent

cliché, clichés (pronounced **klee**-shay)
(noun) an idea or phrase which is no longer effective because it has been used so much.
clichéd (adjective)

click, clicks, clicking, clicked
1 (noun) a short, snapping sound, e.g. *The door shut with a click.*
2 (verb; informal) When something clicks, you suddenly understand it.

client, clients
(noun) someone who pays a professional person or company for a service, e.g. *a solicitor's clients.*
[Latin *cliens* = a dependant]

cliff, cliffs
(noun) a steep, high rock face by the sea.

cliffhanger, cliffhangers
(noun) a situation or story that is exciting because you do not know what is going to happen next, e.g. in a book or film.

climate, climates
(noun) the typical weather conditions of a place e.g. *The tropical climate is hot and very wet.*
climatic (adjective)

climax, climaxes
(noun) The climax of a story, piece of music, etc. is the most exciting part, usually near the end.
[Greek *klimax* = ladder]

climb, climbs, climbing, climbed
(verb) to move upwards.
climber (noun)

Similar words: ascend, scale, mount

climb down
(phrasal verb) If you climb down in an argument, you give in slightly.

Clichés: Last but not least; At this moment in time; Over the moon. Think of some more.

cling, clings, clinging, clung
(verb) to hold on to something or stay closely attached to it, e.g. *She clung tightly to the rope.*

clingfilm
(noun; a trademark) a clear, thin plastic used for wrapping food.

clinic, clinics
(noun) a building, often part of a hospital, where people go for medical treatment.
[Latin *clinicus* = person on sickbed]

clip, clips, clipping, clipped
1 (noun) A clip is used for holding things together.
2 (verb) If you clip something, you cut bits from it to shape it, e.g. *a neatly clipped hedge.*
3 (noun) A clip of a film is a short piece of it shown by itself.
[Old Norse *klippa* = to cut]

clipboard, clipboards
(noun) a board with a clip at the top to keep papers in place.

cloak, cloaks
(noun) a wide, loose coat without sleeves.
[Latin *clocca* = bell]

cloakroom, cloakrooms
(noun) a cloakroom is a room for coats, or a room with toilets and washbasins.

clobber, clobbers, clobbering, clobbered
(verb; informal) If you clobber someone, you hit them.

clock, clocks
1 (noun) an instrument that measures and shows the time.
2 (phrase) If you work **round the clock**, you work all day and night.
[Latin *clocca* = bell]

clock in
(phrasal verb) When workers clock in, they record their time of arrival at work.

clock up
(phrasal verb) To clock up an amount means to achieve it, e.g. *He has clocked up 1000 miles of cycling.*

clockwise
(adjective, adverb) in the same direction as the hands on a clock move.

clockwork
1 (noun) Toys that work by clockwork move when they are wound up with a key.
2 (phrase) If something happens **like clockwork**, it happens with no problems or delays.

clog, clogs, clogging, clogged
1 (verb) to block up, e.g. *The drain was clogged with mud.*
2 (noun) Clogs are heavy wooden shoes.

cloister, cloisters
(noun) a square, covered area of a cathedral or abbey built for monks to walk and sit in.

clone, clones, cloning, cloned
1 (noun) In biology, a clone is an animal or plant that has been produced artificially from the cells of another animal or plant and is therefore identical to it.
2 (informal) a copy, e.g. *This computer is an IBM clone but not as reliable as the real thing.*
3 (verb) To clone an animal or plant means to produce an identical version.
[Greek *klōn* = twig or shoot]

close, closes, closing, closed; closer, closest
1 (verb) to shut or bring to an end.
2 (adjective, adverb) near to something, e.g. *We were close to the stage... Move closer.*
3 (adjective) People who are close to each other are very friendly and know each other well.
4 If a race is close, the competitors are nearly equal.
5 If the atmosphere is close, it is uncomfortably warm with not enough air.
6 (phrase; informal) If something is a **close shave** or a **close call**, there is very nearly an accident or disaster.
closely (adverb) **closeness** (noun)
closed (adjective) **closure** (noun)
[Latin *clausus* = shut up]

Similar words: (adjective, adverb) near, nearby

close down
(phrasal verb) If a business closes down, all work stops there permanently.

close in
(phrasal verb) If people close in on you, they come nearer and nearer, and surround you.

close-up, close-ups
(noun) a close view of something, especially a photograph taken close to the subject.

clot, clots, clotting, clotted
1 (verb) When a substance such as blood clots, it thickens and forms a lump.
2 (noun; informal) If you call someone a clot, you mean they have done something stupid.

cloth, cloths
1 (noun) fabric made by a process such as weaving.
2 a piece of cloth used for wiping or protecting things.

Similar words: (sense 1) material, textile

clothes
(plural noun) Clothes are the things people wear on their bodies.
clothe (verb)

Similar words: clothing, garments, gear, dress

clothing
(noun) the clothes people wear.

cloud, clouds
1 (noun) a mass of water vapour that forms in the air, seen as a white or grey patch in the sky.
2 A cloud of smoke or dust is a mass of it floating in the air.
[Old English *clud* = hill]

cloudburst, cloudbursts
(noun) a sudden, very heavy fall of rain.

Pun. How could you close the mouth of a river? With a lock and quay.

cloudy, cloudier, cloudiest
1 (adjective) full of clouds, e.g. *a cloudy sky*.
2 difficult to see through, e.g. *cloudy water*.

Similar words: (sense 1) dull, overcast

clout, clouts, clouting, clouted
(verb; informal) If you clout someone, you hit them.

clover
(noun) a small plant with leaves made up of 3 lobes, and pink or white flowers in a ball shape. Four-leafed clovers are rare, and thought to be lucky.

clown, clowns, clowning, clowned
1 (noun) a comical circus performer.
2 (verb) If you clown, you do silly things to make people laugh.
clownish (adjective)

Similar words: jester, joker, fool

club, clubs, clubbing, clubbed
1 (noun) an organization of people with a particular interest, who meet regularly; also the place where they meet.
2 a thick, heavy stick used as a weapon.
3 In golf, a club is a stick with a shaped head that a player uses to hit the ball.
4 (verb) to hit someone hard with a heavy object.
5 (noun) Clubs is one of the four suits in a pack of playing cards, marked by a black ♣ symbol.
6 (verb) If people club together, they all join together to give money to buy something.
[noun: senses 2-5 – Old Norse *klubba* = wooden bludgeon]

Similar words: (noun: sense 1) association, society, league
(noun: sense 2) truncheon

cluck, clucks, clucking, clucked
(verb) When a hen clucks, it makes a short repeated high-pitched sound.

clue, clues
(noun) A clue to a problem, mystery or puzzle is something that provides help in solving it.

clueless
(adjective; informal) stupid.

clump, clumps, clumping, clumped
1 (noun) A clump of plants, people or buildings is a small group of them close together.
2 (verb) If you clump about, you walk with heavy footsteps.
[Old English *clympe* = lump or bunch]

clumsy, clumsier, clumsiest
(adjective) moving awkwardly and carelessly.
clumsily (adverb) **clumsiness** (noun)

Similar words: awkward, ungainly

cluster, clusters, clustering, clustered
(noun) a group of things together, e.g. *There were clusters of flowers on the tree.*
[Old English *clyster* = bunch of grapes]

clutch, clutches, clutching, clutched
1 (verb) to hold something tightly or seize it.

2 (plural noun) If you say you are in someone's clutches, you mean they have power or control over you.
3 (noun) In a car, the clutch is the foot pedal that you press when changing gear.
4 A clutch of things, especially hens' eggs, is a group of them produced at one time.
[senses 1-3 – Germanic *klukjan* = to grasp
sense 4 – Old Norse *klekja* = to hatch]

clutter, clutters, cluttering, cluttered
1 (noun) an untidy mess.
2 (verb) Things that clutter a place fill it and make it untidy.

co-
(prefix) together, e.g. *We co-wrote the song.*
[Latin *con* = together]

coach, coaches, coaching, coached
1 (noun) a long passenger motor vehicle.
2 a separate section of a passenger train.
3 a 4-wheeled enclosed vehicle pulled by horses, which people used to travel in.
4 (verb) If someone coaches you, they teach you and help you to get better at a sport or a subject.
5 (noun) Someone's coach is a person who coaches them in a sport or a subject.
[Hungarian *kocsi szekér* = wagon of Kocs (the village where coaches were first made)]

Similar words: (verb) train, instruct
(noun: sense 5) trainer, instructor, tutor

coal, coals
(noun) a hard, black rock from under the earth, burned as a fuel. It consists of decayed vegetation containing carbon.

coalfield, coalfields
(noun) a region where there is coal underground.

coarse, coarser, coarsest
1 (adjective) rough in texture, often consisting of large particles, e.g. *coarse cloth... coarse sand.*
2 Someone who is coarse talks or behaves in a rude or rather offensive way.
coarsely (adverb) **coarseness** (noun)

coast, coasts, coasting, coasted
1 (noun) the edge of the land where it meets the sea.
2 (phrase) If you say that **the coast is clear**, you mean there is no one around who might see you.
3 (verb) A vehicle that is coasting is moving without engine power.
coastal (adjective)
[Latin *costa* = side or rib]

coastguard, coastguards
(noun) an official who watches the sea near a coast to get help for sailors when they need it and to prevent smuggling.

coastline, coastlines
(noun) the outline of a coast, especially as it looks from from the sea or air, e.g. *a rocky coastline.*

coat, coats, coating, coated
1 (noun) a piece of outdoor clothing.
2 fur or hair on an animal's body.
3 a layer of paint or varnish.

Idioms. What are: black diamonds; black sheep; black lists; black looks; black marks?

4 (verb) to cover with a thin layer, e.g. *The nuts are then coated in chocolate.*
coating (noun)
[Germanic *kotta* = garment]

coat hanger, hangers
(noun) a curved piece of wood, metal or plastic that you hang clothes on.

coat of arms, coats of arms
(noun) a shield with a design on it, used as the badge of a noble family, a town or an organization.

coax, coaxes, coaxing, coaxed
(verb) to persuade gently.

Similar words: persuade, wheedle, talk into

cobble, cobbles
(noun) Cobbles or cobblestones are rounded stones, used in the past for road surfaces.
cobbled (adjective)

cobbler, cobblers
(noun; old-fashioned) a person whose job is making or mending shoes.

cobra, cobras (pronounced **koh**-bra)
(noun) a type of large poisonous snake from Africa and Asia.

cobweb, cobwebs
(noun) the net that a spider spins to catch insects.
[Old English *coppe* + *webb* = spider-web]

cocaine
(noun) a preparation made from the leaves of the coca shrub, used in medicine as a local anaesthetic. It is also a highly addictive and dangerous drug, taken illegally by some people as a stimulant.
[Spanish *coca* = preparation of cocoa leaves]

cock, cocks
(noun) an adult male chicken; or any male bird.

cockerel, cockerels
(noun) a young cock.

cockeyed
(adjective; informal) A cockeyed idea or scheme is silly and unlikely to succeed.

cockle, cockles
(noun) a kind of small shellfish.
[Old French *coquille* = shell]

cockney, cockneys
(noun) a person born in the East End of London.
[Middle English *cokeney* = cock's egg]

cockpit, cockpits
(noun) the place where the pilot sits in a plane.

cockroach, cockroaches
(noun) a large dark-coloured insect often found in dirty rooms.
[Spanish *cucaracha* = cockroach]

cocktail, cocktails
(noun) an alcoholic drink made from several ingredients shaken together.

cocky, cockier, cockiest
(adjective; informal) cheeky or too self-confident.
cockily (adverb) **cockiness** (noun)

cocoa
(noun) a brown powder made from the seeds of a tropical tree and used for making chocolate; also a hot drink made from this powder.

coconut, coconuts
(noun) a very large nut with white flesh, milky juice and a hard hairy shell.

cocoon, cocoons
(noun) a silky covering over the silkworm or over the larvae of certain other insects.
[Regional French *coucoun* = eggshell]

cod
(noun) a large, edible fish.

code, codes
1 (noun) a system of replacing the letters or words in a message with other letters or words, so that nobody can understand the message unless they know the system.
2 a group of numbers and letters which is used to identify something, e.g. *The postcode is W1X 3LA.*
3 A code of behaviour is a set of rules about how people should behave.
coded (adjective)
[Latin *codex* = book]

coeducation
(noun) the system of educating boys and girls together at the same school.
coeducational (adjective)

coffee
(noun) a hot drink made from the ground beans of a tropical shrub.
[Arabic *qahwah* = wine or coffee]

coffin, coffins
(noun) a box in which a dead body is buried or cremated.
[Greek *kophinos* = basket]

cog, cogs
(noun) a wheel with teeth which turns another wheel or part of a machine.

coil, coils
(noun) A coil of rope or wire is a length of it wound into loops; also one of the loops.
[Old French *coillir* = to collect up]

coin, coins, coining, coined
1 (noun) a small metal disc used as money.
2 (verb) If you coin a word or a phrase, you invent it.
[Old French *coignier* = to mint]

coincide, coincides, coinciding, coincided
(pronounced co-inside)
1 (verb) If two events coincide, they happen at about the same time.
2 When two people's ideas or opinions coincide, they agree, e.g. *His ideas coincided with mine.*
[Latin *co-* + *incidere* = to occur with]

coincidence, coincidences
1 (noun) the fact that two things are surprisingly the same, e.g. *My name's Egbert Z. Shufflebottom too. What a coincidence!*
2 what happens when two similar things occur at the same time by chance, e.g. *By coincidence she was on the same train.*
coincidental (adjective) **coincidentally** (adverb)

Crack this coded message: YV XQLUD'J TEDU IE QBHUQTO, HUQT JXU IKHLYLQB WKYTU.

coke

1 (noun) a grey fuel produced from coal.
2 an informal name for the drink Coca Cola or similar drinks.

cola

(noun) fizzy drink made from the seed of the cola tree, e.g. *Coca Cola... Pepsi Cola.*

colander, colanders (pronounced kol-an-der)

(noun) a bowl-shaped container with holes in it, for washing or draining food.
[Regional French *colador* = sieve]

cold, colder, coldest; colds

1 (adjective) If it is cold, the air temperature is very low.
2 Someone who has a cold nature does not show much affection.
3 (noun) a minor illness.
coldly (adverb) **coldness** (noun)

cold-blooded

1 (adjective) Someone who is cold-blooded does not show any pity, e.g. *a cold-blooded murderer.*
cold-bloodedly (adverb) **cold-bloodedness** (noun)
2 A cold-blooded animal has a body temperature that changes according to the surrounding temperature.

coleslaw

(noun) a salad of chopped cabbage and other vegetables in mayonnaise.
[Dutch *koolsla* = cabbage salad]

collaborate, collaborates, collaborating, collaborated

1 (verb) When people collaborate, they work together to produce something.
2 In wartime, collaborating means helping an invading enemy.
collaboration (noun) **collaborator** (noun)
[Latin *co- + laborare* = to work together]

collage, collages (pronounced kol-lahj)

(noun) a picture made by sticking pieces of paper or cloth onto a surface.
[French *colle* = glue]

collapse, collapses, collapsing, collapsed

(verb) to fall down suddenly.
[Latin *collapsus* = fallen in ruins]

Similar words: fall down, give way

collapsible

(adjective) A collapsible object can be folded flat when it is not in use, e.g. *a collapsible bed.*

collar, collars, collaring, collared

1 (noun) The collar of a shirt or coat is the part round the neck which is usually folded over.
2 a leather band round the neck of a dog or cat.
3 (verb; informal) If someone collars you, they catch you, e.g. *I was collared by the police.*
[Latin *collum* = neck]

collarbone, collarbones

(noun) one of the two long bones which run from the base of the neck to the shoulders.

colleague, colleagues

(noun) one of the people you work with.
[Latin *com-* = with + *legare* = to choose]

Similar words: associate, workmate

collect, collects, collecting, collected

1 (verb) To collect things means to gather them together for a special purpose or as a hobby, e.g. *collecting firewood... Do you collect antiques?*
2 If you collect someone or something from a place, you call there and take them away, e.g. *I have to collect the children from school.*
collector (noun)
[Latin *colligere* = to gather together]

collection, collections

1 (noun) a group of things acquired over a period of time, e.g. *my stamp collection.*
2 the organized collecting of money, e.g. for charity; or the sum of money collected.

Similar words: (sense 1) anthology, compilation, set

college, colleges

1 (noun) a place where students study after they have left school.
2 one of the institutions into which some universities are divided, e.g. *King's College, Cambridge.*
[Latin *collegium* = band or company]

collide, collides, colliding, collided

(verb) If a moving object collides with something, it hits it.
[Latin *collidere* = to clash together]

collie, collies

(noun) a kind of large, wavy-haired sheepdog.

colliery, collieries

(noun) a coal mine.

collision, collisions

(noun) A collision occurs when a moving object hits something.

Similar words: accident, smash, crash, impact

colloquial (pronounced kol-loh-kwee-al)

(adjective) Colloquial words and phrases are informal and used especially in conversation. e.g. *In the New Forest 'my mush' is a colloquial phrase for 'my friend'.*
colloquially (adverb) **colloquialism** (noun)
[Latin *colloquor* = to talk with]

colon, colons

(noun) the punctuation mark :
[Greek *kōlon* = limb]

colonel, colonels (pronounced kur-nl)

(noun) an army officer.
[Italian *colonnello* = column of soldiers]

colony, colonies

(noun) a country controlled by a more powerful country, e.g. *Australia used to be a colony of the UK.*
colonial (adjective)
[Latin *colere* = to settle]

Similar words: settlement, outpost, province

What do these people collect? a philatelist a numismatist a phillumenist

colossal
(adjective) very large indeed.
colossally (adverb)
[Greek *kolossos* = huge statue]

colour, colours, colouring, coloured
(verb, noun) e.g. *Please colour that picture ...
Red is the colour of post boxes.*
coloured (adjective) **colourful** (adjective)
colourfully (adverb) **colourless** (adjective)
colouring (noun) **coloration** (noun)
[Latin *color* = colour]

Similar words: shade, tint

colour blind
(adjective) not able to distinguish between
certain colours.

colt, colts
(noun) a young male horse.

column, columns
1 (noun) a tall, solid, upright pillar, supporting a
part of a building.
2 a group of people moving in a long line, two or
more abreast.
3 In a newspaper or magazine, a column is a
vertical section of writing; also a regular piece of
writing by the same person or about the same
subject.
[Latin *columen* = peak]

coma, comas
(noun) a state of deep unconsciousness.
[Greek *kōma* = heavy sleep]

comb, combs, combing, combed
1 (verb) to tidy your hair with a comb.
2 to search somewhere thoroughly.

combat, combats, combating, combated
1 (noun) fighting, e.g. *unarmed combat.*
2 (verb) To combat something means to try to
stop it happening or developing, e.g. *the problem
of combating disease.*
[Latin *com-* = together + *battuere* = to hit]

combatant, combatants
(noun) The combatants in a fight or battle are
the people fighting it.

combination, combinations
1 (noun) a mixture, e.g. *The win came from a
combination of luck and skill.*
2 a series of letters or numbers used to open a
combination lock.

combine, combines, combining, combined
1 (verb) to join things together to make a single
thing, e.g. *Two teams were combined into one.*
2 (noun) a group of people or organizations
working or acting together.
[Latin *com-* = together + *bini* = two by two]

combine harvester
(noun) a machine for harvesting corn which cuts
the crop, removes the grain and leaves the straw
behind.

come, comes, coming, came, come
1 (verb) e.g. *Where have you come from... I don't
know what things are coming to!*
2 (phrase) A time or event **to come** is a future
time or event, e.g. *We will see many changes in
the years to come.*

come about
(phrasal verb) The way something comes about
is the way it happens, e.g. *This discovery came
about through a mistake.*

come across
(phrasal verb) to find something by chance.

come by
(phrasal verb) to find or obtain something, e.g.
Jobs were hard to come by.

come into
(phrasal verb) to inherit, e.g. *Brian has come
into money recently.*

come off
(phrasal verb) to succeed, e.g. *I hadn't expected
his plan to come off.*

come on
(phrasal verb) to make progress, e.g. *My project
is coming on well.*

come round
1 (phrasal verb) To come round means to recover
consciousness.
2 To come round to an idea or situation means to
accept it eventually.
3 When a regular event comes round, it happens,
e.g. *Beginning of term came round too quickly.*

come to
(phrasal verb) to recover consciousness,
e.g. *Sarah came to in the middle of the road.*

come up
(phrasal verb) If something comes up in a
conversation or meeting, it is talked about.

come up against
(phrasal verb) If you come up against a problem,
you are faced with it and have to deal with it.

come up with
(phrasal verb) to suggest something, e.g. *Dave
came up with a great idea.*

comeback, comebacks
(noun) To make a comeback means to be popular
or successful again.

comedian, comedians
(noun) an entertainer whose job is to make
people laugh. (female: **comedienne**)

Similar words: humorist, comic, wit, entertainer

comedy, comedies
(noun) a light-hearted play or film with a happy
ending.
[Greek *kōmos* = village festival + *aeidein* = to
sing]

comet, comets
(noun) an object that travels around the sun
leaving a bright trail behind it.
[Greek *komētēs* = long-haired]

comfort, comforts, comforting, comforted
1 (noun) the state of being physically relaxed,
e.g. *She longed to stretch out in comfort.*
2 (plural noun) Comforts are things which make
your life easier and more pleasant, e.g. *I longed
for the comforts of home.*

A hairdresser needs these words: salon perm style scissors.

3 (verb) To comfort someone means to make
them less worried or unhappy.
[Latin *confortare* = to strengthen]

comfortable
(adjective) relaxed, either physically or mentally.
comfortably (adverb)

comic, comics
1 (adjective) funny, e.g. *a comic sight.*
2 (noun) someone who tells jokes.
3 a magazine of stories told in pictures.

comical
(adjective) funny, e.g. *a comical expression.*
comically (adverb)

comma, commas
(noun) the punctuation mark ,
[Greek *koptein* = to cut]

**command, commands, commanding,
commanded**
1 (verb) to order someone to do something.
2 (phrase) Someone who is **in command** of a ship
or part of an army is in charge of it.
3 (noun) Your command of something is your
knowledge of it and your ability to use this
knowledge, e.g. *a good command of French.*
commander (noun)
[Latin *com-* + *mandare* = to entrust with]

Similar words: direct, order

commandment, commandments
(noun) The commandments are 10 rules of
behaviour that, according to the Old Testament,
we should obey. God gave them to Moses.

commando, commandos
(noun) a soldier specially trained for hazardous
missions.

**commemorate, commemorates,
commemorating, commemorated**
(verb) If you commemorate an event, you do
something special to show that you remember it.
commemorative (adjective) **commemoration**
(noun)
[Latin *com-* = with + *memorare* = to remind]

Similar word: celebrate

**commence, commences, commencing,
commenced**
(verb; formal) to begin.
commencement (noun)

**commend, commends, commending,
commended**
(verb) to praise someone or something, e.g. *I was
commended for my work.*
commendation (noun) **commendable** (adjective)
[Latin *com-* + *mandare* = to entrust with]

comment, comments, commenting, commented
1 (verb) If you comment on something, you say
something about it.
2 (noun) a remark about something, e.g. *They
made rude comments about my hair style.*
[Latin *commentum* = invention]

Similar words: (verb) remark, mention, note

commentary, commentaries
(noun) a description of an event broadcast on
radio or TV while the event is taking place.

commentator, commentators
(noun) someone who gives a radio or TV
commentary.

commerce
(noun) the buying and selling of goods.
[Latin *commercium* = trade]

commercial, commercials
1 (adjective) Commercial activities involve
producing goods on a large scale to make money,
e.g. *the commercial breeding of goats.*
2 Commercial TV and radio are paid for by
advertisements between the programmes.
4 (noun) an advertisement on TV or radio.
commercially (adverb)

commercialized; also spelled **commercialised**
(adjective) If something is commercialized, it has
changed and is now used for making money, e.g.
Parts of Spain are now very commercialized.
commercialization (noun)

commit, commits, committing, committed
1 (verb) To commit a crime or sin means to do it.
2 If you commit yourself, you state an opinion or
promise firmly that you will do something.
committed (adjective) **committal** (noun)
[Latin *committere* = to put together]

commitment, commitments
1 (noun) a strong belief in an idea or system.
2 something that regularly takes up some of your
time, e.g. *I have a commitment each Thursday at
Scouts.*

committee, committees
(noun) a group of people who make decisions on
behalf of a larger group.

common, commoner, commonest; commons
1 (adjective) Something that is common exists in
large numbers or happens often, e.g. *It is
common to see foxes here.*
2 If something is common to two or more people,
they all have it or use it, e.g. *We share a common
language with the Americans.*
3 If something is common knowledge or a
common belief, it is widely known or believed.
4 If you describe someone as common, you mean
they do not have good taste or good manners.
5 (noun) an area of grassy land where everyone
can go, e.g. *Clapham Common.*
6 (phrase) If people have something **in common**,
that thing is the same for both of them.
commonly (adverb)
[Latin *communis* = general or universal]

Similar words: (adjective; sense 3) popular
(adjective; sense 4) vulgar, coarse

Common Market
(noun) the European Commission or EC, a group
of countries including the UK who share common
laws and trade agreements.

common sense
(noun) the ability to behave sensibly and make
sound judgments.

These words from Greek have a common ending: magician physician politician musician electrician.

Commonwealth
(noun) an association of countries around the world that are, or used to be, ruled by Britain.

commotion
(noun) a lot of noise and excitement.
[Latin *commovere* = to throw into disorder]

communal
(adjective) shared by a group of people, e.g. *a communal dining-room.*
communally (adverb)
[Old French *comuner* = to hold in common]

communicate, communicates, communicating, communicated
(verb) to exchange information, usually by talking or writing.
communicative (adjective)
[Latin *communicare* = to share]

communication, communications
1 (noun) the process by which people or animals exchange information.
2 (plural noun) Communications are the systems by which people communicate or broadcast information, especially using electricity or radio waves, e.g. *a communications satellite.*

communion
(noun) In Christianity, Communion is a religious service in which people share bread and wine in remembrance of Jesus Christ's death and resurrection.
[Latin *communio* = general participation]

communism
(noun) the political idea that the state should control all industry and agriculture and that there should be no private property.
communist (adjective and noun)
[Old French *commun* = common]

community, communities
(noun) the people living in a particular area; also used to refer to particular groups within a society, e.g. *support from the local community... the black community.*

commute, commutes, commuting, commuted
(verb) People who commute travel a long distance to work every day, e.g.
She commuted to London from Brighton each day.
commuter (noun)

compact, compacts
1 (adjective) taking up very little space, e.g. *a compact kitchen.*
2 (noun) a small, flat, round case containing face-powder and a mirror.
compactly (adverb) **compactness** (noun)
[Latin *com-* + *pangere* = to fasten together]

Similar words: (adjective) dense, solid, compressed

compact disc, discs
(noun) a type of record played using a laser.

companion, companions
(noun) someone you travel or spend time with.
companionship (noun)
[Latin *com-* = together + *panis* = bread; a companion was originally someone you shared a meal with]

company, companies
1 (noun) a business that sells goods or provides a service, e.g. *an oil company.*
2 a group of actors, opera singers or dancers, e.g. *the Royal Shakespeare Company.*
3 If you have company, you have a friend or visitor with you, e.g. *She enjoyed his company.*
4 (phrase) If you **keep someone company**, you spend time with them.
5 If you **part company** with someone, you stop associating with them.
accompany (verb)

Similar words: (sense 3) companionship, society

comparable (pronounced **kom-pra-bl**)
(adjective) similar in size or quality, e.g. *Winning Wimbledon or the Open Golf Championship are comparable achievements.*
comparably (adverb) **comparability** (noun)

comparative
(noun) In grammar, the comparative is the form of an adjective which indicates that the person or thing described has more of a particular quality than someone or something else. For example, **quicker**, **better**, and **easier** are comparatives of 'quick', 'good' and 'easy'.
comparatively (adverb)

compare, compares, comparing, compared
(verb) to consider things together and see in what ways they are different or similar.
comparison (noun)
[Latin *comparabilis* = similar]

compartment, compartments
(noun) a section of something, e.g of a railway carriage.
[Latin *compartiri* = to share]

compass, compasses
1 (noun) an instrument for finding directions.
2 A pair of compasses is a hinged instrument for drawing circles.

compassion
(noun) pity and sympathy for someone who is suffering.
compassionate (adjective) **compassionately** (adverb)
[Latin *compatior* = to suffer with]

compatible
1 (adjective) If people are compatible, they can live or exist together successfully.
2 If computers are compatible, you can transfer files direct from one to the other.
[Latin *compatior* = to be in sympathy with]

Similar words: suited, well-matched

compel, compels, compelling, compelled
(verb) to force someone to do something.
[Latin *compellere* = to drive together]

compensate, compensates, compensating, compensated

What is the difference between a compass and a pair of compasses?

(verb) to give money to replace something lost, damaged or destroyed.
compensatory (adjective) **compensation** (noun)
[Latin *com-* = with + *pendere* = to weigh]

compete, competes, competing, competed
(verb) to take part in a contest or game.
[Latin *competere* = to strive together]

competent
(adjective) able to do something satisfactorily,
e.g. *a competent swimmer.*
competently (adverb) **competence** (noun)

competition, competitions
1 (noun) When there is competition between people or groups, they are all trying to get something that not everyone can have, e.g. *Competition for places was keen.*
2 an event in which people take part to find who is best at something.
competitive (adjective) **competitively** (adverb)

competitor, competitors
(noun) a person or firm that is competing to become the most successful.

compile, compiles, compiling, compiled
(verb) When someone compiles a book, report etc. they make it by putting together several items.
compilation (noun)
[Latin *compilare* = to pile together]

complacent
(adjective) If someone is complacent, they are self-satisfied and not worried about a serious situation, e.g. *Dan was complacent about his poor spelling.*
complacently (adverb) **complacency** (noun)
[Latin *complacens* = very pleasing]

Similar words: self-satisfied, smug

complain, complains, complaining, complained
(verb) to say that you are not satisfied with something.
[Latin *com-* + *plangere* = to bewail greatly]

Similar words: grizzle, groan, grouse, grumble, moan, whine

complaint, complaints
1 (noun) If you make a complaint, you complain about something.
2 an illness, e.g. *She has a minor chest complaint.*

complete, completes, completing, completed
1 (adjective) If something is complete, none of it is missing, e.g. *They found a complete skeleton.*
2 (verb) If you complete something, you finish it.
3 If you complete a form, you fill it in.
completely (adverb) **completion** (noun)
[Latin *completus* = filled up]

Similar words: entire, whole, full

complex, complexes
(adjective) complicated, with many different parts, e.g. *complex patterns.*
complexity (noun)
[Latin *complecti* = to entwine]

Similar words: complicated, intricate, involved

complexion
(noun) the quality of the skin on your face,
e.g. *The model had a beautiful complexion.*
[Latin *complexio* = bodily characteristics]

complicated
(adjective) difficult to understand or deal with, because of its many parts.
complicate (verb) **complication** (noun)
[Latin *complicare* = to fold together]

compliment, compliments, complimenting, complimented
1 (noun) If you pay someone a compliment, you tell them you admire something about them.
2 (verb) If you compliment someone, you pay them a compliment.
[Spanish *cumplir* = to do what is suitable]

complimentary
1 (adjective) If you are complimentary about something, you express admiration for it.
2 A complimentary seat, ticket or publication is given to you free.

component, components
(noun) a part of something, e.g. *The battery is a car component.*
[Latin *componere* = to put together]

compose, composes, composing, composed
1 (verb) If something is composed of particular things or people, it is made up of them.
e.g. *The team is composed of players of all sizes.*
2 to write a piece of music, letter, or speech.
[Latin *componere* = to put together]

composed
(adjective) calm and in control of your feelings.

composer, composers
(noun) someone who writes music.

composition, compositions
(noun) a piece of music or writing.

compost
(noun) a mixture of decaying plants and manure, which is added to soil to help plants grow.
[Latin *compositus* = put together]

compound, compounds
1 (noun) an enclosed area of land with buildings used for a particular purpose, e.g. *a prison compound.*
2 In chemistry, a compound is a substance consisting of two or more different chemical elements.
[Latin *componere* = to put together]

comprehend, comprehends, comprehending, comprehended
(verb; formal) to understand.
comprehension (noun) **comprehensible**
[Latin *comprehendere* = to seize]

comprehensive, comprehensives
1 (adjective) including everything necessary or relevant, e.g. *We had a comprehensive collection of Beatles records.*
2 (noun) a school where children of all abilities are taught together.

compress, compresses, compressing, compressed
(verb) To compress something means to squeeze it or shorten it so that it takes up less space, e.g. *compressed air*.
compression (noun)
[Latin *comprimere* = to squeeze together]

comprise, comprises, comprising, comprised
(verb; formal) What something comprises is what it consists of, e.g. *The team comprised 12 players*.
[French *compris* = included]

compromise, compromises, compromising, compromised
1 (noun) an agreement in which people accept less than they originally wanted, e.g. *At last a compromise was reached*.
2 (verb) When people compromise, they agree to accept less than they oreiginally wanted, e.g *The clubs compromised on a transfer fee of £20,000*. [Latin *compromissum* = joint decision to accept arbiter's judgment]

compulsory
(adjective) If something is compulsory, you have to do it, e.g. *Games are compulsory here.*

Similar word: obligatory

compute, computes, computing, computed
(verb) to calculate.
computation (noun)
[Latin *computare* = to calculate]

computer, computers
(noun) an electronic machine that can quickly make calculations or store, retrieve and process information.
computing (noun)

computerize, computerizes, computerizing, computerized; also spelled **computerise**
(verb) When a system or process is computerized, the work starts being or is done by computers.
computerization (noun)

comrade, comrades
1 (noun) A soldier's comrades are his fellow soldiers, especially in battle.
2 Socialists and communists often address each other as 'comrade'.
comradeship (noun)
[Spanish *camarada* = sharer of a lodging]

con, cons, conning, conned (informal)
1 (verb) If someone cons you, they trick you into doing or believing something.
2 (noun) A con is a trick in which someone deceives you into doing or believing something.
[Con is short for 'confidence trick']

concave
(adjective) curving inwards.
[Latin *concavus* = arched]

conceal, conceals, concealing, concealed
(verb) To conceal something means to hide it, e.g. *He might be concealing his feelings.*
concealed (adjective) **concealment** (noun)
[Latin *con-* + *celare* = to hide thoroughly]

concede, concedes, conceding, conceded
(pronounced kon-**seed**)
1 (verb) If you concede something, you admit that it is true, e.g. *The company conceded that an error had been made.*
2 When someone concedes defeat, they accept that they have lost, for example, an election.
[Latin *concedere* = to yield]

conceited
(adjective) big-headed and too proud of appearance, abilities or achievements.
conceit (noun) **conceitedly** (adverb)

Similar words: cocky, arrogant, vain

conceive, conceives, conceiving, conceived
1 (verb) When a child is conceived, it begins to grow in the mother's womb.
2 If you conceive an idea, you think it up.

concentrate, concentrates, concentrating, concentrated
(verb) to give all your attention to something.
concentration (noun)

concentrated
(adjective) A concentrated liquid has been made stronger by having water removed from it, e.g. *concentrated orange juice.*

concentration camp, camps
(noun) a prison camp, especially one in Nazi Germany during World War Two.

concentric
(adjective) Concentric circles have the same centre.

concept, concepts
(noun) A concept is an idea or abstract principle, e.g. *the concept of justice.*
conceptual (adjective) **conceptually** (adverb)

concern, concerns, concerning, concerned
1 (noun) a feeling of worry about something or someone, e.g. *There was public concern over the number of homeless people.*
2 (verb) If something concerns you or if you are concerned about it, it worries you, e.g. *Her disappearance concerned him deeply.*
3 You also say that something concerns you if it affects or involves you, e.g. *What I have to say concerns all of you.*
4 (noun) If something is your concern, it is your responsibility.
concerned (adjective)
[Latin *concernere* = to mingle together]

concerning
(preposition) about, e.g. *She asked me questions concerning my project.*

concert, concerts
(noun) a public performance by musicians.
[French *concerter* = to bring into agreement]

concerto, concertos or concerti (pronounced kon-**cher**-toe)
(noun) a piece of music for a solo instrument and an orchestra.

concession, concessions
(noun) If you make a concession, you agree to let

someone have or do something, e.g. *As a special concession, we were allowed to go home early.*

conclude, concludes, concluding, concluded
1 (verb) to decide that something is true because of other things you know.
2 to finish or settle finally.
concluding (adjective) **conclusion** (noun)
[Latin *concludere* = to enclose]

concoct, concocts, concocting, concocted
1 (verb) to invent, e.g. an excuse or explanation.
2 If you concoct something, you make it by mixing several things together, e.g. *Nancy had concocted a red wine sauce.*
concoction (noun)
[Latin *con-* + *coquere* = to cook together]

concrete
1 (noun) a building material made by mixing cement, sand and water.
2 (adjective) real and definite, e.g. *We need concrete evidence that she was there at the time of the crime.*
[Latin *concretus* = grown together]

concussed
(adjective) confused or unconscious because of a blow to the head.
concussion (noun)
[Latin *concussus* = violently shaken]

condemn, condemns, condemning, condemned
1 (verb) to say something is bad and unacceptable, e.g. *The archbishop condemned all acts of terrorism.*
2 If someone is condemned to a punishment, they are given it, e.g. *He was condemned to life imprisonment.*
3 When a building is condemned, it is going to be pulled down because it is unsafe.
condemned (adjective) **condemnation** (noun)
[Latin *condemnare* = to condemn]

condensation
1 (noun) a coating of tiny drops formed on a surface by steam or vapour.
2 the changing of gas or vapour to liquid.

condense, condenses, condensing, condensed
1 (verb) If you condense a piece of writing or a speech, you shorten it by removing the less important parts.
2 When a gas or vapour condenses, it changes into a liquid.
[Latin *condensare* = to make thick]

condition, conditions
1 (noun) the state that someone or something is in e.g. *BMW for sale in good condition.*
2 (plural noun) The conditions in which something is done are the location and other factors likely to affect it, e.g. *The experiment was carried out in the most difficult conditions.*
3 a requirement that must be met for something else to be possible, e.g. *The job is yours on the condition that you live here.*
4 an illness or other medical problem, e.g. *a heart condition.*
5 (phrase) **Out of condition** means unfit.
[Latin *condicere* = to discuss or to agree]

conditioner, conditioners
(noun) a thick liquid put on hair after washing to make it soft and shiny.

conduct, conducts, conducting, conducted
1 (verb; pronounced con-**duct**) To conduct an activity or task means to carry it out, e.g. *We are conducting a survey of the region.*
2 (verb) When someone conducts an orchestra or choir, they stand in front of it and direct it.
3 If something conducts heat or electricity, heat or electricity can pass through it.
4 (noun; pronounced **con**-duct) Your conduct is your behaviour.
conduction (noun)
[Latin *conducere* = to draw together]

conductor, conductors
1 (noun) someone who conducts an orchestra or choir.
2 someone who moves round a bus selling tickets (female: **conductress**)
3 A conductor of heat or electricity is a substance that conducts it.

cone, cones
1 (noun) a regular 3D shape with a circular base and a point at the top.
2 the fruit of, e.g. a pine tree, consisting of a cluster of woody scales containing seeds.
conical (adjective)
[Greek *kōnus* = pine cone]

confectionery
(noun) sweets.
[Latin *confectus* = done or made]

confer, confers, conferring, conferred
(verb) When people confer, they discuss something in order to make a decision.
[Latin *conferre* = to gather together]

conference, conferences
(noun) a meeting at which formal discussions take place.

confess, confesses, confessing, confessed
(verb) If you confess to something, you admit it, e.g. *The doctor confessed to the murder.*
[Latin *confiteri* = to admit]

Similar words: admit, come clean, own up

confession, confessions
1 (noun) If you make a confession, you admit you have done something wrong.
2 a religious act in which people confess their sins to a priest.

Similar words: (sense 1) admission, revelation

confetti
(noun) small pieces of coloured paper thrown over the bride and groom at a wedding.
[Italian *confetto* = a sweet]

confide, confides, confiding, confided
(verb) If you confide in someone, you tell them a secret, trusting them to keep it.
confiding (adjective) **confidingly** (adverb)
[Latin *confidere* = to trust]

Concrete poetry uses words and letters to make patterns, shapes and pictures. Have you tried it?

confidence, confidences
1 (noun) If you have confidence in someone, you feel you can trust them.
2 Someone who has confidence is sure of their own abilities, qualities or ideas.

confident
(adjective) sure of your own abilities, qualities or ideas.
confidently (adverb)

Similar word: certain, sure, positive, self-assured

confidential
(adjective) Confidential information is meant to be kept secret.
confidentially (adverb) **confidentiality** (noun)

confine, confines, confining, confined
(verb) If you are confined to a place, you cannot leave it, e.g. *The soldiers were confined to barracks.*
confinement (noun)
[Latin *con-* = with + *finis* = boundary]

confirm, confirms, confirming, confirmed
1 (verb) to say or show that something is true, e.g. *The police confirmed that it was my car they had found.*
2 If you confirm an arrangement or appointment, you say it is definite.
3 When someone is confirmed, they are formally accepted as a member of a Christian church.
confirmation (noun) **confirmatory** (adjective)
[Latin *confirmare* = to establish]

confiscate, confiscates, confiscating, confiscated
(verb) to take something away from someone as a punishment.
confiscation (noun)
[Latin *confiscare* = to seize for the public treasury]

conflict, conflicts, conflicting, conflicted
1 (noun) disagreement and argument, e.g. *They had a conflict of opinions.*
2 a war or battle, e.g. *Never in the field of human conflict was so much owed by so many to so few.*
3 (verb) to differ, e.g. *Your story of what happened conflicts with hers.*
[Latin *confligere* = to fight or to contend]

Similar words: (noun: sense 1) disagreement, clash (verb) disagree

conform, conforms, conforming, conformed
(verb) If you conform, you behave the way people expect you to.
conformist (noun and adjective)

confront, confronts, confronting, confronted
(verb) to meet someone face to face.
[Latin *confrontari* = to stand face to face with]

confrontation, confrontations
(noun) a serious dispute or fight, e.g. *a confrontation with the unions.*

confuse, confuses, confusing, confused
1 (verb) If you confuse two things, you mix them up and think one of them is the other, e.g. *You must be confusing me with my sister.*
2 To confuse someone means to make them uncertain what is happening or what to do.
confused (adjective) **confusing** (adjective)
confusion (noun)
[Latin *confundere* = to pour together]

Similar word: (sense 2) bewilder

congeal, congeals, congealing, congealed
(pronounced kon-**jeel**)
(verb) When a liquid congeals, it becomes very thick and sticky.
[Latin *con-* + *gelare* = to freeze thoroughly]

congested
(adjective) When a road is congested, it is full of traffic.
congestion (noun)
[Latin *congestus* = pressed together]

congratulate, congratulates, congratulating, congratulated
(verb) to praise someone for something they have achieved.
congratulation (noun) **congratulatory** (adjective)
[Latin *con-* + *gratulari* = to rejoice with]

congregation, congregations
(noun) In a church, the congregation are the people attending a service.
congregate (verb)
[Latin *congregare* = to collect into a flock]

congruent
(adjective) Two triangles are congruent if they are exactly the same shape and size.

conical
(adjective) shaped like a cone.

conifer, conifers
(noun) a tree, usually evergreen, that has needle-like leaves and produces brown cones.
coniferous (adjective)
[Latin *conus* = cone + *ferre* = to bear]

conjunction, conjunctions [see page 429]
(noun) In grammar, a conjunction is a word that links two other words or two clauses, e.g. 'and', 'but', 'while', and 'that'.
conjunctive (adjective)
[Latin *conjunctus* = united]

conjurer, conjurers
(noun) someone who does magic tricks.
conjuring (noun)
[Latin *conjurare* = to conspire]

conker, conkers
(noun) a hard, brown nut from a horse chestnut tree.

connect, connects, connecting, connected
(verb) to join together.
[Latin *connectere* = to bind together]

connection, connections; also spelled **connexion**
1 (noun) a link or relationship that exists between things.
2 the point where two wires or pipes are joined together, e.g. *a loose connection.*

conquer, conquers, conquering, conquered
1 (verb) To conquer people means to take control of their country by force.

Can you see why these words confuse some people? chose choose; lose loose; nose noose

2 If you conquer something difficult or dangerous, you succeed in taking control of it, e.g. *the effort to conquer cancer.*
conqueror (noun) **conquest** (noun)
[Latin *conquirere* = to search for]

conscience
1 (noun) the part of your mind that tells you what is right and wrong.
2 If you have a guilty conscience, you feel ashamed because you have done something wrong.
[Latin *conscire* = to know]

Similar word: (sense 1) principles

conscientious (pronounced kon-shee-**en**-shus)
1 (adjective) hard-working.
2 (noun) A **conscientious objector** is someone who, because of their beliefs, refuses to fight in a war.
conscientiously (adverb) **conscientiousness** (noun)

Similar words: (adjective) thorough, painstaking, dedicated

conscious
1 (adjective) awake, rather than asleep or unconscious, e.g. *He was now fully conscious.*
2 aware; knowing, e.g. *She became conscious that something was burning.*
3 A conscious action or effort is done deliberately, e.g. *He made a conscious effort to look happy despite his pain.*
consciously (adverb) **consciousness** (noun)
[Latin *conscius* = sharing knowledge]

consecutive
(adjective) happening one after the other, e.g. *3 consecutive victories... 4 consecutive days.*
consecutively (adverb)
[Latin *consecutus* = having followed]

consent, consents, consenting, consented
1 (noun) permission to do something, e.g. *She married without her parents' consent.*
2 (verb) to agree to something.
[Latin *consentire* = to agree]

consequence, consequences
(noun) The consequence of something is its result or effect.
consequent (adjective) **consequently** (adverb)
[Latin *consequi* = to pursue]

conservation
(noun) work done to preserve for the future important items which are in danger of being destroyed, e.g. buildings, natural habitats.
conservationist (noun and adjective)

Conservative
(adjective) The Conservative Party is one of the three main political parties in Britain. It believes in private enterprise and capitalism.

conservatory, conservatories
(noun) a room with glass walls and a glass roof, often at the back of a house in which plants are kept.

conserve, conserves, conserving, conserved
(verb) to make something last, e.g. *We must conserve our strength.*
[Latin *conservare* = to preserve]

consider, considers, considering, considered
(verb) To consider something means to think about it carefully, e.g. *I stopped to consider what to do next.*
[Latin *considerare* = to inspect]

Similar words: contemplate, ponder, reflect

considerable
(adjective) A considerable amount of something is a lot of it, e.g. *The cost was considerable.*
considerably (adverb)

considerate
(adjective) paying attention to other people's needs, wishes and feelings.
considerately (adverb)

consideration, considerations
1 (noun) careful thought about something, e.g. *After much consideration, they agreed to go.*
2 If you show consideration for someone, you take account of their needs, wishes and feelings.

Similar words: (sense 1) contemplation, reflection

consist, consists, consisting, consisted
(verb) What something consists of is its different parts or members, e.g. *Batter consists of flour, milk and eggs.*

consistent
(adjective) If you are consistent, you react to situations in the same sort of way, every time they occur. So the word can mean reliable, e.g. *Martyn's goalkeeping was very consistent through the season.* It can also mean fair, e.g. *The referee's decisions were consistent during the match.*
consistently (adverb) **consistency** (noun)

console, consoles, consoling, consoled
(verb) To console someone who is unhappy means to try to make them more cheerful, e.g. *I was consoled by the thought of the money.*
consolation (noun) **consolatory** (adjective)
[Latin *consolari* = to comfort]

consolidate, consolidates, consolidating, consolidated
(verb) To consolidate something you have gained or achieved means to make it more secure.
consolidation (noun)
[Latin *consolidare* = to make firm]

consonant, consonants
(noun) any letter of the alphabet which is not a vowel. Consonants are sounds such as 'p' or 'm' made by stopping the air flowing freely through your mouth by making two parts of the mouth touch.
[Latin *consonare* = to sound at the same time]

conspicuous
(adjective) easily seen or noticed.
conspicuously (adverb)
[Latin *conspicere* = to perceive]

We take these words from the Norman invasion: beef pork mutton veal charity humour.

conspiracy, conspiracies
(noun) a secret plan by a group of people, usually illegal.
conspiratorial (adjective) **conspirator** (noun) **conspire** (verb)
[Latin *conspirare* = to plot]

constable, constables
(noun) a police officer of the lowest rank.
constabulary (noun)
[Latin *comes stabuli* = officer of the stable]

constant, constants
1 (adjective) Something that is constant happens all the time or is always there, e.g. *He was in constant pain.*
2 staying the same, e.g. *a constant temperature.*
3 (noun) In maths or science, a constant is a number or quantity that does not change, e.g. pi.
constantly (adverb) **constancy** (noun)
[Latin *constare* = to stand firm]

Similar words: (sense 2) unchanging, consistent

constellation, constellations
(noun) a group of stars.
[Latin *con-* = together + *stellae* = stars]

constipated
(adjective) Someone who is constipated is unable to pass solid waste from their body.
constipation (noun)
[Latin *constipare* = to press together]

constituency, constituencies
(noun) a town or area represented by a Member of Parliament.

constitution, constitutions
1 (noun) The constitution of a country is the system of laws which formally states people's rights and duties.
2 Your constitution is your health, e.g. *He has a strong constitution.*
constitutional (adjective)

construct, constructs, constructing, constructed
1 (verb) to build or make.
2 In geometry, to construct a line, angle or shape means to draw it.
construction (noun)
[Latin *construere* = to heap together or to build]

constructive
(adjective) Constructive criticisms and comments are helpful because they suggest what ought to be done.
constructively (adverb)

consult, consults, consulting, consulted
1 (verb) to ask someone for their opinion or advice.
2 If you consult a book or map, you refer to it for information.
[Latin *consultare* = to consider or to reflect]

consultant, consultants
1 (noun) an experienced doctor who specializes in one type of medicine.
2 someone who gives expert advice, e.g. *a firm of computer consultants.*

consultation, consultations
(noun) discussion or the seeking of advice,

e.g. *The decisions were taken after consultation with the unions.*
consultative (adjective)

consume, consumes, consuming, consumed
1 (verb; formal) to eat or drink.
2 To consume fuel or energy means to use it up.
[Latin *consumere* = to use up entirely]

consumer, consumers
(noun) someone who buys things or uses services, e.g. *The consumer is entitled to value for money.*

consumption
(noun) the using of fuel or the eating of food etc., e.g. *The high fuel consumption of the aircraft worried the airline bosses.*

contact, contacts, contacting, contacted
1 (noun) If you are in contact with someone, you regularly meet, talk to or write to them.
2 When things are in contact, they are touching each other.
3 (verb) If you contact someone, you telephone them or write to them.
4 (noun) someone you know in a place, from whom you can get help or information, e.g. *Peabody is our Hong Kong contact.*
[Latin *contactus* = a touch]

Similar words: (verb) get in touch with, get hold of, reach

contact lens, lenses
(noun) small plastic lenses that you put directly on your eyes instead of wearing glasses.

contagious
(adjective) A contagious disease can be caught by touching people or things infected with it.

contain, contains, containing, contained
1 (verb) If a substance contains something, that thing is a part of it, e.g. *Coffee contains caffeine.*
2 to hold, e.g. *This chest contains buried treasure.*
containment (noun)
[Latin *con-* + *tenere* = to hold together]

container, containers
1 (noun) something that you keep things in, e.g. a box or a bottle.
2 a large sealed metal box for transporting things by road, rail or ship.

Similar words: (sense 1) holder, receptacle, canister, carton, vessel

contaminate, contaminates, contaminating, contaminated
(verb) If something is contaminated by dirt, chemicals or radiation, it is made impure and harmful, e.g. *contaminated drinking water.*
contamination (noun) **contaminant** (noun)
[Latin *contaminare* = to defile]

contemplate, contemplates, contemplating, contemplated
(verb) to think long and hard about something for a long time.
contemplation (noun) **contemplative** (adjective)
[Latin *contemplarie* = to regard]

Advice is seldom welcome; and those who want it the most always like it the least.

contempt
(noun) If you treat someone or something with contempt, you show no respect for them at all, e.g. *Robin Hood looked at the Sheriff of Nottingham with contempt.*
[Latin *contemnere* = to condemn]

contend, contends, contending, contended
1 (verb) To contend with a difficulty means to deal with it, e.g. *I have enough to contend with already.*
2 to compete for something.
contender (noun)
[Latin *contendere* = to stretch or to strive]

content, contents
1 (noun) the proportion of something that a substance contains, e.g. *Spinach has a very high iron content.*
2 (plural noun) The contents of something are the things inside it.
3 (adjective) happy and satisfied.
[Latin *continere* = to contain or to hold back]

contented
(adjective) happy and satisfied.
contentedly (adverb) **contentment** (noun)

contest, contests
(noun) a competition or game, e.g. *a fishing contest.*
[Latin *contestari* = to call to witness]

Similar words: match, championship, tournament, game, competition.

contestant, contestants
(noun) someone taking part in a competition.

Similar words: competitor, participant, player

context, contexts
(noun) The context of a word or sentence consists of the words or sentences before and after it, which make the full meaning clear.
contextual (adjective)
[Latin *contextus* = connected]

continent, continents
1 (noun) One of the 5 largest areas of land: America, Africa, Asia, Europe, Antarctica.
2 The Continent is the mainland of Europe, e.g. *He spent July on the Continent.*
continental (adjective)
[Latin *terra continens* = continuous land]

continual
(adjective) happening again and again, e.g. *continual increases in cost.*
continually (adverb)

Similar words: incessant, persistent, constant, non-stop

continue, continues, continuing, continued
(verb) to carry on doing something.
continuation (noun)
[Latin *continuare* = to join together]

Similar words: go on, proceed

continuous
(adjective) happening or existing without stopping, e.g. *a continuous white line.*
continuously (adverb) **continuity** (noun)

contorted
(adjective) twisted into an unnatural shape, e.g. *His face was contorted with pain.*
[Latin *contortus* = twisted]

contortion, contortions
(noun) Contortions are movements in which you twist your body into unusual positions.

contour, contours
(noun) On a map, a contour is a line joining points of equal height.
[Italian *contornare* = to draw in outline]

contra-
(prefix) against or opposite to.
[Latin *contra* = against]

contraceptive, contraceptives
(noun) a device or pill for preventing pregnancy.
contraception (noun)

contract, contracts, contracting, contracted
1 (noun) a written legal agreement about the sale of something or work done for money.
2 (verb) to get smaller or shorter.
contractual (adjective) **contraction** (noun)
[Latin *contrahere* = to draw together]

contractor, contractors
(noun) a person or company that does work for other people, e.g. *a building contractor.*

contradict, contradicts, contradicting, contradicted
(verb) If you contradict someone, you say the opposite of what they have just said.
e.g. A: *You're always contradicting me.* B: *I most certainly am not!*
contradiction (noun) **contradictory** (adjective)
[Latin *contra-* + *dicere* = to speak against]

contraption, contraptions
(noun) a strange-looking device or machine.

contrary (pronounced **con**-trurry)
1 (adjective) opposite, for example, in opinions, e.g. *Lee's ideas were quite contrary to mine.*
2 (phrase) You say on the contrary when you are contradicting what has just been said, e.g. *'You'll hate the show.'* – *'On the contrary, I'll love it.'*

contrast, contrasts, contrasting, contrasted
(noun) a great difference between things, e.g. *the contrast between day and night.*
2 (verb) If one thing contrasts with another, it is very different from it.
[Latin *contra-* + *stare* = to stand against]

contribute, contributes, contributing, contributed
1 (verb) If you contribute to something, you do something towards it, e.g. *Old people have much to contribute to the community.*
2 If you contribute money, you give it to help to pay for something.
contribution (noun) **contributor** (noun)
contributory (adjective)
[Latin *contribuere* = to bring together]

Similar words: (sense 2) donate, give

A verbal contract isn't worth the paper it's written on. (Samuel Goldwyn)

control, controls, controlling, controlled
1 (noun) Control of a country or organization is the power to decide how it is run.
2 (verb) To control, e.g. a machine or system, means to make it work the way you want it to.
3 If you control yourself, you make yourself behave calmly when you are angry or upset.
4 (noun) The controls on a machine are knobs or other devices used to operate it.
5 (phrase) If something is **out of control**, nobody has any power over it.
controller (noun)

Similar words: (verb: sense 3) restrain, check, hold back

controversial
(adjective) Something that is controversial causes a lot of discussion and argument, because many people disagree about it.
controversy (noun)
[Latin *controversus* = turned in an opposite way]

Similar words: provocative, outrageous

convalesce, convalesces, convalescing, convalesced (pronounced con-val-**ess**)
(verb) to rest and regain health after an illness or operation.
convalescent (adjective) **convalescence** (noun)
[Latin *convalescere* = to become strong]

convection
(noun) the process by which heat travels through gases and liquids.
[Latin *con-* = with + *vectus* = carried]

convector, convectors
(noun) A convector or convector heater is a heater that heats a room using hot air.

convenience, conveniences
(noun) something useful, e.g. *This house has every modern convenience.*

convenient
(adjective) easy to use or to reach.
conveniently (adverb)
[Latin *conveniens* = appropriate]

Similar words: handy, serviceable, useful

convent, convents
(noun) a building where nuns live, or a school run by nuns.
[Latin *conventus* = meeting]

convention
1 (noun) a large meeting of people to discuss their work, e.g. *a convention of cancer surgeons.*
2 a formal agreement between nations, e.g. *the Geneva Convention on the treatment of prisoners of war.*
3 an understanding between, for example a playwright and his audience, e.g. The stage whisper is a dramatic convention. The audience can hear it, but everybody pretends that the other characters cannot hear it.

conventional
(adjective) usual or traditional, e.g. *Mr Brown is very conventional in what he wears, with his pin-stripe suit, bowler hat and rolled umbrella.*

conversation, conversations
(noun) a talk with someone.
conversational (adjective) **conversationally** (adverb) **conversationalist** (noun)

converse, converses, conversing, conversed
1 (verb; formal) to talk to someone.
2 (noun) The converse of something is its opposite, e.g. *The Ugly Sisters fancied the prince. The converse, however, was not true.*
conversely (adverb)
[Latin *conversare* = to turn constantly]

convert, converts, converting, converted
1 (verb) To convert one thing into another means to change it so that it becomes the other thing, e.g. *We're converting the loft into a playroom.*
2 If someone converts you, they persuade you to change your religious or political beliefs.
conversion (noun) **convertible** (adjective)
[Latin *convertere* = to turn round]

convex
(adjective) bulging outwards.
[Latin *convexus* = vaulted or rounded]

convey, conveys, conveying, conveyed
(verb; formal) to transport someone or something.

conveyor belt, belts
(noun) a moving strip used in factories for carrying objects along.

convict, convicts, convicting, convicted
1 (verb; pronounced con-**vict**) To convict someone of a crime means to find them guilty, e.g. *He was convicted of spying.*
2 (noun; pronounced **con**-vict) someone serving a prison sentence.
[Latin *convictus* = convicted of crime]

conviction, convictions
1 (noun) a strong belief or opinion.
2 The conviction of someone is what happens when they are found guilty in a court of law, e.g. *He had 3 previous motoring convictions.*

convince, convinces, convincing, convinced
(verb) To convince someone of something means to persuade them that it is true.
[Latin *convincere* = to demonstrate conclusively]

convincing
(adjective) very believable, e.g. *a convincing explanation.*
convincingly (adverb)

Similar words: persuasive, credible, believable

convoy, convoys
(noun) a group of vehicles or ships travelling together.
[Old French *convoier* = to convey]

cook, cooks, cooking, cooked
(verb) to prepare food by heating it.
cooker (noun)
[Latin *coquere* = to cook]

cook up
(phrasal verb) to invent, e.g. *They cooked up a plan to sell sand to Saharan tribesmen.*

When writing conversation, do not use the word 'said' too often. Notice how authors manage.

cookery
(noun) the activity of preparing and cooking food.

cool, cooler, coolest; cools, cooling, cooled
1 (adjective) Something cool has a low temperature but is not cold.
2 If you are cool in a difficult situation, you stay calm and unemotional.
3 If your behaviour towards someone is cool, you are not friendly to them.
4 (informal) trendy and acceptable, e.g. *Those are cool shoes you're wearing, Gladys.*
5 (verb) to make something cooler.
coolly (adverb) **coolness** (noun)

cooped up
(adjective) kept in a place which is too small or which does not allow enough freedom, e.g. *I hated being cooped up in the flat all day.*

co-operate, co-operates, co-operating, co-operated
(pronounced koh-**op**-er-rate)
1 (verb) When people co-operate, they work or act together.
2 to do what someone asks, e.g. *The gangster said, 'Sid, you'd better co-operate, or else!'*
co-operation (noun)
[Latin *co-* + *operari* = to work with]

co-operative, co-operatives (pronounced koh-**op**-er-ut-tiv)
1 (adjective) A co-operative activity is done by people working together.
2 easy to work with.
co-operatively (adverb)

co-ordinate, co-ordinates, co-ordinating, co-ordinated (pronounced koh-**or**-din-ate)
(verb) To co-ordinate an activity means to organize the people or things involved in it, e.g. *Emergency services were co-ordinated centrally.*
co-ordination (noun) **co-ordinator** (noun)

cope, copes, coping, coped
(verb) to deal successfuly with a problem or task.

copper, coppers
1 (noun) a reddish-brown metal.
2 a brown metal coin of low value.
3 (informal) a policeman.
[Greek *Kupris* = Cyprus, where copper originally came from]

copy, copies, copying, copied
1 (noun) something made to look like something else.
2 A copy of a book, newspaper, etc. is one of many produced.
3 (verb) If you copy something, you make another one like it.
copier (noun)

Similar words: (noun: sense 1) facsimile, reproduction, replica
(verb) duplicate, replicate

---

copyright, copyrights
(noun) If someone has the copyright on a piece of music, writing, etc. it cannot be copied or performed without their permission.

coral, corals
(noun) a hard substance that forms in the sea from the skeletons of tiny animals called corals. Coral is used to make jewellery.
[Greek *korallion* = coral]

cord, cords
1 (noun) strong, thick string.
2 Our vocal cords are pieces of membrane in the windpipe which vibrate to produce the voice
[Greek *khordē* = gut or string]

cordial
1 (adjective) warm and friendly, e.g. *He wrote a cordial reply to my letter.*
2 (noun) a sweet drink made from fruit juice.
cordially (adverb) **cordiality** (noun)

corduroy
(noun) a thick cloth with parallel raised lines on the outside.

cordwangle, cordwangles
(noun) a piece of equipment used to stretch leather in shoemaking; cordwangles are used in a traditional shoemakers' folk dance.
cordwangling (noun)
[Middle English from Old French *corde* = gut of an animal]

core, cores
(noun) the central part, for example of an apple or the earth.

cork, corks
1 (noun) the very light, spongelike bark of a Mediterranean tree.
2 a piece of cork pushed into the end of a bottle to close it.
[Spanish *alcorque* = cork sole or shoe]

corkscrew, corkscrews
(noun) a device for pulling corks out of bottles.

corn, corns
1 (noun) Corn refers to crops such as wheat and barley and to their seeds.
2 a small painful area of hard skin on your foot.

corner, corners, cornering, cornered
1 (noun) a place where two sides or edges of something meet.
2 (verb) To corner a person or animal means to get them into a place they cannot escape from.

cornet, cornets
1 (noun) a small brass instrument like a trumpet used in brass and military bands.
2 an edible cone-shaped holder for a scoop of ice cream.
[Latin *cornu* = horn]

cornflour
(noun) a fine white flour made from maize and used in cooking to thicken soups, gravy and sauces.

corny, cornier, corniest
(adjective) very obvious and not at all original, e.g. *a corny joke.*

coronation, coronations
(noun) the ceremony at which a king or queen is crowned.
[Latin *corona* = crown]

Pun. Why was the farmer cross? Someone trod on his corn.

coroner, coroners
(noun) an official who investigates the deaths of people who have died in a violent or unusual way.

corporal, corporals
(noun) a non-commissioned officer in the army or air force, immediately below sergeant in rank.

corporal punishment
(noun) the punishing of people by beating them.
[Latin *corpus* = body]

corporation, corporations
1 (noun) a group of people, under a mayor, responsible for running a city.
2 a large business, e.g. *British Broadcasting Corporation (BBC)*.

corpse, corpses
(noun) a dead body.
[Latin *corpus* = body]

corpuscle, corpuscles (pronounced kor-pus-sl)
(noun) a red or white blood cell.
[Latin *corpusculum* = little body]

correct, corrects, correcting, corrected
1 (adjective) If something is correct, there are no mistakes in it.
2 (verb) If you correct something which is wrong, you make it right.
correctly (adverb) **correction** (noun)
correctness (noun)
[Latin *corrigere* = to put right]

correspond, corresponds, corresponding, corresponded
1 (verb) to be similar; to match.
2 When people correspond, they write to each other.

correspondence
(noun) the writing of letters; also the letters written.

correspondent, correspondents
(noun) a newspaper, TV or radio reporter on a particular subject or place.

corridor, corridors
(noun) a passage in a building or train.
[Old Italian *corridore* = place for running]

corrugated
(adjective) Corrugated metal or cardboard is rippled to make it stronger.
[Latin *corrugare* = to wrinkle up]

corrupt, corrupts, corrupting, corrupted
1 (adjective) Corrupt people act dishonestly or illegally in return for money or power, e.g. *There are rumours about corrupt politicians*.
2 (verb) To corrupt someone means to make them dishonest or immoral, e.g. *Young prisoners are often corrupted by hardened criminals*.
corruptly (adverb) **corruptible** (adjective)
[Latin *corruptus* = destroyed or weakened]

corruption
(noun) dishonesty and illegal behaviour by people in positions of power.

cosmetic, cosmetics
(noun) Cosmetics are beauty products such as lipstick and face powder.
[Greek *kosmein* = to arrange]

cosmonaut, cosmonauts
(noun) a Soviet astronaut.
[Greek *kosmos* = universe + *nautes* = sailor]

cosmos
(noun) The cosmos is the universe.
cosmic (adjective)

cost, costs, costing, cost
1 (noun) the amount of money needed to buy goods or services.
2 The cost of achieving something is what is lost in achieving it, e.g. *The cost in human life of the First World War was enormous*.
3 (verb) e.g. *What does it cost?*
4 (phrase) If something must be done **at all costs**, it is extremely important.
[Latin *constare* = to cost]

costly, costlier, costliest
(adjective) expensive, e.g. *costly jewels*.

cost of living
(noun) The cost of living in a country is the average amount each person needs to spend on food, housing, and clothing.

costume, costumes
1 (noun) a set of clothes worn by an actor etc.
2 Costume is the clothing worn in a particular place or during a particular period, e.g. *17th-century costume*.

cosy, cosier, cosiest; cosies
(adjective) warm and comfortable.
cosily (adverb) **cosiness** (noun)

cottage, cottages
(noun) a small house, especially in the country.

cotton, cottons, cottoning, cottoned
1 (noun) cloth made from the soft fibres of the cotton plant.
2 thread used for sewing.
3 (verb) If you cotton on to something, you understand or realize it.
[Arabic *qutn* = cotton]

couch, couches
1 (noun) a long, soft piece of furniture which more than one person can sit on.
2 (phrase; informal) A **couch potato** is someone who spends too much time watching TV.
[French *coucher* = to lie down]

cough, coughs, coughing, coughed
(verb) When you cough, you force air out of your throat with a sudden harsh noise.

cough up
(phrasal verb) to hand money over to someone.

could
1 You use 'could' to say that you were able or allowed to do something, e.g. *I could just hear*.
2 You also use 'could' to say that something might happen or might be the case, e.g. *The river could overflow*.
3 You use 'could' when you are asking for something politely, e.g. *Could you pass the salt, please?*

What do these letters stand for: AA, EC, UN, HMS, PC, TNT?

council, councils
(noun) a group of people elected to look after the affairs of a town, district or county, e.g. *Wiltshire County Council*.
[Latin *concilium* = assembly]

councillor, councillors
(noun) an elected member of a local council.

counsel, counsels, counselling, counselled
(verb) to listen to people with problems and give them help.
counselling (noun) **counsellor** (noun)

count, counts, counting, counted
1 (verb) to say numbers in order, or to add up the numbers of things in a group.
2 What counts in a situation is whatever is most important, e.g. *It's the thought that counts*.
3 If you can count on someone or something, you can rely on them.
4 (noun) a European nobleman.
[verb: Latin *computare* = to calculate; noun Latin *comes* = companion or associate]

Similar words: (verb) calculate, reckon, compute, number, tally, tot up (noun) calculation, computation, reckoning, tally

countdown, countdowns
(noun) the counting aloud of numbers in reverse order before something happens.

counter, counters
1 (noun) a small, flat, round object used in board games.
2 a long flat surface in a shop over which goods are sold.
[Latin *computare* = to calculate]

counteract, counteracts, counteracting, counteracted
(verb) To counteract something means to reduce its effect by producing an opposite effect.

counterfeit
(pronounced **kown**-ter-fit)
(adjective) something counterfeit is a fake version made to look like the real thing, e.g. *a counterfeit coin*.
counterfeiter (noun)
[Old French *contrefaire* = to copy]

counterproductive
(adjective) If something is counterproductive, it has the opposite effect from what you intend.

countess, countesses
(noun) the wife of a count or earl.

countless
(adjective) too many to count, e.g. *He sent countless letters to the newspapers*.

country, countries
1 (noun) A country is one of the political areas that the world is divided into.
2 The country is land away from towns and cities.

Similar words: (sense 1) nation, state, land

countryside
(noun) land away from towns and cities.

county, counties
(noun) a region with its own local government.
[Old French *conté* = land belonging to a count]

couple, couples
(noun) A couple of things or people means two of them, e.g. *a couple of years ago*.
[Latin *copula* = bond]

couplet, couplets
(noun) two lines of poetry or verse together.

coupon, coupons
1 (noun) a piece of printed paper which, when you hand it in, entitles you to pay less than usual for something.
2 a form you fill in to ask for information or to enter a competition.
[Old French *colpon* = piece cut off]

courage
(noun) the quality shown by a person who does something knowing it is dangerous or likely to make them unpopular, e.g. *She showed great courage in giving an honest answer*.
courageous (adjective) **courageously** (adverb)

courgette, courgettes (pronounced koor-**jet**)
(noun) a type of small vegetable marrow with dark green skin and pale flesh.
[French *courgette* = little marrow]

courier, couriers (pronounced **koo**-ree-er)
1 (noun) someone employed by a travel company to look after people on holiday.
2 someone employed to deliver special letters quickly.
[Old Italian *correre* = to run]

course, courses
1 (noun) a series of lessons or lectures.
2 a series of medical treatments, e.g. *a course of injections*.
3 one of the parts of a meal.
4 a course of action is one of the things you can do in a situation e.g. *Jumping out of the burning flats was the only course of action left*.
5 a piece of land where sport is played, e.g. *a golf course, a racecourse*.
6 The course of, e.g. a ship, is the route it takes.
7 (phrase) **of course** means certainly.

Similar words: (sense 5) circuit, track

court, courts
1 (noun) a place where legal matters are decided by a judge and jury or a magistrate.
2 a place where a game such as tennis or badminton is played.
3 A king or queen's court is the place where they live and carry out ceremonial duties.

courteous (pronounced **kur**-tee-yuss)
(adjective) Courteous behaviour is polite and considerate.
courteously (adverb)
[Old French *corteis* = courtly-mannered]

courtesy (pronounced **kur**-tus-ee)
1 (noun) polite, respectful, considerate behaviour.
2 (phrase) If something is done **by courtesy of** someone, it is done with their permission.

Pun. Why is a house full of married couples empty? There's not a single person there.

court-martial, court-martials, court-martialling, court-martialled (pronounced court-marshal)
(noun) Soldiers, sailors, etc., if they do something wrong, are tried by a court-martial.

courtyard, courtyards
(noun) a flat area of ground surrounded by buildings or walls.

cousin, cousins
(noun) the child of an uncle or aunt.

cove, coves
(noun) a small bay.

cover, covers, covering, covered
1 (verb) If you cover something, you put something else over it to protect it or hide it.
2 If you cover a particular distance, you travel that distance, e.g. *I covered about 20 miles a day.*
3 An insurance policy that covers something guarantees that money will be paid if that thing is lost or harmed.
4 To cover a topic means to do a full amount of work on it, e.g. *We covered graphs last year.*
5 (noun) e.g. *a book cover... a manhole cover... insurance cover.*
[Latin *cooperire* = to cover completely]

cover up
(phrasal verb) to hide something.
cover-up (noun)

covet, covets, coveting, coveted
(verb; formal) to want something that somebody else owns.
covetous (adjective)

coward, cowards
(noun) someone who is easily frightened and who avoids dangerous or difficult situations.
cowardly (adjective) **cowardice** (noun)

cowboy, cowboys
1 (noun) a man who herds cattle in America.
2 (informal) a tradesman, e.g. a builder, whose work is usually cheap and of low quality, e.g. *Those cowboys left my roof half finished.*

cower, cowers, cowering, cowered
(verb) When someone cowers, they crouch or move backwards because they are afraid.

Similar words: shrink, cringe

coy, coyer, coyest
(adjective) pretending to be shy and modest.
coyly (adverb) **coyness** (noun)

crab, crabs
(noun) a sea creature with 4 pairs of legs, 2 pincers, and a round body covered by a shell.

crack, cracks, cracking, cracked
1 (verb) If something cracks, it becomes damaged, with lines appearing on its surface.
2 If you crack a joke, you tell it.
3 If you crack a problem or code, you solve it.
4 (phrase; informal) If you **have a crack** at something, you try to do it.
5 If you do something **at the crack of dawn**, you do it very early in the morning.
6 (noun) one of the lines appearing on something when it splits.

7 a very dangerous and addictive form of the drug, cocaine.

crack down
(phrasal verb) If the authorities crack down on a group of people, they become stricter in making them obey the law.
crackdown (noun)

crack up
(phrasal verb) If someone cracks up, they become mentally ill as a result of stress.

cracker, crackers
1 (noun) a thin, savoury, crisp biscuit.
2 a paper-covered tube that pulls apart with a bang and usually has a toy and paper hat inside.

crackle, crackles, crackling, crackled
(noun) a short, harsh noise.

crackling
(noun) the crisp, brown skin of roast pork.

cradle, cradles
(noun) a box-shaped bed for a baby.
[Old English *cradol* = little basket]

craft, crafts
1 (noun) an activity such as weaving, carving or pottery.
2 You can also call a boat, plane, etc. a craft.

craftsman, craftsmen
(noun) a man whose job is to make things skilfully with his hands.
craftsmanship (noun)

crafty, craftier, craftiest
(adjective) Someone who is crafty gets what they want by tricking people in a clever way.
craftily (adverb) **craftiness** (noun)
[Old English *cræftig* = skilful]

cram, crams, cramming, crammed
(verb) If you cram people or things into a place, you put more in than there is room for.

Similar words: jam, crowd, overcrowd, stuff, pack

cramp, cramps
(noun) a pain caused by a muscle tightening up.

cramped
(adjective) If a room or building is cramped, it is not big enough for the people or things in it.

crane, cranes, craning, craned
1 (noun) a machine that lifts heavy things.
2 (verb) If you crane your neck, you extend your head in a particular direction to see or hear something better.

crash, crashes, crashing, crashed
1 (noun) an accident in which a moving vehicle hits something violently.
2 a sudden loud noise, e.g. *a crash of thunder.*
3 (verb; informal) If a computer system crashes, it breaks down.

crash helmet, helmets
(noun) a helmet worn by motor cyclists for protection when they are riding.

crate, crates
(noun) a large box used for transporting or storing things.
[Latin *cratis* = wickerwork]

Pat's doing well in the army. He's only been in 3 weeks and already they've made him a court-martial!

crater, craters
(noun) a wide hole in the ground caused by something hitting it or by an explosion, e.g. *the craters of the moon.*
[Greek *kratēr* = mixing-bowl]

crave, craves, craving, craved
(verb) If you crave something, you want it very much, e.g. *She craved big houses and fast cars.*
craving (noun)
[Old English *crafian* = to demand]

crawl, crawls, crawling, crawled
1 (verb) to move forward on hands and knees.
2 (informal) If a place is crawling with people or things, it is full of them, e.g. *The building was crawling with reporters.*
3 (noun) a swimming stroke done on your front.

crayon, crayons
(noun) a coloured pencil or a stick of coloured wax.
[a French word meaning 'pencil']

craze, crazes
(noun) something that is very popular for a short time, e.g. *Yo-yos were a craze in the 1950s and 80s.*

Similar words: fashion, cult, trend

crazy, crazier, craziest
1 (adjective) very strange or foolish, e.g. *They thought I was crazy... a crazy scheme.*
2 If you are crazy about something, you are very keen on it, e.g. *They are crazy about football.*
crazily (adverb) **craziness** (noun)

crazy paving
(noun) irregular, flat pieces of stone made into a path or terrace.

creak, creaks, creaking, creaked
(verb) to make a harsh, squeaking noise.
creaky (adjective) **creak** (noun)

cream, creams
1 (noun) a thick liquid taken from the top of milk.
2 (adjective) yellowish-white.
creamy (adjective)

crease, creases, creasing, creased
1 (noun) Creases are irregular lines that appear on cloth or paper when it is crumpled.
2 Creases are also straight lines on something that has been pressed or folded neatly.
3 In cricket, the crease is a line in front of the wickets and parallel to them.
4 (verb) If something creases, it develops folds in the wrong places.
creased (adjective)

create, creates, creating, created
(verb) To create something means to cause to happen or exist.
creator (noun) **creation** (noun)
[Latin *creare* = to produce or to make]

creative
(adjective) Creative people are able to invent and develop original ideas.
creatively (adverb) **creativity** (noun)

creature, creatures
(noun) Any living thing that moves about can be referred to as a creature.

crèche, crèches (pronounced **kresh**)
(noun) a place where small children are looked after while their parents are busy.
[Old French *crèche* = crib or manger]

credible
(adjective) If someone or something is credible, you can believe or trust them.
credibility (noun)

Similar words: believable, plausible

credit, credits
1 (noun) If you are allowed credit, you can take something and pay for it later, e.g. *We bought the furniture on credit.*
2 If you get the credit for something good, people say you are responsible for it.
3 (phrase) If something **does you credit**, it means you should be praised or admired for it.
4 (plural noun) The list of people who helped make a film, record or TV programme is called the credits.
[sense 1 – Latin *creditum* = loan; senses 2-4 – Latin *credere* = to believe]

credit card, cards
(noun) a card that allows someone to buy goods from shops etc. by paying later on a single bill.

creek, creeks
(noun) a narrow, muddy inlet where the sea comes a long way into the land.
[Old Norse *kriki* = nook]

creep, creeps, creeping, crept
(verb) to move quietly and slowly.

Similar words: sneak, tiptoe

creeper, creepers
(noun) a plant with long stems that wind themselves round things.

creepy, creepier, creepiest
(adjective; informal) strange and frightening, e.g. *a creepy film.*

Similar words: spooky, eerie, scary, frightening

crematorium, crematoriums or **crematoria**
(noun) a building in which the bodies of dead people are burned.
cremate (verb) **cremation** (noun)
[Latin *cremare* = to burn]

crescent, crescents
(noun) a curved shape that is wider in its middle than at the ends, which taper to a point.

cress
(noun) a plant used in salads.

crest, crests
1 (noun) a tuft of feathers on top of a bird's head.
2 a small picture or design that is the emblem of a noble family, a town or an organization.
crested (adjective)
[Latin *crista* = tuft]

Pun. At what time of day was Adam born? A little before Eve.

crevice, crevices
(noun) a narrow crack or gap in rock.
[Latin *crepare* = to crack]

crew, crews
(noun) The crew of a ship, aeroplane or spacecraft are the people who operate it.

crib, cribs, cribbing, cribbed
1 (verb; informal) to copy what someone else has written and pretend it is your own work.
2 (noun; old-fashioned) a baby's cot.
3 A Christmas crib is a model of the Nativity scene.

cricket, crickets
1 (noun) a game played with bat and ball, usually outdoors.
cricketer (noun)
2 a small jumping insect that produces sounds by rubbing its wings together.
[sense 2 – Old French *criquer* = to creak]

crime, crimes
(noun) an action for which you can be punished by law, e.g. *the crime of murder.*
[Latin *crimen* = accusation]

Similar word: offence

criminal, criminals
(noun) someone who has committed a crime.
criminally (adverb)

Similar words: crook, offender,

crimson
(noun, adjective) dark purplish-red.

cringe, cringes, cringing, cringed
(verb) to back away from someone or something because you are afraid or embarrassed.
[Old English *cringan* = to yield in battle]

crinkle, crinkles, crinkling, crinkled
(verb) If something crinkles, it becomes slightly creased or folded.
crinkly (adjective)
[Old English *crincan* = to bend]

cripple, cripples
(noun) someone who cannot move their body properly because it is weak or diseased.
crippled (adjective) **crippling** (adjective)

crisis, crises (pronounced **kry**-seez in the plural)
(noun) a very serious or dangerous situation.
[Greek *krinein* = to decide]

crisp, crisper, crispest; crisps
1 (adjective) pleasantly fresh and firm, e.g. *a crisp lettuce.*
2 (noun) Crisps are thin slices of potato, fried until they are hard and crunchy.
crispy (adjective)

critic, critics
(noun) someone who writes reviews of books, films, plays or musical performances.
[Greek *krites* = a judge]

critical
1 (adjective) A critical situation is a very serious one, e.g. *The patient was in a critical condition.*

2 If you are critical of something or someone, you criticize them.
critically (adverb)

criticism, criticisms
1 (noun) If you make a criticism, you point out a fault you think someone or something has.
2 Criticism of books, plays, and other works of art consists of serious examination and judgment of them, e.g. *literary criticism.*

criticize, criticizes, criticizing, criticized; also spelled **criticise**
(verb) If you criticize someone or something, you say what you think is wrong with them.

Similar words: knock, attack, find fault with

croak, croaks, croaking, croaked
(verb) to make a harsh, low sound.
croaky (adjective) **croak** (noun)
[Old Norse *kraka* = crow]

crockery
(noun) plates, cups and saucers.
[Old English *crocc* = pot]

crocodile, crocodiles
(noun) a large, scaly, meat-eating reptile which lives in tropical rivers.
[Greek *krokodeilos* = lizard]

crocus, crocuses
(noun) crocuses are yellow, purple or white flowers that grow from bulbs in early spring.
[Greek *krokos* = saffron]

croissant, croissants (pronounced **krwus**-on)
(noun) a light, crescent-shaped roll eaten at breakfast.
[a French word meaning '*crescent*']

crook, crooks
1 (noun; informal) a criminal.
2 a long pole with a large hook at the end used by a shepherd for handling sheep.
[sense 2 – Old Norse *krokr* = hook]

crooked (pronounced **kroo**-kid)
1 (adjective) bent or twisted.
2 Someone who is crooked is dishonest.

crop, crops, cropping, cropped
(noun) Crops are plants such as wheat and potatoes that are grown for food.
[Old English *cropp* = something that comes up]

crop up
(phrasal verb; informal) If something crops up, it happens unexpectedly.

cross, crosses, crossing, crossed
1 (verb) e.g. *Why did the chicken cross the road?... Cross your legs and sit down.*
2 to breed one animal with another, e.g. *An ass is a donkey crossed with a horse.*
3 (noun) e.g. *Jesus died on the Cross... If you can't sign, just put a cross here... He looks like a cross between Bugs Bunny and Adolf Hitler.*
4 (adjective) annoyed, e.g. *She was so cross, she slammed the door and the handle fell off.*
crossly (adverb)
[Latin *crux* = a cross]

What verbs match these nouns? e.g. courage — encourage: critic shelf teacher friend ....

cross-country
(noun) the sport of running in towns or the countryside, rather than on a track.

cross-examine, cross-examines, cross-examining, cross-examined
(verb) When someone is cross-examined during a trial in a law court, they are asked questions about evidence they have given.
cross-examination (noun)

cross-legged
(adjective) If you are sitting cross-legged, you are sitting on the floor with your knees pointing outwards and your feet tucked under them.

cross-section, cross-sections
1 (noun) A cross-section of a group of people is a fair sample of them.
2 A cross-section of an object is what you would see if you could cut it through the middle , e.g. *a cross-section of the human brain*.

crossword, crosswords
(noun) a squared word puzzle in which you work out the answers to clues and write them in.

crotchety
(adjective) grumpy and easily irritated.

crouch, crouches, crouching, crouched
(verb) If you are crouching, you are leaning forward with your legs bent under you.

Similar words: huddle, hunch, squat

croûton, croûtons (pronounced **kroo**-ton)
(noun) small pieces of toasted or fried bread added to soup.
[French *croûte* = crust]

crow, crows, crowing, crowed
1 (noun) a large, black bird.
2 (phrase) If a place is a certain distance away **as the crow flies**, that is how far it is when the distance is measured in a straight line.
3 (verb) When a cock crows, it utters a loud squawking sound.
4 If you crow about what you have achieved, you boast about it.

crowbar, crowbars
(noun) a heavy iron bar used as a lever or for forcing things open.

crowd, crowds
(noun) a large group of people.
crowd (verb) **crowded** (adjective)
[Old English *crudan* = to push]

Similar words: flock, mob, host, swarm

crown, crowns
(noun) a circular ornament worn as a royal person's ceremonial headpiece.
[Latin *corona* = crown]

crucial (pronounced **kroo**-shl)
(adjective) If something is crucial, it is very important in determining how something else will be in the future, e.g. *a crucial issue*.
[Latin *crux* = a cross]

Similar words: critical, decisive, vital

crucifix, crucifixes
(noun) a cross with a figure representing Jesus Christ being crucified on it.
[Latin *crucifigere* = to crucify]

crucify, crucifies, crucifying, crucified
(verb) to tie or nail someone to a cross and leave them there to die.
crucifixion (noun)
[Latin *crucifigere* = to crucify]

crude, cruder, crudest
1 (adjective) rough and simple, e.g. *crude farm implements... crude methods*.
2 rude and offensive, e.g. *Do you have to tell such crude jokes?*
crudely (adverb) **crudeness** (noun) **crudity** (noun)
[Latin *crudus* = raw or rough]

Similar words: (sense 1) coarse, rough
(sense 2) tasteless, coarse, vulgar, rude

cruel, crueller, cruellest
(adjective) Cruel people deliberately cause pain or distress to other people or to animals.
cruelly (adverb) **cruelty** (noun)
[Latin *crudelis* = cruel]

Similar words: brutal, heartless, inhuman, vicious, merciless, hard

cruise, cruises, cruising, cruised
1 (noun) a holiday in which you travel on a ship and visit places.
2 (verb) When a vehicle cruises, it moves at a constant moderate speed.
[Dutch *kruisen* = to cross]

cruiser, cruisers
1 (noun) a motor boat with a sleeping cabin.
2 a large, fast warship.

crumb, crumbs
(noun) a very small piece of bread or cake.

crumble, crumbles, crumbling, crumbled
(verb) When something crumbles, it breaks into small pieces.
crumbly (adjective)

crumpet, crumpets
(noun) a round, flat, bread-like cake which you eat toasted with butter.

crumple, crumples, crumpling, crumpled
(verb) To crumple paper or cloth means to squash it so that it is full of creases and folds.
[Middle English *crump* = to bend]

Similar words: crease, crush

crunch, crunches, crunching, crunched
(verb) If you crunch something, you crush it noisily, for example between your teeth or under your feet.
crunchy (adjective)

crusade, crusades
1 (plural noun) In the 11th to 13th centuries, the Crusades were a number of expeditions by Christians who were attempting to recapture the Holy Land from the Muslims.
2 (noun) a long and determined attempt to

.... pleasure obedience prison list bath witch terror

achieve something, e.g. *the great crusade to conquer cancer.*
crusader (noun)
[Spanish *cruzar* = to take up the cross]

crush, crushes, crushing, crushed
1 (verb) to destroy the shape of something by squeezing it.
2 (phrase; informal) If you **have a crush** on someone, you are strongly attracted to them.

crust, crusts
(noun) a hard outside layer, e.g. of bread.
crusty (adjective)
[Latin *crusta* = rind or shell]

crustacean, crustaceans (pronounced kruss-**tay**-shn)
(noun) a creature with a shell and several pairs of legs, e.g. crabs, lobsters, shrimps.

crutch, crutches
(noun) a support which you lean on to help you walk when you have an injured foot or leg.

cry, cries, crying, cried
(verb, noun) e.g *The baby cried all night... We heard their cry for help.*
[Latin *quiritare* = to call for help]

Similar words: bawl, weep, wail, sob

cry off
(phrasal verb) If you cry off, you change your mind and decide not to do something.

cry out for
(phrasal verb) If something is crying out for something else, it needs it very much.

crystal, crystals
(noun) a piece of a mineral that has formed naturally into a regular shape.
crystalline (adjective)
[Greek *krustainein* = to freeze]

crystallize, crystallizes, crystallizing, crystallized; also spelled **crystallise**
(verb) to turn into crystal.
crystallization (noun)

cub, cubs
1 (noun) Some young wild animals are called cubs, e.g. *a lion cub.*
2 The Cubs is an organization for young boys before they join the Scouts.

cubbyhole, cubbyholes
(noun) a small, enclosed space.

cube, cubes, cubing, cubed
1 (noun) a 3-dimensional shape with 6 equal square surfaces.
2 (verb) To cube a number means to multiply it by itself three times, e.g. $6 \times 6 \times 6 = 6$ cubed $= 6^3 = 216.$
[Greek *kubos* = a dice]

cubic
(adjective) used in measurements of volume, e.g. *cubic centimetres* (cm³)*... cubic metres* (m³)*.*

cubicle, cubicles
(noun) a small, enclosed changing area in a place such as a sports centre.

[Latin *cubare* = to lie down; cubicles used to be parts of a dormitory]

cuckoo, cuckoos
(noun) a grey bird with a two-note call, that lays its eggs in other birds' nests.

cucumber, cucumbers
(noun) a long, thin, green-skinned vegetable eaten raw in salads.

cuddle, cuddles, cuddling, cuddled
(verb) to hold someone affectionately in your arms.

cuddly, cuddlier, cuddliest
(adjective) Cuddly people, animals or toys are soft or pleasing in some way so that you want to cuddle them.

cue, cues
1 (noun) In a play etc., a cue is something said or done that is a signal for the performer to begin, e.g. *I nearly missed my first cue.*
2 In snooker and pool, a cue is a long stick used to hit the balls.
[sense 1 – Latin *quando* = when
sense 2 – French *queue* = pigtail]

cuff, cuffs
1 (noun) the end part of a sleeve.
2 (phrase) If you are speaking **off the cuff**, you have not prepared what you are saying.

cul-de-sac, cul-de-sacs (pronounced **kul**-de-sak)
(noun) a road which is a dead end.
[a French phrase meaning 'bottom of the bag']

culprit, culprits
(noun) someone who has done something harmful or wrong, e.g. *The culprits were soon caught and punished.*
[Anglo-French *culpable* = guilty + *prit* = ready (i.e. ready for trial)]

cult, cults
1 (noun) a religious group with special rituals.
2 Cult is used to refer to any situation in which something is very popular with a particular group of people, e.g. *the Heavy Metal cult.*
[Latin *cultus* = a refinement]

cultivate, cultivates, cultivating, cultivated
(verb) To cultivate land means to grow crops on it.
cultivation (noun)
[Latin *cultivare* = to till]

culture, cultures
1 (noun) Culture refers to the arts and to people's appreciation of them.
2 The culture of a particular society is its ideas, customs and art, e.g. *Greek culture.*
cultured (adjective) **cultural** (adjective)
[Latin *cultura* = cultivation]

culvert, culverts
(noun) a water pipe or sewer crossing under a road or railway.

cumbersome
(adjective) large, heavy and difficult to carry or handle.
[Old French *combre* = barrier]

What's the difference between a clothes brush and an iceberg? One brushes coats; the other.....

cunning
(adjective) clever and deceitful.
cunningly (adverb)
[Old Norse *kunna* = to know]

Similar words: wily, sly, crafty, subtle

cupboard, cupboards
(noun) a piece of furniture with doors and shelves.

curable
(adjective) If a disease or illness is curable, it can be cured.
curability (noun)

curate, curates
(noun) a Church of England clergyman who helps a vicar or rector.
curacy (noun)
[Latin *cura* = care]

curator, curators
(noun) The curator of a museum or art gallery is the person in charge of its contents.

cure, cures, curing, cured
(verb) To cure an illness means to heal it.
[Latin *curare* = to attend to or to heal]

Similar words: heal, mend, remedy, restore

curiosity, curiosities
1 (noun) the desire to know about something or about many things.
2 A curiosity is something unusual and interesting.

curious
1 (adjective) eager to know more.
2 unusual and hard to explain, e.g. *a curious thing happened.*
curiously (adverb)
[Latin *curiosus* = taking pains]

Similar words: (sense 1) nosy, inquisitive, prying, inquiring

curl, curls
(noun) Curls are lengths of hair shaped in tight curves and circles.
curly (adjective)

curler, curlers
(noun) Curlers are plastic or metal tubes that women roll their hair round to make it curly.

currant, currants
(noun) Currants are small dried grapes often put in cakes and puddings.
[Middle English *rayson of Corannte* = Corinth raisin]

currency, currencies
(noun) the coins and banknotes of a country, or its monetary system generally, e.g. *On ferries you can pay in UK or French currency.*

current, currents
1 (noun) a strong continuous movement of the water, for example in a river.
2 An electric current is a flow of electricity through a wire or circuit.

3 (adjective) Something that is current is happening, being done or being used now.
currently (adverb)
[Latin *currere* = to run or to flow]

current affairs
(plural noun) political and social events discussed in newspapers and on TV or radio.

curriculum, curriculums or curricula
1 (noun) The curriculum at a school or university consists of the different courses taught there.
2 (adjectival phrase) **Extra-curricular** activities are the things you do beyond the normal school timetable, e.g. stamp collecting, St John Ambulance, playing hockey for the school team.
curricular (adjective)

curry, curries
(noun) an Indian dish made with hot spices.
curried (adjective)
[Tamil *kari* = sauce]

curse, curses, cursing, cursed
1 (verb) to swear because you are angry.
2 (noun) something supernatural that is supposed to cause unpleasant things to happen to someone.
cursed (adjective)

cursive
(adjective) The letters in cursive writing or print are joined together.
[Latin *cursivus* = running]

cursor, cursors
(noun) an indicator on a computer screen which shows where you 'are' on that screen.
[Latin *cursivus* = running]

curtain, curtains
(noun) a hanging piece of material which can be pulled across, a window etc.
[Latin *cortina* = enclosed space]

curtsy, curtsies, curtsying, curtsied; also spelled curtsey
(verb) When a woman curtsies, she lowers her body briefly, bending her knees, to show respect.

curve, curves, curving, curved
1 (noun) a smooth, gradually bending line.
2 (verb) When something curves, it moves in a curve or has the shape of a curve, e.g. *The missile curved towards its target.*
curved (adjective) **curvy** (adjective)
[Latin *curvus* = bent]

cushion, cushions, cushioning, cushioned
1 (noun) a soft object put on a seat to make it more comfortable.
2 (verb) To cushion something means to soften its effect, e.g. *The snow cushioned his fall.*

cushy, cushier, cushiest
(adjective; informal) A cushy job is very easy.

custard
(noun) a sweet yellow sauce made from milk and eggs or milk and a powder.

custody
1 (noun) To have custody of a child means to have the legal right to look after it, e.g. *Divorce courts often award custody to mothers.*

You taught me language; and my profit on't
Is, I know how to curse. (Shakespeare: The Tempest)

2 (phrase) Someone who is **in custody** is being kept in prison until they can be tried in a court.
custodial (adjective)
[Latin *custos* = a guard]

custom, customs
1 (noun) a traditional activity, e.g. *an old English custom.*
2 something usually done at a set time or in particular circumstances by a person or by the people in a society, e.g. *It was his custom to take a walk before breakfast.*
3 Customs is the place at a border, airport or harbour where you have to declare goods that you have brought in from abroad.
customary (adjective) **customarily** (adverb)

Similar words: (sense 2) practice, habit, way

custom-built or **custom-made**
(adjective) Something that is custom-built or custom-made is made to someone's special requirements.

customer, customers
1 (noun) A shop's or firm's customers are the people who buy its goods.
2 (informal) You can use customer to refer to someone when describing what they are like to deal with, e.g. *an awkward customer... a tough customer.*

Similar words: (sense 1) consumer, buyer, purchaser

customize, customizes, customizing, customized; also spelled **customise**
(verb) To customize a car means to alter its appearance to make it look distinctive.

cut, cuts, cutting, cut
1 (verb) e.g. *Please cut the grass... Mum has cut my pocket money.*
2 (noun) e.g. *That looks a nasty cut... The Chancellor has made some cuts in government spending.*
3 In films and TV, a cut is the end of a shot or scene.
4 (verb) If a film director shouts, 'Cut!', it means 'Stop'.

Similar words: (verb, noun) clip, slit, nick, gash, slash

cut back
(phrasal verb) to reduce expenditure, e.g. *Spending on health has been cut back yet again.*
cutback (noun)

cut down
(phrasal verb) to do something less often, e.g. *Try to cut down on smoking.*

cut in
(phrasal verb) If you cut in, you interrupt.

cut off
(phrasal verb) To cut someone or something off means to separate them from things they are

normally connected with, e.g. *We were cut off from the beach by the rising tide.*

cut out
(phrasal verb) to stop doing something, e.g. *He's cut out the drinking ... the engine suddenly cut out.*

cute, cuter, cutest
(adjective) pretty or attractive.

cuticle, cuticles
(noun) the pieces of skin that cover the base of your fingernails and toenails.
[Latin *cuticula* = little skin]

cutlass, cutlasses
(noun) a curved sword once used by sailors.
[Latin *cultellus* = small knife]

cutlery
(noun) knives, forks and spoons.
[Latin *culter* = knife]

cut-price
(adjective) Cut-price things are for sale at a reduced price.

cutting, cuttings
1 (noun) a picture, piece of writing, etc. cut from a newspaper or magazine.
2 A cutting from a plant is a part cut from it and used to grow a new plant.

cyanide (pronounced **sigh**-an-ide)
(noun) an extremely poisonous chemical.

cycle, cycles, cycling, cycled
1 (verb) When you cycle, you ride a bicycle.
2 (noun) a bicycle.
3 a series of events which is repeated again and again in the same order, e.g. *the cycle of the seasons... the water cycle.*
[Greek *kuklos* = ring or wheel]

cyclist, cyclists
(noun) someone who rides a bicycle.

cygnet, cygnets (pronounced **sig**-net)
(noun) a young swan.
[Latin *cygnus* = swan]

cylinder, cylinders
(noun) a regular 3D shape with two equal flat circular ends joined by a curved surface, e.g. a tin can.
cylindrical (adjective)
[Greek *kulindein* = to roll]

cymbal, cymbals
(noun) a circular, brass percussion instrument. Cymbals are clashed together or hit with a stick.
[Greek *kumbē* = something hollow]

Czechoslovak
(pronounced chek-oh-**slow**-vak)
1 (adjective) belonging to Czechoslovakia.
2 (noun) someone who comes from Czechoslovakia (also called a Czech).

Lines of poems and verse usually begin with capitals, but some modern poets ignore this convention.

D

dab, dabs, dabbing, dabbed
1 (verb) to touch with quick light strokes, e.g.
She dabbed the wound with antiseptic.
2 (phrase; informal) If you are a **dab hand** at
something, you are very skilled at it.

dabble, dabbles, dabbling, dabbled
(verb) If you dabble in something, you work or
play at it without being seriously involved in it.
dabbler (noun)

dachshund, dachshunds (pronounced
daks-hoond)
(noun) a small dog with a long body and very
short legs.
[a German word meaning 'badger-dog']

dad, dads or **daddy**, daddies
(noun; informal) father.

daddy-long-legs
(noun) a harmless flying insect with very long
legs (also called a cranefly).

daffodil, daffodils
(noun) a yellow spring flower.

daft, dafter, daftest
(adjective) foolish or slightly insane.
[Old English *gedæfte* = gentle]

dagger, daggers
1 (noun) a weapon like a short knife with a
sharp, pointed blade.
2 (noun) If you **look daggers** at someone, you
glare or scowl angrily at them.

daily, dailies
1 (adjective) occurring every day.
2 (noun) a newspaper that is published every
day except Sunday.

dainty, daintier, daintiest
(adjective) very delicate and pretty.
daintily (adverb) **daintiness** (noun)

dairy, dairies
1 (noun) a shop or company that supplies milk
and milk products.
2 (adjective) A dairy farm is one which keeps
cattle to produce milk and dairy products.

daisy, daisies
(noun) a wild flower with a yellow centre
surrounded by long white petals.
[Old English *dæges eage* = day's eye, because the
daisy opens in the daytime and closes at night]

daisywheel, daisywheels
(noun) a small flat disc used for printing in some
word processors and printers.

dale, dales
(noun) a valley in the north of England.

dalmatian, dalmatians
(noun) a large, spotted breed of dog.

dam, dams
(noun) a barrier, often a concrete wall, built
across a river to hold back water.

damage, damages, damaging, damaged
1 (noun) injury or harm done to something.
2 (verb) To damage something means to harm or
spoil it.
3 (noun) Damages is the sum of money claimed,
or awarded by a court, to repay someone for loss
or harm.
damageable (adjective) **damaging** (adjective)
[Latin *damnum* = injury or loss]

dame, dames
1 Dame is a title given to a woman, e.g. *Dame
Vera Lynn*. It is equal in rank to a man's
knighthood (Sir Fred Bloggs).
2 (noun) The dame in pantomime is the role of a
comic woman, normally played by a man.

damn, damns, damning, damned (pronounced **dam**)
1 (verb) To damn something or someone means to
curse or condemn them to eternal punishment in
hell.
2 'Damn' is a swearword.
damned (adjective)
[Latin *damnare* = to injure]

damp, damper, dampest
(adjective) slightly wet.
dampness (noun) **dampen** (verb)
[Old German *damp* = steam]

damson, damsons
(noun) a small blue-black plum.
[Latin *prunum Damascenum* = Damascus plum]

dance, dances, dancing, danced
1 (verb) to move your feet and body
rhythmically in time to music.
2 (noun) a particular style of dancing, e.g. jiving,
the waltz, the cha-cha.
3 an event at which people are dancing.
dancer (noun) **dancing** (noun)

dandelion, dandelions
(noun) a wild flower with yellow flowers which
form a ball of fluffy seeds.
[Old French *dent de lion* = lion's tooth, referring
to the shape of the leaves]

dandruff
(noun) small, loose scales of dead skin in
someone's hair.

Dane, Danes
(noun) someone who comes from Denmark.

danger, dangers
(noun) something or someone that can hurt or
harm you.

Similar words: peril, jeopardy, hazard

dangerous
(adjective) likely to cause hurt or harm.
dangerously (adverb)

Similar words: unsafe, perilous, hazardous

dangle, dangles, dangling, dangled
(verb) to swing or hang loosely.

Letter D is believed to have been developed from the picture of a door.

Danish
(adjective) belonging to Denmark.

dappled
(adjective) marked with spots or patches of a different or darker shade.

dare, dares, daring, dared
1 (verb) To dare someone means to challenge them to do something to prove their courage.
2 To dare to do something means to have the courage to do it.
[Old English *durran* = to venture or to be bold]

daredevil, daredevils
(noun) a person who is reckless and enjoys doing dangerous things.

daring
(adjective) bold and willing to take risks.
daringly (adverb)

dark, darker, darkest
1 (adjective) If it is dark, there is not enough light to see properly.
2 (phrase) If you are **in the dark** about something, you don't know anything about it.
darkly (adverb) **darkness** (noun) **darken** (verb)

Similar words: gloomy, sombre, dim, murky

dark horse, horses
(noun) If you say that someone is a dark horse, you mean that you suspect that they might have unexpected talents or abilities.

darkroom, darkrooms
(noun) a room where photographs are developed and processed.

darling, darlings
(noun) Someone who is lovable or a favourite may be called a darling.

darn, darns, darning, darned
(verb) to mend a hole in a garment with stitches.
darning (noun)

dart, darts, darting, darted
1 (noun) a small pointed arrow with feathers.
2 Darts is a game in which the players score by throwing darts at numbers on a dartboard.
3 (verb) To dart about means to move quickly and suddenly from one place to another.

dartboard, dartboards
(noun) the target in the game of darts.

dash, dashes, dashing, dashed
1 (verb) To dash somewhere means to rush there.
2 (noun) In writing, a dash is the punctuation mark – which shows a change of subject, or which may be used instead of brackets.

dashboard, dashboards
(noun) the instrument panel in a motor vehicle.

data
(noun) information, usually in the form of facts or figures.
[Latin *data* = things given]

database, databases
(noun) a collection of information stored in a computer.

date, dates, dating, dated
1 (noun) a particular day or year that can be named.
2 If you have a date, you have an appointment to meet someone.
3 (verb) If something dates from a particular time, that is when it happened or was made.
4 (phrase) If something is **out of date**, it is old-fashioned or no longer valid.
5 (noun) a small dark-brown sticky fruit with a stone inside, which grows on palm trees in tropical countries.

dative
(noun, adjective) In the grammar of some languages, the dative is the form of a noun or pronoun when it is the indirect object of a verb, e.g. *He gave me his promise (me = to me)*.

daub, daubs, daubing, daubed
(verb) to smear, for example mud, on a surface.
[Latin *dealbare* = to whitewash]

daughter, daughters
(noun) Someone's daughter is their female child.

daughter-in-law, daughters-in-law
(noun) Someone's daughter-in-law is the wife of their son.

dawdle, dawdles, dawdling, dawdled
(verb) to walk slowly or lag behind.

dawn, dawns, dawning, dawned
1 (noun) the time in the morning when light first appears in the sky.
2 (verb) If an idea or fact dawns on you, it gradually becomes apparent.

day, days
1 (noun) a period of 24 hours, starting and ending at midnight.
2 the time during each 24-hour period when it is light.
3 (phrase) If you **call it a day**, you decide to stop doing something and leave it to be finished later.

daybreak
(noun) the time in the morning when light first appears in the sky.

daydream, daydreams
(noun) a dreamlike fantasy, experienced while you are awake.

daylight
(noun) the light from the sun.

day nursery, nurseries
(noun) a place where children who are too young to go to school are looked after while their parents are at work.

day-to-day
(adjective) happening every day as part of ordinary routine life, e.g. *The arrival of the postman is a very day-to-day event.*

daze
(phrase) If you are **in a daze**, you are confused and bewildered.

Similar words: stunned, stupefied

We take these words from the Viking invasion: clumsy fellow knife outlaw hit clip.

dazzle, dazzles, dazzling, dazzled
(verb) If a bright light dazzles you, it blinds you temporarily.
dazzling (adjective)

de-
(prefix) When de- is added to a noun or verb, it usually changes the meaning to its opposite, e.g. to *demist* a car window.

'dead
(adjective, adverb) no longer living.

deaden, deadens, deadening, deadened
(verb) to make something less intense, e.g. *The injection deadened my gums.*

dead end, ends
1 (noun) a street that is closed off at one end.
2 (adjective) leading nowhere, e.g. *I was in a dead-end job with no chance of promotion.*

dead heat, heats
(noun) In a race a dead heat is where two or more competitors finish at the same time.

deadline, deadlines
(noun) a time or date before which a job or activity must be completed.

deadly, deadlier, deadliest
(adjective) likely or able to cause death.

deadpan
(adjective, adverb) showing no emotion or expression, e.g. *a deadpan face.*

deaf, deafer, deafest
(adjective) partially or totally unable to hear.
deafness (noun)

deaf aid, aids
(noun) a small device fitted into the ear, which helps a deaf person to hear.

deafen, deafens, deafening, deafened
(verb) If you are deafened by a noise, it is so loud that you cannot hear anything else.
deafening (adjective) **deafeningly** (adverb)

deal, deals, dealing, dealt
1 (noun) an agreement or arrangement, especially in business.
2 (verb) If you deal with something, you sort it out, e.g. *I will deal with that problem tomorrow.*
3 If you deal in certain goods, you buy and sell those goods, e.g. *He deals in scrap metal.*
4 If you deal when playing cards, you give out the cards to the players.

dealer, dealers
(noun) a person or firm whose business involves buying or selling things.

dear, dears; dearer, dearest
1 (noun) a sign of affection, e.g. *How are you, dear?*
2 (adjective) much loved, e.g. *a very dear friend.*
3 very costly.
4 You use 'Dear' at the beginning of a letter before the name of the person you are writing to.
dearly (adverb)

Similar words: (adjective: sense 3) costly, pricey, expensive

death, deaths
(noun) the end of life.

debate, debates, debating, debated
1 (noun) argument or discussion, e.g. *There was a great deal of debate about education.*
2 a formal discussion in which opposing views are expressed.
3 (verb) If you are debating whether or not to do something, you are considering it, e.g. *While I was debating what to do, the door opened.*

debris (pronounced **day**-bree)
(noun) fragments or rubble left after something has been destroyed, e.g. *wartime debris.*
[Old French *débrisier* = to shatter]

debt, debts (pronounced **det**)
(noun) money that is owed by one person to another.
[Latin *debitum* = debt]

debtor, debtors
(noun) a person who owes money.

debug, debugs, debugging, debugged
(verb) To debug a computer program means to remove the faults from it.

debut, debuts (pronounced **dayb**-yoo)
(noun) A performer's debut is their first public appearance.
[French *débuter* = to begin the game]

decade, decades
(noun) a period of 10 years.
[Greek *deka* = ten]

decaffeinated (pronounced dee-**kaf**-in-ate-ed)
(adjective) Decaffeinated coffee or tea has had most of the caffeine removed.

decathlon, decathlons (pronounced de-**cath**-lon)
(noun) a sports contest in which athletes compete in 10 different events.
[Greek *deka* = ten + *athlon* = contest]

decay, decays, decaying, decayed
1 (verb) to rot.
2 (noun) damage caused by rotting, e.g. *tooth decay.*
[Latin *decadere* = to fall away]

deceased
1 (adjective; formal) A deceased person is someone who has recently died.
2 (noun) The deceased is someone who has recently died.

deceive, deceives, deceiving, deceived
(verb) If you deceive someone, you make them believe something that is not true, especially by lying or being dishonest.
deceitful (noun) **deceitfully** (adverb)
deceit (noun)
[Latin *decipere* = to cheat]

December
(noun) the 12th and last month of the year.
[Latin *December* = the 10th month; the Romans at first had a 10-month year, which they lengthened to 12 months]

decent
1 (adjective) of an acceptable standard or quality, e.g. *Did you get a decent night's sleep?*

When a syllable rhymes with bee, spell **i** before **e** except straight after **c**: believe receive achieve.

2 Decent people are honest and respectable, e.g. *decent, hard-working citizens.*
decently (adverb) **decency** (noun)

Similar words: (sense 2) respectable, proper

deception, deceptions
(noun) an unpleasant trick, e.g. *The firm's 'free' offer was a total deception.*

deceptive
(adjective) likely to make people believe something that is not true.
deceptively (adverb)

Similar words: misleading, ambiguous

decide, decides, deciding, decided
(verb) to make up your mind.

Similar words: determine, settle, resolve

decided
(adjective) obvious and unmistakable, e.g. *There was a decided improvement.*
decidedly (adverb)

deciduous
(adjective) Deciduous trees lose their leaves every year in the autumn.
[Latin *decidere* = to fall down or to fall off]

decimal, decimals
1 (adjective) The decimal system uses all the figures from 0 to 9.
2 (noun) A decimal is a fraction in which a dot called a decimal point is followed by numbers representing tenths, hundredths, and thousandths, e.g. 0.5 = 5/10 (or 1/2); 0.05 = 5/100 (or 1/20); 0.005 = 5/1000 (or 1/200).
[Latin *decima* = a tenth]

decimal point
(noun) a point which separates whole numbers from decimal fractions.

decipher, deciphers, deciphering, deciphered
(verb) If you decipher a piece of writing or a message, you work out its meaning.

decision, decisions
(noun) a choice or judgement that is made about something, e.g. *the government's decision on the future of the railway.*

Similar words: conclusion, resolution, choice

decisive (pronounced dis-**sigh**-siv)
(adjective) able to make decisions firmly and without unnecessary hesitation.
decisively (adverb) **decisiveness** (noun)

deck, decks, decking, decked
1 (noun) a floor or platform built into a ship, or one of the two floors on a bus.
2 A tape or record deck is the piece of equipment that carries the tape or record in a music system. It does not have power of its own.
3 A deck of cards is a pack of them.
4 (verb) If you deck someone or something or deck them out, you decorate them, e.g. *The rooms had been decked with garlands and flowers.*
[Old Dutch *dec* = a covering]

deckchair, deckchairs
(noun) a light, portable folding chair, made from canvas and wood and used outdoors.

declaration, declarations
(noun) a firm, forceful statement, often an official announcement, e.g. *the Declaration of Independence.*

declare, declares, declaring, declared
1 (verb) to say something firmly and forcefully, e.g. *He declared himself in favour of the motion.*
2 to announce something officially or formally, e.g. *War was declared.*
3 If you declare goods or earnings, you state what you have bought or earned, so that the amount of tax or duty you have to pay can be decided.
4 In cricket, when a team declares, they voluntarily stop their innings.
[Latin *declarare* = to make clear]

Similar words: (sense 1) announce, pronounce

decline, declines, declining, declined
1 (verb) to become smaller, weaker or less important.
2 If you decline something, you politely refuse to accept it or do it.
[Latin *declinare* = to bend away]

decode, decodes, decoding, decoded
(verb) If you decode a coded message, you convert it into ordinary language.

decompose, decomposes, decomposing, decomposed
(verb) to decay through chemical or bacterial action.
decomposition (noun)

decontaminate, decontaminates, decontaminating, decontaminated
(verb) to remove radioactivity or other dangerous substances from an object or place.
decontamination (noun)

decorate, decorates, decorating, decorated
1 (verb) to make something more attractive by adding some ornament or colour to it.
2 to put paint or wallpaper on.
3 A person who is decorated is awarded a medal or other honour, e.g. *He was decorated with the Military Cross for bravery.*

decoration, decorations
1 (noun) features or ornaments added to something to make it more attractive.
2 The decoration in a building or room is the style of the furniture, wallpaper and ornaments.
3 an official honour or medal awarded to someone.
decorative (adjective)

decorator, decorators
(noun) a person whose job is painting and wallpapering rooms and buildings.

decoy, decoys, decoying, decoyed
1 (noun) a person or object that is used to lead someone or something into danger.
2 (verb) To decoy someone or something means

Etymology. Find out how these words are connected: decimal decade December decimetre decimate.

to lead them into a trap or away from the place where they are going, usually by means of a trick.

decrease, decreases, decreasing, decreased
1 (verb) to become less in quantity, size, or strength.
2 (noun) a lessening in the amount of something; also the amount by which something becomes less, e.g. *a 20% decrease in crimes*.
decreasing (adjective) **decreasingly** (adverb)

decrepit
(adjective) broken or worn out by use or old age.
decrepitude (noun)
[Latin *crepare* = to creak]

dedicate, dedicates, dedicating, dedicated
1 (verb) If you dedicate yourself to something, you devote your time and energy to it.
2 If you dedicate a book or piece of music to someone, you address it to them as a sign of respect or affection.
dedication (noun)
[Latin *dedicare* = to announce]

deduce, deduces, deducing, deduced
(verb) to work something out from other facts that you know are true, e.g. *I deduce that it was Mrs White in the kitchen, with the spanner.*
deducible (adjective)
[Latin *deducere* = to lead away or to derive]

deduct, deducts, deducting, deducted
(verb) to take off an amount of money, e.g. *Tax is deducted from your wages.*
deductible (adjective)
[Latin *deducere* = to lead away]

deduction, deductions
1 (noun) an amount which is taken away from a total, e.g. *a 10% deduction for prompt payment.*
2 a conclusion that you have reached because of other things that you know are true.
deductive (adjective)

deed, deeds
1 (noun) something that is done, e.g. *The deeds of Robin Hood live on in legend.*
2 a legal document, especially concerning the ownership of land or buildings.

deep, deeper, deepest
(adjective) e.g. *Look out! The water is deep there... She was lost in deep thought.*
deeply (adverb) **deepen** (verb)

deepfreeze, deepfreezes
(noun) a freezer.

deer
(noun) a large, hoofed mammal that lives wild in parts of Britain.
[Old English *deor* = beast]

deface, defaces, defacing, defaced
(verb) to spoil deliberately the appearance of something, e.g. *Spray cans were used to deface the poster.*

default
(noun) On a computer, the 'default' is what the computer will do unless you give it other instructions.

defeat, defeats, defeating, defeated
1 (verb) to win a victory over someone or something.
2 (noun) the state of being beaten or of failing, e.g. *He finally gave up in defeat.*
[Latin *disfacere* = to undo]

defect, defects, defecting, defected
1 (noun; pronounced **dee**-fect) a fault or flaw in something.
2 (verb; pronounced diff-**ect**) If someone defects they leave their own country or organization and join the opposing one.
defection (noun) **defector** (noun)
[Latin *deficere* = to fail]

defective
(adjective) imperfect or faulty.

defence, defences
1 (noun) action that is taken to protect someone from attack.
2 In a court of law, the defence is the case presented by a lawyer for the person on trial.
3 A country's defences are its military resources, i.e. its army, navy and air force.
defensive (adjective) **defensively** (adverb)
defensiveness (noun) **defensive** (adjective)

defend, defends, defending, defended
1 (verb) To defend someone or something means to protect them from harm or danger.
2 If you defend a person or their ideas and beliefs, you argue in support of them.
3 In a game such as football or hockey, to defend means to try to prevent goals being scored by your opponents.
defender (noun)
[Latin *defendere* = to ward off]

defendant, defendants
(noun) a person who has been accused of a crime in a court of law.

defer, defers, deferring, deferred
(verb) to put something off until later.

defiance
(noun) behaviour which shows that you are not willing to obey someone or behave in the expected way, e.g. *a gesture of defiance.*
defiant (adjective) **defiantly** (adverb)

deficiency, deficiencies
(noun) a lack of something, e.g. *She suffered from a vitamin deficiency.*
deficient (adjective)

define, defines, defining, defined
(verb) to say exactly what something is, e.g. *How would you define art?*
[Latin *definire* = to set limits to]

definite
(adjective) firm, clear and unlikely to be changed, e.g. *a definite date.*
definitely (adverb)
[Latin *definitus* = having fixed limits]

definition, definitions
(noun) a statement explaining the meaning of a word, expression or idea.

Proverbs for acting: Actions speak louder than words. New brooms sweep clean.

deflate, deflates, deflating, deflated
1 (verb) If you deflate, for example, a tyre or balloon, you let out all the air or gas in it.
2 If you deflate someone, you take away their confidence or make them seem less important, e.g. *I felt very deflated after losing the vote.*
deflation (noun)

deflect, deflects, deflecting, deflected
(verb) to turn something aside, divert it or make it change direction.
deflection (noun)
[Latin *deflectere* = to turn aside]

deforestation
(noun) the cutting down of all the trees in an area, e.g. *the deforestation of the Amazon jungle.*

deformed
(adjective) out of shape, e.g. *Her hands were deformed because of arthritis.*
deform (verb) **deformity** (noun)

Similar words: distorted, twisted, warped

defraud, defrauds, defrauding, defrauded
(verb) If you defraud someone, you cheat them out of money, property or a right to something.

defrost, defrosts, defrosting, defrosted
(verb) to remove the ice from a freezer or refrigerator.

deft, defter, deftest
(adjective) quick and skilful in movement.
deftly (adjective) **deftness** (noun)

defuse, defuses, defusing, defused
(verb) To defuse a bomb means to remove its fuse or detonator so that it cannot explode.

defy, defies, defying, defied
(verb) If you defy a person or a law, you openly resist and refuse to obey.

Similar words: challenge, dare

degenerate, degenerates, degenerating, degenerated
(verb) If something degenerates, it becomes worse, e.g. *The political discussion degenerated into an exchange of personal insults.*
degeneration (noun)
[Latin *degener* = departing from its race or kind]

degree, degrees
1 (noun) a unit of measurement of temperature; often written as ° after a number, e.g. *20°C.*
2 a unit of measurement of angles in mathematics, the 360th part of circle; also a measure of latitude and longitude, e.g. *The yacht was 20° off course.*
3 the qualification obtained after passing a course at university or polytechnic, e.g. B.Sc.
4 (phrase) If something happens **by degrees**, it happens very slowly and gradually.

dehydrated
(adjective) If you are dehydrated, you are short of water in your body. This usually happens in hot weather or after exercise.
dehydrate (verb) **dehydration** (noun)

dejected
(adjective) miserable and unhappy.
dejectedly (adverb) **dejection** (noun)
[Latin *de + jacere* = to throw down]

Similar words: downcast, despondent

delay, delays, delaying, delayed
1 (verb) to put something off until a later time.
2 If something delays you, it hinders you or slows you down.
3 (noun) time during which something is delayed, e.g. *There was a short delay before the play began.*

Similar words: (verb: sense 1) postpone, defer, put off, suspend

delete, deletes, deleting, deleted
(verb) To delete something written or on a computer screen means to rub it out or remove it.
deletion (noun)
[Latin *delere* = to destroy]

Similar words: cancel, erase, cross out

deliberate
(adjective) intentional or planned in advance, e.g. *Can you spot the deliberate mistake?*
deliberately (adverb)

Similar words: intentional, wilful, calculated, conscious

delicate
1 (adjective) fine and graceful, e.g. *a delicate floral design.*
2 fragile and needing to be handled carefully, e.g. *delicate fabric.*
3 precise or sensitive, and able to notice very small changes, e.g. *a delicate instrument.*
delicately (adverb)
[Latin *delicatus* = giving pleasure]

delicatessen, delicatessens
(noun) a shop selling unusual or imported foods, e.g. cold meats, that are already cooked or prepared.
[German *Delikatessen* = delicacies]

delicious
(adjective) very pleasing, especially to taste.
deliciously (adverb)
[Latin *delicere* = to entice]

Similar words: scrumptious, mouthwatering, appetizing

delight, delights, delighting, delighted
1 (noun) great pleasure or joy.
2 (verb) If something delights you or if you are delighted by it, it gives you a lot of pleasure.
delighted (adjective)
[Latin *delicere* = to entice]

delightful
(adjective) very pleasant and attractive.
delightfully (adverb)

Cheating is poor business procedure which can lead to loss of all profits. (Wild Bill Hickok)

delinquent, delinquents
(noun) a young person who repeatedly commits minor crimes.
delinquency (noun)
[Latin *delinquens* = offending]

delirious
(adjective) unable to speak or act normally because of illness, fever or happiness.
deliriously (adverb) **delirium** (noun)

deliver, delivers, delivering, delivered
1 (verb) If you deliver something to someone, you take it somewhere and give it to them.
2 To deliver a lecture or speech means to give it.
3 If someone delivers a baby, they help at its birth.
4 (formal) If someone delivers you from something, they rescue you from it.
delivery (noun)
[Latin *liberare* = to set free]

delta, deltas
(noun) a low, flat area at the mouth of a river where the river has split into several branches to enter the sea.
[from the shape of delta (Δ) the 4th letter of the Greek alphabet.]

deluge, deluges
(noun) a sudden, heavy downpour of rain.

delusion, delusions
(noun) a mistaken belief or idea.
delude (verb)

de luxe (pronounced de **luks**)
(adjective) rich, luxurious or of superior quality.
[a French phrase meaning 'of luxury']

demand, demands, demanding, demanded
1 (verb) If you demand something, you ask for it forcefully and urgently.
2 (noun) If there is a demand for something, a lot of people want to buy it or have it.

demanding
1 (adjective) requiring a lot of time, energy or attention, e.g. *He has a demanding job.*
2 difficult to please or satisfy, e.g. *a demanding child.*

Similar word: (sense 1) challenging

demi-
(prefix) half.

demo, demos
(noun; informal) a demonstration (a public protest meeting).

democracy, democracies
(noun) a system of government in which the people choose their leaders by voting in elections.

democrat, democrats
(noun) a person who believes in democracy, personal freedom and equality.

democratic
1 (adjective) having representatives elected by the people, e.g. *This is a democratic society.*
2 favouring or supporting the idea that everyone should have equal rights and should be involved in making decisions that affect them.
democratically (adverb)
[Greek *dēmos* = the people + *kratos* = power]

demolish, demolishes, demolishing, demolished
(verb) To demolish a building means to pull it down or break it up.
demolition (noun)

demon, demons
1 (noun) an evil spirit or devil.
2 (adjective) skilful, keen and energetic, e.g. *She is a demon squash player.*
demonic (adjective)
[Greek *daimōn* = spirit or god]

demonstrate, demonstrates, demonstrating, demonstrated
1 (verb) If you demonstrate something to somebody, you show and explain it by using or doing the thing itself, e.g. *She demonstrated the art of bread-making.*
2 to take part in a march, meeting or rally to show opposition to something or support for something.

demonstration, demonstrations
1 a talk or explanation to show how to do or use something.
2 a public march, meeting or rally in support of or opposition to something, e.g. *an anti-hunting demonstration.*
3 A demonstration of your feelings is a display or expression of them.
demonstrator (noun)

demonstrative
(adjective) People who are demonstrative openly show or express their feelings.

demoralized or demoralised; also spelled demoralized
(adjective) If someone is demoralized, they feel depressed and have lost confidence.
demoralize (verb) **demoralization** (noun)

demote, demotes, demoting, demoted
(verb) A person who is demoted is reduced in rank or position, often as a punishment.
demotion (noun)

den, dens
(noun) the home of some wild animals such as lions or foxes.

denim, denims
(noun) strong cotton cloth, usually blue, used for overalls, jeans and other clothes.
[French *serge de Nîmes in France*, = serge (a type of cloth) from Nîmes]

denominator, denominators
(noun) the bottom part of a fraction.
[opposite: **numerator**]

dense
1 (adjective) very thick, e.g. *a dense crowd... dense fog.*
2 (informal) stupid or dull.
densely (adverb) **denseness** (noun)

density, densities
1 (noun) The density of something is the degree

Do you know the differences between: allusion delusion illusion collusion?

to which it is filled, concentrated or occupied,
e.g. *the high density of buildings in the city.*
2 The density of a substance is its compactness,
measured by comparing its mass to its volume,
i.e. how much weight it packs into its size.

dent, dents, denting, dented
(verb) to damage something by hitting it and
making a hollow in its surface.

dental
(adjective) relating to the teeth.
[Latin *dens* = tooth]

dentist, dentists
(noun) a person who is qualified to examine and
treat people's teeth.

denture, dentures
1 (noun) a plastic 'plate' with false teeth
attached.
2 (plural noun) People call their complete set of
false teeth their dentures, e.g. *I left my dentures
in San Francisco.*

deny, denies, denying, denied
1 (verb) If you deny something that has been
said, you say that it is untrue.
2 If you deny someone something, you refuse to
give it to them or you prevent them from having
it, e.g. *The yobs were denied access to the stand.*
denial (noun)

Similar word: (sense 1) contradict

deodorant, deodorants
(noun) a substance or spray used to hide or
prevent the smell of perspiration.

depart, departs, departing, departed
(verb) to leave, e.g. *The train departing from
Platform 3 is for Leeds.*
departure (noun)

department, departments
(noun) one of the sections into which an
organization is divided, e.g. *the casualty
department of the local hospital.*
departmental (adjective)

department store, stores
(noun) a large shop selling many kinds of goods
in different sections of the shop.

depend, depends, depending, depended
1 (verb) If you depend on someone or something,
you trust them and rely on them.
2 If one thing depends on another, it is influenced
or determined by it, e.g. *Success depends on hard
work.*
dependence (noun)

Similar words: (sense 1) rely on, count on, bank on

dependable
(adjective) reliable and trustworthy.
dependability (noun)

Similar words: sure, trustworthy, trusty

dependant, dependants
(noun) someone who relies on another person for
financial support, e.g. *Granny and I are
dependants of my parents.*

dependent
(adjective) reliant on someone or something.

depict, depicts, depicting, depicted
(verb) To depict someone or something means to
represent them in painting, sculpture, etc., e.g.
Da Vinci's picture depicted a lady with a smile.
[Latin *pingere* = to paint]

deplorable
(adjective) shocking or regrettable, e.g. *He
showed a deplorable lack of taste.*
deplorably (adverb) **deplore** (verb)
[Latin *plorare* = to weep or to lament]

deport, deports, deporting, deported
(verb) If a government deports someone, it sends
them back to their own country because they
have committed a crime or because they do not
have the right to be there.
deportation (noun)
[Latin *deportare* = to carry]

deposit, deposits, depositing, deposited
1 (verb) If something is deposited on a surface, a
layer of it is left there as a result of chemical or
geological action.
2 If you deposit money or valuables, you put
them somewhere for safekeeping.
3 (noun) money given as a first payment for
goods or services.
[Latin *deponere* = to put down]

depot, depots (pronounced **dep**-oh)
(noun) a place where large supplies of materials
or equipment may be stored.
[Latin *depositum* = a deposit]

depressed
1 (adjective) unhappy and gloomy.
2 A place that is depressed has little economic
activity and therefore low incomes and
unemployment, e.g. *Some old coalmining centres
have become depressed areas.*
depress (verb)
[Latin *deprimere* = to press down]

Similar words: (sense 1) doleful, despondent, down

depression, depressions
1 (noun) a state of mind in which someone feels
unhappy and has no energy or enthusiasm.
2 a time of industrial and economic decline.
3 In a weather forecast, a depression is a mass of
air that has low pressure and often causes rain.

deprive, deprives, depriving, deprived
(verb) If you deprive someone of something, you
take it away or prevent them from having it.
deprived (adjective) **deprivation** (noun)

depth, depths
1 (noun) a measurement of how deep something
is.
2 (phrase) If you are **out of your depth**, you
cannot understand or cope with something.

deputize, deputizes, deputizing, deputized; also
spelled **deputise**
(verb) to do someone's job for them temporarily.

deputy, deputies
(noun) a person appointed to act in someone's
place.

Can you think of a four-letter word ending eny?

derail, derails, derailing, derailed
(verb) If a train is derailed, it comes off the tracks.
derailment (noun)

derby, derbies (pronounced **dar**-bee)
(noun) A local derby is a sporting event between two teams from the same area.

derelict, derelicts
(adjective) abandoned and falling into ruin.

derivation, derivations
(noun) The derivation of something is its origin or source, e.g. *Many of the words in this dictionary have their derivations explained.*

derv
(noun) the fuel used by diesel vehicles. It gets its name from 'diesel-engined road vehicle'.

desalinate, desalinates, desalinating, desalinated
(verb) To desalinate seawater means to remove salt from it to make it suitable for drinking or irrigation.
desalination (noun)

descant, descants
1 (noun) The descant to a tune is a series of notes played at the same time and at a higher pitch which harmonize with the main tune.
2 (adjective) A descant musical instrument is the highest one in a range of instruments, e.g. *a descant recorder.*

descend, descends, descending, descended
(verb) to move downwards.

descendant, descendants
(noun) A person's descendants are the people in later generations who are descended from them.

descended
(adjective) If you are descended from someone who lived in the past, your family originally derived from them.

descent, descents
1 (noun) a movement or slope downwards.
2 Your descent is your family's origins, e.g. *He was a jolly good chap of splendid descent.*

describe, describes, describing, described
(verb) To describe someone or something means to give an account or a picture of them in words.
[Latin *describere* = to write down]

description, descriptions
1 (noun) a picture of something in words.
2 (phrase) **Of every description** means of every type or sort, e.g. *reptiles of every description.*
descriptive (adjective)

desert, deserts, deserting, deserted
1 (noun; pronounced **dez**-ert) a region of land with very little plant life, usually because of low rainfall.
2 (verb; pronounced **diz**-ert) to leave or abandon, e.g. *He deserted his family.*
3 (phrase) If someone gets their **just deserts**, they are suitably rewarded or punished.
desertion (noun)

deserter, deserters
(noun) someone who leaves the army, navy or air force without permission.

deserve, deserves, deserving, deserved
(verb) If you deserve something, you are entitled to it or have earned it, e.g. *You deserve a good rest.*

Similar words: merit, justify, earn

deserving
(adjective) worthy of being helped, rewarded or praised, e.g. *a deserving cause.*

design, designs, designing, designed
1 (verb) to plan something especially by preparing a detailed sketch or drawings from which it can be built or made.
2 (noun) The design of something is its shape and style.
designer (noun)

desirable
(adjective) very useful, necessary or popular, e.g. *a desirable neighbourhood.*
desirability (noun)

desire, desires, desiring, desired
1 (verb) to want something very much.
2 (noun) a strong feeling of wanting something.

Similar words: (verb) crave, wish, (noun) appetite

desk, desk
(noun) a piece of furniture, often with drawers, designed for working at or writing on.
[Latin *desca* = table]

desktop
(adjective) of a convenient size to be used on a desk or table, e.g. *a desktop computer.*

desktop publishing
(noun) using a computer to arrange words and pictures etc., before printing out.

desolate
(adjective) deserted and bleak, e.g. *a desolate part of the country.*
desolation (noun)
[Latin *desolare* = to leave alone]

despair, despairs, despairing, despaired
1 (noun) a total loss of hope.
2 (verb) If you despair, you lose hope, e.g. *I despaired of getting anything done.*
despairing (adjective) **despairingly** (adverb)
[Latin *desperare* = to be without hope]

Similar words: (noun) hopelessness, desperation

despatch another spelling of **dispatch**.

desperate
1 (adjective) so worried or frightened that you will try anything to improve your situation, e.g. *a desperate attempt to free herself.*
2 A desperate situation is extremely dangerous, difficult or serious.
desperately (adverb) **desperation** (noun)
[Latin *desperare* = to be without hope]

despise, despises, despising, despised
(verb) If you despise someone, you dislike them and the things they do.
[Latin *despicere* = to look down on]

Main abbreviations are given capital letters, e.g. RSPCA U.S.A. *but* mph vgc ono.

despite
(preposition) in spite of, e.g. *Despite the difference in their ages they were close friends.*

Similar words: regardless of, in spite of

despondent
(adjective) dejected and unhappy.
despondently (adverb) **despondency** (noun)

dessert, desserts (pronounced diz-ert)
(noun) sweet food served after the main course of a meal.
[French *desservir* = to clear a table after a meal]

destination, destinations
(noun) a place to which someone or something is going or is being sent.

destined
(adjective) meant or intended to happen, e.g. *She was destined to be famous.*

destiny, destinies
1 (noun) Your destiny is all the things that happen to you in your life, especially when they are considered to be outside human control.
2 Destiny is the force which some people believe controls everyone's lives.

destitute
(adjective) without money or property, and therefore in great need.
destitution (noun)
[Latin *destituere* = to abandon]

Similar words: down-and-out, broke

destroy, destroys, destroying, destroyed
(verb) To destroy something means to damage it so much that it is completely ruined.

Similar words: annihilate, demolish, devastate, wreck, exterminate, obliterate

destroyer
(noun) a small, fast warship.

destruction
(noun) the act of destroying something or the state of being destroyed.

Similar words: demolition, devastation, obliteration

destructive
(adjective) causing or able to cause great harm, damage or injury.
destructively (adverb) **destructiveness** (noun)

detach, detaches, detaching, detached
(verb) to remove or unfasten, e.g. *The handle can be detached.*
detachable (adjective)

detached
(adjective) separate or standing apart, e.g. *a detached house.*

detail, details
(noun) an individual fact or feature of something, e.g. *He described it in great detail.*
detailed (adjective)
[Old French *detailler* = to cut into pieces]

detain, detains, detaining, detained
1 (verb) To detain someone means to force them to stay, e.g. *They were detained in police cells.*
2 If you detain someone, you delay them, e.g. *I mustn't detain you any longer.*
detainment (noun)

detect, detects, detecting, detected
(verb) If you detect something, you notice it, e.g. *I detected a note of sarcasm in her voice.*
detectable (adjective)

detection
1 (noun) the act of noticing, discovering or sensing something.
2 the work of investigating crime.

detective, detectives
(noun) a person, usually a police officer, whose job is to investigate crimes.

detector, detectors
(noun) an instrument which is used to indicate if something is there, e.g. *a metal detector... a smoke detector.*

detention
1 (noun) the arrest or imprisonment of someone, e.g. *He was sent to a detention centre.*
2 a punishment in which a pupil is made to stay in and do work when other pupils are free.

deter, deters, deterring, deterred
(verb) to discourage or prevent someone from doing something, e.g. *I was deterred from speaking by the teacher's angry look.*
[Latin *deterrere* = to frighten away]

detergent, detergents
(noun) a chemical substance used for washing or cleaning things.
[Latin *detergens* = wiping off]

deteriorate, deteriorates, deteriorating, deteriorated
(verb) If something deteriorates, it gets worse, e.g. *His health deteriorated after the accident.*
deterioration (noun)

determination
(noun) great firmness, after you have made up your mind to do something, e.g. *Her strong determination to win was obvious.*

determined
(adjective) firmly decided, e.g. *I was determined to find out what had happened.*
determinedly (adverb)

deterrent, deterrents
(noun) something that prevents you from doing something by making you afraid of what will happen if you do it, e.g. *Imprisonment is supposed to be a deterrent against committing crime.*
deterrence (noun)

detest, detests, detesting, detested
(verb) If you detest someone or something, you strongly dislike them.
detestation (noun) **detestable** (adjective)
[Latin *detestari* = to curse]

A policeman needs these words: burglar housebreaker statement trial defendant plaintiff witness.

detonate, detonates, detonating, detonated
(verb) to cause a bomb etc. to explode.
detonation (noun) **detonator** (noun)
[Latin *detonare* = to thunder]

detour, detours
(noun) If you are travelling somewhere, a detour is an alternative, less direct route, e.g. *Because of road works, we took a detour round the city.*
[French *détour* = change of direction]

detrimental
(adjective) harmful or disadvantageous.
detriment (noun) **detrimentally** (adverb)

deuce (pronounced **jooce**)
(noun) In tennis, deuce is the score of 40-40.

devastate, devastates, devastating, devastated
(verb) to damage severely or destroy, e.g. *The office was devastated by fire.*
devastation (noun)

devastated
(adjective) very shocked or upset, e.g. *I was devastated when I heard the news.*

develop, develops, developing, developed
1 (verb) When something develops or is developed, it grows or becomes more advanced, e.g. *A bud develops into a flower.*
2 To develop an area of land means to build on it.
3 To develop an illness or a fault means to become affected by it.
4 To develop photographs or film means to treat the film chemically to produce a picture.
developer (noun)
[Old French *desveloper* = to unwrap]

development, developments
1 (noun) gradual growth.
2 The development of land or water is the process of making it more useful or profitable by the expansion of industry or housing, e.g. *the development of the inner cities.*
3 a new stage in a series of events, e.g. *further developments in the industrial dispute.*
developmental (adjective)

device, devices
1 (noun) a machine or tool that is used for a particular purpose, e.g. *a device for getting stones out of horses' hoofs.*
2 (phrase) If you **leave someone to their own devices**, you leave them alone to do as they wish.

devil, devils
(noun) In Christianity, the Devil is the spirit of evil and the enemy of God.
devilish (adjective)
[Greek *diabolos* = enemy, or devil]

devious
1 (adjective) insincere and dishonest.
2 A devious route or course of action is indirect.
deviously (adjective) **deviousness** (noun)
[Latin *devius* = lying to one side of the road]

devise, devises, devising, devised
(verb) to invent or to work something out, e.g. *I have devised a scheme for saving energy.*

devote, devotes, devoting, devoted
(verb) If you devote yourself to something, you give all your time, energy or money to it, e.g. *He devoted himself to his studies.*
[Latin *devovere* = to vow]

devoted
(adjective) very loving and loyal, e.g. *He was devoted to his mother*
devotedly (adverb)

devotion
(noun) great love or affection for someone or something.
devotional (adjective)

devour, devours, devouring, devoured
(verb) If you devour something, you eat it hungrily or greedily.

dew
(noun) drops of moisture that form on the ground and other cool surfaces at night.
dewy (adjective)

dhoti, dhotis (pronounced **doe-tee**)
(noun) a long loose covering for the lower part of the body, worn by Hindu men.
[a Hindi word]

diabetes (pronounced **dy-a-bee-tiss**)
(noun) a disease in which a person has too much sugar in their blood, because they do not produce enough of the body chemical, insulin to absorb it.
diabetic (noun and adjective)

diabolical
1 (adjective; informal) dreadful and very annoying, e.g. *What a diabolical liberty!*
2 devilish; extremely wicked and cruel.
diabolically (adverb)

diagnose, diagnoses, diagnosing, diagnosed
(verb) To diagnose an illness or problem means to spot exactly what is wrong.
diagnosis (noun) **diagnostic** (adjective)
[Greek *diagignōskein* = to distinguish]

diagonal, diagonals
1 (adjective) in a slanting direction.
2 (noun) A diagonal in a 4-sided shape is a straight line joining two of the opposite corners.
diagonally (adverb)
[Greek *diagōnios* = from angle to angle]

diagram, diagrams
(noun) a drawing that shows or explains something in a simplified way.
diagrammatic (adjective) **diagrammatically** (adverb)
[Greek *diagraphein* = to mark out in lines]

dial, dials, dialling, dialled
1 (noun) the face of a clock, meter, radio, etc.
2 (verb) to select a telephone number by pushing the buttons etc.

dialect, dialects
(noun) a form of a language spoken in a particular geographical area.
[Greek *dialektos* = speech]

dialogue
(noun) In a novel, play or film, dialogue is conversation.

English dialect words for a narrow, outside passage: alley entry ginnel snicket giddle-gaddle.

diameter, diameters
(noun) The diameter of a circle is the length of a straight line drawn across it through its centre.

diamond, diamonds
1 (noun) a precious stone made of pure carbon.
2 a shape with 4 straight sides of equal length forming two opposite angles less than 90° and two opposite angles greater than 90°.
3 Diamonds is one of the 4 suits in a pack of playing cards. It is marked by a red symbol ♦.
4 (adjective) A diamond anniversary is the 60th anniversary of an event.

diarrhoea (pronounced dy-a-**ree**-a)
(noun) a stomach illness.
[Greek *diarrhein* = to flow through]

diary, diaries
(noun) a book with a separate space for each day of the year on which to keep a record of appointments or events.
diarist (noun)
[Latin *diarium* = daily allowance]

dice, dices, dicing, diced
1 (noun) a small cube which has each side marked with dots representing the numbers one to six. Its opposite sides add up to 7.
2 (verb) To dice food means to cut it into small cubes.
diced (adjective)

dicey, dicier, diciest
(adjective; informal) risky or uncertain.

dictate, dictates, dictating, dictated
(verb) If you dictate something, you say or read it aloud for someone else to write down.
dictation (noun)
[Latin *dictare* = to order]

dictator, dictators
(noun) a ruler who has complete power in a country, especially one who has taken power by force, e.g. Adolf Hitler.
dictatorial (adjective) **dictatorially** (adverb)

Similar word: tyrant

diction
(noun) Someone's diction is the clarity with which they speak or sing.
[Latin *dictio* = phrase]

Similar word: pronunciation

dictionary, dictionaries
(noun) a book like this in which words are listed alphabetically and explained.
[Latin *dictio* = phrase or word]

diddle, diddles, diddling, diddled
(verb; informal) to cheat or swindle someone.

die, dies, dying, died
1 (verb) When people, animals or plants die, they stop living.
2 (informal) If you are dying to do something, you are longing to do it.

Similar words: (sense 1) pass away, expire, decease, perish

diesel engine, engines
(noun) an engine in which diesel fuel is ignited by hot air. It is named after Rudolf Diesel, who invented it in 1892.

diet, diets, dieting, dieted
1 (noun) Someone's diet is the usual food that they eat, e.g. *a healthy diet.*
2 a restricted selection of foods eaten to improve health or control weight.
3 (verb) to eat a special range of foods, usually to lose weight.
dietary (adjective)
[Greek *diaita* = mode of living]

differ, differs, differing, differed
1 (verb) If two or more things differ, they are unlike each other.
2 If people differ, they have opposing views or disagree about something.

difference, differences
1 (noun) The difference between things is the way in which they are unlike each other.
2 The difference between two numbers is the amount by which one is less than another, e.g. *The difference between 4 and 6 is 2 (6 − 4 = 2).*

Similar words: (sense 1) contrast, dissimilarity, distinction, variation

different
1 (adjective) unlike something else.
2 unusual and out of the ordinary.
differently (adverb)

Similar words: (sense 1) contrasting, unlike

difficult
(adjective) not easy to do, understand or solve.

difficulty, difficulties
(noun) a problem, e.g. *I'm having difficulty with algebra.*

dig, digs, digging, dug
1 (verb) e.g. *Dig those carrots up... Don't dig me in the ribs like that!*
2 (noun) an archaeological excavation.
3 e.g. *She gave me a dig in the ribs.*
4 (informal) a spiteful or unpleasant remark intended to hurt somebody.
5 Digs are lodgings in someone's house.

digest, digests, digesting, digested
1 (verb) to break food down in the gut so that it can be easily absorbed and used by the body.
2 If you digest information or a fact, you understand it and take it in.
digestible (adjective)
[Latin *digerere* = to divide]

digestion, digestions
(noun) the process of digesting food.
digestive (adjective)

digit, digits (pronounced **dij**-it)
1 (noun; formal) a finger or toe.
2 a written symbol for any of the numbers from 0 to 9.

digital
(adjective) displaying information, especially

'Different' should generally be followed by *from* rather than by *to* or *than.*

time, by numbers, rather than by a pointer moving round a dial, e.g. *a digital watch.*
digitally (adverb)

digital recording, recordings
(noun) a sound recording technique that breaks the sound into thousands of very small signals.

dignified
(adjective) serious, calm and controlled.

dignity
(noun) behaviour which is serious, calm and controlled, e.g. *Her quiet dignity impressed us all.*
[Latin *dignus* = worthy]

dilapidated
(adjective) falling to pieces and generally in a bad condition, e.g. *a dilapidated house.*
[Latin *dis-* = apart + *lapides* = stones]

Similar words: broken down, run down, decrepit

dilemma, dilemmas
(noun) a situation where you have to choose between things that are equally difficult or unpleasant.
[Greek *di-* = two + *lemma* = assumption]

diligent
(adjective) hard-working and showing care and perseverance.
diligently (adverb) **diligence** (noun)

dilute, dilutes, diluting, diluted
1 (verb) To dilute a liquid means to add water etc. to it to make it less concentrated.
2 (adjective) thin or weakened because water has been added, e.g. *dilute sulphuric acid.*
dilution (noun)

dim, dimmer, dimmest; dims, dimming, dimmed
1 (adjective) badly lit and lacking in brightness.
2 very vague and unclear in your mind, e.g. *a dim memory.*
3 (informal) stupid or mentally dull, e.g. *She is rather dim when it comes to maths.*
4 (verb) If lights dim or are dimmed, they become less bright.
dimly (adverb) **dimness** (noun)

dimension, dimensions
(noun) The dimensions of something are its measurements, i.e. length, breadth, height.
[Latin *dimensus* = measured out]

dimple, dimples
(noun) a small hollow in someone's cheek or chin.
dimpled (adjective)

din, dins
(noun) a loud and unpleasant noise.

dine, dines, dining, dined
(verb; formal) to eat dinner in the evening, e.g. *We dine at 8 o'clock each night.*

diner, diners
1 (noun) someone who is having dinner in a restaurant.
2 a small restaurant, e.g. *Joe's Diner on 5th Avenue, New York.*

dinghy, dinghies (pronounced **ding**-ee)
(noun) a small boat which is rowed, powered by outboard motor or sailed.

dingy, dingier, dingiest (pronounced **din**-jee)
(adjective) drab and rather depressing, e.g. *We drove through the town's dingiest streets.*

dinner, dinners
(noun) the main meal of the day, eaten either in the evening or at lunchtime.

dinosaur, dinosaurs (pronounced **dy**-no-sor)
(noun) a large, prehistoric reptile.
[Greek *deinos* + *sauros* = fearful lizard]

dip, dips, dipping, dipped
1 (verb) e.g. *I dip my toast in the egg yolk.*
2 (noun) a rich, creamy mixture which you scoop up with biscuits or raw vegetables and eat, e.g. *a cheese dip.*
3 (informal) a swim.
4 (verb) If something dips, it goes downwards.
5 To dip headlights means to point them downwards so that other drivers are not dazzled.
6 To dip into a book means to glance at it or read only parts of it.
7 To dip sheep means to put them into a disinfectant for a short time, to kill harmful insects and germs.

diploma, diplomas
(noun) a certificate awarded to a student who has successfully completed a course of study.
[Greek *diploma* = folded paper or letter of recommendation]

diplomacy
1 (noun) the managing of relationships between countries.
2 skill in dealing with people without offending or upsetting them.
diplomatic (adjective) **diplomatically** (adverb)

diplomat, diplomats
(noun) an official who deals with another country on behalf of his or her own country.

dire, direr, direst
(adjective) disastrous, urgent or terrible, e.g. *dire warnings... people in dire need.*
[Latin *dirus* = fearful]

direct, directs, directing, directed
1 (adjective) in a straight line or by the shortest route, e.g. *a direct flight.*
2 straightforward and without delay or evasion, e.g. *a direct question.*
3 (verb) to guide and control something.
4 To direct people means to show them the way.
directly (adverb)
[Latin *dirigere* = to guide]

Similar words: (adjective: sense 2) frank, straightforward, straight

direction, directions
1 (noun) the general line that someone or something is moving or pointing in.
2 the controlling and guiding of something, e.g. *The team was under the firm direction of the manager.*

Punctuate: *what do you think I will feed you and clothe you for nothing* — Do you notice anything?

3 (plural noun) Directions are instructions that tell you how to do something or get somewhere.

director, directors
1 (noun) a member of the board of a company or institution.
2 the person responsible for, e.g. a play, film or TV programme.
directorial (adjective)

directory, directories
(noun) a book which gives lists of facts, e.g. names and addresses, and is usually arranged in alphabetical order.

dirt
(noun) any unclean substance, such as dust, mud or stains.
[Old Norse *drit* = excrement]

Similar words: filth, grime, muck

dirty, dirtier, dirtiest
1 (adjective) marked or covered with dirt.
2 unfair or dishonest, e.g. *a dirty trick.*
3 referring to sex in a way that many people find offensive, e.g. *a dirty book.*
4 (phrase) If you do someone's **dirty work**, you do something for them that is unpleasant and that they do not want to do themselves.
dirtily (adverb)

Similar words: (sense 1) filthy, grimy, grotty, grubby, mucky

dis-
(prefix) Dis- is added to the beginning of words to form a word that means the opposite, e.g. *obey/disobey*

disability, disabilities
(noun) a physical or mental handicap or illness that restricts someone's way of life.

disabled
(adjective) limited in movement because of injury or illness; differently-abled.
disable (verb) **disablement** (noun)

disadvantage, disadvantages
1 (noun) an unfavourable or harmful circumstance.
2 (phrase) If you are **at a disadvantage**, you have a problem or difficulty that other people do not have, e.g. *A bandaged leg put the runner at a disadvantage.*
disadvantaged (adjective) **disadvantageous** (adjective)

Similar words: drawback, hindrance, handicap

disagree, disagrees, disagreeing, disagreed
(verb) If you disagree with someone, you have a different view or opinion from theirs.
disagreement (noun)

Similar words: differ, dissent

disagreeable
(adjective) unpleasant or unhelpful and unfriendly, e.g. *a disagreeable job... a disagreeable person.*
disagreeably (adverb)

disallow, disallows, disallowing, disallowed
(verb) to refuse to allow or accept something, e.g. *The goal was disallowed by the referee.*

disappear, disappears, disappearing, disappeared
(verb) to go out of sight or become lost.
disappearance (noun)

disappoint, disappoints, disappointing, disappointed
(verb) If something disappoints you, it isn't as good as you expected.
disappointed (adjective) **disappointment** (noun)

disapprove, disapproves, disapproving, disapproved
(verb) to believe something is wrong or bad, e.g. *I disapprove of smoking in trains.*
disapproval (noun) **disapproving** (adjective)
disapprovingly (adverb)

disarm, disarms, disarming, disarmed
(verb) to get rid of weapons.

disaster, disasters
1 (noun) an event or accident that causes great distress or destruction.
2 a complete failure, e.g. *My sponge cake was a disaster.*
disastrous (adjective) **disastrously** (adverb)

Similar word: (sense 1) tragedy, catastrophe

disband, disbands, disbanding, disbanded
(verb) to break up or separate, e.g. *The group disbanded when their record flopped.*

disbelieve, disbelieves, disbelieving, disbelieved
(verb) to refuse to accept that something is true, e.g. *I'm sorry, but I disbelieve their story.*
disbelief (noun) **disbeliever** (noun)

disc, discs; also spelled **disk**
(noun) a flat, round object, e.g. *a compact disc... a floppy disk.*
[Greek *diskos* = quoit or discus]

discard, discards, discarding, discarded
(verb) to get rid of something, because you no longer want it or find it useful.

Similar words: dispose of, ditch, dump, scrap

discerning (pronounced diss-**er**-ning)
(adjective) having good taste and judgement.
discerningly (adverb) **discernment** (noun)

Similar words: discriminating, selective

discharge, discharges, discharging, discharged
1 (verb) If something is discharged, it is sent out, e.g. *Oil was discharged into the sea.*
2 To discharge someone from hospital or the army, RAF, etc means to allow to them to leave.
3 (noun) a substance that is released from the inside of something, e.g. *a radioactive discharge from the nuclear power station.*

disciple, disciples (pronounced dis-**sigh**-pl)
(noun) a follower of someone or something.
[Latin *discipulus* = pupil]

discipline, disciplines, disciplining, disciplined
1 (noun) the imposing of order by making people obey rules and punishing them if they break them.

Don't be at a disadvantage - pass the Survival Test on page v!

2 (verb) If you discipline yourself, you train yourself to behave and work in an ordered way.
disciplinary (adjective) **disciplined** (adjective) **disciplinarian** (noun)
[Latin *disciplina* = teaching]

disc jockey, jockeys
(noun) someone who introduces and plays pop records on the radio, the TV or at a disco.

disclose, discloses, disclosing, disclosed
(verb) to make something known or allow it to be seen, e.g. *The curtains opened to disclose the band.*
disclosure (noun)

disco, discos
1 (noun) a dance club where pop records are played by a disc jockey.
2 the professional equipment that a disc jockey uses to play records etc. at a party or dance.

discolour, discolours, discolouring, discoloured
(verb) to change or spoil the original colour.
discoloured (adjective) **discoloration** (noun)

discomfort
1 (noun) a slight pain.
2 a feeling of worry or embarrassment.

disconnect, disconnects, disconnecting, disconnected
1 (verb) To disconnect something means to detach it from something else.
2 If someone disconnects your telephone or supply of fuel, they cut you off.
disconnection (noun)

discontented
(adjective) unhappy with conditions or with life in general, e.g. *The players were discontented with the way the manager treated them.*
discontent (noun) **discontentedly** (adverb)

discontinue, discontinues, discontinuing, discontinued
(verb) to stop doing something, e.g. *Production of long playing records has been discontinued.*
discontinuation (noun)

discord, discords
1 (noun) argument or unpleasantness between people.
2 a harsh and unattractive combination of musical notes.
discordant (adjective)
[Old French *descorder* = to disagree]

discothèque, discothèques
(pronounced **dis**-ko-tek)
(noun) the original word for a disco.
[a French word]

discount, discounts
(noun) a reduction in the price of something.

discourage, discourages, discouraging, discouraged
(verb) To discourage someone means to take away their enthusiasm or confidence to do something.
discouraging (adjective) **discouragement** (noun)

Similar words: dishearten, demoralize

discover, discovers, discovering, discovered
(verb) When you discover something, you find it or find out about it, especially for the first time.
discovery (noun) **discoverer** (noun)

discreet
(adjective) careful to avoid embarrassment for other people, especially by tactful handling of personal secrets.
discreetly (adverb)

discretion
1 (noun) careful and tactful behaviour.
2 the freedom and authority to make decisions and take action according to your own judgement, e.g. *Use your own discretion about it.*

discriminate, discriminates, discriminating, discriminated
1 (verb) To discriminate between things means to recognize and understand the differences between them, e.g. *He should be able to discriminate between right and wrong.*
2 To discriminate against a person or group means to treat them badly or unfairly, usually because of their race, colour or sex.
discrimination (noun) **discriminatory** (adjective)

discus, discuses
(noun) an athletics event in which contestants throw a heavy disc called a discus.
[Greek *diskos* = discus]

discuss, discusses, discussing, discussed
(verb) When people discuss something, they talk about it.
[Latin *discutere* = to investigate]

discussion, discussions
(noun) a conversation in which a subject is considered in detail.

Similar words: debate, dialogue

disease, diseases
(noun) an unhealthy condition in people, animals or plants.
diseased (adjective)

disembark, disembarks, disembarking, disembarked
(verb) to land or unload from a ship or aircraft, e.g. *Several passengers disembarked early from the QE2 to catch the train.*
disembarkation (noun)

disentangle, disentangles, disentangling, disentangled
(verb) If you disentangle something, you free it from other things that it has become mixed up with or wound round.

disgrace, disgraces, disgracing, disgraced
1 (noun) If something is a disgrace, it is unacceptable, e.g. *Your room is a disgrace!*
2 (verb) If you disgrace yourself or disgrace someone else, you cause yourself or them to be strongly disapproved of by other people.

Similar words: (noun) dishonour, shame, humiliation

disgraceful
(adjective) If something is disgraceful, people

disapprove of it strongly and think that those who are responsible for it should be ashamed.
disgracefully (adverb)

Similar words: shocking, shameful, scandalous, outrageous

disgruntled
(adjective) discontented or in a bad mood.
[from an old word, *gruntle* meaning 'to complain']

disguise, disguises, disguising, disguised
1 (noun) A disguise is something you wear or something you do to alter your appearance so that you cannot be recognized by other people.
2 (verb) To disguise a feeling means to hide it, e.g. *She could not disguise her fear.*

disgusting
(adjective) very unpleasant and offensive.
disgusted (adjective) **disgustingly** (adverb)
disgust (noun and verb)

Similar words: vile, revolting, foul, sickening

dish, dishes
1 (noun) a shallow container for cooking or serving food.
2 a particular kind of food cooked in a particular way.
3 (phrasal verb) If you dish something out, you give it to somebody in a rough way.

dishevelled (pronounced dish-**ev**-ld)
(adjective) untidy or scruffy looking.
[Old French *chevel* = hair]

dishonest
(adjective) not truthful or able to be trusted.
dishonesty (noun) **dishonestly** (adverb)

dishonour
(noun; formal) a feeling of shame because people have lost respect for you, e.g. *He would prefer death to dishonour.*
dishonourable (adjective)

disinfectant, disinfectants
(noun) a chemical that kills germs.
disinfect (verb)

disintegrate, disintegrates, disintegrating, disintegrated
(verb) If something disintegrates, it shatters into many pieces and so is destroyed.
disintegration (noun)

disinterested
(adjective) impartial; not biased, e.g. *For the Newcastle v. Norwich game, the League chose a disinterested referee from Stoke.* [not to be confused with 'uninterested' which means not interested]

disk another spelling of **disc**.

dislike, dislikes, disliking, disliked
(verb) If you dislike something or someone, you do not like them.

dislocate, dislocates, dislocating, dislocated
(verb) To dislocate a bone or joint means to put it out of place, usually in an accident.
dislocation (noun)
[Latin *dis-* = apart + *locare* = to locate]

dislodge, dislodges, dislodging, dislodged
(verb) to move something or force it out of place.

disloyal
(adjective) Someone who is disloyal does not remain firm in their friendship or support for someone.
disloyally (adverb) **disloyalty** (noun)

dismal (pronounced **diz**-mal)
(adjective) rather gloomy and depressing, e.g. *dismal weather.*
dismally (adverb)
[Latin *dies mali* = evil days]

dismantle, dismantles, dismantling, dismantled
(verb) to take something apart.
[Old French *desmanteler* = to take a cloak from]

dismay, dismays, dismaying, dismayed
1 (noun) a feeling of fear and worry.
2 (verb) If someone or something dismays you, it fills you with alarm and worry.

dismiss, dismisses, dismissing, dismissed
1 (verb) If you dismiss something, you decide to ignore it because it is not important enough for you to think about.
2 If you dismiss someone, you sack them from their job.
3 If someone in authority dismisses you, they tell you to leave, e.g. *The teacher dismissed the class.*
dismissal (noun)

dismount, dismounts, dismounting, dismounted
(verb) to get off a horse or bicycle.

disobedient
(adjective) If you are disobedient, you deliberately break a rule or law, or you do not do what someone tells you to do.
disobedience (noun) **disobediently** (adverb)

disobey, disobeys, disobeying, disobeyed
(verb) to refuse deliberately to do what you are told.

disorder, disorders
1 (noun) a state of untidiness.
2 Disorder is violence or rioting in public.
3 A disorder is a disease, e.g. *a kidney disorder.*

Similar words: confusion, chaos, shambles.

disorderly
(adjective) People who are disorderly behave in an uncontrolled or violent way in public, e.g. *drunk and disorderly.*

disorganized
(adjective) confused and inefficient.
disorganization (noun)

disown, disowns, disowning, disowned
(verb) To disown someone or something means to refuse to admit any connection with them or any responsibility for them, e.g. *Her father disowned her after she went to prison.*

dispatch, dispatches, dispatching, dispatched; also spelled **despatch**
1 (verb) To send someone or something for a special reason, e.g. *The cruiser dispatched boats to rescue the survivors.*
2 (noun) an official written message.

Disinterested does not mean the same as uninterested. *Dis* is impartial (like a judge); *un* is bored.

3 a story sent to a newspaper by a journalist who is based overseas.
[Italian *dispacciare* = to hurry things up]

dispense, dispenses, dispensing, dispensed
1 (verb) To dispense medicines means to prepare them and give them out, usually in a hospital or chemist's shop.
dispensary (noun)
2 To dispense with something means to do without it or do away with it, e.g. *We should dispense with all nuclear weapons.*
[Latin *dispendere* = to weigh out]

dispenser, dispensers
(noun) a machine or container which provides an item or a quantity of something, either automatically or by the use of a lever or button, e.g. *a cash dispenser.*

disperse, disperses, dispersing, dispersed
(verb) to scatter over a wide area.
dispersion (noun)
[Latin *dispergere* = to scatter]

displace, displaces, displacing, displaced
(verb) To displace something means to move it from its correct position.

displacement
(noun) In physics, displacement is the weight or volume of liquid displaced by an object that is submerged or floating in it.

display, displays, displaying, displayed
1 (verb) to show something openly.
2 (noun) an arrangement of things designed to attract people's attention.
[Latin *displicare* = to unfold]

displease, displeases, displeasing, displeased
(verb) If something displeases you, it makes you annoyed, dissatisfied or offended.
displeasing (adjective) **displeasure** (noun)

disposable
(adjective) designed to be thrown away after use, e.g. *disposable nappies.*

disposal
1 (noun) the act of getting rid of something.
2 (phrase) If something is **at your disposal**, you can use it in whatever way you want, e.g. *My private jet is at your disposal, Mr Bond.*

dispose, disposes, disposing, disposed
(verb) If you dispose of something, you get rid of it.
[Latin *disponere* = to arrange.]

disprove, disproves, disproving, disproved
(verb) If someone disproves an idea, belief or theory, they show that it is not true.

dispute, disputes, disputing, disputed
1 (noun) an argument.
2 (verb) To dispute a fact or theory means to question the truth of it.

disqualify, disqualifies, disqualifying, disqualified
(verb) If someone is disqualified, their right to take part in a competition etc. is removed, e.g. *He was disqualified from driving.*
disqualification (noun)

disregard, disregards, disregarding, disregarded
(verb) to pay little or no attention to something.

disrespect
(noun) contempt or lack of respect, e.g. *They showed disrespect for the law.*
disrespectful (adjective) **disrespectfully** (adverb)

disrupt, disrupts, disrupting, disrupted
(verb) To disrupt, e.g. an event or system, means to break it up or throw it into confusion, e.g. *The storm disrupted the school fete.*
disruption (noun) **disruptive** (adjective)
[Latin *dirumpere* = to smash to pieces]

dissatisfied
(adjective) not pleased or not contented.
dissatisfaction (noun)

dissect, dissects, dissecting, dissected
(verb) To dissect a plant or a dead body means to cut it up so that it can be scientifically examined.
dissection (noun)
[Latin *dis-* = apart + *secare* = to cut]

dissent
(noun) strong difference of opinion, e.g. *The full back was booked for dissent.*

dissimilar
(adjective) If things are dissimilar, they are unlike each other.
dissimilarity (noun)

dissolve, dissolves, dissolving, dissolved
(verb) If you dissolve something in a liquid, it mixes with the liquid and disappears.
[Latin *dis-* = apart + *solvere* = to release]

dissuade, dissuade, dissuading, dissuaded
(pronounced dis-**wade**)
(verb) to persuade someone not to do something.

distance, distances
(noun) The distance between two points is how far it is between them.

distant
1 (adjective) far away in space or time.
2 A distant relative is one who is not closely related to you.
distantly (adverb)
[Latin *dis-* = apart + *stare* = to stand]

distasteful
(adjective) If you find something distasteful, you think it is unpleasant.

Similar words: displeasing, offensive

distemper
(noun) a dangerous and infectious disease which can affect young dogs.
[Latin *distemperare* = to disrupt the health]

distil, distils, distilling, distilled
(verb) When a liquid is distilled, it is heated until it evaporates and then cooled to enable purified liquid to be collected.
distillation (noun)
[Latin *de-* = down + *stillare* = to drip]

distillery, distilleries
(noun) a place where whisky or other strong alcoholic drink is made by distillation.

Dis used as a prefix becomes diss only as part of a word beginning with s: dissolve disappear.

distinct

(adjective) very clear and plain.
distinctly (adverb) **distinctness** (noun)
[Latin *distinguere* = to separate]

distinction, distinctions

1 (noun) a difference between two things, e.g.
*The distinction between an amateur and a
professional is not always clear in sport.*
2 A distinction is the highest level of
achievement in an examination.

distinctive

(adjective) Something that is distinctive has a
special quality which makes it recognizable, e.g.
The Beatles had a very distinctive sound.
distinctively (adverb) **distinctiveness** (noun)

distinguish, distinguishes, distinguishing, distinguished

1 (verb) to recognize the difference between
things , e.g. *The child could not distinguish
letters 'd' and 'b'.*
2 to make something out by seeing, hearing or
tasting it, e.g. *Few details could be distinguished
in the photograph.*
3 If you distinguish yourself, you do something
that makes people think highly of you.
distinguishable (adjective) **distinguishing**
(adjective)
[Latin *distinguere* = to separate]

distinguished

1 (adjective) dignified and smart in appearance
or behaviour, e.g. *a distinguished-looking
gentleman.*
2 having a very high reputation, e.g. *She is a
distinguished professor.*

distort, distorts, distorting, distorted

1 (verb) If something is distorted, it is changed so
that it seems strange or unclear, e.g. *His voice
was distorted by electronic tricks.*
2 If an object is distorted, it is twisted or pulled
out of shape.
distorted (adjective) **distortion** (noun)
[Latin *dis-* = apart + *torquere* = to twist]

distract, distracts, distracting, distracted

(verb) If something distracts you, your attention
is taken away from what you are doing, e.g. *It
distracted them from their work.*
distracting (adjective) **distraction (noun)**
[Latin *dis-* = apart + *trahere* = to drag]

Similar words: divert, side-track

distress

(noun) great suffering caused by sorrow, danger
etc.
distressing (adjective) **distressed** (adjective)
[Latin *districtus* = divided in mind]

distressing

(adjective) very worrying or upsetting.
distressingly (adverb)

Similar words: upsetting, heart-rending

distribute, distributes, distributing, distributed

(verb) to hand out or deliver something, e.g.

*Harvest gifts were distributed to old people in
the area.*
distribution (noun) **distributor** (noun)

Similar words: dispense, dole out, share out

district, districts

(noun) an area which has special or recognizable
features, e.g. *a working-class district.*

district nurse, nurses

(noun) a specially-qualified nurse who visits and
treats people in their own homes.

distrust, distrusts, distrusting, distrusted

1 (verb) If you distrust someone, you are
suspicious of them because you are not sure
whether they are honest.
2 (noun) a feeling that someone cannot be trusted
distrustful (adjective) **distrustfully** (adverb)

disturb, disturbs, disturbing, disturbed

1 (verb) If you disturb someone, you break their
rest, peace or privacy.
2 If something disturbs you, it makes you feel
upset or worried.
3 If something is disturbed, it is moved out of
position or meddled with.
disturbing (adjective)
[Latin *disturbare* = to drive apart]

Similar words: (sense 2) agitate, fluster, unsettle

disturbance, disturbances

(noun) a violent or unruly incident in public.

disturbed

(adjective) Someone who is disturbed is so
emotionally upset that they need special care or
medical treatment.

disused

(adjective) no longer used.
disuse (noun)

ditch, ditches, ditching, ditched

1 (noun) a channel at the side of a road or field,
usually to drain away excess water.
2 (verb; informal) to get rid of something, e.g. *He
ditched his girl friend.*
3 If an aircraft ditches in the sea, it makes an
emergency landing.
[Old English *dic* = dyke or embankment]

dither, dithers, dithering, dithered

(verb) to be unsure and hesitant.

ditto

Ditto means 'the same'. In written lists, ditto is
represented by a mark („) to avoid repetition,
e.g. Manchester United
    Sheffield   „
    Newcastle   „
[Italian *detto* = said]

divan, divans

(noun) a low bed, or a couch without a back or
arms.

dive, dives, diving, dived

1 (verb) to jump headfirst into water with your
arms held straight in front of you.
2 If an aircraft or bird dives, it flies in a steep
downward path or drops sharply.
diver (noun) **diving** (noun)

Can you distinguish: lightning lightening; morning mourning; dying dyeing; singing singeing?

Similar words: (sense 2) plunge, plummet

diversion, diversions
(noun) a special route arranged for traffic when the usual route is closed.

divert, diverts, diverting, diverted
(verb) To divert something means to change the course or direction it is following.
[Latin *di-* = apart + *vertere* = to turn]

divide, divides, dividing, divided
1 (verb) to split up, e.g. They divided the sweets between them.
2 to separate, e.g. *The Pennines divides Lancashire and Yorkshire.*
3 In maths, dividing can be a form of continuous subtraction, e.g. 6 divided by 3 *(6 ÷ 3)* can mean *'How many lots of 3 in 6?'* or it can also be a form of equal splitting, e.g. *6 ÷ 3* can mean *'If I split 6 into 3 equal lots, how many in each lot?'*
divisible (adjective)

divider, dividers
(noun) a barrier between people or areas of space, e.g. *a room divider.*

divine
(adjective) having the qualities of a god or goddess.
divinely (adverb)
[Latin *divus* = god]

divinity, divinities
(noun) Divinity is the study of religion.

division, divisions
1 (noun) the separation of something into two or more parts.
2 the process of dividing one number by another. (see also the entry for **divide**)
divisional (adjective) **divisible** (adjective)

divisor, divisors
(noun) a number by which another number is divided, e.g. *In the sum of 10 ÷ 2, the divisor is 2.*

divorce, divorces
(noun) the formal and legal ending of a marriage.
divorced (adjective) **divorcee** (noun)
[Latin *divertere* = to separate]

dizzy, dizzier, dizziest
(adjective) having a whirling sensation.
dizzily (adverb) **dizziness** (noun)
[Old English *dysig* = silly]

Similar words: giddy, light-headed, dazed

do, does, doing, did, done
(verb) e.g., *I do like to be beside the seaside.*

do away with
(phrasal verb) To do away with something means to get rid of it or to kill it

do up
1 (phrasal verb) To do something up means to fasten it.
2 To do up something old means to repair and decorate it.

docile
(adjective) quiet, calm and easily controlled.
docilely (adverb) **docility** (noun)
[Latin *docilis* = easily taught]

dock, docks, docking, docked
1 (noun) an enclosed area in a harbour where ships are loaded, unloaded or repaired.
docker (noun)
2 (verb) When a ship docks, it is brought into dock at the end of its voyage.
3 If two spacecraft dock, they join together in space.
4 To dock an animal's tail means to cut part of it off.
5 (noun) In a court, the dock is the place where the accused person stands or sits.

doctor, doctors
(noun) a person who is qualified in medicine and treats people who are ill.
[Latin *doctor* = teacher]

document, documents
(noun) a piece of paper which provides an official record of something.
documentation (noun)
[Latin *documentum* = lesson]

documentary, documentaries
(noun) a factual radio or TV programme or a film providing information on a real-life subject.

doddery
(adjective) unsteady or shaky, especially because of old age.
dodder (verb)

dodge, dodges, dodging, dodged
1 (verb) to move suddenly to avoid being seen, hit or caught.
2 If you dodge something like a problem or an accusation, you avoid dealing with it.
3 (noun) a cunning trick.

dodgy
(adjective; informal) rather risky or unreliable, e.g. *This car's got a dodgy exhaust.*

doe, does
(noun) a female deer, rabbit or hare.

does 3rd person singular, present tense of **do**.

dog
(noun) e.g. *Our dog is called Spike.*

dog collar, collars
(noun; informal) a white collar with no front opening worn by Christian clergy.

dog-eared
(adjective) A book that is dog-eared has the corners of the pages turned down.

doggerel
(noun) funny or silly verse, often written quickly and not intended to be serious.
[Middle English *dogerel* = worthless]

doggo
(phrase; informal) If you **lie doggo**, you keep still and hidden so that people cannot find you.

dogsbody, dogsbodies
(noun) someone who has to do all the unpleasant or boring jobs that no one else wants to do.

Dog proverbs: Let sleeping dogs lie. Every dog has his day. Barking dogs seldom bite.

dolby
(noun; trademark) a Dolby system is used in recording sound to reduce unwanted noise. It is named after R. Dolby, its inventor.

doldrums
1 (plural noun) a region on either side of the equator where light winds and calm seas are common.
2 (phrase; informal) If you are **in the doldrums**, you are depressed or bored.

dole, doles, doling, doled
1 (noun) money given regularly by the government to people who are unemployed.
2 (verb) If you dole something out, you give a certain amount of it to each individual in a group.
[Old English *dal* = share]

doleful
(adjective) miserable and depressed, e.g. *The bloodhound looked really doleful.*
dolefully (adverb) **dolefulness** (noun)
[Latin *dolere* = to lament]

doll, dolls, dolling, dolled
1 (noun) a child's toy.
2 (verb; informal) When a woman dolls herself up, she dresses up smartly.

dollar, dollars
(noun) the main unit of money in the USA, Canada, Australia and some other countries.
(1 dollar [$] = 100 cents)

dollop, dollops
(noun) A dollop of food is an amount of it served casually in a lump.

dolphin, dolphins
(noun) an intelligent sea-mammal with a long pointed snout.

dome, domes
(noun) a round roof, e.g. the dome of St Paul's Cathedral.
domed (adjective)
[Latin *domus* = house]

domestic
1 (adjective) concerned with the home and family, e.g. *domestic chores.*
2 Domestic animals are not wild, but are tamed and kept for work, as pets or for food.
[Latin *domus* = house]

domesticated
1 (adjective) Domesticated wild animals have been brought under control and are used for work, as pets or for food.
2 A person who is domesticated is used to helping with the tasks that need to be done around the house.
domesticate (verb) **domestication** (noun)

dominate, dominates, dominating, dominated
1 (verb) If someone dominates a situation, they are the most powerful or important thing in it and have control over it, e.g. *These issues dominated the election.*
2 If something dominates an area, it towers over

it, e.g. *Docklands is dominated by the Canary Wharf buildings.*
dominating (adjective) **domination** (noun)
[Latin *dominari* = to be lord over]

domino, dominoes
(noun) rectangular block used for playing the game Dominoes.

donate, donates, donating, donated
(verb) To donate something to a charity or organization means to give it as a gift.
donation (noun)
[Latin *donare* = to give]

done past participle of **do.**

donkey, donkeys
1 (noun) an animal related to the horse, but smaller and with longer ears.
2 (phrase) **Donkey's years** means a very long time, e.g. *I haven't seen her for donkey's years.*

donkey jacket, jackets
(noun) a thick warm navy-blue jacket with a waterproof panel along the shoulders.

donkey work
(noun) hard work which is not very interesting.

donor, donors
(noun) someone who gives something; blood donors give blood while they are alive. Others give an organ after their death to be used for medical purposes, e.g. *a kidney donor.*
[Latin *donare* = to give]

donut
another spelling of **doughnut**

doodle, doodles, doodling, doodled
(verb) to make a pattern or a drawing when you are thinking about something else or when you are bored.
doodle (noun)

doom
(noun) a terrible fate or event in the future which you can do nothing to prevent, e.g. *Now meet your doom, Mr Holmes!*

doomed
(adjective) If someone or something is doomed to an unpleasant or unhappy experience, they are certain to suffer it, e.g. *It is doomed to failure.*

doomsday
(noun) the end of the world.

door, doors
(noun) e.g. *Shut the door, please.*

doorway, doorways
(noun) an opening in a wall for a door.

dope, dopes, doping, doped
1 (noun) an illegal drug.
2 (verb) If someone dopes you, they put a drug into your food or drink, e.g. *Horse doping was suspected.*
3 (noun; informal) If you call someone a dope, you mean that they are not acting intelligently.
[Dutch *doop* = sauce]

dopey
1 (adjective; informal) sleepy.
2 silly or stupid.

Learn these words, all of which contain double consonants: occasional paraffin parallel....

dormant

(adjective) If a volcano is dormant, it is neither extinct nor erupting, but might possibly erupt in the future.
[Latin *dormire* = to sleep]

dormitory, dormitories

(noun) a large bedroom where several people sleep, for example in a youth hostel.
[Latin *dormire* = to sleep]

dormouse, dormice

(noun) a rodent with a furry tail which sleeps for several months a year.

DOS

abbreviation for **D**isk **O**perating **S**ystem, a system of commands to make use of a computer possible.

dose, doses

(noun) A dose of a medicine or drug is a measured amount of it.
[Greek *dosis* = giving or gift]

doss, dosses, dossing, dossed

(verb; informal) If you doss or doss down somewhere, you sleep there.

dot, dots

1 (noun) a very small, round mark.
2 (phrase) If you arrive somewhere **on the dot**, you arrive there at exactly the right time.
[Old English *dott* = head of a boil]

dotty, dottier, dottiest

(adjective; informal) slightly mad.

double, doubles, doubling, doubled

1 (adjective) twice the usual size, e.g. *a double portion of chips.*
2 consisting of two parts, e.g. *double doors.*
3 (verb) If something doubles, it becomes twice as large.
4 To double as something means to have a second job or use as well as the main one, e.g. *The bedroom doubles as a study.*
5 (noun) Your double is someone who looks exactly like you.
6 Doubles is a game of tennis etc. which two people play against two other people.
doubly (adverb)

double back

(phrasal verb) to turn and go back in the direction you came from.

double up

(phrasal verb) If you double up with pain or laughter, you bend your body right over.

double agent, agents

(noun) someone who is a spy for one country who is pretending to be an agent of an enemy country.

double bass, basses

(noun) the largest musical instrument in the violin family.

double-cross, double-crosses, double-crossing, double-crossed

(verb) If someone double-crosses you, they cheat you by pretending they are doing what you had planned together, when in fact they are doing the opposite.

double-decker, double-deckers

1 (adjective) having two tiers or layers.
2 (noun) a bus with two floors.

double glazing

(noun) a second layer of glass fitted to windows to keep the building quieter or warmer.

double-jointed

(adjective) having flexible joints so that one's fingers or limbs bend backwards and forwards.

doubt, doubts, doubting, doubted

1 (noun) a feeling of uncertainty.
2 (verb) If you doubt something, you think that it is probably not true or possible.
doubter (noun)
[Latin *dubitare* = to hesitate]

doubtful

(adjective) If you are doubtful about something, you are unsure about it.
doubtfully (adverb)

doubtless

(adverb) probably or almost certainly, e.g. *Many types of animals are already extinct, and there will doubtless be more in the future.*
doubtlessly (adverb)

dough

1 (noun) a mixture of flour, water, etc., used to make bread, pastry or biscuits.
2 (informal) money, e.g. *Hand over the dough!*
doughy (adjective)

doughnut, doughnuts; also spelled donut

(noun) a piece of sweet dough cooked in hot fat covered with sugar, often with jam in the middle.

douse, douses, dousing, doused; also spelled dowse

(verb) If you douse a fire, you stop it burning by throwing water over it.

dove, doves

(noun) a small type of pigeon.

dovetail, dovetails, dovetailing, dovetailed

1 (verb) If two things dovetail together, they fit together closely or neatly.
2 (adjective) A dovetail joint is a wedge-shaped joint used in carpentry for fitting two pieces of wood tightly together.

down

1 (preposition, adverb), e.g., *Down on the farm... we went down the stairs.*
2 (noun) Downs are hilly areas, e.g. *The Berkshire Downs.*

down at heel

(adjective) shabby and in poor condition.

downcast

(adjective) sad and dejected.

downfall

(noun) Something that is someone's downfall is the thing that causes their failure, e.g. *Drink was his downfall.*

downhearted

(adjective) feeling sad and discouraged.

downhill

1 (adverb) moving down a slope.

.... exaggerate embarrass committee mattress address necessary suppose beginning.

2 becoming worse, e.g. *Tabloid newpapers are going downhill nowadays.*

download, downloads, downloading, downloaded
(verb) to take information from a computer, often from a main computer to a smaller terminal.

downpour, downpours
(noun) a heavy fall of rain.

downright
(adjective, adverb) You use downright to emphasize that something is extremely unpleasant or bad, e.g. *That's a downright lie.*

downstairs
(adjective, adverb) on or to a lower floor.

downstream
(adjective, adverb) Something floating downstream on a river is going towards the sea.

downturn
1 (noun) A downturn in trade occurs when people buy less and as a result, there is more unemployment and bankruptcy.
2 a change for the worst, e.g. There was a downturn in trade when interest rates went up.

Similar words: recession, slump

down-to-earth
(adjective) sensible and practical, e.g. *his warm, down-to-earth manner.*

downwards or **downward**
(adverb, adjective) If you look downwards, you look towards the ground or towards a lower level.

doze, dozes, dozing, dozed
(verb) to sleep lightly for a short period.

dozen, dozens
1 (noun) A dozen things are 12 of them.
2 (phrase) A **baker's dozen** consists of 13 things.

dozy, dozier, doziest
1 (adjective) feeling sleepy and not very alert.
2 (informal) If you call someone dozy, you think they are a bit stupid or slow to understand.

drab, drabber, drabbest
(adjective) dull and unattractive.
drabness (noun) **drably** (adverb)

Similar words: dingy, dismal, dreary

draft, drafts
(noun) an early, rough version of a piece of writing.

drag, drags, dragging, dragged
1 (verb) If you drag a heavy object somewhere, you pull it slowly and with difficulty.
2 If an event or a period of time drags, it is boring and seems to last a long time.
3 (noun) an activity or person that is boring.

Similar words: (verb: sense 1) haul, tug, pull, tow

dragon, dragons
(noun) In stories and legends, a dragon is a fierce, fire-breathing animal like a large lizard.
[Greek *drakōn* = serpent]

dragonfly, dragonflies
(noun) a large, brightly-coloured insect with a long, thin body and two pairs of wings.

drain, drains, draining, drained
1 (verb) If you drain something or if it drains, liquid gradually flows out of it.
2 If something drains you, it leaves you feeling physically and emotionally exhausted.
3 (noun) a pipe or channel that carries water or sewage away from a place.
4 (phrase) If you say that something has gone **down the drain**, you mean it is wasted or ruined.

drainage
(noun) the process of draining water away, or the way in which a place drains, e.g. *Bad drainage caused flooding.*

drake, drakes
(noun) a male duck.

drama, dramas
(noun) plays and the theatre in general, or a single serious play.
[Greek *drama* = something performed]

dramatic
1 (adjective) A dramatic change or event happens suddenly and is very noticeable, e.g. *I want to see a dramatic improvement in your work.*
2 Dramatic art or writing is connected with plays and the theatre.
dramatize (verb) **dramatically** (adverb)

dramatist, dramatists
(noun) a person who writes plays; a playwright.

drape, drapes, draping, draped
1 (verb) If you drape a piece of cloth, you arrange it so that it hangs down or covers something in loose folds.
2 (noun) Drapes are curtains, especially in American English.
[Old French *drap* = cloth]

draper, drapers
(noun) a person who sells textiles.

drapery
(noun) cloth and fabrics.

drastic
(adjective) A drastic course of action is very strong and severe and is usually taken urgently, e.g. *drastic steps to cut unemployment.*
drastically (adverb)
[Greek *drastikos* = vigorous or active]

Similar words: dramatic, extreme

draught, draughts (pronounced **draft**)
1 (noun) a current of cold air.
2 Draughts is a game for two people played on a chequered board with round pieces.

draughtsman, draughtsmen
(noun) someone who prepares detailed drawings or plans.
draughtsmanship (noun)

draughty (pronounced **drafty**)
(adjective) A place that is draughty has currents of cold air blowing through it.

A baker's dozen is 13. Bakers used to give an extra loaf when giving short weight was an offence.

draw, draws, drawing, drew, drawn
1 (verb) When you draw, you use a pen, pencil or crayon to make a picture or diagram.
2 to pull, e.g. *Draw the curtains... The coach was drawn by 4 horses... We draw water from the well in the garden... The play drew big audiences.*
3 (noun) the result of a game when the scores are level.
4 (phrase) If something **draws to an end** or **draws to a close**, it finishes.

draw up
1 (phrasal verb) To draw up a plan, document or list means to prepare it and write it out.
2 When a vehicle draws up at a place, it stops there.

drawback, drawbacks
(noun) a problem or disadvantage with something, e.g. *The drawback of nuclear power is the danger of a radioactive leak.*

drawbridge, drawbridges
(noun) a bridge that can be pulled up or lowered, usually over a castle moat.

drawer, drawers
(noun) a sliding box-shaped part of a piece of furniture, used for storage.

drawing, drawings
(noun) a picture made with a pencil, pen or crayon.

drawing pin, pins
(noun) a short type of nail with a broad, flat top, which is pushed in by the thumb.

drawing room, rooms
(noun; old-fashioned) a room in a house where people sit and relax or entertain guests.
[originally a withdrawing room]

drawl, drawls, drawling, drawled
(verb) If someone drawls, they speak slowly with long vowel sounds.

drawn past participle of **draw**.

dread, dreads, dreading, dreaded
1 (verb) If you dread something, you feel very worried and frightened about it, e.g. *I'm dreading the exams.*
2 (noun) a feeling of great fear.
dreaded (adjective)

dreadful
(adjective) very bad or unpleasant.
dreadfully (adverb)

Similar words: terrible, abominable, abysmal, appalling, atrocious, monstrous, deplorable

dream, dreams, dreaming, dreamed or dreamt
1 (noun) a series of pictures or events that you experience in your mind while asleep.
2 (verb) When you dream, you see pictures and events in your mind while you are asleep.
3 When you dream about something happening, you often think about it because you would very much like it to happen.
4 If you would not dream of doing something, you definitely would not do it, e.g. *I wouldn't dream of supporting Leeds United.*

5 (adjective) beautiful or pleasing, e.g. *It was a dream house.*
dreamer (noun)

dreamy, dreamier, dreamiest
(adjective) Someone who is dreamy does things without concentrating, because they are thinking about something else.

dreary, drearier, dreariest
(adjective) dull or boring.
dreariness (noun) **drearily** (adverb)
[Old English *dreorig* = gory or grievous]

dredge, dredges, dredging, dredged
(verb) To dredge a harbour or river means to clear a channel for boats by removing silt or mud from the bed.
dredger (noun)

drench, drenches, drenching, drenched
(verb) If you drench something or someone, you make them soaking wet.
[Old English *drencan* = to cause to drink]

dress, dresses, dressing, dressed
1 (verb) e.g., *She always dresses slowly.*
2 (noun) e.g., *What a pretty dress she has on.*

dressage (pronounced **dres**-ahj)
(noun) the method of training horses to perform manoeuvres as a display of obedience.

dresser, dressers
(noun) a piece of kitchen or dining room furniture with cupboards or drawers in the lower part and open shelves in the top part.

dressing, dressings
1 (noun) a covering put on a wound to protect it while it heals.
2 A salad dressing is a sauce put on salad to enhance its flavour.

dressmaker, dressmakers
(noun) a person who is paid to make clothes.

dribble, dribbles, dribbling, dribbled
1 (verb) If a person or animal dribbles, saliva trickles from their mouth.
2 In sport, to dribble a ball means to move it along by repeatedly tapping it with your hand, your foot or a stick.

drift, drifts, drifting, drifted
1 (verb) When something drifts, it is carried along by the wind or by water.
2 When people drift somewhere, they wander or move there gradually.
3 (noun) A snow drift is a pile of snow heaped up by the wind.
drifter (noun)
[Old Norse *drift* = snow drift]

drill, drills, drilling, drilled
1 (verb) to make a hole in something using a drill.
2 (noun) a tool for making holes, e.g. *an electric drill.*
3 a routine exercise or routine training, e.g. *fire drill.*

drink, drinks, drinking, drank, drunk
1 (verb) e.g. *We drank our cups of tea.*

Shakespeare (1564-1616) died on 23rd April and is believed to have been born on that day as well.

2 To drink also means to drink alcohol, e.g. *He hardly ever drinks now.*
3 (noun) e.g. *Do you want a drink of tea?*
drinker (noun)

drip, drips, dripping, dripped
1 (verb) When liquid drips, it falls in small drops.
2 (noun; informal) If you call someone a drip, you mean they are weak or foolish.
3 A drip is also a device for food to enter the bloodstream of a person who is seriously ill.

drip-dry
(adjective) Drip-dry clothes or fabrics dry without creases if hung up when wet.

dripping
(noun) the fat which comes from meat while it is cooking.

drive, drives, driving, drove, driven
1 (verb) To drive a vehicle means to operate it and control its movements.
driver (noun) **driving** (noun)
2 If something or someone drives you to do something, they force you to do it, e.g. *Losing his job drove him to suicide.*
3 If you drive a post or nail into something, you force it in by hitting it with a hammer.
4 If something drives a machine, it supplies the power that makes it work.
5 (noun) A drive is a private road that leads from a public road to a person's house.
6 Drive is energy and determination.
7 (phrase) If you understand what someone **is driving at,** you understand what they are trying to say.
8 (noun) a campaign for or against something, e.g. *an anti-litter drive.*

drivel
(noun) nonsense, e.g. *Her essay was absolute drivel.*
[Old English *dreflian* = to dribble]

drizzle, drizzles, drizzling, drizzled
(noun) light rain.
[Old English *dreosan* = to fall]

drone, drones, droning, droned
1 (verb) to make a low, continuous humming noise.
2 to keep talking or reading aloud in a boring way.
3 (noun) a male bee.

drool, drools, drooling, drooled
(verb) If someone drools, saliva dribbles from their mouth.

droop, droops, drooping, drooped
(verb) If something droops, it hangs or sags downwards with no strength or firmness.
[Old Norse *drupa* = to hang one's head in sorrow]

drop, drops, dropping, dropped
Selected meanings:
1 (verb) e.g. *I dropped a plate and it smashed... the price of sugar dropped... I was dropped from the school team.*
2 (phrase) If you **drop a hint,** you give someone a hint in a casual way.

3 If you **drop someone a line,** you write them a short letter.

drought, droughts (rhymes with **shout**)
(noun) a long period with no rain.
[Old English *drugath* = dryness]

drove past tense of **drive.**

drown, drowns, drowning, drowned
1 (verb) When someone drowns or is drowned, they die because they have gone under water and cannot breathe.
2 If a noise drowns a sound, it is louder than the sound and makes it impossible to hear it.

drowsy
(adjective) very sleepy.
drowse (verb) **drowsily** (adverb)

drudgery
(noun) hard, uninteresting work.

Similar words: chore, grind, donkey work

drug, drugs, drugging, drugged
1 (noun) a chemical given to people to treat disease.
2 Drugs are substances that some people smoke, swallow, smell or inject because of their stimulating effects. In general, this is usually damaging to their health.
3 (verb) To drug a person or animal means to give them a drug to make them unconscious.
drugged (adjective)

druid, druids (pronounced **droo**-id)
(noun) a priest of an ancient pre-Christian religion in France, Britain and Ireland.

drum, drums, drumming, drummed
1 (noun) a musical instrument consisting of a skin stretched tightly over a round frame.
2 (verb) If you drum something into someone, you keep saying it to them until they understand it or remember it.

drum up
(phrasal verb) If you drum up support, you go round asking people to support you.

drumstick, drumsticks
1 (noun) a stick used for beating a drum.
2 A chicken drumstick is the leg of a chicken, when cooked.

drunk, drunks
1 past tense of **drink.**
2 (adjective) If someone is drunk, they have drunk so much alcohol that they cannot speak clearly or behave sensibly.
3 (noun) A drunk is a person who is drunk or who often gets drunk.
drunken (adjective) **drunkenly** (adverb)
drunkenness (noun)

Similar words: (adjective) intoxicated, tight, tipsy, sloshed, merry.

drunkard, drunkards
(noun) someone who often gets drunk.

Lexicographer: a writer of dictionaries, a harmless drudge. (from Dr Johnson's dictionary)

dry, drier or dryer, driest; dries, drying, dried
1 (adjective) e.g. *We had a hot, dry summer.*
2 (verb) e.g. *I put the clothes on the line to dry.*
dryness (noun) **drily** (adverb)

Similar words: arid, parched, dehydrated

dry up
(phrasal verb) not a very polite way of saying
'Be quiet'.

dry-clean, dry-cleans, dry-cleaning, dry-cleaned
(verb) to clean clothes etc. with a liquid chemical
rather than with water.

dryer, dryers; also spelled **drier**
1 (noun) any device for removing moisture from
something by heating or by hot air, e.g. *a hair
dryer... a tumble dryer.*
2 Dryer and drier are also the comparative forms
of **dry** (dry, **dryer,** driest).

dual
(adjective) having two parts, functions or
aspects, e.g. *a dual-purpose gadget.*
[Latin *duo* = two]

dub, dubs, dubbing, dubbed
(verb) If a film is dubbed, the voices on the
soundtrack are not those of the actors on the
screen but those of other actors. On TV and in
films, singing is often pre-recorded, and singers
mime to their own dubbed voice.

duchess, duchesses
(noun) a woman who has the same rank as a
duke, or who is a duke's wife or widow.

duck, ducks, ducking, ducked
1 (noun) a waterbird.
2 (verb) to move your head quickly downwards
to avoid being hit by something.
3 to push someone briefly under water.
4 (noun) In cricket, if a batsman scores a duck,
he does not score any runs.
[Old English *ducan* = to dive]

duckling, ducklings
(noun) a young duck.

dud, duds
(noun) something which does not function
properly, e.g. *This firework is a dud.*

due
1 (adjective) expected to happen or arrive, e.g.
The bus is due at 3.00 pm.
2 (preposition) because of, e.g. *The fact that the
letter arrived late was due to the postal strike.*
3 (adverb) exactly in a particular direction, e.g.
The hills are due south.
4 (phrase) If you say that something will happen
in due course, you mean it will happen
eventually, when the time is right.

duel, duels
1 (noun) a prearranged fight between two people
using deadly weapons, to settle a quarrel.
2 Any contest or conflict between two people can
be referred to as a duel.

duet, duets
(noun) a piece of music sung or played by two
people.

duffle or **duffel coat**
(noun) a hooded coat made from a rough, heavy,
woollen material, named after the Belgian town
of Duffel.

dugout, dugouts
1 (noun) a canoe made by hollowing out a log.
2 a shelter for soldiers dug in the ground for
protection.

duke, dukes
(noun) a nobleman with a rank just below that of
a prince.
[Latin *dux* = leader]

dull, duller, dullest; dulls, dulling, dulled
1 (adjective) not at all interesting in any way.
2 slow to learn or understand.
3 not bright, sharp or clear.
4 A dull day or dull sky is very cloudy.
dully (adverb) **dullness** (noun)
[Old English *dol* = stupid]

Similar words: (sense 4) overcast, heavy

dumb, dumber, dumbest
1 (adjective) unable to speak.
2 (informal) slow to understand or stupid.

Similar words: (sense 1) mute, speechless

dumbfounded
(adjective) If you are dumbfounded, you are so
surprised that you cannot speak.

dummy, dummies
1 (noun) A baby's dummy is a rubber teat which
it sucks or bites on.
2 an imitation or model of something which is
used for display.

dump, dumps, dumping, dumped
1 (verb) If you dump something, you throw it
down or put it down somewhere in a careless
way.
2 (noun) a place where rubbish is left.
3 (informal) You say a place is a dump when it is
unattractive and unpleasant to live in.

dumpling, dumplings
(noun) a small lump of dough that is cooked and
eaten with meat and vegetables.

dumpy, dumpier, dumpiest
(adjective) short and fat.

dune, dunes
(noun) a hill of sand near the sea or in the desert.

dung
(noun) the excrement (solid waste) from large
animals, sometimes called manure.

dungarees
(plural noun) trousers which have a bib covering
the chest and straps over the shoulders, named
after Dungri in India, where dungaree material
was first made.

dungeon, dungeons (pronounced **dun-jen**)
(noun) an underground prison.

dunk, dunks, dunking, dunked
(verb) to dip something briefly into a liquid, e.g.
He dunked his biscuits in his tea.

Which proverb fits you? Too much bed makes a dull head. All work and no play makes Jack a dull boy.

duo, duos
1 (noun) a pair of musical performers.
2 Any two people doing something together can be referred to as a duo, e.g. *Batman and Robin, the dynamic duo.*

duplicate, duplicates, duplicating, duplicated
1 (verb) to make an exact copy of something.
2 (noun) something that is identical to something else.
duplication (noun)

durable
(adjective) strong and long-lasting.
durability (noun)
[Latin *durare* = to last]

duration
(noun) the length of time during which something happens or exists, e.g. *The airmen were kept in prison for the duration of the war.*

during
(preposition) happening within a particular time, e.g. *Platt was hurt during the match.*

dusk
(noun) the time just before nightfall when it is not completely dark.
[Old English *dox* = dark]

dusky, duskier, duskiest
(adjective) rather dark.

dust, dusts, dusting, dusted
1 (noun) dry, fine, powdery material such as particles of earth, dirt or pollen.
2 (phrase) When something **bites the dust**, it completely fails or stops working.
3 (verb) to wipe the dust off furniture etc.
dusty (adjective) **duster** (noun)

dustbin, dustbins
(noun) a large container for rubbish.

dustjacket, dustjackets
(noun) a paper cover for a hardback book.

dustman, dustmen
(noun) someone whose job is to collect the rubbish from people's houses.

Dutch
1 (adjective) belonging to Holland (Netherlands).
2 (noun) the main language spoken in Holland.

Dutchman, Dutchmen
(noun) a man who comes from Holland.
Dutchwoman (noun)

duty, duties
1 (noun) Duties are things you ought to do or feel you should do, because they are your responsibility.
2 (phrase) If an employed person is **on duty**, they are working. If they are **off duty**, they are not working.
3 (noun) tax paid to the government on some goods, especially imports.
dutiful (adjective) **dutifully** (adverb)

Similar words: (sense 1) responsibility, obligation

duty-free
(adjective) Duty-free goods are goods on which you do not have to pay customs duty. They can be bought at airports or on planes and ships.

duvet, duvets (pronounced **doo**-vay)
(noun) a bed cover consisting of a cotton quilt filled with feathers or other material, used in place of a sheet and blankets.
[a French word]

dwarf, dwarfs, dwarfing, dwarfed
1 (verb) Something that dwarfs another is so much bigger that it makes the other thing look very small.
2 (noun) a person, plant, etc. that is much smaller than average size.

dwell, dwells, dwelling, dwelled or **dwelt**
1 (verb; literary) to live somewhere.
2 If you dwell on something or dwell upon it, you think, speak or write about it a lot.

dwelling, dwellings
(noun; formal) the house or other place where someone lives.

dwindle, dwindles, dwindling, dwindled
(verb) to become less in size, strength or number, e.g. *The number of World War I veterans is dwindling.*

dye, dyes, dyeing, dyed
1 (verb) to change the colour of something by applying coloured liquid to it.
2 (noun) a substance used to change the colour of something such as cloth or hair.

dyke, dykes; also spelled **dike**
(noun) a thick wall that prevents water flooding onto land from a river or from the sea.

dynamic, dynamics
1 (adjective) full of energy, ambition, personality and new ideas.
2 (noun) In physics, dynamics is the study of the forces that change or produce the motion of bodies or particles.
[Greek *dunamis* = strength]

dynamism
(noun) Someone's dynamism is their energy or ability to produce new ideas.

dynamite
(noun) an explosive made of nitro-glycerine.

dynamo, dynamos
(noun) a device that converts mechanical energy into electricity, e.g. on a bicycle.

dynasty, dynasties
(noun) a series of rulers of a country all belonging to the same family.
[Greek *dunasteia* = power]

dyslexia (pronounced dis-**lek**-see-a)
(noun) difficulty with reading, writing and spelling, in some cases caused by a slight disorder of the brain.
dyslexic (adjective and noun)
[Latin *dys-* = bad + Greek *lexis* = word]

We take these words from Dutch: yacht boom yawl blunderbuss skipper smuggle.

E

each
(adjective, pronoun) every one taken separately.
e.g. *Each child was given a sweet... She gave
each a new bag.*

eager
(adjective) keen and full of enthusiasm.
eagerly (adverb) **eagerness** (noun)
[Latin *acer* = sharp or keen]

eagle, eagles
(noun) a large bird which hunts and kills other
animals for food.

eardrum, eardrums
(noun) thin pieces of tightly stretched skin inside
the ears which vibrate so that you can hear
sounds.

earl, earls
(noun) a British nobleman.
[Old English *eorl* = chieftain]

early, earlier, earliest
1 (adverb) before the expected time.
2 (adjective) near the beginning of a day, evening
or other period of time, e.g. *early evening... the
early 1960s.*
3 happening a very long time ago, e.g. *Early Man
lived in caves.*

earmark, earmarks, earmarking, earmarked
(verb) If you earmark something for a special
purpose, you keep it for that purpose, e.g. *These
logs are earmarked for burning next year.*
[from identification marks on the ears of
domestic or farm animals]

earn, earns, earning, earned
(verb) If you earn money, you are paid it in
return for work that you do.
earner (noun) **earnings** (plural noun)

Similar words: make, bring in

earnest
1 (adjective) sincere in what you say or do, e.g.
My earnest wish is to make you happy.
2 (phrase) If you are **in earnest** about something,
you are serious about it, e.g. *She was in earnest
about buying a new handbag.*
earnestly (adverb) **earnestness** (noun)

earphones
(plural noun) small speakers which you wear on
your ears to listen to a radio, tape, etc.

earring, earrings
(noun) jewellery that you wear on your ear lobes.

earth, earths, earthing, earthed
1 (noun) The Earth is the planet on which we live.
2 the dry land on the surface of the earth,
especially the soil in which things grow.
3 An earth is a hole in the ground where an
animal such as a fox lives.
4 The earth in a plug or piece of electrical
equipment is the wire through which electricity
can pass into the ground and so make the
equipment safe for use.

earthquake, earthquakes
(noun) a series of vibrations along the surface of
the earth caused by a build-up of pressure deep
within the earth.

earwig, earwigs
(noun) a small, thin, brown insect which has a
pair of pincers at the end of its body.
[Old English *earwicga* = ear insect; it was
believed to creep into people's ears]

ease, eases, easing, eased
1 (noun) lack of difficulty, worry or hardship,
e.g. *Give me a life of ease, any day!*
2 (verb) When something eases, or when you
ease it, it becomes less, e.g. *She took an aspirin
to ease her headache.*
3 If you ease something somewhere, you move it
there slowly and carefully, e.g. *The QE2 eased
into her berth.*

easel, easels
(noun) an upright frame which supports a
painting or a blackboard.
[Dutch *ezel* = donkey]

easily
1 (adverb) without difficulty.
2 without a doubt, e.g. *She was easily the
prettiest girl in the contest.*

east
1 (noun) the direction in which you look to see
the sun rise.
2 (adjective) An east wind blows from the east.
3 (noun) The Middle East refers to the area
around the eastern Mediterranean and the
Persian Gulf. The Far East refers to south and
east Asia.
eastern (adjective)

Easter
(noun) a Christian religious festival celebrating
the resurrection of Christ.
[Old English *Eostre*, a pre-Christian Germanic
goddess whose festival was at the spring
equinox]

eastward or **eastwards**
(adverb) towards the east.

easy, easier, easiest
(adjective) not difficult, e.g. *an easy task.*

Similar words: simple, straightforward, effortless

easy-going
(adjective) not easily annoyed or worried, e.g.
*The easy-going fellow picked his toes up and
carried on mowing the lawn.*

Similar words: easy, laid-back, tolerant

eat, eats, eating, ate, eaten
(verb) to chew and swallow food.

eaves
(plural noun) The eaves of a roof are the lower
edges which jut out over the walls.

eavesdrop, eavesdrops, eavesdropping, eavesdropped
(verb) to listen secretly to what other people are saying.
[Old English *yfesdrype* = water dripping down from the eaves; people were supposed to stand outside in the rain to hear what was being said inside the house]

ebb, ebbs, ebbing, ebbed
1 (verb) When the sea or the tide ebbs, it flows back.
2 If a person's feeling or strength ebbs, it gets weaker, e.g. *the strength ebbed from his body.*
3 (phrase) If someone or something is **at a low ebb**, they are very weak.

ebony
1 (noun) a hard, dark-coloured wood of a tropical tree, used for making furniture.
2 (noun, adjective) very deep black.

eccentric, eccentrics (pronounced ik-**sen**-trik)
1 (adjective) having habits or opinions which are so different from other people's that you are thought to be odd or peculiar.
2 (noun) An eccentric is someone who behaves oddly.
eccentricity (noun) **eccentrically** (adverb)
[Greek *ekkentros* = off-centre]

echo, echoes, echoing, echoed
(noun) a repeating sound which is caused by sound waves reflecting off a surface.

eclipse, eclipses
(noun) An eclipse occurs when the sun or the moon is hidden from view, wholly or partially, by a planet etc. moving in front.
[Greek *ekleipsis* = abandoning]

ecology
(noun) the relationship between plants, animals, people and their environment; also the study of this relationship.
ecological (adjective) **ecologist** (noun)
[Greek *oikos* = house]

economical
1 (adjective) Something that is economical is cheap to use or operate.
2 Someone who is economical spends money carefully and sensibly.
economically (adverb)

economics
(noun) the study of the production and distribution of goods, services and wealth in a society and the organization of its money, industry and trade.
economic (adjective) **economist** (noun)

economize, economizes, economizing, economized; also spelled **economise**
(verb) If you economize, you save money by being very careful about how you spend it.

economy, economies
1 (noun) The economy of a country is the system it uses to organize and manage its money, industry and trade; also the wealth that a country gets from business and industry.

2 the careful use of things to save money, time or energy.
[Greek *oikonomia* = domestic management]

ecstasy, ecstasies
1 (noun) a feeling of extreme happiness.
2 the name of a certain mixture of drugs which is very addictive and therefore highly dangerous.
ecstatic (adjective) **ecstatically** (adverb)
[Greek *ekstasis* = trance]

eczema (pronounced **ek**-sim-ma)
(noun) a skin disease that causes the surface of the skin to become rough and itchy.
[Greek *ekzein* = to boil over]

edge, edges, edging, edged
1 (noun) The edge of something is a border or line where it ends or meets something else.
2 If you have an edge over someone, you have an advantage over them.
3 (verb) to move very gradually, e.g. *She edged her way towards the front.*
4 (phrase) If you are **on edge**, you are nervous or tense about something.

Similar words: (noun: sense 1) border, brink, margin, fringe

edgeways
1 (adverb) Edgeways means the same as sideways, e.g. *They put the bookcase into the van edgeways.*
2 (phrase) If you cannot get **a word in edgeways**, you do not get a chance to speak because someone else is talking so much.

edgy, edgier, edgiest
(adjective) nervous, anxious and irritable.

edible
(adjective) safe to eat.
[Latin *edere* = to eat]

edit, edits, editing, edited
1 (verb) If you edit a book or a piece of writing, you examine, correct and improve it.
2 To edit a book can also mean to collect pieces of writing by different authors and arrange them ready for publication.
3 To edit a film or a radio or TV programme means to select different parts of it and arrange them in a particular order.
4 Someone who edits a newspaper or magazine is in charge of it.
editor (noun)

edition, editions
1 (noun) a particular version of a book, magazine, etc. printed at one time.
2 An edition of a TV or radio programme is one of a series, e.g. *tonight's edition of Panorama.*
[Latin *edere* = to give out]
editorial (adjective)

educate, educates, educating, educated
(verb) to teach someone so that they acquire knowledge and understanding about something.
[Latin *educere* = to lead out]

Pun. If a girl can't do her homework, why can't her brother help?
He can't be a brother and assist her, too.

education
(noun) the process of acquiring knowledge and understanding through learning.
educational (adjective) **educationally** (adverb)

eel, eels
(noun) a long, thin, snakelike fish.

eerie, eerier, eeriest
(adjective) strange and frightening, e.g. *I had the eerie feeling that someone was watching me.*
eerily (adverb)

effect, effects
1 (noun) a direct result of someone or something on another person or thing, e.g. *The effect of the medicine was to cause drowsiness.*
2 (phrase) If something **takes effect**, it starts to happen or starts to produce results, e.g. *She fell asleep as the potion began to take effect.*
3 (plural noun) In a radio play etc., **sound effects** are noises made to imitate something. In a film, **special effects** are the tricks used to make unreal things look real, e.g. dinosaurs fighting.
[Latin *efficere* = to accomplish]

effective
1 (adjective) working well and producing the intended results.
2 coming into operation or beginning officially, e.g. *The new tax becomes effective from today.*
effectively (adverb) **effectiveness** (noun)

efficient
(adjective) able to do something well without wasting time or energy.
efficiently (adverb) **efficiency** (noun)

Similar words: businesslike, capable, competent, well-organized

effluent, effluents (pronounced ef-loo-ent)
(noun) liquid waste that comes out of factories or sewage works.

effort, efforts
1 (noun) the physical or mental energy needed to do something.
2 an attempt or struggle to do something, e.g. *She made an effort in the exam.*
[Latin *fortis* = strong]

Similar words: (sense 1) endeavour, trouble

effortless
(adjective) done easily.
effortlessly (adverb)

egg, eggs, egging, egged
1 (noun) an oval or rounded object produced by female birds, reptiles, fishes and insects. A new creature develops inside the egg.
2 In a female animal, an egg is a cell produced in its body which can develop into a baby if it is fertilized.
3 (verb) If you egg someone on, you encourage them to do something, especially something foolish or daring.
[noun: an old Norse word
verb: Old Norse *eggja* = to incite]

egocentric
(adjective) only thinking of yourself and your own interests.
[Latin *ego* = I]

eiderdown, eiderdowns
(noun) a thick bed covering that is filled with feathers.
[from the *eider* duck]

eight, eights the number 8.
eighth (adjective and noun)

eighteen the number 18.
eighteenth (adjective and noun)

eighty, eighties the number 80.
eightieth (adjective and noun)

either
(adverb, pronoun, conjunction) e.g. *Do either one thing or the other... Either can have a share... Either come in or go out!*

eject, ejects, ejecting, ejected
(verb) to throw or push out forcefully.
ejection (noun) **ejector seat** (noun)
[Latin *ejicere* = to throw out]

Similar words: expel, throw out

elaborate, elabrates, elaborating, elaborated
1 (adjective; pronounced el-**ab**-or-ut) highly decorated and complicated, e.g. *an elaborate tapestry.*
2 (verb; pronounced el-**ab**-or-ate) to give more details about what you have said, e.g. *Could you elaborate on that, please?*

elastic
(noun) rubber material which stretches and returns to its original shape.
elasticity (adjective)
[Greek *elastikos* = pushing]

elation
(noun) a feeling of great happiness.
elated (adjective)

elbow, elbows, elbowing, elbowed
1 (noun) the joint between the upper part of your arm and your forearm.
2 (verb) If you elbow someone aside, you push them away with your elbow.
3 (phrase) If you clean something using **elbow grease** you do it using only the strength of your hands.

elder, eldest
(adjective) older.

elderly
1 (adjective) An elderly person is rather old.
2 (noun) The elderly are people who are old, e.g. *The elderly need to be cared for.*

elect, elects, electing, elected
(verb) If you elect someone you choose them, usually by voting, e.g. *She was elected captain.*
[Latin *eligere* = to select]

election, elections
(noun) the selection of one or more people for an official position by voting.
electoral (adjective)

Etymology. Find out how these words are connected: octave octagon octopus October octogenarian.

electric
(adjective) powered by electricity.

electrical
(adjective) using, producing or concerning electricity, e.g. *an electrical fault.*
electrically (adverb)

electrician, electricians
(noun) a person whose job is to install, maintain and repair electrical equipment.

electricity
(noun) a form of energy used to provide power for machines, produced by means such as water, sun, coal, oil and nuclear power.
electrify (verb)
[Greek *ēlektron* = amber; in early experiments, scientists rubbed the resin amber to produce an electrical charge]

electrocute, electrocutes, electrocuting, electrocuted
(verb) If someone is electrocuted, they are hurt or killed by receiving an electric shock.
electrocution (noun)

electrode, electrodes
(noun) a small piece of metal which allows an electric current to pass between a source of power and a piece of equipment.
[electric + Greek *hodos* = way]

electromagnet, electromagnets
(noun) a magnet made up of an iron or steel core with a coil of wire round it, through which an electric current is passed.
electromagnetic (adjective)

electronic
(adjective) having transistors, silicon chips or valves which control an electric current.
electronically (adverb)

electronics
(noun) the technology of electronic devices such as radios, TVs and computers; also the study of how these devices work.

elegant
(adjective) pleasing and graceful in appearance, e.g. *an elegant dress.*
elegantly (adverb) **elegance** (noun)
[Greek *elegans* = choosing carefully]

element, elements
1 (noun) An element of something is a part which combines with others to make a whole.
2 The elements of a subject are the basic and most important points.
3 The element in an electric fire, water heater or kettle is the metal part which heats up when electricity passes through it.
4 In chemistry, an element is a substance that is made up of only one type of atom.
5 In maths, an element is a number forming part of a sequence, e.g. one of the figures in a matrix or which make up a set.
6 (phrase) If you are **in your element**, you are in a situation where you are happiest.
[Latin *elementum* = principle]

elementary
(adjective) simple, basic and straightforward, e.g. *The elementary rules are easy to learn.*

elephant, elephants
(noun) a very large mammal with thick, leathery skin, a long trunk and tusks, found in Africa and India.

elevate, elevates, elevating, elevated
(verb) to raise something up.
elevation (noun)
[Latin *levare* = to raise]

elevator, elevators
(noun) In American English, an elevator is a lift.

eleven, elevens
1 the number 11.
2 (noun) An eleven (or XI) is a team of cricket or football players, e.g. *the first eleven (first XI).*
eleventh (adjective and noun)

elevenses
(noun) a small snack eaten in the middle of the morning.

elide, elides, eliding, elided
(verb) If you elidea part of a word, you do not pronounce it when you speak. e.g. o'er *(as in 'The lowing winds slowly o'er the lea')*
elision (noun).
[Latin e*lidere*=to knock]

eligible (pronounced el-lij-i-bl)
(adjective) suitable or having the right qualifications for something, e.g. *He was eligible for unemployment benefit.*
eligibility (noun)
[Latin *eligere* = to choose]

eliminate, eliminates, eliminating, eliminated
1 (verb) to get rid of something, e.g. *Poverty must be eliminated.*
2 If a team or a person is eliminated from a competition, they can no longer take part.
elimination (noun)
[Latin *eliminare* = to turn out of the house]

elite, elites (pronounced ill-eet)
(adjective) the best of its kind, e.g. *an elite club for businessmen.*
[Old French *eslit* = chosen]

elk, elks
(noun) the largest type of deer, found in North Europe, Asia and North America.

ellipse, ellipses
(noun) a regular oval shape
elliptical (adjective).

ellipsis, ellipses
(noun) the leaving out of parts of a sentence, where the sentence can still be easily understood, e.g.: 'You coming too?' instead of 'Are you coming too?'
[Greek *elleipsis* = omission]

elm, elms
(noun) a tall, deciduous tree with broad leaves. Its wood is used for timber and furniture.

Can you explain the differences between: eligible – illegible colonel – kernel jewel – joule?

elocution
(noun) the study of speaking clearly or well with a standard accent.
[Latin *elocutio* = a speaking out]

elongated
(adjective) long and thin.
elongate (verb) **elongation** (noun)

elope, elopes, eloping, eloped
(verb) If someone elopes, they run away secretly with their lover to get married.
elopement (noun)
[Medieval French *aloper* = to run away]

eloquent
(adjective) fluent in speech or writing, e.g. *The speaker gave an eloquent talk on China.*
eloquently (adverb) **eloquence** (noun)
[Latin *eloquens* = speaking out]

else
(adverb, conjunction) e.g. *Let's do something else... Get away or else she'll spot us!*

elsewhere
(adverb) in another place, e.g. *I'd rather do my shopping elsewhere.*

elusive
(adjective) difficult to find, e.g. *'that damned elusive Pimpernel'.*

embankment, embankments
(noun) a man-made ridge built to support a road or railway or to prevent water from overflowing. The Embankment is the north bank of the Thames in central London.

embark, embarks, embarking, embarked
1 (verb) to go onto a ship at the start of a journey.
2 If you embark on something, you start it, e.g. *He embarked upon a new career.*
embarkation (noun)
[French *barque* = boat]

embarrassed
(adjective) shy, ashamed or uncomfortable, e.g. *She felt embarrassed when her wig came off.*
embarrass (verb) **embarrassing** (adjective) **embarrassment** (noun)
[Italian *imbarrazzare* = to impede]

embassy, embassies
(noun) the building in a foreign country where an ambassador and diplomatic staff work, e.g. *the British Embassy in Washington.*

embezzle, embezzles, embezzling, embezzled
(verb) To embezzle money means to steal by fraud from an organization that you work for.
embezzlement (noun) **embezzler** (noun)
[Old French *beseiller* = to make away with]

emblem, emblems
(noun) an object or a design chosen to represent an organization or an idea, e.g. *Hitler's emblem was the swastika.*
emblematic (adjective)
[Latin *emblema* = raised decoration or mosaic]

embrace, embraces, embracing, embraced
(verb) to hug someone when you greet them or to show affection.
[Old French *embracier*, from *brace* = arms]

embroidery
(noun) the sewing of designs onto fabric.
embroider (verb)

embryo, embryos (pronounced **em**-bree-oh)
(noun) an animal or human in the very early stages of development in the womb.
embryonic (adjective)
[Greek *embruon* = new-born animal]

emerald, emeralds
1 (noun) a bright green precious stone.
2 (adjective) bright green.

emerge, emerges, emerging, emerged
(verb) to come out, e.g. *The gunmen emerged from the bank... She is emerging as a star.*
emergence (noun) **emergent** (adjective)
[Latin *emergere* = to rise up from]

emergency, emergencies
(noun) an unexpected and serious event which needs immediate action to deal with it.

Similar word: crisis

emigrate, emigrates, emigrating, emigrated
(verb) to leave your native country and go to live permanently in another one.
emigrant (noun) **emigration** (noun)

eminent
(adjective) well known and respected for what you do, e.g. *an eminent doctor of physics.*
[Latin *eminere* = or to stand out]

emission, emissions
(noun; formal) the release of, for example, gas or radiation into the atmosphere.

emit, emits, emitting, emitted
(verb) to give out or release, e.g. *The food emitted a strong smell.*
[Latin *emittere* = to send out]

emotion, emotions
(noun) a strong feeling, such as love or fear.
[Old French *émouvoir* = to move the feelings]

emotional
1 (adjective) to do with a person's feelings rather than their physical condition, e.g. *She had emotional problems after the divorce.*
2 showing your feelings openly, e.g. *He became very emotional and cried.*
emotionally (adverb)

empathy
(noun) an understanding and imaginative experiencing of how someone is feeling, e.g. *The social worker had a great empathy with the struggling family.*
empathize (verb)
[Greek *empatheia* = affection or passion]

emperor, emperors
(noun) a male ruler of an empire.
[Latin *imperator* = commander-in-chief]

emphasis, emphases
(noun) special importance or extra stress given to something, e.g. *In the name 'Edward', the emphasis is on the first syllable.*
[Greek *emphasis* = significant stress]

Some words change meaning when the emphasis is moved:
conduct convict object present subject suspect.

emphasize, emphasizes, emphasizing, emphasized; also spelled **emphasise**
(verb) If you emphasize something, you make it known that it is very important, e.g. *He emphasized how long the journey would be.*
emphatic (adjective) **emphatically** (adverb)

empire, empires
1 (noun) a group of countries controlled by one country.
2 a powerful group of companies controlled by one person, e.g. *the Hearst newspaper empire.*
[Latin *imperium* = rule]

employ, employs, employing, employed
(verb) If you employ someone, you pay them to work for you.
[Latin *implicari* = to be involved in]

Similar words: hire, take on

employee, employees
(noun) a person who is paid to work for another person or for an organization.

employer, employers
(noun) Someone's employer is the person or company that they work for.

employment
(noun) the position of having a paid job, or the recruiting of people for a job.

empress, empresses
(noun) a woman who rules an empire, or the wife of an emperor.

empty, emptier, emptiest; empties, emptying, emptied
1 (adjective) having nothing inside.
2 (verb) e.g. *He emptied the bin into a rubbish sack.*
emptily (adverb) **emptiness** (noun)

emulsion, emulsions
(noun) a water-based paint for walls.

enable, enables, enabling, enabled
(verb) to make something possible, e.g. *Winning the pools enabled her to retire.*

enamel, enamels
1 (noun) a substance like glass, used to decorate or protect metal, glass or china.
2 The enamel on your teeth is the hard, white substance that forms the outer part.
enamelled (adjective)

enchant, enchants, enchanting, enchanted
1 (verb) If something or someone enchants you, they fascinate or charm you.
2 To enchant someone or something means to put a magic spell on them.
enchanted (adjective)
[Latin *incantare* = to chant a spell]

enchanting
(adjective) attractive, delightful or charming, e.g. *an enchanting smile.*
enchantingly (adverb)

enclose, encloses, enclosing, enclosed
1 (verb) To enclose an object or area means to surround it with something solid.
2 If you enclose something with a letter, you put

it in the same envelope, e.g. *I enclose a cheque for £50 to cover the cost of this order.*
enclosed (adjective)

enclosure, enclosures
(noun) an area of land surrounded by a wall or fence and used for a particular purpose.

encore, encores (pronounced **ong**-kor)
(noun) a short extra performance given by an entertainer because the audience asks for it.
[French *encore* = again]

encounter, encounters, encountering, encountered
1 (verb) to meet something, or be faced with it, e.g. *She encountered problems in her new job.*
2 (noun) a meeting, especially when it is difficult or unexpected, e.g. *a close encounter with death.*

encourage, encourages, encouraging, encouraged
(verb) If you encourage someone, you give them courage and confidence to do something.
encouragingly (adverb) **encouragement** (noun)

Similar words: urge, egg on

encyclopedia, encyclopedias; also spelled **encyclopaedia**
(noun) a book or set of books giving information and facts about many different subjects, places, things and people, and usually arranged in alphabetical order.
[Greek *enkuklios paideia* = general education]

end, ends, ending, ended (noun)
Selected meanings:
1 (verb) e.g. *The meeting started at 2 and ended at 4 o'clock.*
2 (noun) e.g. *at the end of the line stood Oliver Twist... The year 1901 saw the end of Victoria's reign.*
3 (phrase) If you **make ends meet**, you have just enough money to live on.
4 If you are **at a loose end**, you have nothing to do.

endanger, endangers, endangering, endangered
(verb) To endanger something means to cause it to be in a dangerous and harmful situation, e.g. *Insecticides can endanger wildlife.*
endangered (adjective)

endeavour, endeavours, endeavouring, endeavoured (pronounced en-**dev**-er)
1 (verb; formal) to try very hard to do something.
2 (noun) an effort to do or achieve something.
[Middle English *dever* = duty]

endless
(adjective) having or seeming to have no end.

endurance
(noun) the ability to put up with a difficult situation for a period of time.

endure, endures, enduring, endured
1 (verb) If you endure a difficult or unpleasant situation, you put up with it calmly and patiently.
2 to last for a very long time, e.g. *Shakespeare's plays have endured for centuries.*
enduring (adjective)
[Latin *indurare* = to harden]

Have you tried *Bouts-rimés?* Choose three or four pairs of rhyming words and write a verse to fit.

enemy, enemies
(noun) a person or group that is hostile or opposed to another person or group.
enmity (noun)
[Latin *inimicus* = hostile]

Similar words: foe, opponent

energetic
(adjective) showing energy or enthusiasm.
energetically (adverb)

Similar words: lively, vigorous, dynamic, alive

energy, energies
1 (noun) the physical strength to do active things.
2 the power which drives machinery, e.g. *nuclear energy.*
3 In physics, energy is the capacity of a body or system to do work. It is measured in joules.
[Greek *energeia* = activity]

Similar words: (sense 1) vigour, vitality, life, zest, go

enfold, enfolds, enfolding, enfolded
(verb) to cover something or to be wrapped round it, e.g. *Darkness enfolded us.*

enforce, enforces, enforcing, enforced
(verb) If you enforce a law or a rule, you make sure that it is obeyed.
enforceable (adjective) **enforcement** (noun)

engaged
1 (adjective) When two people are engaged, they have agreed to marry each other.
2 occupied or busy, e.g. *The phone was engaged.*
[Old French *gage* = pledge]

engagement, engagements
1 (noun) an appointment that you have with someone.
2 an agreement that two people have made with each other to get married.

engine, engines
1 (noun) any machine designed to convert heat or other kinds of energy into movement.
2 a railway locomotive.
[Latin *ingenium* = ingenious device]

engineer, engineers
1 (noun) a person trained in designing and constructing machinery, engines and electrical devices or roads and bridges.
2 a person who repairs mechanical or electrical devices, e.g. *a service engineer.*

engineering
(noun) the profession of designing and constructing machinery, engines and electrical devices or roads and bridges.

English
1 (adjective) belonging to England.
2 (noun) the main language spoken in the United Kingdom, the USA, Canada, Australia and many other countries.

Englishman, Englishmen
(noun) a man who comes from England.
Englishwoman (noun)

engrave, engraves, engraving, engraved
(verb) to cut marks, such as letters or designs, into a hard surface with a tool.

engraving, engravings
(noun) a picture or design that has been cut into a hard surface; also, a print taken from such a picture or design.
engraver (noun)

engrossed
(adjective) If you are engrossed in something you are giving it all your attention, e.g. *She was engrossed in her book.*
[French *en gros* = in quantity]

Similar words: absorbed, immersed, involved

enhance, enhances, enhancing, enhanced
(verb) to improve and strengthen, e.g. *The herbs enhance the flavour of the meat.*
enhancement (noun)
[Old French *haucier* = to raise]

enjoy, enjoys, enjoying, enjoyed
(verb) If you enjoy something, you find pleasure and satisfaction in it.
enjoyably (adverb) **enjoyable** (adjective)
enjoyment (noun)

enlarge, enlarges, enlarging, enlarged
(verb) When you enlarge something, it gets bigger.
enlargement (noun)

enlist, enlists, enlisting, enlisted
1 (verb) If someone enlists, they join the army, navy or air force.
2 If you enlist someone's help, you persuade them to help you in something you are doing.

enmity
(noun) a feeling of anger or hatred for a person you strongly disagree with.

enormous
(adjective) very large in size, amount or degree.
enormously (adverb)

enough
(adjective, adverb) as much as is needed, e.g. *Do you have enough money?... They had walked enough for the day*

enquire, enquires, enquiring, enquired; also spelled **inquire**
(verb) to ask about something or someone.

enquiry, enquiries; also spelled **inquiry**
1 (noun) a question that you ask to find something out.
2 an investigation into something that has happened and that needs explaining, e.g. *the enquiry into the air crash.*

enrage, enrages, enraging, enraged
(verb) If something enrages you, it makes you very angry.
enraged (adjective)

enrich, enriches, enriching, enriched
(verb) to improve the quality or value of something, e.g. *Travelling enriches one's experience of life.*
enriched (adjective) **enrichment** (noun)

e is the most often used letter in the English language.

enrol, enrols, enrolling, enrolled
(verb) If you enrol, e.g. for a course or a college, you sign your name to become a member of it.
enrolment (noun)

ensign, ensigns
(noun) a flag flown by a ship to show what country that ship belongs to.
[Latin *insignia* = badge of office]

en suite (pronounced on **sweet**)
(adverb) If a bedroom has a bathroom en suite, it has a private bathroom that leads directly off it.
[French *en* + *suite* = in sequence]

ensure, ensures, ensuring, ensured
(verb) to make sure, e.g. *Please ensure that the oven is off before you go out.*

entangle, entangles, entangling, entangled
(verb) If something is entangled in something else, it is caught or tangled up in it.
entanglement (noun)

enter, enters, entering, entered
1 (verb) to go into somewhere.
2 If you enter a competition, race or examination, you take part in it.

enterprise, enterprises
1 (noun) a project or task, especially one involving boldness and effort.
2 Enterprise is having new ideas and being ready to start new projects.
3 An enterprise is a business or company.
[French *entreprendre* = to undertake]

enterprising
(adjective) ready to start new projects and tasks and full of boldness and new ideas, e.g. *an enterprising young architect.*

entertain, entertains, entertaining, entertained
1 (verb) If you entertain people, you keep them amused or interested.
2 If you entertain guests, you receive them into your house and give them food and hospitality.
entertaining (adjective)

entertainer, entertainers
(noun) someone whose job is to amuse and please audiences.

entertainment, entertainments
(noun) anything that people watch for pleasure, for example, shows and films.

enthusiast, enthusiasts (pronounced inth-**yooz**-ee-ast)
(noun) a person who is very interested in something.

enthusiastic
(adjective) showing a lot of excitement, eagerness or approval about something, e.g. *enthusiastic applause.*
enthusiasm (noun) **enthusiastically** (adverb)
[Greek *enthousiasmos* = inspired by the gods]

entice, entices, enticing, enticed
(verb) If you entice someone to do something, you tempt them to do it, e.g. *Tom tried to entice Jerry out of his mousehole.*
enticing (adjective) **enticingly** (adverb)
enticement (noun)

entire
(adjective) all of something, e.g. *He painted the entire fence blue.*
entirely (adverb)
[Latin *integer* = whole]

entitle, entitles, entitling, entitled
(verb) If something entitles you to have or do something, it gives you the right to have or do it, e.g. *Are you entitled to be a member of the club?*
entitlement (noun)

entrance, entrances (pronounced en-**trunss**)
1 (noun) the doorway or gate to a building etc.
2 A person's entrance is their arrival, e.g. *The glamorous star's entrance was spoiled when she tripped and fell down the stairs.*

entrance, entrances, entrancing, entranced (pronounced en-**transs**)
(verb) If something entrances you, it gives you a feeling of wonder and delight.
entranced (adjective) **entrancing** (adjective)

Similar word: fascinate

entrant, entrants
(noun) a person who officially enters a competition or an organization.

entrust, entrusts, entrusting, entrusted
(verb) If you entrust something to someone, you give them the care and protection of it, e.g. *I'm entrusting you with my car while I'm away.*

entry, entries
1 (noun) the act of entering a place.
2 any place through which you enter somewhere.
3 anything which is entered or recorded by writing etc., e.g. *He made an entry in his diary.*

Similar words: (sense 1) access, admission, admittance

enunciate, enunciates, enunciating, enunciated (pronounced in-**un**-see-ate)
(verb) to pronounce words clearly.
enunciation (noun)
[Latin *enuntiare* = to announce]

envelope, envelopes
(noun) a flat, folded paper container for letters.
[French *envelopper* = to wrap around]

envious
(adjective) full of envy, e.g. *She was envious of her neighbour's new car.*
enviously (adverb)

environment, environments
1 (noun) the circumstances, things and conditions that influence you, e.g. *Children need a secure environment.*
2 The environment is the natural world around us, e.g. *We need to protect the environment.*
environmental (adjective)
[Old French *environer* = to surround]

environmentalist, environmentalists
(noun) somebody who is concerned with the problems of the natural environment, such as pollution.

How many vivid expressions can you think of that could be used to describe a football match?

envy, envies, envying, envied
1 (noun) a feeling you have when you wish you could have the same as someone else has.
2 (verb) If you envy someone, you wish that you had the same as they have.

enzyme, enzymes
(noun) a chemical substance, usually a protein, produced by cells in the body.
[Greek *enzumos* = leavened]

epidemic, epidemics
(noun) the occurrence of a disease in one area, spreading quickly and affecting many people.
[Greek *epi* + *demos* = upon the people]

epilepsy
(noun) a condition of the brain which causes fits and periods of unconsciousness.
epileptic (noun and adjective)

epilogue, epilogues (pronounced **ep**-ill-og)
(noun) a passage added to the end of a book or play as a conclusion.

episode, episodes
1 (noun) an incident or event, e.g. *The episode of the mayor's lost wig was most unfortunate.*
2 one of several parts of, e.g. a TV or radio drama. e.g. *an episode of East Enders.*
[Greek *epeisodion* = something added]

epistle, epistles (pronounced ip-**piss**-sl)
1 (noun; formal) a letter.
2 The Epistles are the books in the New Testament originally written as letters.

epitaph, epitaphs (pronounced **ep**-it-ahf)
(noun) a short inscription on a gravestone about the person who has died.
[Greek *epitaphios* = over a tomb]

eponymous (pronounced ip-**on**-im-uss)
(adjective; formal) The eponymous hero or heroine of a play, film or book is the person whose name forms its title, e.g. *Hamlet, the eponymous hero of Shakespeare's play.*
[Greek *eponumos* = given as a name]

equal, equals, equalling, equalled
1 (adjective) having the same size, amount, value or standard.
2 (verb) If one thing equals another, it is as good as the other, e.g. *Nobody can equal her skill on the piano.*
equally (adverb)
[Latin *aequalis* = level]

Similar words: (sense 2) match, parallel

equality
(noun) the same rights etc. for all members of a society, e.g. *There should be equality of opportunity for all.*

equalize, equalizes, equalizing, equalized; also spelled **equalise**
(verb) to make something equal, e.g. *He scored the equalizing goal.*
equalization (noun) **equalizer** (noun)

equation, equations
(noun) a mathematical formula stating that two amounts or values are the same, using the = sign e.g. $3x + 4y = 23.$

equator (pronounced ik-**way**-tor)
(noun) an imaginary line drawn round the middle of the earth, lying halfway between the north and south poles.
equatorial (adjective)

equestrian (pronounced ik-**west**-ree-an)
(adjective) relating to horses.
[Latin *equus* = horse]

equidistant
(adjective) Things that are equidistant are at an equal distance from a central point, e.g. *Perth and Edinburgh are equidistant from Glasgow.*

equilateral
(adjective) An equilateral triangle has sides that are the same length and angles that are the same.

equinox, equinoxes
(noun) one of the two days in the year when the day and night are of equal length. The autumn equinox occurs on about September 22, and the spring equinox occurs on about March 21.
[Latin *aequinoctium* = equal night]

equip, equips, equipping, equipped
(verb If someone equips you with something, or if you equip yourself with it, you obtain it for a particular purpose, e.g. *You will be equipped for the journey... His training equipped him with all the qualities needed for the job.*
[Old French *esciper* = to fit out a ship]

Similar words: outfit, rig, kit out

equipment
(noun) all the things that are needed or used for a particular job or activity.

Similar words: kit, gear, apparatus, tackle

equivalent, equivalents
1 (adjective) equal or nearly equal.
2 (noun) something that has the same use, size, value or effect as something else, e.g. *A quilt is the equivalent of 3 blankets.*
equivalence (noun)

Similar words: (noun) equal, parallel, match

era, eras (pronounced **ear**-a)
(noun) a period of time, usually several years, marked by a particular feature, e.g. *The post-war era was noted for things being in short supply.*
[Latin *aera* = copper counters used for counting, hence for counting time]

Similar words: period, age

eradicate, eradicates, eradicating, eradicated
(verb) to get rid of or destroy something completely.
eradication (noun)
[Latin *eradicare* = to uproot, from *radix* = root]

erase, erases, erasing, erased
(verb) to remove or rub something out.

eraser, erasers
(noun) a rubber used for rubbing out writing.

erect, erects, erecting, erected
1 (verb) to put up, e.g. *He erected the tent.*

Names of cities, towns and villages begin with capital letters, e.g. Aberdeen, Wick, Lower Upham.

2 (adjective) in a straight and upright position, e.g. *She stood on the stage, tall and erect.*
erectly (adverb) **erection** (noun)

Similar words: (adjective) upright, vertical, straight

erode, erodes, eroding, eroded
(verb) If something erodes or is eroded, it is gradually worn or eaten away and destroyed, e.g. *Rocks are eroded by wind, water and ice.*
[Latin *erodere* = to gnaw away]

erosion
(noun) the gradual wearing or eating away and destruction of something, e.g. *soil erosion... the erosion of his authority.*

errand, errands
(noun) a short trip to do a job for someone.
[Old English *ar* = messenger]

erratic
(adjective) not following a regular pattern or a fixed course, e.g. *The bowler's length was erratic.*
erratically (adverb)
[Latin *errare* = to wander]

error, errors
(noun) a mistake.
[Latin *errare* = to wander]

erupt, erupts, erupting, erupted
1 (verb) When a volcano erupts, it violently throws out a lot of hot lava, ash and steam.
2 When a situation erupts, it starts up suddenly and violently, e.g. *Fighting erupted in the city.*
eruption (noun)

escalate, escalates, escalating, escalated
(verb) If a situation escalates, it becomes greater in size, seriousness or intensity.

escalator, escalators
(noun) a mechanical, moving staircase.

escapade, escapades
(noun) an adventurous or daring incident that causes trouble.

escape, escapes, escaping, escaped
(verb) to get free from a person, place or thing.

escort, escorts
(noun) a person or vehicle that travels with another to protect or guide them.

especially
(adverb) specially or particularly, e.g. *He was especially good at athletics.*
especial (adjective)
[Latin *specialis* = individual]

espionage (pronounced **ess**-pee-on-ahj)
(noun) the act of spying to obtain secret information, especially to find out military or political secrets.
[French *espionner* = to spy]

essay, essays, essaying, essayed
(noun) a short piece of writing on a subject.
[French *essai* = try]

essential, essentials
1 (adjective) vitally important and absolutely necessary.

2 (noun) An essential is something that you think is important or necessary.
essentially (adverb)

establish, establishes, establishing, established
1 (verb) to create or set something up in a permanent way.
2 If you establish that something is the case, you find out that it is true, e.g. *They established where the murder had taken place.*
establishment (noun) **established** (adjective)
[Latin *stabilire* = to make firm]

Similar words: (sense 1) to found, set up

estate, estates
1 (noun) a large area of privately-owned land in the country, together with all the property on it.
2 an area of land which has been developed for housing or industry.
[Latin *status* = condition or state]

estate agent, agents
(noun) someone that sells houses and land.

estimate, estimates, estimating, estimated
1 (verb) If you estimate an amount or quantity, you work out an approximate figure.
2 (noun) an approximate calculation of an amount or quantity.
3 a formal statement from a company who you may wish to do some work for you, telling you how much a job is likely to cost, e.g. *Please give us an estimate for painting the walls.*
estimation (noun)
[Latin *aestimare* = to assess the worth of]

estuary, estuaries (pronounced **est**-yoo-ree)
(noun) the wide part of a river near where it joins the sea and where fresh water mixes with salt water.

eternal
(adjective) lasting forever, or seeming to last forever, e.g. *his eternal grumbling.*
eternally (adverb)

Similar words: perpetual, everlasting, endless

eternity, eternities
1 (noun) time without end, especially the state some people believe they will pass into when they die.
2 a period of time which seems to go on for ever, e.g. *This winter seems to be lasting an eternity!*

ethics
(noun) moral beliefs about right and wrong, e.g. *The medical profession has a code of ethics... I don't agree with his business ethics.*
ethical (adjective)
[Greek *ēthos* = custom]

ethnic
1 (adjective) involving different racial groups of people, e.g. *ethnic minorities.*
2 characteristic of a particular racial or cultural group, e.g. *ethnic food.*
ethnically (adverb)
[Greek *ethnos* = race]

ethos (pronounced **eeth**-oss)
(noun) a set of ideas and attitudes that is

We take these words from France: ballet chalet brunette chef fiancé garage.

characteristic of a particular group of people, e.g. *The school had a strong ethos of discipline and work.*
[Greek *ethos* = custom]

etiquette (pronounced et-ik-ket)
(noun) a set of rules for behaviour in a particular social situation.

etymology (pronounced et-tim-ol-loj-ee)
(noun) the study of the origin, development and changes of form in words.
etymological (adjective) **etymologist** (noun)

Eucharist, (pronounced yoo-kar-rist)
(noun) a religious ceremony, also called communion, in which Christians remember and celebrate Christ's last meal with his disciples.
eucharistic (adjective)
[Greek *eucharistia* = thanksgiving]

euphemism, euphemisms (pronounced you-fum-izzum)
(noun) a polite word or expression used instead of one that might offend or upset people, e.g. to 'pass on' is a euphemism for 'to die'.
euphemistic (adjective) **euphemistically** (adverb)
[Greek *eu-* = pleasant + *phēmē* = speech]

European, Europeans
1 (adjective) belonging to Europe.
2 (noun) someone who comes from Europe.

evacuate, evacuates, evacuating, evacuated
(verb) If you evacuate a place, you move out of it for a period of time, usually because it is dangerous, e.g. *The entire building was evacuated... Many children were evacuated to the countryside during the Second World War.*
evacuation (noun) **evacuee** (noun)

evade, evades, evading, evaded
1 (verb) If you evade something or someone, you keep moving to keep out of their way, e.g. *She managed to evade the goal defence.*
2 If you evade a problem or question, you avoid dealing with it.
evasion (noun) **evasive** adjective)

evaluate, evaluates
(verb) If you evaluate something, you decide on its quality, value or significance.
evaluation (noun)

evaporate, evaporates, evaporating, evaporated
1 (verb) When a liquid evaporates, it gradually changes into a gas.
2 If a substance has been evaporated, the liquid has been taken out so that the remainder is dry or concentrated.
evaporation (noun)
[Latin *vapor* = steam]

eve
(noun) The eve of a particular event or occasion is the evening or day before it.

even, evens, evening, evened
1 (adjective) flat and level, e.g. *an even surface.*
2 regular and without variation, e.g. *an even heartbeat.*
3 calm and not easily excited, e.g. *John has an even temper.*

4 In maths, numbers that are even can be exactly divided by two, e.g. 4; 12; 78; 3,486.
5 Scores that are even are exactly the same.
6 (adverb) in spite of, e.g. *Even if it rains I'd like to go to the show jumping.*
7 Even is used to suggest that something is unexpected or surprising, e.g. *She even had to tell him how to make a cup of tea.*
8 Even is also used to say that something is greater in degree than something else, e.g. *She's even better than Sue at swimming.*
9 (verb) If you even things out, you make them level.
evenly (adverb) **evenness** (noun)

Similar words: (adjective: sense 1) level, straight, horizontal
(adjective: sense 5) level, equal, fifty-fifty

evening, evenings
(noun) the part of the day between late afternoon and the time you go to bed.

event, events
1 (noun) something that happens, especially when it is unusual or important.
2 one of the races or competitions that are part of an organized occasion, especially in sports, e.g. *the mile event.*
3 (phrase) If you say **in any event**, you mean whatever happens, e.g. *In any event I'll see her.*
4 If you say **in the event of** something happening, you mean if a thing happens, e.g. *In the event of your missing your train, there is a later bus.*

Similar words: (noun: sense 1) happening, occasion, occurrence, incident, episode

eventful
(adjective) full of interesting, exciting and important events.

eventing
(noun) a name for horse-riding competitions which involve dressage, cross-country and show jumping.

eventual
(adjective) happening in the end, e.g. *Despite their poor start, Manchester City were the eventual winners.*

eventually
(adjective) at last, e.g. *We eventually arrived.*

ever
(adverb) e.g. *Have you ever been to America?*

evergreen, evergreens
(noun) a tree or bush which has green leaves all the year round.

everlasting
(adjective) never coming to an end.

every
1 (adjective) e.g. *He sits in the same place every day.*
2 (phrase) **Every bit as** means equally, e.g. *Jane is every bit as good as you at sports.*
3 **Every other** means alternate, e.g. *Every other day* = *Monday, Wednesday, Friday, Sunday, etc.*

The word 'pen' comes from Latin – *penna* – meaning a feather. Early quill pens were cut from feathers.

everybody
(pronoun) e.g. *Have you told everybody?*

everyday
(adjective) usual or ordinary, e.g. *a normal everyday life... my everyday routine.*

everyone
(pronoun) e.g. *Everyone knows she has got the part.*

everything
(pronoun) e.g. *She remembered everything for the picnic, including the wine.*

everywhere
(adverb) e.g. *There was mud everywhere in the kitchen.*

evict, evicts, evicting, evicted
(verb) to officially force someone to leave a place they are occupying.
eviction (noun)
[Latin *evincere* = to conquer utterly]

Similar words: eject, throw out, kick out

evidence
1 (noun) anything you see, experience, read or are told which gives you reason to believe something.
2 the information used in court to attempt to prove or disprove something.

evident
(adjective) easily noticed or understood, e.g. *It was evident that Fiona was happy.*
evidently (adverb)
[Latin *evidens* = making itself seen]

evil
(adjective) Something that is evil is wrong or bad, e.g. *Frankenstein devised an evil plan.*
evilly (adverb)

evolution (pronounced ee-vol-**oo**-shn)
1 (noun) a process of gradual change and development over a period of time.
2 In biology, evolution is a process of gradual change taking place over many generations during which animals, plants and insects slowly change as they adapt to different environments.

evolve, evolves, evolving, evolved
1 (verb) to grow or develop gradually over a period of time.
2 When plants, animals and insects evolve, they gradually change and develop into different forms over a period of time, e.g. *Darwin suggested that humans have evolved from apes.*
[Latin *evolvere* = to unfold]

ewe, ewes (pronounced **yoo**)
(noun) a female sheep.

ex-
(prefix) former, e.g. *her ex-husband.*

exact
(adjective) accurate and precise as opposed to approximate, e.g. *the exact amount.*

exactly
(adverb) with complete accuracy and precision.

exaggerate, exaggerates, exaggerating, exaggerated
(verb) to say something which is more than the true facts, e.g. *Haven't I told you a million times not to exaggerate?*
exaggeration (noun)
[Latin *exaggerare* = to heap up]

Similar words: magnify, overemphasize

exam, exams
(noun) an official test set to assess your knowledge or skill in a subject. It is an abbreviation of the word 'examination'.

examination, examinations
1 (noun) an official test set to assess your knowledge and skill in a subject.
2 A medical examination is a physical inspection of someone in order to assess the state of their health or to diagnose disease.

examine, examines, examining, examined
1 (verb) If you examine something, you look carefully at it or inspect it in detail.
2 To examine someone means to assess their knowledge or skill in a particular subject by testing them.
examiner (noun)
[Latin *examinare* = to weigh]

Similar words: (sense 1) inspect, analyse, check, test, study

example, examples
1 (noun) something which represents or is typical of a group or set.
2 someone or something special that people can imitate and learn from, e.g. *She was an example to her class.*
[Latin *exemplum* = pattern or model]

Similar words: (sense 1) sample, specimen, illustration, instance

exasperated
(adjective) If you are exasperated with someone, they have made you annoyed and angry, e.g. *The teacher was exasperated with the class.*
exasperating (adjective) **exasperation** (noun)

excavate, excavates, excavating, excavated
1 (verb) to remove earth from the ground by digging.
2 When archaeologists excavate objects, they carefully dig them up from the ground to discover information about the past.
excavation (noun) **excavator** (noun)
[Latin *excavare* = to hollow out]

exceed, exceeds, exceeding, exceeded
(verb) To exceed, for example a limit, means to go beyond it or to become greater than it, e.g. *Do not exceed the speed limit.*

excel, excels, excelling, excelled
(verb) If someone excels in something, they are very good at doing it.
[Latin *excellere* = to rise up]

excellent
(adjective) very good indeed.
excellence (noun) **excellently** (adverb)

Language evolves. For example: *alright, newt, hopefully, finalize, ongoing, academic.*

Similar words: great, fine, superb, outstanding, splendid

except
(preposition, conjunction) apart from, e.g. *I'll eat anything except rice pudding.*
[Old French *excepter* = to leave out]

exception, exceptions
(noun) someone or something not included in a general statement, judgement or rule, e.g. *I never forget a face, but in your case I'll make an exception.*

exceptional
(adjective) very unusual, or unusually talented.
exceptionally (adverb)

excerpt, excerpts
(noun) a short piece of writing or music taken from a larger piece.
[Latin *excerptum* = something picked out]

excess, excesses
1 (noun) a larger amount of something than is needed, permitted or usual, e.g. *The body should not have an excess of sugar.*
2 (adjective) more than is needed, permitted or usual, e.g. *You have to pay to take excess baggage on the plane.*
3 (phrase) **In excess of** a particular amount means more than that amount, e.g. *Her savings are in excess of £10,000.*
4 If you do something **to excess**, you do it too much, e.g. *He drinks to excess.*

excessive
(adjective) beyond the normal limit.
excessively (adverb)

Similar words: extreme, overdone, over the top

exchange, exchanges, exchanging, exchanged
1 (verb) To exchange things means to swap one thing for another, e.g. *They exchanged smiles... exchanging gifts.*
2 (noun) a place where people trade and do business, e.g. *the Stock Exchange.*
3 A telephone exchange is a building where phone calls are connected.
[Latin *cambire* = to trade]

excitable
(adjective) easily excited.

excite, excites, exciting, excited
(verb) If someone or something excites you, they make you feel happy and nervous or interested and enthusiastic.
excited (adjective) **excitedly** (adverb)
exciting (adjective) **excitement** (noun)

Similar words: thrill, electrify, exhilarate

exclaim, exclaims, exclaiming, exclaimed
(verb) to cry out or speak suddenly or loudly.

exclamation, exclamations
(noun) a word or phrase spoken suddenly to express a strong feeling such as surprise, pain, or anger.

exclamation mark, marks
(noun) a punctuation mark ! used in writing to express shock, surprise or anger.

exclude, excludes, excluding, excluded
(verb) If you exclude someone or something, you leave them out or do not consider them.
exclusion (noun)

exclusive
1 (adjective) belonging to or providing for a small, privileged group of people, e.g. *an exclusive night club.*
2 not including, e.g. *The price is exclusive of VAT.*
exclusively (adverb)

Similar words: (sense 1) private, select

excrement (pronounced eks-krim-ment)
(noun) the solid waste matter that is passed out of a person's or animal's body through the bowels.

excrete, excretes, excreting, excreted
(verb) When you excrete waste matter from your body, you get rid of it, for example by going to the lavatory or by sweating.
excretion (noun) **excretory** (adjective)

excruciating (pronounced iks-kroo-shee-ate-ing)
(adjective) unbearably painful.
excruciatingly (adverb)
[Latin *excruciare* = to torture]

excursion, excursions
(noun) a short journey or outing.

excuse, excuses, excusing, excused
1 (noun) a reason which you give to defend something you have done or have failed to do or to avoid doing something.
2 (verb) If you excuse someone for something wrong they have done, you forgive them for it.
4 If you excuse someone from a duty or responsibility, you let them off it.
5 If you ask someone to excuse you, you are asking them to allow you to leave.

execute, executes, executing, executed
1 (verb) to kill someone as a punishment for a crime.
2 If you execute, e.g. a plan, you carry it out.
execution (noun) **executioner** (noun)
[Latin *exsequi* = to follow up, carry out, or punish]

executive, executives
(noun) a person who is employed by a company at a senior level.
[Latin *exsequor* = to carry out]

exempt
(adjective) excused from a rule, duty or obligation, e.g. *He was exempt from taxes.*
exemption (noun)
[Latin *exemptus* = removed or freed]

exercise, exercises, exercising, exercised
1 (verb) to do any activity which helps you to get fit or to remain healthy.
2 (noun) Exercises are also activities which you do to practise and train for a particular skill, e.g. *piano exercises... mathematical exercises.*
[Latin *exercere* = to keep busy or to train]

These words are exceptions to spelling rules and need to be learned: wholly duly truly ninth argument.

exhale, exhales, exhaling, exhaled
(verb) to breathe out.
exhalation (noun)

exhaust, exhausts, exhausting, exhausted
1 (verb) If you exhaust a supply of, for example
money or food, you use it up completely, e.g.
Finally, Scott's team had exhausted their food.
2 (noun) the gas or steam produced by the engine
of a vehicle.
exhaustion (noun)
[Latin *exhaustus* = empty or drained]

exhausted
(adjective) absolutely tired out.

Similar words: worn out, drained, weary, shattered.

exhibition, exhibitions
1 (noun) a public display of works of art,
products, skills or activities.
2 (phrase) If you **make an exhibition of yourself**,
you behave stupidly in public so that people
notice you.
exhibit (verb) **exhibitor** (verb)
[Latin *exhibere* = to hold out]

exhibitionist, exhibitionists
(noun) someone who tries to get people's
attention all the time, especially by stupid
behaviour or boasting.
exhibitionism (noun)

exhilarating
(pronounced ig-**zil**-ler-ating)
(adjective) thrilling and exciting, e.g. *The
Astro-glide was very exhilarating.*
exhilarate (verb) **exhilaration** (noun)
[Latin *exhilarare* = to make cheerful]

exile
1 (noun) If someone is in exile, they live in a
foreign country because they cannot live in their
own country, usually for political reasons.
2 An exile is someone who lives in exile.

exist, exists, existing, existed
(verb) to live or to be real.
[Latin *exsistere* = to come forth or appear]

existence
1 (noun) the state of being or existing, e.g. *The
United Nations has been in existence since 1945.*
2 a way of living or being, e.g. *He led a lonely
existence in his cottage on the moor.*

exit, exits, exiting, exited
1 (noun) a way out of a place.
2 (verb) to leave, e.g. *Exit stage left.*
[Latin *exitus* = a way out]

exorcize, exorcizes, exorcizing, exorcized; also
spelled **exorcise**
(verb) To exorcize an evil spirit means to force it
to leave a person or place by means of prayers.
exorcism (noun) **exorcist** (noun)

exotic
1 (adjective) coming from a foreign country, e.g.
an exotic flower.
2 strange or very unusual, e.g. *exotic paintings.*
[Greek *exotikos* = foreign]

expand, expands, expanding, expanded
(verb) If something expands or you expand it, it
becomes larger in number or size.
expansion (noun)
[Latin *expandere* = to spread out]

expanse, expanses
(noun) a very large or widespread area, e.g. *an
expanse of sand and desert.*
expansive (adjective)

Similar words: area, space, stretch, sweep

expect, expects, expecting, expected
(verb) If you expect something, you believe that
it is going to happen or arrive.

Similar words: anticipate, hope, look forward to

expectant
(adjective) An expectant mother or father is
someone whose baby is going to be born soon.
expectantly (adverb)

expectation, expectations
(noun) a strong belief or hope that something
will happen or should happen.
expectancy (noun)

expecting
(adjective; informal) A woman who is expecting
is pregnant.

expedition, expeditions
(noun) an organized journey made for a special
purpose, e.g. to explore somewhere.
expeditionary (adjective)

expel, expels, expelling, expelled
(verb) If someone is expelled from a school or
club, they are officially told to leave because
they have behaved badly.
expulsion (noun)

expendable
(adjective) no longer useful or necessary, and
therefore able to be got rid of, e.g. *Drink cans
are not as expendable as we used to think.*

expenditure, expenditures
1 (noun) the total amount of money spent on
something.
2 The expenditure of money, energy or time is
the use of it for a particular purpose.

expense, expenses
1 (noun) the money that something costs.
2 (plural noun) Someone's expenses are the
money they spend while doing something
connected with their work, which is paid back to
them by their employers, e.g. *travelling expenses*
3 (phrase) If you do something **at the expense of**
someone or something else, you do it in a way
that harms them, e.g. *Industry has done well
here at the expense of agriculture.*
4 If you do something **at someone's expense**,
they pay the cost, e.g. *She went on the course at
her own expense.*

Similar words: (sense 1) expenditure, outlay

expensive
(adjective) costing a lot of money.
expensively (adverb) **expensiveness** (noun)

experience, experiences, experiencing, experienced
1 (noun) something that happens to you, or something that you do, especially something new or unusual, e.g. *Going on the QE2 for the first time was a terrific experience.*
2 Experience consists of skills or knowledge gained through doing certain things, e.g. *He had 23 years' experience of steam engines.*
3 (verb) If you experience a situation or feeling, it happens to you or you are affected by it.
[Latin *experiri* = to test]

Similar words: (verb) undergo, know, go through

experienced
(adjective) skilled or knowledgeable through doing something for a long time.

experiment, experiments, experimenting, experimented
1 (verb) to test something, either to find out its effect or to prove something.
2 (noun) a scientific test.
experimentation (noun) **experimental** (adjective)
experimentally (adverb) **experimenter** (noun)
[Latin *experimentum* = trial or test]

expert, experts
1 (noun) someone who is very skilled at doing something or very knowledgeable about a particular subject.
2 (adjective) very skilled or knowledgeable, e.g. *He was an expert dancer.*
expertly (adverb)
[Latin *expertus* = known by experience]

Similar words: (noun) authority, master, specialist, ace

expertise (pronounced eks-per-**teez**)
(noun) special skill or knowledge.

expire, expires, expiring, expired
1 (verb) When something expires, it reaches the end of the time for which it is valid, e.g. *My bus pass expires next week.*
2 (literary) to die.
expiry (noun) **expiration** (noun)

Similar words: (sense 1) lapse, run out

explain, explains, explaining, explained
(verb) to give details about something or reasons for it so that it can be understood.
explanation (noun) **explanatory** (adjective)
[Latin *explanare* = to level out]

Similar words: interpret, illustrate, clarify, spell out

explode, explodes, exploding, exploded
1 (verb) to burst open with great violence, often causing damage.
2 When something increases suddenly and rapidly, it can be said to explode, e.g. *The population in India is exploding.*
3 If someone explodes, they react violently or angrily to something.
[Latin *explodere* = to clap hands, from *ex* = out of + *plodere* = to clap]

exploit, exploits, exploiting, exploited
1 (verb) If someone exploits you, they unfairly use your work or ideas for their own purpose, e.g. *In the 19th century, children were exploited in mills and as chimney sweeps.*
exploitation (noun)
2 (noun) An exploit is something brave or interesting that you have done.
[noun: French *exploit* = accomplishment]

explore, explores, exploring, explored
(verb) to travel in a place to find out what it is like.
exploration (noun) **exploratory** (adjective)
explorer (noun)

explosion, explosions
(noun) a sudden violent burst of energy, e.g. one caused by a bomb.

explosive, explosives
1 (adjective) capable of exploding or likely to explode.
2 An explosive situation is one which is in great danger of having serious or damaging effects.
3 (noun) a substance or device that can explode, e.g. *He was an expert with explosives.*

export, exports, exporting, exported
1 (verb) to sell goods to another country and send them there.
2 (noun) Exports are goods which are sold and sent to another country.
exporter (noun)
[Latin *exportare* = to carry away]

expose, exposes, exposing exposed
1 (verb) To expose something means to uncover it and make it visible.
2 To expose a person to something dangerous means to put them in a situation in which it might harm them, e.g. *exposed to radiation.*
3 To expose a person or situation means to reveal the truth about them, especially when it involves dishonest or shocking behaviour, e.g. *The TV preacher was exposed as a liar and a cheat.*
4 To expose a film means to let light reach it.
[Latin *exponere* = to set out]

exposure, exposures
1 (noun) the harmful effect on the body caused by very cold weather, e.g. *After a night on the mountain, they were suffering from exposure.*
2 the length of time a film is exposed to the light, resulting in a single photograph; also the photograph itself.

express, expresses, expressing, expressed
1 (verb) When you express an idea or feeling, you show what you think or feel by saying or doing something.
2 If you express a quantity in a particular form, you write it down in that form, e.g. *0.5 is ½ expressed as a decimal.*
3 (adjective) very fast, e.g. *an express train.*
4 (noun) a fast train or coach which stops at only a few places.
[Latin *expressus* = squeezed out]

expression, expressions
1 (noun) a word or phrase used in communicating, e.g. *slang expressions.*

Idioms. What does it mean to: be an old hand; have the upper hand; have a free hand?

2 The expression of ideas or feelings is the showing of them through words, actions or art.
3 the look on someone's face which shows what they are thinking or feeling.

expressive
1 (adjective) showing feelings clearly.
2 full of expression, e.g. *an expressive dancer.*
expressively (adverb) **expressiveness** (noun)

expulsion, expulsions
(noun) the act of expelling or being expelled, e.g. *His expulsion from school was long overdue.*

expurgate, expurgates, expurgating, expurgated
(verb; formal) If a book or text is expurgated, the parts in it which are obscene or offensive are removed.
expurgation (noun)
[Latin *expurgare* = to clean out]

exquisite
(adjective) extremely beautiful and pleasing.
exquisitely (adverb) **exquisiteness** (noun)

extend, extends, extending, extended
1 (verb) If something extends for a distance, it continues and stretches into the distance.
2 If something extends over a period of time, it continues for that time.
3 If you extend something, you make it larger or longer, e.g. *She extended her visit by 3 weeks.*

extension, extensions
1 (noun) a room or building which is added to an existing building.
2 an extra period of time, e.g. *The pub applied for an extension on New Year's Eve.*
3 an additional phone connected to the same line as another telephone.

extensive
1 (adjective) covering a large area.
2 very great in effect, e.g. *extensive damage.*
extensively (adverb)

extent, extents
(noun) the length, area, size or scale of something.

exterior, exteriors
(noun) the outside, for example of a building.

exterminate, exterminates, exterminating, exterminated
(verb) When animals or people are exterminated, they are deliberately killed in large numbers.
extermination (noun)
[Latin *exterminare* = to drive away]

external, externals
(adjective) existing on the outside of something, e.g. *We had a new external door fitted.*
externally (adverb)

extinct
1 (adjective) An extinct species of animal or plant is no longer in existence.
2 An extinct volcano is no longer likely to erupt.
extinction (noun)

extinguish, extinguishes, extinguishing, extinguished
(verb) to put out, for example a fire.
extinguisher (noun)
[Latin *extinguere* = to quench]

extortionate
(adjective) more expensive than seems fair, e.g. *Most pizzas are extortionate in price for what you get and for the tiny sum they cost to make.*

extra, extras
1 (adjective) more than is usual, necessary or expected.
2 (noun) An extra in a film is a person who is hired to play a very small, non-speaking part in it.

Similar words: (adjective) further, supplementary, additional

extra-
(prefix) outside or beyond, e.g. *extra-curricular activities.*
[Latin *exterus* = outward]

extra-sensory perception or **ESP**
(noun) the apparent ability to know things beyond the reach of the 5 ordinary senses as, for example, in fortune telling and telepathy.

extract, extracts, extracting, extracted
1 (verb) To extract something means to take it out or get it out, often by force.
2 If you extract information from someone, you get it from them with difficulty.
3 (noun) a small section taken from a book, piece of music, play or film.
[Latin *extractus* = drawn forth]

extraction
1 (noun) Your extraction is the country or people that your family originally comes from, e.g. *He's a dentist of Irish extraction.*
2 the process of taking something out of a place, e.g. *a tooth extraction.*

extraordinary (pronounced ex-**tror**-din-erry)
(adjective) unusual or surprising.
extraordinarily (adverb)
[It means literally 'outside the ordinary'.]

Similar words: exceptional, phenomenal, remarkable, rare, unusual

extraterrestrial
(adjective) existing beyond the earth's atmosphere.
[Latin *extra* + *terra* = outside the earth]

extravagant
(adjective) spending or costing too much money, e.g. *The President's wife was an extravagant woman who made shopping a way of life.*
extravagantly (adverb) **extravagance** (noun)
[Latin *extra* + *vagans* = wandering outside]

extreme, extremes
1 (adjective) very great in degree or intensity, e.g. *extreme heat.*
2 at the furthest point or edge of something, e.g. *the extreme edge of the cliff.*
3 (noun) An extreme is the highest or furthest

There is a silent a in each of these words: aisle extraordinary parliament.

degree of something, e.g. *Now, Sidney, shooting your parents just to go on the orphans' picnic is really taking things to the extreme.*
extremely (adverb)
[Latin *extremus* = outermost]

extremist, extremists
(noun) a person who uses severe or unreasonable methods or behaviour, e.g. *The rioters were political extremists.*
extremism (noun)

extrovert, extroverts
1 (noun) a person who is more interested in other people and the world around them than their own thoughts and feelings.
2 (adjective) active, lively and sociable.
[Latin *extra* = outwards + *vertere* = to turn]

exuberant
(adjective) full of energy, excitement and cheerfulness.
exuberantly (adverb) **exuberance** (noun)
[Latin *exuberans* = abundantly fruitful]

eye, eyes, eyeing or **eying, eyed**
1 (noun) the part of the head that you see with.
2 If you have an eye for something, you can recognize it and make good judgements about it.
3 (verb) To eye something means to look at it carefully or suspiciously.
4 (phrase) If two people **see eye to eye**, they agree with each other.

eyeball, eyeballs
(noun) the part of the eye underneath the eyelid.

eyebrows
(plural noun) the two areas of hair on your forehead just above the eyes.

eyelashes
(plural noun) the hairs at the end of your eyelids.

eyelid, eyelids
(noun) the flap of skin which moves up and down over the eye.

eye-opener, eye-openers
(noun) If something you find out is an eye-opener, it is very surprising or revealing, e.g. *Hearing him being so rude to the old lady was a real eye-opener for me.*

eyesight
(noun) the ability to see.

eyesore, eyesores
(noun) Something that is an eyesore is extremely ugly, e.g. *That gasworks is a real eyesore!*

eyewitness, eyewitnesses
(noun) a person who has seen an event and can describe what happened.

eyrie, eyries (pronounced **ear**-ree)
(noun) the nest of an eagle or other bird of prey, usually built on a cliff or mountain.

F

fable, fables
(noun) a story intended to teach a moral lesson, e.g. *Aesop's fables.*
[Latin *fabula* = story]

fabric, fabrics
(noun) cloth, e.g. *a crisp, cotton fabric.*
[Latin *fabrica* = building work]

fabricate, fabricates, fabricating, fabricated
1 (verb) If you fabricate a story or an explanation, you make it up to deceive people.
2 to make or manufacture something, e.g. *Pre-fabricated houses are built in a factory.*
fabrication (noun)
[Latin *fabricare* = to make]

fabulous
1 (adjective) wonderful or very impressive, e.g. *They missed a fabulous opportunity.*
2 not real, but happening or occurring in stories and legends, e.g. *fabulous animals and birds.*
fabulously (adverb)

face, faces, facing, faced
Selected meanings:
1 (noun) e.g. *Wipe that smile off your face.*
2 a surface, e.g. *the 6 faces of a cube... the face of a watch... the north face of Everest.*
3 (verb) to look directly towards something, e.g. *My house faces the church... She faced death with great courage.*
[Latin *facies* = form or appearance]

facetious (pronounced fas-**see**-shus)
(adjective) witty or amusing but in a rather silly or inappropriate way, e.g. *a facetious comment.*
[Latin *facetiae* = witty remarks]

facilitate, facilitates, facilitating, facilitated
(verb) To facilitate something means to make it easier to happen or be done, e.g. *Automatic doors facilitate an easy exit for shoppers.*

facility, facilities
(noun) a service, opportunity or piece of equipment which makes it possible to do something, e.g. *a hotel with sports facilities.*

Similar words: amenity, service

fact, facts
(noun) a piece of knowledge or information that is true or something that has actually happened.
factual (adjective) **factually** (adverb)
[Latin *factum* = something done]

facts of life
(plural noun) details about sexual intercourse and how babies are conceived and born.

factor, factors
1 (noun) something that helps to cause a result, e.g. *The tennis player's tantrums were a major factor in his defeat.*
2 The factors of a number are the whole numbers that will divide exactly into it, e.g. 2 and 5 are factors of 10.
[Latin *factor* = doer]

Letter F seems to have been made from the picture of a long, hooked implement.

factorial, factorials
(noun) In maths, the factorial of a number is the product of all the whole numbers from 1 to that number. For example, factorial 4 is 1 x 2 x 3 x 4.

factory, factories
(noun) a building or group of buildings where goods are made in large quantities.

fad, fads
(noun) a strong, temporary fashion or craze, e.g. *I had a fad on baked beans last month.*

faddy, faddier, faddiest
(adjective) fussy, especially about food.

fade, fades, fading, faded
(verb) If something fades, its colour, brightness or sound is gradually reduced.

fag, fags
1 (noun; informal) a cigarette.
2 If you describe something as a fag, you mean that it is boring or tiring.

fagged or **fagged out**
(adjective; informal) really exhausted.

faggot, faggots
(noun) a ball of chopped meat, bread and herbs.

Fahrenheit (pronounced **far-ren-hite**)
a scale of temperature in which the freezing point of water is 32° and the boiling point is 212°, devised by Gabriel Fahrenheit, a German physicist.

fail, fails, failing, failed
1 (verb) If someone fails to achieve something, they are not successful.
2 If you fail to do something that you should have done, you do not do it, e.g. *She failed to arrive at the time we arranged.*
3 (phrase) **Without fail** means absolutely regularly, e.g. *He comes every week without fail.*
[Latin *fallere* = to deceive or to let down]

Similar words: (sense 1) fall short, flop

failing
1 (noun) a fault or unsatisfactory feature in something or someone.
2 (preposition) used to introduce an alternative, e.g. *Failing that, we could always go to the pictures.*

fail-safe
(adjective) designed so that nothing dangerous can happen if part of a machine or system goes wrong, e.g. *These railway signals are fail-safe.*

failure, failures
1 (noun) a lack of success, e.g. *The attempt ended in failure.*
2 Your failure to do something is not doing something that you were expected to do, e.g. *We noticed his failure to appear at the party.*

Similar words: flop, washout

faint, fainter, faintest; faints, fainting, fainted
1 (adjective) A sound, colour or feeling that is faint has little strength or intensity.
2 (verb) to lose consciousness for a short time.

3 (adjective) If you feel faint, you feel weak, dizzy and unsteady.
faintly (adverb) **faintness** (noun)
[Old French *feint* = weak or sluggish]

Similar words: (verb) pass out, black out, swoon

faint-hearted
(adjective) having little courage and confidence.

fair, fairer, fairest; fairs
1 (adjective) reasonable or equal, e.g. *It's not fair that she should get more than me.*
2 moderately good or likely to be correct, e.g. *I had a pretty fair idea of the answer.*
fairly (adverb) **fairness** (noun)
3 having light-coloured hair or pale skin.
4 (noun) an open-air entertainment with rides, sideshows, etc.
[adjective: Old English *fæger* = lovely
noun: Latin *feria* = festival]

Similar words: (adjective: sense 1) just, impartial, unbiased

fairy, fairies
(noun) In stories, fairies are small, supernatural creatures with magical powers.
[Old French *faerie* = fairyland]

faith, faiths
1 (noun) a feeling of confidence, optimism or trust about something, e.g. *Put your faith in God.*
2 A faith is a particular religion.
3 (phrase) If you do something **in good faith**, your reasons are honest and sincere.
[Latin *fides* = trust]

Similar words: (sense 1) confidence, conviction, trust

faithful
(adjective) loyal to someone or something and remaining firm in support of them.
faithfully (adverb) **faithfulness** (noun)

Similar words: steadfast, loyal, staunch

fake, fakes, faking, faked
1 (noun) an imitation of something, made to trick people into thinking that it is genuine.
2 (verb) to pretend, or to make something which is not genuine to trick people.
e.g. *He faked illness... She faked a painting.*
3 (adjective) e.g. *a fake coin.*

Similar words: (noun) forgery, phoney, fraud, (adjective) bogus, counterfeit, fraudulent, sham, false

falcon, falcons
(noun) a bird of prey.
[Latin *falco* = hawk]

fall, falls, falling, fell, fallen
e.g. *Don't fall over that brick!*

fall out
(phrasal verb) If people fall out, they disagree and quarrel.

fall through
(phrasal verb) If an arrangement or plan falls through, it fails or is abandoned.

Fido, a popular name for a pet dog, comes from a Latin word meaning faithful or loyal.

fallout
(noun) radioactive particles that fall to the earth after a nuclear explosion.

false
(adjective) not real or genuine, e.g. *false teeth.*
falsely (adverb) **falseness** (noun)
[Latin *falsus* = false]

falter, falters, faltering, faltered
(verb) If someone or something falters, they hesitate or become unsure or unsteady, e.g. *His steps faltered as he neared the graveyard.*

fame
(noun) the state of being very well known, e.g. *The young Elvis's fame soon spread.*
[Latin *fama* = reputation]

Similar words: glory, stardom

famed
(adjective) very well known, e.g. *The church is famed for its flower festivals.*

familiar, familiars
1 (adjective) well known or easy to recognize, e.g. *familiar faces... The name sounded familiar.*
2 knowing something well, e.g. *I am, of course, familiar with your poetry.*
3 too informal and friendly in behaviour towards someone, e.g. *The girl was much too familiar with the teacher.*
familiarity (noun) **familiarize** (verb)
[Latin *familiaris* = known in the household]

Similar words: (sense 1) recognizable, well-known

family, families
1 (noun) a group consisting of parents and their children; also the wider group of people related to each other, including aunts and uncles, grandparents and cousins.
2 a group of related species of animals or plants, e.g. *the rose family.*
[Latin *familia* = household]

family tree, trees
(noun) a chart showing all the people in a family and their relationship over many generations.

famine, famines
(noun) a serious, large-scale shortage of food.
[Latin *fames* = hunger]

famished
(adjective; informal) very hungry.

famous
(adjective) very well known.

Similar words: eminent, renowned, legendary

fan, fans, fanning, fanned
1 (noun) a very enthusiastic supporter of someone or something.
2 an object which creates a draught of cool air when it moves.
3 (verb) to waft with cool air.
[noun: sense 1 — a short form of 'fanatic'; noun, verb: sense 2, 3 — Latin *vannus* = winnowing-fan]

Similar words: (noun: sense 1) supporter, enthusiast

fan out
(phrasal verb) If things or people fan out, they move outwards in different directions.

fanatic, fanatics
(noun) a person who is very extreme in their support for a cause or in their enthusiasm for a particular sport or activity.
fanatical (adjective) **fanatically** (adverb) **fanaticism** (noun)
[Latin *fanaticus* = possessed by a god]

fancy, fancies, fancying, fancied; fancier, fanciest
1 (verb) If you fancy something, you want to have it or do it, e.g. *She fancied a flat of her own.*
2 (adjective) Something that is fancy is special and elaborate, e.g. *He prefers good, plain food, nothing fancy.*
fanciful (adjective)
[Greek *phantasia* = imagination]

Similar words: (adjective) elaborate, ornate, flowery

fanfare, fanfares
(noun) a short, loud musical introduction to a special event, usually played on trumpets.

fang, fangs
(noun) Fangs are long, pointed teeth.

fantastic
1 (adjective) wonderful and very pleasing, e.g. *a fantastic film.*
2 strange and difficult to believe, e.g. *The truth is scarcely less fantastic than the fable.*
fantastically (adverb)

Similar words: (sense 1) wonderful, fabulous, marvellous

fantasy, fantasies
(noun) an imagined story or situation.
[Greek *phantasia* = imagination]

far, farther, farthest; further, furthest
(adverb, adjective) e.g. *We travelled far in our search... in a far corner of the room.*

Similar words: distant, remote

farce, farces
1 (noun) a humorous play in which ridiculous and unlikely situations occur.
2 a disorganized and ridiculous situation, e.g. *Your hotel booking system is a farce!*
farcical (adjective)

fare, fares, faring, fared
1 (noun) the amount charged for a journey on a bus, train or plane.
2 (verb) How someone fares in a particular situation is how well they cope, e.g. *They fared badly in the election.*
3 (noun; rather old-fashioned) The fare served in a restaurant is the range of food.
[Old English *faran* = to go]

Far East
(noun) The Far East consists of the countries of East Asia, including China, Japan and Malaysia.

farewell
(interjection) goodbye.

When we say *Goodbye* we are using a shortened form of 'God be with you'.

far-fetched
(adjective) unlikely to be true and difficult to believe, e.g. *Her story was a bit far-fetched.*

farm, farms, farming, farmed
1 (noun) an area of land together with buildings, used for growing crops and raising animals.
2 (verb) to own or manage a farm.
farmer (noun) **farming** (noun)
farmhouse (noun) **farmyard** (noun)
[Old French *ferme* = rented land]

far-out
(adjective; informal) unusual or strange.

farther, farthest
comparative and superlative forms of **far**.

fascinate, fascinates, fascinating, fascinated
(verb) If something fascinates you, it interests and delights you so much that your thoughts concentrate on it and nothing else.
fascinating (adjective)
[Latin *fascinare* = to bewitch]

Similar words: absorb, intrigue

fashion, fashions
1 (noun) a style of dress or way of behaving that is popular at a particular time.
2 (phrase) Something that has been done **after a fashion** has not been done very well.
[Latin *factio* = the making of something]

Similar words: trend, vogue, style, craze, fad

fashionable
(adjective) very popular with a lot of people at the same time.
fashionably (adverb)

Similar words: in, trendy, in vogue, up-to-date

fast, faster, fastest; fasts, fasting, fasted
1 (adjective, adverb) e.g. *Most sports cars are fast... She was sprinting very fast.*
2 (adverb) Something that is held fast is firmly fixed or settled, e.g. *fast asleep.*
3 (adjective) Fast colours or dyes will not run or come out when wet.
4 (noun) a period of time during which someone does not eat food.

Similar words: (adjective: sense 1) quick, speedy (adverb): quickly, rapidly, swiftly

fasten, fastens, fastening, fastened
(verb) to close something, do it up or attach it firmly to something else.
fastener (noun) **fastening** (noun)

Similar words: attach, bind, lock, latch, secure, bolt

fast food
(noun) hot food that is prepared in advance and served quickly after you have ordered it, e.g. burgers, fried chicken, pizzas.

fat, fatter, fattest
(adjective, noun), e.g. *Fat people are usually heavy... You really mustn't eat all the fat from that meat.*
fatness (noun) **fatty** (adjective)

Similar words: overweight, podgy, stout, plump

fatal
1 (adjective) causing death, e.g. *a fatal accident.*
2 very important or significant and likely to have an undesirable effect, e.g. *I made the fatal mistake of accepting the offer.*
fatally (adverb)
[Latin *fatum* = destiny]

Similar words: (sense 1) deadly, lethal, mortal, terminal

fatality, fatalities
(noun) a death caused by accident or violence, e.g. *The fire resulted in 3 fatalities.*

fate, fates
1 (noun) a power that is believed to control events, e.g. *It was fate that I met you.*
2 Someone's fate is what happens to them, e.g. *Several other companies suffered a similar fate.*
[Latin *fatum* = destiny]

Similar word: (sense 1) destiny

fateful
(adjective) having an important, often disastrous effect, e.g. *the fateful day of the election.*

father, fathers
1 (noun) A person's father is their male parent.
2 The father of something is the man who invented or started it, e.g. *King Alfred is sometimes called 'the father of the Navy'.*
3 Father is used to address a priest in some Christian churches.
4 another name for God, e.g. *Our Father.*
fatherly (adjective) **fatherhood** (noun)

father-in-law, fathers-in-law
A person's father-in-law is the father of their husband or wife.

fathom, fathoms
(noun) a unit for measuring the depth of water. (1 fathom = 1.83 metres)

fatigue, fatigues, fatiguing, fatigued (pronounced fat-**eeg**)
1 (noun) extreme tiredness.
2 (verb) If you are fatigued by something, it makes you extremely tired.
[Latin *fatigare* = to make tired]

fatten, fattens, fattening, fattened
(verb) If you fatten animals, you feed them so that they put on weight.

fattening
(adjective) likely to make you put on weight, e.g. *Don't eat cakes – they're fattening.*

fault, faults
1 (noun) If something bad is your fault, you are to blame for it.
2 (phrase) If you are **at fault**, you are mistaken or are to blame for something, e.g. *We failed to explain and are at fault in that.*
3 (noun) something wrong, e.g. in a person's character or a machine.
4 a large crack in rock caused by movement of the earth's crust.

5 In tennis, a fault is an incorrect service. In showjumping, faults are penalty points.
faultless (adjective) **faulty** (adjective)

Similar words: (sense 3) defect, failing, bug

fauna (pronounced **faw**-na)
(noun) The fauna of a particular area is all the animals found in that area, e.g. *the flora (flowers) and fauna of Africa*.
[from Fauna, a Roman goddess of the countryside]

favour, favours, favouring, favoured
1 (noun) If you do someone a favour, you do something helpful for them.
2 (phrase) Something that is **in someone's favour** is a help or advantage to them, e.g. *The wind was in our favour*.
3 If you are **in favour of** something, you agree with it and think it should happen.
4 (verb) If you favour something or someone, you prefer that person or thing.
favourable (adjective) **favourably** (adverb)
[Latin *favor* = goodwill]

favourite, favourites
1 (adjective) Your favourite person or thing is the one you like best.
2 (noun) In a race or contest, the favourite is the animal, person or team expected to win.

favouritism
(noun) behaviour in which someone is unfairly more helpful or more generous to one person than to other people.

fawn, fawns
1 (noun, adjective) pale yellowish-brown.
2 (noun) a very young deer.
[noun: sense 2: Old French *faon* = young deer]

fax, faxes
(noun) an exact copy of a document sent by a telephone fax machine.

fear, fears, fearing, feared
1 (noun) an unpleasant feeling of danger.
2 (verb) If you fear someone or something, you are frightened of them.
fearless (adjective) **fearlessly** (adverb)
[Old English *fær* = danger]

Similar words: (noun) dread, terror, fright, phobia

fearful
1 (adjective) afraid and full of fear.
2 extremely unpleasant or worrying, e.g. *the fearful risks of the operation*.
fearfully (adverb)

fearsome
(adjective) terrible or frightening, e.g. *The dog had a fearsome set of teeth*.

feast, feasts
(noun) a large, special meal for many people.
[Latin *festum* = feast]

feat, feats
(noun) an impressive and difficult achievement, e.g. *an extraordinary feat of strength*.
[Old French *fait* = action]

feather, feathers
(noun) one of the light, fluffy structures covering a bird's body.
feathery (adjective)

Similar words: plume, plumage

feature, features, featuring, featured
1 (noun) an interesting or important part or characteristic of something, e.g. *The silver mascot at the front is a feature of all Rolls Royce cars*.
2 Someone's features are the various parts of their face, e.g. *He had very small features*.
3 a special article or programme dealing with a particular subject; or the main film in a cinema programme.
4 (verb) To feature something means to include it or emphasize it as an important part or subject, e.g. *The circus featured Croako, the Wonder Frog*.
featureless (adjective)

February
(noun) the 2nd month of the year.
[from Februa, a Roman festival of purification]

fed up
(adjective; informal) unhappy or bored.

fee, fees
(noun) a charge or payment for a job, service or activity.

feeble, feebler, feeblest
(adjective) weak and ineffective.
[Latin *flebilis* = pathetic]

feed, feeds, feeding, fed
1 (verb) to give food to a person or animal.
2 to supply what is needed for something to operate, develop or exist, e.g. *Data is fed into the computer... He fed the ball into the scrum*.

feedback
1 (noun) comments and information about the quality or success of something, e.g. *We would like feedback on the course*.
2 an ear-piercing noise when sound from a loudspeaker etc. feeds back in through a microphone.

feel, feels, feeling, felt
(verb) e.g. *I feel happy today... She felt the radiator – it was boiling... He felt that the teacher was being unfair*.

feeler, feelers
(noun) An insect's feelers are the two thin antennae on its head with which it senses things around it.

feeling, feelings
1 (noun) an emotion or reaction, e.g. *strong feelings of jealousy*.
2 a physical sensation, e.g. *a feeling of nausea*.
3 the ability to experience the sense of touch in your body, e.g. *He has no feeling in his left arm*.

feet plural of **foot**.

feline (pronounced **fee**-line)
(adjective) relating to the cat family.
[Latin *feles* = cat]

One name of a month is often misspelt. What mistake do you think people make?

fell, fells, felling, felled
  1 past tense of **fall**.
  2 (verb) To fell a tree means to cut it down.
  [Sense 2: Old English *fellan* = to cause to fall]

fellow, fellows
  1 (noun; rather old-fashioned; informal) a man,
  e.g. *My dear fellow, I really am sorry!*
  2 (adjective) You use fellow to describe people
  who have something in common with you, e.g. *Be
  kind to your fellow men.*
  [Old Norse *felagi* = partner or associate]

felt
  1 past tense and past participle of **feel**.
  2 (noun) thick cloth made from woollen fibres
  matted closely together.

female, females
  1 (noun) a person or animal that belongs to the
  sex that can have babies or young.
  2 (adjective) relating to females.
  [Latin *femina* = woman]

feminine
  1 (adjective) relating to women.
  2 belonging to a particular class of nouns in some
  languages, such as French, German and Latin,
  e.g. '*La porte*' is a feminine noun.
  femininity (noun)
  [Latin *femina* = woman]

feminist
  (noun) someone who believes that women should
  have the same rights, power and opportunities
  as men.
  feminism (noun) **feminist** (adjective)

fence, fences, fencing, fenced
  1 (noun) a wooden or wire barrier between two
  areas of land, or for horses to jump.
  2 (verb) to do sword fencing.

fencing
  (noun) a sport in which two people fight using
  special, thin swords called foils.

fend, fends, fending, fended
  1 (phrase) If you have to **fend for yourself**, you
  have to look after yourself.
  2 (verb) If you fend off an attack or unwanted
  questions or attention, you defend yourself.

ferment, ferments, fermenting, fermented
  (verb) When wine, beer or fruit ferments, the
  sugar in it is converted to alcohol and carbon
  dioxide.
  fermentation (noun)
  [Latin *fermentum* = yeast]

fern, ferns
  (noun) a plant with long feathery leaves, which
  has no flowers and reproduces by spores.

ferocious
  (adjective) violent and fierce
  ferociously (adverb) **ferocity** (noun)
  [Latin *ferox* = like a wild animal]

ferrous
  (adjective) containing or relating to iron, e.g.
  ferrous metals.
  [Latin *ferrum* = iron]

ferry, ferries, ferrying, ferried
  1 (noun) a boat that carries people and vehicles
  across short stretches of water.
  2 (verb) to transport people or goods backwards
  and forwards, e.g. *They ferried groups to and
  from the station in the minibus.*

fertile
  (adjective) capable of producing strong, healthy
  plants, e.g. *fertile land.*
  fertility (noun)
  [Latin *fertilis* = fruitful]

fertilize, fertilizes, fertilizing, fertilized; also
  spelled **fertilise**
  1 (verb) When an egg, plant or female is
  fertilized, the process of reproduction begins by
  sperm joining with the egg, or by pollen touching
  the reproductive part of a plant.
  2 to put manure or chemicals onto land to feed
  plants, crops, etc.

fertilizer, fertilizers; also spelled **fertiliser**
  (noun) a substance put onto soil to improve plant
  growth.

festival, festivals
  1 (noun) an organized series of events and
  performances, e.g. *the Knebworth pop festival.*
  2 a day or period of religious celebration.
  [Latin *festum* = festival]

  Similar words: fiesta, carnival, celebration

---

festive
  (adjective) full of happiness and celebration, e.g.
  at Christmas or other festive occasions.
  [Latin *festum* = festival]

festivity, festivities
  (noun) celebration and happiness, e.g. *He
  enjoyed the wedding festivities.*

fetch, fetches, fetching, fetched
  1 (verb) If you fetch something, you go to where
  it is and bring it back.
  2 If something fetches a particular sum of
  money, it is sold for that amount, e.g. *Her
  paintings always fetch high prices.*

fête, fêtes (rhymes with **date**)
  (noun) an outdoor event with competitions,
  displays and goods for sale, usually to raise
  money for charity.
  [French *fête* = festival]

fetlock, fetlocks
  (noun) the back part of a horse's leg, just above
  the hoof.

fettle
  (phrase) Someone who is **in fine fettle** is in good
  health.

feud, feuds (pronounced **fyood**)
  (noun) a long-lasting and very bitter quarrel,
  especially between families.

fever, fevers
  (noun) a condition in which a sick person has a
  very high temperature.

Pun. Why did the window box? It saw the garden fence.

feverish
1 (adjective) in a state of extreme excitement or agitation, e.g. *a feverish race against time.*
2 suffering from a high temperature.
feverishly (adverb)

Similar words: (sense 2) fevered, flushed, hot

few, fewer, fewest
1 (adjective, noun) not very many.
2 (phrases) **Quite a few** or **a good few** mean a fairly large number of things.

Similar words: (sense 1) some, scattering, handful

fiancé, fiancés (pronounced **fee-on-say**)
(noun) A woman's fiancé is the man to whom she is engaged.
[French *fiancier* = to betroth]

fiancée, fiancées
(noun) A man's fiancée is the woman to whom he is engaged.

fib, fibs, fibbing, fibbed
(verb) If you fib, you tell a small lie.
fibber (noun)

fibre, fibres
1 (noun) a thin thread of a substance used to make cloth.
2 Fibre is also a part of plants that can be eaten but not digested; it helps food pass quickly through the body.
fibrous (adjective)
[Latin *fibra* = strand]

fibreglass
(noun) a material made from thin threads of glass. It can be mixed with adhesives to make boats, cars and furniture.

fickle
(adjective) A fickle person keeps changing their mind about what they like or want.
[Old English *ficol* = treacherous or deceitful]

fiction
(noun) Fiction is stories about imaginary people and events that have been created by the author.
fictional (adjective) **fictitious** (adjective)
[Latin *fictio* = creation or invention]

fiddle, fiddles, fiddling, fiddled
1 (verb) If you fiddle with something, you keep moving it or touching it restlessly.
2 (informal) If someone fiddles, for example their tax, they declare their earnings dishonestly to get money for themselves.
3 (phrase) Someone who is **on the fiddle** is dishonestly obtaining goods or money over a period of time.
4 (noun) a violin.
fiddler (noun)

fiddly, fiddlier, fiddliest
(adjective) small and difficult to do, use or handle, e.g. *It is a very fiddly job.*

fidget, fidgets, fidgeting, fidgeted
(verb) If you fidget, you keep changing your position because of nervousness or boredom.
fidgety (adjective)

field, fields, fielding, fielded
1 (noun) an area of land covered in grass, crops, etc.
2 A coalfield, oilfield or goldfield is an area where coal, oil or gold is found.
3 A particular field is a subject or area of interest, e.g. *She is an expert in the maths field.*
4 (verb) In cricket, when you field the ball, you stop it after the batsman has hit it.

Similar words: (noun: sense 1) meadow, pasture

fielder, fielders
(noun) In cricket, the fielders are the players who stand at various parts of the pitch and try to get the batsmen out.

field marshal, marshals
(noun) an army officer of the highest rank.

fieldwork
(noun) direct study and observation of something in its natural environment.

fiend, fiends (pronounced **feend**)
1 (noun) a devil or evil spirit.
2 a very wicked or cruel person.
3 (informal) You can describe someone who is very keen on a particular thing as a fiend, e.g. *He is a fresh air fiend.*
fiendish (adjective)
[Old English *feond* = enemy]

fierce, fiercer, fiercest
1 (adjective) very aggressive or angry.
2 extremely strong or intense, e.g. *There will be fierce resistance... fierce heat.*
fiercely (adverb)
[Old French *fiers* = brave]

Similar words: (sense 1) ferocious, violent, vicious, savage

fifteen the number 15.
fifteenth (adjective and noun)

fifth, fifths
1 (adjective) first, second, third, fourth, **fifth**.
2 (noun) one of five equal parts (1/5).

fifty, fifties the number 50.
fiftieth (adjective and noun)

fifty-fifty
1 (adverb) divided equally into two portions, e.g. *We'll split the Mars bar fifty-fifty.*
2 (adjective) just as likely not to happen as to happen, e.g. *There is only a fifty-fifty chance.*

fig, figs
(noun) a soft, sweet fruit full of tiny seeds. It grows in hot countries and is often eaten dried.

fight, fights, fighting, fought
1 (verb) When people fight, they take part in a battle, a war, a boxing match or in some other attempt to hurt or kill someone.
2 (noun) a determined attempt to prevent or achieve something, e.g. *the fight against famine.*
fighter (noun)

Similar words: (verb) come to blows, scrap, brawl, scuffle, tussle (noun) skirmish, free-for-all, scrum

What do these fictional characters have in common: Wackford Squeers, Mr Chips?

figure, figures, figuring, figured

1 (noun) a written number.

2 A figure is the shape of a person whom you cannot see clearly, e.g. *We could see several figures on the hilltop.*

3 Your figure is the shape of your body, e.g. *She's got a lovely figure.*

4 A figure is also a person, e.g. *He is a major political figure.*

5 (verb) To figure in something means to appear or be included in it, e.g. *She figured largely in the election victory.*

6 (informal) If you figure that something is the case, you guess or conclude this, e.g. *He figured that it must nearly be dawn.*

[Latin *figura* = shape]

figure of speech, figures of speech

(noun) an expression such as a simile or idiom in which the words are not used in their literal sense.

file, files, filing, filed

1 (noun) a box, folder or cabinet in which a group of papers or records is kept.

2 In computing, a file is a stored set of data with its own name.

3 a long, steel tool with a rough surface, used for smoothing and shaping hard materials.

4 (verb) When someone files a document, they put it in its correct place with similar documents.

5 If you file something, you smooth or shape it with a file.

6 (phrase) To walk **in single file** means to go one behind the other.

fill, fills, filling, filled

(verb) If you fill something or if it fills up, it becomes full.

[Old English *fyllan* = to make full]

fill in

1 (phrasal verb) If you fill in a form, you write information in the appropriate spaces.

2 If you fill someone in, you give them information to bring them up to date.

3 If you fill in for someone, you do their job for them temporarily while they are away.

fillet, fillets, filleting, filleted

1 (noun) a strip of boneless meat or fish.

2 (verb) To fillet meat or fish means to prepare it by cutting out the bones.

filling, fillings

1 (noun) the soft food mixture inside a sandwich etc.

2 a small amount of metal or plastic put into a hole in a tooth by a dentist.

filling station, stations

(noun) a place where petrol and oil for vehicles can be bought.

filly, fillies

(noun) a female horse or pony under the age of 4.

film, films, filming, filmed

1 (noun) a series of moving pictures projected onto a screen and shown at the cinema or on TV.

2 a material used in a camera to take photographs when it is exposed to light.

3 (verb) If you film someone, you use a movie camera or a video camera to record their movements on film.

4 (noun) a very thin layer of powder, liquid etc. on a surface.

5 Clingfilm is a very thin sheet of plastic used for wrapping things.

[Old English *filmen* = membrane]

filter, filters

(noun) a device that allows some substances, lights or sounds to pass through it, but not others, e.g. *a water filter.*

filtration (noun)

[Old French *filtre* = felt]

filth

(noun) disgusting dirt and muck.

filthy (adjective) **filthiness** (noun)

[Old English *fylth* = pus or corruption]

> *Similar words:* grime, squalor

fin, fins

(noun) a thin, angular structure on the body of a fish, to help guide and push it through water.

final, finals

1 (adjective) last in a series or happening at the end of something.

2 (noun) A final is the last game or contest in a series which decides the overall winner.

finalist (noun)

[Latin *finis* = end]

> *Similar words:* (adjective) closing, concluding, ultimate, last

finalize, finalizes, finalizing, finalized; also spelled finalise

(verb) If you finalize something, you complete all the arrangements for it.

finally

1 (adverb) If something finally happens, it happens after a long delay.

2 You use the word finally to introduce a last point, question or topic, e.g. *Finally, I should like to thank...*

> *Similar words:* (sense 1) at last, eventually, in the end, ultimately
> (sense 2) in conclusion, to conclude, lastly

finance, finances

(noun) the money, loans or grants used to pay for something.

financier (noun)

[Old French *finance* = final payment]

financial

(adjective) relating to or involving money.

financially (adverb)

finch, finches

(noun) a small bird with a short, strong beak for crushing seeds.

find, finds, finding, found

1 (verb) to discover.

2 When a court or jury finds a person guilty or not guilty, they decide that the person is guilty or innocent, e.g. *He was found guilty of arson.*

3 (noun) If you describe something or someone as

a find, you mean that you have recently discovered them and they are valuable, interesting or useful, e.g. *Such an excellent restaurant in the middle of nowhere was a real find.*
finder (noun)

Similar words: (verb: sense 1) come across, discover

find out
1 (phrasal verb) to discover something that you did not know.
2 If you find someone out, you discover that they have been doing something wrong.

fine, finer, finest; fines, fining, fined
1 (adjective) very good or very beautiful, e.g *It's a very fine film... a fine palace.*
2 satisfactory or suitable, e.g *If you want to come too, that's fine.*
3 very narrow or thin, e.g. *My hair is too fine.*
4 very delicate, e.g. *a fine detail.*
5 When the weather is fine, it is not raining.
6 (noun) a sum of money paid as a punishment.
7 (verb) If someone is fined, they have to pay money to authority for something they have done wrong.

finger, fingers, fingering, fingered
1 (noun) the 4 long jointed parts of your hands, sometimes including the thumbs.
2 (verb) If you finger something you feel it with your fingers.
3 (phrase) If you are **all fingers and thumbs**, you are very clumsy with your hands.
fingernail (noun)

fingerprint, fingerprints
(noun) a mark made showing the unique pattern on the skin at the tip of a person's finger, often used by police in solving crimes.

finicky
(adjective) extremely fussy, e.g. *He's very finicky about his food.*

finish, finishes, finishing, finished
1 (verb) When you finish something, you reach the end of it and complete it.
2 (noun) the end of something.
[Latin *finis* = end]

Similar words: (verb) complete, conclude, wind up, wrap up, end, close, terminate
(noun) completion, conclusion, close, ending

Finn, Finns
(noun) someone who comes from Finland.

Finnish
1 (adjective) belonging to Finland.
2 (noun) the main language spoken in Finland.

fir, firs
(noun) a tall, pointed evergreen tree that has thin, needle-like leaves and produces cones.

fire, fires, firing, fired
Selected meanings:
1 (noun) e.g. *The fire started in the kitchen.*
2 (verb) e.g. *She fired the gun.*
3 (phrase) If someone **opens fire**, they start shooting.

4 (verb) If you fire questions at someone, you ask them a lot of questions very quickly.
5 (informal) If an employer fires someone, he or she dismisses that person from their job.
6 To fire clay pots means to heat them to a very high temperature in a kiln to harden them.

Similar words: (noun) blaze, inferno

firearm, firearms
(noun) a gun.

fire brigade, brigades
(noun) the organization which has the job of putting out fires.

fire drill, drills
(noun) a practice of what to do if there is a fire in a public building.

fire engine, engines
(noun) a large vehicle that carries equipment for putting out fires.

fire escape, escapes
(noun) an emergency exit or staircase for use if there is a fire.

fire extinguisher, extinguishers
(noun) a metal cylinder containing water, chemical foam, etc. for putting out a fire.

fireguard, fireguards
(noun) a wire screen that can be put around a fire to prevent sparks or burns.

fire hydrant, hydrants
(noun) a pipe in the street used by firemen to obtain water.

firelighter, firelighters
(noun) a small white block of solid fuel that is used to start a fire.

fireman, firemen
(noun) a person whose job is to put out fires and rescue trapped people.

fireplace, fireplaces
(noun) the opening beneath a chimney where a domestic fire can be lit.

fireproof
(adjective) designed to be resistant to fire.

fire station, stations
(noun) a building where fire engines are kept and where firemen wait to be called out.

firetrap, firetraps
(noun) A building that is described as a firetrap would be difficult to escape from in a fire.

firework, fireworks
(noun) a small container of gunpowder and other chemicals which explodes or produces coloured sparks or smoke when lit.

firm, firmer, firmest; firms
1 (adjective) Something that is firm does not move easily when pressed, pushed or shaken, or when weight is put on it.
2 Someone who is firm behaves with authority and shows they will not change their mind, e.g. *The head was a firm lady who stood no arguments.*

Riddle. What will live if fed but die if given water?

3 (noun) a business selling or producing something, e.g. *Which firm do you work for?*
firmly (adverb) **firmness** (noun)
[Latin *firmus* = fixed]

first
(adjective, adverb) an ordinal number: **first, second, third, fourth, fifth.**
firstly (adverb)

first aid
(noun) emergency medical treatment given to an injured person soon after they are hurt.

first-class
(adjective) of the highest quality or standard.

first-hand
(adjective) First-hand knowledge or experience is gained directly, not from books or other people.

first person
(noun) In English grammar, the first person is the 'I' or 'we' form of the pronoun or the verb. The sentence 'I rode my bike' is in the first person.

first-rate
(adjective) excellent.

fish, fishes, fishing, fished
1 (noun) a cold-blooded creature living in water, having a spine, gills, fins and a scaly skin.
2 (verb) to try to catch fish.
3 If you fish for information, you try to obtain it in an indirect way.
(The plural of the noun can be either **fish** or **fishes**, but is normally **fish**.)
fishing (noun) **fisherman** (noun)

fishcake, fishcakes
(noun) a mixture of fish and potato, formed into a flat, round shape and fried.

fish finger, fingers
(noun) a small, oblong piece of chopped fish covered in breadcrumbs.

fishmonger, fishmongers
(noun) a shopkeeper who sells fish.

fishy, fishier, fishiest
1 (adjective) smelling of fish.
2 (informal) suspicious or doubtful, e.g. *Their explanation sounded a bit fishy somehow.*

fist, fists
(noun) a hand with the fingers curled tightly towards the palm.

fit, fits, fitting, fitted; fitter, fittest
1 (verb) e.g. *That coat fits exactly... The doctor can fit you in tomorrow at 3.30.*
2 (adjective) in good condition, e.g. a fit athlete.
3 suitable, e.g. *Is he fit to be in charge?*
4 (noun) If someone has an **epileptic fit** , they are temporarily uncontrollable because of a medical condition, epilepsy.
fitness (noun)

Similar words: meet, match, suit

five, fives the number 5.
fifth (adjective and noun)

fives
(noun) a game played in an enclosed court by hitting a ball with the gloved hand.

fix, fixes, fixing, fixed
Selected meanings:
1 (verb) If you fix something somewhere, you attach it or put it there firmly and securely.
2 If you fix something, you make arrangements for it, e.g. *The meeting is fixed for the 11th.*
3 (noun; informal) Something that is a fix has been unfairly or dishonestly arranged, e.g. *It was proved that the election was a fix.*
4 (informal) If you are in a fix, you are in a difficult situation.
fixed (adjective) **fixedly** (adverb)
[Latin *fixus* = fastened]

Similar words: (verb: sense 2) repair, mend

fixture, fixtures
1 (noun) a piece of furniture or equipment that is fixed into position in a house.
2 a sports event due to take place on a particular date.

fizz, fizzes, fizzing, fizzed
(verb) to make a hissing sound.

fizzle, fizzles, fizzling, fizzled
(verb) to make a weak hissing or spitting sound.

fizzy, fizzier, fizziest
(adjective) bubbly, e.g. *fizzy drinks.*

flab
(noun) large amounts of surplus fat on the body.

flabbergasted
(adjective) extremely surprised.

flabby, flabbier, flabbiest
(adjective) rather fat and unfit, with loose flesh on the body.
flabbiness (noun)

flag, flags, flagging, flagged
1 (noun) a cloth of a particular colour and design, used as the symbol of a nation, or as a signal.
2 (verb) If you or your spirits flag, you start to lose energy or enthusiasm, e.g. *We shall not flag or fail.*

Similar words: (noun) banner, pennant

flagon, flagons
(noun) a large, wide bottle or jug for cider or wine.

flagship, flagships
(noun) a ship carrying the commander of the fleet, e.g. *HMS Victory was Nelson's flagship.*

flagstone, flagstones
(noun) a large, flat rectangular piece of stone used for paving.

flail, flails, flailing, flailed
(verb) If someone's arms or legs flail about, they move in a wild, uncontrolled way.
[Old French *flaiel* = threshing implement]

flair
(noun) a natural ability to do something well or stylishly, e.g. *She had a flair for shop display.*

The first word of a paragraph should be written about 2 cm from the margin.

flak
1 (noun) anti-aircraft fire.
2 (informal) If you get flak for doing something, you get a lot of severe criticism.
[from the first letters of the parts of German *Fliegerabwehrkanone* = anti-aircraft gun]

flake, flakes, flaking, flaked
1 (noun) a small, thin piece of something.
2 (verb) When something such as paint flakes, small, thin pieces of it come off.
flaky (adjective) **flaked** (adjective)

flake out
(phrasal verb; informal) to collapse, go to sleep or lose consciousness.

flame, flames
(noun) a flickering tongue or blaze of fire.
flaming (adjective)
[Latin *flamma* = blazing fire]

flamingo, flamingos or **flamingoes**
(noun) a long-legged wading bird with pink feathers and a long neck.

flammable
(adjective) likely to catch fire and burn easily. The word 'inflammable' is sometimes used to mean the same. (Opposite: **non-flammable**)

flan, flans
(noun) an open sweet or savoury tart with a pastry or cake base.

flank, flanks, flanking, flanked
1 (noun) An animal's flank is its side between the ribs and the hip.
2 (verb) Someone or something that is flanked by a particular thing or person has them at their side, e.g. *a bed flanked by two small tables.*

flannel, flannels
1 (noun) a lightweight woollen fabric.
2 Flannels are men's trousers made of flannel.
3 a small square of towelling, used for washing yourself.
4 (informal) indirect or evasive talk or explanations, e.g. *I wanted to know where the money was, but all I got from her was flannel.*

flap, flaps, flapping, flapped
1 (verb) Something that flaps moves up and down or from side to side with a snapping sound.
2 (noun) A flap of, for example paper or skin, is a loose piece that is attached at one edge.
3 A flap on an aircraft wing is a piece that can be raised or lowered to control the aircraft's movements.
4 (phrase) If you are **in a flap**, you are in a state of panic or agitation.

flapjack, flapjacks
(noun) a type of thick, chewy biscuit made from oats, butter, sugar and syrup.

flare, flares, flaring, flared
1 (noun) a device that produces a very bright flame, used especially as an emergency signal.
2 (verb) If violence or a conflict flares or flares up, it suddenly starts or becomes more serious.
3 Something that flares spreads outwards in a fan shape, e.g. *flared jeans.*

flash, flashes, flashing, flashed
1 (noun) a sudden, short burst of light.
2 If you flash something, you show it briefly, e.g. *She flashed her identity card at the policeman.*
3 (phrase) Something that happens **in a flash** happens suddenly and lasts a very short time.
4 An achievement that is a **flash in the pan** is a fluke and not likely to be repeated.
5 (adjective; informal) Something that is flash looks expensive and fashionable in a vulgar way.

flashback, flashbacks
(noun) a scene in a film, play or book that returns to events in the past.

flashlight, flashlights
(noun) a large, powerful torch.

flash photography
(noun) photography using light from a flash gun or built-in flash.

flashy, flashier, flashiest
(adjective) expensive and fashionable in appearance, in a vulgar way, e.g. *a flashy car.*

flask, flasks
1 (noun) a long-necked, glass bottle with a bowl-shaped base, used especially in laboratories.
2 an insulated container for keeping things hot or cold. Also called a **thermos flask**.

flat, flats; flatter, flattest
1 (noun) a self-contained set of rooms for living in, usually on one level in a bigger building.
2 (adjective) level and smooth.
3 A flat tyre or ball has not got enough air in it.
4 A flat drink has lost its fizziness.
5 A flat battery has lost its electrical charge.
6 Someone with flat feet has feet with very low arches.
7 A flat refusal is complete and firm.
8 Something that is flat is without emotion, variety or interest, e.g. *She spoke in a flat voice.*
9 A flat rate or price is fixed and the same for everyone whatever their circumstances, e.g. *All passengers pay a flat rate of 20p.*
10 A musical instrument or note that is flat is slightly too low in pitch.
11 (noun) In music, a flat is a note or key a semitone lower than that described by the same letter. It is represented by the symbol ♭.
12 (adverb) Something that is done in a particular time flat, takes exactly that time, e.g. *It can reach the target in four minutes flat.*
flatly (adverb) **flatness** (noun)
[Old Norse *flatr* = level]

Similar words: (adjective: sense 2) even, horizontal

---

flatten, flattens, flattening, flattened
(verb) If you flatten something or if it flattens, it becomes flat or flatter.

flatter, flatters, flattering, flattered
1 (verb) to praise someone in an exaggerated way, either to please them or to persuade them to do something.
2 If you flatter yourself that something is the case, you believe, perhaps mistakenly, something

good about yourself or your abilities, e.g. *Don't flatter yourself, Watts. That work is dreadful.*
flatterer (noun) **flattering** (adjective)

Similar words: (sense 1) butter up, cajole, sweet-talk

flattery
(noun) flattering words or behaviour.

flaunt, flaunts, flaunting, flaunted
(verb) If you flaunt your possessions or talents, you display them too obviously or proudly, e.g. *She flaunted her new pencil case.*

flavour, flavours, flavouring, flavoured
1 (noun) The flavour of food is its taste.
2 (verb) If you flavour food with a spice or herb, you add it to the food to give it a particular taste.
flavouring (noun) **flavourless** (adjective)

flaw, flaws
(noun) a fault or weak point in something or someone, e.g. *This cup has a flaw in it.*
flawed (adjective) **flawless** (adjective)

flea, fleas
1 (noun) a small, wingless jumping insect which feeds on blood.
2 (phrase; informal) If you send someone away **with a flea in their ear**, you firmly reject their suggestion and tell them off.

fled past tense and past participle of **flee**.

fledgling, fledglings
(noun) a young bird that is learning to fly.
[Middle English *fledge* = having feathers]

flee, flees, fleeing, fled
(verb) to run away from someone or something.

fleece, fleeces, fleecing, fleeced
1 (noun) A sheep's fleece is its coat of wool.
2 (verb) To fleece someone means to overcharge or swindle them, e.g. *We were fleeced at the car boot sale.*
fleecy (adjective)

fleet, fleets
(noun) a group of ships or vehicles owned by the same organization or travelling together.

fleeting
(adjective) lasting for a very short time, e.g. *a fleeting glimpse.*

flesh
1 (noun) the soft part of the body.
2 (phrase) Your **own flesh and blood** are your relations.
fleshy (adjective)

flew past tense of **fly**.

flex, flexes, flexing, flexed
1 (noun) a length of wire covered in plastic, which carries electricity to an appliance.
2 (verb) If you flex your muscles, you bend and stretch them.
[Latin *flexus* = bent]

flexible
1 (adjective) able to be bent easily without breaking.
2 able to adapt to changing circumstances.

e.g. *Our arrangements had to be flexible, as we didn't know when the plane would land.*
flexibility (noun)
[Latin *flexibilis* = flexible]

flick, flicks, flicking, flicked
1 (verb) If something flicks somewhere, it moves with a short sudden movement, e.g. *Its huge tongue flicked in and out of its mouth.*
2 If you flick something, you move it sharply with your finger.
3 (informal) The flicks are the films showing at a cinema, e.g. *What's on at the flicks?*

flicker, flickers, flickering, flickered
(verb) If a light or a flame flickers, it shines and moves unsteadily.

flight, flights
(noun) a journey made by aeroplane.
2 the action of flying or the ability to fly.
3 a set of stairs or steps.
[Old English *flyht* = flight]

Similar words: (sense 2) flying, aviation

flight lieutenant, lieutenants
(noun) an RAF officer of the rank immediately above flying officer.

flimsy, flimsier, flimsiest
1 (adjective) made of something very thin or weak and not providing much protection.
2 not very convincing, e.g. *a flimsy excuse.*

flinch, flinches, flinching, flinched
(verb) If you flinch, you make a sudden small movement in fear or pain, e.g. *James Bond didn't flinch as the bullet whizzed past.*
[Old French *flenchir* = to turn aside]

Similar words: wince, recoil

fling, flings, flinging, flung
(verb) to throw something with force.

flint, flints
(noun) a hard, greyish-black form of quartz often found in chalk rocks.

flip, flips, flipping, flipped
1 (verb) If you flip something, you turn or move it quickly and sharply, e.g. *flipping through the pages of the magazine.*
2 If you flip something, you hit it sharply with your finger or thumb.
3 (informal) If someone flips, they suddenly become very angry or upset.

flippant
(adjective) showing an unsuitable lack of seriousness, e.g. *a flippant remark.*
flippantly (adverb) **flippancy** (noun)

flipper, flippers
1 (noun) one of the broad, flat limbs of sea animals, e.g. seals or penguins, used for swimming.
2 broad, flat pieces of rubber that you can attach to your feet to help you swim.

float, floats, floating, floated
1 (verb) Something that floats is supported by water or air.

What kind of person is: a cuckoo in the nest; a bear with a sore head; a snake in the grass?

2 (noun) a decorated lorry that is part of a procession.
3 a small amount of money used in a shop etc. for change.
4 a small, buoyant object attached to a fishing line to show, for example, if a fish takes the bait.

flock, flocks, flocking, flocked
1 (noun) a group of birds, sheep, goats, etc.
2 (verb) If people flock somewhere, they go there in large numbers.
[Old English *flocc* = band of people]

flog, flogs, flogging, flogged
1 (verb; informal) to sell something, e.g. *I'm going to flog my car.*
2 to beat someone with a whip or stick.
3 (phrase) To **flog a dead horse** means to keep trying at something when it is a waste of time.
flogging (noun)

flood, floods, flooding, flooded
1 (noun) a large amount of water covering an area that is usually dry.
2 (verb) If people or things flood into a place, they come there in large numbers, e.g. *Calls for help flooded into the AA control room.*

Similar words: (noun) deluge, torrent

floodlight, floodlights
(noun) a very powerful outdoor lamp used to light public buildings and sports grounds.
floodlit (adjective)

floor, floors, flooring, floored
1 (noun) the part of a room that you walk on.
2 A floor of a building is one of the levels in it.
3 (verb) If a remark or question floors you, you are completely unable to deal with it or answer it.
4 (phrase) In a debate, the person who **has the floor** is speaking or has the right to speak.

floorboard, floorboards
(noun) one of the long planks of wood from which a floor is made.

flop, flops, flopping, flopped
1 (verb) If someone or something flops, they fall loosely and rather heavily.
2 (noun; informal) Something that is a flop is completely unsuccessful.

floppy, floppier, floppiest
(adjective) tending to hang downwards in a rather loose way, e.g. *a floppy straw hat.*

Similar words: droopy, limp

floppy disk, disks; also spelled **floppy disc**
(noun) a small magnetic disc on which computer data is stored.

flora
(noun) The flora of a particular area is the plants that grow there, e.g. *the flora and fauna* (animals) *of our countryside.*
[from Flora, a Roman flower goddess]

floral
(adjective) patterned with flowers or made from flowers, e.g. *floral wallpaper.*
[Latin *flores* = flowers]

florist, florists
(noun) a person or shop selling flowers.

flounce, flounces, flouncing, flounced
1 (verb) to walk with exaggerated movements suggesting that you are feeling angry or impatient about something, e.g. *She flounced out of the kitchen in a temper.*
2 (noun) a big frill around the bottom of a dress or skirt.

flounder, flounders, floundering, floundered
(verb) to struggle to move or stay upright, e.g. in water or mud.

flour
(noun) a powder made from finely-ground grain, usually wheat, used for baking and cooking.
floured (adjective) **floury** (adjective)

flourish, flourishes, flourishing, flourished
(pronounced **flurr-ish**)
1 (verb) Something that flourishes continues very successfully.
2 If you flourish something, you wave or display it so that people notice it.
3 (noun) a bold sweeping or waving movement.
[Latin *florere* = to flower]

flow, flows, flowing, flowed
(verb) If something flows, it moves in a steady continuous stream.

flow chart, charts
(noun) a diagram showing the sequence of steps and choices that lead to various results and courses of action.

flower, flowers, flowering, flowered
1 (noun) the part of a plant containing the reproductive organs from which the fruit or seeds develop.
2 (verb) When a plant flowers, its flowers open out and become visible.
[Latin *flos* = flower]

flown past participle of **fly.**

flu
(noun) an illness similar to a very bad cold, which causes headaches, sore throat, weakness and aching muscles. Flu is short for 'influenza'.

fluctuate, fluctuates, fluctuating, fluctuated
(verb) Something that fluctuates is irregular and changeable, e.g. *The TV flickered as the power fluctuated.*
fluctuation (noun)
[Latin *fluctuare* = to toss about or to waver]

flue, flues
(noun) a pipe which takes fumes and smoke away from a stove or boiler.

fluent
(adjective) able to express yourself clearly and without hesitation, e.g. *She was fluent in French.*
fluently (adverb)
[Latin *fluens* = flowing]

Similar words: articulate, eloquent

fluff, fluffs, fluffing, fluffed
1 (noun) soft, light, woolly threads or fibres bunched together.

2 (verb; informal) If an actor fluffs his lines, he forgets them or makes a mistake.
fluffy (adjective)

fluid, fluids
1 (noun) a liquid.
2 (adjective) liquid
fluidity (noun)
[Latin *fluidus* = flowing or loose]

fluke, flukes
(noun) an accidental success or piece of good luck, e.g. *That goal was a complete fluke.*

flung past tense of **fling.**

fluorescent (pronounced floo-er-**ess**-nt)
1 (adjective) having a very bright appearance when light is shone on it, as if it is shining itself, e.g. *fluorescent paint.*
2 A fluorescent light is in the form of a tube and shines with a hard, bright light.
fluorescence (noun)

fluoride
(noun) a chemical compound added to water as a protection against tooth decay.

flush, flushes, flushing, flushed
1 (verb) If you flush, your face goes red.
2 If you flush a toilet or flush out a pipe, you force water through it to clean it.
3 (adjective; informal) Someone who is flush has plenty of money.
4 Something that is flush with a surface is level with it or flat against it.

fluster, flusters, flustering, flustered
1 (verb) If someone flusters you, they make you confused and nervous by rushing you.
2 (noun) If you are in a fluster, you feel confused, nervous and rushed.

flute, flutes
(noun) a wind musical instrument consisting of a long metal tube with holes and keys, held sideways to the mouth.

flutter, flutters, fluttering, fluttered
1 (verb) If something flutters, it flaps or waves with small, quick movements.
2 (noun) If you are in a flutter, you are excited and nervous.
3 (informal) If you have a flutter, you have a small bet.

fly, flies, flying, flew, flown
1 (noun) an insect.
2 (verb) e.g. *Birds fly south for the winter... This plane flies at 600 m.p.h.*
flying (adjective and noun) **flyer** (noun)

fly-fishing
(noun) a method of fishing using imitation flies.

flying officer, officers
(noun) an RAF officer of the rank immediately above pilot officer.

flying saucer, saucers
(noun) a large disc-shaped alien spacecraft. Some people believe in them, but there is no proof of their existence.

flyover, flyovers
(noun) a special bridge structure carrying one road over another.

foal, foals, foaling, foaled
1 (noun) a young horse.
2 (verb) When a female horse foals, she gives birth.

foam, foams, foaming, foamed
1 (noun) a mass of tiny bubbles.
2 Foam is light, spongy material used, for example, in furniture or packaging.
3 (verb) e.g. *to foam at the mouth.*

focus, focuses, focusing, focused
1 (verb) If you focus your eyes or an instrument on an object, you adjust them so that the image is clear.
2 (noun) The focus of something is its centre of attention, e.g. *The Spurs penalty area was the main focus of activity as City attacked.*
focal (adjective)
(The plural of the noun is either **foci** or **focuses**).
[Latin *focus* = hearth. The hearth was seen as the centre of a Roman home]

fodder
(noun) food for farm animals or horses.

foe, foes
(noun) an enemy.

foetus, foetuses; also spelled **fetus** (pronounced **fee**-tus)
(noun) an unborn child or animal in the womb.
foetal (adjective)

fog, fogs
(noun) a thick mist of water droplets in the air.
foggy (adjective)

fogey, fogeys
(noun) If you call someone an old fogey, you mean that they are boring and old-fashioned.

foghorn, foghorns
(noun) a loud horn used to warn ships in fog.

foil, foils, foiling, foiled
1 (verb) If you foil someone's attempt at something, you prevent them from succeeding.
2 (noun) thin, paper-like sheets of metal used to wrap food.

fold, folds, folding, folded
1 (verb) If you fold something, you bend it so that one part lies over another.
2 (informal) If a business folds, it fails and closes down.
3 (noun) a small enclosed area for sheep.

Similar words: (verb: sense 1) crease, double over

folder, folders
(noun) a thin piece of folded cardboard for keeping loose papers together.

foliage
(noun) leaves and plants.
[Latin *folium* = leaf]

folk, folks
1 (noun) Folk or folks are people, often relatives, e.g. *I'm going to visit my folks in Lancashire.*
2 (adjective) Folk music, dance or art is

The main words ending *escent* are: acquiescent adolescent convalescent obsolescent fluorescent.

traditional and comes from the ordinary people of an area.

folklore
(noun) the traditional stories and beliefs of a community.

follow, follows, following, followed
1 (verb) If you follow someone, you move along behind them. If you follow a path or a sign, you move along in that direction.
2 Something that follows a particular thing happens after it.
3 Something that follows is true or logical as a result of something else being the case, e.g. *As he is rich, it follows that he can afford a big car.*
4 If you follow instructions or advice, you do what you are told.

follow up
(verb) If you follow up a suggestion etc., you find out or do something more about it.

follower, followers
(noun) a supporter, e.g. *He's been a follower of Manchester City since 1962.*

Similar word: disciple, fan

following
(adjective) coming afterwards or later, e.g. *the following day.*

fond, fonder, fondest
(adjective) If you are fond of someone or something, you like them.
fondly (adverb) **fondness** (noun)

Similar words: attached, devoted

font, fonts
(noun) a large stone bowl in a church that holds the water for baptisms.
[Latin *fons* = a spring]

food, foods
(noun) any substance consumed by an animal or plant to provide energy.

Similar words: fare, nourishment

food chain, chains
(noun) a series of living things which are linked because each feeds on the next one in the series.

fool, fools, fooling, fooled
1 (noun) Someone who is a fool behaves in a silly and unintelligent way.
2 (verb) to deceive or trick someone, e.g. *You cannot fool all the people all of the time.*

fool around
(phrasal verb) to behave in a silly way.

foolish
(adjective) very silly or unwise.
foolishly (adverb) **foolishness** (noun)

foolproof
(adjective) Something that is foolproof is so well designed or simple to use that it cannot fail.

foot, feet; foots, footing, footed
1 (noun) the part of your body at the lower end of the leg.

2 the bottom, base or lower end of something, e.g. *the foot of the cliffs.*
3 a unit of length. (1 foot = 12 inches = 30.5 centimetres)
4 (phrase) If you **foot the bill** for something, you pay for it.
5 If you **put your foot in it**, you say the wrong thing.

football, footballs
(noun) Football is usually used to mean soccer, a game played by two teams kicking a ball to score goals. There are also rugby football, American football, Gaelic football and others.
footballer (noun)

footnote, footnotes
(noun) a note at the bottom of a page or an additional comment giving extra information.

footpath, footpaths
(noun) a path for people to walk on, usually through countryside.

footprint, footprints
(noun) a mark left by a foot or shoe.

footstep, footsteps
(noun) the sound or mark made by someone walking.

for
1 (preposition) e.g. *I was looking for you.*
2 (conjunction) e.g. *Keep off the road for it's extremely busy.*

forbid, forbids, forbidding, forbade, forbidden
(verb) to order someone not to do something.
forbidden (adjective)

force, forces, forcing, forced
1 (verb) To force someone to do something means to make them do it.
2 To force something means to use violence or great strength to move, push or open it, e.g. *The police forced the door.*
3 (noun) The use of force is the use of violence or great strength.
4 The force of something is its strength or power, e.g. *The force of an earthquake can be measured.*
5 an organized group of soldiers or police, e.g. *The Police Force, the armed forces.*
6 In physics, force is an influence that changes a body from a state of rest to one of motion, or changes its rate of motion, e.g. *The force acting on the particle is constant.*
7 (phrase) A law or rule that is **in force** is valid at present and must be obeyed.
forceful (adjective) **forcefully** adverb)
[Latin *fortis* = strong]

ford, fords
(noun) a shallow place in a river where it is possible to cross on foot or in a vehicle.

fore
(adjective) front, e.g. *the fore and hind wings of the dragonfly.*

forecast, forecasts, forecasting, forecast or forecasted
1 (noun) a prediction of what will happen, e.g. *a weather forecast.*

A closed mouth gathers no feet. (Anon)

2 (verb) To forecast an event means to predict what will happen.

forecourt, forecourts
(noun) an open area at the front of a petrol station or large building.

foreground
(noun) In a picture, the foreground is the part that seems nearest to you.

forehand, forehands
(noun, adjective) a stroke in tennis, squash or badminton made with the palm of your hand facing in the direction that you hit the ball.

forehead, foreheads
(noun) the area at the front of your head, above your eyebrows, and below your hairline.

foreign
(adjective) from or relating to other countries, e.g. *foreign holidays... foreign policy.*
foreigner (noun)

foreman, foremen
(noun) a person in charge of a group of workers, e.g. on a building site.

forename, forenames
(noun) Your forenames are your first names or your Christian names, e.g. Fred Smith's forename is Fred.

foresee, foresees, foreseeing, foresaw, foreseen
(verb) If you foresee something, you predict or expect that it will happen.
foreseeable (adjective) **foresight** (noun)

foreshore, foreshores
(noun) the part of the shore between the points reached by the high and low tides.

forest, forests
(noun) a large area of uncultivated land, mainly covered with trees.

forestry
(noun) the study and work of growing and maintaining forests.

foretell, foretells, foretelling, foretold
(verb) If you foretell something, you predict that it will happen.

forever
(adverb) permanently or continually, e.g. *She was forever asking silly questions.*

foreword, forewords
(noun) a piece of writing at the front of a book recommending it, by an authority on the book's subject.

forfeit, forfeits, forfeiting, forfeited
1 (verb) If you forfeit something, you have to give it up as a penalty.
2 (noun) something that you have to give up or do as a penalty.
[Old French *forfet* = offence]

forge, forges, forging, forged
1 (noun) a place where a blacksmith works making metal goods by hand.
2 (verb) Someone who forges money, documents or paintings makes illegal copies of them.
3 To forge ahead means to progress quickly.

forgery, forgeries
(noun) the crime of faking money, documents, or paintings; also something that has been forged.
forger (noun)

forget, forgets, forgetting, forgot, forgotten
(verb) If you forget something, you fail to remember or think about it.
forgetful (adjective)

forgive, forgives, forgiving, forgave, forgiven
(verb) If you forgive someone for doing something bad, you stop feeling angry and resentful towards them.
forgiveness (noun) **forgiving** (adjective)

Similar words: pardon, absolve

fork, forks
1 (noun) a pronged instrument used for eating.
2 a large garden tool with 3 or 4 prongs.
3 A fork in a road, path, river or branch is a y-shaped junction or division.
[Latin *furca* = pitchfork]

fork out
(phrasal verb; informal) If you fork out for something, you pay for it, often unwillingly.

fork-lift truck, trucks
(noun) a small vehicle with two arms at the front, used to move heavy loads in factories and warehouses.

forlorn
(adjective) lonely, unhappy and uncared for.
forlornly (adverb)

form, forms, forming, formed
1 (noun) A particular form of something is a type or kind of it, e.g. *I never touch alcohol in any form.*
2 The form of something is its shape or pattern, e.g. *the human form.*
3 (verb) The things that form something are the things it consists of, e.g. *Her paintings will form part of a major exhibition.*
4 When someone forms something or when it forms, it is created, organized or started, e.g. *I want you to form a line.*
5 (noun) a sheet of paper with questions and spaces for you to fill in the answers.
6 In a school, a form is a class.
7 a long, low bench.
8 In sport, if you are in form, you are fit and likely to do well.
[Latin *forma* = shape]

formal
1 (adjective) correct and serious, e.g. *The letter was stiff and formal... formal dress.*
2 official and publicly recognized, e.g. *Formal approval has not yet been given.*
formally (adverb).

format, formats, formatting, formatted
1 (noun) the way in which something is arranged or presented.
2 (verb) If you format a computer disk, you prepare it to be used, or you wipe off any data already on it.

Your surname is your family name, e.g. Smith. Your forename is your personal name, e.g. John.

formation, formations
1 (noun) the process of developing and creating something, e.g. *the formation of a pop group.*
2 the pattern or shape of something, e.g. *formation dancing; a rock formation.*
[Latin *formare* = to shape or to make]

former
1 (adjective) happening or existing before now or in the past, e.g. *He was a former army officer.*
2 (noun) You use 'the former' to refer to the first of two things just mentioned, e.g. *If I had to choose between happiness and money, I would have the former.* [Opposite: **latter**]
formerly (adverb)

Formica (pronounced for-**my**-ka)
(noun; trademark) a hard plastic covering used for kitchen worktops and tables.

formidable
(adjective) very difficult to deal with or overcome, and therefore rather frightening or impressive, e.g. *a formidable task.*
[Latin *formido* = terror]

Similar words: threatening, intimidating

formula, formulae or **formulas**
1 (noun) a group of letters, numbers and symbols representing a mathematical or scientific rule, e.g. $E = mc^2$.
2 a list of quantities of substances that when mixed make another substance, for example in chemistry, e.g. H_2SO_4.
3 a plan or set of rules for dealing with a particular problem, e.g. *The United Nations worked out a peace formula.*
formulate (verb)
[Latin *formula* = set form of words]

forsake, forsakes, forsaking, forsook, forsaken
(verb) To forsake someone or something means to desert, give up or abandon them.

fort, forts
1 (noun) a strong building for defence.
2 (phrase) If you **hold the fort** for someone, you manage their affairs while they are away.
[Latin *fortis* = strong]

Similar words: fortress, castle

forth
(adverb; old-fashioned) out and forward from a starting place, e.g. *Page and monarch, forth they went.*

forthcoming
(adjective) planned to happen soon, e.g. *the forthcoming election.*

fortification, fortifications
(noun) Fortifications are buildings, walls and ditches used to protect a place.

fortify, fortifies, fortifying, fortified
1 (verb) to strengthen a place against attack.
2 If something fortifies you, it makes you feel stronger, more determined or better prepared, e.g. *We were fortified by a cup of tea at half time.*
fortification (noun)

fortnight, fortnights
(noun) a period of two weeks.
fortnightly (adverb and adjective)
[an Old English word meaning '14 nights']

fortress, fortresses
(noun) a castle or well-protected town built for defence.

fortuitous
(adjective) happening by chance. (not to be confused with fortunate; fortuitous can refer to unlucky happenings.)

fortunate
(adjective) lucky.
fortunately (adverb)

fortune, fortunes
1 (noun) Fortune or good fortune is good luck.
2 (phrase) If someone **tells your fortune**, they predict your future.
3 (noun) a large amount of money, e.g. *This coat must have cost a fortune.*

forty, forties
the number 40.
fortieth (adjective and noun)

forward, forwards
1 (adverb, adjective) Forward or forwards means in the front or towards the front, e.g. *The seats face forward... the car rolled forwards.*
2 in or towards a future time, e.g. *I look forward to Christmas.*
3 (noun) In a game such as football or hockey, a forward is a player in an attacking position.

fossil, fossils
(noun) the remains or print of an animal or plant of a previous geological age, preserved in rock.
fossilize (verb)
[Latin *fossilis* = dug up]

foster, fosters, fostering, fostered
(verb) If someone fosters a child, they are paid to look after the child for a period, but do not become its legal parents.
foster child (noun) **foster home** (noun)
foster parent (noun)

fought past tense of **fight**.

foul, fouler, foulest; fouls, fouling, fouled
1 (adjective) very unpleasant, especially because it is dirty, wicked or obscene.
2 (verb) To foul something means to make it dirty, e.g. *Dogs must not be allowed to foul the pavement.*
3 (noun) In sport, a foul is an act of breaking the rules.

found, founds, founding, founded
1 past tense and past participle of **find**.
2 (verb) If someone founds an organization or institution, they start it and set it up, e.g. *Baden Powell founded the Boy Scout movement.*
[Latin *fundare* = to lay foundations]

foundation, foundations
(noun) a solid layer of concrete or bricks in the ground, on which a building is built to give it a firm base.

Which is true? 'What must be, must be.' or 'Every man is the architect of his own fortune.'

founder, founders, foundering, foundered
1 (noun) The founder of an institution or organization is the person who sets it up.
2 (verb) to collapse; to sink. e.g. *The Titanic foundered on an iceberg.*

fountain, fountains
(noun) an ornamental feature consisting of a jet of water forced into the air by a pump.
[Latin *fontana* = fountain]

fountain pen, pens
(noun) a pen with a nib supplied with ink from a container inside.

four, fours
1 the number 4.
2 (phrase) If you are **on all fours**, you are on your hands and knees.

fourteen the number 14.
fourteenth (adjective and noun)

fourth
(adjective) first, second, third, **fourth**.

fowl, fowls
(noun) a bird such as a chicken or duck that is kept or hunted for its meat or eggs.

fox, foxes, foxing, foxed
1 (noun) a dog-like wild animal with reddish-brown fur, a pointed face and ears, and a thick tail.
2 (verb) If something foxes you, it is too confusing or puzzling for you to understand.
foxy (adjective)

foyer, foyers (pronounced **foy**-ay)
(noun) a large area just inside the main doors of a cinema, hotel or public building.

fraction, fractions
1 (noun) In arithmetic, a fraction is a part of a whole number e.g. ½ ⅓ ¼.
2 a tiny proportion or amount of something, e.g. *I hesitated for a fraction of a second.*
fractional (adjective) **fractionally** (adverb)
[Latin *frangere* = to break]

fracture, fractures, fracturing, fractured
1 (noun) a crack or break in something, especially a bone.
2 (verb) If something fractures, it breaks.

fragile
(adjective) easily broken or damaged, e.g. *This parcel is fragile. Handle it with care.*
fragility (noun)
[Latin *fragilis* = breakable]

Similar words: brittle, delicate, frail, breakable

fragment, fragments
(noun) a small piece of something, e.g. *Fragments of bone were found in the murderer's car.*
fragmentation (noun) **fragmented** (adjective)

fragrant
(adjective) sweet or pleasant-smelling.
fragrance (noun)
[Latin *fragrans* = sweet-smelling]

frail, frailer, frailest
1 (adjective) Someone who is frail is not strong or healthy.
2 Something that is frail is easily broken or damaged.
frailty (noun)
[Latin *fragilis* = breakable]

fralicate (pronounced **fral**-ik-cut)
(adjective) very easily damaged.

frame, frames, framing, framed
1 (noun) The frame of a door, window or picture is the structure surrounding it.
2 an arrangement of connected bars over which something is formed or built.
3 The frames of a pair of glasses are the wire or plastic parts that hold the lenses.
4 Your frame is your body, e.g. *his sturdy frame.*
5 A frame in snooker is a single game in which all the balls are potted; also the wooden triangle inside which the balls are arranged at the beginning of a game.
7 (verb) To frame a picture means to put it into a frame, e.g. *a framed photograph.*
8 To frame an innocent person is to collect and present false evidence which makes them seem guilty of a crime.
9 (noun) A **zimmer frame** is a walking aid that people with weak legs can hold in front of them for support.

framework, frameworks
(noun) a structure acting as a support or frame.

franc, francs
(noun) the main unit of money in France, Belgium, Switzerland and some other countries. (1 franc = 100 centimes)

frank, franker, frankest
(adjective) If you are frank, you say things in an open and honest way.
frankly (adverb) **frankness** (noun)
[Old French *franc* = free]

Similar words: open, candid

frankfurter, frankfurters
(noun) a type of sausage, originally a speciality of Frankfurt in West Germany.

frantic
(adjective) If you are frantic, you behave in a wild, desperate way because you are anxious or frightened.
frantically (adverb)
[Greek *phrenitikis* = delirious]

fraud, frauds
1 (noun) the crime of getting money by deceit or trickery.
2 Someone who is a fraud is not what they pretend to be.
fraudulent (adjective) **fraudulently** (adverb)
[Latin *fraus* = deception]

fray, frays, fraying, frayed
(verb) If rope frays, its strands become worn and it is likely to break.
[French *frayer* = to rub]

Adverbial pun. 'My first three were wrong,' she said, forthrightly.

freak, freaks
1 (noun) someone whose appearance or behaviour is very unusual.
2 (adjective) A freak event is very unusual and unlikely to happen, e.g. *My mother died in a freak accident, struck by lightning.*

freakish
(adjective) very odd and unusual, e.g. *a freakish-looking man.*
freakishly (adverb) **freakishness** (noun)

freckle, freckles
(noun) Freckles are small, light brown spots on someone's skin, especially their face.
freckled (adjective)

free, freer, freest; frees, freeing, freed
1 (adjective) not restricted in any way, e.g. *The escaped prisoners were free at last.*
2 not costing anything, e.g. *Send for a free sample, today!*
3 (verb) to set someone free.
freely (adverb)

Similar words: (adjective: sense 1) liberated, at liberty, on the loose (adjective: sense 2) complimentary, on the house (verb) release, liberate, turn loose

freebie
(noun; informal) a free gift.

freedom
1 (noun) If you have the freedom to do something, you are allowed to do it, e.g. *Most western countries enjoy freedom of speech.*
2 When prisoners gain their freedom, they escape or are released.
3 When there is freedom from something unpleasant, people are not affected by it, e.g. *freedom from hunger.*

Similar words: (sense 2) liberty, release

freehand
(adjective, adverb) A freehand drawing is done without the help of e.g. a ruler or compasses.

freelance
(adjective, adverb) A freelance journalist, photographer, etc. is not employed by one organization, but is paid for each job they do.

free-range
(adjective) Free-range eggs are laid by hens that can move and feed freely on open ground.

freestyle
(noun) Freestyle refers to sports competitions in which competitors can use any style or method, as, for example, in swimming and wrestling.

free will
(phrase) If you do something **of your own free will**, you do it by choice and not because you are forced to.

freeze, freezes, freezing, froze, frozen
1 (verb) When a liquid freezes, it becomes solid because it is very cold.
2 If you freeze, you suddenly become still and quiet, because there is danger.
freezing (adjective)

freezer, freezers
(noun) a large refrigerator which runs at a specially low temperature.

freight
(noun) goods moved by lorries, ships or other transport.

freighter, freighters
(noun) a ship or plane that carries goods not people.

French
1 (adjective) belonging to France.
2 (noun) the main language spoken in France, and by many people in Belgium, Switzerland and Canada.

French horn, horns
(noun) a brass musical instrument consisting of a tube wound in a circle.

Frenchman, Frenchmen
(noun) a man who comes from France.
Frenchwoman (noun)

french fries
(plural noun) another name for chips.

french window, windows
(noun) glass doors that lead into a garden or onto a balcony.
[This is a rare case of a 'nationality' word not starting with a capital letter].

frenzy, frenzies
(noun) If someone is in a frenzy, their behaviour is wild and uncontrolled.
frenzied (adjective)

frequent
(adjective) often happening, e.g. *His visits were frequent... They move at frequent intervals.*
frequency (noun) **frequently** (adverb)
[Latin *frequens* = occurring often]

fresh, fresher, freshest
1 (adjective) new, e.g. *fresh eggs... fresh instructions.*
2 Fresh water is not salty, e.g. the water in a stream.
3 Fresh weather is fairly cold and windy.
freshly (adverb) **freshness** (noun)

freshen, freshens, freshening, freshened
(verb) to make something cleaner and more pleasant.

freshwater
(adjective) A freshwater lake or pool contains water that is not salty.

fret, frets, fretting, fretted
1 (verb) to worry.
fretful (adjective) **fretfully** (adverb)
2 (noun) The frets on a stringed instrument, e.g. a guitar, are the metal ridges across its neck.
[Old English *fretan* = to gnaw at]

fret saw, saws
(noun) a fine-toothed saw with a narrow blade for cutting designs in thin wood or metal.

friction
1 (noun) the force that prevents things from moving freely when they rub against each other.

We take these words from France: disco souvenir rendezvous leotard pasteurize café.

2 Friction between people is disagreement and quarrels.
[Latin *fricare* = to rub]

Friday, Fridays
(noun) the day between Thursday and Saturday.
[Old English *Frigedæg* = Freya's day. Freya was the Norse goddess of love]

fridge, fridges
(noun; informal) a refrigerator.

friend, friends
(noun) a person you know well and like to spend time with, e.g. *A good book is the best of friends, the same today and for ever.*
friendship (noun)

Similar words: chum, pal, companion

friendly, friendlier, friendliest
(adjective) If you are friendly to someone, you behave in a kind and pleasant way to them.
friendliness (noun)

Similar words: genial, amiable, amicable, cordial

frieze, friezes
(noun) a strip of decoration, carving or pictures along an interior wall.

frigate, frigates
(noun) a small, fast warship.

fright
(noun) a sudden feeling of fear.

frighten, frightens, frightening, frightened
(verb) If something frightens you, it makes you afraid.
frightened (adjective) **frightening** (adjective)

frightful
(adjective) very bad or unpleasant, e.g. *The smell was frightful.*
frightfully (adverb)

frill, frills
(noun) a strip of cloth with many folds, attached to something as a decoration.
frilly (adjective)

fringe, fringes
(noun) If someone has a fringe, their hair is cut to hang over their forehead.

frisk, frisks, frisking, frisked
1 (verb; informal) If someone frisks you, they search you quickly with their hands to see if you are hiding something in your clothes.
2 When animals frisk, they run around in a happy, energetic way, e.g. *His dogs frisked around him.*

frisky, friskier, friskiest
(adjective) energetic and lively.
friskily (adverb) **friskiness** (noun)
[Old French *frisque* = lively]

fritter, fritter, frittering, frittered
1 (noun) Fritters consist of food dipped in batter and fried, e.g. *banana fritters.*
2 (verb) If you fritter away your time or money, you waste it on unimportant things.
[Latin *frigere* = to fry]

frivolous
(adjective) Someone who is frivolous behaves in a silly or light-hearted way, especially when they should be serious or sensible.
frivolously (adverb) **frivolity** (noun)
[Latin *frivolus* = trifling or worthless]

frizzy, frizzier, frizziest
(adjective) Frizzy hair has stiff, wiry curls.

frock, frocks
(noun; old-fashioned) a dress.

frog, frogs
(noun) a small, amphibious creature.

frolic, frolics, frolicking, frolicked
1 (verb) When animals or children frolic, they run around and play in a lively way.
2 (noun) a light-hearted, lively game.
frolicsome (adjective)
[Dutch *vrolijk* = joyful]

Similar words: (verb) frisk, romp, prance

from
(preposition) e.g. *far from home.*

front, fronts
1 (noun) the part of something that faces forward.
2 In a war, the front is the place where two armies are fighting.
3 In meteorology, a front is the line where a mass of cold air meets a mass of warm air.
frontal (adjective)
[Latin *frons* = forehead]

frontier, frontiers
(noun) a border between two countries.

frontispiece, frontispieces
(noun) The frontispiece of a book is a picture opposite the title page.

frost, frosts
(noun) When there is a frost, the temperature outside falls below freezing point (0°C).
frosty (adjective)

frostbite
(noun) damage to your fingers, toes or ears caused by extreme cold.
frostbitten (adjective)

frosted
(adjective) Frosted glass has a rough surface that you cannot see through.

froth, froths, frothing, frothed
1 (noun) a mass of small bubbles on the surface of a liquid.
2 (verb) to form small bubbles.
frothy (adjective)

frown, frowns, frowning, frowned
1 (verb) If you frown, you move your eyebrows closer together, because you are annoyed, worried or concentrating.
2 (noun) e.g. *The sulky girl wore a frown all day.*

froze past tense of **freeze.**

frozen
1 past participle of **freeze.**
2 (adjective) extremely cold.

A faithful friend is the medicine of life. (The Bible)

fruit, fruits
(noun) the part of a plant that develops after the flower and which contains the seeds. Many fruits are edible.
[Latin *fructus* = produce or benefit]

fruitful
(adjective) Something that is fruitful has good and useful results, e.g. *a fruitful discussion.*
fruitfully (adverb) **fruitfulness** (noun)

fruitless
(adjective) Something that is fruitless does not achieve anything, e.g. *their fruitless search.*
fruitlessly (adverb) **fruitlessness** (noun)

fruit machine, machines
(noun) a coin-operated gambling machine which pays out money when a particular series of symbols, usually fruit, appears on a screen.

frustrate, frustrates, frustrating, frustrated
(verb) If something frustrates you, it prevents you doing what you want and makes you upset and angry, e.g. *The lack of money frustrated him.*
frustrated (adjective) **frustrating** (adjective)
frustration (noun)
[Latin *frustrare* = to disappoint]

Similar words: foil, thwart

fry, fries, frying, fried
(verb) to cook food in hot fat or oil.

fuddy-duddy, fuddy-duddies
(noun; informal) someone who is very fixed in their ideas and dull, e.g. *He's a real old fuddy-duddy.*

fudge, fudges
(noun) a soft, brown sweet made from butter, milk and sugar.

fuel, fuels, fuelling, fuelled
1 (noun) a substance, for example coal or petrol, that is burned to provide heat or power.
2 (verb) A machine or vehicle that is fuelled by a substance works by burning the substance as a fuel, e.g. *boilers fuelled by coal.*

fugitive, fugitives (pronounced **fyoo**-jit-tiv)
(noun) someone who is running away or hiding, especially from the police.
[Latin *fugere* = to flee]

fulfil, fulfils, fulfilling, fulfilled
(verb) If you fulfil a promise, hope or duty, you carry it out or achieve it.
fulfilling (adjective) **fulfilment** (noun)

full, fuller, fullest
(adjective) containing as much as it is possible to hold, e.g. *a full bottle of milk.*
fullness (noun) **fully** (adverb)

full-blooded
(adjective) having great commitment and enthusiasm, e.g. *a full-blooded shot at goal.*

full moon
(noun) the moon when it appears as a complete circle.

full stop, stops
(noun) the punctuation mark . used at the end of a sentence and after an abbreviation or initial.

full-time
1 (adjective) involving work for the whole of each normal working week.
2 (noun) In games such as football, full time is the end of the match.

fully-fledged
(adjective) completely developed, e.g. *By the age of 17 he was a fully-fledged life-saver.*

fumble, fumbles, fumbling, fumbled
(verb) to feel or handle something clumsily.

fume, fumes, fuming, fumed
1 (noun) Fumes are unpleasant-smelling gases and smoke, often toxic, that are produced by burning and by some chemicals.
2 (verb) If you are fuming, you are very angry.
[Latin *fumus* = smoke]

fun
1 (noun) pleasant, enjoyable activity.
2 (phrase) If you **make fun** of someone, you tease or ridicule them.

function, functions, functioning, functioned
1 (noun) the purpose or role of something, e.g. *The function of this pedal is to stop the car.*
2 (verb) When something functions, it operates or works, e.g. *Is this mike functioning?*
[Latin *functus* = performed or done]

functional
1 (adjective) designed for practical use rather than for attractiveness, e.g. *The VW Beetle had a very functional design.*
3 working properly, e.g. *How long since the machine was functional?*

fund, funds, funding, funded
1 (noun) an amount of available money, usually for a particular purpose, e.g. *a disaster fund.*
2 (verb) Someone who funds something provides money for it, e.g. *schemes funded by the EC.*
[Latin *fundus* = estate]

Similar words: (verb) finance, support, sponsor, subsidize

fundamental, fundamentals
1 (adjective) basic and central, e.g. *the fundamental principles on which society is based... a fundamental error.*
2 (noun) The fundamentals of something are its most basic and important parts, e.g. *my inability to grasp the fundamentals of physics.*
[Latin *fundamentum* = foundation or base]

funeral, funerals (pronounced **fyoo**-ner-al)
(noun) a religious service or ceremony for the burial or cremation of a dead person.
[Latin *funus* = funeral]

fungus, fungi or **funguses**
(noun) a plant, such as a mushroom or mould, that does not have leaves and reproduces by spores.

Adverbial pun. 'Who ate my apple?' said John, fruitlessly.

funk, funks, funking, funked
1 (noun) a style of music with a strong rhythm based on jazz and blues.
funky (adjective)
2 (verb) to fail to do something you should because you are afraid.

funnel, funnels, funnelling, funnelled
1 (noun) an open cone tapering to a narrow tube, used to pour substances into containers.
2 a metal chimney on a ship or steam engine.
3 (verb) If something is funnelled somewhere, it is directed through a narrow space into that place.
[Latin *fundere* = to pour]

funny, funnier, funniest
1 (adjective) causing amusement or laughter.
2 strange or puzzling.
funnily (adverb)

Similar words: (sense 1) amusing, comical, comic, humorous, witty

funny bone, bones
(noun) a sensitive area near your elbow which can give you a tingling sensation if you hit it accidentally.
[a pun on the anatomical name 'humerus', the elbow bone]

fur, furs
(noun) the soft, thick body hair of many animals.
furry (adjective)

furious
(adjective) extremely angry.
furiously (adverb)
[Latin *furiosus* = raving or raging]

furnace, furnaces
(noun) a container for a very large, hot fire used, for example, in the steel industry for melting ore.
[Latin *furnus* = oven]

furnish, furnishes, furnishing, furnished
(verb) If you furnish a room, you put furniture, carpets, curtains, etc. into it.

furnishings
(plural noun) the furniture and fittings in a room or house.

furniture
(noun) movable objects such as tables, chairs and wardrobes.

furrow, furrows
(noun) a long, shallow trench made by a plough.

further, furthers, furthering, furthered
1 a comparative form of **far**; far **further** furthest.
2 (adjective) additional or more, e.g. *A further £500 is needed.*
3 (verb) If you further something, you help it to progress, e.g. *This success will certainly further your career.*

Similar words: (verb) promote, advance

further education
(noun) education at a college after leaving school, but not at a university or polytechnic. Compare **higher education.**

furthest
a superlative form of **far**; far further **furthest**.

furtive
(adjective) secretive, sly and cautious, e.g. *The shoplifter gave a furtive glance.*
furtively (adverb)
[Latin *furtum* = theft or deceit]

fury
(noun) violent or extreme anger.
[Latin *furia* = madness]

fuse, fuses, fusing, fused
1 (noun) In a plug or electrical appliance, a fuse is a safety device consisting of a wire which melts to stop the electric current if a fault occurs.
2 In some types of simple bomb, a fuse is a long cord which is lit to detonate it.
3 (verb) When an electrical appliance fuses, it stops working because the fuse has melted to protect it.
[Latin *fundere* = to melt]

fuselage, fuselages (pronounced **fyoo**-zil-ahj)
(noun) The fuselage of an aeroplane or rocket is its body.

fuss, fusses, fussing, fussed
1 (noun) unnecessarily anxious or excited behaviour.
2 (verb) If someone fusses, they behave with unnecessary anxiety and concern for unimportant things.
fussy (adjective) **fussily** (adverb)

Similar words: (noun) commotion, bother

futile
(adjective) having no chance of success, e.g. *The attempt to send a rocket to the sun proved futile, even though it was launched at night.*
futility (noun)
[Latin *futilis* = worthless]

Similar words: pointless, useless, vain, worthless

future
1 (noun) the period of time after the present.
2 (adjective) e.g. *a future date.*
[Latin *futurum* = what is yet to be]

future tense
(noun) In grammar, the future tense is the tense of a verb that you use mainly to talk about things that will probably happen after the time of writing or speaking, e.g. *I* **will be reading**... He **will write** books.

fuzz
1 (noun) short, fluffy hair.
2 (informal) a nickname for the police.

fuzzy, fuzzier, fuzziest
(adjective) unclear or blurred, e.g. *The TV picture went fuzzy when the aerial broke.*

What have these books in common: 1984 Brave New World The Time Machine?

G

gabble, gabbles, gabbling, gabbled
(verb) to talk so fast that it is difficult for people to understand you.

gaberdine, gaberdines (pronounced gab-er-**deen**)
(noun) a coat made of thick, heavy gaberdine cloth.
[Old French *gauvardine* = pilgrim's garment]

gadget, gadgets
(noun) a small machine or tool.
gadgetry (noun)

Similar words: appliance, contraption, device

Gaelic (pronounced **gay**-lik in Ireland, **gal**-lik in Scotland)
(noun) a language spoken in some parts of Scotland and Ireland.

gag, gags, gagging, gagged
1 (noun) a strip of cloth that is tied round or put inside someone's mouth to stop them speaking.
2 (verb) to prevent someone from talking by putting a gag on or (informal use) by ordering them not to talk.
3 (noun, informal) a joke told by a comedian.

gain, gains, gaining, gained
1 (noun) an increase, e.g. *a weight gain.*
2 (verb) If you gain from a situation, you get some advantage from it.
3 If a watch gains, it is going too fast.
4 If you gain on someone, you gradually catch them up.

gala, galas
(noun) a special public competition, performance etc., e.g. *a charity gala night... a swimming gala.*
[Old French *galer* = to make merry]

galaxy, galaxies
(noun) an enormous group of stars that extends over many millions of miles. The earth's galaxy is called the Milky Way.
galactic (adjective)
[Greek *gala* = milk]

gale, gales
(noun) an extremely strong wind.

gallant
(adjective) brave and honourable, e.g. *They put up a gallant fight.*
gallantly (adverb) **gallantry** (noun)
[Old French *galer* = to make merry]

galleon, galleons
(noun) a large sailing ship used by the Spanish in the 15th and 16th centuries.

gallery, galleries
1 (noun) a building or room where works of art are exhibited.
2 In a theatre or large hall etc., the gallery is a raised area at the back or sides, e.g. the public gallery in the House of Commons.

galley, galleys
1 (noun) a kitchen in a ship or aircraft.

2 an ancient type of ship, propelled by oars and sometimes sails.

gallon, gallons
(noun) a unit of liquid volume. (1 gallon = 8 pints = 4.55 litres).

gallop, gallops, galloping, galloped
(verb) When a horse gallops fast, all 4 feet are off the ground at the same time.

gallows
(noun) a framework on which criminals used to be hanged.

galore
(adjective) in very large numbers, e.g. *There are restaurants and clubs galore in New York.*
[Irish Gaelic *go leór* = to sufficiency]

gamble, gambles, gambling, gambled
1 (verb) When people gamble, they try to win money by betting on horses etc., or by playing games like roulette or poker.
2 If you gamble something, you risk losing it in the hope of gaining an advantage, e.g. *The company gambled everything on the new factory.*
gambler (noun)

game, games
1 (noun) an enjoyable activity with rules, played by individuals or teams against each other.
2 (adjective; informal) Someone who is game is willing to try something unusual or difficult, e.g. *She's game for a laugh.*
3 (noun) wild animals or birds that are hunted for sport or for food, e.g. pheasants, rabbits.
4 (phrase) To **give the game away** means to reveal a secret.

gamekeeper, gamekeepers
(noun) a person employed to look after game animals and birds on a country estate.

gamesmanship
(noun) the practice of trying to win a game by using methods which are sneaky and unpleasant but not against the rules.

gammon
(noun) cured meat from a pig, similar to bacon.

gander, ganders
(noun) a male goose.

gang, gangs, ganging, ganged
1 (noun) a group of people who join together for some purpose, for example to commit a crime.
2 (verb; informal) If people gang up on you, they join together to oppose you.

gangling
(adjective) tall, thin and clumsy.

gangplank, gangplanks
(noun) a plank used for boarding and leaving a ship or boat.

gangster, gangsters
(noun) a violent criminal who is a member of a gang.

Letter G developed from the same idea of a weapon as letter C.

gangway, gangways
1 (noun) a space between rows of seats for people to walk down, e.g. in a cinema or theatre.
2 A ship's gangway is a gangplank.

gannet, gannets
1 (noun) a large seabird which dives steeply with wings closed to catch fish.
2 (informal) a person who eats greedily.

gaol also spelled **jail**
(noun) a prison.

gap, gaps
(noun) a space between two things.
[Old Norse *gap* = chasm]

Similar words: break, hole, opening, space

gape, gapes, gaping, gaped
1 (verb) If you gape you stare with your mouth open in surprise.
2 Something that gapes is wide open, e.g. *a gaping wound.*

garage, garages
1 (noun) a building where a car can be kept.
2 a place where cars are repaired and where petrol is sold.
[French *garer* = to dock or to park]

garbage
(noun) rubbish, especially household rubbish.
[Anglo-French *garbelage* = removal of rubbish]

garbled
(adjective) Garbled messages are jumbled and the details may be wrong.

Similar words: distorted, confused

garden, gardens
(noun) an area of land next to a house, where flowers, fruit or vegetables are grown.
gardening (noun) **gardener** (noun).
[Old German *gart* = enclosure]

gargle, gargles, gargling, gargled
(verb) to rinse your throat by putting liquid in your mouth, tilting your head back and making a bubbling sound without swallowing the liquid.
[Old French *gargouille* = throat]

gargoyle, gargoyles
(noun) a carved stone water spout on, e.g. a church, in the shape of an ugly person or animal.

garish (pronounced **gair**-ish)
(adjective) bright and harsh to look at, e.g. *The car salesman wore a garish yellow tie.*
garishly (adverb) **garishness** (noun)

garland, garlands
(noun) a circle of flowers and leaves which is worn around the neck or head.

garlic
(noun) the white bulb of an onion-like plant with a strong taste and smell, used in cooking.

garment, garments
(noun) a piece of clothing.
[Old French *garnement* = equipment]

garnish, garnishes, garnishing, garnished
1 (noun) something, e.g. a wedge of lemon or a sprig of parsley, used in cooking for decoration.
2 (verb) To garnish food means to decorate it with a garnish.

garrison, garrisons
(noun) a group of soldiers stationed in a town to guard it.
[Old French *garir* = to defend]

garter, garters
(noun) a piece of elastic worn round the top of a stocking or sock to stop it slipping.
[Old French *garet* = bend of the knee]

gas, gases, gasses, gassing, gassed
1 (noun) any airlike substance that is not liquid or solid, e.g. oxygen, hydrogen, North Sea gas.
2 In American English, gas is petrol.
3 (verb) e.g. *The old man was gassed when his gas fire blew out as he slept in his chair.*
(The form **gases** is the plural of the noun. The verb forms are spelled with a double 's'.)
gaseous (adjective)
[Greek *khaos* = atmosphere]

gash, gashes, gashing, gashed
(noun) a long, deep cut.
[Old French *garser* = to scratch]

gasoline
(noun) In American English, gasoline is petrol.

gasp, gasps, gasping, gasped
(verb) If you gasp, you quickly draw in your breath through your mouth because you are surprised, shocked or in pain.
[Old Norse *geispa* = to yawn]

gassy, gassier, gassiest
(adjective) full of gas, e.g. *My cola is gassy.*

gastric
(adjective) involving the stomach, e.g. *gastric flu.*
[Greek *gaster* = stomach]

gastroenteritis (pronounced gast-roh-en-ter-**eye**-tis)
(noun) an illness in which a person's stomach becomes inflamed.

gate, gates
(noun) a barrier which can open and shut.
gateway (noun)
[Old Norse *gat* = opening or passage]

gateau, gateaux (pronounced **gat**-toe)
(noun) a rich, layered cake with cream in it.

gatecrash, gatecrashes, gatecrashing, gatecrashed
(verb) If you gatecrash a party, you go to it when you have not been invited.

gather, gathers, gathering, gathered
1 (verb) When people gather, they come together in a group.
2 If you gather a number of things, you collect them or bring them together in one place.
3 If you gather that something is true, you learn that it is true, often from what someone says, e.g. *I gather she's leaving.*
4 (plural noun) Gathers are tiny pleats at the waist of a skirt.

Similar words: (verb: senses 1 and 2) assemble, collect, group

A gardener needs these words: organic compost fertilizer shrub lawnmower annual biennial.

gaudy, gaudier, gaudiest (pronounced gaw-dee)
(adjective) very colourful in a vulgar way, e.g.
*The jeweller's window looked very gaudy with
its posters and bright lighting.*
gaudily (adverb) **gaudiness** (noun)

Similar words: flashy, garish, loud

gauge, gauges (pronounced gayj)
1 (noun) a piece of equipment that measures the
amount of something, e.g. *a fuel gauge.*
2 On railways, the gauge is the distance between
the two rails on a railway line. In most countries
this is 4ft. 8½ins (144cm).

gauntlet, gauntlets
1 (noun) Gauntlets are long, thick gloves worn
for protection, for example by motorcyclists.
2 (phrase) If you **throw down the gauntlet**, you
challenge someone.
[French *gant* = glove]

gauze
(noun) very fine cloth with lots of tiny holes in it
often used in bandages.

gave past tense of **give.**

gay, gays; gayer, gayest
1 (adjective) Someone who is gay is homosexual.
2 (old-fashioned) lively and full of fun.

gaze, gazes, gazing, gazed
(verb) If you gaze at something, you look
steadily at it for a long time.

GB Great Britain.

gear, gears, gearing, geared
1 (noun) On a bicycle, gears are special cog
wheels which, when you pedal, control the
number of times the wheels go round. Gears in
vehicles control their speed and power.
2 The gear for an activity is the equipment and
clothes that you need for it.
3 (verb) If someone or something is geared to a
particular event or purpose, they are prepared
or organized for it.

geese plural of **goose.**

gel
(noun) a smooth, soft, jelly-like substance, e.g.
hair gel.

gelding, geldings (pronounced gel-ding)
(noun) a horse which has been neutered.
[Old Norse *geldingr* = *gelding*]

gelignite (pronounced jel-lig-nite)
(noun) an explosive substance similar to
dynamite.

gem, gems
(noun) a jewel or precious stone.
[Latin *gemma* = jewel]

gender, genders
(noun) the sex of a person or animals. Masculine,
feminine, neuter and common are the 4 genders.

gene, genes (pronounced jeen)
(noun) one of the parts of a cell which controls
the physical characteristics of a living thing, e.g.
its eye colour. Genes are passed on from one
generation to the next.

genealogy, genealogies (pronounced
jeen-nee-al-loj-ee)
(noun) the study of the history of families, or the
history of a particular family.
genealogical (adjective) **genealogist** (noun)
[Greek *genea* = race]

general, generals
1 (adjective) relating to the whole of something
or to most things in a group, rather than to
separate parts, e.g. *general household expenses.*
2 (noun) a high-ranking army officer.
3 (phrase) **In general** means usually.
generally (adverb)

Similar words: (adjective) broad, overall

general election, elections
(noun) an election for a new government, which
all the people of a country may vote in. [compare
by-election]

general practitioner, practitioners
(noun) a doctor who works in the local
community rather than in a hospital.

generate, generates, generating, generated
(verb) to create or produce something, e.g. *There
are several methods of generating electricity...
Tourism will generate new jobs.*

generation, generations
(noun) all the people of about the same age; also
the period of time between one generation and
the next, usually considered to be about 25-30
years.

generator, generators
(noun) a machine which produces electricity
from another form of energy such as wind or
water power.

generous
(adjective) A generous person is very willing to
give money, time or gifts.
generously (adverb) **generosity** (noun)

Similar words: lavish, liberal

genetics
(noun) the science of the way that
characteristics are passed on from generation to
generation by means of genes.
genetic (adjective) **genetically** (adverb)

genial
(adjective) cheerful, friendly and kind.
genially (adverb) **geniality** (noun)

genie, genies (pronounced jee-nee)
(noun) In stories from Arabia and Persia (Iran),
a genie is a magical being that obeys the wishes
of the person who controls it.
[Arabic *jinni* = demon]

genitals
(plural noun) Your genitals are your external
sexual organs.

genitive
(noun, adjective) In the grammar of some
languages, the genitive is the form of a noun that
is used to indicate possession or some other kind
of assocation between two things. In English,

nouns show the genitive with an apostrophe, e.g. the lady's hat, the ladies' coats.

genius, geniuses
1 (noun) a highly intelligent, creative or talented person, for example a person who reads the Survival Guide at the front of this dictionary.
2 great intelligence, creativity or talent, e.g. *This dictionary's writers are clearly people of genius.*

genteel
(adjective) excessively polite and refined.
[French *gentil* = well-born]

gentle, gentler, gentlest
(adjective) mild and calm; not violent or rough, e.g. *a gentle dog... gentle breeze...a gentle hint.*
gently (adverb) **gentleness** (noun)

gentleman, gentlemen
(noun) a man who is polite and well-educated; also a polite way of referring to any man.
gentlemanly (adjective)
[French *gentil* = well-born]

gents
(noun; informal) a public toilet for men.

genuflect, genuflects, genuflecting, genuflected
(pronounced **jen**-yoo-flekt)
(verb) to bend the knee, especially in church, as a sign of respect.

genuine (pronounced **jen**-yoo-in)
(adjective) real and not false, e.g. *genuine surprise... a genuine antique.*
genuinely (adverb) **genuineness** (noun)

geography
(noun) the study of the physical features of the earth, together with patterns of climate, natural resources and population in different parts of the world.
geographic or **geographical** (adjective)
geographically (adverb) **geographer** (noun)
[Greek *gēo* = earth + *-graphia* = writing]

geology
(noun) the study of the earth's structure, especially the layers of rock and soil that make up the surface of the earth.
geological (adjective) **geologist** (noun)

geometry
(noun) the branch of mathematics that deals with lines, angles, curves and spaces.
geometric or **geometrical** (adjective)
[Greek *geōmetrein* = to measure the land]

geranium, geraniums
(noun) a garden plant with clusters of red, pink or white flowers.

gerbil, gerbils
(noun) a small rodent with long back legs, from desert regions.

germ, germs
(noun) a micro-organism that causes disease.
[Latin *germen* = sprig, bud, or seed]

German, Germans
1 (adjective) belonging to Germany.
2 (noun) someone who comes from Germany.
3 the main language spoken in Germany and Austria. It is also spoken by many people in Switzerland.

Germanic
(adjective) The Germanic group of languages includes English, Dutch, German, Danish, Swedish and Norwegian.

German measles
(noun) a contagious disease that gives you a cough, sore throat and red spots. It is dangerous to unborn babies if their mothers catch it.

germinate, germinates, germinating, germinated
(verb) When a seed germinates, it starts to grow.
germination (noun)

gestation (pronounced jes-**tay**-shn)
(noun; technical) the time during which a foetus is growing inside its mother's womb, e.g. *The human gestation period is 9 months.*
[Latin *gerere* = to carry]

gesticulate, gesticulates, gesticulating, gesticulated (pronounced jes-**stik**-yoo-late)
(verb) If you gesticulate, you move your hands and arms around while you are talking.
gesticulation (noun)
[Latin *gestus* = action]

gesture, gestures, gesturing, gestured
1 (noun) a movement of your hands or head that conveys a message or feeling.
2 (noun) an action which is more important for what it symbolizes than what it actually does, e.g. *Exchanging shirts was a gesture of friendship from the players.*

get, gets, getting, got
(verb) e.g. *Please get me a pie... Get out of here!*

Similar words: acquire, obtain

get at
1 (phrasal verb) If someone is getting at you, they are criticizing you in an unkind way.
2 If you ask someone what they are getting at, you are asking them to explain what they mean.

get away with
(phrasal verb) If you get away with something dishonest etc, you are not found out.

get by
(phrasal verb) If you get by, you have just enough money, food and clothing to live on.

get on
1 (phrasal verb) If two people get on well together, they like each other's company.
2 If you get on with a job or task, you do it.
3 If you say that someone is getting on, you mean they are old or growing old.
4 (phrase) **Getting on for** means the same as nearly, e.g. *He's getting on for 40.*
5 If someone is getting on in their career, they are doing well and have been promoted.

get over with
(phrasal verb) If you want to get something over with, you want it to be finished quickly.

get through
1 (phrasal verb) If you get through to someone, you make them understand what you are saying.

We take these words from German: blitz lager zinc poodle nickel cobalt quartz sauerkraut.

2 If you get through to someone on the telephone, you succeed in talking to them.

get-together, get-togethers
(noun; informal) an informal meeting or party.

get-up
(noun; informal) a set of clothes, e.g. *Ooh! I really like your get-up, Tracey.*

geyser, geysers (pronounced **gee**-zer)
(noun) a spring through which hot water and steam gush up in spurts.
[Old Norse *geysa* = to gush]

ghastly, ghastlier, ghastliest
(adjective) extremely horrible and unpleasant, e.g. *a ghastly massacre... ghastly curtains.*
[Old English *gaste* = to terrify]

ghost, ghosts
(noun) the spirit of a dead person, believed to haunt people or places.
ghostly (adjective)

Similar words: apparition, phantom, spectre, spirit, spook

ghoul, ghouls (pronounced **gool**)
1 (noun) an evil spirit or demon, believed by Muslims to eat dead bodies.
2 (informal) someone who takes an unpleasant interest in other people's injury or death.
ghoulish (adjective)

giant, giants
1 (noun) In stories and legends, a giant is a huge, very strong person, often cruel or stupid.
2 (adjective) much larger than other similar things, e.g. *a giant doughnut... the giant panda.*
[Latin *gigas* = giant]

gibberish (pronounced **jibb**-er-ish)
(noun) speech that makes no sense at all, e.g. *Don't talk gibberish, boy!*

giddy, giddier, giddiest
(adjective) feeling unsteady on your feet because of illness, tiredness or being overexcited.
giddily (adverb) **giddiness** (noun)
[Old English *gydig* = mad or possessed]

gift, gifts
1 (noun) a present.
2 a natural skill or ability, e.g. *She had a gift for languages.*
[Old English *gift* = dowry]

gifted
(adjective) having a special ability.

gigantic
(adjective) extremely large.

giggle, giggles, giggling, giggled
(verb) to laugh in a nervous or embarrassed way.
giggly (adjective)

gill, gills
(noun) the organs on a fish's sides which it uses for breathing.

gimmick, gimmicks
(noun) a type of advertising trick that is not really necessary but is used to attract interest,

e.g. *Air balloons are often flown over new housing estates as a gimmick.*
gimmicky (adjective)

gin
(noun) a strong, colourless alcoholic drink made from grain and juniper berries.

ginger
1 (noun) a plant root with a hot, spicy flavour, used for flavouring in cooking.
2 (adjective) bright orangey-brown, e.g. *ginger hair.*

ginger beer
(noun) a sweet, fizzy, ginger-flavoured drink, made with sugar and yeast.

gingerbread
(noun) a sweet, ginger-flavoured cake.

gingerly
(adverb, adjective) If you move gingerly, you move cautiously, e.g. *She opened the door gingerly... a gingerly movement.*
[Old French *gensor* = dainty]

gingham
(noun) checked cotton cloth.
[Malay *ginggang* = striped cloth]

gipsy another spelling of **gypsy**.

giraffe, giraffes
(noun) a tall, African mammal with a very long neck and dark patches on its skin.
[Arabic *zarafah* = giraffe]

girder, girders
(noun) a large, metal beam used in the framework of a building, bridge, etc.

girl, girls
(noun) a female child.
girlish (adjective) **girlhood** (noun)

girlfriend, girlfriends
(noun) Someone's girlfriend is the woman or girl with whom they are having a romantic or sexual relationship.

giro, giros (pronounced **jie**-roh)
1 (noun) a system of transferring money through a bank or post office.
2 a cheque received regularly from the government by unemployed or sick people.

gist (pronounced **jist**)
(noun) The gist of a piece of writing or a speech is its general meaning or most important points.

give, gives, giving, gave, given
Selected meanings:
1 (verb) e.g. *I don't know what to give you for your birthday*
2 (phrase) You use **give or take** to indicate that an amount you are mentioning is not exact, e.g. *It took two hours, give or take a few minutes.*

Similar words: (verb) grant, present, provide

give in
(phrasal verb) to admit that you are defeated.

give up
1 (phrasal verb) If you give something up, you stop doing it, e.g. *giving up smoking.*

These words have a hard g and a silent h: aghast ghastly gherkin ghetto ghoul.

2 If you give up, you admit that you cannot do something.

give way
1 (phrasal verb) to collapse, e.g. *Look out, the bridge is giving way!*
2 If you give way to someone, you let them do what they want even though you do not agree.
3 If you give way when you are driving, you let someone else go first.

given
1 past participle of **give**.
2 (adjective) fixed or specified, e.g. *At a given moment we cheered.*
3 (preposition, conjunction) Given a particular fact means taking this fact into account, e.g. *Given his handicap, he did well.*

glacier, glaciers (pronounced glass-yer)
(noun) a huge, frozen mass of slow-moving ice.
[Old French *glace* = ice]

glad, gladder, gladdest
(adjective) happy and pleased, e.g. *I'm glad you can come... I'll be glad to help.*
gladly (adverb) **gladness** (noun) **gladden** (verb)
[Old Norse *glathr* = bright or joyful]

glade, glades
(noun) a grassy space in a forest.

gladiator, gladiators
(noun) At the time of the Roman Empire, gladiators were slaves trained to fight with various weapons, often to the death.
[Latin *gladius* = sword]

glamorous
(adjective) attractive and exciting, e.g. *a glamorous film star.*
glamour (noun)

glance, glances, glancing, glanced
1 (verb) to look at something quickly.
2 If one object glances off another, it hits it at an angle and bounces away in another direction.

gland, glands
(noun) one of several organs in your body, for example the thyroid gland and the sweat glands, which either produce chemical substances for your body to use, or which help to get rid of waste products from your body.
glandular (adjective)

glandular fever
(noun) an infectious disease which causes a fever and swollen glands.

glare, glares, glaring, glared
1 (verb) to look at someone angrily.
2 (noun) extremely bright light.
[Old Dutch *glaren* = gleam]

glaring
(adjective) very obvious, e.g. *a glaring mistake.*
glaringly (adverb)

glass, glasses
(noun) a hard, transparent substance used to make, for example, windows, bottles and lenses.
glassy (adjective)

glaze, glazes, glazing, glazed
1 (verb) To glaze pottery or food means to cover it with a shiny finish.
2 To glaze a window means to fit a sheet of glass into a window frame.
glazier (noun)

glazed
(adjective) Someone who has a glazed expression looks tired and bored.

gleam, gleams, gleaming, gleamed
(verb) to shine and reflect light.
[Old German *glimo* = brightness]

glen, glens
(noun) a deep, narrow valley, especially in Scotland or Ireland.
[Gaelic *gleann* = valley]

glide, glides, gliding, glided
(verb) to move smoothly, e.g. *yachts gliding along the river.*
[Old German *glitan* = to glide]

glider, gliders
(noun) an aircraft, usually without an engine, which flies by floating on air currents.

glimmer, glimmers, glimmering, glimmered
1 (noun) A glimmer of a feeling or quality is a faint sign of it, e.g. *a glimmer of hope.*
2 (verb) to produce a faint, unsteady light.

glimpse, glimpses, glimpsing, glimpsed
(verb) If you glimpse something, you see it very briefly.

glint, glints, glinting, glinted
(verb) If something glints, it reflects quick flashes of light.

glisten, glistens, glistening, glistened
(verb) If something glistens, it shines or sparkles.

glitter, glitters, glittering, glittered
(verb) If something glitters, it shines in a sparkling way, e.g. *glittering stars.*

gloat, gloats, gloating, gloated
(verb) If you gloat, you cruelly show pleasure about your own success or someone else's failure, e.g. *They gloated when I came last.*

global
(adjective) concerning the whole world, e.g. *global issues... protests on a global scale.*

globe, globes
1 (noun) a spherical object, especially one with a map of the earth on it.
2 You can refer to the world as the globe.
[Latin *globus* = ball]

glockenspiel, glockenspiels (pronounced glok-ken-shpeel)
(noun) a percussion instrument consisting of metal bars, bells or tubes played with small hammers.
[German *Glocken* = bells + *Spiel* = play]

gloom
1 (noun) darkness or dimness.
2 a feeling of unhappiness or despair.
gloomy (adjective) **gloomily** (adverb)

What is the difference between a spectacle and a pair of spectacles?

glorious
1 (adjective) very pleasant and giving a feeling of happiness, e.g. *glorious weather*.
2 involving great fame and success, e.g. *Nelson won a glorious victory at Trafalgar*.
gloriously (adverb)

glory, glories
1 (noun) fame and admiration for an achievement, e.g. *Wellington basked in glory after his victory at Waterloo*.
2 something considered splendid or admirable, e.g. *the glory of Venice*.
[Latin *gloria* = glory]

glossary, glossaries
(noun) a list of explanations of specialist words, usually found at the back of a book.

glossy, glossier, glossiest
1 (adjective) smooth and shiny, e.g. *glossy hair*.
2 Glossy magazines and photographs are produced on expensive, shiny paper.
gloss (noun) **glossiness** (noun)

glove, gloves
(noun) a covering for the hands.

glow, glows, glowing, glowed
1 (verb) to shine with a dull, steady light, e.g. *cigarettes glowing in the dark*.
2 If you are glowing, you look very happy or healthy.
3 (noun) e.g. *The fire gave off a warm glow*.

glucose
(noun) a type of sugar found in plants that is also found naturally in the body.
[Greek *glukus* = sweet]

glue, glues, gluing or **glueing, glued**
1 (noun) a substance used for sticking things together.
2 (verb) to stick using glue.
gluey (adjective)

glum, glummer, glummest
(adjective) miserable and depressed.
glumly (adverb) **glumness** (noun)

glutton, gluttons
1 (noun) a person who eats too much.
2 If you are a glutton for something that other people wouldn't like, you seem strangely eager for it, e.g. *She's a glutton for hard work*.
gluttonous (adjective) **gluttony** (noun)
[Latin *gluttus* = greedy]

gnarled (pronounced **nar**-ld)
(adjective) old, twisted and rough, e.g. *gnarled tree trunks*.

gnash, gnashes, gnashing, gnashed (pronounced **nash**)
(verb) If you gnash your teeth, you grind them together because you are angry or in pain.
[Old Norse *gnastan* = gnashing of teeth]

gnat, gnats (pronounced **nat**)
(noun) a tiny flying insect that bites.

gnaw, gnaws, gnawing, gnawed (pronounced **naw**)
(verb) to bite at something repeatedly.

gnome, gnomes (pronounced **nome**)
(noun) a dwarf-like old man in fairy stories.

go, goes, going, went, gone (verb)
Selected meanings:
1 (verb) e.g. *Please may I go to the loo?...There's going to be trouble*.
2 (phrase) If someone is **making a go** of something, they are successful at it.
3 If someone is always **on the go**, they are always busy and active.

go down
1 (phrasal verb) If something goes down well, people like it. If it goes down badly, they do not.
2 If you go down with an illness, you catch it, e.g. *Christopher Robin went down with measles*.

go off
1 (phrasal verb) If you go off someone or something, you stop liking them.
2 If a bomb goes off, it explodes.
3 If food goes off, it becomes unfit to eat.

go on
1 (phrasal verb) If you go on about something, you keep talking about it in a rather boring way.
2 Something that is going on is happening.

go out with
(phrasal verb) If you are going out with someone they are your boyfriend or girlfriend, e.g. *Is she really going out with him?*

go through
1 (phrasal verb) If you go through an unpleasant time, you experience it.
2 If a law etc. goes through, it is approved and becomes official.
3 If you go through with something, you do it even though it is unpleasant, e.g. *As she had promised to go on the roller-coaster, she felt she had to go through with it*.

go-ahead
(noun) If someone gives you the go-ahead for something, they give you permission to do it.

goal, goals
1 (noun) In games like football or hockey, the goal is the space into which the players try to get the ball in order to score.
2 Your goal is something you hope to achieve.

goalkeeper, goalkeepers
(noun) the games player who stands in the goal and tries to stop the other team from scoring.

goalposts
1 (plural noun) the upright posts of a goal.
2 (phrase) If you say someone has **moved the goalposts** you mean they have unfairly changed the basic rules and understandings of a situation.

goat, goats
(noun) an animal with shaggy hair, a beard and horns.
[Old English *gat* = female goat]

gob, gobs
(noun; informal) the mouth.
[Gaelic *gob* = beak or bill]

gobble, gobbles, gobbling, gobbled
1 (verb) to eat very quickly.

These surnames came from jobs our ancestors did: Glover Cook Cooper Draper Mason Shepherd.

2 When a turkey gobbles, it makes a loud gurgling sound.

Similar words: (sense 1) bolt, guzzle, scoff, devour

gobbledygook or **gobbledegook**
(noun) language that is impossible to understand because it is so formal or complicated.

goblet, goblets
(noun) a glass with a long stem and a base.

goblin, goblins
(noun) an ugly, mischievous creature in fairy stories.

gobsmacked
(adjective; very informal!) surprised or shocked.

god, gods
1 (noun) God is the being who is worshipped by Christians, Jews, and Muslims as the creator and ruler of the world. (Jehovah and Allah are the Jewish and Muslim names for God).
2 a supernatural being believed to have power over an aspect of life or a part of the world, e.g. Thor, the Norse god of thunder.

godchild, godchildren
(noun) If you are someone's godchild, they agreed to be responsible for your religious upbringing when you were baptized in a Christian church.
goddaughter (noun) **godson** (noun)

goddess, goddesses
(noun) a female god.

godparent, godparents
(noun) someone who agrees to be responsible for a child's religious upbringing when they are baptized in a Christian church.
godfather (noun) **godmother** (noun)

goggle, goggles, goggling, goggled
1 (verb; informal) to stare in amazement.
2 (plural noun) Goggles are special glasses that fit closely round your eyes to protect them.

going-over, goings-over
(noun; informal) If you give something a going-over, you give it a thorough examination.

goings-on
(plural noun) strange, amusing or improper activities, e.g. *There were some queer goings-on at the manor house.*

go-kart, go-karts
(noun) a very small, low motor vehicle with 4 wheels, used for racing.

gold
1 (noun) a valuable metal used for making jewellery and as an international currency.
2 (adjective) bright yellow.
golden (adjective) **goldsmith** (noun)

golden wedding, weddings
(noun) a 50th wedding anniversary.

goldfinch, goldfinches
(noun) a common, small bird with yellow and black wings and a red, white and black head.

goldfish
(noun) an orange-coloured fish.

golf
(noun) a game played on a golf course with clubs and a small white ball.
golfer (noun)

gone past participle of **go**.

gong, gongs
(noun) a flat, circular piece of metal hit with a hammer to make a loud sound.
[a Malay word]

gooey
(adjective; informal) sticky.

good, better, best
1 (adjective) e.g. *What a good dog you are, Gnasher... Good morning!... I feel really good today.*
2 (phrase) **For good** means for ever.
3 As good as means almost, e.g. *She's as good as blind without her glasses.*
4 If someone **delivers the goods** they do what they are expected to do.
goodness (noun)

goodbye, goodbyes
(interjection, noun) e.g. *We said our goodbyes and left the party.* [short for 'God be with you']

good-natured
(adjective) friendly, pleasant and even-tempered.

goods
(plural noun) objects that people own or that are sold in shops, e.g. *electrical goods.*

goody, goodies; also spelled goodie
1 (noun; informal) Goodies are enjoyable things, often food.
2 You can call a hero in a film or book a goody.

goose, geese
(noun) a fairly large bird with webbed feet and a long neck.
[Old English *gos* = goose]

gooseberry, gooseberries
(noun) a round, green edible berry that grows on a bush and has a sharp taste.

goose pimples
(noun) If you have goose pimples, your skin is bumpy and the hairs are standing up, because you are cold or afraid.

gore, gores, goring, gored
1 (verb) If an animal gores someone, it wounds them badly with its horns or tusks.
2 (noun) clotted blood from a wound.
[noun: Old English *gor* = mud or filth]

gorge, gorges, gorging, gorged
1 (noun) a deep, narrow valley.
2 (verb) If you gorge yourself, you eat a lot of food greedily, e.g. *Bunter gorged himself on Cheddar cheese.*
[Old French *gorge* = throat]

gorgeous
(adjective) extremely pleasant or attractive, e.g. *gorgeous weather... a gorgeous bloke.*
[Old French *gorgias* = elegant or stylish]

gorilla, gorillas
(noun) a very large, strong ape with very dark fur. Gorillas live in forests in central Africa.

Brand names of goods begin with capital letters: Hoover Sellotape Brasso.

[from *Gorillai*, the Greek name for an African tribe with hairy bodies]

gorse
(noun) a dark green, wild shrub that has sharp prickles and small yellow flowers.

gory, gorier, goriest
(adjective) Gory situations involve people being injured in horrible ways.

gosling, goslings (pronounced goz-ling)
(noun) a young goose.
[Old English *gos* + *ling* = little goose]

gospel, gospels
1 (noun) The Gospels are the 4 books in the New Testament which describe the life and teachings of Jesus Christ.
2 (phrase) If you take something as **gospel** or **gospel truth**, you believe that it is true.
[Old English *god* + *spell* = good message]

gossip, gossips, gossiping, gossiped
1 (verb) If you gossip, you chat with someone, especially about other people.
2 (noun) Someone who is a gossip enjoys talking about other people's private affairs.
[Old English *godsibb* = godparent]

gouge, gouges, gouging, gouged (pronounced gowj)
1 (verb) If you gouge a hole in something, you make a hole in it with a pointed object.
2 If you gouge something out, you force it out of position with your fingers or a sharp tool.

govern, governs, governing, governed
(verb) To govern a country means to control it.
e.g. *He that would govern others, first should be the master of himself.*
[Latin *gubernare* = to steer or to direct]

government, governments
1 (noun) the group of people who govern a country, e.g. *a Labour government.*
2 the control and organization of a country, e.g. *sensible government is essential for all countries.*
governmental (adjective)

governor, governors
(noun) a person who controls and organizes a state or an institution, e.g. *the school governors.*

gown, gowns
1 (noun) a long, formal dress.
2 a special long, dark cloak worn by people such as judges and lawyers.
[Latin *gunna* = fur or leather garment]

GP
(noun) a doctor who works in the local community rather than in a hospital.
[an abbreviation for 'general practitioner']

grab, grabs, grabbing, grabbed
1 (verb) to take something quickly or roughly.
2 (informal) If an idea grabs you, it interests you or excites you.
[German *grabben* = to seize or to scramble for]

Similar words: (sense 1) grasp, snatch, seize

grace, graces
1 (noun) an elegant way of moving.
2 a pleasant, kind way of behaving.
3 a short prayer of thanks said before a meal.
e.g. *Please will you say grace, Vicar?*
4 (phrase) If you do something **with good grace**, you do it cheerfully and without complaining.
graceful (adjective) **gracefully** (adverb)
[Latin *gratus* = pleasing]

Similar words: (sense 1) charm, elegance, poise

gracious
1 (adjective) kind, polite and pleasant.
2 'Good gracious!' is an exclamation of surprise.
graciously (adverb)

grade, grades, grading, graded
1 (noun) quality, e.g. *high-grade steel.*
2 A grade in an exam or piece of written work is the mark that you receive for it, e.g. *My dictionary achieved an E-grade.*
3 (verb) To grade a piece of work etc. means to give it a grade; also grading can mean sorting something out into different sizes, colours, etc.
[Latin *gradus* = step]

gradient, gradients
(noun) a slope or the steepness of a slope.

gradual
(adjective) happening or changing slowly over a long period of time rather than suddenly.
gradually (adverb)

graduate, graduates, graduating, graduated
1 (noun) a person who has completed a first degree at a university or college.
2 (verb) to be awarded a first degree, e.g. BA, B.Sc.
graduation (noun)
[Latin *graduari* = to take a degree]

graffiti (pronounced graf-fee-tee)
(plural noun) slogans or drawings scribbled on walls, posters, trains and buses.
[Italian *graffiare* = to scratch a surface]

graft, grafts, grafting, grafted
1 (noun) a piece of healthy flesh etc. used to replace by surgery a damaged or unhealthy part of a person's body, e.g. *a skin graft.*
2 (verb; informal) to work hard.

grain, grains
1 (noun) a cereal plant, for example wheat or corn, that is grown as a crop and used for food.
2 Grains are seeds of a cereal plant.
3 A grain of sand or salt is a tiny particle of it.
4 The grain of a piece of wood is the pattern of lines made by the fibres in it.
5 (phrase) If something **goes against the grain**, you find it difficult to accept because it is against your principles.
[Latin *granum* = corn or grain]

Similar word: (sense 3) speck

gram, grams; also spelled gramme
(noun) a unit of weight (1000g = 1 kilogram).
[Latin *gramma* = small weight]

Proverbs which agree. Empty vessels make most sound. Every ass loves to hear himself bray.

grammar
(noun) the rules of a language relating to the ways you can combine words to form sentences. [Greek *grammatikos* = concerning letters and writing]

grammar school, schools
(noun) a secondary school for pupils of high academic ability.

grammatical
(adjective) following the rules of grammar correctly, e.g. *He speaks grammatical English.*
grammatically (adverb)

gran
(noun; informal) grandmother.

granary, granaries
1 (noun) a building for storing grain.
2 (adjective) Granary bread contains whole grains of wheat.
[Latin *granum* = grain]

grand, grander, grandest
1 (adjective) magnificent in appearance and size, e.g. *a grand palace.*
2 (informal) very pleasant or enjoyable, e.g. *We had a grand time in Huddersfield.*
3 A grand total is the final, complete amount.
4 (noun; informal) A grand is a thousand pounds or dollars.
grandly (adverb) **grandeur** (noun)
[Latin *grandis* = great or large]

Similar words: (adjective: sense 1) imposing, majestic, noble, stately

grandad
(noun; informal) grandfather.

grandchild, grandchildren
(noun) Someone's grandchild is the child of their son or daughter.

granddaughter, granddaughters
(noun) Someone's granddaughter is the daughter of their son or daughter.

grandfather, grandfathers
(noun) Your grandfather is your father's father or your mother's father.

grandfather clock, clocks
(noun) a clock in a tall wooden case that stands on the floor.

grandma
(noun; informal) grandmother.

grandmother, grandmothers
(noun) Your grandmother is your father's mother or your mother's mother.

grandparent, grandparents
(noun) Your grandparents are your parents' parents.

grand piano, pianos
(noun) a large, flat piano with horizontal strings.

grandson, grandsons
(noun) Someone's grandson is the son of their son or daughter.

grandstand, grandstands
(noun) a structure with a roof and seats for spectators at a sports ground.

granite (pronounced **gran**-nit)
(noun) a very hard rock used in building.
[Italian *granito* = grained]

granny
(noun; informal) grandmother.

grant, grants, granting, granted
1 (noun) an amount of money that the government or local council gives to someone for a particular purpose, e.g. *a housing grant.*
2 (verb) If you grant something to someone, you allow them to have it, e.g. *Grant me a wish.*
3 (phrases) If you **take something for granted**, you believe it without thinking about it. If you **take someone for granted**, you assume they will help you, without being grateful for their help.

grape, grapes
(noun) a small green or purple fruit.
[Old French *grape* = bunch of grapes]

grapefruit, grapefruits
(noun) a large, round, yellow citrus fruit.

grapevine, grapevines
1 (noun) a climbing plant which grapes grow on.
2 If you hear some news on the grapevine, it has been passed on from person to person.

graph, graphs
(noun) a diagram which shows how two sets of numbers or measurements are related.
[originally an abbreviation for 'graphic formula']

graphic, graphics
1 (adjective) very detailed and lifelike.
2 (plural noun) Graphics are drawings and pictures composed of simple lines and strong colours, e.g. *computer-generated graphics.*
graphically (adverb)
[Greek *graphein* = to write]

grapple, grapples, grappling, grappled
1 (verb) If you grapple with someone, you struggle with them while fighting.
2 If you grapple with a problem, you try hard to solve it.

grasp, grasps, grasping, grasped
1 (verb) to hold something firmly.
2 If you grasp an idea, you understand it.
[German *grapsen* = to seize]

grass, grasses
(noun) the common green plant that grows on lawns and in parks, fields, etc.
grassy (adjective)

grasshopper, grasshoppers
(noun) an insect with long back legs which it uses for jumping and making a high-pitched vibrating sound.

grass snake, snakes
(noun) a type of harmless British snake with a green or brown body.

grate, grates, grating, grated
1 (noun) a framework of metal bars in a fireplace on which the fire is lit.
2 (verb) to shred food into small pieces by rubbing it against a grater.
3 If something grates on you, it makes you feel uncomfortable.

What does an animal eat if it is a: herbivore carnivore omnivore nucivore?

grateful
(adjective) If you are grateful for something, you are glad you have it and want to thank the person who gave it to you.
gratefully (adverb)
[Latin *gratus* = thankful]

Similar words: appreciative, obliged, thankful

gratitude
(noun) the feeling of being grateful, e.g. *This gift is to show our gratitude.*
[Latin *gratus* = grateful]

Similar words: appreciation, thankfulness, thanks

grave, graves; graver, gravest
1 (noun) a place where a body is buried.
2 (adjective; formal) very serious, e.g. *You have made a grave mistake, Lord Raglan.*
gravity (noun).
[noun: Old English *græf* = grave
adjective: Latin *gravis* = important]

gravel
(noun) small stones used for making roads and paths.

gravestone, gravestones
(noun) a large stone placed over someone's grave.

graveyard, graveyards
(noun) an area of land where bodies are buried.

gravity
(noun) the force that makes things fall when you drop them.
[Latin *gravitas* = weight]

gravy
(noun) a brown sauce made from meat juice.

graze, grazes, grazing, grazed
1 (verb) When animals graze, they eat grass.
2 (noun) a slight injury caused by something scraping against your skin.

grease, greases
1 (noun) an oily substance used for lubricating machines.
2 an oily substance produced by your skin and found in your hair; also in animal fat.
greasy (adjective)

greaseproof paper
(noun) a type of paper which grease cannot pass through, used in cooking and wrapping food.

great, greater, greatest
(adjective) very large, very important or very good. e.g. *a great chunk of ice... a great political figure... a great goal.*
greatly (adverb) **greatness** (noun)

great-grandfather, great-grandfathers
(noun) Your great-grandfather is your father's or mother's grandfather.

great-grandmother, great-grandmothers
(noun) Your great-grandmother is your father's or mother's grandmother.

greedy, greedier, greediest
(adjective) wanting more of something, such as food, than you really need.
greed (noun) **greedily** (adverb)

Greek, Greeks
1 (adjective) belonging to Greece.
2 (noun) someone who comes from Greece.
3 the main language spoken in Greece.
4 In this dictionary, Greek refers to the language used by the ancient Greeks.

green, greener, greenest; greens
1 (adjective, noun) a colour.
2 (noun) an area of grass in the middle of a village usually for public use.
3 an area of smooth short grass used in, for example golf or bowls.
4 (plural noun) Greens are green vegetables.
5 (adjective) used to describe those concerned with environmental issues, e.g. *the Green Party.*
6 (informal) young and inexperienced.

greenfinch, greenfinches
(noun) a common European bird with green and yellow plumage and a strong beak.

green fingers
(noun) someone who has 'green fingers' is good at growing plants.

greengrocer, greengrocers
(noun) a person who sells vegetables and fruit.

greenhouse, greenhouses
(noun) a glass building in which people grow plants that need to be kept warm.

greet, greets, greeting, greeted
(verb) If you greet someone, you say something friendly like 'hello' to them when you meet them.
greeting (noun)

grenade, grenades
(noun) a small bomb thrown by hand.
[Spanish *granada* = pomegranate]

grew past tense of **grow**.

grey, greyer, greyest; greys
(adjective, noun) a colour.
greyness (noun)

greyhound, greyhounds
(noun) a thin, fast-running dog with long legs.

grid, grids
1 (noun) a pattern of lines crossing each other to form squares.
2 The **national grid** is the network of wires and cables by which electricity is distributed throughout a country.
3 an open drain at the roadside for rainwater.

grief, griefs
1 (noun) extreme sadness.
2 (phrase) If someone or something **comes to grief**, they fail or are injured, e.g. *Sir Ralph the Rover came to grief on the Inchcape Rock.*
[Latin *gravis* = concerned with important or sorrowful matters]

Similar words: (noun) anguish, mourning, sadness, sorrow

grieve, grieves, grieving, grieved
(verb) If you grieve, you are extremely sad, especially because someone has died.

Similar words: lament, mourn

Many words from Greek make K with CH: school echo Christmas stomach architect orchid chaos.

grill, grills, grilling, grilled
1 (noun) the part of a cooker where food is cooked by strong heat from above.
2 (verb) If you grill food, you cook it on or under a grill.
3 (verb; informal) If you grill someone, you ask them a lot of questions in a very intense way.

grim, grimmer, grimmest
1 (adjective) If a situation or piece of news is grim, it is very unpleasant and worrying, e.g. *The outlook is grim for the victims of the famine.*
2 unattractive and depressing, e.g. *The streets of Belgrade were grim and sunless.*
3 very serious, e.g. *Her expression was grim.*
grimly (adverb)

grimace, grimaces, grimacing, grimaced
(pronounced grim-**mace**)
1 (noun) a twisted expression of the face indicating annoyance, disgust or pain.
2 (verb) e.g. She grimaced at the weak joke.

grime
(noun) thick dirt.
grimy (adjective)

grin, grins, grinning, grinned
1 (verb) to smile broadly.
2 (phrase) If you **grin and bear it**, you put up with a difficult situation without complaining.

grind, grinds, grinding, ground
1 (verb) to crush into a fine powder.
2 (noun; informal) The daily grind is routine work which is tiring or boring.

Similar words: (verb) crush, powder, pulverize

grip, grips, gripping, gripped
1 (verb) to hold something firmly.
2 (phrase) If you **get to grips with** a situation or problem, you start to deal with it effectively.
3 If you are **losing your grip**, you are becoming less able to deal with things.

gripping
(adjective) A story or film that is gripping is extremely interesting or exciting.

gristle (pronounced **gris**-sl)
(noun) a tough, rubbery substance found in some meat.
gristly (adjective)
[Old English *gristle* = cartilage between bones]

grit, grits, gritting, gritted
1 (noun) very small stones, put on icy roads to make them less slippery.
2 To **grit your teeth** means literally to grind them together; it usually means to carry on bravely doing something unpleasant but necessary.
gritty (adjective)

grizzle, grizzles, grizzling, grizzled
(verb) If a baby or child grizzles, it keeps crying and whining.

groan, groans, groaning, groaned
(verb) to make a long, low sound of pain, unhappiness or disapproval.

grocer, grocers
(noun) a shopkeeper who sells food and household goods.

groceries
(plural noun) Groceries are the goods that you buy in a grocer's shop.

groggy, groggier, groggiest
(adjective) dizzy and sick.

groin
(noun) the area where your legs join the main part of your body at the front.

groom, grooms, grooming, groomed
1 (noun) someone who looks after horses in a stable.
2 At a wedding, the groom is the bridegroom.
3 (verb) To groom an animal means to clean it.

groove, grooves
(noun) a deep line cut into a surface.
grooved (adjective)
[Old Dutch *groeve* = furrow or ditch]

Similar words: channel, hollow, rut

grope, gropes, groping, groped
(verb) If you grope for something you cannot see, you search for it with your hands.

gross, grosser, grossest
1 (adjective) total, e.g. someone's gross income is their total income before any deductions are made. The gross weight of something is its total weight including the weight of its container. Gross stupidity is a state of being totally stupid.
2 (noun) A gross of things is 144 of them.
grossly (adverb)
[Old French *gros* = large]

grotty, grottier, grottiest
(adjective; informal) unattractive or of poor quality, e.g. *a grotty little flat.*

grouchy
(adjective) bad-tempered.

ground, grounds, grounding, grounded
Selected meanings:
1 (noun) the surface of the earth.
2 (verb) the past tense and past participle of **grind**.
3 If a plane is grounded, it cannot take off because of bad weather etc.
4 (informal) If someone is grounded they are not allowed to go out.
5 (phrase) If you **gain ground**, you make progress.
6 If you **get something off the ground**, you get it started.

groundsheet, groundsheets
(noun) a large piece of waterproof material placed on the ground to sleep on when camping.

groundsman, groundsmen
(noun) someone whose job is to look after a sports ground or a park.

group, groups
1 (noun) A group of things or people is a number of them that are linked together in some way.
2 a number of musicians who perform pop music together.

Similar words: (sense 1) assembly, band, bunch, gang, gathering, party

---

Groggy was how British sailors of old felt after drinking their *grog*, a mixture of rum and water.

grovel, grovels, grovelling, grovelled
1 (verb) If you grovel, you behave in an over-humble way towards someone you think is important.
2 to apologize absolutely and completely, e.g. *I forgot the meeting so I had to write and grovel.*
[Middle English *on grufe* = lying on your belly]

grow, grows, growing, grew, grown
1 (verb) to increase in size, amount or degree.
2 (informal) If something grows on you, you gradually get to like it.
3 If you grow out of a type of behaviour, you stop behaving that way.
growth (noun)

Similar words: (sense 1) enlarge, multiply, rise

growl, growls, growling, growled
(verb) When an animal growls, it makes a low rumbling sound, usually because it is angry.
[Old French *grouller* = to grumble]

grown-up, grown-ups
(noun; informal) an adult.

grub, grubs
1 (noun) a worm-like insect that has just hatched from its egg.
2 (informal) another name for food.

grubby, grubbier, grubbiest
(adjective) rather dirty.

grudge, grudges, grudging, grudged
1 (noun) If you have a grudge against someone, you resent them because they have harmed you in the past.
2 (verb) If you grudge someone something, you give it to them unwillingly, or are displeased that they have it.
grudging (adjective) **grudgingly** (adverb)

gruelling
(adjective) difficult and tiring, e.g. *gruelling work.*

Similar words: arduous, strenuous, exhausting

gruesome
(adjective) shocking and horrible, e.g. *Jack the Ripper committed several gruesome murders.*

gruff, gruffer, gruffest
(adjective) If someone's voice is gruff, it sounds rough and unfriendly.
gruffly (adverb)

grumble, grumbles, grumbling, grumbled
(verb) to complain in a bad-tempered way.

grumpy, grumpier, grumpiest
(adjective) bad-tempered and fed-up.
grumpily (adverb) **grumpiness** (noun)

Similar words: gruff, ill-tempered, irritable, surly, touchy, snappy

grunt, grunts, grunting, grunted
(verb) If a person or a pig grunts, they make a short, low, gruff sound.

guarantee, guarantees, guaranteeing, guaranteed
1 (noun) If something is a guarantee of something else, it makes it certain that it will happen.

2 a written promise that if something you buy is faulty, it will be replaced or repaired.
3 (verb) to promise, e.g. *I guarantee it won't happen again, officer.*

Similar words: (noun: sense 2) assurance, pledge

guard, guards, guarding, guarded
1 (verb) If you guard a person or object, you stay near to them to protect them or to make sure they do not escape.
2 If you guard against something, you are careful to avoid it happening.
3 (noun) a person or group of people who guard a person, object or place.
4 a railway official in charge of a train.
5 Any object which covers and protects something can be called a guard, e.g. *a fire guard.*
[Old French *garder* = to protect]

Similar words: (verb) defend, protect, safeguard, watch
(noun) sentry, protector, warden, watchman, lookout

guardian, guardians
(noun) someone who has been legally appointed to look after an orphaned child.

guerrilla, guerrillas (pronounced ger-ril-la); also spelled **guerilla**
(noun) a member of a small, unofficial force of soldiers fighting an official army.
[Spanish *guerrilla* = little war]

guess, guesses, guessing, guessed
1 (verb) If you guess something, you form an opinion without having much information.
2 (noun) an attempt to give an answer to something without having much information.

guest, guests
1 (noun) someone who stays at your home or who visits because they have been invited.
2 a person staying in a hotel.
[Old English *giest* = guest, stranger or enemy]

guest house, houses
(noun) a private house which has rooms where people can pay to stay.

guide, guides, guiding, guided
1 (noun) someone who shows you round places, or leads the way through difficult country.
2 a book which gives you information or instructions. e.g. *a travel guide.*
3 A guide or a girl guide is a girl in the Girl Guides Association.
4 (verb) If you guide someone in a particular direction, you lead them in that direction.
guidance (noun)
[Old French *guider* = to guide]

guided missile, missiles
(noun) a missile which is controlled from the ground during its flight.

guide dog, dogs
(noun) a dog that has been trained to lead a blind person.

guideline, guidelines
(noun) a piece of advice about how something should be done.

'E' and 'i' usually soften 'g', e.g. gents, gin. Putting 'u' in acts as an antidote, e.g. guess, guide.

guillotine, guillotines (pronounced **gil**-lot-teen)
1 (noun) In the past, the guillotine was a machine used for beheading people, especially in France. It was named after Joseph-Ignace Guillotin, who first recommended its use.
2 a piece of equipment with a long sharp blade, used for cutting paper.

guilt
(noun) an unhappy feeling that you have done something wrong.

guilty, guiltier, guiltiest
1 (adjective) If you are guilty of doing something wrong, you did it, e.g. *He was guilty of murder.*
2 If you feel guilty, you are unhappy because you feel you have done something wrong.
guiltily (adverb)

guinea pig, pigs
1 (noun) a small furry animal without a tail.
2 a person used in an experiment, e.g. *She was a guinea pig in tests on a new flu vaccine.*

guitar, guitars
(noun) a musical instrument usually with 6 strings, strummed or plucked with the fingers or a plectrum.
guitarist (noun)
[Spanish *guitarra* = guitar]

Gujarati (pronounced gooj-jer-**rah**-tee); also spelled **Gujerati**
(noun) a language spoken in Gujarat, a state in Western India.

gulf, gulfs
(noun) a very large bay, e.g. *the Persian Gulf.*
[Italian *golfo* = gulf]

gull, gulls
(noun) a seabird with long wings, white and grey or black feathers, and webbed feet.

gullible
(adjective) easily tricked.
gullibility (noun)

Similar words: innocent, naïve

gulp, gulps, gulping, gulped
1 (verb) If you gulp food or drink, you swallow large quantities of it.
2 If you gulp, you swallow air, because you are nervous.

gum, gums, gumming, gummed
1 (noun) a soft, flavoured substance that people chew but do not swallow.
2 glue for sticking paper.
3 Your gums are the firm flesh in which your teeth are set.
[Senses 1-2: Latin *gummi* = gum
sense 3: Old English *goma* = jaw]

gun, guns
(noun) a weapon firing bullets or other missiles propelled by an explosive charge.

gunfire
(noun) the repeated firing of guns.

gunpowder
(noun) an explosive powder made from potassium nitrate and other substances.

gunshot, gunshots
(noun) the sound of a gun being fired.

gurgle, gurgles, gurgling, gurgled
(verb) to make a bubbling sound.
[Latin *gurgulio* = gullet or throat]

gush, gushes, gushing, gushed
(verb) When liquid gushes from something, it flows out of it in large quantities.

Similar words: cascade, flow, spout, spurt

gust, gusts
(noun) a sudden rush of wind.
gusty (adjective)

gut, guts, gutting, gutted
1 (plural noun) Your guts are your internal organs, especially your intestines.
2 (noun; informal) Guts is courage, e.g. *'I'll show them who's got guts', said the man as he jumped off the top of the skyscraper.*
3 (verb) If a building is gutted, the inside of it is destroyed by fire.
4 (informal) If you feel gutted, you feel humiliated usually because you have said or done something wrong.

Similar words: (noun: sense 1) bowels, intestines

gutter, gutters
1 (noun) the edge of a road next to the pavement, where rain collects and flows away, e.g. *We are al in the gutter, but some of us are looking at the sta*
2 a channel fixed to the edge of a roof, where rain collects and flows away.
guttering (noun)

guy, guys
1 (noun) A guy or guy rope is a rope or wire used to keep a pole or a tent fixed in position.
2 (informal) a man or boy, e.g. *That Superman is quite a guy!*

guzzle, guzzles, guzzling, guzzled
(verb) to drink or eat quickly and greedily.

gym, gyms
(noun) a gymnasium.

gymkhana, gymkhanas (pronounced jim-**kah**-na)
(noun) an event in which people take part in horse-riding contests.
[Hindi *gend-khana* = ball house or racket court, because it is where sports were held]

gymnasium, gymnasiums
(noun) a room with special equipment for physical exercises.
[Greek *gumnazein* = to exercise naked]

gymnastics
(noun) physical exercises, especially ones using equipment such as bars and ropes.
gymnast (noun) **gymnastic** (adjective)

gypsy, gypsies; also spelled **gipsy**
(noun) a member of a race of people, originally from India but now found mainly in Europe, who travel around in caravans.
[from 'Egyptian', because people used to think gypsies came from Egypt]

A bird, a man, a loaded gun.
No bird, dead man, Thy will be done.

H

habit, habits
1 (noun) something that you do often, e.g. *The worst boss anyone can have is a bad habit.*
2 a loose garment worn by a monk or nun.
habitual (adjective) **habitually** (adverb)
[Latin *habitus* = custom]

habitat, habitats
(noun) The habitat of a plant or animal is its natural environment where it grows or lives.
[Latin *habitare* = to live or to inhabit]

hack, hacks, hacking, hacked
1 (verb) to cut it using rough strokes.
2 (noun) a long, steady horseride with several horses together.
3 (verb; informal) If you can't hack something, you can't put up with it.

hacker, hackers
(noun; informal) someone who uses a computer to hack or break into the computer system of a company or government.

hackneyed
(adjective) A hackneyed phrase is dull and of little use because it has been used too often.

Similar words: clichéd, overworked

hacksaw, hacksaws
(noun) a small saw with a narrow blade set in a frame. It is used for cutting metal.

haddock
(noun) an edible sea fish.

haemophilia; also spelled **hemophilia**
(pronounced hee-moh-fil-lee-a)
(noun) a condition that some people have from birth in which the blood does not clot, so they bleed for too long when they are injured.
haemophiliac (noun)

haemorrhage; also spelled **hemorrhage**
(pronounced hem-er-rij)
(noun) serious bleeding especially inside a person's body, e.g. *a brain haemorrhage.*
[Greek *haima* + *rhegnunai* = blood burst]

hag, hags
(noun; offensive) an ugly old woman.

haggard
(adjective) looking very tired and ill.

haggle, haggles, haggling, haggled
(verb) If you haggle with someone, you argue with them, usually about the cost of something.

haiku, haikus
(noun) a three part poem of 17 syllables.
[a Japanese word]

hail, hails, hailing, hailed
1 (noun) frozen rain.
2 A hail of things is a lot of them falling together, e.g. *a hail of bullets... a hail of abuse.*
3 (verb) to attract someone's attention, e.g. *to hail a taxi.*

hair, hairs
1 (noun) e.g. *Your hair needs cutting.*
2 (phrase) If you **let your hair down**, you relax completely and enjoy yourself.
3 Someone who is **splitting hairs** is arguing about unimportant details.
4 **A hair's breadth** is a very small amount, e.g. *The bullet missed me by a hair's breadth.*
hairstyle (noun) **haircut** (noun) **hairdo** (noun) **hairdresser** (noun) **hair-grip** (noun)

hairpin
(adjective) A hairpin bend is a U-shaped bend in the road.

hair-raising
(adjective) very frightening or exciting, e.g. *It was a hair-raising journey in the back of the Ferrari sports car.*

hairy, hairier, hairiest
1 (adjective) covered in a lot of hair.
2 (informal) difficult, exciting and rather frightening, e.g. *The ice made driving a bit hairy.*

hake, hakes
(noun) an edible sea fish related to the cod.

half, halves
1 (noun, adjective, adverb), Half refers to one of two equal parts that make up a whole, e.g. *a half-pint... half full.*
2 (phrase) Someone who **never does things by halves** always does things thoroughly and completely.

half-baked
(adjective; informal) not properly thought out, e.g. *half-baked ideas.*

half-brother, half-brothers
(noun) Your half-brother is a boy or man who has either the same mother or father as you but not both parents the same.

half-caste, half-castes
(noun) someone with parents of different races.
[Old English *healf* = half + Portugese *casta* = race]

half-hearted
(adjective) showing no real effort or enthusiasm.
half-heartedly (adverb)

half-mast
(noun) A flag at half-mast is flying halfway down the pole, usually as a signal of mourning for someone who has died.

half-sister, half-sisters
(noun) Your half-sister is a girl or woman who has either the same mother or father as you but not both parents the same.

half-time
(noun) a short break between two parts of a game when the players have a rest.

halfway
(adverb) at a middle point, e.g. *She was halfway up the stairs... halfway through the show.*

Letter H might have begun as a picture of a fence or perhaps a piece of twisted rope.

halibut, halibuts
(noun) a type of large, edible flatfish.
[Old English *halig* = holy + Old Dutch *butte* =
flat fish; halibut was often eaten on holy days]

hall, halls
1 (noun) the small room just inside the front
entrance of a house.
2 a large room or building used for public
meetings, concerts, plays and exhibitions.

hallowed (pronounced **hal**-lode)
(adjective) holy, e.g. *This churchyard is
hallowed ground.*
[Old English *halig* = holy]

Hallowe'en; also spelt **Halloween**
(noun) October 31st, traditionally believed to be
the night on which ghosts and witches can be
seen.
[Old English *halig* + *æfen* = holy evening, the
evening before All Saints' Day]

hallucinations (pronounced
hal-**loo**-sin-ay-shons)
(noun) If you are suffering from hallucinations,
you see strange things in your mind.
hallucinate (verb) **hallucinatory** (adjective)
[Latin *alucinari* = to wander in thought]

halo, haloes or **halos**
(noun) a circle of light around the head of a holy
figure.
[Greek *halos* = disc shape of the sun or moon]

halt, halts, halting, halted
(verb) to stop.

halter, halters
(noun) a strap fastened round a horse's head so
that it can be led easily.

halve, halves, halving, halved (pronounced **hahv**)
(verb) to cut something in half.

ham, hams
1 (noun) meat from the hind leg of a pig, salted,
cured and bought ready-cooked.
2 A radio ham is an amateur radio enthusiast.
3 A ham actor, or ham, is one who overacts
emotions and gestures.

hamburger, hamburgers
(noun) a flat disc of minced meat, seasoned and
fried, often eaten in a bread roll.
[from its city of origin, *Hamburg* in Germany]

hamlet, hamlets
(noun) a small village.
[Old English *ham* = home + *-let* = small]

hammer, hammers, hammering, hammered
1 (noun) a tool for hitting nails into things.
2 (verb) If you hammer something, you hit it
repeatedly, with a hammer or with your fist.
3 In sport, a hammer is a heavy weight attached
to a wire and thrown.

hammer out
(phrasal verb) To hammer out an agreement
means to reach it after a long time discussing it.

hammock, hammocks
(noun) a piece of net or canvas hung between
two supports and used as a bed.

hamper, hampers, hampering, hampered
1 (noun) a wicker food basket with a lid.
2 (verb) If you hamper someone, you make it
difficult for them to move or progress, e.g.
Progress was hampered by the mud on the road.

Similar words: (verb) impede, hinder, obstruct, limit,
handicap

hamster, hamsters
(noun) a small furry rodent, with cheek-pouches
for carrying grain.

hand, hands, handing, handed
1 (noun) e.g. *My hands are freezing... The hands
on the clock said 3.50... Give me a hand to shift
this piano.*
2 (verb) to pass something to someone, e.g. *Hand
me that saw, nurse.*
3 to give someone credit or praise e.g. *You've got
to hand it to her.*
4 (noun) to give someone a hand or a big hand
means to applaud them.
5 In a game of cards, your hand is the cards you
have been dealt.
6 a person's natural style of handwriting, e.g.
and I copied all the letters in a big round hand.
7 a worker doing a physical job, e.g. *All hands on
deck!*
8 a measurement of about 10 centimetres, used to
measure the height of horses.
9 (phrases) Something that is **at hand, to hand,** or
on hand is available, close by and ready for use,
e.g. *Luckily the police were on hand to sort it out.*
10 A situation that is **out of hand** is out of control.
11 If you **wash your hands of something,** you
refuse to have any more involvement with it, e.g.
Pilate washed his hands of Jesus's death.
12 If you **have the upper hand,** you have an
advantage over someone.
13 If you **win hands down,** you win very easily or
by a great amount.

hand down
(phrasal verb) Something that is handed down is
passed from one generation to another.

handbag
(noun) a leather container for personal
belongings, carried by hand.

handbook, handbooks
(noun) a book giving information and
instructions about something.

handcuffs
(plural noun) metal rings used to prevent
prisoners from escaping.

handful, handfuls
1 (noun) a small quantity, e.g. *We employ only a
handful of workers.*
2 Someone who is a handful is difficult to
control, e.g. *She is a bit of a handful.*

handicap, handicaps, handicapping, handicapped
1 (noun) a physical or mental disability.
2 In sport or a competition, a handicap is a
disadvantage or advantage given to competitors
according to their skill, in order to equalize
people's chances of winning.
3 (verb) If something handicaps a person, it

Some surnames come from the places lived near: Hill Wood Hall Ford.

makes it difficult for them to do what they want to do in a satisfactory way.
handicapped (adjective)

Similar words: (noun) disability, impediment

handkerchief, handkerchiefs
(noun) a cloth used for blowing your nose.

handle, handles, handling, handled
1 (verb) If you handle an object, you hold it in your hands to examine it.
2 If you handle something, you deal with it or control it, e.g. *He handled the case very well.*

handlebars
(plural noun) Handlebars are used to steer a bicycle.

hand-picked
(adjective) carefully chosen, e.g. *Scott took a hand-picked team of men to the Antarctic.*

handshake, handshakes
(noun) the grasping and shaking of a person's hand by another person as a greeting etc.

handsome
(adjective) very attractive in appearance, e.g. *a handsome man.*

Similar word: good-looking

handstand, handstands
(noun) balancing upside down on the hands.

handwriting
(noun) Someone's handwriting is their style of writing as it looks on the page.

handy, handier, handiest
1 (adjective) useful and convenient.
2 skilful, e.g. *She's handy with a screwdriver.*

hang, hangs, hanging, hung
1 (verb) e.g. *The washing hangs on the line... The threat of going to prison hung over her.*
2 (phrase) When you **get the hang of** something, you understand it and are able to do it.
3 (verb) If someone hangs, their neck is broken by a sudden drop. For this sense of 'hang', the past tense and past participle is **hanged.**

Similar words: drape, suspend, dangle

hang about or **hang around**
1 (phrasal verb; informal) to wait somewhere.
2 To hang around with someone means to spend a lot of time with them.

hang on
1 (phrasal verb) to hold something tightly or keep it.
2 (informal) to wait.

hang out
(phrasal verb; informal) If you hang out somewhere, you live or spend a lot of time there.

hang up
(phrasal verb) When you hang up, you put down the receiver to end a telephone conversation.

hangar, hangars
(noun) a large building where aircraft are kept.

hanger, hangers
(noun) e.g. *a coat hanger.*

hang-glider, hang-gliders
(noun) an unpowered aircraft consisting of a large frame covered in fabric, from which the pilot is suspended in a harness.

hangover, hangovers
(noun) a feeling of sickness and headache after drinking too much alcohol.

hang-up, hang-ups
(noun) a continual feeling of embarrassment or fear about something, e.g. *She had a hang-up about spiders.*

hanky, hankies
(noun) a handkerchief.

hanky-panky
(verb) naughty or mischievous behaviour.

haphazard (pronounced hap-**haz**-ard)
(adjective) not organized or planned.
haphazardly (adverb)
[Old Norse *hap* = chance + Arabic *azzahr* = gaming dice]

happen, happens, happening, happened
(verb) to occur or take place.
happening (noun)

happiness
(noun) a feeling of great contentment or pleasure.

Similar words: joy, bliss, gladness

happy, happier, happiest
1 (adjective) e.g. *Have a very happy birthday.*
2 (phrase) If someone is **happy-go-lucky**, they are very casual and carefree about life.

harass, harasses, harassing, harassed
(pronounced **harr**-us; Americans say harr-**ass**)
(verb) If someone harasses you, they trouble or annoy you continually.
harassed (adjective) **harassment** (noun)
[Old French *harer* = to set a dog on]

harbour, harbours
(noun) a protected area of deep water where boats can be moored.
[Old English *here* + *beorg* = army shelter]

hard, harder, hardest
1 (adjective, adverb) e.g. *The ice cream was as hard as a brick... It was a hard sum to do... You have to work hard to succeed.*
2 (adjective) Someone who is hard has no kindness or pity, e.g. *Don't be hard on him... She's as hard as nails.*
3 Hard evidence or facts can be proved to be true.
4 Hard water contains a lot of lime, leaves a coating on kettles and does not easily produce a lather.
5 Hard drugs are very strong and dangerous.
6 Hard drink is strong alcohol.
hardness (noun) **harden** (verb)

Similar words: firm, solid, stiff, rigid, set

hard and fast
(adjectival phrase) fixed and not able to be changed,
e.g. *hard and fast rules.*

hardback, hardbacks
(noun) a book with a stiff cover.

Proverbs contradict. Many hands make light work. Too many cooks spoil the broth.

hardboard
(noun) wood fibres pressed together to form a flat sheet.

hard disk, disks
(noun) storage for data inside a computer. The data remains when the machine is off.

hardhearted
(adjective) unsympathetic and uncaring.

hardly
(adverb) almost not or not quite, e.g. *He had hardly any money.*

hard of hearing
(adjectival phrase) not able to hear properly.

hardship, hardships
(noun) a time or situation of suffering and difficulty.

hard shoulder, shoulders
(noun) the area at the edge of a motorway where drivers can stop if their car breaks down.

hard up
(adjective; informal) having hardly any money.

hardware
1 (noun) tools and equipment for use in the home and garden.
2 computer machinery, e.g. computer, printer.

hard-wearing
(adjective) strong, well-made and long-lasting.

hardwood, hardwoods
(noun) strong, hard wood from a deciduous tree e.g. oak, beech, ash, teak.

hardy, hardier, hardiest
(adjective) tough and able to endure very difficult or cold conditions.
[Old French *hardi* = bold]

hare, hares, haring, hared
1 (noun) an animal like a large rabbit.
2 (verb) To hare about means to run very fast, e.g. *He hared off down the corridor.*

harebrained
(adjective) foolish and likely to be unsuccessful, e.g. *harebrained ideas.*

harm, harms, harming, harmed
(verb) to injure or damage someone or something.
[Old German *harm* = injury]

Similar word: wound

harmful
(adjective) having a bad effect on something, e.g. *Too much salt can be harmful to your health.*

harmless
(adjective) safe to use or be near.
harmlessly (adverb) **harmlessness** (noun)

Similar words: inoffensive, safe

harmonica, harmonicas
(noun) a small musical instrument which you play by blowing and sucking.

harmony, harmonies
1 (noun) a state of peaceful agreement and co-operation, e.g. *working together in harmony.*

2 In music, harmony is the pleasant combination of two or more notes played at the same time.
harmonious (adjective) **harmonize** (verb)
[Greek *harmonia* = agreement]

harness, harnesses, harnessing, harnessed
1 (noun) a set of straps and fittings fastened round a horse so that it can pull a vehicle, or fastened round someone's body to attach something, e.g. *a parachute harness.*
2 (verb) If you harness something, you bring it under control to use it, e.g. *harnessing the energy of the sun.*
[Old French *herneis* = military equipment]

harp, harps, harping, harped
1 (noun) a musical instrument consisting of a triangular frame with vertical strings which you pluck with your fingers.
harpist (noun)
2 (verb) If someone harps on about something, they keep talking about it in a boring way.

harpoon, harpoons
(noun) a spear attached to a rope, thrown or fired from a gun to catch whales or large fish.

harsh, harsher, harshest
(adjective) severe, difficult and unpleasant, e.g. *a harsh winter... harsh treatment.*
harshly (adverb) **harshness** (noun)

Similar words: hard, tough, demanding

harvest, harvests
(noun) the cutting and gathering of a crop.
[Old German *herbist* = autumn]

harvest festival, festivals
(noun) a Christian church service held in autumn to give thanks for the harvest.

hash
1 (phrase) If you **make a hash of** a job, you do it badly.
2 (noun) a dish made of small pieces of meat and vegetables cooked together.
3 (informal) another name for cannabis.
[an abbreviation of 'hashish']
[Old French *hacher* = to chop up]

hassle, hassles, hassling, hassled
1 (noun; informal) Something that is a hassle is difficult or causes trouble.
2 (verb) to annoy someone by repeatedly asking them to do something.

hasty, hastier, hastiest
(adjective) done or happening suddenly and quickly, often without enough care or thought.
hastily (adverb) **haste** (noun) **hasten** (verb)
[Old English *hæst* = violence or fury]

hat, hats
1 (noun) e.g. *Lady Pigg's hat blew off.*
2 (phrase) If you say you'll **eat your hat** if something happens, you mean you do not believe it will happen.
3 If you do something **at the drop of a hat**, you do it straight away without hesitation.

hatch, hatches, hatching, hatched
1 (verb) When an egg hatches, it breaks open and a young bird or reptile emerges.

Can you draw these hats: bowler deerstalker fez mitre trilby beret sombrero?

2 (noun) a covered opening in a floor, wall or ceiling.

hatchback, hatchbacks
(noun) a car with a door at the back which opens upwards.

hatchet, hatchets
1 (noun) a small axe.
2 (phrase) To **bury the hatchet** means to sort out a disagreement and become friends again.
[Old French *hachette* = little axe]

hate, hates, hating, hated
(noun) a strong feeling of dislike.

Similar words: loathe, detest, abhor, despise

hateful
(adjective) extremely unpleasant, e.g. *Blackmail is a hateful thing.*

Similar words: abominable, loathsome, detestable, obnoxious

hatred (pronounced **hay**-trid)
(noun) an extremely strong feeling of dislike, e.g. *There is no greater hatred in the world than the hatred of ignorance for knowledge.*

haughty, haughtier, haughtiest (rhymes with **naughty**)
(adjective) big-headed; looking down on other people, e.g. *He gave a haughty wave of the hand.*
haughtily (adverb) **haughtiness** (noun)
[Old French *haut* = high]

Similar words: high and mighty, proud, snooty

haul, hauls, hauling, hauled
1 (verb) to pull with great effort and difficulty.
2 (noun) a quantity of something obtained, e.g. *a good haul of fish... Thieves have made some big hauls in this area.*
3 (phrase) Something that is **a long haul** takes a lot of time and effort to achieve, e.g. *It was a long haul before women got the vote.*

haulage (pronounced **hawl**-lij)
(noun) the business of transporting goods by road.

haunt, haunts, haunting, haunted
1 (verb) If a ghost haunts a place, it is seen or heard there regularly.
2 If a memory or a fear haunts you, it continually worries you.
3 (noun) A person's favourite haunt is a place they like to visit often.
[Old French *hanter* = visit]

haunted
(adjective) regularly visited by a ghost, e.g. *a haunted house.*

have, has, having, had
1 (verb) e.g. *I have a headache... Have a sweet!... The train has left... Has she had a baby?*
2 (phrase) If you **have it in for** someone, you dislike them and are determined to cause them trouble.
3 If you are **having someone on**, you are teasing them by trying to deceive them.

4 If someone is **had up** for something, they are brought before a court for committing an offence.
5 If you have **been had**, you have been tricked.

haversack, haversacks (pronounced **hav**-er-sak)
(noun) a light bag with straps, worn on your back, used for carrying things when you are walking.
[German *Habersack* = oat bag]

hawk, hawks
(noun) a large bird of prey with a short, hooked bill, sharp claws and very good eyesight.

hay
1 (noun) grass which has been cut and dried and is used as animal feed.
2 (phrase) To **make hay while the sun shines** means to do something while you have the chance.

hay fever
(noun) an allergy to pollen and grass causing sneezing, a blocked nose and watering eyes.

hazard, hazards, hazarding, hazarded
1 (noun) something which could be dangerous to you, e.g. *That loose carpet is a safety hazard.*
2 (phrase) If you **hazard a guess**, you make a guess.
hazardous (adjective)
[Arabic *az-zahr* = gaming dice]

haze
(noun) If there is a haze, you can't see clearly because there is moisture, dust or smoke in the air.
hazy (adjective)

he
(third person pronoun) e.g. *He has his bike with him.*

head, heads, heading, headed
Selected meanings:
1 (noun) e.g. *I hit my head on the beam... Sit at the head of the table... He is the Head of Maths here... Heads I win!*
2 (verb) e.g. *They filled up the car and headed out of the city... He headed the ball into the net.*
3 (noun) The heads on a tape recorder etc., are the parts which transmit or receive the electronic signal onto or from the tape.
4 (phrase) If someone **bites** or **snaps your head off**, they speak to you sharply and angrily.
5 If you give some information **off the top of your head**, you give it from memory.
6 If you **lose your head**, you panic.
7 If you **can't make head or tail of something**, you cannot understand it.

headache, headaches
1 (noun) a pain in your head.
2 Something that is a headache is causing a lot of difficulty or worry, e.g. *The child had become a real headache for the teachers.*

heading, headings
(noun) a piece of writing that is written or printed at the top of a page or section.

headlight, headlights
(noun) the large lights at the front of a vehicle.

I should have known that! The words 'should' 'could' and 'would' are followed by *have* not *of*.

headline, headlines
1 (noun) the title of a newspaper article printed in large, bold type.
2 The news headlines are the main points of the radio or TV news.

headmaster, headmasters
(noun) a man in charge of a school.

headmistress, headmistresses
(noun) a woman in charge of a school.

headphones
(plural noun) a pair of small speakers which you wear over your ears to listen to music etc.

headquarters
(noun) the main place from which an organization is run.

headstand, headstands
(noun) If you do a headstand, you balance upside down on your head and your hands.

headteacher, headteachers
(noun) the teacher in charge of a school.

heal, heals, healing, healed
(verb) If something heals or if you heal it, it becomes healthy or normal again, e.g. *His leg needs support while the bone is healing.*
healer (noun)

health
1 (noun) the normally good condition of someone's body, e.g. *Smoking damages your health.*
2 (phrase) To **drink someone's health** means to drink to wish them good health and happiness. [Old English *hælth*, a toast drunk to a person's wellbeing]

health food, foods
(noun) food which is free from added chemicals and is considered to be good for your health.

healthy, healthier, healthiest
1 (adjective) fit and strong with no diseases.
2 Something that is healthy is good for you and likely to make you fit and strong.
healthily (adverb)

heap, heaps
1 (noun) a pile.
2 (informal) Heaps of something means plenty of it, e.g. *We've got heaps of time.*

Similar words: pile, stack, mound, mass

---

hear, hears, hearing, heard
1 (verb) When you hear sounds, you are aware of them because they reach your ears.
2 (interjection) **'Hear, hear!'** is sometimes said to show agreement with a speaker.
hearing (noun)

hearsay
(noun; informal) an account, heard from someone else, of an event which you did not see yourself. It therefore may not be true.

heart, hearts
1 (noun) the organ in your chest that pumps the blood around your body.
2 courage, determination or enthusiasm, e.g. *People were losing heart.*

3 the most central and important part of something, e.g. *Get right to the heart of the matter... deep in the heart of the city.*
4 Hearts is one of the 4 suits in a pack of playing cards. It is marked by a red ♥ symbol.
5 (phrase) If you know something **by heart**, you can remember it all perfectly.
6 If you have a **change of heart**, you change your mind about something.
7 Someone who is a person **after your own heart** shares your own opinions or interests.
8 If your **heart is in your mouth**, you are very frightened.

heart attack, attacks
(noun) a serious medical condition in which the heart suddenly beats unevenly or stops completely.

heartbroken
(adjective) very sad and emotionally upset, e.g. *She would be heartbroken if he died.*
heartbreak (noun) **heartbreaking** (adjective)

hearth, hearths (pronounced **harth**)
(noun) the floor of a fireplace.

heartless
(adjective) cruel and unkind.
heartlessly (adverb)

hearty, heartier, heartiest
1 (adjective) cheerful and enthusiastic, e.g. *hearty applause... a hearty welcome.*
2 A hearty meal is large and satisfying.
heartily (adverb)

heat, heats, heating, heated
1 (noun) warmth.
2 A heat is one of a series of contests in a competition. The winners of a heat go forward to play in the next round of the competition.
3 (verb) to warm something up.

heath, heaths
(noun) an area of open land covered with rough grass or heather.
[Old German *heida* = heather]

heather
(noun) a low, spreading moorland plant with spiky leaves and pink, purple or white flowers.

heatwave, heatwaves
(noun) a period of several weeks during which the weather is much hotter than usual.

heave, heaves, heaving, heaved
1 (verb) to pull, push or throw something with a lot of effort .
2 (noun) If your stomach heaves, you vomit or suddenly feel sick.
3 If you heave a sigh, you sigh loudly.
[Old German *heffen* = to raise]

heaven, heavens
1 (noun) a place of happiness where God is believed to live and where good people are believed to go when they die.
2 If you describe a situation as heaven, you mean that it is wonderful, e.g. *The cottage in the Highlands was just heaven.*

We have five senses through which we experience our environment:
sight, hearing, smell, touch, taste....

3 (phrase) You say **'Good heavens'** to express surprise.
heavenly (adjective)

heavy, heavier, heaviest
1 (adjective) great in weight or force, e.g. *How heavy are you?... heavy rain.*
2 great in degree or amount, e.g. *There were heavy casualties.*
3 solid and thick in appearance, e.g. *glasses with heavy frames.*
4 using a lot of something quickly, e.g. *The van is heavy on petrol.*
5 (informal) serious and difficult to deal with or understand, e.g. *It all got a bit heavy when the police arrived... a heavy speech.*
heavily (adverb) **heaviness** (noun)

heavy-duty
(adjective) strong and hardwearing e.g. *a heavy-duty car battery.*

heavy metal
(noun) a style of loud, fast rock music.

heavyweight, heavyweights
(noun) a boxer in the heaviest weight group (over 13 stone 8 lbs).

Hebrew, (pronounced **hee**-broo)
(noun) an ancient language now spoken in Israel, where it is the official language.
[Hebrew *ibhri* = one from beyond (the river)]

hectare, hectares
(noun) a unit for measuring areas of land. (1 hectare = 10,000 square metres = 2.471 acres)
[Greek *hekaton* = 100 + *area* = piece of ground]

hectic
(adjective) extremely busy and rushed, e.g. *Every day is hectic at Waterloo Station.*
[Greek *hektikos* = habitual]

hedge, hedges
(noun) a row of bushes forming a barrier or boundary.

hedgehog, hedgehogs
(noun) a small, brown, nocturnal animal with sharp spikes covering its back.

heed, heeds, heeding, heeded
(verb) If you heed someone's advice, you pay attention to it.

Similar words: mark, mind, note

heel, heels
1 (noun) the back part of your foot, shoe or sock.
2 (phrase) If you **dig your heels in**, you refuse to be persuaded to do something.
3 If you are left **cooling your heels**, you are being kept waiting.
4 A person or place that looks **down at heel** looks untidy and in poor condition.

hefty, heftier, heftiest
(adjective) of great size, force or weight, e.g. *a hefty profit... a hefty slap on the back.*

heifer, heifers (pronounced **hef**-fer)
(noun) a young cow that has not yet had a calf.

height, heights
1 (noun) The height of an object is its measurement from the bottom to the top.
2 a high position or place.
3 the time when something is most successful or intense, e.g. *the height of the tourist season... Elvis was at the height of his fame.*
heighten (verb)

heir, heirs (pronounced **air**)
(noun) A person's heir is the person who will inherit their property or title.
[Greek *khēros* = bereaved]

heiress, heiresses (pronounced **air**-iss)
(noun) a female with the right to inherit property or a title.

heirloom, heirlooms (pronounced **air**-loom)
(noun) something belonging to a family that has been passed from one generation to another.

helicopter, helicopters
(noun) an aircraft with large rotating horizontal blades.
[Greek *heliko* + *pteron* = spiral wing]

heliport, heliports
(noun) an airport for helicopters.

hell
1 (noun) the place where souls of evil people are believed to go to be punished after death.
2 (informal) If you say that something is hell, you mean it is very unpleasant.
3 If you **raise hell**, you protest angrily about something.
4 If you do something **for the hell of it**, you do it for fun.

hello
(interjection) a greeting .

helmet, helmets
(noun) a hard hat worn to protect the head.

help, helps, helping, helped
1 (verb) e.g. *She helped me feed the ducks.*
2 (noun) e.g. *Thank you for all your help.*
helper (noun)

Similar words: aid, assist

helpful
(adjective) If someone is helpful, they help you by doing something for you.
helpfully (adverb) **helpfulness** (noun)

Similar words: co-operative, obliging

helping, helpings
(noun) the amount of food in a single serving.

helpless
(adjective) without power, strength or protection, e.g. *a helpless child.*
helplessly (adverb) **helplessness** (noun)

helter-skelter, helter-skelters
(noun) a tall, spiral-shaped slide, usually in a fairground.

hem, hems, hemming, hemmed
(noun) an edge of a garment which has been turned over and sewn in place.

....When you write a description, try to make use of all your senses to bring your description to life.

hem in
(phrasal verb) If someone is hemmed in, they are surrounded and prevented from moving.

hemisphere, hemispheres (pronounced **hem**-iss-feer)
(noun) one half of the earth, the brain or a sphere, e.g. *the southern hemisphere*.
hemispherical (adjective)
[Greek *hemi-* + *sphaira* = half a globe]

hemophilia another spelling of **haemophilia**

hemorrhage another spelling of **haemorrhage**

hen, hens
(noun) a female chicken; also any female bird.

henpecked
(adjective; informed) If a married man is henpecked, his wife is always nagging him.

heptagon, heptagons
(noun) a shape with 7 straight sides.
heptagonal (adjective)
[Greek *hepta* + *-gonos* = seven-angled]

her
(pronoun) e.g. *Don't tell her anything.*

heraldry
(noun) the study of coats of arms and the histories of families.
heraldic (adjective)

herb, herbs
(noun) a plant whose leaves are used in medicine or to flavour food.
herbal (adjective) **herbalist** (noun)
[Latin *herba* = grass]

herbivore, herbivores
(noun) an animal that eats only plants.
herbivorous (adjective)
[Latin *herbivora* = grass-eaters]

herd, herds, herding, herded
1 (noun) a large group of animals.
2 (verb) To herd animals or people means to make them move together as a group, e.g. *On the coach trip we were herded around like sheep.*

here
(adverb) e.g. *Please sit here.*

hereditary
(adjective) passed on to a child from a parent, e.g. *Sadly, AIDS can be a hereditary disease.*

heritage
(noun) the possessions, traditions or conditions that have been passed from one generation to another, e.g. *The cathedrals of Britain are part of our heritage.*

hermit, hermits
(noun) a person who lives alone with a simple lifestyle, especially for religious reasons.
[Greek *erēmitēs* = living in the desert]

hero, heroes
1 (noun) the main male character on the side of good in a book, film or play.
2 a person who has done something brave or good, e.g. *Boy hero saves sister from river.*

heroic
(adjective) brave, courageous and determined.
heroically (adverb)

heroin (pronounced **herr**-oh-in)
(noun) a powerful and very addictive drug used as an anaesthetic and now taken illegally by some people for pleasure.

heroine, heroines (pronounced **herr**-oh-in)
1 (noun) the main female character on the side of good in a book, film or play.
2 a woman who has done something brave or good e.g. *Young heroine rescues dog.*

heroism (pronounced **herr**-oh-i-zm)
(noun) great courage and bravery.

heron, herons
(noun) a wading bird with very long legs, broad wings and a long beak and neck.

herring, herrings
(noun) a type of silvery fish that lives in large shoals in northern seas.

hers
(pronoun) e.g. *This book is hers not mine.*

herself
(pronoun) e.g. *She helped herself to salad.*

hesitant
(adjective) If you are hesitant, you do not do something immediately because you are uncertain, worried or embarrassed.
hesitantly (adverb) **hesitance** (noun)
hesitancy (noun)

Similar words: uncertain, doubtful, indecisive

hesitate, hesitates, hesitating, hesitated
(verb) to pause or show uncertainty, e.g. *The soldier hesitated before jumping from the plane.*
hesitation (noun)
[Latin *haesitare* = to be undecided]

Similar words: falter, dither

het up
(adjective; informal) anxious, worried or excited.

hexagon, hexagons
(noun) a shape with 6 straight sides.
hexagonal (adjective)
[Greek *hex* + *-gonos* = six-angled]

hibernate, hibernates, hibernating, hibernated
(verb) Animals that hibernate spend the winter in a resting state in which their temperature, heartbeat and breathing rate become very low.
hibernation (noun)
[Latin *hibernare* = to spend the winter]

hiccup, hiccups
(pronounced **hik**-kup); also spelled **hiccough**
1 (noun) Hiccups are short, uncontrolled choking sounds in your throat that you sometimes get if you have been eating or drinking too quickly.
2 (informal) a minor problem, e.g. *We apologize for the slight hiccup.*

hide, hides, hiding, hid, hidden
1 (verb) to put out of sight.
2 (noun) the skin of a large animal.

Similar words: (verb) conceal, obscure, bury

hideous (pronounced **hid**-ee-uss)
(adjective) extremely ugly or unpleasant.
hideously (adverb)
[Old French *hisdos* = fear]

hideout, hideouts
(noun) a hiding place.

hiding, hidings
(noun; informal) To give someone a hiding means
to beat them severely.

hieroglyphics (pronounced high-ra-**gliff**-iks)
(noun) pictures or symbols used in the writing
system of ancient Egypt.
[Greek *hieros* + *gluphē* = sacred carving]

hi-fi
(noun) a set of stereo equipment on which you
can play records, tapes and compact discs.
[from high fidelity]

higgledy-piggledy
(adjective, adverb; informal) in a great muddle
or disorder.

high, higher, highest
1 (adjective, advert) e.g. *high mountains... We
flew high over the Rockies.*
2 (adjective) e.g. *high prices... a high voice...
high pressure.*
3 Food that is high has an unpleasant smell and
is beginning to go bad.
4 (informal) Someone who is high, or on a high, is
in a very excited and optimistic mood.
5 (phrase) If it is **high time** that something was
done, it should be done immediately.
6 If you are left **high and dry**, you have been
abandoned in a difficult situation.
7 Someone whose behaviour is **high and mighty** is
too confident and full of self-importance.
highly (adverb)

Similar words: (adjective: sense 1) tall, lofty,
towering

higher education
(noun) education at universities, polytechnics
and certain colleges. Compare **further education**

high-fidelity
(adjective) High-fidelity recording equipment
produces very high quality sound.

high jump
1 (noun) an athletics event.
2 (phrase; informal) If you are **for the high jump**,
you are going to be in trouble.

highlands
(noun) mountainous or hilly areas of land,
e.g. *the Highlands of Scotland.*

highlight, highlights, highlighting, highlighted
1 (verb) If you highlight a point or problem, you
draw attention to it.
2 (noun) The highlight of something is the most
interesting part of it, e.g. *Seeing the palace was
the highlight of the trip.*
3 Highlights are also light-coloured streaks in
someone's hair.
4 A highlighter is a pen with bright, transparent
ink which shows things up on a page.

highly strung
(adjective) very nervous and easily upset.

Highness
(noun) Highness is used in titles and forms of
address for members of the royal family other
than a king or queen, e.g. *Her Royal Highness,
Princess Alexandra.*

high-pitched
(adjective) A high-pitched sound or voice is high
and often rather shrill.

high-rise
(adjective) High-rise buildings are very tall, e.g.
a high-rise block of flats.

high school, schools
(noun) a type of secondary school.

high tea
(noun) usually quite a large meal eaten in the
early evening, often with tea to drink.

high technology
(noun) the development and use of advanced
electronics, computers and robots.

high tide
(noun) On a coast, high tide is the time, usually
twice a day, when the sea is at its highest level.

highwayman, highwaymen
(noun) In the past, highwaymen were robbers on
horseback who used to rob travellers at gunpoint.

hijack, hijacks, hijacking, hijacked
(verb) If someone hijacks a plane or vehicle, they
illegally take control of it, forcing the pilot,
driver, etc. to follow their instructions.
hijacker (noun) **hijacking** (noun)

hike, hikes, hiking, hiked
1 (noun) a long country walk.
2 (verb) to walk a long distance.
hiker (noun) **hiking** (noun)

Similar words: ramble, tramp, trek

hilarious
(adjective) very funny.
hilariously (adverb) **hilarity** (noun)
[Greek *hilaros* = cheerful]

Similar words: hysterical, side-splitting

hill, hills
(noun) an area of high land.
hilly (adjective)

hilt, hilts
(noun) the handle of a sword, dagger or knife.

him
(pronoun) e.g. *She told him where to go.*

himself
(pronoun) e.g. *He hid himself in the loo.*

hind, hinds (rhymes with **blind**)
1 (adjective) used to refer to the back part of an
animal, e.g. *the hind legs.*
2 (noun) a female deer.

hinder, hinders, hindering, hindered
(pronounced **hin**-der)
(verb) to get in other people's way and make
something difficult for them.
hindrance (noun)

What nouns match these adjectives, e.g. wise – wisdom; high false sad merry angry anxious?

Hindi (pronounced **hin**-dee)
(noun) a language spoken in northern India.
[Old Persian *Hindu* = the river Indus]

Hindu, Hindus (pronounced **hin**-doo)
(noun) a person who believes in Hinduism, an
Indian religion which has many gods and teaches
that people are reincarnated after death.

hinge, hinges
(noun) the movable joint that a door or window
swings on.

hint, hints, hinting, hinted
1 (noun) a suggestion, clue or helpful piece of
advice e.g. *gardening hints.*
2 (verb; phrase) If you hint at something, or **drop
a hint**, you suggest it without being obvious.

hip, hips
(noun) the part at the side of your body between
your waist and your upper legs.

hippie, hippies; also spelled **hippy**
(noun) a popular name for a person who has
rejected the usual ideas about how to live. They
are associated with long hair and having no
permanent home; also known as travellers.

hippo, hippos
(noun; informal) a hippopotamus.

hippopotamus, hippopotamuses or **hippopotami**
(noun) a large animal from tropical Africa with
thick, wrinkled skin. Hippopotamuses spend a
lot of time in water.
[Greek *hippo* + *potamos* = river horse]

hire, hires, hiring, hired
1 (verb) If you hire something, you pay money to
be able to use it for a period of time.
2 (phrase) Something that is **for hire** is available
for people to hire.

Similar words: rent, lease

hire-purchase
(noun) a way of buying something by making
regular payments over a period of time.

his
(pronoun) e.g. *He took his vorpal sword in hand.*

hiss, hisses, hissing, hissed
(verb) to make a long 's' sound, especially to
show disapproval or aggression, e.g. *We all
hissed when the witch came on.*

histogram, histograms
(noun) a type of bar chart consisting of
rectangles of varying sizes. Histograms show
three sets of information, where graphs and bar
charts show two.
[Greek *histos* + *grammē* = web line]

historian, historians
(noun) a person who studies and writes about
history.

historic
(adjective) important in the past or likely to be
seen as important in the future, e.g. *the historic
occasion when the Pope visited for the first time.*

historical
1 (adjective) occurring in the past, e.g. *historical
events.*

2 describing or representing the past, e.g.
historical novels... historical costumes.
historically (adverb)

history, histories
(noun) the study of the past.
[Greek *historein* = to narrate a story]

hit, hits, hitting, hit
1 (verb) e.g. *If you hit me, I'll hit you back...
Industry was badly hit by the recession.*
2 (noun) e.g. *Give it a hit with that hammer.*
3 a song, play or film that is popular and
successful.
4 (phrase; informal) If you **hit it off** with
someone, you become friendly with them the
first time you meet them.
5 (verb) If you hit on an idea or solution, you
suddenly think of it.

Similar words: (verb: sense 1) knock, strike, bash

hitch, hitches, hitching, hitched
1 (noun) a slight problem or difficulty, e.g. *The
whole thing went without a hitch... There has
been a technical hitch.*
2 (verb; informal) If you hitch, you hitchhike,
e.g. *We tried to hitch a lift to London.*
3 to attach something to something else, e.g.
Hitch your trailer to my car.
4 (phrase; informal) If you **get hitched**, you get
married.

hitchhike, hitchhikes, hitchhiking, hitchhiked
(verb) to travel by getting lifts from passing
vehicles.
hitchhiker (noun) **hitchhiking** (noun)

hi-tech
(adjective) using the most modern methods and
equipment, especially electronic equipment.

hoard, hoards, hoarding, hoarded
1 (verb) to save things even though they may no
longer be useful.
2 (noun) a store of things that has been saved or
hidden, e.g. *a hoard of buried treasure.*

hoarse, hoarser, hoarsest
(adjective) A hoarse voice sounds rough and
unclear.
hoarsely (adverb) **hoarseness** (noun)

Similar words: rough, husky, croaky, gruff

hoax, hoaxes, hoaxing, hoaxed
1 (verb) to trick or deceive someone.
2 (noun) a trick or deception.
hoaxer (noun)

hob, hobs
(noun) a set of gas or electric cooking rings,
either on top of a cooker or in a work surface.

hobble, hobbles, hobbling, hobbled
(verb) to walk awkwardly because of pain or
injury.

hobby, hobbies
(noun) something that you do for enjoyment in
your spare time.

Hobson's choice
(phrase) a situation when you might seem to
have a choice, but actually have no choice.

These nouns end in us: colossus hibiscus octopus hippopotamus papyrus typhus consensus gladiolus.

[Thomas Hobson hired out horses in the 17th century. Customers had to accept the horse offered to them or none at all.]

hock, hocks
(noun) the angled joint in the back leg of a horse.
[Old English *hohsinu* = heel sinew]

hockey
(noun) a game played with sticks and a ball where two teams try to score goals.

hoe, hoes, hoeing, hoed
(noun) a long-handled gardening tool used to remove weeds and break up the soil.

hog, hogs, hogging, hogged
1 (noun) a neutered male pig.
2 (verb; informal) If you hog something, you take more than your share of it, or keep it for too long.
3 (phrase; informal) If you **go the whole hog**, you do something completely or thoroughly in a bold or extravagant way.

Hogmanay (pronounced hog-man-**nay**)
(noun) New Year's Eve in Scotland.

hoist, hoists, hoisting, hoisted
1 (verb) to lift, especially using a crane etc.
2 (noun) a machine for lifting heavy things.

hold, holds, holding, held
1 (verb) To hold something means to carry, support or keep it in place, usually with your hand or arms.
2 to contain, e.g. *This jug holds a pint.*
3 to have, e.g. *Kings used to hold power.*
4 to arrange, e.g. *We're going to hold a meeting.*
5 (noun) a special grip, for example a judo hold.
6 The hold in a ship or plane is the place where cargo or luggage is stored.
7 (phrase) If you **hold your own**, you manage to resist a challenge or attack, especially in an argument.
holder (noun)

Similar words: (verb: sense 1) grasp, grip, clasp, clutch
(verb: sense 4) have, run, conduct

hold out
(phrasal verb) If you hold out, you stand firm and resist opposition in difficult circumstances, e.g. *The rebels held out for 10 years.*

hold up
(phrasal verb) If something holds you up, it delays you.

hold with
(phrasal verb) to agree with something, e.g. *'I don't hold with them new-fangled car phones.'*

holdall, holdalls
(noun) a large, soft bag for carrying clothing.

hold-up, hold-ups
1 (noun) a situation in which someone threatens people with a weapon in order to obtain money or valuables.
2 a delay, e.g. *a traffic hold-up.*

hole, holes, holing, holed
1 (noun) e.g. *The rabbit went down its hole... The golfer putted straight into the hole.*

2 (informal) an unpleasant place, e.g. *I think Minehead is a hole.*
3 a difficult situation, e.g. *I'm sorry, old chap, but I'm in a bit of a hole.*
4 (verb) e.g. *The golfer holed the ball... The ship was holed in the collision.*

Similar words: (noun: sense 1) hollow, cavity

holiday, holidays
(noun) a period of time spent off work or away from home for enjoyment.
[Old English *haligdæg* = holy day]

holidaymaker, holidaymakers
(noun) a person who is away from home on holiday.

holiness
'Your Holiness' and 'His Holiness' are titles used to address or refer to the Pope or to leaders of some other religions.

hollow, hollows
(adjective) something that is hollow has space inside it.
[Old English *holh* = hole or cave]

holly
(noun) an evergreen tree or shrub with spiky leaves. It often has red berries in winter.

hologram, holograms
(noun) a photographic image created by laser beams whick looks three-dimensional.
[Greek *holos* + *gramma* = something completely written or described]

holster, holsters
(noun) a holder for a pistol or revolver, worn at the side of the body or under the arm.

holy, holier, holiest
(adjective) relating to God or to a particular religion, e.g. *the holy book.*

Similar words: divine, sacred, godly

Holy Communion
(noun) a Christian religious service in which people share bread and wine in memory of the death and resurrection of Jesus Christ.

home, homes
1 (noun) the building, place or country in which you live or feel you belong.
2 (phrase) If you feel **at home** somewhere, you feel comfortable because it is familiar or easy to understand, e.g. *The otter is entirely at home in the water.*
3 If a situation or event **brings something home to you**, it makes you realize often for the first time how important or serious that thing is.
4 (adverb) If you press something home, you push it firmly into its correct position.
[Old English *ham* = village]

Similar words: (noun) dwelling, residence

home in
(phrasal verb) If something homes in on a target, it moves directly and quickly towards it.

What creatures live in a: lodge earth form holt drey byre lair burrow eyrie?

homeland, homelands
(noun) Your homeland is the country you were born or brought up in.

homeless
(adjective) having nowhere to live.
homelessness (noun)

homesick
(adjective) unhappy because of being away from home and missing family and friends.
homesickness (noun)

homeward or **homewards**
(adjective, adverb) towards home, e.g. *the homeward journey.*

homework
(noun) work for pupils to do at home, set by teachers for the pupil's benefit.

homing
(adjective) A homing device is able to guide itself to a target. An animal with a homing instinct is able to guide itself home e.g. *a homing pigeon.*

homosexual, homosexuals
(noun) a person who is sexually attracted to someone of the same sex.
homosexuality (noun)
[Greek *homos* = same + Latin *sexus* = sex]

honest
(adjective) truthful and trustworthy.
honestly (adverb) **honesty** (noun)
[Latin *honos* = honour]

Similar words: truthful, honourable, above board

honey
(noun) a sweet, edible, sticky substance produced by bees.

honeycomb, honeycombs
(noun) a wax structure consisting of rows of 6-sided cells made by bees for storage of honey and their eggs.

honeymoon, honeymoons
(noun) a holiday taken by a couple who have just married.

honk, honks, honking, honked
(verb) to make a short, loud sound like that made by a car horn or a goose.

honour, honours, honouring, honoured
1 (noun) Your honour is your good reputation and the respect that other people have for you, e.g. *the family honour.*
2 (phrase) If something is done **in your honour**, it is done specially for you, e.g. *Because she was 100, a party was held in her honour.*
3 (verb) If you honour someone, you give them special praise or attention, or an award.
4 If you honour an agreement or promise, you do what was agreed or promised, e.g. *He honoured his word and the debt was paid.*

hood, hoods
(noun) a loose covering for the head, usually part of a coat or jacket.
hooded (adjective)

hoof, hoofs, or hooves
(noun) the hard bony part of certain animals' feet.

hook, hooks
1 (noun) a curved piece of metal or plastic that is used for catching, holding or hanging things, e.g. *curtain hooks.*
2 (phrase) If you are **let off the hook**, something happens so that you avoid punishment or a difficult situation.
3 If the phone is **off the hook**, the receiver has not been replaced.

hooked
(adjective) addicted to something, e.g. *The boy took the drug twice and was hooked till his death*

hooligan, hooligans
(noun) a noisy, destructive and violent young person.
hooliganism (noun)
[thought to come from the name of a rough Irish family in S.E. London in Victorian times.]

Similar words: delinquent, lout, yob, yobbo

hoop, hoops
(noun) a large ring, usually used as a toy.

hooray another spelling of **hurray.**

hoot, hoots, hooting, hooted
(verb) to make a sound like that made by an owl or a car horn.
hooter (noun)

hoover, hoovers, hoovering, hoovered
1 (noun; trademark) a vacuum cleaner.
2 (verb) e.g. *Oops! I've hoovered my pet mouse up.*

hooves a plural of **hoof.**

hop, hops, hopping, hopped
Selected meanings:
1 (verb) to jump on one leg.
2 (phrase) If you are **caught on the hop**, you are unprepared and surprised by something unexpected.
3 (noun) Hops are flowers of the hop plant, which are dried and used for making beer.

hope, hopes, hoping, hoped
1 (verb) If you hope that something will happen you want it to happen.
2 (noun) a wish or feeling of desire and expectation, e.g. *Don't give up hope!*
hopeful (adjective) **hopefully** (adverb)

hopeless
1 (adjective) having no hope, e.g. *With a hopeless sigh, she turned away.*
2 unable to do something well, e.g. *He's hopeless at games.*
hopelessly (adverb) **hopelessness** (noun)

horde, hordes (rhymes with **bored**)
(noun) a large group or number of people, animals or insects, e.g. *There are hordes of screaming children at most theme parks.*

horizon (pronounced hor-**eye**-zn)
(noun) the distant line where the sky seems to touch the land or sea.
[Greek *horizein* = to limit]

Homonyms are spelled and sound alike but have different meanings: angle post right plot fast.

horizontal (pronounced hor-riz-**zon**-tl)
(adjective) flat and level with the ground .
horizontally (adverb)

hormone, hormones
(noun) a chemical made by one part of your body
that has an effect on another part.
hormonal (adjective)
[Greek *horman* = to stir up]

horn, horns
1 (noun) one of the hard, pointed growths on the
heads of animals, for example sheep, goats.
2 a brass musical instrument, consisting of a pipe
that is narrow at one end and wide at the other.
3 a warning device on a vehicle.

horoscope, horoscopes
(noun) a prediction about what is going to
happen to someone, based on the position of the
stars when the person were born.
[Greek *hora* + *skopos* = hour observer]

horrible
(adjective) causing dislike, shock, fear or
disgust, e.g. *It was a horrible feeling.*
horribly (adverb)

Similar words: horrid, horrific, gruesome, hideous

horrid
(adjective) very unpleasant indeed, e.g. *I didn't
mean to be horrid to you.*

horrify, horrifies, horrifying, horrified
(verb) If something horrifies you, it makes you
feel dismay or disgust, e.g. *They were horrified
at the cost of repairs.*
horrifying (adjective) **horrifyingly** (adverb) **horrific**
(adjective) **horrifically** (adverb)

horror, horrors
1 (noun) a strong feeling of alarm, dismay and
disgust, e.g. *They shrank away in horror.*
2 If you have a horror of something, you dislike
it very much, e.g. *She had a horror of violence.*
[Latin *horrere* = tremble]

horse, horses
1 (noun) a large animal with a mane and a long
tail.
2 In gymnastics, a horse is a piece of equipment
with 4 legs or a solid base, used for jumping over.
3 (phrase) If you get information **straight from
the horse's mouth**, the person directly involved
tells you about it.
4 **To look a gift horse in the mouth** means to be
critical of a gift or ungrateful for it.

horse-box, horse-boxes
(noun) a van or trailer used for transporting
horses.

horse chestnut, chestnuts
(noun) a large tree with big segmented leaves
and tall clusters of flowers in the spring. It
produces a nut called a conker in a green spiky
case.

horseplay
(noun) rough or noisy play.

horsepower
(noun) a unit used for measuring how powerful
an engine is. (1 hp = 746 watts).

horseshoe, horseshoes
(noun) a U-shaped piece of metal, nailed to the
hard surface of a horse's hoof to protect it.

horticulture
(noun) the growing of flowers, fruit and
vegetables.
horticultural (adjective)
[Latin *hortus* + *cultura* = garden cultivation]

hosanna, hosannas (pronounced hoe-**zan**-na)
(noun) a shout of praise to God.
[Hebrew *hoshi ah nna* = save now, we pray]

hose, hoses, hosing, hosed
1 (noun) a long, flexible tube through which
liquid or gas can be passed.
2 (verb) If you hose something, you wash or
water it using a hose, e.g. *Hose down the path.*

hosiery (pronounced **hoze**-yer-ee)
(noun) Hosiery consists of tights, socks,
stockings and similar items, especially in shops.

hospice, hospices (pronounced **hoss**-piss)
(noun) a type of hospital which provides care for
people who are dying.

hospitable
(adjective) friendly, generous and welcoming to
guests or strangers.
hospitably (adverb) **hospitality** (noun)
[Latin *hospes* = guest]

hospital, hospitals
(noun) a place where sick and injured people are
treated and cared for.
[Latin *hospitalis* = relating to a guest]

host, hosts, hosting, hosted
1 (noun) The host of an event is the person or
organization that welcomes guests or visitors
and provides food or accommodation for them,
e.g. *Denton High School were the hosts for the
championships.*
2 (verb) To host an event means to organize it or
act as host at it.
3 (noun) A host of things is a large number of
them, e.g. *We visited a whole host of places.*
[senses 1-2: Latin *hospes* = guest;
sense 3: Old French *hoste* = host]

hostage, hostages
(noun) a person who is illegally held prisoner
and threatened with injury or death unless other
people meet certain demands.
[Latin *obses* = hostage]

hostel, hostels
(noun) a large building in which people can stay
or live, e.g. *a youth hostel.*

hostess, hostesses
(noun) a woman who welcomes guests or visitors
and provides food or accommodation for them.

hostile
(adjective) unfriendly, aggressive and
unpleasant, e.g. *a hostile attitude.*
hostility (noun)
[Latin *hostis* = enemy]

hot, hotter, hottest
1 (adjective) e.g. *a hot summer's day... a hot
curry.*
2 new, recent, and exciting, e.g. *hot off the press.*

A nurse needs these words: syringe transfusion donor casualty ward
theatre hygiene patient ambulance.

3 dangerous or difficult to deal with, e.g. *They're making it too hot for me – I'll have to leave.*
4 (phrase) Someone who has **a hot temper** gets very angry quickly and easily.
5 Someone who is **hot on something** is particularly keen about it, e.g. *Collins are very hot on spelling misteaks!*
6 If you are **in hot water**, you are in trouble.
hotly (adverb) **hotness** (noun)

hot-blooded
(adjective) quick to become angry or emotional.

hot dog, dogs
(noun) a hot sausage served in a roll.

hotel, hotels
(noun) a building where people stay, paying for their room and meals.
[Latin *hospitalis* = relating to a guest]

hound, hounds
(noun) a dog, especially one used for hunting or racing.

hour, hours
(noun) a unit of time (1 hour = 60 minutes; 24 hours = 1 day).
hourly (adverb)
[Greek *hora* = season or time of day]

house, houses, housing, housed
1 (noun) a building, usually with more than one storey, where people live.
2 In a theatre or cinema, the house is the part where the audience sits; also the audience itself, e.g. *The film played to packed houses.*
3 an important family and its ancestors, e.g. *Our Royal Family belongs to the House of Windsor.*
4 (phrase) If someone is offered a drink or meal **on the house**, they do not have to pay for it.
5 (verb) To house something means to keep it, contain it or shelter it, e.g. *The new block will house the library.*

household, households
1 (noun) all the people who live as a group in a house or flat.
householder (noun)
2 (phrase) Someone who is **a household name** is very well known.

housekeeper, housekeepers
(noun) a person who is employed to cook, clean and look after a house.

house martin, martins
(noun) a bird with white and blue-black feathers and a forked tail, which often builds its nest under the eaves of houses.

housewife, housewives
(noun) a married woman who usually does not have a full time job outside the home.

housing
(noun) the buildings in which people live, e.g. *There was a shortage of housing in the city.*

hovel, hovels
(noun) a small hut or house that is dirty or badly in need of repair.

hover, hovers, hovering, hovered
(verb) to stay in the same position in the air.

hovercraft, hovercrafts
(noun) a vehicle which can travel over water or land supported by a cushion of air.

how
(adverb) e.g. *How do you say it in French?*

however
(adverb, conjunction) e.g. *However we add that up, it does not make a dozen!... I had hoped to be offered the job. However, I didn't get it.*

howl, howls, howling, howled
(verb) to make a long, loud wailing noise like that made by a dog when it is upset.

howler, howlers
(noun, informal) a stupid mistake of fact, e.g. Wellington and Napoleon fought a battle at Waterloo Station.

hub, hubs
(noun) the centre part of a wheel.

hubbub
(noun) great noise, fuss or confusion, e.g. *a hubbub of voices.*

huddle, huddles, huddling, huddled
1 (verb) When people or animals huddle together, they sit or stand close to each other, often for warmth.
2 (noun) A huddle of people or things is a small group of them.

huff
(phrase) If you are **in a huff**, you are sulking or offended about something.
huffy (adjective) **huffily** (adverb)

hug, hugs, hugging, hugged
(verb) If you hug someone, you put your arms round them and hold them close to you.
[Old Norse *hugga* = comfort or console]

Similar words: embrace, cuddle

huge, huger, hugest
(adjective) extremely large in amount, size or degree, e.g. *a huge profit... a huge building.*
hugely (adverb)

Similar words: immense, enormous, colossal, gigantic, giant, mammoth, vast

hull, hulls
(noun) the main part of a boat's body that sits in the water.

hullabaloo
(noun) a lot of noise or fuss.

hum, hums, humming, hummed
1 (verb) to sing with your lips closed.
2 (noun) a continuous low noise, e.g. *She could hear the hum of the machine.*

human, humans
(adjective) relating to people, e.g. *This meat is not fit for human consumption.*
humanity (noun) **humanly** (adverb)
[Latin *homo* = man]

human being, beings
(noun) a person.

A politician needs these words: party whip bill act legislation taxation prime minister.

humane
(adjective) showing kindness, thoughtfulness and sympathy towards others.
humaneness (noun) **humanely** (adverb)

humanities
(plural noun) subjects like literature, philosophy and history, which are concerned with people rather than with science.

humble, humbler, humblest
1 (adjective) A humble person is modest and thinks that he or she has very little value.
2 small or not very important, e.g. *My humble cottage is yours to use, sire.*
humbly (adverb) **humbled** (adjective)
[Latin *humilis* = low]

Similar words: modest, unassuming

humbug, humbugs
1 (noun) a hard, black and white, striped sweet that tastes of peppermint.
2 speech or writing that is dishonest, untrue or nonsense.

humid
(adjective) If it is humid, the atmosphere feels damp, heavy and warm.
[Latin *umidus* = wet]

humidity
(noun) the amount of moisture in the atmosphere.

humiliate, humiliates, humiliating, humiliated
(verb) to make someone feel ashamed or appear stupid to other people, e.g. *Mr Bumble humiliated Oliver when the boy asked for more.*
humiliation (noun)

Similar words: embarrass, shame, humble

humility
(noun) the quality of being modest and humble.

humour, humours, humouring, humoured
1 (noun) the quality of being funny, e.g. *The TV version loses all the humour of the original play.*
2 (phrase) If you have a **sense of humour**, you are able to see the funny side of life.
3 (verb) If you humour someone, you do what they want, even if you disagree.
humorous (adjective) **humorously** (adverb)
humorist (noun) **humourless** (adjective)

Similar words: (noun: sense 1) comedy, wit

hump, humps, humping, humped
1 (noun) a small, rounded lump or mound, e.g. *a camel's hump.*
2 (verb; informal) If you hump something heavy, you carry or move it with difficulty.

hunch, hunches, hunching, hunched
1 (noun) a feeling or suspicion about something, not based on facts or evidence, e.g. *PC Jones had a hunch that the thief would return.*
2 (verb) If you hunch your shoulders, you raise your shoulders and lean forwards.

hundred, hundreds
the number 100.
hundredth (adjective and noun)

hundredweight, hundredweights
(noun) a unit of weight. (1cwt [hundredweight] = 112lbs [pounds] = 45.36kg)

Hungarian, Hungarians (pronounced hung-*gair*-ee-an)
1 (adjective) belonging to Hungary.
2 (noun) someone who comes from Hungary.
3 the main language spoken in Hungary.

hunger
1 (noun) the need or the desire to eat.
2 a strong need or desire for something, e.g. *a hunger for power.*

hunger strike, strikes
(noun) a form of protest when people, usually prisoners, refuse to eat.

hungry, hungrier, hungriest
(adjective) needing or wanting to eat.
hungrily (adverb)

hunk, hunks
1 (noun) a large piece of something.
2 (informal) an attractive man, e.g. *Sue thought Tom Cruise was a real hunk.*

hunt, hunts, hunting, hunted
1 (verb) to chase wild animals to kill them for food or for sport.
2 (noun) a group of people who have met together to hunt foxes on horseback.
3 (verb) to search for something.
hunter (noun) **hunting** (adjective and noun)

hurdle, hurdles
1 (noun) one of the barriers that you jump over in an athletics race called hurdles, e.g. *She won the 400 metre hurdles.*
2 a problem or difficulty, e.g. *Getting into college was only the first hurdle.*

hurl, hurls, hurling, hurled
(verb) to throw something with great force.

hurray or hurrah or hooray
(interjection) an exclamation of excitement or approval.

hurricane, hurricanes
(noun) a violent wind or storm.
[Spanish *huracán* = *hurricane*]

hurry, hurries, hurrying, hurried
1 (verb) to move or do something as quickly as possible.
2 (noun) the speed with which you do something quickly, e.g. *He had to leave in a great hurry.*
hurried (adjective) **hurriedly** (adverb)

Similar words: (verb) hasten, rush, fly, scurry
(noun) bustle, rush, haste

hurt, hurts, hurting, hurt
1 (verb) to cause someone physical pain.
2 to make someone unhappy by being unkind or thoughtless towards them, e.g. *I don't want to hurt his feelings.*
3 (adjective) unhappy because of someone's unkindness or thoughtlessness, e.g. *He gave her a hurt look when she ignored him.*
hurtful (adjective)
[Old French *hurter* = to knock against]

Think of a more vivid way to say: He ate hungrily. She had a lovely smile.

hurtle, hurtles, hurtling, hurtled
(verb) to move very fast indeed, especially in an uncontrolled or violent way.

husband, husbands
(noun) A woman's husband is the man she is married to.
[Old English *husbonda* = master of a house]

hush, hushes, hushing, hushed
1 (verb) If you tell someone to hush, you are telling them to be quiet.
2 (noun) If there is a hush, it is quiet and still, e.g. *An expectant hush fell on the crowd.*
3 (verb) To hush something up means to keep it secret, especially something dishonest or disreputable involving important people, e.g. *The council hushed the matter up.*
hushed (adjective)

hush-hush
(adjective; informal) secret, confidential and not to be discussed in public, e.g. *The nuclear tests of the 50s were very hush-hush.*

husky, huskier, huskiest; huskies
1 (adjective) A husky voice is rough or hoarse.
huskily (adverb)
2 (noun) a large, strong dog used in teams to pull sledges across snow.

hustle, hustles, hustling, hustled
(verb) to make someone move by pushing and jostling them, e.g. *Anyone who protested was hustled out of the hall by the stewards.*
[Dutch *husselen* = to shake]

hutch, hutches
(noun) a wooden box with wire mesh at one side, in which small pets can be kept.

hydraulic (pronounced high-**drol**-lik)
(adjective) operated by water, oil or other fluid which is under pressure, e.g. *a hydraulic jack.*
[Greek *hudōr* + *aulos* = water pipe]

hydroelectric
(adjective) powered by electricity generated from the energy of running water.
hydroelectricity (noun)

hydrofoil, hydrofoils
(noun) a boat with a pair of fins like skis which raise the hull above the water when it is moving at speed.

hydrogen
(noun) the lightest gas and the simplest chemical element. It has no colour or smell.

hygiene (pronounced **high**-jeen)
(noun) the practice of keeping yourself and your surroundings clean to prevent disease.
hygienic (adjective) **hygienically** (adverb)
[Greek *hugieinos* = healthful]

Similar words: cleanliness, sanitation

hymn, hymns
(noun) a song in praise of God.

hyper-
(prefix) Hyper- means very much or excessive, e.g. *She's hyper-critical... a hypermarket.*
[Greek *huper* = over]

hyperactive
(adjective) unable to relax and always in a state of restless activity.
[Greek *huper-* = over + Latin *actus* = performance]

hyperbole (pronounced high-**per**-bol-lee)
(noun) a style of speech or writing which uses exaggeration.
hyperbolic (adjective)

hypermarket, hypermarkets
(noun) a very large supermarket.

hyphen, hyphens
(noun) a punctuation mark - used to join together words or parts of words, e.g. in 'left-handed' and 'high-class'.
hyphenate (verb) **hyphenation** (noun)
[Greek *huphen* = together]

hypnotize, hypnotizes, hypnotizing, hypnotized; also spelled **hypnotise**
(verb) to put someone into a state in which they seem to be asleep but can respond to questions and suggestions.
hypnotic (adjective) **hypnosis** (noun)
hypnotism (noun) **hypnotist** (noun)
[Greek *hupnos* = sleep]

Similar words: mesmerize, entrance

hypochondriac, hypochondriacs (pronounced high-pok-**kon**-dree-ak)
(noun) a person who continually worries about their health, and who thinks they are ill when there is actually nothing wrong with them. e.g. *I used to be a hypochondriac, but now I know I'm really ill.*
hypochondria (noun)

hypocrisy, hypocrisies
(noun) pretending to have beliefs that you do not really have, so that you seem a better person than you are.
hypocritical (adjective) **hypocritically** (adverb)
[Greek *hupokrinein* = to pretend]

hypocrite (pronounced **hippo**-krit)
(noun) someone who pretends to believe in something but actually does the opposite.

hypotenuse, hypotenuses (pronounced high-**pot**-tin-yooz)
(noun) In a right-angled triangle, the hypotenuse is the longest side and is opposite the right angle.

hypothermia
(noun) a condition in which a person is very ill because they have become extremely cold.
[Greek *hupo* + *thermē* = under heat]

hysterical
1 (adjective) Someone who is hysterical is in a state of uncontrolled excitement, anger or panic.
2 (informal) extremely funny.
hysterically (adverb) **hysterics** (noun)
hysteria (noun)

Similar words: (sense 1) uncontrollable, frantic, beside yourself

What is the difference between a man-eating chicken and a man eating chicken?

I

(first person pronoun) e.g. *I like your dress.*

ice, ices, icing, iced
1 (noun) water that has frozen solid.
2 (verb) If something ices over or ices up, it becomes covered with a layer of ice.
3 (phrase) If you do something to **break the ice**, you make people feel relaxed and comfortable.
ice cream (noun) **ice cube** (noun) **ice hockey** (noun)

ice age, ages
(noun) a time in the past when a lot of the earth's surface was covered by ice.

iceberg, icebergs
(noun) a large, tall mass of ice floating in the sea.
[Dutch *ijsberg* = ice mountain]

icecap, icecaps
(noun) a layer of ice and snow that permanently covers the North or South Pole.

Icelandic
(noun) the main language spoken in Iceland.

ice-skate, ice-skates, ice-skating, ice-skated
(verb) to move about on ice wearing ice-skates.

icicle, icicles (pronounced **eye**-sikl)
(noun) a piece of ice that hangs down from a surface.

icing
(noun) a mixture of powdered sugar and water or egg whites, used to decorate cakes.

icy, icier, iciest
1 (adjective) freezing cold, e.g. *an icy wind.*
2 Very unfriendly, e.g. *She gave me an icy stare.*
icily (adverb) **iciness** (noun)

ID
(noun) identification; papers, etc. which prove who you are, e.g. *Have you any ID, sir?*

idea, ideas
(noun) a plan, suggestion or thought that you have after thinking about a problem.
[Greek *idea* = model, pattern, or notion]

Similar words: notion, impression, feeling, hunch, thought, concept, image

ideal, ideals
1 (noun) a principle or idea that seems perfect to you and so you try to achieve it, e.g. *My ideal is to live in a world where everybody could trust each other.*
2 (adjective) The ideal person or thing is the best possible person or thing for the situation.
idealist (noun) **idealistic** (adjective)

ideally
1 (adverb) If you say that ideally something should happen, you mean that you would like it to happen but you know that it is unlikely, e.g. *Ideally, everyone would have enough food.*
2 perfectly, e.g. *She's ideally suited for the job.*

I

identical
(adjective) exactly the same, e.g. *identical bags.*
identically (adverb)
[Latin *idem* = the same]

identification
(noun) a document which proves who you are, e.g. a driving licence or passport.

identify, identifies, identifying, identified
1 (verb) To identify someone or something means to recognize them or name them.
2 If you identify with someone, you understand their feelings and ideas.
identifiable (adjective)

identity, identities
(noun) Your identity consists of the characteristics that make you who you are.
[Latin *idem* = the same]

idiom, idioms
(noun) a group of words whose meaning together is different from all the words taken separately, e.g 'It is raining cats and dogs' is an idiom.
idiomatic (adjective)
[Greek *idioma* = special phraseology]

idiot, idiots
(noun) If you call someone an idiot, you mean that they are stupid or foolish.
idiotic (adjective) **idiotically** (adverb)
[Greek *idiōtēs* = private or ignorant person]

Similar words: fool, blockhead, nincompoop, nitwit, moron, imbecile, cretin

idle
1 (adjective) doing nothing, or lazy.
2 Machines that are idle are not being used.
idleness (noun) **idly** (adverb)
[Saxon *idal* = worthless or empty]

idol, idols (pronounced **eye**-doll)
1 (noun) a famous person who is loved, admired, and often imitated by fans.
2 a picture or statue which is worshipped as if it were a god.
[Greek *eidōlon* = image or phantom]

idolize, idolizes, idolizing, idolized; also spelled **idolise**
(verb) If you idolize someone, you admire or love them very much.

if
(conjunction) e.g. *I will stay if you wish.*

igloo, igloos
(noun) a dome-shaped house built out of blocks of snow by the Inuit, or Eskimo, people.
[Inuit *igdlu* = house]

igneous
(adjective) Igneous rocks have been created by volcanic action.

ignition
1 (noun) In a car, the ignition is the part of the engine where the fuel starts to burn.

Letter I was probably made from a picture of a reaching hand.

2 Ignition is the process by which an engine is started, e.g *3... 2... we have ignition... 1... lift off!*
ignite (verb)
[Latin *ignis* = fire]

ignorant
1 (adjective) If you are ignorant of something, you do not know about it.
2 not knowing about things in general, e.g. *How can he be so ignorant at his age?*
ignorantly (adverb) **ignorance** (noun)

Similar words: (sense 1) unaware, oblivious

ignore, ignores, ignoring, ignored
(verb) If you ignore someone or something, you deliberately do not take any notice of them.
[Latin *ignorare* = to not know]

ill
(adjective) unhealthy or sick.
[Norse *illr* = bad]

Similar words: sick, unwell, unhealthy, poorly, off-colour

ill-advised
(adjective) not sensible or wise.

ill at ease
(phrase) unable to relax, e.g. *I felt very ill at ease in the haunted churchyard.*

illegal
(adjective) forbidden by the law.
illegally (adverb) **illegality** (noun)

Similar words: unlawful, criminal

illegible (pronounced il-**lej**-i-bl)
(adjective) Writing which is illegible is unclear and difficult or impossible to read.
illegibly (adverb) **illegibility** (noun)

ill-fated
(adjective) doomed to end unhappily, e.g. *The ill-fated Titanic set sail from Southampton.*

illiterate
(adjective) unable to read or write.
illiterately (adverb) **illiteracy** (noun)

illness
(noun) a medical condition which makes you feel unwell.

Similar words: disease, ailment

illogical
(adjective) not reasonable or sensible.
illogically (adverb)

ill-treat, ill-treats, ill-treating, ill-treated
(verb) to hurt or damage someone or something.
ill-treatment (noun)

illuminate, illuminates, illuminating, illuminated
(verb) to light something up.
[Latin *lumen* = light]

illumination, illuminations
1 (noun) lighting.
2 Illuminations are coloured lights put up to decorate a town, e.g. *Blackpool illuminations.*

illusion, illusions
1 (noun) something which you believe is true, but which is actually false.
2 something which you think you see clearly but is actually different or does not exist, e.g. *an optical illusion.*
illusory (adjective)
[Latin *illusio* = deceit]

illustrate, illustrates, illustrating, illustrated
1 (verb) If you illustrate a point, you explain it or make it clearer, often by using examples.
2 to supply pictures for a piece of writing.
illustrator (noun) **illustrative** (adjective)
[Latin *illustrare* = to make light]

illustration, illustrations
1 (noun) an example or a story which is used to make a point clear.
2 An illustration in a book is a picture.

image, images
1 (noun) a picture or other representation of something or someone, e.g. a sculpture, a photograph.
2 a mental picture of someone or something.
3 the public face of a person, group or organization, e.g. *As overpaid advertising people, we've got to have a trendy image.*
4 In literature, an image is an expression used imaginatively to describe something else, e.g. *His eyes were hollows of madness, his hair like mouldy hay.*
[Latin *imago* = copy or representation]

Similar words: (sense 4) simile, metaphor

imagery
(noun) The imagery of a poem or book is the descriptive language used.

imaginary
(adjective) existing only in the mind, not in reality.

imagination, imaginations
(noun) the ability to form new and exciting ideas, e.g. *a vivid imagination.*
imaginative (adjective) **imaginatively** (adverb)

imagine, imagines, imagining, imagined
(verb) If you imagine something, you form an idea of it in your mind, or you think you have seen or heard it but you have not really.
imaginable (adjective)

Similar words: picture, conceive, visualize

imbecile, imbeciles (pronounced im-bis-seel)
(noun; informal) If you call someone an imbecile, you mean that they are stupid.
[Latin *imbecillus* = physically or mentally feeble]

imitate, imitates, imitating, imitated
(verb) to copy someone or something.
imitator (noun) **imitative** (adjective)
imitation (noun)

Similar words: copy, ape, mimic, impersonate

immaculate (pronounced im-**mak**-yoo-lit)
1 (adjective) completely clean and tidy, e.g. *The room was immaculate.*

Most people ignore most poems; because most poems ignore most people. (Anon)

2 without any mistakes at all, e.g. *Her playing was immaculate.*
immaculately (adverb)
[Latin *im-* = not + *macula* = stain or mark]

immature
1 (adjective) Something that is immature has not finished growing or developing.
2 A person who is immature does not behave in a sensible, adult way.
immaturity (noun)

immediate
1 (adjective) Something that is immediate happens or is done without delay.
2 Your immediate relatives and friends are the ones most closely connected or related to you.

immediately
1 (adverb) straight away; now.
2 very near, e.g. *immediately behind the pub.*

immense
(adjective) very large or huge.
immensely (adverb) **immensity** (noun)
[Latin *im-* = not + *mensus* = measured]

immerse, immerses, immersing, immersed
1 (verb) to cover something completely in a liquid.
2 If you are immersed in an activity you are completely involved in it.
immersion (noun)
[Latin *immergere* = to dip into]

immersion heater, heaters
(noun) an electric heater which provides hot water in the home.

immigrant, immigrants
(noun) someone who has come to live permanently in a new country.
immigrate (verb) **immigration** (noun)
[Latin *immigrare* = to go into]

imminent
(adjective) If something is imminent, it is going to happen very soon.
imminently (adverb) **imminence** (noun)

immobilize, immobilizes, immobilizing, immobilized; also spelled immobilise
(verb) to stop someone or something from moving, e.g. *He immobilized the car by taking the wheels off.*
immobile (adjective)

immoral
(adjective) If you say that someone's behaviour is immoral, you mean that they do not conform with what most people think is right.
immorality (noun)

immortal
(adjective) living or remembered forever, e.g. *Shakespeare's immortal plays.*
immortality (noun)

immovable or **immoveable**
(adjective) fixed and unable to be moved.
immovably (adverb)

immune (pronounced im-yoon)
(adjective) If you are immune to a particular disease, you cannot catch it.
immunity (noun) **immunize** (verb)
immunization (noun)

impact, impacts
1 (noun) the impression that someone or something makes or the effect that they have.
2 the action of one object hitting another, usually with a lot of force, e.g. *The missile exploded on impact.*
[Latin *impactus* = pushed against]

impartial
(adjective) fair and unbiased, e.g. *Referees must be impartial (except when our team is playing).*
impartially (adverb) **impartiality** (noun)

Similar word: objective

impatient
1 (adjective) easily annoyed or quick to become angry when things go wrong, e.g. *He was impatient with students who couldn't follow him.*
2 If you are impatient to do something, you are eager and do not want to wait, e.g. *James was impatient to pass his driving test.*
impatiently (adverb) **impatience** (noun)

impeccable (pronounced im-pek-a-bl)
(adjective) excellent, without any faults.
impeccably (adverb)
[Latin *impeccabilis* = sinless]

impede, impedes, impeding, impeded
(verb) If you impede someone, you get in their way.
[Latin *impedire* = to shackle the feet]

impediment, impediments
(noun) an activity that makes it difficult to do an activity properly, e.g. *a speech impediment.*

imperative
1 (adjective) extremely urgent or important.
2 (noun) In grammar, an imperative is a verb form that is used for giving orders, e.g. *Stop!*
[Compare: **indicative, subjunctive, infinitive**]
[Latin *imperare* = to command]

imperceptible
(adjective) so slight that you hardly notice it, e.g. *an imperceptible darkening of the sky.*
imperceptibly (adverb)

imperfect
1 (adjective) Something that is imperfect has faults or problems.
2 (noun) In grammar, the imperfect is a tense used to describe continuous or repeated actions which happened in the past, e.g. *I was going or We were doing.*
imperfectly (adverb) **imperfection** (noun)

Similar words: (adjective) faulty, flawed, sub-standard

imperial
1 (adjective) relating to an empire or an emperor or empress.
2 The imperial system of measurement is the old

British measuring system, using inches, feet, and yards; ounces and pounds; pints and gallons.
[Latin *imperium* = empire]

impersonate, impersonates, impersonating, impersonated
(verb) to pretend to be somebody else.
impersonation (noun) **impersonator** (noun)

impertinent
(adjective) disrespectful and rude, e.g. *How dare you make impertinent remarks!*
impertinently (adverb) **impertinence** (noun)
[Latin *im-* = not + *pertinens* = relevant]

impetuous
(adjective) If you are impetuous, you act quickly without thinking, e.g. *He regretted his impetuous decision to buy the old banger.*
impetuously (adverb) **impetuosity** (noun)
[Latin *impetuosus* = violent]

implausible
(adjective) very unlikely, e.g. *Don't think I'm going to believe that implausible story!*
implausibly (adverb) **implausibility** (noun)

implement, implements
(noun) a tool.

implore, implores, imploring, implored
(verb) to beg someone to do something.
imploring (adjective) **imploringly** (adverb)

imply, implies, implying, implied
(verb) If you imply that something is the case, you suggest it in an indirect way, e.g. *Are you implying that I am wrong in some way?*
implication (noun)

impolite
(adjective) rude and not polite.

import, imports, importing, imported
1 (verb) If you import something, you bring it into your country, e.g. *BMW cars are imported from Germany.*
2 (noun) a product made in another country and sent to your own country for use there.
importation (noun) **importer** (noun)
[Latin *importare* = to carry in]

important
(adjective) valuable, necessary or significant.
importantly (adverb) **importance** (noun)

impose, imposes, imposing, imposed
1 (verb) If you impose something on people, you force it on them, e.g. *British Rail imposed a ban on smoking in trains.*
2 If someone imposes on you, they unreasonably expect you to do something for them, e.g. *I hope I'm not imposing on you by asking you to do this vanload of washing totally free of charge.*
imposition (noun)
[Latin *imponere* = to place upon]

Similar words: (sense 1) enforce, inflict

imposing
(adjective) impressive in appearance or manner, e.g. *Stormont is an imposing building.*

impossible
(adjective) Something that is impossible cannot happen, be done or be believed.
impossibly (adverb) **impossibility** (noun)

impostor, impostors; also spelled **imposter**
(noun) a person who pretends to be someone else to get things they want.
[Latin *impostor* = deceiver]

impracticable
(noun) Something which is impracticable is impossible to do.

impractical
(adjective) not practical, sensible or realistic.

impregnable
(adjective) A building or other structure that is impregnable is so strong, solid or well-defended that it cannot be broken into or captured.
[Old French *im-* + *prenable* = unable to be taken]

impress, impresses, impressing, impressed
(verb) If you impress someone, you do something to make them admire or respect you.
[Latin *impressio* = emphasis or impression]

impression, impressions
1 (noun) An impression of someone or something is the way they seem to you, e.g. *I got the impression she was scared.*
2 An impression of an object is a mark that it has left in something soft, e.g. a footprint.
3 (phrase) If you are **under the impression** that something is the case, you believe it to be true.
4 If you **make an impression**, you have a strong effect on people you meet.

impressionable
(adjective) easy to influence, e.g. *Many teenagers tend to be impressionable.*

impressive
(adjective) If something is impressive, it impresses you, e.g. *an impressive collection.*

imprint, imprints
(noun) the mark left by the pressure of one object on another.

imprison, imprisons, imprisoning, imprisoned
(verb) to lock someone up against their will.
imprisonment (noun)

improbable
(adjective) not probable or likely to happen.
improbably (adverb) **improbability** (noun)

Similar words: unlikely, far-fetched, implausible, unbelievable

improper
1 (adjective) rude or shocking, e.g. *It was quite improper for the mayor to open the supermarket in his pyjamas.*
2 not correct or not honest, e.g. *The stamp firm had many improper business dealings.*
improperly (adverb)

improve, improves, improving, improved
(verb) to get better or to make something better.
improvement (noun)
[Old French *en prou* = into profit]

Similar words: upgrade, enhance, refurbish

Which proverb is true? Look before you leap. He who hesitates is lost.

improvise, improvises, improvising, improvised
1 (verb) to make or do something without planning in advance, and with whatever materials are available, e.g. *Robinson Crusoe had to improvise a lot on his desert island.*
2 When musicians or actors improvise, they make up the music or words as they go along.
improvised (adjective) **improvisation** (noun)
[Latin *improvisus* = unforeseen]

impudent
(adjective) rude or disrespectful.
impudently (adverb) **impudence** (noun)
[Latin *in-* + *pudens* = not modest]

impulse, impulses
1 (noun) a strong urge to do something, e.g. *I felt a sudden impulse to hit him.*
2 a short, electrical signal that is sent along a wire or nerve or through the air.
3 (phrase) If you do something **on impulse**, you do it without thinking.
impulsion (noun)
[Latin *impulsus* = pushing or incitement]

impulsive
(adjective) If you are impulsive, you do things suddenly, without thinking about them carefully.
impulsively (adverb)

in
1 (preposition, adverb) e.g. *in the sink... We were locked in.*
2 (phrase) If you are **in on** something, you are involved in it.
3 (adjective) fashionable, e.g. *Long hair is in again this year.*

in-
1 (prefix) In- is added to the beginning of some words to form a word with the opposite meaning e.g. *formal/informal.*
2 In- also means in, into, or in the course of, e.g. *invade.*

inability
(noun) a lack of ability to do something, e.g. *The drunk had a complete inability to stand up or to walk in a straight line.*

inaccessible
(adjective) impossible or very difficult to reach, e.g. *The loft was inaccessible without a ladder.*

inaccurate
(adjective) not accurate or correct.
inaccurately (adverb) **inaccuracy** (noun)

inadequate
(adjective) not enough in quantity, or not good enough in quality.
inadequately (adverb) **inadequacy** (noun)

Similar words: insufficient, meagre, poor, sparse

inanimate
(adjective) An inanimate object has no life.

inappropriate
(adjective) not suitable, e.g. *My muddy trainers were inappropriate footwear for the dance.*
inappropriately (adverb) **inappropriateness** (noun)

Similar words: unsuitable, out of place, wrong

inarticulate
(adjective) unable to express yourself well or easily in speech.
inarticulately (adverb)

inattentive
(adjective) not listening properly to what is said.

inaudible
(adjective) not loud enough to be heard, e.g. *I wouldn't describe rock music as inaudible!*
inaudibly (adverb)

incapable
1 (adjective) not able to do something, e.g. *He is incapable of changing a fuse.*
2 weak and helpless.
incapability (noun)

incense, incenses, incensing, incensed
1 (noun) a spicy substance burned to create a sweet smell, especially during religious services.
2 (verb) If you are incensed by something, it makes you extremely angry.
[Latin *incendere* = to light a fire]

incentive, incentives
(noun) something that encourages you to do something, e.g. *In the USA, children were offered free pizzas as an incentive to read books.*
[Latin *incentivus* = the beginning of a song]

incessant
(adjective) continuing without stopping, e.g. *the incessant ringing of telephones.*
incessantly (adverb)

inch, inches, inching, inched
1 (noun) a unit of length. (1 inch = 2.54 centimetres)
2 (verb) to move very slowly indeed.
[Latin *uncia* = twelfth part; 12 inches = 1 foot]

incidence
(noun) The incidence of something is how often it occurs, e.g. *a high incidence of heart disease.*

incident, incidents
(noun) an event, e.g. *a shooting incident.*
[Latin *incidere* = to fall into or to happen]

incidental
(adjective) not very important; playing only a very minor part in an event.

incidentally
(adverb) by the way. 'Incidentally' is used when saying something extra that is not very important, e.g. *He sent me a postcard which, incidentally, hadn't a stamp on.*

incinerator, incinerators
(noun) a furnace for burning rubbish.

incline, inclines, inclining, inclined
1 (noun) a slope.
2 (verb) If you are inclined to behave in a certain way, you often behave that way or you want to behave that way, e.g. *My dad is inclined to make a fool of himself at parties.*
inclination (noun)
[Latin *clinare* = to bend]

Pun. Why is O the only vowel that is sounded? All the others are inaudible.

include, includes, including, included
(verb) If one thing includes another, it has the second thing as one of its parts.
included (adjective) **including** (preposition)
inclusion (noun)
[Latin *in-* + *claudere* = to shut in with]

Similar words: incorporate, cover

inclusive
(adjective) An inclusive price covers everything, with no extras, e.g. £68 *inclusive of VAT.*

incoherent
(adjective) If someone is incoherent, they are talking in an unclear or rambling way, e.g. *He was incoherent with rage.*
incoherently (adverb) **incoherence** (noun)

income, incomes
(noun) the money a person receives on a regular basis.

income tax
(noun) a part of a person's salary which they pay regularly to the government.

incompatible
(adjective) Things or people are incompatible if they are unable to live or work together because they are completely different, e.g. *My computer is incompatible with yours... The husband and wife separated because they were incompatible.*
incompatibly (adverb) **incompatibility** (noun)
[Latin *in-* + *compatibilis* = not in sympathy with]

incompetent
(adjective) Someone who is incompetent does not have the ability to do something properly.
incompetently (adverb) **incompetence** (noun)

incomplete
(adjective) not complete or finished.
incompletely (adverb)

incomprehensible
(adjective) not able to be understood, e.g. *What the teacher said was totally incomprehensible to me.*

inconceivable
(adjective) impossible to believe, e.g. *The idea of aliens living on the moon is inconceivable.*

inconclusive
(adjective) not leading to a decision or to a definite result.

incongruous
(adjective) strange, because it does not fit in to a place or situation, e.g. *It seemed incongruous that Arnold Schwarzenegger should be wearing pink shoes.*
incongruously (adverb) **incongruity** (noun)
[*in-* + Latin *congruere* = to meet or to agree]

inconsiderate
(adjective) If you are inconsiderate, you do not consider other people's feelings.
inconsiderately (adverb)

Similar words: insensitive, thoughtless

inconspicuous
(adjective) not easily seen.
inconspicuously (adverb)

inconvenience, inconveniences, inconveniencing, inconvenienced
1 (noun) If something causes inconvenience, it causes difficulty or problems.
2 (verb) to cause someone difficulty.
inconvenient (adjective) **inconveniently** (adverb)

incorporate, incorporates, incorporating, incorporated
(verb) If something is incorporated into another thing, it becomes part of that thing, e.g. *A lion was incorporated as part of the club badge.*
incorporation (noun)
[*in-* + Latin *corpus* = body]

incorrect
(adjective) wrong or untrue.
incorrectly (adverb)

increase, increases, increasing, increased
(verb) to grow larger in amount, e.g. *The number of fish in the river increased.*
increasingly (adverb)

incredible
(adjective) amazing or impossible to believe.
incredibly (adverb)

Similar words: amazing, unbelievable

incubate, incubates, incubating, incubated
(pronounced **in**-kyoo-bate)
(verb) When eggs incubate, they are kept warm until they are ready to hatch.
incubation (noun)
[Latin *cubare* = to lie down]

incubator, incubators
(noun) a piece of hospital equipment in which sick or weak newborn babies are kept warm.

incurable
(adjective) An incurable disease is one which cannot be cured.
incurably (adverb)

indecent
(adjective) shocking or rude, usually because it concerns nakedness or sex.
indecently (adverb) **indecency** (noun)

indecisive
(adjective) If you are indecisive, you find it difficult to make up your mind.
indecision (noun)

indeed
(adverb) You use indeed to say something strongly, e.g. *You are a very brave girl indeed.*
[Middle English *in dede* = in fact]

indefinite
1 (adjective) If something is indefinite, no time to finish has been decided, e.g. *The union declared an indefinite strike.*
2 vague or not exact, e.g. *The MP gave a very indefinite reply to the awkward question.*
indefinitely (adverb)

indefinite article, articles
(noun) the grammatical term for 'a' and 'an'.

indelible
(adjective) unable to be removed, e.g. *Sadly, the graffiti was indelible.*
indelibly (adverb)
[*in-* + Latin *delere* = to delete]

independent
1 (adjective) If you are independent, you are free from other people's control.
2 not needing other people's help, e.g. *Their children are quite independent.*
independently (adverb) **independence** (noun)

indescribable
(adjective) too intense or extreme to be described, e.g. *The smell from my football socks was indescribable.*
indescribably (adverb)

indestructible
(adjective) unable to be destroyed.

index, indices
1 (noun) an alphabetical list at the back of a book, referring to items in the book.
2 a set of cards with information on them, arranged alphabetically.
3 In maths, an index is a small number placed to the right of another number. It indicates how many times the number is to be multiplied by itself, e.g. in 6^2, the figure ^{2} is the index; so $6^2 = 6 \times 6$; $7^3 = 7 \times 7 \times 7$.
[Latin *index* = forefinger or pointer]

index finger, fingers
(noun) your first finger, next to your thumb.

Indian, Indians
1 (adjective) belonging to India.
2 (noun) someone who comes from India.
3 someone descended from the people who lived in North, South or Central America before Europeans arrived, e.g. *Red Indians.*

indicate, indicates, indicating, indicated
1 (verb) to show that something is true, e.g. *This good work indicates that homework is useful.*
2 to point to something, e.g. *The taxi driver indicated the street I wanted.*
3 If the driver of a vehicle indicates, they give a signal to show which way they are going to turn.
indication (noun) **indicative** (adjective)
[Latin *indicare* = to point out, from *dicare* = to proclaim]

indicative
(noun) If a verb is used in the indicative mood, it is in the form used for making statements.
[**Indicative:** *he goes;* **Imperative:** *Go!;* **Infinitive:** *to go;* the subjunctive, *if he go* is now obsolete.]

indicator, indicators
1 (noun) something which tells you what is happening.
2 A car's indicators are the lights which are used to show when it is turning.

indifferent
1 (adjective) If you are indifferent to something, you have no interest in it.
2 of a poor quality or low standard, e.g. *She was a gifted painter but an indifferent actress.*
indifferently (adverb) **indifference** (noun)

indigestion
(noun) a pain you get when you find it difficult to digest food.
indigestible (adjective)

indignant
(adjective) If you are indignant, you feel angry about something that you think is unfair.
indignantly (adverb) **indignation** (noun)
[Latin *indignari* = to be displeased with]

indirect
(adjective) not direct, e.g. *We went the indirect way to Leeds... It was an indirect free kick so he couldn't score from it.*
indirectly (adverb)

indiscreet
(adjective) If you are indiscreet, you say or do things openly when you should have kept them secret, e.g. *an indiscreet remark.*
indiscreetly (adverb) **indiscretion** (noun)

indispensable
(adjective) If something is indispensable, you cannot do without it, e.g. *In my job, a telephone is indispensable.*

individual, individuals
1 (adjective) relating to one particular person or thing, e.g. *individual tuition.*
2 Someone who is individual behaves quite differently from the way other people behave, e.g. *She dresses in an individual way.*
3 (noun) a person, different from any other person, e.g. *The freedom of the individual.*
individually (adverb) **individuality** (noun)
[Latin *in-* + *dividuus* = not divisible]

indoor
(adjective) situated or happening inside a building, e.g. *an indoor swimming pool.*
indoors (adverb)

indulge, indulges, indulging, indulged
1 (verb) If you indulge in something, you let yourself do something that you enjoy.
2 If you indulge someone, you let them have or do what they want, often in a way that is not good for them.
indulgence (noun)
[Latin *indulgere* = to concede.]

indulgent
(adjective) If you are indulgent, you treat someone with special kindness, e.g. *He was spoilt by an indulgent mother.* [compare: **self-indulgent**]
indulgently (adjective)

industrial action
(adjective) relating to industry.

industrial action
(noun) action taken by workers in protest over pay or working conditions, e.g. a strike, a work-to-rule or an overtime ban.

industrious
(adjective) very hard working.

industry, industries
1 (noun) a general name for the work and processes involved in making things in factories.
2 all the people and processes involved in

We take these words from India: khaki polo bungalow jungle dinghy shampoo loot.

manufacturing a particular thing, e.g. *the plastics industry.*
industrialist (noun)
[Latin *industria* = diligence or hard work]

inedible
(adjective) too nasty or poisonous to eat, e.g. *inedible plants.*

inefficient
(adjective) badly organized, wasteful and slow, e.g. *inefficient farming.*
inefficiently (adverb) **inefficiency** (noun)

ineligible
(adjective) not qualified for something or not entitled to it, e.g *At 13, she was ineligible to be carnival queen.*

inequality
(noun) difference in size, status, wealth or position between different things, groups or people e.g. *There is a great inequality in the way food is distributed in the world.*

inert
1 (adjective) not moving and apparently lifeless, e.g. *We lifted his inert body on to the bed.*
2 In chemistry, an inert gas does not react with other substances.
[Latin *iners* = unskilled or inactive]

inevitable
(adjective) certain to happen.
inevitably (adverb) **inevitability** (noun)
[Latin *in-* = not + *evitare* = to avoid]

inexpensive
(adjective) cheap to buy.

inexperienced
(adjective) lacking experience of a situation or activity, e.g. *The inexperienced swimmer drowned where the currents were strong.*
inexperience (noun)

Similar words: green, raw, unaccustomed

infallible
(adjective) never wrong, e.g. *Teachers aren't infallible, whatever they may say.*
infallibility (noun)

infamous (pronounced in-fe-muss)
(adjective) well known because of something bad or evil, e.g. *He was an infamous villain.*
infamy (noun)
[Latin *infamis* = disreputable]

infant, infants
1 (noun) a baby or very young child.
2 relating to schoolchildren between 4 and 7 years, e.g. *She's with the Infants at present.*
infancy (noun) **infantile** (adjective)
[Latin *infans* = unable to speak]

infantry
(noun) soldiers who fight on foot.
[Italian *infante* = youth or foot-soldier]

infection, infections
(noun) a disease caused by germs, e.g. *a chest infection.*
infect (verb) **infectious** (adjective)
[Latin *inficere* = to dip into or to stain]

Similar words: contagious, catching

infer, infers, inferring, inferred
(verb) to work out that something is true from the information that you already have.
e.g. *She inferred from the way he spoke on the phone that someone was with him.*
inference (noun)
[Latin *inferre* = to bring or carry in]

inferior
(adjective) poorer quality, e.g. *an inferior make.*
inferiority (noun)
[Latin *inferus* = low]

Similar words: bad, poor, shoddy

inferiority complex
(noun) If you have an inferiority complex, you feel less important than other people without any reason to do so.

infertile
(adjective) Infertile soil is of poor quality and plants cannot grow well in it.
infertility (noun)

infest, infests, infesting, infested
(verb) When animals or insects infest something, they spread over it or into it and cause damage, e.g. *My roses are infested with greenfly.*
infestation (noun)
[Latin *infestus* = hostile]

infinite
(adjective) without any limit or end, e.g. *Teachers need infinite patience.*
infinitely (adverb)

Similar words: boundless, endless, limitless

infinitive
(noun) In grammar, the infinitive is the base form of the verb. In modern English it has 'to' in front of it, e.g. to swim, to be.
[Compare **indicative, imperative, subjunctive**]

infinity
1 (noun) a number larger than any other number. It can never be given an exact value.
2 an unreachable point, further away than any other point, e.g. *stars stretching away into infinity... I set my camera at 'infinity'.*

infirmary, infirmaries
(noun) a hospital, e.g. *Manchester Royal Infirmary.*

inflamed
(adjective) red and swollen, usually because of infection.

inflammable
(adjective; old fashioned) An inflammable material burns easily. The modern word for this is **flammable**. [opposite: **non-flammable**]

inflammation
(noun) painful redness or swelling of part of the body.

The first person pronoun: I is always a capital letter, e.g. Mary and I went for a cheap meal.

inflate, inflates, inflating, inflated
(verb) to fill something with air or gas so that it
expands.
inflation (noun) **inflatable** (adjective)
[Latin *in-* + *flare* = to blow into]

inflation
(noun) a general increase in prices, e.g. *Inflation
is now running at 7%*.
inflationary (adjective)

inflection, inflections; also spelled **inflexion**
1 (noun) the way you change the sound of your
voice when you speak.
2 a change in the form of a word that shows its
grammatical function, e.g. a change that makes a
noun plural.

inflexible
(adjective) fixed and unable to be altered.

inflict, inflicts, inflicting, inflicted
(verb) If you inflict something unpleasant on
someone, you make them suffer it.
[Latin *infligere* = to strike against]

influence, influences, influencing, influenced
1 (noun) power that a person has over other
people, e.g. *She was a woman of influence*.
2 the effect that someone or something has, e.g.
driving under the influence of drink.
3 (verb) to have an effect on someone or
something.
influential (adjective)
[Latin *influentia* = power flowing from the stars]

influenza
(noun; formal) flu.

inform, informs, informing, informed
1 (verb) If you inform someone of something, you
tell them about it.
2 If you inform on a person, you tell the police
about a crime they have committed.
informant (noun) **informer** (noun)
[Latin *in-* + *formare* = to describe]

Similar words: (sense 1) notify, tell
(sense 2) sneak, tell on, grass

informal
(adjective) relaxed and casual, e.g. *an informal
interview... informal dress*.
informally (adverb) **informality** (noun)

information
(noun) knowledge, details about something.

Similar words: intelligence, data, facts

informative
(adjective) giving useful information, e.g. *an
informative talk*.

informed
(adjective) knowing a lot about something, e.g.
She is very informed about horses.

infrequent
(adjective) not happening often, e.g. *The sailor's
letters were infrequent*.
infrequently (adverb)

Similar words: occasional, rare

infringe, infringes, infringing, infringed
(verb) If you infringe a law, you break it.
infringement (noun)
[Latin *infringere* = to break off]

infuriate, infuriates, infuriating, infuriated
(verb) to make someone very angry.
infuriating (adjective)

ingenious (pronounced in-**jeen**-yuss)
(adjective) very clever, involving new ideas or
equipment, e.g. *an ingenious gadget*.
ingenuity (noun) **ingeniously** (adverb)
[Latin *ingenium* = natural ability]

ingratitude
(noun) little or no thanks for a gift or for
something that has been done for you.

ingredient, ingredients
(noun) the things that something is made from,
especially in cookery.
[Latin *ingrediens* = going into]

inhabit, inhabits, inhabiting, inhabited
(verb) If a place is inhabited, people live there,
e.g. *The cottage was inhabited by old Mrs Dale*.
inhabitant (noun)
[Latin *in-* + *habitare* = to dwell in]

inhale, inhales, inhaling, inhaled
(verb) to breathe in.
[*in-* + Latin *halare* = to breathe]

inhaler, inhalers
(noun) a container used to breathe in a medicine,
e.g. for asthma.

inherit, inherits, inheriting, inherited
1 (verb) to receive money or property from
someone who has died.
2 If you inherit a quality or characteristic from
someone, it is passed on to you genetically, e.g.
She inherits that temper from her mum.
inheritance (noun) **inheritor** (noun)
[Latin *inhereditare* = to appoint]

inhibited
(adjective) People who are inhibited find it
difficult to relax and to show their emotions.
inhibition (noun)
[Latin *inhibere* = to restrain]

inhospitable
1 (adjective) unpleasant or difficult to live in.
2 If someone is inhospitable, they do not make
people feel welcome when they visit them.

initial, initials, initialling, initialled
(pronounced in-**nish**-l)
1 (noun) the first letter of a name.
2 (verb) to write your initials on something as a
signature.
3 (adjective) first, or at the beginning, e.g. *My
initial reaction was to panic*.
initially (adverb)
[Latin *initium* = beginning]

initiative, initiatives (pronounced
in-**nish**-at-ive)
1 (noun) If you have initiative, you decide what
to do and then do it, without the advice of others.
2 (phrase) If you **take the initiative**, you are the
first person in a group to do something.

T is the most often used initial letter in English.

inject, injects, injecting, injected
(verb) If a doctor or nurse injects you with a substance, they use a needle and syringe to put the substance into your body.
injection (noun)
[Latin *in-* + *jacere* = to throw into]

injure, injures, injuring, injured
(verb) to damage part of someone's body.
injury (noun) **injurious** (adjective)
[Latin *injuria* = injustice, from *jus* = right]

injustice, injustices
1 (noun) unfairness and lack of justice.
2 If you do someone an injustice, you think they are worse than they really are.

ink, inks
(noun) coloured liquid used for writing or printing.
[Greek *enkauston* = purple ink, from *enkaustos* = burnt in]

inland
(adverb, adjective) towards the middle of a country, away from the sea.

in-law, in-laws
(noun) Someone's in-laws are members of their husband's or wife's family.

inlet, inlets
(noun) a narrow bay.

inmate, inmates
(noun) someone who lives in a prison or mental hospital.

inn, inns
(noun) a small, old pub or hotel, often in the country.

inner
(adjective) contained inside a place or object, e.g. *the inner courtyard.*

innings
(noun) In cricket, an innings is a period during which a particular team is batting.

innocent
1 (adjective) not guilty of a crime.
2 without experience of evil or unpleasant things, e.g. *innocent little children.*
innocently (adverb) **innocence** (noun)
[Latin *in-* + *nocens* = not harming]

innovation, innovations
(noun) a completely new idea, product or system of doing things.
innovative (adjective)
[Latin *novus* = new]

innumerable
(adjective) too many to count, e.g. *There are innumerable stars in the night sky.*

inoculate, inoculates, inoculating, inoculated
(verb) to inject a person with a weak form of a disease in order to protect them from that disease.
inoculation (noun)
[Latin *inoculare* = to implant]

input, inputs, inputting, input
1 (noun) In computing, input is information which is fed into a computer.
2 (verb) to feed information into a computer.

inquest, inquests
(noun) an official inquiry to find out what caused a person's death.

inquire, inquires, inquiring, inquired; also spelled **enquire**
1 (verb) to ask for information about something.
2 If you inquire into something, you investigate it carefully.
inquiring (adjective) **inquiringly** (adverb)
inquiry (noun)
[*in-* + Latin *quarere* = to seek]

inquisitive
(adjective) Someone who is inquisitive likes finding out about things.
inquisitively (adverb) **inquisitiveness** (noun)

insane
(adjective) mad; not of sound mind.
insanely (adverb) **insanity** (noun)

inscribe, inscribes, inscribing, inscribed
(verb) If you inscribe words on an object, you write or carve them on it.
[Latin *inscribere* = to write upon]

inscription, inscriptions
(noun) the words that are written or carved on something.

insect, insects
(noun) a small creature with 6 legs and a hard external skeleton. Most insects have wings.
[Latin *insectum* = animal that has been cut into, because of its shape in sections]

insecticide, insecticides
(noun) a poisonous chemical used to kill insects.

insecure
1 (adjective) If you are insecure, you feel unsure of yourself and doubt whether people like you.
2 not safe or well protected, e.g. *These knots look rather too insecure to tie a boat up with.*
insecurity (noun)

insensitive
(adjective) If you are insensitive, you do not notice when you are upsetting people.
insensitively (adverb) **insensitivity** (noun)

inseparable
(adjective) people who are inseparable always seem to be with each other, e.g. *Jane and Fiona are an inseparable pair.*

insert, inserts, inserting, inserted
(verb) If you insert an object into something, you put it inside.
insertion (noun)
[Latin *inserere* = to plant in]

inshore
(adjective, adverb) at sea but close to the shore, e.g. *the R.N.L.I. inshore rescue boat... we kept inshore.*

inside
1 (adverb, preposition) e.g. *Go inside, please... inside the room.*

Think of an original way to say: The house was scary. She felt very cold.

2 (adjective) Inside information is not known to more than the few people involved.

nsignificant
(adjective) small and unimportant.
insignificantly (adverb) **insignificance** (noun)

nsincere
(adjective) Someone who is insincere pretends to have feelings which they do not really have, e.g. *The salesman smiled in an insincere way.*
insincerely (adverb) **insincerity** (noun)

Similar words: two-faced, hypocritical, artificial, false, phoney, shallow

nsinuate, insinuates, insinuating, insinuated
(verb) to hint about something, e.g. *He insinuated I'd been cheating.*
insinuation (noun)
[Latin *insinuare* = to wind your way into, from *sinus* = curve]

nsist, insists, insisting, insisted
(verb) If you insist on something, you demand it emphatically, e.g. *He insists on being let in.*
insistent (adjective) **insistence** (noun)

nsolent
1 (adjective) very rude and disrespectful.
2 (phrase) **dumb insolence**: being rude without saying anything.
insolently (adverb) **insolence** (noun)

nsoluble (pronounced in-**soll**-yoo-bl)
1 (adjective) impossible to solve, e.g. *The missing boat was an insoluble mystery.*
2 impossible to dissolve, e.g. *This ordinary aspirin is insoluble!*

nsomnia
(noun) difficulty in sleeping.
insomniac (noun)
[*in-* + Latin *somnus* = sleep]

nspect, inspects, inspecting, inspected
(verb) to examine something carefully.
inspection (noun)
[Latin *in-* + *specere* = to look into]

nspector, inspectors
1 (noun) someone who inspects things.
2 a senior officer in the police force.

nspire, inspires, inspiring, inspired
(verb) If something inspires you, it gives you new ideas and enthusiasm to do something.
inspired (adjective) **inspiring** (adjective)
inspiration (noun)
[Latin *in-* + *spirare* = to breathe in]

nstall, installs, installing, installed
(verb) If you install a large object in a place, you place it there so it is ready to be used, e.g. *On Monday, we had a boiler installed.*
installation (noun)

nstalment, instalments
1 (noun) If you pay for something in instalments, you pay small amounts of money regularly over a period of time (known as 'hire purchase')
2 one of the parts of a story or TV series that appears regularly over a period of time.

instance
1 (noun) a particular example or occurrence of an event, situation, or person, e.g. *Give me an instance of what you mean.*
2 (phrase) You use **for instance** to give an example of something you are talking about.

instant
1 (noun) a moment or short period of time, e.g. *I'll be with you in an instant.*
2 (adjective) immediate and without delay, e.g. *The song was an instant success.*
instantly (adverb)
[Latin *instans* = being present]

instantaneous
(adjective) happening immediately and without delay, e.g. *Death was instantaneous.*
instantaneously (adverb)

instead
(adverb) in place of.
[Middle English *in stead* = in place]

instep, insteps
(noun) the upper middle part of your foot, e.g. *Always kick the ball with your instep, not your toe.*

instinct, instincts
(noun) a tendency to behave in a certain way that comes naturally, e.g. *Babies have a natural instinct for swimming, but I don't.*
instinctive (adjective) **instinctively** (adverb)
[Latin *instinctus* = roused]

institution, institutions
1 (noun) an old and important tradition, e.g. *the institution of marriage.*
2 a large, important organization, e.g. a university or bank.
institutional (adjective)

instruct, instructs, instructing, instructed
1 (verb) If you instruct someone to do something, you tell them to do it, e.g. *He instructed his bank to give all his money to charity.*
2 to teach someone about a subject or skill.
instructor (noun) **instructive** (adjective)
instruction (noun)
[Latin *struere* = to build]

instrument, instruments
1 (noun) a tool or device used for a particular job, especially for measuring something, e.g. *surgical instruments.*
2 A musical instrument is an object, such as a piano or flute, played to make music.
instrumental (adjective)
[Latin *instrumentum* = tool]

insufficient
(adjective) not enough, e.g. *We had insufficient food.*
insufficiently (adverb) **insufficiency** (noun)

insulate, insulates, insulating, insulated
1 (verb) to keep something warm by covering it in a thick layer of, for example foam or fur.
2 You insulate an electrical or metal object by

A musician needs these words:
orchestra symphony instrument melody harmony sonata concerto baton.

covering it with rubber or plastic. This is to stop it giving you an electric shock.
insulation (noun) **insulator** (noun)
[Latin *insulatus* = made into an island]

insulin (pronounced **inss-yoo-lin**)
(noun) a substance which controls the level of sugar in the blood. Diabetics do not produce insulin naturally and have to take regular doses of it in the form of tablets or injections.

insult, insults, insulting, insulted
1 (verb) to offend someone by being rude to them.
2 (noun; pronounced in-sult) something rude said to you which offends you.
insulting (adjective)
[Latin *insultare* = to jump upon]

Similar words: (verb) abuse, snub, offend

insure, insures, insuring, insured
(verb) If you insure something or yourself, you pay money regularly (a premium) so that if there is an accident or damage, the insurance company will pay for repairs, medical treatment, etc.
insurance (noun)

intact
(adjective) complete, and not changed or damaged in any way, e.g. *They dug up some ancient pots, still intact.*
[Latin *in-* + *tactus* = not touched]

integer, integers
(noun) In maths, an integer is any whole number.
[Latin *integer* = intact or entire]

integral
(adjective) essential, e.g. *This cogwheel is an integral part of the machine.*

integrate, integrates, integrating, integrated
(verb) to combine things so that they become closely linked or form part of a whole idea or system, e.g. *The two companies were integrated.*
integration (noun)

Similar words: assimilate, incorporate

intellectual, intellectuals
1 (noun) someone who spends a lot of time studying and thinking about complicated ideas and theories.
2 (adjective) involving thought, ideas and understanding, e.g. *intellectual stimulation.*
intellectually (adverb) **intellect** (noun)

intelligence
1 (noun) the ability to understand and learn things quickly and well.
intelligent (adjective) **intelligently** (adverb)
2 information received about something, e.g. military intelligence (M.I.5, M.I.6).

Similar words: (sense 1) intellect, cleverness, brains

intelligible
(adjective) able to be understood, e.g. *His scrawled letters were barely intelligible.*

intend, intends, intending, intended
1 (verb) If you intend to do something, you have decided or planned to do it.
2 If something is intended for a particular use, it

should have this use, e.g. *This brush was intended for paint not glue.*
[Latin *intendere* = to extend or to direct]

intense
1 (adjective) very great in strength or amount, e.g. *intense heat... intense interest.*
2 If a person is intense, they take things very seriously and have very strong feelings.
intensely (adverb) **intensity** (noun)
[Latin *intensus* = stretched]

intensive
(adjective) involving a lot of energy or effort over a very short time, e.g. *intensive care.*

intention, intentions
(noun) If you have an intention to do something, you have a plan of what you are going to do.

inter-
(prefix) between, e.g. *an inter-school football match.*
[a Latin word]

intercept, intercepts, intercepting, intercepted
(pronounced in-ter-sept)
(verb) If you intercept someone or something, you stop them from reaching their destination, e.g. *The Post Office intercepted the letter bomb.*
interceptor (noun) **interception** (noun)
[*inter-* + Latin *capere* = to capture]

intercom, intercoms
(noun) a small unit with a microphone and speaker, which you use to speak to people in another room.

interest, interests, interesting, interested
1 (noun) If you have an interest in something, you want to learn or hear more about it.
2 (noun) a sum of money paid as a percentage of a larger sum of money which has been borrowed or invested, e.g. *The building society paid 10% interest on her savings.*
interestingly (adverb)
[Latin *interest* = it concerns]

interface, interfaces
(noun; formal) The interface between two subjects or systems is the area in which they interact with each other or are linked, e.g. an interface between two computers.

interfere, interferes, interfering, interfered
(verb) to involve yourself in a situation which does not really concern you.
interference (noun) **interfering** (adjective)
[Old French *s'entreferir* = to collide]

Similar words: meddle, tamper, poke your nose in

interior
(noun) the inside part of something.
[Latin *inter* = within]

interjection, interjections (see page 429)
(noun) a word or phrase spoken suddenly to express a strong feeling such as surprise, pain or anger.
[Latin *interjicere* = to throw between]

interlude, interludes (rhymes with **rude**)
(noun) a short break from an activity.
[Latin *inter-* + *ludus* = game]

The Survival Guide is an integral part of this dictionary. It will help you.

intermediate
(adjective) at a middle level, e.g. *beginners, intermediate and advanced swimmers.*

intermission, intermissions
(noun) an interval between parts of a film or play.

intermittent
(adjective) happening only occasionally.
intermittently (adverb)

internal
(adjective) happening inside a person, place or object, e.g. *The patient had internal bleeding.*
internally (adverb)

international, internationals
1 (adjective) involving different countries.
2 (noun) a sports match between two countries.
internationally (adverb)

interpret, interprets, interpreting, interpreted
1 (verb) If you interpret what someone says or does, you decide what it means.
2 If you interpret a foreign language that someone is speaking, you translate it.
interpretation (noun) **interpreter** (noun)

interrogate, interrogates, interrogating, interrogated
(verb) to question someone thoroughly to get information from them.
interrogation (noun) **interrogator** (noun)
[Latin *inter-* + *rogare* = to ask]

Similar words: grill, cross-examine, quiz

interrupt, interrupts, interrupting, interrupted
1 (verb) If you interrupt someone, you start talking while they are talking.
2 If an activity is interrupted, it is stopped for a time, e.g. *Train services were interrupted.*
interruption (noun)
[Latin *inter-* + *rumpere* = to break]

intersect, intersects, intersecting, intersected
(verb) When two lines, roads, etc. intersect, they cross each other.
intersection (noun)
[Latin *inter-* + *secare* = to cut between]

interval, intervals
1 (noun) the period of time between two moments or dates.
2 a short break during a play or concert.
3 (phrase) If something happens at intervals, it happens every now and then.
4 If things are placed at intervals, there is a certain amount of space between them.
[Latin *intervallum* = space between ramparts]

Similar words: (sense 2) break, interlude, intermission, gap, pause

intervene, intervenes, intervening, intervened
1 (verb) If you intervene in a situation, you step in to prevent conflict between people, e.g. *The referee intervened to save the boxer from further punishment.*

2 (phrase) The **intervening time** means the time between one event and another.
intervening (adjective) **intervention** (noun)
[Latin *intervenire* = to come between]

interview, interviews, interviewing, interviewed
1 (noun) a meeting at which someone asks you questions about yourself to see if you are suitable for a particular job.
2 a conversation in which a person is asked questions by a newspaper, TV or radio reporter.
3 (verb) If you interview someone, you ask them questions about themselves.
interviewer (noun) **interviewee** (noun)

intestine, intestines
(noun) a long tube which carries food from your stomach through to your bowels, and in which the food is digested.
intestinal (adjective)
[Latin *intestinus* = internal]

intimate
1 (adjective) If two people are intimate, they have a close relationship.
2 An intimate matter is very private and personal.
3 An intimate knowledge of something is very deep and detailed.
intimately (adverb) **intimacy** (noun)
[Latin *intimus* = innermost or deepest]

into
1 (preposition) e.g. *I walked into the room.*
2 (informal) If you are into something, you like it very much, e.g. *He's into American football.*

intolerable
(adjective) If something is intolerable, you can't endure or put up with it.
intolerably (adverb)

intolerant
(adjective) angry about people who are different from you in some way.
intolerance (noun)

intoxicated
(adjective) drunk.
intoxicating (adjective) **intoxication** (noun)
[Greek *toxicon* = arrow poison]

intra-
(prefix) within or inside, e.g. *an intravenous injection.*
[Latin *intra* = within]

intransitive
(adjective) An intransitive verb is one that does not have a direct object, e.g. to smile.

intravenous (pronounced in-trav-**vee**-nuss)
(adjective) Intravenous foods or drugs are given to sick people through their veins.
intravenously (adverb)

intrepid
(adjective) brave, e.g. *intrepid explorers.*
intrepidly (adverb)
[Latin *in-* + *trepidus* = not afraid]

Some poets like to use *internal rhymes* e.g. We were the *first* that ever *burst—*

intricate
(adjective) Something that is intricate has many fine details, e.g. *an intricate design of lace.*
intricately (adverb) **intricacy** (noun)
[Latin *intricatus* = tangled]

intrigue, intrigues, intriguing, intrigued
(verb) If something intrigues you, you are fascinated by it and curious about it.
intriguing (adjective)
[Latin *intricare* = to entangle or to perplex]

introduce, introduces, introducing, introduced
1 (verb) If you introduce one person to another, you tell them each other's name so that they can get to know each other.
2 When someone introduces a radio or TV show, they say a few words at the beginning.
introductory (adjective)
[Latin *introducere* = to bring inside]

introduction, introductions
1 (noun) the act of showing someone or something for the first time.
2 a piece of writing at the beginning of a book, which usually discusses it in some detail.

Similar words: (sense 2) preface, foreword

intrude, intrudes, intruding, intruded
(verb) to disturb or break in, e.g. *I don't want to intrude on your family.*
intruder (noun) **intrusion** (noun)
intrusive (adjective)
[Latin *intrudere* = to thrust in]

Similar words: barge in, gatecrash, trespass

intuition (pronounced int-yoo-**ish**-n)
(noun) a feeling you have about something that you cannot explain, e.g. *My intuition warned me not to trust him.*
intuitive (adjective) **intuitively** (adverb)

inundated
1 (adjective) If you are inundated by letters etc, you receive so many that you cannot deal with them all.
2 flooded, e.g. *The fields were inundated.*
inundation (noun) **inundate** (verb)

Inuit
(adjective) a modern name for Eskimo; belonging to a people living in the Arctic regions of North America and Siberia.

invade, invades, invading, invaded
1 (verb) to enter a country by force.
2 If someone invades your privacy, they disturb you when you want to be alone.
invader (noun) **invasion** (noun)

invalid, invalids (pronounced in-va-lid)
(noun) someone who is so ill that they need to be looked after by someone else.
[Latin *invalidus* = infirm]

invalid (pronounced in-**val**-id)
(adjective) If an election is invalid, it does not count because something has gone wrong.
invalidate (verb)
[Latin *invalidus* = without legal force]

invaluable
(adjective) extremely useful, e.g. *A good map is invaluable if you're crossing London.*
[similar to **priceless**, i.e. you can't put a value on it because it is so useful]

invent, invents, inventing, invented
1 (verb) If you invent a machine, device or process, you are the first person to think of it.
2 If you invent an excuse etc, you make it up.
inventor (noun) **invention** (noun)
inventive (adjective) **inventiveness** (noun)
[Latin *invenire* = to find or to come upon]

Similar words: devise, create

invertebrate, invertebrates
(noun; technical) a creature which does not have a spine, e.g. crab, centipede.

inverted comma, commas
(noun) Inverted commas are the punctuation marks used to show where speech begins and ends e.g. 'Well,' said Fred, 'it all depends.'

invest, invests, investing, invested
1 (verb) If you invest money, you pay it into a bank or buy shares to receive a profit.
2 If you invest in something useful, you buy it because it will help you do something better, e.g. *I invested in a faster printer.*
investor (noun) **investment** (noun)

investigate, investigates, investigating, investigated
(verb) to find out all the facts about something.
investigator (noun) **investigation** (noun)
[Latin *investigare* = to search after, from *vestigium* = track]

Similar words: follow up, look into, make inquiries, explore, probe

invigilate, invigilates, invigilating, invigilated
(pronounced in-**vij**-il-late)
(verb) to supervise an examination.
invigilator (noun)
[Latin *invigilare* = to watch over]

invincible
(adjective) unable to be beaten, e.g. *Manchester City at the moment are invincible.*
invincibly (adverb) **invincibility** (noun)
[Latin *in-* = not + *vincere* = to conquer]

invisible
(adjective) If something is invisible, you cannot see it, e.g.
Patient: Doctor, doctor, I keep thinking I'm invisible!
Doctor: Who said that?
invisibly (adverb) **invisibility** (noun)

invite, invites, inviting, invited
1 (verb) to ask someone to come to e.g. a party.
2 (noun; informal) an invitation.

invoice, invoices
(noun) a bill for services or goods.
[Old French *envois* = messages]

involve, involves, involving, involved
1 (verb) If a situation involves someone or something, it includes them as a necessary part.

We take these words from the Inuit: anorak igloo kayak.

2 If you involve yourself in something, you take part in it, e.g. *He's involved in the school play.*
3 If a film or a book involves you, it makes you feel that you are taking part in events.
involved (adjective) **involvement** (noun)
[Latin *involvere* = to roll in or to surround]

inward or **inwards**
(adjective, adverb) towards the inside or centre of something.
inwardly (adverb) **inwardness** (noun)

IQ, IQs
(noun) Your IQ is your level of intelligence calculated from the results of a special test. (abbreviation for 'intelligence quotient')

Iranian, Iranians (pronounced ir-**rain**-ee-an)
1 (adjective) belonging to Iran.
2 (noun) someone who comes from Iran.
3 the main language spoken in Iran. It is also known as Farsi.

Iraqi, Iraqis (pronounced ir-**ah**-kee)
1 (adjective) belonging to Iraq.
2 (noun) someone who comes from Iraq.

irate (pronounced eye-**rate**)
(adjective) very angry.
[Latin *ira* = anger]

iris, irises (pronounced **eye**-riss)
1 (noun) the round, coloured part of your eye.
2 a type of flower.
[Greek *iris* = rainbow or coloured circle]

Irish
1 (adjective) belonging to Ireland.
2 (noun) Irish or Irish Gaelic is a language spoken in some parts of Ireland.

Irishman, Irishmen
(noun) a man who comes from Ireland.
Irishwoman (noun)

iron, irons, ironing, ironed
1 (noun) a strong, hard metal found in rocks, used in making tools and machines; it is also an important component of blood.
2 (verb) If you iron clothes, you use a hot iron to remove creases from them.
ironing (noun)

iron out
(phrasal verb) If you iron out difficulties, you solve them.

irony
(noun) conveying one meaning with words that seem to suggest a different meaning.

irradiate, irradiates, irradiating, irradiated
(verb) to expose something to radiation. In some countries, food is irradiated to lengthen its life.
irradiation (noun)

irrational
(adjective) Irrational feelings are not based on logical reasons, e.g. *an irrational fear of cats.*
irrationally (adverb) **irrationality** (noun)

irregular
1 (adjective) not smooth or straight; not forming

a regular pattern, e.g. *irregular marks on the wings... feeding them at irregular intervals.*
2 Irregular behaviour is unusual and strange.
irregularly (adverb) **irregularity** (noun)

Similar word: (sense 1) erratic

irrelevant
(adjective) not directly connected with a subject, e.g. *The book was full of irrelevant information.*
irrelevance (noun) **irrelevancy** (noun)

irreparable (pronounced ir-**rep**-rabl)
(adjective) Irreparable damage is so bad that it cannot be repaired.
irreparably (adverb)

irreplaceable
(adjective) If something is irreplaceable, it is so special that it cannot be replaced if it is lost or destroyed.

irresistible
1 (adjective) unable to be controlled, e.g. *I felt an irresistible urge to laugh.*
2 extremely attractive, e.g. *In the 20s, women found Rudolph Valentino irresistible.*
irresistibly (adverb)

irresponsible
(adjective) An irresponsible person does things without considering the consequences, e.g. *The irresponsible driver had been drinking.*
irresponsibly (adverb) **irresponsibility** (noun)

Similar words: thoughtless, reckless

irrigate, irrigates, irrigating, irrigated
(verb) to supply land with water brought through pipes or ditches.
irrigated (adjective) **irrigation** (noun)
[Latin *rigare* = to moisten]

irritate, irritates, irritating, irritated
1 (verb) If something irritates you, it annoys you.
2 If something irritates part of your body, it makes it tender, sore and itchy.
irritable (adjective) **irritant** (noun)
irritation (noun)

Islam
(noun) the religion of the Muslims.
[Arab *islam* = submision (to God)]

island, islands (pronounced **eye**-land)
(noun) a piece of land surrounded by water.
islander (noun)
[Old English *ig* = island + *land*]

isle, isles (rhymes with **mile**)
(noun) an island, e.g. *The Isle of Man.*
[Latin *insula* = island]

isobar, isobars (pronounced **eye**-so-bar)
(noun; technical) a line on a map which joins places of equal air pressure. They are shown on weather charts to help forecasting.
[Greek *isobares* = of equal weight]

isolate, isolates, isolating, isolated
(verb) If you isolate something, you separate it from everything else.

isolated
(adjective) alone
isolation (noun)

isosceles (pronounced eye-**sossy**-leez)
(adjective) An isosceles triangle has two sides of
the same length.
[Greek *iso-* = equal + *skelos* = leg]

Israeli, Israelis (pronounced iz-**rail**-ee)
1 (adjective) belonging to Israel.
2 (noun) someone who comes from Israel.

issue, issues, issuing, issued
(pronounced **ish**-yoo)
1 (noun) an important subject that people are
talking about e.g. *the AIDS issue*.
2 a particular edition of a newspaper or
magazine, e.g. *the June issue of 'Railway World'*.
3 (verb) If someone issues a statement or a
warning, they say it formally and publicly.
4 If someone issues something, they officially
supply it, e.g. *I was issued with a prison uniform*.
[noun: senses 2-4: Latin *exuta* = something that
has gone out]

Similar words: (verb: sense 4) supply, distribute,
give out

it
(pronoun) e.g. *Take it away, it smells*.

Italian, Italians
1 (adjective) belonging to Italy.
2 (noun) someone who comes from Italy.
3 the main language spoken in Italy and also by
some people in Switzerland.

italics
(plural noun) letters printed in a special sloping
way, often used to emphasize something, e.g.
This sentence is printed in italics.
(But this one is printed in roman.)
italic (adjective)

itch, itches, itching, itched
1 (noun) an unpleasant, irritating feeling on your
skin, that you want to scratch.
2 (verb) If you are itching to do something, you
are impatient to do it, e.g. *The showman was
itching to open a flea circus*.
itchy (adjective)
[Old English *giccean* = to itch]

item, items
(noun) one of a collection or list of objects.
[Latin *item* = in like manner; once used to
introduce each item on a list]

itemize, itemizes, itemizing, itemized; also
spelled **itemise**
(verb) to make a list of things.

its
(pronoun) 'Its' refers to something belonging to
things that have already been mentioned, e.g.
The creature lifted its head. [not to be confused
with **it's** which is short for 'it is' or 'it has'.]

itself
(pronoun) e.g. *The bird preened itself*.

ivory
(noun) the creamy-white, bony substance which
forms the tusk of an elephant.
[Latin *ebur* = ivory]

ivy
(noun) an evergreen plant which creeps along
the ground and up walls.

J

jab, jabs, jabbing, jabbed
1 (verb) to poke at something roughly.
2 (noun; informal) an injection, e.g. *a polio jab*.

jabber, jabbers, jabbering, jabbered
(verb; informal) If people jabber, they talk very
fast and you cannot understand them.

jack, jacks, jacking, jacked
1 (noun) a piece of equipment for lifting heavy
objects, especially for lifting a car.
2 (verb) To jack up an object means to raise it,
especially by using a jack.
3 (noun) In a pack of cards, a jack is a face card.
4 Jacks is a game in which you throw up and
catch small, criss-cross shaped objects.
5 (verb) to jack something in means to give it up.
[from the name *Jack*, a nickname for John]

jacket, jackets
1 (noun) a short coat.
2 an outer covering for something, e.g. *a book
jacket*.

3 (adjective) Potatoes cooked in their skins in the
oven are called jacket potatoes.

jackknife, jackknifes, jackknifing, jackknifed
(verb) If an articulated lorry jackknifes, the
trailer skids and swings round out of control
towards the cab.

jackpot, jackpots
(phrase; informal) If you **hit the jackpot**, you win
the top prize or have a stroke of good luck.

jacuzzi
(noun) a type of bath which stimulates the skin
with fine jets of water.

jagged
(adjective) sharp and spiky.

Similar words: ragged, sharp, spiked

jail, jails, jailing, jailed; also spelled **gaol**
1 (noun) a prison.
2 (verb) to lock someone up in a prison.
[Old French *jaiole* = cage]

Letter J developed from letter I by adding a tail.

jam, jams, jamming, jammed
1 (noun) a food made by boiling fruit and sugar together until it sets.
2 a situation which is so crammed that it is impossible to move, e.g. *a traffic jam.*
3 (phrase; informal) If someone is **in a jam**, they are in a difficult situation.
4 (verb) If people or things are jammed into a place, they are squeezed together very closely.
5 If something is jammed, it is stuck or unable to work properly.
6 (informal) When musicians jam, they play together without any planning or rehearsal.

Similar words: (sense 3) fix, pickle

Jamaican, Jamaicans (pronounced jam-**may**-kn)
1 (adjective) belonging to Jamaica.
2 (noun) someone who comes from Jamaica.

jamboree, jamborees
(noun) a party or a gathering of large numbers of people enjoying themselves.

jammy
(adjective; informal) lucky.

jangle, jangles, jangling, jangled
(verb) to make a harsh, metallic ringing noise.

janitor, janitors
(noun) the caretaker of a building.

January
(noun) the first month of the year.
[Latin *Januarius* = the month of Janus, named after a Roman god]

Japanese
1 (adjective) belonging to Japan.
2 (noun) someone who comes from Japan.
3 the main language spoken in Japan.

jar, jars, jarring, jarred
1 (noun) a glass container with a wide top used for storing food.
2 (verb) If something jars on you, you find it unpleasant or annoying.
[noun: Arabic *jarrah* = earthenware container]

jargon
(noun) words or expressions that are used in special or technical ways, often annoyingly.

jaundice
(noun) an illness affecting the liver in which the skin and the whites of the eyes become yellow.
[French *jaune* = yellow]

javelin, javelins
(noun) an athletics event in which contestants throw the javelin, a pointed metal spear, as far as they can.

jaw, jaws
1 (noun) the bone in which the teeth are set.
2 A person's or animal's mouth and teeth are their jaws.

jazz, jazzes, jazzing, jazzed
1 (noun) various styles of music with a forceful rhythm e.g. *modern jazz... trad jazz... big band jazz.*
2 (verb; informal) To jazz something up means to make it more colourful or exciting.

jazzy, jazzier, jazziest
(adjective; informal) bright and flashy.

jealous
1 (adjective) If you are jealous of someone, you feel bitterness and anger towards them because of something they own or something they have achieved.
2 If you are jealous of something you have, you feel you must try to keep it from other people.
jealously (adverb) **jealousy** (noun)

Similar words: (sense 1) covetous, envious
(sense 2) possessive

jeans
(plural noun) casual denim trousers.

jeep, jeeps
(noun) a small army vehicle with 4-wheel drive.
[from G.P. = general purpose]

jeer, jeers, jeering, jeered
(verb) If you jeer at someone, you insult them in a loud, unpleasant way.

Jehovah (pronounced ji-**hove**-ah)
the name of God in the Old Testament.
[from the Hebrew *JHVH*, the sacred name of God]

jelly, jellies
(noun) a clear food made from gelatine and eaten as a dessert.

jeopardy (pronounced **jepp**-er-dy)
(noun) If someone or something is in jeopardy, they are at risk of failing or of being destroyed.
e.g. *The downturn in trade placed many jobs in jeopardy.*
jeopardize (verb)

jerk, jerks, jerking, jerked
1 (verb) to give something a sudden, sharp pull.
2 to move suddenly.
3 (noun; informal) If you call someone a jerk, you mean they are stupid.
jerky (adjective) **jerkily** (adverb)

jersey, jerseys
(noun) a knitted garment for the upper half of the body.
[Knitting is an industry in *Jersey*, one of the Channel Islands]

jest, jests, jesting, jested
1 (noun) a joke, e.g. *There's many a true word spoken in jest.*
2 (verb) to speak jokingly.

jester, jesters
(noun) In the past, a jester was a man who was kept to amuse the king or queen and court.

jet, jets, jetting, jetted
1 (noun) a plane powered by a jet engine.
2 a stream of liquid, gas or flame forced out under pressure, e.g. *a jet of water.*
[French *jeter* = to throw]

jetlag
(noun) intense tiredness or physical confusion that air travellers feel after they have passed through several time zones.

We take these words from Japan: judo karate kimono haiku.

jetty, **jetties**
(noun) a wide, stone wall or wooden platform where boats can be moored.
[Old French *jetee* = something thrown out]

Jew, **Jews**
(noun) a person who practises the religion of Judaism, or who is of Hebrew descent.
(feminine: **Jewess**)
Jewish (adjective)
[from *Judah*, the name of a Jewish patriarch]

jewel, **jewels**
(noun) a precious stone.
jewelled (adjective)

jeweller, **jewellers**
(noun) a person who makes jewellery or who buys, sells and repairs it.

jewellery
(noun) ornaments that people wear, e.g. rings, bracelets, or necklaces, made of valuable metals and sometimes decorated with precious stones.

jiffy
(noun) In a jiffy means very quickly, e.g. *I'll be back in a jiffy.*

jiffy-bag
(noun; trade mark) a padded envelope in which to send fragile things.

jig, **jigs**, **jigging**, **jigged**
1 (noun) a type of lively folk dance; also the music that accompanies it.
2 (verb) If you jig, you dance or jump around in a lively bouncy manner.

jiggle, **jiggles**, **jiggling**, **jiggled**
(verb) If you jiggle something, you move it around with quick jerky movements.

jigsaw, **jigsaws**
(noun) a picture puzzle in small pieces which you have to put together.

jingle, **jingles**, **jingling**, **jingled**
1 (noun) a short, catchy advertising phrase or rhyme set to music, on radio or TV, e.g. *A Mars a day helps you work, rest and play.*
2 (verb) When something jingles, it makes a tinkling sound like small bells.

jinx, **jinxes**
(noun) anything that is thought to bring bad luck, e.g. *There must be a jinx on it.*

jitters
(plural noun; informal) If you have the jitters, you are feeling very nervous.
jittery (noun)

jive
(noun) a lively, energetic dance, first popular in the 1950s, performed to rock'n'roll music.

job, **jobs**
1 (noun) the work someone does for a living.
2 a particular task of work.
3 (phrase) If something is **just the job**, it is exactly right or exactly what you wanted.
4 If you **make the best of a bad job**, you do the best you can in difficult circumstances.
5 If you **give something up as a bad job**, you

abandon it because you feel that you cannot do anything to improve it.

Similar words: occupation, employment, position, trade, profession, situation

job centre, **centres**
(noun) a government office where people can find out about job vacancies.

jobless
(adjective) without any work.

job lot, **lots**
(noun) a collection of items, often cheap and of low quality, that are sold together.

jockey, **jockeys**
(noun) someone who rides a horse in a race.

jodhpurs (pronounced jod-purz)
(plural noun) close-fitting trousers for horse riding.
[from *Jodhpur*, the name of a town in N. India]

jog, **jogs**, **jogging**, **jogged**
1 (verb) to run slowly and rhythmically.
2 (verb) If you jog something, you knock it slightly so that it shakes or moves.
3 If someone or something jogs your memory, they remind you of something.
jogger (noun) **jogging** (noun)

join, **joins**, **joining**, **joined** (verb)
1 (verb) to come together, e.g. *The roads join by the Lamb Inn.*
2 to fasten two things together.
3 to become a member of an organisation.
4 (phrase) If two people **join forces**, they work together to achieve a common aim.
[Latin *jungere* = to yoke]

Similar words: (sense 2) link, connect, unite
(sense 3) enlist, enrol, enter, sign up

join up
(phrasal verb) If someone joins up, they become a member of the army, navy or RAF.

joiner, **joiners**
(noun) a person who makes wooden window frames, door frames or doors.
[compare: **carpenter**]
joinery (noun)

joint, **joints**
1 (adjective) shared by or belonging to two or more people, e.g. *a joint bank account.*
2 (noun) a part of the body where two bones meet and are joined together so that they can move, e.g. a knee or hip.
3 A joint of meat is a large piece suitable for roasting.
4 (informal) any place of entertainment, such as a nightclub or pub, e.g. *What a lousy joint!*
jointly (adverb) **jointed** (adjective)

joke, **jokes**, **joking**, **joked**
1 (noun) something that you say or do to make people laugh.
2 anything that you think is ridiculous and not

A comedian needs these words: parody satire timing humour wit farce slapstick caricature.

worthy of respect, e.g. *The management here is a joke!*
3 (verb) to crack a joke or play a trick.
jokingly (adverb)
[Latin *jocus* = joke]

Similar words: jest, gag, hoax, trick, prank

joker, jokers
(noun) In a pack of cards, a joker is an extra card that does not belong to any of the 4 suits, but is used in some games.

jolliment, jolliments
(noun) a joke, trick, etc. [named after Antoine Jollie, court jester to King Henry II]

jolly, jollier, jolliest; jollies, jollying, jollied
1 (adjective) happy, cheerful and pleasant.
2 (adverb; informal) very, e.g. *It was jolly decent of that chap, wasn't it, Jeeves, old bean?*
3 (verb) If you jolly someone along, you encourage them in a cheerful and friendly way.
jollity (noun)

jolt, jolts, jolting, jolted
1 (verb) to move or shake roughly and violently, e.g. *The carriage jolted as the train started.*
2 (noun) a sudden jerky movement.
3 an unpleasant shock or surprise, e.g. *His death came as a severe jolt.*

Jordanian, Jordanians
1 (adjective) belonging to Jordan.
2 (noun) someone who comes from Jordan.

jostle, jostles, jostling, jostled
(verb) to push or knock roughly against people in a crowd.

jot, jots, jotting, jotted
1 (verb) If you jot something down, you write it quickly in the form of a short informal note.
2 (noun) a very small amount, e.g. *You, sir, won't get one jot of my money.*

jotter, jotters
(noun) a pad or notebook.

journalist
(noun) someone who writes for a newspaper or magazine.
journalism (noun) **journalistic** (adjective)

journalese
(noun) a style of writing like that in newspapers, e.g. *City bigwigs were rocked tonight by a shock police decision to mount a crime probe.*

journey, journeys, journeying, journeyed
1 (noun) the act of travelling.
2 (verb; formal) to travel, e.g. *It got colder as he journeyed north.*
[Old French *journée* = day or a day's travelling]

Similar words: (noun) expedition, voyage

joust, jousts, jousting, jousted
1 (noun) In medieval times, a joust was a competition between knights on horseback, using lances trying to knock each other off.
2 (verb) to take part in a joust.

jovial
(adjective) cheerful and friendly.
jovially (adverb) **joviality** (noun)
[Latin *jovialis* = of Jupiter]

joy, joys
1 (noun) a feeling of great happiness.
2 (informal) success or luck, e.g. *Any joy at the job centre?*
joyful (adjective) **joyfully** (adverb)

joyride, joyrides
(noun) a drive in a stolen car for pleasure.
joyriding (noun) **joyrider** (noun)

joystick, joysticks
1 (noun) a lever in an aircraft which the pilot uses to control height and direction.
2 a lever used to control computer games.

jubilation
(noun) a feeling of great happiness and triumph.
jubilant (adjective) **jubilantly** (adverb)
[Latin *jubilans* = shouting for joy]

jubilee, jubilees
(noun) a special anniversary of an event such as a coronation, e.g. *Queen Elizabeth II's Silver Jubilee in 1977.*
[Hebrew *yobhel* = ram's horn; rams' horns were blown during festivals and celebrations]

Judaism (pronounced joo-day-i-zm)
(noun) the religion of the Jewish people.

judge, judges, judging, judged
1 (noun) the person in a law court who decides how the law should be applied to people on trial.
2 someone who decides the winner in a contest or competition.
3 (verb) If you judge someone or something, you form an opinion about them based on the evidence or information that you have.
judgement or **judgment** (noun)

Similar words: (noun, verb: sense 2) umpire, referee

judo
(noun) a sport in which two people try to force each other to the ground using special throws.
[Japanese *ju do* = gentleness art]

jug, jugs
(noun) a container with a lip or spout.

juggernaut, juggernauts
(noun) a large, heavy lorry.
[from Hindi *Jagannath*, the name of a huge idol of the god Krishna, which every year is wheeled through the streets of Puri in India]

juggle, juggles, juggling, juggled
(verb) to keep several balls etc. in the air, throwing and catching them in sequence.
juggler (noun)
[Old French *jogler* = to perform as a jester]

juice, juices
(noun) the liquid from fruit, vegetables or meat.
juicy (adjective) **juicily** (adverb) **juiciness** (noun)

jukebox, jukeboxes
(noun) a machine found in cafés and pubs which plays selected music when coins are inserted.

The t is silent in: bristle bustle chestnut christen glisten jostle moisten mortgage.

July
(noun) the 7th month of the year. [from Latin *Julius*, the month named after Julius Caesar by the Romans]

jumble, jumbles, jumbling, jumbled
1 (noun) an untidy muddle of things.
2 Jumble consists of articles for a jumble sale.
3 (verb) to mix things up untidily.

jumble sale, sales
(noun) an event at which cheap second-hand clothes and other articles are sold to raise money.

jumbo, jumbos
1 (noun) a Boeing 747 aeroplane that can carry several hundred passengers.
2 (adjective) very large, e.g. *a jumbo packet of soap powder*.
[from *Jumbo*, a famous 19th-century elephant]

jump, jumps, jumping, jumped
(verb) e.g. *She jumped down off the wall.*

Similar words: bound, leap, spring, vault, hurdle

jumped-up
(adjective) If you say someone is jumped-up, you mean that they have risen from a low position, and have now become unpleasant.

jumper, jumpers
(noun) a knitted garment for the upper body.

jump suit, suits
(noun) a one-piece garment combining both top and trousers.

jumpy, jumpier, jumpiest
(adjective) nervous and worried.

junction, junctions
(noun) a place where roads or railway lines meet, join or cross.

June
(noun) the 6th month of the year.
[from Latin *Junius*, the month, probably named after an important Roman family]

jungle, jungles
(noun) a dense tropical forest.
[Hindi *jangal* = wasteland]

junior, juniors
1 (adjective) Someone who is junior to other people has a lower position in an organization.
2 the younger of two people with the same name, usually father and son, e.g. *Harry Connick junior.*
3 relating to school children between 8 and 11 years, e.g. *He goes to a junior school.*
4 (noun) someone who holds an unimportant position in an organization, e.g. *the office junior.*
[Latin *juvenis* = young]

junk, junks
1 (noun) old or second-hand articles sold cheaply or thrown away.
2 a Chinese sailing boat.

[sense 1: Middle English *jonke* = old rope
sense 2: Javanese *jon* = boat]

junk food
(noun) food low in nutritional value which is eaten as well as or instead of proper meals.

junk mail
(noun) advertising leaflets that come in the post when you have not sent for them and do not want them.

junkie, junkies
(noun; informal) a drug addict.

jury, juries
(noun) a group of 12 people (jurors) in a court of law who listen to the facts and decide whether the accused person is guilty or not.
[Old French *jurer* = to swear]

just
1 (adjective) fair and proper, e.g. *She got her just reward for all the hard work she had put in.*
2 (adverb) If something has just happened, it happened a very short time ago.

justice, justices
1 (noun) fairness and reasonableness.
2 The system of justice in a country is the way in which laws are maintained by the courts, e.g. *Justice is truth in action.*
3 (phrase) If you **do yourself justice**, you do something as well as you possibly can.
[Latin *justitia* = justice]

justify, justifies, justifying, justified
1 (verb) If you justify an action or idea, you prove or explain why it is reasonable or necessary, e.g. *How can you possibly justify risking the lives of people in your car?*
2 In printing or word processing, justifying is spacing words out to fill the line. In this dictionary the text is not justified, e.g.
This has been justified.
This has not been justified.
justification (noun) **justifiable** (adjective)
[Latin *justus* + *facere* = to make just]

jut, juts, jutting, jutted
(verb) If something juts out, it sticks out beyond or above a surface or edge.

Similar words: stick out, project, protrude

juvenile, juveniles
1 (noun) a young person not old enough to be considered an adult.
2 (adjective) childish and rather silly.
[Latin *juvenis* = young]

juvenile delinquent, delinquents
(noun) a young person guilty of a crime or of violent behaviour.
juvenile delinquency (noun)

Which ape has a sweet tooth? The meringue-outang.

K

kangaroo, kangaroos
(noun) a large Australian marsupial.

karate (pronounced kar-**rat**-ee)
(noun) a sport in which people fight each other using only their hands, elbows, feet and legs.
[Japanese *kara* + *te* = empty hand]

kayak, kayaks (pronounced **ky**-ak)
(noun) a covered canoe for one person, originally used by Inuits (Eskimos).
[an Inuit word]

kebab, kebabs
(noun) A **shish kebab** is pieces of meat or vegetable stuck on a skewer and grilled. A **doner kebab** is pressed meat heated vertically on a large skewer, then sliced off.
[Arabic *kabab* = roast meat]

keel, keels, keeling, keeled
1 (noun) The keel of a ship is the specially shaped bottom which supports the sides.
2 (verb) If someone or something keels over, they fall down sideways.

keen, keener, keenest
1 (adjective) eager and enthusiastic.
2 If you are keen on someone or something, you are attracted to them.
3 Keen senses let you see, hear, smell and taste things very clearly or strongly.
4 A keen wind is very strong and cold.
keenly (adverb) **keenness** (noun)
[Old English *cene* = fierce or brave]

keep, keeps, keeping, kept
Selected meanings:
1 (verb) e.g. *You can keep warm by jogging... Please keep this in a safe place for me... He kept on going to the end... Samuel Pepys kept a diary.*
2 (noun) Your keep is the cost of the food you eat, your housing, and your clothing, e.g. *I give my mum £20 a week towards my keep.*
3 the stronghold of a castle.

keep in with
(phrasal verb) If you keep in with people, you try to remain friendly with them.

keep up
(phrasal verb) If you keep up with other people, you move or work at the same speed as they do.

keeper, keepers
1 (noun) a person whose job is to look after the animals in a zoo.
2 a goalkeeper in football or hockey.

keg, kegs
(noun) a small barrel.

kennel, kennels
(noun) a shelter for a dog.

Kenyan, Kenyans (pronounced **keen**-yan)
1 (adjective) belonging to Kenya.
2 (noun) someone who comes from Kenya.

kerb, kerbs
(noun) the raised edge of the pavement at the point where it meets the road.

kernel, kernels
(noun) the part of a nut that is inside the shell.

kerosene
(noun) paraffin, e.g. *Most jets fly on kerosene.*

kestrel, kestrels
(noun) a type of small falcon that kills and eats other birds and small animals.

ketchup
(noun) a sauce usually made from tomatoes.
[Chinese *koe* + *tsiap* = seafood sauce]

kettle, kettles
1 (noun) a container with a spout, which you use to boil water in.
2 (phrase) If you call something **a different kettle of fish**, you mean that it is a completely different situation.
[Latin *catillus* = small cooking pot]

key, keys, keying, keyed
1 (noun) a shaped piece of metal to lock and unlock a door, wind a clock, start a car, etc.
2 the buttons on a typewriter, piano or cash register.
3 In music, a key is a scale of notes.
4 On a map or diagram, a key is an explanation of the symbols used.
5 (verb) If you key in information on a computer keyboard, you type it and file it.

keyboard, keyboards
1 (noun) a row of levers or buttons on a piano, organ, typewriter or computer.
2 A musician who plays keyboards plays organ, synthesizer, etc.

khaki (pronounced **kah**-kee)
1 (noun) a strong yellowish-brown material, used especially for military uniforms.
2 (noun, adjective) yellowish-brown.
[Urdu *kaki* = dusty]

kick, kicks, kicking, kicked
Selected meanings:
1 (verb) e.g. *The goalie kicked the ball... We were kicked out of the pool.*
2 (noun; informal) If you get a kick out of doing something, you enjoy doing it very much.

kick off
(phrasal verb) to start a football or rugby match.
kick-off (noun)

kid, kids, kidding, kidded
1 (noun; informal) a child.
2 a young goat.
3 (verb) to tease people by deceiving them in fun, e.g. *You're kidding, aren't you?*

kidnap, kidnaps, kidnapping, kidnapped
(verb) to take someone away by force and

Letter K developed from a picture of a hand, perhaps cupped to receive something.

demand a ransom in exchange for returning them.

kidnapper (noun) **kidnapping** (noun)
[*kid* + *nap* = child stealing; in the 17th century children were kidnapped to work on American plantations]

Similar words: abduct, snatch

kidney, kidneys
(noun) Your kidneys are two organs in your body that remove waste products from your blood.

kill, kills, killing, killed
1 (verb) to make someone or something die.
2 to cause severe pain or discomfort, e.g. *My shoes are killing me.*
3 (phrase) If you **kill time**, you do something unimportant while waiting.

Similar words: (sense 1) murder, slay

kiln, kilns
(noun) an oven for baking china or pottery until it becomes hard and dry.
[Latin *culina* = kitchen or cooking stove]

kilo, kilos
(noun) a kilogram.

kilogram, kilograms
(noun) a unit of mass. (1kg = 1000 grams)

kilometre, kilometres
(noun) a unit of distance. (1km = 1000 metres)

kilowatt, kilowatts
(noun) a unit of power. (1kW = 1000 watts)

kilt, kilts
(noun) a tartan skirt worn as part of Scottish Highland dress, often by men.
[northern English *kilt* = to tuck up]

kimono, kimonos
(noun) a long, loose garment with wide sleeves and a sash, worn in Japan.

kin
(plural noun) Your kin are your relatives.

Similar words: family, relations

kind, kinds; kinder, kindest
1 (noun) a type of something e.g. *a kind of coat.*
2 (adjective) considerate and generous.
3 (phrase) If you pay someone **in kind**, you give them goods as payment instead of money.
kindly (adverb) **kindness** (noun)

Similar words: (noun) breed, species, family, type

kindergarten, kindergartens
(noun) a school for children who are too young to go to primary school.
[German *kinder* + *garten* = children's garden]

kindhearted
(adjective) considerate and sympathetic.

king, kings
1 (noun) a man who, by his birth, is the head of state in the country.
2 In chess, the king is a piece which can only move one square at a time. When a king cannot avoid being taken, the game is lost.
3 In a pack of cards, a king is a face card.

Similar words: (sense 1) monarch, sovereign, ruler

kingdom, kingdoms
1 (noun) a country that is governed by a king or queen.
2 The divisions of the natural world are called kingdoms, e.g. *the animal kingdom.*

king-size or **king-sized**
(adjective) larger than the normal size.

kiosk, kiosks (pronounced **kee**-osk)
(noun) a covered stall on a street where you can buy sandwiches, newspapers, sweets, lottery tickets, etc.
[Turkish *kösk* = pavilion]

kip, kips, kipping, kipped
(verb; informal) to go to sleep; if you kip down somewhere, you make a temporary resting place, for example on a floor.

kipper, kippers
(noun) a smoked herring.

kiss, kisses, kissing, kissed
(verb) to touch someone with your lips as a sign of love or affection.

kiss of life
(noun; informal) a method of reviving someone by blowing air into their lungs.

kit, kits
1 (noun) a collection of things that you use for a sport or other activity.
2 a set of parts that you put together to make something e.g. *a plastic model kit.*

kitchen, kitchens
(noun) a room used for cooking food.
[Latin *coquere* = to cook]

kite, kites
(noun) a frame covered with paper etc. which you fly in the air on a piece of string.

kitten, kittens
(noun) a young cat.
[Old French *chitoun* = small cat]

kitty
(noun) a fund where several people put in money to buy drinks for all who put in.

Kiwi
1 (noun) a flightless New Zealand bird.
2 a nickname for a person from New Zealand.

kiwi fruit, fruits
(noun) a fruit with a hairy skin and green flesh.

knack
(noun) an ability to do something difficult with apparent ease, e.g. *He had the knack of always guessing the right answer.*

knapsack, knapsacks
(noun) a bag which is carried over the shoulder or on the back, used for carrying food etc.
[Old German *knapsack* = bag for food]

A chef needs these words: menu table d'hôte à la carte vegetarian vegan protein carbohydrate.

knead, kneads, kneading, kneaded
(verb) If you knead dough, you press it and squeeze it with your hands before baking it.

knee, knees
(noun) the joint in your leg between your ankle and your hip.

kneel, kneels, kneeling, knelt
(verb) to bend your legs and lower your body until your knees are touching the ground.
[Old English *cneo* = knee]

knickers
(plural noun; old fashioned) underpants worn by women and girls.

knife, knives; knifes, knifing, knifed
1 (noun) a sharp metal tool that you use to cut things.
2 (verb) to stab somebody with a knife.

knight, knights
1 (noun) a man who has been knighted, i.e. given the title 'Sir' by the King or Queen.
2 In medieval Europe, a knight was a man who served a monarch or lord as a mounted soldier.
3 a chess piece that is usually in the shape of a horse's head. It moves one space forward and one space diagonally in any direction.
knighthood (noun) **knight** (verb)
[Old English *cniht* = servant]

knit, knits, knitting, knitted or knit
1 (verb) to make a piece of clothing with wool, using needles or a machine.
2 When broken bones knit, they heal.
[Old English *cnyttan* = to knot]

knob, knobs
1 (noun) a round handle.
2 A knob of butter is a small amount of butter.

knock, knocks, knocking, knocked
(verb) If you knock on something, you strike it with your hand or fist.
knocker (noun)

knockout, knockouts
1 (noun) a punch in boxing which succeeds in knocking a boxer unconscious.
2 a competition in which competitors are

eliminated in each round until only the winner is left.

knot, knots, knotting, knotted
1 (noun) a fastening made by looping a piece of string around itself and pulling the ends tight.
2 (technical) a unit of speed used for ships and aircraft. (1 knot = 1 nautical mile per hour) [from when a ship's speed was measured by trailing a rope with knots in it]
3 (verb) If you knot a piece of string, you tie a knot in it.

know, knows, knowing, knew, known
1 (verb) If you know a fact, you have it in your mind and you do not need to learn it.
2 (phrase) If you are **in-the-know**, you know something which only those closely involved know about.
3 If you have **the know-how**, you know how to do something that might be difficult for others to do.

knowledge
(noun) all the information and facts that you know.

Similar words: learning, know-how

knowledgeable
(adjective) Someone who is knowledgeable knows a lot.

knuckle, knuckles
(noun) Knuckles are the joints on your fingers where they join your hand.

koala, koalas or koala bear
(noun) an Australian marsupial with grey fur and small tufted ears.
[Australian Aboriginal *kula* = Koala bear]

Koran (pronounced kaw-**rahn**)
(noun) the holy book of the Muslim religion.
[Arabic *kara'a* = to read]

kung fu (pronounced kung **foo**)
(noun) a Chinese style of fighting which involves using only your hands and feet.
[Chinese **gong fu** = merit master]

L

lab, labs
(noun; informal) a laboratory.

label, labels, labelling, labelled
1 (noun) a piece of paper or plastic attached to something as an identification.
2 (verb) to put a label on something.
3 to say that someone is a particular type of person, e.g. *She was labelled as a troublemaker.*

laboratory, laboratories
(noun) a place where scientific experiments are carried out.
[Latin *laboratorium* = workshop]

laborious
(adjective) A laborious task involves a lot of hard work.

labour, labours, labouring, laboured
1 (noun) hard work.
2 The working people of a country or industry are sometimes called its labour, e.g. *skilled labour.*
3 Labour or the Labour Party is one of the 3 main political parties in Britain. It believes in social equality.
4 the last stage of pregnancy when a woman gives birth to a baby.
5 (verb; old-fashioned) to work hard.
labourer (noun)

Similar words: (noun: sense 1) industry, toil, slog (verb: sense 5) slave, toil, slog, graft

Letter L might have been a picture of a shepherd's crook.

labrador, labradors
(noun) a large dog with short black or golden hair.

lace, laces
1 (noun) a very fine decorated cloth made with a lot of holes in it.
2 Laces are cords with which you fasten your shoes with laces.

lack, lacks, lacking, lacked
1 (verb) If something is lacking, it is not there when or where it is needed.
2 If you lack something, you do not have it.

lackadaisical (pronounced lakka-**day**-zikl) (adjective) careless and half-hearted.

lacquer, lacquers
1 (noun) thin, clear paint that you put on wood to protect it and make it shiny.
2 Hair lacquer is sprayed onto hair to keep it shiny and in place.
[Old French *lacre* = sealing wax]

lacrosse
(noun) an outdoor ball game in which two teams try to score goals using sticks with nets on the end of them (crosses).
[Canadian French *la crosse* = the hooked stick]

lad, lads
(noun) a boy or young man.

ladder, ladders, laddering, laddered
1 (noun) a long wooden or metal frame with rungs used for climbing.
2 (verb) If you ladder your stockings or tights, you damage a row of threads, causing a hole.

laden (pronounced **lay**-den)
(adjective) To be laden means to be carrying a lot of something, e.g. *She was laden with books.*

ladle, ladles
(noun) a long-handled spoon with a deep, round bowl, which you use to serve soup.

lady, ladies
1 (noun) another name for a woman.
2 the title of the wife of a knight or a lord, e.g. *Sir Derek and Lady Snodgrass.*
ladylike (adjective) **ladyship** (noun)

ladybird, ladybirds
(noun) a small, flying beetle with a round, red body patterned with black spots.

lag, lags, lagging, lagged
1 (verb) To lag behind means to make slower progress than others.
2 to wrap cloth round pipes and tanks to prevent the water inside freezing.
3 (noun) A time lag is a period of time that passes between one event and another.

Similar words: (verb: sense 1) trail, fall behind

lager, lagers
1 (noun) a light-coloured beer.
2 (phrase; informal) A **lager lout** is a person who behaves in an anti-social way when drunk.
[German *Lagerbier* = beer for storing]

lagoon, lagoons
(noun) an area of seawater separated from the sea by a reef or sandbank.
[Latin *lacuna* = pond]

laid past tense and past participle of **lay** e.g. *The hen laid an egg.*

laid back
(adjectival phrase; informal) relaxed, cool and calm.

lain past participle of some meanings of lie, e.g. *We had lain in wait for some hours.*

lair, lairs
(noun) a place where a wild animal lives.

lake, lakes
(noun) an inland area of fresh water.

lamb, lambs
(noun) a young sheep, or the meat from it.

lame, lames
1 (adjective) Someone who is lame has an injured leg and cannot walk easily.
2 A lame excuse is weak and unconvincing.
lamely (adverb) **lameness** (noun)

Similar words: (sense 2) feeble, thin, flimsy

lament, laments, lamenting, lamented
(verb) To lament something means to express sorrow or regret about it.

laminate
(verb) to cover with a layer of plastic film.
[Latin *laminatus* = plated]

lamp, lamps
(noun) a light that works by burning oil or gas, or by using electricity.
[Greek *lampein* = to shine]

lamppost, lampposts
(noun) a tall lighting column in a street.

lampshade, lampshades
(noun) a decorative covering on an electric light.

lance, lances
(noun) a long spear that used to be used by soldiers on horseback.

land, lands, landing, landed
1 (noun) e.g. *He owns 3 acres of land... We sailed 8 days before sighting land... Land of Hope and Glory, mother of the free.*
2 (verb) e.g. *The plane lands at 07.30.*
3 If you land something you have been trying to get, you succeed in getting it, e.g. *I finally landed a job with the BBC.*
4 To land a fish means to catch it while fishing.
5 If someone is landed with something unpleasant, they are left with having to deal with it.

landing, landings
1 (noun) a flat area in a building at the top of a flight of stairs.
2 The landing of an aeroplane is its arrival back on the ground after a flight, e.g. *a safe landing.*

landing stage, stages
(noun) a platform at the edge of a river or lake where boats load and unload.

Names of countries always begin with capital letters, e.g. England, Sweden, Australia.

andlady, landladies
(noun) a woman who runs a pub or who owns a guest house or small hotel.

andlord, landlords
(noun) a man who runs a pub or who owns a guest house or small hotel.

andlubber, landlubbers
(noun; old-fashioned) a person who has no experience of sailing.

andmark, landmarks
1 (noun) a noticeable feature in a landscape, e.g. Blackpool Tower.
2 An important stage in the development of something, e.g. *1993 was a landmark in the history of Europe.*

and mine, mines
(noun) a bomb planted under the ground, which explodes when something passes over it.

andscape, landscapes
(noun) the view over an area of open land.

andslide, landslides
1 (noun) loose earth and rocks falling down a mountainside.
2 In an election, a landslide is a victory won by a large number of votes.

ane, lanes
1 (noun) a narrow road, e.g. *a country lane.*
2 one of the strips in a wide road to guide drivers, e.g. *Don't hog the outside lane.*
3 one strip of a running track; a 10-pin bowling strip.

anguage, languages
1 (noun) the system of words that the people of a country use to communicate with each other.
2 the style in which you express yourself, e.g. *The language of this essay is dull.*
3 a computer language is a set of words or symbols used in writing programs or giving instructions to the computer, e.g. BASIC, COBOL.
[Latin *lingua* = tongue]

anguage laboratory, laboratories
(noun) a classroom equipped with tape recorders where students practise speaking and listening to a foreign language.

anguish, languishes, languishing, languished
(verb) If you languish, you endure an unpleasant situation for a long time.

anky, lankier, lankiest
(adjective) tall and thin and rather awkward in movement.

anolin or **lanoline**
(noun) a fatty substance found in wool, used in making ointments and cosmetics.
[Latin *lana* = wool + *oleum* = oil]

antern, lanterns
(noun) a lamp in a metal frame with glass sides.

anyard, lanyards
(noun) a piece of cord with a whistle or knife attached to it, worn round the neck as part of a uniform, for example by a scout.

lap, laps, lapping, lapped
1 (noun) the flat area formed by your thighs when you are sitting down.
2 one circuit of a running track etc.
3 (phrase) If you say that someone is living **in the lap of luxury**, you mean they are having a very comfortable life.
4 (verb) When an animal laps up liquid, it drinks using its tongue.
5 If you lap someone in a race, you overtake them when they are still on the previous lap.
6 When water laps against something, it gently moves against it in little waves.

lapel, lapels (pronounced lap-**el**)
(noun) a flap which is joined on to the collar of a jacket or coat.
[Old English *læppa* = flap]

lapse, lapses
1 (noun) a moment of bad behaviour by someone who usually behaves well.
2 a period of time between two events.
[Latin *lapsus* = error]

larch, larches
(noun) a deciduous tree which has needle-shaped leaves and bears cones.

lard
(noun) fat from a pig, used in cooking.

larder, larders
(noun) a room in which you store food, often next to a kitchen.

large, larger, largest
1 (adjective) much bigger than average.
2 (phrase) If a prisoner is **at large**, they have escaped from prison.

largely
(adverb) to a great extent, e.g. *The story is largely true.*

lark, larks, larking, larked
1 (noun) a small brown bird with a clear song.
2 If you do something for a lark, you do it in a high-spirited or mischievous way for amusement.
3 (verb) to enjoy yourself in a lively way.

larva, larvae
(noun) an insect at the stage before it becomes an adult. Larvae look like short, fat worms.

laryngitis (pronounced lar-in-**jie**-tiss)
(noun) an infection of the throat which causes you to lose your voice.

lasagne (pronounced laz-**zan**-ya)
(noun) an Italian dish made with wide, flat sheets of pasta, meat and cheese sauce.
[Latin *lasanum* = cooking pot]

laser, lasers
(noun) a machine that produces a powerful concentrated beam of light, used for cutting, in surgery and in telecommunications.
[the first letters of 'Light Amplification by Stimulated Emission of Radiation']

Decay of language is always a symptom of a more serious sickness. (George Mackay Brown)

lash, lashes, lashing, lashed
1 (noun) Your lashes are the hairs growing on the edge of your eyelids.
2 Lashes are blows struck with a whip.
3 (verb) to beat someone with a whip.
4 to tie things together.

lash out
(phrasal verb) to hit or to criticize someone severely.

lashings
(plural noun) a lot, e.g. *lashings of cream.*

lass, lasses
(noun) a girl or young woman.

lasso, lassoes or **lassos** (pronounced las-**soo**)
(noun) a length of rope with a noose at one end, used by cowboys to catch cattle and horses.

last, lasts, lasting, lasted
(adjective, adverb, verb).
e.g. *This is the last train tonight... I ran last in the 100 metres... This will last us for years.*
lastly (adverb)

Similar words: (verb) endure, continue, hold out, survive

last-ditch
(adjective) A last-ditch attempt to do something is a final try when everything else has failed.

latch, latches, latching, latched
1 (noun) a simple door fastening consisting of a metal bar which falls into a hook.
2 a type of door lock which has to be opened with a key.
3 (verb; informal) If you latch onto someone or something, you become attached to them.

latchkey, latchkeys
1 a key which opens a door that has a latch.
2 (phrase) **Latchkey children** are those who have no one at home when they come back from school.

late, later, latest
1 (adjective, adverb) e.g. *the late afternoon... Sorry that I'm late!.*
2 (adjective; formal) dead, e.g. *the late Lord Stockport.*

lately
(adverb) recently.

lathe, lathes
(noun) a machine which holds and turns a piece of wood or metal against a tool to cut and shape it, making, for example, a chair leg.

lather
(noun) the foam that you get when you rub soap in water.
[Old English *leathor* = soap]

Latin
(noun) the language of ancient Rome.
[Latin *Latinus* = of Latium, a region of Italy]

latitude, latitudes
(noun) the latitude of a place is its distance north or south of the equator in degrees, e.g. 30°S.

latter
1 (noun) You use latter to refer to the second of

two things that are mentioned, e.g. *They found a hammer and a crowbar; the latter had been used to force a door.*
2 (adjective) used to describe the later or end part of something, e.g. *the latter half of July.*

laugh, laughs, laughing, laughed
1 (verb) e.g. *Stop laughing at the back, boy!*
2 (phrase) If you **have the last laugh**, you succeed in a situation in which people had thought you were going to fail.
laughter (noun)

laughable
(adjective) quite absurd.

launch, launches, launching, launched
1 (verb) to send a ship into the water for the first time.
2 to send a rocket into space.
3 (noun) a motorboat.

launch pad, pads
(noun) the place where space rockets take off.

Launderette, Launderettes
(noun; trademark) a place where you can wash clothes etc. in coin-operated washing machines.

laundry, laundries
1 (noun) a place where clothes, sheets and towels are taken to be washed and ironed.
2 the dirty clothes, sheets and towels that are being washed, or are about to be washed.
launder (verb)
[Latin **lavare** = to wash]

lava
(noun) the hot, liquid rock that comes out of an erupting volcano, and solidifies as it cools.

lavatory, lavatories
(noun) a toilet.
[Latin *lavare* = to wash]

lavender
(noun) a small bush with bluish-pink flowers that have a strong, pleasant scent.

lavish
(adjective) very generous with your time, money or gifts, e.g. *a lavish party.*
lavishly (adverb)
[Old French *lavas* = profusion]

law, laws
1 (noun) The system of rules developed by the government of a country, which controls what people may and may not do and deals with people who break these rules.
2 a scientific fact which allows you to explain how things work in the physical world, e.g. *the law of gravity.*
3 (informal) The police are sometimes called the law.
lawful (adjective) **lawfully** (adverb)

law-abiding
(adjective) obeying the law.

lawn, lawns
(noun) an area of cultivated grass.

lawnmower, lawnmowers
(noun) a machine for cutting grass.

We take these words from Latin: stamina exit appendix formula index radius alibi.

awyer, lawyers
(noun) a person who is qualified in law, and whose job is to advise people about the law and represent them in court.

ay, lays, laying, laid
1 (verb) e.g. *to lay the table... It laid an egg.*
2 past tense of some senses of lie, e.g. *She lay on the floor.*

lay off
1 (phrasal verb) When workers are laid off, their employers tell them not to come to work for a while because there is a shortage of work.
2 (informal) If you tell someone to lay off, you want them to stop doing something annoying.

lay on
(phrasal verb) If you lay on a meal or entertainment, you provide it.

ayabout, layabouts
(noun; informal) someone who is lazy.

ay-by, lay-bys
(noun) an area by the side of a main road where motorists can stop for a short while.

ayer, layers
(noun) a single thickness of something, e.g. *layers of clothing.*

ayout, layouts
(noun) the pattern in which something is arranged.

azy, lazier, laziest
(adjective) idle and unwilling to work.
lazily (adverb) **laziness** (noun) **laze** (verb)

ead (rhymes with **feed**), **leads, leading, led**
1 (verb) to go in front of someone to show them the way.
2 If one thing leads to another, it causes the second thing to happen.
3 (noun) a length of leather etc. to control a dog.
4 If the police have a lead, they have a clue which might help them to solve a crime.
5 (phrase) If you **take the lead** in something, you are the first to do it.
leading (adjective)

Similar words: (verb: sense 1) conduct, guide

ead (rhymes with **fed**)
(noun) a soft metal.

eader, leaders
1 (noun) someone in charge of a country, an organization or a group of people.
2 the person who is winning a race etc.

eadership
(noun) the ability to be a good leader.

eaf, leaves
(noun) the flat, green growth on the end of a twig, branch of a tree, etc.
leafy (adjective)

eaflet, leaflets
(noun) a piece of folded paper with information or advertising printed on it.

eague, leagues (pronounced **leeg**)
1 (noun) an organization of people or groups who

have joined together because they have a common interest, e.g. *a football league.*
2 (phrase) If you are **in league with** someone, you are working together closely with them.
[Latin *ligare* = to bind]

leak, leaks, leaking, leaked
1 (verb) If a pipe or container leaks, it has a hole which lets gas or liquid escape.
2 If liquid or gas leaks, it escapes from a pipe or container.
3 If someone in an organization leaks information, they give the information to someone who is not supposed to have it, e.g. *The story was leaked to the media.*
leaky (adjective) **leakage** (noun)
[Old Norse *leka* = to drip]

lean, leans, leaning, leant or leaned; leaner leanest
1 (verb) When you lean on something, you rest your body against it for support.
2 (adjective) having little or no fat, e.g. *lean meat.*
3 A lean period is a time when food or money is in short supply.

leap, leaps, leaping, leapt or leaped
(verb) to jump a long distance or high in the air.

leapfrog
(noun) a game in which you jump over people who are squatting with their backs bent.

leap year, years
(noun) a year in which there are 366 days. Every 4th year is a leap year except at century-ends.

learn, learns, learning, learned or learnt
1 (verb) to gain knowledge or a skill through studying or training.
2 If you learn of something, you find out about it, e.g. *She learned of his death from his sister.*
learner (noun)

learned (pronounced ler-nid)
(adjective) a learned person has a lot of knowledge gained from years of study.

learning
(noun) knowledge that has been acquired through serious study.

lease, leases
1 (noun) an agreement to rent a house, flat, shop, car, etc.
2 (phrase) You can say someone has a **new lease of life** if they have been ill or unhappy but are now happier or healthier.

least
1 (noun) the smallest possible amount of something, e.g. *It's the least I can do.*
2 (adjective, adverb; superlative) little, less **least.**
3 (phrase) **At least** refers to the minimum amount of something, and indicates that the true amount is likely to be greater, e.g. *It'll cost at least £10.*

Similar words: (noun) minimum
(adjective) minimal, slightest

leather
(noun) the tanned skin of some animals, used to make shoes, bags, belts and clothes.
leathery (adjective)

leave, leaves, leaving, left
1 (verb) When you leave a place, job, etc. you go away from it.
2 If you leave money to someone in your will, it will be given to them when you die.
3 e.g. *6 take away 2 leaves 4.*
4 (noun) a period of holiday or absence from a job, e.g. *annual leave.*
5 (phrase) If someone **gives you leave** to do something, they allow you to do it.

Similar words: (verb: sense 1) go, depart, withdraw, exit, quit, retire

leave out
(phrasal verb) If you leave someone or something out, you do not include them.

Lebanese
1 (adjective) belonging to the Lebanon.
2 (noun) someone who comes from the Lebanon.

lecture, lectures, lecturing, lectured
1 (noun) a formal talk to teach people about a particular subject.
2 (verb) to give a lecture.
3 to give someone a telling off.

lecturer, lecturers
(noun) a teacher in a college or university.

led past tense and past participle of **lead**, e.g. *We were led into a cave.*

ledge, ledges
(noun) a narrow shelf on the side of a cliff or rock face, or on the outside of a building, e.g. *a window ledge.*

leek, leeks
(noun) a long vegetable of the onion family, white at one end with green leaves at the other; sometimes used as the national symbol of Wales.

leer, leers, leering, leered
(verb) to smile at someone in an unpleasant way.

left
1 (noun, adjective, adverb) e.g. *Drive on the left... Left luggage office... turn left.*
2 past tense and past participle of **leave** e.g. *He left home.*

left-handed
(adjective, adverb) Someone who is left-handed does things such as writing and painting with their left hand.

left wing
(adjective) believing more strongly in socialism, than in capitalism or conservatism e.g. *Arthur holds very left-wing views.*

leg, legs
1 (noun) e.g. *I broke my leg... a trouser leg... a table leg.*
2 A leg of a journey is one part of it.
3 (phrase) If you say that someone **does not have a leg to stand on**, you mean that they cannot justify or prove what they claim.
4 If you **pull someone's leg**, you tell them something untrue as a joke.
5 If you say something is **on its last legs**, you mean it is about to collapse or stop working.

legal
1 (adjective) relating to the law, e.g. *the British legal system.*
2 allowed by the law, e.g. *Is corporal punishment legal in your country?*
legally (adverb)
[Latin *leges* = laws]

legend, legends
1 (noun) an old story which was once believed to be true, but which is probably untrue.
2 If you refer to a person as a legend, you mean they are very famous, e.g. *Elvis Presley was a legend in his own lifetime.*
legendary (adjective)
[Latin *legere* = to read]

legible
(adjective) Writing that is legible is clear enough to be read.
legibly (adverb) **legibility** (noun)

legion, legions
(noun) a large military force, e.g. *the French Foreign Legion... the legions of ancient Rome.*
legionnaire (noun)

legitimate (pronounced lij-it-tim-it)
(adjective) reasonable or acceptable according to our laws or standards, e.g. *a legitimate business deal... a legitimate complaint.*
legitimacy (noun) **legitimately** (adverb)

leisure (rhymes with **measure**)
1 (noun) time when you do not have to work, and can do what you enjoy doing.
2 (phrases) If you do something **at leisure**, or **at your leisure**, you do it without hurrying.
[Latin *licere* = to be allowed]

leisurely
(adjective, adverb) A leisurely action is done in an unhurried and calm way.

Similar words: relaxed, slow

lemon, lemons
(noun) a yellow citrus fruit.

lemonade
(noun) a clear, sweet, fizzy drink.

lend, lends, lending, lent
1 (verb) If you lend someone something, you give it to them for a period of time and then they give it back to you. (opposite: **borrow**)
2 (phrase) If you **lend someone a hand**, you help them.

length, lengths
1 (noun) the horizontal distance from one end of something to the other.
2 The length of an event etc. is the amount of time it lasts for.
3 (phrase) If you **go to great lengths** to achieve something, you try very hard and do extreme things to achieve it, e.g. *I'll go to any lengths to get the job.*

lengthen, lengthens, lengthening, lengthened
(verb) to make something longer.

Similar words: extend, stretch, prolong

Are you sure about the difference between *lend* and *borrow*? May I borrow your pencil?

lengthy, lengthier, lengthiest
(adjective) lasting for a long time, e.g. *Selling your house can be a lengthy business.*

lenient
(adjective) If someone in authority is lenient, they are less severe than expected.
leniently (adverb) **leniency** (noun)
[Latin *lenire* = to soothe]

lens, lenses
1 (noun) a curved piece of glass, for example in a camera, telescope or pair of glasses.
2 the part of your eye behind the iris, which focuses light.
[Latin *lens* = lentil, because of its convex shape]

lent
1 past tense and past participle of **lend**.
2 (noun) Lent is the period of 40 days from Ash Wednesday to Easter, during which Christians fast or give up something they enjoy.

lentil, lentils
(noun) Lentils are small, dried red or brown seeds cooked and eaten in soups and curries.

leopard, leopards
(noun) a large, wild Asian or African animal of the cat family, with yellow fur and dark spots.

leotard, leotards (pronounced lee-oh-tard)
(noun) a tight-fitting costume covering the body and legs, worn for dancing or exercise. It is named after a French acrobat, Jules Léotard.

leper, lepers
(noun) someone who has leprosy.
[Greek *lepros* = scaly]

leprosy
(noun) an infectious disease which attacks the skin and nerves, and which can lead to fingers or toes dropping off.
[Greek *lepros* = scaly]

lesbian, lesbians
(noun) a homosexual woman.
lesbianism (noun)

less
1 a smaller amount, or not as much in quality, e.g. *I've got less than £5 left.*
2 (adjective, adverb; comparative) little, **less**, least.
3 (preposition) e.g. *Eight less two leaves six.*

-less
(suffix) without, e.g. *a colourless sky* = a sky without colour.

lessen, lessens, lessening, lessened
(verb) to reduce in amount, size or quality.

Similar words: decline, decrease, dwindle, diminish, reduce

lesson, lessons
1 (noun) a fixed period of time during which a class of pupils is taught by a teacher.
2 an experience that makes you understand something important which you had not realized before, e.g. *It came as a real lesson to me.*

let, lets, letting, let
1 (verb) to allow, e.g. *Let me do that.*

2 If someone lets a house or flat that they own, they rent it out.
3 If you let yourself in for something, you agree to do it although you do not really want to.
4 (phrase) If you say that something is not the case **let alone** something else, you mean that the second thing is even more unlikely than the first, e.g. *I've never been to London, let alone America.*

let down
(phrasal verb) If you let someone down, you fail to do something you had agreed to do for them.

let go
(phrasal verb) to stop holding something or someone.

let off
1 (phrasal verb) If someone in authority lets you off, they do not punish you for something you have done wrong.
2 If you let someone off a duty, you give them permission not to do it.
3 to light a firework etc.

let on
(phrasal verb) Not to let on about something means to keep it a secret.

let up
(phrasal verb) If something lets up, it stops or becomes less, e.g. *The heat did not let up.*

letdown, letdowns
(noun; informal) a disappointment.

lethal (pronounced lee-thal)
(adjective) able to kill someone, e.g. *a lethal weapon.*
[Latin *letum* = death]

letter, letters
1 (noun) a written symbol — a, b, c, etc.
2 a piece of writing addressed to someone, and usually sent through the post.

lettering
(noun) writing, especially when you are describing the type of letters used, e.g. *This example is in italic lettering.*

lettuce, lettuces
(noun) a vegetable with large green leaves eaten raw in salad.

leukaemia or **leukemia** (pronounced loo-kee-mee-a)
(noun) a serious cancer-like disease in which too many white blood cells are produced by the body.
[Greek *leukos* = white + *haima* = blood]

level, levels, levelling, levelled
1 (adjective) smooth, flat, and parallel to the ground.
2 (verb) To level land means to make it flat.
3 (noun) a point on a scale which measures the amount, importance or difficulty of something, e.g. *'A' levels... sea level.*
4 (adverb) If you draw level with someone, you get closer so that you are moving next to them.

Similar words: (noun) grade, rank, step, stage, degree

There are twelve letters in the Hawaiian alphabet.

level off or **level out**
(phrasal verb) If something levels off or levels out, it stops increasing or decreasing, e.g. *Inflation is starting to level off.*

level crossing, crossings
(noun) a place where road traffic is allowed to drive across a railway track.

level-headed
(adjective) sensible and calm in emergencies.

lever, levers
1 (noun) A lever on a machine is a handle that you pull to make the machine work.
2 a long bar that you wedge underneath a heavy object. When you press down on the lever, it makes the object move.
leverage (noun)

liable
1 (adjective) If you say something is liable to happen, you mean it will probably happen.
2 legally responsible for something you have done, e.g. *She was liable for the damage.*
liability (noun)
[Latin *ligare* = to bind]

liar, liars
(noun) a person who tells lies, e.g. *But liars we can never trust, though they should speak the thing that's true.*

liberal, liberals
1 (adjective) Someone who is liberal is tolerant of a wide range of behaviour, standards or opinions, believing in personal freedom.
2 To be liberal with something means to be generous with it.
3 A **Liberal Democrat** is a member of the Social and Liberal Democrat party, which has views in the political 'centre' between those of the Conservative and Labour parties.
liberally (adverb) **liberalism** (noun)
[Latin *liberalis* = of freedom]

liberate, liberates, liberating, liberated
(verb) to free people from prison or from an unpleasant situation.
liberation (noun) **liberator** (noun)

liberty, liberties
1 (noun) the freedom to choose how you want to live, without government restrictions.
2 (phrase) A criminal who is **at liberty** has not yet been caught or has escaped from prison.
3 If you are **not at liberty** to do something, you are not allowed to do it, e.g. *I'm not at liberty to give you the test results.*
4 Someone who **takes liberties** with someone is too familiar towards them.
[Latin *liber* = free]

librarian, librarians
(noun) a person who works in a library.

library, libraries
(noun) a place where books are kept, usually for people to come and read or borrow.
[Latin *librarius* = relating to books]

Libyan, Libyans
1 (adjective) belonging to Libya.
2 (noun) someone who comes from Libya.

lice plural of **louse**, e.g. *head lice.*

licence, licences
(noun) an official document which entitles you to do a particular thing, e.g. drive a car.
[Latin *licet* = it is allowed]

license, licenses, licensing, licensed
(verb) to give official permission for something to be done, e.g. *A pub is licensed to sell alcohol.*

lichen, lichens (pronounced **lie**-ken)
(noun) a green, moss-like growth on rocks or tree trunks.

lick, licks, licking, licked
1 (verb) e.g. *I licked my lolly.*
2 (phrase) If you **lick your lips**, you are really looking forward to something.
3 If you **lick someone into shape**, you train them in something very quickly.
4 (informal) If you lick someone in a competition, you beat them easily.

lie, lies, lying, lay, lain
1 (verb) e.g. *He lies down before he's hurt... The village lies midway between Norwich and Cromer... At the age of 90, his achievements now lie in the past.*
2 (phrase; informal) If you say that someone **will not take something lying down**, you mean that they will resist it strongly.

lie, lies, lying, lied
(verb) to say something that is not true.

Similar words: fib, falsehood, untruth

lieutenant, lieutenants
(pronounced lef-**ten**-ent)
(noun) a junior officer in the army or navy.
[Old French *lieutenant* = holding a place]

life, lives
1 (noun) the quality of being able to grow and develop in people, plants and animals.
2 your existence from the time you are born until the time you die.
3 the amount of activity in a place, e.g. *There's no life in this town on Sundays.*

life assurance
(noun) an insurance which pays a sum of money if the policy holder dies or reaches a certain age.

lifebelt, belts
(noun) a circular cork belt that you wear to keep afloat if you fall into water.

lifeboat, lifeboats
1 (noun) a boat which goes out to rescue people who are in danger at sea.
2 a small boat kept on a ship, which is used if the ship starts to sink.

life cycle
(noun) The life cycle of an animal or plant is the series of changes it goes through during its life.

lifeguard, lifeguards
(noun) a person whose job is to rescue people who are in difficulty in the sea or in a pool.

life jacket, jackets
(noun) a sleeveless, inflatable jacket that keeps you afloat in water.

A librarian needs these words: fiction non-fiction reference periodicals catalogue browse.

feless
1 (adjective) dead, or seeming to be dead.
2 dull and unexciting, e.g. *Small towns are usually lifeless at night.*

felike
(adjective) looking very real or alive, e.g. *a lifelike statue.*

felong
(adjective) existing throughout someone's life, e.g. *His lifelong passion was trains.*

fespan
(noun) the specific length of time during which someone is alive.

fetime
(noun) the general name for the time during which someone is alive, e.g. *the chance of a lifetime.*

ft, lifts, lifting, lifted
1 (verb) to move something to a higher position.
2 (informal) to lift things means to steal them.
3 (noun) a machine which carries people or goods from one floor to another in a building.
4 If something gives you a lift, it makes you feel happier.
5 If you give someone a lift, you drive them somewhere in a car or on a motorbike.

Similar words: (verb) elevate, hoist, raise, pick up

ftoff
(noun) the act of launching a space rocket.

ght, lights, lighting, lighted or lit; lighter, lightest
Selected meanings:
1 (noun) e.g. *the light of the sun... Have you a light for my cigar, please?*
2 (verb) e.g. *Light the firework and stand well back.*
3 (adjective) e.g. *This box is light to carry.*
4 (phrase) If something **comes to light**, it is discovered.
5 **In the light of** something means taking that thing into consideration, e.g. *In the light of your previous good behaviour, I will let you off this time.*
lightly (adverb) **lightness** (noun)

ghten, lightens, lightening, lightened
1 (verb) to become less dark.
2 To lighten a load means to make it less heavy.

ght-fingered
(adjective) Someone who is light-fingered steals things.

ght-headed
(adjective) If you feel light-headed, you feel slightly dizzy or drunk.

ght-hearted
(adjective) cheerful, with no worries.
light-heartedly (adverb) **light-heartedness** (noun)

Similar words: carefree, happy-go-lucky

ghthouse, lighthouses
(noun) a tower by the sea, which sends out a powerful light to warn ships of danger.

light industry, industries
(noun) industry in which only small items are made and which does not use heavy machinery.

lightning
(noun) the bright flashes of light in the sky from natural electricity during a thunder storm.

lightning conductor, conductors
(noun) a metal rod fixed to the top of a building, which runs into the earth to attract and direct lightning and so protect the building.

light pen, pens
(noun) a pen-like device used to 'read' bar codes electronically.

lightship, lightships
(noun) a ship permanently moored in one place, which acts as a lighthouse.

lightweight
(adjective) something that is lightweight does not weigh very much, e.g. *a lightweight suit.*

light year, years
(noun) a unit to measure distance in space equal to the distance that light travels in a year, i.e. about 6,000,000,000,000 miles.

like, likes, liking, liked
1 (preposition) e.g. *He drove like mad.*
2 (adjective) similar, e.g. *nylon, terylene, and other like materials.*
3 (verb) e.g. *I don't like Mondays.*
4 (conjunction) e.g. *Do it like I do.*

Similar words: (verb) care for, be fond of, enjoy

-like
(suffix) -like means similar to, e.g. *a balloonlike object.*

likeable
(adjective) very pleasant and friendly.

likelihood
(noun) If you say that there is a likelihood that something will happen, you mean that you think it will probably happen.

likely, likelier, likeliest
1 (adjective) Something that is likely will probably happen or is probably true.
2 (phrase; informal) If you describe what someone says as **a likely story**, you mean that you do not believe it.

liken, likens, likening, likened
(verb) If you liken one thing to another, you say they are similar, e.g. *She likened me to a cabbage.*

likeness, likenesses
(noun) If two things have a likeness to each other, they are similar in appearance.

likewise
(adverb) similarly, e.g. *She sat down and he did likewise.*

liking
1 (noun) If you have a liking for someone or something, you like them.
2 (phrase) If something is **to your liking**, you find it pleasant and suitable.

limb, limbs
(noun) Your limbs are your arms and legs.

We take these words from the USA: movie bulldoze elevator automobile highbrow lockout.

lime, limes
1 (noun) a small, green citrus fruit, rather like a lemon.
2 a white powder made from chalk or limestone used in cement, other calcium compounds, in whitewash and as a fertilizer.
[sense 1 – Arabic *lima* = lime fruit
sense 2 – Latin *limus* = slime]

limelight
(noun) If someone is in the limelight, they are getting a lot of attention.
[a limelight was a type of calcium light formerly used for stage lighting]

limerick, limericks
(noun) an amusing nonsense verse of 5 lines, with special rules for the metre and rhyme. The 1st, 2nd, and 5th lines rhyme with each other, while the 3rd and 4th lines rhyme with each other using a different rhyme e.g. *There was a young man from Darjeeling...*

limestone
(noun) a sedimentary rock made up of the shells of sea creatures that died millions of years ago, used as a building stone and in making cement.

limit, limits, limiting, limited
1 (noun) a boundary beyond which something should not go, e.g. *a 40 mph speed limit.*
2 (verb) to prevent something from becoming bigger, e.g. *The government plans to limit spending on education in case it improves.*
3 (phrase) If a place is **off limits**, you are not allowed to go there.
[Latin *limes* = boundary]

Similar words: (sense 1) bound, boundary, extent

limited
1 (adjective) rather small in amount or extent, e.g. *a limited choice.*
2 A limited company is one in which the shareholders are responsible only to a limited extent for the company's debts and losses.

limp, limps, limping, limped; limper, limpest
1 (verb) to walk unevenly because you have hurt your leg or foot.
2 (adjective) soft and floppy, e.g. *a limp lettuce.*
limply (adverb) **limpness** (noun)

linctus, linctuses
(noun) a medicine taken for a sore throat or cough.

line, lines, lining, lined
Selected meanings:
1 (noun) e.g. *Draw a line from A to B... the railway line to Euston... Form a line at the counter... Write 50 lines—'I must read the Survival Guide at the beginning of this dictionary.'*
2 (verb) to make a lining for something, e.g. *The bird lined its nest with feathers.*
3 (noun) Someone's line of work is the kind of work they do, e.g. *What line are you in?*
4 The attitude someone has towards something, e.g. *The head takes a hard line on dishonesty.*
5 (phrase) If you **draw the line** at doing something, you refuse to do it.

6 If you **read between the lines**, you understand what someone really means, even though they do not say or write it openly.

line up
1 (phrasal verb) to join a queue.
2 to make sure something is exactly in line with something else.

linen
1 (noun) a type of cloth made from a plant called flax, used for tea-towels, serviettes, etc.
2 household goods made of cloth, such as sheets, tea-towels and tablecloths.

liner, liners
(noun) a large passenger ship.

linesman, linesmen
(noun) an official at a sports match who watches the lines of the field or court and indicates when the ball goes outside them.

linger, lingers, lingering, lingered
(verb) to remain for a long time, e.g. *Her illness lingered on... We lingered over our meal.*
lingering (adjective)

lingerie (pronounced **lan-jer-ee**)
(noun) women's nightwear and underclothes.

linguist, linguists
(noun) someone who studies foreign languages.
linguistic (adjective) **linguistically** (adverb)

linguistics
(noun) the study of language and how it works.

lining, linings
(noun) any material used to line the inside of something.

link, links, linking, linked
1 (noun) a connection between two things, e.g. *the link between smoking and lung cancer.*
2 (verb) to join together.
linkage (noun)

linoleum or **lino**
(noun) a floor covering and craft material.
[Latin *linum* = flax + *oleum* = oil]

lint
(noun) soft cloth made from linen, used to dress wounds.

lion, lions
(noun) a large member of the cat family which comes from Africa (female: **lioness**).

lip, lips
1 (noun) e.g. *a kiss on the lips.*
2 (phrase) To **give someone lip** means to be cheeky to them.
3 (phrase) Someone who keeps **a stiff upper lip** does not show emotion or fear in a difficult situation.

lip-read, lip-reads, lip-reading, lip-read
(verb) to watch someone's lips when they are talking to understand what they are saying. Deaf people often lip-read.
lip-reading (noun)

lipstick, lipsticks
(noun) a coloured substance which women wear on their lips.

Which animals could you use to help you to describe a very strong person?

liquid, liquids
(noun) any substance which is not a solid or a gas, and which can be poured.
liquefy (verb) **liquidize** (verb)

liquidizer, liquidizers; also spelled **liquidiser**
(noun) a kitchen machine used to make food into a liquid or a pulp.
liquidize (verb)

liquor
(noun) any strong, alcoholic drink.

liquorice (pronounced **lik-ker-iss**)
(noun) a root used to flavour sweets, e.g. *liquorice allsorts.*

lira, lire
(noun) the unit of money in Italy.

lisp, lisps, lisping, lisped
(verb) to speak with a lisp, e.g. *'I'll thqueam until I'm thick,' said Violet Elizabeth.*

list, lists, listing, listed
1 (noun) a set of words or items written one below the other.
2 If a ship has a list, it leans over to one side.
3 (verb) to put things in a list.

Similar words: (noun: sense 1) catalogue

listen, listens, listening, listened
(verb) to hear and pay attention to something.
listener (noun)

listless
(adjective) lacking energy and enthusiasm.
listlessly (adverb)
[Old English *list* = desire]

literacy
(noun) the ability to read and write.
literate (adjective)

literally
(adverb) To take someone literally means to assume they mean **exactly** what they say. e.g. *When I told him to get knotted, he took me literally, and it took us 2 hours to untie him.*
literal (adjective)

Similar word: word for word

literature
(noun) novels, plays and poetry.
literary (adjective)
[Latin *litteratura* = writing]

lithe
(adjective) supple and graceful.

litmus
(noun) In chemistry, litmus is a substance that is turned red by acids and blue by alkalis.

litre, litres
(noun) a unit of liquid volume (1 litre = 1.76 pints).

litter, litters
1 (noun) rubbish in the street etc.
2 a number of baby animals born at the same time to the same mother.

little, littler, littlest; less, lesser, least
(adjective, noun, adverb) e.g. *Little John was*

tall, really... Just a little, please... He little knows my evil plan!

live, lives, living, lived
1 (verb) e.g. *We live in this house... He lived for 93 years.*
2 (phrase) If you **live it up**, you have an exciting and enjoyable time, spending a lot of money.
3 (verb) If something lives up to your expectations, it is as good as you thought it would be.
4 (adjective, adverb; rhymes with **dive**) Live TV or radio is broadcast while the event is taking place, e.g. *a live concert... This show is going out live.*
5 (adjective) directly connected to an electricity supply, e.g. *Careful – those wires are live!*
6 Live ammunition has not yet been exploded.

Similar words: (verb) dwell, inhabit, stay

lively
(adjective) full of life and enthusiasm.
liveliness (noun)

Similar words: active, brisk, frisky, perky, spirited

liven, livens, livening, livened
(verb) To liven things up means to make them more lively, cheerful, or interesting.

liver, livers
1 (noun) a large organ in your body which cleans your blood and aids digestion.
2 Lambs', pigs', or cows' liver may be cooked and eaten.
[Greek *liparos* = fat]

livestock
(noun) farm animals.

live wire, wires
(noun) a bright, lively person.

livid
(adjective) extremely angry.
[Latin *livere* = to be black and blue]

living
(noun) The work you do for a living is the work you do to earn money to live.

lizard, lizards
(noun) a long, thin, dry-skinned reptile.

load, loads, loading, loaded
1 (noun) something being carried.
2 (informal) Loads means a lot, e.g. *loads of food.*
3 (verb) To load a gun means to put a bullet into it. To load a camera means to put a film into it.

loaf, loaves; loafs, loafing, loafed
1 (noun) a large piece of baked bread.
2 (verb) To loaf around means to be lazy.
loafer (noun)

loan, loans, loaning, loaned
1 (noun) a sum of money that you borrow.
2 (verb) If you loan something to someone, you lend it to them.

loathe, loathes, loathing, loathed
(verb) to feel strong dislike or disgust for someone or something.
loathing (noun) **loathsome** (adjective)

lob, lobs, lobbing, lobbed
(verb) to throw or hit something high in the air.

lobby, lobbies
(noun) the main entrance area to a building with corridors and doors leading off it.

lobe, lobes
(noun) The lobe of your ear, or earlobe, is the rounded soft part at the bottom.

lobster, lobsters
(noun) A long edible shellfish with 2 front claws, 8 legs and a tail underneath.

local
1 (adjective) in, near or belonging to the area in which you live, e.g. *the local newspaper*.
2 (noun) A nearby pub is often called 'the local'.
locally (adverb)
[Latin *locus* = place]

Similar words: (adjective) district, neighbourhood, community, regional

locate, locates, locating, located
1 (verb) to find out where something is.
2 If something is located in a place, it is there.

location, locations
1 (noun) a place, or the position of something.
2 (phrase) If a film is made **on location**, it is made away from a studio.

loch, lochs (pronounced **lokh**)
(noun) a lake in Scotland e.g. *Loch Ness*.

lock, locks, locking, locked
1 (verb) to close and fasten with a key.
2 (noun) A lock on a canal is a place where the water level can be raised or lowered to let boats go up or downhill.
3 A lock of hair is a small bunch of hair.
4 (phrase) If, for example, something is sold **lock, stock and barrel**, every little bit of it is sold.

locker, lockers
(noun) a small cupboard for your personal belongings, e.g. in a changing room.

locket, lockets
(noun) a small case which you can keep a photograph in, worn on a chain round your neck.

locomotive, locomotives
(noun) a railway engine.

locust, locusts
(noun) an insect like a large grasshopper. Locusts live in hot countries and usually travel in swarms, eating all the crops they find.

lodge, lodges, lodging, lodged
1 (noun) a small house in the grounds of a large country house.
2 (verb) If you lodge in someone else's house, you live there and pay them rent.
3 If something lodges somewhere, it gets stuck there, e.g. *I had a bone lodged in my throat.*

lodger, lodgers
(noun) a person who lives in someone's house and pays rent.
lodgings (noun)

loft, lofts
(noun) the space immediately under the roof of a house, often used for storing things.

lofty, loftier, loftiest
(adjective) very high, e.g. *lofty treetops*.
loftily (adverb) **loftiness** (noun)

log, logs, logging, logged
1 (noun) a thick branch or piece of tree trunk.
2 the captain's official record of everything that happens on board a ship.
3 (verb) to make an official record of something, for example in a logbook.
4 To log into a computer system or to log on means to gain access to it so that you can use it, usually by giving your name and password. To log out means to finish using the system.

logbook, logbooks
(noun) a book in which you record the details of something, for example on a ship or in a car.

logic
(noun) a way of reasoning involving a series of statements, each of which must follow if the statement before is true.

logical
(adjective) sensible or reasonable in the circumstances, e.g. *When darkness fell, it was logical to stay put and wait for rescue.*
logically (adverb)

logo, logos (pronounced **loh**-goh)
(noun) a badge or design that represents an organization.
[Greek *logos* = reason or speech]

-logy
(suffix) -logy is used to form words that refer to the study of something, e.g. *biology... geology*.
[Greek *logos* = reason, or speech]

loiter, loiters, loitering, loitered
(verb) to stand about idly with no real purpose.

lollipop, lollipops
(noun) a hard sweet on the end of a stick.

lolly, lollies
1 (noun) a sweet or ice cream on a stick.
2 (informal) money, e.g. *The thieves scarpered with the lolly.*

lonely, lonelier, loneliest
1 (adjective) If you are lonely, you are unhappy because you are alone.
2 A lonely place is an isolated one which very few people visit, e.g. *a lonely, windswept moor*.
loneliness (noun)

lonesome
(adjective) lonely and sad.

long, longer, longest; longs, longing, longed
Selected meanings:
1 (adjective, adverb) e.g. *a long time... long hair... Our oil won't last much longer.*
2 **So long** is an informal way of saying goodbye.
3 (verb) If you long for something, you want it very much.
longing (noun) **longingly** (adverb)

Similar words: (verb) yearn, wish, pine

A film director needs these words: pan zoom dolly cut editing camera rushes shot sequence.

ongitude, longitudes
(noun) The longitude of a place is its distance in degrees east or west of a line passing through Greenwich, London.

ong-range
1 (adjective) able to be used over a great distance, e.g. *long-range missiles.*
2 extending a long way into the future, e.g. *a long-range weather forecast.*

ong-standing
(adjective) having existed for a long time, e.g. *The pool game was a long-standing arrangement.*

ong-suffering
(adjective) very patient, e.g. *He was always drunk. I felt sorry for his long-suffering wife.*

ong-term
(adjective) extending a long way into the future, e.g. *GCSEs are a long-term commitment*

ong-winded
(adjective) long and boring, e.g. *The major gave a long-winded speech.*

Similar words: rambling, verbose, wordy

oo, loos
(noun; informal) a toilet.

oofah, loofahs
(noun) a long, rough, spongelike object, used for washing and scrubbing in the bath.

ook, looks, looking, looked
1 (verb) e.g. *Look closely at this.*
2 If you look down on someone, you think that they are inferior to you.
3 If you are looking forward to something, you want it to happen.
4 If you look up to someone, you admire and respect them.
5 (noun) e.g. *Have a look at the Survival Guide in this dictionary... the look on his face.*
6 If you talk about someone's looks, you are talking about how attractive they are, e.g. *Olive Oyl had the looks of a goddess.*

Similar words: (verb) view, glance, peep, glimpse

look after
(phrasal verb) to take care of someone or something.

Similar words: tend, care for, nurse, mind

look up
1 (phrasal verb) to find something out in a book.
2 If you look someone up, you go to see them after not having seen them for a long time.
3 If a situation is looking up, it is improving.

ookalike, lookalikes
(noun) A lookalike is a person who looks very like someone else, e.g. *an Elvis lookalike.*

look-in
(noun; informal) If you do not get a look-in, you do not get the chance to do something, because too many other people are doing it.

lookout, lookouts
1 (noun) someone who is watching for danger, or a place where they watch for danger.
2 (phrase) If you are **on the lookout** for something, you are watching for it.

loom, looms, looming, loomed
1 (noun) a machine for weaving cloth.
2 (verb) If something looms in front of you, it suddenly appears as a tall, unclear shape.
3 If a situation or event is looming, it is likely to happen soon and is rather worrying.

loony
(adjective; informal) People or behaviour can be described as loony if they are mad or eccentric. [from 'lunatic']

loop, loops, looping, looped
(noun) a curved or circular shape in, for example a piece of string, a railway line.
2 (verb) If you loop rope or string around an object, you place it in a loop around the object.

loose, looser, loosest
1 (adjective) not firmly held, fixed or attached.
2 (phrase) If you are **at a loose end**, you have nothing particular to do.
loosely (adverb) **looseness** (noun)

loosebox, looseboxes
(noun) a large stall for a horse.

loose-leaf
(adjective) Loose-leaf folders and binders can be opened and closed for pages to be put in and out.

loosen, loosens, loosening, loosened
(verb) to make something less tight.

Similar words: undo, unfasten, slacken

loot, loots, looting, looted
1 (verb) to steal money and goods from shops, houses etc. during a battle or riot.
2 (noun) stolen money or goods.
looter (noun)
[Hindi *lut* = loot]

Similar words: (verb) raid, ransack, plunder

lopsided
(adjective) uneven because two sides are different sizes or shapes.

lord, lords
1 (noun) a nobleman, e.g. *Lord Palmerston.*
2 In Christianity, 'Lord' is a name given to God and Jesus Christ.

lorry, lorries
(noun) a large road vehicle for carrying goods.

lose, loses, losing, lost
1 (verb) e.g. *I lost my money... He has lost the use of his legs.*
2 If you lose a relative or friend, they die, e.g. *She lost her father when she was six.*
3 to be beaten at a game etc.
4 If a business loses money, it is spending more money than it is earning.
loser (noun) **loss** (noun)

The main words ending OO are: igloo shampoo taboo tattoo too. Do you know any more?

lost

1 (adjective) e.g. *I'm completely lost... My watch got lost at the baths.*
2 past tense and past participle of **lose**.
3 (phrase) If you are **lost for words** you don't know what to say.

Similar words: missing, astray, mislaid, misplaced

lot, lots

1 (noun) e.g. *There is lots of help in the introduction to this dictionary... Put that lot of stuff over there... I like him a lot.*
2 (phrase) You **draw lots** to decide who will do something by each person taking a straw or a piece of paper from a container. The person who takes the straw or piece of paper that is different from the others is chosen.

Similar words: many, heaps, piles, oodles, loads, masses

lotion, lotions

(noun) a liquid that you put on your skin to protect or soften it, e.g. *suntan lotion.*

loud, louder, loudest

(adjective, adverb) e.g. *a loud bang... He sang out loud.*
loudly (adverb) **loudness** (noun)

Similar words: noisy, deafening, ear-piercing

loud-hailer, loud-hailers

(noun) a hand-held loudspeaker.

loudspeaker, loudspeakers

(noun) a piece of equipment that makes your voice louder when you speak into a microphone connected to it.

lough, loughs (pronounced lok)

(noun) a lake in Ireland, e.g. *Lough Neagh.*

lounge, lounges, lounging, lounged

1 (noun) a room in a house or hotel with comfortable chairs where people can relax.
2 (verb) to sit or lie around in a lazy and comfortable way.

louse, lice

(noun) a small insect that lives on people's bodies, e.g. *head lice.*

lousy, lousier, lousiest

(adjective; informal) of bad quality or very unpleasant, e.g. *The hotels are lousy... lousy weather.*

lout, louts

(noun) a boy or young man who behaves in a rude or aggressive way.
loutish (adjective)

Similar words: hooligan, delinquent, lager lout, yob, yobbo

lovable

(adjective) having very attractive qualities and therefore easy to love, e.g. *a lovable little puppy.*

love, loves, loving, loved

1 (verb) e.g. *I love chocolate cake... He loves her.*
2 (noun) e.g. *She's in love with a real drip!*
3 In tennis, love is a score of zero.
loving (adjective) **lovingly** (adverb) **lover** (noun)

lovely, lovelier, loveliest

(adjective) beautiful, attractive and pleasant.
loveliness (noun)

low, lower, lowest; lows, lowing, lowed

1 (adjective, adverb) close to the ground.
2 (adjective) small in value or amount, e.g. *Temperatures will get lower soon.*
3 A low sound is deep and quiet.
4 A light that is low is dim and not bright.
5 If you are feeling low, you are miserable.
6 (verb) When cows low, they make a mooing noise, e.g. *The lowing herd winds slowly o'er the lea.*

lower, lowers, lowering, lowered

1 (verb) to move something downwards.
2 (adjective) below or less important.

Similar words: (adjective) minor, inferior

lower case

(adjective) the small letters used in printing or on a typewriter, e.g. *The poet e.e. cummings always had his initials in lower case letters.*

lowest common denominator, denominators

(noun) In maths, the lowest common denominator is the smallest number that several denominators will go into, e.g. *12 is the lowest common denominator of 3, 4 and 6.*

lowlands

(plural noun) an area of flat, low land.
lowland (adjective)

low profile

(noun) If you keep a low profile, you deliberately avoid attracting attention.

low tide

(noun) the time, usually twice a day, when the sea is at its lowest level.

loyal

(adjective) firm in your friendship or support for someone or something.
loyally (adverb) **loyalty** (noun)

lubricate, lubricates, lubricating, lubricated

(verb) To lubricate a machine means to put oil or grease onto it, so that it moves smoothly.
lubrication (noun) **lubricant** (noun)
[Latin *lubricus* = slippery]

luck

(noun) anything that seems to happen by chance and not through your own efforts, e.g. *The only sure thing about luck is that it will change.*

Similar words: fortune, chance

luckless

(adjective; literary) unsuccessful or unfortunate, e.g. *So our luckless hero went on his weary way.*

lucky, luckier, luckiest

1 Something that is lucky happens by chance and has good effects or consequences.

Idioms. What do we mean by: hard lines hard luck hard times hard up hard words?

2 (adjective) Someone who is lucky has a lot of good luck.
luckily (adverb) **luck** (noun)

Similar words: fortunate, jammy

ludicrous
(adjective) completely foolish, unsuitable or ridiculous, e.g. *What a ludicrous idea!*
ludicrously (adverb)
[Latin *ludicrus* = done in sport]

lug, lugs, lugging, lugged
(verb) to carry something heavy with difficulty.

luggage
(noun) the bags and suitcases that you take with you when you travel.

lukewarm
1 (adjective) slightly warm, e.g. *lukewarm water.*
2 not very enthusiastic or interested, e.g. *My ace dictionary received a lukewarm response.*

lull, lulls, lulling, lulled
1 (noun) a pause in something, e.g. *There was a lull in the conversation.*
2 (verb) To lull someone means to send them to sleep or to make them feel safe and secure, e.g. *We had been lulled into a false sense of security.*

lullaby, lullabies
(noun) a song used for sending a baby to sleep.

lumber, lumbers, lumbering, lumbered
1 (verb) to move heavily and clumsily.
2 (informal) If you are lumbered with something, you are given it to deal with even though you do not want it, e.g. *I was lumbered with producing the school timetable.*
3 (noun) timber which has been sawn up.

lumberjack, lumberjacks
(noun) a man whose job is to chop down trees in forests.

luminous
(adjective) glowing in the dark, e.g. *She can see the luminous hands of her Mickey Mouse clock.*
luminously (adverb) **luminosity** (noun)

lump, lumps, lumping, lumped
1 (noun) a solid piece of something.
2 (informal) If you **have to lump it**, you have to put up with something whether you like it or not, e.g. *Like it or lump it.*
lumpy (adjective)

lunacy
(noun) extremely foolish or eccentric behaviour.

lunar
(adjective) relating to the moon.
[Latin *luna* = moon]

lunatic, lunatics
1 (noun) If you call someone a lunatic, you mean that they are very foolish, stupid and annoying, e.g. *Look at the way he drives – he's a lunatic!*
2 someone who is insane.

lunch, lunches
(noun) a meal eaten in the middle of the day.
luncheon (noun)

lung, lungs
(noun) Your lungs are the two organs inside your ribcage with which you breathe.

lunge, lunges, lunging, lunged
(verb) to make a sudden, deliberate movement in one direction.
[French *allonger* = to stretch out one's arm]

lurch, lurches, lurching, lurched
1 (verb) to make a sudden, jerky movement.
2 (phrase) If someone **leaves you in the lurch**, they leave you in a very difficult situation, instead of helping you.

lure, lures, luring, lured
(verb) to attract someone into going somewhere or doing something.

lurk, lurks, lurking, lurked
(verb) to hang around in a hidden place.

luscious
(adjective) very tasty, e.g. *a luscious peach.*

lust, lusts
(noun) a strong desire to have something, e.g. *a lust for power.*
lustful (adjective)

lusty, lustier, lustiest
(adjective) strong, healthy, and full of energy, e.g *a strong and lusty boy... a lusty hit.*
lustily (adverb)

lute, lutes
(noun) a stringed musical instrument which is plucked like a guitar. It is shaped like half a pear and was popular in the Middle Ages.

luxurious
(adjective) very expensive and full of luxury.
luxuriously (adverb)

luxury, luxuries
1 (noun) great comfort in expensive and beautiful surroundings, e.g. *a life of luxury.*
2 something that you enjoy but do not have often, usually because it is expensive.

Similar words: (sense 2) extra, treat

lying
1 (adjective) A lying person often tells lies.
2 present participle of **lie**, e.g. *lying down.*

Similar words: (adjective) dishonest, untruthful

lyric, lyrics
(noun) The lyric or lyrics of a song are the words, e.g. *I like the tune but the lyrics are dreadful.*
[Greek *lura* = lyre]

Truth is the highest thing that man may keep. (Geoffrey Chaucer)

M

macaroni
(noun) short hollow tubes of pasta.
[an Italian word from Greek *makaria* = food made from barley]

Mach (pronounced **mak**)
(noun) a unit of measurement for aircraft speeds. Mach 1 (770 mph) is the speed of sound.
[named after Ernst Mach, an Austrian physicist.]

machine, machines
(noun) a piece of equipment which uses electricity or power from an engine.

Similar words: apparatus, device

machine-gun, machine-guns
(noun) a gun that works automatically, firing bullets one after the other.

machinery
(noun) machines in general.

macho (pronounced **mat**-show)
(adjective) behaving in an aggressively masculine way.
[Spanish *macho* = male]

mackerel, mackerels
(noun) a sea fish with blue and silver stripes.

mackintosh, mackintoshes, or mac
(noun) a raincoat made from specially treated cloth, named after Charles Mackintosh, who invented it.

mad, madder, maddest
1 (adjective) Someone who is mad has a mental illness which often causes them to behave in strange ways.
2 very foolish, e.g. *You must be mad to go out there alone.*
3 (informal) angry, e.g. *She got pretty mad when she found out I had kidnapped her gerbil.*
4 If you are mad about someone or something, you like them very much.
madness (noun) **madman** (noun) **madly** (adverb)

Similar words: (sense 1) insane, lunatic
(sense 2) crazy, crackers

madam
(noun) a formal name for a lady. You start a business letter to a woman 'Dear Madam', if you do not know her name.
[Old French *ma dame* = my lady]

madden, maddens, maddening, maddened
(verb) If something maddens you, it makes you very angry, irritated or frustrated.
maddening (adjective) **maddeningly** (adverb)

magazine, magazines
1 (noun) a weekly or monthly publication with articles, photographs and advertisements.
2 a compartment in a gun for cartridges.
[Arabic *makhzan* = storehouse]

maggot, maggots
(noun) a creature like a small worm that lives on decaying things and is used for fishing bait. Maggots turn into flies.

magic
1 (noun) In fairy stories, magic is a special power that can make impossible things happen.
2 the art of performing tricks to entertain people.
3 a special quality that makes something seem wonderful and exciting, e.g. *the magic of the theatre.*
magical (adjective) **magically** (adverb)
magician (noun)

Similar words: (sense 2) conjuring, illusion, trickery

magistrate, magistrates
(noun) an official who acts as a judge in a law court that deals with less serious crimes.

magnesium
(noun) a metal which burns with a bright white flame, used in fireworks, flashbulbs and flares.

magnet, magnets
(noun) a piece of iron which attracts iron or steel towards it, and which points towards north if allowed to swing freely.
magnetic (adjective) **magnetically** (adverb)
magnetism (noun) **magnetize** (verb)

magnificent
(adjective) extremely beautiful or impressive.
magnificently (adverb) **magnificence** (noun)
[Latin *magnificus* = great in deeds]

magnify, magnifies, magnifying, magnified
(verb) When something is magnified. it looks bigger than it really is.
magnification (noun)

magnifying glass, glasses
(noun) a lens which makes things appear bigger than they really are.

magpie, magpies
(noun) a large black and white bird.

mahogany
(noun) a reddish-brown, tropical hardwood used for making furniture.

maid, maids
(noun) a female servant.

maiden, maidens
1 (noun; literary) a young woman.
2 (adjective) first, e.g. *the Titanic's maiden voyage.*
3 (noun) In cricket, a maiden is an over in which no runs are scored.

maiden name, names
(noun) A woman's maiden name is the surname she had before she married.

mail
(noun) the letters and parcels delivered to you by the post office.
[Old French *male* = bag]

mail order
(noun) a system of buying goods by post.

Letter M seems to have begun as a picture of the waves of the sea.

maim, maims, maiming, maimed
(verb) to injure someone very badly for life.

main, mains
1 (adjective) most important, e.g. *main road*.
2 (noun) The mains are large pipes or wires that carry gas, water, electricity or sewage.
mainly (adverb)

Similar words: (adjective) chief, premier, major, head, principal, primary

main clause, clauses
(noun) In grammar, a main clause is a clause that can stand alone as a complete sentence.

mainframe
(noun) a large computer with many terminals used by a lot of people at the same time.

mainland
(noun) the main part of a country, in contrast to islands around its coast.

maintain, maintains, maintaining, maintained
1 (verb) to keep something going or keep it at a particular rate or level, e.g. *to maintain standards*.
2 To maintain a machine or a building means to keep it in good condition.
[Latin *manu tenere* = to hold in the hand]

maintenance
(noun) the process of keeping something in good condition.

maisonette, maisonettes
(noun) a flat, usually on two floors of a larger building.

maize
(noun) a tall plant which produces sweetcorn.

majesty, majesties
1 You say 'His Majesty' when you are talking about a king, and 'Her Majesty' when you are talking about a queen.
2 (noun) the quality of great dignity and impressiveness.
majestic (adjective) **majestically** (adverb)

major, majors
1 (adjective) more important or more serious than other things, e.g. *He sustained major injuries in the accident.*
2 (noun) a rank of army officer above a captain and below a colonel.
3 (adjective) A major key is one of the two types of key in which most European music is written.

majority, majorities
1 (noun) The majority of people or things in a group is more than half of the group.
2 In an election, the majority is the difference between the number of votes gained by the winner and the number gained by the runner-up.

make, makes, making, made
Selected meanings:
1 (verb) e.g. *to make a mess... She made us clear up... The Survival Guide makes using this dictionary easy.*
2 (noun) The make of a product is the name of the company that manufactured it, e.g. *'What make is your car?' – 'It's a Rolls Royce'.*

3 (phrase; informal) If someone **makes it**, they are successful.
4 (phrase) If you **make do** with something, you use it because you do not have anything better.
5 If you ask someone what they **make of** something, you are asking what they think of it.

Similar words: (verb) create, form, fashion, manufacture, produce
(noun) brand, type

make off with
(phrasal verb) to steal something and run away.

make out
1 (phrasal verb) If you can make something out, you can see it or hear it. e.g. *I could just make out what she said.*
2 If you make out that something is true, you try to get people to believe it, e.g. *She made out that we had eaten her pet frog, Cecil.*
3 To make out a cheque means to write it.

make up
1 (phrasal verb) If a number of things make up something, they form that thing.
2 If you make up a story, you invent it.
3 If you make yourself up, you put cosmetics on.
4 If two people make it up, they become friends again after a quarrel.
5 To make up for something that you have done wrong means to put it right.
6 If you make up your mind, you decide.

make-up
(noun) coloured creams and powders which women put on their faces. Actors also use make-up on the stage or in films and TV.

maladjusted
(adjective) A maladjusted person has psychological or behaviour problems.

malaria (pronounced mal-**lay**-ree-a)
(noun) a tropical disease caught from mosquitoes which causes fever and shivering.
malarial (adjective)

Malay (pronounced mal-**lay**)
(noun) a language spoken by many people who live in Malaysia and Indonesia.

Malaysian, Malaysians
1 (adjective) belonging to Malaysia.
2 (noun) someone who comes from Malaysia.

male, males
1 (noun) a person or animal belonging to the sex that cannot give birth or lay eggs.
2 (adjective) concerning men rather than women.

male chauvinist, chauvinists
(pronounced **show**-vin-ist)
(noun) a man who thinks that men are better than women.

malfunction, malfunctions
(noun) A malfunction in a machine is when it fails to work properly.

malicious
(adjective) Malicious talk or behaviour is intended to harm someone.
maliciously (adverb) **malice** (noun)
[Latin *malus* = evil]

We take these words from Malaysia: amok bamboo bantam raffia teak.

malignant
(adjective) A malignant disease or tumour could cause death if it is allowed to continue.
malignancy (noun)

mallet, mallets
(noun) a soft hammer made of wood or rubber.
[Latin *maleus* = hammer]

malnutrition
(noun) not eating enough healthy food.

malt
(noun) roasted grain, usually barley, that is used in making beer and whisky.

mammal, mammals
(noun) animals that give birth to live babies and feed their young with milk from the mother's body, e.g. human beings, dogs, lions, whales.
[Latin *mamma* = breast]

mammoth, mammoths
1 (adjective) very large indeed, e.g. *It's a mammoth task.*
2 (noun) an extinct, huge animal that looked like a hairy elephant with long tusks.

man, men; mans, manning, manned
1 (noun) an adult, male human being.
2 (verb) To man something means to be in charge of it or operate it, e.g. *Who's manning the phones?*
manhood (noun)

Similar words: (noun) male, chap, guy, bloke, fellow, gentleman

manage, manages, managing, managed
1 (verb) If you manage to do something, you succeed in doing it, e.g. *However did you manage without looking at the Survival Guide on page v?*
2 If you manage an organization or business, you are responsible for controlling it.
manageable (adjective) **management** (noun)

Similar words: (sense 1) get by, cope, survive

manager, managers
(noun) a person responsible for running a business or organization, e.g. *the bank manager.*
(feminine: **manageress**)

mandarin, mandarins
(noun) a type of small orange.

mane, manes
(noun) the mane of a lion or a horse is the long thick hair growing from its neck.

manger, mangers
(noun) a feeding box in a barn or stable.
[Old French *mangier* = to eat]

mangle, mangles, mangling, mangled
(verb) If something is mangled, it is crushed and twisted.

manhandle, manhandles, manhandling, manhandled
(verb) to treat someone roughly, e.g. *The kidnappers manhandled the man into the car.*

manhole, manholes
(noun) a covered hole in the ground leading to a drain or sewer.

maniac, maniacs
(noun) a mad person, especially one who is violent and dangerous.

manicure, manicures
(noun) a treatment for the hands and nails.
manicurist (noun)
[Latin *manus* = hand + *cura* = care]

manipulate, manipulates, manipulating, manipulated
1 (verb) to control or influence people or events to produce a particular result, e.g. *The spoilt girl was expert at manipulating her parents.*
2 If you manipulate a piece of equipment, you control it in a skilful way.
manipulation (noun) **manipulator** (noun)
manipulative (adjective)
[Latin *manipulus* = handful]

mankind
(noun) You can refer to all human beings as mankind, e.g. *Lister did a service to mankind.*

manly, manlier, manliest
(adjective) having qualities that are typically masculine, e.g. *a strong, manly character.*
manliness (noun)

manner, manners
1 (noun) The manner in which you do something is the way in which you do it.
2 Your manner is the way in which you behave and talk, e.g. *her pleasant manner.*
3 (plural noun) If you have good manners, you behave and speak very politely.

Similar words: (sense 1) way, method, system, fashion, style, technique
(sense 2) behaviour, attitude, approach, conduct

mannerism, mannerisms
(noun) a gesture or a way of speaking which is characteristic of a person, e.g. *Most children enjoy imitating teachers' mannerisms.*

manoeuvre, manoeuvres, manoeuvring, manoeuvred (pronounced man-**noo**-ver)
1 (verb) If you manoeuvre something into a place, you skilfully move it there, e.g. *I manoeuvred the car into a tiny parking space.*
2 (phrase) If you have **room for manoeuvre**, you have the chance to change your plans if you want to.
3 (noun) When military manoeuvres take place, soldiers and equipment are moved around in a large area of countryside as a training exercise.
[Latin *manuopera* = manual work]

manor, manors
(noun) a large country house with land.
[Old French *maneir* = to dwell]

mansion, mansions
(noun) a very large house.

manslaughter
(noun; legal) the accidental killing of a person.

mantelpiece, mantelpieces
(noun) a shelf over a fireplace.

The Venerable Bede (673-735) was the first great writer of Anglo-Saxon prose.

manual, manuals
1 (adjective) Manual work involves physical strength rather than mental skill.
2 operated by hand, e.g. *manual gears.*
3 (noun) an instruction book which tells you how to use a machine, e.g. *a car manual.*
manually (adverb)
[Latin *manus* = hand]

manufacture, manufactures, manufacturing, manufactured
(verb) to make things in a factory.
manufacturer (noun) **manufacturing** (noun)
[Latin *manus* = hand + *facere* = to make]

manure
(noun) animal dung used to fertilize the soil.

manuscript, manuscripts
(noun) a handwritten or typed document, especially a version of a book before it is printed.
[Latin *manus* = hand + *scribere* = to write]

many
(adjective, pronoun), e.g. *How many brothers have you... Many are seated already.*

Maori, Maoris
(noun) someone descended from the people who lived in New Zealand before Europeans arrived.

map, maps, mapping, mapped
1 (noun) a detailed diagram of an area as if seen from above.
2 (verb) to make a map of an area.
[Latin *mappa* = cloth]

maple, maples
(noun) a tree that has large leaves with 5 points. Its wood is used for furniture, its sap for syrup and its leaf shape for the flag of Canada.

marathon, marathons
1 (noun) a race in which people run 26 miles 385 yards (about 42 km) along roads.
2 (adjective) A marathon task is a large one that takes a long time.
[from Marathon, a place in Greece from which a messenger ran to Athens bringing news of a victory in 490 BC]

marble, marbles
1 (noun) a very hard, coloured stone which is polished and used to make statues and decorative features of houses.
2 Marbles is a children's game played with small glass balls.
[Greek *marmairein* = to gleam]

march, marches, marching, marched
1 (noun) March is the 3rd month of the year.
2 (verb) When soldiers march, they walk with quick regular steps in time with each other.
3 to walk quickly in a determined way, e.g. *He slammed the door and marched out.*
4 (noun) an organized protest in which a large group of people walk somewhere together.

mare, mares
(noun) an adult, female horse.

margarine (pronounced mar-jar-reen)
(noun) a substance similar to butter made from vegetable oil and/or animal fats.

margin, margins
1 (noun) the edge of something, e.g. a page.
2 If you win a contest by a small margin, you win it by a small amount.
[Latin *margo* = border]

marigold, marigolds
(noun) a yellow or orange garden flower.

marijuana
(noun) another name for cannabis

marina, marinas
(noun) a harbour for pleasure boats and yachts.

marine, marines
1 (noun) a soldier who serves with the navy.
2 (adjective) relating to the sea, e.g. *marine life.*
[Latin *mare* = sea]

Similar word: (adjective) nautical

mark, marks, marking, marked
Selected meanings:
1 (noun) a small stain, e.g. *I can't get these marks off the carpet.*
2 (verb) If you mark something, you write a symbol on it or identify it in some other way, e.g. *Mark your wellies so you don't lose them.*
3 (noun) a letter or number showing how well you have done in a piece of school work, e.g *I got lousy marks four my speling.*
4 a sign or typical feature of something, e.g. *They removed their hats as a mark of respect.*
5 (noun) The mark or Deutsche Mark is the main unit of money in Germany.
6 (verb) In football or hockey, if you mark your opposing player, you stay close to them, trying to prevent them from getting the ball.

market, markets, marketing, marketed
1 (noun) a place with many small stalls selling different goods.
2 (verb) to plan and supervise the selling of a product.

market research
(noun) finding out what people want, need and buy.

marmalade
(noun) a jam made from oranges, lemons, etc., usually eaten at breakfast.
[Latin *marmelo* = quince]

maroon
(noun, adjective) a dark, reddish-purple colour.

marooned
(adjective) If you are marooned in a place, you cannot leave it. e.g. *I'm marooned on Planet X.*

marquee, marquees (pronounced mar-**kee**)
(noun) a very large tent.

marriage, marriages
(noun) the ceremony when people get married.

marrow, marrows
(noun) a long, thick, green vegetable.

marry, marries, marrying, married
1 (verb) to become someone's husband or wife.
2 to be in charge of a marriage ceremony.

marsh, marshes
(noun) an area of land which is always wet.

Question marks (?) and exclamation marks (!) count as full stops.

marshmallow, marshmallows
(noun) a soft, spongy, pink or white sweet.

marsupial, marsupials (pronounced
mar-**syoo**-pee-al)
(noun) an animal that carries its young in a
pouch, e.g. wombat, koala bear, kangaroo.
[Greek *marsupion* = purse]

martial arts
(plural noun) the techniques of self-defence that
come from the Far East, e.g. karate, judo.

Martian, Martians (pronounced mar-shan)
(noun) an imaginary creature from planet Mars.

martyr, martyrs
(noun) someone who suffers or is killed rather
than change their beliefs.
martyrdom (noun)
[Greek *martus* = witness]

marvel, marvels
(noun) something that makes you feel great
surprise or admiration, e.g. *The Survival Guide
in this dictionary really is a marvel.*

marvellous
(adjective) wonderful or excellent.
marvellously (adverb)

marzipan
(noun) a paste made of almonds, sugar and egg,
put on top of cakes or used to make sweets.

mascara
(noun) a substance that can be used to colour
eyelashes and make them look longer.
[Spanish *mascara* = mask]

mascot, mascots
(noun) an animal or toy which people think
brings them good luck.

masculine
1 (adjective) typical of men, rather than women,
e.g. *a heavy masculine way of walking.*
2 (noun) the male form of a word, e.g. **Duke** is the
masculine of **duchess**. (opposite: **feminine**).
masculinity (noun)

mash, mashes, mashing, mashed
(verb) If you mash vegetables, you crush them
after they have been cooked.

mask, masks
(noun) something worn over the face for
protection or disguise.
masked (adjective)

mason, masons
1 (noun) a person who makes things with stone.
2 a Freemason, member of a society which has
secret rules and ceremonies.
masonic (adjective)

masonry
(noun) pieces of stone which form part of a wall
or building, e.g. *Some masonry fell on me.*

mass, masses
1 (noun) a large amount of something.
2 (adjective) involving a large number of people,
e.g. *mass unemployment.*
3 (noun) The masses are the ordinary people in
society considered as a group, e.g. *Game shows
are entertainment for the masses.*

4 In physics, the mass of an object is the amount
of physical matter that it has.
5 In the Roman Catholic Church, Mass is a
religious service in which people share bread and
wine in remembrance of the death and
resurrection of Jesus Christ.

massacre, massacres, massacring, massacred
(pronounced **mass**-ik-ker)
(noun) the killing of a very large number of
people in a violent and cruel way.

massage, massages, massaging, massaged
(verb) to rub someone's body to help them relax
or to relieve pain.
[French *masser* = to rub]

massive
(adjective) extremely large in size, quantity or
extent, e.g. *a massive task.*
massively (adverb)

mass media
(noun) TV, radio, newspapers and other methods
of giving information to many people at the same
time.

**mass-produce, mass-produces,
mass-producing, mass-produced**
(verb) to make something in large quantities
using a production line, e.g. *Model 'T' Fords were
the first cars to be mass-produced.*
mass-produced (adjective) **mass production**
(noun)

mast, masts
1 (noun) the tall, upright pole that supports the
sails of a boat.
2 A radio or TV mast is a very tall pole for
transmitting sound or television pictures.

master, masters, mastering, mastered
1 (noun) a man who has authority over a servant.
2 a male teacher at a school.
3 (verb) If you master something, you learn how
to do it properly, e.g. *He mastered the language.*
masterful (adjective) **masterly** (adjective)
[Latin *magister* = master]

**mastermind, masterminds, masterminding,
masterminded**
1 (verb) If you mastermind a complicated
activity, you plan and organize it.
2 (noun) The mastermind behind something is
the person responsible for planning it.

masterpiece, masterpieces
(noun) an extremely good painting, novel or
other work of art.

mastery
(noun) Mastery of a skill or art is excellence in it.

matador, matadors
(noun) a man who fights and tries to kill bulls in
a bullfight.
[Spanish *matar* = to kill]

match, matches, matching, matched
1 (noun) e.g. *a hockey match... to strike a match.*
2 (verb) If one thing matches another, the two
things look the same or are similar.
matched (adjective) **matching** (adjective)
3 (phrase) If something is **no match for** something

Can you find out the difference between masculine rhyme and feminine rhyme?

else, the first thing is not as good as the second, e.g. *Halifax Town were no match for Liverpool.*
matchless (adjective)

mate, mates, mating, mated
1 (noun; informal) a friend.
2 The first mate on a ship is the officer who is next in importance to the captain.
3 An animal's mate is its sexual partner.
4 (verb) When a male and female animal mate, they come together sexually in order to breed.
mating (noun)

material, materials
1 (noun) cloth.
2 a substance from which something is made, e.g. *The raw materials of a pancake are flour, milk and eggs.*
3 (adjective) relating to possessions and money, e.g. *the material comforts of life.*
materially (adverb)
[Latin *materia* = matter]

materialistic
(adjective) thinking that money and possessions are the most important things in life.
materialist (noun) **materialism** (noun)

maternal
(adjective) relating to a mother, e.g. *her maternal feelings towards her new baby.*
[Latin *mater* = mother]

maternity
(adjective) relating to pregnant women and birth, e.g. *maternity clothes.*

mathematics or **maths**
(noun) the study of numbers, quantities and shapes.
mathematical (adjective) **mathematically** (adverb) **mathematician** (noun)
[Greek *mathēma* = a science]

matinée, matinées (pronounced **mat**-in-nay).
(noun) an afternoon show of a play or film.

matrices plural of **matrix**.

matrimony
(noun; formal) marriage.
matrimonial (adjective)

matrix, matrices (pronounced **may**-trix)
(noun) In maths, a matrix is a set of numbers or elements set out in rows and columns.
[Latin *matrix* = womb]

matron, matrons
(noun) In a school, the matron is the person who looks after the health of the children.

matt
(adjective) A matt surface is dull rather than shiny, e.g. *I prefer a matt finish on wood.*

matted
(adjective) Hair that is matted is tangled, with the strands sticking together.

matter, matters, mattering, mattered
1 (noun) something that you have to deal with, e.g. *I hope we can sort this matter out soon... What's the matter?*

2 any substance, e.g. *The atom is the smallest divisible particle of matter.*
3 Books and magazines are reading matter.
4 (verb) If something matters to you, it is important.

Similar words: (noun) affair, issue, topic, subject, situation

mattress, mattresses
(noun) a thick pad filled with springs or feathers put on a bed to make it comfortable.

mature, matures, maturing, matured
1 (verb) When a child or young animal matures, it becomes an adult.
2 (adjective) fully developed and grown-up in all ways.
maturely (adverb) **maturity** (noun)
[Latin *maturus* = developed]

maul, mauls, mauling, mauled
(verb) If someone is mauled by an animal, they are savagely attacked and badly injured by it.

mauve (rhymes with **grove**)
(noun, adjective) pale purple.

maxim, maxims
(noun) a rule for good or sensible behaviour in the form of a short saying, e.g. *Be prepared!*

maximum, maximums or **maxing**
(adjective, noun) the most that is possible, e.g. *the maximum daily dose... a maximum of ten people.*
maximize (verb)

may
1 (verb) e.g. *You may help if you wish.*
2 (noun) May is the 5th month of the year.

maybe
(adverb) perhaps, e.g. *I'll come on Tuesday or maybe Wednesday.*

mayonnaise (pronounced may-on-**nayz**)
(noun) a thick salad dressing made with egg yolks and oil.

mayor, mayors
(noun) The mayor of a town is a person who has been elected to lead and represent the people.
[Latin *maior* = greater]

mayoress, mayoresses
(noun) the wife or official partner of a mayor.

maze, mazes
(noun) a system of complicated passages which it is difficult to find your way through, e.g. *a maze of underground tunnels.*

me
(pronoun) e.g. *Page vi really helped me.*

meadow, meadows
(noun) a field of grass.

meagre (pronounced **mee**-ger)
(adjective) very small and poor, e.g. *They couldn't manage on his meagre wages.*
[Old French *maigre* = poor or lean]

meal, meals
(noun) an occasion when people eat food, or the food that they eat then.

mean, means, meaning, meant; meaner, meanest
Selected meanings:
1 (verb) e.g. *What does this mean?... I really mean what I say!... My dog means a lot to me... Giving that goal away means a replay next week... Sorry, I meant to write, but... That dynamite was meant to expl..........*
2 (adjective) unwilling to spend much.
3 unkind or cruel, e.g. *Don't be so mean to him.*
4 (noun) A means of doing something is a way to do it, e.g. *Frankenstein found a means of building people from bits.*
5 In maths, the mean is the average of a set of numbers.
meanness (noun) **meanly** (adverb)

Similar words: (sense 2) stingy, miserly, tight, tight-fisted

meander, meanders, meandering, meandered
(pronounced mee-**an**-der)
(verb) If a river meanders, it has a lot of bends in it.
[from *Maiandros*, the name of a Greek river]

meaning, meanings
(noun) e.g. *This is an example of the meaning of the word 'meaning' – if you see what I mean.*
meaningful (adjective) **meaningfully** (adverb)
meaningless (adjective)

Similar words: significance, gist, content

meantime
(phrase) **In the meantime** means in the period of time between two events, e.g. *The doctor will soon arrive; in the meantime, you must sleep.*

meanwhile
(adverb) at the same time, e.g. *Off the coast of Ireland, the liner Lusitania was sinking. Meanwhile Churchill was dining in Paris.*

measles
(noun) an infectious illness in which you have red spots on your skin.
[Germanic *masele* = spot on the skin]

measly
(adjective; informal) very small or inadequate, e.g. *I only had a measly serving of chips.*

measure, measures, measuring, measured
1 (verb) to find out how big something is by using, for example a ruler or tape measure.
2 (noun) Measures are actions carried out to achieve a particular result, e.g. *Measures have been taken to avoid delay.*
measurable (adjective) **measurement** (noun)

measurement, measurements
1 (noun) the result that you obtain when you measure something.
2 Your measurements are the sizes of your chest, waist and hips that you use to buy clothes.

meat, meats
(noun) the flesh of animals that is cooked and eaten.
meaty (adjective)

mechanic, mechanics
(noun) a person who repairs and maintains engines and machines.

mechanical
(adjective) A mechanical device has moving parts and is used to do a physical task.
mechanically (adverb) **mechanize** (verb)

mechanism, mechanisms
(noun) a part of a machine that does a particular task, e.g. *The steering mechanism is broken.*

medal, medals
(noun) a small disc of metal given as an award for bravery or as a prize for sport.

medallion, medallions
(noun) a round piece of metal worn as an ornament on a chain round the neck.

medallist, medallists
(noun) a person who has won a medal in sport, e.g. *an Olympic medallist.*

meddle, meddles, meddling, meddled
(verb) to interfere and try to change things without being asked.
meddler (noun) **meddlesome** (adjective)

media
(plural noun) You can refer to the TV, radio and newspapers as the media.
[Latin *medius* = middle]

median, medians (pronounced **mee**-dee-an)
1 (noun) The median of a set of numbers is the middle number when the set is arranged in order.
2 In geometry, a median is a straight line drawn from one of the angles of a triangle to the midpoint of the opposite side.
[Latin *mediare* = to be in the middle]

medical, medicals
1 (adjective) relating to the prevention and treatment of illness and injuries.
2 (noun) a thorough examination of your body by a doctor, e.g. *I went for a medical.*
medically (adverb)
[Latin *medicare* = to heal]

medication, medications
(noun) a substance used to treat illness.

medicine, medicines
1 (noun) the treatment of illness and injuries by doctors and nurses.
2 a substance that you drink or swallow to help cure an illness.
medicinal (adjective)

medieval (pronounced med-dee-**ee**-vul; also spelled **mediaeval)**
(adjective) relating to the period between about AD1100 and AD1500, especially in Europe.
[Latin *medium aevum* = the middle age]

mediocre (pronounced mee-dee-**oh**-ker)
(adjective) of rather poor quality, e.g.*This is mediocre work, Mr Bishop. Do it again.*
mediocrity (noun)

Similar words: so-so, indifferent

meditate, meditates, meditating, meditated
1 (verb) If you meditate on something, you think about it very deeply.
2 If you meditate, you remain in a calm, silent state for a period of time.
meditation (noun)

medium
(adjective) neither large nor small, e.g. *a medium sized jacket.*
[Latin *medium* = middle]

medley, medleys
(noun) a number of different songs or tunes sung or played one after the other with no break.
[Old French *medler* = to mix]

meek, meeker, meekest
(adjective) A meek person is timid and does what other people say.
meekly (adverb) **meekness** (noun)

Similar words: submissive, mild

meet, meets, meeting, met
(verb) e.g. *Fancy meeting you here!... She will meet me off the train... We must meet to discuss this... This machine meets all our needs... I've never met such stupidity before... Her speech met with stony silence.*

Similar words: encounter, come across, bump into

meeting, meetings
(noun) an event in which people discuss things and make decisions.

mega-
(prefix) very great, e.g. *megawatt, megastar.*
[Greek *megas* = huge or powerful]

melancholy
(adjective) sad.

mellow, mellower, mellowest; mellows, mellowing, mellowed
1 (adjective) Mellow light is soft and golden.
2 A mellow sound is smooth and pleasant to listen to, e.g. *the mellow tone of the cello.*
3 (verb) If someone mellows, they become more pleasant or relaxed, e.g. *He has mellowed with age... the mellowing effect of wine.*

melodrama, melodramas
(noun) a story or play in which people's emotions are exaggerated.
[Greek *melos* = song + *drama* = action]
melodramatic (adjective)

melody, melodies
(noun) a tune.
melodic (adjective)
[Greek *melōidia* = singing]

melon, melons
(noun) a large, juicy fruit.

melt, melts, melting, melted
(verb) When something melts, it changes from a solid to a liquid because it has been heated.

Similar words: dissolve, liquefy, thaw

member, members
(noun) one of the people or things belonging to a group etc., e.g. *older members of the family.*
membership (noun)
[Latin *membrum* = limb]

Member of Parliament, Members of Parliament
(noun) a person who has been elected to represent people in a country's parliament.

membrane, membranes
(noun) a very thin piece of skin or tissue which connects or covers plant or animal organs or cells, e.g. *the throat membranes.*

memo, memos
(noun) a note from one person to another within the same organization [short for 'memorandum'].

memorable
(adjective) likely to be remembered because it is special or unusual, e.g. *a memorable evening.*
memorably (adverb)

memorial, memorials
(noun) a structure built to remind people of a famous person or event, e.g. *a war memorial.*

memorize, memorizes, memorizing, memorized
(verb) If you memorize something, you learn it off by heart, e.g. *We have to memorize this poem for homework.*

memory, memories
1 (noun) the ability to remember things.
2 something you remember about the past, e.g. *childhood memories.*
3 A computer's memory is the part in which information is stored.

menace, menaces
(noun) someone or something that is likely to cause serious harm, e.g. *Drunken drivers are a menace on the road.*
menacing (adjective) **menacingly** (adverb)

mend, mends, mending, mended
1 (verb) to repair something that is broken.
2 (phrase) If someone **mends their ways,** they begin to behave better than before.

menial
(adjective) Menial work is boring and tiring and the people who do it have low status.

menstruate, menstruates, menstruating, menstruated
(verb) When a woman menstruates, blood comes from her womb. This normally happens monthly.
menstruation (noun) **menstrual** (adjective)
[Latin *mensis* = month]

mental
(adjective) relating to the mind, e.g. *mental arithmetic... mental illness.*
mentally (adverb)
[Latin *mens* = mind]

mention, mentions, mentioning, mentioned
(verb) If you mention something, you talk about it briefly.

Similar words: bring up, refer to

menu, menus
1 (noun) a list of the food you can eat in a restaurant.
2 a list of different options shown on a computer screen which the user can choose from.

MEP, MEPs
(noun) a person who has been elected to represent people at the European Parliament.
[an abbreviation for 'Member of the European Parliament]

mercenary, mercenaries
1 (noun) a soldier who is paid to fight for a foreign country.
2 (adjective) Someone who is mercenary is mainly interested in acquiring money.
[Latin *merces* = wages]

merchandise
(noun; formal) goods that are sold, e.g. *a display of imported merchandise.*

Similar words: products, wares

merchant, merchants
(noun) a trader who imports and exports goods, e.g. *a textile merchant.*
[Latin *mercari* = to trade]

Similar words: dealer, retailer, salesman, trader, -monger (e.g. fishmonger)

merchant navy
(noun) the shipping and seamen involved in carrying goods for trade.

merciful
(adjective) showing kindness and forgiveness.
mercifully (adverb)

Similar words: kind, humane, lenient, compassionate

merciless
(adjective) showing no kindness or forgiveness.
mercilessly (adverb)

Similar words: pitiless, remorseless, ruthless

mercury
(noun) a silver-coloured metal that is liquid at room temperature. It is used in thermometers.

mercy, mercies
(noun) If you show mercy, you show kindness and forgiveness and do not punish someone as severely as you could.
2 (phrase) If you are **at the mercy of** someone or something, they have complete power over you.

Similar words: compassion, pity, leniency

mere, merest
(adjective) used to emphasize how unimportant or small something is, e.g. *He was a mere boy when he rode his first winner.*
merely (adverb)
[Latin *merus* = pure]

merge, merges, merging, merged
(verb) When two companies merge, they combine together to make a larger company.
merger (noun)

meridian, meridians
(noun) one of the lines of longitude drawn on a map running from the North Pole to the South Pole.

meringue, meringues (pronounced mer-**rang**)
(noun) a type of crisp, sweet cake made with egg whites and sugar.

merit, merits, meriting, merited
1 (noun) If something has merit, it is good or worthwhile.
2 an advantage or good quality, e.g. *Her chief merit is that she can keep a secret.*
3 (informal) an exam grade which is better than a pass, but not as good as a distinction, e.g. *I received a merit for my French.*
4 (verb) If something merits a particular treatment, it deserves that treatment, e.g. *Your success merits a celebration.*

mermaid, mermaids
(noun) In stories, a mermaid is a woman with a fish's tail instead of legs, who lives in the sea.
[Middle English *mere* + *maid* = sea maiden]

merry, merrier, merriest
1 (adjective) happy and cheerful, e.g. *his merry smiling face.*
2 (informal) slightly drunk, e.g. *I got a bit merry.*
merrily (adverb) **merriment** (noun)

mesh, meshes
(noun) threads of wire or plastic twisted together like a net, e.g. *a wire-mesh fence.*

mesmerize, mesmerizes, mesmerizing, mesmerized; also spelled **mesmerise.**
(verb) If you are mesmerized by something, you are so fascinated by it that you cannot think of anything else, e.g. *He stood perfectly still, mesmerized by the sound of the waterfall.*
[after F.A. Mesmer, an Austrian doctor who cured people using hypnosis]

mess, messes, messing, messed
1 (noun) If something is a mess, it is untidy.
2 a room or building in which members of the armed forces relax, e.g. *the officers' mess.*
3 (verb) If you mess about or mess around, you do things without any particular purpose.
4 If you mess something up, you spoil it or do it wrong.
messy (adjective) **messily** (adverb)

message, messages
(noun) a piece of information or a request that you send someone or leave for them.
[Latin *missus* = sent]

messenger, messengers
(noun) someone who carries a message.

Messiah (pronounced miss-**eye**-ah)
1 (noun) For Jews, the Messiah is the king of the Jews who will be sent by God.
2 For Christians, the Messiah is Jesus Christ.
[Hebrew *mashiach* = anointed]

metal, metals
(noun) a chemical element, e.g. iron, steel, copper or lead.
metallic (adjective)
[Latin *metallum* = mine]

In poetry and verse, *metre* is the way we measure a line of verse....

metamorphic
(adjective) Metamorphic rocks are sedimentary rocks that have been changed by heat or pressure.

metamorphosis, metamorphoses (pronounced met-am-**mor**-fuss-iss)
(noun; formal) a total change, e.g. *the metamorphosis of a caterpillar into a butterfly*.
metamorphose (verb)
[Greek *meta-* = change + *morphē* = shape]

metaphor, metaphors
(noun) an imaginative way of describing something by saying that it has the typical qualities of something else, e.g. If you wanted to say that someone is greedy, you might say they are a pig or a gannet.
metaphorical (adjective) **metaphorically** (adverb)
[Greek *metapherein* = to transfer]

meteor, meteors
(noun) a piece of rock etc. that burns brightly when it enters the earth's atmosphere from space.
[Greek *meteōros* = lofty]

meteorite, meteorites
(noun) a piece of rock from space that has landed on earth.

meteorological
(adjective) relating to the weather or weather forecasting.
meteorologist (noun) **meteorology** (noun)

meter, meters
(noun) a device that measures and records something, e.g. *a gas meter*.
[Old English *metan* = to measure]

methane (pronounced **mee**-thane)
(noun) a colourless gas with no smell, produced by decaying vegetable matter.

method, methods
(noun) a way of doing something, e.g. *The axe method is not recommended for cutting hair*.

methodical
(adjective) Someone who is methodical does things carefully and in an organized way.
methodically (adverb)

meths
(noun; informal) methylated spirits.

methylated spirits
(noun) a poisonous mixture of alcohol and chemicals, used for cleaning and as a fuel.

metre, metres
1 (noun) a unit of length. (1m = 100 centimetres)
2 In poetry, metre is the regular and rhythmic arrangement of words and syllables.
[Greek *metron* = a measure]

metric
(adjective) relating to the system of measurement that uses metres, grams and litres.

metrication
(noun) the process of changing from measuring things in imperial units (such as feet, inches, pounds and ounces) to measuring in metric units.

metro
(noun) the underground railway system in some cities, e.g. Newcastle, Paris.

metronome, metronomes
(noun) a device that produces a perfectly regular beat for musicians, so they can play or sing at the right speed.

metropolis, metropolises
(noun) a very large city.
[Greek *mētēr* + *polis* = mother city]

metropolitan
(adjective) relating or belonging to a large, busy city, e.g. *the Metropolitan Police*.

mew, mews, mewing, mewed
(verb) to make the short high-pitched sound that a cat makes.

Mexican, Mexicans
1 (adjective) belonging to Mexico.
2 (noun) someone who comes from Mexico.

mice plural of **mouse**.

micro-
(prefix) very small, e.g. *microscopic*
[Greek *micros* = small]

microbe, microbes
(noun) a very small living thing which you can see only if you use a microscope.
[Greek *mikros* = small + *bios* = life]

microchip, microchips
(noun) a small piece of silicon on which electronic circuits for a computer or calculator are printed.

microcomputer, microcomputers
(noun) a small computer.

microfiche, microfiches (pronounced **my**-kro-feesh)
(noun) a small sheet of film on which a lot of information is stored in very small print. It is put into a machine which magnifies it for reading, e.g. *The catalogue is on microfiche*.

microphone, microphones
(noun) a device used to receive sounds which are then made louder or recorded.

microscope, microscopes
(noun) a piece of equipment which magnifies very small objects so that you can study them.

microscopic
(adjective) very small indeed, e.g. *There was a microscopic trace of blood on the car seat*.
microscopically (adverb)

microwave, microwaves
(noun) a type of oven which cooks food very quickly by short-wave radiation.

mid-
(prefix) used to form words that refer to the middle part of a place or period of time, e.g. *mid-Atlantic... the mid-80s*.

midday
(noun, adjective) 12 o'clock in the middle of the day; noon.

middle, middles
(noun, adjective) e.g. *the middle of the night...*

....We generally expect poetry to have a pleasing pattern of stresses in lines of similar length.

I'm just in the middle of washing up... I bowled him middle stump... Of course, she's a middle child, you know.

middle age
(noun) the period of someone's life when they are between about 40 and 60 years old.
middle-aged (adjective)

middle class, classes
(noun) the people in a society who are not working class or upper class, e.g. managers, doctors, and lawyers.

Middle East
(noun) the area around the eastern end of the Mediterranean Sea and the Persian Gulf.

Middle English
(noun) the English language from about AD100 until about AD1450.

middle-of-the-road
1 (adjective) Middle-of-the-road opinions are moderate.
2 Middle-of-the-road (or M.O.R.) music is light, tuneful and rather old-fashioned in style.

middle school, schools
(noun) In Britain, a middle school is for children aged between about 8 and 12.

middling
(adjective) of average quality or ability.

midge, midges
(noun) a small flying insect which can bite people.

midget, midgets
(noun) a very short person.

midnight
(noun, adjective) 12 o'clock at night.

midpoint, midpoints
(noun) In geometry, the midpoint of a line is exactly halfway along it.

midst
(noun) If you are in the midst of a crowd or an event, you are in the middle of it.

midsummer
(adjective) relating to June, July and August, e.g. *a hot midsummer day in July.*

midway
(adverb) in the middle of a distance or period of time, e.g. *We stopped midway for a drink.*

midwife, midwives
(noun) a nurse who is trained to help women at the birth of a baby.
midwifery (noun)

might
1 (verb) e.g. *I might go if I have time... You might write to thank them.*
2 past tense of **may.**
3 (noun; literary) power or strength, e.g. *They pulled with all their might.*

mighty, mightier, mightiest
(adjective; literary) very powerful or strong, e.g. *The smith, a mighty man is he.*
2 very large and impressive, e.g. *two of Asia's mightiest rivers.*

migraine, migraines (pronounced **mee**-grane)
(noun) a severe headache that makes you feel very ill.
[Latin *hemicrania* = pain in half the head]

migrate, migrates, migrating, migrated
(verb) When birds or animals migrate, they move at a particular season to a different place, usually to breed or to find new feeding grounds, e.g. *Swallows migrate to Africa for the winter.*
migration (noun) **migratory** (adjective)

mike, mikes
(noun; informal) a microphone.

mild, milder, mildest.
1 (adjective) not strong and not damaging, e.g. *a mild detergent.*
2 gentle and kind, e.g. *a mild old gent.*
3 Mild weather is warmer than usual, e.g. *We've had two mild winters.*
4 Mild qualities, emotions or attitudes are not very great or extreme, e.g. *He raised an eyebrow in mild surprise.*
mildly (adverb)

mile, miles
1 (noun) a unit of distance.
(1 mile = 1760 yards = 1.6 kilometres).
2 (phrase) If you are **miles away**, you are daydreaming, e.g. *Sorry, I was miles away.*
[Latin *milia passuum* = a thousand paces]

militant, militants
(adjective) very active in trying to bring about extreme political or social change, e.g. *Militant party members handed out leaflets.*
militantly (adverb) **militancy** (noun)

military
(adjective) related to the army, navy or air force of a country, e.g. *military leaders.*
(noun) The military means the armed forces.

milk, milks, milking, milked
1 (noun) the white liquid produced by female cows, goats, etc. to feed their young.
milky (adjective)
2 (verb) to obtain milk from a cow, goat, etc.

milk tooth, teeth
(noun) Your milk teeth are your first teeth, which fall out and are replaced by the permanent set.

mill, mills
1 (noun) a building where grain is crushed to make flour.
2 a factory for making materials, e.g. *a steel mill... a woollen mill... a cotton mill.*
3 a small device for grinding coffee or spices into powder, e.g. *a pepper mill.*
miller (noun)

millennium, millennia or millenniums
(noun; formal) a period of 1000 years.
millennial (adjective)

milli-
(prefix) Milli- is added to some measurement words to form words about measurements a thousand times smaller, e.g. a millimetre is 1000 times smaller than a metre.
[Latin *mille* = thousand]

People's forenames and surnames always begin with capital letters, e.g. John Brown, Michael Stand.

milligram, milligrams
(noun) a unit of weight. (1000mg = 1 gram)

millilitre, millilitres
(noun) a unit of liquid volume. (1000ml = 1 litre)

millimetre, millimetres
(noun) a unit of length. (10mm = 1 centimetre;
1000mm = 1 metre)

million, millions
the number 1,000,000.
millionth (adjective)

millionaire, millionaires
(noun) a very rich person who has property
worth millions of pounds or dollars.

mime, mimes, miming, mimed
(verb) to use movements and gestures to express
something without using speech.
[Greek *mimos* = imitator]

mimic, mimics, mimicking, mimicked
(verb) If you mimic someone's actions or voice,
you imitate them in an amusing way.
mimicry (noun)

mince, minces, mincing, minced
1 (verb) to chop meat etc. into very small pieces
in a mincer.
2 (phrase) If you **do not mince your words**, you
tell someone something unpleasant in a very
forceful and direct way.
mincer (noun)

mincemeat
(noun) a sticky mixture of pieces of dried fruit,
apples and suet used to make mince pies.

mind, minds, minding, minded
1 (noun) Your mind is your ability to think, with
all the thoughts you have and your memory.
2 (phrase) If something is **on your mind**, you
are worrying about it, e.g. *What's on your mind?*
3 (verb) If you do not mind something, you are
not annoyed by it or bothered about it.
4 If you say that you wouldn't mind something,
you mean that you would quite like it, e.g. *I
wouldn't mind a holiday myself.*
5 If you mind a child or mind something for
someone, you look after it for a while, e.g. *I'll
mind your suitcase while you get the tickets.*

mindless
1 (adjective) Mindless actions are stupid and
thoughtless, e.g. *mindless soccer vandalism.*
2 A mindless job or activity is simple, repetitive
and boring.

mine, mines, mining, mined
1 (pronoun) e.g. *That book is mine.*
2 (noun) a series of holes or tunnels in the ground
dug to extract coal or other minerals, e.g. *a gold
mine.*
3 (verb) To mine coal or other minerals means to
obtain them from under the ground.
4 (noun) a bomb hidden in the ground or
underwater.
miner (noun) **mining** (noun)

minefield, minefields
(noun) an area of land or water where mines
have been hidden.

mineral, minerals
(noun) a substance, e.g. tin, salt, uranium or coal,
that is formed naturally in rocks and in the
earth, e.g. *rich mineral deposits.*

mineral water
(noun) water which comes from a natural spring.

minestrone (pronounced min-nes-**strone**-ee)
(noun) soup made from meat stock containing
small pieces of vegetable and pasta.
[Italian *minestrare* = to serve]

mingle, mingles, mingling, mingled
(verb) If things mingle, they become mixed
together, e.g. *The spy mingled with the crowd.*

mini-
(prefix) smaller or less important, e.g. *the
Chancellor's mini-budget.*

miniature, miniatures (pronounced
min-nit-cher)
(adjective) A miniature thing is a tiny copy of
something much larger.

minibus, minibuses
(noun) a van with seats, used as a small bus.

minimal
(adjective) very small, e.g. *Their allies offered
only minimal aid.*
minimally (adverb)

minimize, minimizes, minimizing, minimized
1 (verb) to reduce something to the smallest
amount possible, e.g. *Crop rotation helps to
minimize the risk of disease.*
2 to make something seem smaller or less
important than it really is, e.g. *He minimized the
importance of their contribution.*

minimum
(noun) the smallest amount that is possible, e.g.
Jog for a minimum of ten minutes.

miniskirt, miniskirts
(noun) a very short skirt.

minister, ministers
1 (noun) a person who is in charge of a
government department, e.g. *the Minister of
Health.*
2 A minister in a Protestant church is a member
of the clergy.
ministerial adjective)
[Latin *minister* = servant]

ministry, ministries
1 (noun) a government department that deals
with a particular area of work, e.g. *the Ministry
of Education.*
2 Members of the clergy can be referred to as the
ministry, e.g. *Her son is in the ministry.*

minnow, minnows
(noun) a very small freshwater fish.

minor, minors
1 (adjective) not as important or serious as other
things, e.g. *This is only a minor problem.*
2 A minor key is one of the keys in which most
European music is written.
3 (noun; formal) a young person under the age of
18, e.g. *Alcohol should not be served to minors.*
[Latin *minor* = less or smaller]

Let's not mince words. Take the Survival Test (page v) and minimize the hassle.

minority, minorities
1 (noun) The minority of people or things in a group is a number of them forming less than half of the whole group, e.g. *Only a minority were against the idea.*
2 a group of people of a race or religion living where most people are of a different race or religion, e.g. *Asian people form a large ethnic minority in many northern towns.*

minstrel, minstrels
(noun) a medieval singer and entertainer.

mint, mints, minting, minted
1 (noun) a herb used in cooking.
2 a peppermint flavoured sweet.
3 the place where the coins of a country are made.
4 (verb) When coins or medals are minted, they are made.
5 (adjective) If something is in mint condition, it is in very good condition, like new.
[senses 3-5: Old English *mynet* = coin]

minus
1 subtract or take away, e.g. *Ten minus six equals four* $[10 - 6 = 4]$.
2 (adjective) used for temperatures below 0°C or 0°F, e.g. *It was minus 50 at the Pole* $[-50°F]$

minute, minutes (pronounced **min**-nit)
1 (noun) a unit of time. (1 minute = 60 seconds)
2 The minutes of a meeting are the written records of what was said and decided.

minute (pronounced my-**newt**)
(adjective) extremely small, e.g. *The water contained minute amounts of fluoride.*
minutely (adverb)

miracle, miracles
1 (noun) a wonderful and surprising event, believed to have been caused by God.
2 a very surprising and fortunate event, e.g. *With your brain, it's a miracle you've passed!*
miraculous (adjective) **miraculously** (adverb)
[Latin *mirari* = to wonder at]

mirror, mirrors
(noun) a piece of glass which reflects light and in which you can see your reflection.

mirth
(noun; literary) great amusement and laughter.

misadventure, misadventures
(noun; formal) an unfortunate incident, e.g. *The verdict was death by misadventure.*

misbehave, misbehaves, misbehaving, misbehaved
(verb) to be naughty or behave badly.
misbehaviour (noun)

miscalculate, miscalculates, miscalculating, miscalculated
(verb) to make a wrong judgement or calculation, e.g. *He had miscalculated the time it would take if he didn't read the Survival Guide on page v.*
miscalculation (noun)

miscarriage
(noun) If a women has a miscarriage, she gives birth to a baby before it is properly formed, and it dies.

miscellaneous
(adjective) mixed or assorted, e.g. *She left miscellaneous jobs for him to do.*
miscellaneously (adverb)
[Latin *miscellus* = mixed]

mischief
(noun) eagerness to have fun by teasing people or playing tricks.
mischievous (adjective) [pronounced **mis**-chev-us]

misconduct
(noun) bad or unacceptable behaviour by a professional person, e.g. *He was struck off the medical register for misconduct.*

miser, misers
(noun) a person who enjoys saving money but hates spending it, e.g. *He's such a miser, he refuses to heat the house unless it snows.*
miserly (adjective)
[Latin *miser* = wretched]

miserable
1 (adjective) very unhappy.
2 If a place or a situation is miserable, it makes you feel unhappy, e.g. *a miserable flat.*
miserably (adverb)

Similar words: gloomy, wretched

misery, miseries
(noun) great unhappiness.

misfit, misfits
(noun) a person who is not accepted by other people because of being rather strange or eccentric. e.g. *She felt a misfit in her first term at the school.*

misfortune, misfortunes
(noun) an unpleasant occurrence that is bad luck, e.g. *I had the misfortune to lose my passport.*

misguided
(adjective) A misguided opinion or action is wrong because it is based on a misunderstanding or bad information.

mishap, mishaps (pronounced **miss**-hap)
(noun) an unfortunate but not very serious accident.

misinform, misinforms, misinforming, misinformed
(verb) If you are misinformed, you are given wrong or inaccurate information.
misinformation (noun)

misjudge, misjudges, misjudging, misjudged
(verb) If you misjudge someone or something, you form the wrong opinion about them.
misjudgement (noun)

mislay, mislays, mislaying, mislaid
(verb) to lose something because you have forgotten where you put it.

mislead, misleads, misleading, misled
(verb) to make someone believe something which is not true, e.g. *She misled me into thinking that Mrs Scarlett did it when it was Rev. Green.*
misleading (adjective) **misleadingly** (adverb)

Homographs are spelled the same but sound different: minute refuse sow entrance.

misprint, misprints
(noun) a mistake in somethnig that has been pronted.

misquote, misquotes, misquoting, misquoted
(verb) To misquote someone means to repeat incorrectly something they have said or written.

miss, misses, missing, missed
1 (verb) e.g. *He doesn't miss much... I miss my home... She missed her train... He missed the goal by an inch.*
2 Miss is used before the name of an unmarried woman or girl as a form of address, e.g. *Miss Smith is the new French teacher.*

missile, missiles
(noun) a weapon that moves long distances through the air and explodes when it reaches its target; also any object thrown as a weapon.

mission, missions
(noun) an important task, e.g. *Your mission is to seek out space aliens and blast them to bits.*
[Latin *mittere* = to send]

missionary, missionaries
(noun) a Christian who has been sent to a foreign country to work for the Church.

misspell, misspells, misspelling, misspelt or misspelled
(verb) If you misspell a word, you spell it wrongly.

misspend, misspends, misspending, misspent
(verb) If someone misspends time or money, they waste it or do not use it wisely, e.g. *My misspent youth was spent playing pool.*

mist, mists
(noun) Mist consists of a large number of tiny drops of water in the air, which make it hard to see things clearly.

mistake, mistakes, mistaking, mistook, mistaken
1 (noun) an action or opinion that is wrong or is not what you intended.
2 (verb) If you mistake someone or something for another person or thing, you wrongly think that they are the other person or thing, e.g. *I mistook your wife for your daughter.*
mistaken (adjective) **mistakenly** (adverb)
[Old Norse *mistaka* = to take by mistake]

Similar words: (noun) error, blunder, misunderstanding, slip

mistletoe (pronounced **mis**-sel-toe)
(noun) a plant with white berries which grows on trees. It is used as a Christmas decoration.

mistook past tense of **mistake**.

mistreat, mistreats, mistreating, mistreated
(verb) To mistreat a person or animal means to treat them badly and make them suffer.

mistress, mistresses
1 (noun) A schoolmistress is a female teacher.
2 (old fashioned) A servant's mistress is the woman who is the servant's employer.

mistrust, mistrusts, mistrusting, mistrusted
1 (verb) If you mistrust someone, you do not feel that you can trust them.
2 (noun) a feeling that you don't trust someebody.

misty, mistier, mistiest
(adjective) covered with mist.

misunderstand, misunderstands, misunderstanding, misunderstood
(verb) If you misunderstand someone, you do not properly understand what they say or do, e.g. *He misunderstood my meaning.*

misunderstanding, misunderstandings
(noun) If two people have a misunderstanding, they have a slight quarrel or disagreement.

misuse, misuses, misusing, misused
(verb) to use something wrongly or dishonestly, e.g. *The dictator misused his power by putting lots of his country's money in his Swiss bank acccount.*

mite, mites
1 (noun; old-fashioned) a very small amount, e.g. *Anyone with a mite of common sense would have realized that!*
2 a very tiny creature that lives in animal fur.
3 a small child, especially one you feel sorry for, e.g. *poor little mite.*

mitten, mittens
(noun) a glove with one section for the thumb and another section for the rest of your fingers together; or a glove without fingers.

mix, mixes, mixing, mixed
(verb) e.g. *Mix me a milk shake, please.*

Similar words: blend, mingle, merge

mixed up
1 (adjective) confused.
2 If you are mixed up in a crime or a scandal, you are involved in it.

mixer, mixers
(noun) a machine used for mixing things together, e.g. *a food mixer.*

mixture, mixtures
(noun) several different things together.

Similar words: blend, combination, compound

mix-up, mix-ups
(noun) a mistake in something that was planned, e.g. *There has been a mix-up with the bookings.*

mnemonic, mnemonics (pronounced nim-on-nik)
(noun) a word, phrase or rhyme that helps you remember things like facts and spelling rules, e.g. *'Richard of York gave battle in vain'* for the colours of the rainbow [red, orange, yellow, green, blue, indigo, violet].
[Greek *mnēmōn* = mindful]

moan, moans, moaning, moaned
1 (verb) to make a low, miserable sound because you are in pain or suffering.
2 (informal) to complain.

moat, moats
(noun) a wide, water-filled ditch around a castle.

What are the missing silent letters in each of these: .night .nome thum. .nemonic ha.f .nit?

mob, mobs, mobbing, mobbed
1 (noun) a large, disorganized crowd of people, e.g. *A violent mob attacked the embassy.*
2 (verb) If a lot of people mob someone, they crowd around the person in a disorderly way, e.g. *The pop star was mobbed by fans.*
[Latin *mobile vulgus* = the fickle public]

mobile, mobiles
1 (adjective) able to move or be moved freely and easily, e.g. *Antelopes are fully mobile as soon as they are born.*
2 able to travel or move to another place, e.g. *She's mobile now she's got her scooter.*
3 (noun) a decoration consisting of several small objects which hang from threads and move around when a breeze blows.
mobility (noun) **mobilize** (verb)

mock, mocks, mocking, mocked
1 (verb) If you mock someone, you say something scornful or imitate their foolish behaviour.
2 (adjective) not genuine, e.g. *mock Tudor houses.*
3 A mock examination or a 'mock' is one that you do as a practice before the real examination.
mocking (adjective) **mockingly** (adverb)

Similar words: (verb) ridicule, jeer, sneer, make fun of, scoff, taunt

mockery
1 (noun) the expression of scorn for someone or ridicule of their foolish behaviour.
2 (phrase) If something **makes a mockery of** something else, it makes it appear foolish and worthless, e.g. *The judge's decision made a mockery of justice.*

Similar words: (sense 1) derision, jeering

mock-up, mock-ups
(noun) A mock-up of a building or a machine is a model of it for test or display.

mode, modes
(noun) A mode of life or behaviour is a particular way of living or behaving.

model, models, modelling, modelled
1 (noun, adjective) a miniature version of something real, e.g. *a model railway.*
2 (verb) If you model yourself on someone, you copy their behaviour because you admire them.
3 (noun) A particular model of a machine is a type or version of it, e.g. *the latest model.*
4 a person who poses for a painter or a photographer, e.g. *a fashion model.*
5 (verb) To model clothes means to display them by wearing them.
6 To model shapes or figures means to make them out of clay or wood.

modem, modems (pronounced moe-dem)
(noun) a piece of equipment that links a computer to the telephone system so that data can be transferred from one machine to another via the telephone line.
[from the first letters of 'modulator' and 'demodulator']

moderate, moderates, moderating, moderated
1 (adjective) not extreme.
2 A moderate amount of something is neither large nor small.
3 (verb) If you moderate something or if it moderates, it becomes less extreme or violent, e.g. *The wind moderated.*
4 When teachers moderate, they compare the work of pupils from different classes or schools to decide on a standard for marking.
moderately (adverb) **moderation** (noun)
[Latin *moderari* = to restrain]

moderation
1 (phrase) If you smoke or drink **in moderation**, you do not smoke or drink too much.
2 (noun) the comparing of the exam work of pupils from different classes or schools to decide on a standard for marking.

modern
1 (adjective) relating to the present time, e.g. *the social problems of modern society.*
2 new and involving the latest ideas and equipment, e.g. *modern technology.*
[Latin *modo* = just recently]

Similar words: (sense 1) contemporary, present-day (sense 2) up-to-date

modernize, modernizes, modernizing, modernized; also spelled modernise
(verb) to introduce new methods or equipment.

modest
(adjective) Someone who is modest does not boast about their abilities or possessions.
modestly (adverb) **modesty** (noun)

modify, modifies, modifying, modified
(verb) If you modify something, you change it slightly to improve it.
modification (noun)

module, modules
1 (noun) one of the parts which when put together form a whole unit or object, e.g. *Your course is made up of modules.*
2 a part of a spacecraft, e.g. *the lunar module.*
modular (adjective)

mohair
(noun) very soft wool from angora goats.

moist, moister, moistest
(adjective) slightly wet.
moisten (verb)

moisture
(noun) tiny drops of water.

moisturizer, moisturizers; also spelled moisturiser
(noun) a cream that can be used on dry skin to soften it and restore moisture.

molar, molars
(noun) Your molars are the large teeth at the back of your mouth.

mole, moles
1 (noun) a dark, slightly raised spot on your skin.
2 a small burrowing animal with black fur.
3 (informal) a member of an organization who is working as a spy for a rival organization.

A computer operator needs these words: modem terminal VDU backup cursor database spreadsheet.

molecule, molecules
(noun) the smallest amount of a substance that can exist independently.
molecular (adjective)

molehill, molehills
1 (noun) a small pile of earth left by a mole that has been digging underground.
2 (phrase) If someone is **making a mountain out of a molehill**, they are exaggerating a problem.

molest, molests, molesting, molested
1 (verb) To molest a child means to touch the child in a sexual way. This is illegal.
2 If someone molests you, they annoy you and prevent you from doing something, especially by using physical violence.
molester (noun)

mollusc, molluscs
(noun) an animal with a soft body and no backbone, e.g. snail, slug.
[Latin *mollis* = soft]

mollycoddle, mollycoddles, mollycoddling, mollycoddled
(verb) to do too much to protect someone and make them comfortable, e.g. *Rupert was mollycoddled as a child, and look what a wimp he is now.*

molten
(adjective) Molten rock or metal has been heated to a very high temperature and has become a sticky liquid.

moment, moments
1 (noun) a very short period of time, e.g. *She hesitated for a moment.*
2 (phrase) **At the moment** means now.
momentary (adjective) **momentarily** (adverb)

Similar words: minute, second, instant

momentous
(adjective; formal) very important, often because of its future effect, e.g. *The coronation was a momentous occasion.*

momerath, momeraths
(noun) a dark-coloured, furry mammal related to the mole, e.g. *... and the momeraths outgrabe.*

monarch, monarchs (pronounced **mon**-nark)
(noun) a queen, king or other royal person who reigns over a country.
monarchy (noun)
[Greek *mono-* = one + *arch* = chief]

monastery, monasteries
(noun) a building in which monks live.
monastic (adjective)
[Greek *monazein* = to live alone]

Monday, Mondays
(noun) the day between Sunday and Tuesday.
[Old English *monandæg* = moon's day]

money
(noun) the coins or banknotes that you use to buy something.
monetary (adjective)

Similar words: cash, capital, currency

mongrel, mongrels
(noun) a dog with parents of different breeds.

monitor, monitors, monitoring, monitored
1 (verb) If you monitor something, you regularly check its condition and progress, e.g. *His heartbeat is being monitored.*
2 (noun) the visual display unit of a computer etc.
3 a school pupil chosen to do special duties by the teacher.
[Latin *monere* = to advise]

monk, monks
(noun) a member of a male religious community.

monkey, monkeys
(noun) an animal which has a long tail and climbs trees.

mono
(adjective) used to describe a record or sound system in which the sound is directed through one speaker only. (opposite: **stereo**)

mono-
(prefix) one, e.g. *monosyllable... monopoly.*
[Greek *monos* = single]

monopolize, monopolizes, monopolizing, monopolized; also spelled **monopolise**
(verb) To monopolize something means to control it completely and prevent other people from having a share in it, e.g. *Linda Snell monopolized the conversation.*

monopoly, monopolies
(noun) control of most of an industry by one or two large firms.
[Greek *mono-* = one + *polein* = to sell]

monorail, monorails
(noun) a railway running on a single rail usually raised above ground level.

monosyllable, monosyllables
(noun) If someone speaks in monosyllables, they use only very short words such as 'yes' and 'no'.
monosyllabic (adjective)

monotonous
(adjective) having a regular pattern which is very dull and boring, e.g. *monotonous chores.*
monotony (noun) **monotonously** (adverb)

monsoon, monsoons
(noun) In south-east Asia, the monsoon is the season of very heavy rain which takes its name from the wind which blows at the time.

monster, monsters
1 (noun) a large, imaginary creature that looks very frightening.
2 (adjective) extremely large, e.g. *a monster computer.*
3 (noun) If you call someone a monster, you mean they are cruel, frightening or evil.
[Latin *monstrum* = omen or warning]

monstrosity, monstrosities
(noun) Something that is described as a monstrosity is large and extremely ugly, e.g. *That new shopping precinct is a monstrosity.*

monstrous
(adjective) extremely shocking or unfair, e.g. *The judge's decision was absolutely monstrous...*

The love of money is the root of all evil. (The Bible)
Lack of money is the root of all evil. (George Bernard Shaw)

with monstrous head and sickening cry and ears like errant wings...
monstrously (adverb)

month, months
(noun) one of the 12 periods that a year is divided into.
monthly (adjective)

monument, monuments
(noun) a large stone structure built to remind people of a famous person or event, e.g. *a monument to Queen Victoria.*
[Latin *monere* = to remind]

mooch, mooches, mooching, mooched
(verb; informal) If you mooch about, you walk about slowly with no particular purpose.

mood, moods
1 (noun) the way you are feeling at a particular time, e.g. *I'm in a really good mood.*
2 If you are in a mood, you are angry, sulking or impatient, e.g. *It's no good trying to persuade him. He's in one of his moods.*

moody, moodier, moodiest
(adjective) Someone who is moody often changes their mood for no apparent reason.
moodily (adverb)

Similar words: temperamental

moon, moons
1 (noun) a natural satellite of the earth or other planet, e.g. *Mars has two moons.*
2 (phrase; informal) If you are **over the moon** about something, you are very pleased about it.
3 Something that happens **once in a blue moon** happens very rarely.

moonlight
(noun) the light that comes from the moon.
moonlit (adjective)

moor, moors, mooring, moored
1 (noun) a high area of open and uncultivated land.
2 (verb) If a boat is moored, it is attached to the land or a buoy with a rope.
moorland (noun)

moorhen, moorhens
(noun) a dark-coloured bird with a red bill found in ponds, lakes and canals.
[Old English *mere* + *henn* = lake-hen]

mooring, moorings
(noun) a place where a boat can be tied.

moot, moots, mooting, mooted
(verb; formal) When something is mooted, it is suggested for discussion, e.g. *A holiday in France had been mooted earlier.* [not to be confused with **muted** which means 'made quieter']

mop, mops, mopping, mopped
1 (noun) an implement with a long handle and a soft, shaggy head, for cleaning floors.
2 (verb) to clean with a mop.
3 (noun) A mop of hair is a large amount of loose or untidy hair.

mop up
(phrasal verb) to deal with the remaining parts of a task.

mope, mopes, moping, moped
(verb) to feel miserable and not interested in anything.

moped, mopeds (pronounced **moe**-ped)
(noun) a type of small motorcycle.
[from the first letters of *motor* and *pedal*]

moral, morals
1 (plural noun) Morals are values based on beliefs about the correct way to behave, e.g. *He had no morals at all, judging by the way he cheated the old lady.*
2 (adjective) concerned with whether behaviour is acceptable, e.g. *moral standards.*
3 (noun) The moral of a story is the lesson it teaches about behaviour, e.g. *The moral was clear: never marry for money.*
4 (phrase) If you give **moral support** to someone, you encourage them in what they are doing.
morality (noun) **morally** (adverb)
[Latin *moralis* = relating to customs]

morale (pronounced mor-**rahl**)
(noun) the amount of confidence and optimism that you have, e.g. *The morale of the team was low after recent defeats.*

morbid
(adjective) having too great an interest in unpleasant things, especially death.
morbidly (adverb)
[Latin *morbus* = illness]

more
(adjective, noun, adverb) e.g. *I've got more chips than you... I've got more than you... I liked the second book more than the first... I was more starving than ever.*

morgue, morgues (pronounced **morg**)
(noun) a building where dead bodies are kept before being buried or cremated.

morning, mornings
(noun) the early part of the day.

Moroccan, Moroccans (pronounced mor-**rok**-an)
1 (adjective) belonging to Morocco.
2 (noun) someone who comes from Morocco.

moron, morons
(noun; informal) a stupid person.
moronic (adjective)
[Greek *mōros* meaning foolish]

morose
(adjective) miserable and bad-tempered.
morosely (adverb)

Morse code
(noun) a code used for sending messages in which each letter is represented by a series of dots and dashes, e.g. S.O.S. = $\cdots - - - \cdots$
[named after American inventor, Samuel Morse]

mortal, mortals
1 (adjective) unable to live forever, e.g. *All men think all men mortal, but themselves.*
2 (noun) You can refer to an ordinary person as a mortal, e.g. *I'm only a mere mortal.*

No English word rhymes with month.

3 (adjective) A mortal wound is one that results in death.
[Latin *mors* = death]

mortar, mortars
1 (noun) a short cannon which fires missiles high into the air for a short distance.
2 a mixture of sand, water and cement used to hold bricks firmly together.

mortgage, mortgages (pronounced **mor**-gij)
(noun) a loan which you get from a bank or a building society to buy a house.
[Old French *mort* = death + *gage* = security]

mortuary, mortuaries
(noun) a special room in a hospital where dead bodies are kept before being buried or cremated.

mosaic, mosaics (pronounced moe-**zay**-yik)
(noun) a design made of small coloured stones or pieces of coloured glass set into concrete etc.

Moslem another spelling of **Muslim**.

mosque, mosques (pronounced **mosk**)
(noun) a building where Muslims go to worship.
[Arabic *masjid* = temple]

mosquito, mosquitoes or **mosquitos** (pronounced moss-**kee**-toe)
(noun) a small insect which bites people to suck their blood. Mosquitoes spread disease.
[Spanish *mosquito* = little fly]

moss, mosses
(noun) a soft, low-growing, green plant which grows on damp soil, wood or stone.
mossy (adjective)

most
1 (adjective, noun, adverb) e.g. *Most of us enjoyed the show... That was the most he would say... the most important reason.*
2 (phrase) You say **at most** or **at the most** when stating the maximum number that is likely, e.g. *There will only be 10 people here at the most.*
3 If you **make the most of something**, you get the maximum use or advantage from it, e.g. *Make the most of your talents.*

mostly
(adverb) used to show that a statement is generally true, e.g. *The men at the party were mostly fairly young.*

motel, motels
(noun) a hotel providing sleeping accommodation for people in the middle of a car journey.
[from *motor* + *hotel*]

moth, moths
(noun) an insect like a butterfly which usually flies at night.

moth-eaten
(adjective) Moth-eaten clothes look old and ragged, with holes in them.

mother, mothers
(noun) Your mother is the woman who gave birth to you.
motherly (adjective) **motherhood** (noun)

mother-in-law, mothers-in-law
(noun) Someone's mother-in-law is the mother of their husband or wife.

motion, motions, motioning, motioned
1 (noun) movement, e.g. *the motion of the sea... he made stabbing motions with his spear.*
2 A motion at a meeting is a proposal which people discuss and vote on.
3 (verb) If you motion to someone, you make a movement with your hand to show them what they should do, e.g. *The teacher motioned us to fall into line.*
4 (phrase) If you **go through the motions**, you say or do something that is expected of you without being very sincere or enthusiastic.
[Latin *motio* = moving]

motionless
(adjective) still; not moving at all.

motivate, motivates, motivating, motivated
(verb) If you motivate someone, you make them feel determined to do something, e.g. *Taylor tried hard to motivate his team.*
motivated (adjective) **motivation** (noun)

motive, motives
(noun) a reason for doing something, e.g. *The detective discovered the motive for the crime.*

motor, motors
1 (noun) the part of a vehicle or machine that produces movement so that it can work.
2 (adjective) relating to vehicles with a petrol or diesel engine, e.g. *the motor industry... a motor mechanic.*
[Latin *motor* = mover]

motorcycle, motorcycles
(noun) a two-wheeled vehicle with an engine.

motorist, motorists
(noun) a person who drives a car.

motorway, motorways
(noun) a wide road for fast travel.

mottled
(adjective) covered with patches of different colours, e.g. *a mottled camouflage jacket.*

motto, mottoes or **mottos**
(noun) a short sentence or phrase that expresses a rule for good or sensible behaviour, e.g. *'Be prepared'* is the Scouts' motto.
[Latin *mutum* = utterance]

mould, moulds, moulding, moulded
1 (verb) to influence and change someone or something so they develop in a particular way.
2 to make something into a particular shape, e.g. *clay moulded into pots.*
3 (noun) a container used to shape something, e.g. *a jelly mould.*
4 a soft grey or green substance that can form on old food or damp walls.
mouldy (adjective)

moult, moults, moulting, moulted
(verb) When an animal or bird moults, it loses its hair or feathers to make way for new growth.

mound, mounds
1 (noun) a small man-made hill.
2 a large, untidy pile, e.g. *a mound of dirty washing.*

mount, mounts, mounting, mounted
1 (verb) If something is mounting, it is

What's white and yellow with greasy wings? A bread and butterfly.

increasing, e.g. *The temperature mounted rapidly.*
2 If you mount a horse, you climb on its back.
3 If you mount an object in a particular place, you fix it there to display it.
4 part of the name of a mountain, e.g. *Mount Everest.*

mountain, mountains
1 (noun) a very high piece of land.
2 a large amount of something, often something which there is too much of, e.g. *the European butter mountain.*
mountainous (adjective)

mountaineer, mountaineers
(noun) a person who climbs mountains.
mountaineering (noun)

mourn, mourns, mourning, mourned
(verb) If you mourn for someone who has died, you are very sad and think about them a lot.
mourner (noun)

mournful
(adjective) very sad.
mournfully (adverb)

mourning
(noun) If someone is in mourning, they wear special black clothes or behave in a special way because a member of their family has died.

mouse, mice
1 (noun) a small rodent with a long tail.
2 a small device moved by hand to control the position of the cursor on a computer screen.

mousse, mousses (pronounced **moose**)
(noun) a light, fluffy food made from whipped eggs and cream.
[French *mousse* = froth]

moustache, moustaches (pronounced mus-**stash**)
(noun) hair growing on a man's upper lip.
[Greek *mustax* = upper lip]

mousy
(adjective) Mousy hair is a dull, light brown colour.

mouth, mouths, mouthing, mouthed
1 (noun) e.g. *Don't talk with your mouth full.*
2 The mouth of a cave or a hole is the entrance to it.
3 The mouth of a river is the place where it flows into the sea.
4 (verb; pronounced **mou**-the) If you mouth something, you form words with your lips without making any sound.
mouthful (noun)

mouth-watering
(adjective) looking or smelling delicious.

movable or **moveable**
(adjective) Something that is movable can be moved from one place to another.

move, moves, moving, moved
1 (verb) e.g. *Please move your car, sir... We are moving house today.*
2 (noun) e.g. *Watch every move he makes...*

Accepting that job was a good move... It's my move first in this game.
3 (phrase) If you are **on the move**, you are going from one place to another.
4 (verb) If something moves you, it makes you feel deep emotion, e.g. *The sight of the tiny coffin moved us to tears.*
5 If you move a motion at a meeting, you propose something so that a vote can be taken.

Similar words: (verb: sense 1) budge, shift, stir

movement, movements
1 (noun) changing position or going from one place to another.
2 (plural noun; formal) Your movements are everything you do during a period of time, e.g.*Would you please describe your movements on the night of the 26th January, sir.*
3 (noun) a group of people who share the same beliefs or aims, e.g. *the women's movement.*

moving
(adjective) Something that is moving causes you to feel deep sadness or emotion.

mow, mows, mowing, mowed, mown
1 (verb) to cut grass with a lawnmower.
2 e.g. *Ten people in a bus queue were today mowed down by a runaway lorry.*

mower, mowers
(noun) a machine for cutting grass.

MP, MPs
(noun) a person who has been elected to represent people in a country's parliament. [an abbreviation for 'Member of Parliament']

Mr (pronounced **miss**-ter)
Mr is used before a man's name. [short for 'mister']

Mrs (pronounced **miss**-iz)
Mrs is used before the name of a married woman. [short for 'mistress']

Ms (pronounced **miz**)
Ms can be used before a woman's name when you do not know or do not wish to indicate whether she is married.

much
(adjective, adverb), e.g. *I feel much more confident... It doesn't happen much... It is very much the same... How much string do you need?*

muck, mucks, mucking, mucked
1 (noun; informal) dirt or some other unpleasant substance.
2 manure.
3 (verb; informal) If you muck about, you behave stupidly and waste time.
4 To muck out stables etc. means to clean them.
mucky (adjective)
[Old Norse *myki* = dung]

mud
(noun) wet, sticky earth.
muddy (adjective)

muddle, muddles, muddling, muddled
1 (verb) If you muddle things, you mix them up.
2 If you muddle someone, you confuse them.

Etymology. Can you find out how these words are connected? dentist   indent   dandelion

3 (noun) If things or people are in a muddle, they are confused.
muddled (adjective)
[Dutch *moddelen* = to make muddy]

Similar words: (verb: sense 1) jumble, confuse, mix up

mudguard, mudguards
(noun) the parts on a bike above the tyres which prevent mud from splashing up onto the rider.

muesli (pronounced **myooz**-lee)
(noun) a mixture of chopped nuts, cereal flakes and dried fruit.

muffin, muffins
(noun) a small, round bread bun.

muffle, muffles, muffling, muffled
(verb) If something muffles a sound, it makes it quieter and difficult to hear, e.g. *The snow muffled the sound of our footsteps.*
[Old French *emmouflé* = wrapped up]

mug, mugs, mugging, mugged
1 (noun) a large, deep cup with straight sides.
2 (verb; informal) If someone mugs you, they attack you to steal your money.
mugging (noun) **mugger** (noun)
3 (noun; informal) Someone who is described as a mug is stupid and easily deceived.

muggy, muggier, muggiest
(adjective) Muggy weather is unpleasantly warm and damp.

mule, mules
(noun) the offspring of a female horse and a male donkey.

multi-
(prefix) many, e.g. *a multi-storey car park... a multi-millionaire... a multi-coloured coat... a multi-purpose building.*
[Latin *multus* = much or many]

multiple, multiples
1 (adjective) involving many different things, e.g. *There was a multiple pile-up in thick fog on the M1 today involving cars and lorries.*
2 (noun) The multiples of a number are other numbers that it will divide into exactly, e.g. 6, 9, and 12 are multiples of 3.

multiple-choice
(adjective) In a multiple-choice test, you have to choose the right answer from a list of several possible answers.

multiply, multiplies, multiplying, multiplied
1 (verb) When something multiplies, it increases greatly in number, e.g. *The silkworms multiplied.*
2 Multiplying is a quick way of adding the same number several times, e.g. $4 \times 3 = 4 + 4 + 4$.
[Latin *multus* = many + *plicare* = to fold]

multitude, multitudes
(noun; formal) a very large number of people or things.

mum, mums
1 (noun; informal) mother.
2 (phrase) If you **keep mum** about something, you keep it secret.

mumble, mumbles, mumbling, mumbled
(verb) to speak very quietly and indistinctly.

mummy, mummies
1 (noun; informal, especially by children) mother.
2 a dead body preserved long ago by being rubbed with special oils and wrapped in cloth.
mummified (adjective)
[sense 2: Persian *mum* = wax]

mumps
(noun) a disease that causes painful swelling in the glands of the neck.

munch, munches, munching, munched
(verb) to chew something steadily and thoroughly.

mural, murals
(noun) a picture painted on a wall.
[Latin *murus* = wall]

murder, murders, murdering, murdered
(verb) to kill someone deliberately and unlawfully.
murderer (noun) **murderess** (noun)

murderous
1 (adjective) likely to murder someone, e.g. *a band of murderous pirates.*
2 (informal) very dangerous or difficult, e.g. *a murderous road.*

murky, murkier, murkiest
(adjective) dark or dirty and unpleasant, e.g. *We looked out into the murky streets.*
murk (noun)
[Old Norse *myrkr* = darkness]

murmur, murmurs, murmuring, murmured
1 (verb) to say something very softly.
2 (noun) a continuous, quiet, indistinct sound, e.g. *the murmur of waves on a beach.*

Similar words: (verb) mumble, mutter

muscle, muscles, muscling, muscled
1 (noun) Your muscles are pieces of flesh which you can expand or contract to move parts of your body.
2 (informal) If someone has muscle, they have power or influence.
3 (verb; informal) If you muscle in on something, you force your way into a situation in which you are not welcome.
muscular (adjective)
[Latin *musculus* = little mouse, because muscles were thought to look like mice]

museum, museums
(noun) a building where many interesting or valuable objects are kept and displayed.

mushroom, mushrooms, mushrooming, mushroomed
1 (noun) a type of fungus. Some mushrooms are edible.
2 (verb) If something mushrooms, it appears and grows very quickly, e.g. *Video shops mushroomed in the late 1980s.*

mushy, mushier, mushiest
(adjective) very soft, e.g. *mushy peas.*

music
1 (noun) e.g. *Do you like pop or classical music?*

Can you distinguish between: homicide suicide parricide matricide genocide fratricide patricide?

2 the written symbols that represent musical sounds, e.g. *She can read music.*
musically (adverb)

musical, musicals
(noun) a play or film that uses songs and dance to tell the story, e.g. *Cats; South Pacific.*
2 (adjective) relating to music.
3 good at musical activities.

musician, musicians
(noun) a person who plays a musical instrument as their job or hobby.

musket, muskets
(noun) an old-fashioned gun with a long barrel.

Muslim, Muslims; also spelled **Moslem**
1 (noun) a person who believes in Islam and lives according to its rules.
2 (adjective) relating to Islam.

mussel, mussels
(noun) a kind of shellfish with black shells.

must
1 (verb) e.g. *You must clean your teeth... You must come and stay with us.*
2 (noun) Something that is a must is very necessary, e.g. *Good boots are a must for the hiker.*

mustard
(noun) a hot, spicy flavouring made from the seeds of the mustard plant.

muster, musters, mustering, mustered
1 (verb) to gather together, e.g. *I hit him with all the force I could muster... Muster here at 0900 hours.*
2 (noun) A **muster station** on a ship is where people must gather in an emergency.

musty, mustier, mustiest
(adjective) smelling stale and damp.

mutate, mutates, mutating, mutated
(verb; technical) If an animal or plant mutates, it develops different characteristics as the result of a change in its genes.
mutation (noun) **mutant** (noun and adjective)
[Latin *mutare* = to change]

mute, mutes, muting, muted
1 (adjective; formal) silent, e.g. *She remained mute, completely overwhelmed by the tragedy.*
2 (noun) a person who cannot speak.
3 a device placed in the bell of a trumpet to change its sound.
4 (verb) to make something quieter [not to be confused with **mooted** which means 'suggested'
[Latin *mutus* = silent]

mutilate, mutilates, mutilating, mutilated
1 (verb) If someone is mutilated, their body is badly injured, e.g. *victims mutilated in the blast.*
2 to damage or spoil something deliberately.
mutilation (noun)

mutiny, mutinies
(noun) a rebellion against someone in authority, especially on a ship.
mutineer (noun) **mutinous** (adjective)

mutter, mutters, muttering, muttered
(verb) to speak in a very low and perhaps cross voice, e.g. *He muttered insults under his breath.*

mutton
(noun) the meat of an adult sheep.

muzak (pronounced **myoo**-zak)
(noun; trademark) taped background music played in shops, restaurants, etc.

muzzle, muzzles
1 (noun) the nose and mouth of an animal.
2 a cover for a dog's mouth to prevent it from biting.
3 (noun) the open end of a gun barrel.
[Old French *musel* = little snout]

my
(pronoun) e.g. *I closed my eyes.*

myself
(pronoun) e.g. *I treated myself to a bun.*

mysterious
(adjective) strange and not well understood.
mysteriously (adverb)

mystery, mysteries
(noun) something that is not understood.
mystery (adjective)
[Greek *musterion* = secret rites]

mystify, mystifies, mystifying, mystified
(verb) If something mystifies you, you find it impossible to understand.

myth, myths
1 (noun) an untrue belief or explanation, e.g. *It's a myth that they sing live on 'Top of the Pops'.*
2 a story which was made up long ago to explain natural events and religious beliefs, e.g. *Greek myths and legends.*
mythical (adjective)
[Greek *muthos* = fable]

mythology
(noun) Mythology refers to stories that have been made up about religion or natural events.
mythological (adjective)

N

nag, nags, nagging, nagged
1 (verb) to keep complaining to someone about something.
2 If something nags at you, it keeps worrying you.

nail, nails, nailing, nailed
1 (verb) If you nail something somewhere, you fit it there using a hammer and nails.

2 (phrase) If you **hit the nail on the head**, you say exactly the right thing.
3 (noun) Your nails are the hard ends of your fingers and toes.

naïve (pronounced ny-eev)
(adjective) foolishly believing that things are easier or less complicated than they really are,

Letter N was taken from the shape of a snake. Nahas was an early word for snake.

e.g. *He was rather naïve, at the age of 24, still to believe in the tooth fairy.*
naïvely (adverb) **naïvety** (noun)
[Old French *naif* = native or spontaneous]

naked
(adjective) not wearing any clothes.
nakedness (noun)

name, names, naming, named
1 (noun) e.g. *What's your name?... We must protect our good name... I do this in the name of freedom.*
2 (verb) e.g. *I name this ship H.M.S. Bathtub... Name your price for that fine car.*

name-dropping
(noun) talking about famous people as though they were your friends, in order to impress people, e.g. *As I was saying to Sir Dicky the other day at the Savoy Grill...*

namesake, namesakes
(noun) Your namesake is someone with the same name as you.

nanny, nannies
(noun) a woman whose job is looking after young children.

nap, naps
(noun) a short sleep.

napkin, napkins
(noun) a small piece of cloth etc. used to wipe your hands and mouth after eating.

nappy, nappies
(noun) a piece of towelling or paper worn round a baby's bottom.

narrate, narrates, narrating, narrated
(verb) to tell a story.
narration (noun) **narrator** (noun)
[Latin *narrare* = to tell]

narrative, narratives (pronounced **nar-rat-tiv**)
(noun) a story or an account of events.

narrow, narrows, narrowing, narrowed
1 (adjective) not wide.
2 (verb) to become less wide, e.g. *The river narrowed before the waterfall.*
3 A narrow escape or victory is one that you only just achieve.
narrowly (adverb) **narrowness** (noun)

narrow boat, boats
(noun) a long, thin boat specially built to be used on canals.

narrow-minded
(adjective) unwilling to consider new ideas or opinions.

nasal (pronounced **nay-zal**)
(adjective) relating to the nose, e.g. *I unblocked my nasal passages by blowing my nose.*
[Latin *nasus* = nose]

nasty, nastier, nastiest
(adjective) very unpleasant, e.g. *a nasty smell.*
nastily (adverb) **nastiness** (noun)

nation, nations
(noun) a country; sometimes a tribe, race, etc, e.g. *the English nation... the Zulu nation.*
[Latin *natio* = tribe]

national
1 (adjective) relating to the whole of a country, e.g. *national newspapers.*
2 typical of a particular country, e.g. *dancers in national dress.*
nationally (adverb)

national anthem, anthems
(noun) the official song of a country. England's national anthem is 'God Save The Queen'.

national curriculum
(noun) government guidelines about what should be taught in state schools.

nationality, nationalities
(noun) the fact of belonging to a particular country, e.g. *She is of Swiss nationality.*

nationalize, nationalizes, nationalizing, nationalized; also spelled **nationalise**
(verb) to bring an industry under the control and ownership of the government.
nationalized (adjective) **nationalization** (noun)

nationwide
(adjective, adverb) happening all over a country, e.g. *a nationwide campaign.*

native, natives
1 (adjective) Your native country is the country where you were born.
2 Your native language is the language that you first learned to speak.
3 (noun) A native of a place is someone who was born there, e.g. *She's a native of Yorkshire.*

Nativity
(noun) the birth of Christ or the festival celebrating this.

natter, natters, nattering, nattered
(verb; informal) to talk about unimportant things.

natural, naturals
1 (adjective) normal and to be expected, e.g. *It's only natural that he should feel upset.*
2 existing or happening in nature, e.g. *The destruction of Pompeii was a natural disaster.*
3 (noun) If you are a natural at something, you are good at it without having to try hard.
4 In music, a natural is a note that is not a sharp or a flat.
5 (phrase) If someone dies of **natural causes**, they die because they are ill and not because they are killed or commit suicide.
naturally (adverb)

natural gas
(noun) gas found underground or under the sea and used as a fuel.

natural history
(noun) the study of animals and plants.

naturalist, naturalists
(noun) someone who studies animals and plants.

nature, natures
1 (noun) animals, plants and all the other things in the world not made by people.
2 someone's basic character, e.g. *Molly had a very sweet nature.*
[Latin *natura* = birth]

Word chain: nas**al** alge**bra** rab**bit** Italian....

naughty, naughtier, naughtiest
(adjective) behaving badly.
naughtily (adverb) **naughtiness** (noun)

nautical (pronounced **naw**-tik-kl)
(adjective) relating to ships or navigation.
[Greek *naus* = ship]

naval
(adjective) relating to a navy, e.g. *U.S. naval forces.*
[Latin *navis* = ship]

Similar word: nautical

nave, naves
(noun) the long central part of a church.
[Latin: *navis* = ship]

navel, navels
(noun) the small hollow on the front of your body just above your waist. This is where the umbilical cord joins a baby's body when the baby is in the womb.

navigable
(adjective) wide enough and deep enough to sail on, e.g. *Many canals are now navigable again.*

navigate, navigates, navigating, navigated
1 (verb) to work out the direction a ship, plane or car should go, using maps, instruments, etc.
2 To navigate a stretch of water means to travel safely across it, e.g. *Until then no ship had been large enough to navigate the Atlantic.*
navigation (noun) **navigator** (noun)
[Latin *navigare* = to drive a ship]

navvy, navvies
(noun; old fashioned) a man employed to do hard physical work, e.g. building roads or railways.
[from 'navigator', which used to mean 'builder of navigations' (canals)]

navy, navies
1 (noun) A country's navy is the part of its armed forces that fights at sea.
2 (adjective, noun) dark blue.
[Latin *navis* = ship]

near, nearer, nearest; nears, nearing, neared
1 (preposition, adverb, adjective) e.g. *near the beach... a state of near panic.*
2 (verb) to approach something, e.g. *As they neared the harbour, it began to rain.*

nearby
(adverb, adjective) only a short distance away, e.g. *He lived nearby... a nearby phonebox.*

nearly
1 (adverb) not completely but almost.
2 (phrase) You use **not nearly** to emphasize that something is not the case, e.g. *Your offer for the painting was not nearly enough.*

neat, neater, neatest
1 (adjective) tidy and smart.
2 A neat alcoholic drink does not have anything added to it, e.g. *She takes her whisky neat.*
neatly (adverb) **neatness** (noun)
[Latin *nitidus* = shining or clean]

necessary
(adjective) Something that is necessary is needed or must be done.

necessity (noun) **necessarily** (adverb)
necessitate (verb)
[Latin *necessarius* = essential]

Similar words: essential, vital

neck, necks
1 (noun) e.g. *Your neck is filthy!*
2 (phrase) If you **stick your neck out**, you take a risk and do something that may be criticized or put you in danger.
3 If two competitors are **neck and neck**, they are level with each other.

necklace, necklaces
(noun) a piece of jewellery which is worn around the neck.

nectar
(noun) a sweet liquid produced by flowers and attractive to insects.

need, needs, needing, needed
1 (verb) If you need something, you believe that you must have it or do it.
2 (noun) Your needs are the things that you need to have.
3 (phrase) e.g. *The house was in need of repair.*

Similar words: (noun) necessity, requirement

needle, needles, needling, needled
1 (noun) a thin piece of metal with a pointed end, e.g. a sewing needle, a knitting needle, a needle for injections.
2 On a coniferous tree, needles are its thin green spikes.
3 (verb; informal) If someone needles you, they annoy or provoke you.

needless
(adjective) unnecessary.
needlessly (adverb)

needlework
(noun) sewing or embroidery.

needy, needier, neediest
(adjective) very poor.

negative, negatives
1 (adjective) A negative answer means 'no'.
2 Someone who is negative sees only problems and disadvantages, e.g. *He was very negative about my written work.*
3 A negative number is less than zero, e.g. -2.
4 (noun) the image that is first produced when you take a photograph for a print.
negatively (adverb)

neglect, neglects, neglecting, neglected
1 (verb) If you neglect something, you do not look after it properly.
2 (noun) failure to look after something or someone properly, e.g. *buildings suffering from vandalism and neglect.*
neglectful (adjective)
[Latin *neglegere* = to ignore]

negligent
(adjective) not taking enough care, e.g. *He has been negligent in his duties.*
negligently (adverb) **negligence** (noun)

A sailor needs these words: ship fathom draught admiral submarine frigate merchant.

negotiate, negotiates, negotiating, negotiated
(verb) to have formal discussions to reach an
agreement about something.
negotiation (noun) **negotiator** (noun)
[Latin *negotiari* = to do business]

negro, negroes
(noun) a person with black skin who comes from
Africa or whose ancestors came from Africa.
[Spanish *negro* = black]

neigh, neighs, neighing, neighed
(verb) to make the loud sound of a horse.

neighbour, neighbours
1 (noun) someone who lives near you.
2 someone standing or sitting next to you, e.g.
James turned his head towards his neighbour.
neighbouring (adjective)

neighbourhood, neighbourhoods
(noun) a district where people live, e.g. *Wilmslow
is a wealthy neighbourhood.*

neither
(adverb, adjective, pronoun) e.g. *neither here
nor there... neither boy is lying... neither was
having any luck.* [note that neither is singular
referring to only one thing]

neon (pronounced **nee**-yon)
(noun) a gas found in the atmosphere, used in
glass tubes to make electric lights and signs.

nephew, nephews
(noun) Someone's nephew is the son of their
sister or brother.

nerve, nerves
1 (noun) a long, thin fibre that transmits
messages between your brain and other parts of
your body.
nervous system (noun)
2 If you talk about someone's nerves, you mean
how well they can remain calm in a difficult
situation, e.g. *She had strong nerves.*
3 courage or impudence, e.g. *Nobody had the
nerve to criticize him... What a nerve!*
4 (phrase; informal) If someone **gets on your
nerves**, they annoy you.

nerve-racking
(adjective) making you feel very worried and
tense, e.g. *a nerve-racking experience.*

nervous
1 (adjective) worried and frightened.
2 A nervous illness affects your emotions and
mental health.
nervously (adverb) **nervousness** (noun)

Similar words: (sense 1) jittery, jumpy, edgy, on
edge, uptight

---

nervous breakdown, breakdowns
(noun) an illness in which someone suffers from
depression and worry and feels unable to cope
with life.

nest, nests, nesting, nested
1 (noun) a place that a bird makes to lay its eggs
in; also a place that some insects and other
animals make to rear their young in.
2 (verb) to make a nest and settle in it.

nestle, nestles, nestling, nestled
(pronounced **ness**-sl)
(verb) to settle comfortably somewhere, often
pressing up against someone else.

nestling, nestlings
(noun) a young bird that has not yet learned to
fly and so has not left the nest.

net, nets
1 (noun) a mesh of string, lace, rope, etc., e.g. *a
fishing net... net curtains.*
2 (adjective) A net result or amount is final, after
everything has been considered, e.g. *The
company made a net profit of just over 23%.*
3 The net weight of something is its weight
without its wrapping.
4 (noun) The two-dimensional shape from which
a 3D structure is made.

netball
(noun) a game in which two teams try to score
goals by throwing a ball through a net on a pole.

netting
(noun) woven fence material, e.g. *wire netting.*

nettle, nettles
(noun) a wild plant covered with stinging hairs.

network, networks
1 (noun) a large number of lines or roads which
cross each other at many points, e.g. *New York
has a vast network of streets.*
2 A network of people or organizations is a large
number of them that work together as a system,
e.g. *the public telephone network.*
3 A TV network is a group of linked broadcasting
stations that all transmit the same programmes
at the same time, e.g. *the ITV network.*

neuter, neuters, neutering, neutered
(pronounced **nyoo**-ter)
1 (adjective) In some languages, a neuter noun or
pronoun is one not masculine or feminine.
2 (verb) When an animal is neutered, its
reproductive organs are removed.

neutral, neutrals
1 (adjective) People who are neutral do not
support either side in a disagreement or war.
neutrality (noun)
2 The neutral wire in an electric plug is the one
that is not earth or live.
3 A neutral colour is not definite or striking, for
example pale grey.
4 In chemistry, a neutral substance is neither
acid nor alkaline.

neutralize, neutralizes, neutralizing, neutralized;
also spelled **neutralise**
(verb) to prevent something from working or
taking effect, e.g. *Bond neutralized the bomb
with just 3 seconds left.*

neutron, neutrons
(noun) an atomic particle that has no electrical
charge.

neutron bomb, bombs
(noun) a bomb that is designed to kill people by
radiation and without destroying buildings.

Don't have a nervous breakdown — take the Survival Test instead (page v).

never
(adverb) at no time, e.g. *I never watch situation comedies. They stunt your growth.*

nevertheless
(adverb) in spite of what has just been said, e.g. *She saw Jane immediately. Nevertheless she pretended to look around for her.*

new, newer, newest
(adjective) e.g. *They are building new houses.*
newness (noun) **newly** (adverb)

Similar words: brand-new, latest, novel

newborn
(adjective) born recently.

new moon, moons
(noun) The moon is new when it is a thin crescent shape at the start of its 4-week cycle.

news
1 (noun) information about things that have happened very recently.
2 (phrase) If you say **that's news to me**, you mean that you did not know about it before.

newsagent, newsagents
(noun) a person or shop that sells newspapers and magazines.

newsletter, newsletters
(noun) a printed sheet of paper containing information about an organization and sent regularly to its members.

newspaper, newspapers
(noun) e.g. the Independent, the Daily Mirror.

newt, newts
(noun) a small amphibious creature with a moist skin, short legs and a long tail.
[from mistaken division of Middle English *an ewt*]

New Testament
(noun) the second part of the Bible, about the life of Jesus Christ and the early Church.

New Year
(noun) the start of a year.

New Zealander, Zealanders
(noun) someone who comes from New Zealand.

next
(adjective, adverb) e.g. *Stop at the next lay-by... What's next?*

Similar words: subsequent, following

next of kin
(noun) Your next of kin is your closest relative.

nibble, nibbles, nibbling, nibbled
1 (verb) to take small bites of something.
2 (noun) Nibbles are small things to eat with drinks, e.g. crisps, nuts.

nice, nicer, nicest
(adjective) pleasant or attractive.
nicely (adverb) **niceness** (noun)

niche, niches (pronounced neesh)
1 (noun) a hollow area in a wall, e.g. *The little statue of the saint stood in its niche.*
2 If you say that you have found your niche, you

mean that you have found a job or way of life that is exactly right for you.
[Old French *nichier* = to nest]

nick, nicks, nicking, nicked
1 (verb) If you nick something, you make a small cut in its surface, e.g. *He nicked himself shaving.*
2 (noun) a small cut in the surface of something.
3 (verb; informal) to steal something.
4 (phrase) If something happens **in the nick of time**, it only just happens in time.
5 (informal) If something is **in good nick**, it is in good condition.

nickel, nickels
(noun) a silver-coloured metal used in alloys, for example, for coins.

nickname, nicknames
(noun) an informal name given to someone.
[Middle English *an ekename* = an additional name]

nicotine
(noun) an addictive substance found in tobacco, named after Jacques Nicot, who first brought tobacco to France.

niece, nieces
(noun) Someone's niece is the daughter of their sister or brother.

Nigerian, Nigerians (pronounced nie-*jeer*-ee-an)
1 (adjective) belonging to Nigeria.
2 (noun) someone who comes from Nigeria.

niggle, niggles, niggling, niggled
1 (verb) If something niggles you, it worries you slightly and for some time.
2 to criticize someone continually.

night, nights
(noun) the time between sunset and sunrise.

nightdress, nightdresses or **nightie**
(noun) a loose dress that a woman or girl wears to sleep in.

nightly
(adjective, adverb) happening every night, e.g. *theatre performances twice nightly.*

nightmare, nightmares
(noun) a very frightening dream; also any very unpleasant or frightening situation, e.g. *My first day at work was a nightmare.*
nightmarish (adjective)
[night + Middle English *mare* = evil spirit]

nil
(noun) zero or nothing.

nimble, nimbler, nimblest
1 (adjective) able to move quickly and easily.
2 able to think quickly and cleverly, e.g. *The interviewer had a nimble mind.*
nimbleness (noun) **nimbly** (adverb)

nimcompoop, nincompoops
(noun; informal) a foolish person.

nine the number 9.
ninth (adjective and noun)

nineteen the number 19.
nineteenth (adjective and noun)

The word NICE is one of the the most overused in English. Try to avoid using it when you are writing.

ninety, nineties
the number 90.
ninetieth (adjective and noun)

nip, nips, nipping, nipped
1 (verb; informal) to go somewhere quickly.
2 (noun) a light pinch.

nipper, nippers
(noun; informal) a child.

nippy
(adjective; informal) quite cold, e.g. *The air was nippy outside.*

nit, nits
1 (noun; informal) a stupid person.
2 Nits are the eggs of a kind of louse that sometimes lives in people's hair.

nitrate, nitrates
(noun) a chemical compound that includes nitrogen and oxygen, used as a fertilizer in agriculture.

nitrogen
(noun) a chemical element usually found as a gas, forming about 78% of the earth's atmosphere.

nitty-gritty
(noun; informal) the most important facts about something, e.g. *Let's get down to the nitty-gritty.*

no
(interjection, adjective, adverb) e.g. *No! This must stop... He gave no reason... no later than Monday.*

noble, nobler, noblest
(adjective) honest and brave, and deserving admiration.
nobly (adjective)
[Latin *nobilis* = well-known]

nobody, nobodies
1 (pronoun) e.g. *There was nobody in.*
2 (noun) Someone who is a nobody is not at all important.

nocturnal
(adjective) active at night, e.g. *The badger is a nocturnal animal.*

nod off
(phrasal verb) to fall asleep.

noise, noises
(noun) a sound, especially one that is loud or unpleasant.
[Old French *noise* = disturbance]

Similar words: din, racket, row

noisy, noisier, noisiest
(adjective) making a lot of noise or full of noise.
noisily (adverb) **noisiness** (noun)

nomad, nomads
(noun) a person who belongs to a tribe which travels from place to place rather than living in just one place.
nomadic (adjective)
[Latin *nomas* = wandering shepherd]

nominate, nominates, nominating, nominated
(verb) If you nominate someone for a job or position, you formally suggest that they have it.
nomination (noun)
[Latin *nominare* = to call by name]

Similar words: propose, suggest, recommend

nominative
(noun, adjective) In the grammar of some languages, the nominative is the form of a noun when it is the subject of a verb.

non-
(prefix) not, e.g. *non-industrial societies.*

nonchalant (pronounced **non**-shal-nt)
(adjective) seeming calm and not worried.
nonchalance (noun) **nonchalantly** (adverb)
[Old French *nonchalant* = not concerned]

non-commissioned officer, officers or **NCO**
(noun) an officer in the army or RAF, such as a sergeant or corporal who has worked his way up from the lower ranks, rather than by receiving a commission.

none
(pronoun) e.g. *There was none left.*
[N.B. None is short for 'not one' and so is singular]

non-existent
(adjective) Something that is non-existent does not exist.

non-fiction
(noun) writing that gives facts and information rather than telling a story.

non-flammable
(adjective) not capable of burning.

nonsense
(noun) foolish and meaningless words or behaviour.
nonsensical (adjective)

Similar words: rubbish, rot

non-stick
(adjective) coated with a special substance to stop food from sticking, e.g. *a non-stick frying pan.*

non-stop
(adjective, adverb) continuing without any pauses or breaks, e.g. *non-stop noise.*

noodles
(plural, noun) a kind of pasta shaped into long, thin pieces.

nook, nooks
(noun; literary) a small sheltered place.

noon
(noun) 12 o'clock midday.

no one
(pronoun) e.g. *There was no one there.*

noose, nooses
(noun) a loop at the end of a piece of rope, with a knot that tightens when the rope is pulled.

nor
(conjunction) e.g. *Neither Margaret nor Angus was there.*

Notice the difference between these nouns and their verbs: advice – advise; licence – license....

normal
(adjective) usual and ordinary.
normally (adverb)
[Latin *norma* = carpenter's rule]

Similar words: natural, usual, typical

north
(noun, adverb, adjective) a direction, e.g. *Go north for 3 miles... Are you from the North?... It's a north wind.*
North Pole (noun)

north-east
(noun, adverb, adjective) a direction halfway between north and east.
north-eastern (adjective)

northern
(adjective) in or from the north, e.g. *the mountains of northern Japan.*

northward or northwards
(adverb) towards the north.

north-west
(noun, adverb, adjective) a direction halfway between north and west.
north-western (adjective)

Norwegian, Norwegians (pronounced nor-**wee**-jn)
1 (adjective) belonging to Norway.
2 (noun) someone who comes from Norway.
3 the main language spoken in Norway.

nose, noses, nosing, nosed
1 (noun) e.g. *Blow your nose — it's dripping.*
2 (verb) to move very slowly, e.g. *The liner nosed into the harbour.*
3 (phrase) If you **pay through the nose** for something, you pay a very high price for it.
4 If someone **turns their nose up at** something, they reject it because they think it is not good enough for them.

nosedive, nosedives
(noun) a sudden downward plunge by an aircraft.

nostalgia (pronounced nos-**tal**-ja)
(noun) a feeling of affection for the past, and sadness that things have changed.
nostalgic (adjective) **nostalgically** (adverb)

nostril, nostrils
(noun) the two openings in your nose.
[Old English *nosu* = nose + *thyrel* = hole]

nosy, nosier, nosiest
(adjective) trying to find out about things that do not concern you.

not
(adverb) e.g. *We are not amused.*

notable
(adjective) important or interesting, e.g. *Fleet Street used to be notable for newspaper offices.*
notably (adverb)

notch, notches
(noun) a small V-shaped cut in a surface.
[a mistaken division of Middle English *an otch*]

note, notes, noting, noted
1 (noun) a short letter etc.
2 a piece of paper money.

3 a musical sound of a particular pitch, or a written symbol that represents it.
4 (verb) If you note a fact, you become aware of it or you mention it, e.g. *His audience, I noted, were looking bored.*
5 If you note something down, you write it down so that you will remember it.
6 (phrase) If you **take note** of something, you pay attention to it, e.g. *The detective took note of the man's dirty hands.*
[Latin *nota* = mark or sign]

notebook, notebooks
(noun) a small book for writing notes in.

noted
(adjective) well-known and admired, e.g. *F. Scott Fitzgerald was a noted American writer.*

nothing
(pronoun) e.g. *It's nothing to worry about.*

Similar words: zero, nought, nil, zilch

notice, notices, noticing, noticed
1 (verb) to become aware of something.
2 (noun) a written announcement.
3 advance warning about something, e.g. *She could have gone if she'd had more notice.*
4 (phrase) If you **hand in your notice**, you tell your employer that you intend to leave your job.
[Latin *notitia* = knowledge]
noticeable (adjective) **noticeably** (adverb)

Similar words: (verb) note, observe, detect, perceive

noticeboard, noticeboards
(noun) a board for notices.

notion, notions
(noun) an idea or belief.

notorious
(adjective) well-known for something bad, e.g. *The area was notorious for murders.*
notoriously (adverb) **notoriety** (noun)
[Latin *notorius* = well-known']

Similar words: disreputable, infamous

nought the number 0.

noun, nouns
(noun) a word which refers to a person, thing or idea, e.g. president, table, sun, beauty.
[Latin *nomen* = name]

nourish, nourishes, nourishing, nourished
(pronounced **nur**-rish)
(verb) To nourish people or animals means to provide them with food.
nourishing (adjective) **nourishment** (noun)
[Old French *norir* = to feed]

novel, novels
1 (noun) a book that tells an invented story.
2 (adjective) A novel idea is unusual and new.
[Old French *novelle* = new story]

novelist, novelists
(noun) a person who writes novels.

November
(noun) the 11th month of the year.
[Latin *November* = the 9th month; the Romans

at first had a 10-month year which they lengthened to 12 months.]

novice, novices
(noun) someone who is not yet experienced at something.

now
1 (adverb, conjunction) e.g. *Where is she now?... I like him a lot now he's older.*
2 (phrase) **Just now** means very recently, e.g. *I was talking to him just now.*
3 If something happens **now and then**, it happens sometimes but not regularly.

nowadays
(adverb) at the present time, e.g. *Nowadays most babies are born in a hospital.*

nowhere
(adverb) e.g. *She was nowhere to be seen.*

nozzle, nozzles
(noun) a spout fitted onto the end of a pipe or hose to control the flow of a liquid.

nuclear
1 (adjective) relating to the energy produced when the nuclei of atoms are split, e.g. *nuclear power... the nuclear industry.*
2 relating to weapons that explode using the energy released by atoms, e.g. *nuclear war.*

nucleus, nuclei (pronounced **nyoo**-klee-uss)
1 (noun) The nucleus of an atom is the central part of it.
2 the part of a cell that contains the chromosomes and controls its growth and reproduction.
[Latin *nucleus* = kernel]

nude, nudes
1 (adjective) naked.
2 (noun) a picture or statue of a naked person.
nudity (noun) **nudist** (noun)

nudge, nudges, nudging, nudged
(verb) If you nudge someone, you push them gently, usually with your elbow.

nuisance, nuisances
(noun) someone or something that is annoying or inconvenient.

Similar words: pest, inconvenience, bother, drag

numb
(adjective) unable to feel anything, e.g. *My leg had gone numb... She was numb with shock.*
[Middle English *nomen* = paralysed]

number, numbers, numbering, numbered
1 (noun) a word or a symbol used for counting or calculating.
2 a quantity of things, e.g. *There are large numbers of children in care.*
3 (verb) If things number a particular amount, there are that many of them, e.g. *The force numbered almost a quarter of a million men.*
4 (phrase) If **someone's days are numbered**, they will not live much longer.

Similar words: (noun: sense 1) figure, numeral, digit

numeral, numerals
(noun) a symbol that represents a number, e.g. *6, 274, XIII, MMIV.*

numerate (pronounced **nyoo**-mer-rit)
(adjective) able to do arithmetic.
numeracy (noun)

numerator, numerators
(noun) In maths, the numerator is the top part of a fraction. (opposite: **denominator**)

numerical
(adjective) expressed in numbers or relating to numbers, e.g. *in numerical order.*

numerous
(adjective) many, e.g. *numerous phone-calls.*

numismatics (pronounced nyoo-miz-**mat**-tiks)
(noun) the study of coins.
numismatist (noun)
[Latin *nomisma* = coin]

nun, nuns
(noun) a woman who has taken religious vows and lives in a convent.

nurse, nurses, nursing, nursed
1 (verb) If you nurse someone, you look after them when they are ill.
2 (noun) a person whose main job is to care for sick people.

nursery, nurseries
1 (noun) a room in which young children sleep and play.
2 A nursery or day nursery is a place where young children are looked after while their parents are working.
3 a place where plants are grown and sold.

nursery rhyme, rhymes
(noun) a short verse or song for young children.

nursery school, schools
(noun) a school for children from 3 to 5 years old.

nursing home, homes
(noun) a privately-run hospital for people who are ill or recovering from illness.

nut, nuts
1 (noun) the fruit of a tree, with a hard shell and an edible centre.
2 a piece of metal with a hole in the middle which a bolt screws into.
3 (informal) a mad or very foolish person.

nutrition
(noun) the food that you eat, considered from the point of view of how it helps you to grow and be healthy, e.g. *Because of poor nutrition, many refugees have grown weaker.*

nutritious
(adjective) containing substances that help you to grow and remain healthy.

nutty, nuttier, nuttiest
1 (adjective) tasting of nuts.
2 (informal) mad or very foolish.

nylon, nylons
(noun) a type of strong artificial material, e.g. *nylon stockings.*
[from the first letters of New York and London]

The nut came off the bolt, NOT the nut came off of the bolt.
Off and *of* hardly ever go together.

O

oaf, oafs
(noun) a clumsy and stupid person.
[Old Norse *alfr* = elf]

Similar word: lout

oak, oaks
(noun) a large, deciduous hardwood tree.

oar, oars
(noun) a wooden pole used for rowing a boat.

oasis, oases (pronounced oh-**ay**-siss)
(noun) a small area in a desert where water and
plants are found.

oats
(plural noun) a type of grain.

oath, oaths
(noun) a formal promise, especially a promise to
tell the truth in a court of law.

Similar words: vow, pledge

oatmeal
(noun) a coarse flour made from oats.

obedient
(adjective) doing what you are told to do.
obediently (adverb) **obedience** (noun)

obey, obeys, obeying, obeyed
(verb) If you obey a person or an order, you do
what you are told to do.

object, objects, objecting, objected
1 (noun) An object is anything solid that you can
touch or see and that is not alive.
2 Someone's object is their aim or purpose.
3 In grammar, the object of a verb or preposition
is the word or phrase which follows it and
describes the person or thing affected, e.g.
in *I kicked the ball*, 'ball' is the object of the verb
'kicked'.
4 (verb; pronounced ob-**ject**) If you object to
something, you dislike it or disapprove of it.

Similar words: (verb) oppose, protest

objection, objections
(noun) If you have an objection to something,
you dislike it or disapprove of it.

objective, objectives
1 (noun) An objective is a specific aim, e.g. *Our
objective is to capture that ridge.*
2 (adjective) If you are objective, you are not
influenced by personal feelings or prejudices,
e.g. *Scientific evidence must be objective.*
objectively (adverb) **objectivity** (noun)

obligation, obligations
(noun) something that you must do because it is
your duty.

oblige, obliges, obliging, obliged
1 (verb) If you are obliged to do something, you
have to do it.
2 If you oblige someone, you help them.

3 (phrase) When someone says '**much obliged**'
they mean 'Thank you very much'.
obliging (adjective)

oblique (pronounced o-**bleek**)
(adjective) Oblique lines slope, e.g. / or \.

obliterate, obliterates, obliterating, obliterated
(verb) to destroy something completely.
obliteration (noun)
[Latin *oblitterare* = to erase or cancel]

oblong, oblongs
(noun) a 4-sided shape with 2 parallel short
sides, 2 parallel long sides, and 4 right angles.
[Latin *oblongus* = oblong]

obnoxious (pronounced ob-**nok**-shuss)
(adjective) extremely unpleasant, e.g. *The
obnoxious politician had a smart answer for
everything, yet showed he knew nothing.*
[Latin *obnoxiosus* = exposed to harm]

oboe, oboes
(noun) a woodwind musical instrument.
oboist (noun)
[French *haut bois* = high wood, a reference to
the instrument's high note]

obscene
(adjective) indecent and offensive.
obscenely (adverb) **obscenity** (noun)

Similar words: filthy, foul, indecent, pornographic

obscure, obscures, obscuring, obscured
1 (adjective) known by only a few people, e.g.
This is one of Mozart's obscure operas.
2 difficult to see or to understand, e.g. *She gave
an obscure answer to a simple question.*
3 (verb) to make something difficult to see or
understand, e.g. *Please don't obscure my view of
the stage.*
obscurity (noun)
[Latin *obscurus* = dark]

observant
(adjective) Someone who is observant notices
things that are not easy to see.

observation, observations
1 (noun) the act of watching something carefully,
e.g. *The police had the house under observation.*
2 the ability to notice things.

observatory, observatories
(noun) a room or building containing telescopes
etc. for studying the sun, moon and stars.

observe, observes, observing, observed
1 (verb) to watch something carefully, e.g. *From
the hide, we could observe the birds nesting.*
2 to notice something, e.g. *She observed that he
had forgotten his wig.*
observer (noun) **observable** (adjective)
[Latin *observare* = to watch]

Letter O seems to have begun as a picture of an eye.

obsession, obsessions
(noun) If someone has an obsession about
something, they cannot stop thinking about it.
obsessed (adjective) **obsessive** (adjective)
[Latin *obsidere* = to sit down before]

obsolete
(adjective) out of date and no longer used.
[Latin *obsoletus* = worn out]

obstacle, obstacles
(noun) something which is in your way.
[Latin *ob-* = against + *stare* = to stand]

Similar words: hurdle, barrier

obstinate
(adjective) stubborn and unwilling to change.
obstinately (adjective) **obstinacy** (noun)

obstruct, obstructs, obstructing, obstructed
1 (verb) to block a road, path etc..
2 To obstruct justice or progress means to
prevent it from happening.
obstruction (noun) **obstructive** (adjective)
[Latin *obstruere* = to build against]

obtain, obtains, obtaining, obtained
(verb) If you obtain something, you get it.
obtainable (adjective)
[Latin *obtinere* to take hold of]

obtuse
(adjective) An obtuse angle is between 90° and
180°. (An **acute** angle is less than 180°; a **reflex**
angle is between 180° and 360°.)

obvious
(adjective) easy to see or understand.
obviously (adverb)

Similar words: blatant, apparent, evident, clear,
conspicuous, plain

occasion, occasions
(noun) a time when something happens, e.g. *I
met him on only one occasion.*

occasional
(adjective) happening sometimes but not often,
e.g. *He took an occasional trip to Aberdeen.*
occasionally (adverb)

occupation, occupations
1 (noun) a job or profession.
2 a hobby or something you do for pleasure, e.g.
Her favourite occupation was chasing the cat.
occupational (adjective)
3 The occupation of a country is the act of
invading it and taking control of it.

occupy, occupies, occupying, occupied
1 (verb) The people who occupy a building are
the people who live or work there.
2 to move into and take control of something, e.g.
The protesters occupied the missile base.
3 If something occupies you, you spend your time
doing it, e.g. *That work occupied him all day.*
occupier (noun) **occupant** (noun)
[Latin *occupare* = to seize hold of]

occur, occurs, occurring, occurred
1 (verb) to happen, e.g. *The attack occurred six
days ago.*

2 If something occurs to you, you suddenly think
of it.
occurrence (noun)

ocean, oceans
(noun) a very large area of sea, e.g. *the Atlantic
Ocean.*
oceanic (adjective)

o'clock
(adverb) e.g. *12 o'clock.* (an abbreviation of 'of
the clock')

octagon, octagons
(noun) a shape with 8 straight sides.
octagonal (adjective)
[Greek *okto* + *gonos* = eight angled]

October
(noun) the 10th month of the year.
[Latin *October* = the 8th month; the Romans at
first had a 10-month year which they lengthened
to 12 months]

octopus, octopuses
(noun) a sea creature with 8 long tentacles.
[Greek *okto* + *pous* = 8 feet]

odd, odder, oddest; odds
1 (adjective) strange or unusual.
2 Odd numbers are numbers that cannot be
divided exactly by 2, e.g *3, 7, 25, 641.*
3 not matching, e.g. *odd socks.*
4 (phrase) The **odd one out** in a group is the one
that is different from all the others.
5 (adverb) You use odd after a number to
indicate that it is approximate, e.g. *We met
twenty-odd years ago.*
6 (plural noun) In gambling, the probability of
something happening is referred to as the odds
e.g. *The odds are 10 to 1 for 'Lucky Lad' in the
3.30 at Doncaster Races.*
oddly (adverb) **oddness** (noun)

oddity, oddities
(noun) something very strange.

oddment, oddments
(noun) Oddments are things that are left over
after other things have been used.

Similar words: remnants, odds and ends

odds and ends
(noun) a collection of small unimportant things.

ode, odes
(noun) a poem written in praise of someone or
something.
[Greek *oide* = song]

odour, odours
(noun; formal) a strong smell.

of
(preposition) e.g. *a cup of tea.*

off
1 (preposition, adverb) e.g. *He took his hand off
her arm... The train stopped and people got off...
The boat sank off the coast of China... The
railway was fenced off.*
2 not working, e.g. *Tonight is his night off.*
3 (adverb, adjective) not switched on, e.g. *She
turned the radio off.*

Idioms. What is a: dead language dead heat dead weight dead letter dead ringer?

4 (adjective) cancelled or postponed, e.g.
Tonight's match is off.
5 Food that is off has gone sour or bad.

off colour
(adjective) feeling slightly ill.

offence, offences
1 (noun) a crime, e.g. *They were arrested for drug offences.*
2 (phrases) If something **gives offence**, it upsets people. If you **take offence**, you are upset by someone or something.

offend, offends, offending, offended
(verb) If you offend someone, you upset them.
[Latin *offendere* = to strike against]

offender, offenders
(noun) someone who commits a crime.

offensive, offensives
1 (adjective) rude and upsetting, e.g. *an offensive remark.*
2 Offensive actions or weapons are used in attacking someone.
offensively (adverb)

offer, offers, offering, offered
1 (verb) If you offer something to someone, you ask them if they would like it, e.g. *He offered her his chair... She offered to take us home.*
2 (noun) something that someone asks if you would like or agree to, e.g. *She accepted the offer of £5,000 for the painting.*
3 An offer in a shop is a specially low price for a product, e.g. *This item is on special offer today.*
[Latin *offere* = to present]

office, offices
1 (noun) a room where people work at desks.
2 a government department which deals with a particular area of administration, e.g. *your local education office.*
[Latin *officium* = performance of a task]

officer, officers
(noun) a person holding a position of authority in the armed forces, the police or a government organization.

official, officials
1 (adjective) approved by the government or by someone in authority, e.g. *the official figures.*
2 (noun) a person who holds a position of authority in an organization.
officially (adverb)

offing
(phrase) If something is **in the offing**, it is likely to happen soon, e.g. *A wedding is in the offing.*

off-licence, off-licences
(noun) a shop which sells alcoholic drinks.

offshore
(adjective, adverb) towards or in the sea, e.g.
offshore breezes... offshore oil terminals.

offside
(adjective) If a football, rugby or hockey player is offside, they have broken the rules by moving too far forward. [N.B. not to be confused with **in touch** or **out of play**]

offspring
(noun) the children of a person or animal.

often
(adverb) frequently or a lot of the time.

ogre, ogres (pronounced **oh**-gur)
(noun) a cruel, frightening giant in a fairy story.

oil, oils
1 (noun) a thick, sticky liquid, e.g. *engine oil... cooking oil.*
2 Oils are oil paintings or oil paints.
oily (adjective)
[Latin *oleum* = (olive) oil]

oil paint, paints
(noun) thick paint used by artists, made from a coloured powder and linseed oil.

oilskin, oilskins
(noun) a piece of clothing made from a thick, waterproof material, worn especially by fishermen.

ointment, ointments
(noun) a smooth, thick substance that you put on sore skin to heal it.

OK
1 (adjective, adverb; informal) all right, e.g. *Was the trip OK?... Did things go OK?*
2 (verb; informal) To OK something means to agree to it officially.

Similar words: (adjective) passable, not bad

okra (pronounced **oh**-kra)
(noun) tropical plant with long, green, edible pods.

old, older, oldest
1 (adjective) e.g. *an old lady... an old joke.*
2 former, e.g. *our old teacher.*

Similar words: (sense 1) ancient (sense 2) ex-

old boy, boys
(noun) a former male pupil of a school.

olden
(phrase; literary) **In the olden days** means long ago.

Old English
(noun) the English language from the 5th century AD until about 1100; also known as Anglo-Saxon.

old-fashioned
1 (adjective) no longer fashionable, e.g.
old-fashioned shoes.
2 believing in the values and standards of the past, e.g. *My Dad's a bit old-fashioned.*

Similar words: antiquated, fuddy-duddy

old girl, girls
(noun) a former female pupil of a school.

old master, masters
(noun) a famous painter of the past, or a painting by such a painter.

Old Norse
(noun) a language spoken in Scandinavia and Iceland from about AD 700 to about AD 1350. Many English words are derived from it.

Very few words begin with the sound oi: oil ointment oyster

Old Testament
(noun) the first part of the Christian Bible. It is also the holy book of the Jewish religion and relates to the history of the Jews.

olive, olives
(noun) a small Mediterranean green or black fruit containing a stone. Olives are pickled and eaten as a snack or crushed to produce oil.
[Latin *oliva* = olive]

-ology
(suffix) -ology is used to form words that refer to the study of something, e.g. biology, geology.
[Greek *logos* = reason or speech]

omelette, omelettes (pronounced **om**-lit)
(noun) a dish made by beating eggs together and cooking them in a flat pan.

omen, omens
(noun) something thought to be a sign of what will happen in the future, e.g. *The albatross was a bad omen for the old sailor.*

Similar words: sign, warning

ominous
(adjective) suggesting that something unpleasant is going to happen, e.g. *an ominous silence.*
ominously (adverb)

Similar words: menacing, threatening, unfavourable, sinister

omission, omissions
(noun) something that has been left out or not done, e.g. *The reports were full of errors and omissions... The omission of Platt from the team left a gap in midfield.*

omit, omits, omitting, omitted
1 (verb) If you omit something, you leave it out.
2 (formal) If you omit to do something, you do not do it.
[Latin *ob-* = away + *mittere* = to send]

omnivorous
(adjective) eating all kinds of food, including meat and plants.
omnivore (noun)
[Latin *omni-* = all + *vorare* = to eat greedily]

on
1 (preposition, adverb) e.g. *They were sitting on chairs... He had his boots on... What's on TV?*
2 (phrase) **On and off** means occasionally.
3 If you say that something is **not on**, you mean that it is unacceptable or impossible.

once
1 (adverb) happening one time only.
2 formerly, e.g. *She was once a prefect here.*
3 (conjunction) after, e.g. *I'll see you once I've seen him.*
4 (phrase) If you do something **at once**, you do it immediately. If several things happen **at once**, they all happen at the same time.
5 **Once and for all** means completely or finally.

one, ones
1 the number 1.
2 (adjective) single, e.g. *Their one aim in life is to go to university.*

3 (pronoun) a particular thing or person, e.g. *That's a difficult one to answer.*
4 people in general, e.g. *One can eat well here.*
[Greek *oinē* = ace]

one-off
(noun) something that happens or is made only once.

oneself
(pronoun) Oneself is used when you are talking about people in general, e.g. *One should keep such thoughts to oneself.* It is also used as an alternative to 'myself'.

one-sided
(adjective) not balanced or fair, e.g. *a one-sided conversation... a one-sided argument.*

one-way
1 (adjective) One-way streets are streets along which vehicles can drive in only one direction.
2 A one-way ticket is one that you can use to travel to a place, but not to travel back again.

onion, onions
(noun) a small, round vegetable with a brown, papery skin and a very strong taste.

onlooker, onlookers
(noun) someone who is watching an event.

only
1 (adverb) e.g. *Only mother knows... Don't worry, it's only a slight crack.*
2 (adjective) e.g. *It was the only way out.*
3 If you are an only child, you have no brothers or sisters.
4 (conjunction) e.g. *Snake is just like chicken only it's tougher.*
5 (adverb) e.g. *He broke off, only to resume almost at once.*
6 (phrase) **Only too** means extremely, e.g. *She remembered that sad night only too clearly.*

onomatopoeia (pronounced on-o-mat-o-**pee**-a)
(noun) the use of words which sound like the thing that they represent, e.g. hiss, buzz.
[Greek *onoma* = name + *poiein* = to make]

onto or **on to**
(preposition) e.g. *Put it onto the table... The police were on to the thief.*

onwards or **onward**
1 (adverb) continuing to happen from a particular time, e.g. *From that time onwards he had never spoken to her again.*
2 travelling forwards, e.g. *Onward Christian soldiers!*

ooze, oozes, oozing, oozed
(verb) to flow slowly and thickly, e.g. *Blood oozed from his wounds.*
[Old English *wos* = juice]

opaque (pronounced oh-**pake**)
(adjective) If something is opaque, you cannot see through it, e.g. *opaque windows.*

open, opens, opening, opened
1 (verb) e.g. *She opened the door... The shop opened... We opened a bank account.*
2 (adjective) e.g. *He tore open the envelope.*

Can you continue this word chain? school olive vest stripe petal alone neat atom ominous

3 If you have an open mind, you are willing to consider new ideas or suggestions.
4 honest and frank, e.g. *Please be open in what you say.*
openly (adverb)
5 (adjective) e.g. *The office was open... We walked in the open countryside.*
6 (phrase) **In the open** means outside.
7 (adjective) If something is open to you, it is possible for you to do it, e.g. *The competition is open to all.*

open-ended
(adjective) An open-ended question does not dictate the answer in advance, e.g. *How did you like Spain?* rather than *Was Spain interesting?*

opening, openings
1 (adjective) coming first, e.g. *the opening scene of the play.*
2 (noun) The opening of a book or film is the first part of it.
3 a hole or gap.
4 a chance, e.g. *an opening into show business.*

open-minded
(adjective) willing to consider new ideas and suggestions.

opera, operas
(noun) a dramatic performance in which the words are sung rather than spoken.
operatic (adjective)
[Latin *opera* = works]

operate, operates, operating, operated
1 (verb) to work or make something work, e.g. *Secret agents operate in enemy countries... How does this machine operate?... How do I operate the lift?*
2 When surgeons operate, they cut open the body of a patient to remove or repair a damaged part.
operator (noun)
[Latin *operare* = to work]

operation, operations
1 (noun) a complex, planned event, e.g. *a rescue operation... military operations.*
2 a form of medical treatment in which a surgeon cuts open a patient's body to remove or repair a damaged part.
3 (phrase) If something is **in operation**, it is working or being used, e.g. *The plans were put into operation at once.*

operator
(noun) A telephone operator helps people make their phonecalls.

opinion, opinions
(noun) Your opinion is what you think about something, e.g. *The students were eager to express their opinions.*
[Latin *opinio* = belief]

Similar words: attitude, belief, view

opponent, opponents
(noun) someone who is against you in an argument, a contest or a game.

opportunity, opportunities
(noun) a chance to do something, e.g. *This will be an opportunity to meet people.*

oppose, opposes, opposing, opposed
(verb) to disagree with something and try to prevent it, e.g. *I oppose the idea of building more motorways as it just makes things worse.*
[Latin *ob-* = against + *ponere* = to place]

opposed
1 (adjective) If you are opposed to something, you disagree with it, e.g. *I am opposed to hanging.*
2 (phrase) If you refer to one thing **as opposed to** another, you are saying that it is the first thing not the second which concerns you, e.g. *The green/yellow wire is safe, as opposed to the blue or brown ones which would fry you instantly.*

opposite, opposites
1 (preposition, adverb) facing, e.g. *The hotel is opposite a railway station... the house opposite.*
2 (adjective) e.g. *on the opposite side of the street.*
3 completely different, e.g. *the opposite direction... the opposite point of view.*
4 (noun) If two things are completely different, they are opposites.
[Latin *ob* = against + *ponere* = to place]

Similar words: (noun) contrast, reverse

opposition
1 (noun) If there is opposition to something, people disagree with it and try to prevent it.
2 The main political party which is not in power is referred to as the Opposition.
3 In a game, the opposition is the person or team that you are competing against.

oppress, oppresses, oppressing, oppressed
1 (verb) to treat people cruelly or unfairly, e.g. *The wicked Sheriff oppressed the peasants.*
2 If something oppresses you, it makes you feel depressed and worried.
oppression (noun) **oppressor** (noun)
oppressive (adjective) **oppressively** (adverb)
[Latin *ob-* = against + *premere* = to press]

opt, opts, opting, opted
(verb) If you opt for something, you choose it. If you opt out of something, you choose not to be involved in it.

optical
(adjective) concerned with vision, light or images, e.g. *an optical microscope... an optical illusion.*

optician, opticians
(noun) someone who tests people's eyes, and makes and sells glasses and contact lenses.

optimism
(noun) a feeling of hopefulness about the future.
optimist (noun) **optimistic** (adjective)
optimistically (adverb)
[Latin *optimus* = best]

Not only strike while the iron is hot, but make it hot by striking. (Oliver Cromwell)

ption, options
(noun) a choice, e.g. *He had two options open to him, to burn or to jump.*
optional (adjective)
[Latin *optare* = to choose]

r
(conjunction) e.g. *Take it or leave it... Look out or you'll fall off.*

racle, oracles
(noun) a priest or priestess in ancient Greece, who made predictions about the future by interpreting messages from the gods.
[Latin *orare* = to pray]

ral, orals
1 (adjective) spoken, e.g. *an oral examination.*
2 related to the mouth, e.g. *an oral antiseptic.*
3 (noun) a spoken exam, e.g. *When is your oral?*
orally (adverb)
[Latin *oralis* = of the mouth]

Similar words: (adjective) spoken, verbal

range, oranges
1 (noun) a citrus fruit.
2 (adjective, noun) reddish-yellow.
[Sanskrit *naranga* = orange]

rangeade
(noun) a drink made from, or flavoured with, oranges.

rang-utan, orang-utans; also spelled **orang-utang**
(noun) a large ape with reddish-brown hair.
[Malay *orang* = man + *hutan* = forest]

rator, orators
(noun) someone who is skilled at making speeches.

rbit, orbits, orbiting, orbited
(verb) If something orbits a planet or the sun, it goes round and round it.
[Latin *orbita* = course]

rbital
1 (adjective) relating to the orbit of an object in space.
2 An orbital road goes all the way round a city, e.g. *The M25 is London's orbital motorway.*

rchard, orchards
(noun) land on which fruit trees are grown.

rchestra, orchestras (pronounced **or**-kess-tra)
(noun) a large group of musicians who play together.
orchestral (adjective)
[Greek *orkhestra* = the area in a theatre reserved for musicians]

rdeal, ordeals
(noun) a difficult and extremely unpleasant experience, e.g. *He described his terrible ordeal.*

rder, orders, ordering, ordered
1 (noun) a command given by someone in authority.
2 (verb) to tell someone firmly to do something.
3 When you order something, you ask for it to be brought or sent to you.
4 (noun) a sequence, e.g. *alphabetical order.*

5 a situation in which everything is in the correct place or done at the correct time.
6 (phrase) **in order to:** e.g. *The child shot his parents in order to go on the orphans' picnic.*
7 If a machine or device is in **working order**, it works and is not broken. If it is **out of order**, it is broken and does not work.

Similar words: (noun: sense 4) arrangement, grouping, series

ordinal number, numbers
(noun) a number which tells you what position something has in a group or series, e.g. 3rd, 5th (opposite: **cardinal number**)

ordinary
1 (adjective) not special or different in any way.
2 (phrase) Something **out of the ordinary** is unusual or different.
ordinarily (adverb)

Similar words: average, common, everyday

Ordnance Survey
(noun) the organization that produces detailed maps of Britain and Ireland.
[Ordnance is a term for big army guns. In the 19th century, gunnery officers used to be responsible for making the maps.]

ore, ores
(noun) rock or earth from which metal is extracted.

organ, organs
1 (noun) Your organs are parts of your body that have a particular function, e.g. heart, lungs.
2 a keyboard musical instrument with pipes of different lengths through which air is forced.
organist (noun)
[Greek *organon* = tool]

organic
1 (adjective) produced by or found in plants or animals, e.g. *The rocks were searched for organic remains.*
2 Organic food is produced without the use of artificial fertilizers or pesticides.
organically (adverb)

organism, organisms
(noun) any living animal or plant.

organization, organizations
1 (noun) any group, society, club or business.
2 the act of planning and arranging something.
organizational (adjective)

Similar words: (sense 1) association, network, corporation

organize, organizes, organizing, organized; also spelled **organise**
(verb) to plan and arrange something.
organized (adjective) **organizer** (noun)

Orient
(noun; literary) The Orient is eastern and south-eastern Asia.
[Latin *oriens* = rising (sun)]

Notice the spelling of these ordinal numbers: fifth eighth ninth twelfth twentieth hundredth.

oriental
(adjective) belonging to eastern or south-eastern Asia.

orientate, orientates, orientating, orientated
1 (verb) When you orientate yourself, you find out where you are by looking at a map, or by looking around for familiar places.
2 If you orientate yourself to a new situation, you learn about it and adjust to it.
orientation (noun) **orientated** (adjective)
[sense 1: Old French *orienter* = to face east]

orienteering
(noun) a sport in which people run from one place to another in the countryside, using a map and compass to guide them.

origami
(noun) the Japanese art of paper folding.
[Japanese *ori* = a folding + *kami* paper]

origin, origins
1 (noun) the beginning or cause of something.
2 someone's family background, e.g. *a woman of Pakistani origin... His origins were humble.*
[Latin *origo* = beginning or birth]

Similar words: (sense 1) root, source

original, originals
1 (adjective) Original describes things that existed at the beginning, rather than being added later, or things that were the first of their kind to exist, e.g. *They will restore the house to its original state... The Stockton to Darlington was the original passenger railway.*
2 (noun) a work of art or a document that is the one that was first produced, and not a copy.
3 (adjective) imaginative and clever, e.g. *a daring and original idea.*
originally (adverb) **originality** (noun)

originate, originates, originating, originated
(verb) to begin to happen or exist, e.g. *The Trades Union movement originated in a small Dorset village called Tolpuddle.*
originator (noun)

ornament, ornaments
1 (noun) a small, attractive object that you display in your home or that you wear to look attractive.
2 decoration on a building, a piece of furniture, or a work of art.
[Latin *ornare* = to adorn]

ornamental
(adjective) designed to be attractive rather than useful, e.g. *an ornamental pond.*

ornithology
(noun) the study of birds.
ornithologist (noun)
[Greek *ornis* = bird + *-logia* = study of]

orphan, orphans, orphaning, orphaned
1 (noun) a child whose parents are dead.
2 (verb) If a child is orphaned, its parents die.

orthodox
1 (adjective) Orthodox methods are the standard ones that most people use, e.g. *He's an orthodox seam bowler.*

2 People who are orthodox believe in the older, more traditional ideas of their religion or political party, e.g. *orthodox Jews.*
[Greek *orthos* + *doxa* = correct belief]

orthography
(noun; formal) the way words are spelled or should be spelled.
[Greek *orthos* + *-graphos* = correct writing]

osteopath, osteopaths
(noun) someone who treats illnesses by manipulating people's bones, especially the spine.
osteopathy (noun)
[Greek *osteon* + *pathos* = bone suffering]

ostrich, ostriches
(noun) the largest bird in the world. They live in Africa and cannot fly.

other, others
1 (adjective, pronoun) e.g. *On the other hand... Wait until the others come back.*
2 (phrases) **The other day** or **the other week** means recently, e.g. *I saw him the other day.*
3 **Other than** means except, e.g. *She never discussed it with anyone other than Derek.*
4 **Every other day** or **every other week** means every alternate day or week.

otherwise
(adverb) e.g. *Wash five times a day. You're not really clean otherwise... I've a fractured skull and scarlet fever but otherwise I'm fine.*

otter, otters
(noun) a small, furry animal with a long tail. Otters swim well and eat fish.

ought (pronounced **awt**)
(verb) e.g. *She ought to see a doctor... I ought to have called... It ought to be quite easy.*

ounce, ounces
(noun) a unit of weight. [1 oz (ounce) = 28.3 grams; 16 oz = 1 pound.]

our
(pronoun) e.g. *Our new car is a Skoda.*

ours
(pronoun) e.g. *There's no school like ours.*

ourselves
(pronoun) e.g. *We almost made ourselves ill.*

out
1 (adverb) e.g. *She rushed out... He came when I was out... The lights went out.*
2 (adjective) on strike, e.g. *The men stayed out for nearly a month.*
3 unfashionable or unacceptable e.g. *Long skirts are out this year... Chewing gum is out, young man!*
4 incorrect, e.g. *It's only a couple of degrees out.*

out of
1 (preposition) If you do something out of a feeling, that feeling makes you do it, e.g. *She kicked the door out of sheer rage.*
2 If you are out of something, you no longer have any of it, e.g. *We're out of milk again.*

out-of-date
(adjective) old-fashioned and no longer useful.

Some men are wise.
And some are otherwise.

outback
(noun) In Australia, the outback is the remote parts where very few people live.

outboard motor, motors
(noun) a motor that can be fixed to the back of a small boat.

outbreak, outbreaks
(noun) a sudden occurrence, e.g. *an outbreak of war... an outbreak of measles.*

outburst, outbursts
(noun) a sudden, strong expression of an emotion, especially anger, e.g. *I apologize for my outburst just now.*

outcast, outcasts
(noun) someone who is rejected by others.

outclass, outclasses, outclassing, outclassed
(verb) If you outclass someone, you are a lot better than they are at doing something, e.g. *I was outclassed in the sprint finals.*

outcome, outcomes
(noun) a result, e.g. *I predicted the outcome of the election.*

outcry, outcries
(noun) If there is an outcry about something, a lot of people are angry about it, e.g. *Despite the public outcry, hunting was still allowed on National Trust property.*

outdated
(adjective) no longer in fashion.

outdoor
(adjective) happening or used outside.

outdoors
(adverb) outside, e.g. *Classes were held outdoors.*

outer
(adjective) The outer parts of something are the parts furthest from the centre, e.g. *the castle's outer walls.*

outer space
(noun) everything beyond the Earth's atmosphere.

outfit, outfits
1 (noun) a set of clothes.
2 (informal) an organization, e.g. *Who runs this outfit?*

outgoing, outgoings
1 (adjective) Outgoing describes someone who is leaving a job or place, e.g. *the outgoing President.*
2 friendly and not shy.
3 (plural noun) Your outgoings are the amount of money that you spend.

outgrow, outgrows, outgrowing, outgrew, outgrown
(verb) to grow too big for something, e.g. *She outgrew bedtime stories... I outgrew my favourite pullover.*

outing, outings
(noun) a pleasure trip.

outlandish
(adjective) very unusual or odd, e.g. *I thought his fur-lined jeans were a bit outlandish.*

outlaw, outlaws, outlawing, outlawed
1 (verb) If something is outlawed, it is made illegal.
2 (noun) In the past, an outlaw was a criminal.

outlay, outlays
(noun) an amount of money spent on something, e.g. *I had an outlay of £500 to start off with.*

outlet, outlets
1 (noun) a way of expressing your feelings or ideas.
2 a hole or pipe through which water or air can flow away.

outline, outlines, outlining, outlined
1 (verb) If you outline a plan or idea, you explain it in a general way.
2 (noun) a general explanation or description of something.
3 The outline of something is its shape.

Similar words: (noun: sense 3) contour, profile

outlive, outlives, outliving, outlived
(verb) to live longer than someone else, e.g. *Victoria outlived Albert by 40 years.*

outlook
1 (noun) Your outlook is your general attitude towards life.
2 The outlook of a situation is the way it is likely to develop, e.g. *The economic outlook is bright.*
3 the view from a place.

outnumber, outnumbers, outnumbering, outnumbered
(verb) to be more in number, e.g. *In 1940, the Luftwaffe outnumbered the RAF by over a thousand planes.*

outpatient, outpatients
(noun) a person who receives treatment in hospital without staying overnight.

outplay, outplays, outplaying, outplayed
(verb) If you outplay someone, you play better than they do.

output, outputs
(noun) the amount of something produced by a person or organization.

outrage, outrages, outraging, outraged
1 (verb) If something outrages you, it angers and shocks you, e.g. *I was outraged by his cruelty.*
2 (noun) a feeling of anger and shock.
3 something very shocking or violent, e.g. *The terrorist bombing was an outrage.*
outrageous (adjective) **outrageously** (adverb)

outright
1 (adjective) absolute, e.g. *an outright winner.*
2 (adverb) in an open and direct way, e.g. *If I ask the boss outright I will get nowhere.*
3 completely and totally, e.g. *The government has banned the drug outright.*

outside
1 (noun) the part of something which surrounds or encloses the rest of it.
2 (adverb, adjective, preposition) not inside, e.g. *a demonstration outside the embassy... Let's go outside... an outside toilet... outside office hours.*

Every time he opens his mouth he puts his foot in it. What does this mean? Anyone you know?

3 (adjective) On a motorway, the outside lanes are the overtaking ones closest to its centre.
4 (phrase) If there is **an outside chance** of something happening, it could happen, but is not very likely.

outsider, outsiders
1 (noun) someone who does not belong to a particular group.
2 a competitor considered unlikely to win, e.g. *Coventry City were outsiders to win the F.A. Cup but they won it just the same.*

outskirts
(plural noun) the parts around the edge of a city or town.

outspoken
(adjective) Outspoken people give their opinions openly, even if they shock other people.

outstanding
1 (adjective) extremely good, e.g. *an outstanding war record.*
2 Money that is outstanding is still owed, e.g. *There is £50 outstanding on your car loan.*

outstay, outstays, outstaying, outstayed
(phrase) If you **outstay your welcome**, you stay longer than your host wishes.

outstretched
(adjective) stretched out as far as possible, e.g. *She ran into his outstretched arms.*

outward
(adjective) The outward feelings or qualities of someone are the ones they appear to have, rather than the ones they actually have, e.g. *I said it with outward calm, but inside I was blazing.*
outwardly (adverb)

outwards
(adverb) away from a place or towards the outside, e.g. *The door opens outwards.*

outweigh, outweighs, outweighing, outweighed
(verb) If the advantages of something outweigh its disadvantages, you mean that the advantages are more important than the disadvantages.

outwit, outwits, outwitting, outwitted
(verb) If you outwit someone, you cleverly get the better of them.

oval, ovals
(noun) egg-shaped.
[Latin *ovalis* = egg shaped]

ovary, ovaries (pronounced oh-var-ree)
(noun) A woman's ovaries are the two organs in her body that produce human eggs.
[Latin *ovum* = egg]

ovation, ovations
1 (noun) a long burst of applause.
2 (phrase) If someone gets **a standing ovation**, the audience stands up and applauds them.

oven, ovens
(noun) the part of a cooker used for baking.

over, overs
1 (preposition) e.g. *the picture over the fireplace... Her hair hung down over her eyes... the view over the park... over the road... a quarrel over money... She spent over £100.*

2 (adverb) Over is used to indicate a position, e.g. *Come over here... She tipped the pan over... His search was over.*
3 (adverb, preposition) e.g. *Pat leaned over and picked it up... bent over his desk.*
4 (phrase) **Over and over again** means many times, e.g. *I read it over and over again.*
5 (phrase, adjective) If you go **over the top**, you do something too extremely, e.g. *The chap playing Hamlet went right over the top when he took 20 minutes to die... an over-the-top performance.*
6 (noun) In cricket, an over is a set of 6 balls bowled from the same end of the pitch.

over-
(prefix) too much, e.g. *an over-confident young man... They overfed their dog.*

overact, overacts, overacting, overacted
(verb) If you overact, you perform your part in an exaggerated manner.

overall, overalls
1 (adjective, adverb) general or generally, e.g. *The overall impression was of a smoky industrial city... Overall, the chances are good.*
2 (plural noun) Overalls are a piece of clothing worn to protect your other clothes when working.
3 (noun) a piece of clothing like a coat that you wear to protect your other clothes when working.

overarm
(adverb) If you throw or hit a ball overarm, your arm is raised above your shoulder as you throw.

overboard
1 (adverb) over the side of a ship, e.g. *Man overboard!*
2 (phrase; informal) If you **go overboard**, you are excessively enthusiastic, e.g. *I think you've gone a bit overboard on the sunflowers, Vincent.*

overcast
(adjective) An overcast sky is covered by cloud.

overcoat, overcoats
(noun) a thick, warm coat.

overcome, overcomes, overcoming, overcame
1 (verb) If you overcome a problem or a feeling, you manage to deal with it or control it.
2 (adjective) If you are overcome by a feeling, you feel it very strongly, e.g. *She was overcome by the fumes.*

overcrowded
(adjective) If a place is overcrowded, there are too many things or people in it.

overdo, overdoes, overdoing, overdid, overdone
(verb) If you overdo something, you do it too much, e.g. *Take some gentle exercise, but don't overdo it.*

overdose, overdoses
(noun) a dangerous amount of a drug.

overdraft
(noun) money that someone draws out of their bank when they have no money in the account.
overdrawn (adjective)

What are: a maiden over a maiden speech a maiden name a maiden voyage?

overdue
(adjective) late, e.g. *Tom is half an hour overdue... long overdue changes.*

overestimate, overestimates, overestimating, overestimated
(verb) to think something is bigger than it really is, e.g. *You are overestimating the problem.*

overflow, overflows, overflowing, overflowed
1 (verb) to spill over.
2 When people overflow a place, there are too many of them in it and some have to go outside.

overgrown
(adjective) covered with weeds because of neglect, e.g. *the overgrown path.*

overhang, overhangs, overhanging, overhung
(verb) If one thing overhangs another, it sticks out above it, e.g. *A tree overhung the lake.*

overhaul, overhauls, overhauling, overhauled
(verb) If you overhaul something, you examine it thoroughly and repair any faults.

overhead
(adverb, adjective) above, e.g. *Seagulls were circling overhead.*

overhear, overhears, overhearing, overheard
(verb) to hear what someone is saying to someone else.

overjoyed
(adjective) extremely pleased.

Similar words: jubilant, delighted, thrilled

overland
(adjective, adverb) travelling across land, not by sea or air, e.g. *an overland march... They are going overland to India in a bus.*

overlap, overlaps, overlapping, overlapped
(verb) If one thing overlaps another, one part of it covers part of the other thing.

overleaf
(adverb) on the next page, e.g. *Some of the animals are illustrated overleaf.*

overload, overloads, overloading, overloaded
(verb) If you overload someone or something, you give them too much to do or to carry.

overlook, overlooks, overlooking, overlooked
1 (verb) If a building or window overlooks a place, it has a view over that place.
2 If you overlook something, you ignore it, do not notice it or do not realize its importance, e.g. *They overlooked the enormous risks involved... I decided to overlook his unkindness.*

overnight
1 (adjective, adverb) during the night, e.g. *You can leave your bike here overnight.*
2 (adverb) sudden or suddenly, e.g. *an overnight success... The colonel became a hero overnight.*

overpower, overpowers, overpowering, overpowered
1 (verb) If you overpower someone, you seize them despite their struggles, because you are stronger than they are.

2 If a feeling overpowers you, it affects you very strongly.
overpowering (adjective)

overrated
(adjective) If you think something is overrated, you think it is not as good as people say it is.

overrule, overrules, overruling, overruled
(verb) To overrule a person or their decisions means to have your own way because their decisions are incorrect or inappropriate.

overrun, overruns, overrunning, overran, overrun
1 (verb) If an army overruns a country, it occupies it very quickly.
2 If animals or plants overrun a place, they spread quickly over it.
3 If an event overruns, it continues for longer than it was meant to.

overseas
(adjective, adverb) abroad or from abroad, e.g. *travelling overseas... overseas students.*

oversight, oversights
(noun) something which you forget to do or fail to notice.

oversleep, oversleeps, oversleeping, overslept
(verb) to sleep for longer than you meant to.

overstep, oversteps, overstepping, overstepped
(phrase) If you **overstep the mark**, you go too far and behave in an unacceptable way.

overtake, overtakes, overtaking, overtook, overtaken
(verb) to pass someone because you are moving faster than they are.

overthrow, overthrows, overthrowing, overthrew, overthrown
(verb) If a government is overthrown, it is removed from power by force.

overtime
(noun) extra time that someone works over their normal working hours.

overture, overtures
(noun) a piece of music at the start of an opera or play.
[Latin *apertura* = opening]

overturn, overturns, overturning, overturned
(verb) to turn something upside down or onto its side, e.g. *Overturned lorries filled the road.*

overweight
(adjective) too fat and heavy.

overwhelm, overwhelms, overwhelming, overwhelmed
1 (verb) If you are overwhelmed by something, it affects you very strongly, e.g. *The horror of the motorway crash overwhelmed me.*
2 If one group of people overwhelms another, they gain complete control or victory over them.
overwhelming (adjective) **overwhelmingly** (adverb)

overwork, overworks, overworking, overworked
(verb) to work too hard.

ovum, ova (pronounced **oh**-vum)
(noun) a reproductive cell of a woman or female

animal, which when fertilized by a male sperm produces young.
[a Latin word meaning 'egg']

owe, owes, owing, owed
1 (verb) If you owe someone money, they have lent it to you and you have not yet paid it back.
2 If you say that you owe someone thanks, respect or loyalty, you mean that they deserve it from you.
3 (phrase) **Owing to** something means because of, e.g. *I was late owing to a traffic jam.*

owl, owls
(noun) a bird of prey that hunts at night.

own, owns, owning, owned
1 (adjective) If something is your own, it belongs to you.
2 (phrase) **On your own** means alone.
3 If you **get your own back**, you take revenge on someone for something they did to you.
4 (verb) If you own something, it belongs to you.

own up
(phrasal verb) to admit that you did something wrong.

pace, paces, pacing, paced
1 (noun) the speed at which something moves.
2 a step; also used as a measurement of distance.
3 (verb) If you pace up and down, you keep walking about because of anxiety or impatience.
[Latin *passus* = a step]

pacifist, pacifists
(noun) someone who is completely opposed to all violence and war.
pacifism (noun)
[Latin *pax* = peace + *facere* = to make]

pacify, pacifies, pacifying, pacified
(verb) If you pacify someone who is angry, you calm them down.

pack, packs, packing, packed
1 (verb) to fill, e.g. *I'll pack your case... The house was packed full.*
2 (noun) a group, e.g. *a pack of cards... a pack of dogs... a pack of lies.*
3 (phrase) If you **send someone packing**, you send them away, perhaps angrily.

pack in
(phrasal verb; informal) If you pack something in, you stop doing it.

pack up
1 (phrasal verb; informal) If you pack up, you stop what you are doing and go away.
2 If a machine packs up, it breaks down.

package, packages
1 (noun) a small parcel.
2 In computing, a package is a set of programs to help carry out several related operations.

package holiday, holidays
(noun) a complete holiday, including travel, that is bought from a travel company.

owner, owners
(noun) the person that something belongs to.
ownership (noun)

ox, oxen
(noun) cattle which are used for carrying or pulling things.

oxide, oxides
(noun) a compound of oxygen and another chemical element, e.g. *ferrous oxide.*

oxygen
(noun) a colourless gas which makes up about 21% of the Earth's atmosphere.

oyster, oysters
(noun) a large, flat, edible shellfish.
[Greek *ostrakon* = shell]

ozone layer
(noun) a layer of ozone gas high above the Earth's surface that absorbs ultraviolet rays from the sun.
[Greek *ozein* = smell]

P

packaging
(noun) the container or wrapping in which an item is sold or sent.

packet, packets
(noun) a thin cardboard box or paper container in which something is sold.

pad, pads, padding, padded
1 (noun) e.g. *nappy pads... cricket pads... a writing pad... a rocket launch pad.*
2 (verb) to move around softly.
padding (noun)

paddle, paddles, paddling, paddled
1 (verb) If someone paddles a canoe or boat, they move it using a special pole with flat ends.
2 to walk in shallow water.

paddle steamer, steamers
(noun) a boat with large revolving wheels at each side powered by a steam engine.

paddock, paddocks
(noun) a small field.

padlock, padlocks
(noun) a detachable lock with a U-shaped bar.

page, pages, paging, paged
1 (noun) one of the pieces of paper in a book etc.
2 (verb) To page someone means to call their name out on a loudspeaker system to give them a message.
3 (noun) In medieval times, a page was a young boy servant who was learning to be a knight.

pageant, pageants (pronounced **paj-jent**)
(noun) a grand, colourful show or parade, especially one with a historical theme.
pageantry (noun)
[Latin *pagina* = scene of a play]

Letter P might have begun as a picture of a mouth. Later, a hook was added and the shape turned around.

pain, pains
1 (noun) an unpleasant feeling of physical hurt or deep unhappiness.
2 (phrase) If you **take pains** to do something, you are careful to do it properly.
3 (noun; informal) If you say that someone is a pain, you mean they are a nuisance or a bore.
painless (adjective) **painlessly** (adverb)
[Latin *poena* = punishment]

Similar words: ache, hurt, twinge

painful
(adjective) causing emotional or physical pain.
painfully (adverb)

painkiller, painkillers
(noun) a drug that relieves pain.

painstaking
(adjective) very careful and thorough.

paint, paints, painting, painted
(noun, verb) e.g. *oil paint... emulsion paint... to paint a picture... to paint a house.*
painter (noun) **painting** (noun)

pair, pairs, pairing, paired
1 (noun) two of something, e.g. *a pair of scissors... a pair of shoes.*
2 (verb) If you pair up with someone, you agree to do something together.

Pakistani, Pakistanis
1 (adjective) belonging to Pakistan.
2 (noun) someone who comes from Pakistan.

palace, palaces
(noun) a large, grand house, often the residence of a king, queen, bishop, etc.

palate, palates (pronounced **pal**-lat)
(noun) the top of the inside of your mouth.

pale, paler, palest
(adjective) rather white and without much colour or brightness.

Palestinian, Palestinians
(noun) an Arab from the region formerly called Palestine between the River Jordan and the Mediterranean.

palette, palettes
(noun) a flat piece of wood on which an artist mixes colours.

palindrome, palindromes
(noun) a word or phrase that is the same whether you read it forwards or backwards, e.g. *refer... Madam, I'm Adam.*

pallet, pallets
(noun) a wooden platform on which goods are stacked to be moved by a fork-lift truck.
[Old French *pallette* = little spade]

palm, palms
1 (noun) a tropical tree with no branches and a crown of long leaves.
2 the flat surface of your hand.

pamper, pampers, pampering, pampered
(verb) If you pamper someone, you give them too much kindness and comfort, e.g. *She was very pampered as a child, and at 40 she's helpless.*

pamphlet, pamphlets
(noun) a very thin book in paper covers.

pan, pans, panning, panned
1 (noun) a round container used for cooking.
2 (verb) When a film camera pans, it moves in a wide sweep.
3 to search for gold in mud and water.
4 (informal) to criticize someone strongly, e.g. *The film 'Rocky V' really got panned!*

pancake, pancakes
(noun) a thin, flat round of cooked batter.

pancreas (pronounced **pang**-kree-ass)
(noun) an organ in the body situated behind the stomach which produces insulin and enzymes that help digestion.

panda car, cars
(noun) a police patrol car.

pandemonium (pronounced pan-dim-**moan**-ee-um)
(noun) a state of noisy confusion.
[from *Pandemonium*, the capital of Hell in Milton's 'Paradise Lost']

pane, panes
(noun) a flat sheet of glass in a window or door.

panel, panels
1 (noun) a small group of people who are chosen to do something, e.g. *He was on the panel for 'Any Questions'.*
panellist (noun)
2 a flat piece of wood forming part of a larger object, e.g. *door panels.*
3 A control panel is a surface containing switches and instruments to operate a machine etc.
panelled (adjective) **panelling** (noun)

panic, panics, panicking, panicked
1 (noun) an overwhelming feeling of fear or anxiety.
2 (verb) If you panic, you become so afraid or anxious that you cannot act sensibly.
panic-stricken (adjective)

panorama, panoramas
(noun) an extensive view over a wide area of land.
panoramic (adjective)

pansy, pansies
(noun) a small garden flower.

pant, pants, panting, panted
(verb) to breathe quickly and loudly through your mouth.

panther, panthers
(noun) a large wild animal belonging to the cat family, especially the black leopard.

pantomime, pantomimes
(noun) an entertainment with music, usually based on a fairy story, performed at Christmas.

pantry, pantries
(noun) a small room where food is kept.
[Old French *paneterie* = bread store]

pants
1 (plural noun) a piece of underwear.
2 In American English, pants are trousers.

Fleet Street in London is known as the home of England's newspapers, but none are now printed there.

paper, papers, papering, papered
1 (noun) a material made from wood pulp and used for writing on or wrapping things.
2 a newspaper.
3 (plural noun) Papers are official documents, e.g. passport, ID card.
4 (noun) part of a written examination.
5 (verb) to put wallpaper on.
[from *papyrus*, the plant from which paper was made in ancient Egypt, Greece and Rome]

paperback, paperbacks
(noun) a book with a thin, cardboard cover.

paperweight, paperweights
(noun) a small, heavy object placed on papers to keep them in place.

paperwork
(noun) the part of a job that involves dealing with letters, reports etc.

papier-mâché (pronounced pap-yay **mash**-ay)
(noun) mashed, wet paper mixed with glue and moulded into shape to make models etc.
[French *papier-mâché* = chewed paper]

papyrus (pronounced pap-**eye**-russ)
(noun) a type of paper made in ancient Egypt, Greece and Rome from the stems of a tall water plant called papyrus.

par
1 Something that is **below par** or **under par** is below its normal standard.
2 (noun) In golf, par is the number of strokes which a good player should take for a hole or for all the holes on a golf course.
[Latin *par* = equal]

parable, parables
(noun) a short story with moral or religious meaning.

parachute, parachutes (pronounced **par**-rash-oot)
(noun) a device made of fabric to enable people to fall safely from an aircraft.

parade, parades
(noun) a line of people or vehicles standing or moving together as a display.

paradise
(noun) another name for heaven.
[Greek *paradeisos* = garden]

paraffin
(noun) a strong-smelling liquid made from petrol, used as a fuel and for cleaning [also called **kerosene**].

paragraph, paragraphs
(noun) a section of a piece of writing. Paragraphs begin on a new line.

parallel, parallels, paralleling or **parallelling, paralleled** or **parallelled**
1 (adjective) If two lines are parallel, they are the same distance apart along their whole length.
2 (verb) If something parallels something else, it is as good as or similar to it.
[Greek *parallēlos* = alongside one another]

parallelogram, parallelograms
(noun) a 4-sided shape in which each side is parallel to the opposite side.

paralyse, paralyses, paralysing, paralysed
(verb) If something paralyses you, it causes loss of feeling and movement in your body.
paralysis (noun)

Similar words: immobilize, freeze

parapet, parapets
(noun) a low wall along the edge of a bridge or roof.
[Italian *parapetto* = chest-high wall]

paraphernalia (pronounced par-raf-fan-**ale**-yah)
(noun) Someone's paraphernalia consists of all their belongings or equipment.
[Latin *parapherna* = personal property of a married woman]

paraphrase, paraphrases, paraphrasing, paraphrased
1 (verb) to say the same thing in a different way.
2 (noun) something said in a different way.

Similar words: (verb) reword, rephrase, restate

parasite, parasites
(noun) a small animal or plant that lives on or inside a larger animal or plant.
parasitic (adjective)
[Greek *parasitos* = someone who eats at someone else's table]

parasol, parasols
(noun) a type of umbrella that provides shelter from the sun.

paratroops or **paratroopers**
(plural noun) soldiers trained to be dropped by parachute.

parcel, parcels
(noun) something wrapped up in paper.

parched
1 (adjective) If the ground is parched, it is very dry and in need of water.
2 If you are parched, you are very thirsty.

parchment
(noun) thick, yellowish paper of very good quality.

pardon, pardons, pardoning, pardoned
1 You say **pardon** or **beg your pardon** to apologize in small matters, or when you have not heard what someone has said.
2 (verb) If you pardon someone, you forgive them for doing something wrong.

parent, parents
(noun) Your parents are your father and mother.
parental (adjective)

parenthesis, parentheses (pronounced par-**renth**-iss-iss)
1 (noun) a phrase or remark inside brackets, dashes or commas that is inserted into a piece of writing or speech.
2 Parentheses are a pair of brackets put round a word or phrase.

The cruel sun beat down. This kind of expression is called a *pathetic fallacy*. The sun cannot be cruel.

parish, parishes
(noun) an area with its own church and clergyman, and often its own council.

park, parks, parking, parked
1 (noun) a public area with grass and trees.
2 a private area of grass and trees around a large country house.
3 (verb) to drive a vehicle into a position where it can be left.
[Latin *parricus* = enclosure]

parka, parkas
(noun) a jacket with a quilted lining and fur round the hood.

parking meter, meters
(noun) a machine in which you put coins to pay for parking a vehicle in the street.

parliament, parliaments
(noun) A country's parliament is the group of elected representatives who make its laws.
parliamentary (adjective)

parody, parodies
(noun) an amusing imitation of the style of an author or of a familiar situation.

Similar words: send-up, take-off, spoof

parole
(noun) When prisoners get parole, they are let out early, on condition that they behave well.
[French *parole d'honneur* = word of honour]

parrot, parrots
1 (noun) a brightly-coloured tropical bird.
2 (phrase) If you learn or repeat something **parrot fashion**, you do it accurately without understanding it or thinking about what it means.

parse, parses, parsing, parsed
(verb) If you parse a sentence, you decide the grammatical type of each word and clause.

parsley
(noun) a herb used in cooking.

parsnip, parsnips
(noun) a long, pointed root vegetable.

parson, parsons
(noun) a vicar or other clergyman.

part, parts, parting, parted
1 (noun) a piece of something e.g. *It's easy to get parts for this car... I've got a small part in the school play.*
2 (phrase) **Parts of speech** are the different types of word, e.g. noun, verb, adjective.
3 If you **take part** in an activity, you do it together with other people.
4 (verb) to move away or separate, e.g. *The Red Sea waters parted in the middle... The couple decided to part... The rope parted and the boat was adrift.*
5 (phrase) Example: *It was a mistake* **on your part** means that you made the mistake.
partly (adverb)
[Latin *partire* = to divide]

Similar words: (noun) component, element, member

partial
1 (adjective) not complete, e.g. *I could give it only partial support.*
partially (adverb)
2 liking something very much, e.g. *The vicar is very partial to roast pheasant.*
3 favouring one side in a dispute etc.

participate, participates, participating, participated
(verb) to take part in something.
participant (noun) **participation** (noun)

participle, participles
(noun) In grammar, a participle is a form of a verb. English has two participles: the present participle, e.g. crying — *The child was crying; a crying child:* the past participle, e.g. stolen — *They have stolen my TV; a stolen car.*

particle, particles
(noun) a very small piece of something.

particular, particulars
1 (adjective) relating to only one thing or person, e.g. *Each person had his own particular mug.*
2 Someone who is particular demands high standards and is not easily satisfied.
3 (plural noun) Particulars are facts or details, e.g. *Please give me particulars of that cooker.*
particularly (adverb)

parting, partings
1 (noun) an occasion when one person leaves another, e.g. *Such parting is sweet sorrow.*
2 The line of visible scalp created when someone combs their hair into two parts.

partition, partitions
(noun) a screen separating one part of a room or vehicle from another.

partner, partners, partnering, partnered
1 the person you are doing something with, e.g. in a dance or a game, in marriage, in business.
2 (verb) If you partner someone, you are their partner for a game or social occasion.
partnership (noun)

part-time
(adjective) involving work for only a part of the working day or week.

party, parties
1 (noun) an enjoyable private, social event.
2 A political party is an organization whose members share similar political beliefs and campaign for elections.
3 a group of people who are doing something together, e.g. *a coach party.*

pass, passes, passing, passed
1 (verb) e.g. *I pass the bus stop each day... Pass me the sugar, please... He passed the time in reading... several days passed... She passed her driving test.*
2 (noun) A pass in a ball game is sending the ball to another player in the same team.
3 A pass is an official document that allows you to go somewhere, e.g. *a bus pass.*
4 a narrow route between mountains.
5 A pass in an exam is a satisfactory mark.

The word *cemetery* comes from a Greek word *koimeterion* which meant 'a sleeping room'.

pass away or **pass on**
(phrasal verb) to die.

pass out
(phrasal verb) to faint.

pass up
(phrasal verb) If you pass up an opportunity, you do not take advantage of it.

passable
(adjective) of a fair standard; not bad. e.g. *This is a passable wine, Obadiah.*

passage, passages
1 (noun) a long, narrow corridor.
2 a section of a book or piece of music.
3 A sea passage is a journey by ship.
[Old French *passage* = act of passing]

passenger, passengers
1 (noun) a person travelling in a vehicle, aircraft, or ship.
2 (informal) If you say that a member of a team is a passenger, you mean that they are not much use to the team, perhaps because of injury.

passer-by, passers-by
(noun) someone who is walking past someone or something.

passionate
(adjective) expressing very strong feelings about something, e.g. *a passionate romance.*
passion (noun)

Similar words: hot-blooded, fiery, intense

passive
1 (adjective) remaining calm and showing no feeling when provoked.
2 (noun) In grammar, the passive voice is the form of the verb in which the object of an action becomes the subject of the sentence, e.g. The passive version of *He kicked the ball* is *The ball was kicked by him.* [opposite: **active**]
passively (adverb)

Passover
(noun) an 8-day Jewish festival in spring.

passport, passports
(noun) an official identification document which you need to travel abroad.

password, passwords
(noun) a word you need to know to get into a protected computer file, or into a special place.

past
1 (noun) the period of time before the present, e.g. *Even God cannot change the past.*
2 (adjective) Past things are things that happened or existed before the present.
3 (preposition, adverb) e.g. *It is ten past six... the car went past the house.*

past tense
(noun) In grammar, the past tense is the tense of a verb used to refer to things that happened or existed in the past, e.g. *I* **spoke** *to him just a second ago... She* **taught** *me many years ago.*
[compare: **present** tense; **future** tense].

pasta
(noun) a dried mixture of flour, eggs and water, formed into different shapes, e.g. spaghetti.

paste, pastes, pasting, pasted
1 (noun) a soft, rather sticky mixture that can be easily spread.
2 (verb) If you paste something onto a surface, you stick it with glue.

pastel, pastels
1 (adjective) Pastel colours are pale and soft.
2 (noun) Pastels are small sticks of coloured crayon, used for drawing pictures.

pasteurized also spelt **pasteurised** (pronounced **past**-yoor-ized)
(adjective) Pasteurized milk has been treated with a special heating process to kill bacteria.
[named after Louis Pasteur (1822-95) who invented the process]

pastille, pastilles (pronounced **pass**-till)
(noun) a small, soft sweet with a fruit flavour.

pastime, pastimes
(noun) a hobby or something you do for pleasure.

Similar words: pursuit, interest, recreation, play

past participle, past participles
(noun) In grammar, the past participle of a verb is the form, usually ending in 'ed' or 'en', that is used to make some past tenses and the passive, e.g. *baked, taken, swum.*

pastry, pastries
1 (noun) a mixture of flour, fat and water, rolled flat and used for making pies.
2 a small cake, e.g. *a Danish pastry.*

pasture, pastures
(noun) an area of grass for animals to graze.

pasty, pasties
1 (adjective; rhymes with **hasty**) pale and unhealthy looking.
2 (noun; pronounced **pass**-tee) a small pie containing meat and vegetables.

pat, pats, patting, patted
(verb) e.g. *Don't pat the dog. It will eat you.*

patch, patches, patching, patched
1 (noun) a piece of material used to cover a hole in something.
2 an area of a surface that is different from the rest, e.g. *a damp patch on the ceiling.*
3 (verb) to put a patch on something.
4 (phrase) Something that is **not a patch on** something else is not nearly as good.

patchy
(adjective) uneven; spread around in patches, e.g. *patchy fog.*

pâté (pronounced **pa**-tay)
(noun) a mixture of meat, fish or vegetables with various flavourings, blended into a paste.

patent, patents
(noun) an official right given to an inventor to be the only person or company allowed to make or sell a new product.

path, paths
(noun) a strip of ground for people to walk on.

pathetic
1 (adjective) weak, inadequate or helpless.
2 (informal) a word used scornfully to say that
something is of very poor quality.
pathetically (adverb)
[Greek *pathetikos* = sensitive]

Similar words: forlorn, pitiful, moving, sorry

pathology
(noun) the study of diseases and the way they
develop.
pathological (adjective) **pathologist** (noun)

patience
1 (noun) the ability to stay calm in a difficult or
irritating situation.
2 a card game for one player.
[Latin *patienta* = endurance]

patient, patients
1 (adjective) If you are patient, you stay calm in
a difficult or annoying situation.
2 (noun) a person receiving medical treatment
from a doctor or in a hospital.
patiently (adverb)

patio, patios
(noun) a paved area close to a house.

patriotic (adjective)
Someone who is patriotic loves their country and
feels very loyal towards it.
patriot (noun) **patriotism** (noun)
[Latin *patria* = native land]

patrol, patrols, patrolling, patrolled
(verb) When soldiers, police or guards patrol an
area, they walk or drive around to make sure
there is no trouble.
[French *patouiller* = to flounder in mud]

patron, patrons
1 (noun) a person who supports or gives money
to artists, writers or musicians.
2 The patrons of a hotel, pub or shop are the
people who use it.
[Latin *patronus* = protector]

patronize, patronizes, patronizing, patronized;
also spelled **patronise**
1 (verb) If someone patronizes you, they treat
you kindly, but in a way that suggests that you
are less intelligent or inferior to them.
patronizing (adjective)
2 If you patronize a hotel, pub or shop, you are a
customer there.

patron saint, saints
(noun) a saint who is believed to look after a
group of people, a place, etc.

patter, patters, pattering, pattered
1 (verb) to make quick, light, tapping sounds.
2 (noun) quick, light, tapping sounds, e.g. *the
patter of tiny feet.*

pattern, patterns
1 (noun) the way something is usually done or
happens, e.g. *This crime doesn't fit the pattern.*
2 a decorative design of repeated shapes.
patterned (adjective)
3 a diagram or shape used as a guide for making
something, e.g. clothes.

pause, pauses, pausing, paused
(verb) to stop what you are doing for a short
time.

pave, paves, paving, paved
1 (verb) When an area of ground is paved, it is
covered with flat blocks of stone or concrete.
2 (phrase) If something **paves the way** for a
change, it makes things right for change to
happen.

pavement, pavements
(noun) a surfaced path at the side of a road.
[Latin *pavimentum* = hard floor]

pavilion, pavilions
(noun) a building at a sports ground where
players can wash and change.
[Old French *pavillon* = tent]

paw, paws, pawing, pawed
1 (noun) the feet of an animal, e.g. cat, dog.
2 (verb) If an animal paws something, it hits it or
scrapes at it with its paws.

pawn, pawns, pawning, pawned
1 (verb) If you pawn something, you leave it with
a pawnbroker in return for a loan of money. If
you do not pay back the money within a certain
time, the item is sold.
pawnshop (noun)
2 (noun) In chess, a pawn is the smallest and
least valuable playing piece.

pay, pays, paying, paid
1 (verb) e.g. *Pay me what you owe... It will pay
you to read lots of books... You'll pay for this, you
villain!... Pay attention, Smithers!... Let's pay a
visit to Grandad.*
2 (noun) Someone's pay is their salary or wages.

payable
1 (adjective) Money that is payable has to be
paid or can be paid, e.g. *Fees are payable in
advance here at St Trinian's.*
2 If a cheque is made payable to you, you are the
person who should receive the money.

payment, payments
(noun) a sum of money paid.

PC, PCs
1 (noun) a police constable.
2 a personal computer.

PE
(noun) a lesson in which gymnastics or sports
are taught [an abbreviation for physical
education].

pea, peas
(noun) a small, round, green vegetable in a pod.

peace
1 (noun) undisturbed calm and quiet.
2 When a country is at peace, it is not at war.

Similar words: (sense 1) tranquillity, quiet, calm

peaceful
(adjective) quiet, calm and free from noise.
peacefully (adverb)

Similar words: serene, tranquil

....Write 2 short descriptions of the start of the school day. Use the active voice then the passive.

peach, peaches
1 (noun) a soft, round, juicy fruit.
2 (adjective, noun) pale pinky-orange.

peacock, peacocks
(noun) a large bird with green and blue feathers. The male has a long tail which it can spread out in a fan. [feminine: **peahen**]

peak, peaks, peaking, peaked
1 (noun) The peak of an activity or process is the point at which it is strongest or most successful.
2 (verb) When something peaks, it reaches its highest value or its greatest level of success.
3 (noun) the pointed top of a mountain.
4 The peak of a cap is the part that sticks out over your eyes.

Similar words: height, summit

peal, peals, pealing, pealed
(verb) When bells peal, they ring one after the other.

peanut, peanuts
1 (noun) a small, oval nut eaten as a snack.
2 (informal) If you describe an amount of money as peanuts, you mean that it is very small, e.g. *If you pay peanuts, you get monkeys!*

pear, pears
(noun) a fruit.

pearl, pearls
(noun) a hard, round, creamy-white object grown inside an oyster and used in jewellery.

peasant, peasants
(noun) a person who works on the land, especially in a poor country.

peat
(noun) dark-brown, decaying plant material found in cool, wet regions, used as fuel or in gardening.

pebble, pebbles
(noun) a smooth, round stone.

peck, pecks, pecking, pecked
1 (verb) If a bird pecks something, it bites at it quickly with its beak.
2 (noun) a quick kiss on the cheek.

peckish
(adjective; informal) hungry.

peculiar
(adjective) strange and perhaps unpleasant.
peculiarly (adverb) **peculiarity** (noun)

pedal, pedals, pedalling, pedalled
1 (noun) a control lever on a machine or vehicle that you press with your foot.
2 (verb) When you pedal a bicycle, you push the pedals round with your feet to move along.

peddle, peddles, peddling, peddled
(verb) to go round selling something, e.g. *The man was caught peddling drugs.*
peddler (noun) **pedlar** (noun)

pedestal, pedestals
(noun) a base on which a statue stands.

pedestrian, pedestrians
(noun) someone who is walking.
pedestrian crossing (noun)
[Latin *pedester* = on foot]

pedigree
(adjective) A pedigree animal is descended from a single breed and its ancestors are known and recorded.

peek, peeks, peeking, peeked
(verb) to have a quick look at something.

peel, peels, peeling, peeled
1 (verb) to remove the skin of fruit or vegetables.
2 If, after being in the sun, you are peeling, your sunburnt skin is flaking off.

peep, peeps, peeping, peeped
1 (verb) to have a look at something, sometimes when you should not.
2 (noun) If you have not heard a peep out of someone, they have not said or done anything.

peer, peers, peering, peered
1 (verb) to look at something very hard.
2 (noun) Lords, dukes, earls, etc. are peers.
3 Your peers are the people who are of the same age and social background as you.

peerage, peerages
(noun) the rank of being a peer (a baroness, lord, duke etc.), e.g. *She was given a life peerage.*

peevish
(adjective) irritable and complaining.

peg, pegs
(noun) a fastener, e.g. *a clothes peg... a tent peg.*

pelican crossing, crossings
(noun) a place where you can cross the road by operating traffic lights.

pellet, pellets
(noun) a small ball of paper, lead, etc.

pelt, pelts, pelting, pelted
1 (verb) If you pelt someone, you throw things violently at them, e.g. *pelted with snowballs.*
2 If you pelt along, you run very fast.
3 (noun) the skin and fur of an animal.

pelvis, pelvises
(noun) the wide framework of bones at hip-level at the base of the spine.
[Latin *pelvis* = basin]

pen, pens, penning, penned
1 (noun) e.g. *fountain pen... ballpoint pen... animal pen.*
2 (verb) to write, e.g. *I will pen a brief note.*
3 If you are penned up, you have to remain in an uncomfortably small area.
[Latin *penna* = feather; pens used to be made from feathers]

penalize, penalizes, penalizing, penalized; also spelled penalise
(verb) If you are penalized, you are punished in some way, e.g. *The full back was penalized for tripping his opponent.*

penalty, penalties
(noun) a punishment or disadvantage that someone is made to suffer, e.g. *a fixed penalty for parking... a last minute penalty for United.*

Etymology. Find out how these words are connected: scribble inscribe inscription describe.

ence a plural form of **penny**.

encil, pencils
(noun) e.g. *HB pencils are used for most writing.*
[Latin *pencillus* = painter's brush]

endant, pendants
(noun) a piece of jewellery on a chain, worn round the neck.
[French *pendre* = to hang down]

endulum, pendulums
(noun) a rod in a clock with a weight at one end which swings regularly from side to side to control the clock.
[Latin *pendere* = to hang down]

enetrate, penetrates, penetrating, penetrated
(verb) to work your way into something, e.g. *He penetrated the enemy lines.*
penetration (noun)

en friend, friends
(noun) someone living in a different place or country to whom you write regularly.

enguin, penguins
(noun) a black and white Antarctic bird with webbed feet and small wings like flippers.

enicillin
(noun) a powerful antibiotic from the fungus penicillium, used to treat infections.

eninsula, peninsulas
(noun) an area of land almost surrounded by water, e.g. *the Ards Peninsula in Ireland.*
[Latin *paene* + *insula* = almost an island]

enis, penises
(noun) the part of a man's body used when urinating and having sexual intercourse.

enknife, penknives
(noun) a small, folding knife.

en-name, pen-names
(noun) a name used by a writer instead of his or her own name, e.g. 'Boz' was a pen-name of Charles Dickens.

ennant, pennants
(noun) a triangular flag, especially one used by ships as a signal.

enniless
(adjective) having no money.

enny, pennies or **pence**
(noun) a unit of money in Britain and some other countries. (100p = £1)

ension, pensions (pronounced **pen-shn**)
(noun) a regular sum of money paid to an old, retired, disabled or widowed person.
[Latin *pensio* = a payment]

ensioner, pensioners
(noun) an old, retired person receiving a pension paid by the state.

ensive
(adjective) deep in thought.
[French *penser* = to think]

Similar words: thoughtful, dreamy

pentagon, pentagons
(noun) a shape with 5 straight sides.
pentagonal (adjective)
[Greek *pente* = five + *gōnius* = angled]

pentathlon, pentathlons (pronounced pen-**tath**-lon)
(noun) a sports contest in which athletes compete in 5 different events.
[Greek *pente* = five + *athlon* = contest]

pent-up
(adjective) Pent-up emotions have been held back for a long time without release.

Similar words: suppressed, bottled-up

penultimate
(adjective) the one before the last.
[Latin *paene* = almost + *ultimus* = last]

people, peoples
1 (plural noun) men, women and children.
2 (noun) A people is all the men, women and children of a particular country or race.

Similar words: (sense 1) folk, persons, human beings (sense 2) nation, race, population, public

pepper, peppers, peppering, peppered
1 (noun) a hot-tasting spice used for cooking.
2 a hollow green, red or yellow vegetable.
3 (verb) e.g. *The gamekeeper lifted his gun and peppered the poacher with pellets.*

peppermint, peppermints
(noun) a mint-flavoured sweet.

pep talk, talks
(noun; informal) a speech intended to encourage people, e.g. *The manager gave the team a pep talk at half time.*

per
(preposition) Per is used to mean 'each' in rates and ratios, e.g. *The rent is £200 per month... travelling at 40 miles per hour.*

per annum
(adverb) each year, e.g. *£2000 per annum.*
[Latin *per annum* = each year]

perceive, perceives, perceiving, perceived
(verb) to notice or realize.

Similar words: make out, distinguish

per cent
(phrase) You use **per cent** to talk about amounts as a proportion of a hundred. e.g. *64 per cent of Americans voted 'Yes'* means that out of every 100 people, 64 voted 'Yes'.
(64 per cent = 64% = 64/100 = ·64)
[Latin *per* = each + *centum* = hundred]

percentage, percentages
(noun) a fraction expressed as a number of hundredths, e.g. *56%... A high percentage of schoolchildren own calculators.*

perception
1 (noun) Someone who has perception notices or understands things that are not obvious.
2 Your perception of something or someone is the way you see them.

Saki's real name was H. H. Munro. George Eliot's real name was Mary Ann Evans.

perceptive

(adjective) Someone who is perceptive realizes or notices things that are not obvious.
perceptively (adverb)

Similar word: observant, sensitive

perch, perches, perching, perched

1 (verb) If you perch on something, you sit on the edge of it.
2 When a bird perches, it stands on something.
3 (noun) an edible freshwater fish.

percolate, percolates, percolating, percolated

(verb) To percolate coffee means to make it in a percolator, where hot water passes through the coffee grains.
percolator (noun)
[Latin *per* = through + *colare* = to strain]

percussion

(noun, adjective) Percussion instruments are instruments that you hit to produce sounds, e.g. cymbals, drums.
percussionist (noun)

perennial, perennials

1 (adjective) continually occurring or never ending, e.g. *The harvest festival is a perennial feature of the school year.*
2 (noun) a plant that flowers for several years.
[Latin *per* = each + *annus* = through the years]

perfect, perfects, perfecting, perfected

1 (adjective) of the highest standard and without fault, e.g. *I used to be boastful, but now I'm perfect.*
2 absolute, e.g. *They were perfect strangers.*
3 In grammar, the perfect tense of a verb is normally formed with the present tense of 'have' and the past participle of the main verb, e.g. *He has gone.*
4 (verb; pronounced per-**fect**) If you perfect something, you make it as good as it can possibly be.
perfectly (adverb) **perfection** (noun)

Similar words: (adjective: sense 1) faultless, flawless, immaculate, ideal

perfectionist, perfectionists

(noun) someone who always tries to do everything perfectly.

perforated

(adjective) Something that is perforated has small holes in it, e.g. stamps, tea bags, eardrums.
perforation (noun)

perform, performs, performing, performed

1 (verb) To perform a task, action or service means to do it.
2 to act, dance in front of an audience.
performer (noun)

performance, performances

1 (noun) an entertainment for an audience.
2 Someone's or something's performance is how successful they are, e.g. *Her performance in the exams was disappointing.*

perfume, perfumes

(noun) a pleasant-smelling liquid which people put on their bodies.
perfumed (adjective)

perhaps

(adverb) maybe, e.g. *It is perhaps her best film.*

peril, perils

(noun; formal) great danger.
perilous (adjective) **perilously** (adverb)

perimeter, perimeters

(noun) the outer edge of an area or shape.

period, periods

1 (noun) a length of time.
2 one of the parts of the school day.
3 the monthly bleeding from a woman's womb.
4 In American English, a period is a full stop. It is sometimes used like this: *He's no good, period*, meaning *He's no good and there's nothing more to be said about it.*
5 (adjective) relating to a historical period of time, e.g. *period costumes.*
periodic (adjective) **periodically** (adverb)
[Greek *periodos* = circuit]

periodical, periodicals

(noun) a magazine or journal.

periscope, periscopes

(noun) a tube with mirrors used in a submarine to see above the surface of the water.
[Greek *periskopein* = to look around]

perish, perishes, perishing, perished

1 (verb; formal) If someone or something perishes, they are killed or destroyed.
2 If fruit, rubber or fabric perishes, it rots.
perishable (adjective)

perk, perks, perking, perked

1 (noun) an extra advantage which comes with a job, e.g. *Free use of the pool is one of the perks of working in a hotel.*
[an abbreviation for 'perquisite']
2 (verb; informal) When someone perks up, they become more cheerful.
perky (adjective)

perm, perms

(noun) If you have a perm, your hair is curled and treated with chemicals to keep the curls for several months. [short for 'permanent wave']

permanent

(adjective) lasting for ever, or present all the time, e.g. *a permanent job.*
permanently (adverb) **permanence** (noun)

permissible

(adjective) allowed by the rules.

Similar words: legitimate, permitted

permission

(noun) If you have permission to do something, you are allowed to do it.

Similar words: consent, clearance, leave, licence, authorization

People who acted in medieval plays were given surnames from their roles: King, Knight.

permissive
(adjective) A permissive society allows things which some people disapprove of.
permissiveness (noun)

permit, permits, permitting, permitted
1 (verb; pronounced per-**mit)** to allow something.
2 (noun; pronounced **per**-mit) an official document which says that you are allowed to do something.

Similar words: (verb) allow, authorize, let, grant

perpendicular
(adjective) upright, or at right angles to a horizontal line.
[Latin *perpendiculum* = a plumb line]

perpetual
(adjective) never-ending.
perpetually (adverb) **perpetuity** (noun)

perplexed
(adjective) puzzled and confused.
perplex (verb) **perplexity** (noun)
[Latin *perplexus* = entangled]

persecute, persecutes, persecuting, persecuted
(verb) to treat someone with continual cruelty and unfairness.
persecution (noun) **persecutor** (noun)
[Latin *persecutor* = pursuer]

Similar words: victimize, pick on

persevere, perseveres, persevering, persevered
(verb) to keep trying to do something and not give up.
perseverance (noun)

Similar words: persist, carry on, keep going, stick at

persist, persists, persisting, persisted
(verb) If you persist in doing something, you continue in spite of opposition or difficulty.
persistence (noun) **persistent** (adjective)

person, people or **persons**
1 (noun) a man, woman or child.
2 (phrase) If you do something **in person**, you do it yourself rather than getting someone else to do it for you.
3 (noun) In grammar, the first person is the speaker (I, we), the second person is the person being spoken to (you), and the third person is anyone else being referred to (he, she, it, they).
[Latin *persona* = actor's mask]

Similar words: human being, individual, character

personal
1 (adjective) relating to someone in particular, e.g. *a personal stereo.*
2 Personal matters relate to your feelings, relationships, and health which you may not wish to discuss with most other people.
3 Personal comments refer to someone's appearance or character in an offensive way, e.g. *She was becoming very personal about me.*
personally (adverb)

Similar words: own, individual, private, exclusive

personality, personalities
1 (noun) someone's character and nature.
2 a famous person, e.g. *a sports personality.*

personalized; also spelled **personalised**
(adjective) designed specially for someone.

personnel (pronounced per-son-**nell)**
(noun) The personnel of an organization are the people who work for it.
personnel officer (noun)

perspective, perspectives
(noun) In art, perspective is a method by which things in the distance are made to look further away than things in the foreground.
[Latin *perspicere* = to inspect carefully]

perspiration
(noun) sweat.
perspire (verb)

persuade, persuades, persuading, persuaded
(verb) to make someone do something or believe something by giving very good reasons.
persuasion (noun) **persuasive** (adjective)

Similar words: get, coax, win over

perturbed
(adjective) worried.
perturb (verb)

Peruvian, Peruvians (pronounced per-**roo**-vee-an)
1 (adjective) belonging to Peru.
2 (noun) someone who comes from Peru.

perverse
(adjective) Someone who is perverse deliberately does things that are unreasonable or harmful.
perversely (adverb) **perversity** (noun)
[Latin *perversus* = turned the wrong way]

pervert, perverts
(noun) a person whose sexual behaviour is disgusting or harmful.
perverted (adjective)
[Latin *pervertere* = to turn the wrong way]

peseta, pesetas (pronounced pes-**say**-ta)
(noun) the main unit of money in Spain.

pessimistic
(adjective) believing that bad things will happen.
pessimist (noun) **pessimism** (noun)
pessimistically (adverb)
[Latin *pessimus* = worst]

pest, pests
1 (noun) an insect or small animal which damages plants or food supplies.
2 Someone who is a pest keeps bothering you.
[Latin *pestis* = plague]

pester, pesters, pestering, pestered
(verb) If you pester someone, you keep bothering them or asking them to do something.

Similar words: harass, badger, hassle

pesticide, pesticides
(noun) a chemical sprayed onto plants to kill insects and grubs.

pet, pets, petting, petted
1 (noun) a tame animal kept at home.

Two men look out through the same bars;
One sees mud – and one sees stars.

2 (adjective) Someone's pet theory or pet project is something that they particularly support or feel strongly about.
3 (verb) If you pet a person or animal, you stroke them affectionately.

petal, petals
(noun) the coloured outer parts of a flower.
[Greek *petalon* = leaf]

petition, petitions
(noun) a document demanding official action signed by a lot of people.

petrified
(adjective) very frightened.
[It literally means 'turned to stone']

petrol
(noun) a fuel obtained from oil.
[from **petroleum**, a thick oil found under the earth; Latin *petra* = rock + *oleum* = oil]

petticoat, petticoats
(noun) a piece of underclothing like a very thin skirt or dress.

petty, pettier, pettiest
1 (adjective) small and unimportant.
2 Petty behaviour consists of doing small things which are selfish or unkind.

petty officer, officers
(noun) a non-commissioned officer in the navy.

pew, pews
(noun) a long, wooden seat in a church.

phantom, phantoms
(noun) a ghost.

pharaoh, pharaohs (pronounced **fair**-oh)
(noun) a king of ancient Egypt.

pharmacist, pharmacists
(noun) a person who is qualified to prepare and sell medicines, often called a chemist.

pharmacy, pharmacies
(noun) a shop where medicines are sold, often called the chemist's.
[Greek *pharmakeia* = the making of drugs]

phase, phases
(noun) a particular stage in the development of something or someone, e.g. *It's just a phase he's going through.*

pheasant, pheasants
(noun) a large, long-tailed game bird.

phenomenal (pronounced fin-**nom**-in-nal)
(adjective) extraordinarily great or good.
phenomenally (adverb)

phenomenon
(noun) something or someone special and unusual, e.g. *the U.F.O. phenomenon... The Beatles were a phenomenon of the 60s.*

philately (pronounced fil-**lat**-tel-ee)
(noun) the collection and study of postage stamps.
philatelist (noun)

phlegm (pronounced **flem**)
(noun) the thick liquid which comes up from your throat, especially when you have a cold.
[Greek *phlegma* = inflammation]

phobia, phobias
(noun) an abnormal fear or hatred of something, e.g. *She has a phobia about spiders, and the spiders aren't too keen on her either.*
[Greek *phobos* = fear]

phone, phones, phoning, phoned
(noun, verb) e.g. *a mobile phone... Phone me later on.*
[abbreviation of 'telephone']

phonetics
(noun) the study of speech sounds.
phonetic (adjective)
[Greek *phone* = sound or voice]

phoney, phonier, phoniest; phoneys
1 (adjective; informal) false or fake.
2 (noun; informal) Someone who is a phoney pretends to be something they are not.

phosphate, phosphates
(noun) a chemical containing phosphorus, often used in fertilizers.

photo, photos
(noun; informal) a photograph.

photocopier, photocopiers
(noun) a machine which makes instant copies.
photocopy (noun) **photocopy** (verb)

photogenic
(adjective) Someone who is photogenic always looks attractive in photographs.

photograph, photographs, photographing, photographed
1 (verb) to take a picture with a camera.
2 (noun) a picture taken with a camera.
photographer (noun) **photography** (noun)
photographic (adjective)

phrasal verb, verbs
(noun) a verb, e.g. 'take over' or 'break in', made up of a verb + an adverb or preposition.

phrase, phrases, phrasing, phrased
(noun) a group of words considered as a unit, especially a saying.
2 (verb) If you phrase something in a particular way, you choose those words to express it.
[Greek *phrasis* = speech]

phrase book, books
(noun) a book of useful words and expressions in a foreign language with translations.

physical
(adjective) concerning the body not the mind.
physically (adverb)
[Greek *phusis* = nature]

physical education
(noun) P.E. consists of the sport, gymnastics and athletics that you do at school.

physics
(noun) the scientific study of the nature and properties of matter, energy, gravity, electricity, heat and sound.
physicist (noun)

physiotherapy
(noun) medical treatment which involves exercise and massage.
physiotherapist (noun)

These phrases are always written as two separate words: in case; a lot; as well; no one.

physique, physiques (pronounced fiz-**zeek**)
(noun) the shape and size of someone's body and the tone of their muscles.

pi (rhymes with **fly**)
(noun) a number, approximately 3.14, shown by the Greek letter π. Pi is the ratio of the circumference of a circle to its diameter.

piano, pianos
(noun) a large, keyboard musical instrument.
pianist (noun)
[originally called 'pianoforte', from Italian *piano e forte* = soft and loud]

piccolo, piccolos
(noun) a small, high-pitched wind instrument like a small flute.
[Italian *piccolo* = small]

pick, picks, picking, picked
1 (verb) to take or choose, e.g. *She picked the winning number... Pick your own strawberries... Don't pick a fight with me... He picked his way through the nettles.*
2 (noun) a pickaxe.

pick on
(phrasal verb) to criticize someone unfairly or treat them unkindly.

pick out
(phrasal verb) to recognize someone or something when it is difficult to see, e.g. *I could just pick out the spire in the distance.*

pick up
(phrasal verb) e.g. *Pick me up at 9 o'clock... I'm picking up an S.O.S. message.*

pickaxe, pickaxes
(noun) a tool with a curved, pointed iron bar on a long handle, used for breaking up rock etc.

picket, pickets, picketing, picketed
(verb) When a group of people picket a factory etc., they stand outside to persuade other workers to join or support a strike.

pickle, pickles
1 (noun) vegetables or fruit preserved in vinegar or salt water, often with additional flavouring.
2 (phrase; informal) If you are **in a pickle**, you are in a difficult situation.

pickpocket, pickpockets
(noun) a thief who steals from people's pockets or handbags.

pick-up, pick-ups
(noun) a small truck with low sides.

picnic, picnics, picnicking, picnicked
1 (noun) a light meal made to be eaten out of doors.
2 (verb) to eat a picnic.

pictorial
(adjective) relating to pictures.
pictorially (adverb)

picture, pictures, picturing, pictured
1 (noun) a drawing, painting or photograph.
2 (plural noun) If you go to the pictures, you go to the cinema.
3 (verb) If you picture something, you think of it and imagine it clearly.

[Latin *pictura* = painting]

Similar words: (noun) illustration, sketch, figure

picturesque (pronounced pik-chur-**esk**)
(adjective) A place that is picturesque is very attractive, e.g. *a picturesque village.*
[Italian *pittoresco* = in the style of a painter]

pie, pies
(noun) e.g. *apple pie... chicken pie.*

piece, pieces, piecing, pieced
1 (noun) e.g. *a piece of cake... a piece of music... a 10p piece... a chess piece.*
2 (verb) If you piece together a number of things, you gradually put them together.

pier, piers
(noun) a structure sticking out into the sea at a seaside town, which people can walk along.

pierce, pierces, piercing, pierced
(verb) If a sharp object pierces something, it goes through it, making a hole.

Similar words: penetrate, perforate, prick, puncture

piercing
(adjective) A piercing sound is high-pitched, sharp and unpleasant, e.g. *a piercing scream.*

Similar words: shrill, ear-splitting, sharp

pig, pigs
1 (noun) a farm animal.
2 (phrase) If you **make a pig of yourself**, you eat too much.

pigeon, pigeons
(noun) a plump bird with grey feathers.

piggyback, piggybacks
(noun) If you give someone a piggyback, you carry them on your back.

pig-headed
(adjective) Someone who is pig-headed is stubborn and refuses to change their mind.

piglet, piglets
(noun) a young pig.

pigsty, pigsties
1 (noun) a hut and run where pigs are kept.
2 If you describe a room as a pigsty, you mean it is very untidy and dirty.

pigtail, pigtails
(noun) a length of plaited hair.

pike, pikes
(noun) a large freshwater fish.

pilchard, pilchards
(noun) a small, edible sea fish.

pile, piles, piling, piled
1 (verb) If you pile things somewhere, you put them one on top of the other.
2 (noun) a heap of something.
[Latin *pila* = pillar or pier]

pile-up, pile-ups
(noun; informal) a road accident involving several vehicles.

Many words of French origin make K sound with QUE: antique unique physique picturesque grotesque.

pilfer, pilfers, pilfering, pilfered
(verb) Someone who pilfers steals small things, often over a period of time.
[Old French *pelfre* = booty]

pilgrim, pilgrims
(noun) a person who travels to a holy place for religious reasons.
pilgrimage (noun)

pill, pills
(noun) a small, round, hard tablet.
[Latin *pilula* = little ball]

pillar, pillars
1 (noun) a tall, narrow, solid structure, usually supporting part of a building.
2 A **pillar box** is a free-standing, cylindrical red box in which you post letters.

pillow, pillows
(noun) a rectangular cushion on a bed.

pillowcase, pillowcases
(noun) a cover for a pillow.

pilot, pilots, piloting, piloted
1 (noun) a person trained to fly an aircraft.
2 a person who goes on board ships to guide them through local waters to a port.
3 (verb) To pilot something means to control its movement or to guide it.

pimple, pimples
(noun) a small spot on the skin.
pimply (adjective)

pin, pins, pinning, pinned
Selected meanings :
1 (noun) a sharp, thin piece of metal used as a fastener.
2 (verb) If someone pins you in a particular position, they hold you there so that you cannot move.
3 If you try to pin something or somebody down, you try to get the details of something clear.

pinafore, pinafores
(noun) a dress with no sleeves, worn over a blouse.

pincers
(plural noun) a tool used for gripping and pulling things. It consists of two pieces of metal hinged at the end which grips.

pinch, pinches, pinching, pinched
1 (noun, verb) e.g. *a pinch of salt... Pinch me, I'm dreaming.*
2 (verb; informal) to steal something.
3 (phrase; informal) **At a pinch** means if absolutely necessary, e.g. *He could do the part at a pinch, but he's not much good as an actor.*

pine, pines, pining, pined
1 (noun) an evergreen tree with very thin leaves.
2 (verb) If you pine for something, you are sad because you cannot have it.

pineapple, pineapples
(noun) a large, yellow, oval fruit.

pink, pinker, pinkest; pinks
(adjective, noun) pale, reddish-white colour.

pinpoint, pinpoints, pinpointing, pinpointed
(verb) to explain or discover exactly what or where something is, e.g. *The garage man pinpointed the fault straight away.*

pint, pints
(noun) a unit of liquid volume. (1 pint = 0.57 litres; 8 pints = 1 gallon).

pin-up, pin-ups
(noun) a picture of an attractive woman or man.

pioneer, pioneers, pioneering, pioneered
(pronounced pie-on-**ear**)
1 (noun) one of the first people to do something, e.g. *Charles Rolls and Henry Royce were pioneers of motor car manufacture.*
2 (verb) Someone who pioneers a new process or invention is the first person to develop it.

pious (pronounced **pie**-uss)
(adjective) very religious and moral.
piously (adverb) **piety** (noun)

pipe, pipes, piping, piped
1 (noun) a long, round, hollow tube.
2 an object used for smoking tobacco.
3 (plural noun) The pipes are another name for bag pipes.
4 (verb) to play the bagpipes.
5 to send something by pipe. Piped music or TV, for example in a hotel, comes by cable from a central source.
piper (noun)

pipeline, pipelines
1 (noun) a large underground pipe that carries oil or gas over a long distance.
2 (phrase) If something is **in the pipeline**, it is already planned.

pipette, pipettes
(noun) a thin glass tube used for measuring or carrying small amounts of liquid.

piranha, piranhas (pronounced pir-**rah**-nah)
(noun) a small, fierce fish with sharp teeth, which lives in rivers in South America.
[a Portuguese word]

pirate, pirates, pirating, pirated
1 (noun) Pirates were sailors who attacked and robbed other ships.
2 (verb) Someone who pirates video tapes, cassettes or books makes illegal copies for sale.
piracy (noun)
[Greek *peiratēs* = attacker]

pirouette, pirouettes (pronounced pir-roo-**et**)
(noun) In ballet, a pirouette is a fast spinning step done on the toes.

pistol, pistols
(noun) a small gun held in the hand.

piston, pistons
(noun) a cylinder or disc that slides up and down inside a tube. Pistons in an engine have rods attached to them, and their movement causes other parts of the engine to move.

pit, pits, pitting, pitted
1 (noun) a large hole in the ground.
2 a coal mine.
3 (plural noun) In motor racing, the pits are the areas where drivers stop for fuel and repairs.

Television? No good will come of this device. The word is half Greek and half Latin. (C. P. Scott)

4 (phrase) If you **pit your wits** against someone, you compete against them.
5 (informal) If something is **the pits**, it is really dreadful.

pitch, pitches, pitching, pitched
1 (noun) an area for playing games, e.g. *a football pitch... a cricket pitch.*
2 The pitch of a sound is how high or low it is.
3 (verb) to throw something with a lot of force.
4 If you pitch something at a particular level of difficulty, you set it at that level.
5 When you pitch a tent, you put it up and fasten it to the ground.

pitiful
(adjective) in such a sad or weak situation that you feel pity, e.g. *The lost dog was a pitiful sight.*

pity, pities, pitying, pitied
(verb) If you pity someone, you feel very sorry for them.

pivot, pivots, pivoting, pivoted
(noun) the central point on which something balances or turns.

pizza, pizzas (pronounced **peet**-sah)
(noun) a flat piece of dough covered with cheese, tomato and other savoury food.

place, places, placing, placed
1 (noun) a position somewhere, e.g. *Save me a place... Exeter's a good place to live... She was given a place at college.*
2 (phrase) When something **takes place**, it happens.
3 (verb) If you place something somewhere, you put it there.
4 If you place an order, you order something.
5 If you cannot place someone, you cannot remember exactly who they are or where you met them before.
[French *place* = square or courtyard]

Similar words: (noun) site, spot, situation, location

placenta (pronounced plas-**sen**-tah)
(noun) the organ that develops inside a mother's womb during pregnancy. It consists of a mass of veins and tissues which supply food and oxygen to the baby from the mother's blood and remove waste products.

placid
(adjective) calm and not easily excited or upset.
placidly (adverb) **placidity** (noun)
[Latin *placidus* = peaceful]

plague, plagues, plaguing, plagued
(pronounced **playg**)
1 (noun) a very infectious disease that kills large numbers of people.
2 (verb) If problems plague you, they keep causing you trouble.

plaice
(noun) an edible, flat seafish.

plain
1 (adjective) e.g. *a plain dress... It's plain to see... You're just plain stupid... She's a plain girl.*
2 (noun) a large, flat area of land with few trees.
3 Plain is the basic knitting stitch.
plainly (adverb)

Similar words: (adjective) bare, basic, simple, natural

plain-clothes
(adjective) Plain-clothes police officers are wearing ordinary clothes instead of a uniform so that they are not identified.

plait, plaits, plaiting, plaited (pronounced **plat**)
1 (verb) If you plait 3 lengths of hair or rope together, you twist them over each other in turn to make one thick length.
2 (noun) a length of hair that has been plaited.
[Old French *pleit* = a fold]

plan, plans, planning, planned
1 (noun) a detailed diagram or drawing of something e.g. a room or a building.
2 (verb) If you plan something, you decide in detail what it is to be and how to do it.
3 If you are planning to do something, you intend to do it.

Similar words: scheme, strategy, design, formula, policy

plane, planes
1 (noun) a vehicle with wings and engines that enable it to fly. (abbreviation of 'aeroplane')
2 a flat surface.
3 a tool used to make wood smooth.

planet, planets
(noun) a round body in space which moves in orbit around the sun or a star and is lit up by light from it.
planetary (adjective)
[Greek *planētēs* = wanderer]

plank, planks
(noun) a long, rectangular piece of wood.

plant, plants, planting, planted
1 (noun) a living thing that grows in the earth and has stems, leaves and roots.
2 a factory or power station.
3 large industrial machinery or equipment.
4 (verb) e.g. *to plant a seed... to plant your feet firmly on the ground... to plant a bomb.*
[Latin *planta* = shoot or cutting]

plantation, plantations
(noun) a large area of land where crops, for example tea, cotton or sugar are grown.

plaque, plaques (rhymes with **black**)
1 (noun) a flat piece of metal which is fixed to a wall and has an inscription in memory of a famous person or event.
2 a substance which forms around your teeth and consists of bacteria, saliva and food.

plaster, plasters, plastering, plastered
1 (noun) a paste made of sand, lime and water, which is used to form a smooth surface for inside walls and ceilings.
plasterer (noun)

From the names of which places do these words come? attic bayonet bedlam bunkum
canter indigo jersey

2 (noun) a strip of sticky material with a small pad, used for covering cuts on your body.
3 (phrase) If a person's leg is **in plaster**, it is covered with plaster of Paris to protect a broken bone.
4 (verb) to cover something thickly with a sticky substance, e.g. *He plastered mousse on his hair.*

plastered
1 (adjective) If something is plastered with things, they are all over its surface.
2 (informal) very drunk.

plastic, plastics
(noun) a substance, made by a chemical process, that can be moulded when soft to make a wide range of objects.

Plasticine
(noun; trademark) a soft, coloured substance which can be used for modelling.

plastic surgery
(noun) operations to replace or repair damaged skin or to improve a person's appearance by changing the shape of their features.

plate, plates
(noun) e.g. *a plate of mushy peas... dishes of gold plate... a plate glass window.*

platform, platforms
(noun) a raised structure on which someone or something can stand.

platinum
(noun) a valuable silver-coloured metal.

plausible
(adjective) An explanation that is plausible seems likely to be true.

play, plays, playing, played
(verb, noun) e.g. *Let's play football... In this film, Mel Gibson plays a stuntman... She plays the piano... I'll play this Mozart tape... Hamlet is an amazing play.*
playful (adjective) **playfully** (adverb)
player (noun)

play up
(phrasal verb) If something is playing up, it is not working or behaving as it should.

playground, playgrounds
(noun) an area for children to play in.

playgroup, playgroups
(noun) an informal kind of school for very young children.

playing card, cards
(noun) Playing cards are cards printed with numbers or pictures, used to play various games.

playing field, fields
(noun) an area of grass for playing sports.

playpen, playpens
(noun) a small structure with bars etc. round the sides in which a young child can play safely.

playwright, playwrights
(noun) a person who writes plays; a dramatist.

plead, pleads, pleading, pleaded
1 (verb) to beg someone to do something.
2 When a person pleads guilty or not guilty in

court, they say if they did or did not commit a crime.
plea (noun)

pleasant
(adjective) enjoyable, likeable or attractive.
pleasantly (adverb)

Similar words: good, agreeable, pleasing, enjoyable

please, pleases, pleasing, pleased
(verb) e.g. *Some chips, please... This gift pleases me greatly... She does just what she pleases.*
pleased (adjective)

Similar words: satisfy, suit, delight

pleasing
(adjective) attractive, satisfying or enjoyable.

pleasure, pleasures
(noun) a feeling of happiness, satisfaction or enjoyment.
pleasurable (adjective)

pleat, pleats
(noun) a permanent fold in, for example, a skirt.

plectrum, plectrums
(noun) a small, flat piece of plastic or metal for plucking the strings of a guitar etc.

pledge, pledges, pledging, pledged
1 (noun) a solemn promise.
2 (verb) If you pledge something, you promise that you will do it or give it.

plentiful
(adjective) existing in large amounts and available, e.g. *Sand is plentiful in the desert.*
plentifully (adverb)

plenty
(noun) a lot, e.g. *plenty of money.*

pliers
(plural noun) a small tool with metal jaws for holding small objects and bending wire.

plight
(noun) Someone's plight is the very difficult or dangerous situation that they are in.

plimsolls
(plural noun) canvas shoes with flat rubber soles

Similar words: gymshoes, pumps

plod, plods, plodding, plodded
1 (verb) to walk slowly and heavily.
2 If you plod through a piece of work, you work slowly without enthusiasm.

plonk, plonks, plonking, plonked
1 (verb) to put something down carelessly.
2 (noun; informal) cheap wine.

plot, plots, plotting, plotted
1 (noun) the secret plan of a group of people.
2 The plot of a novel or play is the story.
3 A plot of land is a small piece of it.
4 (verb) If someone plots the course of ship etc. on a map, or plots a graph, they mark the points in the correct places.

Similar words: (noun: sense 1) conspiracy, scheme

plough, ploughs, ploughing, ploughed
1 (noun) a large farming tool that is pulled across a field to turn the soil.
2 (verb) If you plough on, you keep moving or keep trying to complete something with a lot of effort.

pluck, plucks, plucking, plucked
1 (verb) to give a sharp pull, e.g. *plucking a flower... a chicken... a guitar.*
2 (noun) courage.
3 (phrase) If you **pluck up courage** to do a frightening thing, you make an effort to do it.
plucky (adjective)

plug, plugs, plugging, plugged
1 (noun) an electrical connector.
2 (verb) If you plug a hole, you block it with something.
3 (informal) If someone plugs a book, record, etc., they praise it to persuade people to buy it.

plum, plums
(noun) a small fruit with a red or yellow skin.

plumage (pronounced **ploom**-mage)
(noun) a bird's plumage is its feathers.
plume (noun)
[French *plume* = feather]

plumber, plumbers
(noun) a person who connects and repairs water pipes, baths and toilets.
plumbing (noun)
[Old French *plommier* = worker in lead]

plummet, plummets, plummeting, plummeted
(verb) to fall very quickly, e.g. *The burning Spitfire plummeted to earth.*

plump, plumper, plumpest; plumps, plumping, plumped
1 (adjective) rather fat.
2 (verb; informal) When you plump for a particular thing, you choose it.

Similar words: (adjective) chubby, stout, tubby

plunder, plunders, plundering, plundered
(verb) If someone plunders a place, they steal many things from it.

plunge, plunges, plunging, plunged
1 (verb) to fall suddenly.
2 If you plunge an object into something, you push it in quickly.
3 (noun) a sudden fall.

Similar words: (verb: sense 1) dive, swoop

plural, plurals
(noun) the form of a word that is used for two or more people or things, e.g. one mouse (singular), two mice (plural); the plural of 'mouse' is 'mice'.
[Latin *pluralis* = concerning many]

plural noun, nouns
(noun) In this dictionary, 'plural noun' is the name given to a noun normally used only in the plural, e.g. 'scissors' or 'police'.

plus
(preposition) added to, e.g. *Four plus three equals seven.* (4+3 = 7)
[Latin *plus* = more]

plush
(adjective) very expensive and smart, e.g. *a plush restaurant.*

plutonium
(noun) a radioactive element used in nuclear weapons and in the generation of nuclear power.

plywood
(noun) wooden board made from several thin sheets of wood glued together under pressure.

pneumatic (pronounced new-**mat**-ik)
(adjective) operated by or filled with compressed air, e.g. *a pneumatic drill... pneumatic tyres.*
[Latin *pneumaticus* = of air or wind]

pneumonia (pronounced new-**moan**-ee-ah)
(noun) a serious disease which affects a person's lungs and makes breathing difficult.
[Greek *pneumōn* = lung]

poach, poaches, poaching, poached
1 (verb) to catch animals, fish, etc. illegally.
poacher (noun)
2 When you poach food, you cook it gently in hot liquid, e.g. *poached eggs.*

pocket, pockets, pocketing, pocketed
1 (noun) e.g. *My trouser pockets were full of coins.*
2 a small area of something, e.g. *The army met pockets of resistance from the enemy.*
3 (verb) If someone pockets something that does not belong to them, they take it secretly.
4 (phrase) If you are **out of pocket**, you have less money than you should have.
pocket money (noun)

pod, pods
(noun) a long, narrow seed container that grows on plants such as peas or beans.

podgy, podgier, podgiest
(adjective) rather fat.

poem, poems
(noun) a piece of writing arranged in rhythmic lines, often with a rhyme.

poet, poets
(noun) a person who writes poems.

poetry
(noun) a word for poems in general.
poetic (adjective) **poetically** (adverb)

point, points, pointing, pointed
1 (verb) e.g. *Don't point your finger at me!*
2 (noun) e.g. *The needle had a sharp point.*
3 an opinion or fact, e.g. *I want to make several points about your handwriting.*
4 a quality, e.g. *Your strong points are speed and accuracy.*
5 The point of something is its purpose or meaning, e.g. *You have missed the point.*
6 a position or time, e.g. *At some point, I must have dropped the key.*
7 The decimal point in a number is the dot separating the whole number from the fraction.
8 (plural noun) On a railway track, the points are the levers and rails which enable a train to move from one track to another.

point out
(phrasal verb) If you point something out to

Poetry – the best words in the best order. (Samuel Taylor Coleridge)

someone, you draw their attention to it by
pointing to it or explaining it.

point-blank
(adjective) Something that is shot at point-blank
range is shot with a gun held very close to it.

pointless
(adjective) Something that is pointless has no
use, sense or purpose.
pointlessly (adverb)

point of view, **points of view**
1 (noun) Your point of view is your opinion about
something or your attitude towards it.
2 A point of view is also one way of thinking
about something, e.g. *From the business point of
view, fax machines are useful.*

poison, **poisons, poisoning, poisoned**
1 (noun) a substance that can kill people or
animals if they swallow it or absorb it.
2 (verb) to kill or attempt to kill by poisoning.
poisonous (adjective)
[Old French *puison* = potion]

poke, **pokes, poking, poked**
(verb) If you poke someone, you push at them
quickly with your finger or a sharp object.

Similar words: jab, prod, dig

poker, **pokers**
1 (noun) a card game in which the players make
bets on the cards dealt to them.
2 a rod used for moving coals or logs in a fire.

poky, **pokier, pokiest**
(adjective) A poky room or house is
uncomfortably small.

polar
(adjective) relating to the area around the north
and south poles, e.g. *polar expeditions.*

Polaroid camera, **cameras**
(noun; trademark) a camera that can take a
photograph and print it in a few seconds, within
the camera.

pole, **poles**
1 (noun) a long, rounded piece of wood or metal.
2 The earth's poles are the two ends of its axis
(its top and bottom).
3 The poles of a magnet are the two opposite
ends where magnetic forces are concentrated.
[senses 2-3: Greek *polos* = pivot or axis]

Pole, **Poles**
(noun) someone who comes from Poland.

pole vault
(noun) an athletics event in which people jump a
high bar using a long flexible pole.

police
(plural noun) the people who are responsible for
making sure that people obey the law.

policeman, **policemen**
(noun) a man who is a member of a police force.
[feminine: **policewoman**]

policy, **policies**
1 (noun) a set of plans used as a basis for action,
especially in politics or business.

2 an insurance policy is a document which shows
that you are insured.
[sense 1: Latin *politia* = administration
sense 2: Old French *police* = certificate]

polio
(noun) an infectious disease that is caused by a
virus and often results in paralysis [short for
'poliomyelitis'].

polish, **polishes, polishing, polished**
1 (noun) a substance that you put on an object to
clean it and make it shine.
2 (verb) to rub a surface to make it shine.

polish off
(phrasal verb; informal) If you polish something
off, you finish it completely.

Polish (pronounced **pole**-ish)
1 (adjective) belonging or relating to Poland.
2 (noun) the main language spoken in Poland.

polished
(adjective) If someone gives a polished
performance, it is slick and well-rehearsed.

polite
(adjective) Someone who is polite has good
manners and behaves considerately to others.
politely (adverb) **politeness** (noun)
[Latin *politus* = polished]

Similar words: courteous, well-behaved,
well-mannered, respectful

politician, **politicians**
(noun) a person involved in the government of a
country.

politics
(noun) the activity and planning concerned with
achieving power and control in a country.
political (adjective) **politically** (adverb)

polka, **polkas**
(noun) a fast dance.

poll, **polls, polling, polled** (pronounced **pole**)
1 (noun) a survey in which people are asked their
opinions about something.
2 (verb) If you are polled on something, you are
asked your opinion about it as part of a survey.
3 (plural noun) A political election can be called
the polls.
4 (noun) A **polling station** is a place where people
go to vote in an election.

pollen
(noun) a fine, yellow powder produced by
flowers, which can fertilize other flowers, of the
same species when it is transferred by insects.
[Latin *pollen* = powder]

pollen count, **counts**
(noun) a measurement of the amount of pollen in
the air at a particular time.

pollinate, **pollinates, pollinating, pollinated**
(verb) to fertilize a plant with pollen.
pollination (noun)

pollutant, **pollutants**
(noun) a substance that causes pollution.

Adjectives of nationality usually begin with capital letters, e.g. British, Dutch, French, Swedish.

pollute, pollutes, polluting, polluted
(verb) To pollute water or air means to make it dirty and dangerous to use or live in.
pollution (noun) **polluted** (adjective)

polo
(noun) a game played between two teams of four on horseback who try to score goals, using long wooden hammers to hit the ball.

polo-necked
(adjective) A polo-necked jumper has a deep fold of material at the neck.

poly-
(prefix) many or much.
[Greek *polus* = many or much]

polyester
(noun) a man-made fibre, used especially to make clothes.

polygon, polygons
(noun) any two-dimensional shape whose sides are all straight.

polystyrene
(noun) a very light, plastic substance, used as insulating material or to make containers.

polytechnic, polytechnics
(noun) a college where people of 18 or over study after leaving school.
[Greek *polutekhnos* = skilled in many arts]

polythene
(noun) a type of plastic that is used to make thin sheets or bags.

polyurethane (pronounced pol-lee-**yoo**-rath-ane)
(noun) a plastic material used especially to make paint or types of foam.

pom or **pommy**
(noun; informal; Australian) the nickname that Australians have for English people.
[The origins of this use are uncertain]

pompous
(adjective) behaving in a way that is too serious and self-important.
pomposity (noun)

pond, ponds
(noun) a small, usually man-made area of water.

ponder, ponders, pondering, pondered
(verb) to think about something deeply.
[Latin *ponderare* = to consider]

pony, ponies
(noun) a small horse.

ponytail, ponytails
(noun) a hairstyle in which hair is tied at the back of the head and hangs down like a tail.

ponytrekking
(noun) a leisure activity in which people ride across country on ponies.

poodle, poodles
(noun) a breed of dog with curly hair.

pool, pools, pooling, pooled
1 (noun) a small area of still water.
2 a game similar to snooker played with numbered balls on a smaller table.

3 (verb) If people pool their resources, they gather together the things they have so that they can be shared or used by all of them.
4 (plural noun) The pools is a competition in which people try to guess football results.

poop, poops, pooping, pooped
(verb, informal) If a dog poops on your lawn, it leaves its excrement there.
pooper scooper (noun)

pooped
(adjective; informal) very tired.

poor, poorer, poorest
(adjective) e.g. *The old man was very poor... You poor thing!... This is a poor piece of work.*
[Latin *pauper* = poor]

poorly
1 (adjective) feeling ill.
2 (adverb) badly, e.g. *It was poorly planned.*

pop, pops, popping, popped
(noun, adjective, verb) e.g. *Have a drink of pop... The cork came out with a pop... Do you like classical or pop music?... 'Pop' goes the weasel... My eyes popped with amazement... Pop out and get me some sugar.*

popcorn
(noun) a snack consisting of grains of maize heated until they puff up and burst.

Pope
(noun) The Pope is the head of the Roman Catholic Church.
[Latin *Papa* = bishop or father]

poplar, poplars
(noun) a type of tall, thin tree.

poppadum, poppadums
(noun) a large, circular crisp made of flour and spices, eaten with Indian food.

popper, poppers
(noun) a device for fastening clothes.

poppy, poppies
(noun) a plant with a large, red flower.

popular
(adjective) liked by a lot of people.
popularly (adverb) **popularity** (noun)
[Latin *popularis* = belonging to the people]

Similar words: in, fashionable, well-liked

population, populations
(noun) the people who live in a place or the number of people living there.

porch, porches
(noun) a covered area at the entrance to a building.
[Latin *porticus* = portico]

pore, pores
(noun) Pores are very small holes in your skin which allow moisture to pass through.

pork
(noun) meat from a pig which has not been salted or smoked.
[Latin *porcus* = pig]

Idioms. What are: white horses a white lie a white elephant a white flag a white feather?

pornography

(noun) magazines and films designed to cause sexual excitement by showing naked people and sexual acts.
pornographic (adjective)
[Greek *pornos* = prostitute + *graphein* = to write]

porous

(adjective) containing many holes through which water and air can pass, e.g. *a porous rock.*

porridge

(noun) a thick, sticky food made from oats cooked in water or milk.

port, ports

1 (noun) a town or area with a harbour or docks.
2 a kind of sweet, strong red wine.
3 (adjective, noun) The port side of a ship is the left side when you are facing the bow (front).
[Latin *portus* = harbour; ships paddled by a steerboard (starboard) always had to dock with the left side to the harbour]

portable

(adjective) easily carried, e.g. *a portable TV.*

portcullis, portcullises

(noun) a large, metal gate above the entrance to a castle, which was lowered to keep out enemies.
[Old French *porte coleice* = sliding gate]

porter, porters

(noun) a person whose job is to carry or move things in a station, airport, hospital, etc.
[Latin *portator* = one who carries]

porthole, portholes

(noun) a small, circular window in the side of a ship or aircraft.

portion, portions

(noun) a part or amount of something.
[Latin *portio* = portion or share]

Similar words: helping, share

portrait, portraits

(noun) a picture or photograph of someone.

portray, portrays, portraying, portrayed

(verb) When an actor, artist or writer portrays someone or something, they represent or describe them.
portrayal (noun)

Portuguese (pronounced por-tyoo-**geez**)

1 (adjective) belonging to Portugal.
2 (noun) someone who comes from Portugal.
3 the main language spoken in Portugal and Brazil.

pose, poses, posing, posed

1 (verb) to stay in a particular position so that someone can photograph or paint you.
2 If you pose as someone else, you pretend to be them to deceive people.
3 If something poses a problem, it is the cause of the problem.
4 (noun) the particular position of the subject of a photograph or painting.
[French *poser* = to put in place]

poser, posers; also spelled poseur.

1 (noun) someone who behaves or dresses in an exaggerated way to impress people.
2 a difficult problem or question.

posh, posher, poshest

(adjective; informal) smart, fashionable and expensive. [On the old liners to and from India, rich people had cabins away from the sun, hence P(ort) O(ut), S(tarboard) H(ome)]

position, positions, positioning, positioned

1 (noun) the place where someone or something is.
2 the situation that someone is in, e.g. *You are in the fortunate position of having no debts.*
3 (verb) To position something means to put it somewhere exactly.

positive

1 (adjective) completely sure about something, e.g. *I'm positive she said she would come.*
2 showing approval, agreement, or encouragement, e.g. *Public response was positive.*
3 A positive number is greater than zero.
4 If a medical test is positive, it shows something is present, e.g. *a positive pregnancy test.*
[opposite: **negative**]
positively (adverb)
[Latin *positivus* = positive or agreed]

Similar words: affirmative, categorical, definite, certain

possession, possessions

1 (noun) If something is in your possession or if you are in possession of it, you have it.
2 Your possessions are the things that you own or that you have with you.
possess (verb)
[Latin *possidere* = to own or to occupy]

Similar words: (sense 2) property, belongings, effects

possessive

1 (adjective) A person who is possessive about something wants to keep it to themselves.
2 (noun) In grammar, the possessive is the form of a noun or pronoun used to show possession. e.g. *my, his, Fiona's, theirs.*

possibility, possibilities

(noun) something that might be true or might happen.

Similar words: chance, likelihood, prospect

possible

(adjective) able to be done or to be true.
possibly (adverb)
[Latin *possibilis* = that may be, and the verb *posse* = to be able]

Similar words: feasible, practicable, viable, workable

post, posts, posting, posted

1 (verb) If you post a letter, you send it to someone by putting it into a postbox.
postal (adjective)
2 (noun) a job, e.g. *the post of Team Manager.*

We take these words from Portuguese: marmalade veranda albatross.

3 (verb) If you are posted somewhere, you are sent by your employers to work there.
4 (noun) a strong upright pole in the ground.
[senses 1-3: Latin *posita* = something placed
sense 4: Old English *post* = pole]

post-
(prefix) after, e.g. *the post-war years... a post-exam party.*
[Latin *post* = after]

postage
(noun) the money that you pay to send letters and parcels by post.

postal order, orders
(noun) a piece of paper representing a sum of money which you buy at a post office to send through the post.
postbox (noun) **postcard** (noun) **postcode** (noun) **postman** (noun) **post office** (noun)

poster, posters
(noun) a large notice or picture.

postmark, postmarks
(noun) a mark printed on letters showing when and where they were posted.

post-mortem, post-mortems
(noun) a medical examination of a dead body to find out how the person died.
[Latin *post mortem* = after death]

postpone, postpones, postponing, postponed
(verb) to put something off until later, e.g. *The match was postponed because of rain.*
postponement (noun)
[Latin *postponere* = to put after]

postscript, postscripts
(noun) an extra message at the end of a letter, after your signature, which starts 'P.S.'.
[Latin *post scriptum* = written after]

posture, postures
(noun) the way you sit, stand and walk.
[Latin *positura* = position]

posy, posies
(noun) a small bunch of flowers.

pot, pots, potting, potted
(noun, verb) e.g. *Warm the pot before making the tea... I potted these pansies last week... He needs to pot the black for the game.*

potassium
(noun) a soft, silver-coloured chemical element used in making soap, detergents, fertilizers and glass.

potato, potatoes
(noun) an edible root vegetable.

potent
(adjective) effective, powerful or strong, e.g. *a potent drink.*
potency (noun)
[Latin *potens* = able]

potential
1 (adjective) capable of becoming the kind of thing mentioned, e.g. *a list of potential MPs.*
2 (noun) Your potential is your ability to achieve a particular level of success in the future.
potentially (adverb)

pothole, potholes
1 (noun) a hole in the surface of a road.
2 an underground cavern.

potholing
(noun) the activity of exploring underground caverns; also called caving.
potholer (noun)

potion, potions
(noun) a drink containing medicine, poison, etc.
[Latin *potio* = a drink]

pot luck
(noun) If you take pot luck, you have whatever is available without being able to choose.

potter, potters, pottering, pottered
1 (noun) a person who makes pottery.
2 (verb) If you potter about, you pass the time doing pleasant, unimportant things.

pottery, potteries
(noun) pots, dishes, etc. made from clay and fired in a kiln; also the place where they are made.

potty, potties; pottier, pottiest
1 (noun) a bowl which a small child uses instead of a toilet.
2 (adjective; informal) crazy or foolish.

pouch, pouches
1 (noun) a small, soft container with a fold-over top, e.g. *a tobacco pouch.*
2 Marsupials, e.g. kangaroos, have a pouch, a pocket of skin in which they carry their young.
[Old French *poche* = bag]

pouffe, pouffes (rhymes with **hoof**)
(noun) a low, soft piece of furniture used for sitting on or resting your feet on.

poultry
(noun) chickens, turkeys and other birds kept for their meat or eggs.

pounce, pounces, pouncing, pounced
(verb) to leap forward and grab something.

pound, pounds, pounding, pounded
1 (noun) the main unit of money in Britain.
2 a unit of weight [450 grams = 1lb (pound) = 16 ounces = .45kg].
3 (verb) If you pound something, you hit it repeatedly with your fist.
4 If your heart is pounding, it is beating very strongly and quickly.
5 If you pound somewhere, you run there with heavy noisy steps.
6 (noun) an enclosure for animals.

pour, pours, pouring, poured
(verb) e.g. *Pour me a cup of tea... Sweat began to pour down his face... It is pouring outside.*

Similar words: teem, pelt, bucket, stream

pout, pouts, pouting, pouted
(verb) to stick out your lip to show disappointment or annoyance, e.g. *Julia always pouted when she didn't get her way.*

poverty
(noun) the state of being very poor.

Never put off today what you can put off tomorrow.

powder, powders, powdering, powdered
(noun) many tiny particles of a solid substance,
e.g. *gunpowder.*
2 (verb) If you powder a surface, you cover it
with powder, e.g. *to powder your face.*
powdery (adjective)

powder room, rooms
(noun) a ladies' toilet.

power, powers, powering, powered
1 (noun) control over people and activities, e.g.
The Prime Minister came to power in 1992.
2 the ability to do something, e.g. *the power of
speech.*
3 physical strength, e.g. *power lifting.*
4 energy, e.g. *Water power... wind power...
electric power.*
5 In maths, e.g. $6^4 = 6 \times 6 \times 6 \times 6 = 6$ **to the
power of** 4.
6 In physics, power is the rate of doing work. It is
measured in watts or horsepower.
7 (verb) Something that powers a machine
provides the energy for it to work.
powerful (adjective) **powerfully** (adverb)

Similar words: (noun: sense 3) force, potency,
strength

power boat, boats
(noun) a large, fast boat driven by motor.

powerless
(adjective) unable to control or influence events.

Similar word: helpless

power station, stations
(noun) a place where electricity is generated.

practical, practicals
1 (adjective) relating to real situations not ideas
or theories.
2 Ideas, methods, tools or clothes that are
practical are sensible and likely to be effective.
3 Someone who is practical is able to deal
effectively and sensibly with problems.
4 (noun) a non-written exam in which you work
with real things to show you understand them,
e.g. *a chemistry practical.*
practicality (noun)
[Greek *praktikos* = concerned with action]

practical joke, jokes
(noun) a trick intended to make someone look a
fool.

practically
(adverb) almost, e.g. *He was practically dead
when we found him.*

practice, practices
1 (noun) regular training or exercise.
2 A doctor's or lawyer's practice is their business.
3 (phrase) What happens **in practice** is what
actually happens, in contrast to what is
supposed to happen, e.g. *The timetable says 3.30,
but in practice, the bus always comes at 3.45.*
[Greek *praktikē* = practical work]

practise, practises, practising, practised
1 (verb) to do something regularly in order to
improve.

2 People who practise a religion, custom or craft
regularly take part in the associated activities.

prairie, prairies
(noun) a large area of grassland, especially in
North America.

praise, praises, praising, praised
1 (verb) If you praise someone, you say 'well
done' to them.
2 (noun) e.g. *You deserve praise for your hard
work on your GCSE project.*

Similar words: commend, compliment, applaud

praiseworthy
(adjective; formal) deserving praise, e.g. *It was a
praiseworthy effort of hers to finish 5th.*

pram, prams
(noun) a baby's cot on wheels. [short for
'perambulator']

prance, prances, prancing, pranced
(verb) Someone who is prancing around is
walking with exaggerated bounding movements.

prank, pranks
(noun) a childish trick.

prannock, prannocks
(noun) If you say someone is a prannock, you
mean they are not very intelligent and easily
fooled.
[Anglo-Saxon *prann* = person easily taken in]

prawn, prawns
(noun) a small, pink, edible shellfish.

pray, prays, praying, prayed
(verb) When someone prays, they speak to God
to give thanks or to ask for help.

prayer, prayers
(noun) the words said when someone prays.

prayer rug, rugs
(noun) a small carpet on which Muslims kneel to
pray.

prayer shawl, shawls
(noun) a white shawl worn by Jewish men
during religious ceremonies.

pre-
(prefix) before, e.g. *the pre-Christmas period... a
pre-school playgroup.*
[Latin *prae* = before]

preach, preaches, preaching, preached
1 (verb) to give a short talk (a sermon) on a
religious or moral subject as part of a church
service.
2 to lecture someone on what they should do.
preacher (noun)
[Latin *praedicare* = to proclaim]

precaution, precautions
(noun) an action intended to prevent something
from happening, e.g. *As a precaution against
getting wet, take your umbrella.*
precautionary (adjective)

Similar words: safety measure, safeguard

precede, precedes, preceding, preceded
(verb) Something that precedes another thing
happens or occurs before it.
preceding (adjective)

precinct, precincts
(noun) A shopping precinct is a pedestrian
shopping area.

precious
1 (adjective) valuable or very important.
2 (phrase) If there is **precious little** of something,
there is only a very small amount.
[Latin *pretiosus* = valuable]

precipice, precipices (pronounced
press-sip-iss)
(noun) a very steep rock face.

précis (pronounced **pray**-see)
(noun) a short piece of writing which sums up
the main points of a book or article.

precise
(adjective) exact and accurate in every detail.
precisely (adverb) **precision** (noun)
[French *précis* = precise]

predator, predators (pronounced **pred**-dat-tor)
(noun) an animal that kills and eats other
animals.
predatory (adjective)

predict, predicts, predicting, predicted
(verb) If someone predicts an event, they say
that it will happen in the future.
prediction (noun)
[Latin *praedicere* = to say before]

Similar words: forecast, foretell, prophesy, foresee

preen, preens, preening, preened
(verb) When a bird preens its feathers, it cleans
them and arranges them using its beak.

prefabricated
(adjective) A prefabricated building is made in
sections in a factory, then put together where it
is needed.

preface, prefaces (pronounced **pref**-iss)
(noun) an introduction at the beginning of a book
explaining what the book is about or why it was
written.
[Latin *prae* + *fari* = to say before]

prefect, prefects
(noun) a school pupil who has special duties.
[Latin *praefectus* = someone put in charge]

prefer, prefers, preferring, preferred
(verb) If you prefer one thing to another, you
like it better than the other thing.
preferable (adjective) **preferably** (adverb)

preference, preferences (pronounced
pref-er-enss)
1 (noun) If you have a preference for something,
you like it more than other things.
2 When making a choice, if you give preference
to one type of person or thing, you try to choose
that type.
preferential (adjective)

prefix, prefixes
(noun) a letter or group of letters added to the
beginning of a word to make a new word, e.g.
'semi-', 'pre-', 'un-'.

pregnant
(adjective) A woman who is pregnant has a baby
developing in her womb.
pregnancy (noun)
[Latin *prae* = before + *nasci* = to be born]

prehistoric
(adjective) living at a time in the past before
anything was written down.

prejudice, prejudices
(noun) an unreasonable and unfair like or dislike
of someone or something, e.g. *racial prejudice*.
prejudiced (adjective)
[Latin *prae* = before + *judicium* = trial]

preliminary, preliminaries
(adjective) Preliminary activities take place
before an event, in preparation for it.

premature (pronounced prem-mat-**yoor**)
(adjective) happening too early, or earlier than
expected, e.g. *The baby was a month premature*.
prematurely (adverb)
[Latin *prae* + *maturus* = ripe in advance]

premier, premiers
(noun) another name for prime minister.

première, premières (pronounced **prem**-mee-er)
(noun) the first public performance of a new
play or film.
[French *premier* = first]

premises (pronounced **prem**-isses)
(plural noun) The premises of an organization
are the buildings it occupies, e.g. *P.C. Boot
caught the burglar on the premises*.

premium bond, bonds
(noun) numbered tickets that you can buy at a
post office. Each month a computer selects
several ticket numbers, and the people with
those tickets win money.

preoccupied
(adjective) deep in thought or totally involved
with something.

preparatory school or **prep school**
(noun) a private school for children up to 13.

prepare, prepares, preparing, prepared
(verb) to get ready.
preparation (noun)

prepared
(adjective) willing, e.g. *The fool was so desperate
for cash that he was prepared to do anything*.

preposition, prepositions [see page 428]
(noun) a word showing the relationship between
people or things, e.g. *The cat sat on the mat... He
ran into the wall... She took it from him*.
[Latin *prae* + *positum* = placed before]

prescribe, prescribes, prescribing, prescribed
(verb) When doctors prescribe treatment, they
state what treatment a patient should have.
[Latin *prae* + *scribere* = to write before]

prescription, prescriptions
(noun) a piece of paper on which the doctor has
written a medicine needed by a patient.

a is an Anglo-Saxon prefix meaning on, in, at; e.g. abed, aboard, around, asleep, apiece.

presence, presences
(noun) being in a place, e.g. *His presence would not be welcome.* [opposite: **absence**]

present, presents, presenting, presented
1 (adjective) If someone is present somewhere, they are there.
2 (noun) The present is the period of time that is taking place now.
3 (adjective) Example: *the present moment* means now.
4 (noun) a gift.
5 (verb; pronounced pre-**zent**) If you present someone with something, you give it to them.
6 The person who presents a radio or TV show introduces each part or each guest.
presentation (noun) **presenter** (noun)

Similar words: (adjective) current, present-day, existing

presently
(adverb) soon, e.g. *He will be here presently.*

present participle, participles
(noun) In grammar, the present participle of an English verb is the form that ends in '-ing'. It is used to form some tenses, and can be used to form adjectives and nouns from a verb, e.g. *She was* **looking**... *the* **winning** *team.*

present tense
(noun) In grammar, the present tense is the tense of a verb that you use mainly to talk about things that happen at the time of writing or speaking, e.g. *I* **am reading**... *He* **writes** *books.*

preservative, preservatives
(noun) a substance or chemical that prevents food etc. from decaying.

preserve, preserves, preserving, preserved
1 (verb) to take action to make sure that something is not changed, damaged or ended.
2 If you preserve food, you treat it to prevent it from decaying so that it can be stored.
[Latin *prae* = before + *servare* = to keep safe]

president, presidents
1 (noun) In a country which has no king or queen, the president is the elected leader.
2 The president of, for example, a company is the person who has the highest position.
presidency (noun) **presidential** (adjective)
[Latin *praesidens* = ruler]

press, presses, pressing, pressed
1 (verb) e.g. *Press the button... Please press my skirt... They pressed for action on the new road.*
2 (noun) Newspapers and the journalists who work for them are called the press.
3 A printing press is a machine used for printing newspapers and books.

press on
(phrasal verb) If you press on, you continue with something in spite of difficulties or tiredness.

press-up, press-ups
(noun) When you do press-ups, you lie with your face towards the floor and repeatedly raise your body by pushing down with your hands.

pressure, pressures
1 (noun) the force that is produced by pushing on something.
2 If you are under pressure, you have too much to do and not enough time, or someone is trying hard to persuade you to do something.

presumably
(adverb) e.g. If you say 'Presumably she will do her homework tonight', you assume that she will.

presume, presumes, presuming, presumed
(pronounced priz-**yoom**)
(verb) e.g. *When Stanley said 'Dr Livingstone, I presume', he thought it was the Doctor, but he had no proof.*
presumption (noun)
[Latin *praesumere* = to anticipate]

Similar words: assume, suppose

pretence, pretences
(phrase) If you do something **under false pretences**, you allow people to believe that you are doing it for a different reason.

pretend, pretends, pretending, pretended
(verb) e.g. *He pretended to be dead and the lion went away.*
[Latin *praetendere* = to claim]

Similar words: bluff, simulate

pretty, prettier, prettiest
1 (adjective) attractive to look at.
prettily (adverb) **prettiness** (noun)
2 (adverb; informal) quite, e.g. *I thought the concert was pretty good.*
[Old English *prættig* = clever]

prevent, prevents, preventing, prevented
(verb) to stop something from happening.
preventable (adjective) **prevention** (noun)
[Latin *praevenire* = to hinder]

Similar words: avert, stop

preventive
(adjective) intended to help prevent things such as disease or crime, e.g. *preventive medicine.*

preview, previews
(noun) A preview of e.g. a film or exhibition is a chance to see it before it is shown to the public.

previous
(adjective) happening before something else, e.g. *a previous marriage... the previous night.*
previously (adverb)
[Latin *praevius* = leading the way]

Similar words: former, past, ex-, old

prey, preys, preying, preyed (rhymes with **say**)
1 (noun) The creatures that an animal hunts and eats are called its prey.
2 (verb) An animal that preys on a particular kind of animal lives by hunting and eating it.

price, prices
(noun) the amount of money you have to pay to buy something.
pricey (adjective)

A journalist needs these words: copy editor column headline byline feature editorial.

Similar words: charge, cost, rate

priceless
(adjective) Something priceless is so valuable that it is difficult to say how much it is worth.

prick, pricks, pricking, pricked
1 (verb) If you prick something, you stick a sharp pointed object into it.
2 (phrase) If you **prick up your ears**, you listen carefully.
[Old English *prica* = point or puncture]

prickle, prickles, prickling, prickled
1 (noun) a small, sharp point on a plant.
2 (verb) If your skin prickles, it feels as if a lot of sharp points are being stuck into it.
prickly (adverb)

pride, prides, priding, prided
1 (noun) a feeling of satisfaction you have when you have done something well.
2 a feeling of being better than other people, e.g. *Pride comes before a fall.*
3 (verb) If you pride yourself on a quality or skill, you are proud of it.

Similar words: (noun: sense 1) honour, self-respect, dignity

priest, priests
(noun) a person who has special duties and responsibilites in a church, temple, etc.

prim, primmer, primmest
(adjective) always very correctly behaved and easily shocked by anything rude.

primary, primaries
(adjective) extremely important, e.g. *One of Europe's primary requirements was minerals.*
[Latin *primarius* = principal]

primary colour, colours
(noun) In art, the primary colours are red, yellow and blue, from which other colours can be mixed.

primary school, schools
(noun) a school for children from 5 to 11.

primate, primates
(noun) a member of the group of animals which includes humans, monkeys and apes.

Prime Minister, Ministers
(noun) the leader of a government.

prime number, numbers
(noun) a whole number greater than one that cannot be divided exactly by any number except itself and one, e.g. 2, 3, 17, 59.

primitive
(adjective) very simple, basic or old-fashioned, e.g. *a primitive tribe... At the camp, the washing facilities were primitive.*
[Latin *primitivus* = earliest of its kind]

primrose, primroses
(noun) a small, yellow plant.
[Latin *prima rosa* = first rose]

prince, princes
(noun) a male member of a royal family, especially the son of a king or queen.
[Latin *princeps* = chief or ruler]

princess, princesses
(noun) a female member of a royal family, usually the daughter of a king or queen, or the wife of a prince.

principal, principals
1 (adjective) most important, e.g. *Women were the principal organizers of the campaign.*
2 (noun) The principal of a college etc. is the person in charge of it.
principally (adverb)

principle, principles
1 (noun) a belief you have about the way you should behave, e.g. *He stuck to his principles... She was a woman of principle and wouldn't give in.*
2 a general rule or scientific law which explains how something happens or works, e.g. *the principle of levers.*
3 (phrase) If you agree with something **in principle**, you agree with the idea but may be doubtful about some of the details.

Similar words: (sense 1) value, standard, ideal, moral

print, prints, printing, printed
1 (verb) To print a newspaper or book means to reproduce it in large quantities.
2 (phrase) If a book is **out of print**, it is no longer available from the publisher.
printable (adjective) **printer** (noun)
3 (noun) a photograph or a printed copy of a painting.
4 Footprints and fingerprints can be referred to as prints.
5 (verb) If you print when you are writing, you do not join the letters together.

print-out, print-outs
(noun) a printed copy of information from a computer.

priority, priorities
(noun) Something that has priority is the most important thing and needs to be dealt with first.

prison, prisons
(noun) a jail, e.g. *Dartmoor Prison.*

prisoner, prisoners
(noun) someone who is kept in prison or held in captivity against their will.

private, privates
1 (adjective) for the use of one person rather than people in general, e.g. *a private bathroom.*
2 secret from other people, e.g. *private talks.*
3 (noun) a soldier of the lowest rank.
privacy (noun) **privately** (adverb)
[Latin *privatus* = belonging to one person]

private school, schools
(noun) a school that is not supported financially by the government, and where parents pay for their children to attend.

privatize, privatizes, privatizing, privatized; also spelled **privatise**

I hate definitions. (Benjamin Disraeli)

(verb) If the government privatizes a state-owned industry or organization, it allows it to be owned and controlled by a private individual or group. [opposite: **nationalize**]

privet
(noun) a type of evergreen shrub, used to make hedges.

privilege, privileges
(noun) a special right or advantage given to a person or group.
privileged (adjective)

prize, prizes, prizing, prized
1 (noun) a reward given to the winner of a competition or game.
2 (verb) If you prize something that you own, you are very proud of it.

Similar words: award, trophy, jackpot, winnings, reward

pro, pros
1 (noun; informal) a professional, e.g. *a golf pro.*
2 (phrase) The **pros and cons** of a situation are its advantages and disadvantages.
[sense 2: Latin *pro* = for; *contra* = against]

pro-
(prefix) in favour of, e.g. *pro-government newspapers.*
[Latin *pro* = for, or on behalf of]

probable
(adjective) Something that is probable is likely to be true or correct, or likely to happen.
probability (noun)

probably
(adverb) Something that is probably the case is likely but not certain.

probation
1 (noun) a period of time during which a person convicted of a crime is supervised by a probation officer instead of being sent to prison.
2 a trial period after someone has started a job.
probationary (adjective) **probationer** (noun)

probe, probes, probing, probed
1 (verb) to ask a lot of questions to discover the facts about something.
2 If you probe something, you gently push a long thin object into it, usually to find something.
3 (noun) an investigation, e.g. *a space probe.*
[Latin *probare* = to test]

problem, problems
1 (noun) an unsatisfactory situation that causes difficulties.
2 a puzzle or question that you solve using logical thought or mathematics.
[Greek *problēma* = something put forward]

Similar words: (sense 1) hitch, snag, difficulty, hiccup

procedure, procedures
(noun) a way of doing something, especially the correct or usual way.

proceed, proceeds, proceeding, proceeded
1 (verb) If you proceed to do something, you start doing it or continue doing it, e.g. *He came in and proceeded to explain why he was late.*

2 (plural noun) The proceeds from a fund-raising event are the money obtained from it.
[Latin *pro* + *cedere* = to go onward]

process, processes, processing, processed
1 (noun) a series of actions intended to achieve a particular result.
2 (phrase) If you are **in the process** of doing something, you have started doing it but have not yet finished.
3 (verb) When, for example, food is processed, it is treated and cooked in a factory.

procession, processions
(noun) a group of people moving in a line, often as part of a ceremony.

processor, processors
(noun) the central chip in a computer which controls its operations.

proclaim, proclaims, proclaiming, proclaimed
(verb) If someone proclaims something, they formally announce it or make it known.
proclamation (noun)
[Latin *proclamare* = to shout out]

procure, procures, procuring, procured
(verb) to obtain something.

prod, prods, prodding, prodded
(verb) If you prod something, you give it a push with your finger or with something pointed.

prodigy, prodigies (pronounced **prod-dij-ee**)
(noun) someone who shows an extraordinary natural ability at an early age.
[Latin *prodigium* = unnatural happening]

produce, produces, producing, produced
1 (verb) to make or cause something, e.g. *artists producing works of great beauty... headaches produced by tension.*
2 to bring something out so it can be seen, e.g. *He produced a rabbit from a hat.*
3 When someone produces a play, record, etc. they organize it and decide how it will be performed and presented.
4 (noun) food that is grown to be sold.

producer, producers
(noun) The producer of a film or show is the person in charge of making it or putting it on.

product, products
1 (noun) something that is made to be sold.
2 Example: $2 \times 3 = 6$; 6 is the product of 2 and 3 ; 12 is the product of 3 and 4.

production, productions
1 (noun) the process of manufacturing or growing something in large quantities, e.g. *methods of production.*
productive (adjective)
2 A production of a play, opera or other show is a series of performances of it.

productivity
(noun) the rate at which things are produced or dealt with, e.g. *The workforce got a rise in return for greater productivity.*

profession, professions
(noun) a type of job that requires advanced education or training, e.g. *the medical profession*

Titles of books, plays, films, records, TV and radio programmes take capital letters for main words.

[Latin *professio* = taking of vows (when becoming a monk)]

professional, professionals
1 (noun) a person who has been trained in a profession.
2 someone who, for example, plays a sport to earn money rather than as a hobby.
3 (adjective) Professional describes a job rather than a hobby, e.g. *professional football.*
4 For professional advice, you go to someone trained in a particular job.
5 A professional piece of work is of a very high standard.

professor, professors
(noun) In a British university, a professor is the most senior teacher in a department.

proficient
(adjective) If you are proficient at something, you can do it well.
proficiency (noun)
[Latin *proficere* = to make progress]

profile, profiles
1 (noun) the outline of your face seen from the side.
2 a short description of someone's life and character.
3 At school, a profile is a summary of your ability and achievements in different subjects.
[Italian *profilare* = to sketch lightly]

profit, profits
(noun) When someone sells something, the profit is the amount they gain by selling it for more than it cost them to buy or make.
profitable (adjective)

Similar words: gains, proceeds

program, programs, programming, programmed
1 (noun) a set of instructions that a computer follows to perform a particular task.
2 (verb) When someone programs a computer, they write a program and install it.
programmer (noun)

programme, programmes
1 (noun) a planned series of events, e.g. *a programme of work.*
2 e.g. *a TV programme.*
3 a booklet giving information about a play, concert or show that you are attending.
[Greek *programma* = public notice]

progress, progresses, progressing, progressed
1 (noun) the process of gradually improving or moving forward.
2 (phrase) Something that is **in progress** is happening, e.g. *Examinations in progress.*
3 (verb) If you progress, you become more advanced or skilful.
progression (noun)
[Latin *progressus*, past participle of *progredi* = to advance]

Similar words: advance, development

progressive
(adjective) having modern ideas about how things should be done.

prohibit, prohibits, prohibiting, prohibited
(verb) to forbid something or make it illegal, e.g. *Selling alcohol to under-18s is prohibited.*
prohibition (noun) **prohibitive** (adjective)
[Latin *prohibere* = to prevent]

Similar words: prevent, ban, stop

project, projects
(noun) a carefully planned attempt to achieve or to study something over a period of time.
[Latin *proicere* = to throw down]

projector, projectors
(noun) a piece of equipment which shows slides, films, etc. on a screen.

prolific
(adjective) producing a lot of something, e.g. *a prolific bush... a prolific writer.*

prologue, prologues
(noun) a speech or section that introduces a play or book, e.g. the Prologue to the Canterbury Tales.

prolong, prolongs, prolonging, prolonged
(verb) to make something last longer, e.g. *The MP deliberately prolonged his speech so that there would be no time to vote.*
prolonged (adjective)
[Latin *prolongare* = to extend]

promenade, promenades (pronounced prom-en-**ahd**)
(noun) At a seaside resort, the promenade is a road or path along the sea front.
[French word, from *se promener* = to go for a walk]

prominent
1 (adjective) very noticeable, e.g. *Big Ben is a prominent landmark in London.*
2 Prominent people are well-known, e.g. *film stars and other prominent personalities.*
prominence (noun) **prominently** (adverb)
[Latin *prominere* = to stick out]

promise, promise, promising, promised
1 (verb) e.g. *I promise not to run away... Next season promises to be a good one for the team.*
2 (noun) Someone or something that shows promise seems likely to be very successful.
promising (adjective)

Similar words: (verb) give your word, vow, pledge, swear

promote, promotes, promoting, promoted
1 (verb) If someone promotes something, they try to make it happen, increase or become more popular, e.g. *the need to promote peace.*
2 If someone is promoted, they are given a more important job.
promotion (noun)

prompt, prompts, prompting, prompted
1 (verb) If you prompt someone when they stop speaking, you tell them what to say next.

Education is discipline for the adventure of life. (A. N. Whitehead)

2 (adjective) without any delay, e.g. *She received a prompt reply.*
3 (adverb) exactly at the time mentioned, e.g. *The meeting will start at 8 o'clock prompt.*
promptly (adverb)

prone
(adjective) If you are prone to something, you are easily affected by it, e.g. *Athletes are prone to infections.*
[Latin *pronus* = bent forward]

prong, prongs
(noun) one of the pointed parts of a fork.

pronoun, pronouns
(noun) In grammar, a pronoun is a word that is used to replace a noun, e.g. *he, she, them.*

pronounce, pronounces, pronouncing, pronounced
(verb) When you pronounce a word, you say it.
[Latin *pronuntiare* = to announce]

pronounced
(adjective) very noticeable, e.g. *The dog had a pronounced limp.*

pronunciation, pronunciations (pronounced pron-nun-see-**ay**-shn)
(noun) The pronunciation of a word is the way it is usually pronounced.

proof, proofs
(noun) evidence which shows that something happened, is true or exists.

prop, props, propping, propped
1 (verb) If you prop an object somewhere, you support it or rest it against something.
2 (noun) a stick or other object used to support something, e.g. *a clothes prop.*
3 The props in a play are all the objects and furniture used by the actors. [an abbreviation for 'properties']

propaganda
(noun) exaggerated or false information that is published or broadcast to influence people.

propel, propels, propelling, propelled
(verb) to make something move in a particular direction.
propulsion (noun)
[Latin *pro* + *pellere* = to drive onwards]

propeller, propellers
(noun) a device with blades, turned by an engine, that makes a boat or aircraft move.

proper
1 (adjective) real, e.g. *Why don't you get a proper job?*
2 correct, e.g. *Put it in its proper place.*
properly (adverb)
[Latin *proprius* = special]

proper noun, nouns
(noun) the special name of a person, place, etc., e.g. *John, Tuesday, Manchester, July.*

property, properties
1 (noun) A person's property is the things that belong to them.
2 A property is a building and the land belonging to it, e.g. *She arranged to rent the property.*

3 A property of something is a characteristic or quality that it has, e.g. *the properties of a rectangle.*
[Latin *proprietas* = something personal]

prophecy, prophecies
(noun) a statement about what someone believes will happen in the future.
prophesy (verb)

prophet, prophets
(noun) a person who predicts what will happen in the future.
prophetic (adjective)

proportion, proportions
1 (noun) a part of something.
2 The proportion of one amount to another is its size compared with the other amount, e.g. *In most sausages, the proportion of real meat to other stuff is very small indeed.*
3 (phrase) If one thing increases in **proportion to** another, it does so at the same rate or to the same degree, e.g. *Mr Bacon got fatter in proportion to the amount of beer he drank.*
4 If a part of something is **in proportion** to the whole of it, it is the correct size compared with the whole thing.

proportional or **proportionate**
(adjective) If one thing is proportional to another, it remains the same size compared with the other, e.g. *Death rates are generally proportional to the size of the city.*
proportionally (adverb) **proportionately** (adverb)

proportional representation or **PR**
(noun) a system of voting in elections in which the number of MPs of each party is in proportion to the number of people who voted for that party

proposal, proposals
1 (noun) a plan that has been suggested.
2 When someone asks another person to marry them, this request is called a proposal.

propose, proposes, proposing, proposed
1 (verb) to suggest a plan or idea.
2 If you propose to do something, you intend to do it.
3 The person who proposes a motion in a debate introduces it and says why they believe it should be accepted.
4 When someone proposes a toast to somebody, they ask people to drink to that person's health.
5 If someone proposes to another person, they ask that person to marry them.
[Latin *proponere* = to put forward]

proprietor, proprietors
(noun) The proprietor of a business is the owner.

prose
(noun) ordinary written language, not poetry.
[Latin *prosa oratorio* = straightforward speech]

prosecute, prosecutes, prosecuting, prosecuted
(verb) If someone is prosecuted, they are charged with a crime and have to stand trial.
prosecutor (noun)

prosecution
(noun) The lawyers who try to prove a person on trial is guilty are called the prosecution.

One merit of poetry few persons will deny: it says more and in fewer words than prose. (Voltaire)

prospect, prospects, prospecting, prospected
1 (noun) Someone's prospects are their chances of being successful in the future.
2 (verb) to search for gold, oil, etc.
prospector (noun)
[Latin *prospectus* = distant view]

Similar words: (noun) future, outlook

prospective
(adjective) used to say that someone wants to be or is likely to be something; e.g., the prospective buyer of a house is the person who wants to buy it.

prospectus, prospectuses
(noun) a booklet giving details of, for example, a college or a company.

prosper, prospers, prospering, prospered
(verb) When people or businesses prosper, they are successful and make a lot of money.
prosperous (adjective) **prosperity** (noun)
[Latin *prosperare* = to succeed]

prostitute, prostitutes, prostituting, prostituted
(noun) a person, usually a woman, who has sex with men in exchange for money.
prostitution (noun)
[Latin *prostituere* = to succeed]

protect, protects, protecting, protected
(verb) To protect someone or something means to prevent them from being harmed or damaged.
protection (noun) **protective** (adjective)
[Latin *protegere* = to cover]

protein, proteins
(noun) a natural chemical found in many foods, e.g. meat, fish. It is essential for all living things.
[Greek *proteios* = primary]

protest, protests, protesting, protested
1 (verb) to say publicly that you disagree with something.
2 (noun) a demonstration or statement showing that you disagree with something.
[Latin *protestari* = to make a formal declaration]

protestant, Protestants
(noun, adjective) a member of one of the Christian churches which separated from the Catholic church in the 16th century.

prototype, prototypes
(noun) a first model of something, made so that the design can be tested and improved.
[Greek *protos* = first]

protractor, protractors
(noun) a flat, semicircular piece of plastic used for measuring angles.

protrude, protrudes, protruding, protruded
(verb; formal) to stick out from a surface or edge.
protrusion (noun)
[Latin *protrudere* = to thrust forward]

proud, prouder, proudest
1 (adjective) feeling pleasure and satisfaction at something you own or have achieved, e.g. *They were proud of their success.*
2 having great dignity and self-respect, e.g. *Don't be too proud to ask for advice.*
proudly (adverb)

prove, proves, proving, proved, proven
(verb) to provide evidence that something is definitely true.

proverb, proverbs
(noun) a short sentence which gives advice or makes a comment about life, e.g. *Too many cooks spoil the broth.*
proverbial (adjective)

provide, provides, providing, provided
(verb) If you provide something for someone, you give it to them or make it available for them.
provision (noun)

Similar words: cater for, supply

provided
(conjunction) on condition that, e.g. *I will vac the floor, provided you wash the dishes.*

province, provinces
1 (noun) one of the areas into which some large countries are divided.
2 You can refer to the parts of a country which are not near the capital as the provinces.
provincial (adjective)
[Latin *provincia* = a conquered territory]

provisional
(adjective) A provisional arrangement has not yet been made definite and so might be changed.

provocation, provocations
(noun) an act done deliberately to annoy someone.
provocative (adjective)

provoke, provokes, provoking, provoked
(verb) If you provoke someone, you deliberately try to make them angry.
[Latin *provocare* = to call forth]

prowess
(noun) outstanding ability, e.g. *His prowess at sports earned their respect.*
[Old French *proesce* = bravery]

prowl, prowls, prowling, prowled
(verb) If a person or animal prowls around, they move around quickly and secretly, as if hunting.

proximity
(noun; formal) nearness, e.g., *We were in close proximity to the watch tower.*
[Latin *proximitas* = nearness]

prune, prunes, pruning, pruned
1 (noun) a dried plum.
2 (verb) When someone prunes a tree or shrub, they cut back some of the branches.

pry, pries, prying, pried
(verb) If someone is prying, they are trying to find out about something secret or private.

psalm, psalms (pronounced **sahm**)
(noun) one of the 150 songs, poems and prayers which form the Book of Psalms in the Bible.
[Greek *psalmos* = song accompanied on the harp]

pseudo- (pronounced **syoo**-doh)
(prefix) not real, e.g. *a pseudo-Tudor house... pseudonym.*
[Greek *pseudes* = false]

French proverbs. A fool writes his name everywhere.
When it is fine, take your umbrella. In rain, please yourself.

pseudonym, pseudonyms (pronounced **syoo**-doe-nim)
(noun) A writer who uses a pseudonym uses another name as an author rather than their real name, e.g. Mark Twain was the pseudonym of Samuel Langhorn Clemens.
[Greek *pseudōnumon* = false name]

psychiatry
(noun) the branch of medicine concerned with mental illness.
psychiatrist (noun) **psychiatric** (adjective)
[Greek *psukhē* = mind + *iatros* = healer]

psychic
(adjective) having unusual mental powers, e.g. able to read people's minds or predict the future.
[Greek *psukhikos* = of the mind]

psychology
1 (noun) the scientific study of the mind and of the reasons for people's behaviour.
2 The psychology of a person is the kind of mind they have and the way they think.
psychological (adjective) **psychologist** (noun)

psychopath, psychopaths
(noun) a mentally ill person who behaves violently without feeling guilt.
psychopathic (adjective)

PTA, PTAs
(noun) an organization for parents of the children at a school to discuss school matters with the teachers and to raise funds. [an abbreviation for 'Parent-Teacher Association']

pterodactyl, pterodactyls (pronounced ter-ro-**dak**-til)
(noun) a prehistoric flying reptile.
[Greek *pteron* = wing + *daktulos* = finger]

pub, pubs or **public house**
(noun) a building where people go to drink alcoholic or soft drinks and talk with their friends. [short for 'public house']

puberty (pronounced **pyoo**-ber-tee)
(noun) the stage when a person's body changes from that of a child into that of an adult.
[Latin *pubertas* = maturity]

pubic (pronounced **pyoo**-bik)
(adjective) relating to the area around and above a person's genitals, e.g. *pubic hair*.

public
1 (adjective) relating to people in general, e.g. *The campaign attracted public support*.
2 provided for everyone to use, or open to anyone, e.g. *public transport... public toilets*.
publicly (adverb)
[Latin *poplicus* = of the people]

Similar words: civil, civic, communal, unrestricted

publication, publications
1 (noun) The publication of a book is the act of printing it and making it available.
2 A publication is a book or magazine.

public convenience, conveniences
(noun) a toilet that anyone can use.

publicity
(noun) information or advertisements about an item or event.

publicize, publicizes, publicizing, publicized; also spelled **publicise**
(verb) When someone publicizes a fact or event, they advertise it and make it widely known.

public school, schools
(noun) a school that is privately run and that charges fees for the pupils to attend.

publish, publishes, publishing, published
(verb) When a company publishes a book etc., they arrange for copies to be printed and distributed.
publisher (noun) **publishing** (noun)
[Latin *publicare* = to make public]

pudding, puddings
1 (noun) a sweet cake mixture cooked with fruit etc., e.g. *treacle pudding*.
2 the sweet course of a meal.

puddle, puddles
(noun) a small, shallow pool of liquid.

puerile (pronounced **pyoo**-rile)
(adjective) silly and childish.
[Latin *puerilis*, from *puer* = boy]

puff, puffs, puffing, puffed
(verb) e.g. *to puff at a pipe... After two miles I was really puffing... My face puffed up after the insect bit me.*

puffin, puffins
(noun) a black and white sea bird with a large brightly-coloured striped beak.

pull, pulls, pulling, pulled
1 (verb) e.g. *Watch the huskies pull that sledge.*
2 (phrase) If you **pull someone's leg**, you play a trick on them by pretending something is true when it isn't.

pull off
(phrasal verb) If you pull something off, you succeed in doing it, e.g. *The businessman pulled off a big deal with Japan.*

pull out
(phrasal verb) If you pull out of something, you withdraw from it or leave it, e.g. *You will lose your money if you decide to pull out.*

pull through
(phrasal verb) to recover from a serious illness.

pull together
1 (phrasal verb) When people pull together, they co-operate with each other to achieve something
2 If someone tells you to pull yourself together, they are telling you to control yourself.

pull up
(phrasal verb) When a vehicle pulls up, it stops.

pulley, pulleys
(noun) a device for lifting heavy weights, consisting of a wheel or series of wheels over which a rope passes.

pullover, pullovers
(noun) a woollen garment that covers the top part of your body.

Reference book: Brewer's Dictionary of Phrase and Fable is full of 'words that have a tale to tell'.

pulp
(noun) If something is turned into a pulp, it is crushed until it is soft, smooth and moist.

pulpit, pulpits
(noun) the small, raised platform in a church where people stand to preach.
[Latin *pulpitum* = platform]

pulsate, pulsates, pulsating, pulsated
(verb) If something is pulsating, it is vibrating regularly, e.g. *a pulsating rhythm.*
[Latin *pulsare* = to push]

pulse, pulses
1 (noun) the regular beating of blood through your body.
2 pulses are the edible seeds of certain types of plant, e.g. peas, beans, lentils.

pulverize, pulverizes, pulverizing, pulverized; also spelled **pulverise**
(verb) to crush into very small pieces.
[Latin *pulvus* = dust]

pump, pumps, pumping, pumped
1 (noun) a machine that is used to force a liquid or gas to move in a particular direction.
2 (plural noun) Pumps are canvas shoes with flat soles which people wear for sport or leisure.
3 (verb) If you pump someone about something, you ask them a lot of questions.

pumpkin, pumpkins
(noun) a very large, round, orange-coloured vegetable.

pun, puns
(noun) a clever and amusing use of words so that what you say has two different meanings, e.g. *There are plenty of puns about trees but if I put them here you might not twig them.*

punch, punches, punching, punched
1 (verb) to hit someone hard with your fist.
2 (noun) a drink made from wine, spirits, fruit, sugar and spices.

punch line, lines
(noun) The punch line of a joke is the last sentence which makes the joke funny.

punctual
(adjective) arriving at the correct time.
punctually (adverb) **punctuality** (noun)
[Latin *punctualis* = of detail]

Similar words: prompt, on time

punctuation
(noun) the marks in writing : full stops, question marks, commas, etc.
punctuate (verb)
[Latin *punctum* = point]

puncture, punctures, puncturing, punctured
1 (noun) If a tyre has a puncture, a small hole has been made in it and it has become flat.
2 (verb) to make a small hole in something.
[Latin *punctum* = point]

punish, punishes, punishing, punished
(verb) To punish someone who has done wrong means to make them suffer because of it.
punishment (noun)
[Latin *punire* = to punish]

Similar words: chastise, penalize

Punjabi, Punjabis (pronounced pun-**jah**-bee)
1 (adjective) belonging to the Punjab, a state in north-western India.
2 (noun) someone who comes from the Punjab.
3 a language spoken in the Punjab.

punk, punks
(noun) a name for a young person who dresses in a certain way popular in the late 1970s. Punks are associated with black dress, pins in the skin and brightly-coloured shaven hair.

punt, punts
(noun) a long, flat-bottomed boat, moved along by pushing a pole against the river bottom.

puny, punier, puniest
(adjective) very small and weak.

pupa, pupae (pronounced **pyoo**-pa)
(noun) an insect that is at the stage between a larva and a fully developed adult.

pupil, pupils
1 (noun) The pupils at a school are the children who go there.
2 Your pupils are the small, round openings in the centre of your eyes.
[sense 1: Latin *pupillus* = orphan]

puppet, puppets
(noun) a doll or toy animal moved by pulling strings or by putting your hand inside its body.
[Old French *poupette* = little doll]

puppy, puppies or **pup**
(noun) a young dog.

purchase, purchases, purchasing, purchased
1 (verb) to buy something.
2 (noun) something you have bought.
purchaser (noun)

pure, purer, purest
1 (adjective) not mixed with anything else, e.g. *pure silk... pure white.*
2 complete, e.g. *We met by pure chance.*
purity (noun) **purely** (adverb)

Similar words: (sense 1): clean, spotless

purge, purges
(noun) a campaign to remove unwanted things or to change undesirable behaviour, e.g. *We're going to have a purge on lateness this week.*
[Latin *purgare* = to purify]

purify, purifies, purifying, purified
(verb) to remove all dirty or harmful substances from something.
purification (noun)
[Latin *purificare* = to cleanse]

purl
(noun) one of the two main knitting stitches.

purple
(noun, adjective) reddish-blue.

purpose, purposes
1 (noun) the reason for something.
2 (phrase) If you do something **on purpose**, you do it deliberately.
purposeful (adjective)

Punctuate this sentence: *the boy said the teacher is a fool* — Do you notice anything?

purpose-built
(adjective) specially made for a particular purpose, e.g. *This car was purpose-built for handicapped people.*

purr, purrs, purring, purred
(verb) to make the low noise that a cat makes.

purse, purses
(noun) a small leather or fabric container for carrying money.
[Latin *bursa* = bag]

pursue, pursues, pursuing, pursued
(verb) If you pursue someone, you follow them to try to catch them.
pursuer (noun) **pursuit** (noun)

pursuit, pursuits
(noun) a hobby or occupation, e.g. *My favourite pursuit is vole watching.*

pus
(noun) a thick, yellowish liquid that forms in an infected wound.

push, pushes, pushing, pushed
1 (verb) e.g. *Push the door and it will open... He is pushing to be made a prefect.*
2 (informal) Someone who pushes drugs sells them illegally.
3 (phrase; informal) If someone is **given the push**, they are dismissed from their job.
4 If, for example, you say someone is pushing 40, you mean they are nearly that age.
[French *pousser* = to push]

Similar words: (sense 1) shove, thrust, jog, jostle

push off
(phrasal verb; informal) If you tell someone to push off, you are telling them rudely to go away.

pushchair, pushchairs
(noun) a small, folding chair on wheels in which a toddler can be wheeled around.

put, puts, putting, put
(verb) e.g. *Put it over there... He didn't put it quite as crudely as that!... This puts me in a difficult position... The cost is put at £2,000.*

Similar words: place, set, position, lay

put away
(phrasal verb) If someone is put away, they are sent to prison or mental hospital for a long time.

put down
1 (phrasal verb) If soldiers or police put down a rebellion, they stop it by using force.
2 To put someone down means to criticize them and make them appear foolish.
3 If an animal is put down, it is killed because it is very ill, dangerous or unwanted.
4 If you put something down to a particular thing, you believe it is caused by that thing, e.g. *The illness was put down to dirty food handling.*

put forward
(phrasal verb) If you put something forward, you want it to be considered, e.g. *She put forward a suggestion.*

put off
1 (phrasal verb) to delay something.
2 To put someone off means to discourage them, e.g. *He tried to put me off by making rude noises.*

put on
(phrase) If someone is behaving or speaking in a false way, you can say they are **putting it on.**

put out
1 (phrasal verb) e.g. *Put the light out.*
2 If you put your back, hip or shoulder out, you injure it by dislocating a bone etc.
3 If you are put out, you are annoyed or upset e.g. *I was very put out when she wouldn't speak to me.*
4 If you put yourself out for someone, you go to a lot of trouble to help them.

put up
1 (phrasal verb) If someone puts you up, you stay at their home for one or more nights.
2 If someone puts you up to something wrong or foolish, they encourage you to do it.
3 If you put up with something, you tolerate it even though you disagree with it or dislike it.

putt, putts
(noun) In golf, a putt is a gentle stroke made when the ball is on the green.
putting (noun)

putty
(noun) a paste of linseed oil, chalk, etc., used to fix panes of glass into frames.

puzzle, puzzles, puzzling, puzzled
1 (verb) If something puzzles you, it confuses you and you do not understand it.
2 (noun) a game, toy or question that requires a lot of thought to complete or solve.
puzzled (adjective)

Similar words: (verb) baffle, bewilder, stump, perplex

pygmy, pygmies (pronounced **pig**-mee)
(plural noun) a very small person, especially one who belongs to a race in which all the people are small.
[Greek *pugmaios* = undersized]

pyjamas
(plural noun) a type of nightwear.
[Persian *pay jama* = leg clothing]

pylon, pylons
(noun) Pylons are very tall metal structures which carry overhead electricity cables.
[Greek *pulon* = gateway]

pyramid, pyramids
(noun) a 3D shape, usually with a square base and flat triangular sides sloping upwards to a point.
[Greek *puramis* = pyramid]

Pyrex
(noun; trademark) a type of glass used for making dishes that are ovenproof.

python, pythons
(noun) a large snake that kills animals by squeezing them with its body.
[from Greek *Puthon*, a huge mythical serpent]

It is a man's kindly acts that are remembered of him in the years after his life.

Q

quack, quacks, quacking, quacked
1 (verb) to make the sound made by a duck.

quad, quads (pronounced **kwod**)
1 (noun) Quads are 4 children born at the same time to the same mother. [an abbreviation for **quadruplet**]
2 A quad is a courtyard with buildings all round it. [an abbreviation for **quadrangle**]

quadrangle, quadrangles (pronounced **kwod**-rang-gl)
1 (noun) a courtyard with buildings all round it.
2 In geometry, a quadrangle is a 4-sided figure.

quadrant, quadrants (pronounced **kwod**-rant)
(noun) a quarter of a circle, or a quarter of the circumference of a circle.
[Latin *quadrans* = quarter]

quadri-
(prefix) 4 e.g. *quadrilateral*
[a Latin word]

quadrilateral, quadrilaterals (pronounced kwod-ril-**lat**-ral)
(noun) a shape with 4 straight sides.
[Latin *quadri-* = 4 + *latus* = side]

quadruped, quadrupeds (pronounced **kwod**-roo-ped)
(noun) any animal with 4 legs.
[Latin *quadri-* + *pes* = four feet]

quadruple, quadruples, quadrupling, quadrupled (pronounced kwod-**roo**-pl)
1 (verb) When a number quadruples, it becomes 4 times as large as it was.
2 (adjective) 4 times as large as normal, e.g. *'A quadruple whisky, please', said the drunk.*

quadruplet, quadruplets (pronounced kwod-**roo**-plet)
(noun) Quadruplets are 4 children born at the same time to the same mother.

quagmire, quagmires (pronounced **kwag**-mire)
(noun) a soft, wet area of land which you sink into if you walk on it.

quail, quails, quailing, quailed
1 (noun) a type of small game bird.
2 (verb) If you quail, you feel or look afraid.

quaint, quainter, quaintest
(adjective) attractively old-fashioned or unusual, e.g. *quaint little houses... quaint ideas.*
quaintly (adverb) **quaintness** (noun)

quake, quakes, quaking, quaked
1 (verb) to shake and tremble because you are very frightened.
2 (noun; informal) an earthquake.
[Old English *cwecian* = to quake]

qualification, qualifications
(noun) Your qualifications are your skills and achievements, especially as officially recognized at the end of a course of training or study.

qualify, qualifies, qualifying, qualified
1 (verb) When you qualify, you pass the examinations that you need to pass to do a particular job, e.g. *I qualified as a doctor.*
2 If you qualify for something, you become eligible for it, e.g. *Manchester City qualified for the F.A. Cup Final.*

quality, qualities
1 (noun) The quality of something is how good it is, e.g. *The quality of the photograph was poor.*
2 a personal characteristic, e.g. *We look for certain qualities in a teacher.*
[Latin *qualitas* = state or nature]

quantity, quantities
(noun) an amount, e.g. *What quantity of grain did you harvest?*
[Latin *quantus* = how much]

quarantine, quarantines, quarantining, quarantined (pronounced **kwor**-an-teen)
(noun) If an animal is in quarantine, it is kept away from other animals for a time because it might have an infectious disease.
[Italian *quarantina* = 40 days]

quarrel, quarrels, quarrelling, quarrelled
1 (verb) If people quarrel, they have an angry argument.
2 (verb) to disagree with something, e.g. *I would quarrel with your suggestion that we do not care.*
[Latin *queri* = to complain]

Similar words: (verb) fight, dispute, bicker, fall out, squabble

quarrelsome
(adjective) often quarrelling, e.g. *His brothers were greedy and quarrelsome.*

quarry, quarries
(pronounced **kwor**-ree)
(noun) a place where stone is removed from the ground by digging or blasting.

quart, quarts (pronounced **kwort**)
(noun) a unit of liquid volume. (1 qt = 2 pints = 1.14 litres)
[Latin *quartus* = 4th; 4 quarts = 1 gallon]

quarter, quarters
1 (noun) one of 4 equal parts.
2 You can refer to a particular area in a city as a quarter, e.g. *the Chinese quarter.*
3 (plural noun) A soldier's or a servant's quarters are the rooms that they live in.
4 (phrase) **At close quarters** means very close, e.g. *Oswald was shot at close quarters.*
[Latin *quartarius* = a 4th part]

quarterly, quarterlies
(adjective, adverb) happening regularly every 3 months, e.g. *a quarterly magazine.*

quartet, quartets (pronounced kwor-**tet**)
(noun) a group of 4 musicians.

quartz
(noun) a kind of mineral. Quartz crystal is used

Letter Q is a puzzle. It seems to have had connections with K or might have been a monkey!

in making electronic equipment and very accurate watches and clocks.

quaver, quavers, quavering, quavered
(pronounced **kway**-ver)
(verb) If your voice quavers, it sounds unsteady, usually because you are nervous.
[Middle English *quaven* = to tremble]

quay, quays (pronounced **kee**)
(noun) a place where boats are tied up and loaded or unloaded.

queasy, queasier, queasiest (pronounced **kwee**-zee)
(adjective) feeling slightly sick.
queasiness (noun)

queen, queens
1 (noun) a female monarch or a woman married to a king.
2 a female bee, ant, etc. which can lay eggs.
3 In chess, the queen is the most powerful piece, which can move in any direction.
[Old English *cwen* = queen]

queer, queerer, queerest
(adjective) very strange.

quench, quenches, quenching, quenched
(verb) If you quench your thirst, you have a drink so that you are no longer thirsty.
[Old English *acwencan* = to extinguish]

query, queries, querying, queried (pronounced **qweer**-ee)
1 (noun) a question.
2 (verb) If you query something, you ask about it because you think it might not be right, e.g. *He queried the accuracy of the figures.*
[Latin *quaerere* = to ask]

quest, quests
(noun) a long search for something.
[Latin *quaesita* = a thing people seek]

question, questions, questioning, questioned
1 (noun) a sentence which asks for information.
2 (verb) to ask someone questions.
3 (noun) If there is some question about something, there is doubt about it.
4 a problem that needs to be discussed, e.g. *The death raised the question of speeding in town.*
5 (phrase) If something is **out of the question**, it is impossible.
6 The time, place or thing **in question** is the one that you have just been talking about, e.g. *Did you see him on the night in question?*

Similar words: (sense 1) query, inquiry

question mark, marks
(noun) the punctuation mark **?** used at the end of a question, e.g. *Do you understand?*

questionnaire, questionnaires
(noun) a list of questions which asks for information for a survey.

queue, queues, queueing, queued
(pronounced **kyoo**)
(verb) When people queue, they stand in a line waiting for something.

quibble, quibbles, quibbling, quibbled
(verb) If you quibble, you argue about something unimportant.

quiche, quiches (pronounced **keesh**)
(noun) a tart with a savoury filling.
[a French word, from German *Kuchen* = cake]

quick, quicker, quickest
(adjective) fast, e.g. *Quick march!... She's really quick at French.*
quickly (adverb)
[Old English *cwicu* = alive]

quicksand, quicksands
(noun) an area of deep, wet sand that you sink into if you walk on it.

quid
(noun; informal) a pound.

quiet, quieter, quietest
1 (adjective) e.g. *Be quiet!... a quiet evening at home... a quiet wedding.*
2 (noun) e.g. *a bit of peace and quiet*
quietly (adverb) **quietness** (noun) **quieten** (verb)
[Latin *quies* = calm or rest]

quilt, quilts
(noun) a padded cover for a bed.
quilted (adjective)
[Latin *culcita* = stuffed item of bedding]

quin, quins
(noun) one of 5 children born at the same time to the same mother [an abbreviation for quintuplet]

quintet, quintets (pronounced kwin-**tet**)
(noun) a group of 5 musicians
[Italian *quinto* = 5th]

quintuplet, quintuplets (pronounced kwin-**tyoo**-plit)
(noun) one of 5 children born at the same time to the same mother.
[Latin *quintus* = 5th]

quit, quits, quitting, quit or quitted
1 (verb) to leave or stop doing something, e.g. *Anthony said he was going to quit teaching.*
2 (phrase; informal) If two people **are quits**, neither of them owes the other anything.

quite
1 (adverb) fairly e.g. *She was quite young.*
2 completely, e.g. *I stood quite still.*
3 (phrase; informal) You use **quite a** to emphasize that something is large or impressive, e.g. *The New York skyline was quite a sight.*

quiver, quivers, quivering, quivered
1 (verb) If something quivers, it trembles.
2 (noun) a container for arrows.

quiz, quizzes, quizzing, quizzed
1 (noun) a game in which competitors are asked questions to test their knowledge.
2 (verb) If you quiz someone, you question them closely about something.

quizzical (pronounced **kwiz**-ik-kl)
(adjective) amused and questioning, e.g. *He gave me a quizzical look when I told him I was an alien from Mars.*

Whenever Q is used in an English word it must be followed by U ('U' must join the queue).

quotation, quotations or quote
1 (noun) an extract from a book or speech which is used by someone else.
2 A quotation is also a written estimate of how much a piece of work will cost.

quotation mark, marks
(noun) the punctuation marks '...' that show where a speech or quotation begins and ends, e.g. *'I've started so I'll finish,' said Magnus.*

quote, quotes, quoting, quoted
1 (verb) If you quote what someone has written or said, you repeat their exact words.
2 If you quote a fact, you state it because it supports what you are saying.
[Latin *quotare* = to mark passages in a book with reference numbers or notes]

quotient, quotients (pronounced **kwoh**-shent)
(noun) Example: $6 \div 3 = 2$; 2 is the quotient of 6 and 3; 4 is the quotient of 20 and 5.
[Latin *quotiens* = how often]

R

rabbi, rabbis (pronounced **rab**-bye)
(noun) a Jewish religious leader.
[Hebrew *rabh* + *-i* = my master]

rabbit, rabbits
(noun) a small animal with long ears.

rabble
(noun) a noisy, disorderly crowd.

rabies (pronounced **ray**-beez)
(noun) an infectious disease which causes people and animals, especially dogs, to go mad and die.
[Latin *rabies* = madness]

race, races, racing, raced
1 (noun) a competition to see who is fastest.
2 (verb) If you race somewhere, you go there as quickly as possible, e.g. *She raced downstairs.*
3 (noun) one of the major groups that human beings can be divided into according to their physical features.

racecourse, racecourses
(noun) a grass track where horses race.

racehorse, racehorses
(noun) a horse trained to run in races.

racial
(adjective) relating to the different races that people belong to, e.g. *racial discrimination.*
racially (adverb)

racism or racialism
(noun) the treatment of some people as inferior because of their race.
racist (noun and adjective)

rack, racks, racking, racked
1 (noun) a piece of equipment for holding things or hanging things on.
2 (phrase; informal) If you **rack your brains**, you try hard to think of or remember something.

racket, rackets
1 (noun) a lot of noise.
2 an illegal way of making money.
3 a bat with strings across it used in tennis, squash, and badminton (also spelled **racquet**)
[Arabic *rahat* = palm of the hand]

radar
(noun) equipment used to track ships, aircraft etc. by using radio signals that are reflected back from the object and shown on a screen.
[from *RA(dio) D(etecting) A(nd) R(anging)*]

radial (pronounced **ray**-dee-al)
(adjective) Radial lines come out in different directions from a central point.
[Latin *radius* = ray or spoke]

radiant
1 (adjective) Someone who is radiant is so happy that it shows in their face, e.g. *a radiant bride.*
2 glowing brightly, e.g. *radiant heat.*
radiantly (adverb) **radiance** (noun)
[Latin *radiare* = to shine]

radiate, radiates, radiating, radiated
1 (verb) If things radiate from a place, they spread out from a central point, e.g. *Roads radiated from the city centre.*
2 If you radiate a quality or emotion, it shows clearly in your face and behaviour, e.g. *She radiated confidence.*

radiation
(noun) the stream of particles given out by a radioactive substance, e.g. *Radiation leaks are the constant worry of nuclear engineers.*

radiator, radiators
1 (noun) a hollow metal panel for heating a room.
2 A car's radiator is the part that is filled with water to cool the engine.

radii the plural of radius.

radio, radios, radioing, radioed
1 (noun) a piece of equipment for listening to radio programmes and messages.
2 (verb) To radio someone means to send them a message by radio, e.g. *The pilot radioed for help.*
[a shortened form of *radiotelegraphy*]

radioactive
(adjective) giving off powerful and harmful rays.
radioactivity (noun)

radiography
(noun) the process of taking X-rays.
radiographer (noun)

radio telescope, telescopes
(noun) an instrument that can pick up radio waves from space and so detect things that cannot be seen using ordinary telescopes.

radish, radishes
(noun) a small salad vegetable with a red skin.
[Latin *radix* = root]

Letter R began as a picture of a human head, perhaps a man with a beard.

radium
(noun) a radioactive element used in the treatment of cancer and other diseases.

radius, radii
(noun) The radius of a circle is the length of a straight line drawn from its centre to its circumference.
[Latin *radius* = ray or spoke]

raffia
(noun) a material made from palm leaves and used for making mats and baskets.

raffle, raffles
(noun) a competition in which people buy numbered tickets and win a prize if they have the ticket that is chosen.

raft, rafts
(noun) a floating platform made from long pieces of wood tied together.

rafter, rafters
(noun) Rafters are the sloping pieces of wood that support a roof.

rage, rages, raging, raged
1 (noun) great anger.
2 (verb) If a storm or battle is raging, it is continuing with great force or violence, e.g. *Outside, the tempest raged.*
4 (phrase; informal) Something that is **all the rage** is popular or fashionable.

ragged
(adjective) Ragged clothes are old and torn.

raid, raids, raiding, raided
1 (verb) To raid a place means to enter it by force to attack it or steal something.
2 (noun) an attack, e.g. *an air raid.*
[Old English *rad* = military expedition]

rail, rails
1 (noun) a fixed horizontal bar used as a support or for hanging things on.
2 Rails are the steel bars which trains run along.
3 the railway, e.g. *I usually go by rail.*

railing, railings
(noun) Railings are a fence made from metal bars.

railway, railways
(noun) a route along which trains travel.

rain, rains, raining, rained
1 (noun) water falling from the clouds in drops.
2 (verb) If something rains from above, it falls in large quantities, e.g. *Ash rained from the sky.*
rainy (adjective) **raindrop** (noun) **raincoat** (noun)

rainbow, rainbows
(noun) an arch of different colours caused by the sun shining through raindrops.

rainfall
(noun) the amount of rain that falls in a place during a particular period.

rainforest, rainforests
(noun) a dense forest of tall trees in a tropical area where there is a lot of rain.

raise, raises, raising, raised
1 (verb) to make something higher, e.g. *He tried to raise the window... We must raise our standards by taking the Survival Test on page v.*
2 If you raise your voice, you speak more loudly.
3 To raise money means to obtain it from several people or organizations.
4 To raise a child means to look after it until it is grown up.
5 If you raise a subject, you mention it.

raisin, raisins
(noun) Raisins are dried grapes.
[French *raisin* = grape]

rake, rakes
(noun) A rake is a garden tool with a row of metal teeth and a long handle.

rally, rallies, rallying, rallied
1 (noun) a large public meeting held to show support for something, e.g. *a Greenpeace rally.*
2 a competition in which vehicles are raced over public roads, e.g. *the RAC rally.*
3 In tennis or squash, a rally is a continuous series of shots.
4 (verb) When people rally round, they work as a group to support someone at a difficult time.

ram, rams, ramming, rammed
1 (verb) to crash into something deliberately.
2 To ram something somewhere means to push it there firmly, e.g. *He rammed tobacco in his pipe.*
3 (noun) an adult male sheep.

RAM
(noun) In computing, RAM is a temporary storage space which can be filled with data by the user but which loses its contents when the machine is switched off. [RAM stands for 'random access memory']

Ramadan
(noun) the 9th month of the Muslim year, during which Muslims eat and drink nothing during daylight.
[Arabic *Ramadan* = the hot month]

ramble, rambles, rambling, rambled
1 (noun) a long walk in the countryside.
2 (verb) to talk in a confused and lengthy way, e.g. *I listened to him rambling on.*
3 to walk in the countryside.
rambler (noun)

rambling
(adjective) A rambling building is large and spreads out in many directions.

ramp, ramps
(noun) a sloping surface connecting two different levels.

rampage, rampages, rampaging, rampaged
1 (verb) to rush about wildly causing damage.
2 (phrase) To **go on the rampage** means to rush about in a wild or violent way.

Similar words: go berserk, run amok, run riot

rampart, ramparts
(noun) Ramparts are earth banks, often with a wall on top, built to protect a castle or city.

ramshackle
(adjective) A ramshackle building is in poor condition, and likely to fall down.

Similar words: rickety, tumbledown, dilapidated

ranch, ranches
(noun) a large farm where cattle, sheep or horses are reared, especially in the USA.
rancher (adjective)
[Mexican Spanish *rancho* = small farm]

rancid (pronounced **ran**-sid)
(adjective) Rancid food has gone bad.
[Latin *rancere* = to stink]

random
(phrase) If you do something **at random**, you do it without any definite plan, e.g. *As it didn't matter, he chose a number at random.*

Similar words: haphazard, unplanned

range, ranges, ranging, ranged
1 (noun) The range of something is the maximum distance over which it can work, e.g. *We kept out of range of their guns.*
2 a number of different things of the same kind, e.g. *a wide range of TV sets.*
3 e.g.*The age range is from 5 to 11.*
4 a line of mountains, e.g. *the Pennine range.*
5 a place where people practise shooting at targets, e.g. *a rifle range.*
6 (verb) e.g. *prices ranging from £6 to £16.*
[Old French *range* = row]

Similar words: (sense 2) variety, scope, spectrum

ranger, rangers
(noun) someone whose job is to look after a forest or park.

rank, ranks, ranking, ranked
1 (noun) Someone's rank is their official level in a job or profession.
2 The ranks are the ordinary members of the armed forces, rather than the officers.
3 a row of people or things, e.g. *a taxi rank.*
4 (verb) To rank as something means to have that position compared with others, e.g. *Brighton ranks as one of the top seaside resorts.*

ransack, ransacks, ransacking, ransacked
(verb) Ransacking a room means disturbing everything to search for or steal something.
[Old Norse *rann* = house + *saka* = to search]

ransom, ransoms
(noun) money that is demanded to free someone who has been kidnapped.

rant, rants, ranting, ranted
(verb) to talk loudly in an excited or angry way.

rap, raps, rapping, rapped
1 (verb) to hit something with a series of quick blows, e.g. *to rap on the door.*
2 (noun) a style of poetry spoken to music with a strong rhythmic beat.

rape, rapes, raping, raped
1 (verb) If a man rapes a woman, he violently forces her to have sex with him against her will.
rapist (noun)
2 (noun) a plant with bright yellow flowers, grown as a farm crop to provide oil and fodder.

[verb: Latin *rapere* = to seize
noun: Latin *rapum* = turnip]

rapid, rapids
1 (adjective) happening or moving very quickly, e.g. *rapid industrial expansion.*
2 (plural noun) Rapids are parts of a river where water moves extremely fast over rocks.
rapidly (adverb) **rapidity** (noun)

rapier, rapiers
(noun) a long, thin sword with a sharp point.

rare, rarer, rarest
1 (adjective) Something that is rare is not common or does not happen often, e.g. *rare wild flowers... Cases of smallpox are rare.*
2 Rare meat has been lightly cooked.
rarely (adverb) **rarity** (noun)

rascal, rascals
(noun) a friendly word for someone who does bad or mischievous things.
[Old French *rascaille* = rabble]

rash, rashes
1 (adjective) hasty and foolish, e.g. *You are rash to rush after her like that.*
2 (noun) an area of red spots that appear on your skin when you are ill or have an allergy.
rashly (adverb) **rashness** (noun)

Similar words: (adjective) impetuous, reckless, irresponsible, foolish

rasher, rashers
(noun) a thin slice of bacon.

rasp, rasps, rasping, rasped
(verb) to make a harsh unpleasant sound.

raspberry, raspberries
(noun) a small, soft red fruit.

rate, rates, rating, rated
1 (noun) speed or frequency, e.g. *the rapid rate of change... the divorce rate.*
2 The rate of interest is its level, e.g. *Interest rates dropped to 6%.*
3 The rates were local taxes paid by people who owned buildings.
4 (phrase) If you say **at this rate** something will happen, you mean it will happen if things continue in the same way, e.g. *At this rate I will have gone round the twist by Christmas.*
5 (verb) The way you rate someone or something is your opinion of them, e.g. *I don't rate heavy metal music because I'm old and boring.*

rather
(adverb) e.g. *He looked rather sad... I'm in rather a hurry... I would rather be on holiday... We could go by train rather than wait hours in a jam... We walked, or rather staggered, home.*

ratio, ratios
(noun) a relationship which shows how many times one thing is bigger than another, e.g. *There is a ratio of 1 teacher to 18 pupils.*
[Latin *ratio* = a reckoning]

Similar words: rate, proportion, relation

ration, rations, rationing, rationed
1 (verb) When something is rationed, you are

....Focus is where the sun's rays meet. (Think about it!)

only allowed a limited amount of it, because there is a shortage.
2 (noun) Rations are the food supplied each day to a soldier or member of an expedition.

rational
(adjective) When people are rational, their judgements are based on reason, not emotion.

rat race
(noun) If you refer to a way of life as a rat race, you mean that it is fiercely competitive e.g. *They decided to leave the London rat race, and bought a small farm in the Shetlands.*

rattle, rattles, rattling, rattled
1 (verb) to make short, regular knocking sounds.
2 (noun) a baby's toy.
3 (verb) If something rattles you, it upsets you, e.g. *His questions obviously rattled her.*

rattle off
(phrasal verb) If you rattle off a number of things, you say or produce them quickly and easily, e.g. *She rattled off the answers without even thinking.*

rattlesnake, rattlesnakes
(noun) a poisonous American snake with rattling, horny rings in its tail

ratty, rattier, rattiest
(adjective; informal) cross and irritable.

rave, raves, raving, raved
1 (verb) to talk in an angry, uncontrolled way, e.g. *He started raving about his dented car.*
2 (informal) If you rave about something, you talk about it very enthusiastically.

raven, ravens
1 (noun) a large, black bird of the crow family.
2 (adjective) Raven hair is black and shiny.

ravenous
(adjective) very hungry.
ravenously (adverb)

ravine, ravines
(noun) a deep, narrow valley with steep sides.

raving, ravings
(adjective) If someone is raving, they are mad, e.g. *I think you're a raving lunatic.*

ravioli, (pronounced rav-ee-oh-lee)
(noun) small squares of pasta filled with meat and served with a sauce.

raw
1 (adjective) uncooked, e.g. *raw meat.*
2 in its natural state, e.g. *raw cotton.*
3 If part of your body is raw, the skin has come off or been rubbed away.
4 (phrase; informal) If you have had a **raw deal**, you have been treated unfairly.

raw material, materials
(noun) Raw materials are the natural substances used to make something.

ray, rays
1 (noun) a beam of light or radiation.
2 A ray of hope is a small amount that makes an unpleasant situation seem slightly better.

razor, razors
(noun) an object used for shaving.
razor blade (noun)

re-
(prefix) Re- is used to form nouns and verbs that refer to the repeating an action or process, e.g. to reread something means to read it again, and to remarry means to marry again.

reach, reaches, reaching, reached
1 (verb) e.g. *We reached Leeds at 2.30... I reached for the TV control box... She wore a skirt reaching to the ground... Unemployment has reached 3 million... We reached an agreement about pay.*
2 (phrase) If a place is **within reach**, you can go there.
3 If something is **out of reach**, you cannot get it by stretching out your arm.

react, reacts, reacting, reacted
1 (verb) When you react to something, you behave in a particular way because of it, e.g. *I wondered how he would react to this news.*
2 If one substance reacts with another, a chemical change takes place when they are put together.

reaction, reactions
1 (noun) Your reaction to something is what you feel, say or do because of it, e.g. *My immediate reaction was one of horror.*
2 the ability to move quickly in response to something that happens, e.g. *Alcohol slows your reactions down.*
3 If there is a reaction against something, it becomes unpopular, e.g. *There was a huge reaction against the poll tax in 1990.*
4 In a chemical reaction, a chemical change takes place when two substances are put together.

Similar words: (sense 1) response
(sense 3) backlash

reactor, reactors
(noun) a device used to obtain nuclear energy.

read, reads, reading, read
1 (verb) e.g. *to read a book... She can read my mind... He's come to read the gas meter.*
2 (phrase) To **read between the lines** means to understand a meaning that is not expressed directly, e.g. *Reading between the lines, it was easy to see she was unhappy.*
reader (noun)

readily
1 (adverb) willingly, e.g. *She readily accepted the invitation.*
2 easily done or quickly obtainable, e.g. *Food was readily available.*

ready
(adjective) e.g. *The crop was ready for harvesting... We were ready to leave... He was ready to go anywhere to get a job.*
readiness (noun)

ready-made
(adjective) already made and therefore able to be used immediately.

Find out the Christian names of these authors: Austen Dahl Carroll Stevenson Grahame.

real
(adjective) e.g. *It was made of real gold... the real reason for his visit was to ask for help.*
reality (noun)

Similar words: actual, authentic, original

realistic
1 (adjective) accepting the true nature of a situation, e.g. *Look, Joan, let's be realistic — you're too old to try to look 16 when you're pushing 60.*
2 true to life, e.g. *The Jorvik museum gives a realistic impression of Viking life.*
realistically (adverb)

realize, realizes, realizing, realized; also spelled realise
1 (verb) to become aware of something, e.g. *He realized his hair had gone green overnight.*
2 (formal) If your hopes or fears are realized, what you hoped for or feared actually happens, e.g. *My worst fears were realized when Marv Hammerman came round the corner.*
realization (noun)

really
(adverb) e.g. *It was really good... I want to know what really happened.*

reap, reaps, reaping, reaped
1 (verb) To reap a crop such as corn means to cut and gather it.
2 When people reap rewards, they get them as a result of hard work or careful planning.

reappear, reappears, reappearing, reappeared
(verb) to come back into sight, e.g. *The waiter reappeared... The mini-skirt reappeared for a year or two.*
reappearance (noun)

rear, rears, rearing, reared
1 (noun) the back part, e.g. *the rear of the horse.*
2 (verb) To rear children or young animals means to bring them up until they are able to look after themselves.
3 When a horse rears, it raises the front part of its body, so that its front legs are in the air.

rearrange, rearranges, rearranging, rearranged
(verb) to organize something in a different way.
rearrangement (noun)

reason, reasons, reasoning, reasoned
1 (noun) the explanation for something, e.g. *The reason for her absence was that she had flu.*
2 good sense and logic.
3 (verb) If you reason that something is true, you decide it is true after considering all the facts.
4 If you reason with someone, you persuade them by using sensible arguments.
5 (phrase) If something **stands to reason**, it is sensible and logical.

Similar words: (noun: sense 1) cause, motive

reasonable
1 (adjective) fair and sensible, e.g. *That seems reasonable to me... We agreed on a reasonable price.*
2 A reasonable amount is a fairly large amount, e.g. *We had a reasonable amount of work to do.*
reasonably (adverb)

reassemble, reassembles, reassembling, reassembled
(verb) to put something back together after it has been taken apart.

reassure, reassures, reassuring, reassured
(verb) If you reassure someone, you say or do things that make them less worried.
reassuring (adjective) **reassuringly** (adverb) **reassurance** (noun)

rebel, rebels, rebelling, rebelled
1 (verb) to fight against authority and reject accepted values.
2 (noun) someone who fights against authority
[Latin *rebellis* = insurgent]

rebellion, rebellions
(noun) organized and often violent opposition to authority.

Similar words: uprising, mutiny, revolt, revolution

rebellious
(adjective) unwilling to obey and likely to rebel against authority.
rebelliously (adverb)

rebound, rebounds, rebounding, rebounded
(verb) to bounce or spring back after hitting a solid surface.

rebuild, rebuilds, rebuilding, rebuilt
(verb) When a town or building is rebuilt, it is built again after being damaged or destroyed.

recall, recalls, recalling, recalled
(verb) to remember something.

recap, recaps, recapping, recapped
(verb) to repeat and summarize the main points of an explanation or discussion.

recapture, recaptures, recapturing, recaptured
(verb) When animals or prisoners are recaptured, they are caught after they have escaped.

recede, recedes, receding, receded
1 (verb) to move away into the distance.
2 If a man's hair is receding, he is starting to go bald at the front.
[Latin *recedere* = to go back]

receipt, receipts (pronounced ris-*seet*)
1 (noun) a piece of paper to say that money or goods have been received.
2 In a shop, theatre box office, etc., the money received is often called the receipts, e.g. *Receipts are down this month.*
3 (formal) The receipt of something is the receiving of it, e.g. *We await the receipt of further information from you.*
[Latin *recipere* = to receive]

receive, receives, receiving, received
(verb) e.g. *She received a present from Aunt Jane... He received a kick on the shin... Her latest novel has been very well received.*
[Latin *recipere* = to take back]

How did Vikings send messages to each other? .... Norse Code!

receiver, receivers
1 (noun) the part of a telephone you hold near to your ear and mouth.
2 a TV or radio set.

recent
(adjective) If something is recent, it happened a short time ago.
recently (adverb)
[Latin *recens* = fresh]

reception, receptions,
1 (noun) In a hotel, office or hospital, the reception is the place near the entrance where appointments and enquiries are dealt with.
2 a formal party, e.g. *a wedding reception*.
3 The reception someone or something gets is the way people react to them, e.g. *Q.P.R. received a sporting reception from the Arsenal crowd*.
4 If your radio or TV gets good reception, the sound or picture is clear.

receptionist, receptionists
(noun) The receptionist in a hotel, office or surgery deals with people when they arrive, answers the telephone and arranges reservations or appointments.

recess, recesses
(noun) a period when no work is done by a committee or parliament, e.g. *the summer recess*.
[Latin *recessus* = retreat]

recession, recessions
(noun) a period when a country's industrial production goes down and more people become unemployed.

Similar words: downturn, slump, decline

recharge, recharges, recharging, recharged
(verb) To recharge a battery means to charge it with electricity again after it has been used.

recipe, recipes (pronounced **res**-sip-ee)
(noun) a list of ingredients and instructions for cooking something.

recipient, recipients
(noun) a person who receives something.

recite, recites, reciting, recited
(verb) If you recite a poem or something you have learned, you say it aloud.
recitation (noun)

reckless
(adjective) totally careless about danger or damage, e.g. *a reckless driver*.
recklessly (adverb) **recklessness** (noun)

reckon, reckons, reckoning, reckoned
1 (verb; informal) to think something is true, e.g. *I reckon he's lost*.
2 (informal) to claim, e.g. *They reckon to double their output each year*.
3 to calculate, e.g. *Reckon up that total, Jim*.
4 to rely on something, e.g. *He reckoned on getting a large reward for finding the wallet*.
5 If you had not reckoned with something, you had not expected it, e.g. *She had not reckoned with her father's disapproval*.
6 (phrase) If something is **to be reckoned with**, it has to be dealt with and will be difficult.

reclaim, reclaims, reclaiming, reclaimed
1 (verb) When you reclaim something, you collect it after leaving it somewhere or losing it.
2 to make land suitable for use, for example by draining or clearing it.
reclamation (noun)

recline, reclines, reclining, reclined
(verb) to lie or lean back at an angle, e.g. *a reclining chair*.

recognize, recognizes, recognizing, recognized; also spelled **recognise**
1 (verb) to realize that you know someone or something, e.g. *I thought I recognized that perfume – it's 'Midnight in Walsall' isn't it?*
2 to accept and acknowledge, e.g. *We recognize the need for more money in the Health Service*.
recognition (noun) **recognizable** (adjective)
recognizably (adverb)
[Latin *recognoscere* = to know again]

Similar words: (sense 1) know, identify, place

recollect, recollects, recollecting, recollected
(verb) to remember something.
recollection (noun)

recommend, recommends, recommending, recommended
(verb) If you recommend something to someone, you praise it and suggest they try it.
recommendation (noun)

reconditioned
(adjective) A reconditioned machine etc. has been repaired, its worn parts replaced and it is nearly as good as new.

reconnaissance (pronounced rik-**kon**-iss-sanss)
(noun) the gathering of military information by sending out soldiers, planes or satellites.

reconsider, reconsiders, reconsidering, reconsidered
(verb) to think about something again after you have made a decision.
reconsideration (noun)

reconstruct, reconstructs, reconstructing, reconstructed
1 (verb) to rebuild something that has been damaged.
2 To reconstruct a past event means to obtain a complete description of it from small pieces of information.
reconstruction (noun)

Similar words: rebuild, reform, re-create

record, records, recording, recorded
1 (noun) If you keep a record of something, you keep a written account or store information in a computer, e.g. *medical records*.
2 (verb) To record sound means to put it on tape.
3 (noun) a round, flat piece of black plastic on which music has been recorded.
4 an achievement which is the best of its type, e.g. *a world record*.
5 (adjective) higher, lower, better or worse than ever before, e.g. *Inflation was at a record low*.
6 (noun) Your record is what is known about

A rock musician needs these words: guitar amplifier keyboards bass vocals rhythm gig audience

your achievements or past activities, e.g. *He has a distinguished record... a police record.*
[Latin *recordari* = to remember]

recorder, recorders
(noun) a woodwind instrument.

record player, players
(noun) a machine for playing records.

recover, recovers, recovering, recovered
1 (verb) To recover from an illness or unhappy experience means to get well again or get over it.
2 If you recover a lost object, you get it back.
recovery (noun)

Similar words: (sense 1) convalesce, recuperate
(sense 2) regain, retrieve, reclaim

recreation, recreations
(noun) all the things that you do for enjoyment in your spare time.
recreational (adjective)

recreation ground, grounds
(noun) a piece of public land where people can play sports and games.

recruit, recruits, recruiting, recruited
1 (verb) To recruit people means to get them to join a group or help with something.
2 (noun) someone who has just joined an organization, for example the army.
recruitment (noun)
[French *recrute* = new growth]

rectangle, rectangles
(noun) a 4-sided shape with 4 right angles.
rectangular (adjective)
[Latin *rectus* = straight + *angulus* = angle]

rectify, rectifies, rectifying, rectified
(verb; formal) If you rectify something that is wrong, you put it right.
[Latin *rectus* + *facere* = to make straight]

rector, rectors
(noun) a Church of England priest in charge of a parish.
[Latin *rector* = ruler or guide]

rectory, rectories
(noun) a house where a rector lives.

recuperate, recuperates, recuperating, recuperated
(verb) to recover gradually after being ill or injured.
recuperation (noun)
[*re-* + Latin *capere* = to take]

recur, recurs, recurring, recurred
(verb) If something recurs, it happens again, e.g. *The symptoms might recur.*
recurrence (noun) **recurrent** (adjective)

recurring
(adjective) occurring many times, e.g. *a recurring problem... 10 ÷ 3 = 3.3333333333 3333333333333333333...... = 3.3 recurring.*

recycle, recycles, recycling, recycled
(verb) to process products so that they can be used again, e.g. *recycled paper.*

red, redder, reddest; reds
1 (adjective, noun) a colour.

2 (phrase; informal) If you **see red**, you get very angry.
3 If your bank account is **in the red**, you have spent more than you had in the account.
4 (noun) People with strong left wing views are sometimes called Reds.
redden (verb)

red blood cell, cells
(noun) The red cells in your blood carry oxygen, carbon dioxide and haemoglobin all over your body.

redeploy, redeploys, redeploying, redeployed
(verb) To redeploy forces or workers means to give them new positions or tasks.
redeployment (noun)

redevelop, redevelops, redeveloping, redeveloped
(verb) When part of a town is redeveloped, buildings are demolished and new ones are built.
redevelopment (noun)

red-handed
(phrase) To catch someone red-handed means to catch them in the act of doing something wrong.

red herring, herrings
(noun) Something that is a red herring is irrelevant and distracts people's attention from what is important. [A red herring was formerly used to provide a scent for exercising hunting hounds]

red tape
(noun) official rules and procedures that seem unnecessary and cause delay. [In the 18th century, red tape was used to bind official government documents.]

reduce, reduces, reducing, reduced
(verb) to make something smaller.

Similar words: compress, condense, cut, trim

reduction, reductions
(noun) When there is a reduction in something, it is made smaller, e.g. *a price reduction.*

redundant
(adjective) When people are made redundant, they lose their jobs because there is no more work for them or no money to pay them.
redundancy (noun)
[Latin *redundans* = overflowing]

reed, reeds
1 (noun) Reeds are hollow stemmed plants that grow in shallow water or marshy ground.
2 a thin piece of cane or metal in some wind instruments, which vibrates when air is blown over it.

reef, reefs
(noun) a long line of rocks or coral close to the surface of the sea, e.g. *The Great Barrier Reef.*

reef knot, knots
(noun) a type of double knot that does not slip.

reek, reeks, reeking, reeked
(verb) to smell strongly and unpleasantly.

reel, reels, reeling, reeled
1 (noun) a cylindrical object around which you wrap something, e.g. *a hose reel... a reel of film.*

We take these words from the North American Indians: moccasin tomahawk wigwam papoose tepee.

2 (verb) When someone reels, they move unsteadily as if they are going to fall.
3 If your mind is reeling, you are confused because you have too much to think about.
4 (noun) a fast Scottish dance.

reel off
(phrasal verb) If you reel off information, you repeat it from memory quickly and easily.

refer, refers, referring, referred
1 (verb) If you refer to something, you mention it, e.g. *You must be referring to my brother, Dave.*
2 If you refer to a book, document or record, you look at it to find something out.
3 When a problem or issue is referred to someone, they are formally asked to deal with it, e.g. *Her case was referred a higher court.*
[Latin *referre* = to carry back]

referee, referees
1 (noun) the official who controls a football game or a boxing or wrestling match.
2 someone who gives a reference to a person who is applying for a job etc.

reference, references
1 (noun) A reference to something or someone is a mention of them, e.g. *When Scrooge talked about very adequate heat and light it was a reference to the candle on Cratchit's desk.*
2 the act of referring to something or someone for information or advice, e.g. *a reference book.*
3 a number or name that tells you where to obtain information or identifies a document.
4 If someone gives you a reference when you apply for a job, they write a letter about your character and abilities.

refine, refines, refining, refined
(verb) To refine a raw material, e.g. oil or sugar, means to process it to remove impurities.

refinery, refineries
(noun) a factory where, for example, oil or sugar are refined.

reflect, reflects, reflecting, reflected
1 (verb) If something reflects an attitude or situation, it shows what it is like, e.g. *The choice of school reflected Dad's hopes for us.*
2 If something reflects light or heat, the light or heat bounces off it.
3 When something is reflected in a mirror or water, you can see its image in it.
4 to think about something.
reflection (noun) **reflective** (adjective)
[Latin *reflectere* = to bend back]

reflector, reflectors
(noun) a piece of glass or plastic which glows when light shines on it.

reflex, reflexes
1 (noun) If you have good reflexes, you respond quickly when something unexpected happens.
2 (adjective) A reflex angle is between 180° and 360°.

reflexive, reflexives
(adjective, noun) In grammar, a reflexive verb or pronoun is one that refers back to the subject of the sentence, e.g. In the sentence *I banged myself*, the word 'myself' is a reflexive.

reform, reforms, reforming, reformed
1 (noun) a major change to laws, systems, or institutions, e.g. *the reform of the divorce laws.*
2 (verb) When laws, systems, or institutions are reformed, major changes are made to them.
3 When people reform, they stop committing crimes or doing other unacceptable things, e.g. *'Scarface' Malone is a reformed character now. He just loves doing embroidery.*

Similar words: (verb: sense 3) go straight, turn over a new leaf, mend your ways

refrain, refrains, refraining, refrained
(verb; formal) If you refrain from doing something, you do not do it, e.g. *Kindly refrain from smoking.*
[Latin *refrenare* = to restrain (a horse) with a bridle]

refresh, refreshes, refreshing, refreshed
1 (verb) If something refreshes you when you are hot or tired, it makes you feel cooler or more energetic, e.g. *a refreshing swim.*
2 (phrase) To **refresh someone's memory** means to remind them of something they had forgotten.

refreshments
(plural noun) drinks and small amounts of food.

refrigerator, refrigerators
(noun) an electrically or gas-cooled container in which you store food to keep it fresh.
refrigeration (noun) **refrigerated** (adjective)
refrigerate (verb)
[Latin *frigerare* = to make cool]

refuel, refuels, refuelling, refuelled
(verb) When an aircraft or vehicle is refuelled, it is filled with more fuel.

refuge, refuges
1 (noun) a place where you go for safety.
2 If you take refuge, you go somewhere for safety or behave in a way that will protect you, e.g. *Fred Flintstone took refuge in a cave.*
[Latin *refugere* = to flee]

refugee, refugees
(noun) Refugees are people who have been forced to leave their country and live elsewhere.

refund, refunds, refunding, refunded
1 (noun) money returned to you because you have paid too much for something, or because you have returned goods.
2 (verb) To refund someone's money means to return it to them after they have paid for something with it.

Similar words: (verb) reimburse, repay, pay back

refurbish, refurbishes, refurbishing, refurbished
(verb; formal) to decorate a building and repair damage.
refurbishment (noun)

refuse, refuses, refusing, refused
(pronounced rif-**yooz**)
1 (verb) If you refuse to do something, you say or decide firmly that you will not do it.

George Bernard Shaw believed that the apostrophe was unnecessary and he refused to use it.

2 If someone refuses something, they do not allow it or do not accept it, e.g. *The council refused him a loan... I offered him wine but he refused it.*
refusal (noun)

refuse (pronounced **ref**-yoose)
(noun) rubbish or waste.

regain, regains, regaining, regained
(verb) To regain something means to get it back.

regal
(adjective) very grand and suitable for a king or queen, e.g. *a regal staircase.*
regally (adverb)
[Latin *regalis*, from *rex* = king]

regard, regards, regarding, regarded
1 (verb) To regard someone or something in a particular way means to think of them in that way, e.g. *I regard it as one of my masterpieces... His friends regarded him with envy.*
2 (noun) If you have a high regard for someone, you respect and admire them.
3 (phrases) **Regarding, as regards, with regard to**, and **in regard to** are all used to indicate what you are talking or writing about, e.g. *There was always some question regarding education... As regards the car, we have decided not to sell it.* [These can often be better expressed by a simple preposition, e.g. about, in, of.]
4 Regards is used in various expressions to express friendly feelings, e.g. *Give my regards to Mo... With best regards, Jim.*
[French *regarder* = to look]

regatta, regattas
(noun) a race meeting for sailing boats.

reggae
(noun) a type of music, originally from the West Indies, with a strong and distinctive rhythm.

regiment, regiments
(noun) a large group of soldiers commanded by a colonel.
regimental (adjective)
[Latin *regimentum* = government]

region, regions
1 (noun) a large area of land.
2 You can refer to any area or part as a region, e.g. *He has pains in the shoulder region.*
3 (phrase) **In the region of** means approximately, e.g. *temperatures in the region of 500°C.*
regional (adjective) **regionally** (adverb)

Similar words: (sense 1) district, province, territory

register, registers, registering, registered
1 (noun) an official list or record of things, e.g. *the class register.*
2 (verb) When something is registered, it is recorded on an official list, e.g. *The car was registered in my name.*
3 If your face registers a feeling, it shows it.
registration (noun)

registered
(adjective) If you send a registered letter, you pay extra to insure it in case it is not delivered.

registration number, numbers
(noun) the number on a vehicle's number plate.

registry office, offices
(noun) a place where births, marriages and deaths are recorded, and where people can marry without a religious ceremony.

regret, regrets, regretting, regretted
1 (verb) If you regret something, you are sorry that it happened.
2 You can say that you regret something as a way of apologizing, e.g. *We regret any inconvenience to passengers.*
3 (noun) a feeling of sorrow that something has happened.
regretful (adjective) **regretfully** (adverb)

regrettable
(adjective) unfortunate and undesirable, e.g. *It was a regrettable error on our part.*
regrettably (adverb)

regular, regulars
1 (adjective) even and equally spaced, e.g. *deep, regular breathing.*
2 happening often and according to a pattern, for example each day or each week, e.g. *regular Sunday concerts.*
3 (noun) People who go to a place often are known as its regulars.
4 (adjective) usual or normal, e.g. *It's way past his regular bedtime... Who's your regular doctor?*
regularly (adverb) **regularity** (noun)

Similar words: (adjective: sense 1) even, steady

regulate, regulates, regulating, regulated
(verb) to control, e.g. *How do you regulate this boiler? It's glowing red-hot!*
regulator (noun)
[Latin *regulare* = to control]

regulation, regulations
(noun) Regulations are official rules.

rehearse, rehearses, rehearsing, rehearsed
(verb) To rehearse a performance means to practise it in preparation for the actual event.
rehearsal (noun)

reign, reigns, reigning, reigned (pronounced **rain**)
1 (verb) When a king or queen reigns, they rule a country.
2 (noun) The reign of a king or queen is the period during which they reign.
3 (verb) You can say that something reigns when it is a noticeable feature of a situation, e.g. *Peace reigned in Europe.*
[Latin *regnum* = kingdom]

reimburse, reimburses, reimbursing, reimbursed
(verb) to pay someone back money they have spent out on your behalf.
reimbursement (noun)

rein, reins
(noun) the thin leather straps which you hold when you are riding a horse.

reincarnation
(verb) People who believe in reincarnation

Motorists travelling abroad put their country's International Vehicle Registration sticker on their car....

believe that when you die, you are born again as another person or as a creature.
reincarnated (adjective)

reindeer
(noun) a deer with large antlers, that lives in northern areas of Europe, Asia and America.

reinforce, reinforces, reinforcing, reinforced
(verb) to strengthen.
reinforcement (noun)

reinforced concrete
(noun) Reinforced concrete has rods of metal inside to make it stronger.

reiterate, reiterates, reiterating, reiterated
(pronounced ree-**it**-er-ate)
(verb; formal) to say something again.
reiteration (noun)
[*re-* + Latin *iterare* = to do again]

reject, rejects, rejecting, rejected
1 (verb; pronounced re-**ject**) If you reject a proposal or request, you do not accept it or agree to it.
2 (noun; pronounced **ree**-ject) a product that cannot be used, because there is something wrong with it.
rejection (noun)
[Latin *reicere* = to throw back]

rejoice, rejoices, rejoicing, rejoiced
(verb; literary) to be very pleased about something, e.g. *We rejoiced in his success.*
rejoicing (noun)

relapse, relapses
(noun) If a sick person has a relapse, their health suddenly gets worse after improving.
[Latin *relabi* = to slip back]

relate, relates, relating, related
1 (verb) If something relates to something else, it is connected with it, e.g. *In a sentence, the words all relate to each other.*
2 If you are related to someone, they are a relation of yours.
3 If you can relate to someone, you can understand their thoughts and feelings.
4 To relate a story means to tell it.

relation, relations
1 (noun) a connection or similarity, e.g. *The boy's story bears no relation to what happened.*
2 Your relations are the members of your family.
3 Relations between people are their feelings and behaviour towards each other, e.g. *an improvement in East-West relations.*

Similar words: (sense 1) correspondence, relationship

relationship, relationships
1 (noun) The relationship between two people or groups is the way they feel and behave towards each other.
2 a close friendship.
3 the way in which things are connected, e.g. *The relationship between 25 and 100 is that 100 is four times bigger.*

relative, relatives
1 (adjective) compared to other things or people

of the same kind, e.g. *I prefer the relative peace of my home village... He is a relative newcomer.*
2 You use relative when comparing the size or quality of two things, e.g. *the relative naval strengths of Britain and Japan.*
3 (noun) a member of your family.

relatively
(adverb) fairly or quite, e.g. *relatively easy.*

relax, relaxes, relaxing, relaxed
1 (verb) If you relax, you become calm and your muscles lose their tenseness.
2 to make something less strict or controlled, e.g. *The rules on school dress were relaxed.*
relaxation (noun) **relaxed** (adjective)
relaxing (adjective)
[*re-* + Latin *laxare* = to loosen]

Similar words: (sense 1) unwind, rest, loosen up (sense 2) slacken, loose, ease

relay, relays, relaying, relayed
1 (noun) A relay race or relay is a race between teams, with each team member running one part.
2 (verb) To relay a message means to pass it on.

release, releases, releasing, released
1 (verb) to let go or set free.
2 (noun) A new release is a new record or video that has just become available.

relegate, relegates, relegating, relegated
(verb) To relegate something or someone means to give them a less important position or status, e.g. *Wimbledon were relegated to Division 3.*
relegation (noun)

relent, relents, relenting relented
(verb) If someone relents, they agree to something they had previously not allowed, e.g. *Sally was told not to go to the party, but her mum relented at the last minute.*

relentless
(adjective) never stopping and never reducing in severity, e.g. *the relentless beating of the sun.*
relentlessly (adverb) **relentlessness** (noun)

Similar words: unrelenting, unyielding, uncompromising

relevant
(adjective) If something is relevant, it is connected with and suitable for what is being discussed, e.g. *Please bring all relevant documents for a meeting about maths.*
relevance (noun)

reliable
1 (adjective) Reliable people and things can be trusted to do what you want.
2 If information is reliable, you can assume that it is correct.
reliably (adverb) **reliability** (noun)

relic, relics
(noun) Relics are objects or customs that have survived from an earlier time.
[Latin *reliquiae* = remains]

relief
1 (noun) If you feel relief, you are glad and

thankful because a bad situation is over or has been avoided.
2 money, food or clothing provided for poor or hungry people.

relief map, maps
(noun) A relief map shows, by shading, the shape of mountains and hills.

relieve, relieves, relieving, relieved
1 (verb) If something relieves an unpleasant feeling, it makes it less unpleasant, e.g. *They gave me an injection to relieve the pain.*
2 (formal) If you relieve someone, you do their job or duty for a period.

religion, religions
1 (noun) the belief in a god or gods and all the activities connected with this belief.
2 a system of religious belief.

religious
1 (adjective) connected with religion, e.g. *Religious services are held every day here.*
2 Someone who is religious has a strong belief in a god or gods.

relish, relishes, relishing, relished
(verb) If you relish something, you enjoy it, e.g. *The aggressive lady relished arguments.*
2 (noun) a savoury sauce or pickle.

reluctant
(adjective) If you are reluctant to do something, you don't want to do it.
reluctance (noun) **reluctantly** (adverb)
[Latin *reluctari* = to resist]

rely, relies, relying, relied
1 (verb) If you rely on someone or something, you need them and depend on them, e.g. *She is forced to rely on social security money.*
2 If you can rely on someone to do something, you can trust them to do it.
[Old French *relier* = to fasten together]

remain, remains, remaining, remained
1 (verb) to stay as you are, e.g. *Suzie remained sure she was right... He remained at home.*
2 (plural noun) The remains of something are the parts that are left after most of it has been destroyed, e.g. *the remains of the castle.*
3 You can refer to a dead body as remains, e.g. *Human remains were found in a shallow grave.*
remaining (adjective)
[Latin *remanere* = to stay behind]

Similar words: (sense 2) debris, remnants, traces

remainder
(noun) The remainder of something is the part that is left, e.g. *Pay the remainder next month.*

remand
(phrase) If someone is **on remand**, they are usually in prison waiting for their trial to begin.

remark, remarks, remarking, remarked
(verb) to mention or comment on something, e.g. *He remarked on the weather.*

Similar words: comment, talk about

remarkable
(adjective) impressive and unexpected, e.g. *You've made remarkable progress.*
remarkably (adverb)

Similar words: notable, significant, outstanding

remarry, remarries, remarrying, remarried
(verb) to get married again.

remedial
(adjective) Remedial exercises are designed to improve someone's ability in something, e.g. *I've put her in the remedial reading group.*

remedy, remedies
(noun) a way of dealing with a problem, e.g. *a good remedy for a sore throat.*

remember, remembers, remembering, remembered
1 (verb) e.g. *I remember our first car... Remember to send off the application forms.*
2 If you ask someone to remember you to a person, you are asking them to send your greetings to that person, e.g. *Remember me to your parents.*
[Latin *rememorari* = to remember]

Similar words: recollect, recall, commemorate

remembrance
(noun) If you do something in remembrance of a dead person, you are showing that they are remembered with respect and affection.

remind, reminds, reminding, reminded
1 (verb) If someone reminds you of something, they jog your memory e.g. *Remind me to phone Pete later, will you?*
2 If someone reminds you of another person, you notice that they are similar.
reminder (noun)

remittance, remittances
(noun; formal) a payment sent by post etc.

remnant, remnants
(noun) a small part of something left after the rest has been used or destroyed.
[Old French *remenant* = remaining]

remorse
(noun; formal) a strong feeling of guilt.
remorseful (adjective) **remorsefully** (adverb)
[Latin *remorsus* = a gnawing]

Similar words: repentance, regret

remorseless
(adjective) determined; with no feeling of guilt, e.g. *The sheriff's remorseless pursuit of the bandits.*

remote, remoter, remotest
1 (adjective) far away, e.g. *a remote island.*
2 If there is only a remote possibility of something happening, it is unlikely to happen.
remoteness (noun)
[Latin *remotus* = distant]

remote control
(noun) a system of controlling a machine, model, etc. from a distance, using radio or electronic signals.

Few words are best. (16th-century proverb)

remove, removes, removing, removed
1 (verb) to take something away.
2 to move from living in one home to living in another.
removal (noun) **removable** (adjective)

rename, renames, renaming, renamed
(verb) to give something a new name.

rendezvous (pronounced ron-day-voo)
1 (noun) a meeting or a place for a meeting e.g. *They met at a secret rendezvous near the river.*
2 (verb; informal) to meet up, e.g. *Right, men! We will rendezvous at the crossroads at 06.30 hours.*
[a French word, meaning 'present yourselves!']

renew, renews, renewing, renewed
1 (verb) To renew an activity or relationship means to begin it again.
2 To renew a licence, library book, etc. means to extend the period of time for which it is valid.
renewable (adjective) **renewal** (noun)

renovate, renovates, renovating, renovated
(verb) to repair and restore something old.
renovation (noun)
[Latin *renovare* = to renew]

renowned
(adjective) well known for something good, e.g. *The cafe is renowned for its excellent food.*
renown (noun)

rent, rents, renting, rented
1 (verb) If you rent something, you pay the owner a regular sum of money in return for being able to use it.
2 (noun) the amount of money you pay regularly to rent a house, flat, etc.
rented (adjective) **rental** (noun and adjective)

reorganize, reorganizes, reorganizing, reorganized; also spelled **reorganise**
(verb) to organize something in a new way.

repair, repairs, repairing, repaired
(verb) If you repair something, you mend it.
[Latin *reparare* = to restore]

repay, repays, repaying, repaid
(verb) to give money back to the person who lent it to you.
repayment (noun)

repeat, repeats, repeating, repeated
1 (verb) to do or say something again.
2 If you repeat what someone has said, you tell someone else about it, e.g. *Please don't repeat what I've just told you.*
3 (noun) a TV programme that has been shown before.
repeated (adjective) **repeatedly** (adverb)

repellent, repellents
(noun) chemical used to keep insects etc. away.

repent, repents, repenting, repented
(verb; formal) If you repent, you are sorry for something bad you have done.
repentance (noun) **repentant** (adjective)

repetition, repetitions
(noun) If there is a repetition of something, it happens again, e.g. *I don't want a repetition of yesterday's terrible work.*
repetitive (adjective) **repetitively** (adverb)

replace, replaces, replacing, replaced
(verb) e.g *She replaced her as captain... I must replace that broken mug... Sam Spade replaced the phone on the hook.*
replacement (noun)

replay, replays
1 (noun) a second match, played after the first match has ended in a draw.
2 a rerun of a sound or video tape, to hear or see something again.

replica, replicas
(noun) an accurate copy of something.
[an Italian word meaning 'a reply']

reply, replies, replying, replied
(verb) to answer.

report, reports, reporting, reported
1 (verb) If you report that something has happened, you tell someone about it or give an official account of it, e.g. *He rushed back to report the news.*
2 (noun) A report is an account of an event, a situation or a person's progress.
3 (verb) To report someone to an authority means to make an official complaint about them.
4 If you report to a person or place, you go there and say you have arrived.
[Old French *reporter* = to carry back]

Similar words: (noun: sense 2) statement, write-up

reporter, reporters
(noun) someone who writes news articles or broadcasts news reports.

repossess, repossesses, repossessing, repossessed
(verb) If a shop or company repossesses goods that have not been paid for, they take them back

represent, represents, representing, represented
1 (verb) to do things on someone else's behalf, e.g. *lawyers representing the victims of the disaster.*
2 If a sign or symbol represents something, it stands for it.
representation (noun)

representative, representatives
(noun) a person chosen to do things on behalf of another person or a group.

reprieve, reprieves, reprieving, reprieved
(pronounced rip-**preev**)
(verb) If someone who has been sentenced to death is reprieved, their sentence is changed and they are not killed.

reprimand, reprimands, reprimanding, reprimanded
1 (verb) to tell someone off officially.
2 (noun) an official telling-off for something you have done wrong.

reprint, reprints, reprinting, reprinted
(verb) If a book is reprinted, further copies are printed because the others have been sold.

reprisal, reprisals
(noun) violent actions taken by one group of people in revenge against another group that has harmed them.

Nothing is said that has not been said before. (Terence, 185-159 B.C.)

reproach, reproaches, reproaching, reproached
1 (verb; formal) If you reproach someone, you tell them, rather sadly, that they have done something wrong.
2 (noun) a quiet telling-off.
reproachful (adjective) **reproachfully** (adverb)

reproduce, reproduces, reproducing, reproduced
1 (verb) to make a copy of something.
2 When people, animals or plants reproduce, they produce more of their own kind, e.g. *Bacteria reproduce by splitting into two.*

reproduction, reproductions
1 (noun) a modern copy of a painting or piece of furniture.
2 The reproduction of sound, art or writing is the copying of it, e.g. *Compact discs give marvellous reproduction.*
3 the process by which a living thing produces more of its kind, e.g. *We're studying human reproduction in Biology.*
reproductive (adjective)

reptile, reptiles
(noun) a cold-blooded animal which has scaly skin and lays eggs, e.g. snake, lizard.
reptilian (adjective)
[Latin *reptilis* = creeping]

republic, republics
(noun) a country which has a president rather than a king or queen, e.g. *the Irish Republic.*
republican (noun and adjective)
[Latin *res publica* = literally public thing]

repulsive
(adjective) horrible and disgusting.
repulsively (noun) **repulsion** (noun)

reputable
(adjective) known to be good and reliable, e.g. *A reputable company should give a guarantee.*
reputably (adjective)

reputation, reputations
(noun) The reputation of something or someone is the opinion that people have of them, e.g. *She had built up a reputation as a creative designer.*

Similar words: good name, honour

request, requests, requesting, requested
1 (verb) to ask for something politely or formally.
2 (noun) e.g. *I made a request for 3 days' leave.*

require, requires, requiring, required
1 (verb) If you require something, you need it.
2 If you are required to do something, you have to do it because someone says you must, e.g. *Children are required to study R.E. at school.*

requirement, requirements
(noun) A requirement is something that you must have or must do, e.g. *GCSE maths is a requirement for this job.*

rescue, rescues, rescuing, rescued
1 (verb) to save someone from a dangerous or unpleasant situation.
2 (noun) e.g. *The lifeboat crew carried out a courageous rescue.*
rescuer (noun)

research, researches, researching, researched
1 (noun) work that involves studying something and trying to find out facts about it.
2 (verb) to find out about something by study and enquiry.

resemble, resembles, resembling, resembled
(verb) To resemble something means to be similar to it, e.g. *The dog resembled his master.*
resemblance (noun)
[Old French *resembler* = to be like]

resent, resent, resenting, resented
(verb) If you resent something, you feel bitter and angry about it, e.g. *She resented washing up when her son had sat around all day.*
resentment (noun) **resentful** (adjective)

reservation, reservations
1 (noun) If you have reservations about something, you are not sure that it is right.
2 If you make a reservation, you book a place in advance, e.g. *a flight reservation.*

reserve, reserves, reserving, reserved
1 (verb) If something is reserved for a particular person or purpose, it is kept specially for them.
2 (noun) a supply of something for future use.
3 In sport, a reserve is someone who is available to play in case one of the team is unable to play.
4 A nature reserve is an area of land where animals, birds or plants are officially protected.
[Latin *reservare* = to save up]

Similar words: (verb) save, preserve

reserved
(adjective) quiet and shy.

reservoir, reservoirs (pronounced **rez-ev-wahr**)
(noun) a lake used for storing water before it is supplied to people.
[French *réservoir*; from *réserver* = to keep]

reshuffle, reshuffles
(noun) a reorganization of people or things, e.g. *a Cabinet reshuffle.*

residence, residences
1 (noun; formal) a house.
2 (phrase) If you **take up residence** somewhere, you go and live there.
reside (verb)

resident, residents
1 (noun) A resident of a house or area is someone who lives there.
2 (adjective) living in a particular place, e.g. *He is a resident of Westminster.*

residential
1 (adjective) A residential area contains mainly houses rather than offices or factories.
2 providing accommodation, e.g. *a residential home for the elderly.*

resign, resigns, resigning, resigned
1 (verb) If you resign from a job, you formally announce that you are leaving it.
2 If you resign yourself to an unpleasant situation, or are resigned to it, you realize that you have to accept it, e.g. *He was resigned to spending two more months in West Bromwich.*

resignation, resignations
(noun) a formal statement of someone's intention to leave a job.

resist, resists, resisting, resisted
(verb) to fight back against someone or something, e.g. *He resisted all attempts to modernize the system.*
[Latin *resistere* = to remain standing]

Similar word: oppose

resistance, resistances
1 (noun) a refusal to accept something.
2 Resistance to an attack consists of fighting back, e.g. *The invaders met with little resistance.*
3 The power of a substance to resist the flow of an electrical current through it.

resistant
(adjective) If something is resistant to a particular thing, it is not harmed by it, e.g. *This anorak is water-resistant.*

resolution, resolutions
1 (noun) determination.
2 If you make a resolution, you promise yourself to do something, e.g. *Resolutions are like eels – easy to catch, but hard to hang on to.*
3 a formal decision taken at a meeting.

resolve, resolves, resolving, resolved
(verb) to decide firmly to do something.

resort, resorts, resorting, resorted
1 (verb) If you resort to doing something, you do it because you have no alternative.
2 (phrase) If you do something **as a last resort**, you do it because you can find no other way of solving a problem.
3 (noun) a place where people spend holidays.

resource, resources
(noun) Resources are materials, money or skills available for use.

respect, respects, respecting, respected
1 (verb) If you respect someone, you admire their character or ideas.
2 If you respect someone's rights or wishes, you do not do things that they would not like, or would consider wrong, e.g. *We respected the Muslim custom and took our shoes off to enter the mosque.*
3 (phrase) You can say **in this respect** to refer to something in particular, e.g. *Time for maths has been limited and we are behind in this respect.*
respectful (adjective)

respectable
1 (adjective) thought to be acceptable and morally correct, e.g. *respectable families.*
2 adequate or reasonable, e.g. *a respectable amount of work.*
respectability (noun) **respectably** (adverb)

respectively
(adverb) in the same order as the items just mentioned, e.g. *United and City are 4th and 5th respectively.*

resplendent
(adjective; formal) very impressive.

respond, responds, responding, responded
(verb) When you respond to something, you react to it by doing or saying something.
response (noun) **responsive** (adjective)
[Latin *respondere* = to return like for like]

responsibility, responsibilities
1 (noun) If you have responsibility for something, it is your duty to deal with it or look after it, e.g. *The garden is Paul's responsibility.*
2 If you accept responsibility for something that has happened, you agree that you caused it or were to blame, e.g. *The company will not accept responsibility for any loss or damage.*

Similar words: (sense 2) obligation, liability

responsible
1 (adjective) If you are responsible for something, it is your duty to deal with it and you are to blame if it goes wrong.
2 If you are responsible to someone, that person is your boss and tells you what you have to do.
3 A responsible person behaves properly and sensibly without needing to be supervised.
4 A responsible job involves making careful judgements about important matters.
responsibly (adverb)

rest, rests, resting, rested
(noun, verb) e.g. *Eat the rest of your meal... Rest after your meal.*
restful (adjective)

Similar words: (noun) breather, stop, break, time off

restaurant, restaurants
(noun) a place where you can buy and eat a meal
[a French word; from *restaurer* = to restore]

restless
(adjective) finding it difficult to remain still or relaxed as a result of boredom or impatience.
restlessness (noun) **restlessly** (adverb)

Similar words: jumpy, unsettled, fidgety

restore, restores, restoring, restored
(verb) To restore an old building or a work of art means to clean and repair it.
restoration (noun)

Similar words: refurbish, renovate, do up

restrain, restrains, restraining, restrained
(verb) to hold someone or something back or prevent them from doing what they want to.
restraint (noun)
[Latin *restringere* = to draw back tightly]

restrained
(adjective) behaving in a controlled way.

restrict, restricts, restricting, restricted
1 (verb) to prevent something becoming too large or varied, e.g. *Speed is restricted here.*
2 To restrict people or animals means to limit their movement or actions.
restrictive (adjective)

restriction, restrictions
(noun) a rule or situation that limits what you can do, e.g. *speed restrictions.*

Similar word: limitation

result, results, resulting, resulted
1 (verb) If something results in a particular
event, it causes that event to happen, e.g. *The
cutbacks resulted in long waiting lists.*
2 If something results from a particular event, it
is caused by that event.
3 (noun) the final situation, e.g. *I tripped and got
a cut head as a result... football results... What
do you make the result?*
resultant (adjective)
[Latin *resultare* = to rebound]

Similar words: (noun) consequence, outcome

resume, resumes, resuming, resumed
(pronounced riz-**yoom**)
(verb) If you resume an activity or position, you
return to it again after a break.
resumption (noun)
[Latin *resumere* = to take up again]

resurrection
(noun) In Christian belief, the Resurrection is the
coming back to life of Jesus Christ 3 days after
he had been killed.

**resuscitate, resuscitates, resuscitating,
resuscitated** (pronounced ris-**suss**-it-tate)
(verb) to make someone conscious again after
their breathing has stopped.
resuscitation (noun)
[Latin *resuscitare* = to revive]

retail, retails, retailing, retailed
1 (adjective) The retail price is the price at which
something is sold in the shops.
2 (verb) To retail goods means to sell them to the
public. (opposite: **wholesale**)
retailer (noun)

retain, retains, retaining, retained
(verb) to keep.
retention (noun)

retaliate, retaliates, retaliating, retaliated
(verb) to fight back in revenge.
retaliation (noun) **retaliatory** (adjective)

retarded
(adjective) If someone is retarded, their mental
development is much less advanced than average.

reticent
(adjective) shy and unwilling about things.
reticence (noun)
[*re-* + Latin *tacere* = to be silent]

retire, retires, retiring, retired
1 (verb) to give up work because of age or
sickness.
2 To drop out of a race, sports match, etc.,
usually because of injury.
retired (adjective) **retirement** (noun)

retiring
(adjective) a retiring person is shy and avoids
meeting other people.

retort, retorts, retorting, retorted
1 (verb) to reply angrily.
2 (noun) a glass container with a long neck and a
round bulb that is used in laboratories,
especially for distilling substances.

retrace, retraces, retracing, retraced
(verb) If you retrace your steps, you go back
along the same route to where you started.

retract, retracts, retracting, retracted
1 (verb) If you retract something you have said,
you say that you did not mean it.
2 When something is retracted, it moves inwards
or backwards, e.g. *The plane's undercarriage
retracted as the 747 soared skywards.*
retraction (noun) **retractable** (adjective)

Similar words: (sense 1) withdraw, take back

retreat, retreats, retreating, retreated
1 (verb) to move backwards away from
something or someone.
2 (noun) If an army moves away from the enemy,
this is referred to as a retreat.

retrieve, retrieves, retrieving, retrieved
(verb) to fetch something back, e.g. *The dog
retrieved the stick ... I retrieved the file from the
hard disk.*
retrieval (noun)
[*re-* + French *trouver* = to find]

retriever, retrievers
(noun) a large dog often used by hunters to bring
back birds etc. which have been shot.

retrospective
1 (adjective) looking back to the past, e.g. *a
retrospective view at the war years.*
2 taking effect from a date in the past.
retrospectively (adverb)

return, returns, returning, returned
1 (verb) to go back.
2 to give something back.
3 (noun) The return on an investment is the
profit or interest you make on it.
4 A return is a ticket for the journey to a place
and back again.
5 (phrase) If you do something **in return** for a
favour, you do it to repay the favour.
6 You say **many happy returns** to wish someone a
happy birthday.
7 To reply **by return** means to send a reply
immediately in the next post.

reunite, reunites, reuniting, reunited
(verb) If people are reunited, they meet again
after they have been separated for some time.

rev, revs, revving, revved
1 (verb; informal) When you rev a car engine,
you press the accelerator to increase the engine
speed when the car is out of gear.
2 (noun) The speed of an engine is measured in
revolutions per minute, often called revs.

reveal, reveals, revealing, revealed
1 (verb) To reveal something means to tell people
about it, e.g. *Police revealed the culprit's name.*
2 If you reveal something that has been hidden,
you uncover it.
[Latin *revelare* = to unveil]

A shopkeeper needs these words: wholesale turnover stock customer service courtesy
cash and carry.

revel, revels, revelling, revelled
(verb) If you revel in a situation, you enjoy it very much.

Similar words: relish, thrive on

revelation, revelations
1 (noun) a surprising or interesting fact made known to people.
2 If an experience is a revelation, it makes you realize or learn something.

revenge
(noun) Revenge involves hurting someone who has hurt you, e.g. *Revenge is always the delight of a mean spirit.*
revengeful (adjective)

Similar words: retaliation, vengeance

Reverend
(adjective) a title used before the name of a member of the clergy, e.g. *the Revd W. Alnut.*
[Latin *reverendus* = venerable]

reverent
(adjective) showing great respect.
reverently (adverb) **reverence** (noun)

reverse, reverses, reversing, reversed
1 (verb) If you reverse the order of things, you arrange them in the opposite order.
2 to drive a car backwards.
3 (noun) The reverse is the opposite of what has just been said or done.
reversal (noun)
[Latin *revertere* = to turn back]

reversible
(adjective) Reversible clothing can be worn with either side on the outside.

revert, reverts, reverting, reverted
(verb; formal) to go back to a former situation.
e.g. *Kevin reverted to his bad behaviour only a week after seeing the headteacher.*
reversion (noun)

review, reviews, reviewing, reviewed
1 (noun) an article or an item on TV or radio, giving an opinion of a new book or play.
2 (verb) To review a play or book means to write an account expressing an opinion of it.
3 To review something means to examine it to decide whether changes are needed.
reviewer (noun)

Similar words: (sense 3) criticize, evaluate

revise, revises, revising, revised
1 (verb) to change, improve or correct something, for example a decision or a piece of work.
2 When you revise for an examination, you go over your work to learn things thoroughly.
revision (noun)
[Latin *revisere* = to look back at]

revival
(noun) If something which is out of fashion has a revival, it becomes popular again.

revive, revives, reviving, revived
(verb) When you revive someone who has fainted, they become conscious again.
[Old French *revivre* = to live again]

revolt, revolts, revolting, revolted
(verb) When people revolt, they fight against the authority that governs them.

revolting
(adjective) horrible and disgusting, e.g. *a revolting smell of rotten vegetables.*

revolution, revolutions
1 (noun) a violent attempt by a large group of people to change the political system of their country, e.g. *the French Revolution.*
2 an important change in an area of human activity, e.g. *the Industrial Revolution... the computer revolution.*
3 one complete turn in a circle (360°).

revolutionary, revolutionaries
1 (adjective) involving great changes, e.g. *revolutionary changes in the design of cars.*
2 (noun) a person who takes part in a revolution.

revolutionize, revolutionizes, revolutionizing, revolutionized; also spelled **revolutionise**
(verb) To revolutionize an activity means to cause great changes in the way that it is done, e.g. *Electrical machines have revolutionized the modern home.*

revolve, revolves, revolving, revolved
1 (verb) If something revolves round something else, it centres on that as the most important thing, e.g. *Her life revolves around her family.*
2 to turn in a circle, e.g. *The earth revolves round the sun.*
[Latin *revolvere* = to roll back]

revolver, revolvers
(noun) a small hand gun.

reward, rewards
(noun) something you are given because you have done something good.

rewarding
(adjective) Something that is rewarding gives you a lot of satisfaction, e.g. *a rewarding job.*

rewind, rewinds, rewinding, rewound
(verb) If you rewind a tape on a tape recorder or video, you make the tape go backwards.

rewrite, rewrites, rewriting, rewrote
(verb) to write something again in a different way.

rhetorical
(adjective) A rhetorical question is one which is asked in order to make a statement rather than to get an answer, e.g. *Do you want to die of cold?*
rhetorically (adverb)

rheumatism (pronounced **room-at-izm**)
(noun) an illness that makes your joints and muscles stiff and painful.
rheumatic (adjective)
[Latin *rheumatismus* = catarrh]

Reverse spellings. These words make new words when read backwards:
lever knits evil time meet parts.

rhinoceros, rhinoceroses
(noun) a large African or Asian animal with one or two horns on its nose.
[Greek *rhin* = of the nose + *keras* = horn]

rhombus, rhombuses or rhombi
(noun) a shape with 4 equal sides and no right angles.

rhubarb
(noun) an edible plant with long, red stems.

rhyme, rhymes, rhyming, rhymed
1 (verb) If two words rhyme, they have a similar sound, e.g. *Sally* rhymes with *valley*.
2 (noun) a word that rhymes with another.
3 a short poem with rhyming lines.

rhythm, rhythms
1 (noun) a regular movement or beat.
2 a regular pattern of changes, e.g. *the rhythm of the seasons*.
rhythmic (adjective) **rhythmically** (adverb)

Similar words: (sense 1) tempo, pulse, time, beat

rib, ribs
(noun) Your ribs are the curved bones that go from your backbone to your chest.

ribbon, ribbons
1 (noun) a long, narrow piece of cloth used for decoration.
2 A printer ribbon is a long, narrow piece of cloth containing a special ink for printing letters.

rice
(noun) a tall grass that produces edible grains.

rich, richer, richest; riches
1 (adjective) wealthy, e.g. *a rich merchant*.
2 containing a lot of something, e.g. *The sea bed is rich in minerals*.
3 Rich food contains a lot of fat, oil or sugar.
4 Rich colours, smells, etc. are strong and pleasant.

richly
(adverb) If someone really deserves something, you can say it is richly deserved.

rickety
(adjective) likely to collapse, e.g. *a rickety bridge*.

riddance
(phrase; informal) If you say **good riddance** when someone leaves, you mean you are glad they have gone.

riddle, riddles
(noun) a puzzle which seems to be nonsense, but which has an entertaining solution.

Similar words: puzzle, poser

riddled
(adjective) full of something undesirable, e.g. *This sideboard's riddled with woodworm*.
[Old English *hriddel* = sieve]

ride, rides, riding, rode, ridden
1 (verb) e.g. *to ride a bike*.
2 (noun) e.g. *Have a ride on my camel!*

3 (phrase; informal) To **take someone for a ride** means to deceive them.
rider (noun)

ridge, ridges
1 (noun) a long, narrow piece of high land.
2 In meteorology, a ridge of high pressure is a line of high pressure from an anticyclone.

ridicule, ridicules, ridiculing, ridiculed
(verb) To ridicule someone means to make fun of them in an unkind way.

ridiculous
(adjective) very foolish.
ridiculously (adverb)
[Latin *ridere* = to laugh]

riff-raff
(noun) You can refer to worthless, badly-behaved people as riff-raff.

rifle, rifles
(noun) a gun with a long barrel.

rig, rigs, rigging, rigged
1 (verb) If someone rigs an election or contest, they dishonestly arrange for a particular person to win.
2 (noun) a large structure used for extracting oil or gas from the ground or sea bed.

rig up
(phrasal verb) If you rig up a device or structure, you make it quickly and fix it in place, e.g. *We rigged up a temporary mast*.

rigging
(noun) The rigging of a sailing ship is the ropes supporting its mast and sails.

right, rights, righting, righted
1 (adjective, adverb) e.g. *Is that clock right?... Did I pronounce that right?... It isn't right to steal*.
2 (noun) correct behaviour, e.g. *She knew the difference between right and wrong*.
3 If you have a right to something, you are entitled to it, e.g. *I have a right to see my lawyer*.
4 (adjective, adverb) e.g. *In the USA they drive on the right hand side*.
5 (adverb) e.g. *I'm staying right here... I'll be right back*.
rightly (adverb) **right-handed** (adjective, adverb)

right angle, angles
(noun) an angle of 90°.

right-handed
(adjective, adverb) Someone who is right-handed does things such as writing or painting with their right hand.

right-hand man
(noun) Someone's right-hand man is the person who helps them most in their work.

right of way, rights of way
1 (noun) When a vehicle has right of way, all other traffic must stop for it.
2 a public path across private land.

right-wing
(adjective) believing more strongly in capitalism or conservatism, than in socialism, e.g. *Norman holds very right-wing views*.

A poet needs these words: ballad epic lyric ode sonnet metre rhyme scansion stanza laureate.

rigid
1 (adjective) Rigid laws or systems cannot be changed and are strict.
2 A rigid object is stiff and does not bend easily.
rigidly (adverb) **rigidity** (noun)
[Latin *rigere* = to be stiff]

rigmarole, rigmaroles
(noun; informal) a way of doing something that seems too complicated.

rim, rims
(noun) the outside or top edge of, e.g. a cup.

rind, rinds
(noun) the outer skin of fruit, cheese or bacon.

ring, rings, ringing, rang, rung
1 (verb, noun) e.g. *Ring me later on... When the bell rings, answer the door... a wedding ring... a boxing ring.*
2 (phrase) If a statement **rings true**, it sounds likely to be true.
3 an organized group of criminals, e.g. *The police have uncovered a drugs ring.*
4 (verb) e.g. *The lake was ringed with trees.*

ringleader, ringleaders
(noun) the leader of a group of troublemakers or criminals.

ringlet, ringlets
(noun) Ringlets are long, hanging curls of hair.

ringworm
(noun) an infection of the skin that causes itching circular patches.

rink, rinks
(noun) a large indoor area for ice-skating or roller-skating.

rinse, rinses, rinsing, rinsed
(verb) to wash something in clean water.

riot, riots, rioting, rioted
1 (noun) When there is a riot, a crowd of people behave noisily and violently.
2 (verb) If a crowd riots, they are out of control in their behaviour.
3 (phrase) To **run riot** means to behave in a wild and uncontrolled way.
riotous (adjective)

rip, rips, ripping, ripped
(verb) e.g. *Don't rip your shirt.*

ripe, riper, ripest
(adjective) When fruit or grain is ripe, it is fully developed and ready to be eaten.
ripeness (noun) **ripen** (verb)

rip-off, rip-offs
(noun; informal) If you say that something you bought was a rip-off, you mean it was not worth what you paid.

ripple, ripples, rippling, rippled
(noun) Ripples are little waves on the surface of calm water.

rise, rises, rising, rose, risen
1 (verb) e.g. *The balloon rises... I rise at 7 in the morning... the sun rises at 6... The sound rose to a deafening level... Taxes rose to a new high.*
2 The place where a river rises is where it begins.
3 (noun) A rise is an increase.

4 Someone's rise is the way they grow more powerful or successful, e.g. *her rise to fame.*
5 (phrase) To **give rise to** something means to cause it to happen, e.g. *Cancer treatment can give rise to hair loss.*

risk, risks, risking, risked
1 (noun) a chance that something unpleasant or dangerous might happen.
2 (verb) If you risk something unpleasant, you d something knowing that the unpleasant thing might happen as a result, e.g. *If you don't go to training, you risk losing your place in the team.*
risky (adjective)
[Italian *rischiare* = to be in danger]

Similar words: (noun) chance, venture, gamble

ritual, rituals
(noun) a fixed series of actions which are part o a custom or tradition, e.g. *the rituals of greeting*

rival, rivals, rivalling, rivalled
1 (noun) the person you are competing with.
2 (verb) If something rivals something else, it is of the same high standard or quality, e.g. *Nothing can rival the first sight of Venice.*

Similar words: (noun) competitor, opponent, contender

rivalry, rivalries
(noun) competition between people.

river, rivers
(noun) e.g. *the River Amazon.*

road, roads
1 (noun) e.g. *Is this the road to London?*
2 (phrase) If someone is **on the road to** something they are likely to achieve it, e.g. *He's well on the road to success.*

roadworks
(noun) repairs being done on a road.

roadworthy
(adjective) A roadworthy car is in good conditio

roam, roams, roaming, roamed
(verb) to wander around.

roar, roars, roaring, roared
1 (verb) to make a very loud noise.
2 (noun) a very loud noise, e.g. *the roar of a lion... the roar of an aircraft.*

roaring
(phrase) When someone is doing a **roaring trade**, they are selling a lot of goods.

roast, roast, roasting, roasted
(verb, adjective) to cook in a very hot oven or over a fire, e.g. *to roast a pig... roast beef and Yorkshire pudding.*

robbery, robberies
(noun) the stealing of money or property using force or threats.
robber (noun)

robe, robes
(noun) a long, loose piece of clothing which covers the body, e.g. *priests in ceremonial robes*

robin, robins
(noun) a small bird with a red breast.

▶bot, robots
(noun) a machine programmed to move and perform tasks automatically.
[Czech *robota* = work]

▶bust
(adjective) very strong and healthy.
[Latin *robur* = oak or strength]

▶ck, rocks, rocking, rocked
1 (noun) the hard mineral substance that forms the surface of the earth.
rocky (adjective)
2 (verb) to move regularly backwards and forwards or side to side, e.g. *She gently rocked the cradle.*
3 (noun) 'heavy' music with simple tunes and a very strong beat, e.g. *a rock concert.*
4 a sweet shaped into long, hard sticks, sold in holiday resorts.

▶ck and roll or **rock 'n' roll**
(noun) music with a strong beat that became popular in the 1950s.

▶ck-bottom
(adjective) at the lowest price or level, e.g. *videos at rock-bottom prices.*

▶cker
(phrase; informal) If you say that someone is **off their rocker**, you mean they are mad.

▶ckery, rockeries
(noun) a raised area of garden, built of rocks and soil, where small plants are grown.

▶cket, rockets, rocketing, rocketed
1 (noun) a space vehicle, a missile or a type of firework.
2 (verb) If prices rocket, they go up very quickly.

▶d, rods
(noun) a long, thin pole or bar, e.g. *a fishing rod.*

▶dent, rodents
(noun) a small mammal with sharp front teeth used for gnawing, e.g. mice, rats, squirrels.
[Latin *rodere* = to gnaw]

▶deo, rodeos
(noun) a show in which cowboys try their skills, for example, lassoing, riding a bucking bronco.

▶e
(noun) the eggs of a fish.

▶gue, rogues
(noun) a friendly word for a man who behaves dishonestly.

▶le, roles
1 (noun) Someone's role is their position and function in a situation or society.
2 An actor's role is the part that they play, e.g. *She played the leading role.*

▶ll, rolls, rolling, rolled
1 (verb) e.g. *The coin rolled along the floor... She rolled her eyes and made a face... She rolled up the poster.*
2 (noun) e.g. *a roll of cloth... a roll of film... a bread roll.*
3 A roll on a drum is a long, rumbling sound made on it.

roll up
(phrasal verb; informal) If you roll up, you arrive.

roll-call, roll-calls
(noun) If you take a roll-call, you call a register of names to see who is present.

roller, rollers
1 (noun) a cylinder that turns round in a machine or piece of equipment.
2 Rollers are tubes for curling hair.

roller-coaster, roller-coasters
(noun) a funfair ride, consisting of a small railway that goes up and down very steep slopes.

roller-boots or **roller-skates**
(plural noun) shoes with small wheels underneath.

rolling
(phrase; informal) If someone is **rolling in it**, they are very rich.

ROM
(noun) In computing, ROM is a storage device that holds data permanently [short for 'read only memory'].

Roman Catholic, Catholics
(noun) someone who belongs to the branch of the Christian church that accepts the Pope in Rome as its leader.

romance, romances
1 (noun) a relationship between two people who are in love with each other.
2 the pleasure and excitement of doing something new and unusual, e.g. *the romance of foreign travel.*
3 a story, especially one about love.
romantic (adjective)

Romanian, Romanians
1 (adjective) belonging to Romania.
2 (noun) someone who comes from Romania.
3 the main language spoken in Romania.

Roman numeral, numerals
(noun) Roman numerals are the letters used by the ancient Romans to write numbers, e.g. $V = 5$; $VI = 6$; $IV = 4$; $X = 10$; $L = 50$; $C = 100$; $D = 500$; $M = 1000$; $MCMXCIV = 1994$

romp, romps, romping, romped
(verb) to play and jump around in a happy, noisy way.
[Old French *ramper* = to crawl or to climb]

roof, roofs
1 (noun) the covering on top of a building.
2 the highest part of your mouth or of a cave.
3 (phrase; informal) If someone **hits the roof** or **goes through the roof**, they get very angry indeed.
rooftops (noun)

roof rack, racks
(noun) a carrying frame placed on top of a car.

rook, rooks
1 (noun) a large, black bird of the crow family.
2 a chess piece which can move any number of squares in a straight, but not diagonal, line.

Roman numerals. Can you read: Henry VIII; The First XI; XXV; CXLIV (a gross); MCMXCIII?

room, rooms
(noun) e.g. *the living room... Have you room for a passenger?*

roost, roosts, roosting, roosted
1 (verb) When birds roost, they settle down somewhere for the night.
2 (phrase) Someone who **rules the roost** is in charge of the people in a particular place.

rooster, roosters
(noun) an adult male chicken; a cockerel.

root, roots, rooting, rooted
1 (noun) the part of a plant that is underground.
2 You can say that the place you grew up in is your roots, e.g. *My roots are in Manchester.*
3 The root of something is its original cause or basis, e.g. *We traced the root of the problem.*
4 (verb) To root through things means to search through them, pushing them aside.

root out
(phrasal verb) to find something or someone and force them out, e.g. *She rooted out the troublemakers.*

rope, ropes, roping, roped
1 (noun) a thick, strong length of cord.
2 (phrase) If someone **knows the ropes**, they are experienced and know how a job should be done.

rope in
(phrasal verb) If you rope someone in to do something, you persuade them to help.

ropey, ropier, ropiest
(adjective; informal) not very good, e.g. *It was a pretty ropey film.*

rosary, rosaries
(noun) a string of beads that Roman Catholics use for counting prayers.

rose, roses
1 (noun) a large garden flower.
2 (noun, adjective) reddish-pink.
rosy (adjective)

rosette, rosettes
(noun) a large, circular badge made of coloured ribbons and card, worn as a prize etc.
[Old French *rosette* = little rose]

rot, rots, rotting, rotted
1 (verb) to decay and break up.
2 (noun) decay, e.g. *Our floorboards were full of rot.*
3 nonsense, e.g. *Don't talk rot, Kenneth!*

Similar words: (verb) decompose, perish

rota, rotas
(noun) a list of people who take turns to do a job.
[Latin *rota* = wheel]

rotary
(adjective) moving in a circular direction, e.g. *a rotary lawn mower.*

rotate, rotates, rotating, rotated
(verb) to turn with a circular movement.
rotation (noun)

rotor, rotors
(noun) The rotors or rotor blades of a helicopter

are the 4 long, flat pieces of metal on top of it which rotate and lift it off the ground.
[short for 'rotator']

rotten
(adjective) e.g. *The fabric was rotten and fell to pieces... What a rotten song! You're being rotten to me!... I've got a rotten headache.*

rouble, roubles (pronounced **roo**-bl)
(noun) the main unit of money in the Soviet Union. (1 rouble = 100 kopecks)
[Russian *rubl* = silver bar]

rough, rougher, roughest; roughs, roughing, roughed
1 (adjective) uneven and not smooth, e.g. *a rough road... a rough sea.*
2 not using enough care or gentleness, e.g. *Don't be so rough or you'll break it.*
3 difficult or unpleasant, e.g. *Molly's having a rough time in her new job.*
4 approximately correct, e.g. *a rough guess.*
5 A rough area has a lot of crime or violence.
6 A rough sketch is a drawing that shows the main features but not the details.
7 (phrasal verb) If you have to rough it, you have to put up with very basic living conditions.
roughly (adverb) **roughness** (noun) **roughen** (verb)

roughage
(noun) the fibre in food that makes digestion easier and helps your bowels work properly.

roulette (pronounced roo-**let**)
(noun) a gambling game in which a ball is dropped onto a revolving wheel with numbered and coloured holes in it.
[French *roue* = wheel]

round, rounder, roundest; rounds
1 (adjective, preposition, adverb) e.g. *a round window... It goes round the hole... It's quiet round here... round the corner... Turn round a minute... We went round the castle... The Smiths are coming round for tea.*
2 (adjective) complete or whole, e.g. *round numbers.*
3 (noun) A round is one of a series of events, e.g. *the first round of the F.A. Cup.*
4 a song which several people sing together, each starting after the other.
5 e.g. *a round of drinks... a round of applause... a round of golf... rounds of ammunition.*

round up
(verb) If you round up people or animals, you gather them together.

roundabout, roundabouts
1 (noun) a circular road junction.
2 a rotating platform which children ride on in a playground etc.

rounders
(noun) a team game in which rounders are scored by hitting a ball and running around 4 sides of a square pitch.

rouse, rouses, rousing, roused
(verb) to wake someone up, or get them excited.
rousing (adjective)

Do you know what is meant by: a storm in a teacup; a windfall; seeing red; feeling blue?

ute, routes
(noun) a way from one place to another.

utine, routines
1 (noun) the usual way or order in which you do things.
2 (adjective) ordinary and regular.
routinely (adverb)
[Old French *route* = usual way]

ve, roves, roving, roved
(verb; literary) to wander, far and wide.

w, rows, rowing, rowed (rhymes with **snow**)
1 (noun) a line of people or things.
2 (verb) When you row a boat, you use oars to make it move through the water.
rowing boat (noun)

Similar words: (noun) column, line, rank

w, rows (rhymes with **now**)
1 (noun) a serious argument.
2 If someone is making a row, they are making too much noise.

wdy, rowdier, rowdiest
(adjective) rough and noisy.
rowdily (adverb)

yal
1 (adjective) belonging to or involving a queen, a king, or a member of their family.
2 (noun; informal) a member of the royal family

Similar words: regal, imperial, sovereign

yalty, royalties
1 (noun) the members of a royal family.
2 Royalties are payments made to authors and musicians for sales of their books or records.

b, rubs, rubbing, rubbed
1 (verb) e.g. *Fagin rubbed his hands together in greedy anticipation... I rubbed out my mistakes.*
2 (phrase) If you **rub someone up the wrong way**, you annoy or offend them without meaning to.

bber, rubbers
1 (noun) a strong, elastic substance made from the sap of a tropical tree or produced chemically.
2 (noun) a small piece of rubber used to rub out pencil mistakes.
rubbery (adjective)

bbish
1 (noun) unwanted things or waste material.
2 nonsense or something of very poor quality.

Similar words: (sense 1) junk, trash, garbage, litter, refuse, waste
(sense 2) rot, nonsense, trash, piffle, twaddle

bble
(noun) bits of old brick and stone etc.

by, rubies
(noun) a type of red jewel.
[Latin *ruber* = red]

cksack, rucksacks
(noun) a bag with shoulder straps and a frame for carrying things on your back.

dder, rudders
(noun) a piece of metal or wood attached to the stern of a boat or the back of a plane, used for steering.

rude, ruder, rudest
(adjective) not polite.
rudely (adverb) **rudeness** (noun)

ruff, ruffs
1 (noun) a stiff circular collar with many pleats in it, worn especially in the 16th century.
2 a thick band of fur or feathers around the neck of a bird or animal.

ruffle, ruffles, ruffling, ruffled
1 (verb) If you ruffle someone's hair, you move your hand quickly backwards and forwards over their head.
2 If something ruffles you, it makes you annoyed or upset.

rugby or **rugger**
(noun) a game played by two teams, who try to kick, throw or carry an oval ball to their opponents' end of the pitch. [named after Rugby School where it was first played]

rugged
(adjective) rocky, wild and unsheltered, e.g. *the rugged Cornish coastline.*

ruin, ruins, ruining, ruined
1 (verb) to destroy or spoil something completely.
2 (plural noun) The ruins of something refers to the parts that are left after it has been severely damaged, e.g. *the ruins of a Norman castle.*
3 (verb) If someone is ruined, they have lost all their money.

rule, rules, ruling, ruled
1 (noun) Rules are statements which tell you what you can and can't do.
2 (verb) To rule a country means to have power over it and be in charge of it.
3 To rule lines means to draw them with a ruler.
4 (phrase) If something is **the rule**, it is the normal state of things.
5 As a rule, means usually, e.g. *We have lunch, as a rule, around 1 o'clock.*

Similar words: (noun) law, regulation, principle

rule out
(phrasal verb) to reject something, e.g. *The head ruled out the idea of a school trip to Las Vegas.*

ruler, rulers
1 (noun) a person who rules a country.
2 a piece of equipment for measuring and drawing lines.

rum
(noun) a strong alcoholic drink from the West Indies made from sugar cane juice.

rumble, rumbles, rumbling, rumbled
(verb) to make a continuous low noise, e.g. *The traffic rumbled past all day.*

rummage, rummages, rummaging, rummaged
(verb) to search for something, moving things about carelessly.

rumour, rumours
(noun) a story that people are talking about, which may or may not be true.

Pun. Why is an archaeologist a failure? ...His career is in ruins.

[Latin *rumor* = common talk]

Similar words: hearsay, gossip, report

rump, rumps
(noun) An animal's rump is its rear end.

rumpus
(noun) a lot of noise or argument.

run, runs, running, ran
1 (verb) e.g. *He's running for President... Can you run me home, please?... Let's run through the details again... Unemployment is running at 10%... The bus is running late.*
2 (noun) e.g. *The batsmen scored only one run... The play is booked for a long run.*
runner (noun)

Similar words: dash, sprint, bolt

run into
to meet unexpectedly, e.g. *I ran into my ex-wife yesterday.*

run off
(phrasal verb) to make copies of a document on a printer or photocopier e.g. *Run me off a few more sheets, please.*

run through
(phrasal verb) to rehearse or practise something.

run down
1 (adjective) tired and not well.
2 neglected and in poor condition.

runaway, runaways
(noun) a person who has escaped from a place or left it secretly and hurriedly.

rung, rungs
(noun) The rungs on a ladder are the wooden or metal bars that form the steps.

runner bean, beans
(noun) a long, green pod eaten as a vegetable.

runner-up, runners-up
(noun) a person or team that comes 2nd in a race or competition.

runny, runnier, runniest
(adjective) more liquid than usual, e.g. *If there's one thing I hate, it's a runny boiled egg.*

runway, runways
(noun) a long strip of ground used by aeroplanes for taking off or landing.

rupee, rupees (pronounced roo-**pee**)
(noun) the main unit of money in India, Pakistan and some other countries.

rural
(adjective) relating to the countryside.
[Latin *ruralis*, from *rus* = the country]

rush, rushes, rushing, rushed
1 (verb) to move fast or do something quickly.
2 (noun) a long, thin, waterside plant.

rush hour, hours
(noun) one of the busy parts of the day when most people are travelling to or from work.

Russian, Russians
1 (adjective) belonging to Russia.
2 (noun) someone who comes from Russia.
3 the main language spoken in the U.S.S.R.
[As Russia is by far the largest republic in the U.S.S.R., we tend to use it in describing the whol[e] nation although, strictly, this is not correct]

rust
(noun) a reddish-brown, flaky coating that form[s] on iron or steel when it gets wet.

rustic
(adjective) of a simple type thought to be typica[l] of the countryside, e.g. *a rustic stone wall.*
[Latin *rus* = the country]

rustle, rustles, rustling, rustled
(verb) When something rustles, it makes soft sounds as it moves.

rusty, rustier, rustiest
1 (adjective) affected by rust, e.g. *a rusty bike.*
2 If someone's knowledge is rusty, it is not as good as it used to be, e.g. *My French is a bit rust[y]*

rut, ruts
1 (noun) a deep, narrow groove in the ground made by the wheels of a vehicle.
2 (phrase) If someone is **in a rut**, they have become fixed in their way of doing things or tired of their job etc.

ruthless
(adjective) very harsh or cruel, e.g. *Ruthless gangsters sold my granny as a slave girl.*
ruthlessness (noun) **ruthlessly** (adverb)

S

Sabbath
(noun) the day of rest for members of some religions, e.g. Jews and Christians.
[Hebrew *shabbath* = to rest]

sabotage, (pronounced **sab**-ot-ahj)
(noun) the deliberate damaging of things like machinery and railway lines.
saboteur (noun)
[French *saboter* = to spoil through clumsiness]

sabre, sabres
(noun) a type of sword.

saccharin (pronounced sak-er-rin)
(noun) a chemical used instead of sugar to sweeten things.
[Greek *sakkharon* = sugar]

sachet, sachets (pronounced **sash**-ay)
(noun) a small, closed packet, containing a small amount of, for example sugar or shampoo.
[Old French *sachet* = little bag]

sack, sacks, sacking, sacked
1 (noun) a large bag.
2 (verb; informal) If someone is sacked, they are dismissed from their job.

Letter S might have been a picture of an extracted tooth. Shin was a word for tooth.

3 (phrase; informal) If someone **gets the sack**, they are sacked by their employer.

Similar words: (verb) fire, discharge, dismiss

acred (pronounced **say**-krid)
(adjective) holy, or connected with religion or religious ceremonies, e.g. *sacred music*.
[Latin *sacer* = holy]

acrifice, sacrifices, sacrificing, sacrificed
(pronounced **sak**-riff-ice)
1 (verb) to give up something valuable or important.
2 To sacrifice an animal means to kill it as an offering to a god or gods.
3 (noun) A sacrifice is something important that you give up for a good cause.
sacrificial (adjective)

ad, sadder, saddest
(adjective) unhappy.
sadly (adverb) **sadness** (noun)

Similar words: glum, melancholy, down in the dumps

adden, saddens, saddening, saddened
(verb) If something saddens you, it makes you feel sad.

addle, saddles, saddling, saddled
1 (noun) a seat that you sit on when you are riding a horse or bicycle.
2 (verb) If you saddle a horse, you put a saddle on it.
3 To saddle someone with a problem means to give it to them to deal with.

addlebag, saddlebags
(noun) a bag fastened to the saddle of a horse, bicycle or motorcycle.

afari, safaris
(noun) an expedition for hunting or observing wild animals, especially in East Africa.
safari park (noun)
[Swahili *safari* = journey]

afe, safer, safest; safes
1 (adjective) e.g. *You are safe here... The bomb is safe now... It is safe to say that Stockport County won't win the Cup this year.*
2 (noun) a strong metal box with special locks, in which you can keep valuable things.
safely (adverb) **safety** (noun)
[Latin *salvus* = uninjured or healthy]

Similar words: (sense 1) unharmed, unhurt, secure, safe and sound

afeguard, safeguards
(noun) a rule or law designed to protect something or someone.

afekeeping
(noun) If you give a person something for safekeeping, you give it them to look after, e.g. *I gave the P.E. teacher my watch for safekeeping, but he sold it to the Head.*

afety catch, catches
(noun) The safety catch on a gun is a catch that stops the gun from being fired accidentally.

safety pin, pins
(noun) a pin with a covered point.

sag, sags, sagging, sagged
(verb) When something sags, it hangs down loosely or sinks downwards in the middle.
sagging (adjective)

saga, sagas (pronounced **sah**-ga)
(noun) a very long story, usually with many different adventures, e.g. *the Norse sagas.*
[Old Norse *saga* = story]

sage, sages
(noun) a herb used for flavouring in cooking.
[Latin *salvus* = healthy, because the plant is supposed to help healing]

sago (pronounced **say**-go)
(noun) a starchy substance obtained from palm trees, used for making puddings and sauces.

sail, sails, sailing, sailed
1 (noun) e.g. *Our new boat had a blue sail.*
2 (verb) e.g. *The ship sails tonight.*
3 (noun) The sails on a windmill are the long arms that move round in the wind.

sailboard, sailboards
(noun) a board like a surfboard with a mast and sail attached, used for windsurfing.

sailor, sailors
(noun) a member of a ship's crew.

saint, saints
(noun) Saints are people honoured, after their death, by the Church because of their holiness.
saintly (adjective)
[Latin *sanctus* = holy]

sake, sakes
1 (phrase) You use **for the sake of** to say why you are doing something, e.g. *I usually check from time to time, just for the sake of safety.*
2 If you do something **for someone's sake**, you do it to help or please them.

salad, salads
(noun) a mixture of raw vegetables or fruit.
[Reginal French *salar* = to season with salt]

salami (pronounced sal-**lah**-mee)
(noun) a kind of spicy sausage.

salary, salaries
(noun) a regular monthly payment to a worker.
[Latin *salarium* = money given to soldiers to buy salt]

sale, sales
1 (plural noun) The sales of a product are the numbers that are sold.
2 (noun) A sale is an occasion when a shop sells things at reduced prices; also an auction.

salesman, salesmen
(noun) someone who sells products for a company.

salient (pronounced **say**-lee-ent)
(adjective; formal) The salient points or facts are the important ones.

saliva (pronounced sal-**live**-a)
(noun) the watery liquid in your mouth that helps you chew and digest food.

Homophones: ail ale; aisle isle; brake break; cent scent sent; berry bury; desert (verb) dessert

salmon (pronounced **sam-on**)
(noun) a large, edible fish with pink flesh.

salon, salons
(noun) a place where hairdressers or beauticians work.
[French *salon* = reception room]

saloon, saloons
1 (noun) a car with a fixed roof and a separate boot.
2 In America, a saloon is a building or bar where alcoholic drinks are sold and drunk.
[sense 2: French *salon* = reception room]

salt, salts
1 (noun) a white substance, sodium chloride, found in sea water and underground, used to flavour and preserve food.
2 a chemical compound formed from an acid base.
3 (phrase) If you **take something with a pinch of salt**, you do not believe it completely.
salty (adjective)
[Latin *sal* = salt]

salt cellar, cellars
(noun) a small container for salt.

salute, salutes, saluting, saluted
(verb) to give a formal sign of respect. In the army, soldiers salute by raising their right hand to their forehead.
[Latin *salutare* = to greet]

salvage, salvages, salvaging, salvaged
(verb) If you salvage things, you save them, e.g. from a wrecked ship or a destroyed building.
[Latin *salvare* = to save]

salvation
(noun) When someone's salvation takes place, they are saved from harm or evil.
[Latin *salvare* = to save]

same
1 (adjective, pronoun) e.g. *We come from the same place... This badge is the same.*
2 (phrase) **All the same** means in spite of what has just been said, e.g. *He wasn't listening, but she went on all the same.*

samosa, samosas
(noun) a small pastry case filled with a spicy meat or vegetable mixture, eaten as a snack.

sample, samples, sampling, sampled
1 (noun) a small amount of something that you can try or test, e.g. *free samples of shampoo.*
2 (verb) If you sample something, you try it, e.g. *Next Bunter sampled ten slices of roast beef.*
[Latin *exemplum* = example]

sanction, sanctions, sanctioning, sanctioned
1 (verb) To sanction something means to approve of it or allow it officially.
2 (noun) a severe punishment or penalty intended to make people obey the law. Sanctions are sometimes taken by countries against a country that has broken international law.
[Latin *sancire* = to decree]

sanctuary, sanctuaries
(noun) a place where someone or something is safe from harm or danger, e.g. *a bird sanctuary.*
[Latin *sanctus* = holy]

sand, sands, sanding, sanded
1 (noun) Sand consists of tiny pieces of stone.
2 (verb) If you sand something, you rub sandpaper over it to make it smooth.
sandy (adjective)

sandal, sandals
(noun) light shoes with straps.

sandbag, sandbags
(noun) a sack filled with sand and used as a protection against floods or explosives.

sandbank, sandbanks
(noun) a ridge of sand in the sea or a river.

sandpaper
(noun) strong paper with a coating of sand on it used for rubbing wooden or metal surfaces to make them smooth.

sandstone
(noun) a type of rock formed from compressed sand.

sandwich, sandwiches, sandwiching, sandwiched
1 (noun) two slices of bread with a filling between them.
2 (verb) If one thing is sandwiched between two others, it is squashed between them.
[noun: named after the 4th Earl of Sandwich (1718-92), for whom sandwiches were invented so that he could eat and gamble at the same time]

sandwich course, courses
(noun) a course of study between periods of work in industry or business.

sane, saner, sanest
1 (adjective) If someone is sane, they have a normal and healthy mind.
2 sensible and reasonable, e.g. *It was the only sane thing to do.*
[Latin *sanus* = healthy]

sanitary towel, towels
(noun) Sanitary towels are pads of thick, soft material which women wear during their period.

sanitation
(noun) the process of keeping places clean and hygienic, especially by providing a sewage system and water supply.
sanitary (adjective)
[Latin *sanitas* = health]

sanity
(noun) a person's ability to think and act reasonably, e.g. *The teacher's sanity was in some doubt after he had taken 10G.*

Sanskrit
(noun) an ancient language of India.

sap, saps, sapping, sapped
1 (verb) If something saps your strength or confidence, it gradually weakens and destroys it.
2 (noun) the watery liquid in plants.

sapling, saplings
(noun) a young tree.

sapphire, sapphires
(noun) a blue precious stone.

sarcastic
(adjective) saying or doing the opposite of what you really mean in order to mock or insult

What are the full versions of these forenames: Sandy Bess Bill Ben Dot Paddy Peggy Ike Bert?

someone, e.g. *a sarcastic smile... God forbid that I should be sarcastic!*
sarcasm (noun) **sarcastically** (adverb)
[Greek *sarkazein* = to tear the flesh]

sardine, sardines
(noun) a small, edible sea fish.

sari, saris (pronounced **sah**-ree)
(noun) a long piece of material folded around the body, worn mainly by Indian women.
[a Hindi word]

sash, sashes
(noun) a long piece of cloth worn round the waist or over one shoulder.
[Arabic *shash* = muslin]

Satan
(noun) the Devil.
satanic (adjective)
[Hebrew *satan* = to plot against]

satchel, satchels
(noun) a bag with a long strap, traditionally used by children for carrying school books.

satellite, satellites
1 (noun) an object sent into orbit round the earth to collect information or as part of a communications system.
2 a natural object in space that moves round a planet or star, e.g. the moon.

satin
(noun) a kind of smooth, shiny silk.

satire, satires
(noun) the use of mocking humour, for example in plays or literature, to show how foolish or wicked some people or ideas are.
satirical (adjective)

satisfaction
(noun) the feeling of pleasure you get when you do something you wanted or needed to do.
[Latin *satis* = enough + *facere* = to make]

satisfactory
(adjective) acceptable or adequate, e.g. *You will find the Survival Guide on pages v to vii very satisfactory.*
satisfy (verb) **satisfied** (adjective) **satisfactorily** (adverb)

Similar words: fulfilling, rewarding, enriching

satsuma, satsumas (pronounced sat-**soo**-ma)
(noun) a fruit like a small orange.

saturated
(adjective) as wet as it is possible to be.
saturation (noun)

Saturday, Saturdays
(noun) the day between Friday and Sunday.
[Latin *Saturni dies* = day of Saturn]

sauce, sauces
(noun) a liquid eaten with food.
[Latin *salsus* = salted]

saucepan, saucepans
(noun) a cooking pot with a handle and a lid.

saucer, saucers
(noun) a small curved plate for a cup.
[Old French *saussier* = a container for sauce]

saucy, saucier, sauciest
(adjective) cheeky in an amusing way.

Saudi, Saudis (rhymes with **cloudy**)
1 (adjective) belonging to Saudi Arabia.
2 (noun) someone who comes from Saudi Arabia.

sauna, saunas (pronounced **saw**-na)
(noun) to have a sauna, you sit in a very hot room to sweat, then have a cold bath or shower.
[a Finnish word]

saunter, saunters, sauntering, sauntered
(verb) to walk slowly and casually, e.g. *We sauntered along the promenade at Rhyl.*

sausage, sausages
(noun) a mixture of minced meat, herbs, etc. formed into a tube and cooked.

savage, savages, savaging, savaged
1 (adjective) cruel and violent, e.g. *two weeks of savage rioting.*
2 (verb) If a dog or other animal savages you, it attacks you and bites you.
3 (noun) someone who is cruel, violent or uncivilized.
savagely (adverb) **savagery** (noun)

Similar words: (adjective) bloodthirsty, murderous, brutal, uncivilized

save, saves, saving, saved
1 (verb) e.g. *She saved him from drowning... They had saved enough money to buy a house... She saved time by catching train.*
2 (preposition; formal) except, e.g. *The stage was empty save for a piano.*
savings (noun)

saviour, saviours
1 (noun) If someone saves you from danger, you can refer to them as your saviour.
2 In Christianity, the Saviour is Jesus Christ.

savoury
(adjective) salty or spicy.

saw, saws, sawing, sawed, sawn
1 past tense of **see**.
2 (noun) a tool for cutting wood.
3 (verb) to cut something with a saw.
sawdust (noun)

saxophone, saxophones
(noun) a curved, metal wind instrument often played in jazz bands. [named after Adolphe Sax (1814-94), who invented it]

say, says, saying, said
1 (verb) e.g. *I'll say a few words.*
2 Say is used to give an example, e.g. *Compare, say, a Ford with a Volvo.*
3 (noun) If you have a say in something, you can give your opinion and influence decisions.
4 (phrase) You use **that is to say** to express the same idea in a different way, e.g. *She had angina pectoris, that is to say, heart trouble.*
5 If something **goes without saying**, it is obvious.

Similar words: (verb) utter, remark, comment

saying, sayings
(noun) a well-known sentence or phrase that

What do we call a witch on a broomstick? A flying sorcerer.

tells you something about human life.

Similar words: axiom, motto, proverb, maxim

scab, scabs
(noun) a hard, dry covering forming over a wound.

scabbard, scabbards
(noun) a cover for a sword.

scaffold, scaffolds
(noun) a platform on which criminals used to be hanged or beheaded.
scaffolder (noun)

scaffolding
(noun) a temporary structure erected around buildings being built or repaired.

scald, scalds, scalding, scalded (pronounced **skawld**)
(verb) If you scald yourself, you burn yourself with very hot liquid or steam.
[Latin *excaldare* = to wash in warm water]

scale, scales, scaling, scaled
1 (noun) The scale of something is its size, e.g. *The scale of change is enormous.*
2 a set of levels or numbers used for measuring things, e.g. *the Beaufort Scale* (of windspeed).
3 The scale of a map is the ratio of measurements on the map to measurements in the real world, e.g. *a scale of 1:50,000.*
4 an upward or downward sequence of musical notes, e.g. *the scale of C.*
5 (verb) If you scale something high, you climb it.
6 (noun) The scales of a fish or reptile are the small pieces of hard skin covering its body.
7 (plural noun) Scales are a piece of equipment used for weighing things.
scaly adjective)
[senses 2-5: Latin *scala* = ladder]

scalene
(adjective) A scalene triangle has sides which are all of different lengths.

scalp, scalps
(noun) the skin under the hair on your head.

scamper, scampers, scampering, scampered
(verb) to move quickly and lightly.

scampi
(noun) large prawns fried in batter.

scan, scans, scanning, scanned
1 (verb) to look all over something carefully, e.g. *The lifeguards scanned the sea for shark fins.*
2 If a machine scans something, it examines it quickly by means of a beam of light or x-rays.
scanner (noun)
3 (noun) a search or examination by a scanner, e.g. *Paddy went for a brain scan but it proved negative because they couldn't find it.*
4 (verb) If the words of a poem scan, they fit into a regular, rhythmical pattern.

scandal, scandals
(noun) a situation or event that people think is shocking.
scandalous (adjective) **scandalously** (adverb) **scandalize** (verb)

Scandinavian (pronounced skan-din-**nay**-vee-an)
(adjective) relating to a group of countries in Northern Europe, including Norway, Sweden, Denmark, and sometimes Finland and Iceland.

scansion
(noun) the rhythmic arrangement of syllables in lines of poetry.

scanty, scantier, scantiest
(adjective) small in size or amount, e.g. *There was a rather scanty audience in the cinema.*
scantily (adverb)

scapegoat, scapegoats
(noun) If someone is made a scapegoat, they are blamed for something, although it may not be their fault [In an ancient Jewish ritual, a priest would symbolically transfer the sins of the people to a goat, which would then be allowed to escape.]

scar, scars, scarring, scarred
1 (verb) If an injury scars you, it leaves a permanent mark on your skin.
2 (noun) the permanent mark from an injury.
[Greek *eskhara* = scab]

scarce, scarcer, scarcest
1 (adjective) If something is scarce, there is not very much of it.
2 (phrase) If you **make yourself scarce**, you leave quickly.
scarcity (noun)

scarcely
(adverb) hardly, e.g. *He was scarcely ever in.*

scare, scares, scaring, scared
1 (verb) If something scares you, it frightens you.
2 (noun) If there is a scare about something, people are worried about it, e.g. *a rabies scare.*
scared (adjective)

Similar words: (verb) frighten , alarm, startle

scarecrow, scarecrows
(noun) an object resembling a person put in a field to scare birds away.

scarf, scarfs or **scarves**
(noun) a piece of cloth worn round your neck or head to keep you warm.

scarlet
(adjective, noun) bright red.

scarlet fever
(noun) an infectious disease.

scarper, scarpers, scarpering, scarpered
(verb; informal) to run away.
[Cockney rhyming slang – *Scapa Flow:* to go.]

scary, scarier, scariest
(adjective; informal) frightening.

scatter, scatters, scattering, scattered
1 (verb) To scatter things means to throw or drop them all over an area.
2 If people scatter, they suddenly move away in different directions.

Similar words: (sense 2) disperse

Rhyming slang. What do these mean: a butcher's; apples and pears; mince pies; dog and bone; the Sweeney, trouble and strife?

scatty, scattier, scattiest
(adjective; informal) rather absent-minded.

scavenge, scavenges, scavenging, scavenged
(verb) If you scavenge for things, you search for them among waste and rubbish.

scene, scenes
1 (noun) part of a play, film or book in which a series of events happen in one place.
2 Pictures and views are sometimes called scenes, e.g. *a village scene*.
3 The scene of an event is the place where it happened.
4 (phrase) If you **make a scene**, you embarrass people by losing your temper in public.
5 **Behind the scenes**, means in secret.
[Latin *scena* = theatrical stage]

scenery
1 (noun) the views in the countryside.
2 the painted cloth etc. for a play.
scenic (adjective)

scent, scents, scenting, scented
1 (noun) a smell, especially a pleasant one.
2 (verb) to catch the smell of something.
3 If, for example, you scent victory, you start to think you are going to win.
[Old French *sentir* = to sense]

sceptical (pronounced **skep**-tik-kl)
(adjective) doubtful, e.g. *She was sceptical about his promises.*
sceptically (adverb) **scepticism** (noun)

sceptre, sceptres (pronounced **sep**-ter)
(noun) an ornamental rod carried at ceremonies by a king or queen as a symbol of power.

schedule, schedules, scheduling, scheduled
(pronounced **shed**-yool)
1 (noun) a plan that gives a list of events or tasks, and the times when they should be done.
2 (verb) If something is scheduled to happen, it has been planned and arranged, e.g. *A meeting had been scheduled for that day.*

scheme, schemes, scheming, schemed
1 (noun) a plan or arrangement.
2 (verb) to make secret plans.
scheming (adjective)
[Greek *skhēma* = form]

scholar, scholars
1 (noun) a person who studies an academic subject and knows a lot about it.
2 a pupil or student who has a scholarship.
scholastic (adjective)

scholarship, scholarships
(noun) If you get a scholarship to a school or university, your studies are fully or partly paid for by the school, university, etc.

school, schools
1 (noun) a place where children are educated.
2 a large group of dolphins or fish.
schoolboy (noun) **schoolgirl** (noun)
[sense 1: Latin *schola* = school
sense 2: Old English *scolu* = shoal]

school-leaver, school-leavers
(noun) a young person who has just left school or is about to leave.

science, sciences
(noun) the study of nature and natural things and the knowledge obtained about them.
[Latin *scientia* = knowledge]

science fiction
(noun) stories about events happening in the future or in other parts of the universe.

scientific
1 (adjective) relating to science or to a particular science, e.g. *scientific instruments*.
2 done in a systematic way, using experiments or tests, e.g. *a scientific study of language*.
scientifically (adverb)

scientist, scientists
(noun) an expert in one of the sciences.

scissors
(plural noun) a cutting tool with two blades.

scoff, scoffs, scoffing, scoffed
1 (verb) to speak in a scornful, mocking way about something.
2 (informal) to eat quickly and greedily.

scold, scolds, scolding, scolded
(verb) to tell someone off.

Similar words: chastise, tick off, reprimand

scone, scones (pronounced **skone** or **skon**)
(noun) a small cake made from flour and fat, usually eaten with butter.

scoop, scoops, scooping, scooped
1 (verb) to pick something up using a spoon or the palm of your hand.
2 (noun) an object like a large spoon used for picking up food, e.g. *an ice cream scoop*.
[Old Dutch *schope* = vessel for baling]

scooter, scooters
1 (noun) a light motorcycle with platforms.
2 a simple type of cycle which a child rides by standing on it and pushing with one foot.

scorch, scorches, scorching, scorched
(verb) to burn something slightly.

score, scores, scoring, scored
1 (verb) to get a goal, run or point in a game.
2 to keep the score in a game.
scorer (noun)
3 (noun) The score in a game is the number of goals, runs or points obtained by the two teams.
4 Scores of things means very many of them, e.g. *We received scores of letters.*
5 (old-fashioned) A score is 20.
6 (verb) to cut a line into a surface.
[Old Norse *skor* = notch, tally, or 20]

scornful
(adjective) If you are scornful about something you say it is useless and pathetic.
scorn (noun) **scornfully** (adverb)

Scot, Scots
1 (noun) a person who comes from Scotland.
2 (adjective) Scots means the same as Scottish.
Scotsman (noun) **Scotswoman** (noun)

scotch, scotches
(noun) whisky made in Scotland.

A teacher needs these words: lesson patience humour tolerance motivation encouragement examination.

scot-free
(adverb) If you get away scot-free, you get away without being punished.
[Old English *scot* = payment; hence payment-free]

Scottish
(adjective) relating to Scotland.

scoundrel, scoundrels
(noun; old-fashioned) a man who cheats and deceives people.

scour, scours, scouring, scoured
1 (verb) to look all over a place for something. e.g. *I scoured the shop for a book on worms.*
2 If you scour a pan, you clean it by rubbing it with something rough.
[Latin *excurare* = to cleanse]

scout, scouts, scouting, scouted
1 (noun) a member of the Scout Association.
2 (verb) If you scout around for something, you look around for it.
[Old French *ascouter* = to listen to]

scowl, scowls, scowling, scowled
(verb) to frown because you are angry.

scrabble, scrabbles, scrabbling, scrabbled
1 (verb) If you scrabble at something, you scrape at it with your hands or feet.
2 (noun; trademark) Scrabble is a word game played with letters on a board.
[Old Dutch *schrabbelen* = to scrape repeatedly]

scraggy, scraggier, scraggiest
(adjective) thin and bony, e.g. *a scraggy neck.*

scramble, scrambles, scrambling, scrambled
1 (verb) If you scramble over something, you climb over it using your hands to help you.
2 To scramble a radio or phone message means to interfere with it so that it can only be received by special equipment.

scrambled egg, eggs
(noun) eggs mixed with milk and cooked in a pan.

scrap, scraps, scrapping, scrapped
1 (noun) a very small piece, e.g. *a scrap of paper.*
2 (plural noun) Scraps are pieces of leftover food.
3 (verb) to get rid of something, e.g. *The GCE has been scrapped.*
4 (adjective, noun) Scrap metal or scrap is metal from old machinery or cars that can be re-used.
5 (noun; informal) a fight, e.g. *Want a scrap?*
scrappy (adjective)

scrapbook, scrapbooks
(noun) a book in which you stick things, for example pictures or newspaper articles.

scrape, scrapes, scraping, scraped
(verb) If you scrape something off a surface, you remove it by pulling a knife over it, e.g. *She scraped the mud off her boots.*

scratch, scratches, scratching, scratched
1 (verb) to make a small cut.
2 to rub your skin with your nails because it is itching.
3 If you scratch from a game, you say that you cannot play in it.

4 (phrase; informal) If you do something **from scratch**, you do it right from the start.
5 If something is **up to scratch**, it is satisfactory.

scrawl, scrawls, scrawling, scrawled
1 (verb) to write in a careless and untidy way.
2 (noun) careless, untidy writing.

scream, screams, screaming, screamed
1 (verb) to shout or cry in a loud, high-pitched voice.
2 (noun; informal) You can say that someone is a scream when you think they are very funny.

Similar words: (verb) screech, shriek

screech, screeches, screeching, screeched
1 (verb) to make an unpleasant, high-pitched noise.
2 (noun) an unpleasant, high-pitched noise.

screen, screens, screening, screened
1 (noun) a flat, vertical surface on which a picture is shown, e.g. *a TV screen.*
2 a vertical panel used to separate different parts of a room.
3 (verb) To screen people for a disease means to examine them to make sure they have not got it, e.g. *Women were screened for breast cancer.*

screw, screws, screwing, screwed
(verb) e.g. *He screwed the lid onto the jar... I screwed the paper up into a tiny ball.*

screwdriver, screwdrivers
(noun) a tool for turning screws.

scribble, scribbles, scribbling, scribbled
(verb) to write quickly and roughly or to make meaningless marks, e.g. *Someone's scribbled all over the wall.*

script, scripts
(noun) The script of a play, film or TV programme is the written version of it.
scriptwriter (noun)
[Latin *scriptum* = something written]

scripture, scriptures
(noun) sacred writings, e.g. the Bible.
[Latin *scriptura* = written material]

scroll, scrolls
(noun) a long roll of paper or parchment with writing on it.

scrounge, scrounges, scrounging, scrounged
(verb; informal) to obtain something by asking for it rather than by earning or buying it.
scrounger (noun)

Similar words: cadge, sponge

scrub, scrubs, scrubbing, scrubbed
1 (verb) to clean with a stiff brush and water.
2 (informal) to cancel, e.g. *I've scrubbed the game.*
3 (noun) Scrub consists of low trees and bushes.

scruff
(noun) The scruff of your neck is the back of your neck or collar.

scruffy, scruffier, scruffiest
(adjective) dirty and untidy, e.g. *a scruffy child.*

Strange anagrams. Eleven + Two = Twelve + One; No more stars = astronomers.

scrum, scrums
(noun) When rugby players form a scrum, they form a group and push against each other with their heads down in an attempt to get the ball.

scuba diving
(noun) swimming underwater with tanks of compressed air on the back.
[from *S(elf)-C(ontained) U(nder water) B(reathing) A(pparatus)*]

scuff, scuffs, scuffing, scuffed
(verb) If you scuff your shoes, you mark them by scraping or rubbing them.

scuffle, scuffles, scuffling, scuffled
(verb) When people scuffle, they fight roughly.

sculptor, sculptors
(noun) someone who makes sculptures.
sculpt (verb)
[Latin *sculpere* = to carve]

sculpture, sculptures
(noun) a work of art produced by carving or shaping stone, wood or clay.
[Latin *sculptura* = carving]

scum
1 (noun) a layer of a dirty substance on the surface of a liquid.
2 an insulting name for people thought to be worthless.

scurry, scurries, scurrying, scurried
(verb) to run quickly with short steps.

scuttle, scuttles, scuttling, scuttled
1 (verb) to run quickly.
2 To scuttle a ship means to sink it deliberately by letting water in.
3 (noun) a container for coal.

scythe, scythes
(noun) a tool with a long handle and a curved blade used for cutting grass or grain.

sea, seas
1 (noun) the salty water that covers much of the earth's surface.
2 (noun) If you are **at sea**, you are baffled.
3 (noun) A sea of people or things is a very large number of them, e.g. *a sea of faces.*
seaside (noun) **seashore** (noun) **seaweed** (noun)

seafront
(noun) the part of a seaside town next to the sea or beach.

seagull, seagulls
(noun) a common type of seabird.

seal, seals, sealing, sealed
1 (verb) If you seal an envelope, you stick down the flap.
2 (phrase) If you give something your **seal of approval**, you say officially that you approve of it.
3 (noun) a large mammal with flippers.
[sense 1-2: Latin *sigillum* = little picture]

sea level
(noun) the average level of the surface of the sea in relation to the land.

seam, seams
1 (noun) a line of stitches joining two pieces of cloth.
2 A coal seam is a layer of coal between other rocks.

seaman, seamen
(noun) a sailor.

search, searches, searching, searched
(verb) to look for something in several places.
[Latin *circare* = to go around]

Similar words: comb, scour, hunt, look for, seek

searchlight, searchlights
(noun) a powerful light whose beam can be turned in different directions.

seasick
(adjective) feeling sick on board a moving boat.
seasickness (noun)

season, seasons, seasoning, seasoned
1 (noun) a period of the year, e.g. spring, summer, autumn, winter... *the football season... the holiday season.*
2 (verb) If you season food, you add salt, pepper or spices to it.
[Latin *satio* = sowing (of crops)]

seasonal
(adjective) happening during one season or one time of the year, e.g. *Ploughing is seasonal work.*

seasoning
(noun) flavouring, e.g. salt, pepper, herbs.

season ticket, tickets
(noun) a train or bus ticket that you can use as often as you like for a certain period.

seat, seats, seating, seated
1 (noun) e.g. *Have a seat!... the seat of your trousers.*
2 (verb) e.g. *Please be seated.*
3 If a place seats a particular number of people, it has enough seats for that number, e.g. *The hall seats 400.*
4 (noun) If someone wins a seat in Parliament, they are elected as an MP.

seat belt, belts
(noun) a strap that you fasten across your body for safety in a car or aircraft.

seaward or **seawards**
(adjective, adverb) moving or facing towards the sea.

seaworthy
(adjective) A seaworthy ship is in good condition and can go to sea safely.

secluded
(adjective) quiet and hidden from view.
[Latin *secludere* = to shut off]

second, seconds, seconding, seconded
1 (adjective) first, **second**, third, fourth, fifth.
2 (noun) a unit of time. (60 seconds = 1 minute)
3 (verb) If you second a proposal, you formally agree with it so it can be discussed or voted on.
secondly (adverb)
[Latin *secundus* = second]

The letters of CHESTY can be rearranged to form only one other word. What is it?

secondary school, schools
(noun) a school for pupils from 11 to 16 or 18.

second cousin, cousins
(noun) the children of your parents' cousins.

second-hand
1 (adjective, adverb) Something that is second-hand has already been owned by someone else, e.g. *second-hand clothes.*
2 If you hear a story second-hand, you hear it indirectly, rather than from the people involved.

second nature
(noun) If something is second nature to you, you have done it so often that you do it without thinking about it.

second-rate
(adjective) of poor quality.

second thoughts
(plural noun) If you have second thoughts about something you have said or done, you have doubts about it and wonder if it was right.

secret, secrets
(adjective, noun) e.g. *a secret agent... a secret meeting... Tell me your secret.*
secretly (adverb) **secrecy** (noun) **secretive** (adjective)
[Latin *secretus* = concealed]

Similar words: confidential, hush-hush

secretary, secretaries
1 (noun) a person employed to keep records, type letters and do other office work.
2 Some government ministers are called secretaries, e.g. *the Foreign Secretary.*
secretarial (adjective)
[Latin *secretarius* = confidential officer]

secrete, secretes, secreting, secreted
(pronounced sik-**kreet**)
(verb) When a plant or animal secretes a liquid, it produces it.
secretion (noun)

sect, sects
(noun) a religious or political group.

section, sections
(noun) one of the parts something is divided into, e.g. *the first-class section of the ship.*
[Latin *secare* = to cut]

Similar words: portion, segment

sector, sectors
(noun) a part of something large, e.g. *the private sector of the economy.*
[Latin *sector* = cutter]

secure, secures, securing, secured
1 (adjective) If a place is secure, it is tightly locked or well protected.
2 If an object is secure, it is firmly fixed in place.
3 If you feel secure, you feel safe and confident.
4 (verb) To secure something means to fasten it firmly, e. g. *A plastic box was secured to the wall.*
securely (adverb)
[Latin *securus* = free from care]

security, securities
(noun, adjective) all the precautions taken to protect a place, e.g. *Security forces were patrolling the streets.*
2 (noun) a feeling of being safe.

sedate (pronounced sid-**date**)
(adjective) quiet, calm and dignified.
sedately (adverb)
[Latin *sedare* = to soothe]

sedative, sedatives (pronounced **sed**-at-tiv)
(noun) a drug that calms you down or makes you sleep.

sedimentary
(adjective) Sedimentary rocks are formed from fragments of shells or rocks that have become compressed, e.g. sandstone, limestone.

see, sees, seeing, saw, seen
(verb) e.g. *I see what you mean... See a doctor soon... What does she see in him?... Seeing as you're here, you'd better have a cup of tea.*

Similar words: spy, catch sight of, spot, sight, perceive, notice

seed, seeds
1 (noun) The seeds of a plant are the small, hard parts from which new plants can grow.
2 a tennis player who is ranked according to ability and recent results, e.g. *She's top seed at Wimbledon this year.*

seedling, seedlings
(noun) a young plant grown from a seed.

seedy, seedier, seediest
(adjective) untidy and shabby.

seek, seeks, seeking, sought
(verb; formal) to try to find or achieve something, e.g. *Both countries are seeking peace.*

seem, seems, seeming, seemed
(verb) to appear to be, e.g. *It seems like a good idea to mix these chemicals togeth......*

seep, seeps, seeping, seeped
(verb) If a liquid or gas seeps through something, it flows through very slowly.

seesaw, seesaws
(noun) a piece of play equipment for children.

seethe, seethes, seething, seethed
1 (verb) If you seethe, you feel very angry but do not show it, e.g. *I seethed with secret rage.*
2 If a place is seething with people, there are a lot of them moving about.

segment, segments
(noun) one part of something, e.g. *grapefruit segments.*
[Latin *secare* = to cut]

segregate, segregates, segregating, segregated
(verb) To segregate two groups of people means to keep them apart from each other, e.g. *In some Belfast streets, walls have been built to segregate Protestant and Catholic people.*
segregated (adjective) **segregation** (noun)
[Latin *se* = apart + *grex* = flock]

seismograph, seismographs (pronounced **size**-moh-grahf)

English is the most widely used language in the world and by far the most popular second language.

(noun) an instrument for measuring the strength of earthquakes.

seismic (adjective)
[Greek *seismos* = earthquake + *graphein* = to write]

seize, seizes, seizing, seized
(verb) to grab something firmly, e.g. *I seized him by the collar.*

seize up
(phrasal verb) If an engine seizes up, it becomes jammed and stops working.

seldom
(adverb) not very often, e.g. *Things are seldom what they seem.*

select, selects, selecting, selected
(verb) to choose something, e.g. *Atherton was selected to play for England.*
selector (noun)
[Latin *seligere* = to choose]

selection, selections
(noun) The selection of goods in a shop is the choice of goods available, e.g. *They have a good selection of beds in the showroom.*

self, selves
(noun) Your self is your basic personality or nature, e.g. *Soon she was her normal self again.*

self-
1 (prefix) done to yourself or by yourself, e.g. *self-inflicted injury... a self-service shop.*
2 doing something automatically, e.g. *self-locking doors.*

self-addressed
(adjective) A self-addressed envelope (or s.a.e) is one on which you have written your own name and address.

self-assured
(adjective) confident.

self-catering
(adjective) In self-catering accommodation, you provide your own meals.

self-centred
(adjective) thinking only about yourself and not about other people.

self-confident
(adjective) confident of your own abilities.
self-confidence (noun)

self-conscious
(adjective) nervous and easily embarrassed, and worried about what other people think of you.
self-consciously (adverb) **self-consciousness** (noun)

self-control
(noun) the ability to restrain yourself and not show your feelings.

self-defence
(noun) the use of violence or special physical techniques to protect yourself when someone attacks you.

self-employed
(adjective) working for yourself, not an employer.

self-indulgent
(adjective) allowing yourself to do or have things you enjoy, especially as a treat.
self-indulgence (noun)

selfish
(adjective) caring only about yourself, and not about other people.
selfishly (adverb) **selfishness** (noun)

selfless
(adjective) the opposite of selfish, e.g. *She gave years of selfless care to her aged mother.*
selflessly (adverb) **selflessness** (noun)

self-made
(adjective) rich and successful through your own efforts, e.g. *Bernard was a self-made millionaire.*

self-raising
(adjective) Self-raising flour contains baking powder to make it rise.

self-reliant
(adjective) able to do things by yourself rather than depending on other people.
self-reliance (noun)

self-respect
(noun) a feeling of confidence and pride in your own abilities.

self-righteous
(adjective) convinced that you are better or more virtuous than other people.
self-righteousness (noun)

self-sacrifice
(noun) the giving up of things for the sake of other people.

self-satisfied
(adjective) feeling smug and satisfied with yourself.

self-sufficient
1 (adjective) producing or making everything you need, and so not needing to buy things.
2 able to live in a way in which you do not need other people.

self-willed
(adjective) stubborn and obstinate.

sell, sells, selling, sold
1 (verb) e.g. *Do you sell flowers?... These little books sell for 95p each.*
2 (informal) If you sell someone an idea, you convince them that it is a good idea.
3 If you sell yourself, you present yourself well. e.g. *You've got to sell yourself at the interview.*
[Old English *sellan* = to lend or to deliver]

Similar words: (sense 1) market, peddle, retail

sell up
(phrasal verb) If you sell up, you sell everything you have because you need the money.

Sellotape
(noun; trademark) transparent sticky tape.

sellout
(noun; informal) If an event is a sellout, all the tickets for it have been sold.

Is it ie or ei: ach..ve dec..ve th..f n..ce fr..nd c..ling w..rd Sh..la K..th s..ze?

semaphore (pronounced **sem**-ma-for)
(noun) a system of sending messages using two flags.
[Greek *sēma* + *-phoros* = signal bearing]

semen (pronounced **see**-men)
(noun) the liquid containing sperm produced by a man's or male animal's sex organs.
[Latin *semen* = seed]

semi-
(prefix) half or partly, e.g. *semi-skilled workers*.
[Latin *semi-* = half]

semicircle, semicircles
(noun) a half of a circle.
semicircular (adjective)

semicolon, semicolons
(noun) the punctuation mark ; used to separate different parts of a sentence; it can also, as here, indicate a pause.

semi-detached
(adjective) A semi-detached house is one of a pair, joined to each other on one side.

semifinals
(noun) the two matches in a knock-out competition played to decide who plays in the final.
semifinalist (noun)

semolina
(noun) Semolina consists of the hard parts of wheat grains that are left after flour is made. It is often used for making puddings.
[Italian *semola* = bran]

senator, senators
(noun) a member of the senate, an elected body which forms part of the USA government.

send, sends, sending, sent
(verb) e.g. *I'm sending you a card... She sent for me and then sacked me... We sent off for the free offer... The ref sent Jones off.*

send up
(phrasal verb) If you send someone up, you imitate them and make fun of them.

senile
(adjective) If old people become senile, they become confused and cannot look after themselves.
senility (noun)
[Latin *senex* = old man]

senior, seniors
1 (adjective) The senior people in an organization are those who have the most important jobs.
2 (noun) Someone who is your senior is older than you.
seniority (noun)
[Latin *senior* = older]

senior citizen, citizens
(noun) someone receiving an old-age pension.

sensation, sensations
1 (noun) a feeling, especially a physical feeling, e.g. *a dizzy sensation*.
2 If something is a sensation, it causes great excitement and interest.

sensational
1 (adjective) causing great excitement and interest.
2 (informal) extremely good, e.g. *'Guys and Dolls' was a sensational show.*
sensationally (adverb)

sense, senses, sensing, sensed
1 (noun) Your senses are your ability to see, hear, smell, touch and taste.
2 (verb) If you sense something, you become aware of it.
3 (noun) a feeling, e.g. *a sense of failure... She has a strong sense of justice.*
4 A sense of a word is one of its meanings.
5 the ability to think and behave sensibly, e.g. *common sense.*
6 (phrase) If something **makes sense**, you can understand it or it seems sensible.
[Latin *sentire* = to feel]

senseless
1 (adjective) A senseless action has no meaning or purpose, e.g. *a senseless act of vandalism.*
2 unconscious, e.g. *He was knocked senseless.*
senselessly (adverb) **senselessness** (noun)

sense of humour
(noun) an ability to see the funny side of things.

sensible
(adjective) showing good sense and judgment.
sensibly (adverb)

Similar words: practical, logical, wise, realistic, sound, rational, balanced, level-headed

sensitive
1 (adjective) If you are sensitive to other people's feelings, you understand them.
2 If you are sensitive about something, you are worried or easily upset about it, e.g. *Don't be so sensitive about your wooden leg, Long John.*
3 A sensitive subject needs to be handled carefully because it can make people angry or upset.
sensitively (adverb) **sensitivity** (noun)

sentence, sentences, sentencing, sentenced
1 (noun) a group of words which makes sense on its own, begins with a capital letter and ends with a full stop.
2 (verb) When a guilty person is sentenced, they are told officially what their punishment will be.
[Latin *sententia* = feeling, opinion or judgment]

sentiment, sentiments
(noun) feelings such as tenderness, romance or sadness, e.g. *He scorns sentiment and emotion.*
sentimental (adjective)
[Latin *sentire* = to feel]

sentry, sentries
(noun) a soldier who keeps watch and guards a camp or building.

separate, separates, separating, separated
1 (adjective) If something is separate from something else, the two things are not connected.
2 (verb) To separate people or things means to cause them to be apart from each other.

A sentence always begins with a capital letter and ends with a full stop.

3 If a married couple separate, they decide to live apart.
separately (adverb) **separation** (noun)

September
(noun) the 9th month of the year.
[Latin *September* = the 7th month; the Romans at first had a 10-month year which they lengthened to 12 months.]

septic
(adjective) If a wound becomes septic, it becomes infected with poison.
[Greek *sēpein* = to rot]

sequel, sequels
(noun) A sequel to a book or film is another book or film which continues the story e.g. Jaws II.

sequence, sequences
1 (noun) A sequence of events is a number of them coming one after the other, e.g. *the strange sequence of events that led up to the murder.*
2 The sequence in which things are arranged is the order in which they are arranged, e.g. *paintings exhibited in chronological sequence.*
[Latin *sequi* = to follow]

sequin, sequins
(noun) Sequins are small, shiny, coloured discs sewn on clothes to decorate them.

serene
(adjective) peaceful and calm.
serenely (adverb) **serenity** (noun)

serf, serfs
(noun) Serfs were a class of people in medieval Europe who had to work on their master's land and could not leave without his permission.
serfdom (noun)
[Latin *servus* = slave]

serge
(noun) a type of strong woollen cloth used to make coats and suits.

sergeant, sergeants
1 (noun) a non-commissioned officer of middle rank in the army or air force.
2 a police officer just above a constable in rank.
[Latin *serviens* = serving]

sergeant major, majors
(noun) a non-commissioned army officer of the highest rank, e.g. *Regimental Sergeant Major.*

serial, serials
(noun) a story in a number of parts told over a period of time, e.g. *a TV serial.*

serial number, numbers
(noun) a number on a product, for example a computer, which identifies it and distinguishes it from other objects of the same kind.

series
1 (noun) a number of things coming one after the other, e.g. *a series of lessons on careers.*
2 A radio or TV series is a set of programmes with the same title.
[Latin *serere* = to link]

Similar words: succession, sequence, string, chain

serious
1 (adjective) very bad and worrying, e.g. *a serious accident.*
2 important and worth thinking about, e.g. *Career choice is a serious matter.*
3 If you are serious about something, you are sincere about it, e.g. *You cannot be serious!*
4 People who are serious are thoughtful, quiet, and do not laugh easily.
seriously (adverb) **seriousness** (noun)

Similar words: (sense 1) grave, severe, critical (sense 4) solemn, sombre, stern, grim

sermon, sermons
(noun) a talk on a religious or moral subject given as part of a church service.
[Latin *sermo* = talk]

serpent, serpents
(noun; literary) a snake.
[Latin *serpere* = to creep]

servant, servants
(noun) someone who is employed to work in another person's house.
[Old French *servir* = to serve]

serve, serves, serving, served
1 (verb) e.g. *He served his country well... She served me with ice cream instead of soup... What purpose does this serve?... He served 5 years in jail... Agassi to serve, first set.*
2 (phrase) If you say that something unpleasant **serves someone right**, you mean that it is their own fault and they deserve it.
[Latin *servus* = slave]

service, services, servicing, serviced
1 (noun) a system organized to provide something for the public, e.g. *the postal service.*
2 The services are the army, navy and air force.
3 In a shop or restaurant, service is the process of being served, e.g. *The service here is poor.*
4 (phrase; formal) To be **of service** to someone means to help them in some way, e.g. *May I be of service to you?*
5 If a vehicle or piece of equipment is **in service**, it is being used or is available for use, e.g. *New trains were now coming into service.* If it is **out of service**, it is not being used.
6 (verb) When a machine or vehicle is serviced, it is examined, adjusted and cleaned so that it will continue working efficiently.
7 (noun) a religious ceremony.
8 When it is your service in a game of tennis or badminton, it is your turn to start.
[Latin *servus* = slave]

service charge
(noun) an amount added to your bill to pay for the service in a restaurant (instead of a tip).

serviceman, servicemen
(noun) a man in the army, navy or air force.

service station, stations
(noun) a place that sells petrol, oil, etc.

serviette, serviettes
(noun) a cloth or paper used when eating to protect the clothes or to wipe the mouth.
[Old French *serviette* = small towel]

Can you make an alphabetical series using only words that have a silent letter? aplomb ballet—

serving, servings
(noun) a helping of food.

session, sessions
1 (noun) a meeting of an official group, e.g. *an emergency session of the Council.*
2 one continuous period of activity, e.g. *a recording session... He ate 96 burgers at a session, then exploded.*
[Latin *sessio* = sitting]

set, sets, setting, set
1 (noun) e.g. *a set of encyclopaedias... a TV set.*
2 In maths, a set is a collection of numbers or other things which are treated as a group.
3 (verb) e.g. *The sun sets in the west... Set the table, please... Set your watches, gentlemen... It is important to set an example... I'm setting you an essay to do... Has the jelly set yet?*
4 (adjective) e.g. *'1984' is a set book for GCSE this year... You can park for a set time only... She is set on becoming a ballet dancer... The play is set in France.*
5 (noun) The set for a play, film, etc. is the scenery or furniture on the stage or in the studio.
6 In tennis, a set is a group of six or more games. There are usually several sets in a match.

set back
(phrasal verb; informal) If something sets you back a lot of money, it costs you that much.

set in
(phrasal verb) If something unpleasant sets in, it begins and seems likely to continue.

set up
(phrasal verb) to make the preparations for something, e.g. *It took a long time to set up the experiment.*

setback, setbacks
(noun) something that delays or hinders you, e.g. *My plan to be an ace rally driver suffered a setback when my car failed its MOT.*

set square, squares
(noun) a triangular piece of plastic or metal used for drawing angles and lines.

settee, settees
(noun) a sofa; a long comfortable seat for a small number of people to sit on.

setting, settings
(noun) The setting of something is its surroundings or circumstances, e.g. *The castle provided the perfect setting for a horror story.*

settle, settles, settling, settled
1 (verb) to sort out and finish, e.g. *The strike was finally settled... She settled the deal... He settled for chips instead.*
2 When you settle a bill, you pay it.
3 to make your permanent home somewhere, e.g. *The Pilgrim Fathers settled in America.*
4 to sit down and make yourself comfortable.

settle down
1 (phrasal verb) When someone settles down, they start living a quiet life in one place. It is particularly used about someone getting married.
2 to become quiet or calm.

settle up
(phrasal verb) When you settle up, you pay a bill.

settlement, settlements
1 (noun) an official agreement between people who have been in conflict, e.g. *There was no real chance of a peaceful settlement with Hitler.*
2 a place where people have settled and built homes.

settler, settlers
(noun) someone who settles in a new country, e.g. *The first white settlers in South Africa were Dutch.*

seven the number 7.
seventh (adjective and noun)

seventeen the number 17.
seventeenth (adjective and noun)

seventy, seventies
the number 70.
seventieth (adjective and noun)

sever, severs, severing, severed
(verb) to cut something off or cut right through it, e.g. *He severed his finger in the machine.*
[Latin *separare* = to separate]

several
(adjective, pronoun) a small number of people or things, e.g. *several days later... I'll have several.*

severe
1 (adjective) extremely bad or unpleasant, e.g. *The blast caused severe damage.*
2 stern and harsh, e.g. *The headteacher was very severe in his punishment.*
severely (adverb) **severity** (noun)
[Latin *severus* = stern or harsh]

sew, sews, sewing, sewed, sewn (pronounced so)
(verb) to join things using a needle and thread.

sewage
(noun) dirty water and waste matter which is carried away in sewers.

sewer, sewers
(noun) a large underground channel that carries sewage to a sewage works.
[Old French *essever* = to drain]

sex, sexes
1 (noun) The sexes are the two groups, male and female, into which people and animals are divided.
2 The sex of a person or animal is their identity as a male or female.
3 the physical activity by which people and animals produce young.

sexism
(noun) discrimination against the members of one sex, usually women.
sexist (adjective and noun)

sextant, sextants
(noun) an instrument used to navigate a ship by the stars.

sextet, sextets
(noun) a group of 6 musicians.
[Latin *sex* = six]

Seven words become plural by changing the main vowel. This is known as the mutated plural....

exual
1 (adjective) connected with the act of sex or with people's desire for sex, e.g. *sexual attraction.*
2 relating to the difference between males and females, e.g. *sexual equality.*
sexually (adverb)

exual intercourse
(noun) the physical act of sex between a man and a woman.

habby, shabbier, shabbiest
(adjective) old and worn in appearance, e.g. *shabby clothes.*
shabbily (adverb) **shabbiness** (noun)
[Old English *sceabb* = scab]

Similar words: threadbare, worn, faded

hack, shacks
(noun) a small hut.

hade, shades, shading, shaded
1 (noun) an area of darkness and coolness which the sun does not reach.
2 (verb) If a place is shaded by trees etc, they prevent the sun from shining on it.
3 (noun) The shades of a colour are its different forms, e.g. *olive is a shade of green.*
4 (plural noun; informal) Shades are another name for sunglasses.

hadow, shadows, shadowing, shadowed
1 (noun) the darkness made by an object when it gets in the way of the light.
2 (verb) To shadow someone means to follow them and watch them closely.
shadowy (adjective)
[Old English *sceadu* = shade]

hadow Cabinet
(noun) The Shadow Cabinet is made up of the leaders of the main opposition party, e.g. *the Shadow Minister of Health.*

hady, shadier, shadiest
1 (adjective) sheltered from sunlight.
2 (informal) Shady people and activities are slightly dishonest and not to be trusted.

haft, shafts
1 (noun) a vertical passage, e.g. *a lift shaft... a mine shaft.*
2 A shaft of light is a beam of light.

haggy, shaggier, shaggiest
(adjective) Shaggy hair or fur is long and untidy.
[Old English *sceacga* = rough hair or wool]

hake, shakes, shaking, shook, shaken
(verb) e.g. *I was shaking like a leaf... He shook her hand... My voice shook as I began to read... The news really shook me... She shook her head.*
shaky (adjective)

Similar words: quake, quiver, tremble, shudder, tremor, shiver

hale
(noun) a smooth soft rock, which breaks easily into flakes.
[Old English *scealu* = shell]

shall
(verb) e.g. *You shall go to the ball, Cinderella... Shall we go to the pictures?*

shallow, shallower, shallowest
(adjective) not deep, e.g. *shallow water... shallow thinking... shallow breathing.*
shallowness (noun)

sham, shams
(noun) a fake, e.g. *The election was a sham.*

shambles
(noun) If an event is a shambles, it is confused and badly organized, e.g. *The rehearsal for the village play was a shambles.*
[Old English *shamble* = meat-seller's table]

shame, shames, shaming, shamed
1 (noun) the feeling of guilt or embarrassment you get when you know you have done something wrong or foolish.
2 (verb) If you shame someone into doing something, you force them to do it by making them feel ashamed not to, e.g. *My brother was shamed into helping with the washing-up.*
3 (noun) If you say something is a shame, you mean you are sorry about it, e.g. *It's a shame he didn't come.*

shameful
(adjective) If someone's behaviour is shameful, they ought to be ashamed of it.
shamefully (adverb)

shameless
(adjective) behaving badly in some way but not being ashamed, e.g. *She was a shameless liar.*
shamelessly (adverb)

shampoo, shampoos
(noun) a liquid for washing hair.
[Hindi *champna* = to knead]

shamrock, shamrocks
(noun) a plant with three round leaves on each stem; the national emblem of Ireland.
[Irish Gaelic *seamrog* = little clover]

shandy, shandies
(noun) a mixed drink of beer and lemonade.

shanty, shanties
(noun) A sea shanty is a song sailors used to sing.
[French *chanter* = to sing]

shape, shapes, shaping, shaped
1 (noun) The shape of something is the form or pattern of its outline.
2 (verb) If you shape an object, you form it into a particular shape, e.g. *He began to shape the dough into rolls.*
3 (phrase) **In good shape** means in good condition.
[Old English *gesceap* = creation or form]

Similar words: (noun) form, formation, line, mould

shape up
(phrasal verb) The way that something is shaping up is the way that it is developing.

share, shares, sharing, shared
1 (verb) If two people share something, they both use it, do it or have it, e.g. *I share a bedroom with my brother, and I don't like it.*
2 (noun) A share of something is a portion of it.

....foot - feet; goose - geese; louse - lice; man - men; mouse - mice; tooth - teeth; woman - women.

3 The shares of a company are the equal parts into which its ownership is divided. People can buy shares as an investment.
[Old English *scearu* = cutting or division]

Similar words: (noun) allocation, ration, lot, cut, portion

shareholder, shareholders
(noun) a person who owns shares in a company.

shark, sharks
1 (noun) a large, powerful fish.
2 a person who cheats people out of money, e.g. *That photocopier salesman was a real shark.*

sharp, sharper, sharpest; sharps
1 (adjective) e.g. *a sharp knife... a sharp movement... a sharp pain.*
2 quick to notice or understand things.
3 sudden and significant, e.g. *a sharp corner.*
4 If you say something in a sharp way, you say it firmly and rather angrily.
5 A sharp taste is slightly sour.
6 (adverb) exactly, e.g. *His train came in at 8 sharp.*
7 (noun) In music, a sharp is a note or key a semitone higher than that described by the same letter, represented by the symbol #.
sharply (adverb) **sharpen** (verb) **sharpness** (noun) **sharpener** (noun)

Similar words: (sense 2) keen, acute

shatter, shatters, shattering, shattered
1 (verb) to break into a lot of small pieces.
2 If you are shattered by an event or piece of news, you are shocked and upset by it.

shattered
(adjective; informal) completely exhausted.

shave, shaves, shaving, shaved
1 (verb) When a man shaves, he removes hair from his face with a razor.
2 to cut very thin pieces from something.
3 (phrase; informal) A **close shave** is a narrow escape.
shaver (noun) **shavings** (plural noun)

shavings
(plural noun) the money placed in a bank account by a person who tends to drink too much.
[Old Norse *shavva* = to put by]

shawl, shawls
(noun) a piece of cloth worn round a woman's head or shoulders or used to wrap a baby in.
[Persian *shal* = shawl]

she
(pronoun) e.g. *She walks in beauty, like the night.*

sheaf, sheaves
(noun) a bundle, for example of papers or corn.

shear, shears, shearing, sheared, shorn
1 (verb) to cut the wool off a sheep.
2 (plural noun) Shears are a tool like a large pair of scissors, used for cutting hedges etc.

shear off
(phrasal verb) If metal shears off, it breaks because it is too weak or under too much strain.

sheath, sheaths
(noun) a covering for the blade of a knife.
sheathe (verb)

shed, sheds, shedding, shed
1 (noun) a small building used as a store.
2 (verb) When an animal sheds hair or skin, some of its hair or skin drops off. When a tree sheds its leaves, its leaves fall off.
3 If you shed tears, you cry.
4 To shed blood means to kill people violently.
[verb: Old English *sceadan* = to drop]

sheep
(noun) a farm animal.
sheepskin (noun)

sheepdog, sheepdogs
(noun) a breed of dog often used for herding sheep.

sheepish
(adjective) If you look sheepish, you look embarrassed because you feel shy or foolish.
sheepishly (adverb)

sheer, sheerest
1 (adjective) complete and total, e.g. *The hotel was sheer luxury... a sheer waste of time.*
2 A sheer cliff or drop is vertical.

sheet, sheets
(noun) e.g. *bed sheets... a sheet of paper... a sheet of glass.*

sheikh, sheikhs (pronounced **shake**)
(noun) an Arab chief or ruler.
[Arabic *shaykh* = old man]

shelf, shelves
(noun) a level piece of wood etc. fixed to a wall and used for putting things on.
[Old English *scylfe* = compartment]

shell, shells, shelling, shelled
1 (noun) a hard, outer covering, e.g. *an egg shell... a snail's shell.*
2 a container filled with explosives that can be fired from a gun.
3 (verb) to fire shells at a place, e.g. *Whitby Abbey was shelled in World War I.*

shellfish
(noun) a small sea creature with a shell.

shelter, shelters, sheltering, sheltered
1 (noun) a small building made to protect people from bad weather or danger.
2 (verb) If you shelter in a place, you stay there and are safe. If you shelter someone you look after them.

shepherd, shepherds
(noun) a person who looks after sheep.
[Old English *scep* = sheep + *hierde* = keeper of a herd]

shepherd's pie, pies
(noun) a dish of minced meat covered with mashed potatoes and baked in an oven.

sherbet
(noun) a sweet, fizzy powder in sweets and drinks.
[Arabic *sharbah* = drink]

The sound SH can be spelled: ship ocean nation version procession magician machine.

sheriff, sheriffs
1 (noun) In the USA, a sheriff is a person elected to enforce the law in a county.
2 In Scotland, a sheriff is a senior judge.
[Old English *scir* = shire + *gerefa* = reeve, an official]

sherry, sherries
(noun) a kind of strong wine.
[from *Jerez* in Spain where it was first made]

shield, shields, shielding, shielded
1 (noun) A shield is a large piece of metal that soldiers used to carry to protect themselves.
2 (verb) to protect, e.g. *She shielded her child from the death ray.*

shift, shifts, shifting, shifted
1 (verb) to move, e.g. *He shifted the chair closer to the bed.*
2 (noun) a set period during which people work in a factory, e.g. *the night shift.*

shifty, shiftier, shiftiest
(adjective) looking sly and deceitful.
shiftiness (noun)

shimmer, shimmers, shimmering, shimmered
(verb) If something shimmers, it shines with a faint, flickering light, e.g. *The sea shimmered in the sunlight.*

shin, shins, shinning, shinned
1 (noun) the front part of your leg.
2 (verb) If you shin up a tree or pole, you climb it quickly by gripping it with your hands and legs.

shine, shines, shining, shone
1 (verb) e.g. *The sun shone all day... His eyes shone like stars... Shine your torch in there.*
2 If you shine at something, you are very good at it, e.g. *He shines at hockey.*
shiny (adjective)

shingle, shingles
(noun) small pebbles on the seashore.

ship, ships, shipping, shipped
1 (noun) a large boat.
2 (verb) If people or things are shipped somewhere, they are transported there.

shipping
1 (noun) the transport of cargo on ships.
2 You can also refer to ships generally as shipping, e.g. *Attention all shipping!*

shipshape
(adjective) neat and tidy.

shipwreck, shipwrecks, shipwrecking, shipwrecked
1 (noun) When there is a shipwreck, a ship is destroyed at sea.
2 (verb) If someone is shipwrecked, they survive a shipwreck and manage to reach land.

shipyard, shipyards
(noun) a place where ships are built and repaired.

shirk, shirks, shirking, shirked
(verb) To shirk a job means to avoid doing it.
shirker (noun)

shirt, shirts
(noun) a piece of clothing.

shirty
(adjective; informal) bad-tempered.

shiver, shivers, shivering, shivered
1 (verb) When you shiver, you tremble slightly because you are cold or frightened.
2 (noun) e.g. *The howling sent a shiver down my spine.*
shivery (adjective)

shoal, shoals
(noun) a large group of fish.

shock, shocks, shocking, shocked
1 (noun) If you have a shock, you have a sudden, upsetting experience.
2 (verb) If something shocks you, it upsets you because it is unpleasant and unexpected, e.g. *She was deeply shocked by her husband's death.*
[Old French *choquier* = to meet violently]

shocking
(adjective; informal) very bad, e.g. *His liver was in a shocking state because of all the drink.*

shoddy, shoddier, shoddiest
(adjective) badly done, e.g. *shoddy work.*

shoe, shoes
(noun) e.g. *High-heeled shoes damage your feet.*

shoot, shoots, shooting, shot
1 (verb) to fire a gun, arrow, etc.
2 to move very quickly e.g. *She shot back into the room.*
3 When a film is shot, it is filmed, e.g. *Most of the film was shot in Spain.*
4 In games, to shoot means to kick or hit the ball towards the goal.
5 (noun) a plant that is beginning to grow, or a new part growing from a plant.

shoot up
(phrasal verb) If something shoots up, it grows or increases very quickly, e.g. *Prices shot up.*

shooting star, stars
(noun) a meteor.

shop, shops, shopping, shopped
1 (verb, noun) e.g. *Where do you shop for your groceries?... I bought my suit at the Oxfam shop.*
shopper (noun)
2 (verb; informal) To shop someone means to tell e.g. the police what the person has done wrong.
[Old French *eschoppe* = stall or booth]

shop around
(phrasal verb) If you shop around, you compare goods in several shops before you buy them.

shopfloor
(noun) the part of a factory where the product is made.

shopkeeper, shopkeepers
(noun) someone who owns or manages a small shop.

shoplifting
(noun) stealing goods from shops.
shoplifter (noun)

shopsoiled
(adjective) Shopsoiled goods are slightly dirty or damaged.

shore, shores
(noun) land along the edge of a sea, lake etc.
[Old Dutch *schore*]

short, shorter, shortest; shorts
1 (adjective) e.g. *a short talk... a short hair cut... the short way home... a short temper... We are short of money... 'Mr' is short for 'mister'.*
2 (noun) Shorts are trousers with short legs.
3 If something is **cut short**, it is stopped before it has finished.
4 A **short cut** is a quick way of doing something.
shorten (verb)

shortage, shortages
(noun) If there is a shortage of something, there is not enough of it.

shortbread or **shortcake**
(noun) a crumbly biscuit made from flour and butter.
[*short* used to mean crumbly]

short circuit, circuits
(noun) an electrical fault, when two points accidentally become connected and the electricity travels directly between them, not through the complete circuit.

shorthand
(noun) a very quick way of writing in which signs represent words or syllables.

shortly
(adverb) soon, e.g. *She's leaving shortly.*

short-sighted
1 (adjective) If you are short-sighted, you cannot see things clearly when they are far away.
2 A short-sighted decision does not take account of the way things may develop in the future.

short-tempered
(adjective) Someone who is short-tempered loses their temper easily.

short-term
(adjective) happening only for a short time.

shot, shots
1 (verb) the past tense and past participle of **shoot**.
2 (noun) e.g. *She fired a shot... He's a good shot with a gun... a 25-yard shot at goal... The film included good shots of New York.*
3 (informal) If you have a shot at something, you try to do it.
4 (informal) A shot of a drug is an injection of it.
5 (phrase; informal) If you do something **like a shot**, you do it quickly and eagerly.

shotgun, shotguns
(noun) a gun that fires a lot of small pellets.

shot put
(noun) an athletics event in which the contestants throw a heavy ball called a shot.
shot putter (noun)

should
(verb) e.g. *Crimes should be punished... She should have won... We should be there by 8... I should like to say a few words... If we should be seen together, they might get suspicious... It's strange that you should come today... I should think it was about 12 years ago.*

shoulder, shoulders
(noun) Shoulders are the parts of your body immediately below your neck.
shoulder blade (noun)

shout, shouts, shouting, shouted
(verb) e.g. *She shouted at us for breaking the window.*

Similar words: call, cry, yell, roar, bellow, bawl

shove, shoves, shoving, shoved
(verb) to push roughly, e.g. *He shoved the man through the door.*
[Old English *scufan* = to push]

shove off
(phrasal verb; informal) If you tell someone to shove off, you are telling them angrily and rudely to go away.

shovel, shovels
(noun) a tool like a wide, curved spade.

show, shows, showing, showed, shown
1 (verb) e.g. *This fingerprint shows the man must have been here... The picture shows two cats fighting... Let me show you the garden... Show me how it works... He showed great kindness... Your slip is showing.*
2 (noun) e.g. *a TV show... a flower show.*
3 (phrase) If something is **on show**, it is being exhibited for the public to see.

Similar words: (verb) demonstrate, reveal, exhibit
(noun) exhibit, exhibition, spectacle, performance, presentation, display

show off
(phrasal verb; informal) If someone is showing off, they are trying to impress people.
show-off (noun)

show up
1 (phrasal verb; informal) to arrive.
2 to be seen clearly, e.g. *Light colours will show up well.*
3 (informal) If someone shows you up, they embarrass you by behaving badly.

show business
(noun) entertainment in the theatre, films and TV.

shower, showers, showering, showered
1 (noun) a device which sprays you with water so that you can wash yourself.
2 a short period of rain.
3 (verb) If you are showered with a lot of things, they fall on you or you receive them.
showery (adjective)

show-jumping
(noun) a horse-riding competition in which the horses jump over walls and fences.

showroom, showrooms
(noun) a shop where goods, for example cars or electrical machines, are displayed.

shred, shreds, shredding, shredded
1 (verb) If you shred something, you cut or tear it into very small pieces.
2 (noun) a small piece of something.
shredder (noun)

Do you know where these bones are? mandible scapula sternum femur pelvis

shrew, shrews (pronounced **shroo**)
1 (noun) a small mouse-like animal.
2 a bad-tempered woman, e.g. Katharina in *The Taming of the Shrew*.

shrewd, shrewder, shrewdest
(adjective) Someone who is shrewd is intelligent and makes good judgements.
shrewdly (adverb) **shrewdness** (noun)

shriek, shrieks, shrieking, shrieked
(verb) to make a high-pitched scream.

shrill, shriller, shrillest
(adjective) A shrill sound is unpleasantly high-pitched and piercing.

shrimp, shrimps
(noun) a small, edible shellfish.

shrine, shrines
(noun) a place of worship linked with a sacred person or object.
[Latin *scrinium* = bookcase; originally it referred to a container of sacred relics]

shrink, shrinks, shrinking, shrank, shrunk
(verb) to become smaller.
shrunken (adjective)

shrivel, shrivels, shrivelling, shrivelled
(verb) to become dry and withered, e.g. *The grapes shrivelled in the sun.*

shrub, shrubs
(noun) a low, bushy plant.

shrubbery, shrubberies
(noun) part of a garden where there are a lot of shrubs.

shrug, shrugs, shrugging, shrugged
(verb) If you shrug your shoulders, you raise them slightly as a sign of not caring.

shrug off
(phrasal verb) If you shrug something off, you ignore it or treat it as unimportant e.g. *She shrugs off any criticism of her methods.*

shudder, shudders, shuddering, shuddered
(verb) to tremble with fear or horror, or to shake violently.
[Old German *schoderen* = to shake]

shuffle, shuffles, shuffling, shuffled
1 (verb) to walk without lifting your feet properly off the ground.
2 If you shuffle about, you move about and fidget because you feel uncomfortable.
3 to mix up a pack of cards.

shun, shuns, shunning, shunned
(verb) If you shun someone or something, you deliberately avoid them.

shut, shuts, shutting, shut
(verb, adjective) e.g. *Shut that door!... The shop is shut.*

shut down
(phrasal verb) When a factory or business is shut down, it is closed permanently.

shutter, shutters
1 (noun) a hinged wooden or metal cover fitted on the outside or inside of a window.
2 The shutter in a camera is the part which opens to allow light through the lens.

shuttle, shuttles
1 (adjective) A shuttle service or shuttle is an air, bus or train service which makes frequent journeys between two places.
2 the part of a loom which takes a thread backwards and forwards over other threads to weave cloth.
3 A **space shuttle** is a spacecraft for travelling out into space and back again many times.
[Old English *scytel* = bolt or dart, from the shape and movement of the shuttle of a loom]

shuttlecock, shuttlecocks
(noun) the feathered object which is hit in the game of badminton.

shy, shyer, shyest; shies, shying, shied
1 (adjective) nervous and uncomfortable in the company of other people.
2 (verb) When a horse shies, it moves away suddenly because something has frightened it.
shyly (adverb) **shyness** (noun)

Similar words: (adjective) timid, retiring, reserved

sibling, siblings
(noun; formal) Your siblings are your brothers and sisters.
[Old English *sibling* = relative]

sick, sicker, sickest
1 (adjective) ill, e.g. *He's off sick.*
2 angry or fed up, e.g. *It makes me sick!... I'm sick of doing this day after day.*
3 (informal) A sick joke deals with death or suffering in an unpleasantly light-hearted way.
sickness (noun)

sick bay, bays
(noun) an area, for example, on a ship, where people who are ill can receive treatment.

sicken, sickens, sickening, sickened
(verb) If something sickens you, it makes you feel disgusted.
sickening (adjective)

sickle, sickles
(noun) a tool with a short handle and a curved blade used for cutting grass or grain.
[Latin *secare* = to cut]

sickly, sicklier, sickliest
(adjective) weak and unhealthy.

side, sides, siding, sided
1 (noun) e.g. *the left-hand side... Will you play on my side?*
2 (verb) If you side with someone in an argument, you support them.
3 If you keep **on the right side** of someone, you stay friends with them. If you get **on the wrong side** of someone, you annoy them and make them dislike you.

sideboard, sideboards
(noun) a long, low cupboard for plates etc.

sideburns
(plural noun) A man's sideburns are areas of hair growing on his cheeks in front of his ears.
[from a 19th-century US army general called *Burnside* who wore his whiskers like this]

Idioms. What kinds of persons are: self-conscious self-made self-possesed self-seeking

side effect, effects
(noun) The side effects of a drug are the effects
it has in addition to its main purpose, e.g. *A side
effect of taking too much aspirin is ringing in
the ears* (True!).

sidelong
(adverb, adjective) out of the corner of your eye,
e.g. *a sidelong look.*

sideshow, sideshows
(noun) a stall at a fairground.

sidetrack, sidetracks, sidetracking, sidetracked
(verb) If you are sidetracked, you forget what
you are supposed to be doing or saying and start
doing or talking about something else.

sideways
(adverb, adjective) e.g. *She turned sideways and
her nose stuck out... a sideways glance.*

sidle, sidles, sidling, sidled
(verb) to walk cautiously and slowly, as if you
do not want to be noticed.

siege, sieges (pronounced **seej**)
(noun) a military operation in which an army
surrounds a place and prevents food or help
from reaching the people inside.

sieve, sieves, sieving, sieved (pronounced **siv**)
(noun) a kitchen implement used for sifting or
straining things.

sift, sifts, sifting, sifted
(verb) If you sift a powdery substance, you pass
it through a sieve to remove lumps.

sigh, sighs, sighing, sighed
(verb) to let out a deep breath.

sight, sights, sighting, sighted
1 (noun) the ability to see, e.g. *Her sight is
failing.*
2 something you see, e.g. *an amazing sight.*
3 (verb) If you sight someone or something, you
see them briefly or suddenly, e.g. *The missing
woman has been sighted in Birmingham.*
4 (phrases) If something is **in sight**, you can see
it. If it is **out of sight**, you cannot see it.
5 If you **set your sights** on something, you decide
you want it and try hard to obtain it.

sight-read, sight-reads, sight-reading, sight-read
(verb) If you can sight-read, you can play or sing
music from a printed sheet without practice.

sightseeing
(noun) visiting the interesting places that
tourists usually visit.
sightseer (noun)

sign, signs, signing, signed
1 (noun) a mark, gesture, etc. that has a
particular meaning, e.g. *The 'equals' sign... a 'V'
sign... a road sign.*
2 If there are signs of something, there is
evidence that it exists or is happening.
3 (verb) to write your name, e.g. *Please sign my
autograph book.*
[Latin *signum* = mark]

sign up
(phrasal verb) If you sign up for a job or course,
you officially agree to do it by signing a contract.

signal, signals, signalling, signalled
1 (verb) If you signal to someone, you make a
gesture or sound to give them a message.
2 (noun) A railway signal is a piece of equipment
which tells train drivers whether to stop or not.
[Latin *signum* = sign or mark]

signature, signatures
(noun) If you write your signature, you write
your name the way you usually write it.
[Latin *signare* = to sign]

signature tune, tunes
(noun) the tune which is played at the beginning
or end of a particular TV or radio programme.

significant
1 (adjective) important, e.g. *a significant
discovery.*
2 A significant action or gesture has a special
meaning, e.g. *With a significant look at her
husband, she went out.*
significance (noun) **significantly** (adverb)
signify (verb)
[Latin *significare* = to mean]

sign language
(noun) a way of communicating using your
hands, used especially by the deaf.

signpost, signposts
(noun) an old-style road sign giving directions
and distances.

Sikh, Sikhs (pronounced **seek**)
(noun) a person who believes in Sikhism, an
Indian religion.
[Hindi *sikh* = disciple]

silage (pronounced **sigh**-lij)
(noun) grass for cattle food, which is harvested
when it is green and kept in a silo.

silence, silences, silencing, silenced
1 (noun) absolute quietness.
2 (verb) To silence someone or something means
to stop them talking or making a noise.

Similar words: (verb) muffle, gag, hush, muzzle

silencer, silencers
(noun) a device on a car exhaust or a gun which
makes it quieter.

silent
1 (adjective) If you are silent, you are not saying
anything.
2 When something is silent, it makes no noise.
[Latin *silere* = to be quiet]

Similar words: (sense 1) mute, dumb

silhouette, silhouettes (pronounced sil-loo-**ett**)
(noun) the outline of a dark shape against a light
background.

silicon
(noun) a chemical found in sand, clay and stone,
used to make glass and also silicon chips in
computers.

silk, silks
(noun) a fine, soft cloth made from a substance
produced by silkworms.
silky (adjective)

The word 'silly' once meant happy and blessed. It came to mean innocent, then simple and now foolish.

sill, sills
(noun) a ledge at the bottom of a window.

silly, sillier, silliest
(adjective) foolish or childish.

Similar words: daft, senseless

silo, silos (pronounced **sigh**-low)
1 (noun) a tall, metal tower on a farm in which silage is stored.
2 a place underground where a nuclear missile is kept ready to be launched.
[Greek *siros* = pit to store corn in]

silt, silts, silting, silted
1 (noun) fine sand or soil carried by a river.
2 (verb) If a river or lake silts up, it becomes blocked with silt.

silver
1 (noun) valuable metal used for making jewellery and ornaments.
2 coins made from silver or from silver-coloured metal, e.g. *My float was £5 in silver.*
silvery (adjective)

silver jubilee, jubilees
(noun) the 25th anniversary of an important event.

silver paper
(noun) thin, metal foil used for wrapping.

silver wedding, weddings
(noun) the 25th anniversary of a wedding.

similar
1 (adjective) alike, e.g. *Trevor is similar in looks to Janet.*
2 In maths, two triangles are similar if the angles in one match exactly the angles in the other.
similarly (adverb)

similarity, similarities
(noun) If there is a similarity between things, they are alike in some way.

Similar words: likeness, resemblance

simile, similes (pronounced **sim**-ill-ee)
(noun) an expression in which a person or thing is described as being similar to someone or something else. e.g. *He has a nose like Concorde... She had a face like a bag of spanners.*
[Latin *simile* = something similar]

simmer, simmers, simmering, simmered
(verb) When food simmers, it cooks gently at just below boiling point.

simple, simpler, simplest
1 (adjective) easy to understand or do.
2 plain, e.g. *a simple brown dress.*
3 A simple way of life is uncomplicated.
4 Someone who is simple is mentally retarded.
simplicity (noun)
[Latin *simplex* = plain]

simplify, simplifies, simplifying, simplified
(verb) to make something easier to do or understand.
simplification (noun)
[Latin *simplus* = simple + *facere* = to make]

simply
1 (adverb) e.g. *It's simply a question of hard work... I simply can't believe it.*
2 If you say or write something simply, you do it in a way that makes it easy to understand.

simulate, simulates, simulating, simulated
(verb) to imitate something, e.g. *The wood is carved to simulate hair... This machine simulates an aircraft flight.*
simulation (noun)
[Latin *simulare* = to copy]

simulator, simulators
(noun) a device designed to imitate actual conditions, e.g. to train pilots or astronauts.

simultaneous
(adjective) Things that are simultaneous happen at the same time.
simultaneously (adverb)
[Latin *simul* = at the same time]

sin, sins, sinning, sinned
(verb) to do something wicked and immoral.
sinful (adjective) **sinner** (noun)
[Old English *synn* = wrongdoing]

since
(preposition, adverb, conjunction) e.g. *I've been wearing glasses since I was three... He used to be an art student. He has since become a lawyer... Noise is a problem since we're close to the airport.*
[Old English *siththan* = after that]

sincere
(adjective) If you are sincere, you say things that you really mean, e.g. *The apology was sincere.*
sincerity (noun)

Similar words: genuine, honest

sincerely
(phrase) You write **yours sincerely** before your signature at the end of a formal letter.
[Latin **sincerus** = genuine; from *sine cera* = without wax; a scroll containing a truthful message did not need wax to seal it.]

sing, sings, singing, sang, sung
(verb) e.g. *Singing in the Rain.*

singe, singes, singeing, singed
(verb) to burn something slightly so that it goes brown.

single, singles, singling, singled
1 (adjective) only one and not more, e.g. *We heard a single shot.*
2 not married, e.g. *a single woman.*
3 A single bed or bedroom is for one person.
4 A single ticket is a one-way ticket.
5 (noun) A single is a small record, tape or CD with one or two songs on it.
6 Singles is a game of tennis, badminton, or squash between just two players.
7 (phrase) If a group of people walk **in single file**, they walk in a line, one behind the other.
singly (adverb)
[Latin *singulus* = individual]

single out
(phrasal verb) If you single someone out from a

A paragraph is made up of one or more sentences dealing with a single main idea.

group, you give them special treatment, e.g. *Three people were singled out for praise.*

single-handed
(adverb) on your own, without any help.

single-minded
(adjective) A single-minded person has only one aim and is determined to achieve it.

singlet, singlets
(noun) a sleeveless vest.

singular
(noun) In grammar, the singular is the form of a word that refers to just one person or thing. [opposite: **plural**]

sinister
(adjective) seeming harmful or evil, e.g. *A sinister figure appeared.* [Latin *sinister* = left-hand side, because the left side was considered unlucky]

sink, sinks, sinking, sank, sunk
1 (noun) e.g. *the kitchen sink.*
2 (verb) e.g *The boat sank to the bottom of the lake... The U-boat sank the destroyer... The value of the pound sank today... He sank his teeth into an apple.*

sink in
(phrasal verb) When a fact sinks in, you realize it, e.g. *It took a moment for her words to sink in.*

sip, sips, sipping, sipped
(verb) to drink very slowly.

siphon, siphons, siphoning, siphoned (pronounced **sigh**-fn)
(verb) If you siphon off a liquid, you draw it out of a container through a tube and transfer it to another place. [Greek *siphōn* = tube]

sir
e.g. *Good morning, sir... Sir John Betjeman.* [Latin *senior* = an elder]

siren, sirens
(noun) a warning device, for example on a police car, which makes a loud, wailing noise. [The Sirens in Greek mythology were sea nymphs who had beautiful voices and sang to lure sailors to their deaths on the rocks where they lived.]

sirloin
(noun) a cut of beef from a cow's back. [Old French *sur* = above + *longe* = loin]

sissy, sissies; also spelled **cissy**
(noun; informal) a weak, cowardly boy.

sister, sisters
1 (noun) Your sister is the girl or woman who has the same parents as you. Your **half-sister** has one parent the same as you, and one parent different. If your parents get divorced and remarry other people, your **stepsister** would be a child of the people they marry.
2 a member of a female religious order.
3 a senior nurse in charge of a hospital ward.
4 (adjective) closely related to something or very similar to it, e.g. *Her sister ship was sunk by a torpedo.*

sister-in-law, sisters-in-law
(noun) Your sister-in-law is the wife of your brother, the sister of your husband or wife, or the woman married to your wife's or husband's brother.

sit, sits, sitting, sat
1 (verb) e.g. *Please sit down... I'm sitting an exam tomorrow... May I sit in on your meeting... Parliament is sitting tonight.*
2 (phrase) If you **sit tight**, you remain where you are, do nothing, and wait.
3 (phrasal verb) If you **sit back,** you relax and do not become involved in something.

sitcom, sitcoms
(noun; informal) a TV comedy series which shows characters in amusing situations similar to everyday life. [from *situation comedy*]

site, sites
(noun) a piece of ground where a particular thing happens or is situated, e.g. *a caravan site... the site of the murder.* [Latin *situs* = situation]

sit-in, sit-ins
(noun) a protest in which people sit in a public place for a long time.

sitting, sittings
(noun) one of the times when a meal is served e.g. *First sitting for lunch is at 12 noon.*

situated
(adjective) If something is situated somewhere, that is where it is, e.g. *The control centre is situated between Southampton and Portsmouth.* [Latin *situare* = to position]

situation, situations
1 (noun) what is happening in a particular place at a particular time, e.g. *the economic situation... the Hong Kong situation.*
2 The situation of a building etc. is its place.
3 a job, e.g. *Situations vacant.*

Similar words: (sense 1) circumstances, position, state, condition

six, sixes
1 the number 6.
2 (phrase) To be **at sixes and sevens** means to be completely disorganized.
sixth (adjective and noun)

sixteen the number 16.
sixteenth (adjective and noun)

sixth sense
(noun) You say that someone has a sixth sense when they know something by instinct without having any proof of it.

sixty, sixties
the number 60.
sixtieth (adjective and noun)

size, sizes
1 (noun) The size of something is how big or small it is, e.g. *The population increased in size.*
2 The size of something is also the fact that it is very large, e.g. *The sheer size of the world is amazing.*

Do you know where these bones are? tibia humerus clavicle patella rib

Similar words: (sense 1) dimension, proportions, measurement

size up
(phrasal verb) If you size up situations, you look at them carefully and make judgements about them.

sizeable
(adjective) fairly large, e.g. *a sizeable amount.*

sizzle, sizzles, sizzling, sizzled
(verb) to make a hissing sound like the sound of frying food, e.g. *Chinese-style sizzling beef.*

skate, skates, skating, skated
1 (verb) If you skate, you move about on ice wearing ice skates.
2 (noun) Skates are shoes for ice or roller skating.

skateboard, skateboards
(noun) a narrow board on wheels which people stand on and ride for pleasure.
skateboarder (noun) **skateboarding** (noun)

skeleton, skeletons
(noun) the framework of bones in the body.
[Greek *skeleton* = dried up]

sketch, sketches, sketching, sketched
1 (verb) If you sketch something, you draw it quickly and roughly.
2 (noun) a quick, rough drawing.
3 a short, humorous piece of acting, usually forming part of a comedy show.
[Latin *schedius* = hastily made]

sketchy, sketchier, sketchiest
(adjective) giving only a rough description, e.g. *a sketchy outline.*

ski, skis, skiing, skied
1 (verb) When you ski, you move on snow wearing skis, especially as a sport.
2 (noun) Skis are long thin platforms, made to be clamped on to the boots for travelling on snow.
[Old Norse *skith* = snowshoes]

skid, skids, skidding, skidded
(verb) If a vehicle skids, it slides sideways or forwards in an uncontrolled way.

skilful
(adjective) If you are skilful at something, you can do it very well.
skilfully (adverb)

Similar words: able, skilled, deft, expert, proficient, adept

skill, skills
1 (noun) the knowledge and ability that enables you to do something well.
2 A skill is a type of work or technique which requires special training and knowledge.
skilled (adjective)
[Old Norse *skil* = distinction or knowledge]

Similar words: (sense 1) ability, artistry, craft, proficiency

skimmed milk
(noun) milk which has had the cream removed.

skimp, skimps, skimping, skimped
(verb) If you skimp on a task, you do it carelessly or using less material than you should.

skimpy, skimpier, skimpiest
(adjective) inadequate in size or amount, e.g. *skimpy cotton frocks.*

skin, skins, skinning, skinned
1 (noun) an outer covering, for example, of the body or of fruit.
2 (verb) If you skin a dead animal, you remove its skin.
3 (phrase) If you do something **by the skin of your teeth**, you only just manage to do it.
[Old English *scinn* = skin]

skin diving
(noun) the sport of swimming underwater using breathing apparatus.
skin-diver (noun)

skinflint, skinflints
(noun; informal) a very mean person.

skinhead, skinheads
(noun) usually one of a group of youths who wear heavy boots and have their hair closely shaved.

skinny, skinnier, skinniest
(adjective) extremely thin.

skint
(adjective; informal) having no money [from 'skinned'].

skip, skips, skipping, skipped
1 (verb) e.g. *Violet Elizabeth skipped along.*
2 If you skip something, you miss it out or avoid doing it, e.g. *I decided to skip lunch.*
3 (noun) a large, transportable metal container for holding rubbish.

skipper, skippers
(noun; informal) the captain of a ship.
[Old Dutch *schipper* = shipper]

skirt, skirts
(noun) a piece of woman's clothing.
[Old Norse *skyrta* = shirt]

skirting board, boards
(noun) a narrow strip of wood running along the bottom of a wall in a room.

skittles
(noun) a game in which players roll a ball and try to knock down wooden pins called skittles.

skive, skives, skiving, skived
(verb; informal) to avoid working by staying away from a place.
skiver (noun)

skull, skulls
(noun) the bony part of your head.

skunk, skunks
(noun) a small black and white animal from North America which gives off an unpleasant smell when it is frightened.
[a North American Indian word]

sky, skies
(noun) the space around the earth.
[Old Norse *sky* = cloud]

Can you make anagrams of: skin life dare parts verse north south east west deaf smile mean?

skyscraper, skyscrapers
(noun) a very tall building.

slab, slabs
(noun) a thick, flat piece of something.

slack, slacker, slackest
1 (adjective) loose and not firmly stretched.
2 A slack period is one in which there is not much work to do.
3 If you are slack in your work, you do not do it properly or thoroughly.
slackly (adverb) **slackness** (noun) **slacken** (verb)

slag, slags, slagging, slagged
1 (verb; informal) To slag someone off means to criticize them in an unpleasant way, usually behind their back.
2 (noun) the waste material from the smelting of metals. A **slag heap** is a large mound of this.

slam, slams, slamming, slammed
(verb) to shut noisily and with great force.

slander
(noun) something said about someone which is untrue and malicious.

slang
(noun) very informal words and expressions.
[possibly from s(ecret) lang(uage)]

slant, slants, slanting, slanted
(verb) If something slants, it slopes, e.g. *The old wooden roof slanted a little.*

slap, slaps, slapping, slapped
(verb) e.g. *She slapped his face... He slapped some paper on the wall.*
[German *Schlappe*, an imitation of the sound]

slapdash
(adjective) done quickly and carelessly, e.g. *Why is your homework so slapdash, James?*

slapstick
(noun) rough, boisterous comedy.

slash, slashes, slashing, slashed
1 (verb) to make a long, deep cut in something, e.g. *Her tyres had been slashed.*
2 (noun) a diagonal line that separates letters, words or numbers, e.g. in 340/21/K.
[**backslash**: e.g. 340\21\K]

slate, slates, slating, slated
1 (noun) a dark grey rock that splits easily into thin layers, used for roofs.
2 (verb) If critics slate a play, film or book, they criticize it severely.
[Old French *esclat* = fragment or splinter]

slaughter, slaughters, slaughtering, slaughtered
1 (noun) the killing of many people.
2 (verb) To slaughter farm animals means to kill them for meat.

Similar word: (noun) massacre

slaughterhouse, slaughterhouses
(noun) a place where farm animals are killed for meat.

slave, slaves, slaving, slaved
1 (noun) someone who is owned by another person and must work for them for no money.

2 (verb) If you slave for someone, you work very hard, e.g. *Look at me, slaving over a hot stove.*

slavery (noun)
[Latin *Sclavus* = a Slav, because Slavonic races were frequently conquered and made into slaves]

slave-driver, slave-drivers
(noun; informal) someone who makes people work very hard.

slay, slays, slaying, slew, slain
(verb; literary) to kill.

sleazy, sleazier, sleaziest
(adjective) dirty, run-down and not respectable, e.g. *a sleazy bar.*

sledge, sledges or **sled**
(noun) a vehicle on runners used for travelling over snow.

sledgehammer, sledgehammers
(noun) a heavy hammer with a long handle.
[Old English *slecg* = large hammer]

sleek, sleeker, sleekest
(adjective) Sleek hair is smooth and shiny.

sleep, sleeps, sleeping, slept
1 (verb, noun) e.g. *To sleep: perchance to dream... For in that sleep of death what dreams may come?*
2 (verb) If a house sleeps a particular number of people, it has beds for that number.
3 (phrase) If a sick or injured animal is **put to sleep**, it is painlessly killed.
sleepy (adjective)

Similar words: doze, snooze, nap, slumber, forty winks

sleeping bag, bags
(noun) a large, warm bag for sleeping in.

sleepwalk, sleepwalks, sleepwalking, sleepwalked
(verb) to walk around while asleep.

sleet
(noun) a mixture of rain and snow.
[Old German *sloten* = hail]

sleeve, sleeves
1 (noun) The sleeves of a piece of clothing are the parts that cover your arms.
2 the stiff envelope in which a record is kept.
sleeveless (adjective)

sleigh, sleighs (pronounced **slay**)
(noun) a sledge.
[Old Dutch *slee* = sledge]

slender
(adjective) attractively thin and graceful.

slice, slices, slicing, sliced
1 (noun) a piece of cake, bread, etc. cut from a larger piece.
2 a kitchen tool with a broad, flat blade, e.g. *a fish slice.*
3 (verb) to cut food into thin pieces.
[Old French *esclice* = piece split off]

slick, slicker, slickest; slicks
1 (adjective) A slick action is done quickly and smoothly, e.g. *There was some slick baton-changing in the 400m relay.*

2 (noun) An oil slick is a layer of oil floating on the surface of the sea or a lake.

slide, slides, sliding, slid
1 (verb) to move smoothly over or against something else.
2 (noun) a piece of film used in a projector.
3 a small piece of glass on which you put something that you want to examine through a microscope.
4 a slope for children to slide down.

slight, slighter, slightest
1 (adjective) small in amount or degree, e.g. *He had a slight German accent.*
2 (phrase) **Not in the slightest** means not at all, e.g. *My tennis hadn't improved in the slightest.*
slightly (adverb)

slim, slimmer, slimmest; slims, slimming, slimmed
1 (adjective) attractively thin.
2 (verb) If you are slimming, you are trying to lose weight.
3 If there is only a slim chance that something will happen, it is unlikely to happen.
slimmer (noun) **slimness** (noun)

slime
(noun) an unpleasant, thick, slippery substance.
slimy (adjective)
[Old English *slim* = soft sticky mud]

sling, slings, slinging, slung
1 (verb; informal) If you sling something somewhere, you throw it there.
2 If you sling a rope between two points, you attach it so that it hangs loosely between them.
3 (noun) a device made of ropes or cloth used for carrying things, e.g. *Many mothers carry their babies around in slings.*
4 a piece of cloth tied round a person's neck to support a broken or injured arm.

slink, slinks, slinking, slunk
(verb) to move in a slow, quiet, secretive way.
[Old English *slincan* = to creep]

slip, slips, slipping, slipped
1 (verb) e.g. *He slipped and fell... She slipped out of the room... I slipped it into my pocket... Production has slipped by 12% in a year.*
2 (phrase) If something **slips your mind**, you forget about it.
3 If you **give someone the slip**, you manage to escape from them.
4 (noun) a small mistake.
5 A slip of paper is a small piece of paper.
6 a piece of clothing worn under a dress or skirt.

slip up
(phrasal verb; informal) to make a mistake.
slip-up (noun)

slippers
(noun) loose, soft shoes worn indoors.

slippery
(adjective) smooth, wet or greasy, and difficult to hold or walk on.

slipshod
(adjective) done in a careless or untidy way, e.g. *a slipshod piece of work.*

[originally meant wearing slippers or loose shoes; hence carelessly dressed]

slipway, slipways
(noun) a platform sloping down into the water, on which ships are built and launched.

slit, slits, slitting, slit
(verb) to make a long, narrow cut in something.
[Old English *slitan* = to slice]

slither, slithers, slithering, slithered
(verb) to slide along the ground in an uneven way, e.g. *A huge snake slithered under my bed.*
[Old English *slidan* = to slide]

slob, slobs
(noun; informal) a lazy, untidy person.

slog, slogs, slogging, slogged
(verb; informal) to work hard and steadily, e.g. *slogging away at revision.*

slogan, slogans
(noun) a short, easily-remembered phrase used in advertising or by a political party, e.g. *Beanz meanz Heinz.*
[Gaelic *sluagh-ghairm* = war cry]

Similar words: catchphrase, motto

slop, slops, slopping, slopped
1 (verb) to spill over in a messy way.
2 (plural noun) Dirty water or liquid waste is often called the slops.

slope, slopes, sloping, sloped
1 (verb) If a surface slopes, it is at an angle.
2 (noun) The slope of something is the angle at which it slopes, e.g. *a slope of 10°.*
[Old English *aslope* = slanting]

Similar words: incline, tilt, slant, gradient

sloppy, sloppier, sloppiest
1 (adjective; informal) very messy or careless, e.g. *a sloppy piece of work.*
2 foolishly sentimental, e.g. *sloppy love scenes.*
sloppily (adverb) **sloppiness** (noun)

slot, slots, slotting, slotted
1 (noun) a narrow opening in a machine or container, for example to put coins in.
2 (verb) When you slot something into something else, you put it into a space where it fits.
slot machine (noun)

slouch, slouches, slouching, slouched
(verb) to stand or sit with your shoulders and head drooping forwards.

slovenly (pronounced sluv-ven-lee)
(adjective) untidy and careless.

slow, slower, slowest; slows, slowing, slowed
1 (adjective, verb) e.g. *slow music... slow changes... the car slowed down... He's rather slow at school.*
2 If a clock or watch is slow, it shows a time earlier than the correct one.
slowly (adverb) **slowness** (noun)
[Old English *slaw* = sluggish]

slowcoach, slowcoaches
(noun; informal) If you call someone a slowcoach, you mean they do things very slowly.

The man who makes no mistakes does not usually make anything.

slow motion
(noun) movement which is much slower than
normal, especially in a film, e.g. *I dreamed I was
falling off a cliff in slow motion.*

sludge
(noun) thick mud or sewage.

slug, slugs, slugging, slugged
1 (noun) a small, slimy slow-moving creature.
2 (verb; informal) to hit someone hard.
3 (noun) a bullet.

sluggish
(adjective) moving slowly and without energy.
sluggishly (adverb)

slums
(plural noun) In a city 'the slums' refers to an
area of poor, run-down housing.

slumber, slumbers
(noun; literary) sleep.
[Old English *sluma* = sleep]

slump, slumps, slumping, slumped
1 (verb) to fall heavily, e.g. *She slumped to the
ground... the price of oil slumped.*
2 (noun) A slump is a time when prices drop,
industry declines and unemployment rises.

slurp, slurps, slurping, slurped
(verb) If you slurp a drink, you drink it noisily.
[Old Dutch *slorpen* = to sip]

slush
(noun) wet, melting snow.
slushy (adjective)

sly, slyer or slier, slyest or sliest
(adjective) cunning and good at deceiving people.
slyly (adverb)
[Old Norse *slægr* = clever or cunning]

Similar words: sneaky, devious, underhand, shifty

smack, smacks, smacking, smacked
(verb) to hit someone with your open hand.
[Old German *smacken*, an imitation of the sound]

small, smaller, smallest
(adjective) e.g. *a small child.*

Similar words: little, slight, tiny, minor, trivial,
unimportant

**smart, smarter, smartest; smarts, smarting,
smarted**
1 (adjective) clean and neatly dressed.
2 clever, e.g. *a smart idea.*
3 (verb) If a wound smarts, it stings.
4 (noun) A smart card looks like a banker's card
but is fitted with a microchip. It is used in
business, communications, etc.
smartly (adverb) **smartness** (noun) **smarten**
(verb)

smash, smashes, smashing, smashed
1 (verb) If you smash something, you break it
into a lot of pieces by hitting it or dropping it.
e.g. *I have smashed your best vase... The sea
smashed the boat against the rocks.*
2 (noun; informal) If a play or film is a smash or
a smash hit, it is very successful.
3 a car crash.

4 In tennis, a smash is a stroke in which the
player hits the ball downwards very hard.

smashing
(adjective; informal) really good.

smattering
(noun) A smattering of knowledge or
information is a very small amount of it,
e.g. *Jane spoke a smattering of Greek.*

smear, smears, smearing, smeared
(verb) If something smears a surface, it makes
dirty, greasy marks on it, e.g. *The windows were
smeared with fingermarks.*
[Old English *smierwan* = to rub with grease or
oil]

smell, smells, smelling, smelled or smelt
(noun, verb) e.g. *the smell of fresh bread... The
dog smelled awful.*
smelly (adjective)

Similar words: (noun) odour, whiff

smelt, smelts, smelting, smelted
(verb) To smelt a metal ore means to heat it until
it melts, so that the metal can be extracted.

smile, smiles, smiling, smiled
(verb) e.g. *The Mona Lisa smiles mysteriously.*

smirk, smirks, smirking, smirked
(verb) to smile in a sneering way, e.g. *'That's
where you're wrong,' said Ellen, smirking.*
[Old English *smearcian* = to smile]

smith, smiths
(noun) someone who makes things out of iron,
gold, etc. e.g. *goldsmith, blacksmith.*
[Old English *smith* = craftsman]

smithy, smithies
(noun) a place where a blacksmith works.

smock, smocks
(noun) a loose garment like a long blouse.

smog
(noun) a mixture of fog and smoke which occurs
in some industrial cities.
[a combination of *smoke* and *fog*]

smoke, smokes, smoking, smoked
1 (noun) a mixture of gas and small particles sent
into the air when something burns.
2 (verb) e.g. *to smoke a cigar... smoked salmon...
Our chimney is smoking.*
smoker (noun) **smoking** (noun) **smoky** (adjective)

smokeless
(adjective) Smokeless fuel burns without smoke.

**smooth, smoother, smoothest; smooths,
smoothing, smoothed**
1 (adjective) A smooth surface has no roughness
and no holes in it.
2 A smooth movement or process happens evenly
and steadily, e.g. *the smooth flow of the river.*
3 If you say a man is smooth, you mean he is
smart, confident and polite in a way you don't
trust.
4 (verb) to make things smoother.
smoothly (adverb) **smoothness** (noun)

What kind of person would you be if you were: sluggish waspish shrewish catty mulish?

smother, smothers, smothering, smothered
1 (verb) to cover someone's face with something so that they cannot breathe.
2 to give children too much love and protection, e.g. *Parents should love their children without smothering them.*
[Old English *smorian* = to suffocate]

smoulder, smoulders, smouldering, smouldered
(verb) to burn slowly, producing smoke but no flames.

smudge, smudges, smudging, smudged
(verb) If you smudge something, you make it dirty or messy by touching it or marking it.

smug, smugger, smuggest
(adjective) Someone who is smug is very pleased with how good or clever they are.
smugly (adverb) **smugness** (noun)

smuggle, smuggles, smuggling, smuggled
(verb) To smuggle things into or out of a place means to take them there illegally or secretly.
smuggler (noun)

snack, snacks
(noun) a light, quick meal.

snag, snags
(noun) a small problem or disadvantage, e.g. *Spot is a lovely dog; the only snag is that he eats postmen for breakfast.*

snail, snails
1 (noun) a small, slow-moving creature with a long, shiny body and a shell on its back.
2 (phrase) If you do something **at a snail's pace**, you do it very slowly.

snake, snakes
(noun) a long, thin, scaly reptile with no legs.

snap, snaps, snapping, snapped
1 (verb, noun) e.g. *My shoelace has snapped... The dog snapped at the postman... The boss snapped at me for being late... I snapped her with my new camera... The branch broke with a snap... Please take a snap of me.*
2 (adjective) A snap decision or action is taken suddenly without careful thought.
[Old German *snappen* = to seize]

snappy, snappier, snappiest
(adjective) Someone who is snappy speaks to people in a sharp, unfriendly way.

snare, snares, snaring, snared
1 (noun) a trap for catching birds or small animals.
2 (verb) to trap something or someone.

snarl, snarls, snarling, snarled
(verb) When an animal snarls, it bares its teeth and makes a fierce growling noise.

snarled up
(adjective) When traffic is snarled up, it is totally jammed.
snarl-up (noun)

snatch, snatches, snatching, snatched
1 (verb) to reach out quickly and take something.
2 (noun) A snatch of conversation or song is a very small piece of it.

sneak, sneaks, sneaking, sneaked
1 (verb) If you sneak somewhere, you go there quietly, trying not to be seen or heard.
2 If you sneak something somewhere, you take it there secretly.
sneaky (adjective) **sneakily** (adverb)
[Old English *snican* = to creep]

sneakers
(plural noun) casual shoes with rubber soles.

sneer, sneers, sneering, sneered
(verb) If you sneer at someone or something, you show by your face and by what you say that you think they are stupid or inferior.

sneeze, sneezes, sneezing, sneezed
(verb) e.g. *People sneeze when they have a cold.*

sniff, sniffs, sniffing, sniffed
(verb) e.g. *Sniff this new perfume.*

sniffle, sniffles, sniffling, sniffled
(verb) to sniff a lot, e.g. because you have a cold.

snigger, sniggers, sniggering, sniggered
(verb) to laugh quietly and disrespectfully, e.g. *They all sniggered as Mr Ripman fell over.*

snip, snips, snipping, snipped
(verb) to cut something with scissors or shears in a single quick action.
[Old German *snippen*, an imitation of the sound]

snob, snobs
1 (noun) someone who admires upper-class people and looks down on lower-class people. An **inverted snob** is someone who has an unreasoning dislike of all upper-class people.
2 someone who believes that they are better than other people.
snobbery (noun) **snobbish** (adjective)

snooker
(noun) a game played with cues and coloured balls on a large, purpose-built table.

snoop, snoops, snooping, snooped
(verb; informal) Someone who is snooping is secretly looking round a place to find out things.
[Dutch *snoepen* = to eat furtively]

snooty, snootier, snootiest
(adjective; informal) A snooty person behaves as if they are better than other people.

snooze, snoozes, snoozing, snoozed
(verb; informal) to sleep lightly for a short time.

snore, snores, snoring, snored
(verb) When a sleeping person snores, they make a loud noise each time they breathe.

snorkel, snorkels
(noun) a tube you can breathe through when you are swimming just under the water.
snorkelling (noun)
[German *Schnorchel*, originally an air pipe for a submarine]

snort, snorts, snorting, snorted
(verb) When people or animals snort, they force breath out through their nose in a noisy way, e.g. *My sister snorts when she laughs.*

snout, snouts
(noun) An animal's snout is its nose.

Examples of onomatopoeia: hiss buzzer clang splatter hoot neigh booming. What does it mean?

snow, snows, snowing, snowed
1 (noun) flakes of ice crystals which fall from the sky in cold weather.
2 (verb) e.g. *The north wind doth blow, and we shall have snow.*
3 (phrase) If you are **snowed in** or **snowed up**, you cannot go anywhere because of heavy snow.
4 If you are **snowed under** with work, you have a lot of it to deal with.
snowman (noun) **snowfall** (noun)

snowball, snowballs, snowballing, snowballed
1 (noun) a ball of snow made for throwing.
2 (verb) When something, for example a project, snowballs, it grows rapidly.

snowdrift, snowdrifts
(noun) a deep pile of snow formed by the wind.

snowdrop, snowdrops
(noun) a small, white flower of early spring.

snowplough, snowploughs
(noun) a vehicle used to push snow off roads or railway lines.

snub, snubs, snubbing, snubbed
1 (verb) To snub someone means to behave rudely towards them, especially by making an insulting remark or ignoring them.
2 (adjective) A snub nose is short and turned-up.
[verb: Old Norse *snubba* = to scold]

snuffle, snuffles, snuffling, snuffled
(verb) When people or animals snuffle, they make sniffing noises.
snuffly (adjective)

snug
(adjective) warm and comfortable.
snugly (adverb)
[from an old use which describes a ship made secure and ready for a storm]

snuggle, snuggles, snuggling, snuggled
(verb) If you snuggle somewhere, you cuddle up more closely to something or someone.

so
(adverb, conjunction) e.g. *I was so scared... Do you like reading? If so, try this... They went on foot, so as not to be heard.*

soak, soaks, soaking, soaked
(verb) To soak something or leave it to soak means to put it in a liquid and leave it there.

Similar words: drench, saturate

soap, soaps
(noun) a substance made of natural oils and fats used for washing yourself.
soapy (adjective)

soap opera, operas
(noun) A soap opera or soap is a popular TV drama serial about people's daily lives.
[The first examples in America were sponsored by a soap company]

soar, soars, soaring, soared
(verb) to go up very quickly, e.g. *House prices soared... The jet soared into the sky.*

sob, sobs, sobbing, sobbed
(verb) to cry in a noisy way, breathing in short breaths.

sober, soberer, soberest
(adjective) the opposite of drunk.

so-called
(adjective) Example: '*her so-called friend Jane*' means that Jane isn't a real friend.

soccer
(noun) football.
[from *Association Football*]

sociable
(adjective) Sociable people are friendly and enjoy talking to other people.

social
1 (adjective) to do with society or life within a society, e.g. *children from different social backgrounds.*
2 to do with leisure activities that involve meeting other people, e.g. *a social event.*
socially (adverb)
[Latin *socialis* = companionable]

socialism
(noun) the political belief that the state should own industries on behalf of the people and that everyone should have an equal opportunity to develop their talents.
socialist (adjective and noun)

social science, sciences
(noun) the scientific study of society.

social security
(noun) a system by which the government pays money regularly to people who have no other income or only a very small income. The money paid can also be called social security, e.g. *Are you claiming social security?*

social services
(plural noun) the services provided by a local authority to help people who have social and money problems.

social worker
(noun) someone who gives help and advice to people with serious money or family problems.

society, societies
1 (noun) the people in a particular country or region, e.g. *Women must have equal status in society.*
2 an organization for people who have the same interest or aim, e.g. *the school film society.*
[Latin *societas* = companion]

Similar words: (sense 1) culture, community, civilization

sociology
(noun) the study of human societies.
sociological (adjective) **sociologist** (noun)
[Latin *socius* = companion + *-ology*]

sock, socks
(noun) e.g. *Your socks smell!*
[Old English *socc* = light shoe]

What do these musical terms mean: piano forte allegro stave clef pitch?

socket, sockets
1 (noun) a place on a wall etc. where you plug in electrical equipment.
2 Any hollow part or opening into which another part fits can be called a socket, e.g. *eye sockets.*

soda water
(noun) a type of fizzy water used for mixing with alcoholic drinks or fruit juice.

sodium
(noun) a silvery-white chemical which combines with other chemicals; e.g. salt is a sodium compound.

sofa, sofas
(noun) a long, comfortable seat with a back and arms for a small number of people.
[Arabic *suffah* = an upholstered platform]

soft, softer, softest
1 (adjective) e.g. *a soft brush... a soft breeze... a soft voice... a soft light.*
2 weak or not strict enough.
softly (adverb) **soften** (verb)

soft drink, drinks
(noun) any cold, non-alcoholic drink.

software
(noun) computer disks, programs, etc.

soggy, soggier, soggiest
(adjective) unpleasantly wet or full of water.
[American dialect *sog* = marsh]

soil, soils, soiling, soiled
1 (noun) the top layer of the earth's surface.
2 (verb) If you soil something, you make it dirty.
e.g. *soiled nappies.*
[Anglo-French *soil* = land]

solar
(adjective) relating to the sun, e.g. *a solar-heated swimming pool.*
[Latin *sol* = sun]

solar system
(noun) the sun and all the planets, comets and asteroids that orbit round it.

sold past tense of **sell.**

solder, solders, soldering, soldered
(verb) To solder two pieces of metal together means to join them with molten metal.
soldering iron (noun)
[Latin *solidare* = to join together]

soldier, soldiers, soldiering, soldiered
1 (noun) a person in an army.
2 (phrasal verb) To **soldier on** means to keep going for a long time in difficult conditions.
[Old French *soude* = army pay]

sole, soles
1 (adjective) only or single, e.g. *Her sole reason for going was to see him.*
2 (noun) the underneath part of a foot or shoe.
3 an edible, flat sea fish.
[adjective: Latin *solus* = alone;
noun: Latin *solea* = sandal; the fish is called this because of its shape]

solemn
(adjective) very serious, e.g. *Funerals are solemn occasions.*
solemnly (adverb) **solemnity** (noun)

solicitor, solicitors
(noun) a lawyer who gives advice about the law and prepares legal documents and court cases.
[Latin *sollicitare* = to harass]

solid, solids
1 (adjective) hard or firm, not liquid or gas.
2 without stopping, e.g. *I worked for 3 hours solid.*
solidly (adverb) **solidity** (noun)

solidarity
(noun) If a group of people show solidarity, they show unity and support for each other.

solidify, solidifies, solidifying, solidified
(verb) When a liquid solidifies, it becomes solid.

solitaire, solitaires
(noun) a game with small pegs for one person.
[Old French *solitaire* = solitary]

solitary
1 (adjective) A solitary person or animal spends a lot of time alone.
2 If there is a solitary person or object somewhere, there is only one.
solitude (noun)
[Latin *solus* = alone]

Similar words: lonely, isolated, secluded

solo, solos
(adjective, noun) A solo performance or solo is done by one person alone, e.g. *a flute solo.*
[Latin *solus* = alone]

soloist, soloists
(noun) a person who performs on their own, perhaps with an orchestra.

solstice, solstices
(noun) one of the two times in the year when the sun is furthest away from the equator (21 June and 21 December).
[Latin *sol* = sun + *sistere* = to stand still]

soluble
(adjective) able to dissolve in liquid.
[Latin *solvere* = to dissolve]

solution, solutions
1 (noun) the answer to a problem or difficult situation, e.g. *The only solution is for us all to go in the same car.*
2 a liquid in which a solid substance has been dissolved, e.g. *a salt solution.*

solve, solves, solving, solved
(verb) If you solve a problem or a question, you find a solution or answer to it.

Similar words: answer, decipher, crack, work out, get to the bottom of

solvent, solvents
(noun) a liquid that can dissolve other substances, e.g. white spirit, methylated spirits.
[Latin *solvere* = to dissolve, or to loosen]

Planets begin with capitals: Mercury Venus Earth Mars Jupiter Saturn Uranus Neptune Pluto.

sombre
(adjective) serious, sad or gloomy.
[Latin *sub* + *umbra* = under shade]

some
(adjective, pronoun, adverb) e.g. *Please may I have some cake?... Do you want some?... The bookshelves were some 8 metres high.*

somebody
(pronoun) e.g. *Are you looking for somebody?*

some day
(adverb) e.g. *Some day I'll get my revenge!*

somehow
(adverb) e.g. *We'll manage somehow.*

someone
(pronoun) e.g. *Someone has taken my pencil.*

somersault, somersaults
(noun) a forwards or backwards roll, or handspring.
[Regional French *sobre* = over + *saut* = jump]

something
(pronoun) e.g. *It goes something like this.*

sometime
(adverb) e.g. *Come up and see me sometime.*

sometimes
(adverb) e.g. *She sometimes smiles but not often.*

somewhat
(adverb) a little bit, e.g. *I was somewhat tired.*

somewhere
(adverb) e.g. *There's a pen around somewhere... It's a number somewhere between 80 and 100.*

son, sons
(noun) Someone's son is their male child.

sonar
(noun) equipment on a ship which calculates, using sound waves, the depth of the sea or the position of an underwater object.
[from *So(und) Na(vigation) R(anging)*]

song, songs
(noun) e.g. *Which song was their first hit?*

sonic boom, booms
(noun) the loud noise caused by an aircraft travelling faster than the speed of sound.
[Latin *sonus* = sound]

son-in-law, sons-in-law
(noun) Someone's son-in-law is the husband of their daughter.

sonnet, sonnets
(noun) a poem with 14 lines, in which lines rhyme according to fixed patterns.
[Regional French *sonet* = little poem]

soon, sooner, soonest
(adverb) e.g. *Please come back soon.*

soot
(noun) black powder which rises in the smoke from a fire.
sooty (adjective)

soothe, soothes, soothing, soothed.
(verb) to make someone calmer, or to relieve pain.
soothing (adjective)

sophisticated
1 (adjective) Sophisticated people have more complicated or cultured tastes or habits, e.g. *In the city, people's tastes tend to be more sophisticated than in rural areas.*
2 A sophisticated machine or device is capable of using advanced and complicated methods.
sophistication (noun)

sopping
(adjective) soaking wet.

soppy, soppier, soppiest
(adjective; informal) silly or foolishly sentimental, e.g. *I hate all that soppy kissing in some films.*

sorbet, sorbets (pronounced **sor**-bay)
(noun) water ice made from fruit.
[Turkish *serbet* = sherbet]

sorcerer, sorcerers (pronounced **sor**-ser-er)
(noun) a person who performs magic by using the power of evil spirits.
sorcery (noun) **sorceress** (noun)

sordid
(adjective) dirty, dishonest or immoral, e.g. *This is a sordid business.*
[Latin *sordere* = dirty]

sore, sorer, sorest; sores
1 (adjective) If part of your body is sore, it causes you pain and discomfort.
2 (noun) an area of skin which is painful.
sorely (adverb) **soreness** (noun)

Similar words: raw, tender, sensitive, painful

sorrow, sorrows
(noun) deep sadness or regret.
sorrowful (adjective) **sorrowfully** (adverb)

sorry, sorrier, sorriest
1 (adjective) e.g. *I'm sorry to hear that you failed the exam.*
2 in a bad physical or mental state, e.g. *I've never seen him in such a sorry state.*

Similar words: (sense 1) apologetic, repentent

sort, sorts, sorting, sorted
1 (verb) To sort things means to arrange them into different groups or sorts.
2 (noun) a type or kind of something, e.g. *What sort of beetle is that?*

sort out
(phrasal verb) If you sort out a problem, you deal with it and find a solution to it.

SOS
(noun) a signal that you are in danger and need help. [from *Save Our Souls*, the old distress call]

so-so
(adjective) neither good nor bad, e.g. *'What's the food like?'–'So-so.'*

soul, souls
1 (noun) Our soul is the spirit part of us that is supposed to live on after we die.
2 'Soul' can be used to mean person, e.g. *She's a happy soul... not a soul in sight.*

Some surnames mean *son of*: Richardson O'Brian MacDonald Wilson Wills Fitzjohn.

sound, sounds, sounding, sounded; sounder, soundest
1 (noun) every noise that can be heard.
2 (verb) e.g. *The bell sounded for the lesson.*
3 (adjective) reliable and of good quality, e.g. *a sound report... The car is in sound condition.*
soundly (adverb) **soundness** (noun)
[senses 1-2: Old French *soner* = to make a sound sense 3: Old English *gesund* = uninjured]

sound out
(phrasal verb) If you sound someone out, you ask their opinion on something.

sound barrier
(noun) the sudden increase in the force of the air against an aircraft that occurs as it passes the speed of sound (approximately 770 m.p.h.).

sound effect, effects
(noun) sounds created to make a play on film more realistic.

soundproof
(adjective) If a room is soundproof, sound cannot get into it or out of it.

soup, soups
(noun) liquid food made by boiling meat, fish or vegetables in water.

sour
1 (adjective) If something is sour, it has a sharp, acid taste, e.g. lemons.
2 Sour milk has an unpleasant taste because it is no longer fresh.
3 A sour person is bad-tempered and unfriendly.

source, sources
1 (noun) The source of something is the person, place or thing that it comes from, e.g. *They're trying to trace the source of the trouble.*
2 the place where a river begins.
[Old French *sourdre* = to spring forth]

south
(noun, adjective, adverb) a direction, e.g. *Do you live in the South?... We headed south... the south wall of the church... a south wind.*
southern (adjective)

south-east
(noun, adverb, adjective) a direction halfway between south and east.
south-eastern (adjective)

southward or **southwards**
(adverb) towards the south.

south-west
(noun, adverb, adjective) a direction halfway between south and west.
south-western (adjective)

souvenir, souvenirs
(noun) something you keep to remind you of a holiday, place or event.
[French *se souvenir* = to remember]

sou'wester, sou'westers
(noun) a waterproof hat with a wide brim at the back to keep your neck dry.

sovereign, sovereigns (pronounced **sov**-rin)
1 (noun) a king, queen or royal ruler of a country.

2 (noun) In the past, a sovereign was a gold coin worth £1. Now it is rare and worth much more.

Soviet (pronounced soe-vee-et)
(adjective) relating to the Soviet Union.

sow, sows, sowing, sowed, sown (rhymes with **go**)
(verb) to plant seeds.

sow, sows (rhymes with **now**)
(noun) an adult, female pig.

soya bean, beans
(noun) a type of edible Asian bean.

spa, spas
(noun) a place where water containing minerals bubbles out of the ground. People drink or bathe in the water to improve their health.
[from the Belgian town *Spa*]

space, spaces
(noun) e.g. *empty space... outer space... The door had spaces at the top and bottom... It happened twice in the space of 3 weeks.*
spacecraft (noun) **spaceship** (noun)

space capsule, capsules
(noun) the part of a spacecraft which astronauts travel in.

space probe, probes
(noun) a small spacecraft sent into space to transmit information about space.

space shuttle, shuttles
(noun) a spacecraft for travelling out into space and back again many times.

space station, stations
(noun) a large satellite that orbits the earth, used as a base by astronauts or scientists.

spacesuit, spacesuits
(noun) a protective suit for an astronaut.

spacious
(adjective) having or providing a lot of space, e.g. *a very spacious dining room.*
spaciousness (noun)

spade, spades
1 (noun) a tool used for digging.
2 one of the 4 suits in a pack of playing cards. It is marked by a black symbol ♠.

spaghetti (pronounced spag-**get**-ee)
(noun) long, thin pieces of pasta.
[Italian *spago* = string]

span, spans, spanning, spanned
1 (noun) a period of time, e.g. *in the short span that man has been on earth.*
2 In maths, your span is the distance between the tips of your outstretched thumb and little finger.
3 (noun) the total length of something, e.g. *the span of a bridge.*
4 (verb) A bridge that spans something stretches right across it.

Spaniard, Spaniards (pronounced **span**-yard)
(noun) someone who comes from Spain.

spaniel, spaniels
(noun) a gundog with long drooping ears and a silky coat.
[Old French *espaigneul* = Spanish dog]

Homophones sound alike but are spelled differently: fair fare there their hear here aloud allowed.

Spanish
1 (adjective) belonging to Spain.
2 (noun) the main language spoken in Spain, and by many people in Central and South America.

spank, spanks, spanking, spanked
(verb) If a child is spanked, it is punished by being slapped, usually on its leg or bottom.

spanner, spanners
(noun) a tool with a specially shaped end that fits round a nut to turn it.

spare, spares, sparing, spared
1 (adjective) extra, e.g. *a spare tyre.*
2 (verb) If you spare something for a particular purpose, you make it available, e.g. *Nowadays more land can be spared for planting trees.*
3 If someone is spared an unpleasant experience, they are prevented from suffering it, e.g. *He was spared the shame of being told off.*
4 (phrase) If you **spare no expense** in doing something, you do it as well as possible, without trying to save money.
[Old English *sparian* = to refrain from injuring or using]

spare-ribs
(noun) pork ribs with most of the meat trimmed off.

sparing
(adjective) If you are sparing with something, you use it in very small quantities.
sparingly (adverb)

spark, sparks, sparking, sparked
1 (noun) a tiny, bright piece of burning material thrown up by a fire; or a small flash of light caused by electricity.
2 (verb) If one thing sparks another thing off, it causes the second thing to start happening, e.g. *The letter sparked off a friendship between them.*

sparkle, sparkles, sparkling, sparkled
(verb) to shine with a lot of small, bright points of light.
sparkling (adjective) **sparkler** (noun)

Similar words: glisten, glitter, twinkle

sparrow, sparrows
(noun) a very common, small bird.

sparse, sparser, sparsest
(adjective) small in number or amount and spread out over an area, e.g. *sparse white hair.*
sparsely (adverb)
[Latin *spargere* = to scatter]

spastic, spastics
(adjective, noun) A spastic person or spastic is born with a disability which makes it difficult for them to control their muscles.
[Greek *spasmos* = cramp]

spatter, spatters, spattering, spattered
(verb) If something spatters a surface, it covers the surface with drops of liquid.

spatula, spatulas
(noun) a knife-like object with a wide, flat blade, used in cooking and by doctors.
[Latin *spatha* = flat wooden implement]

spawn, spawns, spawning, spawned.
1 (noun) a jelly-like substance containing the eggs of fish or amphibians, e.g. *frog spawn.*
2 (verb) When fish or amphibians spawn, they lay their eggs.
[Old French *spandre* = to spread out]

spay, spays, spaying, spayed
(verb) When a female animal is spayed, it has its ovaries removed so it cannot become pregnant.
[Old French *espeer* = to cut with a sword]

speak, speaks, speaking, spoke, spoken
(verb) e.g. *I speak fluent Welsh, boyo.*

speaker, speakers
1 (noun) a person who is speaking.
2 A speaker on a radio or hi-fi is a loudspeaker.
3 In Parliament, the Speaker is an MP elected to control meetings of the House of Commons.

spear, spears
(noun) a long, pointed weapon.

spearmint, spearmints
(noun) a mint-flavoured herb.

spec, specs
(plural noun; informal) Someone's specs are their glasses.
[shortened form of *spectacles*]

special
1 (adjective) more important or better than other things of its kind, e.g. *a special guest... a special event.*
2 particular, e.g. *You need special permission to marry a foreigner... the special needs of children with learning difficulties.*
specially (adverb)
[Latin *specialis* = individual]

specialist, specialists
(noun) someone who has a particular skill or who knows a lot about a particular subject, e.g. *an eye specialist.*
2 (adjective) e.g. *a specialist teacher of maths.*

speciality, specialities
(noun) A person's speciality is something they are especially good at or know a lot about.

specialize, specializes, specializing, specialized; also spelled specialise
(verb) If you specialize in something, you make it your speciality, e.g. *a shop specializing in camping equipment.*
specialization (noun)

species (pronounced **spee**-sheez)
(noun) a class of plants, animals, birds, insects, etc., e.g. *a species of butterfly.*

specific
1 (adjective) particular, e.g. *Education should not be restricted to any one specific age group.*
2 precise and exact, e.g. *Try to be more specific.*
[This word tends to be confused with 'pacific' which means something entirely different]
specifically (adverb)

Similar words: precise, exact, certain

specify, specifies, specifying, specified
(verb) to state or describe something clearly and precisely, e.g. *Please specify what it is you want*

We take these words from Spanish: poncho patio siesta cockroach cork sherry mosquito rodeo.

ecimen, specimens
noun) an example or small amount of something
vhich gives an idea of what the whole is like, e.g.
a specimen of his work.
[Latin *specimen* = mark or evidence]

eck, specks
noun) a very small piece, e.g. *a speck of dust.*

eckled
adjective) covered with small marks or spots.

ectacle, spectacles
1 (plural noun) Spectacles are glasses.
2 (noun) a strange or interesting sight or scene,
e.g. *a tragic spectacle.*
3 a grand and impressive event.
[Latin *spectaculum* = a show]

ectacular, spectaculars
1 (adjective) very impressive or dramatic.
2 (noun) a grand and impressive show or
performance, e.g. *an ice spectacular.*

Similar words: (adjective) breathtaking, dazzling,
stunning, sensational

ectator, spectators
noun) a person who is watching something.
[Latin *spectare* = to watch]

Similar words: observer, watcher, viewer, onlooker

ectre, spectres
noun) a ghost.
[Latin *spectrum* = appearance]

ectrum, spectra or spectrums
1 (noun) the range of different rainbow colours
produced when light passes through a prism or a
drop of water.
2 a range of opinions or emotions.
[Latin *spectrum* = appearance or image]

eech, speeches
1 (noun) speaking or the ability to speak.
2 a formal talk given to an audience.
Old English *spec* = speech]

eechless
(adjective) Someone who is speechless is unable
to speak for a while because something has
shocked them.

eed, speeds, speeding, sped or speeded
1 (noun) e.g. *a speed of 60 m.p.h.... the speed of
change.*
2 (verb) Someone who is speeding is driving a
vehicle faster than the legal speed limit.
3 (noun) a name for a type of amphetamine drug.
This has medical uses but is also taken illegally,
causing dangerously hyperactive behaviour.
speedy (adjective) **speedily** (adverb)
[Old English *sped* = success]

Similar words: (noun) pace, rate, tempo, velocity

eedboat, speedboats
(noun) a small, fast motorboat.

eed limit, limits
(noun) the maximum speed at which vehicles are
allowed to drive on a particular road.

speedometer, speedometers
(noun) an instrument which measures how fast a
vehicle is moving.

speedway
(noun) the sport of racing light motorcycles on
special dirt tracks.

spell, spells, spelling, spelled or spelt
1 (verb) e.g. *Spell your name, please... D O G
spells dog... Nuclear war would spell the end of
civilization.*
2 (noun) a short period, e.g. *a spell of mild
weather.*
3 words used to perform magic.
[sense 1: Old French *espeller* = to spell
sense 2: Old English *spelian* = to take the place
of someone for a short time
sense 3: Old English *spell* = speech]

spell out
(phrasal verb) to explain something in detail,
e.g. *Do I have to spell it out to you?*

spellbound
(adjective) absolutely fascinated by something,
e.g. *We were spellbound as we listened to her.*

spend, spends, spending, spent
1 (verb) to buy things.
2 To spend time or energy means to use it.
[Latin *expendere* = to spend]

spendthrift, spendthrifts
(noun) a person who spends money in a wasteful
way.

sperm, sperms
(noun) a cell produced in the sex organ of a male
animal which can fertilize a female animal's egg.
[Greek *sperma* = seed]

sphere, spheres
(noun) a perfectly round object, e.g. a ball.
spherical (adjective)
[Latin *sphaera* = globe]

sphinx, sphinxes (pronounced **sfingks**)
(noun) a huge, stone, ancient Egyptian statue
with the head of a man and the body of a lion.

spice, spices
(noun) powder or seeds from a plant added to
food to give it flavour.
spicy (adjective)
[Old French *espice* = spice]

spick and span
(adjective) very clean and tidy.

spider, spiders
(noun) an insect-like creature with 8 legs.
[Old English *spinnan* = to spin]

spike, spikes
1 (noun) a long, pointed piece of metal.
2 The spikes on a sports shoe are the pointed
pieces of metal attached to the sole.
spiky (adjective)

spill, spills, spilling, spilled or spilt
(verb) If you spill something or if it spills, it
accidentally falls or runs out of a container.
[Old English *spillan* = to destroy]

spin, spins, spinning, spun
1 (verb) e.g. *This washer also spins clothes dry.*

Nouns of assembly. Can you make up your own nouns for a collection of: teachers spiders vampires?

2 When spiders spin a web, they give out a sticky substance and make it into a web.
3 When people spin, they make thread by twisting together pieces of fibre using a machine.
4 If your head is spinning, you feel dizzy.

spin out
(phrasal verb) If you spin something out, you make it last longer than it otherwise would.

spina bifida (pronounced spy-na biff-id-a)
(noun) a condition of the spine which some people are born with, sometimes causing paralysis.
[Latin *spina* + *bifidus* = spine split into 2 parts]

spinach (pronounced spin-ij)
(noun) a vegetable with large green, leaves.

spindly
(adjective) long, thin and weak-looking.

spin dryer, dryers; also spelled **spin drier**
(noun) a machine for drying clothes by spinning.
spin-dry (verb)

spine, spines
1 (noun) the backbone.
2 the narrow, stiff part of a book that holds the pages together.
3 long, sharp points on an animal or plant.
spiny (adjective)

spine-chilling
(adjective) very frightening.
spine-chiller (noun)

spineless
(adjective) cowardly.

spinning wheel, wheels
(noun) a wooden machine for spinning wool etc.

spin-off, spin-offs
(noun) A spin-off is something useful that unexpectedly results from an activity, e.g. *The digital watch was a spin-off from the Apollo space programme of the late 60s.*

spinster, spinsters
(noun) a woman who has never married.
[originally a person who spent time spinning]

spiral, spirals, spiralling, spiralled
1 (noun) a continuous curve which winds round and round, with each curve above or outside the previous one.
2 (adjective) e.g. *a spiral staircase.*
3 (verb) If an amount or level spirals, it rises or falls quickly at an increasing rate, e.g. *Prices had continued to spiral upward.*
[Latin *spira* = coil]

spire, spires
(noun) the tall cone-shaped structure on top of a church.
[Old English *spir* = blade]

spirit, spirits
1 (noun) Your spirit is the part of you that is not physical and that is connected with your deepest thoughts and feelings.
2 The spirit of a dead person is a non-physical part that is believed to remain alive after death.
3 a ghost etc.

4 liveliness, energy, and self-confidence, e.g. *a performance full of spirit.*
5 a strong alcoholic drink, e.g. whisky, gin.
[Latin *spiritus* = breath or spirit]

spirit level, levels
(noun) a device for finding out if a surface is level using an air bubble sealed in a tube of liquid.

spiritual, spirituals
1 (adjective) to do with people's thoughts and beliefs, rather than their bodies and physical surroundings.
2 (noun) a religious song originally sung by black slaves in America.

spit, spits, spitting, spat
(verb) If you spit, you force saliva or some other substance out of your mouth.
[Old English *spittan* = to spit]

spite
1 (phrase) **In spite of:** e.g. *In spite of poor health, my father was always cheerful.*
2 (verb) If you do something to spite someone, you do it deliberately to hurt or annoy them.
3 (noun) If you do something out of spite, you do it to hurt or annoy someone.

spiteful
(adjective) A spiteful person does or says nasty things to people deliberately to hurt them.
spitefully (adverb)

Similar words: malicious, vicious, mean, nasty, vindictive, catty, bitchy

spitting image
(noun) If someone is the spitting image of someone else, they look just like them.

splash, splashes, splashing, splashed
(verb) e.g. *My rubber duck and I splashed around in the bath.*

splash out
(phrasal verb) To splash out on something mean to spend a lot of money on it.

splatter, splatters, splattering, splattered
(verb) When something is splattered with a substance, the substance is splashed all over it.

spleen
(noun) an organ near your stomach which controls the quality of your blood.

splendid
1 (adjective) very good indeed.
2 beautiful and impressive, e.g. *a splendid Victorian building.*
splendidly (adverb) **splendour** (noun)

Similar words: (sense 2) magnificent, grand, gloriou

splint, splints
(noun) a piece of wood or metal fastened to a broken limb to hold it in place.

splinter, splinters, splintering, splintered
1 (noun) a thin, sharp piece of wood or glass which has broken off a larger piece.
2 (verb) to break into splinters, e.g. *The old pier splintered when the ferry crashed into it.*

In *The Rivals* Sheridan created Mrs Malaprop, who confused words that look alike....

split, splits, splitting, split
(verb) to divide into two or more parts.
[Old Dutch *splitten* = to break up]

split second
(noun) an extremely short period of time.

splitting
(adjective) A splitting headache is very painful.

splodge, splodges
(noun; informal) a large messy mark or stain.

splutter, splutters, spluttering, spluttered
(verb) If someone splutters, they speak in a confused way because they are embarrassed.
If something splutters, it makes a series of short, sharp sounds, e.g. *a spluttering engine*.

spoil, spoils, spoiling, spoiled or spoilt
1 (verb) If you spoil something, you prevent it from being successful or satisfactory.
2 To spoil children means to give them everything they want, with harmful effects on their character.
3 If you are spoiling for a fight, you are eager to have one.
[Latin *spoliare* = to strip or to plunder]

Similar words: (sense 1) ruin, wreck
(sense 2) pamper, indulge, mollycoddle, pet

spoiled or spoilt
(adjective) Someone who is spoiled is used to having their own way and cannot accept anything else.

spoilsport, spoilsports
(noun) someone who spoils people's fun.

spoke, spokes
(noun) The spokes of a wheel are the bars which connect the edge to the centre.

sponge, sponges, sponging, sponged
1 (noun) a sea creature with a porous body.
2 part of the very light skeleton of a sponge, used for bathing and cleaning.
spongy (adjective)
3 a very light cake.
4 (verb) Someone who sponges gets money from people without giving anything in return.
sponger (noun)
[Greek *spoggia* = sponge]

sponsor, sponsors, sponsoring, sponsored
1 (verb) To sponsor something, for example an event, means to support it with money, e.g. *My trip was sponsored by ICI... I sponsored Pam in the charity swim.*
2 (noun) a person or organization sponsoring something or someone.
sponsorship (noun)
[Latin *spondere* = to promise solemnly]

spontaneous
(adjective) If you do something spontaneous, you don't plan it but do it because you feel like it.
spontaneously (adverb) **spontaneity** (noun)
[Latin *sponte* = voluntarily]

spook, spooks
(noun; informal) a ghost.
[a Dutch word]

spooky, spookier, spookiest
(adjective) eerie and frightening.

spoon, spoons
(noun) e.g. *knife, fork and spoon.*

spoonerism, spoonerisms
(noun) a mistake made when speaking, in which the first sounds of two words are changed over, e.g. *'I saw her fighting a liar'* instead of *'I saw her lighting a fire'*. [named after the Revd W. A. Spooner (1844-1930), who made frequent slips of this kind]

spoonful, spoonfuls or spoonsful
(noun) the amount held by a spoon.

spoor, spoors
(noun) The spoor of an animal is the trail it leaves as it moves along.
[Afrikaans *spoor* = trail]

spore, spores
(noun; technical) cells produced by bacteria and non-flowering plants, e.g. fungi, which develop into new bacteria or plants.
[Greek *spora* = sowing]

sport, sports
1 (noun) games etc.
2 You say that someone is a sport when they accept defeat or teasing cheerfully, e.g. *Be a sport, Martin!*
sporting (adjective) **sportsman** (noun)
sportswoman (noun)
[Middle English *disport* = to amuse oneself]

sports car, cars
(noun) a low, fast car, usually for two people.

sports jacket, jackets
(noun) an informal jacket for men.

sportsmanship
(noun) the behaviour and attitudes of a good sportsman, for example being fair, generous and cheerful when you lose and when you win.

sportswear
(noun) clothes worn for sport.

spot, spots, spotting, spotted
1 (noun) e.g. *Zitto cures spots on the face... spots of rain... How about a spot of lunch?... It's a lovely spot for a picnic.*
2 (verb) If you spot something, you notice it.
3 (phrase) If you do something **on the spot**, you do it immediately.

spotless
(adjective) perfectly clean.
spotlessly (adverb)

Similar words: immaculate, impeccable

spotlight, spotlights
(noun) a powerful light directed to light up a small area.

spot-on
(adjective; informal) exactly correct.

spotted
(adjective) e.g. *Leopards are spotted.*

spotter, spotters
(noun) a person whose hobby is looking out for particular things, e.g. *a train spotter.*

....Malapropism: I've never been so insulated in all my life!

spotty, spottier, spottiest
(adjective) Someone who is spotty has spots or pimples on their skin, especially on the face.

spouse, spouses
(noun) Someone's spouse is the person they are married to.

spout, spouts, spouting, spouted
1 (verb) When someone spouts about something they say it in a boring way.
2 (noun) a tube with an end for pouring liquid, e.g. *the spout of a kettle.*

sprain, sprains, spraining, sprained
(verb) If you sprain a joint, you accidentally damage it by twisting it violently.

sprawl, sprawls, sprawling, sprawled
1 (verb) If you sprawl somewhere, you sit or lie there with your legs and arms spread out.
2 A place that sprawls is spread out over a large area, e.g. *The town sprawls along the coastline.*
3 (noun) anything that spreads in an untidy and uncontrolled way, e.g. *London's urban sprawl.*

spray, sprays, spraying, sprayed
1 (noun) many drops of liquid splashed or forced into the air, e.g. *sea spray... hair spray.*
2 (verb) To spray a liquid over something means to cover it with drops of the liquid.
3 A spray of flowers consists of several of them on one stem.
[senses 1-2: Old Dutch *spraien* = spray]

spread, spreads, spreading, spread
1 (verb) e.g. *He spread the map over the table... I spread butter very thickly... News of the wreck spread quickly.*
2 (noun) A spread is soft food put on bread, e.g. *sandwich spread.*

sprightly, sprightlier, sprightliest
(adjective) lively and active.

spring, springs, springing, sprang, sprung
1 (noun) the season between winter and summer.
2 a coil of wire which returns to its natural shape after being pressed or pulled.
3 a place where water comes up through the ground.
4 (verb) to jump upwards or forwards, e.g. *She sprang to her feet.*
5 If one thing springs from another, it is the result of it, e.g. *These problems spring from different causes.*
6 (phrase) If a boat or container **springs a leak**, water starts coming in through a crack.
7 (verb) If you spring some news or a surprise on someone, you tell them something unexpected.
springy (adjective)

springboard, springboards
(noun) a flexible board on which a diver or gymnast jumps to gain height.

spring-clean, -cleans, -cleaning, -cleaned
(verb) to clean something very thoroughly, perhaps only once a year.

sprinkle, sprinkles, sprinkling, sprinkled
(verb) If you sprinkle a liquid or powder over something, you scatter it over it.

sprinkler, sprinklers
(noun) a device used to spray water, especially to water lawns or put out fires in emergency.

sprint, sprints, sprinting, sprinted
1 (verb) to run fast over a short distance.
2 (noun) a short, fast race, e.g. *100m sprint.*
sprinter (noun)

sprite, sprites
(noun) a type of fairy.
[Latin *spiritus* = spirit]

sprout, sprouts, sprouting, sprouted
1 (verb) to grow quickly.
2 (noun) a vegetable like a small cabbage.

spruce, spruces; sprucer, sprucest
1 (noun) an evergreen tree.
2 (adjective) very neat and smart.

spud, spuds
(noun; informal) a potato.

spur, spurs, spurring, spurred
1 (verb) If something spurs you to do something or spurs you on, it encourages you to do it.
2 (phrase) If you do something **on the spur of the moment**, you do it suddenly, without planning it
3 (noun) Spurs are metal points attached to the heels of a rider's boots, used to urge a horse on.

spurt, spurts
1 (noun) A spurt of liquid or flame is a thick powerful stream of it, e.g. *a spurt of blood.*
2 a sudden, brief period of activity or effort, e.g. *The runner put in a spurt near the finish.*

spy, spies, spying, spied
1 (noun) a person sent to find out secret information about a country or organization.
2 (verb) to watch someone secretly.
[Old French *espier* = to espy]

squabble, squabbles, squabbling, squabbled
(verb) to quarrel about something trivial.

squad, squads
(noun) a small group chosen to do something, e.g. *the Flying Squad... the England squad.*
[Old Spanish *escuadra* = square, because of the square formation used by soldiers]

squadron, squadrons
(noun) a section of one of the armed forces, especially the air force.
[Italian *squadrone* = soldiers drawn up in a square formation]

squander, squanders, squandering, squandered
(verb) To squander money or resources means to waste them, e.g. *He squandered all his money o clothes and drink.*

square, squares, squaring, squared
1 (noun) a shape with 4 equal sides and 4 right angles.
2 In a town or city, a square is a flat, open place bordered by buildings or streets.
3 The square of a number is the number multiplied by itself. e.g., the square of 3, writte 3^2, is $3 \times 3 = 9$.
4 (adjective) Square is used before units of length when talking about the area of somethin, e.g. an area 2 metres wide and 4 metres long ha an area of 8 square metres, written 8m².

5 (verb) If you square a number, you multiply it by itself, e.g. *6 squared is 36.*
[Latin *quadra* = square]

square root, roots
(noun) Example: *3 is the square root of 9 because 3 × 3 = 9; 5 is the square root of 25 (5 × 5 = 25)*

squash, squashes, squashing, squashed
1 (verb) to press something, so it becomes flat or loses its shape.
2 (noun) a game where two players hit a small rubber ball against the walls of a closed indoor court using rackets.
3 a drink made from fruit juice, sugar and water.
squashy (adjective)
[Latin *quassare* = to shatter]

squat, squats, squatting, squatted
1 (verb) If you squat down, you crouch, balancing on your feet with your legs bent.
2 A person who squats in an unused building lives there uninvited and without paying.
squatter (noun)
[Old French *esquater* = to crouch]

squawk, squawks, squawking, squawked
(noun) a loud, harsh noise made by a bird.

squeak, squeaks, squeaking, squeaked
(noun) a short, high-pitched sound.
squeaky (adjective)

squeal, squeals, squealing, squealed
(noun) e.g. *a squeal of brakes.*

squeeze, squeezes, squeezing, squeezed
1 (verb) to press something firmly from two sides.
2 If you squeeze something into a small amount of time or space, you manage to fit it in.
3 If you squeeze something out of someone, you persuade them to give it to you, e.g. *I managed to squeeze £5 out of Ebenezer.*
[Middle English *queysen* = to press]

squelch, squelches, squelching, squelched
(verb) to make a wet, sucking sound e.g. *We squelched through the mud in our wellies.*

squid, squids
(noun) a sea creature with a long soft body and 10 tentacles.

squiggle, squiggles
(noun) a wiggly line.

squint, squints, squinting, squinted
1 (verb) If you squint at something, you look at it with your eyes screwed up.
2 (noun) If someone has a squint, their eyes look in different directions from each other.

squirm, squirms, squirming, squirmed
(verb) to wriggle and twist your body about, because you are nervous, uncomfortable, etc.

squirrel, squirrels
(noun) a small, furry animal with a bushy tail.
[Greek *skia* = shadow + *oura* = tail]

squirt, squirts, squirting, squirted
(verb) If a liquid squirts, it comes out of a narrow opening in a thin, fast stream.

Sri Lankan, Sri Lankans (pronounced sree-**lang**-kan)
1 (adjective) belonging to Sri Lanka.
2 (noun) someone who comes from Sri Lanka.

stab, stabs, stabbing, stabbed
1 (verb) to wound somebody by pushing a knife into their body.
2 (phrase; informal) If you **have a stab** at something, you try to do it.
[Middle English *stabbe* = stab wound]

stable, stables
1 (adjective) not likely to change or come to an end suddenly, e.g. *a stable marriage.*
2 firmly fixed or balanced and not likely to move, wobble or fall.
3 (noun) a building in which horses are kept.
stability (noun) **stabilize** (verb)
[Latin *stabilis* = steady]

stack, stacks, stacking, stacked
1 (noun) a pile of things, one on top of the other.
2 (plural noun; informal) If someone has stacks of something, they have a lot of it.
3 (verb) to put several things in a pile, one on top of the other.
[Old Norse *stakkr* = haystack]

stadium, stadiums
(noun) a sports ground with rows of seats around it.
[Greek *stadion* = racecourse]

staff, staffs
(noun) The staff of an organization is the people who work for it.

stag, stags
(noun) an adult, male deer.

stage, stages, staging, staged
1 (noun) a part of a process that lasts for a period of time, e.g. *the final stage of building.*
2 In a theatre, the stage is the area where the actors or entertainers perform.
3 (verb) If someone stages a play or event, they organize it and present it or take part in it.
[Old French *estage* = position]

stagecoach, stagecoaches
(noun) a large carriage pulled by horses which used to carry passengers and mail.

stagger, staggers, staggering, staggered
1 (verb) to walk unsteadily because you are ill or drunk.
2 If something staggers you, it amazes you.
staggering (adjective)
3 If events are staggered, they are arranged so that they do not all happen at the same time.
staggered (adjective)
[Old Norse *staka* = to push]

Similar words: (verb: sense 1) reel, totter, lurch

stagnant
1 (adjective) Stagnant water is not flowing and is unhealthy and dirty.
2 If business or society is stagnant, there is a lack of activity or development.
[Latin *stagnum* = pool]

An actor needs these words: cue dialogue proscenium prompt script
rehearsal wings comedy tragedy.

stagnate, stagnates, stagnating, stagnated
(verb) If a business or society stagnates, it becomes dead and unchanging.
stagnation (noun)

stain, stains, staining, stained
(noun) a mark on something that is difficult to move.
(verb) e.g. *That tomato has stained my jeans.*
[Old French *desteindre* = to discolour]

stained glass
(noun) coloured pieces of glass held together with strips of lead, as found in churches.

stainless steel
(noun) a metal made from steel and chromium which does not rust.

stairs
(plural noun) a set of steps inside a building.
staircase (noun)

stake, stakes, staking, staked
1 (noun) A stake is a bet, e.g. *He had a stake of £5 on 'Lucky Lady' to win in the 2.30 race.*
2 (phrase) If something is **at stake**, it might be lost or damaged if something else is not successful, e.g. *We must fight to save the company – there are thousands of jobs at stake.*
3 (verb) If you say you would stake your money, life or reputation on the success or truth of something, you mean you would risk it, e.g. *I wouldn't like to stake my life on that being true.*
4 (noun) If you have a stake in, for example, a business, you own part of it.
5 (phrase) If you **stake a claim** to something, you state that it is or should be yours.
6 (noun) a pointed wooden post that can be hammered into the ground.
[noun: sense 6: Old English *staca* = pin]

stalactite, stalactites
(noun) a piece of rock like a huge icicle hanging from the roof of a cave.
[Greek *stalaktos* = dripping]

stalagmite, stalagmites
(noun) a large pointed piece of rock sticking up from the floor of a cave.
[Greek *stalagmos* = dripping]

stale, staler, stalest
(adjective) no longer fresh.

stalemate
(noun) a situation in which neither side in an argument or contest can win [a chess term].

stalk, stalks, stalking, stalked (pronounced **stawk**)
1 (noun) the stem of a flower or leaf.
2 (verb) To stalk a person or animal means to follow them quietly.
3 If someone stalks out of a room, they walk out in a stiff, proud or angry way.
[noun: Old English *stalu* = upright piece of wood; verb: Old English *bestealcian* = to walk stealthily]

stall, stalls, stalling, stalled
1 (noun) a large table containing goods for sale or information.

2 (plural noun) In a theatre, the stalls are the seats at the lowest level, in front of the stage.
3 (verb) When a vehicle stalls, the engine suddenly stops.
4 If you stall when someone asks you to do something, you try to avoid doing it until later.
[senses 1-3: Old English *steall* = place for standing; sense 4: Anglo-French *estale* = bird used as a decoy, hence avoidance]

stallion, stallions
(noun) an adult, male horse that can be used for breeding.

stamen, stamens
(noun) the small, delicate stalks which grow inside a flower's blossom and produce pollen.
[Latin *stamen* = thread, because stamens are like the upright threads in weaving]

stamina
(noun) the physical or mental energy needed to do something for a very long time.

stammer, stammers, stammering, stammered
(verb) to speak with difficulty, repeating words and sounds and hesitating awkwardly.
(noun) e.g. *George VI mastered his stammer bravely when he unexpectedly became king.*

stamp, stamps, stamping, stamped
1 (noun) e.g. *I collect stamps... They used a rubber stamp to date my library book.*
2 (verb) e.g. *to stamp an envelope... to stamp a library book.*
3 e.g. *to stamp your foot.*

stamp out
(phrasal verb) to put an end to something e.g. *We are determined to stamp out crime.*

stampede, stampedes, stampeding, stampeded
(verb) When animals stampede, they run in a wild, uncontrolled way.
[Spanish *estampida* = crash or din]

stand, stands, standing, stood
Selected meanings:
1 (verb) e.g. *I was so tired I could hardly stand.*
2 If a decision or offer stands, it is still valid e.g. *Fifty years later, the rule still stands.*
3 e.g. *Unemployment stands at 38 per cent.*
4 If you say you will not stand for something, you mean you will not put up with it.
5 If you stand by someone who is in trouble, you continue to give them support.
6 If you stand by an earlier promise, you continue to keep to it.
7 If you cannot stand something, you cannot bear it, e.g. *I can't stand the din any longer.*
8 If you stand to win something, you are likely to win it.
9 If you stand in an election, you are one of the candidates.
10 (phrase) If it **stands to reason** that something is the case, it is obvious and logical.
11 (noun) e.g. *a hat stand... We sat in the main stand at the football match.*
12 (phrases) If you **make a stand** or **take a stand** you defend your beliefs or ideas against criticism
[Latin *stare* = to stand]

What is the feminine of: dog fox boar gander lion stag?

stand by
(phrasal verb) to be ready, e.g. *The St John Ambulance were standing by in case of injuries.*
stand-by (noun)

stand in
(phrasal verb) If you stand in for someone, you take their place while they are ill or away.
stand-in (noun)

stand out
(phrasal verb) If something stands out, it can be easily noticed, e.g. *He stood out from the rest.*

stand up
1 (phrasal verb) If something stands up to rough treatment, it remains undamaged or unharmed.
2 If you stand up to someone who is criticizing or attacking you, you defend yourself.

standard, standards
1 (noun) a level of quality, achievement or behaviour, e.g. *His work is below the standard required.*
2 (adjective) usual, normal and correct, e.g. *This is the standard way to do it.*

standard of living, standards of living
(noun) The standard of living in a country or a family is its level of comfort and wealth.

standstill
(noun) If something comes to a standstill, it stops completely.

stanza, stanzas
(noun) a verse of a poem
[an Italian word meaning 'stopping place']

staple, staples, stapling, stapled
1 (verb) If you staple sheets of paper, you fasten them together with a stapler.
stapler (noun)
2 (adjective) A staple food forms a regular and basic part of someone's everyday diet.
[verb: Old English *stapol* = prop; adjective: Old Dutch *stapel* = warehouse]

star, stars, starring, starred
1 (noun) a large ball of burning gas in space.
2 a regular, pointed shape.
3 Famous actors, sports players and musicians are called stars.
4 (verb) e.g. *The first James Bond films starred Sean Connery.*
stellar (adjective) **starry** (adjective)

starboard
(adjective, noun) the starboard side of a ship is the right side when you are facing the bow (front). (opposite: **port**)
[Old English *steorbord* = steering side, because boats were formerly steered with a paddle over the right-hand side]

starch, starches
1 (noun) a substance used for stiffening fabric.
2 a carbohydrate found in foods such as bread, potatoes, and rice.

stare, stares, staring, stared
1 (verb) to look at something for a long time.
2 (noun) a long, piercing look.

Similar words: gape, gaze, goggle

stark
(phrase) If someone is **stark-naked**, they have no clothes on at all.
[Old English *stearc* = stiff]

starling, starlings
(noun) a common European bird.

start, starts, starting, started
1 (verb) e.g. *I started to do my homework... The car started first time.*
2 (noun) If you do something with a start, you do it with a sudden jerky movement because of surprise or fear, e.g. *He awoke with a start.*

startle, startles, startling, startled
(verb) If something sudden and unexpected startles you, it surprises you and makes you slightly frightened.
[Old English *steartlian* = to stumble]

starve, starves, starving, starved
(verb) If people are starving, they are suffering from a serious lack of food and are likely to die.
starvation (noun)
[Old English *steorfan* = to die]

state, states, stating, stated
1 (noun) the condition of something, e.g. *The R.S.P.C.A. man found the dog in a dreadful state.*
2 (phrase) If you are **in a state**, you are nervous or upset and unable to control your emotions.
3 (noun) a country, e.g. *the state of Denmark.*
4 Some big countries are divided into states with their own laws, e.g. *New York State.*
5 You can refer to the government of a country as the State, e.g. *The Tower of London is owned by the State.*
6 (verb) to say or write something formally.
[Latin *status* = standing or condition]

stately, statelier, stateliest
(adjective) impressive, graceful and dignified.

stately home, homes
(noun) a very large and grand old house.

statement, statements
(noun) something you say or write when you give facts or information in a formal way.

state school, schools
(noun) a school maintained and financed by the local authority and/or government.

static
1 (adjective) never moving or changing.
2 (noun) an electrical charge caused by friction.
[Greek *statikos* = causing to stand]

station, stations, stationing, stationed
1 (noun) e.g. *a railway station... a bus station... a radio station... a work station.*
2 (verb) Someone who is stationed somewhere is sent there to work or do a particular job, e.g. *He was stationed at Biggin Hill during the war.*
[Latin *statio* = a standing still]

stationary
(adjective) not moving, e.g. *stationary vehicles.*

Similar words: immobile, motionless, static, standing

Are your sure about the differences between: astrology and astronomy; biology and biography?

stationery
(noun) paper, pens and other writing equipment.
[Not to be confused with stationary; remember: 'e' is for envelopes]

statistic, statistics
(noun) an item of numerical information.
statistical (adjective) **statistically** (adverb)
[Latin *statisticus* = concerning state affairs]

statue, statues
(noun) a sculpture of a person.
[Latin *statua* = statue or image]

status (pronounced **stay**-tuss)
(noun) A person's status is their position and importance in society.
[Latin *status* = position]

Similar words: rank, position

staunch, stauncher, staunchest
(adjective) A staunch supporter is a strong and loyal supporter, e.g. *Berry's staunchest ally.*
[Old French *estanche* = watertight]

stave, staves, staving, staved
1 (noun) In music, a stave is the 5 lines used for recording musical notes on paper.
2 (verb) If you stave something off, you try to delay or prevent it.

stay, stays, staying, stayed
1 (verb) e.g. *We stayed on the beach all day... She is staying with friends... I stayed awake till 12.*
2 (phrase) If you **stay put**, you remain in the same place.

Similar words: remain, linger

steady, steadier, steadiest
1 (adjective) continuing gradually without big changes, e.g. *a steady rise in prices.*
2 firm and not shaking or wobbling, e.g. *He held it with a steady hand.*

Similar words: (sense 2) firm, secure, sure, fixed

steak, steaks
(noun) a good-quality cut of meat or fish.
[Old Norse *steik* = roast]

steal, steals, stealing, stole, stolen
(verb) to take something without permission, and keep it.
2 to move quietly and secretively, e.g. *We stole up the stairs.*

stealthy (rhymes with **healthy**)
(noun) If you do something stealthy, you do it quietly and secretively, e.g. *The burglar made a stealthy exit.*
stealth (noun) **stealthily** (adverb)

steam, steams, steaming, steamed
1 (noun) the vapour formed when water boils.
2 (phrase; informal) If you **let off steam**, you get rid of your energy or emotions by behaving noisily or energetically.
3 If you **run out of steam**, you have no more energy or enthusiasm left to do anything.
4 (verb) e.g. *The ship steamed out of the port... The car came steaming along at 70 m.p.h.*
5 (verb; informal) Steaming is a word for

attacking or stealing by a group of people in a crowd.
steamy (adjective) **steamer** (noun)

steam engine, engines
(noun) any engine that uses the energy of steam to produce mechanical work.

steel, steels
(noun) a very strong metal containing mainly iron with a small amount of carbon.

steel band, bands
(noun) a group of people who play music on special metal drums.

steelworks
(noun) a factory where steel is made.

steep, steeper, steepest
(adjective) e.g. *a steep slope... a steep increase in prices.*
steeply (adverb)
[Old English *steap* = high or towering]

steeple, steeples
(noun) a tall, pointed structure on top of a church tower.

steeplechase, steeplechases
(noun) a long horse race in which the horses jump over hedges, water jumps, etc.
[originally a race with a church steeple in sight as the finishing point]

steeplejack, steeplejacks
(noun) a person who climbs up very high buildings to repair or paint them.

steer, steers, steering, steered
1 (verb) To steer a vehicle or boat means to control it so that it goes in the right direction.
2 (noun) a neutered bull.

Similar words: (verb) pilot, guide, direct

stellar
(adjective) relating to the stars.
[Latin *stella* = star]

stem, stems, stemming, stemmed
1 (noun) the long, thin, central part of a plant that carries the leaves and flowers.
2 (verb) to originate from, e.g., *Long hospital waiting lists stem from a lack of money in the health service.*
[Old English *stemn* = stem or stalk]

stench, stenches
(noun) a very strong, unpleasant smell.

stencil, stencils
(noun) a piece of card or metal with a design cut out of it which can be painted over to make copies of the design.
[Middle English *stanselen* = to decorate with bright colours]

step, steps, stepping, stepped
1 (verb) e.g. *She stepped out of the car.*
2 (phrase) If someone tells you to **watch your step**, they are warning you to behave.
3 (noun) one of a series of actions that you take in order to achieve something, e.g. *The police took steps to see that there was no more trouble.*

How many anagrams can you make from STEP?

4 (verb) If someone steps down from an important position, they resign.

step in
(phrasal verb) If you step in, you become involved in a difficult situation to help sort it out.

step up
(phrasal verb) to increase, e.g. *The company has stepped up production this week.*

stepbrother, stepbrothers
(noun) Someone's stepbrother is a son of their stepmother or stepfather.

stepchild, stepchildren
(noun) a stepdaughter or stepson.

stepdaughter, stepdaughters
(noun) Someone's stepdaughter is a daughter their husband or wife had by an earlier marriage.

stepfather, stepfathers
(noun) Someone's stepfather is the man who is married to their mother but who is not their natural father.

stepladder, stepladders
(noun) a ladder in two parts that stands on its own.

stepmother, stepmothers
(noun) Someone's stepmother is the woman who is married to their father but who is not their natural mother.

stepping stones
(plural noun) a line of large stones that you walk on to cross a shallow river.

stepsister, stepsisters
(noun) Someone's stepsister is a daughter of their stepmother or stepfather.

stepson, stepsons
(noun) Someone's stepson is a son their husband or wife had by an earlier marriage.

stereo
1 (adjective) A stereo recording is one in which the sound is directed through two speakers.
2 (noun) A **personal stereo** is a small portable cassette recorder with headphones.
stereophonic (adjective)
[Greek *stereos* + *phōnē* = solid sound]

sterile
(adjective) completely clean and germ free.
[Latin *sterilis* = barren]

Similar words: antiseptic, disinfected

sterilize, sterilizes, sterilizing, sterilized; also spelled **sterilise**
(verb) to make something completely clean and free from germs.

stern, sterner, sternest; sterns
1 (adjective) very serious and strict, e.g. *stern parents... a stern warning.*
2 (noun) the back part of a boat.
[adjective: Old English *styrne* = severe or harsh noun: Old Norse *stjorn* = steering]

steroid, steroids
(noun) organic compounds that occur naturally in your body, e.g. as hormones. They are sometimes used and misused as a drug.

stethoscope, stethoscopes
(noun) a device used by a doctor to listen to a patient's heart and breathing.
[Greek *stēthos* = chest + *skopein* = to look at]

stew, stews, stewing, stewed
1 (verb) To stew meat, vegetables or fruit means to cook them slowly in a liquid.
2 (noun) a meat or vegetable dish cooked slowly in liquid.
[Middle English *stuen* = to take a very hot bath]

steward, stewards
1 (noun) a man who works on a ship or plane looking after passengers and serving meals.
2 a person who helps to direct the public at a race, march or other event.
[Old English *stigweard* = hall protector]

stewardess, stewardesses
(noun) a woman who works on a ship or plane looking after passengers and serving meals.

stick, sticks, sticking, stuck
1 (noun) e.g. *a stick of dynamite.*
2 (verb) e.g. *It sticks like glue... Stick it in the cupboard... You must stick to our agreement.*
3 (phrase) If someone gets **the wrong end of the stick**, they completely misunderstand a situation.
sticky (adjective)

stick out
1 (phrasal verb) e.g. *Don't his ears stick out!*
2 If someone doing a difficult thing sticks it out, they do not leave or give up.
3 If you stick out for something, you continue to demand it and do not accept anything less, e.g. *The ambulancemen stuck out for a better deal.*

stick insect, insects
(noun) an insect with a long, cylindrical body and long legs, which looks like a twig.

stick-in-the-mud, stick-in-the-muds
(noun; informal) someone who does not like doing anything new or adventurous.

stiff, stiffer, stiffest
1 (adjective) firm and not easily bent.
2 difficult or severe, e.g. *Competition is stiff.*
3 (adverb; informal) If you are bored stiff or scared stiff, you are very bored or very scared.
stiffly (adverb) **stiffness** (noun) **stiffen** (verb)

stile, stiles
(noun) a step on either side of a wall or fence to enable you to climb over.

still, stiller, stillest
1 (adverb) e.g. *It is still raining... We could still win... You may not want to wash up but you've still got to do it.*
2 (adverb, adjective) *Try to keep still... Still waters run deep.*
stillness (noun)

stilts
(plural noun) two long pieces of wood or metal on which people balance and walk.
[Middle English *stilte* = crutch or plough handle]

stilted
(adjective) formal, unnatural and rather awkward, e.g. *After some stilted efforts at*

Repeat quickly: Does this shop still sell shiny, silk shirts?

conversation, he gave up.

Similar words: wooden, stiff

stimulate, stimulates, stimulating, stimulated
1 (verb) to encourage something to begin or develop, e.g. *Rising prices will stimulate demands for higher wages.*
2 If something stimulates you, it gives you new ideas and enthusiasm.
stimulating (adjective) **stimulation** (noun)

Similar words: (sense 1) inspire, arouse, rouse

sting, stings, stinging, stung
(verb) If a creature or plant stings you, it pricks your skin and injects a substance causing pain.

stingy, stingier, stingiest (pronounced stin-jee)
(adjective; informal) very mean.

stink, stinks, stinking, stank, stunk
1 (verb) to smell very unpleasant.
2 (verb; informal) If you say that a situation stinks, you mean there is something very unpleasant or suspicious about it.

Similar words: stench, reek, pong

stint, stints
(noun) a period of time spent doing a particular job, e.g. *She's doing a 3-month stint as a waitress.*

stir, stirs, stirring, stirred
1 (verb) e.g. *to stir a cup of tea... The trees stirred in the breeze.*
2 (noun) If an event causes a stir, it causes general excitement or shock, e.g. *Her latest speech has caused a huge stir.*

stir up
(phrasal verb) To stir up trouble or emotion means to cause it.
stirrer (noun)

stir-fry, stir-fries, stir-frying, stir-fried
(verb) to fry small pieces of meat or vegetables quickly in oil over a high heat.

stirrup, stirrups
(noun) Stirrups are two metal loops which you put your feet in when riding.
[Old English *stig* = step + *rap* = rope]

stitch, stitches, stitching, stitched
1 (verb) to use a needle and thread to sew things, for example material or wounds, together.
2 (noun) one of the pieces of thread that can be seen where a wound has been stitched, e.g. *I had to have 3 stitches in my leg.*
3 a sharp, muscular pain at the side of your abdomen, usually felt while running.
4 (phrase; informal) Someone who is **in stitches** is laughing and cannot stop.

stoat, stoats
(noun) a wild animal with a long body, brown fur and a black tip to its tail.

stock, stocks, stocking, stocked
1 (noun) Stocks are shares bought as an investment in a company.
2 (verb) A shop that stocks particular goods keeps a supply of them to sell.

3 (noun) A shop's stock is the total amount of goods it has for sale.
4 (phrases) If goods are **in stock** in a shop, you can buy them now. If they are **out of stock**, they have all been sold and are unavailable.
5 (verb) If you stock a shelf or cupboard, you fill it with food or other things.

stock up
(phrasal verb) to buy a big supply of something.

stockbroker, stockbrokers
(noun) a person whose job is to buy and sell shares for people who want to invest money.

stock car, cars
(noun) an old car converted for racing on tracks where the cars often collide.

stock exchange, exchanges
(noun) a place where there is trading in stocks and shares, e.g. *Prices on the London Stock Exchange fell heavily today.*

stocking, stockings
(noun) Stockings are long pieces of clothing that cover a woman's legs.

stock market, markets
(noun) the organization and activity involved in buying and selling stocks and shares.

stock-still
(adverb) absolutely still.
[Old English *stock* = tree trunk or log + *still*]

stocktaking
(noun) the counting and checking of all a shop's or a business's goods.

stocky, stockier, stockiest
(adjective) A stocky person is rather short, but broad and solid-looking.

stodgy, stodgier, stodgiest
(adjective) Stodgy food is solid and filling.

stoke, stokes, stoking, stoked
(verb) to put more fuel on a fire.
[Old Dutch *stoken* = to push or to poke]

stomach, stomachs
1 (noun) the organ inside the body where food is digested.
2 You can refer to the front part of your body below your waist as your stomach.

Similar words: abdomen, tummy, belly

stomp, stomps, stomping, stomped
(verb; informal) If you stomp around, you walk with heavy steps, often because you are angry.

stone, stones, stoning, stoned
1 (noun) the hard, solid substance found in the ground and used for building.
2 the large seed in the centre of some fruits.
3 (verb) to throw stones at someone e.g. *the stoning of St Stephen.*
4 Someone who is stoned is under the influence of drink or drugs.
5 (noun) a unit of weight. (1 st. = 6.35kg = 14lbs)
stony (adjective)

stone-cold
(adjective) completely without warmth.

Repeat quickly: A library likes to lend literature that a bookshop might not stock.

stone-deaf
(adjective) completely deaf.

stool, stools
(noun) a seat with legs but no back or arms.

stoop, stoops, stooping, stooped
1 (verb) to stand or walk with your shoulders bent forwards.
2 If you would not stoop to something, you would not disgrace yourself by doing it.
[Old English *stupan* = to bow down]

stop, stops, stopping, stopped
1 (verb) e.g. *I stopped at the kerb to look for traffic... This stereo has stopped working.*
2 (phrase) To **put a stop to** something means to prevent it from happening or continuing.

Similar words: cease, discontinue, quit, leave off, pack in

stop off
(phrasal verb) If you stop off somewhere on a journey, you stay there for a short while.

stop up
(phrasal verb) If you stop up a hole or gap in something, you fill it.

stopper, stoppers
(noun) a piece of glass, plastic or cork that fits into the neck of a jar or bottle.

stopwatch, stopwatches
(noun) a watch, used to time events, that can be started and stopped by pressing buttons.

storage
(noun) The storage of something is the keeping of it somewhere until it is needed.

storage heater, heaters
(noun) a heater containing special bricks that can store heat.

store, stores, storing, stored
1 (noun) a shop.
2 (verb) When you store something somewhere, you keep it there until it is needed.
3 (noun) a supply of something kept for future use, e.g. *I kept a store of envelopes just in case.*
4 a place where things are kept while they are not used, e.g. *a meatstore.*
5 (phrase) Something that is **in store** for you is going to happen to you in the future.
[Latin *instaurare* = to restore or to renew]

Similar words: (noun: sense 3) reserve, stockpile, stock, reservoir, supply

storeroom, storerooms
(noun) a room where things are kept until they are needed.

storey, storeys
(noun) one of the floors of a building.

stork, storks
(noun) a very large, white and black bird with long red legs and a long bill.

storm, storms, storming, stormed
1 (noun) a time of high wind and heavy rain.
2 (verb) If someone storms out, they leave quickly, noisily and angrily.
3 If people storm a place, they attack it.
stormy (adjective)

story, stories
(noun) e.g. *Tell me a story... She's writing her life story.*
[Latin *historia* = narrative or history]

Similar words: yarn, anecdote, tale, narrative, saga

stout, stouter, stoutest
1 (adjective) rather fat.
2 thick, strong and sturdy, e.g. *stout shoes.*
[Old French *estout* = bold]

stove, stoves
(noun) a piece of equipment which provides heat for a room or for cooking.

stow, stows, stowing, stowed
(verb) If you stow something somewhere or stow it away, you store it until it is needed.
[Old English *stowian* = to keep back from]

stowaway, stowaways
(noun) someone who hides in a ship or plane to go somewhere secretly without paying.
stow away (verb)

straddle, straddles, straddling, straddled
(verb) If you straddle something, you stand or sit with one leg on either side of it.

straggle, straggles, straggling, straggled
(verb) to move slowly in irregular and disorganized groups, e.g. *As Mr Bishop strode on, the children behind him straggled more and more.*
straggly (adjective) **straggler** (noun)

straight, straighter, straightest
1 (adjective, adverb) continuing in the same direction, e.g. *a straight road... The car came straight at me.*
2 (adverb) immediately, e.g. *Go straight to bed.*
3 (adjective) neat and tidy, e.g. *I must get the house straight this weekend.*
4 honest, frank and direct, e.g. *Give me a straight answer... I'll be straight with you.*
5 (phrase) To **get something straight** means to understand it properly and correctly.
6 To **keep a straight face** means to manage not to laugh even when something funny happens.
7 A criminal who is **going straight** is no longer involved in crime.
straighten (verb)
[Middle English *streccan* = to stretch]

straightaway
(adverb) immediately.

straightforward
1 (adjective) easy and involving no problems, e.g. *It was a straightforward operation.*
2 honest, open and frank, e.g. *He is a straightforward sort of chap.*

strain, strains, straining, strained
1 (noun) worry and nervous tension.
2 (verb) To strain something means to force it or use it more than is reasonable or normal.
3 If you strain a muscle, you injure it.

4 To strain food means to pour away the liquid from it.
[Old French *estreindre* = to press together]

Similar words: (verb: sense 4) sieve, sift, filter

strained
(adjective) worried and anxious.

strait, **straits**
(noun) a narrow strip of sea; difficult circumstances, e.g. *the Menai Straits... the company is in dire financial straits.*
[Old French *estreit* = tight]

stranded
(adjective) If someone or something is stranded somewhere, they are stuck and cannot leave.

strange, **stranger**, **strangest**
(adjective) unusual or unexpected.
strangely (adverb) **strangeness** (noun)
[Latin *extraneus* = foreign]

Similar words: peculiar, odd, queer, curious, funny, zany, freakish, unfamiliar, alien, foreign

stranger, **strangers**
(noun) someone you have never met before.

strangle, **strangles**, **strangling**, **strangled**
(verb) to kill someone by squeezing their throat.
strangulation (noun)
[Greek *straggein* = to squeeze]

strap, **straps**
(noun) a narrow piece of leather or cloth, used to fasten or hold things together.

strapping
(adjective) tall, strong and healthy-looking.

strategy, **strategies**
(noun) a plan for achieving something.
[Greek *stratēgia* = the function of a general]

straw, **straws**
1 (noun) the dry, yellowish stalks from cereal crops.
2 a hollow tube of paper or plastic which you use to suck a drink into your mouth.
3 (phrase) If something is **the last straw**, it is the latest in a series of bad events and makes you feel you cannot tolerate any more.

strawberry, **strawberries**
(noun) a small red fruit.

stray, **strays**, **straying**, **strayed**
1 (verb) When people or animals stray, they wander away from where they should be.
2 (adjective) e.g. *a stray dog.*
3 (noun) A stray is a stray dog or cat.

streak, **streaks**, **streaking**, **streaked**
1 (verb) If something is streaked with a colour, it has lines of the colour in it.
streaky (adjective)
2 to move very quickly.
3 (noun) A lucky streak is a series of successes.
[Old English *strica* = mark or stroke of a pen]

stream, **streams**, **streaming**, **streamed**
1 (noun) a small river.
2 a steady flow of something, e.g. *a stream of traffic.*
3 (verb) to move in a continuous flow in large quantities, e.g. *Tears streamed down his face.*

streamer, **streamers**
(noun) a long, narrow strip of coloured paper used for decoration.

streamlined
(adjective) A streamlined plane, train etc. has a pointed shape which helps it to move quickly and efficiently.

street, **streets**
1 (noun) a road in a city, town or village, usually with buildings along it.
2 (phrase) Someone who is **streets ahead** has made much more progress than others.
3 If something is **right up your street**, you are very interested in it or know a lot about it.
[Latin *via strata* = paved way]

streetwise
(adjective; informal) A person who is streetwise knows the tricks and dodges of how to get by in the city.

strength, **strengths**
1 (noun) Your strength is your physical energy and the power of your muscles.
2 Someone's strengths are their good qualities and abilities, e.g. *Her great strength was her ability to listen to others.*
3 e.g. *The toy must have had great strength to stand up to the way it was treated... Make sure you mix the squash to the correct strength.*

Similar words: (sense 1) might, force, intensity, muscle

strengthen, **strengthens**, **strengthening**, **strengthened**
(verb) to make something stronger.

Similar words: fortify, reinforce, toughen

strenuous (pronounced **stren**-yoo-uss)
(adjective) involving a lot of effort or energy, e.g. *It was a very strenuous walk.*
strenuously (adverb)
[Latin *strenuus* = brisk]

stress, **stresses**, **stressing**, **stressed**
1 (noun) worry and nervous tension.
2 (verb) If you stress a point, you emphasize it and draw attention to its importance.
3 (noun) emphasis put on a word or part of a word when it is pronounced, making it slightly louder, e.g. In the word 'cowboy' the stress is on 'cow'.
stressful (adjective)
[a shortened form of *distress*]

Similar words: (noun: sense 1) strain, pressure, tension
(verb) emphasize, highlight, underline
(noun: sense 3) accent, emphasis

stretch, **stretches**, **stretching**, **stretched**
1 (verb) e.g. *Elastic stretches to twice its size...*

Names of streets, roads, avenues, etc. begin with capital letters, e.g. High Street, Dover Road.

*Stretch your arms as wide as you can... The
water stretches as far as you can see.*
2 (noun) A stretch of land etc. is an area of it.
3 A stretch of time is a period of time.
4 If someone's money or resources are stretched,
they hardly have enough for their needs.

stretcher, stretchers
(noun) a long piece of material with a pole along
each side, used to carry an injured person.

strict, stricter, strictest
(adjective) in very firm control, e.g. *a strict
teacher... a strict diet.*
[Latin *stringere* = to draw tight]

strictly
1 (adverb) only for a particular purpose, e.g.
This meeting is strictly for members only.
2 (phrase) You say **strictly speaking** to correct a
statement or add more precise information, e.g.
*This is my friend Paul – well, strictly speaking,
he's my sister's friend.*

stride, strides, striding, strode
1 (verb) to walk quickly with long steps.
2 (noun) The length of your stride is the distance
between your footmarks when you walk.
3 (phrase) To **make strides** means to make rapid
progress.
4 To **take a problem in your stride** means to deal
with it calmly.

strike, strikes, striking, struck
1 (noun) If there is a strike, people stop working
as a protest.
2 A hunger strike is a refusal to eat anything as a
protest. A rent strike is a refusal to pay rent.
3 (verb) To strike someone means to hit them.
4 e.g. *A thought struck me... DISASTER STRIKES
VILLAGE!... The clock struck 3... We struck a
match in the cave.*
5 If you are struck by something, you are
impressed by it.
6 To strike a deal with someone means to come to
an agreement with them.
7 If someone strikes oil or gold, they discover it
in the ground.
8 (phrase) If you **strike lucky**, you have good luck.

striker, strikers
1 (noun) a person refusing to work as a protest.
2 In football, a striker is a central attacking
player.

string, strings
1 (noun) thin cord for tying things up.
2 The strings of a musical instrument are tight
lengths of wire or nylon which vibrate to
produce notes.
3 (plural noun) The section of an orchestra with
stringed instruments is called the strings.

string out
(phrasal verb) If things are strung out, they are
spread out in a long line.

stringed
(adjective) A stringed instrument is one with
strings, e.g. a guitar or violin.

strip, strips, stripping, stripped
1 (noun) A strip of something is a long, narrow
piece of it.
2 (verb) If you strip, you take off all your clothes.
3 To strip something means to remove whatever
is covering its surface, e.g. *to strip wallpaper.*
4 To strip someone of their property or rights
means to take them away officially.
5 (noun) A comic strip is a series of drawings
which tell a story.
6 A football team's strip is the clothes worn by
the team when playing a match.
7 (phrase; informal) To **tear someone off a strip**
means to tell them off severely.
[noun: sense 1 – Old Dutch *stripe* = stripe;
verb: senses 2-4: Old English *bestriepan* = to
plunder]

stripe, stripes
1 (noun) Stripes are long, thin lines, usually of
different colours.
2 Stripes are also narrow bands of material sewn
onto a uniform to indicate someone's rank.
striped (adjective)

strive, strives, striving, strove, striven
(verb) If you strive to do something, you make a
great effort to achieve it.

strobe lighting
(noun) high-intensity flashing light.
[Greek *strobos* = twisting or spinning]

stroke, strokes, stroking, stroked
1 (verb) to move your hand smoothly and gently
over something.
2 (noun) If someone has a stroke, they suddenly
lose consciousness as a result of a blockage or
break in a blood vessel in the brain.
3 When you swim or row, the strokes are the
movements you make with your arms or the
oars; also the style of swimming, e.g. *backstroke.*
4 In games such as tennis, a stroke is a particular
way of hitting the ball.
5 e.g. *At the stroke of 12 the ghost emerged.*

stroll, strolls, strolling, strolled
1 (verb) to walk slowly in a relaxed way.
2 (noun) a slow, pleasant walk.

Similar words: amble, saunter

strong, stronger, strongest
1 (adjective) e.g. *a strong weightlifter... She has
a strong personality... a strong toy... a strong
wind... a strong smell... a strong drink... Troops
nearly 50,000 strong were stationed in Germany.*
2 Your strong points are the things you are good
at.
3 (adverb) If someone or something is still going
strong, they are still healthy or working well
after a long time.

Similar words: (sense 1) mighty, muscular, powerful

stroppy, stroppier, stroppiest
(adjective; informal) bad-tempered or annoyed.

structure, structures, structuring, structured
1 (noun) something that has been built or
constructed.

Do you know what these are? granny sheepshank bowline clove hitch reef

2 (verb) To structure something means to arrange it into an organized pattern or system.
structural (adjective) **structurally** (adverb)
[Latin *structura* = building or arrangement]

struggle, struggles, struggling, struggled
1 (verb) If you struggle to do something, you try hard to do it in difficult circumstances.
2 When people struggle, they twist and move violently during a fight.
3 (noun) a fight.

strum, strums, strumming, strummed
(verb) To strum a guitar means to play it by moving your fingers across all the strings.

strut, struts, strutting, strutted
(verb) To strut means to walk in a stiff, proud way with your chest out and your head high.
[Old English *strutian* = to walk stiffly]

Similar words: swagger, parade

stub, stubs, stubbing, stubbed
1 (noun) The stub of a pencil is the short piece that is left when the rest has been used.
2 The stub of a cheque or ticket is the small part that you keep when the rest is handed in.
3 (verb) If you stub your toe, you hurt it by accidentally kicking something.
[Old English *stubb* = stump]

stubble
1 (noun) the short stalks remaining in the ground after a crop is harvested.
2 the short hair on a man's face because he has not shaved recently.
[Latin *stipula* = stalk or stem]

stubborn
(adjective) determined not to change or give way.
stubbornly (adverb) **stubbornness** (noun)

Similar words: obstinate, persistent, pig-headed

stubby, stubbier, stubbiest
(adjective) short and thick, e.g. *stubby fingers.*

stuck
(adjective) e.g. *The lift is stuck between the second and third floors... I got stuck with my German.*

stuck-up
(adjective; informal) proud and conceited.

studded
(adjective) decorated with small pieces of metal or precious stones.

student, students
(noun) a person studying at university or college.
[Latin *studens* = hard-working]

studio, studios
1 (noun) a room where a photographer or painter works.
2 a room with special equipment where records, films, radio or TV programmes are made.
[Italian *studio* = study]

study, studies, studying, studied
1 (verb) If you study a particular subject, you spend time learning about it.

2 (noun) Studies are subjects which are studied, e.g. *European Studies.*
3 (verb) to look at something carefully, e.g. *I studied the map for a while.*
4 (noun) a room used for writing, reading and studying, e.g. *the vicar's study.*
studious (adjective)
[Latin *studere* = to study]

stuff, stuffs, stuffing, stuffed
1 (noun) a general word for a substance or group of things, e.g. *This paint is good stuff... There was stuff lying everywhere.*
2 (verb) to push something in quickly and roughly, e.g. *I stuffed my clothes in the drawer.*
[Old French *estoffer* = to furnish or to provide]

stuffing
(noun) a savoury filling, e.g. sage and onion, put inside poultry or a vegetable before cooking.

stuffy, stuffier, stuffiest
1 (adjective) very formal and old-fashioned.
2 If it is stuffy in a room, there is not enough fresh air.

Similar word: (sense 2) close

stumble, stumbles, stumbling, stumbled
(verb) to trip and almost fall.

stump, stumps, stumping, stumped
1 (noun) a small part of something that is left when the rest has been removed, e.g. *the stump of an old tree.*
2 In cricket, the stumps are the 3 upright sticks that support the bails to make the wicket.
3 (verb) If a question or problem stumps you, you cannot think of an answer or solution.

stumpy, stumpier, stumpiest
(adjective) short and thick.

stun, stuns, stunning, stunned
(verb) If you are stunned by something, you are very shocked by it.
[Old French *estoner* = to daze]

stunning
(adjective) very beautiful or impressive, e.g. *The film is visually stunning... a stunning victory.*

stunt, stunts, stunting, stunted
1 (noun) an unusual or dangerous and exciting action that someone does to get publicity or as part of a film.
stunt man (noun)
2 (verb) To stunt the growth of something means to prevent it from growing as it should.

stupid, stupider, stupidest
(adjective) lacking in intelligence and sense.
stupidity (noun)
[Latin *stupidus* = senseless]

Similar words: dull, dim, dumb, simple, thick

sturdy, sturdier, sturdiest
(adjective) strong and firm and unlikely to be damaged or injured, e.g. *a sturdy oak table.*

stutter, stutters, stuttering, stuttered
1 (verb) When someone stutters, they hesitate or repeat sounds when speaking.
2 (noun) a difficulty in speaking smoothly.

Can you spell and define these words? geology archaeology psychology palaeontology biology

sty, sties
1 (noun) a shed and run for a pig.
2 an infection in the form of a small red swelling on a person's eyelid.
[sense 1: Old English *stig* = pig pen
sense 2: Old English *stigend* = swelling + *ye* = eye]

style, styles
1 (noun) The style of something is the general way in which it is done or presented.
2 A person or place that has style is smart, elegant and fashionable.
[Latin *stilus* = writing implement, hence styles of writing]

Similar words: (sense 2) flair, elegance

stylish
(adjective) smart, elegant and fashionable.
stylishly (adverb)

suave (pronounced **swahv**)
(adjective) charming, polite and confident, e.g. *a suave young man.*
[Latin *suavis* = sweet or agreeable]

sub-
(prefix) under, e.g. *substandard... subconscious... subset.*
[Latin *sub* = under or below]

subconscious
1 (noun) the part of your mind that can influence you without your being aware of it.
2 (adjective) e.g. *a subconscious wish to get revenge.*
subconsciously (adverb)

subcontinent, subcontinents
(noun) a large mass of land, forming part of a continent, e.g. *the Indian subcontinent.*

subdivision, subdivisions
(noun) something which is part of something larger, e.g. *InterCity is a subdivision of British Rail.*

subdued
1 (adjective) rather quiet and sad.
2 not very bright, e.g. *subdued lighting.*

subject, subjects, subjecting, subjected
1 (noun) The subject of writing or a conversation is the thing being discussed.
2 In grammar, the subject is the person or thing doing the action expressed by the verb, e.g., In the sentence *My cat keeps catching birds,* 'my cat' is the subject.
3 an area of study, e.g. history.
4 (verb; pronounced sub-**ject**) To subject someone to something means to make them experience it, e.g. *I'm sorry to subject you to all these tests.*
5 (noun) The subjects of a country are the people who live there.
6 (adjective) **Subject to** means affected by, e.g. *These prices are subject to VAT* (which means VAT will be added on).
[Latin *subjectus* = brought under]

subjective
(adjective) influenced by personal feelings and opinion, not fact or logic.

subjunctive
(noun) In grammar, the subjunctive mood is one of the forms a verb can take. It is used to express wishes and doubts or purposes – anything but a fact, e.g. *I should be grateful if you would send me a catalogue.* With most English verbs it is obsolete.
[compare: **indicative, infinitive, imperative**]

submarine, submarines
(noun) a ship that can travel beneath the surface of the sea.

submerge, submerges, submerging, submerged
1 (verb) to go beneath the surface of a liquid.
2 If you submerge yourself in an activity, you become totally involved in it.
[Latin *submergere* = to plunge under]

submit, submits, submitting, submitted
1 (verb) If you submit to something, you accept it because you are not powerful enough to resist.
submissive (adjective)
2 If you submit an application etc., you send it to someone for consideration.
submission (noun)
[Latin *submittere* = to place under]

subnormal
(adjective) Someone who is subnormal has less intelligence than a normal person of their age.

subordinate
(adjective) If one thing is subordinate to another, it is less important, e.g. *All other questions are subordinate to this one.*
[Latin *subordinare* = below in rank]

subordinate clause, clauses
(noun) In grammar, a subordinate clause is a group of words which adds details to the main clause of a sentence e.g. In the sentence: *This is our house, which has a green door,* 'which has a green door' is the subordinate clause.

subscribe, subscribes, subscribing, subscribed
(verb) If you subscribe to a charity or campaign, you send money to it regularly.
subscriber (noun)
[Latin *subscribere* = to write underneath]

subscription, subscriptions
(noun) a sum of money that you pay regularly to belong to an organization or to receive regular copies of a magazine.

subsequent
(adjective) happening afterwards, e.g *Subsequent tests have given better results.*
subsequently (adverb)
[Latin *subsequi* = to follow after]

subset, subsets
(noun) A subset of a larger set or group is a smaller set or group contained within it.

subside, subsides, subsiding, subsided
1 (verb) to become less intense or quieter, e.g. *The pain subsided... the noise subsided.*
2 If the ground subsides, it sinks down.
subsidence (noun)
[Latin *subsidere* = to settle or to sink down]

Etymology. Find out how these words are connected: mariner mermaid submarine.

subsidiary, subsidiaries (pronounced
sub-**sid**-yer-ee)
1 (adjective) less important than the main thing.
2 (noun) a company which is part of a larger
company.

subsidize, subsidizes, subsidizing, subsidized;
also spelled **subsidise**
(verb) to provide part of the cost of something,
e.g. *Many governments subsidize their railways.*
subsidy (noun)

subsist, subsists, subsisting, subsisted
(verb) If people are subsisting on a particular
food, they are just managing to stay alive on it.
subsistence (noun)
[Latin *subsistere* = to stand firm]

substance, substances
(noun) anything which is a solid; a powder, a
liquid or a paste can be called a substance.
[Latin *substantia* = substance or property]

Similar words: matter, stuff, material, fabric

substandard
(adjective) below a required standard and
therefore unacceptable.

substantial
(adjective) very large in degree or amount, e.g. *a
substantial increase... substantial damage.*
substantially (adverb)

substitute, substitutes, substituting, substituted
1 (verb) to replace one person or thing with
another.
2 (noun) a replacement.
substitution (noun)
[Latin *substituere* = to set in place]

subterranean (pronounced sub-ter-**rain**-ee-an)
(adjective) underground.
[Latin *subterraneus* = under the earth]

subtitle, subtitles
(noun) A film or TV programme with subtitles
has a printed version of the spoken words at the
bottom of the screen.

subtle, subtler, subtlest (pronounced **sut**-tl)
(adjective) very fine, delicate or small in degree,
e.g. *a subtle change... a subtle joke.*
2 using quiet, hidden ways to achieve something.
e.g. *Iago was a subtle troublemaker.*
subtly (adverb) **subtlety** (noun)
[Latin *subtilis* = finely woven]

subtract, subtracts, subtracting, subtracted
(verb) to take away one number from another,
e.g. *5 subtract 3 = 5 − 3 = 2.*
subtraction (noun)
[Latin *subtrahere* = to draw away]

subtropical
(adjective) relating to areas of the world
between the tropical and the milder regions.

suburb, suburbs
(noun) an area of a town or city that is away
from its centre.
suburban (adjective) **suburbia** (noun)
[Latin *suburbium* = close to a city]

subway, subways
(noun) a footpath under a road.

succeed, succeeds, succeeding, succeeded
1 (verb) to achieve the result you want e.g., *If at
first you don't succeed, Try, try again.*
2 To succeed someone means to be the next
person to have their job.
[Latin *succedere* = to follow after]

Similar words: (sense 1) prosper, thrive, do well

success, successes
(noun) the achievement of something you have
been trying to do.
successful (adjective) **successfully** (adverb)

succession, successions
1 (noun) A succession of things is a number of
them occurring one after the other.
2 (phrase) Example: *She went to Rome for the
third year* in succession means she went three
years running, without a break.
3 A member of the royal family who is first in
succession to the throne is the person who will
be the next king or queen.

successive
(adjective) occurring one after the other without
a break, e.g. *two successive Saturdays.*

successor, successors
(noun) Someone's successor is the person who
takes their job when they leave.

succulent
(adjective) Succulent food is juicy and delicious.
[Latin *sucus* = juice]

such
(adjective, pronoun) e.g. *It was Brighton or
Bournemouth or some such place... a game of
chance such as roulette... It was such a lovely
day.*

suck, sucks, sucking, sucked
(verb) e.g. *This vac isn't sucking properly.*
suction (noun)

sucker, suckers
1 (noun; informal) someone who is easily fooled
or cheated.
2 Suckers are pads on the bodies of some animals
and insects which they use to cling to a surface.
3 A sucker on a plant is a new shoot that grows
from an underground stem or root.

Sudanese (pronounced soo-dan-**neez**)
1 (adjective) belonging to the Sudan.
2 (noun) someone who comes from the Sudan.

sudden
(adjective) happening quickly and unexpectedly
e.g. *a sudden drop in temperature.*
suddenly (adverb) **suddenness** (noun)
[Latin *subitus* = unexpected]

sue, sues, suing, sued
(verb) If you sue someone, you start a legal case
against them, usually to claim money from them
for something they have done to you.
[Latin *sequi* = to follow]

suede (pronounced **swayd**)
(noun) leather with a soft, roughened surface.
[French *gants de Suède* = gloves from Sweden]

suffer, suffers, suffering, suffered
(verb) to be badly affected by something, e.g. *He*

A prefix may be added at the start of a root word and a suffix at the end. General name: *affixes.*

*is suffering terrible pain... Her work is suffering
because of these late nights.*
sufferer (noun) **suffering** (noun)
[Latin *sufferre* = to bear]

sufficient
(adjective) enough, e.g. *We had sufficient food
for 3 days.*
sufficiently (adverb) **suffice** (verb)
[Latin *sufficiens* = supplying the needs of]

suffix, suffixes
(noun) a group of letters which is added to the
end of a word to form a new word, e.g. '-ology'.
[Latin *suffigere* = to fasten or to fix below]

suffocate, suffocates, suffocating, suffocated
(verb) to die as a result of having too little air or
oxygen to breathe.
suffocation (noun)
[Latin *suffocare* = to strangle]

sugar
(noun) a sweet substance used to sweeten food
or drinks, obtained from cane or beet.
[Arabic *sukkar* = sugar]

sugar beet
(noun) a plant with white roots from which
sugar is obtained.

sugar cane
(noun) a tall, tropical plant with thick stems
from which sugar is obtained.

suggest, suggests, suggesting, suggested
(verb) If you suggest a plan or idea you mention
it as a possibility.
[Latin *suggerere* = to bring up]

Similar words: propose, recommend

suggestion, suggestions
1 (noun) a plan or idea that is mentioned as a
possibility.
2 A suggestion of something is a very slight
indication of it, e.g. *He replied with the merest
suggestion of a smile.*

Similar words: (sense 1) motion, proposal,
recommendation

suicide, suicides
1 (noun) People who commit suicide deliberately
kill themselves.
2 If you say that to do something would be
suicide, you mean that it would ruin someone's
career or future.
suicidal (adjective) **suicidally** (adverb)
[Latin *sui* = of oneself + *caedere* = to kill]

suit, suits, suiting, suited
1 (noun) a matching jacket and trousers or skirt.
2 (verb) If a situation or course of action suits
you, you are quite happy about it.
3 If a piece of clothing or a colour suits you, you
look good when you are wearing it.
4 (noun) one of 4 different types of card in a
pack of playing cards: hearts, clubs, diamonds,
spades.
5 (phrase) To **follow suit** means to do what

someone else has just done, e.g. *He bowed his
head. Mother and Jenny followed suit.*
[Old French *sieute* = set of things]

suitable
(adjective) right for a particular purpose, e.g.
suitable clothes for winter.
suitability (noun) **suitably** (adverb)

Similar words: appropriate, apt, proper

suitcase, suitcases
(noun) a case in which you carry your clothes
when you are travelling.

suite, suites (pronounced **sweet**)
1 (noun) In a hotel, a suite is a set of rooms.
2 a set of matching furniture or bathroom
fittings, e.g. *a 3-piece suite.*
[Old French *sieute* = set of things]

suited
(adjective) right or appropriate for a particular
purpose or person, e.g. *ideally suited for the job.*

sulk, sulks, sulking, sulked
1 (verb) Someone who is sulking is showing their
annoyance by being silent and moody.
2 (noun) a sulky mood.
sulky (adjective)

sullen
(adjective) behaving in a bad-tempered and
disagreeably silent way, e.g. *a sullen boy.*
sullenly (adverb)

sulphate, sulphates
(noun) a salt or compound containing sulphuric
acid.

sulphur
(noun) a pale yellow, non-metallic chemical
which burns with a very unpleasant smell.

sultan, sultans
(noun) In some Muslim countries, the ruler of the
country is called the sultan.
[Arabic *sultan* = rule]

sultana, sultanas
(noun) Sultanas are dried grapes.

sultry, sultrier, sultriest
(adjective) Sultry weather is unpleasantly hot
and humid.

sum, sums, summing, summed
1 (noun) an amount of money, e.g. *a sum of £10.*
2 In arithmetic, a sum is a calculation.
3 The sum of something is the total amount of it,
e.g. *The sum of 3 and 4 = 3 + 4 = 7.*
4 (verb) If you sum something up, you briefly
describe its main points.
[Latin *summus* = highest or total]

**summarize, summarizes, summarizing,
summarized**; also spelled **summarise**
(verb) To summarize something means to give a
short account of its main points.

summary, summaries
(noun) A summary of something is a short
account of its main points.

Similar words: outline, précis

Portmanteau words are formed when writers combine two words,
e.g. brunch = breakfast and lunch.

summer, summers
(noun) the season between spring and autumn.

summit, summits
1 (noun) The summit of a mountain is its top.
2 A summit is a meeting between leaders of major countries to discuss important issues.

summon, summons, summoning, summoned
1 (verb) If someone summons you, they order you to go to them.
2 If you summon up strength or energy, you make a great effort to be strong or energetic.
[Latin *summonere* = to remind discreetly]

summons, summonses, summonsing, summonsed
1 (noun) an official order to appear in court.
2 (verb) If someone is summonsed, they are officially ordered to appear in court.

sun
(noun) the star providing heat and light for the planets in our solar system.
sunshine (noun) **sunlight** (noun) **sunlit** (adjective)

sunbathe, sunbathes, sunbathing, sunbathed
(verb) to sit in the sunshine to get a suntan.

sunburn
(noun) sore red skin on someone's body caused by too much exposure to the rays of the sun.
sunburnt (adjective)

sundae, sundaes (pronounced **sun**-day)
(noun) a dish of ice cream, cream and fruit or nuts.

Sunday, Sundays
(noun) the day between Saturday and Monday.
[Old English *sunnandæg* = day of the sun]

sundial, sundials
(noun) a device used for telling the time, by the sun; a pointer casts a shadow on a flat base marked with the hours.

sundry
1 (adjective) Sundry is used to refer to several things or people of various sorts, e.g. *The pilot pressed sundry switches.*
2 (phrase) **All and sundry** means everyone.
[Old English *syndrig* = separate]

sunflower, sunflowers
(noun) a tall plant with large, yellow flowers.

sunglasses
(plural noun) Dark spectacles that you wear to protect your eyes from the sun.

sunken
(adjective) When something has sunk, it is then sunken, e.g. *a sunken wreck.*

sunny, sunnier, sunniest
(adjective) When it is sunny, the sun is shining.

sunrise, sunrises
(noun) the time in the morning when the sun first appears.

sunroof, sunroofs
(noun) an opening part in the roof of a car.

sunset, sunsets
(noun) the time in the evening when the sun disappears below the horizon.

sunshade, sunshades
(noun) anything which is used as a protection from the sun, e.g. a parasol.

sunstroke
(noun) an illness caused by spending too much time in hot sunshine.

suntan, suntans
(noun) brown skin from light of the sun.
suntanned (adjective)

super
1 (adjective) very nice or very good, e.g. *We had a super holiday.*
2 used to describe something that is larger or better than similar things, e.g. *a superplastic, resistant to high temperatures.*
[Latin *super* = above]

superb
(adjective) very good indeed.
superbly (adverb)
[Latin *superbus* = distinguished]

superficial
(adjective) not very deep, e.g. *Trivial Pursuit tests our superficial knowledge... a superficial interest... superficial wounds.*
superficially (adverb)

superfluous (pronounced soo-per-floo-uss)
(adjective) unnecessary or no longer needed.
[Latin *superfluus* = overflowing]

superhuman
(adjective) stronger or more able than a normal human, e.g. *superhuman strength.*

superintendent, superintendents
(noun) a senior police officer.
[Latin *superintendere* = to oversee]

superior, superiors
1 (adjective) better or of higher quality than other similar things.
2 (noun) Your superiors are people who are in a higher position than you in e.g. an organization.
[Latin *superus* = higher]

superlative, superlatives (pronounced soo-per-lat-tiv)
1 (noun) In grammar, the superlative is the form of adjective which indicates that the person or thing described has more of a particular quality than anyone or anything else. For example, **quickest**, **best** and **easiest** are superlatives of 'quick', 'good' and 'best'.
2 (adjective; formal) very good indeed, e.g. *She is a superlative actress.*
[Latin *superlatus* = extravagant]

supermarket, supermarkets
(noun) a large self-service store.

supernatural
(adjective) Something that is supernatural, e.g. ghosts or witchcraft, cannot be explained by normal scientific laws.
2 (noun) e.g. *She studied the supernatural.*

supersonic
(adjective) A supersonic aircraft can travel faster than the speed of sound (770 m.p.h).
[Latin *super-* + *sonus* = above sound]

Become a superhuman in the dictionary world. Take the Survival Test on page v.

superstitious
(adjective) If you are superstitious, you believe in things like magic and powers that bring good or bad luck.
superstition (noun)
[Latin *superstitio* = dread of the supernatural]

supervise, supervises, supervising, supervised
(verb) to check and direct what someone is doing to make sure they do it correctly.
supervision (noun) **supervisor** (noun)
[Latin *super-* = above + *videre* = to see]

supper, suppers
(noun) a meal eaten in the evening or a snack eaten before you go to bed.
[Old French *soper* = supper]

supple
(adjective) able to bend and move easily, e.g. *You polish leather regularly to keep it supple.*
[Latin *supplex* = bowed]

supplement, supplements, supplementing, supplemented
1 (noun; pronounced **supp**-li-munt) something that is added to something else to improve it.
2 A newspaper or magazine supplement is a separate extra part of it.
3 (verb; pronounced supp-li-**ment**) to add on to.
supplementary (adjective)

supplier, suppliers
(noun) a firm which provides particular goods, e.g. *an electrical supplier.*

supply, supplies, supplying, supplied
1 (verb) To supply someone with something means to provide it or send it to them.
2 (noun) A supply of something is an amount available for use, e.g. *a hot water supply.*
3 (plural noun) Supplies are food and equipment for a particular purpose.
[Latin *supplere* = to complete]

support, supports, supporting, supported
1 (verb) If you support someone, you agree with their aims and want them to succeed, e.g. *We support Newcastle United.*
2 If you support someone who is in difficulties, you are kind, encouraging and helpful to them.
3 If something supports an object, it is underneath it and holding it up.
4 (noun) Financial support is money that is provided for someone or something.
supporter (noun)
[Latin *supportare* = to bring]

supportive
(adjective) kind, encouraging and helpful to someone who is in difficulties.

suppose, supposes, supposing, supposed
1 (verb) to think that something is likely, e.g. *I suppose they will come tomorrow.*
2 (phrase) You can say **I suppose** when you are not entirely certain about something, e.g. *We could take him with us, I suppose.*
3 (conjunction) You can use 'suppose' or 'supposing' when you are considering a possible situation, e.g. *Suppose something goes wrong – what then?*
4 (verb) e.g. *You are supposed to report it to the police... The party was supposed to be tonight... It's supposed to be the best hairdresser's in town.*
supposition (noun)

suppress, suppresses, suppressing, suppressed
(verb) to keep under control or to prevent something completely, e.g. *The army suppressed the demonstrations... I suppressed my urge to smack him on the nose.*

supreme
(adjective) Supreme is used to emphasize the greatness of something, e.g. *a supreme achievement.*
supremacy (noun) **supremely** (adverb)
[Latin *supremus* = highest]

Similar words: superlative, foremost

surcharge, surcharges
(noun) an extra charge, on what you normally pay, e.g. *Taxis have a surcharge after midnight.*

sure, surer, surest
(adjective) certain, e.g. *I was sure she would come... She made sure it was locked... Those holes are a sure sign of woodworm.*
[Latin *securus* = secure]

surely
1 (adverb) e.g. *Surely you don't mean that!*
2 (phrase) Something happening **slowly but surely**, is happening gradually and cannot be stopped.

surf
(noun) the white foam that forms on the top of waves when they break near the shore.

surface, surfaces, surfacing, surfaced
1 (noun) the top or outside area of something.
2 (verb) to come up from under water to the surface.
3 To surface an area means to give it a surface, e.g. *They've been surfacing the road all morning.*
[French *sur* = on + *face* = face or side]

surfboard, surfboards
(noun) a long, narrow board for surfing.

surfing
(noun) a sport which involves riding towards the shore on the top of a large wave while standing on a surfboard.

surge, surges, surging, surged
1 (noun) a sudden great increase in the amount of something, e.g. *a surge of electricity.*
2 (verb) to move suddenly and powerfully, e.g. *The crowd surged forwards.*
[Latin *surgere* = to rise]

surgeon, surgeons
(noun) a doctor who performs operations.

surgery, surgeries
1 (noun) medical treatment involving the cutting open of the body to treat the damaged part.
surgical (adjective)
2 The room or building where a doctor or dentist works is called a surgery.

surly, surlier, surliest
(adjective) rude and bad-tempered.
surliness (noun)

A doctor needs these words: prescription stethoscope anatomy physiology diagnosis infection.

surname, surnames
(noun) your family name, e.g. *Smith, Jones.*

surplus, surpluses
(noun) If there is a surplus of something there is more of it than is needed.
[Latin *super-* = over + *plus* = more]

surprise, surprises, surprising, surprised
1 (noun) an unexpected event.
2 (verb) *He surprised us with a quickly-taken free kick.*
3 (adjective) e.g. *a surprise party.*
surprising (adjective)
[Old French *surprendre* = to overtake]

surrender, surrenders, surrendering, surrendered
(verb) to stop fighting and agree that the other side has won.
[Old French *surrendre* = to yield]

Similar words: yield, submit, give in, give up

surround, surrounds, surrounding, surrounded
(verb) To surround someone or something means to be situated all around them.
[Old French *suronder* = to overflow]

Similar words: circle, encircle, enclose

surrounding, surroundings
1 (adjective) The surrounding area of a place is the area around it.
2 (plural noun) The area and environment around a place or person can be called the surroundings.

Similar words: (sense 2) environment, habitat

survey, surveys, surveying, surveyed
1 (verb; pronounced sur-**vay**) To survey something means to look carefully at the whole of it.
2 (noun; pronounced **sur**-vay) a detailed examination of something, often as a report.
surveyor (noun)
[Old French *surveoir* = to oversee]

Similar words: (verb) view, scan, look over

survival, survivals
(noun) being able to continue existing in spite of great danger or difficulties, e.g. *What are the chances of survival in the jungle?*

survive, survives, surviving, survived
(verb) to continue to live in spite of great danger or difficulties, e.g. *Very few people near Chernobyl survived the explosion for very long.*
survivor (noun)

susceptible (pronounced suss-**sep**-tibl)
(adjective) If you are susceptible to something, you are likely to be influenced or affected by it.
e.g. *Children are particularly susceptible to advertising.*

suspect, suspects, suspecting, suspected
1 (verb; pronounced sus-**pect**) If you suspect something or someone, you have doubts about their reliability, e.g. *I have my reasons for suspecting these reports.*

2 (noun; pronounced **sus**-pect) someone who is thought to be guilty of a crime.
3 (adjective) If something is suspect, it cannot be trusted or relied upon, e.g. *The M.O.T. certificate for that old banger is very suspect.*
[Latin *suspicere* = to mistrust]

suspend
1 (verb) to hang, e.g. *A model aeroplane was suspended above the stage.*
2 To suspend an event etc. means to stop it for a while, e.g. *Play was suspended for rain.*
3 If someone is suspended from school, they are prevented from going there for a time.
suspension (noun)
[Latin *sub-* = under + *pendere* = hang]

suspense
(noun) a state of excitement or anxiety caused by having to wait for something.

suspension bridge, bridges
(noun) a bridge that is supported from above by cables attached to towers.

suspicious
1 (adjective) If you are suspicious of someone, you do not trust them.
2 Suspicious is used to describe things that make you think there is something wrong with a situation, e.g. *Suspicious aircraft were spotted.*
suspicion (noun) **suspiciously** (adverb)

Similar words: (sense 2) fishy, shady, doubtful, suspect

sustain, sustains, sustaining, sustained
1 (verb) to continue or maintain something for a period of time, e.g. *They do not have enough food to sustain a sit-in.*
2 If something sustains you, it gives you energy and strength, e.g. *They had had nothing to sustain them except two cups of coffee.*
[Latin *sustinere* = to hold up]

swagger, swaggers, swaggering, swaggered
(verb) to walk in a boastful way.

Swahili (pronounced swa-**hee**-lee)
(noun) a language of eastern Africa.

swallow, swallows, swallowing, swallowed
1 (verb) If you swallow something, you make it go down your throat and into your stomach.
2 If you swallow your feelings, you stop yourself from showing them.
3 (noun) a migrating bird with a long, forked tail.

swamp, swamps, swamping, swamped
1 (noun) an area of permanently wet land.
swampy (adjective)
2 (verb) If you are swamped by things, you have more than you are able to deal with, e.g. *We've been swamped with letters after the appeal.*

swan, swans
(noun) a large water-bird with a very long neck.

swank, swanks, swanking, swanked
(verb; informal) to show off something that you have.
swanky (adjective)

swap, swaps, swapping, swapped (rhymes with **stop**); also spelled **swop**

The Latin root word *viv* means 'live'. From it we make: revive vivid vital vivisection survive.

(verb) to exchange, e.g. *He swapped his referee's kit for a pair of glasses.*

swarm, swarms, swarming, swarmed
1 (noun) a large group of flying insects.
2 (verb) If people swarm somewhere, a lot of people go there quickly and at the same time, e.g. *On bank holidays, people swarm to the coast.*
3 If a place is swarming with people, there are many people there.

Similar words: (verb: sense 3) seethe, teem

swarthy, swarthier, swarthiest
(adjective) A swarthy person has a dark complexion.
swarthiness (noun)

swastika, swastikas (pronounced **swoss**-tik-ka)
(noun) a symbol, formerly used by the Nazis in Germany; but in India it is a good luck sign.
[Sanskrit *svasti* = prosperity]

swat, swats, swatting, swatted
(verb) To swat an insect means to hit it sharply with something to kill it.

sway, sways, swaying, swayed
1 (verb) to lean or swing slowly from side to side.
2 If something sways you, it influences your thinking about something, e.g. *The judge was swayed by the girl's pleas for mercy.*

swear, swears, swearing, swore, sworn
1 (verb) to say words that are considered to be rude or blasphemous.
swearword (noun)
2 If you swear to something, you promise solemnly that you will do it or that it is true.
3 If you swear by something, you firmly believe it is a reliable cure or solution, e.g. *He swears by Vitamin C and zinc to cure colds.*

sweat, sweats, sweating, sweated
1 (noun) the salty liquid produced by your sweat glands when you are hot or afraid.
2 (verb) to perspire when you are hot or afraid.
sweaty (adjective)

sweater, sweaters
(noun) a knitted piece of clothing covering your upper body and arms.

sweatshirt, sweatshirts
(noun) a piece of clothing made of thick cotton.

swede, swedes
(noun) a large, round root vegetable.
[from *Swedish turnip* because it was introduced from Sweden in the 18th century]

Swede, Swedes
(noun) someone who comes from Sweden.

Swedish
1 (adjective) belonging to Sweden.
2 (noun) the main language spoken in Sweden.

sweep, sweeps, sweeping, swept
1 (verb) e.g. *I'll sweep the floor... She swept my books off the desk... Cold winds sweep over the plain... She was swept out to sea... the craze that is currently sweeping America.*
2 (noun) a chimney sweep.

sweet, sweeter, sweetest; sweets
(adjective, noun) e.g. *a cup of sweet tea... Toffees are my favourite sweets... We'll have beef for a main course and trifle as a sweet... a sweet smell... a sweet kitten.*
sweetly (adverb) **sweetness** (noun) **sweeten** (verb)

sweetcorn
(noun) a long stalk covered with juicy, yellow seeds, eaten as a vegetable.

sweetener, sweeteners
(noun) a very sweet, artificial substance that can be used instead of sugar.

sweetheart, sweethearts
(noun) You can call someone whom you are very fond of 'sweetheart'.

sweet tooth
(noun) If you have a sweet tooth, you like sweet food very much.

swell, swells, swelling, swelled, swollen
(verb) If something swells, it becomes larger and rounder, e.g. *Pauline's foot began to swell.*

swelling, swellings
(noun) an enlarged area on your body as a result of injury or illness.

sweltering
(adjective) Sweltering weather is so hot that it is uncomfortable.
[Old English *sweltan* = to die]

swerve, swerves, swerving, swerved
(verb) to change direction suddenly to avoid colliding with something.

swift, swifter, swiftest; swifts
1 (adjective) happening or moving very quickly, e.g. *We need a swift decision.*
2 (noun) a migrating bird with narrow crescent-shaped wings, which can fly very fast.
swiftly (adverb) **swiftness** (noun)
[Old English *swifan* = to turn]

swig, swigs, swigging, swigged
1 (verb; informal) to drink in large mouthfuls, usually from a bottle.
2 (noun) e.g. *Have a swig of this lemonade.*

swill, swills, swilling, swilled
(verb) To swill something means to pour water over it to clean it, e.g. *Go and swill the bucket out.*
[Old English *swilian* = to wash out]

swim, swims, swimming, swam, swum
(verb, noun) e.g. *Unfortunately, I swim like a brick... Come for a swim in the pool.*
swimmer (noun) **swimming costume** (noun) **swimming pool** (noun) **swimming trunks** (plural noun)

swimsuit, swimsuits
(noun) a swimming costume.

swindle, swindles, swindling, swindled
1 (verb) to trick someone for money or property.
2 (noun) e.g. *This raffle is a swindle!*
swindler (noun)
[German *Schwindler* = cheat]

swine, swines
1 (noun; old-fashioned) Swine are pigs.

Here's a little proverb you surely ought to know;
Horses sweat and men perspire, but ladies only glow.

2 (informal) If you call someone a swine, you mean they are nasty and spiteful.
[Old English *swin* = pig]

swing, swings, swinging, swung
1 (verb) If something swings, it moves repeatedly from side to side from a fixed point.
2 (noun) a piece of play equipment for a child.
3 (phrase) If something is **in full swing**, it is operating fully and no longer in its early stages, e.g. *The party was in full swing.*
4 (informal) If you get **into the swing** of something, you become familiar with it and understand what you are doing.

swipe, swipes, swiping, swiped
(verb) to try to hit something making a curving movement with the arm.
2 (informal) to steal something.

swirl, swirls, swirling, swirled
(verb) to move quickly in circles, e.g. *Bath water swirled down the plughole.*

Swiss
1 (adjective) belonging to Switzerland.
2 (noun) someone who comes from Switzerland.

switch, switches, switching, switched
1 (noun) a small control for an electrical device or machine.
2 (verb) To switch to a different task or topic means to change to it.
3 If you switch things, you swap them over.

switchboard, switchboards
(noun) the part of an organization where all phone calls are received and connected.

swivel, swivels, swivelling, swivelled
1 (verb) to turn round on a central point.
2 (adjective) A swivel chair or lamp is made so that you can move the main part of it while the base is fixed.
[Old English *swifan* = to turn]

swollen
(adjective) something swollen has swelled up, e.g. *He gave me a swollen lip.*

Similar words: bloated, puffy

swoon, swoons, swooning, swooned
(verb; literary) to faint because of strong emotion or shock.
[Old English *geswogen* = insensible]

swoop, swoops, swooping, swooped
1 (verb) to move downwards through the air in a fast, curving movement, e.g. *Planes swooped low over the village.*
2 (phrase) If you do something in **one fell swoop**, you do it in a single action.
[Old English *swapan* = to sweep or to move in a curving movement]

swop another spelling of **swap.**

sword, swords
(noun) a weapon with a long blade.

swot, swots, swotting, swotted
1 (noun; informal) someone who people think spends a lot of time studying.
2 (verb; informal) to study or revise very hard.

3 If you swot up on a subject you find out as much about it as possible in a short time.

sycamore, sycamores (pronounced **sik**-am-mor)
(noun) a deciduous tree.

syllable, syllables
(noun) a part of a word that contains a single vowel sound and is pronounced as a unit, e.g. 'book' has one syllable, 'reading' has two.

syllabus, syllabuses
(noun) details of the things that are studied for a course or examination, e.g. *'The Romans' is in our history syllabus.*

symbol, symbols
(noun) a shape, design or idea that is used to represent something, e.g. *Communion wine is a symbol of Christ's blood.*
symbolic (adjective) **symbolize** (verb)
[Greek *sumbolon* = mark or token]

Similar words: emblem, token, sign, logo

symmetrical
(adjective) If something is symmetrical, it has two halves which are exactly the same, except that one half is the mirror image of the other.
symmetry (noun) **symmetrically** (adverb)
[Greek *summetria* = proportion]

sympathetic
(adjective) A sympathetic person shows kindness and understanding to other people.

sympathize, sympathizes, sympathizing, sympathized; also spelled **sympathise**
(verb) to show understanding and care to someone who is in difficulties.

sympathy, sympathies
1 (noun) kindness and understanding towards someone who is in difficulties.
2 (phrase) If you do something **in sympathy** with someone, you do it to show support for them.
[Greek *sumpathēs* = sharing a feeling]

symphony, symphonies
(noun) a piece of music for an orchestra, e.g. *Beethoven's Pastoral Symphony.*
[Greek *sumphōnos* = harmonious]

symptom, symptoms
(noun) something wrong with your body that is evidence of an illness, e.g. *A sore throat is often the first symptom of a cold.*

synagogue, synagogues (pronounced **sin**-a-gog)
(noun) a Jewish place of worship.
[Greek *sunagōgē* = meeting]

synchronize, synchronizes, synchronizing, synchronized (pronounced **sing**-kron-nize; also spelled **synchronise)**
(verb) To synchronize watches means to set them at exactly the same time as each other.

syndrome, syndromes
(noun) a medical condition known by a particular set of symptoms, e.g. *Down's syndrome.*
[Greek *sun-* = together + *dramein* = to run]

synonym, synonyms
(noun) If two words have the same or a very
similar meaning, they are synonyms, e.g. *'Aid' is
a synonym of 'help'; 'sufficient' is a synonym of
'enough'.*

synopsis, synopses
(noun) a summary of a book, play or film.

syntax
(noun) the grammatical rules of a language and
the way its words are arranged.
[Greek *suntassein* = to arrange]

synthesizer, synthesizers; also spelled
synthesiser
(noun) an electronic machine that creates music
or speech sounds from electronic signals.

synthetic
(adjective) made from artificial substances
rather than natural ones.

Syrian, Syrians (pronounced sirr-ee-an)
1 (adjective) belonging to Syria.
2 (noun) someone who comes from Syria.

syringe, syringes (pronounced sir-inj)
(noun) a hollow tube with a plunger and a fine
hollow needle, used for injecting or extracting
liquids.
[Greek *surinx* = pipe or tube]

syrup, syrups
(noun) a thick, sweet liquid made by boiling
sugar with water.
[Arabic *sharab* = drink]

system, systems
1 (noun) an organized way of doing something
from a fixed plan or set of rules.
2 You can also refer to a set of equipment as a
system, e.g. *a stereo system.*
3 In biology, a system is a set of organs that
performs a function, e.g. *the digestive system.*
[Greek *sustēma* = organized whole]

Similar words: (sense 1) process, procedure, routine

systematic
(adjective) following a fixed plan and done in an
efficient way, e.g. *a systematic search.*
systematically (adverb)

T

tabs
(phrase; informal) If you **keep tabs on** someone,
you make sure that you always know where they
are and what they are doing.

tabby, tabbies
(noun) a cat whose fur has grey, brown or black
stripes.
[Old French *tabis* = striped silk cloth]

tabernacle, tabernacles (pronounced
tab-er-nak-kl)
(noun) a place of worship used by some religious
groups including the Mormons.
[Latin *tabernaculum* = tent]

table, tables
Selected meanings:
1 (noun) a piece of furniture.
2 Your multiplication tables are the facts about
multiplying numbers from 0 to 10. e.g. *I know my
8 times table.*
3 a chart of figures in a book.
4 (phrase) If you **turn the tables** on someone, you
change the situation completely, so that they
have the problems they were causing you.

tablecloth, tablecloths
(noun) a cloth used to cover a table.

tablespoon, tablespoons
(noun) a large spoon used for serving food.

tablet, tablets
1 (noun) a small, round, solid pill made of
powdered medicine.
2 A tablet of soap is a flattish block of it.
3 a slab of stone with words cut into it.

table tennis
(noun) a game for 2 or 4 people in which you use
bats to hit a small hollow ball over a low net
across a table.

tabloid, tabloids
(noun) a newspaper with small pages, big
headlines, short news stories and lots of
photographs. [opposite: **broadsheet**]

taboo, taboos
1 (noun) a religious or social custom that forbids
people to do something.
2 (adjective) forbidden or disapproved of, e.g. *a
taboo subject.*

tack, tacks, tacking, tacked
1 (noun) a short nail with a broad, flat head.
2 (verb) If you tack a piece of fabric, you sew it
with long loose stitches.
3 (noun) If you change tack, you start to use a
different method for dealing with something.
4 the equipment used for horseriding.
[senses 1-3: Middle English *tak* = nail
sense 4: short for tackle]

tackle, tackles, tackling, tackled
1 (verb) If you tackle a difficult task, you start
dealing with it in a determined way.
2 If you tackle someone in a game, e.g. football,
you try to get the ball away from them.
3 (noun) the equipment for fishing or for a job.

tacky, tackier, tackiest
1 (adjective) slightly sticky to touch, e.g. *the
paint was still tacky.*
2 (informal) badly made and unpleasant, e.g. *The
star's room was filled with tacky furniture.*

tact
(noun) the ability to see when a situation is
difficult or delicate and to handle it without
upsetting or offending people.

T began as an X. This became an upright cross and later the top of the cross was removed.

tactful (adjective) **tactfully** (adverb) **tactless** (adjective) **tactlessly** (adverb)

Similar words: discretion, diplomacy

tactics
1 (plural noun) the methods you use to achieve what you want.
2 the ways in which troops and equipment are used in order to win a battle.
tactical (adjective)

tadpole, tadpoles
(noun) the larva of a frog or a toad.
[Middle English *tadde* = toad + *pol* = head]

tag, tags, tagging, tagged
1 (noun) a small label made of cloth, paper, plastic or leather, e.g. *a name tag.*
2 (verb) If you tag along with someone, you go with them or behind them.

tail, tails, tailing, tailed
1 (noun) e.g. *The dog wagged its tail.*
2 (verb; informal) If you tail someone, you follow them to find out where they go.
3 (adjective, adverb) The tails side of a coin is the side which does not have a person's head.

tail off
(phrasal verb) If something tails off, it becomes gradually less.

tailback, tailbacks
(noun) a long queue of traffic.

taillight, taillights
(noun) a red light at the back of a car or lorry.

tailor, tailors, tailoring, tailored
1 (noun) a person who makes, alters and repairs clothes, especially for men.
2 (verb) If something is tailored for a particular purpose, it is specially designed for it.
[Old French *tailleur* = cutter]

tailor-made
(adjective) suitable for a particular person or purpose, or specially designed for them.

take, takes, taking, took, taken
(verb) e.g. *He took a bath... What exams are you taking?... She took an interest in us... It all takes time... Take me to your leader... Let me take your case... She took my wallet!... Take three pills daily... I can't take her criticism... take my advice... take my temperature... take a train.*

take after
(phrasal verb) If you take after someone in your family, you look or behave like them.

take down
(phrasal verb) If you take down what someone is saying or has written, you write it down.

take in
1 (phrasal verb) If someone is taken in, they are deceived, e.g. *You took me in with that wig.*
2 If you take something in, you understand it.

take off
(phrasal verb) When a plane takes off, it leaves the ground.
takeoff (noun)

take on
1 (phrasal verb) If you take on a job or responsibility, you accept it.
2 If you take on a person, you fight them or compete against them.

take over
(phrasal verb) To take something over means to start controlling it.
takeover (noun)

take to
1 (phrasal verb) If you take to someone or something, you like them immediately.
2 If you take to doing something, you begin to do it regularly, e.g. *She took to eating oranges daily.*

takeaway, takeaways
1 (noun) a shop that sells hot food to be eaten elsewhere, e.g. *a Chinese takeaway.*
2 a meal bought from a takeaway.

takings
(plural noun) the money that a shop, theatre or cinema gets from selling its goods or tickets, e.g. *The boss counted the day's takings.*

talcum powder or talc
(noun) Talcum powder is a soft perfumed powder used for absorbing moisture on the body.

tale, tales
(noun) a story.

talent, talents
(noun) the natural ability to do something well.
talented (adjective)
[from *talanton*, a Greek coin in the Bible parable (Matthew 25:14-30); Jesus uses the example of the man who buried a talent to show that we should use our natural gifts, not hide them]

Similar words: knack, gift, flair

talk, talks, talking, talked
(verb, noun) e.g. *She just can't stop talking!... She gave us a talk on Health Education.*

talk down to
(phrasal verb) If someone talks down to you, they talk in a way that shows they think they are more important or clever than you.

talkative
(adjective) talking a lot.

talking-to
(noun; informal) If you give someone a talking-to, you tell them off.

tall, taller, tallest
1 (adjective) of more than average height.
2 (phrase) If someone tells you a **tall story** it is very difficult to believe.

tallboy, tallboys
(noun) a tall chest of drawers made in two sections placed on top of one another.

tally, tallies, tallying, tallied
1 (noun) an informal count, e.g. *Are you keeping a tally of the score?*
2 (verb) If numbers or statements tally, they are exactly the same or they give the same results or conclusions, e.g. *The stories of both witnesses tallied.*

Talk is cheap because supply exceeds demand. (Anon)

3 In maths, tallying is recording a count in bundles of 5, e.g. ⅢⅢ III = 8.

Talmud (pronounced **tal**-mood)
(noun) the books containing the ancient Jewish ceremonies and civil laws.
[Hebrew = instruction]

talon, talons
(noun) Talons are sharp, hooked claws, for example of an eagle.
[Latin *talus* = heel]

tambourine, tambourines
(noun) a percussion instrument.
[Old French *tambourin* = little drum]

tame, tamer, tamest; tames, taming, tamed
1 (adjective) A tame animal or bird is not afraid of people and is not violent towards them.
2 Something that is tame is uninteresting and lacks excitement or risk, e.g. *It was a tame film.*
3 (verb) If you tame people, animals or things, you bring them under control.

tamper, tampers, tampering, tampered
(verb) If you tamper with something, you interfere or meddle with it.

tampon, tampons
(noun) a firm, specially shaped piece of cotton wool that a woman places inside her vagina to absorb the blood during her period.
[a French word meaning 'plug']

tan, tans, tanning, tanned
(verb, noun) When you tan, your skin becomes darker because it is exposed to a lot of sun; you then have a tan.

tandem, tandems
(noun) a bicycle designed for two riders.

tandoori (pronounced tan-**doo**-ree)
(noun) an Indian method of cooking meat in a clay oven, e.g. *tandoori chicken.*
[an Urdu word]

tang, tangs
(noun) a strong, sharp smell or flavour, e.g. *This sauce has a real tang to it.*
tangy (adjective)

tangent, tangents
1 (noun) A tangent of a curve is any straight line that touches the curve at one point only.
2 (phrase) If you **go off at a tangent**, you start talking or thinking about something that is not completely relevant to what has gone before.
[Latin *tangere* = to touch]

tangerine, tangerines
(noun) a type of small, sweet orange with a loose rind. [named after Tangier in Morocco]

tangible (pronounced **tan**-jib-bl)
(adjective) clear or definite enough to be easily seen, felt or noticed, e.g. *tangible evidence.*
[Latin *tangere* = to touch]

tangle, tangles, tangling, tangled
1 (noun) a mass of things knotted or coiled together and difficult to separate.
2 (verb) If you are tangled in wires or ropes, you are caught or trapped in them so that it is difficult to get free.

tango
(noun) a dance with a very dramatic beat.

tank, tanks
1 (noun) a container for storing liquid or gas.
2 an armoured military vehicle.

tankard, tankards
(noun) a large mug used for drinking beer.

tanker, tankers
(noun) a ship, lorry or aeroplane designed to carry large quantities of gas or liquid, e.g. *an oil tanker.*

tantalize, tantalizes, tantalizing, tantalized; also spelled tantalise
(verb) to tease someone by making them feel hopeful and then not allowing them to have what they want. [from a Greek myth: Tantalus, son of Zeus, was punished for his lies and theft by being put in a lake, everlastingly just out of reach of food and drink.]
tantalizing (adjective) **tantalizingly** (adverb)

tantrum, tantrums
(noun) a noisy outburst of temper.

Tanzanian, Tanzanians (pronounced tan-zan-**nee**-an)
1 (adjective) belonging to Tanzania.
2 (noun) someone who comes from Tanzania.

tap, taps, tapping, tapped
1 (noun) e.g. *a water tap.*
2 (phrase) If something is **on tap**, it is ready to be used immediately.
3 (verb) If you tap a resource or situation, you make use of it by getting what you want from it.
4 If a telephone is tapped, a device is fitted to it so that someone can listen secretly to the calls.
5 to hit lightly, e.g. *She tapped the rhythm.*

tap-dancing
(noun) a type of dancing with special shoes which make clicking noises as the dancers move their feet.

tape, tapes, taping, taped
1 (noun) plastic ribbon covered with a magnetic substance, used to record sounds, pictures and computer information.
2 (verb) to record music, TV pictures etc.
3 (noun) a long, thin strip of fabric etc., e.g. *sticky tape... the finishing tape.*

tape measure, measures
(noun) a strip of plastic, cloth or metal used for measuring things.

taper, tapers, tapering, tapered
1 (verb) Something that tapers gradually becomes thinner towards one end.
2 Something that tapers off becomes gradually smaller, e.g. *The baby boom is tapering off.*
3 (noun) a thin candle.

tape recorder, recorders
(noun) a machine used for recording and playing back sounds on magnetic tape.

tapestry, tapestries
(noun) a piece of heavy cloth with designs embroidered on it.
[Old French *tapisserie* = carpeting]

Anger is short madness. (Horace)

tar
(noun) a thick, black, sticky substance which comes from distilling coal, wood or peat.

tarantula, tarantulas
(noun) a large, hairy, poisonous spider.

target, targets
1 (noun) something which you aim at when firing weapons.
2 the result that you are trying to achieve.
[Old French *targette* = little shield]

tarmac
(noun) a material consisting of crushed stones mixed with tar used for making road surfaces.
[short for *tarmacadam*, from the name of John MacAdam, the Scottish engineer who invented it]

tarpaulin, tarpaulins
(noun) a sheet of heavy, waterproof material used as a protective covering.

tart, tarts; tarter, tartest
1 (noun) a pastry case with a sweet filling.
2 (adjective) sour or sharp to taste.
[noun: Old French *tarte*
adjective: Old English *teart* = rough]

tartan, tartans
(noun) a woollen fabric from Scotland with checks of various colours and sizes.

task, tasks
(noun) a piece of work which has to be done.

Similar words: chore, assignment, mission

taste, tastes, tasting, tasted
1 (noun) e.g. *The taste of this cheese is terrific.*
2 (verb) e.g. *I can just taste the garlic.*
3 (noun) A person's taste is their choice in the things they like to buy or have around them, e.g. *Wally's taste in clothes is appalling.*
tasty (adjective)

tasteful
(adjective) attractive and elegant, e.g. *a tasteful wallpaper.*
tastefully (adverb)

tasteless
1 (adjective) vulgar and unattractive.
2 A tasteless remark or joke is offensive.
3 Tasteless food has very little flavour.
tastelessly (adverb)

tattered
(adjective) looking scruffy, with torn clothing.

tattoo, tattoos
1 (noun) a picture or design tattooed on someone's body.
2 a public military display of exercises and music, e.g. *the Edinburgh Tattoo.*

tatty, tattier, tattiest
(adjective) worn out or untidy and rather dirty.

taught past tense and past participle of **teach**.

taunt, taunts, taunting, taunted
(verb) To taunt someone means to speak offensively to them about their weaknesses or failures in order to make them angry or upset.

taut
(adjective) stretched very tight, e.g. *a taut rope.*

tautology, tautologies
(noun) using different words to say the same thing twice in the same sentence, e.g. *a joint partnership... to continue on... to revert back.*
tautological (adjective)

tax, taxes, taxing, taxed
1 (noun) an amount of money that people have to pay to the government for public services, e.g. health care and education.
2 (verb) If goods are taxed, a proportion of their price has to be paid to the government.
taxable (adjective) **taxation** (noun) **taxpayer** (noun)

taxi, taxis, taxiing, taxied
1 (noun) a car with a driver which you hire to take you to where you want to go.
2 (verb) When an aeroplane taxis, it moves slowly before taking off or after landing.

tea, teas
(noun) e.g. *a cup of tea... What's for tea?*
teapot (noun)

teacake, teacakes
(noun) a type of large currant bun.

teach, teaches, teaching, taught
(verb) e.g. *Please teach me to swim... My mum teaches cookery... That'll teach you to keep out of here!*
teacher (noun) **teaching** (noun)

Similar words: educate, instruct, train

team, teams, teaming, teamed
1 (noun) a group of people who play or work together.
2 (verb) If you team up with someone, you join them and work together with them.

Similar words: (noun) company, crew, squad

teamwork
(noun) the ability of a group of people to work well together.

tear, tears (rhymes with **peer**)
(noun) a drop of salty liquid when you cry.

tear, tears, tearing, tore, torn (rhymes with **hair**)
1 (verb) If you tear something, it is damaged by being pulled so that a hole appears in it.
2 (noun) e.g. *a tear in your shirt.*
3 (verb) If you tear something from somewhere, you remove it roughly and violently, e.g. *He tore the book out of her hands.*
4 to rush around, e.g. *He tore out of the house.*

tearaway, tearaways
(noun) someone who is wild and uncontrollable.

teardrop, teardrops
(noun) a single tear that falls from your eye.

tearful
(adjective) about to cry, or crying gently.
tearfully (adverb) **tearfulness** (noun)

tease, teases, teasing, teased
1 (verb) to make fun of someone.
2 (noun) e.g. *Ooh Kev! You're a real tease!*

teaspoon, teaspoons
(noun) a small spoon for stirring drinks.

Some famous people's names have become part of our language:
R. W. Diesel; J. L. Macadam; L. and A. Biro.

teat, teats
(noun) a piece of rubber or plastic on a feeding bottle for a baby to suck.

technical
1 (adjective) involving machines, processes and materials used in industry, transport, etc.
2 involving a specialized activity, e.g. *the technical jargon of computer science.*
technical college (noun)
[Greek *tekhnē* = art or skill]

technician, technicians
(noun) someone whose job involves skilled practical work with scientific equipment.

technique, techniques
(noun) a special way of doing something, e.g. *the different techniques of printing.*

technology, technologies
(noun) the study of the application of science and scientific knowledge for practical purposes in industry, farming, medicine, business, etc.
technological (adjective) **technologically** (adverb) **technologist** (noun)

teddy, teddies
(noun) a stuffed toy [named after the U.S. President Theodore (Teddy) Roosevelt, who hunted bears]

tedious (pronounced **tee**-dee-uss)
(adjective) boring and lasting for a long time, e.g. *Mr. Day gave a rather tedious history lesson.*
tediously (adverb)

teem, teems, teeming, teemed
1 (verb) to rain very heavily, e.g. *It's teeming down.*
2 If a place is teeming with people, there are a lot of them moving about.

teenage
(adjective) aged from 13 to 19 years of age.
teenager (noun)

teens
(plural noun) the period of life from 13 to 19 years of age.

teenybopper, teenyboppers
(noun; informal) a youngster who is very interested in pop music and fashion.

teeshirt or **T-shirt**
(noun) a short-sleeved cotton shirt with no collar.
[from the "T" shape of the shirt]

teeth plural of **tooth.**

teetotal (pronounced tee-**toe**-tl)
(adjective) never drinking alcohol.
teetotaller (noun)

teleclamy (pronounced tell-**eck**-lam-ee)
(noun) the act of shouting over a long distance, e.g. *The farmer's wife used teleclamy to tell her son it was time for bed.*
teleclamous (adjective) **teleclamate** (verb)
[Greek *tele* = far + Latin *clamare* = to shout]

telecommunications
(noun) the science and activity of sending signals and messages over long distances.

telegram, telegrams
(noun) a message sent by telegraph.

telegraph
(noun) a system of sending messages over long distances by electrical or radio signals.
[Greek *tele* = far + *graphein* = to write]

telepathy (pronounced tel-**lep**-ath-ee)
(noun) the ability to know what someone is thinking without being told.
telepathic (adjective)

telephone, telephones, telephoning, telephoned
(noun, verb) e.g. *Portable telephones can be useful, but don't give you much peace... Telephone me tomorrow.*

telephone exchange, exchanges
(noun) a building where telephone calls are connected.

telephonist, telephonists (pronounced tel-**lef**-on-ist)
(noun) someone who works in a telephone exchange.

telescope, telescopes
(noun) an instrument which make distant objects appear larger and nearer.
telescopic (adjective)

teletext
(noun) an electronic system that broadcasts pages of information onto a TV set.

televise, televises, televising, televised
(verb) If an event is televised, it is shown on TV.

television, televisions or **TV**
(noun) e.g. *The first televisions for public use were sold in the 30s... She has always wanted to work in television.*

telex, telexes
(noun) a system of sending written messages electronically; also a message sent this way.

tell, tells, telling, told
1 (verb) e.g. *Tell me all about it... I'm telling you to do it... I could tell she was unhappy.*
2 If an unpleasant or tiring experience begins to tell, it begins to have a serious effect, e.g. *The strain was beginning to tell on the boss.*

telltale, telltales
1 (noun) a person who reveals something meant to be secret.
2 (adjective) A telltale sign reveals information, e.g. *The car showed telltale signs of conking out.*

telly, tellies
(noun; informal) a television.

temper, tempers
1 (noun) the mood you are in, e.g. *a good temper.*
2 a sudden outburst of anger.
3 (phrase) If you **lose your temper**, you become very angry.

temperament, temperaments (pronounced tem-pra-ment)
(noun) a person's nature or personality, e.g. *She has a very cheerful temperament.*

temperamental
(adjective) moody and unpredictable, e.g. *The footballer was too temperamental to do well.*
temperamentally (adverb)

Idioms. What are: second sight second wind second thoughts second nature second-best?

temperate
(adjective) A temperate place has weather that is neither extremely hot nor extremely cold.

temperature, temperatures
1 (noun) The temperature of something is how hot or cold it is.
2 (phrase) If you **have a temperature**, the temperature of your body is higher than it should be (98.4°F), usually because you are ill.

template, templates
(noun) a shape or pattern cut out in wood, metal, plastic or card which you draw or cut around to reproduce that shape or pattern.

temple, temples
1 (noun) a building used for the worship of a god in various religions, e.g. *a Hindu temple.*
2 Your temples are the flat parts on each side of your forehead.

tempo
(noun) The tempo of a piece of music is its timing and rhythm.

temporary
(adjective) lasting for only a short time.
temporarily (adverb)

tempt, tempts, tempting, tempted
(verb) If you tempt someone, you try to persuade them to do something by offering them something they want.
tempting (adjective) **tempter** (noun)

Similar words: lure, entice, lead on

temptation, temptations
(noun) something that you want to do or have, even though you know it might be wrong or harmful, e.g. *It was such a temptation to leave.*

ten the number 10.
tenth (adjective and noun)

tenant, tenants
(noun) someone who pays rent for the place they live in, or for buildings etc. that they use.

tend, tends, tending, tended
1 (verb) If something tends to happen, it happens usually or often.
2 If you tend someone, you look after them.
[sense 1: Latin *tendere* = to stretch
sense 2: short for *attend*]

tendency, tendencies
(noun) a habit, trend or type of behaviour that happens very often, e.g. *He has a tendency to become irritated.*

tender, tenderest
1 (adjective) Someone who is tender has gentle and caring feelings.
2 Tender meat is easy to cut or chew.
3 painful and sore, e.g. *a tender spot.*
tenderness (noun) **tenderly** (adverb)

Similar words: (sense 1) affectionate, loving

tendon, tendons
(noun) a strong cord of tissue which joins a muscle to a bone.

tennis
(noun) a game played by 2 or 4 players on a court, hitting a ball over a net with rackets.

tenor, tenors
(adjective, noun) A tenor has the highest voice in the normal male range. A tenor recorder, saxophone, etc plays notes in the middle range.

tense, tenser, tensest; tenses, tensing, tensed
1 (adjective) If you are tense, you are worried and nervous and cannot relax.
2 (verb) If you tense, or if your muscles tense, your muscles become tight and stiff.
3 (noun) The tense of a verb is the form which shows whether you are talking about the past, present or future, e.g. *I am* (present tense) *I was* (past tense) *I will be* (future tense).
[senses 1-2: Latin *tensus* = stretched
sense 3: Latin *tempus* = time]

Similar words: (adjective) strained, uptight, keyed up

tension, tensions
1 (noun) a feeling of nervousness or worry.
2 The tension in a rope or wire is how tightly it is stretched.

tent, tents
(noun) a shelter made of canvas, etc.

tentacle, tentacles
(noun) the long, thin parts of, e.g. an octopus.
[Latin *tentare* = to feel]

tenterhooks
(plural noun) If you are on tenterhooks, you are nervous and excited about something that is going to happen.
[from the hooks called *tenterhooks* which were used to stretch cloth tight while it was drying]

tepid
(adjective) Tepid liquid is only slightly warm.

term, terms
1 (noun) a period of time, e.g. *His term of office lasts one year... a school term.*
2 a word used for a particular thing, e.g. *forte* is a musical term.
3 (plural noun) The terms of an agreement are the conditions that have been accepted by the people involved in it, e.g. *She wouldn't meet him on those terms.*
4 (phrase) e.g. *It was a bad year in terms of money, but a good year in terms of happiness.*
5 If you **come to terms with** something difficult or unpleasant, you learn to accept it.

terminal, terminals
1 (adjective) A terminal illness or disease cannot be cured and causes death gradually.
2 (noun) a place where people begin or end a journey, e.g. *Terminal 4 at Heathrow Airport.*
3 A computer terminal is a keyboard and a VDU linked to a mainframe computer elsewhere.
terminally (adverb)
[Latin *terminus* = end]

terminate, terminates, terminating, terminated
(verb) When you terminate something or when it terminates, it stops or ends.
termination (noun)

Verbs have three main tenses, Past (I ran), Present (I run) and Future (I shall run)....

terminology, terminologies
(noun) The terminology of a subject is the set of special words and expressions used in it.

terminus, terminuses (pronounced **ter**-min-uss)
(noun) a place where a bus or train route ends.

terrace, terraces
1 (noun) a row of houses joined together by their side walls.
2 a flat area next to a building where people can sit.
3 one of a series of flat areas of ground built like steps so that crops can be grown there.
[Old French *terrasse* = platform]

terrible
1 (adjective) serious and unpleasant, e.g. *a terrible accident.*
2 (informal) very bad or of poor quality, e.g. *The weather was terrible.*
terribly (adverb)

terrier, terriers
(noun) a small, short-bodied dog.
[Old French *chien terrier* = earth dog]

terrific
1 (adjective; informal) very pleasing or impressive, e.g. *We had a terrific holiday.*
2 great in amount, degree or intensity, e.g. *There was a terrific explosion.*
terrifically (adverb)

terrify, terrifies, terrifying, terrified
(verb) If something terrifies you, it makes you feel extremely frightened.
[Latin *terrificare* = to terrify]

territory, territories
1 (noun) The territory of a country is the land that it controls.
2 An animal's territory is an area which it thinks of as its own and defends when other animals try to enter it.
territorial (adjective)

terror, terrors
(noun) great fear or panic.

terrorist
(noun) someone who uses violence for political reasons.
terrorism (noun) **terrorize** (verb)

tessellate
(verb) When a shape tessellates, it fits together exactly with other shapes which are the same.
[Latin *tessella* = small stone cube]

test, tests, testing, tested
1 (verb) to try something out.
2 (noun) a set of questions or tasks given to someone to find out what they know or can do.

testament, testaments
(noun) a copy of either the Old or the New Testament of the Bible.
[Latin *testari* = to bear witness]

testicle, testicles
(noun) A man's testicles are the two sex glands that produce sperm.

testify, testifies, testifying, testified
(verb) When someone testifies, they make a formal statement, especially in a court of law, e.g. *Three witnesses testified against him.*

test match, matches
(noun) one of a series of international cricket or rugby matches.

test tube, tubes
(noun) a small, cylindrical, glass container used in chemical experiments.

tetanus (pronounced **tet**-nuss)
(noun) a painful, infectious disease caused by germs getting into wounds.
[Greek *tetanos* = stretched]

tether, tethers, tethering, tethered
1 (verb) If you tether an animal, you tie it to a post.
2 (phrase) If you are **at the end of your tether**, you are extremely tired and have no more patience or energy left to deal with problems.

text, texts
(noun) The text of a book is the main written part of it, rather than the pictures or index.
[Latin *textus* = something woven or composed]

textbook, textbooks
(noun) a book about a particular subject intended for students to use.

textile, textiles
(noun) a woven cloth or fabric.
[Latin *texere* = to weave]

texture, textures
(noun) The texture of something is the way it feels when you touch it.

Thai, Thais (pronounced **tie**)
1 (adjective) belonging to Thailand.
2 (noun) someone who comes from Thailand.
3 the main language spoken in Thailand.

than
(preposition, conjunction) e.g. *She is older than I am... He'd rather do things by himself than ask for help.*

thank, thanks, thanking, thanked
(verb) e.g. *Thank you very much.*
[Note that 'thank you' is always two words.]

thankful
(adjective) happy and relieved that something has happened.
thankfully (adverb)

thanks
(plural noun) e.g. *Many thanks for your help... Thanks to you I'm going to be late.*

that, those
1 (adjective, pronoun, conjunction,) e.g. *That film came out years ago... Who is that?... She suggested that I wrote to him.*
2 (phrase) You use **that is** (or i.e.) when you are giving further details about something, e.g. *We deal with social matters, that is, everything from housing to education.*

thatch, thatches, thatching, thatched
1 (noun) straw and reeds used to make roofs.
2 (verb) to make a thatched roof.
[Old English *theccan* = to cover]

....Can you write the main tenses of: to have; to do; to be; to think; to fly?

thaw, thaws, thawing, thawed
(verb) When snow or ice thaws, it melts.

the
(definite article) e.g. *Shut the door.*

theatre, theatres
1 (noun) a building where plays and other entertainments are performed on a stage.
2 An operating theatre is a room in a hospital for surgical operations.
theatrical (adjective) **theatrically** (adverb)
[Greek *theatron* = viewing place]

thee
(pronoun; old-fashioned) you.

theft, thefts
(noun) the crime of stealing.

their
(pronoun) e.g. *They lost their way.*

theirs
(pronoun) e.g. *It was his fault, not theirs.*

them
(pronoun) e.g. *He took off his glasses and put them in his pocket.*

theme, themes
1 (noun) a main idea or topic in writing, painting, film, or music, e.g. *The theme of the poem is love.*
2 a tune, especially one played at the beginning and end of a TV or radio programme.
[Latin *thema* = something laid down]

theme park, parks
(noun) an area which people pay to visit in which displays, buildings and activities on a particular subject have been set up.

themselves
(pronoun) e.g. *They hurt themselves in the crash.*

then
(adverb) e.g. *I'll never get there by then... If you haven't got the money, then don't buy it.*

theology
(noun) the study of religion and God.
theological (adjective)

theorem, theorems
(noun) a statement in maths that can be proved to be true by reasoning.
[Greek *theorema* = something to be looked at]

theory, theories
1 (noun) an idea or set of ideas that is meant to explain something, e.g. *Darwin's theory of evolution.*
2 the set of rules, principles and ideas that a particular subject or skill is based upon, e.g. *musical theory.*
3 (phrase) You use **in theory** to say that although something is supposed to happen, it may not in fact happen, e.g. *In theory, the car should start. In practice, it won't.*
theoretical (adjective) **theoretically** (adverb)
theorize (verb)
[Greek *theoria* = speculation]

therapy
(noun) the treatment of mental or physical

illness, often without the use of drugs or operations.
therapist (noun)

there
(adverb pronoun) e.g. *I'm going there... I agree with you there... There was no school bus today.*

therefore
(adverb) consequently, e.g. *You have failed me, Bond, therefore you must die!*

thermal
(adjective) to do with or caused by heat, e.g. *thermal energy... a thermal vest.*
[Greek *therme* = heat]

thermo-
(prefix) related to, caused by or measuring heat.

thermometer, thermometers
(noun) an instrument for measuring the temperature of a room or a person's body.

Thermos flask, flasks
(noun; trademark) a container used to keep drinks either hot or cold by means of a vacuum.

thermostat, thermostats
(noun) a device used to control temperature, e.g. on a central heating system.

thesaurus, thesauruses (pronounced this-**saw**-russ)
(noun) a reference book which you use to find words with similar meanings.
[Greek *thesauros* = treasure]

these plural of **this**.

they
(third person pronoun) e.g. *They found the body in a dustbin.*

thick, thicker, thickest
1 (adjective) e.g. *concrete two metres thick... thick undergrowth... thick milk shake... thick smoke... .*
2 (informal) e.g. *Im thik at Inglish.*
thickly (adverb) **thickness** (noun)

thicken, thickens, thickening, thickened
(verb) If something thickens, it becomes thicker, e.g. *The fog thickened.*

thickset
(adjective) Someone who is thickset is broad and heavy with a solid-looking body.

thief, thieves
(noun) a person who steals.

thigh, thighs
(noun) the front part of the leg above the knee.

thimble, thimbles
(noun) a small metal or plastic cap that you put on the end of your finger to protect it when you are sewing.
[Old English *thuma* = thumb]

thin, thinner, thinnest; thins, thinning, thinned
1 (adjective) e.g. *She's looking thin since she was poorly... a thin coat of paint.*
2 (verb) If you thin paint, you add water or other liquid to it to make it thinner.
thinness (noun) **thinly** (adverb)

Similar words: skinny, scraggy, lean, spindly

thing, things
1 (noun) an object, rather than a plant, an animal, a human being or something abstract.
2 (plural noun) Your things are your clothes or possessions.

Similar words: (sense 1) item, article, object

think, thinks, thinking, thought
(verb) e.g. *Just think about it... I think dogs are better than cats.*

Similar words: meditate, consider, believe, feel, reckon, suppose

third, thirds
1 (adjective) first, second, **third**, fourth, fifth.
2 (noun) A third is one of three equal parts.
thirdly (adverb)

Third World
(noun) the poorer countries of Africa, Asia and South America.

thirsty
(adjective) needing to drink something.
thirst (verb and noun) **thirstily** (adverb)

thirteen the number 13.
thirteenth (adjective and noun)

thirty, thirties
the number 30.
thirtieth (adjective and noun)

this, these
(adjective, adverb, pronoun) e.g. *this Tuesday... Do you want these?... This is David... We've got this far.*

thistle, thistles
(noun) a wild plant with prickly-edged leaves and purple flowers.

thorn, thorns
(noun) one of many sharp points growing on some plants and trees.
thorny (adjective)

thorough (pronounced **thur**-ruh)
1 (adjective) done very carefully and completely, e.g. *a thorough examination.*
2 A thorough person is very careful and methodical in what they do.
thoroughly (adverb) **thoroughness** (noun)

those plural of that.

thou
(pronoun; old-fashioned) you (meaning one person) e.g. *Thou art a rogue, Blackadder.*

though
(conjunction, adverb) e.g. *She arrived on time, even though she'd missed her bus... He looked as though he'd just got up.*

thought, thoughts
1 (verb) past tense and past participle of **think**.
2 (noun) an idea that you have in your mind.
3 the activity of thinking, e.g. *lost in thought.*

Similar words: (noun: sense 3) consideration, contemplation, reflection, thinking

thoughtful
1 (adjective) When someone is thoughtful, they are quiet and serious because they are thinking.
2 A thoughtful person remembers what other people want or need, and tries to be kind to them.
thoughtfully (adverb)

thoughtless
(adjective) A thoughtless person forgets or ignores what other people want, need or feel.
thoughtlessly (adverb) **thoughtlessness** (noun)

thousand, thousands
the number 1000.
thousandth (adjective and noun)

thrash, thrashes, thrashing, thrashed
1 (verb) to beat someone by hitting them with something.
2 To thrash someone in a game, contest or fight means to defeat them completely.
3 To thrash out a problem or an idea means to discuss it in detail until a solution is reached.

thread, threads, threading, threaded
1 (noun) a long, fine piece of cotton, silk, nylon or wool.
2 (verb) e.g. *to thread a needle.*
3 If you thread your way through a crowd, you carefully make your way through it.

threadbare
(adjective) Threadbare clothes are clothes that are old and thin.

threat, threats (pronounced thret)
1 (noun) a statement that someone will harm you, especially if you do not do what they want.
2 If there is a threat of something unpleasant happening, it is very possible that it will happen.

threaten, threatens, threatening, threatened
1 (verb) If you threaten to harm someone or to do something that will upset them, you say that you will do it.
2 If something threatens a person or thing, they are likely to harm them, e.g. *danger threatened.*
threatened (adjective) **threatening** (adjective)

Similar words: (sense 2) intimidate, menace

three
the number 3.
third (adjective)

three-dimensional or 3D
(adjective) solid, not flat.

thresh, threshes, threshing, threshed
(verb) When people thresh corn, wheat, or rice, they beat it in order to separate the grains from the rest of the plant.

thrifty, thriftier, thriftiest
(adjective) A thrifty person saves money and does not waste things.
thrift (noun)
[Old Norse = prosperity]

thrill, thrills, thrilling, thrilled
(noun, verb) If something thrills you or you thrill to it, it gives you a feeling of great pleasure and excitement.
thrilled (adjective) **thrilling** (adjective)
[Old English *thyrlian* = to pierce]

Say: There are thirty thousand feathers on every thrush's throat.

thriller, thrillers
(noun) an exciting book, film or play about dangerous, frightening or mysterious events.

thrive, thrives, thriving, thrived or **throve**
(verb) When people or things thrive, they are healthy, happy, successful or strong.

throat, throats
(noun) the back of your mouth and the top part of the passages inside your neck.

throb, throbs, throbbing, throbbed
1 (verb) If a part of your body throbs, you feel a series of strong beats or dull pains.
2 If something throbs, it vibrates and makes a loud, rhythmic noise, e.g. *The engine throbbed.*

throne, thrones
(noun) a ceremonial chair used by a king or queen on important official occasions.

throttle, throttles, throttling, throttled
(verb) to kill or injure someone by squeezing their throat.
[Middle English *throte* = throat]

through
(preposition, adjective) e.g. *a path through the garden... She failed the exam through lack of study... We keep the heating on through the winter... I'm through with delivering papers.*

throughout
(preposition, adverb) e.g. *She fidgeted throughout the film... The house was carpeted throughout.*

throw, throws, throwing, threw, thrown
1 (verb) e.g. *Throw me the ball... He threw himself onto the floor... He always throws me into confusion.*
2 If you throw a fit or tantrum, you suddenly begin behaving in an uncontrolled way.
3 (informal) If something throws you, it confuses or surprises you because it is unexpected, e.g. *Your phone call really threw me.*

Similar words: (sense 1) bowl, hurl, fling, cast, catapult, chuck, pelt

thrush, thrushes
(noun) a small, brown songbird.

thrust, thrusts, thrusting, thrust
1 (verb) If you thrust something somewhere, you push or move it there quickly with a lot of force.
2 (noun) a sudden, forceful movement.

thud, thuds
(noun) a dull sound, usually made by a solid, heavy object hitting something soft.
[Old English *thyddan* = to strike]

thug, thugs
(noun) a very rough and violent person.
[Hindi *thag* = thief]

thumb, thumbs, thumbing, thumbed
1 (noun) a short, thick digit
2 (verb) If someone thumbs a lift, they stand at the side of the road and stick out their thumb until a driver stops and gives them a lift.
3 If you thumb through a book, you look through it quickly.

thump, thumps, thumping, thumped
1 (verb) to hit someone or something hard with your fist.
2 (noun) a fairly loud, dull sound.

thunder, thunders, thundering, thundered
1 (noun) a loud cracking or rumbling noise caused by expanding air which is suddenly heated by lightning.
thundery (adjective)
2 (verb) If something thunders, it makes a loud, continuous noise, e.g. *The traffic thundered by.*
thunderous (adjective)

Thursday, Thursdays
(noun) the day between Wednesday and Friday.
[Old English *Thursdæg* = Thor's day; Thor was the Norse god of thunder]

thus
1 (adverb; formal) in this way, e.g. *You tie the knot thus.*
2 therefore, e.g. *He failed. Thus he must try again.*

thwart, thwarts, thwarting, thwarted
(verb) To thwart someone means to prevent them from doing or getting what they want.
[Old English *thweorh* = crooked or perverse]

thy
(pronoun; old-fashioned) your, e.g. *Thy will be done.*

thyme (pronounced **time**)
(noun) a herb used in cooking.

Tibetan, Tibetans
1 (adjective) belonging to Tibet.
2 (noun) someone who comes from Tibet.

tick, ticks, ticking, ticked
1 (noun, verb) e.g. *She put a tick by the wrong answer... I ticked my own work after that... I wish that clock would stop ticking.*
2 (verb) If you talk about what makes someone tick, you are talking about what makes them behave the way they do.

tick off
(phrasal verb; informal) If you tick someone off, you speak angrily to them because they have done something wrong.

ticket, tickets
1 (noun) a piece of paper or card which shows that you have paid for a journey, seat, etc.
2 When drivers get a ticket, they are given an official piece of paper which says that they have committed a driving or parking offence.
[Old French *estiquier* = to stick on]

tickle, tickles, tickling, tickled
1 (verb) to move your fingers lightly over someone's skin.
2 If something tickles you, it amuses you or gives you pleasure, e.g. *I was tickled by her remark.*
ticklish (adjective)

tidal
(adjective) to do with or produced by tides, e.g. *tidal energy.*

tiddler, tiddlers
(noun) a very small fish, e.g. a stickleback or minnow.

The i sound can be spelled: tie sigh by buy guide either.

tiddly, tiddlier, tiddliest
(adjective) slightly drunk.

tiddlywinks
(noun) a game in which players try to flick small plastic discs into a cup.

tide, tides
(noun) the regular change in the level of the sea on the shore, caused by the pull of the sun and the moon's gravity.
[Old English *tid* = time]

tide over
(phrasal verb) If something will tide someone over, it will help them through a difficult period of time, e.g. *Have this cash to tide you over.*

tidings
(plural noun; formal) news, e.g. *The angel bought glad tidings.*
[Old English *tidan* = to happen]

tidy, tidier, tidiest; tidies, tidying, tidied
1 (adjective) neat and orderly.
2 (verb) To tidy a place means to make it neat.
3 (adjective; informal) A tidy sum of money is a fairly large amount of it.

Similar words: (adjective: sense 1) trim, shipshape, spick and span
(verb) neaten, clear, straighten, spruce up

tie, ties, tying, tied
1 (verb) e.g. *Tie your laces before you trip up.*
2 (noun) e.g. *a school tie.*
3 a connection or feeling that links you with a person, place, or organization, e.g. *This company has strong ties with Germany.*
4 (verb) If you tie with someone in a competition or game, you have the same number of points.

Similar words: (verb: sense 1) bind, rope, tether, lash

tiebreak, tiebreaks
(noun) In tennis, a tiebreak is a long extra game to decide who wins a set.

tied up
(adjective) If you are tied up, you are busy.

tiger, tigers
(noun) a large animal of the cat family.

tight, tighter, tightest
1 (adjective) e.g. *These shoes are too tight... a tight knot... I have a very tight schedule.*
2 (adverb) e.g. *She held him tight.*
tightly (adverb) **tightness** (noun) **tighten** (verb)

Similar words: (adjective) taut, tense

tightrope, tightropes
(noun) a tightly-stretched rope on which an acrobat balances and performs tricks.

tights
(plural noun) legwear worn by women, ballet dancers and acrobats.

tile, tiles
(noun) a small, flat, square piece of e.g. slate, carpet or cork, used to cover surfaces.

till, tills, tilling, tilled
(preposition, conjunction) until, e.g. *I can't wait till we meet again.*
2 (noun) a drawer or box in a shop where money is kept, usually in a cash register.
3 (verb) To till the ground means to plough it for raising crops.

tiller, tillers
(noun) In a boat, the tiller is the handle fixed to the top of the rudder for steering.

tilt, tilts, tilting, tilted
(verb) If you tilt an object or it tilts, one end or side is higher than the other.

timber, timbers
(noun) wood that is cut ready for building and making furniture.

time, times, timing, timed
1 (noun) e.g. *What time is it?... I enjoyed my time in France... 'Time for bed,' said Mother... I play games three times a week... 3 times 4 is 12.*
2 (verb) e.g. *He timed his visit for 11.00 am... Mrs Churchill timed the race for us.*
3 (phrase) Someone who is **behind the times** is old-fashioned.
4 If you **have no time for** someone, you do not like them and cannot put up with them.

Similar words: (noun) spell, stretch, phase, term, period, space, interval

timer, timers
(noun) a device that measures time, e.g. *I've set the timer on the cooker.*

timetable, timetables
1 (noun) a plan of the times when particular activities or jobs should be done.
2 a list of the times when trains, boats, buses or planes arrive and depart.

timid
(adjective) shy and having no courage or self-confidence.
timidly (adverb) **timidity** (noun)
[Latin *timere* = to fear]

Similar words: cowardly, faint-hearted

timing
1 (noun) the skill to judge the right moment to do something, e.g. *The batsman's timing was good.*
2 The timing of an event is when it happens, e.g. *I didn't agree with the timing of the Summer Fête for the first week in December.*

tin, tins
1 (noun) a soft silvery-white metal used in alloys.
2 a metal container for food.
tinned (adjective)

tinfoil
(noun) sheet aluminium as thin as paper, used for wrapping and covering food.

tinge, tinges
(noun) a small amount of something, e.g. *a tinge of blue... a tinge of sadness.*
[Latin *tingere* = to colour]

What did the sardine say when her baby saw a submarine? Don't cry. It's only a tin of people.

tingle, tingles, tingling, tingled
1 (verb) When a part of your body tingles, you feel a slight prickling feeling in it
2 (noun) e.g. *I felt a tingle up my spine.*

tinker, tinkers, tinkering, tinkered
1 (verb) If you tinker with something, you make a lot of small adjustments to it to repair or improve it, e.g. *He's tinkering with the car.*
2 (old fashioned) a mender of kettles, pots, etc.

tinkle, tinkles, tinkling, tinkled
(verb) If something tinkles, it makes a sound like a small bell ringing.

tinsel
(noun) long threads with strips of shiny paper attached, used as a decoration at Christmas.

tint, tints, tinting, tinted
1 (noun) a small amount of a particular colour, e.g. *Your hair has a tint of auburn in it.*
2 (verb) If a person tints their hair, they change its colour by adding a weak dye to it.

tiny, tinier, tiniest
(adjective) extremely small.

tip, tips, tipping, tipped
1 (noun) The tip of something long and thin is the end of it, e.g. *a fingertip.*
2 (verb) e.g. *We tipped the wardrobe to get it up the stairs... You can't tip that rubbish here!*
3 (phrasal verb) If you tip someone off, you warn them that something is going to happen.
4 (noun) a place where rubbish is dumped.
5 If you give someone, e.g. a waiter, a tip, you give them money to thank them for their services.
6 a useful piece of advice or information.
tip-off (noun)

tipsy, tipsier, tipsiest
(adjective) slightly drunk.

tiptoe, tiptoes, tiptoeing, tiptoed
(verb) to walk quietly on your toes.

tire, tires, tiring, tired
1 (verb) If something tires you, it makes you use a lot of energy so that you want to rest or sleep.
2 If you tire of something, you become bored with it.
tired (adjective) **tiredness** (noun)

tireless
(adjective) Someone who is tireless has a lot of energy and never seems to need a rest.

tiresome
(adjective) A person or thing that is tiresome makes you feel irritated or bored.

tissue, tissues (pronounced **tiss-**yoo)
1 (noun) a general word for the substances which make up animals and plants; e.g. skin is human tissue.
2 thin paper used for wrapping, wiping, handkerchiefs, etc.
[Old French *tissu* = woven cloth]

titbit, titbits
(noun) a small, tasty piece of food.

title, titles
1 (noun) the name of a book, play or piece of music.

2 a word that describes someone's rank, status or job, e.g. *My Dad's title is Area Manager.*
3 A title in a sports competition is the position of champion, e.g. *He's won the heavyweight title.*

titled
(adjective) Someone who is titled has a high social rank and has a title e.g. 'Princess', 'Lord', 'Lady', or 'Sir'.

titter, titters, tittering, tittered
(verb) to laugh in a way that shows you are nervous or embarrassed.

tizz or **tizzy**
(noun; informal) If you get into a tizz, you get excited, worried or nervous.

to
1 (preposition) e.g. *Jill's going with us to London.*
2 (adverb) If you push or shut a door to, you close it but do not shut it completely.
3 (phrase) When you **come to**, you regain consciousness after fainting.

toad, toads
(noun) an amphibian that looks like a frog but has a drier skin and lives less in the water.

toadstool, toadstools
(noun) a type of poisonous fungus.

toast, toasts, toasting, toasted
1 (noun) cooked bread.
2 (verb) To toast someone means to drink an alcoholic drink in honour of them.
toaster (noun)
[Latin *tostus* = parched]

tobacco
(noun) the dried leaves of the tobacco plant which people smoke in pipes and cigarettes.
[Spanish *tabaco* = tabacco]

tobacconist, tobacconists
(noun) a person who runs a shop that sells tobacco, cigarettes and cigars; also the shop itself.

toboggan, toboggans, tobogganing, tobogganed
1 (noun) a small sledge.
2 (verb) e.g. *I tobogganed downhill.*
[an American Indian word]

today
(adverb, noun) e.g. *It's my birthday today... The car of today is very different from vintage cars.*

toddler, toddlers
(noun) a small child who has just learned to walk.
toddle (verb)

to-do, to-dos
(noun) a situation in which people are very agitated, confused or annoyed, e.g. *There was an awful to-do about her leaving college.*

toe, toes, toeing, toed
1 (noun) e.g. *Don't step on my toes.*
2 (phrase) If you **toe the line**, you behave in the way that people in authority expect you to.

toffee, toffees
(noun) a sticky, chewy sweet.

toga, togas
(noun) a long loose robe, worn in ancient Rome.

Try not to confuse *to, too* and *two. Two* miles is *too* far *to* walk. Are you tired, *too?*

together
(adverb) e.g. *We are all going together... Fix the two ends together.*

toggle, toggles
(noun) a small rod which is pushed through a loop or hole, as a fastener, e.g. on a duffle coat.

togs
(plural noun; informal) clothes.

toil, toils, toiling, toiled
1 (verb) to work hard doing unpleasant, difficult or tiring tasks.
2 (noun) unpleasant, difficult or tiring work.

toilet, toilets
(noun) e.g. *Is there a ladies' toilet here?*
[French *toilette* = dress]

toiletries
(plural noun) the things you use when cleaning and taking care of your body, e.g. soap and deodorant.

token, tokens
1 (noun) a card, paper, etc. that is worth a particular amount of money and can be exchanged for goods, e.g. *book tokens*.
2 a flat, round piece of metal or plastic used instead of money, for example in a car wash.
3 a way of showing something, e.g. *These flowers are a token of my love for you, Ethel.*

told
1 past tense and past participle of **tell**.
2 (phrase) You use **all told** when you want to emphasize that everything has been counted, e.g. *There are five of us all told going to the play.*

tolerance
(noun) A person's tolerance is their ability to accept or put up with something which may not be enjoyable or pleasant for them or that they might not agree with.
tolerant (adjective)

tolerate, tolerates, tolerating, tolerated
1 (verb) If you tolerate things that you do not approve of or agree with, you allow them.
2 If you can tolerate something, you accept it, even though it is unsatisfactory or unpleasant.
toleration (noun) **tolerable** (adjective)
[Latin *tolerare* = to endure]

Similar words: bear, endure, put up with, stand

toll, tolls, tolling, tolled
1 (verb) to ring a bell slowly.
2 (noun) The death toll in an accident is the number of people who have died in it.
3 (phrase) If something **takes its toll**, it has a serious effect and causes a lot of suffering, e.g. *The plague took its toll in London in 1665.*
4 (noun) a sum of money that you have to pay to use a particular bridge or road.
[noun: Greek *telos* = tax]

tomato, tomatoes
(noun) a small, round, red fruit, used as a vegetable.
[Spanish *tomate* = tomato]

tomb, tombs
(noun) a large grave for one or more corpses.

tomboy, tomboys
(noun) a girl who likes playing rough or noisy games.

tomorrow
(adverb, noun) e.g. *Tomorrow is New Year's Eve... But how will it be for the children of tomorrow.*

tom-tom, tom-toms
(noun) an African or Asian drum.
[Hindi *tamtam* = drum]

ton, tons
1 (noun) a unit of weight. (1 ton = 1016kg = 2240 pounds)
2 (plural noun; informal) If you have tons of something, you have a lot of it.

tone, tones, toning, toned
1 (noun) Someone's tone is the way they say or write something, e.g *I don't like your tone, Smithers... The tone of the newspaper article was offensive.*
2 The tone of a musical instrument or a singer's voice is the kind of sound it has.
3 a lighter, darker or brighter shade of the same colour, e.g. *You need to match the skirt with a blouse of a darker tone.*

tone down
(phrasal verb) If you tone down something, you make it more moderate.

tone-deaf
(adjective) unable to sing in tune or to recognize different tunes.

tongs
(plural noun) a tool for picking things up, e.g. *coal tongs... sugar tongs.*

tongue, tongues
1 (noun) the soft part in your mouth that you can move and use for tasting, licking and speaking.
2 a language, e.g. *Her native tongue was Gaelic.*
3 the cooked tongue of an ox.
4 The tongue of a shoe or boot is the piece of leather underneath the laces.
5 (phrase) If you **have your tongue in your cheek**, you are not being sincere or serious, although you may pretend to be.
6 A **slip of the tongue** is a small mistake that you make when you are speaking.

tongue twister, twisters
(noun) a sentence that is very difficult to say properly, especially when you are saying it quickly, e.g. *She sells sea shells on the sea shore.*

tonic, tonics
1 (noun) Tonic or tonic water is a colourless, fizzy drink that has a slightly bitter flavour and is often mixed with alcoholic drinks.
2 a medicine that makes you feel stronger, healthier and less tired.

tonight
(adverb, noun) e.g. *I'm going out tonight.*

tonne, tonnes (pronounced **tun**)
(noun) a unit of weight. (1 tonne = 1000kg)

There are about three thousand different languages spoken throughout the world.

tonsils
(plural noun) Your tonsils are the two small, soft lumps in your throat at the back of your mouth.
tonsillitis (noun)

too
(adverb) e.g. *You come too... There's too much salt in the rice.*

tool, tools
(noun) any hand-held instrument or piece of equipment that you use to help you do a job.

Similar words: implement, utensil

tooth, teeth
1 (noun) e.g. *The dentist filled my tooth.*
2 The teeth of a comb, saw or zip are the parts that stick out in a row on its edge.

toothpaste
(noun) a substance used to clean teeth.

top, tops, topping, topped
Selected meanings:
1 (noun) e.g. *the table top... a bottle top.*
2 (adjective) e.g. *He was on the top step.*
3 (verb) e.g. *The band has topped the charts for three weeks... Money raised by the marathon topped £5000.*

top-heavy
(adjective) heavier at the top than at the bottom and so, likely to tip over.

topic, topics
(noun) a particular subject that you write about or discuss.

topical
(adjective) involving events that are happening now, e.g. *It was very topical of Mrs. Stephenson to teach us about European farming when the Brussels conference was being held.*

topography, topographies
(noun) the study and description of the physical features of an area, e.g. the hills, valleys or rivers.
[Greek *topos* = place + *graphein* = to write]

topple, topples, toppling, toppled
(verb) to become unsteady and fall over.

top-secret
(adjective) meant to be kept completely secret.

topsy-turvy
(adjective) in a confused state, e.g. *Her room was all topsy-turvy.*

torch, torches
1 (noun) a portable, battery-powered light.
2 a long stick with burning material wrapped around one end.
torchlight (noun)
[Old French *torche* = handful of twisted straw]

torment, torments, tormenting, tormented
1 (noun) extreme pain or unhappiness.
2 (verb) If someone torments you, they annoy you in a playful and rather cruel way, e.g. *Jan is always tormenting her younger sister.*
[Latin *tormentum* = torture]

torn
1 past participle of **tear**.

2 (adjective) If you are torn between two or more things, you cannot decide which one to choose and this makes you unhappy, e.g. *He was torn between his job and his family.*

tornado, tornadoes
(noun) a violent storm with strong, circular winds around a funnel-shaped cloud.

torpedo, torpedoes
(noun) a tube-shaped bomb that travels underwater and explodes when it hits a target.

torrent, torrents
(noun) a lot of water in a flood.
[Latin *torrens* = burning]

torrential
(adjective) Torrential rain pours down very rapidly and in great quantities.

torso, torsos
(noun) the main part of your body, excluding your head, arms and legs.
[an Italian word]

tortoise, tortoises
(noun) a slow-moving reptile with a shell.

torture, tortures, torturing, tortured
(noun, verb) If someone tortures another person, they deliberately cause that person great pain to punish them or get information.
torturer (noun).

Tory, Tories
(noun) a supporter of the Conservative Party.
[Irish *toraidhe* = outlaw]

toss, tosses, tossing, tossed
1 (verb) to throw something lightly and carelessly.
2 If you toss your head, you move it suddenly backwards.
3 If you toss a coin, you decide something by throwing a coin into the air and guessing which side will face upwards when it lands.
4 To toss means to move repeatedly from side to side, e.g. *She tossed restlessly in her sleep.*

Similar words: (sense 1) lob, flip, flick

toss-up
(noun; informal) If it is a toss-up whether you do one thing or another, you could do either, but it doesn't matter which one.

tot, tots, totting, totted
1 (noun) a very young child.
2 a small amount of strong drink, e.g. whisky.
3 (verb) To tot up means to count.

total, totals, totalling, totalled
1 (noun) the number you get when you add several numbers together.
2 (verb) e.g. *If you total these figures up... The cost totalled £3.*
3 (adjective) complete, e.g. *a total disaster.*
totally (adverb)

totem pole, poles
(noun) a long, wooden pole with symbols and pictures carved and painted on it, made by North American Indians.

otter, totters, tottering, tottered
(verb) to walk in an unsteady way.

ouch, touches, touching, touched
1 (verb) to put your fingers or hand on something.
2 When two things touch, their surfaces come into contact, e.g. *the wires are touching.*
3 (noun) Your sense of touch is your ability to tell what something is like by touching it.
4 a detail which is added to improve something, e.g. *finishing touches.*
5 The way someone does something can be called their touch, e.g. *He hasn't got your touch, David, when it comes to painting watercolours.*
6 a small amount of something, e.g. *'Do you take milk?' – 'Just a touch.'*
7 (verb) If you are touched by something, you are emotionally affected by it, e.g. *I was touched by her kind words.*
8 (phrase) If you are **in touch** with someone, you are in contact with them.
9 If something is **touch and go**, you are not sure whether it will happen or succeed.
10 (noun) In football, rugby, etc. touch is the area at the side of the pitch, e.g. *The ball went into touch* means it went out of play.

ouchdown, touchdowns
(noun) the landing of an aircraft.
touch down (verb)

touching
(adjective) causing someone to feel pleasant emotions, e.g. *a very touching gift.*

touchline, touchlines
(noun) In football, rugby, etc., the touchline is a line marking the side of the pitch.

touchy, touchier, touchiest
1 (adjective) easily upset, offended or irritated.
2 A touchy subject is one that needs to be dealt with carefully, as it might upset or offend people.

tough, tougher, toughest
1 (adjective) strong and independent, e.g *You've got to be tough in the Arctic.*
2 e.g. *a tough plastic... a tough problem... We need to get tough with muggers.*
3 (phrase) If you say someone is a **tough cookie**, you mean they have a strong, sturdy character.
4 If you say someone is a **tough customer**, you mean they are strong and maybe violent.
toughly (adverb) **toughness** (noun)
toughen (verb)

Similar words: (sense 2) durable, sturdy

tour, tours, touring, toured
1 (verb) If you tour a place, you go on a journey or a trip round it.
2 (noun) a circular trip, either on foot, e.g. *a guided tour,* or in a car or a coach, e.g. *a mystery tour.*
[French *tour* = a turn]

tourist, tourists
(noun) a person who visits places for pleasure or interest.

tournament, tournaments
(noun) a knock-out sports competition.
[Old French *tourneier* = to fight on horseback]

tousled
(adjective) Tousled hair is untidy.

tow, tows, towing, towed
(verb) If a car tows another car, it pulls it along behind it.
2 (phrase) If a car is **on tow** it is being towed. If a Lada has a Rolls Royce **in tow**, the Lada is towing the Rolls Royce.

towards
(preposition) e.g. *He saw his mother running towards him... Dad gave me £20 towards my new bike... We sat towards the back.*

towel, towels
(noun) a piece of thick, soft cloth that you use to dry yourself with.

tower, towers, towering, towered
1 (noun) a tall, narrow building, sometimes part of a larger building, e.g. a castle or church.
2 (phrase) Someone who is **a tower of strength** gives help and support.
3 (verb) Someone or something that towers over other people or things is much taller than them.

town, towns
1 (noun) e.g. *Towns are smaller than cities... We went into town to do some Christmas shopping.*
2 (phrase) If you **go to town on** an activity, you put a lot of effort and enthusiasm into it.

towpath, towpaths
(noun) a path along the side of a canal or river.

toxic
(adjective) poisonous.
[Greek *toxikon* = poison used on arrows from *toxon* = arrow]

toy, toys, toying, toyed
1 (noun) any object made to play with.
2 (verb) If you toy with an idea, you consider it without being too serious about it, e.g. *We both toyed with the idea of joining the Air Force.*

trace, traces, tracing, traced
1 (verb) to find something after looking for it, e.g. *They were trying to trace the missing child.*
2 to copy a drawing etc. by covering it with a piece of transparent paper and drawing over the lines of the original.
tracing paper (noun)
3 (noun) a sign which shows you that someone or something has been in a place, e.g. *There were traces of blood on the floor.*

track, tracks, tracking, tracked
1 (noun) a narrow road or path.
2 e.g. *a railway track... a race track.*
3 (plural noun) Tracks are marks left on the ground by a person or animal.
4 (verb) If you track animals or people, you follow their footprints or other signs that they have left behind.
5 (noun) one of the songs or pieces of music on a tape, CD, etc, e.g. *This is my favourite track.*

....William Caxton set up his printing press near Westminster Abbey about 1476. He died in 1491.

track down
(phrasal verb) If you track down someone or something, you find them by searching for them.

tracksuit, tracksuits
(noun) a loose, warm suit of trousers and a top, worn for outdoor sports.

traction engine, engines
(noun) a large, heavy steam vehicle used in the past for pulling heavy loads.

tractor, tractors
(noun) a vehicle with large rear wheels that is used on a farm.

trade, trades, trading, traded
1 (noun) the activity of buying, selling or exchanging goods or services between people, firms or countries.
2 (verb) to buy, sell or exchange goods or services.
3 (noun) Someone's trade is the kind of work they do, especially when it needs special training in practical skills.

Similar words: (noun) commerce
(verb) bargain, barter, haggle, deal

trade in
(phrasal verb) If a person trades in, for example, a car, they hand it over to the dealer who is selling them a new one and its value is taken off the price of the new car.

trademark, trademarks
(noun) a name or symbol that a manufacturer uses on its products. Trademarks are protected by law so that no one else can use them.

trader, traders
(noun) a person whose job is to deal in goods, e.g. *market traders.*

tradesman, tradesmen
(noun) a person, e.g. a shopkeeper, whose job is to sell goods; also someone who has learned a trade, e.g. a plumber.

trade union, unions
(noun) an organization that tries to improve the pay and conditions of workers in a particular industry.

tradition, traditions
(noun) a custom or belief that has existed for a long time without changing.
traditional (adjective) **traditionally** (adverb)
[Latin *traditio* = a handing down]

Similar words: custom, convention

traffic, traffics, trafficking, trafficked
1 (noun) the movement of vehicles or people along a route.
2 (verb) Someone who traffics in drugs or other goods buys and sells them illegally.
[Italian *traffico* = trade]

traffic lights
(plural noun) the set of lights at a road junction which controls the flow of traffic.

traffic warden, wardens
(noun) a person whose job is to make sure that cars are parked correctly.

tragedy, tragedies (pronounced traj-id-ee)
1 (noun) an event or situation that is disastrous or very sad.
2 a serious play that usually ends with the death of the main character.
[Greek *tragoidia* = tragically]

tragic
(adjective) very sad because it involves death, suffering or disaster, e.g. *He had a tragic accident and lost both legs.*
tragically (adverb)

trail, trails, trailing, trailed
1 (noun) a rough path across open country etc.
2 a series of marks or other signs left by someone or something as they move along.
3 (verb) If you trail something or it trails, it drags along behind you as you move, or it hangs down loosely, e.g. *She trailed her fingers through the water.*
4 If someone trails along, they move slowly, without any energy or enthusiasm, e.g. *I used to trail around after him like a child.*
5 If a voice trails away or trails off, it gradually becomes more hesitant until it stops completely.
[Latin *trahere* = to drag]

trailer, trailers
1 (noun) a small vehicle which can be loaded with things and pulled behind a car or lorry.
2 A trailer for a film or a TV or radio programme is a set of short extracts from it, shown or broadcast to advertise it.

train, trains, training, trained
1 (noun) e.g. *an Inter-City express train.*
2 The train of a bride's dress is a long part at the back of it that rests on the ground.
3 (verb) If you train, you learn how to do a particular job, e.g. *She is trained as a nurse.*
4 If you train for a sports match or a race, you prepare for it by doing exercises.

trainee, trainees
(noun) someone who is being taught how to do a job, e.g. *a trainee accountant.*

trainers
(plural noun) special shoes worn for running or jogging; also for fashion wear.

traitor, traitors
(noun) someone who betrays their country or the group which they belong to.
traitorous (adjective), **traitorously** (adverb).
[Latin *traditor* = traitor]

tram, trams
(noun) a type of bus which runs on rails along the street and is powered by electricity from an overhead wire.

tramp, tramps, tramping, tramped
1 (noun) a person who has no home, no job and very little money.
2 (verb) If you tramp from one place to another, you walk with slow, heavy footsteps.

trample, tramples, trampling, trampled
1 (verb) If you **trample on** something, you tread heavily on it so that it is damaged.

Working from memory, how many road and traffic signs can you draw and explain?

2 If you trample on someone, you behave in a way that shows you don't care about them.

trampoline, trampolines
(noun) a piece of gymnastic apparatus.

trance, trances
(noun) a mental state in which someone seems to be asleep but is conscious.
[Old French *transir* = to faint]

tranquil (pronounced **trang**-kwil)
(adjective) calm and peaceful.
tranquillity (noun)

tranquillize, tranquillizes, tranquillizing, tranquillized; also spelled **tranquillise**
(verb) If people or animals are tranquillized, they are given a drug to make them become calm, sleepy or unconscious.
tranquillizer (noun)

trans-
(prefix) across, through or beyond, e.g. *transatlantic.*

transaction
(noun) a business deal.

transcript, transcripts
(noun) A transcript of something that is spoken is a written copy of it.
transcribe (verb)

transfer, transfers, transferring, transferred
1 (verb; pronounced trans-**fer**) to move something from one place to another, e.g. *She transferred her savings to a special account.*
2 If you transfer to a different place or job, or are transferred to it, you move to a different place or job, e.g. *The goalkeeper transferred from Q.P.R. to Arsenal.*
3 (noun; pronounced **trans**-fer) The transfer of something is the movement of it from one place to another.
4 a piece of paper with a design on one side which can be ironed or pressed onto cloth, paper or china.
transferable (adjective) **transference** (noun)

transform, transforms, transforming, transformed
(verb) If something is transformed, it is changed completely, e.g. *Her appearance was transformed by her new hairdo.*
transformation (noun)

transformer, transformers
(noun) a piece of electrical equipment which changes the voltage of a current.

transfusion, transfusions
(noun) A blood transfusion is a process in which blood from a healthy person is injected into another person who is badly injured or ill.
[Latin *trans-* = across + *fundere* = to pour]

transistor, transistors
1 (noun) a small electrical part in, for example a TV or radio.
2 A transistor or a transistor radio (or 'trannie') is a small portable radio.

transit
(noun) the carrying of goods or people by vehicle from one place to another.
[Latin *transire* = to pass over]

transition, transitions
(noun) a change, e.g. *We made the transition from imperial to metric measurement.*
transitional (adjective)

transitive
(adjective) In grammar, a transitive verb is a verb which has an object, e.g. In 'I hit the ball', 'hit' is a transitive verb. (An **intransitive** verb has no object.)

translate, translates, translating, translated
(verb) To translate something means to say or write it in a different language.
translation (noun) **translator** (noun)
[Latin *translatus* = transferred]

transmission, transmissions
1 (noun) passing or sending something to a different place or person, e.g. *the transmission of diseases.*
2 The transmission of TV or radio programmes is the broadcasting of them.

transmit, transmits, transmitting, transmitted
1 (verb) When a message or an electronic signal is transmitted, it is sent by radio waves.
2 to pass or send something to a different place or person, e.g. *a way of transmitting energy.*
transmitter (noun)
[Latin *trans-* = across + *mittere* = to send]

transparency, transparencies
(noun) a photographic slide.

transparent
(adjective) If an object or substance is transparent, you can see through it.
[Latin *trans-* = across + *parere* = to appear]

Similar words: clear, see-through

transplant, transplants, transplanting, transplanted
1 (noun) the process of removing something from one place and putting it in another, e.g. *I'm putting you down for a brain transplant, Watts.*
2 (verb) When something is transplanted, it is moved to a different place.

transport, transports, transporting, transported
1 (noun) vehicles that you travel in, e.g. *public transport.*
2 the moving of goods or people from one place to another, e.g. *rail transport.*
[Latin *trans-* = across + *portare* = to carry]

trap, traps, trapping, trapped
1 (noun) a piece of equipment or a hole to catch animals or birds.
trapper (noun)
2 (verb) e.g. *She trapped him into admitting to the murder... We were trapped in the cave.*

trap door, doors
(noun) a small, horizontal door in a floor, ceiling or stage.

trapeze, trapezes
(noun) a bar hanging from two ropes on which

John Wycliffe (1320-1384) was the first to translate the New Testament into English.

acrobats and gymnasts swing and perform skilful movements.

trapezium, trapeziums or **trapezia** (pronounced trap-**pee**-zee-um)
(noun) a 4-sided shape with two sides parallel to each other.

trash
1 (noun) rubbish, e.g. *The pavement was littered with trash.*
2 If you say that, for example, a book, painting or film is trash, you mean it is not very good.

trashy, trashier, trashiest
(adjective) of very poor quality.

traumatic
(adjective) A traumatic experience is very upsetting.
trauma (noun)

travel, travels, travelling, travelled
1 (verb) to go from one place to another.
2 (noun) the act of travelling, e.g. *air travel.*
traveller (noun) **travelling** (adjective)

Similar words: (verb) journey, commute, go

trawler, trawlers
(noun) a fishing boat; fish are caught in a large net dragged behind the boat.
trawl (verb)

tray, trays
(noun) a board used for carrying food or drinks.

treacherous (pronounced **tretch**-er-ous)
1 (adjective) A treacherous person is likely to betray you and cannot be trusted, e.g. *The Sheriff of Nottingham was a treacherous type.*
2 The ground or the sea can be described as treacherous when it is dangerous or unreliable, e.g. *The currents are treacherous.*
treacherously (adverb) **treachery** (noun)
[Old French *trechier* = to cheat]

treacle
(noun) a thick, sweet, sticky syrup obtained by refining sugar, e.g. *treacle tart.*

tread, treads, treading, trod, trodden
1 (verb) If you tread on something, you step on it.
2 (noun) A person's tread is the sound they make with their feet as they walk, e.g. *She could hear the light tread of footsteps on the carpet.*
3 The tread of a tyre is the pattern of ridges on it that stops it slipping.

treason
(noun) the crime of betraying your country, by helping its enemies.

treasure, treasures, treasuring, treasured
1 (noun) a collection of gold, silver, jewels, etc., especially one that was hidden, e.g. *buried treasure.*
2 valuable works of art, e.g. *the sale of art treasures.*
3 (verb) If you treasure something, you are very pleased that you have it, e.g. *I treasure my memories.*

treasurer, treasurers
(noun) a person who is in charge of the money and accounts of an organization.

treat, treats, treating, treated
1 (verb) e.g. *Oliver was treated in a cruel way at the workhouse... Don't treat it as some sort of joke... Let me treat you to a cake.*
2 When doctors treat patients or an illness, they give them medical care and attention.
3 If something like wood or cloth is treated, a special substance is put on it to protect it, e.g. *The floorboards have been treated for woodworm.*
treatment (noun)
4 (noun) If you give someone a treat, you buy or arrange something special for them which they will enjoy.
5 (verb) If you treat someone, you buy or arrange something special for them, e.g. *As it's your birthday, I'll treat you to lunch.*
[Latin *tractare* = to manage]

treaty, treaties
(noun) a written agreement between countries, e.g. *The Treaty of Rome 1957.*
[Latin *tractatus* = handling]

treble, trebles, trebling, trebled
1 (verb) to become 3 times greater in number or amount.
2 (adjective) 3 times bigger, e.g. *The price is treble the amount it was last year.*
3 (noun) a boy with a singing voice in the highest range of musical notes.
4 an instrument which uses a high range of musical notes, e.g. *This recorder is a treble.*

tree, trees
(noun) e.g. *Forests are made up of trees.*

trek, treks, trekking, trekked
1 (noun) a long and difficult journey.
2 (verb) e.g. *Scott trekked across Antarctica.*
[an Afrikaans word]

trellis, trellises
(noun) a frame used to support climbing plants.

tremble, trembles, trembling, trembled
(verb) to shake slightly, because you are frightened or cold.

tremendous
1 (adjective) large or impressive, e.g. *The film was a tremendous success.*
2 (informal) very good or pleasing, e.g. *We had a tremendous holiday.*
tremendously (adverb)

tremor, tremors
(noun) a small earthquake.

trench, trenches
(noun) a long, narrow channel in the ground.

trend, trends
(noun) a change towards doing or being something different, e.g. *the trend towards more single-parent families.*

trendy, trendier, trendiest
(adjective; informal) fashionable.

∴ is a short way of writing 'therefore' when you are taking notes.

respass, trespasses, trespassing, trespassed
1 (verb) to go onto someone's land or property without their permission.
2 (old fashioned) a bad deed.
trespasser (noun)
[Old French *trespasser* = to pass through]

restle, trestles
(noun) a wooden or metal structure that is used as one of the supports for a table.

ri-
(prefix) 3, *e.g. tricycle, tripod, triangle.*

rial, trials
1 (noun) the legal process in which a judge and jury decide whether a person is guilty of a crime after listening to all the evidence about it.
2 an experiment in which something is tested, e.g. *After many trials the new drug has proved to be successful.*
3 (phrase) If you do something **by trial and error**, you try different methods of doing it until you find one that works well.

riangle, triangles
1 (noun) a shape with 3 straight sides.
2 a percussion instrument consisting of a thin steel bar bent in the shape of a triangle.
triangular (adjective)
[*tri-* + Latin *angulus* = corner]

ribe, tribes
(noun) a group of people of the same race who have the same customs, religion, language or land. It is usually used of people in less developed countries.
tribal (adjective)
[Latin *tribus* = division of the (Roman) people]

ributary, tributaries
(noun) a stream or river that flows into a larger river.

ribute, tributes
(noun) something said or done to show admiration and respect for someone, e.g. *The MP paid tribute to the soldiers.*

rice
(noun) If someone does something in a trice, they do it very quickly.

rick, tricks, tricking, tricked
1 (verb) If someone tricks you, they deceive you.
2 (noun) Tricks are clever or skilful actions done to entertain people, e.g. *magic tricks.*
3 In card games, a trick is a batch of cards, one from each player, won by the person who plays the card with the highest value.
5 (adjective) intended to deceive people for a joke or for entertainment, e.g. *a trick question.*

rickery
(noun) deception, e.g. *Othello suspected trickery from Cassio, but not Iago.*

rickle, trickles, trickling, trickled
1 (verb) When a liquid trickles somewhere, it flows slowly in a thin stream.
2 When people or things trickle somewhere, they move there slowly in small groups or amounts.
3 (noun) e.g. *There was a trickle of water in the stream.*

trickster, tricksters
(noun) a person who deceives or cheats people.

tricky, trickier, trickiest
(adjective) difficult to do or deal with, e.g. *Wiring this plug is a tricky job.*

tricycle, tricycles
(noun) a 3-wheeled version of the bicycle.
[*tri-* + Greek *kyklos* = wheel]

trident, tridents
(noun) a 3-pronged spear, e.g. the one carried by the sea god Neptune in Greek mythology.
[*tri-* + Latin *dentes* = teeth]

trifle, trifles
1 (noun) something that is not very important or valuable.
2 a cold pudding made of layers of sponge cake, fruit, jelly, and custard.

trigger, triggers, triggering, triggered
1 (noun) the lever which is pulled to fire a gun.
2 (verb) If something triggers an event or triggers it off, it causes it to happen.
[Dutch *trekken* = to pull]

trigonometry (pronounced trig-gon-**nom**-it-ree)
(noun) the branch of maths concerned with calculating the angles of triangles or the lengths of their sides.
[Greek *trigonon* = triangle]

trill, trills, trilling, trilled
(verb) If a bird trills, it sings with short high-pitched repeated notes.
[Italian *trillo* = trill]

trillion, trillions
(noun; informal) Trillions of things means an extremely large number of them. A trillion used to mean a million million million.

trilogy, trilogies
(noun) a series of 3 books or plays that have the same characters or are on the same subject.
[Greek *trilogia* = group of 3 tragedies]

trim, trimmer, trimmest; trims, trimming, trimmed
1 (adjective) neat, tidy and attractive.
2 (verb) To trim something means to clip small amounts off it, e.g. *to trim a hedge.*

trinity
(noun) In the Christian religion, the Holy Trinity is God the Father, the Son and the Holy Spirit.
[Latin *trinus* = triple]

trinket, trinkets
(noun) a cheap ornament or piece of jewellery.

trio, trios
1 (noun) a group of 3 musicians who sing or play together.
2 Any group of 3 things or people together can be referred to as a trio.
[an Italian word]

trip, trips, tripping, tripped
1 (noun) a journey made to a place.
tripper (noun)
2 (verb) If you trip, you catch your foot on something and fall over.

Similar words: (noun) outing, excursion

What kind of animal can jump higher than a house? ... All kinds. Houses can't jump.

tripe
1 (noun) the stomach lining of a pig, cow or ox, which is cooked and eaten.
2 (informal) anything that you consider to be silly or worthless, e.g. *I wish you wouldn't read tripe like that.*

triple, triples, tripling, tripled
1 (adjective) consisting of 3 things or 3 parts, e.g. *a triple somersault.*
2 (verb) If you triple something or if it triples, it becomes 3 times greater in number or size.

triple jump
(noun) an athletics event in which you do a hop, step and jump after taking a long run.

triplet, triplets
(noun) one of 3 children born at the same time to the same mother.

triplicate
(noun) If a document is in triplicate, there are 3 copies of it.

tripod, tripods (pronounced **try**-pod)
(noun) a stand with 3 legs used to support something like a camera or telescope.
[*tri-* + Greek *podes* = feet]

triumph, triumphs, triumphing, triumphed
1 (noun) a great success or achievement, e.g. *The over 60s egg and spoon race was a triumph for my granny.*
2 (verb) If you triumph, you win a victory or succeed in overcoming something.
triumphant (adjective)

trivia
1 (plural noun) unimportant or uninteresting things, e.g. *the trivia of gossip.*
2 unimportant items of general knowledge.

trivial
(adjective) unimportant.
triviality (noun)
[Latin *trivialis* = found everywhere]

troll, trolls
(noun) an imaginary creature in Scandinavian mythology that lives in caves or mountains.

trolley, trolleys
1 (noun) a small table on wheels.
2 a small cart on wheels used for carrying heavy objects, e.g. *supermarket trolleys.*

trolley bus, buses
(noun) a public transport vehicle powered by overhead electricity wires.

trombone, trombones
(noun) a brass wind instrument.
[an Italian word]

troop, troops, trooping, trooped
1 (verb) If people troop somewhere, they go there in a group.
2 (noun) Troops are soldiers.
3 a group of people or animals.

trophy, trophies
(noun) a cup or shield given as a prize to the winner of a competition.
[Greek *tropē* = defeat of the enemy]

tropical
(adjective) belonging to or typical of the tropics, the hot zone of the Earth on either side of the equator, e.g. *tropical rainforest.*

tropics
(plural noun) The tropics are the hottest parts of the world between the Tropic of Cancer, 23½°F north of the equator, and the Tropic of Capricorn, 23½°F south of the equator.

trot, trots, trotting, trotted
1 (verb) When a horse trots, it moves at a speed between a walk and a canter, lifting its feet quite high off the ground.
2 (phrase) If things happen **on the trot**, they happen one after the other.

trot out
(phrasal verb) If you trot out information or ideas, you repeat them in a boring way, e.g. *Old Parkie trotted out all his old history notes.*

trouble, troubles, troubling, troubled
1 (noun) e.g. *Are you looking for trouble?... You're in trouble now!... Share your troubles with a friend.*
2 (phrase) If you **take the trouble** to do something, you do it although it requires time and effort.
3 (verb) If something troubles you, it makes you feel worried or anxious.
4 If you trouble someone for something, you disturb them to ask them for it, e.g. *I'm sorry to trouble you, but do you have the time?*

troublesome
(adjective) causing problems or difficulties, e.g. *She has a very troublesome aunt.*

trough, troughs (pronounced **troff**)
(noun) a long, narrow container from which animals drink or feed.

trounce, trounces, trouncing, trounced
(verb) If you trounce someone, you beat them completely, e.g. *Leeds United were trounced by Manchester City.*

trousers
(plural noun) a piece of men's clothing.
[Gaelic *triubhas* = trews (tartan trousers)]

trout
(noun) a type of freshwater fish.

trowel, trowels
1 (noun) a small garden tool with a curved, pointed blade used for planting or weeding.
2 a tool with a flat, diamond-shaped blade used for spreading cement or plaster.
[Latin *trulla* = ladle]

truant
(phrase) If children **play truant**, they stay away from school without permission.
truancy (noun)

truce, truces
(noun) an agreement between two people or groups to stop fighting for a short time.

truck, trucks
(noun) a lorry or a wheeled carrying device.

truculent (pronounced **truk-yoo-lent**)
(adjective) bad-tempered and aggressive.
truculently (adverb) **truculence** (noun)

trudge, **trudges**, **trudging**, **trudged**
(verb) to walk with slow, heavy steps.

true, **truer**, **truest**
1 (adjective) A true story or statement is based on facts and is not made up.
2 (phrase) If something **comes true**, it actually happens.
3 (adjective) real, e.g. *He's a true friend.*
truly (adverb)

trump, **trumps**, **trumping**, **trumped**
1 (noun) In a game of cards, trumps is the suit with the highest value.
2 (verb) To trump a card means to beat it by playing a trump.
[from *triumph*]

trumpet, **trumpets**, **trumpeting**, **trumpeted**
1 (noun) a brass wind instrument.
2 (verb) When an elephant trumpets, it makes a sound like a very loud trumpet.
trumpeter (noun)
[French *trompette* = trumpet]

truncheon, **truncheons**
(noun) a short, thick stick that policemen carry as a weapon.
[Old French *tronchon* = stump]

trundle, **trundles**, **trundling**, **trundled**
(verb) If you trundle something or it trundles somewhere, it moves or rolls along slowly.

trunk, **trunks**
1 (noun) the main stem of a tree.
2 the main part of your body, excluding your head, neck, arms and legs.
3 An elephant's trunk is its long, flexible nose.
4 a large, strong case or box with a hinged lid used for storing things.
5 (plural noun) a man's bathing shorts.
[Latin *truncus* = lopped]

trust, **trusts**, **trusting**, **trusted**
1 (verb) If you trust someone, you believe that they are honest and will not harm you.
2 to rely on, e.g. *I trust Bond to complete the mission... She's not a person I can trust with this sort of secret... I don't trust old cars.*
3 (noun) the responsibility to deal with or look after important, valuable or secret things, e.g. *To be school librarian is a position of trust.*
trustful (adjective) **trusting** (adjective)

trustworthy
(adjective) A trustworthy person is reliable and responsible and can be trusted.

trusty, **trustier**, **trustiest**
(adjective) Trusty things and animals are thought to be reliable because they have always worked well in the past, e.g. *I mounted my trusty old bike and rode to the Post Office.*

truth, **truths**
(noun) the facts about something, not things that are imagined or made up, e.g. *I think he's telling the truth.*

truthful
(adjective) A truthful person is honest and tells the truth.
truthfully (adverb) **truthfulness** (noun)

try, **tries**, **trying**, **tried**
1 (verb) e.g. *You must try harder!*
2 (noun) e.g. *I had a try at starting the car.*
3 In rugby, a try is scored by carrying the ball over the opponents' goal line and touching the ground with it.
4 (verb) When a person is tried, they appear in court and a judge and jury decide if they are guilty after hearing the evidence.

Similar words: (verb) attempt, endeavour, strive (noun: sense 2) go, shot, endeavour, bid

trying
(adjective) A trying person is difficult to deal with and makes you feel impatient or annoyed.

tsar, **tsars** (pronounced **zar**); also spelled **czar**
(noun) a Russian emperor or king.

tuba, **tubas**
(noun) a large, brass musical instrument.
[an Italian word]

tubby, **tubbier**, **tubbiest**
(adjective) rather fat.

tube, **tubes**
1 (noun) a round, hollow pipe.
2 a container, e.g. *a tube of toothpaste.*
3 The Tube is the London underground railway.
tubular (adjective)

tuck, **tucks**, **tucking**, **tucked**
1 (noun) a small pleat in a piece of clothing.
2 (verb) e.g. *Tuck your shirt in... He tucked the books under his arm... She had money tucked away... a pretty cottage tucked away in the hills.*

tuck shop, **shops**
(noun) a small shop in a school that sells snacks and sweets to the pupils.

Tuesday, **Tuesdays**
(noun) the day between Monday and Wednesday.
[Old English *tiwesdæg* = Tiw's day; Tiw was the Scandinavian god of war and the sky]

tuft, **tufts**
(noun) A tuft of hair is a bunch of it growing closely together.
tufted (adjective) **tufty** (adjective)

tug, **tugs**, **tugging**, **tugged**
1 (verb) To tug something means to give it a quick, hard pull.
2 (noun) a small, powerful boat which tows large ships.

tug of war
(noun) a sport in which two teams test their strength by pulling against each other on opposite ends of a rope.

tuition
(noun) the teaching of a subject, especially to one person or to a small group.
[Latin *tuitio* = guarding]

Truth needs not many words. (16th century proverb)

tulip, tulips
(noun) a brightly-coloured spring flower.
[Turkish *tulbend* = turban, because of its shape]

tumble, tumbles, tumbling, tumbled
(verb) to fall.

tumble dryer, dryers; also spelled **drier**
(noun) a machine that dries washing with heat.

tumbler, tumblers
(noun) a drinking glass with straight sides.

tummy, tummies
(noun; informal) the stomach.

tumour, tumours (pronounced **tyoo**-mur)
(noun) a mass of diseased or abnormal cells that
has grown in a person's or animal's body.

tuna (pronounced **tyoo**-na)
(noun) a type of edible fish living in warm seas.

tundra
(noun) a vast, treeless Arctic region with
permanently frozen subsoil.
[a Russian word]

tune, tunes, tuning, tuned
1 (noun) an organized sequence of musical notes,
e.g. *Play that tune again*.
2 (verb) To tune a musical instrument means to
adjust it so that it produces the right notes.
piano tuner (noun)
3 To tune an engine or machine means to adjust it
so that it works well.
4 e.g. *Tune in to Radio 1 FM*.
5 (phrase) If your voice or an instrument is **in
tune**, it produces the right notes.

tuneful
(adjective) having a pleasant and easily
remembered tune.

tunic, tunics
(noun) a long, sleeveless garment covering the
top part of the body.

Tunisian, Tunisians (pronounced
tyoo-**niz**-ee-an)
1 (adjective) belonging to Tunisia.
2 (noun) someone who comes from Tunisia.

tunnel, tunnels, tunnelling, tunnelled
1 (noun) a long, underground passage.
2 (verb) to make a tunnel.

turban, turbans
(noun) a long piece of cloth wound round the
head of a Hindu, Muslim or Sikh man.
[Turkish *tulbend* = turban]

turbine, turbines
(noun) an engine in which power is produced
when a stream of air, gas, water or steam pushes
the blades of a wheel and makes it revolve.
[Latin *turbo* = whirlwind]

turbo, turbos
(noun) a fan in an engine that improves its
performance.

turbulent
1 (adjective) A turbulent period of history is one
where there is much confusion, uncertainty and
possibly violent change.

2 Turbulent air or water currents make sudden
changes of direction.
turbulence (noun) **turbulently** (adverb)

turf, turves
(noun) short, thick, even grass and the layer of
soil beneath it.

turf out
(phrasal verb; informal) To turf someone out
means to force them to leave a place.

Turk, Turks
(noun) someone who comes from Turkey.

turkey, turkeys
(noun) a large bird reared for food.

Turkish
1 (adjective) belonging to Turkey.
2 (noun) the main language spoken in Turkey.

turkish delight
(noun) a jelly-like sweet covered with powdered
sugar or chocolate.

turn, turns, turning, turned
1 (verb) e.g. *Turn round so I can see you... Let's
turn our thoughts to the next meeting... He
turned to her for help... With heat, water turns
into steam*.
2 (noun) e.g. *Make a turn to the left here... She
took a turn for the worse... It's your turn to wash
up*.
3 (phrase) If you do someone **a good turn**, you do
something that helps or benefits them.

turn down
(phrasal verb) If you turn down someone's
request or offer, you refuse or reject it.

turn up
(phrasal verb) If someone or something turns up,
they arrive or appear somewhere.

turning point, points
(noun) a moment in time when events start to
move in a different direction, e.g. *Getting a job
was the turning point in my life*.

turnip, turnips
(noun) a round root vegetable.

turnout, turnouts
(noun) The turnout at an event is the number of
people who go to it.

turnstile, turnstiles
(noun) a revolving barrier at the entrance to
places like football grounds or theme parks.

turntable, turntables
(noun) the flat, round part of a record player.

turps
(noun) turpentine, a white spirit used for
cleaning and thinning paint.

turquoise (pronounced **tur**-kwoyz)
(noun, adjective) light bluish-green.
[Old French *turqueise* = Turkish]

turret, turrets
1 (noun) a small, narrow tower on top of a larger
tower or other buildings.
2 a revolving structure on tanks and warships,
on which guns are mounted.

We take these words from Turkish: tulip kiosk coffee horde turban.

turtle, turtles
(noun) a large reptile with a thick shell.

tusk, tusks
(noun) The tusks of an elephant, wild boar, etc. are the pair of long, curving, pointed teeth it has.

tussle, tussles
(noun) an energetic fight, struggle, or argument between two people, especially about something they both want.

tutor, tutors, tutoring, tutored
1 (noun) a teacher at a college, university, etc., or a private teacher.
2 (verb) If someone tutors a person or subject, they teach that person or subject.
[Latin *tueri* = to watch over]

tutu, tutus (pronounced **too**-too)
(noun) a short, stiff ballet skirt.

TV, TVs
(noun) television.

twaddle (pronounced **twod**-dl)
(noun) meaningless or silly talk or writing.

twang, twangs, twanging, twanged
(verb) If a tight wire or string twangs or you twang it, it makes a sound as it is pulled and then released.

tweak, tweaks, tweaking, tweaked
1 (verb) to twist or pull something.
2 (noun) e.g. *I gave her nose a tweak.*

tweed, tweeds
(noun) a thick, woollen cloth.

tweet, tweets, tweeting, tweeted
(verb) When a small bird tweets, it makes a short, high-pitched sound.

tweezers
(plural noun) a small tool used for pulling out hairs or picking up small objects.

twelve the number 12.
twelfth (adjective and noun)

twenty, twenties
the number 20.
twentieth (adjective and noun)

twice
(adverb) two times.

twiddle, twiddles, twiddling, twiddled
(verb) to twist or turn something quickly, or to mess about with it.

twig, twigs, twigging, twigged
1 (noun) a very small, thin branch.
2 (verb; informal) to realize or understand something e.g. *Suddenly she twigged what the joke was and started to laugh.*

twilight (pronounced **twy**-lite)
(noun) the time after sunset when it is just getting dark.
[Old English *twi-* = half + *light*]

twin, twins, twinning, twinned
1 (noun) If two people are twins, they have the same mother and were born on the same day.
2 (adjective) double, e.g. *a twin-engined plane.*
3 (verb) A town that is twinned with another

town in a different country has agreed to exchange visits of groups of its people.

twine, twines, twining, twined
1 (noun) strong, smooth string.
2 (verb) If you twine one thing round another, you twist or wind it round, e.g. *The snake twined itself around my body.*

twinge, twinges
(noun) a sudden, unpleasant feeling, e.g. *a twinge of fear... I've got a twinge in my leg.*

twinkle, twinkles, twinkling, twinkled
1 (verb) to sparkle or seem to sparkle with an unsteady light, e.g. *The lights twinkled... Her eyes twinkled.*
2 (noun) e.g. *My grandad always had a twinkle in his eye.*

twirl, twirls, twirling, twirled
(verb) to spin or twist round and round.

twist, twists, twisting, twisted
1 (verb) e.g. *Stop twisting my ear!... I've twisted my ankle... the road twisted through the valley.*
2 (phrase) If you **twist someone's arm**, you persuade them to do something.
3 (verb) If you twist something that someone has said, you change the meaning slightly.
4 (noun) A twist in a story or film is an unexpected development or event, especially at the end, e.g. *There was an odd twist to the story.*
5 (phrase; informal) If you say someone is **round the twist** you mean that they are slightly or completely mad.

Similar words: (verb) wind, coil

twisted
1 (adjective) Something twisted has been bent or moved into a strange shape, e.g. *They were trapped under the twisted steel girders.*
2 If someone's mind or behaviour is twisted, it is unpleasantly abnormal, e.g. *He has become bitter and twisted since his wife's death.*

twister, twisters
(noun) someone who is dishonest and deliberately deceives people.

twisty
(adjective) having a lot of sharp bends and corners, e.g. *a twisty road.*

twit, twits
(noun; informal) a silly person.

twitch, twitches, twitching, twitched
1 (verb) If you twitch, you make little jerky movements which you cannot control.
2 (noun) a little jerky movement.

twitter, twitters, twittering, twittered
1 (verb) When birds twitter, they make short high-pitched sounds.
2 to speak very fast in a high-pitched voice, e.g. *The old girl was really twittering on!*

two the number 2.

two-faced
(adjective) A two-faced person pretends to be honest while treating their victims dishonestly.

What is the difference between cardinal and ordinal numbers?

tycoon, tycoons
(noun) a person who is successful in business and has become rich and powerful.
[Chinese *tai* + *chun* = great ruler]

type, types, typing, typed
1 (noun) e.g. *What type of cheese would you prefer?... He's one of these quiet, intelligent types.*
2 (verb) If you type something, you use a typewriter or word processor to write it.
3 (noun) the printing used in a book or newspaper, e.g. **bold type**; *italic type*; roman type.
[Greek *tupos* = image]

typewriter, typewriters
(noun) a writing machine with a keyboard.
typewritten (adjective)

typhoid (pronounced **tie**-foyd)
(noun) a serious infectious disease caused by contaminated water or food.

typhoon, typhoons
(noun) a very violent tropical storm.
[Chinese *tai fung* = great wind]

typical
(adjective) showing the most usual behaviour or characteristics, e.g. *He's a typical Leo.*
typically (adverb)

Similar words: characteristic, standard, conventional

typist, typists
(noun) a person who types, especially as part of their job.

tyrannosaurus, tyrannosauruses (pronounced tir-ran-oh-**saw**-russ)
(noun) a very large, meat-eating dinosaur.
[Greek *turannos* = tyrant + Latin *saurus* = lizard]

tyrant, tyrants
(noun) someone who treats the people they are in charge of cruelly and unjustly.
tyranny (noun) **tyrannical** (adjective) **tyrannize** (verb)
[from Greek *turannos*]

tyre, tyres
(noun) e.g. *a bicycle tyre... a car tyre.*

U

udder, udders
(noun) A cow's udder is the baglike organ that hangs below its body and produces milk.

UFO, UFOs
(noun) a strange object seen in the sky, which some people believe to be a spaceship from another planet. [an abbreviation for 'unidentified flying object']

Ugandan, Ugandans (pronounced yoo-**gan**-dan)
1 (adjective) belonging to Uganda.
2 (noun) someone who comes from Uganda.

ugly, uglier, ugliest
(adjective) very unattractive in appearance.
[Old Norse *uggligr* = terrifying]

Similar words: (sense 1) unsightly, hideous, unattractive

UK United Kingdom [Great Britain]

ulcer, ulcers
(noun) a sore area on the skin or inside the body, e.g. *stomach ulcers.*
[Latin *ulcus* = sore]

ultimate
1 (adjective) final or eventual, e.g. *the ultimate success of the revolution.*
2 most important or powerful, e.g. *Professor Hammond-Knight is the ultimate authority on fossil hunting.*
3 (noun) You can call the best or most advanced example of something the ultimate, e.g. *This Jaguar car is the ultimate in luxury.*
ultimately (adverb).
[Latin *ultimus* = last]

ultimatum, ultimatums
(noun) a final warning, e.g. *Britain gave Germany an ultimatum in 1939 that unless they withdrew from Poland, war would be declared.*

ultra-
(prefix) very, very, e.g. *She stayed ultra-cool... an ultra-modern building.*
[Latin *ultra* = beyond]

ultraviolet
(adjective) Ultraviolet or UV light is not visible to the human eye. It is a form of radiation that causes your skin to tan with sunlight.

umbilical cord, cords (pronounced um-**bil**-lik-kl)
(noun) the tube of blood vessels which connects an unborn baby to its mother.
[Latin *umbilicus* = navel]

umbrella, umbrellas
(noun) a folding device to keep the rain off.

umpire, umpires
(noun) the person in charge of a tennis or cricket match.

umpteen
(adjective; informal) very many, e.g. *I've told you umpteen times before!*
umpteenth (adjective)

un-
(prefix) e.g. *an uncomfortable chair... He regretted his unkindness... He unlocked the door... The hedges remained uncut.*

unable
(adjective) If you are unable to do something, you cannot do it.

unacceptable
(adjective) very bad or of a very low standard.

unaccompanied
(adjective) alone, e.g. *She sang unaccompanied.*

unaccustomed
(adjective) not used to doing something, e.g. *The Amazonian natives are unaccustomed to wearing suits and ties.*

What goes up a chimney down but can't go down a chimney up?

unaffected
(adjective) not changed in any way by a particular thing, e.g. *Ted was strangely unaffected by his wife's death.*

unaided
(adverb, adjective) without help, e.g. *The baby was sitting up unaided.*

unaltered
(adjective) still in the original form, e.g. *The house survives unaltered since Tudor times.*

unanimous (pronounced yoon-**nan**-nim-mus)
(adjective) When people are unanimous, they all agree about something.
unanimously (adverb)
[Latin *unanimus* = of one mind]

unarmed
(adjective) not carrying any weapons.

unassuming
(adjective) modest and quiet.

unattached
(adjective) An unattached person is not married and is not in a steady relationship with anyone.

unattended
(adjective) not being watched or looked after, e.g. *Keep a lookout for unattended baggage.*

unauthorized; also spelled unauthorised
(adjective) done without official permission, e.g. *Unauthorized entry not permitted.*

unavoidable
(adjective) unable to be prevented or avoided, e.g. *He could see that a crash was unavoidable.*

unaware
(adjective) If you are unaware of something, you do not know about it.

unbearable
(adjective) so unpleasant or upsetting that you feel unable to put up with it, e.g. *I think that most Australian soap operas are unbearable.*
unbearably (adverb)

Similar words: intolerable, unacceptable

unbeatable
(adjective) Something that is unbeatable is the best thing of its kind.

unbelievable
1 (adjective) extremely good or surprising, e.g. *an unbelievable bargain.*
2 so unlikely that you cannot believe it.
unbelievably (adverb)

Similar words: fantastic, incredible, astonishing, staggering

unborn
(adjective) not yet born.

unbroken
(adjective) continuous or complete, e.g. *The sky was an unbroken sheet of grey.*

unbutton, unbuttons, unbuttoning, unbuttoned
(verb) to undo the buttons on something.
unbuttoned (adjective)

uncalled-for
(adjective) If something that is said is uncalled-for, it is unkind and undeserved.

uncanny
(adjective) strange and difficult to explain, e.g. *an uncanny resemblance between the two men.*
[Scottish *uncanny* = unreliable or not safe to deal with]

unceasing
(adjective) continuing without stopping, e.g. *Ron's unceasing talk about his health.*
unceasingly (adverb)

uncertain
(adjective) not sure or certain, e.g. *She hesitated, uncertain whether to continue... The cause of death remains uncertain.*
uncertainty (noun)

uncivilized; also spelled uncivilised
1 (adjective) unacceptable, for example by being very cruel or rude, e.g. *the uncivilized behaviour of louts, swearing in the streets.*
2 (phrase) If something happens **at an uncivilized hour**, it happens very early in the morning.

uncle, uncles
(noun) the brother of your mother or father, or the husband of your aunt.
[Latin *avunculus* = mother's brother]

unclear
(adjective) confusing and not obvious.

uncomfortable
(adjective) not comfortable, e.g. *an uncomfortable seat... I had an uncomfortable feeling I had forgotten something.*
uncomfortably (adverb)

uncommon
(adjective) not usual, e.g. *Vultures are an uncommon sight in Trafalgar Square.*

unconcerned
(adjective) not interested in something or not worried about it, e.g. *He acted unconcerned.*
unconcernedly (adverb)

unconditional
(adjective) with no conditions or limits, e.g. *The sponsors offered unconditional support.*
unconditionally (adverb)

unconscious
1 (adjective) in a state similar to sleep as a result of a shock, accident or injury.
2 unaware, e.g. *He walked to the cliff edge, unconscious of the danger.*

unconventional
(adjective) not behaving in the same way as most other people, e.g. *Punks like to look unconventional.*

uncooperative
(adjective) An uncooperative person makes no effort to help or work with other people.

uncoordinated
(adjective) Uncoordinated movements are jerky and not controlled.

The Survival Guide in this dictionary is unbelievably useful.

uncover, uncovers, uncovering, uncovered
1 (verb) If you uncover a secret, you find it out.
2 to remove the cover or lid from something.

undecided
(adjective) If you are undecided, you have not yet made a decision about something.

undeniable
(adjective) certainly true, e.g. *It was undeniable that they were still fond of each other.*
undeniably (adverb)

under
(preposition) e.g. *Under the spreading chestnut tree... We were working under difficult conditions... Emily Bronte wrote under the name of Ellis Bell... You'll find it under O in the dictionary... under £10... under 16 years old.*
2 (phrase) **Under way** means already started, e.g. *The match was under way when I arrived.*

underachieve, underachieves, underachieving, underachieved
(verb) If you underachieve, you do not perform as well as you could.
underachiever (noun)

underarm
1 (adjective) e.g. *an underarm deodorant.*
2 If you throw a ball underarm, you do not raise your arm over your shoulder.

undercarriage, undercarriages
(noun) The undercarriage of an aircraft is the part, including the wheels, that supports it when it is on the ground.

underclothes
(plural noun) the clothes you wear next to your skin.

undercover
(adjective) involving secret work to obtain information, e.g. *undercover police work.*

underdeveloped
(adjective) An underdeveloped country does not have modern industries, and usually has a low standard of living.

underdog, underdogs
(noun) The underdog in a game, competition etc, is the person or team who seems likely to lose.

underdone
(adjective) not cooked for long enough, e.g. *It is risky for pork to be underdone.*

underestimate, underestimates, underestimating, underestimated
1 (verb) If you underestimate someone, you do not realize how much they can do.
2 e.g. *I underestimated the number of plates we would need.*

underfed
(adjective) not getting enough to eat, e.g. *Underfed children are more open to infection.*

underfoot
1 (adjective, adverb) under your feet, e.g. *the grass underfoot... The ground was spongy underfoot.*
2 (phrase) To be **trampled underfoot** means to be trodden on.

undergo, undergoes, undergoing, underwent, undergone
(verb) If you undergo something unpleasant, it happens to you, e.g. *He underwent an operation.*

underground
1 (adjective) below the surface of the ground.
2 secret, unofficial and usually illegal.
3 (noun) The underground is a railway system in which trains travel in tunnels below ground.

undergrowth
(noun) small bushes and plants growing under trees.

underhand
(adjective) secret and dishonest.

underlay
(noun) a thick material that you place between a carpet and the floor.

underline, underlines, underlining, underlined
(verb) to draw a line under a word or sentence.

underneath
(preposition, adjective, adverb) e.g. *underneath the arches... Underneath, he is rather shy... the underneath part... I ran underneath the bridge.*

undernourished
(adjective) weak and ill because of not eating enough food.

underpants
(plural noun) a piece of boys' and men's clothing.

underpass, underpasses
(noun) a road or footpath that goes under a road or railway.

underprivileged
(adjective) Underprivileged people have much less money and fewer opportunities than other people in their society.

underrate, underrates, underrating, underrated
(verb) If you underrate someone, you do not realize how clever or valuable they are.

understand, understands, understanding, understood
(verb) e.g. *He understood what I meant... I understand you're new here.*

understandable
(adjective) If something is understandable, people can easily understand it, e.g. *With his brain, it's understandable that he only got 12%.*
understandably (adverb)

understanding
(adjective) kind and sympathetic, e.g. *Thank you for being so understanding.*

understudy, understudies
(noun) someone who has learnt a part in a play so that they can act it if the main actor or actress is ill.

undertake, undertakes, undertaking, undertook, undertaken
(verb) When you undertake a task or job, you agree to do it.

undertaker, undertakers
(noun) someone whose job is to prepare bodies for burial and arrange funerals.

undervalue, undervalues, undervaluing, undervalued
(verb) If you undervalue something, you think it is less important than it really is.

underwater
(adverb, adjective) e.g. *We swam underwater ... She used an underwater camera.*

underwear
(noun) the clothing that you wear next to your skin.

underworld
(noun) You can refer to organized crime and the people who are involved in it as the underworld, e.g. *Al Capone led the Chicago underworld.*

undesirable
(adjective) unwelcome and likely to cause harm, e.g. *Cuts in education are very undesirable.*

undeveloped
1 (adjective) An undeveloped country has little industry and does not use modern farming methods.
2 Undeveloped land has not yet been built on.

undignified
(adjective) foolish and embarrassing, e.g. *The Minister made an undignified exit with egg all over his suit.*

undisputed
(adjective) definite and without any doubt, e.g. *Buck was the undisputed leader of the pack.*

undistinguished
(adjective) without any really good qualities or features, e.g. *He had an undistinguished political career.*

undivided
(adjective) If you give something your undivided attention, you concentrate on it totally.

undo, undoes, undoing, undid, undone
1 (verb) to unfasten, e.g. *Undo that zip.*
2 If you undo something that has been done, you reverse the effect of it, e.g. *We'll never undo the harm you have done.*

undoubted
(adjective) a word used to emphasize something, e.g. *The record was an undoubted hit.*
undoubtedly (adverb)

undress, undresses, undressing, undressed
(verb) to take off your clothes.

unearth, unearths, unearthing, unearthed
(verb) to discover something that is hidden.

uneasy
(adjective) to feel worried that something may be wrong.
uneasily (adverb) **uneasiness** (noun)

uneconomic or **uneconomical**
(adjective) Something uneconomic produces little profit or wastes time or energy, e.g. *British Coal wants to close uneconomic coal mines.*

unemotional
(adjective) not showing any feelings.

unemployed
1 (adjective) without a job.

2 (noun) The unemployed are all the people who are without a job.
unemployment (noun)

unequal
(adjective) Unequal things are different in size, strength or ability, e.g *unequal pieces of cake.*

uneven
1 (adjective) not regular or consistent, e.g. *uneven breathing.*
2 An uneven surface is not level or smooth.
unevenly (adverb)

uneventful
(adjective) During an uneventful time nothing interesting happens.

unexpected
(adjective) surprising because it is not expected, e.g. *The Emperor of Japan was an unexpected visitor at 13B, Gasworks Street, Crewe.*
unexpectedly (adverb)

unfair
(adjective) not right, fair or just.
unfairly (adverb)

unfamiliar
(adjective) If something is unfamiliar to you, or if you are unfamiliar with it, you have not seen or heard it before.

unfasten, unfastens, unfastening, unfastened
(verb) If you unfasten something, you undo its buttons, straps or clips.

unfit
1 (adjective) not in good condition, e.g. *Smoking often makes you unfit.*
2 not suitable, e.g. *This meat is unfit even for the dog to eat.*

unfold, unfolds, unfolding, unfolded
(verb) to open out something that has been folded.

unforeseen
(adjective) happening unexpectedly, e.g. *The fortune teller's tent was closed due to unforeseen circumstances.*

unforgettable
(adjective) Something unforgettable is so good or so bad that you are unlikely to forget it.
unforgettably (adverb)

unforgivable
(adjective) Something unforgivable is so bad or cruel that it can never be forgiven or justified.
unforgivably (adverb)

unfortunate
1 (adjective) unlucky.
2 If you describe an event as unfortunate, you mean that it is a pity that it happened, e.g. *That was an unfortunate remark you made to the hotel inspector, Mr Fawlty.*
unfortunately (adverb)

unfurnished
(adjective) containing no furniture.

ungainly
(adjective) awkward or clumsy.
[Old Norse *ungegn* = not straight]

....*Recto* means the right-hand page of an open book, having an odd number.

ungrateful
(adjective) not thankful, e.g. *That ungrateful girl won't receive any more presents from me.*

unhappy, unhappier, unhappiest
(adjective) e.g. *The orphan looked really unhappy... Parents were unhappy about the lack of information... an unhappy state of affairs.*
unhappily (adverb) **unhappiness** (noun)

unhealthy
1 (adjective) likely to cause illness, e.g. *the unhealthy life we lead in the cities.*
2 An unhealthy person is often ill.
3 Unhealthy attitudes are thought of as extreme or unnatural, and possibly harmful, e.g. *He had an unhealthy interest in guns.*

unheard-of
(adjective) never having happened before and therefore surprising or shocking, e.g. *It was unheard-of for Lisa to get less than full marks.*

unicorn, unicorns
(noun) an imaginary animal that looks like a white horse with a straight horn growing from its forehead.
[Latin *unicornis* = having one horn]

unidentified
(adjective) something is unidentified when nobody knows what it is.

uniform, uniforms
1 (noun) a special set of clothing worn by members of an organization.
2 (adjective) Something that is uniform does not vary, but is regular and even throughout.
[Latin *uniformis* = of one kind]

unify, unifies, unifying, unified
(verb) If you unify a number of things, you bring them together to form a single unit, e.g. *Bismarck unified Germany in the 19th century.*
unification (noun)
[Latin *unificare* = to make one]

unimaginative
(adjective) rather dull and without any imagination, e.g. *an unimaginative story.*

unimportant
(adjective) having very little importance.

Similar words: insignificant, trivial, petty

uninhabited
(adjective) An uninhabited place is a place where nobody lives, e.g. *an uninhabited island.*

uninhibited
(adjective) If you are uninhibited, you behave freely and naturally and show your true feelings.

unintentional
(adjective) not done deliberately, e.g. *Although the trip was unintentional, the ref gave a penalty.*

uninterested
(adjective) If you are uninterested in something, you are not interested in it. [not to be confused with 'disinterested' which means impartial]

uninterrupted
(adjective) continuing without breaks or interruptions, e.g. *uninterrupted reading.*

uninvited
(adjective) arriving or doing something without being asked, e.g. *Gerald sat down uninvited.*

union, unions
(noun) an organization of workers that aims to improve the working conditions, pay and benefits of its members.
[Latin *unus* = one]

unique (pronounced yoo-**neek**)
(adjective) being the only one of its kind, e.g. *Lowry had a unique style of painting.*
uniquely (adverb)
[Latin *unicus* = one and only]

unisex
(adjective) designed for both men and women, e.g. *a unisex hairdresser's... unisex jeans.*

unit, units
1 (noun) a single, complete thing.
2 a group of people who work together at a particular job, e.g. *the intensive-care unit.*
3 a machine or piece of equipment which does a particular job, e.g. *a waste-disposal unit... kitchen units.*
4 A unit of measurement is a fixed standard that is used for measuring things, e.g. the metre, the litre and the gram.
[Latin *unus* = one]

unite, unites, uniting, united
(verb) If a number of people unite, they join together and act as a group, e.g. *Workers of the world unite!*
[Latin *unire* = to form into one]

unity
(noun) Where there is unity, people are in agreement and act together.
[Latin *unitas* = oneness]

universal
1 (adjective) concerning everyone or every part of the world.
2 A universal truth is something that is true at all times and in all situations.
universally (adverb)

universe
(noun) the whole of space, including all the stars and planets.
[Latin *universum* = whole world]

university, universities
(noun) a place of advanced education where students study for degrees and research is done.
[Latin *universitas* = group of scholars]

unjust
(adjective) not fair or reasonable.
unjustly (adverb)

unjustified
(adjective) If a belief or action is unjustified, there is no good reason for it.

unkempt
(adjective) untidy and not looked after properly, e.g. *Why is your hair so unkempt?*
[Old English *uncembed* = not combed]

What six-letter word means the opposite if the two middle letters are reversed?

unkind
(adjective) unpleasant and rather cruel.
unkindly (adverb) **unkindness** (noun)

unknown
(adjective) If someone or something is unknown, people do not know about them or have not heard of them.

unlawful
(adjective) not legal, e.g. *unlawful deals*.

unless
(conjunction) e.g. *You can't get into that club unless you are a member.*

unlike
1 (preposition) If one thing is unlike another, the two things are different.
2 e.g. *It's unlike Fred to get so angry.*

unlikely
1 (adjective) If something is unlikely, it is probably not true or probably will not happen.
2 strange and unexpected, e.g. *They make an unlikely couple.*

unlimited
(adjective) If a supply of something is unlimited, you can have as much as you need.

unload, unloads, unloading, unloaded
(verb) to remove things from a container or vehicle.

unlock, unlocks, unlocking, unlocked
(verb) to open by turning a key in a lock.

unlucky
(adjective) e.g. *You were really unlucky to fall when you were winning... It's unlucky to walk under a ladder.*
unluckily (adverb)

Similar words: luckless, unfortunate, wretched

unmanageable
(adjective) difficult or impossible to use, deal with or control, e.g. *unmanageable hair*.

unmanned
(adjective) An unmanned spacecraft has no people inside it.

unmarked
1 (adjective) with no marks of damage or injury.
2 with no signs or marks of identification, e.g. *Unmarked police cars were used for the raid.*

unmentionable
(adjective) too embarrassing or unpleasant to talk about.

unmistakable
(adjective) Something unmistakable is so obvious that it cannot be mistaken for something else.
unmistakably (adverb)

unnatural
1 (adjective) strange and rather frightening because it is not usual, e.g. *the unnatural light that comes before a storm*.
2 artificial and not typical, e.g. *Her voice sounded strained and unnatural.*
unnaturally (adverb)

unobserved
(adjective) If you do something unobserved, you do it without being seen.

unobtrusive
(adjective) If you want to be unobtrusive, you keep as quiet and as far out of the way as possible.
unobtrusively (adverb)

unoccupied
(adjective) If a house is unoccupied, there is nobody living in it.

unofficial
(adjective) without the approval or authorization of a person in authority, e.g. *an unofficial strike*.
unofficially (adverb)

unorthodox
(adjective) unusual and not generally accepted, e.g. *Murphy has an unorthodox batting style, holding it handle downwards.*

unpack, unpacks, unpacking, unpacked
(verb) to take everything out of a suitcase or bag.

unpaid
1 (adjective) If you do unpaid work, you do not expect to receive any money for doing it.
2 An unpaid bill has not yet been paid.

unpleasant
1 (adjective) Something unpleasant causes you to have bad feelings.
2 An unpleasant person is unfriendly or rude.

unplug, unplugs, unplugging, unplugged
(verb) If you unplug something electrical, you take its plug out of the socket.

unpopular
(adjective) disliked by most people, e.g. *The idea of the new tax proved amazingly unpopular.*

unprecedented (pronounced un-**press**-id-en-tid)
(adjective; formal) Something that is unprecedented has never happened before or is the best of its kind so far.

unpredictable
(adjective) If someone is unpredictable, you never know how they will behave or react.

unprepared
(adjective) not prepared, e.g. *We were unprepared for the storms.*

unproductive
(adjective) not producing anything useful.

unprovoked
(adjective) An unprovoked attack is one that is made without any cause.

unqualified
(adjective) having no qualifications or the wrong qualifications for a job, e.g. *Many childminders are unqualified.*

unravel, unravels, unravelling, unravelled
1 (verb) If you unravel something such as a knotted piece of string, you untie and unwind it so that it is straight.

Which proverb do you prefer? Out of sight, out of mind. Absence makes the heart grow fonder.

2 If you unravel a mystery, you work out the answer to it.
[Dutch *ravelen* = to unpick]

unreal
(adjective) so strange that it is hard to believe.

unrealistic
1 (adjective) An unrealistic person does not face the truth about something or deal with it in a practical way.
2 Something unrealistic is not true to life, e.g. *The plot of the film was completely unrealistic.*
unrealistically (adverb)

unreasonable
(adjective) unfair and difficult to deal with or justify, e.g. *an unreasonable request.*
unreasonably (adverb)

unrelated
(adjective) Things that are unrelated have no connection with each other.

unreliable
(adjective) If a machine is unreliable, you cannot be sure it will work.

unrest
(noun) If there is unrest, people are angry and dissatisfied.

unroll, unrolls, unrolling, unrolled
(verb) If you unroll a roll of cloth or paper, you open it up and make it flat.

unruffled
(adjective) calm and not affected by something surprising or frightening.

unruly
(adjective) difficult to control or keep tidy, e.g. *unruly children... unruly hair.*
[*un-* = not + the obsolete word *ruly* = orderly]

unsatisfactory
(adjective) not good enough.

unscathed (pronounced un-**skaythed**)
(adjective) not injured or harmed as a result of a dangerous experience.
[*un-* = not + Old German *skado* = injury or harm]

unscrew, unscrews, unscrewing, unscrewed
(verb) e.g. *to unscrew a jam jar.*

unseen
(adjective) You use unseen to describe things that you cannot see or have not seen, e.g. *The unseen enemy... an unseen translation.*

unselfish
(adjective) An unselfish person is concerned about other people's wishes and needs, rather than their own.
unselfishly (adverb)

unsettle, unsettles, unsettling, unsettled
(verb) If something unsettles you, it makes you restless, dissatisfied or rather worried.

unshaven
(adjective) If a man is unshaven, he has not shaved recently.

unskilled
(adjective) Unskilled work does not require any special training.

unsociable
(adjective) An unsociable person does not enjoy meeting and talking to other people.

unsophisticated (pronounced un-sof-**fist**-tik-kay-tid)
1 (adjective) An unsophisticated person has simple tastes and does not have a lot of experience or knowledge.
2 An unsophisticated method is simple and basic.

unspecified
(adjective) You say that something is unspecified when you are not told exactly what it is, e.g. *at some unspecified time in the future.*

unstable
1 (adjective) likely to change suddenly and create difficulty or danger, e.g. *the unstable political situation in the Middle East.*
2 likely to wobble or fall.

unsteady
1 (adjective) having difficulty in controlling the movement of your legs or hands, e.g. *unsteady on her feet... an unsteady hand.*
2 not held or fixed securely; likely to fall over.
unsteadily (adverb)

unstuck
1 (adjective) If something comes unstuck, it comes away from the thing it was stuck to.
2 (informal) If someone or something comes unstuck, they fail.

unsuccessful
(adjective) If you are unsuccessful, you do not succeed in what you are trying to do.
unsuccessfully (adverb)

unsuitable
(adjective) not right or appropriate, e.g. *Fifi the poodle is unsuitable as a guard dog.*
unsuitably (adverb)

unsuited
(adjective) not appropriate for a situation, e.g. *Goldfish are unsuited to life in a kennel.*

unsure
(adjective) uncertain or doubtful.

unsuspecting
(adjective) having no idea of what is happening or going to happen, e.g. *Police lay in wait for the unsuspecting thieves.*

untangle, untangles, untangling, untangled
(verb) to undo the knots and twists in something.

untidy, untidier, untidiest
(adjective) not neat or well arranged.

untie, unties, untying, untied
(verb) If you untie something, you undo the knots in the string or rope round it.

until
(preposition, conjunction) e.g. *I stayed until 10... He kept working until he had finished.*

The hand that gives, gathers. (James Howell)

untouched
1 (adjective) not changed, moved or damaged, e.g. *a Norman chapel, untouched since* AD1079.
2 not used, e.g. *He left his food untouched.*

untried
(adjective) not yet used, done or tested.

untrue
(adjective) not true.

untruthful
(adjective) Someone who is untruthful tells lies.

unused
1 (adjective; pronounced un-**yoozd**) not used.
2 (pronounced un-**yoost**) If you are unused to something, you have not often done or experienced it.

unusual
(adjective) Something that is unusual does not occur very often.
unusually (adverb)

Similar words: abnormal, irregular, strange

unveil, unveils, unveiling, unveiled
1 (verb) When in a special ceremony someone unveils a new statue or plaque, they draw back a curtain that is covering it.
2 If someone unveils something that has been secret, they tell about it for the first time.

unwelcome
(adjective) not wanted, e.g. *an unwelcome visitor... unwelcome news.*

unwell
(adjective) If you are unwell, you are ill.

unwilling
(adjective) not wanting to do something.
unwillingly (adverb)

Similar words: reluctant, hesitant

unwind, unwinds, unwinding, unwound
1 (verb) to relax after working hard.
2 to undo something that is wound up.

unwise
(adjective) foolish or not sensible.

unworthy
(adjective; formal) Someone who is unworthy of something does not deserve it.

unwrap, unwraps, unwrapping, unwrapped
(verb) When you unwrap something, you take off the paper or covering round it.

up
1 (adverb, preposition, adjective) e.g. *up in Scotland... He walked up the road... Are you up yet?.*
2 (informal) If someone is up to something, they are secretly doing something they should not be doing.
3 (informal) If something **is up**, something is wrong or something unexpected might happen, e.g. *What's up, Doc?*

up-and-coming
(adjective) likely to be successful, e.g. *She's an up-and-coming show jumper.*

upbringing
(noun) Your upbringing is the way that your parents have taught you to behave.

update, updates, updating, updated
(verb) If you update something, you make it more modern or bring new information into it, e.g. *Our records are regularly updated.*

upgrade, upgrades, upgrading, upgraded ·
(verb) to replace what you already have with something better, e.g. *upgrading your computer.*

upheaval, upheavals
(noun) a big change which causes a lot of trouble.

uphill
1 (adverb) If you go uphill, you go up a slope.
2 (adjective) An uphill task requires a lot of effort and determination.

upholstery
(noun) the soft covering on chairs and sofas that makes them comfortable.

upkeep
(noun) The upkeep of something is the continual process and cost of keeping it in good condition.

Similar words: maintenance, running

upland, uplands
(noun) an area of high land.

upon
(preposition) e.g. *sitting with the cat upon her knee... Upon entering the cabin, she sat down... The festive season is upon us.*

upper
(adjective) higher, e.g. *an upper shelf... the upper half of his face.*

upper case
(adjective) Upper case letters are the capital letters used in printing or on a typewriter.

upper class, classes
(noun) belonging to the highest social class, i.e. very rich or aristocratic people *(e.g. Lord X, the Duchess of Y).*

upright
(adjective, adverb) standing or sitting up straight.

uprising
(noun) a rebellion or revolt against a government.

uproar
(noun) a lot of shouting and noise, often because people are angry.
[Dutch *oproer* = revolt]

Similar words: commotion, pandemonium

uproot, uproots, uprooting, uprooted
(verb) to pull a plant etc. out of the ground.

upset, upsets, upsetting, upset
1 (adjective) unhappy and disappointed.
2 (verb) If something upsets you, it makes you feel worried or unhappy.
3 (noun) A stomach upset is a slight stomach illness.

upside down
1 (adjective, adverb) the wrong way up.

The uplands of Southern England are called downs, from the Anglo-Saxon word *dun* meaning 'hill'.

2 (phrase) If you **turn a place upside down**, you make it untidy by moving everything.

upstairs
(adverb, noun) e.g. *I went upstairs to my bedroom... What is the upstairs of the house like?*

upstream
(adverb) towards the source of a river, e.g. *He was making his way upstream.*

uptight
(adjective; informal) tense or annoyed.

up-to-date
1 (adjective) very new; the latest fashion.
2 having the latest information.

upturned
upside down, e.g. *an upturned bucket.*

upwards
1(adverb) e.g. *He happened to glance upwards... The world population is rocketing upwards.*
2 (phrase) **Upwards of** a particular number means more than that number, e.g. *There were upwards of 20,000 at the match.*
upward (adjective)

uranium (pronounced yoo-**ray**-nee-um)
(noun) a radioactive metallic element used in the production of nuclear power and weapons.

urban
(adjective) relating to a town or city, e.g. *urban development.*
[Latin *urbs* = city]

urchin, urchins
(noun) a young child who is dirty and poorly dressed can be called an urchin.
[Latin *ericius* = hedgehog]

Urdu (pronounced **oor**-doo)
(noun) the official language of Pakistan, also spoken by many people in India.

urge, urges, urging, urged
1 (noun) If you have an urge to do something, you have a strong wish to do it.
2 (verb) If you urge someone to do something, you try hard to persuade them to do it.
[Latin *urgere* = to insist]

urgent
(adjective) needing to be dealt with as soon as possible, e.g. *an urgent message.*
urgently (adverb) **urgency** (noun)
[Latin *urgens* = pressing or insistent]

urinate, urinates, urinating, urinated
(pronounced **yoor**-rin-ate)
(verb) When you urinate, you get rid of urine from your body.

urine (pronounced **yoor**-rin)
(noun) the waste liquid that you get rid of from your body when you go to the toilet.
[Latin *urina* = urine]

us
(pronoun) e.g. *Why didn't you tell us?*

US or **USA** United States of America.

use, uses, using, used
1 (verb) e.g. *He wants to use the phone.*

2 (noun) e.g. *the use of fertilizers... We'll find a use for it.*
3 (phrase) Something that is **of use** is useful.
usable (adjective) **user** (noun) **usage** (noun)

Similar words: (verb) apply, employ, utilize
(noun) utilization, employment

used
1 (verb; pronounced **yoost**) e.g. *We used to train spot here.*
2 (phrase) e.g. *You'll soon get used to it.*
3 (adjective; pronounced **yoozd**) e.g. *a used car.*

useful
(adjective) If something is useful, you can use it to do something or to help you in some way.
usefully (adverb) **usefulness** (noun)

useless
1 (adjective) If something is useless, you cannot use it because it is not suitable or helpful.
2 (informal) Someone who is useless at something is very bad at it.

user-friendly
(adjective; informal) A user-friendly machine has been designed to be easy to use.

usher, ushers
(noun) a person who shows people where to sit at a wedding or a concert.
[Latin *ostiarius* = doorkeeper]

usherette, usherettes
(noun) a woman who shows people where to sit in a cinema or theatre.

USSR Union of Soviet Socialist Republics.

usual
(adjective) happening, done or used most often, e.g. *He sat in his usual chair... As usual Mrs Stephenson was late.*
usually (adverb)
[Latin *usualis* = ordinary]

utensil, utensils (pronounced yoo-**ten**-sil)
(noun) Utensils are tools, e.g. *cooking utensils.*
[Latin *utensilis* = available for use]

uterus, uteruses (pronounced **yoo**-ter-rus)
(noun; formal) A woman's uterus is her womb, the place where a baby develops.
[a Latin word]

utility room
(noun) a room in a house which is used for washing and other household jobs.

utilize, utilizes, utilizing, utilized; also spelled **utilise**
(verb; formal) to use.
utilization (noun)

utter, utters, uttering, uttered
1 (verb) When you utter sounds or words, you make or say them.
2 (adjective) complete or total, e.g. *You're talkin utter nonsense!*
utterly (adverb)
[verb: Dutch *uiteren* = to speak
adjective: Old English *utera* = extreme]

'Urk' used to be a word for a small, undergrown child. An urchin was even smaller.

V

vacant
1 (adjective) empty; not being used, e.g. *The room is vacant now.*
2 If a job is vacant, no one holds it at present.
3 A vacant look on a person's face might show that they do not understand something or are not very intelligent.
vacancy (noun) **vacantly** (adverb)
vacate (verb)
[Latin *vacare* = to be empty]

vacation, vacations
(noun) In American English, a vacation is a holiday.

vaccinate, vaccinates, vaccinating, vaccinated
(pronounced **vak**-sin-ate)
(verb) to give someone a vaccine, usually by injection, to protect them against a disease.
vaccination (noun)

vaccine, vaccines (pronounced **vak**-seen)
(noun) a substance made from the germs that cause a disease, given to people to make them immune to that disease.
[Latin *vacca* = cow, because smallpox vaccine, the first invented, is based on cowpox]

vacuum, vacuums, vacuuming, vacuumed
(pronounced **vak**-yoom)
1 (noun) a space containing no air, gases, etc.
2 (verb) If you vacuum or vac something, you clean it using a vacuum cleaner.
[Latin *vacuum* = empty space]

vacuum cleaner, cleaners
(noun) an electric machine which cleans by sucking up dirt (also called a **hoover**).

vagina (pronounced vaj-**jie**-na)
(noun) the passage that connects a woman's outer sex organs to her womb.
[Latin *vagina* = sheath]

vague, vaguer, vaguest (pronounced **vayg**)
1 (adjective) If something is vague, it is not clear, e.g. *vague instructions... a vague memory of my first home.*
2 Someone looks or sounds vague if they are not concentrating or thinking clearly.
vaguely (adverb) **vagueness** (noun)

Similar words: (sense 1) indefinite, woolly

vain, vainer, vainest
1 (adjective) not successful, e.g. *The lady made a vain attempt to revive the drowned child.*
2 A vain person is very proud of their looks, intelligence or other qualities.
3 (phrase) If you do something **in vain**, you do not succeed in achieving what you intend.
vainly (adverb)

vale, vales
(noun; literary) a valley.

valency or valence
(noun; technical) The valency of an atom or chemical group is the number of atoms it has available to combine with atoms of hydrogen and so form compounds.

valentine, valentines
(noun) the card you send on St Valentine's Day, February 14th, to the person you love.
[St Valentine was a 3rd-century martyr]

valiant
(adjective) very brave.
valiantly (adverb)

valid
1 (adjective) based on sound reasoning, e.g. *That's a valid point you are making.*
2 A valid ticket or document is one which is officially accepted.
validity (noun)

valley, valleys
(noun) a stretch of land between hills, often with a river flowing through it.

valour
(noun) great bravery.

valuable, valuables
1 (adjective) Something that is valuable has great value.
2 (plural noun) Valuables are things that you own that cost a lot of money, e.g. jewellery.

Similar words: (adjective) prized, valued, precious

value, values, valuing, valued
1 (noun) the importance or usefulness of something, e.g. *the value of friendship.*
2 the amount of money that something is worth.
3 The values of a group or a person are the moral principles and beliefs that they think are important, e.g. *the traditional values of politeness and good manners.*
4 (verb) If you value something, you think it is important and you appreciate it.
5 When experts value something, they decide how much money it is worth.

value-added tax or VAT
(noun) a tax which is added to the cost of many goods and services.

valve, valves
(noun) a part attached to a pipe or tube which controls the flow of gas or liquid.
[Latin *valva* = folding door]

vampire, vampires
(noun) In horror stories, vampires are corpses that come out of their graves at night and suck the blood of living people.
[Hungarian *vampir* = vampire]

vandal, vandals
(noun) someone who deliberately damages or destroys things, particularly public property.
vandalize or **vandalise** (verb)
vandalism (noun)
[from the Germanic tribe the *Vandals* who sacked Rome in AD 455]

Letters U, V and W. U and W were developed from V, which seems to have been another form of a hook.
Do you know what these words ending id mean? valid livid acrid putrid morbid rancid candid.

vanilla
(noun) a flavouring for food, e.g. ice cream,
which comes from the pods of a tropical plant.
[Spanish *vainilla* = pod]

vanish, vanishes, vanishing, vanished
(verb) to disappear or cease to exist, e.g. *The car
vanished from sight... We must protect vanishing
species of animals, birds and fish.*

vanity
(noun) a feeling of excessive pride about your
looks or abilities.

vapour
(noun) a mass of tiny drops of water or other
liquids in the air, which looks like mist.
vaporize or **vaporise** (verb)
[Latin *vapor* = steam]

variable, variables
1 (adjective) likely to change at any time, e.g.
variable winds.
2 (noun) In maths, a variable is a symbol which
can represent any value, e.g. x.

variation, variations
(noun) a change from the normal pattern.

varied
(adjective) of different types, quantities or sizes,
e.g. *Many varied plants were on sale.*

variety, varieties
1 (noun) a number of different kinds of things,
e.g. *for a whole variety of reasons.*
2 a particular type of something, e.g. *a new
variety of rose.*
3 Variety is a form of entertainment consisting of
short, unrelated acts, such as singing, dancing
and comedy, e.g *the Royal Variety Performance.*

Similar words: (sense 1) assortment, array

various
(adjective) of several different types, e.g. *sweets
of various kinds.*

Similar words: varied, miscellaneous

varnish, varnishes
(noun) a liquid which when painted onto a
surface gives it a hard, clear, shiny finish.
[Latin *veronix* = fragrant resin]

vary, varies, varied, varying
1 (verb) to be different or to change, e.g. *The
price of vegetables varies with the seasons.*
2 If you vary something, you introduce changes
in it, e.g. *He varied his daily routine.*

vase, vases
(noun) a jar for flowers.

vast
(adjective) extremely large, e.g. *a vast desert... a
vast aircraft hangar.*
vastly (adverb) **vastness** (noun)

vault, vaults, vaulting, vaulted
(rhymes with **salt**)
1 (noun) a strong, secure room where valuables
are stored.
2 a small room, usually underneath a church
where people are buried.

3 (verb) If you vault over something, you jump
over it using your hands or a pole to help.

VDU, VDUs
(noun) a monitor screen attached to a computer
or word processor [an abbreviation for 'visual
display unit'].

veal
(noun) the meat from a calf.
[Latin *vitellus* = little calf]

vegan, vegans (pronounced **vee**-gn)
(noun) someone who does not eat any food made
from animal products, such as meat, eggs, cheese
or milk.
veganism (noun)

vegetable, vegetables
1 (noun) edible roots or leaves, e.g. carrots,
cabbage, potatoes.
2 (adjective) Vegetable is used to refer to any
plants–in contrast to animals or minerals, e.g.
vegetable matter.
3 (noun; informal) If you call someone a
vegetable you mean they are not at all lively.
[Latin *vegetabilis* = enlivening]

vegetarian, vegetarians
(noun) a person who does not eat meat.
vegetarianism (noun)

vegetation
(noun) the plants in a particular area.

vehicle, vehicles (pronounced **vee**-ik-kl)
(noun) a machine, often with an engine, used for
transporting people or goods, e.g. car, bicycle,
lorry, tank.

veil, veils (rhymes with **male**)
(noun) a piece of cloth worn by a woman as part
of a hat or headdress, or to cover her face.
[Latin *vela* = curtains]

vein, veins (rhymes with **rain**)
(noun) Your veins are the tubes in your body
through which the blood flows to the heart.

velocity, velocities
(noun) speed; rate of motion.
[Latin *velox* = swift]

velvet
(noun, adjective) a very soft material which has
a thick layer of fine short threads on one side.
velvety (adjective)
[Latin *villus* = shaggy hair]

vending machine, machines
(noun) a machine for selling drinks, sweets, etc.

Venetian blind, blinds
(pronounced vin-**nee**-shn)
(noun) a type of adjustable window blind made
of thin, horizontal strips.

vengeance
1 (noun) the act of harming someone because
they have harmed you, e.g. *I set out to wreak
vengeance on the evil gang that stole my false
teeth and sold them to foreign teeth traders.*
2 (phrase) If something happens **with a
vengeance**, it happens far worse than was
expected, e.g. *The hurricane struck the coast
with a vengeance.*

Dracula was published in 1897. Written by Bram Stoker, it is the world's best known vampire story.

venison
(noun) the meat from a deer.
[Latin *venatio* = hunting]

Venn diagram, diagrams
(noun) In mathematics, a Venn diagram is a drawing which uses circles to show the relationships between different sets [named after John Venn (1834-1923) who invented them].

venom
(noun) the poison of a snake, scorpion, etc.
venomous (adjective) **venomously** (adverb)
[Latin *venenum* = love potion or poison]

vent, vents
(noun) a hole in something through which gases and smoke can escape and fresh air can enter, e.g. *air vents*.

ventilator, ventilators
(noun) a device which allows fresh air into a building and lets stale air out.
ventilation (noun) **ventilate** (verb)

ventriloquist, ventriloquists (pronounced ven-**trill**-o-kwist)
(noun) an entertainer who can speak without moving the lips so that the words seem to come from the dummy person etc. they carry.
ventriloquism (noun)
[Latin *venter* = belly + *loqui* = to speak]

venture, ventures, venturing, ventured
1 (noun) something new which involves the risk of failure or of losing money, e.g. *a scientific venture*.
2 (verb) If you venture somewhere that might be dangerous, you go there.

Similar words: (noun) enterprise, endeavour, project

venue, venues (pronounced **ven**-yoo)
(noun) the place where an event will happen, e.g. *Wembley is the venue for the F.A. Cup Final.*

veranda, verandas (pronounced ver-**ran**-da; also spelled **verandah)**
(noun) a platform with a roof, around the outside wall of a house at ground level.

verb, verbs
(noun) In grammar, a verb is a word that expresses actions and the way things are, e.g. *'is', 'become', 'take', 'ran', 'likes'.*

verbal
1 (adjective) connected with words and their use, e.g. *a contest of verbal skills.*
2 spoken, not written, e.g. *a written exam followed by verbal questions.* [Note that this is strictly incorrect; 'oral' is the correct word.]
verbally (adverb)

verbose
(adjective) using more words than is necessary.
verbosely (adverb) **verbosity** (noun)

verdict, verdicts
1 (noun) the decision in a court which states whether a prisoner is guilty or not guilty.
2 If you give a verdict on something, you give your opinion after thinking about it.

Similar words: judgment, finding, conclusion, opinion

verge, verges, verging, verged
1 (noun) the narrow strip of grassy ground at the side of a road.
2 (phrase) If you **are on the verge** of something, you are going to do it soon or it is likely to happen soon, e.g. *on the verge of starvation.*
3 (verb) Something that verges on something else is almost the same as it, e.g. *Your behaviour is verging on the lunatic.*

verify, verifies, verifying, verified
1 (verb) If you verify something, you check that it is true, e.g. *evidence that could be verified.*
2 On a computer, verifying a disk checks that the data on it has been recorded properly.
verification (noun)

vermin
(plural noun) small animals or insects, such as rats and cockroaches, which carry disease and damage crops or food.

verruca, verrucas (pronounced ver-**roo**-ka)
(noun) a small, hard, infectious growth rather like a wart, usually on the foot.

versatile
(adjective) If someone is versatile, they have many different skills.
versatility (noun)

verse, verses
1 (noun) Verse is often used to mean poetry, but more accurately refers to any lines written in metrical form. Thus a limerick is a form of verse rather than poetry.
2 one part of a poem, song or Bible chapter.

version, versions
1 (noun) a revised form of something in which some details are different from earlier or later forms, e.g. *the final version of my project.*
2 Someone's version of an event is their personal description of what happened.

versus
(preposition) used to indicate that two people or teams are competing against each other, e.g. *Arsenal versus QPR = Arsenal v. QPR.*

vertebra, vertebrae (pronounced **ver**-tib-bra)
(noun) Vertebrae are the small bones which form a person's or animal's backbone.

vertebrate, vertebrates
(noun) any creature which has a backbone.

vertex, vertexes or **vertices**
(noun) The vertex of something like a triangle or pyramid is the point opposite the base.

vertical
(adjective) Something that is vertical points straight up and forms a 90 degree angle with the surface on which it stands.
vertically (adverb)

very
(adjective, adverb) e.g. *a very small child... the very top of the hill.*

vessel, vessels
1 (noun) a ship or large boat, e.g. *Like a sheeted ghost, the vessel swept towards the reef of Norman's woe.*

The word *verse* originally meant line but it has come to mean several *lines*, i.e. a stanza.

2 any bowl or container in which a liquid can be kept.
3 a thin tube along which liquids move in animals and plants, e.g. *a blood vessel*.

vest, vests
(noun) a piece of underclothing.
[Latin *vestis* = clothing]

vet, vets, vetting, vetted
1 (noun) a doctor for animals [an abbreviation of veterinary surgeon].
2 (verb) If you vet someone or something, you check them carefully to see if they are acceptable, e.g. *He was vetted by security*.

veteran, veterans
1 (noun) someone who has served in the armed forces, particularly during a war.
2 someone who has been involved in doing something for many years, e.g. *a veteran marathon runner*.
3 (adjective) A veteran car was made before 1918.
[Latin *vetus* = old]

veterinary surgeon, surgeons
(noun) A veterinary surgeon is the same as a vet.
[Latin *veterinae* = animals used for pulling carts and ploughs]

veto, vetoes, vetoing, vetoed
1 (verb) If someone in authority vetoes something, they reject or forbid it.
2 (noun) e.g. *The Chinese used their veto at the United Nations*.
[Latin *veto* = I forbid]

via
1 (preposition) by way of, e.g. If you go from Derby to London via Birmingham, you travel to Birmingham before going to London.
2 done by using a particular thing or person, e.g. *TV pictures via satellite*.
[Latin *via* = way or road]

viable (pronounced **vy**-a-bl)
(adjective) capable of doing what it is intended to do without extra help or money, e.g. *It seemed a viable project to the bank manager*.
viability (noun)

viaduct, viaducts
(noun) a long, high bridge that carries a road or railway across a valley.
[Latin *via* = road + *ducere* = to bring]

vibrate, vibrates, vibrating, vibrated
(verb) If something vibrates, it moves a tiny amount backwards and forwards very quickly.
vibration (noun)

vicar, vicars
(noun) a priest in the Church of England.
[Latin *vicarius* = deputy; in medieval times, vicars were bishops' representatives]

vicarage, vicarages
(noun) a house where a vicar lives.

vice, vices
1 (noun) a serious moral fault in someone's character, e.g. greed; or a weakness, e.g. smoking.
2 Vice is criminal activities connected with drugs, prostitution, pornography or gambling.

3 a tool with a pair of jaws that hold an object tightly while it is being worked on.
[senses 1-2 – Latin *vitium* = defect
sense 3 – Old French *vis* = screw]

vice-
(prefix) Example: a vice-chairman of a company is deputy to the chairman.

vice versa
(phrase) used to show that the reverse of what you have said is also true, e.g. *Boys tease girls, and vice versa*.
[Latin *vice versa* = relations being reversed]

vicinity (pronounced vis-**sin**-it-ee)
(noun) If something is in the vicinity of a place, it is near it.
[Latin *vicus* = village]

vicious
(adjective) cruel and violent.
viciously (adverb) **viciousness** (noun)

vicious circle, circles
(noun) a situation in which a difficulty leads to a new difficulty which then causes the original difficulty to occur again.

victim, victims
(noun) someone who has been harmed or injured by someone or something.

victimize, victimizes, victimizing, victimized; also spelled **victimise**
(verb) If someone is victimized, they are deliberately treated unfairly.
victimization (noun)

victor, victors
(noun) The victor in a fight or contest is the person who wins.

Victorian
(adjective) Victorian describes things that happened or were made during the reign of Queen Victoria (1837-1901).

victory, victories
(noun) a success in a battle or competition.
victorious (adjective) **victoriously** (adverb)

Similar words: conquest, win, triumph

video, videos, videoing, videoed
1 (noun) e.g. *We're making a video at school... Dad says we can't have a video.*
2 (verb) e.g. *We'll video the late film.*
[Latin *videre* = to see]

video recorder, recorders or **VCR**
(noun) a machine for recording and playing back programmes from TV.

video tape, tapes
(noun) magnetic tape that can be used to record sound and pictures.

Vietnamese (pronounced vyet-nam-**meez**)
1 (adjective) belonging to Vietnam.
2 (noun) someone who comes from Vietnam.
3 the main language spoken in Vietnam.

view, views, viewing, viewed
1 (noun) Your views are your personal opinions, e.g. *He went to jail for his political views.*
2 (verb) If you view something in a particular

Pair these up with words on this page: roll president innocent automobile pot-bellied pig Albert.

way, you think of it in that way, e.g. *He viewed the future with gloom.*
3 (noun) A view is everything you can see from a particular place.
4 (phrase) **in view of**: e.g. *In view of the fact that the rest of the group are going, I think you should go too.*
5 If something is **on view**, it is being shown to the public.

Similar words: (noun; sense 3) landscape, scene

iewer, viewers
1 (noun) a person who watches TV.
2 a box with a magnifying lens for looking at photographic slides.

iewfinder, viewfinders
(noun) a small square of glass in a camera that you look through to see what you are about to photograph.

iewpoint, viewpoints
1 (noun) Your viewpoint is your attitude towards something.
2 a place from which you get a good view of an area or event.

Similar words: (sense 1) outlook, point of view, position

igilant
(adjective) careful and alert to danger or trouble.
vigilance (noun) **vigilantly** (adverb)

igorous
(adjective) energetic or enthusiastic.
vigorously (adverb) **vigour** (noun)

ile, viler, vilest
(adjective) unpleasant or disgusting, e.g. *vile weather... vile language.*

illa, villas
(noun) a house, especially a pleasant holiday home in a country with a warm climate.

illage, villages
(noun) a community of houses and other buildings in the countryside.
villager (noun)
[Old French *ville* = farm]

illain, villains
(noun) A name for someone who harms others or breaks the law.
villainous (adjective) **villainy** (noun)
[Old French *vilein* = serf]

Similar words: scoundrel, rogue, blackguard

indictive
(adjective) deliberately hurtful towards someone, often as an act of revenge.
vindictively (adverb) **vindictiveness** (noun)

ine, vines
(noun) a trailing or climbing plant, especially one which produces grapes.

inegar
(noun) a sharp-tasting liquid made from sour wine, beer or cider, used for salad dressing, on chips and for pickling.
vinegary (adjective)
[French *vin* = wine + *aigre* = sour]

vineyard, vineyards (pronounced **vin**-yard)
(noun) an area of land where grapes are grown.

vintage, vintages
1 (adjective) Vintage describes something which is the best or most typical of its kind, e.g. *vintage rock 'n' roll.*
2 (noun) A vintage is a grape harvest of one particular year and the wine produced from it.
3 (adjective) A vintage car is one made 1918-30.
[Old French *vendage* = grape harvest]

vinyl
(noun) a strong plastic used to make things such as furniture and floor coverings.

viola, violas (pronounced vee-oh-la)
(noun) a musical instrument with 4 strings, larger than a violin and lower in sound.

violate, violates, violating, violated
(verb) If you violate an agreement, law or promise, you break it.
violation (noun)

violence
(noun) behaviour intended to hurt or kill.

violent
1 (adjective) If someone is violent, they try to hurt or kill people.
2 A violent event happens unexpectedly and with great force, e.g. *a violent storm.*
violently (adverb)

violet, violets
1 (noun) a plant with dark, purple flowers.
2 (noun, adjective) bluish purple.

violin, violins
(noun) a musical instrument with 4 strings, played with a bow.
violinist (noun)
[Italian *violino* = little viola]

VIP, VIPs
(noun) a famous or important person [an abbreviation for 'very important person'].

viper, vipers
(noun) an adder, a type of poisonous snake.

virgin
1 (noun) The Virgin, or the Blessed Virgin, is a name given to Mary, the mother of Jesus Christ.
2 (adjective) unspoiled or untouched, e.g. *virgin forest.*

virtually (pronounced vur-tyoo-lee)
(adverb) almost; as good as, e.g. *We had virtually won, when they scored the equalizer.*
virtual (adjective)

Similar word: practically, nearly

virtue, virtues
1 (noun) a good quality in someone's character, e.g. *Honesty is a real virtue.*
2 A virtue of something is an advantage, e.g. *The plan has the virtue of simplicity.*

Similar word: (sense 1) goodness, morality

Any name used for God or Jesus must begin with a capital letter, e.g. Pray to God and His Son.

virtuous
(adjective) thinking and doing what is morally right and avoiding what is wrong.

virus, viruses (pronounced vie-russ)
1 (noun) a kind of germ that often causes disease; or the disease itself.
2 A computer virus is a bug deliberately put into software which damages or destroys data.
viral (adjective)
[Latin *virus* = slime or poisonous liquid]

visa, visas
(noun) an official stamp put in your passport, that allows you to visit a particular country.
[Latin *visa* = things seen]

visibility
(noun) how far or how clearly you can see, e.g. *Because of fog, visibility is down to 10 metres.*

visible
(adjective) able to be seen.
visibly (adverb)

vision, visions
1 (noun) the ability to see clearly.
2 a mental picture, in which you imagine how things might be different, e.g. *I have a vision of a future world at peace.*

visit, visits, visiting, visited
1 (verb) to go to see someone or somewhere.
2 (noun) a trip to see a person or place.
visitor (noun)

visor, visors (pronounced vie-zor)
(noun) a transparent shield attached to a helmet, which is pulled down to protect the eyes or face.

visual
(adjective) relating to sight.
visually (adverb)

visual aid, aids
(noun) something you look at to help you learn and remember things, e.g. maps, slides, films.

visualize, visualizes, visualizing, visualized
(pronounced viz-yool-eyes; also spelled visualise)
(verb) If you visualize something, you form a picture of it in your mind.

vital
(adjective) necessary or very important, e.g. *vital repair work.*
vitally (adverb)
[Latin *vita* = life]

Similar words: essential, crucial, imperative, indispensable, necessary

vitality
(noun) People who have vitality are energetic and lively.

vitamin, vitamins
(noun) Vitamins are organic compounds in food which you need in order to remain healthy.

vivacious (pronounced viv-vay-shuss)
(adjective) A vivacious person is attractively lively and high-spirited.

Similar words: animated, sparkling, lively

vivid
(adjective) very bright in colour or clear in detail, e.g. *a vivid green dress... a vivid dream.*
vividly (adverb)

vivisection
(noun) the act of cutting open living animals for medical research.
[Latin *vivus* = living + *secare* = to cut]

vixen, vixens
(noun) a female fox.
[Old English *fyxe* = female fox]

vocabulary, vocabularies
(noun) Someone's vocabulary is the total number of words they know in a particular language.

vocal
(adjective, noun) connected with the human voice, e.g. *vocal cords... vocal by Frank Sinatra.*
vocalist (noun) vocally (adverb)

vocation, vocations
1 (noun) a strong wish to do a particular job, e.g. *Fiona had a vocation for nursing.*
2 a profession or career.

vocational
(adjective) used to describe the skills needed for a job, e.g. *vocational training.*

vocative
(noun, adjective) In the grammar of some languages, the vocative is the form of a noun or name used when the person it refers to is being spoken or written to.

vodka, vodkas
(noun) a strong, clear, alcoholic drink.
[Russian *vodka* = little water]

voice, voices, voicing, voiced
1 (noun) the sounds produced by your vocal cords, e.g. *Opera singers have powerful voices.*
2 (verb) If you voice an opinion you say what you think, e.g. *The workers voiced their anger.*

volcanic
1 (adjective) A volcanic region has many volcanoes or was created by volcanoes.
2 In geology, volcanic rocks come from the cooled lava of volcanoes.

volcano, volcanoes
(noun) a mountain with an opening through which lava, gas and ash are shot out from inside the earth's crust.
[named after *Vulcan*, the Roman god of fire]

vole, voles
(noun) a small animal like a mouse with a short tail.
[a shortened form of *volemouse*; from Old Norse *vollr* + *mus* = fieldmouse]

volley, volleys
(noun) In games, a volley is a stroke or kick in which the player hits the ball before it bounces.
[French *volée* = flight]

volleyball
(noun) a game in which two teams hit a large ball

We take these words from Russia: vodka steppe tundra samovar commissar.

over a high net with their hands, trying to keep it off the ground.

volt, volts
(noun) a unit of electrical force [named after the Italian, Count Alessandro Volta (1745-1827)].
voltage (noun)

volume, volumes
1 (noun) a book, or one of a series of books.
2 The volume of something is the amount of space it contains or occupies, measured in, for example cubic feet or cubic metres (m³).
3 The volume of a radio, TV, etc. is the strength of the sound that it produces.
[Latin *volumen* = roll or book]

voluntary
1 (adjective) Voluntary actions are ones that you do because you choose to do them and not because you have been forced to do them.
2 Voluntary work is done by people who are not paid for what they do.
voluntarily (adverb)
[Latin *voluntas* = will]

volunteer, volunteers, volunteering, volunteered
1 (noun) someone who does work for which they are not paid.
2 (verb) If you volunteer to do something, you offer to do it rather than being forced into it.

vomit, vomits, vomiting, vomited
(verb) to be sick.

vote, votes, voting, voted
1 (noun) When a group of people have a vote, they make a decision by allowing each person in the group to say what they would prefer.
2 In an election, the vote is the total number of people who have made their choice, e.g. *Labour increased its total vote by a million.*
3 (verb) When people vote, they indicate their choice, usually by writing on a piece of paper or by raising their hand.
voter (noun)

vouch, vouches, vouching, vouched
(verb) If you say that you can vouch for

someone, you mean that you are sure that you can guarantee their good behaviour or support, e.g. *He said you'd vouch for him.*

voucher, vouchers
(noun) a piece of paper used instead of money to pay for something, e.g. *a gift voucher.*

vow, vows, vowing, vowed
1 (verb) to make a solemn promise, e.g. *She vowed never to let it happen again.*
2 (noun) a solemn promise.
[Latin *votum* = solemn promise]

vowel, vowels
(noun) The vowels are a, e, i, o, u, and y (as used in 'story'). They are sounds made without your tongue touching the roof of your mouth or your teeth.

voyage, voyages, voyaging, voyaged
1 (noun) a long journey on a ship or in a spacecraft.
2 (verb; old-fashioned) e.g. *Columbus voyaged to the shores of the New World.*
voyager (noun)
[Latin *viaticus* = concerning a journey]

vulgar
(adjective) unacceptable or offensive, e.g. *vulgar remarks.*
vulgarity (noun)

vulnerable
(adjective) weak and without protection, e.g. *When the drawbridge is down a castle is more vulnerable to attack.*
vulnerably (adverb) **vulnerability** (noun)
[Latin *vulnerare* = to wound]

Similar words: susceptible, defenceless, unprotected

vulture, vultures
(noun) a large bird which lives in hot countries and eats the flesh of dead animals.

vulva, vulvas or vulvae
(noun) the outer part of a woman's sexual organs.

W

wacky, wackier, wackiest
(adjective; informal) odd or crazy, e.g. *a wacky new comedy.*

wad, wads (pronounced wod)
(noun) a thick bundle, e.g. *a wad of banknotes.*

wadding (pronounced wodd-ing)
(noun) soft material used for stuffing things or packing round things to protect them.

waddle, waddles, waddling, waddled
(pronounced wod-dl)
(verb) When a duck or a fat person waddles, they walk with short, quick steps, swaying slightly from side to side.

wade, wades, wading, waded
1 (verb) to walk slowly through water or mud.
2 If you wade through a book, you spend a lot of

time and effort reading it because you find it dull or difficult.

wader, waders
1 (noun) a long-legged and long-necked bird that lives near water and feeds on fish.
2 Waders are long, waterproof, rubber boots worn by fishermen.

wafer, wafers
(noun) a thin, crisp, sweet biscuit often eaten with ice cream.
[Old French *waufre* = wafer]

wafer-thin
(adjective) extremely thin.

waffle, waffles, waffling, waffled (pronounced wof-fl)
1 (verb) to talk or write a lot without being clear or without saying anything of importance.

When were there only two vowels? In the days of No-a before U and I were born.

2 (noun) vague and wordy speech or writing, e.g. *This essay is a load of waffle!*
3 a thick, crisp pancake with squares marked on it, often eaten with syrup on it.

waft, wafts, wafting, wafted (pronounced **woft**)
(verb) If a scent wafts through the air, it moves gently through it.

wag, wags, wagging, wagged
1 (verb) to move something repeatedly up and down, or side to side, e.g. *The dog wagged its tail... Don't wag your finger at me!*
2 (phrase; informal) When **tongues wag**, people are gossiping, e.g. *He dared not visit her, because tongues might wag.*
3 (noun; old-fashioned) A wag is someone who tells or plays jokes.
[verb: Old English *wagian* = to shake]

wage, wages, waging, waged
1 (noun) A wage or wages is the regular payment made to someone each week for the work they do, especially for manual or unskilled work.
2 (verb) If a person wages a campaign or a country wages war, they start it and carry it on over a period of time.
[Old French *wagier* = to pledge]

waggle, waggles, waggling, waggled
(verb) to move something repeatedly up and down or side to side, e.g. *He waggled his eyebrows... Marilyn waggled her bottom.*

wagon, wagons; also spelled **waggon**
1 (noun) a strong 4-wheeled cart for carrying heavy loads, pulled by a horse or tractor.
2 Wagons are also the containers for freight pulled by a railway engine.
[Dutch *wagen* = wagon]

wagtail, wagtails
(noun) a small bird with a long tail.

wail, wails, wailing, wailed
1 (verb) to cry loudly with sorrow or pain.
2 (noun) e.g. *He let out a wail of fear*

waist, waists
(noun) the middle part of the body where it narrows slightly above your hips.

waistcoat, waistcoats
(noun) a sleeveless, buttoned piece of men's clothing, often worn under a suit or jacket.

wait, waits, waiting, waited
1 (verb) e.g. *Wait a minute!*
2 (noun) e.g. *We had a long wait for the bus.*
3 (verb) If you wait on people in a restaurant, it is your job to serve them.
4 (phrase) If you **wait on** someone **hand and foot**, you do everything for them.

waiter, waiters
(noun) a man who works in a restaurant, serving people with food and drink.

waiting room, rooms
(noun) a room where people can sit and wait in, for example, a station or a doctor's surgery.

waitress, waitresses
(noun) a woman who works in a restaurant, serving people with food and drink.

wake, wakes, waking, woke, woken
1 (verb) e.g. *Wake up, James, then get up!*
2 (noun) The wake of a boat moving in water is the track of waves it leaves behind it.

Similar words: (verb) arouse, awake, waken, stir

walk, walks, walking, walked
1 (verb) e.g. *Walk sensibly across the road.*
2 (informal) If someone walks off with something, they take it without asking the person who owns it.
3 (noun) e.g. *He went for a long walk... His walk was more like a stagger.*
walker (noun)
[Old English *wealcan*]

walk out
(phrasal verb) If you walk out on someone, you leave them suddenly.

walkie-talkie, walkie-talkies
(noun) a small, portable radio for sending and receiving messages.

walking stick, sticks
(noun) a wooden stick which people can lean on while walking.

Walkman
(noun; trademark) a small cassette player with lightweight headphones.

walk of life, walks of life
(noun) the position you have in society and the kind of job you have, e.g. *In your walk of life, you must meet many rich people.*

walkover, walkovers
(noun; informal) a very easy victory in a competition or contest, especially when your opponent is forced to withdraw from the game.

wall, walls
1 (noun) e.g. *Most rooms have 4 walls.*
2 (phrase) If you are **banging your head against a brick wall**, you are not making any progress in something you are trying to do.
[Old English *weall* = wall]

wallet, wallets
(noun) a small, flat case made of leather or plastic, used for keeping money, stamps, credit cards, etc.

wallflower, wallflowers
(noun) a garden plant.

wallop, wallops, walloping, walloped
1 (verb; informal) to hit someone very hard.
2 (noun) e.g. *She gave me a wallop round my ear.*
[Old French *galoper* = to gallop]

wallow, wallows, wallowing, wallowed
(verb) When an animal wallows in mud or water, it lies or rolls about in it slowly for pleasure.
[Old English *wealwian* = to roll (in mud)]

wallpaper, wallpapers
(noun) thick paper in a roll for pasting onto the walls of rooms to decorate them.

Repeat quickly: I like to hike from early to late whatever the weather may be.

walnut, walnuts
(noun) the edible nut of the walnut tree.
[Old English *walh-hnutu* = foreign nut]

waltz, waltzes, waltzing, waltzed
1 (noun) a piece of music with a rhythm of 3 beats to the bar, which people can dance to.
2 (verb) If you waltz with someone, you dance a waltz with them.
[Old German *walzen* = to revolve]

wand, wands
(noun) a long, thin rod that magicians wave when they are performing tricks and magic.

wander, wanders, wandering, wandered
1 (verb) to walk around in a casual way.
2 If your mind wanders or your thoughts wander, you lose concentration and start thinking about other things.
wanderer (noun)
[Old English *wandrian*]

Similar words: (sense 1) ramble, stray, roam, rove

wangle, wangles, wangling, wangled
(verb; informal) If you wangle something that you want, you manage to obtain it by being crafty or persuasive.

want, wants, wanting, wanted
(verb) e.g. *He wants a bike for his birthday... He wants a good hiding... She is wanted for murder.*
[Old Norse *vanta* = to be lacking]

war, wars
1 (noun) a period of fighting between countries.
2 competition between groups of people, or a campaign against something, e.g. *a price war... the war against drugs.*
3 (phrase; informal) If you say someone has been **in the wars**, you mean they look as if they have been in a fight.
[French *guerre* = war]

Similar words: (sense 1) battle, warfare, conflict

warble, warbles, warbling, warbled
(verb) When a bird warbles, it sings with high notes and many variations.
warbler (noun)

ward, wards, warding, warded
1 (noun) a room or group of rooms in a hospital with beds for people who need similar treatment.
2 A ward or a ward of court is a child who is officially put in the care of an adult or a court of law, because their parents are dead or because they need protection.
3 (verb) If you ward off a danger or an illness, you do something to prevent it from affecting or harming you.

ward or **-wards**
(suffix) -ward and -wards form adverbs or adjectives that show the way something is moving or facing, e.g. *skyward... homewards.*
[Old English *-weard* = towards]

warden, wardens
1 (noun) a person in charge of a building or institution, e.g. a youth hostel or prison.
2 an official who makes sure that certain laws or rules are obeyed, e.g. *traffic wardens.*

warder, warders
(noun) a person who works in a prison and is in charge of prisoners.

wardrobe, wardrobes
1 (noun) a tall cupboard for clothes.
2 Someone's wardrobe is their collection of clothes.
[Old French *garder* + *robes* = to guard robes]

ware, wares
(noun) manufactured goods of a particular kind, e.g. *kitchenware... glassware... hardware.*

warehouse, warehouses
(noun) a large building where raw materials or manufactured goods are stored.

warfare
(noun) the activity of fighting a war.

warhead, warheads
(noun) the front end of a bomb or missile, where the explosives are carried.

warm, warmer, warmest; warms, warming, warmed
1 (adjective) fairly hot.
2 A warm person is friendly and affectionate.
3 (verb) If you warm something, you heat it up gently so that it stops being cold.
[Old English *wearm* = warm]

warm up
1 (phrasal verb) If you warm up for an event or an activity, you practise or you exercise gently to prepare for it.
2 When an engine etc. warms up, it becomes ready for use a little while after being started.
warm-up (noun)

warm-hearted
(adjective) friendly and affectionate.

warmth
1 (noun) a moderate amount of heat.
2 Someone who has warmth is friendly and affectionate.

warn, warns, warning, warned
(verb) to tell someone about a possible problem or danger, e.g. *I did warn you it was expensive... I warned him not to lose his temper.*
warning (noun)
[Old English *wearnian* = to warn]

Similar words: caution, alert, give notice, tip off

warp, warps, warping, warped
1 (verb) If something warps or is warped, it becomes bent, often because of heat or water.
2 (noun) A time warp is an imaginary break or sudden change in normal experience.
[Old English *wearp* = a throw]

warpath
(noun) If someone is on the warpath, they are angry and getting ready for a fight or argument.

warrant officer, officers
(noun) the highest rank of non-commissioned officer in the army or the RAF.

War is delightful to those who have had no experience of it. (Erasmus)

warren, warrens
(noun) a group of holes under the ground connected by tunnels, which rabbits live in.

warrior, warriors
(noun) a fighting man or soldier, especially in ancient times.

warship, warships
(noun) a ship built with guns and used for fighting in wars.

wart, warts
(noun) a small, hard piece of skin which can grow on someone's face or hands.

wary, warier, wariest
(adjective) cautious and on one's guard, e.g. *Our dog Molly was very wary of next door's cat.*
warily (adverb)

wash, washes, washing, washed
1 (verb) e.g. *Please wash your hands.*
2 (noun) e.g. *Whizzo gives you a whiter wash.*
3 (verb) e.g. *The body was washed up on the shore.*
4 (phrase) If you **wash your hands of** something, you refuse to have anything more to do with it.
[Old English *wæscan* = to wash]

washable
(adjective) able to be washed without being damaged, e.g. *washable wallpaper.*

washbasin, washbasins
(noun) a bowl, usually fixed to a wall, with taps for hot and cold water.

washer, washers
(noun) a thin, flat ring of metal etc. screwed on with a nut and bolt to make a tighter connection.

washing
(noun) e.g. *Mum put the washing on the line.*
washing machine (noun) **washing powder** (noun)

washing-up
(noun) the washing of plates, cups, pans, etc.

washout, washouts
(noun; informal) If an event or project is a washout, it is a complete disaster or failure.

wasp, wasps
(noun) a striped insect which can sting.

wastage
(noun) loss and misuse of something, e.g. *Here there is a terrible wastage of paper and glass.*

waste, wastes, wasting, wasted
1 (verb) If you waste time, money or energy, you use too much of it on something that is not important or necessary.
2 If you waste a chance, you do not take advantage of it while it is available.
3 If you say that something is wasted on someone, you mean that it is too good for them, e.g. *New clothes are wasted on her – she does not take care of them.*
4 (noun) the use of more money or some other resource than is necessary.
5 material that has been used and is no longer wanted, or material left over, e.g. *radioactive waste.*
6 (adjective) e.g. *waste paper... waste land.*

7 (phrase) If something **goes to waste**, it is unused, goes bad or is thrown away.
[Latin *vastus* = empty]

waste away
(phrasal verb) If someone is wasting away, they are becoming very thin and weak because they are ill or not eating properly.

wasteful
(adjective) extravagant or causing waste by using resources in a careless and inefficient way.
wastefully (adverb) **wastefulness** (noun)

watch, watches, watching, watched
1 (noun) a small clock usually worn on the wrist.
2 (verb) e.g. *Watch my hands closely... I'll watch her progress with interest.*
[Old English *wæccan* = to be awake]

watch out
(phrasal verb) e.g. *Watch out for the Perth turn-off... Watch out for that broken step.*

watchdog, watchdogs
(noun) a dog used to guard property.

watchful
(adjective) careful to notice everything that is happening, e.g. *Dogs tend to keep a watchful eye on anyone who is eating food.*
watchfully (adverb) **watchfulness** (noun)

watchman, watchmen
(noun) a person whose job is to guard property.

water, waters, watering, watered
1 (noun) e.g. *Water, water every where. Nor any drop to drink.*
2 (verb) e.g. *Water your plants regularly... My eyes watered during the sad film... My mouth waters at the sight of chips.*
3 (phrase) When you **pass water**, you urinate.
4 If you say that an event or incident is **water under the bridge**, you mean that it is past and done with and cannot now be changed.
5 If you **pour** or **throw cold water on** a suggestion you show that you do not think it is a very good one.

water down
(phrasal verb) If you water something down, you make it weaker.
watered-down (adjective)

watercolour, watercolours
1 (noun) Watercolours are paints for painting pictures which are mixed with water.
2 a picture which has been painted using watercolours.

watercress
(noun) a small, edible plant which grows in streams and pools. It is eaten in salads.

waterfall, waterfalls
(noun) water from a river or stream as it flows over the edge of a steep cliff and falls to the ground below.

watering can, cans
(noun) a container with a handle and a long spout, which you use to water plants.

Many place names are connected with water: aber = river mouth; burn = stream....

waterlogged

1 (adjective) Waterlogged land is so wet that some water remains on the surface of the ground.
2 A waterlogged boat is so full of water that it might soon sink.

water main, mains

(noun) a large, underground pipe supplying water to houses and factories.

watermark, watermarks

(noun) a design put into paper as it is being made, which is only visible when held up to the light, e.g. in banknotes and in notepaper.

watermelon, watermelons

(noun) a large, round, green fruit with red juicy flesh and a lot of black seeds.

waterproof, waterproofs, waterproofing, waterproofed

1 (adjective) not letting water pass through, e.g. *waterproof trousers*.
2 (verb) To waterproof something means to make it waterproof.
3 (noun) a coat which is waterproof.

waterside

(noun) an area of land next to a river, lake, etc.

water-skiing

(noun) the sport of skimming over the water on skis while being pulled by a boat.

watertight

1 (adjective) Something that is watertight does not allow water to pass through because it is tightly sealed.
2 An agreement or an argument that is watertight has been so carefully put together that nobody should be able to find a fault in it.

water vapour

(noun) steam formed by water when it boils.

waterway, waterways

(noun) a canal, river or narrow channel of sea which ships or boats can sail along.

waterworks

1 (noun) the system of pipes, tanks, etc., where public water is stored and cleaned, and from where it is piped to houses.
2 (informal) used to describe the parts in someone's body which form their urinary system, e.g. *I don't like to gossip, Mavis, but he's had trouble with his waterworks. Say no more!*
3 (phrase; informal) If someone **turns on the waterworks**, they start crying.

watery

1 (adjective) pale or weak, e.g. *a watery smile*.
2 Watery food or drink contains a lot of water or is thin like water, e.g. *watery milk*.

watt, watts (pronounced **wot**)

(noun) a unit of power [named after James Watt (1736-1819) the inventor of the modern steam engine.]

wave, waves, waving, waved

1 (verb) e.g. *As the train left, Debbie waved to her parents... The policeman waved them on... He waved the photographs in the air.*
2 (noun) e.g. *After the storm, the waves on the beach were huge.*

3 part of someone's hair that forms a gently curving shape.
wavy (adjective)
4 the form in which some types of energy such as heat, light or sound travel, e.g. *sound waves... radio waves.*
5 a sudden, large amount of something, e.g. *a wave of panic swept the shop... There was a wave of crime against banks.*

waveband, wavebands

(noun) a group of radio waves used for particular types of radio transmission, e.g *the FM waveband.*

wavelength, wavelengths

1 (noun) the size of radio wave which a particular radio station uses to broadcast its programmes.
2 (phrase) If two people are **on the same wavelength**, they have a lot in common and get on very well together.

wax, waxes

1 (noun) a solid, slightly shiny substance made of fat or oil, used to make candles and polish.
2 the sticky yellow substance in your ears.
waxy (adjective)
[Old English *weax* = wax]

waxworks

(plural noun) a place where wax models of famous people are displayed for the public to look at, e.g. *Madame Tussaud's Waxworks.*

way, ways

Selected meanings:
1 (noun) e.g. *Which way do I go?*
2 (phrase) Example: *The chocolate went a long way to making the boy feel better*, means that the chocolate helped a lot.
3 If you **go out of your way** to do something, you make a special effort to do it.
4 (informal) If someone is **in a bad way**, they are in a poor state of health or state of mind.
5 If an event is **under way**, it has already started.
6 Your **way of life** is how you live, e.g. *Our way of life changed completely when we moved to the country.*

way-out

(adjective; informal) unusual, odd or very modern, e.g. *That coat's way-out, man!*

we

(pronoun) e.g. *We could hear the birds singing.*

weak, weaker, weakest

1 (adjective) not having much strength, e.g. *weak from hunger... a weak voice.*
2 If you describe someone as weak, you mean they are easily influenced by other people.
3 e.g. *I was weak in maths.*
weakly (adverb)
[Old English *wac* = soft and miserable]

Similar words: (sense 1) feeble, puny, weedy

weaken, weakens, weakening, weakened

1 (verb) If someone weakens something, they make it less strong, powerful or certain.

2 If someone weakens, they become less certain about something they had previously decided.

weak-kneed
(adjective) Someone who is weak-kneed is not able or willing to make their own decisions or stand up for themselves.

weakling, weaklings
(noun) a person who lacks physical strength or who is weak in character or health.

weakness, weaknesses
1 (noun) lack of strength.
2 If you have a weakness for something, you like it a lot, e.g. *She has a weakness for chocolate.*

wealth
1 (noun) the large amount of money, property, etc. which someone owns.
2 If someone has a wealth of something, they have a lot of it, e.g. *a wealth of knowledge.*

Similar words: (sense 1) fortune, riches, prosperity

wealthy, wealthier, wealthiest
(adjective) very rich.

Similar words: affluent, prosperous, rich, well-off

wean, weans, weaning, weaned
1 (verb) To wean a baby or animal means to start feeding it other food than its mother's milk.
2 If you wean someone from something, you help them gradually to stop doing it.
[Old English *wenian* = to accustom]

weapon, weapons
(noun) an object used to kill or hurt people in a fight or war.

wear, wears, wearing, wore, worn
1 (verb) e.g. *She was wearing jeans... He wore a stupid grin on his face.*
2 (noun) clothes that are suitable for a particular time or occasion, e.g. *evening wear.*
3 (verb) If something wears, it becomes thinner, weaker or worse in condition.

wear down
(phrasal verb) If you wear people down, you weaken them by being more persistent than they are.

wear off
(phrasal verb) to disappear gradually, e.g. *The effect of the dentist's injection wore off.*

wear on
(phrasal verb) If time wears on, it seems to pass very slowly or boringly.

wear out
(phrasal verb) e.g. *My old shoes wore out... These toddlers are wearing me out.*

wear and tear
(noun) the damage caused to something by normal use.

weary, wearier, weariest; wearies, wearying, wearied
1 (adjective) very tired.

2 (verb) If you weary of something, you become tired of it and lose your enthusiasm for it.
wearily (adverb) **weariness** (noun)
[Old English *werig* = tired]

weasel, weasels
(noun) a small, wild animal with a long, thin body and short legs.

weather, weathers, weathering, weathered
1 (noun) the condition of the atmosphere, e.g. *a weather forecast.*
2 (verb) If rock or wood weathers, it changes colour or shape as a result of being exposed to the wind, rain or sun.
3 (phrase) If you say that someone is making **heavy weather** of doing something, you mean they are making it much more difficult for themselves than it needs to be.
4 If you are **under the weather**, you feel slightly ill.
[Old English *weder* = weather]

weather-beaten
(adjective) rough or damaged because of being outside for a long time.

weathercock, weathercocks
(noun) a metal object, often in the shape of a cockerel, fixed to the roof of a building to show the direction of the wind.

weather forecast, forecasts
(noun) a statement saying what the weather will be like the next day or for the next few days.
weather forecaster (noun)

weatherproof
(adjective) able to keep out or resist wind and rain.

weather vane
(noun) a metal pointer on a roof which shows which way the wind is blowing.

weave, weaves, weaving, wove, woven
1 (verb) To weave cloth means to make it by crossing threads over and under each other, especially by using a machine called a loom.
weaver (noun)
2 If you weave your way somewhere, you go there by moving from side to side through and round the obstacles.
3 (phrase; informal) If you tell someone to **get weaving**, you are telling them to hurry up and start what they are supposed to be doing.
[Old English *wefan* = to weave]

webbed
(adjective) An animal's webbed feet have the toes connected by a piece of skin.

wedding, weddings
(noun) a marriage ceremony.

wedge, wedges, wedging, wedged
1 (verb) If you wedge something, you force it to remain there by fixing something next to it to prevent it from moving, e.g. *Wedge the door open with a book.*
2 (noun) a piece of wood, etc. with one pointed edge and one thick edge used to wedge something
3 a piece of something that has a thick, triangular shape, e.g. *a wedge of cake.*

I can resist everything except temptation. (Oscar Wilde)

Wednesday, Wednesdays
(noun) the day between Tuesday and Thursday.
[Old English *Wodnes dæg* = Woden's day; Woden
was the Anglo-Saxon sky-god.]

wee, weer, weest
(adjective; Scottish) very small.

weed, weeds, weeding, weeded
1 (noun) a wild plant.
2 (verb) to remove weeds.
3 (noun; informal) If you call someone a weed,
you mean they are physically weak or have a
weak character.
weedy (adjective)

week, weeks
1 (noun) a period of 7 days. The week begins on
Sunday and ends on Saturday.
2 the number of hours you spend at work during
a week, e.g. *He works a 40-hour week.*
3 the part of a week that does not include
Saturday and Sunday, e.g. *I don't go out during
the week.*
[Old English *wice* = week]

weekday, weekdays
(noun) any of the days of the week except
Saturday and Sunday.

weekend, weekends
(noun) Saturday and Sunday.

weekly, weeklies
1 (adjective, adverb) happening once a week.
2 (noun) a newspaper or magazine that is
published once a week, e.g. *Woman's Weekly.*

weep, weeps, weeping, wept
(verb) to cry.
weepy (adjective)

weigh, weighs, weighing, weighed
(verb) e.g. *She weighs 8 stone... Please weigh the
fish that I have caught.*

weigh down
1 (phrasal verb) If a load weighs you down, it
stops you moving easily.
2 If you are weighed down by a difficulty, it is
making you very worried.

weigh up
(phrasal verb) to assess a person or a situation,
e.g. *They weighed up the chances of escaping at
night.*

weight, weights, weighting, weighted
1 (noun) e.g. *The weight of the boxer was 15 stone
3 lbs... a 10kg weight... This sack is a weight to
carry!*
2 (verb) If you weight something or weight it
down, you make it heavier, often so that it
cannot move.
3 (phrase) If you **pull your weight**, you do your
fair share of the work.
4 If you **throw your weight about**, you act in an
aggressive or bossy way.

weightless
(adjective) Something that is weightless has no
weight or very little weight, e.g. because it is in
space and not affected by the Earth's gravity.
weightlessness (noun)

weightlifting
(noun) the sport of lifting heavy weights in
competition or for exercise.
weightlifter (noun)

weir, weirs (rhymes with **near**)
(noun) a low dam built across a river to raise the
water level, control the flow of water or change
its direction.
[Old English *wer* = river-dam]

weird, weirder, weirdest (pronounced **weerd**)
(adjective) strange; very odd.
weirdly (adverb) **weirdness** (noun)
[Old English *wyrd* = destiny]

Similar words: grotesque, outlandish

weirdo, weirdos (pronounced **weer**-doe)
(noun; informal) If you call someone a weirdo,
you mean they behave in a strange way.

welcome, welcomes, welcoming, welcomed
1 (verb) If you welcome a visitor, you greet them
in a friendly way when they arrive.
2 e.g *'Welcome, good friend, to Camelot!'*
3 (noun) e.g. *a warm welcome.*
4 (adjective) e.g. *a welcome gift... a welcome
guest.*
5 If you tell someone they are welcome to
something, you mean you are willing for them to
have it; you may also mean that you don't like it.
6 (verb) If you welcome something, you approve
of it and support it, e.g. *I welcomed his idea.*
welcoming (adjective)
[Old English *wilcuma* = welcome guest]

weld, welds, welding, welded
(verb) to join two pieces of metal together by
heating their edges and fixing them together so
that when they cool they harden into one piece.
welder (noun)
[Old English *weallan* = to boil or melt]

welfare
1 (noun) someone's welfare is their general state
of health, comfort and prosperity.
2 Welfare is used to describe activities concerned
with the health, living conditions and financial
problems of people in society.

welfare state
(noun) a system in which the government uses
money from taxes to provide health and
education services, and to give benefits to people
who are old, unemployed or sick.

well, better, best
1 (adverb) e.g. *The party went well... It may well
happen... They stood well back.*
2 (adjective) e.g. *I'm very well, thank you.*
3 (noun) a hole drilled in the ground from which
water, oil or gas is obtained.
[senses 1-2 – Old English *wel* = well
noun: Old English *weallan* = to boil or to melt]

well-advised
(adjective) sensible or wise, e.g. *You would be
well-advised to leave while you can.*

well-balanced
(adjective) sensible and without serious

The long 'a' sound can be spelled: bake raid say gaol gauge break rein grey reign weight.

emotional problems, e.g. *He is mature and well-balanced.*

wellbeing
(noun) Someone's wellbeing is their health and happiness.

well-bred
(adjective) having good manners.

well-earned
(adjective) thoroughly deserved, e.g. *a well-earned round of applause.*

well-groomed
(adjective) neat and tidy in appearance.

well-informed
(adjective) having a great deal of knowledge about a subject or subjects.

wellingtons or **wellies**
(plural noun) long, waterproof rubber boots. [Long boots were made popular by the 1st Duke of Wellington.]

well-intentioned
(adjective) Something that is well-intentioned is meant to be helpful but often goes wrong.

well-meaning
(adjective) A well-meaning person tries to be helpful but is often unsuccessful.

well-off
(adjective; informal) quite wealthy.

well-thought-of
(adjective) admired and respected, e.g. *He was very well-thought-of in the area.*

well-to-do
(adjective) quite wealthy.

well-worn
1 (adjective) A well-worn expression or saying has been used too often and has become boring.
2 A well-worn piece of clothing has been worn so much that it looks old and shabby.

Welsh
1 (adjective) belonging to Wales.
2 (noun) a language spoken in parts of Wales.

Welshman, Welshmen
(noun) a man who comes from Wales.
Welshwoman (noun)

wend, wends, wending, wended
(verb; literary) If you wend your way somewhere, you walk slowly in that direction. [Old English *wendan* = to turn or go]

wept past tense and past participle of **weep**.

werewolf, werewolves
(noun) In horror stories, a werewolf is a person who sometimes changes into a wolf. [Old English *wer* + *wulf* = man wolf]

west
1 (noun) the direction in which you look to see the sun set.
2 (adjective) A west wind blows from the west.
3 (noun) The West refers to the countries of North America and western and southern Europe.

western, westerns
1 (adjective) in or from the west.

2 associated with the countries of North America and western Europe, e.g. *western-style housing.*
3 (noun) a book or film about cowboys etc. who lived in the American West in the 19th century.

West Indian, Indians
1 (adjective) belonging to the West Indies, a group of islands between North and South America.
2 (noun) someone who comes from the West Indies.

westward or **westwards**
(adverb) towards the west.

wet, wetter, wettest; wets, wetting, wet or **wetted**
1 (adjective) e.g. *Rain tends to be wet.*
2 (informal) If you say someone is wet, you mean they are weak and lack enthusiasm, energy or confidence, e.g. *Don't be so wet, Martin.*
3 (verb) to put water or some other liquid over something.
wetness (noun)

wet blanket, blankets
(noun; informal) a person whose lack of enthusiasm has a depressing effect on others.

wet suit, suits
(noun) a close-fitting rubber suit which a diver or someone taking part in water sports wears to keep their body warm.

whack, whacks, whacking, whacked
1 (verb) If you whack someone or something, you hit them hard.
2 (noun; informal) If someone gets their whack of something, they get their fair share of it.

whacked
(adjective; informal) extremely tired, e.g. *By 9 o'clock, I was whacked.*

whacking
(adjective; informal) very big.

whale, whales
1 (noun) a very large sea mammal.
2 (phrase; informal) If you say that you had a **whale of a time**, you mean that you enjoyed yourself very much.

whaling
(noun) the work of hunting and killing whales for oil or food.

wham
(interjection) e.g. *Wham! Mrs T's handbag hit me right on the ear.*

wharf, wharves or **wharfs** (pronounced **worf**)
(noun) a platform along the side of a river, etc., where ships load or unload. [Old English *hwearf* = heap]

what
1 (pronoun, adjective, adverb) e.g. *What is your name?... I've spent what money I had... What does it matter?*
2 (phrase; informal) **What's what** means the important things that need to be known about a situation, e.g. *There'll be a meeting to find out what's what.*

Adverbial pun. 'What a whale!' said Captain Ahab, superficially.

whatever
(pronoun, conjunction, adverb) e.g. *I'll do whatever I can to help... I have to return whatever happens... There is no proof whatever that she is guilty.*

whatsoever
(adverb) You use whatsoever to emphasize a negative statement, e.g. *There is no proof whatsoever that she is guilty.*

wheat
(noun) a cereal plant grown for its grain.
[Old English *hwæte* = wheat]

wheatmeal
(noun) a brown flour made from wheat grains.

wheedle, wheedles, wheedling, wheedled
(verb) to persuade someone into doing something, very gently and cleverly.

wheel, wheels, wheeling, wheeled
1 (noun) e.g. *Most cars have 4 wheels.*
2 (verb) e.g. *He wheeled his barrow along.*
3 If you wheel round, you turn round to face someone or something.

wheelbarrow, wheelbarrows
(noun) a small carrying cart with a single wheel at the front.

wheelchair, wheelchairs
(noun) a chair with wheels for sick, injured or disabled people.

wheeze, wheezes, wheezing, wheezed
(verb) If someone wheezes, they breathe with difficulty, making a whistling sound.
wheezy (adjective)

when
(adverb, conjunction) e.g. *When are you getting married?... I first met him when I was 13.*
[Old English *hwanne* = when]

whence
(adverb, conjunction; old-fashioned) from where, e.g. *Go back whence you came.*

whenever
(conjunction) at any time, or every time that something happens, e.g. *I avoid fights whenever possible.*

where
(adverb, conjunction, pronoun) e.g. *Where is Jane?... I know where we are... Where do you come from?*
[Old English *hwær* = where]

whereabouts
1 (noun) The whereabouts of a person or thing is the place where they are.
2 (adverb) You use whereabouts when you are asking where something approximately is, e.g. *Whereabouts in Spain will you be going?*

wherever
1 (conjunction) in every place or situation, e.g. *Wherever you go, you see poverty.*
2 You use wherever to show that you do not know where a place or person is, e.g. *John lived in Denton, wherever that is.*

whet, whets, whetting, whetted
(phrase) To **whet someone's appetite** for something, means to increase their desire for it.
[Old English *hwettan* = sharpen]

whether
(conjunction) e.g. *I can't tell whether he loves me or not.*

which
(adjective, pronoun) e.g. *I don't know which team she played for... Which of the two do you prefer?... the awful conditions which exist in our prisons.*

whichever
(adjective, pronoun) e.g. *Write or phone, whichever you prefer... Use whichever is best.*

whiff, whiffs
(noun) a slight smell of something.

while
1 (conjunction) e.g. *Nero fiddled while Rome burned... Fred gambled his money while Julia spent hers on clothes.*
2 (noun) a period of time, e.g. *a little while ago.*
3 (phrase) If doing something is **worth your while**, it will be useful to you if you do it.

while away
(phrasal verb) If you while away the time doing something, you have little else to do.

whilst
(conjunction) Whilst means the same as while.

whim, whims
(noun) a sudden desire or fancy.

whimper, whimpers, whimpering, whimpered
1 (verb) When children or animals whimper, they make soft, low, unhappy sounds.
2 (noun) e.g. *I heard a whimper from the kennel.*

whine, whines, whining, whined
1 (verb) to make a long, high-pitched noise, especially one which sounds sad or unpleasant, e.g. *The jet engine whined.*
2 (noun) the noise made by someone whining.
3 If someone whines about something, they complain about it in an annoying way.

whinge, whinges, whinging or **whingeing, whinged**
(verb) If someone whinges about something, they complain about it in an annoying way.
[Old English *hwinsian* = to whine]

whinny, whinnies, whinnying, whinnied
(verb) When a horse whinnies, it neighs softly.

whip, whips, whipping, whipped
1 (noun) a thin piece of leather etc. on a handle, used for hitting animals or people.
2 (verb) If you whip something out, you take it out very quickly, e.g. *He whipped out a gun.*
3 If you whip cream or eggs, you beat them until they are thick and frothy or stiff.

whippet, whippets
(noun) a small, thin dog used for racing.

whip-round, whip-rounds
(noun; informal) When people have a whip-round, money is collected from each

person, for example, to help someone in trouble or to buy them a present.

whir, whirs, whirring, whirred; also spelled whirr
(verb) e.g. *The helicopter whirred overhead.*

whirdle, whirdles, whirdling, whirdled
(verb) to shake something violently, e.g. *The musician lost his temper and whirdled his banjo at the band.*
whirdlesome (adjective)

Similar word: agitate

whirl, whirls, whirling, whirled
1 (verb) When something whirls, or when you whirl it round, it turns round very fast.
2 (noun) You can refer to a lot of intense activity as a whirl of activity.
3 (verb) If you say that your head is whirling, you mean you are very confused or excited by something.
[Old Norse *hvirfla* = to turn about]

whirlpool, whirlpools
(noun) a small, circular area in a river or the sea where water is moving quickly round and round.

whirlwind, whirlwinds
1 (noun) a tall column of air which spins round and round very fast while moving across the land or sea.
2 (adjective) more rapid than usual, e.g. *a whirlwind romance.*

whisk, whisks, whisking, whisked
1 (verb) If you whisk someone or something somewhere, you take them there quickly, e.g. *I was whisked into hospital.*
2 If you whisk eggs or cream, you stir air into them quickly.
3 When an animal whisks its tail, it makes quick sweeping movements with it.
4 (noun) a kitchen tool used for quickly stirring air into eggs or cream.
[Old Norse *visk* = wisp]

whisker, whiskers
1 (noun) The whiskers of, for example a cat or mouse, are the long, stiff hairs near its mouth.
2 You can refer to the hair on a man's face, especially on his cheeks, as his whiskers.
3 (phrase; informal) By a whisker means by a very small amount, e.g. *We won by a whisker.*

whisky, whiskies
(noun) a strong, alcoholic drink made from grain such as barley or rye. [In Ireland and the USA, **whiskey** is the usual spelling .]
[Scottish Gaelic *uisge beatha* = water of life]

whisper, whispers, whispering, whispered
1 (verb) to talk very quietly, using your breath.
2 (noun) a low, quiet sound which can just be heard, e.g. *the whisper of wind in the trees.*

whist
(noun) a card game for 4 players in which one pair of players tries to win more tricks than the other pair.

whistle, whistles, whistling, whistled
1 (verb) e.g. *He whistled a tune... The kettle whistled... Bullets whistled past his head.*

2 (noun) a small metal tube that you blow into to produce a whistling sound.

white, whiter, whitest; whites
(adjective) e.g. *Snow is white when it falls... a white South African... She turned white with shock.*
2 (noun) The white of an egg is the transparent liquid (albumen) surrounding the yolk.
whiteness (noun) **whiten** (verb)
[Old English *hwit* = white]

white blood cell, cells
(noun) White blood cells are the cells in your blood that cannot carry oxygen.

white elephant, elephants
(noun) an expensive but useless possession, e.g. *The non-compatible computer system turned out to be a total white elephant.*
[from the pale-coloured elephants of parts of South Asia which are regarded as sacred]

white-hot
(adjective) extremely hot.

white lie, lies
(noun) a harmless lie, especially one told to prevent someone's feelings from being hurt.

white spirit
(noun) a colourless liquid made from petrol and used, e.g., to thin paint or to clean surfaces.

whittle, whittles, whittling, whittled
(verb) If you whittle a piece of wood, you shape it by shaving or cutting small pieces off it.
[Middle English *thwittle* = large knife]

whittle away or **whittle down**
(phrasal verb) To whittle away at something or to whittle it down means to make it smaller over a period of time, e.g. *The value of the £ was whittled down over the years.*

whizz, whizzes, whizzing, whizzed (also spelled whiz)
1 (verb; informal) If you whizz somewhere, you move there quickly, e.g. *The cars whizzed by.*
2 (noun; informal) If you are a whizz at something, you are very good at it.

whizz-kid, whizz-kids; also spelled whiz-kid
(noun; informal) a fairly young person who is very good at their job and extremely successful for their age.

who
(pronoun) e.g. *Who was that masked stranger?*

whoever
(pronoun) e.g. *Whoever finds the treasure should share it.*

whole, wholes
1 (noun, adjective) e.g. *the whole of Europe... the whole thing.*
2 (adverb) in one piece, e.g. *He swallowed a plum whole.*
3 (phrase) You use as a whole to emphasize that you are talking about all of something, e.g. *Is that just in India, or in the world as a whole?*
4 You say on the whole to mean that something is generally true, e.g. *On the whole, I enjoyed school.*

Six words that will help you with all your studies are: who, when, where, why, what, how....

wholefood, wholefoods
(noun) Wholefoods are foods which have been processed as little as possible, do not contain additives and are eaten in their natural state.

wholehearted
(adjective) enthusiastic and totally sincere, e.g. *She had the wholehearted support of her staff.*
wholeheartedly (adverb)

wholemeal
(adjective) Wholemeal flour is made from complete wheat grain, including the husk.

whole number, numbers
(noun) an exact number, not a fraction or a decimal, e.g. 1, 5, 12, 300.

wholesale
1 (adjective, adverb) Wholesale refers to the activity of buying goods cheaply in large quantities and selling them again, especially to shopkeepers, e.g. *A rise in wholesale prices will soon be reflected in the shops.* [opposite: **retail**]
2 (adjective) done to an excessive extent, e.g. *The wholesale slaughter of whales is unforgivable.*
wholesaler (noun)

wholesome
(adjective) good and likely to improve your life, behaviour or health, e.g. *a wholesome diet.*

wholly (pronounced **hoe**-lee)
(adverb) completely.

whom
(pronoun) the object form of 'who', e.g. *Of whom were you thinking?*

whooping cough (pronounced **hoop**-ing)
(noun) an acute infectious disease which makes people cough violently and produce a loud sound when they breathe.

whopper, whoppers
1 (noun; informal) an unusually large example of something, e.g. *This potato's a whopper!*
2 (informal) If you tell whoppers, you tell lies.

whopping
(adjective; informal) unusually large.

whose
(pronoun) e.g. *Whose car is this?... Barbara, whose father had just died, did not want to come.* [not to be confused with **who's** which means 'who is' or 'who has']

why
(adverb, pronoun) e.g. *Why did it happen?... He explained why... Why, he's only just learned to swim himself!*

wick, wicks
1 (noun) the cord in the middle of a candle, oil lamp, etc., which you set alight.
2 (phrase; informal) If someone **gets on your wick**, they irritate you.

wicked
(adjective) very bad, e.g. *the wicked witch... By the pricking of my thumbs, Something wicked this way comes.*
wickedly (adverb) **wickedness** (noun)
[Old English *wicce* = witch]

wickerwork
(noun) Wickerwork is used to make baskets and furniture and is made by weaving twigs, canes or reeds together.

wicket, wickets
(noun) In cricket, the wicket is one of the two sets of stumps and bails at which the bowler aims the ball; also the grass between the wickets.

wicketkeeper, wicketkeepers
(noun) In cricket, the wicketkeeper is the padded fielder who stands behind the wicket.

wide, wider, widest
1 (adjective) e.g. *the wide River Amazon... a wide range of books*
2 (adverb) e.g. *The dentist said, 'Open wide'... The bullet went wide.*
widen (verb)

wide-awake
(adjective) completely awake.

wide-ranging
(adjective) extending over a variety of different things or over a large area, e.g. *a wide-ranging discussion... a wide-ranging search.*

widespread
(adjective) existing over a large area or to a great extent, e.g. *a widespread belief... a widespread belt of rain.*

widow, widows
(noun) a woman whose husband has died and who has not remarried.

widowed
(adjective) If someone is widowed, their husband or wife has died.

widower, widowers
(noun) a man whose wife has died and who has not remarried.

width, widths
(noun) The width of something is the distance from one side or edge to the other.

wife, wives
(noun) A man's wife is the woman he is married to.
[Old English *wif* = woman]

wig, wigs
(noun) a false head of hair.
[short for *periwig* from Italian *perrucca* = wig]

wiggle, wiggles, wiggling, wiggled
(verb) e.g. *I got the axe out of the log by wiggling it about.*
wiggly (adjective)
[Old German *wiggelen* = to wiggle]

wild, wilder, wildest; wilds
1 (adjective) natural and untamed, e.g. *wild animals... the wilder parts of Scotland.*
2 (noun) The wild is a free and natural state of living, e.g. *Most zoo-bred animals could not survive in the wild.*
3 (adjective) Wild weather or sea is stormy and rough.
4 A wild guess is made without much thought and is unlikely to be right.

.....Try to think of questions beginning with these words about any subject you are studying.

5 (informal) If you are wild about something, you like it very much, e.g. *I'm just wild about Harry!*
wildly (adverb)

wilderness, wildernesses
1 (noun) a desert or other area of land where there are very few plants or animals.
2 An area where grass or plants grow thickly in a confused, uncontrolled mass, e.g. *The garden turned into a wilderness while we were away.*
[Old English *wildeor* + *nes* = wild animal state]

wildfire
(noun) If something spreads like wildfire, it spreads very quickly, e.g. *The news spread like wildfire round the school.*

wildfowl
(noun) birds such as ducks, pheasants and quails which are hunted and shot.

wild-goose chase, chases
(noun) a hopeless or useless search for something you have little chance of finding.

wildlife
(noun) wild animals and plants.

wilful
1 (adjective) deliberate and often intended to hurt someone, e.g. *wilful damage.*
2 obstinate and determined to get their own way, e.g. *a wilful child.*
wilfully (adverb)

will, wills, willing, willed
1 (verb) e.g. *She will turn up soon.*
2 (noun) the determination to do something, e.g. *The young joiner had the will to succeed.*
3 If something is the will of a person or group, they want it to happen, e.g. *the will of the people.*
4 (phrase) If you can do something **at will**, you can do it whenever you want.
5 (verb) If you will something to happen, you try to make it happen by mental effort, e.g. *I willed my legs to walk a bit farther.*
6 (noun) a legal document in which you say what you want to happen to your money and property when you die.

willies
(noun; informal) If something gives you the willies, it makes you nervous and uncomfortable.

willing
1 (adjective) prepared to do something, e.g. *I am willing to get married right now.*
2 eager and enthusiastic, e.g. *a willing helper.*
willingly (adverb) **willingness** (noun)

Similar words: (sense 1) game, ready

willow, willows
(noun) a type of tree whose wood is used for making baskets and cricket bats.

willowy
(adjective) A willowy person is tall, slim and graceful.

willpower
(noun) strong determination to do something and the mental strength to control one's actions, e.g. *She stayed calm by sheer willpower.*

wilt, wilts, wilting, wilted
(verb) If a plant wilts, it gradually droops downwards and becomes weak.

wily, wilier, wiliest (pronounced **wie**-lee)
(adjective) clever and cunning.

wimp, wimps
(noun; informal) If you call someone a wimp, you mean they are feeble and timid.
wimpish (adjective)

win, wins, winning, won
Selected meanings:
1 (verb) e.g. *She won the 100m race.*
2 (informal) If you say that someone **can't win** in a situation, you mean they are certain to fail whatever they do.
3 (phrase; informal) A **no-win situation** is one in which you are bound to fail.

win over or **win round**
(phrasal verb) If you win someone over or win them round, you persuade them to support you or agree with you.

wince, winces, wincing, winced
(verb) When you wince, the muscles of your face tighten suddenly because of pain, fear, etc.

winch, winches, winching, winched
1 (noun) a machine used to lift heavy objects, by winding them in with a cable on a drum.
2 (verb) If you winch an object, you lift, lower or pull it using a winch.
[Old English *wince* = pulley]

wind, winds (rhymes with **tinned**)
1 (noun) a moving current of air.
2 the ability to breathe easily, e.g. *I got my second wind and carried on running.*
3 air swallowed with food or drink, or gas produced in your stomach, which causes discomfort.
4 The wind section of an orchestra is the group of musicians who play wind instruments.
5 (phrase; informal) If you **get wind of** something, you begin to suspect it or become aware of it.
6 If something **takes the wind out of your sails**, it makes you much less confident about what you are doing.
windy (adjective)

wind, winds, winding, wound (rhymes with **mind**)
1 (verb) to twist and turn, e.g. a river.
2 to wrap something round something else.
3 When you wind a clock up, you turn a key or handle several times to make it work.
[Old English *windan* = wind]

wind up
1 (phrasal verb) When someone winds up a business, they close it forever.
2 If you wind up in a particular place, you end up there.
3 (informal) If you wind someone up, you deliberately annoy or tease them.

winded
(adjective) out of breath because of exercise or because you have been hit in the stomach.

Names of companies and shops begin with capital letters, e.g. Marks & Spencer, British Aerospace.

windfall, windfalls
1 (noun) a sum of money that you receive
unexpectedly.
2 a fruit, usually an apple, that has been blown
from a tree by the wind.

wind instrument, instruments
(noun) an instrument you play by using your
breath, e.g. a flute, oboe, trumpet.

windmill, windmills
(noun) a machine for grinding grain or pumping
water, driven by the wind.

window, windows
(noun) a space in a wall, etc., usually with glass
in it.
windowsill (noun)
[Old Norse *vindauga* = wind eye]

window-dressing
(noun) the arranging of goods attractively in a
shop window.
window-dresser (noun)

window-shopping
(noun) looking in shop windows without actually
buying anything.

windpipe, windpipes
(noun) the tube which carries air into your lungs
when you breathe.

windscreen, windscreens
(noun) the glass at the front of a vehicle.
windscreen wiper (noun)

windsurfing
(noun) the sport of moving on water by standing
on a sailboard equipped with a mast and sail.
windsurfer (noun)

windswept
(adjective) blown by the wind, e.g. *a windswept
hillside... windswept hair.*

windward
(adjective, adverb) facing into the wind, or
moving into the wind.

windy, windier, windiest
1 (adjective) If it is windy, there is a lot of wind.
2 (informal) If someone gets windy, they become
nervous or worried about something.

wine, wines
(noun) the red or white alcoholic drink made
from grapes, but also from fruits and vegetables.
[Latin *vinum* = wine]

wing, wings
1 (noun) e.g. *the wings of a bird... an aeroplane
wing.*
2 A wing of a building is a part which sticks out
from the main part.
3 part of an organization, with a particular role
or particular beliefs, e.g. *the political wing of the
IRA... the left wing of the Labour Party.*
4 (plural noun) The wings in a theatre are the
sides of the stage which are hidden from the
audience by curtains or scenery.
5 (noun) In football, hockey, etc., the wing is the
left or right edge of the pitch.
6 A car's wings are the parts around and above
its wheels.

7 If you **take someone under your wing**, you help
and guide them.
[Old Norse *vængir* = wing]

wing commander, commanders
(noun) a senior RAF officer.

winger, wingers
(noun) In football or hockey, the wingers are
attacking players who play mainly on the far
right or left of the pitch.

wingspan
(noun) The wingspan of a bird, insect or
aeroplane is the distance from the end of one
wing to the end of the other.

wink, winks, winking, winked
1 (verb) to close one eye briefly, often as a signal
that something is a joke or a secret.
2 (phrase; informal) If you have **forty winks**, you
sleep for a short while.
[Old English *wincian* = to close your eyes]

winkle-pickers
(plural noun) shoes or boots with long pointed
toes.

winner, winners
(noun) The winner of a prize, race or competition
is the person or thing that wins it.

Similar words: victor, champion, champ

winter, winters, wintering, wintered
1 (noun) the season between autumn and spring.
2 (verb) to live somewhere else in the winter, e.g.
Swallows winter in Africa.
wintry (adjective)

wipe, wipes, wiping, wiped
1 (verb) e.g. *He wiped the tears from his eyes.*
2 (phrase; informal) If you **wipe the floor with**
someone, you defeat them totally.

wipe out
(phrasal verb) To wipe out people or places
means to destroy them completely.

wire, wires, wiring, wired
1 (noun) metal in the form of a long, thin, flexible
thread used for fastening things or conducting
electric current.
2 (verb) If you wire one thing to another, you
fasten them together using wire.
3 If you wire something or wire it up, you
connect it so that electricity can pass through it.
4 (phrase; informal) If two people **get their wires
crossed**, they become confused and
misunderstand each other.

wireless, wirelesses
(noun; old-fashioned) a radio

wiring
(noun) The wiring in a building is the system of
wires that supplies electricity to the rooms.

wiry, wirier, wiriest
1 (adjective) Wiry people are thin but have
strong muscles.
2 Wiry things are stiff and rough to the touch,
e.g. *wiry black hair.*

wisdom
(noun) the ability to use experience and

Proverbs from the Bible: Wisdom is better than rubies. A soft answer turneth away wrath.

knowledge in order to make sensible decisions or judgements.
[Old English *wis* + *-dom* = wise condition]

wise, wiser, wisest

1 (adjective) Someone who is wise can use their experience and knowledge to make sensible decisions and judgements.
2 If you say that someone is **none the wiser** or **no wiser**, you mean they know no more about something than they did before, e.g. *I read the professor's article, but I'm none the wiser.*
3 (phrase; informal) If you **get wise** to a situation, you find out about it.

-wise

1 (suffix) -wise means behaving like someone or something, e.g. *I edged crabwise to my seat.*
2 (informal) -wise can also mean with reference to one particular thing, e.g. *Football-wise, we're all Rangers fans.*

wisecrack, wisecracks

(noun) a clever remark, intended to be amusing but often unkind, e.g. *He made some wisecrack about her clothes.*

wish, wishes, wishing, wished

1 (noun) a longing or desire for something, e.g. *His dying wish was for a pint of beer.*
2 (plural noun) e.g. *My parents send their best wishes.*
3 (verb) to want something, e.g. *We wish to marry next month, papa.*
[Old English *wyscan* = to have a desire for]

wishful thinking

(noun) If someone's hope or wish is wishful thinking, it is unlikely to come true.

wishy-washy

(adjective; informal) feeble and half-hearted, e.g. *They supported us in a rather wishy-washy way.*

wisp, wisps

1 (noun) A wisp of grass or hair is a small, thin, untidy bunch of it, e.g. *birds carrying wisps of hay in their beaks.*
2 A wisp of smoke is a long, thin streak of it.
wispy (adjective)

wit, wits

1 (noun) the ability to use words or ideas in an amusing and clever way.
2 common sense, e.g. *No one had the wit to bring a bottle-opener.*
3 (plural noun) Your wits are the ability to think and act quickly in a difficult situation, e.g. *She used her wits when the chair caught fire.*
4 (phrase) If someone is **at their wits' end**, they are so worried and exhausted by problems or difficulties that they do not know what to do.

witch, witches

(noun) a woman who claimed to have magic powers. [masculine: **warlock**]
[Old English *wicca* = witch]

witchcraft

(noun) the skill or art of using magic powers, especially evil ones.

Similar words: wizardry, sorcery, black magic

with

1 (preposition) e.g. *Walk home with me.*
2 (phrase; informal) **With it** means fashionable and up-to-date.

withdraw, withdraws, withdrawing, withdrew, withdrawn

1 (verb) If you withdraw something, you remove it or take it out, e.g. *I withdrew all my money from the bank.*
2 to go away from a place or situation, e.g. *The British army withdrew from France in 1940... She withdrew from the argument.*
3 If you withdraw a remark, you say that you wish to change or deny it.
withdrawal (noun)

withdrawn

1 past participle of **withdraw**.
2 (adjective) unusually shy or quiet.

wither, withers, withering, withered

1 (verb) If a plant withers, or if heat or lack of water withers it, it wilts or shrivels up and dies.
2 (plural noun) A horse's withers are the highest part of its back behind its neck.

within

(preposition, adverb) e.g. *Within these walls lies hidden treasure...*

without

(preposition) e.g. *He did it without any help.*

withstand, withstands, withstanding, withstood

(verb) When something withstands a force, it survives it or does not give in to it, e.g. *The walls had to withstand high winds.*

witness, witnesses, witnessing, witnessed

1 (noun) someone who has seen an event such as an accident and can describe what happened.
2 someone who appears in a court of law to say what they know about a crime or other event.
3 someone who writes their name on a document that someone else has signed, to confirm that it is really that person's signature.
4 (verb; formal) If you witness an event, you see it.
[Old English *witan* = to know]

Similar words: (noun: sense 1) bystander, onlooker, eyewitness

witter, witters, wittering, wittered

(verb; informal) If you say that someone is wittering on about something, you mean they are saying a lot of silly and boring things.

witty, wittier, wittiest

(adjective) amusing in a clever way.
wittily (adverb) **witticism** (noun)

wives plural of wife.

wizard, wizards

1 (noun) a man with magic powers, usually in a fairy story.
2 an expert at something, e.g. *a wizard with cars*

wizardry

(noun) something that is very cleverly done, e.g. *technological wizardry.*

wobble, wobbles, wobbling, wobbled

(verb) If something wobbles, it shakes or moves

from side to side because it is loose or unsteady,
e.g. *She wobbled and then fell.*
wobbly (adjective)
[German *wabbeln* = waver]

wodge, wodges
(noun; informal) a large amount or thick lump of
something, e.g. *I cut myself a wodge of cheese.*

wok, woks
(noun) a large, bowl-shaped, metal pan used for
Chinese-style cooking.
[a Chinese word]

woke past tense of **wake.**

woken past participle of **wake.**

wolf, wolves; wolfs, wolfing, wolfed
1 (noun) a wild animal related to the dog that
hunts in packs and kills other animals for food.
2 (verb; informal) If you wolf food or wolf it
down, you eat it up quickly and greedily.
3 (phrase) If someone **cries wolf,** they ask for
help so often when they do not need it that
people do not believe them when they really are
in danger or trouble.
4 A **wolf in sheep's clothing** is someone who
appears to be pleasant or harmless, but is in fact
rather dangerous.

wolf-whistle, wolf-whistles
(noun) a two-note whistle usually made by a man
to show he likes a woman's appearance.

woman, women
(noun) an adult, female human being.
womanly (adjective)
[Old English *wifmann* = woman human being]

womanhood
1 (noun) the state of being a woman rather than
a girl.
2 women in general, e.g. *a perfect specimen of
English womanhood.*

womb, wombs (pronounced **woom**)
(noun) A woman's womb is the part inside her
body where her unborn baby grows. Womb is a
non-technical word for **uterus.**

wonder, wonders, wondering, wondered
1 (verb) If you wonder about something, you
think about it with curiosity or doubt.
2 (noun) something or someone that surprises
and amazes people, e.g. *the wonders of modern
technology.*
3 a feeling of surprise and amazement.
4 (adjective) extremely clever or skilful, e.g.
Hendry was the wonder boy of snooker.

Similar words: (noun: sense 2) marvel, miracle

wonderful
1 (adjective) making you feel very happy and
pleased, e.g. *It was wonderful to breathe fresh
air again.*
2 very impressive, e.g. *The moon landings were a
wonderful achievement.*
wonderfully (adverb)

Similar words: (sense 2) miraculous, marvellous

wonky, wonkier, wonkiest
1 (adjective; informal) unsteady, e.g. *a wonky
table.*
2 unreliable and likely to break down, e.g. *My
knee is wonky since I banged it.*
[Old English *wancol* = wavering or unsteady]

wood, woods
1 (noun) e.g. *Trees give us wood.*
2 a large area of trees growing near each other.
3 (phrase) If you **can't see the wood for the trees,**
you are so involved with the details of a
situation that you have lost track of what are the
important things about it.

wooded
(adjective) covered in trees, e.g. *a wooded valley.*

wooden
1 (adjective) made of wood, e.g. *a wooden box.*
2 Behaviour which is wooden is stiff and shows
little life, e.g. *Many amateur actors are wooden
on stage.*
woodenly (adverb)

woodland, woodlands
(noun) land that is mostly covered with trees.

woodlouse, woodlice
(noun) a very small, grey crustacean that looks
rather like an insect, with 14 legs.

woodpecker, woodpeckers
(noun) a climbing bird with a long, sharp beak.

wood pulp
(noun) wood that has been crushed to a pulp to
be used to make paper.

woodwind
(adjective) Woodwind instruments are musical
instruments that are played by being blown into
but not made of brass, e.g. flute, oboe, clarinet,
and bassoon.

woodwork
(noun) the craft of making things out of wood.

woodworm, woodworm or **woodworms**
(noun) the larva of a kind of beetle. Woodworms
make holes in wood by feeding on it.

wool, wools
1 (noun) the hair that grows on sheep, goats, etc.
2 yarn spun from the wool of animals which is
used to knit, weave, etc.
3 (phrase) If you **pull the wool over someone's
eyes,** you tell them something that is not true to
deceive them.

woollen, woollens
1 (adjective) made from wool.
2 (noun) Woollens are clothes made of wool.

woolly, woollies; woollier, woolliest
1 (adjective) made of wool, e.g. *a woolly cap.*
2 (noun) a woollen garment, e.g. *I must put my
winter woollies on.*
3 (adjective) If you describe people or their
thoughts as woolly, you mean they seem
confused and unclear.

woozy, woozier, wooziest
(adjective; informal) dazed, unsteady and unable
to think clearly.

These words end MB. Can you add to the list? lamb climb limb bomb comb tomb crumb dumb.

word, words, wording, worded
  1 (noun) e.g. *What word shall I write?... Can we have a word?... The word got out that he was leaving... I give you my word... Give the word, and I'll go.*
  2 (verb) to choose your words carefully, e.g. *How would you word the advertisement?*
  wording (noun)
  3 (phrase) If you **have words** with someone, you have an argument with them.
  4 If someone **has the last word** in an argument or discussion, they make the final comment that settles the issue.
  5 If something is **the last word** in, for example, fashion, it is the latest in design, e.g. *The car was the last word in luxury.*

word-perfect
  (adjective) If you are word-perfect, you are able to repeat from memory the exact words of something you have learned.

word processing
  (noun) the production, storage and organization of documents, letters, etc. with a word processor.

word processor, word processors
  (noun) an electronic machine with a keyboard and a VDU, used to produce, store and organize letters, documents, etc.

work, works, working, worked
  1 (verb) e.g. *I was working as a waitress in a cocktail bar.*
  2 (noun) e.g. *I can't find work.*
  3 (noun) something done or made as a result of effort, e.g. *a work of art.*
  4 e.g. *Can you work this machine?... The clock won't work... the rope worked loose... She worked herself into a rage.*
  5 (noun) A works is a place where a number of people are employed to make something or where an industrial process is carried out, e.g. *the locomotive works.*
  6 (plural noun) Works are large-scale building, digging or general construction activities, e.g. *Civil engineering works caused a traffic jam.*

work off
  (phrasal verb) If you work off a feeling, you gradually overcome it by doing something energetic or violent, e.g. *He worked off his anger by chopping wood all afternoon.*

work out
  1 (phrasal verb) If you work out a solution to a problem, you find the answer.
  2 e.g. *Don't worry, it will work out OK in the end.*
  3 If you work out, you practise physical exercises or do athletics training.

work up
  1 (phrasal verb) If you work up to something, you gradually progress towards it.
  2 If you work yourself up or work someone else up, you make yourself or the other person very upset or angry about something.
  worked-up (adjective)

workable
  (adjective) Something workable can operate successfully, e.g. *Is it a workable system?*

workaholic, workaholics
  (noun) a person who finds it difficult to stop working and to enjoy their leisure.

workday, workdays
  (noun) a day on which work is done, usually for an agreed number of hours.

worker, workers
  1 (noun) a person employed in a particular industry or business and who has no responsibility for it.
  2 someone who does a particular kind of job, e.g. *a research worker.*
  3 a female member of a colony of ants, bees or wasps that cannot produce any young but searches for food and cares for the colony's larvae.

workforce, workforces
  (noun) the number of people who work in a particular industry, company, region or country.

working, workings
  1 (adjective) Working people have jobs which they are paid to do.
  2 A working day or week is the number of hours that are worked during a day or a week.
  3 (noun) In maths, your working is a record of the steps by which the solution is reached, e.g. *Show your working for all questions.*

working class, classes
  (noun) The working class or working classes are the group of people in society who do not own much property and who do jobs which involve physical rather than mental skills.

workman, workmen
  (noun) a man whose job involves using physical rather than mental skills.

workmanship
  (noun) the skill with which something is made or a job completed.

workout, workouts
  (noun) a session of physical exercise or training.

workshop, workshops
  1 (noun) a room or building used for making or repairing things, e.g. *an engineering workshop.*
  2 A workshop on a subject is a period of discussion or practical work in which a group of people learn about the subject, e.g. *a drama workshop.*

world, worlds
  1 (noun) The world is the earth, the planet we live on.
  2 You can use world to mean people generally, e.g. *In the eyes of the world, I'm a do-nothing kind of a guy.*
  3 a division of the earth, its history or its people, e.g. *the Arab World; the Ancient World.*
  4 a field of activity and the people involved in it, e.g. *the world of television.*
  5 (adjective) e.g. *world famous... a world power.*
  6 (phrase) If you **think the world** of someone, you like or admire them very much.
  [Old English *weorold* from *wer* = man + *ald* = age]

Every English word includes a vowel sound; a, e, i, o, u, are the vowels
but y often makes a vowel sound....

world war, wars
(noun) a war that involves countries all over the world, e.g. *World War II.*

worldwide
(adjective) throughout the world, e.g. *a worldwide economic depression.*

worm, worms
1 (noun) a small, boneless, legless animal with a long, thin body which lives in the soil or off other creatures.
2 (phrase) If you **worm your way into** someone's confidence, you gradually make them trust you, often to gain some advantage.

worm out
(phrasal verb) If you worm information out of someone, you gradually find it out from them by constant questioning, even though they had wanted to keep it secret.

worn
1 past participle of **wear.**
2 (adjective) damaged or thin due to long use.

worn-out
1 (adjective) too old or too damaged to be useful any more, e.g. *a worn-out sofa.*
2 extremely tired, e.g. *Sit down, headteacher, you look worn-out.*

worried
(adjective) unhappy and anxious about a problem or about something unpleasant that might happen.

Similar words: uneasy, concerned, anxious

worry, worries, worrying, worried
1 (verb) to feel anxious, fearful and uneasy about a problem or about something unpleasant that might happen.
2 (noun) e.g. *Housing was their main worry.*
[Old English *wyrgan* = strangle]

Similar words: fret, bother, concern, trouble

worse
1 (adjective, adverb; comparative) e.g. *bad worse worst; badly worse worst.*
2 (phrase) If someone is **none the worse** for something that has happened to them, they have not been harmed by it, e.g. *He was none the worse for his fall.*

worsen, worsens, worsening, worsened
(verb) to get worse, e.g. *Oil pollution seems to be worsening.*

Similar words: deteriorate, decline, aggravate,

worse off
1 (adjective) having less money than before or than someone else, e.g. *The budget made the elderly worse off.*
2 e.g. *We had food for two days. Tim's lot were worse off than us with no food at all.*

worship, worships, worshipping, worshipped
1 (verb) If you worship a god, you show your love and respect by praying or singing hymns.
2 If you worship someone, you love them or admire them very much so that often you do not notice their faults or weaknesses.
3 (noun) a general name for church services.
4 great love or admiration for someone or something, e.g. *hero worship.*
worshipful (adjective) **worshipper** (noun)
[Old English *weorth* = worth + *-ship* = rank or position]

Similar words: (sense 2) adore, idolize

worst
1 (adjective, adverb; superlative) e.g. *bad, worse worst; badly, worse, worst.*
2 If you say that something might happen **if the worst comes to the worst,** you mean that it might happen if the situation is as bad as it possibly could be, e.g. *If the worst comes to the worst, I'll have to sell the house.*

worth
1 (preposition) e.g. *It's worth £50,000... This job's worth doing properly.*
2 (noun) e.g. *£5's worth of sweets.*
[Old English *weorth* = worth]

worthless
(adjective) having no real value or use, e.g. *The goods were worthless when they finally arrived.*
worthlessness (noun)

worthwhile
(adjective) important enough or valuable enough to justify the time, money or effort spent on it, e.g. *Taking time to look around you is always worthwhile.*

worthy, worthier, worthiest
(adjective) If someone or something is worthy of something, they deserve it, e.g. *He was a worthy winner of the singles title.*

would
1 (verb) e.g. *I felt confident that everything would be all right.*
2 e.g. *If you can manage to help I would be very grateful... Would you like a drink?*

wound, wounds, wounding, wounded
1 (noun) an injury to part of your body, especially a cut in your skin and flesh, caused by a knife, gun or other weapon.
2 (verb) If someone wounds you, they damage your body using a gun, knife or other weapon.
3 If you are wounded by what someone says or does, your feelings are hurt.

wrap, wraps, wrapping, wrapped
1 (verb) If you wrap something, you fold a piece of paper or cloth tightly around it to cover or enclose it.
2 (phrase) If you **keep something under wraps,** you keep it secret.
wrapper (noun) **wrapping** (noun)

wrap up
1 (verb) e.g. *Wrap up well. It's cold today.*
2 (informal) If you wrap up, for example, a deal, you complete it in a satisfactory way.

wrath (pronounced **roth**)
(noun; literary) great anger, e.g. *The wrath of God.*

....shy fly cry hymn crypt gypsy.

wreath, wreaths (pronounced **reeth**)
(noun) an arrangement of flowers and leaves, often in the shape of a circle, put on a grave as a sign of remembrance for the dead person.
[Old English *writha* = coil or twisted band]

wreck, wrecks, wrecking, wrecked
1 (verb) If someone wrecks something, they break it, destroy it or spoil it completely.
2 (noun) a ship, car, plane, etc which has been badly damaged in an accident.
3 If you say someone is a wreck, you mean that they are in a very poor physical or mental state of health and cannot cope with life, e.g. *You'll end up a wreck if you don't rest.*

wreckage
(noun) Wreckage is what remains after something has been badly damaged or destroyed.

wren, wrens
(noun) a very small, brown songbird.

wrench, wrenches, wrenching, wrenched
1 (verb) If you wrench something, you give it a sudden and violent twist or pull, especially to remove it from something, e.g. *The firemen wrenched the door off its hinges.*
2 (noun) a metal tool with parts which can be adjusted to fit around nuts or bolts to loosen or tighten them, e.g. *a monkey wrench.*
[Old English *wrencan* = turn or twist]

wrestling
(noun) a sport in which two people fight and try to throw or pin their opponent to the ground.
wrestler (noun) **wrestle** (verb)

wretch, wretches
(noun; old-fashioned) someone who is thought to be wicked or very unfortunate, e.g. *The poor wretch in the cell groaned and fell down.*
[Old English *wrecca* = exile or despised person]

wretched (pronounced **ret**-shid)
(adjective) very unhappy or unfortunate, e.g. *How that wretched woman suffered!*

wriggle, wriggles, wriggling, wriggled
1 (verb) to twist and turn the body or a part of the body using quick movements, e.g. *They wriggled their toes.*
2 If you wriggle out of doing something that you do not want to do, you manage to avoid doing it.
[Old German *wriggelen* = to wriggle a lot]

-wright, -wrights (pronounced **rite**)
(suffix) -wright is used to form nouns that refer to a person who makes something, e.g. *a playwright... a wheelwright... a shipwright.*
[Old English *wryhta* = craftsman]

wring, wrings, wringing, wrung
1 (verb) When you wring a wet cloth or wring it out, you squeeze the water out of it by twisting it.

2 If you wring your hands, you hold them together and twist and turn them, usually because you are worried or upset.
wrinkled (adjective) **wrinkly** (adjective)
[Old English *wringan* = to wring]

wrinkle, wrinkles
(noun) Wrinkles are lines in someone's skin.
wrinkled (adjective)
[Old English *wrinclian* = to wind around]

Similar words: crease, fold

wrist, wrists
(noun) the joint between your hand and your arm.

wristwatch, wristwatches
(noun) a watch with a strap etc., which you wear round your wrist.

write, writes, writing, wrote, written
(verb) e.g. *Please write your name here.*
[Old English *writan* = to scratch marks in wood]

write off
(phrasal verb; informal) If you write off a vehicle, you damage it so badly in a crash that it is not worth repairing.
write-off (noun)

write up
(phrasal verb) If you write something up, you write a full account of it, often using notes that you have made previously.

writer, writers
(noun) a person who writes books, stories or articles; an author.

writhe, writhes, writhing, writhed (pronounced rie-th)
(verb) If you writhe, you twist and turn your body, often because you are in pain.

writing, writings
(noun) e.g. *Your writing is very neat... The book contains some very witty writing.*

written past participle of **write.**

wrong, wrongs
1 (adjective) e.g. *the wrong answer... It is wrong to steal... There was something wrong with my brain – I kept thinking I was a spiny anteater called Alfie.*
2 (noun) an unjust action or situation, e.g. *Two wrongs do not make a right.*
wrongly (adverb)
[Old English *wrang* = injustice]

Similar words: (adjective) false, inaccurate, incorrect

X

Xmas
(noun; informal) Xmas means the same as Christmas.
[in Greek *X* is the first letter of *Christos* = Christ]

X-ray, X-rays, X-raying, X-rayed
1 (noun) X-rays are used by doctors to examine the bones or organs inside a person's body.

Some surnames come from the jobs our ancestors did: Smith Taylor Wright Butcher Baker.

2 (verb) to make a picture of the inside of the body by passing X-rays through it.

xylophone, xylophones (pronounced **zy**-lo-fone) (noun) a musical instrument made of a row of wooden bars of different lengths, played by hitting the bars with special hammers.
[Greek *xulon* + *phōnē* = wood sound]

Y

yacht, yachts (pronounced **yot**)
(noun) a boat with sails or an engine, used for racing or for pleasure trips.
yachting (noun) **yachtsman** (noun)
yachtswoman (noun)

yam, yams
(noun) a root vegetable which grows in tropical regions, also called a sweet potato.
[Portuguese *inhame* = yam]

yank, yanks, yanking, yanked
1 (verb) to pull or jerk something suddenly with a lot of force.
2 (noun; informal) an American.

yap, yaps, yapping, yapped
(verb) If a dog yaps, it barks a lot with a high-pitched sound.

yard, yards
1 (noun) a unit of length. (1 yard = 36 inches = 3 feet = 91cm)
2 an enclosed area that is usually next to a building, e.g. *a builder's yard.*
[sense 1: Old English *gierd* = twig or rod; sense 2: Old English *geard* = enclosure]

yarn, yarns
1 (noun) thread used for knitting or making cloth.
2 (informal) a story that someone tells, often with invented details to make it more interesting or exciting, e.g. *And all I ask is a merry yarn from a laughing fellow rover.*

yawn, yawns, yawning, yawned
(verb) e.g. *She was so tired, she couldn't stop yawning... A great gap yawned between the two ships.*

ye (an old word)
1 (pronoun) you, e.g. *O come all ye faithful.*
2 (definite article) the, e.g. *Ye olde tea shoppe.*

year, years
1 (noun) a period of 12 months or 365 days (366 days in a leap year), the time taken for the earth to make one revolution around the sun.
2 (phrase) If something happens **year in, year out**, it happens every year, e.g. *They went to Blackpool in September year in, year out.*
yearly (adjective and adverb)

yearn, yearns, yearning, yearned (rhymes with **learn**)
(verb) If you yearn for something, you want it very much indeed, e.g. *She yearned to go home.*
yearning (noun)

yeast, yeasts
(noun) a kind of fungus which is used to make bread rise, and to make liquids ferment to produce alcohol, e.g. in beer making.

yell, yells, yelling, yelled
1 (verb) to shout loudly.
2 (noun) a loud shout.

yellow, yellower, yellowest
1 (noun, adjective) a colour.
2 (adjective; informal) If you say someone is yellow, you mean they are cowardly.

Yellow Pages
(plural noun) a telephone directory in which businesses are listed under headings describing the kinds of goods or services provided.

yelp, yelps, yelping, yelped
(verb) When people or animals yelp, they give a sudden, short cry.

yen
(noun) the main unit of money in Japan.
[Japanese *en* = round thing or dollar]

yesterday
1 (noun, adverb) the day before today.
2 the past, e.g. *The worker of today is different from the worker of yesterday.*

yet
(adverb, conjunction) e.g. *Have you had your lunch yet?... I am sorry to bring up this subject yet again... Everything was blown to pieces, yet he escaped unharmed.*

yeti, yetis (pronounced **yet**-tee)
(noun) A yeti, or 'abominable snowman', is a large, hairy, apelike animal which some people believe exists in the Himalayas.
[a Tibetan word]

yew, yews
(noun) an evergreen tree with bright red berries.

yield, yields, yielding, yielded
1 (verb) to give in, e.g. *The only way to get rid of a temptation is to yield to it.*
2 to break or give way, e.g. *The rusty lock yielded to a blow from my hammer.*
3 to produce, e.g. *One acre yielded only 500 pounds of rice.*

yippee
(exclamation) an exclamation of happiness.

yob, yobs or **yobbo**
(noun; informal) a noisy, badly behaved boy or young man.

yoga (pronounced **yoe**-ga)
(noun) a Hindu method of mental and physical exercise or discipline.
[a Sanskrit word meaning 'union']

yoghurt, yoghurts (also spelled **yoghourt** or **yogurt**; pronounced **yog**-gurt)
(noun) a slightly sour, thick liquid made from milk that has had bacteria added to it.
[a Turkish word]

Letter Y probably began as a picture of a hook, possibly a thumbstick – or perhaps even a tree.

yokel, yokels (pronounced **yoe**-kl)
(noun; informal) If you call someone a yokel, you mean they live in the country, and you think they are rather slow-witted and old-fashioned.

yolk, yolks (rhymes with **joke**)
(noun) the yellow part in the middle of an egg.
[Old English *geoloca*, from *geolu* = yellow]

yonder
(adverb, adjective; an old word) over there, e.g. *over that hill yonder... Look yonder, shepherds.*

you
1 (second person pronoun) e.g. *You are better than me at tennis.*
2 'You' can be used to mean people in general e.g. *You can buy these anywhere.*

young, younger, youngest
1 (adjective) a young person, animal or plant has not lived very long and is not yet mature.
2 (noun) The young of an animal are its babies.

Similar words: (adjective) youthful, juvenile
(noun) offspring.

youngster, youngsters
(noun) a child or young person.

your
(pronoun) e.g. *Where's your father?... The system is geared to taking your GCSE when you're 16... I am grateful for your coming so soon, doctor.*

yours
(pronoun) e.g. *Our house is older than yours.*

yourself, yourselves
(pronoun) e.g. *You'll have to do it yourself.*

youth, youths
1 (noun) Someone's youth is the period of their life before they are a fully mature adult.
2 A youth is a boy or young man.
3 young people, e.g. *the youth of today.*
youthful (adjective) **youthfully** (adverb)

youth hostel, hostels
(noun) a place where mainly young people can stay cheaply when they are on holiday.

yo-yo, yo-yos
(noun) a round wooden or plastic toy attached to a piece of string.

Yugoslav, Yugoslavs (pronounced **yoo**-goe-slahv)
1 (adjective) belonging to Yugoslavia.
2 (noun) someone who comes from Yugoslavia.

yuppie, yuppies
(noun) If you say people are yuppies, you think they are young, middle-class, and earn a lot of money which they spend on themselves. Yuppie stands for 'Young urban professional'.

Z

Zambian, Zambians (pronounced **zam**-bee-an)
1 (adjective) belonging to Zambia.
2 (noun) someone who comes from Zambia.

zany, zanier, zaniest
(adjective) funny in an odd and ridiculous way, e.g *The Marx Brothers' films were really zany.*
[Italian *zanni* = clown]

zap, zaps, zapping, zapped
1 (verb; informal) to do something quickly or suddenly; e.g. *We zapped into action.*
2 to hit or kill with a gun, e.g. *We zapped the androids with our space blasters.*

zebra, zebras
(noun) a type of African wild horse with black and white stripes over its body.

zebra crossing, crossings
(noun) a place, marked with black and white stripes, where people can cross the road safely.

zero, zeros or **zeroes, zeroing, zeroed**
1 the number 0.
2 freezing point, 0° Centigrade.
3 (adjective) e.g. *Its running costs were zero.*
4 (verb) to home in on something, e.g. *The missile zeroed in on the tank.*
[Arabic *sifr* = empty]

zero hour
(noun) the time at which something is planned to begin, for example a military operation.

zest
(noun) a feeling of pleasure and enthusiasm, e.g. *She had a zest for life.*

zigzag, zigzags, zigzagging, zigzagged
(verb) to move forward by going at an angle first right and then left, e.g. *We zigzagged up the hill.*

zilch
(noun; informal) nothing.

Zimbabwean, Zimbabweans (pronounced **zim**-bahb-wee-an)
1 (adjective) belonging to Zimbabwe.
2 (noun) someone who comes from Zimbabwe.

zimmer frame
(noun) a walking aid that people with weak legs can hold in front of them for support.
[German *zimmer* = room]

zinc
(noun) a bluish-white metal used in alloys and to coat other metals to stop them rusting.

zip, zips, zipping, zipped
1 (noun) a long, narrow fastener, e.g. *My zip is stuck.*
2 (verb) When you zip something or zip it up, you fasten it using a zip.
3 (phrase) If you zip into action, you move very quickly to start something.

zipper, zippers
(noun) the same as a zip.

zodiac (pronounced **zoe**-dee-ak)
1 (noun) an imaginary belt in the sky which

Letter Z was a weapon, probably one using two sticks. Zayin was a word meaning weapon.

contains the planets and stars which astrologers think are important influences on people.
2 a diagram used by astrologers to represent the positions of the planets and stars. It is divided into 12 sections, each with a special name and symbol, e.g. Taurus, Leo, Pisces.
[Greek *zōidiakos kuklos* = circle of signs]

zombie, zombies
(noun; informal) someone who is unaware of what is going on around them and seems to act without thinking about what they are doing.
[In African witchcraft, a zombie is a dead body said to be revived by magic]

zone, zones
(noun) an area that has particular features or properties, e.g. *a no-parking zone.*
[Latin *zona* = belt]

zoo, zoos
(noun) a place where live animals are kept so that people can look at them.

zoology (pronounced zoo-ol-loj-jee)
(noun) the scientific study of animals.
zoological (adjective) **zoologist** (noun)
[Greek *zōion* = animal + *-logy* = study of]

zoom, zooms, zooming, zoomed
1 (verb) to move very quickly, e.g. *They zoomed down on their bikes.*
2 If a camera zooms in on something, it gives a close-up picture of it.

zoom lens
(noun) a camera lens that allows the user to move quickly between wide angle and close-up shots.

Remember that the words in this dictionary are only a small proportion of the 800,000 or so words in the English language. To find many words that you come across, you will need to use bigger or more specialist dictionaries. Make sure you know what dictionaries are available in your library.

Parts of speech

Every word in the English language, when used in a sentence, can be classified into one of the 8 parts of speech:

verb
noun
pronoun
adjective
adverb
conjunction
preposition
interjection

Many words can be more than one part of speech, depending on how they are used, e.g. *play* is a noun in 'We watched the Shakespeare play'.
play is a verb in 'Let's play cricket'.

Action

Use each of these words in at least two sentences as a different part of speech each time:

cheer   aged   park   brown   match

love   tomorrow   common   horse   glass

Verbs

'Verb' is from the Latin *verbum* meaning 'a word'. This gives us a clue that the verb is the most important type of word in human speech. Every sentence must have one before it can 'say' anything.

We can think of verbs as 'doing' or 'being' words, e.g. I *am*, she *runs*, he *thought*, we *were sitting*, they *have returned*.

There are three main tenses of verbs: Past, Present and Future

PAST	PRESENT	FUTURE
I ran	I run	I shall run
I thought	I think	I shall think
I was	I am	I shall be

The word 'tense' comes from the Latin *tempus* meaning 'time'.

If you are studying a foreign language, it might be helpful to know the full list of major tenses:

Present: *I do*
Continuous present: *I am doing*
Future: *I shall do*
Continuous future: *I shall be doing*
Imperfect: *I was doing, I used to do*
Perfect: *I have done*
Continuous perfect: *I have been doing*

Past: *I did*
Continuous past: *I was doing*
Pluperfect: *I had done*
Continuous pluperfect: *I had been doing*
Future perfect: *I shall have done*
Continuous future perfect: *I shall have been doing*
Conditional: *I would do*

When the verb has 'to' before it, it is called an infinitive, e.g. *to run, to cry*. Placing a word between *to* and its verb is called splitting the infinitive. Split infinitives should be avoided if possible.

Wrong: I want *to quickly find* him.
Right: I want *to find* him *quickly*.

Wrong: *To boldly go* where no man has gone before.
Right: *To go boldly* ... or *Boldly to go* ...

The present and past participles of a verb can be very useful to add variety to your sentence structure, as they can begin a sentence.

e.g. *Running* along the road, I bumped into a lamppost.
(present participle)
Knocked down for the seventh time Fred still got up.
(past participle)

careful, though, that the subject of the participle must be the subject of the next main verb. Otherwise, we have this sort of thing:

Running along the road, a lamppost hit me.

Action

What is wrong with these?
1 The boy done well!
2 I walk up to the house, knock on the door and went inside.
3 The man catched the ball and throwed it to the dog.

Nouns

Nouns are the names we give to all the things we can experience or identify.

Common nouns name objects which exist in reasonable numbers, e.g. *table, boy, apple, ship, town*.

Proper nouns name particular persons, things or places, e.g. *Peter, Buckingham Palace, Watford*.

Abstract nouns name what we can experience through our minds and emotions but not through the five senses, e.g. *love, goodness, hope, friendship*.

Collective nouns name groups of things, e.g. *a flock of birds*. They can be used as singular and plural, but not at the same time, e.g. It is wrong to say '*A crowd is coming and they will soon be here*'. Use either 'is' and 'it' or 'are' and 'they'.

Action

1 Can you name a common noun and a proper noun beginning with each letter of the alphabet?
2 Try the same for collective and abstract nouns. How many letters can you do?

Pronouns

Pronouns are words that stand in place of nouns. They cut down repetition of the same words, e.g. instead of:

Mrs Brown cleaned Mrs Brown's car then drove Mrs Brown's son Philip to Philip's football match;

we have:

Mrs Brown cleaned her car then drove her son Philip to his football match.

Main pronouns: *I, me, you, him, her, we, us, he, she, it, they, them, one, someone, somebody, anyone, anybody, no one, nobody, none, both, all, everyone, everybody*.

A common confusion is whether to say 'I' or 'me' in sentences like:

Sid and I like going to the pictures.
Please give *Sid and me* some money for the pictures.

The rule is very simple. Ignore the other person and use the pronoun that would be correct if you were the only one involved.

Remember that 'none' is singular, being short for 'not one', e.g

The horsebox overturned, but of the six ponies none was injured.

Only use 'you' in your essays if you are giving direct advice to the reader. The sentence you are reading is a perfect example.

Adjectives

Adjectives add descriptive force to a noun, but they need to be used thoughtfully. Vague ones like *exciting, great* and *super* mean very little unless you explain why you feel this way.

Try not to use 'nice', which has lost almost all its meaning. Use 'good' very carefully, too.

This example shows how adjectives can affect the meaning of a sentence:

The man fell from the window.
The desperate man fell from the moonlit window.
The drunken man fell from the open window.

NB Adjectives of nationality (*Welsh American, Dutch,* etc.) normally begin with a capital letter (exception: *french window*).

Action

1 Write the story of a picnic using the word *nice* as often as possible. Exchange it with a partner, and rewrite their story, replacing *nice* throughout with more precise adjectives.

2 From the dictionary find as many adjectives of nationality as you can, putting them in alphabetical order under their continents – America, Europe, Asia, Africa, others.

Adverbs

An adverb adds to the sense of a verb or of another adverb. It usually answers one of the questions **how, when** or **where** about the verb,

e.g. He ran (*well, yesterday, home*)

Adverbs which tell **how** usually end '*ly*'. This sometimes causes spelling problems, but it does not need to.

Take care when you use comparative and superlative adverbs.

Wrong: *She spoke louder.*
Right: *She spoke more loudly.*

Wrong: *He ran quickest.*
Right: *He ran most quickly.*

Action

1 Look at these correct spellings, then write down the rule in your own words

sincere – sincerely
faithful – faithfully
definite – definitely
helpful – helpfully
temporary – temporarily
happy – happily

2 Explain how the meaning of this sentence is changed if the word 'only', is moved about:

Only boxers may enter the ring.

3 What went wrong with this conversation? How could the mistake have been avoided?

A: *Your hair needs cutting badly.*
B: *Really? Can you recommend a bad hairdresser?*

Conjunctions

Some young writers make their work monotonous to read by stringing simple sentences together with words like 'and', 'but', then', 'so'. These conjunctions (co-ordinating) can often be replaced by others (subordinate) which make the relationships between your ideas clearer. Try using conjunctions such as:

when   before   because   as   if

whether   although   while

e.g. He was tired *and* went to bed.
(co-ordinate)
As he was tired, he went to bed.
(subordinate)

If you are asked a question, do not begin your answer with 'because' unless the answer has two parts.

e.g. Question: *Why did you go out?*
    Answer: Wrong: *Because I felt sick.*
        Right: *I felt sick.*

The first one is quite acceptable in spoken English, but is not correctly constructed and should not be written.

Action

The question is: *Are you coming out this evening?* Make up eight answers, each containing a subordinate conjunction.

Prepositions

A preposition shows the relationship of one noun to another. The most common ones are:

after   around   at   beside   between

by   from   in   off   over   through

to   under   up   with

Certain words always take the same preposition:

e.g. different *from* (not 'than' or 'to')
    I live *in* Southampton (not 'at')
    We went *to* Manchester (not 'up' or 'over')

Do not use 'like' to mean as if:

e.g. Wrong: *I looked like I had been painted.*

e.g. Right: *I looked as if I had been painted.*

Some writers will not end a sentence with a preposition. This is not a rule. Sir Winston Churchill mocked the style caused by this practice when he said:

'This is the kind of nonsense up with which I shall not put.'

However, as prepositions are usually short and not emphasized, they do give sentences a weak ending.

Action

Write sentences containing all the main prepositions listed above.

Interjections

An interjection is the only part of speech that stands alone, grammatically unconnected with the words around it. Examples are:

Hello.   Ha! ha!   Hurray!   Alas!

Oh!   Bravo!   Pooh!   Tut-tut!

Hush!   Encore!   Hear, hear!

Action

1 The origin of 'interjection' will help you remember its function. Find out where it comes from and what its literal meaning is.
2 When might you use these: *Alas! Bravo! Tut tut! Encore! Hear-hear! Oh! ?*

Basic words

List A

These 205 words are used so often that they make up about half of all reading. If you know these, half your spelling will be right.

a	about	after	again	all	always	am	an	and	another
any	are	as	ask	at	away	back	bad	be	because
been	before	best	big	bird	black	blue	boy	bring	but
by	call	came	can	come	could	day	did	do	dog
done	down	eat	every	far	fast	father	fell	find	first
five	fly	for	four (4)	found	from	gave	get	girl	give
go	going	good	got	green	had	hand	has	have	he
head	held	help	her	hero	him	home	house	how	I
if	in	into	is	it	jump	just	keep	know	last
left	let	like	little	live	long	look	made	make	man
many	may	me	men	more	mother	Mr	Mrs	much	must
my	never	new	next	no	not	now	of	off	old
on	once	one	only	open	or	other	our	out	over
own	play	put	ran	right	road	rod	room	round	run
said	sat	saw	say	school	see	she	should	sing	sit
so	some	soon	stop	take	tell	than	that	the	their
them	then	there	these	they	thing	think	this	three	time
to	too	tree	two	under	up	us	very	walk	want
was	we	well	went	were	what	when	where	which	white
who	why	will	wish	with	woman	women	work	would	year
yellow	yes	yet	you	young	your				

List B

Here are some 300 words that are often misspelt. Make sure you know their meanings as well as how to spell them.

absence	accelerator	accent	accidentally	accommodate
achieved	acknowledge	acquainted	address	advertisement
aerial	aggravate	agreeable	all right	amateur
among	answer	Antarctic	anxiety	apparent
appearance	appropriate	Arctic	argument	arrangements
article	ascend	athletic	aunt	autumn
awful	bachelor	beautiful	because	beginning
believed	benefited	bicycle	breakfast	breathe
Britain	build	business	café	calm
captain	careful	catalogue	cemetery	certain
character	chemistry	chocolate	choice	Christmas
clothes	college	colour	coming	committee
comparative	comparison	competent	completely	conscience
conscientious	conscious	consistent	convenience	copies
course	courteous	courtesy	crept	criticism

cupboard	cylindrical	deceive	decide	decision
definite	descend	describe	desirable	desperate
different	dinghy	disappeared	disappointed	disastrous
discipline	disease	dissatisfied	doctor	does
efficiency	eighth	eliminated	embarrassed	emphasize
encyclopaedia	enjoy	enquire	enthusiasm	envelope
equipped	especially	essential	etc.	everybody
exaggerated	excellent	except	exciting	exercise
exhausted	exhibition	existence	expenses	experience
familiar	fashion	favourite	February	fictitious
financial	forecast	foreign	formerly	forty
friend	gauge	genius	geography	government
grammar	grievance	guarantee	guard	guardian
guess	handkerchief	height	heroes	humour
hungry	hurriedly	hygiene	hypocrisy	imagination
immediately	immigrate	incidentally	independent	indispensable
influential	instance	intelligence	interest	irresistible
jewellery	jewelry	kept	knowledge	laboratory
led	library	licence	lightning	literature
longitude	lose	losing	lying	maintenance
marriage	mathematics	meant	mechanical	medicine
Mediterranean	meringue	miniature	minute	minutes
mischievous	murmur	mysterious	mystery	necessarily
necessary	neighbour	niece	noticeable	nuisance
occasional	occurred	occurrence	omitted	opinion
opportunity	originally	parallel	parliament	pastime
people	perhaps	permanent	permissible	perseverance
pharmacy	physical	physics	physique	planning
pleasant	police	possesses	preference	prejudice
present	privilege	probably	procedure	proceeding
proceeds	professional	professor	pronunciation	psychology
quiet	quite	really	received	recognized
recommended	referred	refrigerator (but fridge)		remember
repetition	restaurant	rhyme	rhythm	said
satellite	scarcely	science	secondary	secretaries
seize	sentence	separate	sergeant	severely
Shakespeare	shining	siege	similar	sincerely
speak	speech	squirrel	straight	strength
successful	suppression	surprise	syllable	sympathy
symphony	synonym	taught	television	temporarily
temporary	tendency	themselves	thorough	through
tongue	tragedy	transferred	trouble	twelfth
unconscious	unnecessary	until	usually	vacuum
valuable	veterinary	view	Wednesday	went
whole	wholly	woollen	write	
yacht	you're (= you are)			

Note that this list is in strict alphabetical order, reading across the page. Study the order of words to help you to remember the correct spellings and to improve your understanding of alphabetical sequences.

Earth, Air, Fire, Water
Some words for creative writing

Dungeons and Dragons

adventure
ambush
ancient
bravery
captive
castle
cauldron
cavern
caves
chamber
charm
chest
cloak
combat
creatures
cunning
demons
dwarves
enchantment
enemy
evil
exorcism
fantasy
foe
forest
fortress
ghost
giant
gnome
goblin
good
Hallowe'en
hero
heroine
hobgoblin
imagination
incantation
invisible
jewels
knight
labyrinth
lore
magic
master
maze
mercenaries
mermaid
minotaur

mission
monster
nightmare
ogress
ordeal
passage
prison
power
pursuit
quest
riddle
runes
sandals
shadows
shield
skeleton
slime
sanctuary
slave
sorceress
spear
spell
spirit
subterranean
supernatural
superstitious
swamp
sword
talisman
time
tower
treasure
trolls
tunnel
tunic
underworld
unicorn
vampire
villain
warden
warlock
watchdog
weapon
weird
werewolf
wisdom
witch
wizard

Environment

accident
acid
additives
aerosol
agriculture
Antarctic
atmosphere
biodegradable
biosphere
carbon monoxide
chlorofluorocarbons
climate
conservation
contamination
desert
destruction
disease
disposal
domestic
earthquake
ecology
electricity
energy
epidemic
extinct
farming
fumes
gamekeeper
global warming
greenhouse effect
habitat
health
heathland
hygiene
incineration
industry
jungle
lead
litter
luxuriant
malnutrition

nature
noise
nuclear power
oceans
organic
ozone layer
pesticide
petrol
plastic
poacher
poison
pollution
population
radiation
rain
rare
reclamation
recycling
refuse
reserve
resource
rubbish
sanitation
sewage
slick
smog
stress
surplus
tobacco
toxic
transport
tropical
tundra
urbanization
vegetation
volcanoes
waste
water
weather
wildlife
woodland

Shipwreck

cabins
captain
cargo
castaway
coral
Cornwall
crew
crow's-nest
current
deck
disaster
diver
emergency
fathom
flotsam
gales
hulk
hurricane
iceberg
insurance
island
jetsam
knots
lagoon
lifeboat
lighthouse
lightning
mariner
marooned
mast

nautical
ocean
octopus
passengers
pirate
porpoise
port
prow
reef
rescue
rigging
rocks
sail
sailors
seamen
shark
smuggler
squall
squid
starboard
stern
thunder
underwater
voyage
waves
whale
whirlwind
wreckage
yacht

Space

abort
alien
Apollo
asteroid
astronaut
black hole
boosters
buggy
comet
computer
cosmonaut
countdown
crater
data
discovery
docking
Earth
exploration
galaxy
helicopter
interplanetary
interstellar
Jupiter
kaleidoscope
laser
launchpad
lift-off
light year
Mars
meteorite
Mercury
Milky Way
missile
module

moonbase
NASA
nebula
Neptune
nova
observatory
orbit
origins
planet
Pluto
pressure
propellants
quasars
radio
robot
rocket
satellite
saucer
Saturn
shuttle
solar system
spacesuit
Skylab
telescope
timewarp
tracking
UFO
universe
unknown
velocity
Venus
vortex
weightlessness
zero

Finding books in a library

Libraries often contain many thousands of books. If readers are to find the information they want quickly and easily, all these books need to be arranged in a way that makes sense to everybody.

There are many ways that books might be arranged, but in 1876 an American, Melvil Dewey, published a method which is still used in most libraries. The Dewey Decimal System of Classification is extremely flexible. Because the system uses decimal numbers, new subjects that had not even been considered in 1876 can always be added; it can never run out of numbers.

The system divides all books into ten major **classes,** numbered 0-9, according to their subjects. Each class is divided into ten **divisions,** the first division being used for general works and the other nine for related areas of knowledge. Each of the ten divisions is divided into ten **sections** and each section can have as many **subsections** as are needed, each one identified by a decimal point followed by one or more figures.

For example:

800-899 is one of the ten main classes: *Literature.*
820-829 is the division devoted to *English* literature.
821 identifies the English *poetry* section.
821.08 is a subsection containing poetry *anthologies.*

The Dewey Decimal classification

Fiction (novels and short stories) is arranged in alphabetical order under the names of authors. All fiction books by the same author will be found together.

Biography (920) is arranged in alphabetical order of the names of persons written about. Common practice is to mark biographies with B/ followed by the first three letters of the subject's surname. Alternatively, biographies are often placed in the section relating to the sphere of activity for which the subject is best known, e.g. film stars might be found among books on the cinema (791.430....).
Non-Fiction works means all other types of book. These are arranged in numerical order of class and division numbers as shown below. Libraries will have catalogues on computer, microfiche, cards, posters, folders, etc. to help you locate the sections and subsections you need.

Libraries are usually divided into **Reference** and **Lending** rooms. In each room the books will be arranged in the same numerical system and you should look in the Reference room for books you cannot find in the Lending area. Books in the Reference section are for study in the library and may not normally be borrowed to take away.

How books are arranged

000 General works
010 Bibliography
020 Library and information sciences
030 General encyclopaedias
040 General collections
050 General periodicals
060 General societies and museums
070 Journalism
080 Collected works
090 Manuscripts and rare books

100 Philosophy and psychology
110 Metaphysics: ways of knowing
120 Theories of knowledge
130 The paranormal; unexplained phenomena
140 Philosophical topics
150 Psychology
160 Logic: ways of reasoning
170 Ethics: morals and behaviour

180 Ancient and medieval philosophy	630 Agriculture: farming and food
190 Modern philosophy	640 Home economics
	650 Business and business methods
200 Religion	660 Chemical technology
210 Religious viewpoints	670 Manufactures in specific materials
220 The Bible	680 Manufactures of products
230 Christian teachings	690 Building technology
240 Christian prayer and practice	
250 Christian organizations	**700 Arts, recreations, hobbies and**
260 Work of the Christian Church	**sports**
270 History of the Christian Church	710 Town and country planning
280 Christian Churches and sects	720 Architecture
290 Other religions	730 Sculpture
	740 Drawing, decoration and design
300 Social sciences	750 Painting
310 Statistics: social surveys	760 Prints and print making
320 Politics	770 Photography
330 Economics	780 Music
340 Law	790 Hobbies, performing arts and sports
350 Public administration	
360 Social problems and services	**800 Literature**
370 Education	810 American literature
380 Commerce and communications	820 English literature
390 Customs and folklore	830 Germanic literature
	840 French literature
400 Language and linguistics	850 Italian literature
410 Comparative: common and distinctive	860 Spanish and Portuguese literature
features of languages	870 Latin literature
420 English language	880 Greek literature
430 Germanic languages	890 Other literatures
440 French language	
450 Italian language	**900 History and geography**
460 Spanish and Portuguese	910 Geography and travel
470 Latin	920 Biography
480 Greek	930 Ancient world history
490 Other languages	940 European history
	950 Asian history
500 Pure sciences	960 African history
510 Mathematics	970 North American history
520 Astronomy: space and the universe	980 South American history
530 Physics	990 History of Oceania and polar regions
540 Chemistry	
550 Geology: earth sciences	
560 Palaeontology: prehistoric life and	
fossils	Some of the terms used in this
570 Biology and physical anthropology	classification have been updated to reflect
580 Botanical sciences: plants	current library practice and to make it
590 Zoological sciences: animals	easier for readers to find the areas of
	study they need.
600 Applied sciences (technology)	
610 Medical sciences	
620 Engineering	

Words often mispronounced

There will always be disagreement about how some words should be pronounced. Regional differences exist as well as differences of class. People will argue passionately about how words should be said and what is correct often changes through custom. Some words are mispronounced, however, because users have a wrong idea of how they should be spelled or because they insist on a strictly phonetic pronunciation. In some cases mispronunciation causes users to spell words wrongly. Discuss these words in class and decide on the correct ways of saying them.

advertisement	aerate	again	aitch
Antarctic	Arctic	ate	café
certificate	comparable	controversy	deteriorate
either	envelope	escape	et cetera
extraordinary	February	finances	forehead
formidable	garage	grievous	harass
kilometres	laboratory	length	library
longitude	maintenance	magistrate	mischievous
particularly	Prime Minister	probably	pronunciation
recognize	secretary	scone	specific
strength	superfluous	tortoise	utmost

Words with interesting origins

amok	anorak	armadillo	assassin	average
avocado	balaclava	barbarian	bead	berserk
bicycle	biochemistry	blurb	bonfire	bowel
boycott	bungalow	bus	candidate	chapel
checkmate	claustrophobia	coach	coleslaw	crater
dandelion	denim	dilapidated	dirt	dismal
eavesdrop	electricity	era	flak	galaxy
gorilla	graffiti	grenade	grovel	gull
gymnasium	gypsy	harass	helicopter	hooligan
isosceles	jodhpurs	jubilee	judo	juggernaut
kidnap	kiosk	lens	magazine	marathon
marsupial	mesmerize	migraine	mob	muscle
newt	nickname	nylon	oboe	October
pandemonium	parasite	patrol	person	posh
pupil	pyjamas	quarantine	radar	ransack
red tape	red herring	robot	safari	salary
sandwich	sarcastic	scapegoat	scarper	scuba diving
shampoo	sideburns	sincerely	sinister	siren
slave	smack	soggy	spaghetti	squadron
starboard	suede	tadpole	talent	tantalize
Tory	toxic	trek	tulip	tyrannosaurus
ugly				